BUSINESS REORGANIZATION IN BANKRUPTCY

CASES AND MATERIALS

Third Edition

By

Mark S. Scarberry
Professor of Law
Pepperdine University

Kenneth N. Klee
Professor of Law, UCLA School of Law
Partner, Klee, Tuchin, Bogdanoff & Stern LLP

Grant W. Newton
Professor Emeritus, Pepperdine University
Executive Director,
Association of Insolvency & Restructuring Advisors

Steve H. Nickles
C.C. Hope Chair in Law and Management
Wake Forest University

AMERICAN CASEBOOK SERIES®

Mat #40130672

American Casebook Series and West Group are trademarks
registered in the U.S. Patent and Trademark Office.

COPYRIGHT © 1996 WEST PUBLISHING CO.
© West, a Thomson business, 2001
© 2006 Thomson/West
     610 Opperman Drive
     P.O. Box 64526
     St. Paul, MN 55164–0526
     1–800–328–9352

Printed in the United States of America

ISBN–13: 978–0–314–14564–2
ISBN–10: 0–314–14564–8

*TEXT IS PRINTED ON 10% POST
CONSUMER RECYCLED PAPER*

THIRD EDITION
DEDICATION

This third edition is dedicated to the memory of a great and inspiring
bankruptcy teacher, scholar, editor, and legislative advisor; a guide
to generations of practitioners, judges and law teachers;
a mentor who is greatly missed.

In Memoriam

Professor Lawrence P. King
1929 – 2001

PREFACE TO THIRD EDITION

Another five years have passed, and again much has happened since the publication of the previous edition. The Supreme Court issued important pronouncements on bankruptcy issues, including state sovereign immunity and cramdown interest rates. Lower courts continued to produce bankruptcy precedent at a prodigious rate, on issues from recoupment to "critical vendor" orders to recharacterization of debt as equity. In 2005 Congress finally passed a bankruptcy bill: the long awaited—or feared—Bankruptcy Abuse Prevention and Consumer Protection Act (the "2005 BAPCPA") that, despite its consumer focus, will have a substantial effect on chapter 11 cases. Practitioners have adapted chapter 11 further as a tool for selling distressed companies, whether by way of a § 363(b) nonordinary course sale or by way of a confirmed plan. Chapter 11 petitions were filed by some very large (and in some cases notorious) public companies, including WorldCom, Enron, Conseco, Global Crossing, Pacific Gas & Electric, Calpine, Adelphia, United Airlines, and Mirant. Sadly, the past five years also saw the passing of a bankruptcy giant, Professor Lawrence P. King. As the second edition was dedicated to the memory of Professor Vern Countryman, this third edition is dedicated to the memory of Professor King.

The book has been thoroughly updated and, in our view, strengthened. It now includes, for example, a section in Chapter Three on bankruptcy and arbitration; coverage in Chapter Ten of deepening insolvency; a more thorough treatment of valuation in Chapter Twelve (including exhibits presented by the experts in the Exide Technologies reorganization); an expanded note in Chapter Fifteen on the scholarly debate over how to reorganize distressed companies; and more explanatory text (which we suspect students will like).

But the book's thrust remains the same, and prior users will find that it has very substantial continuity with past editions. Thus we include the Prefaces to the First and Second Editions and invite the reader's attention to them. As before, the book presents a hypothetical financially distressed manufacturer, Foam Corporation, in some detail, and then tells its chapter 11 story—and the broader story of chapter 11 reorganization—with explanatory text, carefully chosen judicial opinions, and numerous problems.

It remains true, as we said in the Preface to the First Edition and echoed in the Preface to the Second Edition, that

> [w]hen a business's survival is at stake—along with its employees' jobs—the bankruptcy lawyer must draw on all of his or her skills and creativity in a crisis environment. Chapter 11 business reorganizations combine litigation, negotiation, and transactional planning into one process—an intense microcosm of legal practice.

We again invite you to join us in exploring this intense microcosm.

Additional materials related to this book are available on Professor Scarberry's web page at http://law.pepperdine.edu/scarberry. We hope you will visit it and make use of the resources there.

The second edition included excerpts placed throughout the book from Judge Wizmur's fine 2000 opinion in the *Greate Bay* case. To fit in the developments of the past five years, and the expanded notes and textual discussions, something had to be taken out, and thus only one *Greate Bay* excerpt remains.

* * * * * * * * * *

Professor Klee gratefully acknowledges the assistance of his able research assistant William Holzer of the UCLA School of Law Class of 2007 and the support of his assistant Tal Grietzer. Professor Scarberry thanks his talented research assistants Jennifer T. Purpero and Scott Siemer (of the Pepperdine University School of Law Classes of 2006 and 2007, respectively) and wishes to express appreciation for the capable volunteer assistance of Gunnar B. Gundersen (Pepperdine University School of Law Class of 2007). A team working in the Dean's Office at the Pepperdine University School of Law provided substantial last-minute help with the book's tables. For their diligent and tireless assistance Professor Scarberry thanks Rian Schoeffling (Executive Assistant to the Dean), Taneekia C. Collymore (Pepperdine University, Seaver College, Class of 2005), and in particular Emily Montgomery (Pepperdine University, Seaver College, Class of 2006).

* * * * * * * * * *

Citation and editing practices are the same in this third edition as in the second edition, and substantially the same as in the first edition. Please see the prefaces to the first and second editions, reprinted below. As before, code section references in this book are to the Bankruptcy Code, Title 11 U.S.C., unless otherwise noted. References to "Rules" are to the Federal Rules of Bankruptcy Procedure unless otherwise noted. Footnotes and citations are omitted without notation. References to the "2005 BAPCPA" are to the Bankruptcy Abuse Prevention and Consumer Protection Act of 2005, Pub. L. 109-8, 119 Stat. 23 (2005). References to Resnick & Sommer, COLLIER ON BANKRUPTCY ¶ ___ are to the fifteenth edition, revised, of which Professor Alan N. Resnick and consumer bankruptcy law expert Henry J. Sommer, Esq. are the principal editors. We continue to use three asterisks (" * * * ") to indicate our editorial deletions. We did not always retain the exact paragraph structure of the source when edits encompassed several paragraphs, and thus three asterisks at the end of a paragraph may indicate not only the omission of the remainder of the paragraph but also the omission of succeeding paragraphs.

This book is intended for educational purposes and does not constitute the rendering of legal advice. Any reader with an actual legal problem should consult an attorney. As was the case with the earlier editions, positions taken in the book do not necessarily represent the views of all of the authors or of any of their clients, and sometimes positions are taken for pedagogical purposes. The authors continue to disagree—productively, we think—on the appropriate approach to many issues and on the appropriate emphasis to be given to different points of view. As with earlier editions, the disagreements made the writing of the book more interesting, and enjoyable, but often are not reflected in the final text. The authors will gladly receive any comments on the book or suggestions for its improvement.

PREFACE TO SECOND EDITION

A lot has happened in the five years since the first edition came out. There is substantially more Supreme Court authority on various bankruptcy issues—new opinions on the new value "exception," on equitable subordination, on valuation of collateral in a cramdown, and on preferences, among other issues. We expected Congress to amend the Bankruptcy Code this past year, and we held up final work on this edition so that the amendments could be included. But that did not happen—at least it has not yet happened as of late October, 2000.

One of the saddest occurrences of the past five years was the passing of Professor Vern Countryman in 1999. This book is dedicated to his memory.

The thrust of this book remains the same. Thus we include the Preface to the First Edition and invite the reader's attention to it. In addition to updating the cases and materials, we have shortened the book by about a hundred pages and included several excerpts from a remarkable bankruptcy court opinion that came out this year, In re Greate Bay Hotel & Casino, 251 B.R. 213 (Bankr. D.N.J. 2000). Judge Judith Wizmur's opinion is unusually rich in interwoven issues, and her writing is unusually clear. We have included excerpts from the opinion dealing with classification of claims and impairment of classes, with the voting process, with the fair and equitable standard, with the "no unfair discrimination" standard, and with the choice of which plan to confirm if two meet all the statutory requirements. We hope that *Greate Bay* will help students to integrate the materials as they see the relationship of the issues in one very interesting case.

For materials related to this book, the reader is invited to visit Professor Scarberry's web page at http://law.pepperdine.edu/scarberry. As the first paragraph of the Preface to the First Edition states,

> When a business's survival is at stake—along with its employees' jobs—the bankruptcy lawyer must draw on all of his or her skills and creativity in a crisis environment. Chapter 11 business reorganizations combine litigation, negotiation, and transactional planning into one process—an intense microcosm of legal practice.

We invite you to join us in exploring this intense microcosm.

* * * * * * * * *

Professor Klee would like to thank his research assistant, Lisa-Jane Hooper, for her help in updating the book. Professor Scarberry would like to thank his research assistants, Karen Chapman Gilkeson, Timothy Spence, and Paul Taylor, for their important help with this Second Edition. Several first year students from Professor Scarberry's Fall 2000 Contracts class worked unselfishly as volunteers to help with cite checking and other important but time-consuming matters; for that help we gratefully thank Tammie Carpenter, Brett Fenoglio, Gary Gaston, Brigette Gorelick, Jennifer Grossman, Sherry Kohan, Louis Pacella, Megan Peitzke, Michael Perkins, Stephanie Rettier, and Court Will.

* * * * * * * * * *

With a few exceptions, citation and editing practices are the same in this second edition as in the first. Please see the Preface to the First Edition, reprinted below. Code section references in this book are to the Bankruptcy Code, Title 11 U.S.C., unless otherwise noted. References to "Rules" are to the Federal Rules of Bankruptcy Procedure unless otherwise noted. Footnotes and citations are omitted without notation. We continue to use three asterisks ("* * *") to indicate our editorial deletions. In the interests of space and aesthetics, we did not always retain the exact paragraph structure of the source when edits encompassed several paragraphs. Thus three asterisks at the end of a paragraph may indicate not only the omission of the remainder of the paragraph but also the omission of succeeding paragraphs.

This book is intended for educational purposes and does not constitute the rendering of legal advice. Any reader with an actual legal problem should consult an attorney. Positions taken in the book do not necessarily represent the views of all of the authors (or of any of their clients); sometimes positions are taken for pedagogical purposes. The authors often disagreed on the appropriate approach to issues or on the appropriate emphasis to be given to different points of view. Those disagreements made the writing of the book much more interesting, but often are not reflected in the final text.

The authors welcome comments on the book and suggestions for its improvement.

Preface to First Edition

When a business's survival is at stake—along with its employees' jobs—the bankruptcy lawyer must draw on all of his or her skills and creativity in a crisis environment. Chapter 11 business reorganizations combine litigation, negotiation, and transactional planning into one process—an intense microcosm of legal practice.

In this book, the student will follow that process from beginning to end through the hypothetical experiences of a financially distressed manufacturer, Foam Corporation. Chapter Two of this book presents Foam Corporation in realistic detail and presents its start on the road to reorganization. Most of the problems in the rest of the book build on Foam Corporation's attempt to reorganize.

Along with problems and cases, we include a substantial amount of explanatory text, much of which uses Foam Corporation to illustrate the application of the law. We do not seek to "hide the ball," but to let the student see it, consider it thoughtfully, and use it creatively. Our goal is to present not just the theory of chapter 11 bankruptcy law, but its practical application in creative, ethical lawyering.

Of course, lawyers do not work in a vacuum. To help a business reorganize—or to oppose a reorganization on behalf of a creditor who does not believe the business can be saved—the lawyer must know something about business, and about what must be done to turn around a failing business and make it profitable. Thus we have integrated business and financial issues into this book. We seek to give the student—especially the student with no business background—enough of an introduction to these issues so that the student will be able to communicate with financial and business advisors intelligently. We provide ample explanatory text written with the business novice in mind. We believe that the business orientation provided in this book will help the student in dealing with business clients, whether or not the student ever practices bankruptcy law.

Two other major threads weave their way through the book. First, we often ask the student to think about how bankruptcy law changes the nonbankruptcy rights of the parties; we often ask whether bankruptcy law changes their rights too much (or too little) for the sake of helping the debtor to reorganize. Second, we often ask (and we encourage the student always to ask) the "so what" question. Do not settle for an abstract understanding of the law. For example, the court is supposed to allow a secured creditor (e.g., a creditor with a lien on the debtor's business equipment) to foreclose on the collateral if its lien is not "adequately protected." See Bankruptcy Code (Title 11 U.S.C.) § 362(d)(1). So what? Well, if the creditor is permitted to foreclose, the debtor will be unable to continue its business, and the reorganization will fail; as a result, the debtor's employees will lose their jobs. On the other hand, if the creditor is not permitted to foreclose (as it could outside bankruptcy if the debtor were in default), the equipment may drop in value or be damaged or destroyed. As a result, the creditor may lose a lot of money. How much risk should the law place on the creditor in order to let a debtor who is in default continue to use the equipment in an attempt to reorganize? This example brings the two threads together, as will often happen. The practical consequence of the court's ruling—the answer to the "so what" question—raises the issue of how much we are willing to change the creditor's nonbankruptcy rights in order to help the debtor reorganize.

* * * * * * * * * *

Professor Scarberry wishes to thank the students who have worked with him as research assistants in preparing this book: Joshua M. Fried, Brian D. Kahn, Holly R. Randall, Scott M. Reddie, and Deborah R. Smotrich. He also thanks Therese Barron for typing and cite checking portions of the manuscript.

* * * * * * * * *

Code section references in this book are to the Bankruptcy Code, Title 11 U.S.C., unless otherwise noted. References to "Rules" are to the Federal Rules of Bankruptcy Procedure unless otherwise noted. References to Epstein, Nickles & White, BANKRUPTCY § __ without a volume number are to the one volume student edition written by David G. Epstein, Steve H. Nickles, and James J. White, and published in 1993 as part of the West Hornbook Series.® If a volume number is given, the reference is to the three volume West Practitioner Treatise Series ® edition published in 1992. References to King, COLLIER ON BANKRUPTCY ¶ __ are to the fifteenth edition, of which Lawrence King is the principal editor. We cite the House and Senate Reports on the bankruptcy bills which became the Bankruptcy Reform Act of 1978 simply as H.R. Rep. No. 595, 95th Cong., 1st Sess.

(1977), and S. Rep. No. 989, 95th Cong., 2d Sess. (1978); those reports are reprinted in 1978 U.S. Code Cong. & Admin. News at 5963 and 5787 respectively. They also can be found easily in a special legislative history database on Westlaw (BANKR78-LH).

We omitted footnotes and citations from cases and other reprinted material without noting the omissions. Otherwise, we used asterisks (* * *) to indicate omissions. Footnotes are consecutively numbered in each Chapter, including any footnotes which we did not omit from the cases and other reprinted material; the original footnote number of such footnotes is indicated in brackets.

We used WESTLAW® extensively in preparing the text. We also used the West CD Rom Bankruptcy Library and found it to be helpful.

This book is intended for educational purposes and does not constitute the rendering of legal advice. Any reader with an actual legal problem should consult an attorney. Positions taken in the book do not necessarily represent the views of all of the authors (or of any of their clients); sometimes positions are taken for pedagogical purposes. The authors often disagreed on the appropriate approach to issues or on the appropriate emphasis to be given to different points of view. Those disagreements made the writing of the book much more interesting, but often are not reflected in the final text.

The authors welcome comments on the book and suggestions for its improvement.

ACKNOWLEDGMENTS

We thank the authors and publishers who have permitted us to reproduce portions of their copyrighted works, including these:

Kenneth N. Klee and Laine Mervis, "Recharacterization in Bankruptcy," in CHAPTER 11 BUSINESS REORGANIZATIONS, 211 (2005). Copyright © 2005 by the American Law Institute. Reproduced with the permission of American Law Institute-American Bar Association Continuing Professional Education.

Lynn M. LoPucki and William C. Whitford, *Corporate Governance in the Bankruptcy of Large, Publicly Held Companies*, 141 UNIVERSITY OF PENNSYLVANIA LAW REVIEW 669 (1993). Copyright © 1993 University of Pennsylvania Law Review, William C. Whitford, and Lynn M. LoPucki.

John C. McCoid, *Setoff: Why Bankruptcy Priority?*, 75 VIRGINIA LAW REVIEW 15 (1989). Copyright © 1989 by the Virginia Law Review Association.

Sally S. Neely, "Investing in Troubled Companies and Trading in Claims and Interests in Chapter 11 Cases—A Brave New World," in FUNDAMENTALS OF CHAPTER 11 BUSINESS REORGANIZATIONS, 109 (1993). Copyright © 1993 by the American Law Institute and Sally S. Neely. Reprinted with the permission of the American Law Institute-American Bar Association Committee on Continuing Professional Education and with the permission of Sally S. Neely.

Howard J. Steinberg, Contractual Subordination, in 2 Steinberg, BANKRUPTCY LITIGATION § 10:44 (1989 & Supp. 2005). Reprinted from BANKRUPTCY LITIGATION, by Howard J. Steinberg, with permission of West, a Thomson business. Copyright © 2005. For further information about this publication, please visit www.west.thomson.com/store, or call 800-328-9352.

SUMMARY OF CONTENTS

TABLE OF CONTENTS

PART III
TURNING THE BUSINESS AROUND

PART V
RESTRUCTURING THE DEBTS AND DIVIDING
THE ENTERPRISE'S VALUE

TABLE OF CASES

Names of principal cases are in bold type. The page number at which the opinion in a principal case begins is also in bold type. Cases merely cited or discussed in the text are in ordinary type. Cases cited only in principal cases or within other quoted materials are not included. For convenience, opinions in adversary proceedings generally are indexed not only under their full name—e.g., "Smith v. Jones (In re Smith)"—but also under the name of the related chapter 11 case—e.g., "Smith, In re"—if the debtor is not the first named party.

B

C

D

F

G

H

K

L

M

N

O

P

Q

R

S

U

W

X

Y

Z

TABLE OF BANKRUPTCY CODE SECTIONS CITED
(nonexhaustive)

---

11 U.S.C.

Section	Page	Section	Page
101	78	106(a)(3)	170
101(2)(A)	44	106(a)(4)	170
101(5)(A)	304, 486, 491, 492, 523, 518	108(b)	343, 679
		109	10, 64
101(5)(B)	352, 368, 486, 944	301	486, 504, 807
101(9)	254	302	807
101(9)(A)(v)	804	303	29, 807
101(10)	486, 493, 504	303(a)	926
101(10)(A)	942	303(b)(3)	64
101(10)(B)	486	303(h)(1)	10
101(12)	305, 944	307	74
101(14)	31	322(e)	254
101(15)	88, 98, 160, 804	323(a)	244
101(16)	283	325(g)	951
101(17)	283	327	79, 86, 505
101(27)	89, 98	327(a)	76, 78, 86
101(31)	31, 443, 682	328	505
101(31)(E)	44	328(a)	287
101(32)	10	328(c)	79
101(32)(A)	440, 722	330	505
101(37)	427	330(a)	76, 284
101(41)	170, 804	331	505
101(51)	428	361	18, 136
101(51)(B)	95	361(1)	93
101(51C)	639, 642	361(2)	20, 93
101(51D)	639, 642	361(3)	136, 548
101(54)	440	362	13, 90, 99, 342, 480, 482
102(1)	153, 175, 188	362(a)	11, 88, 89, 96, 98, 99, 111, 134, 160, 485
102(2)	493		
102(3)	36, 682	362(a)(1)	89, 96, 98, 108
105	955	362(a)(2)	89
105(a)	18, 73, 90, 91, 98, 108, 109, 170, 207, 291, 587, 624, 626, 796, 904, 915, 942, 952, 955, 957	362(a)(3)	18, 88, 96, 97, 98, 112, 116, 125, 129, 957
		362(a)(4)	18, 88, 96, 98, 99, 430
		362(a)(5)	18, 98
		362(a)(6)	88, 90, 98, 99, 508
105(d)	73, 174, 246	362(a)(7)	116, 471
–(2)(B)(vi)	769, 770	362(b)	98, 99, 125
106	160, 170	362(b)(1)	98
106(a)	170, 415	362(b)(3)	430

PART I

INTRODUCTION

Chapter One

Introduction to Chapter 11 Business Reorganizations

Chapter 11 of the federal Bankruptcy Code[1] gives financially distressed businesses an opportunity to reorganize and to avoid liquidation. Liquidation of a business's assets can be very costly to the persons directly involved and to society. "The fundamental purpose of reorganization is to prevent a debtor from going into liquidation, with an attendant loss of jobs and possible misuse of economic resources." NLRB v. Bildisco & Bildisco, 465 U.S. 513, 528, 104 S. Ct. 1188, 1197, 79 L. Ed. 2d 482 (1984).

A. THE BENEFITS OF REORGANIZATION

Creating a business is costly. It takes time and money to create the business entity (typically by forming a corporation, partnership, or limited liability company), to obtain the necessary start-up financing, to purchase or lease the necessary tangible assets, to integrate those physical assets together into a productive plant, to recruit and train a work force, to build relationships with customers and suppliers, and to build name recognition.

If the business is liquidated piecemeal, the assets and the work force will be dispersed; whatever value was created by bringing them together and forging them into a productive whole will be lost. The value of the relationships and name recognition will also be destroyed. The value of other intangible assets will be diminished; for example, it is generally much more difficult to collect the accounts receivable of a business that is in liquidation than of one that is a going concern. The liquidation sale price of tangible assets is often very low compared to the value they would have as part of a productive whole.

---

1. The Bankruptcy Code itself is *title* 11 of the United States Code; *chapter* 11 of the Bankruptcy Code is the series of sections in the Bankruptcy Code from § 1101 to § 1174.

The cost to society of business liquidations is high. The destruction of value caused by business liquidations reduces the total wealth of our society. The loss of jobs causes additional social costs, such as increased unemployment insurance payments, increased use of other social welfare programs, and decreased tax revenues. Increased unemployment may have other social costs, such as an increase in poverty and crime. If overall demand for the products of the kind made by a liquidated business does not decrease, many of the workers and managers eventually may be hired by other firms for similar positions, but this does not happen quickly, and it is not cost-free. It does not happen at all if jobs are lost to foreign competition. Society pays a price for the liquidation of businesses.

For the workers, the managers, the creditors, and the owners of a liquidated business, the effect is more direct and, in some cases, devastating. The workers and managers lose their jobs, with the accompanying financial and emotional stress on them and their families.[2] On liquidation the assets may be insufficient to repay creditors more than a small fraction of their debts; unsecured creditors (those who do not have liens on any particular assets of the debtor) often will receive nothing. If creditors are not paid in full in the liquidation, then the stockholders, partners or other owners of the business will receive nothing.

Keeping the business in operation will therefore often be much more desirable than liquidating it. The fundamental premise of chapter 11 of the Bankruptcy Code is that reorganization is desirable.[3]

---

2.   There is, however, the possibility that a purchaser of some or all of the assets in the liquidation may hire them.

3.   In this book (1) the term "liquidation" generally means the sale of the business's assets in such a way that the business ceases to operate; and (2) the terms "reorganization" and "rehabilitation" generally are used synonymously to mean the restructuring of the debtor and its debts so that the business can continue in operation under the ownership of its creditors or former owners. Writers do not always use these terms in exactly these ways. For example, a sale of the business's assets as a whole to a buyer who will continue to operate the business is a kind of "liquidation"—it turns the assets into liquid funds that can be paid to creditors. Some writers would call such a sale a kind of "reorganization," because it allows the business operations to continue. A few writers might even call it a "rehabilitation" because it keeps the business going despite past difficulties. Indeed, it is even possible (just barely) to call a piecemeal liquidation a "reorganization;" after all, chapter 11, which is entitled "Reorganization," permits confirmation of a plan providing for sale of the business as a going concern or even for its piecemeal liquidation. See § 1123(a)(5)(D). Our intent is to use the terms as we have defined them, and we trust that the context will make clear any deviation from such usage.

Sale of the business as a going concern does not disperse the assets or necessarily cost workers their jobs. Unless the identity of the business's owner is important—as with a dentist's or accountant's professional practice, for example—the going concern value of the business may be preserved. Such a sale may yield many of the benefits that a true reorganization would yield. State law makes sale of a distressed business as a going concern difficult outside of bankruptcy for the same reasons that it makes true reorganization difficult. (We detail those reasons later in this chapter of the book.) Thus it may be much easier to accomplish such a sale in a chapter 11 plan under § 1123(a)(5)(D) than outside of bankruptcy. Many courts will allow such a sale in chapter 11 under the procedurally much easier § 363(b)(1), if there are good reasons for doing so. See Chapter Four, section B.2. below.

However, not all distressed businesses should be kept in operation; sometimes a business has no going concern value or a going concern value less than its liquidation value. In such cases, the creditors will be harmed by the continuation of the business.

Later in this chapter we will consider a financially distressed shoe manufacturer (Acme), which manufactures shoes worth $9.50 per pair and uses up $10 in resources for every pair of shoes it manufactures. Thus Acme has a 50 cent per pair "negative cash flow from operations." Such a business is worth nothing as a going concern, unless its operating costs can be cut or the value of its products increased. A business that creates less value than it consumes diminishes the wealth of society and of the business's owners. A business sometimes can survive negative cash flow in the short run, but not in the long run. Unless a business can be turned around so that it has sustainable "positive cash flow from operations," it has no going concern value and should be liquidated.

Even if the business has some going concern value because it can be turned around so that it has positive cash flow from operations, its value as a going concern may still be less than its liquidation value. Should Acme be reorganized or, on the other hand, liquidated if (1) its positive cash flow from operations will be $1,000 per year for the foreseeable future, and (2) its assets could be sold in a piecemeal liquidation for $150,000? No one would pay $150,000 for the right to get $1,000 per year; even in a very safe investment like U.S. treasury securities, a $150,000 investment will yield more than $1,000 per year. Thus Acme's going concern value would be less than its liquidation value. If it were kept in operation there would be only $1,000 per year that could be distributed to the creditors on account of their prepetition debts, even if all the positive cash flow were distributed to the creditors and none to the present stockholders.

That represents much less than $150,000 in total "present value" for the creditors, in fact, less than $100,000, as the following analysis shows. If the creditors were given $100,000 cash they could buy U.S. treasury bonds or even deposit the money at a bank and earn more than $1,000 per year;[4] thus they

---

Congress could have required that a business in chapter 11 be sold quickly as a going concern, so as to avoid many of the complexities discussed in this book. But Congress did not do so, probably for good reason. There could be severe practical problems with requiring a sale of the assets, especially a quick sale. The owners or managers of a distressed business would probably wait longer than they do now before filing a chapter 11 bankruptcy petition, if they knew that the business would be sold out from under them in bankruptcy. If so, the going concern value of the debtor could be diminished substantially before the filing of a petition as employees, customers, and suppliers abandon the distressed business and as its productive assets become depleted. The distress nature of a quick sale of the assets in bankruptcy might lead to a low price being paid for the assets. Even if a quick sale were not required, the debtor's managers would have little incentive to be diligent or loyal during the bankruptcy case; they would know that a sale was in prospect and that they had little prospect of long term employment with the debtor. Today, however, the high cost of chapter 11 and aggressive debtor in possession financing orders have increased the frequency of sales of businesses as going concerns under § 363 rather than under a plan.

4.   Currently, 10 year treasury bonds yield well over 4%; their yield has exceeded 3% every year at least since 1962. See Bd. of Govs. of Fed. Reserve Sys., *Fed. Res. Statistical Release: Selected Interest Rates—Historical Data*, http://www.federalreserve.gov/releases/H15/data.htm

would prefer to have $100,000 rather than the $1,000 per year from the shoe manufacturer; and thus the right to get the $1,000 per year from Acme is worth less than $100,000. Since the creditors as a group could receive $150,000 cash if Acme were liquidated, the creditors will lose more than $50,000 in present value if Acme is reorganized rather than liquidated. Whether such a business should be reorganized or liquidated involves a choice between maximizing the economic return for creditors and saving the jobs of the workers and managers.[5]

Generally, a chapter 11 plan of reorganization cannot be confirmed over the objection of even one creditor unless that creditor will receive at least as much value under the plan as it would receive in a liquidation. See § 1129(a)(7).[6] Thus most businesses for whom liquidation value exceeds going concern value cannot successfully reorganize under chapter 11.

Problem 1-1

Ernestine Entrepreneur paid $1000 to attend a workshop put on by PostHaste National Corp. ("PHNC," a hypothetical business, not the direct mail firm). PHNC sells franchises for PostHaste locations, at which people can send and receive mail and faxes, obtain copying services, and buy business supplies. At the workshop Ernestine learned how to open and operate a PostHaste location. She thought it was a great opportunity and thus purchased a franchise from PHNC for $15,000.

PostHaste National provided Ernestine with its standard, mandatory plans for a PostHaste location, including floor plan layout and color scheme: orange and green. She then leased space from Lester Lessor under a commercial lease.

Ernestine and Lester spent three hours negotiating the terms of the proposed lease. Each of them then spent $300 having the lease reviewed by their attorneys before signing the lease. Ernestine purchased two photocopy machines, a fax machine, an electronic cash register, a postal metering machine, a personal computer, an accounting software package, and a set of 100 post office boxes, for a total cost of $22,000. Ernestine purchased stationery and other office supplies for sale to her customers, at a cost of $3,000. Ernestine paid Cornell Contractor $12,000 to remodel the space to PostHaste National's specifications, including

---

(scroll down to "Treasury Constant Maturities, 10-year," and follow "annual" hyperlink) (last visited Feb. 26, 2006). The national average rate for negotiable 6 month certificates of deposit in the secondary market was 4.69% for January, 2006; for every month since at least mid-1964 that average rate has exceeded 1% (though only slightly in 2003 and early 2004). Id. (scroll down to "Treasury bills (secondary market), 6-month," and follow "monthly" hyperlink) (last visited Feb. 26, 2006).

5. This may be a false choice. It is possible that receipt by the creditors of the higher liquidation value could result in additional investment or lending by them, which in turn could result in creation of additional jobs, perhaps more jobs than would be saved by not liquidating the business.

6. As noted in section D.2. of this chapter, the liquidation value for purposes of § 1129(a)(7) is determined as of the effective date of a proposed plan of reorganization. For several reasons, that may be less than the liquidation value on the date the petition was filed. Thus, creditors are not assured of getting value equal to the liquidation value that the debtor's assets had on the petition date. Of course, even a liquidation takes time; creditors are not assured even in a chapter 7 case that the assets will not depreciate before liquidation is completed.

- installation of a customer service counter,

- installation of the post office boxes on one wall,

- construction of an internal wall with a locking door so that customers could have access to their post office boxes even if the rest of the premises were closed,

- construction of storage cabinets,

- relocation of electric outlets to serve the photocopy and fax machines and the personal computer,

- construction of a distinctive PostHaste sign on the outside of the premises, and

- painting of the premises in orange and green.

Ernestine advertised in the local newspaper at a cost of $150 for one full time and two part time employees. She spent thirteen hours interviewing potential employees before making the hiring decisions. She then spent $1500 for a PostHaste National "employee training program" for them. Ernestine paid $4000 for an advertisement in the "Yellow Pages" and $3000 for a grand opening advertisement in the local newspaper. She also paid a local radio station $6000 to produce and air a commercial promoting the new PostHaste location. Pursuant to the franchise agreement, at its expense PostHaste National featured the new PostHaste location in several of its own magazine advertisements. Finally, Ernestine was ready to open her PostHaste location to the public. All of the money she had was invested in the business, plus $25,000 she had borrowed from First Bank.

The grand opening was a success, and business was brisk at the new PostHaste location. However, Ernestine forgot to obtain liability insurance. Two days after the grand opening, one of the employees mistakenly waxed the floor instead of just mopping it; thus it was extremely slippery. Carl Customer slipped and fell, injuring his back. Ernestine's attorney believes the case can be settled for $75,000. Ernestine does not have and cannot borrow that kind of money. Ernestine cannot even afford to pay the costs of defending Carl's lawsuit.

Should Ernestine's business be liquidated? What losses would be caused by a liquidation?

B. THE MAJOR OBSTACLES TO REORGANIZATION OUTSIDE OF CHAPTER 11

A financially distressed business can be reorganized outside of chapter 11, in what is called an "out-of-court workout" or simply a "workout." In a workout, the creditors typically agree to a moratorium on debt collection activities while a workout agreement is negotiated. The workout agreement may give the debtor extra time to pay its debts (an "extension" agreement), may provide that each creditor's debt is reduced by a certain percent (a "composition" agreement), or may provide for both an extension and a composition. If the creditors forgive debt, they are sometimes given shares of the debtor's stock in exchange, so that they become equity owners in the debtor.

However, three major obstacles stand in the way of successful reorganization outside of chapter 11.

First, the state law of creditors' rights puts a premium on diligent collection activity. The first creditor to obtain a lien on an asset will typically have priority in that asset over the other creditors.[7] When the debtor fails to pay a debt, the creditor will therefore have a strong incentive to obtain a lien on some or all of the debtor's assets, if the creditor does not already have a lien. Thus, if, for example, a creditor, Finance Co., can obtain an attachment or execution lien on the debtor's punch press before any other creditors obtain a lien on it, then whatever value can be obtained from liquidation of the punch press will go first to Finance Co.; other creditors will not receive any of that value unless there is a surplus left over after Finance Co.'s debt is fully paid. State law therefore encourages a race of diligence to obtain liens on the debtor's assets by judicial process. State law makes it dangerous for creditors to wait while the debtor attempts to reorganize.

Second, the obtaining of a judicial lien on an asset other than real property typically involves a seizure of the asset, so that the debtor no longer has the use of it. After obtaining a judgment for the debt, the creditor will obtain as a matter of right a writ of execution authorizing the sheriff or some other governmental officer to seize specific assets belonging to the debtor.[8] That seizure (called a "levy") creates a judicial lien—an "execution lien"—in favor of the creditor on whatever assets were seized. Real property is typically only "constructively" seized; to levy, the sheriff simply records the appropriate notice in the county real property records.[9] Tangible personal property, however, usually is physically seized.

Whether the asset is real or tangible personal property, the *enforcement* of the execution lien typically results in the execution sale of the asset, which makes it permanently unavailable to the debtor (absent a right of redemption). Intangible personal property, such as a bank account or a debt owed to the debtor by a customer for goods sold or services rendered (an "account receivable"), effectively will be seized when it is "garnished." Garnishment

---

7.   For an introduction to liens and to the general law of debtor-creditor relations, and for other supplemental material, see http://law.pepperdine.edu/scarberry.

8.   In some cases it is possible for a creditor to obtain a prejudgment writ of attachment, which will authorize the sheriff to seize assets of the debtor and hold them as security for any judgment that ultimately may be obtained.

9.   A creditor who has obtained a judgment can obtain a judicial lien—called a "judgment lien"—on whatever real property the debtor may own in a particular county in the state where the judgment was entered, simply by recording the appropriate notice of the judgment in the county real property records. In many states, mere docketing of the judgment, without any recording of a notice of the judgment, is sufficient to create such a lien on real property in the county where the judgment was entered. Levy under a writ of execution is not therefore needed for the judgment creditor to obtain a lien on real property, but it still is used in some states as one step in foreclosure of the judgment lien. In a few states, filing of a notice of judgment lien in the appropriate personal property records creates a judgment lien on certain personal property.

is accomplished under the writ of execution or under other procedures depending on the jurisdiction. Garnishment occurs when the sheriff or other officer serves appropriate papers on the persons who owe the money to the debtor. Those persons then must pay the debts to the sheriff rather than the debtor, thus diverting cash that otherwise would have gone to the debtor.

The debtor cannot stay in business for very long if it has no inventory to sell (because its inventory was seized), or if its production equipment cannot be used (because its equipment was seized), or if it has no cash to pay wages and other expenses (because its bank accounts and accounts receivable were garnished). Once the business ceases operations, much of its going concern value will evaporate quickly; workers will leave, customers will find other companies to supply their needs, and the goodwill of the business will erode. Thus, state law not only makes it dangerous for creditors to wait but also encourages creditor activity that as a practical matter will bring the debtor's business to a halt and destroy its going concern value.

Third, outside chapter 11 the creditors as a group may not be able to give the debtor the chance it needs to reorganize, even if most of the creditors want to give the debtor that chance. Dissenting creditors, those who oppose the reorganization, generally cannot be forced to cooperate. The existence of even a few dissenters may doom the workout for the following reasons.

Out-of-court workouts are entirely voluntary from the creditors' point of view and require almost unanimous creditor support to succeed. Only creditors who agree to the workout agreement are bound by it; even if 99 out of 100 creditors agree to it, the one dissenting creditor can demand full payment and pursue legal remedies. The debtor typically will pay that dissenting creditor to avoid the disruption that would be caused if the dissenter exercised its state law creditor's rights. The 99 creditors may be willing to give the debtor concessions even if the other creditor is immediately paid in full, but, depending on the size of the debt owed to the dissenter, the lack of equal treatment may be troubling to them. Creditors will not give concessions to the debtor unless substantially all the other similarly situated creditors also give concessions; no one wants to bear much more than a fair share of the burden. Thus most workout agreements expressly require a very high degree of participation by creditors (e.g., 95% in dollar amount) before becoming effective. If there is too much dissent to obtain that high degree of participation, then the workout will fail. *Outside of chapter 11, a few dissenting creditors can prevent reorganization.*

The question is not only whether enough creditors will eventually sign a workout agreement for it to become effective, but whether the moratorium on debt collection activity will hold while the debtor is trying to obtain those signatures. Usually creditors agree to forbear from pursuing or enforcing their state law remedies for a limited time period only, and only on condition that other creditors not receive preferred treatment. There typically will not be a binding agreement to abide by the moratorium; creditors who abide by it do so because they believe that immediate payment is not attainable, because they believe the workout may succeed, because they believe they will receive more in a successful workout than in a liquidation, and because they believe that the workout agreement will treat them fairly as compared with other creditors.[10] If any of those beliefs are shaken, the moratorium will fall apart.

The beliefs that underlie the moratorium will be shaken if there is significant dissent. Creditors can dissent not only by refusing to agree to a proposed workout agreement but also by refusing to abide by the moratorium. If, to avoid disruption of the business, the debtor pays even a few dissenters who refuse to abide by the moratorium, then other creditors will decide that dissent pays; they may abandon the moratorium, hoping to be paid off. And dissent by even a few creditors, who either show an unwillingness to agree to a workout agreement or who go further and abandon the moratorium, may convince other creditors that too few creditors will participate in the workout agreement for it to succeed; those other creditors may then abandon the moratorium. Finally, immediate payment to even a few dissenters will undermine the other creditors' belief that they will be treated fairly in the workout. If that belief is shaken, then more creditors will abandon the moratorium. Each additional dissenter created in one of these ways will further shake the beliefs that underlie the moratorium, thus potentially creating more dissent. The chain reaction of shaken belief and resulting dissent will destroy the moratorium.

Without the moratorium to protect the debtor, there will be little chance of a workout succeeding; engaging in the state law race of diligence, the creditors will have the debtor's tangible assets seized (under writs of execution or attachment) and will eliminate the debtor's sources of cash by garnishing the debtor's bank accounts and accounts receivable. The debtor's business will not be able to survive the disruption.

---

10. Trade creditors—those whom the debtor owes for goods or services—have an additional interest in seeing a workout succeed; a rehabilitated debtor probably will buy goods and services from them in the future. The workout will save a customer for them. They generally will not, however, provide goods or services to the debtor on unsecured credit during the moratorium. Instead, they will require "cash on delivery" or even prepayment. (They are also likely to try to raise the prices they charge the debtor, so as to obtain, in effect, some repayment of the existing debt.) Note that such a debtor *already* has announced its inability to pay unsecured debts. The debtor is also not likely to obtain trade credit on a purchase money secured basis during a workout. If, as is often the case, there is an existing Article 9 secured party whose security agreement extends to the debtor's present and after-acquired inventory and accounts receivable, the debtor may be unwilling to buy inventory from trade creditors on purchase money secured credit. The granting of such a security interest in the newly purchased inventory is a default under most well-drafted security agreements. And to obtain purchase money priority a trade creditor would generally need to notify the existing secured party of the proposed purchase money financing. See U.C.C. § 9-324. All of this would alienate further the existing secured party, who is counting on having priority in new inventory, and would provide an additional basis for that secured party to accelerate the debt and move against the collateral. Even if the debtor is willing to take that risk, a trade creditor often still cannot safely sell inventory to the debtor on purchase money secured credit; the purchase money priority will not extend to any accounts receivable generated when the debtor resells the inventory to its customers. Id.

This picture is not entirely realistic, because it ignores the secured creditors. In many cases, all or nearly all the debtor's assets are subject to consensual liens securing debts. By agreement, the debtor will have given liens—called "security interests" by § 101(51) and U.C.C. § 1-201(37) (§ 1-201(b)(35) in 2001 Official Text)—on personal property and fixtures to one or more creditors under U.C.C. Article 9. By agreement, the debtor also will have given liens on its real property to one or more creditors by executing mortgages or deeds of trust (also within the definition of "security interest" under Bankruptcy Code § 101(51) but not within the U.C.C. definition of that term). The debts secured by the liens typically will exceed the liquidation value of the assets. If so, the unsecured creditors will have little incentive to seek judicial liens; there is no available value in the assets, at least not if the debtor's assets are liquidated. The only real hope the unsecured creditors have is for the debtor to continue in business and earn enough money to pay something on their debts. Thus, beyond the question whether unsecured creditors will abide by the moratorium is another question: whether the secured creditors—especially the Article 9 secured parties—will abide by the moratorium.[11]

The effect on the debtor if Article 9 secured parties do not abide by the moratorium may be immediate. The secured party is entitled to take possession of tangible collateral if the debtor is in default. U.C.C. § 9-609. The secured party can take possession using self-help without even going to court if the repossession can be accomplished without a breach of the peace. Id. Even if court action is needed, provisional relief under a writ of replevin (or "claim and delivery") often will result in immediate seizure of the collateral. If the collateral is intangible, like accounts receivable, the secured party may not need to go to court to realize on the collateral; the secured party can demand payment from the "account debtors" who owe the accounts receivable. U.C.C. § 9-607. Any of these actions will quickly destroy the business.[12]

Problem 1-2

> Going back to the facts in Problem 1-1, assume Carl Customer obtains a judgment against Ernestine Entrepreneur for $200,000. Assume Ernestine does not pay the judgment, that she misses a payment on her loan from First Bank, and that she fails to pay rent to Lester Lessor. Assume First Bank has a security interest in all of Ernestine's "inventory, accounts receivable, equipment and fixtures." What actions are likely to be taken by Carl, First Bank, and Lester? Will they benefit if Ernestine's business ceases operations?

---

11. Indeed, if secured creditors support the workout attempt, they may be able to assert "third party" claims and defeat attempts by unsecured creditors to execute upon or attach the assets.

12. By contrast, unless an unsecured creditor can obtain an attachment lien, the unsecured creditor must obtain a judgment before obtaining a judicial lien. Even if the debtor permits a default judgment to be entered, there will be at least several weeks between filing of the complaint and the obtaining of such a post-judgment judicial lien. Unfortunately for debtors, in many states prejudgment attachment liens often can be obtained for business debts.

C. THE CHAPTER 11 SOLUTION

The problems, then, are (1) that state law gives each creditor an incentive to attack the debtor's assets diligently, (2) that the use of state law creditors' rights against the debtor—including U.C.C. Article 9 default rights of secured parties—will disrupt and destroy the debtor's business, and (3) that a few dissenting creditors can prevent a reorganization from occurring outside of bankruptcy. How does the Bankruptcy Code deal with these problems?

First, the Bankruptcy Code mildly discourages creditors from pressuring the debtor and from engaging in the race of diligence. Unsecured creditors who pressured an insolvent[13] debtor for payment or obtained payment through judicial action usually must return any payments made within 90 days before the filing of the bankruptcy petition; the payments will be "avoidable preferences." See § 547 (especially § 547(c)(2), which permits many creditors to keep payments made by the debtor in the "ordinary course" rather than in response to pressure). Section 547 also avoids (eliminates) most liens obtained by unsecured creditors within 90 days before the date the bankruptcy petition is filed. Section 542 (the "turnover" section) usually permits the debtor to recover possession of its property that is held by others, including property seized under writs of attachment or execution and property seized by Article 9 secured parties. These provisions provide some incentive for the creditors not to take actions that simply will be reversed if the debtor files a bankruptcy petition. In addition, by reversing the actions, the provisions can cause creditors to return resources to the debtor that may be needed for the reorganization. The provisions also advance the bankruptcy policy of equality of distribution among general—that is, nonpriority—unsecured creditors.

---

13. There are two main kinds of insolvency, "balance sheet" insolvency and "equity" insolvency. Usually the term insolvency refers to balance sheet insolvency. A debtor is insolvent in the balance sheet sense if the sum of the debtor's debts exceeds the value of the debtor's assets. "Insolvent on a liquidation basis" means that the debtor's debts exceed the value that would be obtained in a liquidation of the assets; "insolvent on a going concern basis" means that the debtor's debts exceed the value of the business as a going concern. For debtors other than municipalities, the Bankruptcy Code defines insolvency in the balance sheet sense, § 101(32), and requires use of a "fair valuation," which for a business debtor means going concern value unless the debtor was (on the relevant date) "on its deathbed," so that liquidation was "clearly imminent." See In re DAK Indus., 170 F.3d 1197, 1199 (9th Cir. 1999); In re Trans World Airlines, Inc., 134 F.3d 188, 193 (3d Cir. 1998); In re Taxman Clothing Co., 905 F.2d 166, 170 (7th Cir. 1990). Also, under the Bankruptcy Code definition, the value of any assets that are exempt is not counted in determining whether the debtor is insolvent. (Only human beings have exemptions; corporations, partnerships, LLCs, and other artificial persons do not. See § 522.) The Bankruptcy Code definition is not as important as it might seem. A debtor (other than a municipality) need not be insolvent to file a petition in bankruptcy. See § 109.

A debtor is insolvent in the "equity" sense if the debtor is unable to pay debts as they become due. Regardless of the debtor's *ability* to pay, if the debtor generally *fails* to pay debts as they become due, creditors can commence and maintain an involuntary bankruptcy case against the debtor. See § 303(h)(1). In this book, "insolvent" and "insolvency" refer to balance sheet insolvency, unless otherwise specified.

Second, the Bankruptcy Code provides a much stronger substitute for the fragile workout moratorium. The filing of a bankruptcy petition creates an automatic stay of almost all creditor actions to collect prepetition debts. Section 362(a). Creditors are prohibited from trying to obtain judicial liens, from trying to take possession of property away from the debtor, and from engaging in any other collection activity; they cannot even send letters to the debtor demanding payment. The debtor is permitted to retain possession of and use its property,[14] subject to the need to provide adequate protection of the property interests of others, such as secured creditors. See §§ 362(a) & (d), 363(c)(1) & (e).

Third, the Bankruptcy Code (specifically chapter 11) provides a more workable substitute for the workout agreement. Dissenting creditors cannot be bound in a workout, but they can be bound in chapter 11. Chapter 11 permits a plan of reorganization to be confirmed even if some creditors oppose it. The debtor, its stockholders (or other owners), and all the creditors then will be bound to the terms of the confirmed plan. Chapter 11 thus imposes a collective solution.

The impact of chapter 11 extends beyond the cases in which a chapter 11 petition actually is filed. Creditors know that the debtor can file a chapter 11 petition if necessary; that strongly affects the negotiations in out-of-court workouts. Because creditors know that chapter 11 is an option, they often give concessions in out-of-court workouts that they would not give if chapter 11 did not exist. The threat, implicit or explicit, is always there; if the creditors do not cooperate, the debtor can file a chapter 11 petition. That gives the debtor considerable leverage in workout negotiations.

If the leverage given by the existence of chapter 11 permits the reorganization to occur out of court, that usually will be preferable to reorganizing in chapter 11. The advantages of an out-of-court workout (if one can be accomplished) are considerable:

1. Attorneys' fees and other professionals' fees will usually be much lower in a workout than in a chapter 11 case.

2. Workouts usually can be accomplished and consummated much faster than the more formal chapter 11 reorganizations.

3. Workouts minimize some of the pressures that are present in a chapter 11 case. The very commencement of a chapter 11 case may create additional pressures on a debtor that is undergoing financial difficulties. Often, customers will find reasons to avoid paying for products or services supplied by the debtor or to cease dealing with the debtor. They may fear or claim to fear that the debtor will not be

---

14. It is not quite accurate to say that the property is the debtor's. The filing of the bankruptcy petition creates an "estate." See § 541(a). The debtor's property becomes property of that estate. Unless the court orders appointment of a trustee, the debtor in a chapter 11 case is thus permitted to retain and use the property *of the estate* as the "debtor in possession." See §§ 1101(1), 1107, 1108, 1115(b).

able to honor warranties or service contracts. They may believe that the debtor will not have the resources to pursue uncollected accounts. They may question whether the debtor will survive and may simply prefer to pay accounts owed to those with whom they believe they will be continuing to transact business. These problems usually are less intense in workouts than in chapter 11.

4. Workouts usually also cause much less damage than the filing of a chapter 11 petition to the debtor's general reputation.

As a result, most reorganizations are accomplished in out-of-court workouts. Creditors often recognize that it is not in their best interest to force the debtor to file in chapter 11; the debtor can use the explicit or implicit threat of chapter 11 as leverage to negotiate a workout agreement.

However, there are situations in which the mere threat of chapter 11 is not sufficient to allow a workout to be accomplished out-of-court:

1. Creditors may have taken actions that, if not reversed, would disrupt or destroy the debtor's business, such as having the debtor's assets seized or garnished.

2. One or more creditors may have obtained an advantage by obtaining liens on the debtor's assets; the other creditors may refuse to agree to a workout that leaves that advantage in place. If a bankruptcy petition is filed within ninety days after creation of the lien, it may be possible to eliminate that advantage as a preference under § 547.

3. Outside bankruptcy, the debtor may not be able to borrow the funds needed for the business to stay afloat. Lenders will want assurances that the new loans will be repaid, even if the debtor cannot pay its old debts; in chapter 11 the lenders can obtain (at a minimum) an administrative priority over the prepetition creditors. See § 364. Likewise, trade creditors may not ship needed goods on credit unless they receive the chapter 11 administrative priority or other protection available only in bankruptcy. Id.

4. The debtor also may need the power that bankruptcy law gives to deal with executory contracts and with leases. See § 365. For example, if the debtor has failed to pay rent on its business premises, the debtor in possession may need more time to cure the default than nonbankruptcy law would provide.

5. The debtor may need the special tax treatment that is given to debtors only in bankruptcy. One of the debtor's major "assets" may be its "net operating loss" from past years, which can save the debtor huge amounts of taxes on income from future profitable years. Special tax law provisions applicable only in bankruptcy cases may help the debtor to preserve the benefit of its past net operating loss.

6. The debtor may need the special securities law exemption provided in chapter 11. As part of its reorganization, the debtor may need to issue new securities that could not be issued (or could be issued only at a prohibitive cost) under the securities laws outside chapter 11. See §§ 1125(d), 1145.

7. Most importantly, the mere threat of a chapter 11 filing may not be enough for the debtor to obtain the unanimous or near unanimous support needed for an out-of-court workout to succeed. The debtor may need the protection of the automatic stay during negotiation of the reorganization plan. See § 362. The debtor may also need

to be able to bind dissenting creditors to the terms of the plan; confirmation of the chapter 11 plan will bind all the creditors, including dissenters. See § 1141(a). That power to bind dissenting creditors generally is available only in bankruptcy.[15]

In such cases, the benefits of chapter 11 may outweigh the burdens, from the debtor's standpoint; thus the debtor may choose to file in chapter 11.

In addition, chapter 11 is now often used, not as a substitute for a workout, but to facilitate a sale of the debtor's business. See Baird & Rasmussen, *Chapter 11 at Twilight*, 56 STAN. L. REV. 673, 674 (2003) (noting that "in 84% of all large Chapter 11s from 2002, the investors entered bankruptcy with a deal in hand or used it to sell the assets of the business"). We will consider the implications of that use of chapter 11 frequently in this book.

Problem 1-3

> Going back to the facts in problems 1-1 and 1-2, what should Ernestine consider in deciding whether to file a chapter 11 petition?

---

15. There are at least two possible exceptions to this rule. First, it may be possible to bind dissenting public bondholders or tort claimants to a workout outside of bankruptcy by use of a non-opt out class action. If the bondholders or tort claimants are made part of a class in a class action under Federal Rule of Civil Procedure 23(b)(1), it may be possible to bind dissenters to a settlement of the class action as part of a workout. Class members do not have the right to "opt out" of a class if it is certified under Rule 23(b)(1). See Issacharoff, *Class Action Conflicts*, 30 U.C. DAVIS L. REV. 805 (1997); Spiotto, *Exchange Offers,* in THE PROBLEMS OF INDENTURE TRUSTEES AND BONDHOLDERS 759, 770-76 (409 PLI Real Estate Law & Practice Course Handbook Series No. 4591, 1995), available at 409 PLI/Real 759 (Westlaw); Kraemer & Paige, *Consensual Workouts—Bankruptcy Alternative for the 1990s?,* in BANKING AND COMMERCIAL LENDING LAW 419 (Annual Advanced ALI-ABA Course of Study, No. R182, 1994),available at R182 ALI-ABA 419 (Westlaw); Edwards, Herbst & Hewitt, *Mandatory Class Action Lawsuits As a Restructuring Technique*, 19 PEPP. L. REV. 875 (1992). The Supreme Court has held that class certification under Rule 23(b)(1) is not proper in an asbestos injury action filed for settlement purposes where the traditional features of a "common fund" case are not present. Ortiz v. Fibreboard Corp., 527 U.S. 815, 119 S. Ct. 2295, 144 L. Ed. 2d 715 (1999). The court did not hold that such a mass tort class could never be certified under Rule 23(b)(1). But the Court did (1) catalogue numerous obstacles to such certification, (2) question whether Rule 23(b)(1) should ever be so used, and (3) note that settlement of monetary claims in a mandatory non-opt-out class action in federal court may violate the Seventh Amendment right to jury trial. For a discussion of *Ortiz*'s effect on use of class actions to resolve mass tort litigation, see Vairo, *Mass Torts Bankruptcies: The Who, the Why and the How*, 78 AM. BANKR. L.J. 93, 95-98 (2004).

The second possible exception, as implemented by attorney Lincoln Brooks, is described in LoPucki & Weyrauch, *A Theory of Legal Strategy*, 49 DUKE L.J. 1405, 1477-78 (2000). The debtor grants a security interest in all assets to the Credit Managers' Association (CMA) as trustee for all creditors, with CMA then "opposing the levy [of any creditor who attempts to seize the assets] on the novel ground that it violates the newly minted secured creditors' right to priority." Id. Audio files of an extended interview of Mr. Brooks and his partner David Caplan are available at http://www.cfo-connection.com/radio_show/pgradio_show.htm#052201 (program 14) (last visited Jan. 23, 2006). It is possible that such a scheme is fraudulent under the principles stated by Justice Cardozo in Shapiro v. Wilgus, 287 U.S. 348, 53 S. Ct. 142, 77 L. Ed. 355 (1932).

D. THE BENEFITS OF REORGANIZATION VERSUS THE BURDENS ON CREDITORS AND OTHERS

Of course, chapter 11 does not impose burdens only on the debtor. There is a question in many cases whether the burdens imposed by chapter 11 on creditors (or others) are justified by its benefits. There are several kinds of burdens imposed by chapter 11. The automatic stay forces creditors to use the collective bankruptcy process to collect their debts rather than the state law race of diligence; some creditors may see this as a burden, although others will welcome the equality provided by bankruptcy law. Property interests also are affected by the stay; the secured creditor who is prevented from foreclosing and the landlord who is prevented from evicting the delinquent debtor suffer a burden on their property rights. In this section we discuss two additional effects of bankruptcy, one that creditors may perceive as a burden even though it is not, and one that may create an actual burden.

1. Recognition of Existing Loss

Most people do not like to be forced to face the fact that they have lost money. Creditors are no exception. Chapter 11 (and other forms of bankruptcy) may force them to face that fact, and they may see that as a burden. Assume a corporation owes $1,000,000 in debts, all unsecured. Assume the corporation's assets are worth $400,000 on a going concern basis and $300,000 on a liquidation basis. In the aggregate, the creditors already have lost at least $600,000, plus the costs of negotiating a workout. If the corporation is not reorganized successfully, it will not continue as a going concern and creditors will have lost $700,000, plus the costs of liquidating the assets. Suppose the corporation files a chapter 11 petition, creditors receive $360,000 in cash or other forms of value in the reorganization, and the remaining $640,000 of debt is discharged. The creditors may feel that bankruptcy law cost them $640,000, but most or all of that money was lost with or without bankruptcy. In fact, it is difficult to say that chapter 11 created a burden on the creditors as long as they receive at least $300,000 minus the costs of liquidation, the amount they would have received if there had been a liquidation.

2. Risk of Further Losses To Creditors

The creditors could more justifiably complain of a burden if they received less than $300,000 (minus costs of liquidation) in value as a result of the attempt to reorganize. That may indeed happen if the debtor suffers further losses.

If the debtor continues to lose money after filing its chapter 11 petition, it may use up much of its assets and incur additional business debts as administrative expenses of the reorganization. Attorneys' fees and other professional fees in a chapter 11 case will also be considered administrative expenses and may consume a substantial part of the value of the debtor. If the debtor manages to reorganize, the value of the business may be less than $300,000 due to the consumption of assets. Further, the administrative expense claims will have to be paid in full, thus reducing the value available for the unsecured creditors. They may end up with much less than the amount they could have received in a prompt liquidation.

Some reorganization attempts fail. If the debtor's property ultimately is liquidated after a failed reorganization attempt, there may be few remaining assets to liquidate. Administrative expenses from the failed reorganization will be paid ahead of the prepetition unsecured debts, so there may be little or nothing left for the prepetition unsecured creditors.

The delay in payment in a chapter 11 case also causes further losses. A chapter 11 reorganization often takes much longer to consummate than does a workout, although "prepackaged" chapter 11 reorganizations sometimes can be accomplished very quickly.[16] (The procedures in chapter 11 are much more formal—and thus time-consuming—and the automatic stay reduces the debtor's sense of urgency.) The value of whatever the creditors ultimately receive will be diminished by the delay in receiving it; that diminishment is a further loss imposed by chapter 11. In our example, a liquidation would yield $300,000 (minus costs) for creditors. Creditors could insist on at least that much value in a quick out-of-court workout. During the time spent in a chapter 11 reorganization, they lose the interest or other return they could have earned on the $300,000. If the creditors have to wait a year or two or three during a chapter 11 case before receiving value, they thus will have to receive more than $300,000 to be even. The delay in receiving payment may cause some creditors to be unable to pay their own obligations, which may cause serious loss to them. (Note, however, that even chapter 7 liquidations often do not produce quick cash for creditors; a chapter 7 trustee might take several months or more to sell the assets in an orderly way and make distributions to creditors.)

Chapter 11 therefore creates a serious risk of loss to the creditors. Chapter 11 prevents creditors from forcing the liquidation of the debtor's property, thus preventing them from receiving the liquidation value of the assets. Chapter 11 allows the debtor to risk that liquidation value in an attempt to reorganize. In a sense then, chapter 11 forces the creditors to finance the reorganization venture and to bear the risk of losses from it. It might be said that the debtor is gambling with the creditors' money.[17]

---

16. For a description of an extraordinarily quick "prepack," see Elman, *Blue Bird Could Herald Quicker Prepacks*, DAILY DEAL, Feb. 10, 2006, available at 2006 WLNR 2322894 (Westlaw) (describing four-day reorganization of bus manufacturer Blue Bird Body Co.). It is not clear that the court should permit the kind of expedited process allowed in the Blue Bird case. Notice periods in Rules 2002(b), 3017(a), and 3020(b) require at least 50 days between filing of a plan and the confirmation hearing, absent a Rule 9006(c) order shortening time. Rule 3020(e) normally stays the confirmation order for ten days to provide an opportunity for a party to file a notice of appeal and seek a stay of the confirmation order.

17. Note, however, that a creditor ordinarily is not considered to have an interest in the debtor's property unless and until it obtains a lien. See Grupo Mexicano de Desarollo v. Alliance Bond Fund, 527 U.S. 308, 119 S. Ct. 1961, 144 L. Ed. 2d 319 (1999). On the other hand, under modern fraudulent transfer law, an unsecured creditor may simultaneously seek a judgment and seek to restrain or reverse a fraudulent transfer of the debtor's property; thus the unsecured creditor could be said to have some corresponding very limited interest in that property. See id. at 324 n.7, 119 S.

Because the creditors in a sense provide the financing for the attempted reorganization, the following key questions demand answers. Should the creditors or at least someone other than the debtor's managers control whether and how an attempt to reorganize is made? How can the danger of further losses be balanced against the potential benefits of reorganization? How much support from creditors should be required before a plan of reorganization can be confirmed?

Chapter 11 answers those questions in a way that does not give great comfort to creditors:

- No creditor consent is needed for the filing of a chapter 11 petition; even if none of the creditors believes the debtor can successfully reorganize, the debtor still can file a chapter 11 petition and continue to operate its business.

- The debtor's management typically continues to operate its business during the reorganization, even if it is the same management whose mismanagement caused the financial distress; the debtor is called the "debtor in possession" because the debtor stays in possession of the property of the estate unless the court orders appointment of a trustee. See §§ 1101(1), 1104(a) (including "gross mismanagement" but not simple mismanagement as a cause for appointment of a trustee), 1107(a), 1108, 1115(b).

- Indeed, even if the debtor continues to lose money during the chapter 11 case, that by itself is not a ground for dismissal of the case or for conversion to a chapter 7 liquidation as long as there is a reasonable likelihood that the business can be rehabilitated. See § 1112(b)(1) & (4)(A).

- Some creditor support is needed for confirmation of a plan of reorganization, but unanimity is not needed; in some cases a plan can be confirmed over the objection of most of the creditors. See §§ 1126(c), 1129(a)(10), 1129(b).

- The plan generally must give a dissenting creditor at least as much value as it would receive in a chapter 7 liquidation as of the effective date of the reorganization plan. See § 1129(a)(7)(A). That provides small comfort. The debtor may have suffered losses and piled up large administrative expenses during the reorganization. Thus the creditor's share of liquidation value as of the effective date of the plan may be much less than it would have been before the attempted reorganization.

- Further, the creditors may not receive what the plan provides; if the reorganized debtor again falls into financial distress, it may be unable to make the payments required by the plan, and any stock or other securities given to the creditors under the plan may turn out to be worth little or nothing. (Under § 1129(a)(11) the plan cannot be confirmed unless the court determines under a preponderance of the evidence standard that confirmation is not likely to be followed by an unplanned liquidation or the need for further financial reorganization; but the court is sometimes wrong.)

On the other hand most creditors voluntarily chose to extend credit to the debtor knowing that the debtor someday could utilize chapter 11. Most creditors chose to do so on an unsecured basis under nonbankruptcy law that

---

Ct. at 1970. Cf. Kirkeby v. Super. Ct., 33 Cal. 4th 642, 15 Cal. Rptr. 3d 805 (2004) (holding that filing of lis pendens was proper in action by unsecured creditor who sought money judgment and also sought to avoid fraudulent transfer).

affords them no rights other than the right to sue for nonpayment. They did so to make a profit. Perhaps the bankruptcy law should require them to bear some risk in an attempt to preserve jobs and rehabilitate the business.

In a more realistic case there will be not only unsecured creditors but also secured creditors. Secured creditors who are prevented from foreclosing on their collateral during an attempted reorganization also run several risks of loss. See Section E.1.a immediately below.

E. THE FOUR INGREDIENTS FOR A SUCCESSFUL REORGANIZATION IN CHAPTER 11

Four ingredients usually are needed for a chapter 11 reorganization to be successful. This book is organized around those four ingredients. Following this introductory Part I, the book is divided into four Parts:

Part II: **Keeping the Ship Afloat**

Part III: **Turning the Business Around**

Part IV: **Determining Claims by and Against the Estate**

Part V: **Restructuring the Debts and Dividing the Enterprise's Value**

Chapter 11 helps to provide each of those ingredients, but at the cost of denying various persons the rights they would have had outside of bankruptcy. In each case there is a question whether chapter 11 strikes an appropriate balance between the benefits and burdens of reorganization.

It is important for the student to keep the larger picture in mind during the course. To help the student do that, we provide the following overview of Parts II through V of this text. *We strongly urge the student to reread the relevant portions of the overview as the course moves into each Part, and to reread the entirety of this chapter several times during the course. We also strongly urge the student to reread this entire chapter at the end of the course; we believe it will prove to be very helpful to the student in integrating the material and crystallizing an understanding of it.*

1. Keeping the Ship Afloat

The first ingredient is keeping the ship afloat—keeping the business in operation. If the business ceases operations, even for a short time, key employees will be lost, and relationships with customers and suppliers will be damaged severely.

a. Preventing Disruptive Interference

To keep the ship afloat, the debtor in possession will need protection from disruptive interference with its business. Most importantly, the debtor needs protection from having its assets seized. As we have seen, the automatic stay enjoins creditors from attempting to collect their debts once the petition is filed; that includes a ban on seizure of assets. See § 362(a)(3), (4), (5). The respite from having to defend suits and respond to collection activities also allows the debtor to concentrate on reorganizing its business.

The automatic stay does not provide total protection against disruptive interference with the debtor's business. There are important questions as to the scope of the automatic stay. For example, may a supplier refuse to sell goods to the debtor on a cash basis because the debtor has not paid for goods delivered before the bankruptcy petition was filed? Does the automatic stay prevent creditors from harassing or suing the debtor's managers, who may have guaranteed the debts or may be alleged co-tortfeasors? May a bank place an administrative freeze on the debtor's bank account to protect the bank's right to set off those accounts against debts owed to the bank? There are also explicit statutory exceptions to the automatic stay. In particular there is an important exception for governmental regulatory actions; if the debtor, for example, is violating air pollution regulations, the automatic stay will not prevent the state or federal regulatory agencies from shutting down the debtor's business. Query: if the automatic stay does not provide sufficient protection for the debtor, does § 105(a) empower the court to provide additional protection?

Even if the automatic stay initially provides sufficient protection to the debtor, creditors can seek relief from the automatic stay. See § 362(d). Secured creditors often seek relief from the stay so that they can foreclose on their collateral; much of the litigation in the bankruptcy courts consists of such motions for relief from the automatic stay. In many cases the reorganization will be doomed if the court grants relief. On the other hand, if relief is not granted, the secured creditor's property rights may be damaged.

The collateral may depreciate in value. The secured party may be entitled to "adequate protection" against such a decline—see §§ 361, 362(d)(1), 363(e)—but sometimes the protection turns out to be inadequate. See § 507(b). Further, if the value of the collateral is less than or equal to the amount of the debt secured by the collateral, the secured creditor generally will not be entitled to accrue postpetition interest on the debt (although interest ultimately may have to be paid if the debtor is solvent on a liquidation basis). See §§ 502(b) (fixing amount of claim as of date of filing of petition, not including unmatured interest), 506(b) (permitting postpetition interest to accrue only to extent collateral value exceeds amount of secured debt). Outside bankruptcy the secured creditor could foreclose and then earn interest by reinvesting the foreclosure proceeds. The automatic stay deprives it of that reinvestment opportunity. The "undersecured" creditor is not entitled to postpetition interest or any other compensation for that loss. See United Sav. Ass'n v. Timbers of Inwood Forest Assocs., 484 U.S. 365, 108 S. Ct. 626, 98 L. Ed. 2d 740 (1988) (reprinted below).

The risks and costs imposed on secured creditors must be balanced against the policy of facilitating reorganization. We will see that the Code and the courts balance them by demanding good faith on the part of the debtor, by demanding (as we have seen) "adequate protection" of the secured creditor's property interest, and demanding (in some cases) that there be a reasonable possibility of a successful reorganization within a reasonable time.

Problem 1-4

Return to the continuing saga of Ernestine and her PostHaste franchise from the earlier problems in this chapter. Assume Ernestine files a chapter 11 petition. Apply § 362(a) to answer the following basic questions:

1. Is Lester Lessor entitled to evict Ernestine for nonpayment of rent?
2. Is First Bank entitled to repossess the cash register and other items of equipment in which it has a security interest?
3. Is Carl Customer entitled to have the sheriff levy on Ernestine's bank accounts or otherwise attempt to enforce his $200,000 judgment?

---

b. Finding the Cash To Continue Operations

There is one other major factor that is needed to keep the ship afloat beyond prevention of interference with the business: the business will need cash to operate. Businesses cannot be operated without cash. If workers are not paid for their continuing services, they will strike or simply leave (perhaps taking inventory or other property with them in an unlawful but understandable form of self-help wage recovery). If raw materials or inventory cannot be purchased, the business cannot continue for long. Without access to cash, the debtor cannot continue in business.

The debtor's business operations will generate some cash,[18] but there may be an obstacle in the way of the debtor using the cash. The cash often will be subject to a lien;[19] if so, it will be "cash collateral," and the debtor will not be permitted to use it unless the lienholder consents or the court authorizes its use. See § 363(a), (c)(2).

---

18. This is not to say that the debtor's operations will generate enough cash to pay all the expenses of operations; many chapter 11 debtors do not have net positive cash flow from operations, at least not at first. However, some cash should come in that can at least be used to pay part of the postpetition expenses of operations.

19. An Article 9 secured party who has a security interest in the debtor's accounts receivable and inventory will claim a lien on the cash collections from the accounts receivable and on the proceeds of sale of inventory; the cash will be "proceeds" of the accounts or of the inventory, and Article 9 gives the secured party a lien on "proceeds" of its collateral. See U.C.C. § 9-315. Similarly, real property mortgagees with mortgages on rental property (such as apartments and office buildings) typically will claim a lien on the rents under provisions in the mortgages. Section 552(b) protects these liens on proceeds and rents except to the extent the "equities of the case" otherwise require.

If the court does not authorize use of cash collateral, the business probably will not be able to continue in operation, and the reorganization will fail. If the court does authorize use of the cash collateral, the debtor in possession will spend the cash, and the business's operations might not generate enough new cash to replace it. That may result in losses to the lienholder. The question will be to what extent the law should place that risk on the lienholder in order to facilitate reorganization.

Problem 1-5

> Ernestine filed her chapter 11 petition and continued to operate her PostHaste business. She then sold stationery and other office supplies to a customer for $250 cash. First Bank had a security interest in the stationery and office supplies (which were inventory); hence, under § 552(b) and U.C.C. § 9-315, First Bank has a security interest in the $250 as proceeds of its collateral. Is Ernestine entitled to use the $250 in her business, for example to pay her utility bill or pay her employees' wages or buy more office supplies? See § 363(a) and (c)(2). Which of those uses for the $250 would help Ernestine provide adequate protection of First Bank's security interest? See § 361(2).

Access to cash collateral may be enough to keep the business operating, but in many cases the debtor needs to borrow additional cash or obtain additional credit for purchases of goods and services. No one will extend credit to a financially distressed business on a nonpriority, unsecured basis. In most cases the debtor in possession will not be able to pay prepetition creditors in full; if the new, postpetition creditors were placed on an equal footing with the prepetition creditors, then they would not be repaid in full, either. No one would willingly extend credit knowing that full repayment will not occur. Special protection for the new creditors is essential.[20] Outside of bankruptcy, the debtor could give the new creditors a security interest in unencumbered assets, or junior liens on assets that were already encumbered,[21] but there usually is not enough unencumbered asset value to secure the needed credit. A subordination agreement by some of the existing creditors might suffice; so might a guarantee of the new credit by a financially sound person (such as the debtor's principal stockholder). In many cases none of these is available, and the debtor cannot obtain the needed credit outside of chapter 11.

In chapter 11, if new credit is obtained properly, it will be considered an administrative expense (an expense of reorganizing the debtor) and will have priority over the prepetition general unsecured claims held by the other

---

20. In many cases one or more of the old creditors will be the best source of new credit. To the extent that they extend new credit, the discussion here applies to them as if they were "new creditors."

21. This often would be an event of default under existing security agreements, which would entitle the existing secured party to accelerate its debt and move against the collateral. See footnote 10, supra, this Chapter.

creditors. See § 364(a)-(b). (Note, however, that §§ 503(b)(9) and 546(c) may give administrative priority to the claim of a trade creditor who delivered goods to the debtor shortly before bankruptcy, or even allow the creditor to reclaim the goods in kind.) Each holder of an administrative expense claim is entitled to be paid in full in cash on the effective date of the chapter 11 plan of reorganization, unless it agrees otherwise. See § 1129(a)(9)(A). Even if the case is converted to a chapter 7 liquidation, the administrative expenses of the attempted reorganization will be entitled to be paid ahead of the prepetition general unsecured claims. See §§ 507(a)(2), 726(a)(1).

In effect, the prepetition unsecured creditors are involuntarily subordinated to the postpetition creditors. This helps create an incentive for the new creditors to extend credit, but it carries great risks for the prepetition creditors. The new credit may merely permit the debtor to operate at a loss for a longer time and lose even more money. Then, when the debtor's assets are finally liquidated, the new credit and all the other administrative expenses built up during that longer period of time will have to be paid in full before the prepetition unsecured creditors receive anything.[22]

If needed credit cannot be obtained by offering the new lender an administrative priority, the debtor can seek court approval to give the postpetition creditor a superpriority over all the other administrative claims. See § 364(c)(1). The debtor also can seek court approval to offer liens on unencumbered property or junior liens on already encumbered property. See § 364(c)(2)-(3). If even that is not enough to induce the potential postpetition creditor to extend credit, the debtor in possession can seek court approval to give the postpetition creditor a senior, "priming" lien on property on which prepetition creditors already have liens. See § 364(d). The subordination of existing liens by a "priming" lien given to the new lender creates a grave danger that the existing lienholders' property interests will be damaged. Again there is a question of the extent to which this risk should be placed on the existing lienholders in order to facilitate reorganization.

---

22. Eastern Airlines suffered operating losses of more than $1.5 billion from the time it filed its chapter 11 petition—in March 1989—up to the time it stopped flying—in January 1991. More than a billion dollars generated from asset sales were set aside initially in an escrow account to pay unsecured creditors, who were owed about a billion dollars. During a long and unsuccessful attempt to turn the business around, the court allowed Eastern to spend about $900 million from the escrow account to fund its continued operations. A liquidating plan was confirmed in late 1994. See O'Brian & Pae, *Judge Rebuffs Call to Liquidate Eastern Airlines*, WALL ST. J., Nov. 15, 1990, at A3; O'Brian & Pae, *Eastern Air Bid For $135 Million Cleared by Court*, WALL ST. J., Nov. 28, 1990, at A3; In re Ionosphere Clubs, Inc., 113 B.R. 164 (Bankr. S.D.N.Y. 1990); Abel v. Shugrue (In re Ionosphere Clubs, Inc.), 184 B.R. 648 (S.D.N.Y. 1995). Under the plan, holders of smaller unsecured claims received 11% of their claims in cash. Holders of larger unsecured claims were to receive between 9% and 16% over time from sale of remaining assets. *Business Brief: Eastern Air Lines: Some Creditors' Settlements Are Planned for 1st Quarter*, WALL ST. J., Dec. 23, 1994, at A4.

2. Turning the Business Around

A business "turnaround" is a necessary part of most chapter 11 cases. Management must try to cut costs, increase revenues, and otherwise deal with the problems that led to financial distress. Unprofitable divisions or product lines must be made profitable, sold, or shut down. As we have seen, if the business cannot be turned around so that there is a "positive cash flow from operations," there will be no point in trying to reorganize the debtor. The debtor's revenues from its business operations (typically the amount of its sales) must exceed what it costs the debtor to generate those revenues (not including interest or principal payments on prepetition debts). If the debtor cannot generate any extra cash even when it is not paying its debts, then there is no earning power in the business, and it is worthless as a going concern. As low as liquidation value might be, it would be more than the zero reorganization value. Reorganization would not make sense.

The business turnaround may require cash outlays, such as payments to purchase new, efficient manufacturing equipment to replace old, failing, inefficient equipment, or to purchase more inventory for the debtor's stores so that there will be something to draw customers to the stores. The cash to take those steps will need to be found. Again, the debtor in possession will look to cash collateral, and if necessary to new credit, as discussed above. If the reorganization ultimately fails, the expenditures may add little to the liquidation value of the debtor's assets, but the new debts will be paid ahead of the prepetition unsecured creditors.

As we have seen, the creditors are in effect forced to finance the reorganization attempt, because chapter 11 places on them the risk of further losses during the reorganization. Normally, the owners of an enterprise put at least some resources into the enterprise as equity capital. Creditors thus normally are protected to some extent by that equity capital, in that the enterprise will not become insolvent until it has lost all of the equity capital that the owners contributed. In effect the owners lose their equity capital before the creditors lose what they have lent. By contrast, in chapter 11, at least if the debtor is insolvent, every dollar of further loss will be at the expense of the creditors. In a sense they are thus providing the "equity capital" for the enterprise as it attempts to reorganize. Outside bankruptcy, those who provide the equity capital—the owners—typically have the right to control the enterprise, or at least to choose whether to contribute the equity capital. Should the unsecured creditors thus have some control over the reorganization, including some control over whether nonordinary course expenditures are made in the chapter 11 case?

It is true that the debtor in possession must seek court approval for nonordinary course borrowings. See § 364(b). Also, before the debtor in possession takes other nonordinary course actions, the creditors usually must be given notice and an opportunity to seek a court hearing on the proposed actions. See § 363(b)(1). However, the courts have tended to defer to the decisions of debtors in possession if the decisions result from the exercise of business judgment. The creditors may thus have little control over whether the expenditures are made.

If creditors believe the reorganization will be unsuccessful, and if the debtor is continuing to lose money, they can move to have the case dismissed or converted to a chapter 7 liquidation case. See § 1112. As a less drastic step, the creditors can ask the court to order appointment of a trustee to oust the debtor's management, which the creditors may believe is incompetent or dishonest. See § 1104(a). Creditors may prefer to have an independent trustee running the business, supervising the attempt to turn it around, and making the decision as to whether it is worth the risk to attempt to rehabilitate the business.

Some of the steps in the business turnaround may require the termination, continuation, or assignment of existing contracts and leases. Outside bankruptcy this can be impossible or very burdensome. The other party may have a right to specific performance of a contract that effectively prevents the debtor from avoiding performance. Even if an award of damages is the only remedy, the creditors' remedies that the non-breaching party can use to collect the damages will disrupt the business. The debtor may have a long term lease at a low rent on premises it no longer needs; others might pay handsomely for an assignment of the lease, but a provision in the lease may bar assignment. Alternatively the rent on the long term lease on the unneeded premises might be well above a market rate; if the debtor wishes to close that unprofitable business location, the debtor may incur enormous damages from a breach of the lease, damages so large as to dwarf the other claims. The debtor may need relief from high labor costs under a collective bargaining agreement. Finally, because of the debtor's default or for other reasons, other parties may have taken steps to terminate or may have threatened to terminate contracts or leases that are needed for the debtor's reorganization. It may be possible to handle each of these problems advantageously in chapter 11. See §§ 365 and 1113. That can help the debtor's management substantially in turning around the business. Of course, in assisting the reorganization in this way, chapter 11 denies the nondebtor parties their normal nonbankruptcy rights. Again the question is whether chapter 11 strikes an appropriate balance between the benefits of reorganization and the burdens placed on the nondebtor parties.

Problem 1-6

Assume Ernestine's financial problems stemmed from more than just the slip and fall accident. After her PostHaste business was going well, she decided to open a frozen yogurt shop next door to the PostHaste location. That was a mistake; there were already two frozen yogurt shops and three ice cream parlors in the vicinity, so Ernestine's yogurt shop had few customers. Compounding the problem, she had few repeat customers; people who did buy her yogurt generally did not like it as well as the yogurt and ice cream available elsewhere. The yogurt shop did not come close to bringing in enough money to pay the expenses of operating it, such as lease payments, utilities, and wages for the employees. Whether or not Ernestine files a chapter 11 petition, what business step should she take? Assume Ernestine did not incorporate either of her businesses but was simply a sole proprietor.

---

3. Determining Claims By and Against the Debtor

The starting point for determining claims by and against the debtor will be nonbankruptcy law. Nonbankruptcy law determines property interests and the general, substantive rights of the parties—such as whether a creditor has a lien or whether a person owes money to the debtor. See Raleigh v. Ill. Dept. of Revenue, 530 U.S. 15, 120 S. Ct. 1951, 147 L. Ed. 2d 13 (2000) (recognizing that nonbankruptcy law creates a substantive right in favor of taxing authorities when it places burden of proof on taxpayers in tax claim disputes, and thus holding that taxpayer retains burden of proof even when disputing a tax claim in taxpayer's bankruptcy). However, bankruptcy changes the procedures used to enforce those property interests and other rights, and sometimes it even changes their substance. In some cases, the litigation costs of determining the claims against the debtor are a major factor in the debtor's financial distress; the question is whether those claims can be determined efficiently in a chapter 11 case. If not, then the process of determining them may use up much of the value that otherwise could go to pay them. Always, there is the question whether bankruptcy policies justify the burdens imposed on the creditors.

The debtor typically will have claims against others when it files a petition in bankruptcy; for example, most debtors have some accounts receivable that are owed to them by their customers. Determining what debts are owed to the debtor (and collecting them) will be an important part of gathering the resources needed for the reorganization. Nonbankruptcy law will provide the rule of decision for these claims by the debtor, but bankruptcy procedures—such as nationwide service of process and the possible curtailment of jury trial rights in bankruptcy—may change important procedural rights of the defendants. See, e.g., 28 U.S.C. §§ 157, 1334(e); Rule 7004(d).

We already have seen that the filing of a bankruptcy petition will result in preference claims arising against creditors under § 547. The power to avoid preferences is one of the "avoiding powers" that may give the debtor in possession (or trustee if one is appointed or elected) claims against others, claims that do not exist under nonbankruptcy law. Other avoiding powers permit the debtor in possession to bring claims for the recovery of fraudulent transfers, for the recovery of unauthorized postpetition transfers, and for the recovery of some setoffs. See §§ 548, 544(b) (which allows the debtor in possession to assert unsecured creditors' rights under nonbankruptcy fraudulent transfer law), 549, 553. The proceeds of these avoiding power claims may provide the needed value to permit a plan to succeed. In other cases the claims provide leverage for the debtor in negotiating the plan. As we have seen, some of these provisions also advance the bankruptcy policy of equal distribution among unsecured creditors. In each case we will want to consider whether the avoiding powers change the nonbankruptcy rights of the parties more than is justified, or whether, on the other hand, the avoiding powers should be strengthened.

The avoiding powers also can operate to modify the claims that creditors have against the debtor. Creditors who have obtained liens to secure their pre-existing claims may lose those liens under the preference section; this may slightly discourage creditors from destroying the debtor's business by obtaining such liens, and it furthers the policy of equal distribution among general unsecured creditors. Creditors with statutory liens may lose them as well, under § 545, resulting in a more equal distribution to creditors. Creditors who *failed* to give public notice of their liens may lose them under the "strong arm" avoiding power found in § 544(a); creditors who *delayed* in giving public notice of their liens may lose them under an arcane part of the preference section, § 547(e). These provisions also further the policy of equal distribution in cases in which the failure to give public notice of liens may have misled other creditors.

Creditors' claims against the debtor are also modified in other ways in bankruptcy. Claims of undersecured creditors are bifurcated into secured and unsecured claims; the creditor has a secured claim equal to the lesser of the amount of the debt and the value of the collateral.[23] See § 506(a). Sometimes the lien on the collateral is effectively stripped down to the value of the collateral.[24] As we have seen, postpetition interest does not accrue on prepetition unsecured claims, see § 502(b), nor does it accrue on prepetition secured claims except to the extent that they are oversecured. See § 506(b). Defaults under loan agreements often can be cured in bankruptcy even though they could not be cured under nonbankruptcy law. See §§ 1123(a)(5)(G), 1124(2). Claims for punitive damages or for high "default interest rates" may in some cases be eliminated or subordinated to other claims. See §§ 365(b)(2)(D), 510(c). The dollar amount of claims of landlords and of employees with employment contracts is limited. See § 502(b)(6)-(7). Late filed claims may be disallowed. See § 502(b)(9).

Of course the major substantive change bankruptcy makes to claims is to discharge them. Confirmation of the plan discharges almost all of a business entity's debts, if the debtor stays in business after consummation of the plan; thus the reorganized debtor owes only the obligations set forth in the plan. See § 1141(d).[25]

---

23. As we will see, if the estate retains the collateral, § 1111(b)(2) gives the undersecured creditor an election to have the entire debt treated as secured, but the benefits of such an election are not as substantial as it might seem.

24. The Supreme Court in Dewsnup v. Timm, 502 U.S. 410, 112 S. Ct. 773, 116 L. Ed. 2d 903 (1992), held that liens could not be stripped down in chapter 7 liquidation cases absent redemption under § 722. *Dewsnup* is unlikely to affect strip down of liens in chapter 11 plans. See § 1123(b)(5) (added in 1994); Wade v. Bradford, 39 F.3d 1126, 1128-29 (10th Cir.1994).

25. Under § 1141(d)(6) (added in 2005), a few debts of a corporate debtor might not be discharged. For individual debtors—human beings—the chapter 11 discharge is not effective until sometime after confirmation of the plan, unless the court orders otherwise for cause. See § 1141(d)(5) (added in 2005). Note that an individual debtor will not receive a discharge in chapter 11 of debts that the individual could not discharge in a chapter 7 case. See §§ 523(a), 1141(d)(2).

In addition to these substantive changes in claims against the debtor, there are serious procedural changes. The automatic stay prevents creditors from taking action to collect their claims; creditors are limited to the bankruptcy claims and distribution procedure. In some cases the bankruptcy judge has the power to "estimate" a claim, rather than determining it after a full hearing. See § 502(c); 28 U.S.C. § 157(b)(2)(B), (b)(5). Jury trial rights for those with claims against the debtor are abridged, except in cases of personal injury or wrongful death. Novel approaches to determining claims have been attempted in chapter 11 cases involving mass tort liability, such as the Manville and A.H. Robins cases.[26]

Administrative claims against the estate are key claims that must be determined. Attorneys' fees often make up the bulk of the administrative claims and implicate important ethical and practical issues.

Finally, creditor misconduct can give the debtor claims against the creditors or affect their claims against the debtor. The debtor may have state law "lender liability" claims against institutional creditors on various theories, including breach of loan agreements. The debtor may also seek "equitable subordination" under § 510(c) or other remedies against creditors who have engaged in misconduct. In particular, the purchasing or selling of claims against the debtor ("trading in claims") occasionally may constitute misconduct. It may be that the way in which chapter 11 changes the rights of dissenting creditors—by permitting them to be bound to a plan of reorganization by the vote of other creditors—requires limits to be placed on trading in claims, so that votes in effect cannot be bought.

4. The Restructuring of the Debts and the Division of the Enterprise's Value

The final ingredient for a successful reorganization is that the debts must be restructured so that the debtor will be able to pay them, and the value of the reorganized debtor must be divided among the creditors and the stockholders (or other owners).

a. The Need for Restructuring of the Debts

The debtor will need to have the debts that it owes reduced or the time for payment extended, or more likely both. It will do no one any good if the debtor finishes the reorganization still owing debts that it cannot pay. In fact, it will often be to the creditors' advantage to agree to reduce their debts enough so that the

---

26. In reaction to the approaches taken in two asbestos manufacturers' cases, Manville and UNR, Congress in 1994 added subsections (g) and (h) to § 524. Subsection (g) supplements the existing authority of the court and was modeled on the Manville approach; subsection (h) is an attempt to ensure the validity of the channeling injunctions entered in the Manville and UNR cases, which require asbestos personal injury actions to be prosecuted only against the trusts set up in the plans of reorganization and not against the reorganized debtors. See Pub. L. 103-394, § 111 (1994); 140 Cong. Rec. H10765-66 (daily ed. Oct. 4, 1994) (analyzing subsections (g) and (h)).

debtor is in a good, solvent financial position; as a result, the debtor will very likely be able to pay the reduced debts as they come due. If the debts are reduced that much, the shares of stock (or other ownership interests) in the now solvent debtor will have value. The question then will be who will get those valuable shares, which will represent part of the value of the reorganized debtor.

b.   How Value Can Be Given to Creditors in the Plan of Reorganization

Creditors can receive value in an out-of-court workout or a chapter 11 reorganization in three ways. First, any cash or other property that is not needed for continuing operations can be distributed immediately to creditors when the reorganization or workout agreement is consummated. Surprisingly, debtors often are able to build up cash. Because of the moratorium or the automatic stay, the debtor will not be making payments on at least some, and perhaps most, of its prepetition debts; if the debtor has positive cash flow from operations, cash may build up. In fact, in chapter 11 a substantial amount of cash may be needed in order to put the plan of reorganization into effect; unpaid administrative expenses of the reorganization, including attorneys' and accountants' fees, will have to be paid in full on the effective date of the reorganization or shortly afterwards. However, there still may be excess cash that can be used to make some immediate payments to prepetition creditors on the effective date.[27]

Second, the workout agreement or chapter 11 plan will not wipe out completely the debts owed to the creditors; the agreement or plan will provide for debts to be owed to the creditors by the reorganized debtor, though typically in a reduced amount and with a longer time for payment. Those debts will be valuable assets owned by the creditors. The debts will represent a commitment of part of the value of the debtor's business to the creditors, since cash generated from the operations of the business will have to be used to pay interest and principal on the debts. The value of the debts to the creditors will depend on the amount of interest and principal to be paid, the payment schedule, the risk that the debtor may fail to make the payments, and whether the debts are secured. The concept of the time value of money requires that the future payments be discounted by an appropriate yearly discount rate. For example, if in the reorganization or workout a particular creditor receives a thirty-year unsecured promissory note for $1000, with 2% interest payable each year and the entire principle payable at the end of the thirty years, the debt's value will much less than its face value, because the appropriate discount rate will be much more than the note's 2% interest rate. If in addition the debtor is not financially sound even after the reorganization, the value of the debt will be even less, because the risk of nonpayment will increase the appropriate discount rate.

---

27.   If the debtor does not have enough cash to make the needed payments on the effective date, it may be able to borrow it. See Chapter Four.

Third, the creditors can be given shares of stock (or other kinds of ownership interests) in the reorganized debtor, which will have value, assuming the debts were reduced enough to make the debtor solvent.[28] Near the end of this introductory chapter we discuss how the value of the shares can be determined.

c. Determining the Value to which Creditors Are Entitled—Liquidation Value vs. Reorganization Value

When value is given out in the plan of reorganization, a key question will be how much of the debtor's reorganization (going concern) value the creditors are entitled to receive. Chapter 11's approach to this question is based to some extent on the nonbankruptcy rights of the parties and on the way those rights could be exercised in an out-of-court workout.

As we have seen, dissenting creditors generally cannot be bound against their will to take less than full cash payment in satisfaction of their debts outside of bankruptcy. If some creditors refuse to take less than full cash payment, then the other creditors likely will refuse, as well, being unwilling to make sacrifices for the reorganization unless all or almost all creditors share the burden. The dissenting creditors are entitled to demand full payment, even if that prevents out-of-court reorganization. If there were no chapter 11, liquidation would result. In liquidation, creditors would receive payment ahead of stockholders (or other owners) out of the value of the debtor's assets. That follows from a basic corporation law principle: creditors are entitled to the value of a company ahead of owners, such as stockholders.[29] The creditors have first claim to the liquidation value of a corporation's assets, ahead of the stockholders, who, as equity owners, have the residual rights to the corporation's liquidation value if it exceeds the creditors' claims.

On the other hand, if in a workout the creditors refuse to agree to reduce the debts sufficiently or if they demand too much of the stock of the debtor in exchange for reducing their debts, then the debtor's management, acting on behalf of the existing stockholders, can refuse to consent to an out-of-court workout agreement. (The stockholders themselves may even have the right to vote on whether stock will be issued to the creditors; the agreement may call for issuance of more shares than are authorized in the corporation's articles, requiring a shareholder vote to amend the articles.) Thus either dissenting creditors or dissenting stockholders may be able to prevent a workout from succeeding and therefore force a liquidation of the business. In fact, the

---

28. A plan that would leave the reorganized debtor insolvent is not feasible and should not be confirmed, because there would likely be need for further reorganization. See § 1129(a)(11).

29. For simplicity, we refer in general simply to stockholders in the remainder of this section 4.c. A similar analysis would apply to partners (as owners of a partnership) and to "members" (as owners of a limited liability company).

debtor's managers—with approval of the shareholders—usually can choose to liquidate the debtor. Apart from the bankruptcy laws,[30] the creditors cannot prevent a liquidation. (However, if a corporate debtor is insolvent, its officers and directors may owe fiduciary duties to the creditors, which would prevent them from liquidating the debtor simply to spite the creditors.)

Outside of bankruptcy, then, neither the creditors nor the stockholders nor the debtor's management are absolutely entitled to keep the business in operation and preserve the going concern value of the debtor. Creditors are entitled to the entire value that can be obtained from the debtor's assets in a liquidation (if all of it is needed to pay their claims), so they are entitled to the full liquidation value of the debtor. However, if the debtor is reorganized, and if the reorganization value exceeds the liquidation value, then what should happen to the excess value? In other words, the creditors should at least get the liquidation value (if all of it is needed to pay their claims), but who should get the rest, the difference between the liquidation value and the reorganization value? Neither creditors alone nor stockholders alone have any entitlement to that excess value outside of chapter 11, so who should get it in chapter 11? Further, how does chapter 11 assure that creditors receive at least the liquidation value they could obtain outside bankruptcy?

Initially, at least, chapter 11 leaves the result up to negotiations among the parties. The negotiations occur under ground rules for the eventual confirmation of the plan that are designed to give creditors and stockholders (directly and through the debtor's management) appropriate bargaining power. Thus, how the debtor's value is divided is determined in the first instance by negotiations. Typically the debtor's management negotiates with a committee made up of unsecured creditors, see §§ 1102, 1103, and with the major secured creditors; sometimes there are several committees of unsecured creditors, and occasionally there are one or more committees of stockholders (or other owners, such as limited partners).

Under chapter 11, a plan of reorganization can be confirmed without unanimous creditor or stockholder support, and the confirmed plan will bind all the creditors and stockholders, including those who opposed it. The debtor can file a plan without negotiating with creditors, but some creditor support generally will be needed for confirmation. Thus chapter 11 plans are usually the result of negotiations; to that extent the process of formulating the chapter 11 plan is like the formulation of an out-of-court workout agreement. The dynamics of the negotiations are, however, very different. The negotiations likely will result in the

---

30. If the debtor attempts to liquidate outside bankruptcy, the creditors could try to prevent the liquidation by filing an involuntary chapter 11 petition against the debtor. See § 303. If the debtor files a chapter 7 petition seeking liquidation in bankruptcy, the creditors could move to convert the case to chapter 11. See § 706(b).

successful confirmation of the plan in chapter 11 if *most* of the interested parties can come to agreement, since neither unanimous creditor support nor, in many cases, substantial stockholder support is needed. That makes the negotiations much easier to conclude and takes away much of the leverage that assertive individual creditors would have in an out-of-court workout.

A key factor in the negotiations is that, for a period of time (usually at least 120 days but not more than twenty months), the debtor has the exclusive right to file a proposed plan of reorganization. See § 1121 (as amended by the 2005 BAPCPA to incorporate twenty month limit). This "exclusivity" gives the debtor some leverage in negotiations, since the creditors must either come to agreement with the debtor or face delay. The automatic stay protects the debtor during the negotiations, so the debtor does not have the fear that is always present during workout negotiations, that the moratorium will break down if negotiations do not proceed swiftly. However, "exclusivity" must end no later than twenty months from the petition date; when it ends, any party can file a plan (unless the debtor already has confirmed a plan). The debtor is not supposed to be able to say to creditors, "Accept this plan or there will be no reorganization." Thus, the debtor's leverage is limited.

Any plan that is proposed must place the creditors' claims into classes and state, for each class, what the creditors will receive on account of those claims. See § 1123(a)(1)-(3). Similarly, the proposed plan must place the interests of stockholders (or other owners) into classes of "interests," and state what, if anything, they will receive on account of those interests. Id. No claim or interest can be put into a class with any other claim or interest that is not substantially similar to it, see § 1122(a),[31] because the creditors and interest holders will vote on the plan by classes; the vote of a class should represent the collective decision of a group of creditors or stockholders with similar entitlements. However, the statute does not require that all substantially similar claims be put in the same class; most courts give the drafter of the plan some discretion to separate substantially similar claims into two or more classes if there is a legitimate reason for doing so.

A class of creditors' claims accepts a plan if the holders of two thirds in amount and over one half in number of the claims (out of the claims that are voted) vote to accept the plan. See § 1126(c). A class of stockholders' interests accepts a plan if holders of two thirds in amount (out of the stock that is voted) vote to accept the plan. See § 1126(d).

It is easiest to have the plan confirmed if all classes accept the plan; it will be a "consensual plan," which needs to meet the requirements only of § 1129(a). If not all classes accept, the plan still may be confirmed in a

---

31. Section 1122(b) provides an exception to this rule; it permits small claims to be classified together for administrative convenience even if they are dissimilar.

"cramdown" if the requirements of *both* § 1129(a)—except for § 1129(a)(8)—*and* § 1129(b) are met. Generally, in either case, the plan cannot be confirmed unless at least one class of claims accepts the plan *not counting the acceptances of "insiders"* such as directors, officers, controlling stockholders, their relatives, and affiliated corporations who may hold claims against the debtor. See §§ 101(31), 1129(a)(10).[32] This last requirement is designed to ensure that the plan has at least some support from "disinterested" creditors—that is, creditors who will likely accept or reject the plan on the basis of what is best for them as creditors.[33] An insider, such as a major stockholder in the debtor who also lent money to the debtor, may vote the resulting claim in favor of the plan not because the plan is in the best interest of the insider as a creditor, but because it is in the insider's best interest as a stockholder.

The debtor might be tempted to engage in "gerrymandering" of the classes created by its plan. The debtor will try to place the claims in classes in such a way that a sufficient majority in each class will support the plan; the debtor will want to be sure, however, that there is a sufficient noninsider majority in at least one class of claims. Most courts restrict such gerrymandering, at least if it obviously is done for the purpose of satisfying § 1129(a)(10). Debtors usually are able to give other reasons for their classification schemes, which often will be accepted by the courts. The requirement that at least one class of claims accept the plan *not counting the acceptances of insiders* places some limit on the most effective form of gerrymandering: the strategic placement of insiders' claims in classes. Insiders' claims still can be placed strategically in various classes to affect the outcome in each class, so long as one class of claims can be constructed that will accept the plan not counting insiders' acceptances.

The debtor's ability to gerrymander the classes adds to the negotiating leverage that the exclusivity period gives the debtor. Obviously, it reduces to some extent the negotiating leverage of creditors; their threats to vote against the plan have reduced force due to the debtor's ability to construct the classes in the plan proposed by the debtor.

Of course chapter 11 provides protections for dissenting creditors and interest holders beyond their right merely to engage in negotiations over the plan. In fact, the negotiating leverage of creditors and interest holders comes in large part from the protections they receive if they dissent. Thus, even if

---

32. The class that accepts not counting acceptances by insiders must be an "impaired" class of claims, if there is at least one "impaired" class of claims. As we discuss more fully in Chapter Eleven of this text, a class is impaired unless the rights of holders of claims in the class are left untouched or nearly untouched. See § 1124. Of course, if no class of claims is impaired, then there is no need to obtain acceptance of an impaired class of claims. See § 1129(a)(10).

33. Note that here we are not using the term "disinterested" as it is used in the definition of "disinterested person" in § 101(14), though the usages are related.

a plan ultimately may be confirmed with little or no dissent, the negotiations over the terms of the plan will be dominated by the rights that the parties are guaranteed if they dissent.

The extent of the protections for dissenters depends on the breadth of the dissent. If a dissenter votes against the plan, but the dissenter's class accepts the plan, then confirmation of the plan rather than liquidation is probably in the economic interest of all the class members; at least, most of the class members holding most of the debt (out of those who bothered to vote) think so. As added insurance, however, chapter 11 imposes what is called the "best interests" test: the value to be received under the plan by a dissenter (with a claim in an impaired class[34]) must equal at least what the dissenter would receive if the debtor were liquidated in a chapter 7 case on the effective date of the plan. See § 1129(a)(7). If the test is met, then the plan can be confirmed despite the dissenter's objection. The dissenter will then be at least no worse off under the plan than the dissenter would be if reorganization were blocked and the debtor were liquidated.[35] If the "best interests" test is not met, then the plan cannot be confirmed even if there is only one dissenter with respect to whom the test is not met. This guarantees at least that the bankruptcy judge believes dissenters will obtain the liquidation value that is their right.

On the other hand, if an impaired *class* does not accept the plan, then there is likely either significant collective dissent or dissent by a holder of a major claim or interest. Then it is not a case of a few obstructive dissenters with relatively small claims or interests trying to block a reorganization that similarly situated creditors or interest holders in general find acceptable. A forced reorganization under the proposed plan (a "cramdown") may then do too much violence to the rights that the dissenting class would have outside of bankruptcy. Chapter 11 therefore sets two requirements (in addition to the "best interests" test) that then must be met for the plan to be confirmed in a cramdown. First, the plan must be "fair and equitable" with respect to the dissenting class or classes. Second, the plan must not "unfairly discriminate" against the dissenting class or classes in favor of other classes. See § 1129(b).

---

34. See footnote 32, supra, and Chapter Eleven of this text for the meaning of "impaired."

35. This is not to say that the dissenting creditor must receive an amount equal to what it would have received had the debtor's assets been liquidated promptly at the beginning of the case. See section D.2. of this chapter. Note also that the best interests test does not require that the plan be the best one possible from the dissenter's point of view or require that the dissenter receive full value equal to the amount of the debt. The major reason for reorganizing a debtor is to avoid the diminution in value of its assets that would occur in a liquidation. Because only the debtor can propose a plan during the exclusivity period, creditors may be faced with voting for a plan that is better than liquidation would be, but that is not as good for them as some other plan might be. Creditors may decide to vote for the debtor's plan rather than wait and hope that eventually a better plan might be brought forward. This is part of the leverage that exclusivity gives to the debtor.

The requirement that the plan not unfairly discriminate against the dissenting class probably means that the dissenting class must receive value approximately equal to the same percentage of its claims as other classes whose claims have equal priority. Whether deviation from that principle of equality can ever be justified, and thus not be "unfair" discrimination, is the subject of some controversy. See Chapter Fifteen below, and Markell, *A New Perspective on Unfair Discrimination in Chapter 11*, 72 AM. BANKR. L.J. 227 (1998).

However, it is in the "fair and equitable" requirement—with respect to dissenting classes of general unsecured claims—that chapter 11 answers the large question left unanswered above: if negotiations fail to allocate it, who will receive the excess of the going concern value of the reorganized debtor over its liquidation value? Here chapter 11 comes down on the side of the holders of claims in a dissenting class. In the end, when negotiations fail, the theory of chapter 11 is that holders of claims in a dissenting class are entitled to the full going concern value of the debtor company ahead of the stockholders (or other interest holders), including the excess of reorganization value over liquidation value, if that much is needed to provide them with full repayment. Thus chapter 11's "fair and equitable" standard is an absolute priority rule in favor of dissenting classes of general unsecured claims.

Section 1129(b)(2)(B) explains the treatment that a dissenting class of general unsecured claims must receive under the fair and equitable requirement. The plan must treat the class in one of two ways. The plan can give the holders of claims in the dissenting class property (which can include stock in the reorganized debtor) with a present value equal to the full amount of their claims—a kind of full payment. If that is not done, the plan *must* provide that holders of claims in classes "junior" to the dissenting class neither retain nor receive anything at all—no cash, no promissory notes, no stock—on account of their junior claims or interests. Those junior classes typically would include classes of claims held by creditors who agreed to subordinate their debt to the dissenting class's debt (e.g., subordinated notes or debentures), any classes of preferred stockholders' interests, and the class of common stockholders' interests.

One important result is that if there is a dissenting class of general unsecured claims that will not receive value equal to 100% of its claims, then the debtor's stockholders (or other interest holders) will receive nothing on account of their interests; their stock will be canceled, and they will cease to have any ownership interest in the company. As we will see, however, some courts have permitted interest holders in such cases to receive some or all of the ownership of the reorganized debtor, not "on account of" their prior ownership interests, but on account of a contribution of new value. The Supreme Court has hinted that this is permissible under strict conditions, but the law on this matter is still unclear.[36]

---

36. See Bank of Am. Nat'l Trust and Sav. Ass'n v. 203 North LaSalle St. P'ship, 526 U.S. 434, 119 S. Ct. 1411, 143 L. Ed. 2d 607 (1999), reprinted in Chapter Fifteen below.

Section 1129(b)(2)(A)(i) explains the treatment that a dissenting class of *secured* claims usually must receive under the fair and equitable requirement if the debtor retains the collateral. The plan must let the holders of claims in the dissenting class keep their liens for the amount of their secured claims and must provide for them to receive cash payments that have a present value equal (in the usual case) to the amount of their secured claims.[37] Note that under § 1129(b)(2)(A)(i) a dissenting class of secured claims is entitled to monetary payment and cannot be forced to take stock in the debtor or other property as part of the value received for purposes of the fair and equitable requirement. However, under § 1129(b)(2)(A)(iii) there is an alternative way to satisfy the fair and equitable standard with respect to a dissenting class of secured claims: the plan may provide for the "realization" by the secured claim holders of the "indubitable equivalent" of their claims. As strong as that language sounds, its vagueness creates uncertainty in the rights of secured creditors. See Chapter Fifteen, section A.2.a.(2).

> d. Determining the Value of the Debtor and of Property Distributed Under the Plan

> *(1) Why Valuation Is Critical*

Valuation issues are critically important in chapter 11. Suppose that, under the proposed plan of reorganization for a debtor, creditors with general unsecured claims in a certain class (say, Class V) are to receive the following property for each $100 of claims: $10 cash, a $20 five-year promissory note, and one share of common stock in the reorganized debtor. Suppose creditors with general unsecured claims in Class VI are to receive $5 cash and a $30 ten-year promissory note, but no stock, for each $100 of claims. Consider the number of valuation questions that may have to be answered.

First, suppose a creditor with a claim in Class V dissents. The "best interests" test will require the court to determine how much value the creditor would receive on account of the claim in a liquidation,[38] determine how much

---

37. The language of § 1129(b)(2)(A)(i)(II) is complex because of the possibility that the class will make the § 1111(b)(2) election. If the class makes the § 1111(b)(2) election then a holder of an undersecured claim in the class will be considered to have an allowed secured claim for the entire amount of its debt, rather than just for the value of its collateral, which is the usual allowed amount under § 506(a). In a cramdown, despite the election, the secured creditor still is entitled only to present value equal to the value of its collateral; it is, however, entitled to receive payments over time totaling at least the amount of its debt. See Chapter Fifteen of this text.

38. To determine what the creditor would receive in a liquidation for each $100 of claim, the court will have to determine the liquidation value of the debtor's assets, subtract the amount of any valid liens and of any priority claims, and divide the remaining amount by the total amount of general unsecured claims. That will yield a percentage that would be paid on unsecured claims in a liquidation. (If, for example, the liquidation value minus liens and priority claims is $250,000, and total general unsecured claims are $1,000,000, then dividing the two yields a payment percentage of 25%. The creditor therefore would receive $25 in a liquidation for each $100 of allowed general unsecured claim.)

value the creditor will receive on account of the claim under the plan (including the value of the note and stock),[39] and compare the two values to ensure that the creditor receives at least as much under the plan as in a liquidation.

Second, suppose Class V rejects the plan, but Class VI accepts it. The plan can be confirmed only if it does not unfairly discriminate against Class V. Assuming the two classes are of equal priority (neither one subordinate to the other) that probably means that holders of claims in Class V must at least receive approximately the same percentage repayment that holders of claims in Class VI will receive. To determine whether that standard is met, the court will have to determine the value of the $20 five-year promissory notes, the value of the $30 ten-year promissory notes, and the value of the shares of common stock.

Third, suppose again that Class V rejects the plan and that Class VI accepts it, but now suppose that Class V is senior to Class VI. (For example, the holders of claims in Class VI may be the owners of "subordinated debentures"—long term unsecured debt securities issued by the debtor, which, according to their terms, are subordinated to some or all of the debtor's other debts. Debentures often are subordinate to "institutional debt" but not to trade debt. In this case we assume the Class V claims are claims of institutional creditors such as banks and finance companies, and that the Class VI claims of the debentureholders are thus subordinated to the Class V claims by agreement between the debtor and the debentureholders.) Now, under the fair and equitable standard, the plan cannot be confirmed unless the plan either (1) gives holders of claims in Class V value equal to 100% of their claims, or else (2) gives the holders of claims in Class VI (and holders of claims in all other junior classes) nothing. Here the plan gives something to the junior Class VI, and thus the plan cannot be confirmed unless the property received by holders of claims in Class V for each $100 of claim—the $10 cash, the $20 promissory note, and the share of stock—is worth at least $100. Once again the court will have to determine the value of the promissory note and of the common stock to determine whether the plan can be confirmed.[40]

---

39. To determine how much value the creditor will receive under the plan for each $100 of claim, the court will have to determine what the $20 promissory note is worth and what the share of stock is worth. If the promissory note carries a fair market interest rate, it will be worth its face value, $20. If it carries a below market interest rate, it will be worth less than $20, and its value can be calculated, as we explain below. Also as we explain below, in order to determine the value of one share of common stock, the court will need to determine the reorganization value (also called the going concern value) of the debtor, then subtract the present value of all of the debt that the reorganized debtor will have, and then divide by the total number of shares that will be outstanding.

40. There also may be a question whether holders of claims in Class V are entitled under the fair and equitable requirement or under § 510(b) to receive full payment *including postpetition interest* before the holders of claims in Class VI are entitled to receive anything. Another serious question is whether, under the terms of the plan, the senior class (Class V) is treated fairly and equitably where it is forced to take the risk of owning common stock but the junior class (Class VI) is not forced to take that risk. The stock to be received by holders of claims in Class V would be junior to the $30

Of course the negotiations of the parties will be influenced by the power of the debtor to have a plan confirmed over the dissent of creditors, just as it will be influenced by the creditors' ability to block a plan that does not meet the legal standards. Thus the parties will need the best valuation information they can get to help them determine their negotiating positions. Beyond the question of legal requirements, the creditors need valuation information to decide whether to accept or reject a proposed plan. A creditor with a claim in Class V will need to know what the share of common stock will be worth to know how much value it will receive under the plan. Obviously the creditor will be more likely to accept the plan if the share of stock will be worth $50 than if it will be worth only $2. The creditor will also want to know what it would get in a liquidation of the debtor's assets; if liquidation would give the creditor as much or nearly as much value as the plan would give, then the creditor will likely prefer to receive cash in a liquidation rather than to be subject to the delays and future uncertainties involved in owning a five year promissory note and common stock. Finally, the creditor will want to know what the reorganization value of the debtor is. If the reorganization value is $80 million and the total debts are $100 million, all unsecured, the creditor might well support a plan that gave it and other creditors value equal to 75% of their claims (thus leaving something, but not too much, for the old stockholders). The creditor probably would balk at a plan that gave it only a 50% recovery.

Thus valuation issues are critically important.[41]

(2) The Valuation Process

The basic principle of valuation is that the reorganization value of the debtor's business depends on its earning power, on the amount of cash that it will be able to generate in excess of its operating expenses. To the extent the debtor can generate such excess cash, there will be value that can be given out to the parties.

An analogy to liquidation value is helpful. It is easy to see how the liquidation value of a debtor's assets can be determined and then distributed in a chapter 7 liquidation; the liquidation creates a one-time pool of money (received from sale of the debtor's assets) that simply is used to pay the costs of administration of the chapter 7 case and then divided among the creditors,

---

promissory notes to be received by the holders of claims in Class VI. Section 1129(b)(2) does not expressly prohibit this arrangement, but that does not mean that it is fair and equitable. The fair and equitable requirement "includes" the requirements of § 1129(b)(2) but is not limited to them. See §§ 102(3), 1129(b)(1)-(2). And finally there is a question whether the plan could provide less than 100% value to Class V claimholders and still be fair and equitable, if the Class V claimholders retain their state law rights to sue the Class VI claimholders under the subordination agreement.

41. It is also often critically important to be able to determine a value for an individual asset, when the asset is subject to a lien. As noted above, under § 506(a) a secured creditor ordinarily has an allowable secured claim to the extent of the lesser of the amount of the debt or the value of the collateral, and an allowable unsecured claim for the rest of the debt. Thus, the valuation of the collateral determines the amount of secured and unsecured claims.

all by application of the rules in § 726. In the beginning it may be harder for the student to see how the reorganization value of a going business can be determined and distributed, but it is actually fairly simple. If the debtor's assets are not going to be sold, then the debtor will use its assets to make money year after year. Instead of a one-time pool of money, a pool of money is created each year, which can be distributed;[42] the reorganization value of the debtor lies precisely in those yearly pools of available cash. In order to distribute the reorganization value of the debtor, we simply need to find a way to allocate that future cash among the existing creditors and stockholders. To determine the reorganization value, we must find a way to determine the total value of a series of yearly cash amounts.

Allocation of the future cash is handled by the chapter 11 plan of reorganization. Most plans allocate the cash in two ways. First, they provide that the creditors will receive scheduled payments in the future; often this is done by providing that the creditors will receive promissory notes or other debt instruments payable by the reorganized debtor. As a result, the creditors who were owed money before the reorganization will end up again as creditors of the reorganized debtor (although typically with a reduced amount owed to them). Second, the plan of reorganization typically will provide that the creditors will receive shares of stock (or other ownership interests) in the debtor. The plan also may allocate some of the future cash to the existing stockholders of the debtor by providing for them to receive shares in the reorganized debtor. Through dividends, or in other ways, the owners of the stock in the reorganized debtor will share in the future cash flows.

To determine the value of the yearly cash flows, it may be helpful to think about the assets of an operating business as the contents of a sealed box. Imagine a box that has two slots, one marked "cash in," and one marked "cash out." Consider Acme, a shoe manufacturer that pays out $10 per pair of shoes for the raw materials, labor, rent, utilities, and other expenses necessary to make and sell a pair of shoes. Assume Acme has enough cash at present to operate its business, but no excess cash and no other excess assets. Acme's assets can be considered as the contents of a box with the following characteristics: (1) when you put $10 in the "cash in" slot, a certain amount of money comes out of the "cash out" slot; (2) the box is capable of being operated a certain number of times each year, so that the cycle of putting the $10 in and getting some cash out can occur that many times each year; and (3) a few $10 bills are in an envelope attached to the box.

---

42. Instead of being distributed directly, some of the excess cash may be reinvested in the business so that the business will generate more cash in the future than previously projected. The expectation of future cash flow will make the shares of stock more valuable. That will increase the wealth of whoever owns the stock, without any cash being given directly to the owners. Thus, the cash flow does not have to be distributed directly for its value to be given to the stockholders.

What is the value of the box? In other words, what would an investor pay for the box? That depends on how much money comes out of the "cash out" slot for each $10 put in the "cash in" slot and on how many times per year the box can be operated—how many times per year it can go through the cycle of taking in a $10 bill and ejecting cash.

Suppose the best price Acme can get on sale of its shoes is $9.50 per pair, and that Acme can make 10,000 pairs per year. What would an investor pay for a box that takes in and consumes $10 and in return ejects $9.50 for the investor 10,000 times during the year? An investor would pay nothing if the investor had to leave the box sealed and had to operate it. Every cycle of the box would use up 50 cents of the money in the envelope. Soon that money would be gone, and the owner would have to use other money to keep the box operating. The only value of the box would be for the investor to open it quickly, sell off its contents, and pocket any money that might still be in the envelope. Similarly, Acme's assets would be worthless as a going concern, and would have no reorganization value (at least no positive value).[43] Of course the equipment and raw materials and other assets could be sold off for some amount of money; if there were any cash in Acme's bank account (the "envelope" attached to the box), that would add to the total in the liquidation. Thus the only value of the assets would be their liquidation value. It would make no sense to try to reorganize Acme, since the only valuable use of its assets is in a liquidation. In fact, a business cannot be successfully reorganized if it cannot bring in enough revenues to pay for its operating costs. Even if the business is relieved of all of its debts it eventually will run up more debts, and be unable to pay them.

It may be that with better management or with an infusion of cash, Acme can take steps to cut its costs or to increase the price it receives for its product, so that its revenues will more than cover its operating costs. If Acme may succeed in such a business "turn around," the assets may have a going concern value, and an attempt to reorganize may make sense.

Suppose that Acme cuts its costs of operation to $8.50 per pair of shoes, based upon manufacture and sale of 10,000 pairs per year, which it can sell for $9.50 per pair. Suppose that likely will continue for the foreseeable future, although with some "ups" and some "downs." Acme's average cash flow from operations will be a dollar per pair of shoes, for a total of $10,000 per year ($1 times 10,000 pairs of shoes).[44]

---

43. The owner of a business that efficiently produced leather and other shoe manufacturing raw materials, and that thus could provide the needed resources for Acme's business at a cost of less than $9.50 per pair, might, however, be interested in acquiring Acme as a going concern. That would give the new owner a "captive market" for its products and would create a vertically integrated manufacturing enterprise.

44. Of course the shoe stitching machinery and the other equipment eventually will wear out and have to be replaced. Each year, therefore, to maintain its capacity and efficiency, Acme will probably have to replace some of its equipment. Therefore some amount of the cash generated from

Think of Acme's assets again as a sealed box. What would you pay for a box that, on average, would give you $10,000 per year?

The amount you would pay for the box would depend on the rate of return that you would demand on your investment. Assume you can get at least a 4% return on government bonds, a much safer investment than money invested in a shoe manufacturer. (After all, you do not *know* that you will receive $10,000 each year if you buy the shoe manufacturer's assets, although that is your expectation for an average year. You might do better and you might do worse; typically investors demand a higher rate of return when the outcome is less predictable, because most investors are *risk averse*.) Thus you will ask for more than a 4% return. You will compare the investment in the shoe manufacturer's assets with other investments you could make, and you will not settle for a lower rate of return than what you could get from other investments that involve a similar risk.

Suppose you decide that you will not settle for less than a 20% return (before taxes) each year on your investment in Acme's assets; what would you be willing to pay for those assets? If you believe that the assets will give you average net cash flow of $10,000 per year for the foreseeable future, then you would be willing to pay $50,000 for the assets. Then you would expect to make an average of $10,000 per year on your $50,000 investment, which is the 20% return (before taxes) that you demanded.[45]

Note that this assumes that Acme will continue to have the same cash flow year after year. However, a debtor coming out of chapter 11 may be able to do better each year for the first few years. As time goes on, the debtor will regain more of the confidence of its customers, and the "stain" of having been in chapter 11 will fade. Or for other reasons we may anticipate that the reorganized debtor's

---

sale of the shoes will have to go to equipment replacement to maintain Acme's cash generating abilities. That amount of "capital expenditure" will have to be subtracted from the $10,000 per year to determine how much net cash is actually available to be paid out to the investor. For simplicity, the example in the text assumes that no capital expenditures will be needed.

In the real world, businesses start with what they paid for an item of equipment and allocate part of that amount each year as an "expense" of using the equipment. That expense is called "depreciation." For purposes of figuring out the business's profits for a year, depreciation is treated as an expense, just as payment of wages to employees is treated as a expense; all the business's expenses are subtracted from its revenues to come up with a profit figure. See Appendix A at the end of this text. Depreciation expense does not require the business to expend any more cash; all the cash needed to buy the equipment was spent when it was first purchased. Eventually, though, the equipment will have to be replaced (unless the business reduces its operations), which will use up cash. A buyer of the business would take into account that need to spend cash in the future in deciding how much the business is worth.

45. In the example, it is possible to "eyeball" the problem and figure out that a 20% return is one fifth per year, so the value of the business must be five times the yearly payout, or $50,000. In other cases a formula is helpful. In general, if an investment will pay P dollars per year in perpetuity (with the first payment being made one year from today), and if the investor demands a return of r percent per year on the investment, then the investment is worth P divided by r and then multiplied by 100. In the example, X is $10,000, and r is 20; thus the value of the business to the investor is $10,000 divided by 20 and then multiplied times 100, which equals 500 times 100, which equals $50,000. If r is expressed as a decimal instead of as a whole number (e.g., .20 instead of 20), then the formula is simply P divided by r. Note that $10,000 divided by .20 equals $50,000.

cash flows will increase over time. Thus we need more sophisticated methods of giving a value to the cash that the debtor will generate, methods that can take into account the projected increase in cash flows. Earlier years may be more important, because the longer the investor will have to wait to receive cash, the greater the discount due to the time value of money. However, larger cash flows in later years can have a substantial effect on the value of the business. We discuss more sophisticated methods of valuation in Chapter Twelve.

Now we can compare the liquidation value to going concern value. As a going concern, the assets are worth $50,000, if investors will demand a 20% rate of return. Suppose an appraisal shows that the assets would probably sell in a liquidation for $30,000. The going concern value then would be greater than the liquidation value. (Presumably this would be due to the time and money Acme's owners put into assembling the assets, training the workers, building good relations with customers and suppliers, and developing a good reputation for the company's shoes.) It would make no sense to liquidate the company, when that would destroy $20,000 of the assets' value along with the employees' jobs.

If the value of the cash that will be generated by the debtor is $50,000, then that is the value of the debtor's assets as a going concern, and that is the total amount of value that can be given out in the plan in the form of stock in the reorganized debtor and debts to be owed by the reorganized debtor.[46] You can understand that, if you consider that the value of the stock in the reorganized debtor and the value of the debts to be owed by the reorganized debtor depend on the amount of cash Acme can generate in the future. Acme's future cash flows will be used to make interest and principal payments on debts of the reorganized debtor and to pay dividends or in some other way give value to the reorganized debtor's stockholders. Imagine that a person bought all the debts of the reorganized Acme and all its stock; that person then would get all of Acme's future cash flows. Since those cash flows are worth $50,000, the person likely would pay $50,000 for all the debts and stock of the debtor. *That means that the total value of all the debts and stock of the reorganized debtor equals $50,000, the value of the cash flows.[47]*

---

46. If the debtor has built up unencumbered surplus cash during the reorganization—cash beyond the amount needed to run its business and beyond the amount that must be paid to holders of administrative expense claims on the effective date of the plan—then the debtor can give out some cash to creditors in its plan of reorganization. Similarly, if the debtor has surplus assets—such as equipment that it does not need—the assets can be sold to generate cash to give to creditors.

47. We make the assumption that the total value of the debts and the stock is the same whether they are all owned by the same person or are owned by many different people. Thus, we assume that if an investor would pay $50,000 for all of the debt and stock, the total value of the debt and stock is $50,000, whether or not it is all owned by one person. Consider the result if the total value of the debt and stock were less than $50,000 simply because many different people owned the debts and the stock. A smart investor would buy all the debts and all the stock, paying less than $50,000, would end up with $50,000 in value, and would have made a profit. We do not observe many cases in which investors buy up all the stock *and* all the debts of companies. That is some indication that they are not worth less simply because they are not all owned by the same person.

Using that principle, we can determine the value of Acme's stock. If the reorganized Acme will end up owing $35,000 in debts, then the stock will be worth $15,000, because the value of the debts and the value of the stock must total $50,000. That does assume something; it assumes that the $35,000 in debts is worth $35,000. (Remember we have determined that an investor would pay a total of $50,000 for all of the stock and all of the debts; if an investor would pay less than $35,000 for the debts alone, then the stock is worth more than $15,000.) If the interest rate on the debts is lower than a fair market rate, given the risk and the length of time before payment, then the debts will not be worth $35,000. Suppose the interest rate is so low that an investor would only pay $33,000 for the $35,000 in face amount of the debts; if so, the stock in the debtor should be worth $17,000, because the value of the stock and debts together should be $50,000. If the interest rate is an above-market rate, so that the debts are worth $40,000 instead of their face amount of $35,000, the stock will be worth $10,000.

This is just common sense. A company that pays a higher rate of interest on its debts has less cash left to benefit the stockholders. Thus the stock is not as valuable. A company that pays a lower interest rate on its debts has more cash for the stockholders. Thus the stock is more valuable.[48]

Therefore, if we can determine Acme's total reorganization value, and if we can determine the value of the debt that Acme will have after reorganization, we can determine the value of Acme's stock—the total value of all the shares of stock in the reorganized debtor. If we divide that value by the number of shares of stock that will be outstanding in the reorganized Acme, we will get the value of each share. For example, if the total value of Acme's stock is $37,000, and if there will be 1,000 shares of stock outstanding after the reorganization, then each share will be worth $37.[49] That then allows us to determine how much value a proposed plan of reorganization will give to each

---

48.   Note that if the debt payments are too high, then the value of the reorganized company may suffer. If the company has to pay so much on its debts that a downturn in business will cause the company to default on its debts, then there is a risk of another bankruptcy. The risky nature of the business would lead investors to demand a higher rate of return, causing the value of the company's projected future cash flows to be reduced. As we have seen, the business is worth $50,000 if investors demand a 20% return. If investors demand a 25% return, then the same expected $10,000 per year cash flows are worth only $40,000 total, because a buyer who paid $40,000 for the business would receive a 25% per year return on the investment. Thus it is in everyone's interest to leave the reorganized debtor in a strong financial position, not with too much debt, so that its value will not be diminished by the risk of future financial distress. But if the amount of debt is low, the company may be forgoing tax advantages. Interest payments are usually tax deductible, but dividends paid to stockholders are not. The company may reduce its taxes by paying out some of its cash flows in the form of interest on debts. See generally Appendix B at the end of this text; Miller, *The Modigliani-Miller Propositions after Thirty Years*, 2 J. ECON. PERSP. 99, 111-18 (1988).

49.   For the sake of simplicity we assume the reorganized Acme will have only one class of stock, rather than a complex financial structure with different classes of common and preferred shares. We also ignore control premiums and minority share discounts.

party. In turn, that will allow the parties to decide whether they wish to accept or reject the plan. It will also then allow the court to decide whether the "best interests" test has been satisfied, and, if a cramdown is necessary, to decide whether the plan is "fair and equitable" and whether it "unfairly discriminates."

Problem 1-7

Suppose Acme was doing fine making shoes, but got into trouble by opening an unprofitable metal fabrication operation. Acme then filed a chapter 11 petition and proposed the plan of reorganization that is reproduced at the beginning of Chapter Eleven of this text. Under the plan, Acme will sell the assets of its metal fabrication division to Metalmatic Corp. for cash. Assume that the cash that Metalmatic will pay, plus the cash Acme has built up during the reorganization, will be sufficient for Acme to make the cash payments that must be made on the effective date of the plan and to have enough cash left to run its shoe business. Assume the amount of the unpaid priority tax claims (plan paragraph III.B.) and the amount of the small claims in Class 4 (plan paragraph I.D. and II.D.) are small enough to be ignored for financial purposes.

First Bank has a $50,000 first mortgage on Acme's shoe factory, consisting of real property and fixtures worth $90,000. The interest rate on First Bank's mortgage is 6% (slightly less than the current 6.5% fair market interest rate for such loans), and the mortgage has twenty years to run. The plan leaves First Bank's fully secured claim unaltered. See plan paragraphs I.A. and II.A. Using a financial calculator or a book of mortgage tables, you can determine that the monthly payment on First Bank's mortgage is about $358, for a total of about $4,300 per year.

Second Finance Company has a $100,000 second mortgage on the factory. The court has determined under § 506(a) that Second Finance Company has a $40,000 secured claim (the value of the factory beyond the amount of First Bank's first mortgage), and a $60,000 general unsecured claim. The plan places Second Finance Company's $40,000 secured claim in Class 2, and provides that the reorganized debtor will pay off the $40,000 secured claim, with 10% annual interest, by making 120 equal monthly payments. See plan paragraphs I.B. and II.B. Again, using a financial calculator or a book of mortgage tables, you can determine that the monthly payment to Second Finance under the plan will be about $529 per month, or about $6,300 per year.

Class 3 in the plan consists of all general unsecured claims other than the small claims in Class 4. See plan paragraph I.C. Thus Second Finance Company has a $60,000 claim in Class 3. The rest of the Class 3 claims are unpaid trade debts totaling $440,000 for goods and services provided to Acme on credit before it filed its chapter 11 petition. Thus the total amount of claims in Class 3 is $500,000.

Under paragraph II.C of the plan, each holder of a claim in Class 3 will receive a promissory note in an amount equal to 25% of the claim; the notes will carry a 12% annual interest rate and will be paid off in five equal yearly payments. The total amount of the promissory notes to be given to holders of claims in Class 3 will therefore be $125,000 (25% of $500,000). Mortgage tables or a financial calculator let us determine that for each $1000 of notes given out to holders of Class 3 claims, the reorganized Acme will pay about $277 per year for the five year term of the notes; thus the reorganized Acme will have to pay $34,625 per year on the notes for five years.

Holders of claims in Class 3 will also receive one share of common stock in the reorganized Acme for each $100 of claim; thus they will receive a total of 5,000 shares of stock in the reorganized Acme, one for each $100 of the $500,000 in claims. (In addition, each holder will receive 5% payment in cash on the effective date; as noted above, we assume that the cash payment from Metalmatic and the cash Acme has built up during the plan are sufficient for Acme to make the cash payments that are to be made on the effective date.)

The plan provides that the existing owners of Acme stock (whose stock interests are classified in Class 5 under plan paragraph I.E) will have their stock canceled but will receive one share of stock in the reorganized Acme for each five shares they currently hold. See plan paragraph II.E. There are now 10,000 shares of Acme stock outstanding; thus the existing stockholders will own 2,000 shares in the reorganized Acme after the plan is put into effect.

Acme will owe, as of the effective date of the plan, $20,000 in unpaid administrative expense claims to trade creditors for goods purchased on credit during the reorganization. Administrative expense claims must be paid in full in cash on the effective date of the plan, unless the holder of a particular claim agrees to other treatment. See § 1129(a)(9)(A). Because the postpetition trade debts were incurred under agreements that allowed Acme time to pay, paragraph III.A. of Acme's plan provides that they will be paid at the agreed time rather than on the effective date.

Assume Acme is expected to generate $60,000 of cash flow from operations each year and that the interest rates set forth in the plan are fair market interest rates for the various obligations (except for First Bank's mortgage, which is left unaltered by the plan). Assume an appropriate discount rate for determining the value of the cash flows is 18%, because the court has concluded that 18% is the annual return a typical investor who was going to purchase Acme's assets would demand. Ignore any effect of taxes. Assume Acme's liquidation value is $250,000 (including the $90,000 of value in the factory real property—all of which would go to First Bank and Second Finance Company—and including the value of the metal fabrication assets).

1. What will be the going concern value of Acme's assets immediately after the plan goes into effect (and therefore after the metal fabrication assets have been sold and after the cash payments have been made that must be made on the effective date of the plan)? What will each share of stock in the reorganized Acme be worth?

2. Will Acme be able to make the payments required by the plan after the effective date?

3. If all classes accept the plan, but one trade creditor with a claim in Class 3 votes against the plan, can the plan be confirmed? See § 1129(a)(7)(A) (the best interests of creditors test).

4. Assume there are twenty-seven creditors (including Second Finance Co.) each holding one allowed claim in Class 3. If twenty vote their claims, how many must vote in favor of the plan for Class 3 to accept the plan? If the twenty who vote have claims totaling $450,000, what dollar amount of claims must be voted in favor of the plan for Class 3 to accept the plan? See § 1126(c).

5. Assume the court considers all of the requirements of § 1129(a) except for paragraphs (8) and (10), and finds that all of them are satisfied.

    a. If Classes 2, 3, and 5 vote to accept the plan, can the plan be confirmed consensually under § 1129(a)? See § 1129(a)(8) and (a)(10). (Note that unimpaired classes, such as classes 1 and 4, are conclusively presumed to have accepted the plan. See § 1126(f).) What if Second Finance Company owned 20% of Acme's stock? See § 101(2)(A) ("affiliate") and (31)(E) ("insider"); § 1129(a)(10). *For the rest of this Problem, assume that no creditor is an insider.*

    b. Assume Class 3 votes to accept the plan, but Class 2 votes to reject it. Can the plan be confirmed in a cramdown under § 1129(b), or does the plan violate the fair and equitable standard that applies in favor of dissenting classes of secured claims? See § 1129(b)(2)(A)(i).

    c. Assume Class 2 votes to accept the plan, but Class 3 votes to reject it. Can the plan be confirmed in a cramdown, or does it violate the fair and equitable standard that applies in favor of dissenting classes of unsecured claims? See § 1129(b)(2)(B).

    d. Suppose the plan divided the unsecured claims (other than Class 4 claims) into two classes, 3A and 3B. Class 3A includes claims (totaling $250,000) of those trade creditors with whom Acme wishes to continue doing business. Class 3B contains the other $250,000 of unsecured claims, other than the small Class 4 claims but including Second Finance Company's unsecured claim. Suppose the plan provided that, for each $100 of claim, holders of claims in Class 3A would receive $5 in cash, $20 in notes, and two shares of common stock; holders of claims in Class 3B would receive $5 in cash, $30 in notes, and no stock. (Thus there still will be 7,000 shares of stock of the reorganized Acme outstanding after the reorganization—5,000 shares owned by holders of claims in Class 3A, and 2,000 owned by the existing shareholders of Acme.) Assume Class 3A votes to accept the amended plan, but Class 3B rejects it. Is there a reason other than the fair and equitable standard why this version of the plan might not be confirmable? See § 1129(b)(1).

Chapter Two

Introduction To Foam Corporation
and Its Chapter 11 Case

We cannot duplicate all the complexities of the reorganization of a real debtor corporation in this book. However, we can present an extended hypothetical case that embodies many of the key features of an actual business and of an actual reorganization. Thus, we present Foam Corporation, a somewhat realistic candidate for chapter 11 reorganization. In this book we follow Foam Corporation through the stages of a typical business reorganization, from the realization that there is a financial problem to the consummation of a plan of reorganization.

Section A of this chapter gives background information on Foam Corporation and its financial problems. At the end of section A we provide simplified, summary financial statements for Foam Corporation. Business reorganization is at least as much a financial process as it is a legal process. A lawyer who does not understand a financially distressed company's financial situation cannot deal with the legal problems of reorganizing it. A lawyer who works in any aspect of business-related law must know enough to be able to talk to the accountants and financial advisers. Thus, in Appendix A near the end of this book, Chief Financial Officer Deborah Bell explains Foam Corporation's financial statements to President Gruff. The explanation is designed for students who have no prior knowledge of accounting, but it may be useful for others.

Section B of this chapter recounts Foam Corporation's attempt to work out its financial problems outside of bankruptcy. We hate to give away the ending of this part of the story, but, given the title of this book, most students will have guessed that the workout attempt fails; it does, and Foam Corporation is forced to file a chapter 11 petition.

Section C discusses who is eligible to be a chapter 11 debtor and what must be filed along with or shortly after the filing of the petition.

Section D introduces the various players who will be important in Foam Corporation's chapter 11 case. These include Foam Corporation as debtor in possession, the United States trustee, the creditors' committee, and the major secured creditors.

Finally, Section E discusses the retention of professionals such as attorneys and accountants by Foam Corporation as debtor in possession and by the creditors' committee. We focus on questions of conflict of interest.

A. BACKGROUND INFORMATION ON FOAM CORPORATION AS OF FEBRUARY 1, 2006

Foam Corporation is a California corporation that manufactures polyurethane foam for distribution in bulk and in products. The foam is made by combining chemicals in large machines and cutting the resulting foam buns to size. Some of the foam is sold in bulk to manufacturers of automobiles and furniture for use in seat cushions. Other foam is used as baffles to reduce the wave action in water beds manufactured in Foam Corporation's water bed division. A good portion of the foam is glued to paper and used as insulation in construction products. Residual scraps of foam are rebonded and sold as carpet underlay padding. In the last two years Foam Corporation has used some of its foam in its manufacture of children's pillows, which it has sold to consumers by way of the Internet. The cloth coverings for the pillows feature popular cartoon characters, used under license from the characters' owner, Miramin Studios, Inc.

Foam Corporation's five "western" plants are in Los Angeles, Fresno, and Richmond, California; Seattle, Washington; and Denver, Colorado. Foam Corporation's four "eastern" plants are in Philadelphia, Pennsylvania; Camden, New Jersey; Cleveland, Ohio; and Detroit, Michigan. In addition, Foam Corporation owns 100% of a North Carolina subsidiary, U Foam, which owns and operates a foam plant in North Carolina.

William Gruff owns 90% of Foam Corporation's shares. Gruff's sister, Marilyn Simmons, owns the other 10% as the result of an investment she made in the company when Gruff started it in 1987. Gruff is in the second year of a five year employment contract with Foam Corporation and serves as its Chief Executive Officer and Chairman of its Board of Directors. The board consists of Gruff, Simmons, and Foam Corporation's attorney, Carlos Mendoza. Mendoza also serves as general counsel to Foam Corporation.

Foam Corporation was profitable for many years, when its only operations were in the west. Gruff owned the original plant (in Richmond, California). In 2003 he transferred it to the Gruff Family Trust, an irrevocable trust; he is the trustee and his children are the beneficiaries. Originally Gruff, and now the Trust, have leased the plant to Foam Corporation since 1987. Foam Corporation owns two of the California plants (Los Angeles and Fresno, both of which went into service in 1993. There are no real estate mortgages on the Los Angeles or Richmond plants. First Bank financed the acquisition of the land for the Fresno plant and has a $550,000 real estate mortgage on it. The remaining western plants (in Denver and Seattle) are leased to Foam Corporation by Imperial Insurance Company. Imperial purchased the land and built the buildings for the Denver and Seattle plants in 1997 under an agreement that bound Foam Corporation to lease them on a long term basis.

In 1998 Foam Corporation purchased the assets of a foam manufacturer in North Carolina for $2 million. The assets (land, buildings, equipment, inventory, etc.) were appraised at that time item by item; the total appraised value was $1.5 million. Foam Corporation then formed its North Carolina subsidiary, U Foam, Inc., and contributed the assets to it. U Foam owns the land, free and clear, on which its one plant stands.

In 2001 Gruff loaned Foam Corporation $3.2 million to expand the business by opening the four eastern plants. First Bank financed purchase of the land for the Philadelphia and Camden plants and holds a $700,000 real estate mortgage covering both of them. Imperial Insurance purchased the land and built the buildings for the Cleveland and Detroit plants and leased them to Foam Corporation under an agreement similar to the ones covering the Denver and Seattle plants. The leases of all four plants from Imperial are now subject to the terms of a single master lease with a cross-default clause that provides that a default as to any of the plants is a default as to all.

The $3.2 million lent by Gruff covered the cost of building on the Philadelphia and Camden sites, and some of the cost of equipment for the new sites, but Foam Corporation needed more financing. Thus Foam Corporation began its relationship with Kick Credit Corporation.

In late 2001 Kick Credit lent Foam Corporation $1.5 million on a term loan basis, with interest only payable until 2008, when the entire $1.5 million of principal was to be due. Kick Credit also set up a revolving line of credit arrangement under which Foam Corporation could borrow up to 80% of the amount of its eligible accounts receivable, up to a maximum of $4.5 million. These loans are described more fully below.

The North Carolina subsidiary, U Foam, is profitable due in part to low non-union labor costs. By contrast, Foam Corporation's eastern operations have been and remain very unprofitable, so much so that Foam Corporation is trying to sell the business operations at each of its four eastern locations. Two of the eastern plants (Philadelphia and Camden) have union contracts that last through 2007 with local chapters of the Foam Union International ("FUI"). The union contracts have obligated Foam Corporation to pay large pension benefits, health benefits for current employees and retirees, and wages that are above the current market wage for foam industry labor. Foam Corporation's attempts to convince the union to agree to wage and benefit concessions have all failed, with the Foam Corporation and FUI representatives accusing each other of acting in bad faith. The eastern locations are each losing $1 million to $2 million per year (not counting interest expense) due to declining demand and increased competition, as well as high labor costs at the two union locations. Gruff is confident that if Foam Corporation can sell its eastern operations quickly, it can reverse its losses.

Foam Corporation's water bed division is a pioneer in the industry with a patented process and a trademark ("Waveless") that are very valuable. To raise capital, in 2003 Foam Corporation granted a twenty year nonexclusive license in the water bed patent and "Waveless" trademark to More Foam, Inc., a North Carolina corporation, in return for a one time payment of $200,000. More

Foam manufactures and distributes water beds in North Carolina and has done quite well due in part to a covenant not to compete given by Foam Corporation and U Foam. The covenant not to compete was given at the same time as the license, runs for the same period, and covers the same area (North Carolina) but is contained in a separate document. More Foam paid $50,000 to Foam Corporation and U Foam for the covenant not to compete. More Foam has covenanted not to misuse or sublicense the patent or trademark or to sell products incorporating either unless the license is in force. Gruff would like Foam Corporation or U Foam to enter the North Carolina water-bed market but cannot do so due to the covenant not to compete.

Nevertheless, Gruff hopes to expand water bed sales nationally from $1 million to $10 million yearly. At a net pre-tax profit of 10% of gross sales, Foam Corporation could increase pre-tax income by $900,000 per year. Unfortunately, Foam Corporation lacks the $2 million in additional capital needed to expand its manufacturing facilities, upgrade its equipment, and advertise its product in order to achieve Gruff's projected results.

In fact, Foam Corporation's trade creditors recently refused to extend trade credit to Foam Corporation. In the past, Foam Corporation's suppliers have been willing to sell chemicals and other materials to Foam Corporation on credit; that has been a very important source of financing for Foam Corporation. Now the trade creditors will deliver goods only for cash on delivery; occasionally they even demand prepayment. The trade creditors are also pressing Foam Corporation to pay its trade debt of $8 million, most of which is past due. Although most of the trade debt was due on thirty day terms, Foam Corporation has been paying 120 days past delivery on its old trade debt, well beyond the sixty-day industry custom. Now that trade creditors have stopped selling to Foam Corporation on credit, Foam Corporation cannot afford to use its cash to pay trade debts, even to pay them late. Foam Corporation needs that cash to pay for the new goods that it must have in order to keep its plants running. When the trade creditors realize that Foam Corporation has stopped paying any of its trade debts, they will be upset, to say the least; if they are not handled correctly, many of them may refuse to sell goods to Foam Corporation even if orders are prepaid. That could prevent Foam Corporation from obtaining the raw materials it needs.

Two years ago, when Foam Corporation encountered temporary financial problems, Gruff gave an unsecured continuing guaranty of Foam Corporation's debts to its two largest suppliers, the Tina Chemical Company and the Swenson Chemical Company; those debts now stand at $3 million and $2 million, respectively. Recently Tina and Swenson stopped selling to Foam Corporation on credit, despite Gruff's guarantee, and Swenson has been pressing Gruff himself for payment. For that reason, and because Tina and Swenson are the largest suppliers, Gruff is especially concerned about their reaction to the cutoff of payments.

Gruff also gave an unsecured guaranty to Kick Credit Corporation. He guaranteed both loans made by Kick Credit, the $1.5 million term loan and the $4.5 million line of credit, in 2001, when the loans were originated. To secure both the term loan and the line of credit, Kick Credit holds a first lien on Foam Corporation's (and U Foam's) personal property assets, including deposit accounts, accounts receivable, inventory, machinery and equipment, intangibles, and the U Foam common stock. (U Foam also guaranteed Foam Corporation's debts to Kick Credit.) Both loans carry a variable interest rate of prime plus 2%.

As noted above, the $1.5 million term loan was to be due in 2008, with only monthly interest payments to be made until then. However, Kick Credit recently accelerated the term loan and demanded payment within sixty days. Kick Credit claimed that Foam Corporation violated a financial covenant in the term loan agreement by failing to maintain a $1 million net worth.

The revolving line of credit agreement provides that Kick Credit will "in its sole discretion" lend Foam Corporation up to $4.5 million (in addition to the term loan), but not more than 80% of the value of the "eligible accounts receivable." "Eligible accounts receivable" are defined as debts owed by "customers" of Foam Corporation for goods delivered to them on credit, but does not include any accounts (1) owed by customers who are not, in Kick Credit's opinion, creditworthy, or (2) with respect to which there is a dispute (such as a breach of warranty claim), or (3) that are more than fifteen days overdue. (The term "customers" is defined to exclude retail purchasers such as consumers who buy the children's pillows by credit card over the Internet.)

When the line of credit was set up a little more than four years ago (in late 2001), Foam Corporation requested and received an initial advance of $3.5 million, which was 80% of the eligible accounts at that time. Foam Corporation then instructed its customers to send payments on their accounts to Foam Corporation at an address that was actually a "lock box" under Kick Credit's control. Kick Credit applied those payments against the debt owed on the line of credit (including interest). In this way, each payment by a Foam Corporation customer on an account paid off a portion of the line of credit.

The line is a "revolving" line; as payments were made on it and as new accounts receivable were generated, Kick Credit made additional advances to Foam Corporation under the line of credit. Foam Corporation received orders for foam and for water beds to be sold on credit to its customers. When Foam Corporation shipped the goods to a customer and sent the customer an invoice, a new account receivable was earned, increasing the total amount of Foam Corporation's accounts receivable by the amount of the invoice. Foam Corporation regularly sent copies of invoices and shipping confirmations to Kick Credit as water beds or foam were shipped to customers; Kick Credit reviewed the documents and added the amount of the invoices to the total of the "eligible" accounts if the customers appeared to be creditworthy.

Weekly (and sometimes daily) Kick Credit compared the amount owed (including interest) on the line of credit with the "maximum total loan amount" for the line of credit. By agreement the maximum total loan amount for the line was 80% of the amount of the eligible accounts, but not more than $4.5 million. If the amount owed under the line of credit exceeded the maximum total loan amount, Kick Credit demanded payment of the difference from Foam Corporation. If the amount owed under the line of credit was less than the maximum total loan amount, Kick Credit advanced the difference as an additional loan under the line of credit. The amount owed on the line of credit increased as the amount of accounts receivable increased and as Kick Credit made further advances; the full $4.5 million is now owed. The eligible accounts total $5.488 million; almost $1 million of the $6.35 million in total accounts (as of the end of 2005) are overdue, disputed, or owed by customers whose creditworthiness is doubtful.[1] The $4.5 million loan is 82% of the eligible accounts and thus is slightly larger than the loan amount to which Foam Corporation would be entitled under the 80% formula. Several of the accounts owed to Foam Corporation recently became overdue; that reduced the amount of the eligible accounts and increased the percentage from 80% to 82%.

When Kick Credit accelerated the term loan, it also demanded repayment of the entire line of credit in sixty days. Kick Credit stated that it would make no further advances after the sixty days expired and would pursue its legal remedies if payment were not made. Kick Credit also exercised its "discretion" to reduce the amount that it would lend against new accounts. Now only 70%, rather than 80%, of the amount of new eligible accounts receivable will be used in determining the maximum total loan amount under the line of credit. That will reduce the amount of any further advances Kick Credit will give to Foam Corporation on new eligible receivables. In turn that will hurt Foam Corporation, which is losing over $400,000 per month and needs all the cash it can get. Worse yet, Foam Corporation cannot pay off the term loan and the line of credit in sixty days unless it can find a lender to take Kick Credit's place. Foam Corporation would need to borrow at least $6 million from the new lender. Given the difficult financial situation of Foam Corporation, it will be practically impossible to find a new lender.

Gruff knows he must negotiate with the trade creditors and with Kick Credit if Foam Corporation is to avoid bankruptcy. Before setting up those negotiations, Gruff asked the company's chief financial officer, Deborah Bell, to bring him the latest summaries of Foam Corporation's financial statements, which appear on pages 52 and 53. Gruff has never been very comfortable with financial statements, and he hoped Bell could explain them.

---

1.   The $6.35 million also includes $50,000 in credit card receivables for consumer purchases of children's pillows at Foam Corporation's Internet website. As noted above, these receivables are not "eligible accounts" as that term is defined in the revolving loan agreement.

Appendix A near the end of this book contains Bell's full explanation. In brief, she pointed out that the balance sheet shows that Foam Corporation owes $4.6 million more than the book value of its assets (the value at which its assets appear on the balance sheet, which may not be a very accurate valuation). That means Foam Corporation has lost all of the $5 million that its shareholders invested in it (see the Common Stock line on the balance sheet) and also has lost another $4.6 million that it got from its creditors. Other bad news contained in the balance sheet is the low level of current assets (cash and other assets that will be turned into cash within a year) as compared to current liabilities (debts that are due within a year). Foam Corporation has only $11 million in current assets out of which it will have to pay about $15 million in current liabilities, for a "current ratio" of 11 to 15, or about .73 to 1. A current ratio of 2 to 1 is often considered good for a manufacturing company; Foam Corporation's current ratio of less than 1 to 1 indicates real financial problems.

Bell also pointed out that, as accountants figure revenues and expenses, the statement of operations shows that Foam Corporation's expenses for 2005 exceeded its revenues by $5 million. The picture is only a little less bleak when actual cash inflows and outflows are considered; the statement of cash flows shows that Foam Corporation spent $2.1 million more in cash during 2005 than it took in. The statement of cash flows also shows that Foam Corporation's negative cash flow from its operations was even greater, $3.9 million (which would have been $5.4 million but for the tax refund). The overall net cash outflow was "only" $2.1 million because during 2005 Foam Corporation received $800,000 cash from selling surplus equipment and borrowed an extra $1 million from Kick Credit. None of those factors is likely to help Foam Corporation during 2006. Finally, the statement of cash flows and the balance sheet show that Foam Corporation only has $800,000 in cash left as of the end of 2005. At the rate Foam Corporation is losing cash, that $800,000 will be gone in a few months, and Foam Corporation will be unable to pay its employees, pay for raw materials, and pay other expenses that must be paid in order to keep its business going.

It became obvious to Gruff that drastic action was needed. Gruff asked Mendoza, Foam Corporation's general counsel, for advice. Mendoza suggested getting a bank loan by mortgaging the L.A. plant. When contacted, several banks refused; they doubted Foam Corporation could repay any loan and were concerned that the land might be polluted with toxic chemicals used in foam manufacturing.

SUMMARY OF CONSOLIDATED FINANCIAL STATEMENTS
FOAM CORPORATION (UNAUDITED)
(in thousands of dollars)

CONSOLIDATED BALANCE SHEET
December 31, 2005

Assets			Liabilities		
Current			Current		
Cash	$	800	Trade Payables	$	8,000
Receivables		6,350	Kick Credit Line		
Taxes Receivable		1,100	and Term Loan		6,000
Inventory and Raw			Withholding Taxes		1,000
Materials		2,700	Mortgages Payable		21
Prepaid Expenses		50	Other		50
		11,000			15,071
Property, Plant, Equipment			Long Term		
and Certain Intangibles			Mortgages Payable		1,229
P.P. & E. (at cost)		6,500	Notes to Gruff		3,200
Goodwill, Patent,					4,429
and Trademark		1,000			
		7,500	Total Liabilities		19,500
Less Accumulated					
Depreciation and			**Shareholders' Equity**		
Amortization		(3,600)	Common Stock (100,000		
Net P.P. & E. and			shares–no par)		5,000
Intangibles		3,900	Retained Earnings		
			(Deficit)		(9,600)
					(4,600)
Total		$ 14,900	Total		$ 14,900

CONSOLIDATED STATEMENT OF OPERATIONS
For the Year Ended December 31, 2005

Revenue:	
Net Sales	$ 30,000
Expenses:	
Cost of Goods Sold	20,000
Selling Expenses	6,000
General and Administrative Expense	8,000
Interest Expense	1,500
Loss on Sale of Equipment	600
Taxes (refund)	(1,100)
Net Loss	$ (5,000)

CONSOLIDATED STATEMENT OF CHANGES
IN RETAINED EARNINGS
For the Year Ended December 31, 2005
(in thousands of dollars)

Retained Earnings (Deficit), January 1, 2005	$ (4,600)
Net Loss for 2005	(5,000)
Retained Earnings, December 31, 2005	$ (9,600)

CONSOLIDATED STATEMENT OF CASH FLOWS
For the Year Ended December 31, 2005
(in thousands of dollars)

Cash Flows from operating activities:	
Cash received from customers	$ 29,000
Cash paid to suppliers and employees	(33,000)
Interest paid	(1,400)
Tax refund	1,500
Net cash provided by operating activities	(3,900)
Cash flows from investing activities:	
Sale of equipment	800
Cash flows used by financing activities:	
Net borrowings from Kick	1,000
Net decrease in cash and cash equivalents	(2,100)
Cash and cash equivalents at beginning of year	2,900
Cash and cash equivalents at end of year	$ 800

B. THE WORKOUT ATTEMPT

Mendoza then recommended that Gruff contact Smith, Martinez & Johnson, a law firm that specialized in workouts and chapter 11 reorganizations. After an initial consultation, Ed Johnson asked for and received a $75,000 retainer from Foam Corporation. Foam Corporation paid Johnson an additional$25,000 that would be kept untouched in a trust account, to be added to the $75,000 retainer if Foam Corporation decided to file a chapter 11 petition. Johnson then accompanied Gruff to two brief meetings: one with Kathryn Kerns, a representative from Kick Credit's workout department, and one with Gruff's friend Margaret Taggart, the president of Tina Chemical Company. Johnson and Gruff attempted to meet with Imperial Insurance Company, but it refused to discuss Foam Corporation's problems and stated that it expected Foam Corporation to live up to its responsibilities under the leases. Gruff then sent this letter to all the trade creditors:

February 9, 2006

Dear _____:

 Foam Corporation needs your support. We have been and still can be a good customer of yours, but we are currently experiencing difficulties. We have a difficult choice. If we continue to pay our trade payables, we will not have enough cash to continue buying from you COD. We can close the plants--then you will lose a customer and we won't be able to earn the money to repay you--or we can temporarily suspend payments on our trade debt. Our eastern operations are not profitable, and we are trying to sell them. When that occurs, we will be able to generate substantial positive cash flow from operations. Meanwhile, we are taking every possible step to cut costs. I will not receive a paycheck this month; the other managers are taking a 20% pay cut; and we are laying off 10% of our work force.
 We are currently negotiating with Kick Credit, and we would like to meet with representatives of the trade creditors. To that end Tina Chemical Company has agreed to call a meeting of the trade creditors to choose an informal trade creditors' committee. The meeting will be at Tina Chemical's offices at 10 a.m. on February 20. We need your patience; please do not act precipitously pending the meeting.

                    Very truly yours,

                    Bill Gruff

                President and Chairman
                Foam Corporation

At their meeting on February 20, the trade creditors elected the following creditors to the committee:

- Tina Chemical Company
- Swenson Chemical Company
- Albert Cochran (sole proprietor of Allchem Industrial Supply, one of the smaller trade creditors)
- VinylCo (which sold Foam Corporation most of the vinyl for the water bed shells), and
- Plumbing Contractors, Inc.

The committee asked Tina Chemical's attorney, Pat Gray, to represent it and demanded that Foam Corporation immediately pay Gray a $50,000 retainer.

Foam Corporation's attorney, Johnson, then arranged a meeting on February 23 that included Johnson, Gruff, Bell, Gray, Kerns, and representatives of the members of the trade creditors' committee, including Taggart. At the meeting, Gruff expressed his regrets that Foam Corporation had not been able to meet its commitments to the trade. He explained that Foam Corporation was committed to taking the necessary steps to turn its business around so that it could generate cash to pay debts, and that Foam Corporation needed the trade creditors to be patient in this difficult time. He also explained that he thought Kick Credit's position was safe unless Foam Corporation was liquidated; he said he hoped Kick Credit would assist in turning the situation around. Gruff then handed out copies of the 12/31/05 unaudited financial statements and made the following points orally:

- Foam Corporation was in the process of cutting its payroll by 10% and had taken other steps to cut costs, including deferring indefinitely payment of Gruff's salary and cutting other managers' salaries by 20%. Payments to creditors were temporarily suspended, except that regular payments to First Bank on its first mortgages would be made, necessary payments for utilities, rent, and for insurance would be made, and Foam Corporation planned to make the quarterly interest payments on the Kick Credit term loan. Foam Corporation did not have complete control over payments on the line of credit since Kick Credit was receiving the collections on the accounts receivable through the "lock box."
- Foam Corporation's eastern operations were on the market and Foam Corporation would aggressively seek to sell them. Foam Corporation was informed that it probably would take six months to sell them at a reasonable price, which likely would be $4 million net cash for the four plants. If the eastern operations were shut down and liquidated, only about

$1.5 million could be realized, of which very little could go to trade creditors or other unsecured creditors. Proceeds from sale of the real estate would probably pay off First Bank's mortgage on the Camden and Philadelphia plants with only about $50,000 to spare, and the proceeds from sale of the personal property would all go to Kick Credit. If the eastern operations were shut down and no one could be found to assume the Cleveland and Detroit leases with Imperial Insurance Company, Foam Corporation would have to default on those leases, which could result in a large claim for breach of the long term leases and could affect the leases of the Denver and Seattle plants under the cross-default clause. Although the rent under the Cleveland and Detroit leases was slightly more than fair market rental value, the rent under the Denver and Seattle leases was substantially below fair market rental value. The Denver and Seattle leaseholds were therefore of substantial value.

- All creditors (except First Bank) would lose substantial amounts in a liquidation. By the time a liquidation could be accomplished, Foam Corporation would have little or no cash left. The debt for withholding taxes and the tax refund entitlement would offset each other with $100,000 left over for Foam Corporation and its unsecured creditors. A net amount of $5.8 million likely would be realized from sale and collection of Kick Credit's collateral (including all of U Foam's assets other than its real estate), leaving a loss—a deficiency—of at least $200,000 for Kick Credit. (Anticipated difficulties in collecting the accounts during a liquidation would cut the realizable value of Foam Corporation's $6.3 million in accounts receivable nearly in half, and the chemicals and bulk foam in Foam Corporation's inventory would bring little in a forced sale.) The Los Angeles real estate (on which there is no real estate mortgage) would sell for about $1 million—or less if it turns out that there has been significant chemical pollution of the premises, as Gruff fears. The Fresno real estate would bring $800,000, leaving $250,000 for unsecured creditors after payment of First Bank's $550,000 mortgage. The Philadelphia and Camden real estate would bring about $750,000; First Bank's $700,000 mortgage on them would be paid off with perhaps $50,000 left for unsecured creditors. U Foam's real estate could probably be sold for about $350,000, all of which would be available to pay U Foam's $800,000 trade debt and the deficiency of $200,000 or more owed to Kick Credit. (Recall that U Foam guaranteed Foam Corporation's debt to Kick Credit.) Thus U Foam's creditors would receive 35 cents or less on the dollar.

- The total available for unsecured creditors of Foam Corporation then would be about $1.4 million ($100,000 plus $1 million plus $250,000 plus $50,000). The trade debt plus Kick Credit's deficiency plus the long term notes payable to Gruff would total $10.6 million,[2] not counting the large claim Imperial would assert for breach of the Cleveland and Detroit leases. Thus, Gruff argued, if his claims, the claims of Foam Corporation's trade creditors, and Kick Credit's deficiency claim were paid on a pro rata basis, the payments would be about 13 cents on the dollar.[3]

- Foam Corporation had $800,000 cash on hand as of 12/31/05, but that would be down to $150,000 by March 1, 2006. Foam Corporation's future cash position was projected on the assumption that the status quo would be maintained with regard to Kick Credit.[4] On that basis Foam Corporation's losses from operations would give it a negative cash balance of $100,000 at the end of March, a negative cash balance of $325,000 at the end of April, and a negative cash balance $200,000 more in the red at the end of each of the following months until sale of the eastern operations. Assuming sale of the eastern operations in six months (late August, 2006), Foam Corporation's cash account would be "overdrawn" at that time by more than $1.1 million. Commerce Bank, where Foam Corporation has its bank accounts, would not allow Foam Corporation to be overdrawn by that much (or at all), so Foam Corporation's checks would start bouncing sometime in March unless more cash is found. Without an infusion of extra cash, Foam Corporation could not then buy materials to keep its plants in operation or pay its employees; it could not continue in business. The ensuing liquidation would result in substantial losses to all creditors except First Bank. If

---

2. The consolidated balance sheet shows the total trade debt to be $8 million. $800,000 of that represents the trade debt owed by U Foam, leaving $7.2 million owing by Foam Corporation. Adding in Kick Credit's $200,000 deficiency and the $3.2 million owed to Gruff on the long term notes, we obtain a figure of $10.6 million.

3. $1.4 million in available value divided by $10.6 million in debts equals only a little more than 13%. Thus, if the creditors each received a pro rata share of the $1.4 million, each would receive slightly more than 13% repayment.

4. Kerns asked for an explanation of the term "status quo." Bell said it meant that Foam Corporation would make its regular quarterly payments of interest to Kick Credit on the term loan. With respect to the line of credit, each week the amount of money (if any) that Kick Credit would advance to Foam Corporation would be calculated so that (1) the credit line debt would not increase beyond the present $4.5 million, and (2) the amount of the credit line debt would not exceed the present figure of 82% of the eligible accounts. This would mean that Foam Corporation would receive an advance equal to the payments on accounts by Foam Corporation's customers during the week minus the interest on the $4.5 million debt for the week. However, Foam Corporation could only receive that amount if enough new accounts receivable were generated during the week to replace the accounts that were paid off, so that the percentage would stay at 82%. Otherwise, Kick Credit would reduce the advance enough to reduce the debt enough to keep the percentage at 82%.

extra cash could be found so that Foam Corporation could continue operations, and the eastern operations were sold, Foam Corporation would begin generating net cash, starting at $100,000 per month and increasing (Foam Corporation hoped) to $250,000 per month within another six months (by early 2007).

- The separate corporate existence of U Foam would be strictly observed. Although Foam Corporation had used a centralized cash management approach in the past, from this point on no cash would be provided to or withdrawn from U Foam except for its share of Foam Corporation's management expenses. Other assets of U Foam also would be kept separate from the assets of Foam Corporation. Creditors with claims only against Foam Corporation or only against U Foam would be expected to look only to their particular debtor for eventual payment.

Johnson then made the following proposal on behalf of Foam Corporation:

1. All creditors should observe a moratorium on debt collection activities against Foam Corporation, U Foam, and Gruff for 180 days—they should refrain from taking legal action or otherwise acting to collect their debts while negotiations would go forward on a workout agreement. Trade creditors should continue to sell to Foam Corporation on a COD basis.

2. Beyond maintaining the status quo, Kick Credit should lend an additional $1.1 million to Foam Corporation over the next six months, secured by all the assets of Foam Corporation. Foam Corporation would execute a first mortgage on its real property in Los Angeles, second mortgages on the Philadelphia and Camden real estate, and leasehold mortgages on the four Imperial Insurance leases; and would execute any other required documents to give Kick Credit security in all of Foam Corporation's assets for the $1.1 million. The security held by Kick Credit for the term loan and the $4.5 million line of credit would not be increased; the mortgages on the real property and the leaseholds would not secure the old loans but only the new $1.1 million loan.

3. All creditors would be assured of equality of treatment. No unsecured creditor would be given security in advance of a permanent financial solution. No undersecured creditor would be given additional security. No creditors other than utilities and insurance companies would be paid in advance of others, pending agreement. Pending agreement, no payments would be made on any other existing debts except for interest payments to Kick Credit on the term loan, on the line of credit, and on the new $1.1 million loan. Kick Credit would continue to collect the accounts receivable through the lock box, but would not use that position to do more than maintain the status quo on the line of credit.

The trade creditors' committee representatives expressed general support for the proposal, but insisted that Gruff should subordinate his $3.2 million claim to the trade creditors' claims. Speaking for Kick Credit, Kerns rejected Foam Corporation's proposal out of hand. Kerns proposed an additional loan of only $100,000 from Kick Credit (which would get Foam Corporation through March), suggested that Kick Credit would consider near the end of March whether a further loan was justified, and in exchange demanded:

- that Foam Corporation give Kick Credit a lien on all of Foam Corporation's assets as proposed by Johnson but that all the assets would secure all of Kick Credit's loans, not just the additional loan; and

- that Gruff personally guarantee the new loan and give Kick Credit a mortgage on the Richmond, California, plant to secure the guaranty of the new loan and to secure his existing guaranty of the existing term loan and line of credit.

The trade creditors' representatives objected that $100,000 was not enough money to give Foam Corporation a chance to succeed and that the proposal was an attempt by Kick Credit to ensure that it would receive full payment from Foam Corporation in a liquidation at the expense of the trade creditors. Gruff objected that he had already sunk enough money and other value into Foam Corporation, by way of his $3.2 million loan to Foam Corporation and his existing guaranties. Gruff threatened to have Foam Corporation file a chapter 11 petition; Johnson pointed out that the court in a chapter 11 case could permit Foam Corporation to use Kick Credit's cash collateral and to collect the accounts itself, outside of the lock box agreement. Johnson also pointed out that Foam Corporation would have various ways to borrow money in chapter 11; he stated that Kick Credit was oversecured on a going concern basis and that Foam Corporation could ask the court in a chapter 11 case to authorize a priming lien—in other words to give a new lender priority over Kick Credit in Kick Credit's existing collateral. Gruff added that as he understood it, a chapter 11 filing would stop all creditor collection activity. Gruff did not point out that he had conveyed the Richmond plant to the Gruff Family Trust and thus no longer owned it personally.

After much discussion, Johnson's original proposal was agreed to with some major changes:

1. Kick Credit would lend Foam Corporation an additional $425,000 in installments through mid-May (assuming no unexpected adverse change in the situation) and would *consider* making additional advances then if it appeared that the eastern operations were going to be sold in a timely way and if Foam Corporation's financial situation had not deteriorated;

2. Kick Credit would receive a lien on all of Foam Corporation's assets to secure the additional $425,000, but would not receive additional security for its existing loans;

3. Gruff would personally guarantee on an unsecured basis the last $200,000 of the new loan;

4. $1 million of Gruff's claim under the long term notes would be subordinated to the trade debt (so that Gruff could not collect any part of that $1 million unless and until the trade creditors had been paid in full);

5. Foam Corporation would pay a $25,000 retainer to the creditors' committee's counsel, Pat Gray, and a $15,000 retainer to accountants to be selected by the creditors' committee;

6. Foam Corporation would provide the creditors' committee information on all payments and other transfers over $5,000 made by Foam Corporation within the previous 90 days; and

7. The creditors' committee would send a letter to the trade creditors stating that Foam Corporation was taking good faith steps to get its house in order, strongly recommending that all the trade creditors observe a moratorium on collection activities, and strongly recommending that they not cut off supplies to Foam Corporation but rather continue to sell goods and services to Foam Corporation on a COD basis.

The creditors' committee sent the letter, and it was generally well received by the trade creditors, who observed the moratorium on debt collection activities at first. Foam Corporation, Kick Credit, and the trade creditors' committee held several negotiating sessions at which they attempted to negotiate the terms of a workout agreement. In broad strokes, Foam Corporation proposed that the trade debt be turned into five year promissory notes, with a principal amount equal to 65% of the trade debt. The notes would carry an 8% interest rate. Interest would be payable yearly; 6% of the principal would be payable at the end of two years, another 10% at the end of three years, another 10% at the end of four years, and the remaining 74% at the end of five years. The committee insisted that the five year notes should have a face amount of 100% of the trade debt, that they should carry a 12% interest rate, and that at least 15% of the principal should be paid each year, so that no more than 40% would be left to be paid at the end of the fifth year. Foam Corporation said that was unrealistic, and that there would not be sufficient cash flows to make such high payments.

Problem 2-1

Suppose Foam Corporation sweetened its offer by raising the proposed interest rates on the notes from 8% to 10%, and by raising the proposed percentage of repayment from 65% to 70%. Assume—contrary to what "actually" happens later in this Chapter—that trade creditors holding 98% of the dollar amount of the trade debt signed a formal workout agreement embodying those new terms. (The agreement provided that it would become effective once signed by Foam Corporation and by holders of at least 95% of the dollar amount of the trade debt.) A few days later, ChemSales, one of the trade creditors who had signed, changed its mind and filed suit, seeking a judgment for the full original amount of the debt owed to it. Foam Corporation pled the workout agreement in defense. Is there consideration for ChemSales' agreement to discharge the entire debt for 70% payment and for its agreement to give Foam Corporation five years to pay? Is ChemSales liable for breach of contract to Foam Corporation, to other trade creditors who signed the workout agreement, or to Kick Credit? If Dexter Engineering Co., one of the few trade creditors who had refused to sign the workout agreement, files suit against Foam Corporation, will the workout agreement provide Foam Corporation a defense?

When negotiations appeared to be going slowly, DistCo, a trade creditor with a $200,000 claim, sued Foam Corporation and properly obtained an ex parte prejudgment writ of attachment. When DistCo attached (garnished) Foam Corporation's bank accounts at Commerce Bank, Foam Corporation's checks began to bounce. Kick Credit interposed a third-party claim seeking return of the money to the accounts, claiming that its security interest was superior to DistCo's attachment lien. Kerns (from Kick Credit) told Gruff that the funds might be tied up for fifteen days even if DistCo did not oppose the third-party claim. Gruff decided he had to do something. He offered to have Foam Corporation pay $50,000 of DistCo's debt immediately if DistCo would release the attachment, even though that would violate Foam Corporation's commitment not to pay any of the unsecured creditors.

DistCo told a few other creditors about that offer. Many of the trade creditors then began to consider violating the moratorium. Some were frustrated with the slow pace of the negotiations. Others were outraged at Foam Corporation's offer to pay DistCo. Still others thought that if DistCo could get an offer of substantial payment by violating the moratorium then perhaps they should try the same tactic. Others heard that Foam Corporation checks had been dishonored and thought that this spelled the end for the workout attempt. As a result, a few more creditors sued; publicity about those suits caused still more creditors to abandon the moratorium.

In short order Foam Corporation was the defendant in seventeen collection actions, and five creditors with prejudgment writs of attachment were searching for assets to attach. Swenson Chemical and Tina Chemical sued Gruff on his personal guaranties. Kick Credit decided that the situation had gotten out of control; it refused to make the next scheduled advance of funds to Foam Corporation.

Johnson met with Gruff and Bell; he advised them that it was time to file a chapter 11 petition or to throw in the towel and allow Foam Corporation to be liquidated. Gruff said Foam Corporation would file a chapter 11 petition. Johnson and Gruff (with Bell's help) then got down to the business of taking Foam Corporation into chapter 11.

C. FOAM CORP.'S CHAPTER 11 FILING (APRIL 10, 2006)

For the remainder of this book, we will assume that Foam Corporation files its chapter 11 petition on April 10, 2006. To make that filing, Johnson and Gruff will have to go through four steps. First, they have to determine whether Foam Corporation is eligible to be a chapter 11 debtor. Second, they must obtain proper authorization from Foam Corporation to file the chapter 11 petition. Third, they must determine where the petition should be filed; that includes issues of jurisdiction and venue. Fourth, they must prepare and file the petition and the voluminous lists and schedules that must accompany the petition or be filed shortly after it.[5]

1. Eligibility for Chapter 11

How will Johnson and Gruff determine whether Foam Corporation is eligible to be a chapter 11 debtor? Read § 109(a), (b), and (d). Is Foam Corporation eligible? Is U Foam? Is Gruff?

What if U Foam had not guaranteed any of Foam Corporation's debts and had not given its assets as collateral for any of Foam Corporation's debts—would U Foam be eligible even though it would be solvent? See In re Johns-Manville Corp., 36 B.R. 727 (Bankr. S.D.N.Y. 1984) (holding that insolvency is not required because open access policy of bankruptcy law helps to encourage debtors to file before their condition deteriorates so much that they cannot be reorganized). Note that a lack of good faith in the filing of a chapter 11 petition is cause for dismissal (or conversion to chapter 7) under § 1112(b), even though lack of good faith is not one of the kinds of cause specifically listed in that section. See In re SGL Carbon Corp., 200 F.3d 154 (3d Cir. 1999) (stating that "[i]t is well established that a debtor need not be insolvent before filing for bankruptcy protection," but holding, under a "totality of facts and circumstances" test, that a healthy business's chapter

---

5. Foam Corporation also must pay the filing fee required by 28 U.S.C. § 1930(a)(3). See Rule 1006(a). Congress apparently intended to raise the chapter 11 filing fee from $1,000 to $2,750 by the 2006 amendment to § 1930, but the amendment mistakenly references § 1930(a)(2) rather than § 1930(a)(3), and thus, for now, the court clerks will be asking only for $1,000. See the Deficit Reduction Act of 2005, Pub. L. No. 109-171, § 11101(a) (2006) ("striking '$1,000' and inserting '$2750' " in § 1930(a)(2)); Fee Issues in Bankruptcy Courts, http://www.uscourts.gov/fedcourtfees/bankruptcyfee2006.pdf (Admin. Office of U.S. Courts, eff. 4/9/06). There is also a $39 administrative fee imposed by the Judicial Conference pursuant to 28 U.S.C. § 1930(b). See Bankruptcy Court Miscellaneous Fee Schedule, at 2 (Oct. 17, 2005), http://www.uscourts.gov/fedcourtfees/101705bankruptcyFee.pdf.

11 petition should be dismissed for lack of good faith due to lack of a valid reorganizational purpose, where the debtor had suffered neither financial nor managerial difficulties and filed the petition only to gain a tactical advantage in settling price-fixing claims brought by numerous customers). A filing ordinarily will not be in good faith absent some level of present or anticipated financial distress; some courts require the financial difficulties to be fairly severe or imminent. See id.; In re Liberate Technologies, 314 B.R. 206 (Bankr. N.D. Cal. 2004); In re Bus. Info. Co., 81 B.R. 382, 385 (Bankr. W.D. Pa. 1988) (dismissing petition of solvent corporation after review of "all pertinent facts and circumstances," because amount of judgment on appeal was not "so large as to single-handedly vitiate the debtor's existence," and thus filing of petition as a litigation tactic indicated a lack of good faith). Some courts require not only that the debtor suffer from "some degree of financial distress" but also that the filing serve one or both of the two main purposes of chapter 11: (1) preserving the business as a going concern (either by reorganization or by sale of the business as a going concern) and (2) maximizing the value of the estate for creditors.[6] But a petition may nevertheless be considered to be filed in good faith if it is filed primarily not for one of those two purposes but rather to obtain the benefits of a specific provision of the Code (such as the cap on lessors' claims under § 502(b)(6)).[7]

A few courts have suggested that a more lenient good faith standard should apply where a debtor is a member of a corporate group and "[w]here * * * the need for rehabilitation of the corporate family enterprise is obvious;" in such a case a filing by a "key and integrated member of the * * * corporate group" should be considered to be in good faith without regard to the subsidiary's particular need for bankruptcy relief. In re Mirant Corp., 2005 WL 2148362 (Bankr. N.D. Tex. Jan. 26, 2005) (relying on Heisley v. U.I.P. Engineered Prods. Corp. (In re U.I.P. Engineered Prods. Corp.), 831 F.2d 54 (4th Cir. 1987)). In any event, the filing by affiliated corporations often will constitute a default under contracts to which the subsidiary may be a party; in *Mirant*, for example, such defaults might have deprived the debtor subsidiary of the access to the electrical grid that it needed in order to deliver the electricity that it generated. Thus, where the parent (or another important member of a corporate group) files in chapter 11 due to financial distress, the consequences to other members of the group usually will be sufficient to allow them to file chapter 11 petitions in good faith, even if a more lenient good faith standard is not applied. See *Mirant*.

---

6. See NMSBPCSLDHB, L.P. v. Integrated Telecom Express, Inc. (In re Integrated Telecom Express, Inc.), 384 F.3d 108, 121 (3d Cir. 2004) (reversing and remanding for dismissal where debtor was a "highly solvent and cash rich" corporation that sought to use chapter 11 to reduce a lessor's claim under § 502(b)(6)).

7. See Solow v. PPI Enters. (U.S.), Inc. (In re PPI Enters. (U.S.), Inc.), 324 F.3d 197 (3d Cir. 2003).

Is Gruff eligible even if he only owns shares in Foam Corporation and does not otherwise own any business? See Toibb v. Radloff, 501 U.S. 157, 111 S. Ct. 2197, 115 L. Ed. 2d 145 (1991) (individual who was not in business was eligible for chapter 11 relief). Suppose Gruff operated a business as a sole proprietor under the name FoamScraps Company, selling foam scraps he purchased from Foam Corporation; could he file a petition on behalf of FoamScraps Company and keep his nonbusiness assets out of the bankruptcy estate? Suppose Gruff operated FoamScraps Company as a partnership with Simmons; then could FoamScraps be a debtor in its own chapter 11 case? What if Foamscraps were a limited liability company (LLC), a form of business entity so little known in 1978 that it is not mentioned in § 109?

2. Authorization of the Filing

The Bankruptcy Code and the Rules are silent as to who must authorize a chapter 11 petition on behalf of a corporation. The Supreme Court has held that "local law" determines who has authority to act for a corporation in filing a bankruptcy petition. Price v. Gurney, 324 U.S. 100, 65 S. Ct. 513, 89 L. Ed. 776 (1945) (rejecting argument that shareholders had right to file bankruptcy petition for corporation). Thus, whatever law determines who has authority to act for the corporation in other matters—generally the corporation law of the state of incorporation—also determines who must authorize the filing of a petition.[8]

---

8.   Section 303(b)(3) provides that an involuntary bankruptcy petition may be filed against a partnership by "fewer than all of the general partners." It would seem, then, that a voluntary petition could be filed for a partnership only with consent of all the general partners, as Rule 1004(a) provided until its amendment in 2002. But the Advisory Committee concluded that no provision of the Code requires consent of all general partners, and that it was beyond the proper scope of the Rules to require it. Thus Rule 1004 was amended to delete that requirement. Unless a court disagrees with the Advisory Committee and finds such a requirement by implication from § 303(b)(3), authorization to file partnership petitions will be governed by nonbankruptcy law, under the principles of Price v. Gurney, with the result that the provisions of the partnership agreement are likely to be dispositive.

There is little authority on authorization of voluntary petitions for LLCs. They almost certainly are "persons" eligible to file bankruptcy petitions and probably are "corporations" as that term is defined in § 101. See Gilliam v. Speier (In re KRSM Props., LLC), 318 B.R. 712 (B.A.P. 9th Cir. 2004); In re Midpoint Dev. LLC, 313 B.R. 486 (Bankr. W.D. Okla. 2004). It is possible to argue that LLCs should be treated like partnerships, and then, by implication from § 303(b)(3), to argue that all members must consent to authorize the filing. More likely, though, authority to file will be governed by nonbankruptcy law, again under the principles of Price v. Gurney. Specific provisions in the articles of organization or operating agreement likely will be given effect. See, e.g., In re Avalon Hotel Partners, LLC, 302 B.R. 377 (Bankr. D. Or. 2003) (construing LLC Operating Agreement to allow filing of petition with consent or ratification of holders of 75% of ownership interests). Absent such specific provision, nonbankruptcy law may require consent of all the members to authorize filing of a voluntary petition, but it is possible that a majority vote or a 2/3 vote may be sufficient. See generally Murray, *Limited Liability Companies—Bankruptcy Issues*, in MODERN REAL ESTATE TRANSACTIONS 2955 (Annual Advanced ALI-ABA Course of Study, No. SL004, 2005), available at SL004 ALI-ABA 2955 (Westlaw) (not noting, however, the 2002 amendment to Rule 1004); Comm. on Bankr. & Corp. Reorg. of the Ass'n of the Bar of the City of N.Y., *Limited Liability Companies and Bankruptcy*, in THE BEST ENTITY FOR DOING THE DEAL 747, 768-69 (937 PLI

Under state corporation laws, corporations are to be managed by or under the direction of their boards of directors. See, e.g., Del. Gen. Corp. Law § 141(a). In practice, the chief executive officer and the other executives may run a company, and the board may delegate day-to-day decision-making authority to the officers, but the legal authority to manage the corporation's affairs and to make major corporate decisions, such as the decision to file a chapter 11 petition, must remain with the board, which, depending on the provisions of the corporation's charter and by-laws, may or may not need to obtain shareholder approval for the chapter 11 filing.[9]

Johnson and Gruff will therefore either need to call a meeting of Foam Corporation's board of directors for approval of a resolution authorizing the chapter 11 filing, or else obtain the written consent of each director—Gruff, Simmons, and attorney Mendoza. Whoever the board authorizes to sign the actual petition (probably Gruff) must declare under penalty of perjury that the filing of the petition has been authorized. See Official Form 1.[10]

Corp. Law & Practice Course Handbook Series No. 7143, 1996), available at 937 PLI/Corp 747, 768-69 (Westlaw); JTB Enters. v. D & B Venture, 194 B.R. 79, 87 n.12 (Bankr. E.D. Va. 1996); Blakemore, *Limited Liability Companies and the Bankruptcy Code: A Technical Review*, 13 AM. BANKR. INST. L.J. 12 (1994); Kornberg, Shorr, & Antonoff, *Treatment of LLCs Under Chapter 11 of the Bankruptcy Code*, 1 J. LTD. LIAB. COS. 17 (1994), reprinted at 869 PLI/Corp 285 (Westlaw).

9. Secured creditors sometimes attempt to use contracts and other consensual arrangements to prevent debtors from utilizing the protections of the bankruptcy laws. For example, financing arrangements often now include creation of a "Special Purpose Vehicle" (SPV), which is a separate business entity (typically an LLC or a corporation), created to hold title to the collateral. The SPV is designed to be "bankruptcy remote," which means steps are taken to try in advance to make sure that the SPV will not be able to file a bankruptcy petition. See generally Weissburg & Trott, *Special Purpose Bankruptcy Remote Entities*, in COMMERCIAL REAL ESTATE FINANCING 2005: WHAT BORROWERS & LENDERS NEED TO KNOW NOW 237 (512 PLI Real Estate Law & Practice Course Handbook Series No. 6179, 2005), available at 512 PLI/Real 237 (Westlaw); Klee & Butler, *Asset-Backed Securitization, Special Purpose Vehicles and Other Securitization Issues*, in CHAPTER 11 BUSINESS REORGANIZATIONS 55 (Annual Advanced ALI-ABA Course of Study, No. SJ082, 2004) available at SJ082 ALI-ABA 55 (Westlaw); 4 Dunaway, LAW OF DISTRESSED REAL ESTATE §§ 56:1-121 (2005), available at LAWDRE § 56:1 (Westlaw). If the SPV is a corporation, its charter may require (1) unanimous approval of its board of directors for the filing of a bankruptcy petition, and (2) that one of its directors at all times be an independent director owing fiduciary duties primarily to the SPV's creditors. See, e.g., LoPucki, *Contract Bankruptcy: A Reply to Alan Schwartz*, 109 YALE L.J. 317, 334-37 (1999). Thus the rules for authorization of a bankruptcy filing have become quite important to the secured finance industry. The extent to which the law should permit such contractual avoidance of bankruptcy protections is one of the most important issues in current bankruptcy scholarship. See id. at 317-19. Note that nothing in the corporation's charter can prevent creditors from filing an involuntary petition in bankruptcy; thus the special purpose vehicle may end up in chapter 11 even if the charter provisions keep it from filing a voluntary petition. See In re Kingston Square Assocs., 214 B.R. 713 (Bankr. S.D.N.Y. 1997) (refusing to find filing to be in bad faith even though debtors orchestrated filing of involuntary petition by creditors to evade corporate charter "bankruptcy remote" provisions).

10. If Foam Corporation is organized as a "close corporation," board authorization may not be needed. Under California law, which applies to Foam Corporation as a California corporation, Foam Corporation will be a close corporation if its articles of incorporation provide that its shares shall not be held by more than a specified number of persons (not exceeding 35), and if the articles include the statement, "This corporation is a close corporation." Cal. Corp. Code § 158; cf. Del. Gen. Corp. Law

3. Timing of the Filing, and the Concept of "Deepening Insolvency"

Suppose Gruff delays the chapter 11 filing. Instead he causes Foam Corporation, which he effectively controls, to continue its losing operations, so that it becomes ever deeper mired in debt. He will not be personally liable for those debts merely as a stockholder, because of the principle of limited liability. But he may have violated his fiduciary obligations to the corporation or to its creditors by deepening the insolvency of Foam Corporation. As a result, he may be personally liable to the corporation or to the creditors. See generally Official Comm. of Unsec. Cred. v. R.F. Lafferty & Co., 267 F.3d 340 (3d Cir. 2001) (noting "soundness" of deepening insolvency theory and holding that cause of action belonged to bankruptcy estate, but affirming dismissal based on in pari delicto defense); Limor v. Buerger (In re Del-Met Corp.), 322 B.R. 781 (Bankr. M.D. Tenn. 2005) (reprinted below in Chapter Ten); Heaton, *Deepening Insolvency*, 30 J. CORP. L. 465 (2005); Willett, *The Shallows of Deepening Insolvency*, 60 BUS. LAW. 549 (2005).

This relatively new concept of liability for "deepening insolvency" has two interrelated bases. First, corporate directors and officers owe fiduciary duties of loyalty and care to the corporation. Ordinarily the focus of those duties is on protecting the interests of the corporation's shareholders, not its creditors. See, e.g., Gevurtz, CORPORATION LAW § 4.1.5 (2000). But the corporation itself, and not just its creditors, may be harmed when directors and officers cause the corporation to deplete its assets while building up unnecessary, excessive, unpayable debt.[11] "Whether a firm is solvent or insolvent, it—and not a constituency such as its stockholders or its creditors—owns a claim that a director has, by failing to exercise sufficient care, mismanaged the firm and caused a diminution to its economic value." Prod. Res. Group v. NCT Group, 863 A.2d 772 (Del. Ch. 2004).

Second, as the court in *Production Resources Group* notes, when a corporation has become insolvent—and perhaps even when it is nearly insolvent and thus in the "zone of insolvency"—the focus of the fiduciary obligations shifts

---

§ 342 (limiting the specified number of shareholders to no more than 30 and requiring that no public offering of the corporation's stock be made). A written agreement among the stockholders of a close corporation can remove management authority from the board of directors and place it elsewhere, such as in the stockholders themselves. See Cal. Corp. Code § 300(b); Del. Gen. Corp. Law § 350. If such an agreement is in place, then action by the board of a close corporation is neither necessary nor sufficient to authorize a chapter 11 filing; the shareholders, or whoever is authorized to manage the business under the shareholders' agreement, will need to authorize it.

11. Cf. Smith v. Arthur Andersen LLP, 421 F.3d 989, 1004 (9th Cir. 2005) (holding that corporation suffered "cognizable harm," and thus that trustee had standing to assert claim "that the defendants 'prolonged' the firm's existence, causing it to expend corporate assets that would not have been spent 'if the corporation [had been] dissolved in a timely manner, rather than kept afloat with spurious debt,' " but not reaching questions whether complaint stated a valid claim or whether incurring of unpayable debt constituted a harm to the corporation) (quoting *R.F. Lafferty & Co.*, 267 F.3d at 350).

to the interests of creditors. 863 A.2d at 787-91. See also Lin, *Shift of Fiduciary Duty upon Corporate Insolvency: Proper Scope of Directors' Duty to Creditors*, 46 VAND. L. REV. 1485 (1993). Further losses harm the creditors financially, and may cause little or no harm to the shareholders (because their shares already may be valueless or nearly so). Directors then have a duty of care to protect the corporation and the creditors from further unnecessary losses. They must take into account the harm that further losses will cause to creditors. It is not clear, though, that the duty to try to avoid losses that harm the creditors of an insolvent or nearly insolvent corporation is any different from the duty to avoid losses that harm the shareholders of a clearly solvent corporation:

> The directors continue to have the task of attempting to maximize the economic value of the firm. That much of their job does not change. But the fact of insolvency does necessarily affect the constituency on whose behalf the directors are pursuing that end. By definition, the fact of insolvency places the creditors in the shoes normally occupied by the shareholders—that of residual riskbearers.

Production Resources Group, 863 A.2d at 791 (footnote omitted). On the other hand, as the omitted footnote states, maximizing the value of an insolvent firm might

> require the directors to undertake the course of action that best preserves value in a situation when the procession of the firm as a going concern would be value-destroying. In other words, the efficient liquidation of an insolvent firm might well be the method by which the firm's value is enhanced in order to meet the legitimate claims of its creditors.

Id. at 791, n. 60.

Corporate charter provisions exculpating directors and officers from liability for certain breaches of the duty of care may provide some comfort. See *Production Resources Group*, 863 A.2d at 793-95; Pereira v. Farace, 413 F.3d 330, 342 (2d Cir. 2005). There is also authority that the business judgment rule protects the decision of directors and officers to continue operation of an insolvent corporation—and the decision of lenders and others to assist in such continued operation[12]—absent bad faith or fraudulent intent. See In re Global Serv. Group, 316 B.R. 451 (Bankr. S.D.N.Y. 2004). Nevertheless, the question whether Gruff may breach his fiduciary duties to Foam Corporation by failing to shut down the losing operations, or by failing to seek timely chapter 11 protection for the corporation, is one that Gruff should consider carefully.

4. Jurisdiction and Venue

The bankruptcy judges for a particular district "shall constitute a unit of the district court to be known as the bankruptcy court for that district." 28 U.S.C. § 151. Bankruptcy cases are commenced by the filing with the bankruptcy court

---

12. We discuss the "deepening insolvency" concept further, with respect to its potential use against lenders, in Chapter Ten of this text.

of a petition. Sections 301-304. Thus Johnson and Gruff will have to file the petition with the bankruptcy court. There are two questions, however.

First, what court has jurisdiction to handle the case? Under § 301 the petition must be filed in the *bankruptcy court*, but under 28 U.S.C. § 1334(a), the federal *district courts* have original and exclusive jurisdiction of all cases under title 11 of the United States Code (which is the Bankruptcy Code). Of course, that includes chapter 11 cases such as Foam Corporation's. The apparent confusion is resolved by 28 U.S.C. § 157(a), which authorizes the district courts to refer any or all cases under the Bankruptcy Code to the bankruptcy judges for the district. Under 28 U.S.C. § 157(d) a district court may withdraw the reference and handle any case itself. Not surprisingly, given the heavy workload of the district courts, almost all cases are referred to the bankruptcy judges, and seldom is the reference withdrawn. Thus a bankruptcy judge will handle Foam Corporation's case. Jurisdiction over various proceedings and related cases that may arise during the chapter 11 case is more complex. See generally Brubaker, *On the Nature of Federal Bankruptcy Jurisdiction: A General Statutory and Constitutional Theory*, 41 WM. & MARY L. REV. 743 (2000); Epstein, Nickles & White, BANKRUPTCY §§ 12-1 to 12-5; 1 NORTON BANKR. L. & PRAC. 2D §§ 4:1-145. For now it is enough to see that the bankruptcy judge has jurisdiction of the chapter 11 case.

The second question is venue; in which district should Foam Corporation file its bankruptcy petition? 28 U.S.C. § 1408 governs venue for bankruptcy cases:

> Except as provided in section 1410 of this title [dealing with venue of chapter 15 cases ancillary to foreign proceedings], a case under title 11 may be commenced in the district court for the district—
>
> (1) in which the domicile, residence, principal place of business in the United States, or principal assets in the United States, of the person or entity that is the subject of the case have been located for the one hundred and eighty days immediately preceding such commencement, or for a longer portion of such one-hundred-and-eighty day period than the domicile, residence, or principal place of business, in the United States, or principal assets in the United States, of such person were located in any other district; or
>
> (2) in which there is pending a case under title 11 concerning such person's affiliate, general partner, or partnership.

Corporations are domiciled in the state of their incorporation. See Hoffman v. Bullmore (In re Nat'l Warranty Ins. Risk Retention Group), 384 F.3d 959, 962 (8th Cir. 2004); In re Ocean Props. of Del., Inc., 95 B.R. 304 (Bankr. D. Del. 1988). But see In re Indus. Pollution Control, Inc, 137 B.R. 176, 180 (Bankr. W.D. Pa. 1992) ("Domicile and residence … generally apply to individuals and not to corporations."). What if the state of incorporation contains more than one district? In which district or districts would the corporation be domiciled? The answer is unclear. Presumably, if a corporation can be said to have a "residence," it is the same as its domicile. However, by analogy to 28 U.S.C. § 1391(c) (which applies to corporations as defendants), a corporation might be considered to be a resident of any district in which it is subject to personal jurisdiction, which for many corporations would be virtually every district in the nation.

Problem 2-2

U Foam, Foam Corporation's wholly owned subsidiary, is a North Carolina corporation, which does business throughout North Carolina but nowhere else. U Foam's plants, executive offices, and most of its assets are located in the Eastern District of North Carolina. If Foam Corporation properly files a chapter 11 petition in the Central District of California, what choices of venue would U Foam have for its petition? See § 101 (definition of "affiliate").

If U Foam filed a chapter 11 petition in the Eastern District of North Carolina before Foam Corporation filed its petition, what choices of venue would Foam Corporation have? Assume a court will find Foam Corporation's principal place of business to be its executive offices. Assume Foam Corporation moved its executive offices 85 days ago from Richmond, California (which is in the Northern District of California) to Los Angeles (which is in the Central District of California). Because Foam Corporation's assets are spread out over so many states, assume there is no district in which its principal assets are located. If Gruff wants to file Foam Corporation's petition in the Central District of California, what should he do?

Suppose Gruff wants to file Foam Corporation's petition in the (mythical) Northern District of the State of Oklabraska, because he has heard that the sole bankruptcy judge for that district is very sympathetic to debtors. What could Gruff do? You may have noticed that case names for opinions in many chapter 11 cases are not the names of the principal corporations involved. See, e.g., In re Chateaugay Corp., 924 F.2d 480 (2d Cir. 1991) (involving LTV, the large steel company); In re Ionosphere Clubs, Inc., 922 F.2d 984 (2d Cir. 1990) (involving Eastern Airlines). What do you think debtors (or their lawyers) who wish to file in a particular district may be doing? See LoPucki, COURTING FAILURE (2005); Epstein, Nickles & White, BANKRUPTCY § 12-7; Eisenberg & LoPucki, *Shopping for Judges: An Empirical Analysis of Venue Choice in Large Chapter 11 Reorganizations*, 84 CORNELL L. REV. 967 (1999); LoPucki & Whitford, *Venue Choice and Forum Shopping in the Bankruptcy Reorganization of Large, Publicly Held Companies*, 1991 WIS.L.REV. 11 (1991).

5. Filing the Petition and Accompanying Forms

The various forms that Foam Corporation must file are set forth in § 521, Rule 1007, any applicable local bankruptcy court rules, and any applicable United States trustee guidelines. The Judicial Conference of the United States has promulgated Official Forms that must be used, although they may be altered as appropriate. Rule 9009.

Foam Corporation must "file *with the petition* a list containing the name and address of each creditor unless the petition is accompanied by a schedule of liabilities." Rule 1007(a) (emphasis added). The list or schedule will permit the court to send notice of the filing to the creditors. The burden of compiling such a list can delay a desired filing, especially if the debtor's records are in poor shape, as is often true of financially distressed companies. Under Rule 1007(d) the debtor also must file *with the petition* a list (Official Form 4) containing the name, address, and claim of the holders of the twenty largest unsecured claims, excluding insiders.[13] Unless it obtains an extension from the court, Foam Corporation will be required to file its Schedules (Official Form 6) and its Statement of Financial Affairs (Official Form 7) within fifteen days after filing the petition. Gruff and Johnson will need to gather a substantial amount of information to complete those forms.

The United States trustee (a Justice Department official described below) will require Foam Corporation to submit additional information. If Foam Corporation does not provide the required information, the United States trustee may move for dismissal of the case or conversion of it to chapter 7.

D. AN INTRODUCTION TO THE "PLAYERS" IN FOAM CORPORATION'S CHAPTER 11 CASE

At this point it will be helpful to introduce the "players" who will be important in the chapter 11 case that Foam Corporation has just commenced.

1. The Debtor in Possession

Foam Corporation probably will stay in control of its business and keep possession of the property of the estate as a "debtor in possession." See § 1115(b). So long as there is no trustee serving in the case, the debtor is called the "debtor in possession" or "DIP." See § 1101. The court can order appointment of a trustee for the case if there is "cause" or if it is in the interests of the creditors, stockholders, and estate. Section 1104(a) (discussed in Chapter Six of this text). It is unusual for the court to order appointment of a trustee in a chapter 11 case. If, however, such an order is entered, the United States trustee will appoint a trustee for the case (subject to the court's approval). The appointed trustee will take over control of the business and possession of the property of the estate, unless creditors demand to elect a trustee within 30 days after entry of the order. See § 1104(b) and (d).

The debtor in possession has almost all of the rights that a trustee would have, including (unless the court orders otherwise) the right to operate the business. See §§ 1107(a), 1108. The debtor in possession has the right to enter into transactions in the ordinary course of its business and may use the property of the estate (other than cash collateral) in the ordinary course of its

---

13. Until a creditors' committee is appointed, the creditors on the Rule 1007(d) list serve some of the watchdog functions that the committee ordinarily would serve. See Rule 4001 (providing for notice of certain important motions—such as motions for relief from stay and motions for authority to obtain credit—to be given to the creditors on the Rule 1007(d) list, if no creditors' committee has been appointed); see generally infra section D.3. of this Chapter (discussing creditors' committees). The court is prohibited from allowing the debtor to delay the filing of the Rule 1007(d) list. Rule 9006(b)(2).

business without seeking permission from the court. Section 363(c). The debtor typically will need to use cash collateral and may need to take steps that are outside (or at least arguably outside) the ordinary course of its business. In Chapter Four we consider the circumstances under which the court should approve use of "cash collateral" and under which the court should approve nonordinary course transactions, such as a sale of all or a substantial part of the assets. In Chapter Six we discuss more fully how courts distinguish between ordinary course and nonordinary course transactions.

For most purposes, the debtor in possession should not be seen as a new entity; it is simply the same debtor that existed before the chapter 11 petition was filed. (This is controversial, but under § 1101 "debtor in possession" simply means the debtor so long as there is no trustee serving in the case.) The debtor manages but no longer owns the property it previously owned; the property is now part of an estate. As long as the debtor keeps possession of that property—that is, as long as a trustee is not serving after appointment or election—the debtor is a debtor in possession of the estate's property and hence a "debtor in possession."

Unless the debtor is a natural person (an individual human being), it will need to act through agents, and it will need to have a process for internal governance. If the debtor is a corporation it will continue to be managed under the direction of its board of directors (at least if it is not a close corporation). Outside of bankruptcy the directors generally have the duty to manage the debtor in the best interests of the shareholders. When a company nears insolvency, the directors' duties are expanded so that duties are also owed to creditors, perhaps primarily to them. In particular, in bankruptcy the debtor in possession and the directors and others who act on its behalf are bound by duties of loyalty and care as fiduciaries for all those who may be entitled to some of the value of the estate's assets. That includes creditors and stockholders. The interests of the creditors and stockholders may conflict; the debtor and its directors may have difficulty balancing those conflicting interests. In Chapter Six we consider corporate governance issues, such as the extent of the fiduciary duties owed by the directors, the circumstances under which the court should limit the control exercised by the board, and the circumstances under which the court should limit the shareholders' ability to remove and elect directors.

Unfortunately, debtors in possession do not always carry out their duties competently and honestly. Sometimes the court should order appointment of a trustee[14] to take possession of the property of the estate, to manage the business, and to decide whether the business should continue in operation. See § 1104(a) & (e) (discussed below in Chapter Six).

---

14. As noted above, if the court orders appointment of a trustee, the creditors may demand to elect the trustee instead of having the United States trustee appoint one. See § 1104(b).

Most business decisions made by the debtor in possession or trustee are entitled to deference, but neither is permitted to run the business without supervision. The "supervisors" include the United States trustee, the creditors' committee (or committees), any equity security holders' committee (or committees), and, typically, the major secured creditor (or creditors). Ultimately, through its function of resolving legal disputes, the bankruptcy court gives the debtor a kind of supervision.

2. The United States Trustee (and the Bankruptcy Judge in an Administrative Role)

Do not confuse the United States trustee with a trustee for the case. The United States trustee is a Justice Department official who is responsible for supervising the administration of bankruptcy cases within a region. The United States is divided into twenty-one regions, most of which include more than one federal judicial district. See 28 U.S.C. § 581(a). (In Alabama and North Carolina, cases are supervised by judicially appointed bankruptcy administrators rather than United States trustees.[15]) In the ordinary chapter 11 case, the court does not order appointment of a trustee for the case, and the debtor in possession will operate the business, but the United States trustee (or an assistant United States trustee) still will be involved in administration of the case.

The United States trustees were created in an attempt to remove the bankruptcy judges further from the administration of chapter 11 cases. This is a continuation of a process that was begun in 1938. At that time bankruptcy "referees" (they were not called judges) were primarily administrative officers, who supervised and administered bankruptcy cases, and who decided only a limited range of disputes that arose in such cases. In 1938 the Chandler Act removed many of the referees' administrative functions and gave them a larger judicial role. The Rules of Bankruptcy Procedure promulgated in 1973 changed their title from "referee" to "bankruptcy judge" and again expanded their judicial power. See H.R. Rep. No. 595, 95th Cong., 1st Sess. 7-9 (1977).

The Bankruptcy Reform Act of 1978 (the "1978 BRA")[16] continued the process of removing the bankruptcy judges from administration of cases and expanding their duties as judicial officers.[17] The 1978 BRA designated

---

15. See the Bankruptcy Judges, United States Trustees, and Family Farmer Bankruptcy Act of 1986, Pub. L. 99-554, § 302, 100 Stat. 3088, 3121-23 (1986).

16. Pub. L. 95-598, 92 Stat. 2549 (1978).

17. In fact, the 1978 BRA went too far; the Supreme Court held unconstitutional the BRA's broad grant of jurisdiction to the bankruptcy judges. Northern Pipeline Constr. Co. v. Marathon Pipe Line Co., 458 U.S. 50, 102 S. Ct. 2858, 73 L. Ed. 2d 598 (1982), judgment stayed temporarily, 459 U.S. 813, 103 S. Ct. 199, 74 L. Ed. 2d 160 (1982). The Bankruptcy Amendments and Federal Judgeship Act of 1984, Pub. L. 98-353, 98 Stat. 333 (1984), subjects bankruptcy judges' decisions in "non-core" cases to de novo district court review, thus probably resolving the constitutional problem.

eighteen pilot districts in which United States trustees would supervise and administer bankruptcy cases. In 1986, the United States trustee system was extended to cover the entire nation, except for Alabama and North Carolina.[18]

Nevertheless, even as Congress was creating a nationwide United States trustee program to administer bankruptcy cases, Congress reversed the trend toward removing the judge from administration of cases, with bankruptcy judges reclaiming the power to act *sua sponte* rather than only on request of a party in interest. See § 105(a) (as amended in 1986). That reversal continued in the Bankruptcy Reform Act of 1994,[19] which codified in § 105(d) the power of bankruptcy judges to hold status conferences, at which judges may learn about their cases outside the context of an adversarial dispute. The reversal intensified in the Bankruptcy Abuse Prevention and Consumer Protection Act of 2005 (the "2005 BAPCPA"),[20] which amended § 105(d) to state that a bankruptcy judge "shall hold such status conferences as are necessary to further the expeditious and economical resolution of the case."

In a chapter 11 case, the United States trustee (or an assistant United States trustee acting on behalf of the United States trustee)

- appoints the unsecured creditors' committee and any other committees that may be needed;

- in the absence of an election appoints the trustee for the case if the court orders the appointment of one, and presides over the election of a trustee if the creditors request an election;

- moves for appointment of a trustee, as required by the 2005 amendments, in certain cases involving fraud, dishonesty, or criminal conduct;

- monitors the case to be sure that the debtor files the required reports and pays the required fees;

- monitors the applications for compensation made by the attorneys and other professionals; and

- generally monitors the progress of the case, including the plans and disclosure statements that are filed.

See §§ 1102(a), 1104(b) & (d), 1104(e) (added in 2005); 28 U.S.C. § 586. As we have seen, the United States trustee may demand various kinds and amounts of information from the debtor.

---

18. The Ninth Circuit has held that the exclusion of the districts in Alabama and North Carolina violates the constitutional requirement (U.S. CONST. art. I, § 8, cl. 4) that bankruptcy laws be uniform. See St. Angelo v. Victoria Farms, Inc., 38 F.3d 1525 (9th Cir. 1994), opinion amended, 46 F.3d 969 (9th Cir. 1995) (holding that the infirmity can be cured by striking the exclusion of the Alabama and North Carolina districts). Neither the Department of Justice nor the federal courts in Alabama and North Carolina have given effect to the Ninth Circuit's "striking" of the exclusion.

19. Pub. L. 103-394, § 104(a), 108 Stat. 4106, 4108-09 (1994).

20. Pub. L. 109-8, § 440, 119 Stat. 23, 114 (2005).

The United States trustee also has standing to raise any issue, appear in court on any issue, and be heard on any issue in the case; the only exception is that the United States trustee may not file a plan of reorganization. Section 307. For example, the United States trustee has standing to ask the bankruptcy court to order appointment of a trustee for the case and standing to move for dismissal of the case or conversion to a chapter 7 liquidation case. Sections 1104(a), 1112(b). That gives the debtor a strong incentive to cooperate with the United States trustee. However, the debtor or any other party in interest may go to court to challenge the actions (or the inaction) of the United States trustee. See Rule 2020.

Unfortunately, due to budgetary constraints and to a burdensome case load, it is difficult for the United States trustees to supervise effectively all the chapter 11 cases that are filed.

3. Creditors' Committees[21]

Creditors' committees also supervise the debtor in possession. If unsecured creditors are willing to serve, the United States trustee ordinarily appoints at least one creditors' committee in each chapter 11 case; typically the committee consists of those creditors willing to serve that hold the seven largest unsecured claims. See § 1102. In Foam Corporation's case, the United States trustee may decide to appoint the members of the prepetition creditors' committee who were elected by the creditors during the workout attempt, if the requirements of § 1102(b)(1) and Rule 2007 are met.

The members of the creditors' committee owe fiduciary duties to the general unsecured creditors whom they represent. In Chapter Six we consider the nature of those duties, and also whether certain creditors should be excluded from the creditors' committee because of the likelihood that a conflict of interest would cause them to breach their duties. For example, Gruff holds the largest unsecured claim against Foam Corporation—$3.2 million. Of course he is also the president, chairman of the board, and majority stockholder in Foam Corporation. If he were permitted to serve on the creditors' committee, he would be privy to the creditors' committee's strategy and confidential discussions, which would hinder the committee from representing the interests of unsecured creditors.

Sometimes more than one creditors' committee should be appointed so that the various kinds of unsecured creditors will be adequately represented in the chapter 11 case. In Foam Corporation's case, the unsecured creditors (other than Gruff) are almost entirely trade creditors, whose concerns will be similar, so one creditors' committee probably can adequately represent the body of unsecured creditors.

---

21. See generally Klee & Shaffer, *Creditors' Committees Under Chapter 11 of the Bankruptcy Code*, 44 S. CAR. L. REV. 995 (1993).

In some cases one or more committees should be appointed to represent shareholders or other equity security holders. See § 1102(a)(2). In Foam Corporation's case, there are only two stockholders (Gruff and Simmons), and the majority stockholder is president and chairman of the board, so there is probably no need for an equity security holders' committee to make sure that stockholders' interests are protected.

The most important function of the creditors' committee is to negotiate with the debtor in possession over the plan of reorganization and to advise the creditors as to any plan that may be filed. See In re Structurlite Plastics, 91 B.R. 813 (Bankr. S.D. Ohio 1988); § 1103(c)(3). Instead of having to negotiate with hundreds or thousands of individual creditors, the debtor can negotiate with the committee. That greatly simplifies the negotiation of a plan. If the negotiations result in a plan that the committee can support, then most of the creditors are likely to follow the committee's recommendation and support the plan as well.

The creditors' committee also has a role to play in supervising the business's operations. The committee should not try to take over management of the debtor, but it has the right to consult with the debtor in possession concerning the business operations and any other facet of the administration of case. See § 1103(c)(1). It has the right to perform a broad investigation of the debtor, including an investigation of whether the debtor's business should continue in operation and of "any other matter relevant to the case or to the formulation of a plan." Section 1103(c)(2). If its investigation leads it to conclude that the business should not be continued, the creditors' committee can move under § 1112 for dismissal of the case or conversion to a chapter 7 liquidation case, or under § 1108 for an order limiting or closing down operation of the business. Section 1103(c)(4) specifically gives the committee the right to seek appointment of a trustee to displace the debtor in possession or of an examiner to conduct an investigation of the debtor.[22]

In performing these functions, the committee must provide information (or access to information) to the creditors whom it represents. See § 1102(b)(3) (added in 2005). It must also "seek and receive comments" from the represented creditors. Id.

The members of the creditors' committee are not paid for their work, although they can seek reimbursement for expenses, such as expenses to travel to attend meetings. See § 503(b)(3)(F). They run the risk of being sued for alleged breach of fiduciary duty to other creditors. Thus it is often difficult to

---

22. More generally, a creditors' committee has the right as a "party in interest" to raise any issue in court and to appear and be heard on any issue. Section 1109(b). (Nevertheless, as discussed in Chapter Six below, the committee does not necessarily have the right to file motions or actions that the Code authorizes only the debtor in possession—or trustee—to pursue.) Notices sent to all creditors under Rule 2002 also must be sent to the committee, see Rule 2002(i). More importantly, the committee receives notice under Rule 4001 of some important motions, notice of which may not be sent to all creditors, such as motions for relief from stay and motions for authority to obtain credit.

find creditors who are willing to serve actively on a creditors' committee.[23] As a result, especially in small cases, there may be no creditors' committee, or the creditors' committee may provide little or no supervision of the debtor.

Even when there is an active committee, it will require professional assistance to be effective. The committee will need an attorney to investigate legal matters, to represent it in court, and to assist with negotiations. The committee will usually need an accountant or other financial adviser to investigate and evaluate the debtor's business. With the court's approval, the committee can hire such professionals, who may be paid out of the estate as an expense of administration. See §§ 330(a), 503(b)(2), 1103(a).

Of course the debtor will have professionals working with it, who may also be paid out of the estate as an administrative expense pursuant to the same provisions of the Code. See §§ 327(a), 330(a), 503(b)(2), 1107(a). The total administrative expenses for professionals in a chapter 11 case can consume a substantial part of the value of the business. Not surprisingly, courts and the United States trustee take this into account in deciding how many committees should be formed; every additional committee means at least an extra lawyer to pay, and perhaps other expenses as well.

4. Major Secured Creditors

Major secured creditors often play important roles in monitoring the debtor in possession and in shaping the outcome of the case. In many cases there is one major secured creditor who holds a lien on all or nearly all the property of the estate for a debt that is more than the liquidation value of all the property. If there are further losses from business operations in the chapter 11 reorganization, and if the reorganization ultimately fails, the losses will fall on the secured creditor. That gives the secured creditor a great incentive to monitor the debtor and act to prevent those losses. If the liquidation value is substantially less than the debt owed to the secured creditor, the secured creditor may want to give the debtor a chance to reorganize—that may result in a higher payout to the secured creditor than would occur in a liquidation. However, the secured creditor will still have an incentive to monitor the debtor carefully to minimize losses and maximize the chances of a successful reorganization.

Foam Corporation's case is typical. Kick Credit has a security interest in Foam Corporation's personal property. In a liquidation (according to Gruff's analysis, supra, this chapter, section B), Kick Credit might not be fully paid off; thus it may be in Kick Credit's interest for Foam Corporation to

---

23. Small business creditors may be especially reluctant to devote the needed time, and to run the accompanying risk, of serving on the committee. On the other hand, small businesses may be more likely than larger concerns to suffer ruin when a debtor who is a large customer fails to pay; that may provide the needed motivation. The Code now permits the court to order that such a small business creditor be added to the committee. See § 1102(a)(4) (added in 2005).

reorganize so that a larger amount can be paid. However, if, in attempting to reorganize, Foam Corporation depletes its assets, Kick Credit may suffer a larger loss than it would in an immediate liquidation.

As we have seen already, secured creditors have special rights. Those rights give them a great deal of leverage in monitoring the debtor and affecting the outcome of the case.

Secured creditors can demand adequate protection of their interest in the estate's property; if, for example, Foam Corporation is not adequately maintaining its manufacturing equipment, Kick Credit can demand that the debtor take appropriate remedial steps and threaten to seek relief from the automatic stay if the steps are not taken. See § 362(d)(1). To the extent the debtor is using the secured creditor's cash collateral, the secured creditor can monitor the debtor's efficiency; if Foam Corporation is unable to generate as much new cash collateral as it uses up, Kick Credit will likely be able to block Foam Corporation from obtaining an order authorizing use of the cash collateral, and the court may grant Kick Credit relief from the automatic stay for lack of adequate protection. See id. and § 363(c)(2) & (e). Thus the debtor will be under strong pressure to turn its operations around quickly, so that there are no substantial losses from continuing operations.

Secured creditors also have a strong bargaining position in negotiations over a plan of reorganization. If a secured creditor does not accept the plan, the secured creditor ordinarily must be given its collateral, or a substitute that is the "indubitable equivalent," or else cash payments under the plan that have a present value equal to the lesser of the amount of the debt or the value of the collateral. If the debtor needs to keep the collateral but is unable to fund such payments (and unable to provide an "indubitable equivalent"), then no plan of reorganization can be confirmed over the secured creditor's opposition. See § 1129(b)(2)(A). Absent a § 1111(b)(2) election, and assuming the collateral is retained by the debtor, an undersecured creditor will hold a secured claim equal to the value of the collateral and an unsecured claim for the rest of the debt; often that unsecured claim is large enough so that if the undersecured creditor votes against the plan, the plan will not be confirmable. As we will see, an undersecured creditor can sometimes make confirmation of a plan more difficult by making the § 1111(b)(2) election, even though it will not then hold an unsecured claim that can be voted against the plan.

The debtor therefore needs to gain the confidence of the major secured creditors. If the debtor cannot convince them that it is taking effective action to turn its business around, they often will be able to block progress in negotiation of a plan. That may result in the secured creditors obtaining relief from the automatic stay under § 362(d)(2) or (d)(3), on the ground that a successful reorganization within a reasonable time is not likely. It also may result in the appointment of a trustee, or in the dismissal of the case or conversion of the case to a chapter 7 liquidation case.

If a secured creditor is oversecured, then the secured creditor has a different kind of ability to monitor the debtor and take action. Most loan agreements provide that the creditor is entitled to recover attorneys' fees against the debtor. Under § 506(b), an oversecured creditor can add its reasonable attorneys' fees and other costs to the amount of its secured claim if the loan agreement so provides. That gives oversecured creditors somewhat the same benefit that creditors' committees have in supervising the debtor—their attorneys are paid, at least to some extent, by the estate. Individual creditors, including secured creditors, are "parties in interest" with the right to raise issues and appear and be heard in court on issues involved in the case. Section 1109(b). An oversecured creditor's right to have reasonable attorneys' fees added to the secured claim gives the oversecured creditor an incentive to raise issues and make its voice heard in court whenever it believes it is needed. First Bank (with its real estate mortgages on Foam Corporation's Los Angeles, Philadelphia, and Camden plants) appears to be oversecured, and thus is likely to be able to add its reasonable attorneys' fees to the amount of its secured claim.[24]

E. RETENTION OF PROFESSIONALS

Foam Corporation will need the help of attorneys, accountants, and other professionals to reorganize under chapter 11. The creditors' committee will also need professional assistance to play an active and effective role. Sections 327(a), 1103(a), and 1107(a) permit Foam Corporation and the committee to retain needed professionals, with the court's approval. Under § 327(a), the debtor in possession's attorney (and other professionals retained by the debtor in possession) must not "hold or represent an interest adverse to the estate" and must be "disinterested," a term defined in § 101. Under § 1103(b), the committee's attorney (and its other

---

24. Even an undersecured or unsecured creditor may be entitled to have reasonable postpetition attorneys' fees added to the allowed amount of its unsecured claim if the credit contract provides for fees. See United Merchs. & Mfrs. v. Equitable Life Assurance Soc'y (In re United Merchs. & Mfrs.), 674 F.2d 134 (2d Cir. 1982) (holding that the old Bankruptcy Act gave unsecured creditors such a right); In re New Power Co., 313 B.R. 496 (Bankr. N.D. Ga. 2004); In re Byrd, 192 B.R. 917, 919 (Bankr. E.D. Tenn. 1996) (allowing such fees as prepetition, contingent, unliquidated claims). But see In re FINOVA Group, 304 B.R. 630 (D. Del. 2004) (affirming denial of allowance of unsecured creditors' postpetition fees and costs, and describing such denial as the majority approach); cf. Adams v. Zimmerman, 73 F.3d 1164 (1st Cir. 1996) (stating that unsecured creditors' postpetition attorneys' fees generally are not allowed as a part of their claims, and applying that rule by analogy in an FDIC receivership case). There are two reasons why unsecured and undersecured creditors will be more reluctant than oversecured creditors to incur attorneys' fees in the bankruptcy case, even if their contract provides for them, and even if the bankruptcy court will allow them. First, unsecured claims typically are not paid in full; the addition of postpetition attorneys' fees to a creditor's unsecured claim typically will not result in those fees being paid in full out of the property of the estate. Thus the creditor will bear at least some of the cost of the fees. By contrast, attorneys' fees allowed to an oversecured creditor under § 506(b) ordinarily will be paid in full. Second, some courts that allow postpetition fees to be added to unsecured claims pursuant to contract nevertheless refuse to allow addition of fees incurred in litigating bankruptcy law issues rather than contract law issues. Oversecured creditors, on the other hand, are probably entitled to allowance of reasonable fees under § 506(b) even if the fees are incurred in litigating purely bankruptcy law issues. See Kord Enters. II v. Cal. Commerce Bank (In re Kord Enters. II), 139 F.3d 684 (9th Cir. 1998).

professionals) "may not, while employed by such committee, represent any other entity having an adverse interest in connection with the case." Under § 328(c) the court may refuse to permit payment of any professional employed under § 327 or § 1103 if "at any time during [the] employment" the professional is not disinterested or holds or represents an adverse interest.

One of the first actions Foam Corporation should take in its chapter 11 case is to apply for court approval to employ Johnson's firm (Smith, Martinez & Johnson) as its attorneys. (Foam Corporation cannot appear except by an attorney; thus Johnson will file the application and appear on Foam Corporation's behalf to obtain court approval of his firm's employment.) Once the United States trustee appoints the creditors' committee, its members will decide whether to continue to use the services of Pat Gray (who is also representing Tina Chemical) or to hire someone else. Whoever the committee selects should promptly file an application on behalf of the committee for court approval of the employment. Under Rule 2014 Foam Corporation and the committee must disclose in their respective applications to the best of their knowledge all of the attorneys' connections with Foam Corporation, creditors of Foam Corporation, any other party in interest, the attorneys or accountants for any of those persons, the United States trustee, and anyone employed by the United States trustee. The attorneys must provide verified statements of any such connections.

In re White Glove, Inc.
United States Bankruptcy Court, E.D. Pennsylvania, 1998
1998 WL 226781

MEMORANDUM OPINION

SIGMUND, Bankruptcy J.

Before the Court are the Applications for Retention of Counsel for Debtor in Possession (the "Applications") in the Chapter 11 cases of White Glove, Inc. ("Inc.") and White Glove Enterprises, Inc. ("Enterprises") (together "White Glove"). In each, an Order is sought authorizing the retention of the Law Firm of Robert T. Cohen and Associates ("Cohen Firm" or "Cohen"), and to each objections have been filed by the United States Trustee ("UST") and the Official Committee of Unsecured Creditors (the "Committee").

The objections may be summarized as follows: (1) The Cohen Firm is not "disinterested" in either case as it has and continues to represent White Glove's principal Anthony D. Baker ("Baker"); (2) Moreover, it is not "disinterested" in the Inc. case for the additional reason that it has not waived its outstanding prepetition claim against Inc. in the amount of $39,000; and (3) Inc. and Enterprises have claims against each other and have made transfers to each other in the past twelve months so that the same counsel has an actual conflict in representing both.[25] * * *

---

25. [Footnote 2 in original:] Additionally the UST raised the potential problem raised by the marriage of an associate of the Cohen Firm who will be involved in this bankruptcy case to an associate at the law firm of the Committee. Counsel to the Committee indicated that his associate

Since 1978 Baker has been the sole shareholder and chief executive officer of Inc. which operates car wash facilities in Flourtown and Norristown, Pennsylvania. As owner of the real estate on which the businesses are located, he is also Inc.'s landlord. Moreover, among the assets of Inc. are 50% interests in each of White Glove Chandler, Arizona and Chicago, Illinois and a 1% interest in White Glove Exton, Pennsylvania; the balance of interests in these companies is owned by Baker. For the past seven years, Baker has also been sole shareholder and chief executive officer of Enterprises which operates car wash facilities in Montgomeryville, Bryn Mawr and Westchester, Pennsylvania. These properties are owned by independent third parties. Baker has also guaranteed Inc.'s and Enterprises' obligations to Main Line Bank and PNC Bank, respectively.

Prior to the filing, there was an agreement to sell all the Inc. and Enterprises locations other than Montgomeryville ("Sale Transaction")[26] but an Internal Revenue Services' ("IRS") seizure for back taxes precluded a closing and necessitated the bankruptcy filings. The first event in these cases was the recovery by White Glove of its assets through a consent order with the IRS which provided interim payments for the release of its levy.

White Glove has sought the retention of the Cohen Firm which has represented Inc. and Enterprises and Baker in the past. Specifically Robert Cohen acted on their behalfs [sic] in the negotiation of the Sale Transaction and in meetings with the IRS about the tax arrears for which Baker is also responsible. Indeed the Cohen Firm is owed $39,000 by Enterprises on account of past legal services rendered. Because the "affairs of the two companies and Baker are related," he has sought the continued retention of the Cohen Firm in these bankruptcy cases on economic and practical grounds. "It is easier and more expedient to have one counsel," Baker explained. It is clear that Baker expects that the Cohen Firm will represent his personal interests along with those of the two Debtors.[27] It is also clear that Cohen came into the hearing on the Applications expecting the same.

---

would not work on this case nor would he have any access to information about it. On the other hand, the Cohen firm only has the one associate and therefore [she] must work on the case. As indicated on the record, I believe this problem can be remedied by putting into place certain safeguards, including the restriction on communication between the married partners. This solution is acceptable to the Committee but must be memorialized by an appropriate document to be signed by the partners in charge of the engagement of both firms and the marital partners.

26. [Footnote 3 in original:] Upon cross examination as to how the purchase price for the locations was determined, Baker indicated that the buyer determined the allocation between the real estate and the business based on tax considerations, and he usually was compliant. He stated that real estate appraisals had never been secured since value is derived from the going concern, and moreover that he didn't care what the allocation was. However, since ownership of the real estate and business diverges with respect to Flourtown and Norristown, it is apparent that the interests of Baker and Inc. are adverse as to allocating a purchase price upon sale.

27. [Footnote 6 in original:] Specifically when Baker was asked who would represent his interests as landlord in connection with the Debtors' determinations as to assumption or rejection of the Flourtown and Norristown leases, he indicated that Cohen would represent both him and the Debtors. Moreover, Baker is scheduled as a creditor of Enterprise with an unsecured claim of $1,800,000, having unpaid rent and sizeable loan balances. Enterprises has not paid Baker rent since the filing nor has Inc. paid him a salary for over one year, although he testified that he does not intend to demand either. But see n. 14 infra.

While prior to the hearing, Cohen recognized and so advised Baker that he could not maintain his claim against Enterprises to qualify under the "disinterested" standard of § 327(a), his resolution of that impediment was to ask Baker to guarantee payment of that claim. Thus, it was understood by Cohen and Baker that the Cohen Firm would be paid the $39,000 by Baker or one of his other companies.

Baker also testified as to the intercompany claims set forth in the Debtors' Schedules. The Enterprise Schedule B reflects a note receivable from Inc. in the amount of $1,658,353 and, not surprisingly, the Inc. Schedule F reflects an unsecured claim by Enterprises in a like amount. Apparently seven or eight years ago Enterprises borrowed this amount from Copelco with the intention of it being utilized by Inc. Copelco was replaced by Main Line Bank which is scheduled by Enterprises as secured with a claim of $1.9 million, $1.1 million of which Baker attributes to the Copelco transaction. According to Baker, Enterprise has made payments in reduction of the original indebtedness but Inc. has not done likewise. Moreover, in the twelve months preceding the bankruptcy filing, Enterprises made a transfer of $195,989 to Inc., a $58,361.00 transfer to Exton and a $21,662.00 transfer to White Glove Glick, companies controlled by Baker. Baker was unable to explain the nature of any of these transfers, deferring to his chief financial officer for the details. * * *

The term "disinterested person" is defined by the Code, in pertinent part, as a person who "is not a creditor, an equity security holder or an insider" and "does not have an interest materially adverse to the interest of the estate or of any class of creditors or equity security holders, by reason of any direct or indirect relationship to, connection with, or interest in the debtor ... or for any other reason." Id. § 101[(14)(A), (C)]. While the concept of disinterestedness overlaps with the other prong of [§ 327(a)], i.e., that the professional not hold an interest adverse to the estate, the adverse interest prohibition standing alone is broader, also prohibiting the representation of an interest adverse to the estate.

The proper application of these terms to cases in this Circuit has recently been enunciated by the Third Circuit Court of Appeals in In re Marvel Entertainment Group, [140 F.3d 463] (3d Cir. 1998) * * * as follows:

> Section 327(a), as well as § 327(c), imposes a per se disqualification as trustee's counsel of any attorney who has an actual conflict of interest; (2) the * * * court may within its discretion—pursuant to § 327(a) and consistent with § 327(c)—disqualify an attorney who has a potential conflict of interest; and (3) the district court may not disqualify an attorney on the appearance of conflict alone.

[Id. at 476.] * * *

A. The Cohen Firm's Representation of Both Debtors

The UST, while acknowledging the absence of an actual conflict between the Debtors, urges the appointment of separate counsel for the Debtors based on a potential for conflict given the existence of intercompany claims and transfers.[28] The Committee does not press for separate counsel for each Debtor, at least not at this stage of the case when the facts surrounding the relationship have not been developed. In *Marvel*, the Third Circuit * * * stated:

[t]he court should generally disapprove employment of a professional with a potential conflict, with certain possible exceptions. First of all, ... there may occasionally be large cases where every competent professional in a particular field is already employed by a creditor or a party in interest.... The other exception is where the possibility that the potential conflict will become actual is remote, and the reasons for employing the professional in question are particularly compelling. This court will not attempt here to define the parameters of this exception, which necessarily will depend upon the facts of a particular case. I will, however, note that even in such situations, employment of a professional with a potential conflict is disfavored.

We do not find error in the bankruptcy court's articulation of the standard governing conflict of interest applicable to professionals.... As we have said, denomination of a conflict as "potential" or "actual" and the decision concerning whether to disqualify a professional based upon that determination in situations not yet rising to the level of an actual conflict are matters committed to the bankruptcy court's sound exercise of discretion.

[140 F.3d at 476] (quoting *BH & P*, 949 F.2d at 1316-1317). From this pronouncement, I understand that while potential conflicts are disfavored, I have discretion to allow the dual representation of these related Debtors where there is a compelling reason to do so and the likelihood of the conflict is remote.

Adopting the "wait and see" approach advocated here by the Committee, the Court in OPM Leasing Services, Inc., 16 B.R. 932, 939 (Bankr. S.D.N.Y. 1982) stated:

For that matter, "the apparent conflict of interest might be resolved in a number of ways," In re General Economics Corporation, 360 F.2d 762, 766 (2d Cir. 1966), including the appointment of special counsel. [Citations omitted.] It is only at this later time that the alleged conflict will reveal itself as real or merely apparent and imaginary. To act earlier in a preemptive manner could result in confusion and interruption of the orderly administration of the OPM and Cali bankruptcy proceedings and cause them to incur unnecessary great expense.

---

28. [Footnote 10 in original:] The UST could not explain its decision to appoint one official creditors' committee for both estates given its view of the potential conflict. Indeed the appointment of two committees minimizes the risk of allowing debtors with related managements and business affairs to engage one set of professionals.

I too find it too early to discern whether the intercompany claim arising out of the Copelco transaction presents a likely conflict. Based on the preliminary testimony of Baker, I cannot state that I understand the economics of that transaction. Moreover, since neither Enterprises nor Inc. has paid the monies borrowed, and it appears that both are obligated to the lender, the claim may at this stage be contingent. Finally, while there are a number of transfers between the Debtors and other entities owned or controlled by Baker, it is not clear to me how they present a potential for conflict that requires at this stage the prophylactic and costly step of appointing two separate counsel.

Moreover, given Baker's testimony that the plan of reorganization that he envisions involves the bundling of certain locations, a joint plan may be proposed by the Debtors.[29] Thus, there may be a utility to having one counsel for both estates.

Based on the preliminary facts that I have gleaned, I will for now allow one counsel to serve both Debtors. If, as the cases develop, it should appear that all relevant facts were not disclosed or that the intercompany claims are disputed, I will not hesitate to revisit this issue. Debtors' counsel is charged with the continuing responsibility of bringing to the attention of the Court, the UST and the Committee any facts that bear on the issue of whether these estates are adverse to each other.

B. The Cohen Firm's Representation of Baker

In his testimony, Baker made clear that he considers Cohen to be representing both him and the Debtors in these Chapter 11 proceedings. Yet there are already and will be in the future issues in which the interests of Baker and the Debtors are adverse. They include the terms of assumption of the leases in which Baker is the landlord, Baker's compensation package,[30] and the terms of any contemplated sales of assets.[31] These are actual conflicts which prohibit engagement of the Cohen Firm as Debtors' counsel where there is simultaneous representation of Baker.

The conflict presented here is exacerbated by the fact that Baker has guaranteed payment of the Cohen Firm's prepetition claim against Inc. Mindful of the bright line rule in this Circuit that a debtor's attorney with outstanding fees as of the petition date is a creditor and therefore not "disinterested" as is required for employment under § 327, Cohen sought to cure that disability without suffering the consequence of the one accepted means of gaining employment in

---

29. [Footnote 12 in original:] The Debtors have each requested and been granted joint administration in order to more efficiently and economically manage these cases.

30. [Footnote 13 in original:] The Committee has filed an objection to the compensation proposed to be paid to Baker by the Debtors. In negotiating and then defending that compensation package, Cohen has already been presented with a conflict between the interests of his two clients.

31. [Footnote 14 in original:] While Baker expressed no interest or concern on how the values for the assets would be allocated in a sale of the business with the real estate, obviously that allocation is of significant interest to creditors as the estate only recovers proceeds from sale of the business. Thus, his view, which may have been appropriate outside of Chapter 11, is insensitive to the fiduciary obligations that obtain in bankruptcy. Since he is apparently not making the distinction, it is all the more important that the Debtors be represented by counsel who can advance the interests of the Debtors without regard to Baker's personal interests. Cohen cannot do this.

that situation, i.e. waiving the prepetition claim. Rather than waive the claim, Cohen represented that he will not look to the Debtors for payment and rather secured Baker's agreement to guarantee payment, although at this point it is unclear whether he or one of his other entities will actually satisfy the debt.[32] While the $39,000 claim and waiver of payment were disclosed in Inc.'s Application for Retention, there is no mention of Baker's promise to pay. Clearly this arrangement should have been disclosed. Reliance on Baker to pay this claim from his own resources or entities which he controls (but to whom Cohen provided no service) further compromises Cohen's independence.

Having concluded that the Cohen Firm may not represent Baker and the Debtors, the question remains as to whether it may represent the Debtors if Baker secures his own counsel.[33] Stated another way, is the relationship between Cohen and Baker so close that Cohen is unable to provide independent representation to the Debtors. In answering my own question, I begin with the recognition that in a closely held corporation a debtor's counsel must take direction from an officer whose self interest is frequently not distinguished by that officer from the interests of the corporation. * * * Because of this potential for conflict, the debtor's attorney must be especially vigilant to ensure that the debtor acts as a fiduciary with the interests of creditors paramount at all times.

There is nothing in this record that causes me to conclude that Cohen, shed of his duty to Baker and the promise of compensation therefrom, must be disqualified from representation of the Debtors. There is no actual conflict and the potential for conflict arises, as stated above, because of the closely held nature of businesses and not by reason of any particular attribute of the Cohen Firm. The Third Circuit in *Marvel* has made clear that an appearance of impropriety, such as the one that might obtain because of the past relationship between Baker and Cohen, is not sufficient to disqualify counsel. In balancing the likelihood of an impropriety and the importance of honoring a debtor's right to counsel of its own choosing, the scale tips in favor of the latter. Moreover, while these cases are not very advanced, they are presently active and contentious. Bringing in replacement counsel without the Cohen Firm's knowledge of the Debtors' businesses and reorganization strategy could be harmful to the Debtors.

My decision to allow the Cohen Firm to represent the Debtors is made easier by two important safeguards in this case. One, there is an active and vigilant Creditors' Committee. Presumably, if it appears to the Committee that the

32. [Footnote 16 in original:] Notably the Debtors hold equity interests in certain other White Glove entities. Since Baker had not determined how Cohen would be paid, presumably he could have been paid by an entity partially owned by a Debtor.

33. [Footnote 17 in original:] At the conclusion of the hearing, I suggested that given my preliminary ruling that Cohen could not represent both Baker and the Debtors that Cohen and Baker discuss whether the Debtors wished to withdraw the application to retain Cohen, presumably leaving Cohen free to represent Baker. There has been no move in that direction. Indeed the Cohen Firm had recently filed an application to sell one of the Debtor locations. However, if, as it appears, Cohen is to represent the Debtors, he must secure the consent of Baker. See Rules of Professional Conduct, Rule 1.9.

Debtors' and Baker's separate interests are not being maintained, it will take appropriate action. Two, this Court's review of every professional's services in connection with the awarding of fees provides a mechanism to ensure that the services that are rendered are not adverse to but indeed benefit the estate. See 11 U.S.C. §§ 328(c), 330(a)(3)(C). Finally, to be perfectly clear, the granting of the Debtors Application is conditioned on the Cohen Firm not at any time advancing the interests of Baker and not accepting payment from him or any of his businesses of its prepetition claim. * * *

NOTES

1. In addition to ABA Model Rule of Professional Conduct 1.9, cited by the court in its footnote 17, several other Model Rules are particularly important in the context of retention of professionals for a business reorganization. The Annotated Model Rules are available on Westlaw in the ABA-AMRPC database. For purposes of analyzing the White Glove opinion and Problems 2-3, 2-4, and 2-5, the student should consider Rule 1.2(a) and (d); Rule 1.6 (and the Comment on "Withdrawal"); Rule 1.7; Rule 1.9(a) and (b); Rule 1.13 (and the Comment); and Rule 1.16 (and the Comment on "Mandatory Withdrawal").

2. Professionals who fail to disclose facts relevant to their eligibility to serve have often been denied payment or forced to disgorge payments already made. See, e.g., In re Kendavis Indus. Int'l, 91 B.R. 742 (Bankr. N.D. Tex. 1988) (requiring attorneys to disgorge several million dollars in fees); In re Roberts, 75 B.R. 402 (Bankr. D. Utah 1987) (en banc) (reversing denial of all fees and holding that fees should be partially disallowed).

3. If the debtor in possession's managers instruct the debtor in possession's lawyer to take steps that the lawyer believes are not in the best interest of the estate, what should the lawyer do? If the lawyer ultimately decides to seek permission from the court to withdraw, must the court grant that permission? What should the lawyer do if the court asks why the lawyer is seeking to withdraw? What will be the likely result if the lawyer tells the court that ethical considerations require withdrawal? Note that if a trustee is appointed or elected, the trustee will have the power to waive the attorney-client privilege with respect to communications between the debtor's agents and its lawyers. Commodity Futures Trading Comm'n v. Weintraub, 471 U.S. 343, 105 S. Ct. 1986, 85 L. Ed. 2d 372 (1985). In light of all of this, what kinds of warnings or disclaimers should the lawyer give to the owner of a closely held corporation when he or she asks the lawyer to represent the debtor in possession? If the lawyer gives the owner an accurate picture of the lawyer's ethical responsibilities and of the possible consequences for the owner, will the owner likely look for another lawyer who may be less concerned about ethics?

Problem 2-3

Assume Johnson did not receive a retainer before undertaking to represent Foam Corporation in the workout attempt. Thus, when Foam Corporation filed its chapter 11 petition on April 10, 2006, it owed Johnson's firm $15,500 for expenses incurred and services rendered. Should the court approve Foam Corporation's application to employ Johnson's firm? See §§ 327(a) and 1107(b). How could the existence of the debt influence Johnson's advice? Would it matter if the amount were $50? Does it matter that $15,500 is relatively small compared to Foam Corporation's other debts or total debts? If the court refuses to approve employment of Johnson's firm, what can the firm do to change the court's mind? Does this difficulty completely explain why debtor's attorneys typically demand retainers? Would it have helped matters if Foam Corporation had paid the $15,500 with a cashier's check shortly before filing its chapter 11 petition? What if neither Foam Corporation nor Johnson's firm disclose the $15,500 debt to the court, and the existence of the debt is disclosed only when Johnson's firm seeks payment from the estate for substantial postpetition services rendered? If the court would have approved the employment of Johnson's firm even if the debt had been disclosed, is there any harm from the nondisclosure?

Problem 2-4

If Foam Corporation and Gruff each file chapter 11 petitions, can Johnson's firm represent both? Does § 327 absolutely preclude Johnson from representing both because Foam Corporation owes $3.2 million to Gruff? Are their interests adverse? What obligations do Foam Corporation and Johnson's firm have to disclose to the court in Foam Corporation's case that Gruff is also seeking approval to employ Johnson's firm in Gruff's case? What consequences may follow if no disclosure is made? If the same person—Gruff—is going to "call the shots" in both cases anyway, why might there be a need for two law firms? Would your analysis differ if Foam Corporation and its subsidiary U Foam (rather than Gruff) were to file chapter 11 petitions and Johnson's firm sought to represent both?

Problem 2-5

Assume only Foam Corporation files a petition, and the court approves Foam Corporation's application to employ Johnson's firm. Gruff then instructs Johnson that all of Foam Corporation's actions and positions in the chapter 11 case must be designed to protect the interests of Gruff and Simmons (Gruff's sister who owns 10% of the stock of Foam Corporation), no matter what the consequences for the creditors. Should Johnson follow Gruff's instructions? What are the consequences if Johnson does follow those instructions? What are the consequences if Johnson does not follow those instructions? Who is the client?

PART II

KEEPING THE SHIP AFLOAT

The reorganization of Foam Corporation will succeed only if business continues. Keeping the ship afloat—continuing the business—is the first ingredient of a successful reorganization, because much of the value of Foam Corporation will disappear if business stops. The work force will disperse. Customers will find other sources of supply. Restarting operations will be comparatively more difficult and expensive.

This part of the book deals with the major threats to continuing the debtor's business. Chapter Three deals with the threat of outside interference. Creditors (and some others) who wish to interfere with the reorganization have powerful weapons at their disposal outside of bankruptcy that may force an end to the operation of the business. To what extent does the filing of a bankruptcy petition prevent that interference, especially the interference caused by secured creditors foreclosing on their collateral? Will Kick Credit be permitted to foreclose on Foam Corporation's equipment, inventory, and accounts receivable?

Chapter Four deals with the threat that the debtor will run out of cash that can be used to fund its operations. The filing of a petition in bankruptcy does not magically permit a business to run without cash; the continuing operations of a business require cash. Where will the debtor get the cash for operations? Will the bankruptcy laws permit Foam Corporation to spend cash in which Kick Credit has a security interest or in other ways violate the nonbankruptcy rights of creditors in order to get usable cash? Will the bankruptcy laws permit Foam Corporation to borrow money or to obtain needed goods and services on credit during the chapter 11 case? Will the bankruptcy laws permit Foam Corporation to give incentives—such as priorities or liens—to potential lenders or credit sellers to convince them to extend credit, even if those incentives create risks for existing creditors? May Foam Corporation even give incentives in the form of liens that are superior to existing liens?

In each instance, a key issue is the extent to which the potential benefits of reorganization justify a denial of the nonbankruptcy rights of the parties.

Chapter Three

Preventing Interference with the Debtor's Operations: The Automatic Stay

A. OVERVIEW

1. Creditors' Nonbankruptcy Rights To Interfere With Reorganization

Reorganization outside of bankruptcy, through an out-of-court workout, is possible only if creditors exercise self-restraint. Nonbankruptcy law gives creditors ample power to destroy the debtor's operations, even before the debtor has an opportunity to negotiate a workout agreement with the creditors and to seek their agreement to it.

Of course, outside bankruptcy the creditors cannot be required to agree to a workout agreement that extends the time for payment or provides that debts will be satisfied for less than full payment. Most creditors will not be willing to bear more than their share of the sacrifice in any case, so a workout agreement will not be possible unless almost all the creditors participate. That permits a few dissenting creditors to block the out-of-court workout agreement. Sections 1126 and 1129 (dealing with acceptance of a plan of reorganization by creditors and equity owners and with confirmation of the plan) respond to the problem that out-of-court workouts require near unanimity. More on this point later in the book.

The main problem dealt with here is that creditor *interference* (as opposed to mere nonagreement) may end the attempt to reorganize before the debtor has an opportunity to negotiate a workout agreement and to seek agreement from the creditors. The automatic stay and the other aspects of bankruptcy law discussed here respond to the breakdown of the debt-collection moratorium in a workout situation (or to the refusal of the creditors even to set up a moratorium initially). See Chapter One, Section B, and Chapter Two, Section B, supra.

2. The Automatic Stay in Bankruptcy

The filing of the bankruptcy petition automatically enjoins creditor activity because the filing itself "operates as a stay." Section 362(a). The automatic stay prohibits creditors with liens from enforcing them. Section 362(a)(4). U.C.C. Article 9 secured parties like Kick Credit cannot seize their collateral, nor can they sell off collateral that was seized before the bankruptcy petition was filed. Sections 362(a)(3), (4), (6). Real estate mortgagees cannot foreclose, nor can they obtain appointment of receivers to oust the debtor from possession of the real estate. Id. Landlords like Imperial Insurance cannot evict debtors for any prepetition failure to pay rent or for other breaches. Section 362(a)(3).

"All entities" are prohibited from suing the debtor on prepetition claims, from continuing to prosecute suits filed prepetition, and from enforcing judgments entered prepetition. Section 362(a)(1), (2).[1] The prohibition applies nationally without regard to the venue of the bankruptcy case. If a debtor has filed a case in Delaware, the stay is effective against "all entities" there and in every other state. The stay is not explicitly limited to actions or entities with a U.S. connection. Congress may have intended the stay to apply worldwide, extraterritorially,[2] though its effect may be limited due to foreign sovereign immunity, the practical difficulties[3] of enforcing the stay against non-U.S. entities, and uncertain reception[4] of U.S. court decrees in foreign courts.[5] At least with regard to actions of U.S. citizens, the automatic stay applies to actions taken in foreign countries.[6]

---

1.   The automatic stay does not, of course, prohibit the bankruptcy case from proceeding. A creditor's filing of a proof of claim in the bankruptcy case might violate several paragraphs of § 362(a) under a literal reading, but the Code expressly permits such a filing. See § 501(a). Neither does the automatic stay prohibit interested parties from filing motions or adversary proceedings adverse to the debtor in the bankruptcy court where the bankruptcy case is pending. See Civic Ctr. Square, Inc. v. Ford (In re Roxford Foods, Inc.), 12 F. 3d 875 (9th Cir. 1993); In re Toyota of Yonkers, Inc., 135 B.R. 471, 477 (Bankr. S.D.N.Y. 1992) ("A party is never stayed [by § 362(a)]from litigating with the debtor in the debtor's bankruptcy forum."). Mere ministerial acts taken in nonbankruptcy court proceedings may not violate the automatic stay. See Soares v. Brockton Credit Union (In re Soares), 107 F.3d 969 (1st Cir. 1997) (holding, however, that state court's issuance of order of default and later entry of default judgment against debtor were not ministerial acts, and thus the resulting judgment was void). Acts in such proceedings that simply maintain the status quo may also not violate the automatic stay. See Mason-McDuffie Mortgage Corp. v. Peters (In re Peters), 101 F.3d 618 (9th Cir. 1996) (holding that postponement of foreclosure sale did not violate the stay).

On the other hand, "all entities" does include a bankruptcy court that purports to issue orders affecting a separate bankruptcy case in another court. An automatic stay emanating from a "home bankruptcy court" applies to all other bankruptcy courts. In re Miller, 397 F.3d 726 (9th Cir. 2005).

2.   See § 362(a) (providing for stay applicable to "all entities", thus even including foreign governments per § 101(15) & (27), and for stay as to certain acts with regard to property of the estate); § 541(a) ("Such estate is comprised of all of the following property, wherever located and by whomever held * * * "); 28 U.S.C. § 1334(e) (granting the district court "exclusive jurisdiction—(1) of all the property, wherever located, of the debtor as of the commencement of [the bankruptcy] case, and of property of the estate"); Lykes Bros. S.S. Co. v. Hanseatic Marine Serv., GmBH (In re Lykes Bros. S.S. Co.), 207 B.R. 282 (Bankr. M.D. Fla. 1997) (holding that automatic stay prohibited actions taken in Belgian court, by German assignee of Singapore company's claims, that resulted in seizure of debtor's ship in Belgian port); Nakash v. Zur (In re Nakash), 190 B.R. 763 (Bankr. S.D.N.Y. 1996). Cf. In re Aerovias Nacionales de Colombia S.A., 303 B.R. 1, 6 (Bankr. S.D.N.Y. 2003) ("Since the extraterritorial reach of the automatic stay of § 362 of the Bankruptcy Code is uncertain, the Debtors also sought authority to pay foreign creditors who might otherwise be able to take action against Avianca in a non-U.S. jurisdiction. Similar orders have been entered in other international airline and shipping bankruptcies * * *.").

3.   See, e.g., In re Cenargo Int'l, PLC, 294 B.R. 571 (Bankr. S.D.N.Y. 2003).

4.   See, e.g., Sinatra v. Gucci (In re Gucci), 309 B.R. 679, 683-84 (S.D.N.Y. 2004).

5.   The 2005 BAPCPA enacted chapter 15 of the Bankruptcy Code, incorporating the Model Law on Cross-Border Insolvency into the Code. See § 1501. As other nations adopt the Model Law, coordination problems in cross-border insolvencies should be eased. See Westbrook, *Chapter 15 at Last*, 79 AM. BANKR. L.J. 713 (2005). For a negative view of the Model Law, see LoPucki, *Global and Out of Control?*, 79 Am. Bankr. L.J. 79 (2005), and LoPucki, *Universalism Unravels*, 79 Am. Bankr. L.J. 143 (2005).

6.   See Underwood v. Hilliard (In re Rimsat, Ltd.), 98 F.3d 956, 961 (7th Cir. 1996) ("Hilliard is a U.S. citizen, incontestably within the jurisdiction of the Congress of the United States, which can by statute (the automatic stay) forbid him to conduct proceedings anywhere in the world that would affect the debtor's

Creditors cannot take any steps to collect prepetition debts—they cannot even telephone the debtor to demand, encourage, or beg for repayment. See § 362(a)(6). If creditors have set collection activity in motion, they may be obligated to take affirmative steps to stop the collection activity from continuing.[7]

This comprehensive and expansive injunction springs into being solely because the debtor chooses to file a bankruptcy petition. The debtor is not required to make the showing typically needed for entry of a preliminary injunction; no court action at all is needed for the stay to be created. Congress itself has determined that the stay should be created to further the policies of the bankruptcy laws:

> The automatic stay is one of the fundamental debtor protections provided by the bankruptcy laws. It gives the debtor a breathing spell from his creditors. It stops all collection efforts, all harassment, and all foreclosure actions. It permits the debtor to attempt a repayment or reorganization plan, or simply to be relieved of the financial pressures that drove him into bankruptcy.

H.R. Rep. No. 595, 95th Cong., 1st Sess. 340; S. Rep. No. 989, 95th Cong., 2d Sess. 54.

3. Supplemental Injunctive Relief Under Section 105(a)

The automatic stay may not be enough by itself to give the debtor the needed "breathing spell."

If the debtor's managers guaranteed some or all of the debtor's debts or are otherwise liable for those debts, the automatic stay will not stay collection activity directed at those managers. Unless the managers are also given a "breathing spell," creditors may be able to suffocate the debtor indirectly by suffocating the managers—the persons responsible for the debtor's operations and for moving the reorganization forward. Gruff, the majority shareholder, chief executive officer, and chairman of the board of Foam Corporation, has guaranteed the $11 million of debt that Foam Corporation owes to Kick Credit, Tina Chemical, and Swenson Chemical. If Gruff is forced to fight for his financial life against collection activities by those creditors, will he be able to devote the time and attention that is needed to reorganize Foam Corporation?

The § 362 automatic stay ordinarily does not protect guarantors or other co-debtors. Chapters 12 and 13 provide limited stays of actions against co-debtors, see §§ 1201 & 1301, but chapter 11 does not. Section 105(a) gives the court seemingly broad power—in every bankruptcy case—to enter "any order * * * necessary or appropriate to carry out the provisions of this title." Does § 105(a) give the court power to enjoin actions against guarantors

---

property. * * * There is no authority for allowing the presumption against the extraterritorial application of U.S. statutes (EEOC v. Arabian American Oil Co., 499 U.S. 244, 248, 111 S. Ct. 1227, 1230-31, 113 L. Ed. 2d 274 (1991)) to defeat application of the automatic stay to a U.S. citizen to prevent his interfering with a U.S. bankruptcy proceeding in which the debtor is a corporation headquartered in the United States.").

7.   See, e.g., In re Timbs, 178 B.R. 989 (Bankr. E.D. Tenn. 1994) (awarding compensatory and punitive damages against creditor's attorney for failing to take affirmative steps to stop garnishment of debtor's wages); but see Gouveia v. IRS (In re Quality Health Care), 215 B.R. 543 (Bankr. N.D. Ind. 1997) (holding that IRS had no duty to notify bank that it should not transfer debtor's funds to IRS postpetition pursuant to prepetition levy), appeal denied and cause remanded, 228 B.R. 412 (N.D. Ind. 1998).

and co-debtors in order to prevent interference with the reorganization? Would that provide the benefits of bankruptcy protection to Gruff without requiring him to pay the price for that protection—the filing of a bankruptcy petition himself? Creditors demand guarantees to protect themselves against losses in the event the debtor becomes financially distressed. Use of § 105(a) to prevent collection from the guarantors would deny them their nonbankruptcy rights at the very moment they most need those rights. Does the need for reorganization justify such a denial of nonbankruptcy rights?

Creditors are not the only persons with the power to disrupt Foam Corporation's operations. A federal, state, or local government may destroy the debtor's business operations by regulating it. For example, the federal Food and Drug Administration can destroy the operations of a pharmaceutical company by banning sales of its major product. Similarly, enforcement of environmental laws may regulate the debtor out of business; if Foam Corporation is required to cut the formaldehyde emissions from its foam manufacturing plants by 90%, Foam Corporation may not have the money to purchase the necessary pollution control equipment and may therefore be forced to close down.

Can Foam Corporation or other debtors avoid the effect of government regulation by filing a chapter 11 petition? Congress has required chapter 11 debtors to obey valid state laws, so state regulatory laws are not preempted by the Bankruptcy Code. See 28 U.S.C.A. § 959(b). There is an explicit exception to the automatic stay for governmental (state and federal) enforcement of police and regulatory powers, so the automatic stay does not fully protect the debtor. See § 362(b)(4). How wide are these exceptions? Does § 105(a) give the court power to enjoin regulatory actions—and thereby shrink the exceptions—so that a reorganization can occur? Would that be too great a denial of the nonbankruptcy rights of the people (acting through federal, state, or local governments)? Should a bankruptcy court allow Foam Corporation to pollute the air in violation of the law if that is necessary for a reorganization to succeed?

4. How Long The Stay Continues

The automatic stay does not last forever. It is temporary. It is a rest period from creditors, not a means of escape in itself. On the other hand, while its temporary freeze is in effect, other Code provisions can come into play that directly or indirectly provide permanent or longer lasting relief. Unless relief from the stay is sooner granted, the general rules are:

(1) the stay of an act against property of the estate under subsection (a) of this section continues until such property is no longer property of the estate; and

(2) the stay of any other act under subsection (a) of this section continues until the earliest of —

(A) the time the case is closed;

(B) the time the case is dismissed; or

(C) if the case is a case under chapter 7 of this title concerning an individual or a case under chapter 9, 11, 12, or 13 of this title, the time a discharge is granted or denied. * * *

Section 362(c). In a chapter 11 case, the discharge occurs when the plan of reorganization is confirmed. Section 1141(d). Significantly, the discharge itself, like the automatic stay, operates as an injunction. See § 524(a). In some respects, the discharge picks up where the automatic stay leaves off.

5. Relief From The Automatic Stay

Just as the automatic stay can sometimes be augmented by a stay issued under § 105(a), it can be reduced in scope or effect by the granting of "relief" from the stay. See § 362(d). Motions for relief from the automatic stay are a very large part of the bankruptcy courts' dockets. Most motions for relief from the stay are made by secured creditors who seek permission to repossess their collateral or otherwise foreclose their liens. The granting of such a motion will deprive the debtor of the property involved and usually end the reorganization.

Keeping the automatic stay in force deprives secured creditors of their nonbankruptcy rights; granting relief often will end the attempt to reorganize. Here, in its starkest form, is the question whether the need for reorganization justifies denial to the creditor of its nonbankruptcy rights. Chapter 11 gives a four part answer to this question: § 362(d)(1), § 362(d)(2), § 362(d)(3), and § 362(d)(4). Only two of these provisions, subsections (d)(1) and (d)(2), are generally applicable.

Under § 362(d)(1), relief from the stay will be granted "for cause." The most important kinds of cause are lack of adequate protection of a parties' property interest and lack of good faith in the filing of the petition. Lack of good faith is also grounds for dismissal of the petition; it will be discussed in Chapter Fifteen below, in which we consider creditors' remedies where the debtor is unable to confirm a plan. The primary feature, however, of a lack of good faith that is cause for relief is that the petition was filed not for the purpose of reorganizing the debtor, but for some other purpose. Where the debtor did not file its chapter 11 petition for the purpose of reorganizing, denial of creditors' nonbankruptcy rights would be to no purpose (unless (1) the debtor changes its mind and decides to use the chapter 11 case as a vehicle for a reorganization or (2) some other party is able to use the chapter 11 case as a vehicle to reorganize the debtor despite the debtor's management's lack of good faith intent to reorganize).

As § 362(d)(1) says, lack of adequate protection of a party's property interest is "cause" for granting relief from the automatic stay. Sections 361(1) and (2) give specific examples of how adequate protection can be provided. They suggest that the adequate protection requirement is designed to protect the value of the party's property interest. Thus, for example, if Foam Corporation's equipment is depreciating in value after the filing of the chapter 11 petition, the value of Kick Credit's property interest—the security interest in the collateral—may also drop. If Foam Corporation had not filed a bankruptcy petition, Kick Credit could take action to seize the equipment and sell it, thus preventing further losses to Kick Credit from the depreciation. The automatic stay prevents Kick Credit from doing that and thus will cause injury to Kick Credit's property rights unless Kick Credit either (1) is protected against losses from the depreciation, or (2) is given relief from the automatic stay so that it can seize and sell the collateral. Under § 362(d)(1), Kick Credit is entitled to one or the other. Kick Credit will be entitled to relief from the stay to permit it to foreclose on the collateral unless Foam Corporation provides—or unless Kick Credit already has—"adequate protection" against losses from the drop in value.

Section 361(1) and (2) allows Foam Corporation to provide adequate protection to Kick Credit by making periodic payments to Kick Credit equal to the depreciation or by giving Kick Credit an additional lien on other property sufficient to make up for the depreciation. There may be other creative ways as well by which the debtor could provide adequate protection. See § 361(3). Or Kick Credit's property interest may already be adequately protected against losses if there is no serious danger that the passage of time will result in reduction of the value of Kick Credit's lien. For example, Kick Credit's property interest could be adequately protected if the value of the collateral is substantially greater than the debts it secures (not counting debts secured by liens junior to Kick Credit's lien). Such an "equity cushion,"[8] if present, may protect Kick Credit from losses even if the collateral suffers some depreciation. The meaning of adequate protection has been the subject of much controversy, and we will consider it in some detail. It is one of the primary concepts used by chapter 11 to balance the need for reorganization against the nonbankruptcy rights of secured creditors.

Section 362(d)(2) is more straightforward. If the sum of all the liens on an item or a parcel of property is greater than its value, then the debtor has no "equity" in it. It has no excess value to which the debtor or the unsecured creditors could look, so in that sense they have no interest in it that needs protection under the bankruptcy laws. If, in addition, the debtor does not need to keep possession of the property to reorganize successfully, there would be little point in preventing the secured creditors from foreclosing on it. The bankruptcy policy of encouraging reorganization would have no application, and there would be no reason to deny the secured creditors their nonbankruptcy rights. Thus § 362(d)(2) requires the court to grant relief from the stay with regard to acts against property if the debtor does not have any equity in the property and if it is not necessary to an effective reorganization.

Valuation of property is a crucial and difficult issue under § 362(d)(2) and throughout bankruptcy law. Assuming the court resolves the battle of expert witness appraisers in favor of a finding that the debtor has no equity, then the secured creditor will be entitled to relief from the automatic stay if the property is "not necessary to an effective reorganization." As the Supreme Court stated in what may have been dictum—but if so, extremely influential dictum—collateral is not considered to be necessary to an effective reorganization simply because

---

8.   The excess of the value of the collateral over the amount of the secured creditor's lien, not including junior liens, is perhaps more correctly called a "value cushion," because the debtor need not have any equity in the property for a senior secured creditor to be adequately protected by the value of the collateral. But the term "equity cushion" is commonly used.

the collateral will be essential or functionally important to any reorganization that conceivably may occur. There also must be an effective reorganization "in prospect"—there must be "a reasonable possibility of an effective reorganization [being accomplished] within a reasonable time." United Sav. Ass'n v. Timbers of Inwood Forest Assocs., 484 U.S. 365, 375-76, 108 S. Ct. 626, 632-33, 98 L. Ed. 2d 740, 751 (1988). If no reorganization is in prospect, the collateral cannot be necessary for an effective reorganization, because it does not seem that there is going to *be* an effective reorganization.

Section 362(d)(3), which was added to the Code in 1994, responds to the Supreme Court's *holding* in *Timbers,* that adequate protection for an undersecured creditor does not include the right to be paid postpetition interest on the value of its lien. Undersecured creditors do not accrue postpetition interest on their claims. See § 506(b). The automatic stay prevents them from foreclosing, getting their money out of the collateral, and reinvesting it, thus costing them the interest they could have earned on the money if there were no stay. But that loss of interest is a price the law forces the undersecured creditor to pay in order to facilitate reorganization, according to *Timbers.* To a limited degree—and only with respect to "single asset real estate"—§ 362(d)(3) effectively reverses the holding in *Timbers,* but at the same time it makes use of the insight in *Timbers* that secured creditors' rights should not be sacrificed for the goal of facilitating reorganization if there is no reorganization in prospect.

Where it applies, § 362(d)(3) forces the debtor to take one of two actions as soon as 90 days after the order for relief in order to keep the stay in effect. The debtor must either file a plan "that has a reasonable possibility of being confirmed within a reasonable time," or else begin paying secured creditors monthly an amount equal to interest on the value of their liens. Interest is calculated according to the "then applicable nondefault contract rate of interest," § 362(d)(3)(B)(ii), and the debtor may make the monthly payments from the rents and profits or other income of the collateral whether the income is generated before or after the case is filed, § 362(d)(3)(B)(i).

Note that § 362(d)(3) applies both to oversecured and undersecured creditors. Under § 506(b), oversecured creditors already had the right to *accrue* postpetition interest on their claims. Under § 362(d)(3) they now have the right (as do undersecured creditors) to be *paid* an amount equal to postpetition interest on a current basis or to obtain relief from the stay, if the debtor does not propose a reasonably confirmable plan within 90 days after the order for relief.[9]

---

9.   There is a question whether any such payments to undersecured creditors should be treated as interest on their claims or instead credited against the principal amount of their claims. See In re Star Trust, 237 B.R. 827 (Bankr. M.D. Fla. 1999) (crediting payments against principal). There is also a question whether § 362(d)(3) may affect the application of § 362(d)(1) and (2) to single asset real estate cases. See id. (noting that § 362(d)(3) does not create a 90 day "safe harbor" during which the stay may not be lifted under § 362(d)(1) or (2) in single asset real estate cases but that it may change the emphasis some courts give to certain factors in deciding whether there is bad faith); In re Jacksonville Riverfront Dev., Ltd., 215 B.R. 239 (Bankr. M.D. Fla. 1997) (holding that, by enacting § 362(d)(3), "Congress has clearly expressed its intention that the automatic stay not be lifted, and the case not be dismissed, simply

Section 362(d)(3) also responds to the concern that real estate owners and developers may use bankruptcy simply to hold off mortgagees while waiting and praying for a revival of the real estate market. Such a debtor may lack good faith, so that there is cause for relief from stay. Whether or not that is true, § 362(d)(3)—where it applies—will force the debtor to speed up the reorganization or else compensate secured creditors for the delay.

However, § 362(d)(3) applies narrowly, because it applies only with respect to stays of actions against "single asset real estate." Real property is "single asset real estate" only if it is a single property or project from which the debtor derives substantially all of the debtor's gross income. Section 101(51B); see In re The McGreals, 201 B.R. 736, 742 (Bankr. E.D. Pa. 1996) (holding that debtor's properties were not "single asset real estate" where debtor owned two contiguous parcels that were not "linked together in some fashion in a common plan or scheme involving their use"). It is not "single asset real estate" if the debtor operates any substantial business on the property other than the business of operating the property and other than activities incidental to operating the property. Section 101(51B); see Centofante v. CBJ Dev. Inc. (In re CBJ Dev., Inc.), 202 B.R. 467 (B.A.P. 9th Cir. 1996) (holding that full service hotel was not single asset real estate, but noting that apartment building would be, even if it were called a hotel).[10]

The application of § 362(d)(3) may also be avoided if debtors convey two or more small distressed properties to a single entity and then have it file a petition. With two properties generating gross income for the debtor, neither property would be "single asset real estate." Alternatively, before filing a chapter 11 petition, a debtor may commence operation of a business on the premises—one that is not just incidental to operation of the real property—and then assert that the property is not "single asset real estate;" the debtor may argue either that the business is a substantial business or that it generates enough revenue that the operation of the debtor's real property does not generate substantially all of the debtor's gross income. See § 101(51B). It remains to be seen whether such schemes will permit avoidance of § 362(d)(3), and whether courts will treat such schemes as strong evidence of lack of good faith—which independently would be cause for relief from the stay.

Section 362(d)(4) is among several provisions added to the Code in 2005 that are congressionally-intended and designed to reduce "abusive filings." This cause for relief, however, like § 362(d)(3), is targeted and narrow.

---

because the case is a single asset real estate case"); In re Midway Invs., Ltd., 187 B.R. 382 (Bankr. S.D. Fla. 1995) (holding that addition of § 362(d)(3) does not limit creditors' rights under § 362(d)(1) & (2)); State St. Houses, Inc. v. N.Y. State Urban Dev. Corp. (In re State St. Houses, Inc.), 356 F. 3d 1345 (11th Cir. 2004) (abrogating *Jacksonville Riverfront* at least with regard to issue of dismissal for bad faith).

10.   A triplex held as rental property is not "single asset real estate," because it has "fewer than 4 residential units." Section 101(51B). Note also that prior to the 2005 amendment of § 101(51B), the term "single asset real estate" did not include cases in which the debtor's noncontingent, liquidated secured debts exceeded $4 million. The $4 million limit no longer applies, with the result that § 362(d)(3) has broader application than before the 2005 amendment.

Under subsection (d)(4), relief from the automatic stay with respect to acts against collateral is limited to a creditor whose claim is secured by an interest in real property; relief is triggered only if the court finds that the filing of the bankruptcy case was part of a scheme to delay, hinder and defraud creditors and that the scheme involved either: (1) a transfer of all or part of an ownership interest in real property without such creditor's consent or without court approval; or (2) multiple bankruptcy filings affecting the real property.

If the court makes these findings and orders relief on this basis, and if the creditor records the order in compliance with applicable state law governing notice of an interest in or a lien on real property, the recorded order is binding in any other bankruptcy case for two years from the date of entry of such order. Any government unit that accepts any notice of interest or lien in real property for any purpose must also accept for filing a certified copy of a bankruptcy court order entered under § 362(d)(4).

The availability of relief from stay under subsection (d)(4) on the basis of fraud discourages abusive filings. Giving the relief a two-year effect in subsequent cases prevents an end run around the relief and also discourages multiple filings, which are themselves an independent evil that the 2005 amendments aim to reduce.

B. THE SCOPE OF THE AUTOMATIC STAY (AND SECTION 105 INJUNCTIONS)

The greatest importance of the stay in keeping the debtor afloat is that it allows the debtor, temporarily, to keep property in which other people have overriding interests, especially including secured creditors and lessors. Ordinarily, without the stay blocking them, these people could repossess the property and, in the typical case, leave the debtor nothing with which to do business. Moreover, the stay keeps unsecured creditors from getting liens. Actions and proceedings against the debtor on prepetition claims are stopped under § 362(a)(1), which prevents creditors from obtaining judgments and from obtaining judicial liens. Section 362(a)(4) also prevents them from obtaining liens.

Section 362(a) is redundant in providing this protection. Virtually every subsection contributes in one way or another, directly or indirectly. One of the most potentially expansive provisions is § 362(a)(3). It stays "any act to obtain possession of property of the estate or of property from the estate or to exercise control over property of the estate." The meaning of (a)(3), especially the meaning of "property of the estate," largely affects the width of the stay, the size of the protection it gives the debtor, and the odds of a successful reorganization. The more property that the stay protects, the more property the debtor gets to keep during the bankruptcy, at least during the critical early days of the case.

Significantly, "property of the estate" is defined very broadly to include "all legal or equitable interests of the debtor in property as of the commencement of the case." Section 541(a). Also, the courts generously define the other terms of § 362(a)(3). For example, if the debtor's rights under a contract are property of the estate,[11] § 362(a)(3) prevents the other party to the contract from freely cancelling it because of the debtor's bankruptcy. Cancellation would be an act to "obtain * * * property from the estate or to exercise control over property of the estate," as that phrase is broadly construed. Thus, if Foam Corporation's suppliers are contractually bound before bankruptcy to provide property or services, they usually cannot escape the contract after bankruptcy because of the filing or any increased risk of nonpayment. This reasoning equally applies to sellers or lessors of property and providers of services, including insurance.

Large problems remain in keeping the business afloat. The biggest problem is that the stay does not extinguish liens and other property interests. It only suspends their enforcement. The suspension will eventually end, even early in the bankruptcy if relief from the stay is appropriate then. Also, the debtor's bankruptcy does not enslave contract obligors. The debtor eventually must provide protection for obligors whose contracts the debtor wishes to continue; the debtor will need to cure defaults under such contracts (or provide adequate assurances that defaults will be cured) and then assume the contracts, thus making the debtor's obligations under the contracts into obligations of the estate. See § 365. This problem, which is the eventual fading of the stay's protection, is fundamental but is something to worry about later. The immediate object is to keep the business going today—right now.

In trying to stay alive after having filed bankruptcy, the debtor commonly faces four major problems that the stay does not neatly solve:

* First, the debtor needs cash to operate. Much of its cash is often in the bank. The debtor usually is obligated to the bank. State law allows the bank to set off the debtor's accounts in satisfaction of the debtor's obligation to the bank. The stay stops the setoff but does not necessarily stop the bank from blocking the account. The debtor's business is strangled without free access to the funds.

* Second, suppliers are not always bound to the debtor by contract. Many of them, even most, have dealt with the debtor on an open or running account under which neither party is legally obligated to continue doing business with the other. Such a supplier can freely decide not to do business with the

---

11. Contractual rights that the debtor has earned (by performing its obligations) are property of the estate. If both the debtor and the other party still owe substantial obligations under the contract, the contract is considered "executory" and thus is governed by § 365. We discuss in Chapter Seven of this text how executory contracts are treated in bankruptcy. It is not clear whether the debtor's rights under an executory contract become property of the estate when the case is commenced or only become property of the estate if and when the debtor in possession assumes the contract for the estate under § 365(a). See Chapter Seven of this text, infra, at 347. As indicated there, even if the debtor's rights under the contract are not property of the estate—and thus § 362(a)(3) does not apply—there is another reason why the other party in most instances could not cancel the contract.

debtor in bankruptcy, not even on a C.O.D. basis, unless the refusal violates the stay. The debtor's reorganization is sometimes doomed from the start if a critical supplier makes this decision.

- Third, the stay usually protects only the debtor. The problem is that the debtor is usually a corporation, partnership, or limited liability company, which naturally acts through others (human beings), and creditors sometimes go after *them*. Other common targets are other entities that the debtor owns or that are otherwise closely connected to the debtor. The possible result is, indirectly, to hamper reorganization.

- Fourth, government, as creditor or regulator, may take actions that make reorganization difficult. Federal, state, and local governments are "entities" subject to the stay of § 362(a). See § 101(15), (27). However, the Code excepts from the stay a variety of governmental actions, including criminal prosecutions, police and regulatory power enforcement actions (except for enforcement of any money judgment), tax audits, tax assessments, and imposition of liens on real property for postpetition real property taxes. See § 362(b)(1), (4), (9), (18). Until recently, states could argue that sovereign immunity principles protected them to some degree from the effects of the stay, but the Supreme Court has now rejected those arguments.[12]

These problems force us to ask just how far we are willing to go to provide the best chance for a successful reorganization. Answering in the debtor's favor—by interpreting the automatic stay's coverage very broadly or by authorizing § 105(a) supplemental injunctions that prohibit governmental action not otherwise stayed—requires subordinating some very big competing concerns.

Problem 3-1

Seventeen collection actions were pending against Foam Corporation when the company filed bankruptcy. The filing itself automatically stayed these actions anywhere in the country in any federal or state court. Section 362(a)(1). No notice to anyone is required. (Any results of further steps taken in these cases will be void or voidable—unless (i) an exception in § 362(b) applies or (ii) the bankruptcy court grants relief from the stay under § 362(d). We discuss below in Section E the question whether actions taken in violation of the stay are void or merely voidable.)

1. What ultimately becomes of these actions that are stayed?

2. Five of the creditor-plaintiffs were armed with writs of attachment and were searching for assets to attach. Once the petition is filed, the creditors must cease attempting to attach assets. In any event, continuation of the attempts would be pointless. The stay would void (or render voidable) any lien resulting from postpetition attachment efforts. See § 362(a)(3-6). Voiding the lien does not affect the creditor's claim, except that the claim is transformed from secured to unsecured. So what?

---

12. See Cent. Va. Cmty. Coll. v. Katz, __ U.S. __, 126 S. Ct. 990, 163 L. Ed. 2d 945 (2006) (reprinted below); Tenn. Student Assist. Corp. v. Hood, 541 U.S. 440, 124 S. Ct. 1905, 158 L. Ed.2d 764 (2004).

In contrast, neither the bankruptcy filing nor the stay terminates prepetition encumbrances. Therefore, Kick Credit's security interest and First Bank's mortgages survive commencement of the case. It is possible that the debtor in possession will avoid these encumbrances because of other bankruptcy law or that the bankruptcy court will subordinate them to other creditors' claims, but the stay itself does not threaten their existence. The stay nevertheless affects these encumbrances. It forbids doing anything to perfect or enforce them so long as the stay is effective, § 362(a)(4), unless an exception applies or relief is granted. Section 362(b), (d).

Thus, the debtor and the bankruptcy estate are fairly well insulated from creditors' debt-collection efforts. The protection is so wide that even routine dunning letters and similar requests of the debtor to pay its bills are stayed. Section 362(a)(6). By so restraining creditors and keeping them silent, § 362(a) creates the "breathing spell" that allows the debtor to plan for reorganization in peace and quiet. During this interim period § 362(a) also preserves the estate by preventing seizure of assets by creditors.

There is, however, a threat to the calm. The debtor usually is dependent on third parties. Creditors pursuing them can dilute the resources and attention they devote to the debtor and thereby undermine the debtor's reorganization efforts.

3. William Gruff, who runs Foam Corporation, personally guaranteed millions of dollars in debts that it owes its two largest suppliers, Tina Chemical and Swenson Chemical, and also debts that it owes to Kick Credit. It is possible that suing Gruff personally on his suretyship commitments will distract him, disrupt the debtor's reorganization efforts, and indirectly circumvent the insulating effects of the stay. Such suits may also strip Gruff of assets that he might be willing to contribute to Foam Corporation to help it reorganize. Yet, by the terms of § 362(a), the stay protects only the debtor, not third parties. Is there any way—should there be some way—to protect third parties if actions against them would adversely (albeit indirectly) affect the debtor? Consider *Piccinin* and *F.T.L., Inc.* (below) and the notes that follow them.

4. Even though the attachments against Foam Corporation itself are stayed, could a creditor garnish the account debtors who owe money to Foam Corporation? Does the stay in Foam Corporation's bankruptcy affect the garnishment of its bank accounts by DistCo, a trade creditor, in a state court proceeding? If Foam Corporation raises the automatic stay in that state court proceeding, does the state court have authority to interpret § 362 to determine whether the stay applies? Does the state court have authority to grant DistCo relief from the automatic stay? Would a state court final judgment on that issue have res judicata effect? See Gruntz v. County of Los Angeles (In re Gruntz), 202 F.3d 1074 (9th Cir. 2000) (en banc).

5. U Foam is a North Carolina subsidiary of Foam Corporation. They are separate corporations, but Foam Corporation owns 100% of U Foam's stock, the same persons are the officers and directors of both corporations, and the corporations' cash was managed centrally before the workout was attempted. Does the stay in Foam Corporation's bankruptcy insulate U Foam and its property? See In re Two Appeals Arising out of the San Juan Dupont Plaza Hotel Fire Litig., 994 F.2d 956 (1st Cir. 1993); In re Winer, 158 B.R. 736 (N.D. Ill. 1993); but see B.F. Goodrich v. Betkoski, 99 F.3d 505, 535 (2d Cir. 1996), clarified on other grounds and reh'g denied, 112 F.3d 88 (2d Cir. 1997).

A. H. Robins Co. v. Piccinin
United States Court of Appeals, Fourth Circuit, 1986
788 F.2d 994

Donald Russell, Circuit Judge:

Confronted, if not overwhelmed, with an avalanche of actions filed in various state and federal courts throughout the United States by citizens of this country as well as of foreign countries seeking damages for injuries allegedly sustained by the use of an intrauterine contraceptive device known as a Dalkon Shield, the manufacturer of the device, A.H. Robins Company, Incorporated (Robins) filed its petition under Chapter 11 of the Bankruptcy Code, 11 U.S.C.A. §§ 101 et seq., in August, 1985. * * *

The filing of the Chapter 11 petition automatically stayed all suits against Robins itself under section 362(a) of the Bankruptcy Code, even though no formal order of stay was immediately entered. But a number of plaintiffs in suits where there were defendants other than Robins, sought to sever their actions against Robins and to proceed with their claims against the co-defendant or co-defendants. Robins responded to the move by filing an adversary proceeding in which it named as defendants the plaintiffs in eight such suits pending in various state and federal courts. In that proceeding, the debtor sought (1) declaratory relief adjudging that the debtor's products liability policy with Aetna Casualty and Insurance Company (Aetna) was an asset of the estate in which all the Dalkon Shield plaintiffs and claimants had an interest and (2) injunctive relief restraining the prosecution of the actions against its co-defendants. * * *

[T]he district court granted Robins' request for a preliminary injunction. * * *

Section 362 is broken down into several subsections, only two of which are relevant on this appeal. The first of such subsections is (a)(1), which imposes an automatic stay of any proceeding "commenced or [that] could have been commenced against the debtor" at the time of the filing of the Chapter 11 proceeding; the second is (a)(3), which provides similar relief against suits involving the possession or custody of property of the debtor, irrespective of whether the suits are against the debtor alone or others. * * *

(a)

Subsection (a)(1) is generally said to be available only to the debtor, not third party defendants or co-defendants. * * * However, * * * "there are cases [under 362(a)(1)] where a bankruptcy court may properly stay the proceedings against non-bankrupt co-defendants" but, * * * in order for relief for such non-bankrupt defendants to be available under (a)(1), there must be "unusual circumstances" and certainly "'[s]omething more than the mere fact that one of the parties to the lawsuit has filed a Chapter 11 bankruptcy must be shown in order that proceedings be stayed against non-bankrupt parties.'" This "unusual situation," it would seem, arises when there is such identity between the debtor and the third-party defendant that the debtor may be said to be the real party defendant and that a judgment against the third-party defendant will in effect be a judgment or finding against the debtor. An illustration of such a situation would be a suit against a third-party who is entitled to absolute indemnity by the debtor on account of any judgment that might result against them in the case. To refuse application of the statutory stay in that case would defeat the very purpose and intent of the statute. This fact was recognized by the court in In Re Metal Center, 31 B.R. 458 (D. Conn. 1983).

In *Metal Center* the third-party plaintiff had been sued, along with the debtor, on his guaranty of the debtor's obligation. The third-party was entitled to be indemnified by the debtor on account of any judgment rendered against him because of his guaranty. While the action against both the debtor and the guarantor was pending, the debtor filed its Chapter 11 petition. The action was stayed against the debtor but the plaintiff sought to continue his suit against the guarantor. The guarantor at this point moved to stay the action as against him. The bankruptcy court reviewed the motion because of the possible "effect upon the debtor of a state court judgment against Gardner [the guarantor]." In discussing the issue, the court first dismissed as inapplicable to the facts of this case the situation where the third-party defendant was "independently liable as, for example, where the debtor and another are joint tortfeasors or where the nondebtor's liability rests upon his own breach of duty." It noted that in such a case "the automatic stay would clearly not extend to such non debtor." But, in contrast to those situations, it declared that "where, however, a debtor and nondebtor are so bound by statute or contract that the liability of the nondebtor is imputed to the debtor by operation of law, then the Congressional intent to provide relief to debtors would be frustrated by permitting indirectly what is expressly prohibited in the Code." It concluded with the statement: "Clearly the debtor's protection must be extended to enjoin litigation against others if the result would be binding upon the debtor's estate," and this is so, whether the debtor is a party or not. 31 B.R. at 462.

It is true that, although the third-party defendant in *Metal Center* was found to be entitled to indemnity from the debtor, the court held that the situation was not such as to qualify for a stay under section 362(a)(1). The court reached this conclusion because in its opinion the judgment in the suit against the third-party would not be binding on the bankruptcy court. Of course, if the indemnitee, who has suffered a judgment for which he is entitled to be absolutely indemnified by the debtor, cannot file and have allowed as an adjudicated claim the actual amount of the judgment he has secured [sic] but must submit his claim for allowance in the bankruptcy proceeding with the prospect that his claim may not be allowed in the full amount of the judgment * * * , the indemnitee will be unfairly mulcted by inconsistent judgments and his contract of indemnity in effect nullified. We do not accept such reasoning with its shocking result and would find a stay under (a)(1) acceptable. Apparently the court in *Metal Center* recognized the inconsistency and the injustice resulting from its refusal to sustain a stay under (a)(1) for *it did grant a stay* of the action against the third-party but *on equitable grounds,* finding in justification that "severing and remanding [the plaintiff's action against the indemnitee to the state court for trial and judgment * * *] ... potentially expose[s] Gardner [the indemnitee] to inconsistent judgments." 31 B.R. at 463. While, as we have said, it seems that a ruling sustaining the stay in that case under section 362(a)(1) would have been more logical and appropriate, it is unimportant whether the stay is granted under section 362(a)(1) or on equitable grounds: the result is the same; a stay is proper in such a situation. * * *

(b)

But (a)(1), which stays actions against the debtor and arguably against those whose interests are so intimately intertwined with those of the debtor that the latter may be said to be the real party in interest, is not the only part of section 362 providing for an automatic stay of proceedings. Subsection (a)(3) directs stays of any action, *whether against the debtor or third-parties,* to obtain possession or to exercise control over property of the debtor. A key phrase in the construction and application of this section is, of course, "property" as that term is used in the Act. Section 541(a)(1) of the Bankruptcy Act defines "property" in the bankruptcy context. It provides that the "estate is comprised of all the following property, wherever located ... all legal or equitable interests of the debtor in property as of the commencement of the case." The Supreme Court in construing this language in United States v. Whiting Pools, Inc., 462 U.S. 198, 205, n. 9, 103 S. Ct. 2309, 2313, n. 9, 76 L. Ed. 2d 515, quoted this language in the legislative history of the Section:

> The scope of this paragraph [541(a)(1)] is broad. It include[s] all kinds of property including tangible or intangible property, causes of action (see Bankruptcy Act § 70a(6)), and all other forms of property currently specified in section 70a of the Bankruptcy Act.

Under the weight of authority, insurance contracts have been said to be embraced in this statutory definition of "property." For example, even the right to cancel an insurance policy issued to the debtor has uniformly been held to be stayed under section 362(a)(3). A products liability policy of the debtor is similarly within the principle: it is a valuable property of a debtor, particularly if the debtor is confronted with substantial liability claims within the coverage of the policy in which case the policy may well be, as one court has remarked in a case like the one under review, "the most important asset of [i.e., the debtor's] estate," In re Johns Manville Corp., 40 B.R. 219, 229 (S.D.N.Y. 1984). Any action in which the judgment may diminish this "important asset" is unquestionably subject to a stay under this subsection. Accordingly actions "related to" the bankruptcy proceedings against the insurer or against officers or employees of the debtor who may be entitled to indemnification under such policy or who qualify as additional insureds under the policy are to be stayed under section 362(a)(3).

(c)

The statutory power of the bankruptcy court to stay actions involving the debtor or its property is not, however, limited to section 362(a)(1) and (a)(3). It has been repeatedly held that 11 U.S.C. § 105 which provides that the bankruptcy court "may issue any order, process, or judgment that is necessary or appropriate to carry out the provisions of this title," "empowers the bankruptcy court to enjoin parties other than the bankrupt" from commencing or continuing litigation. In re Otero Mills, Inc., 25 B.R. 1018, 1020 (D.N.M. 1982). In that case, the Court said:

> * * * Under the new Bankruptcy Code, the jurisdictional statute provides that the bankruptcy court shall have jurisdiction "of all civil proceedings arising under title 11 or arising in or related to cases under title 11." 28 U.S.C.A. § 1471 (Supp.1982). This broader jurisdictional statute, combined with § 105(a), grants the bankruptcy court power to enjoin parties from proceeding in state court against non-bankrupts where the state proceeding is related to a case arising under Title 11.

25 B.R. at 1020.

In stating the same scope for section 105, the Court in Johns-Manville Corp., 26 B.R. 420, 425 (S.D.N.Y. 1983), quoting from 2 COLLIER ON BANKRUPTCY §§ 362.02 and 362.05 (15th ed. 1982), put the matter thus:

> [Section 362 of the Code] does not attempt to state the jurisdiction of the bankruptcy court with respect to stays and injunctive relief or to determine the boundaries of the exercise of the court's injunctive power.
>
> Section 105 which is the successor to Section 2A(15), gives the court the power to issue any order, process or judgment that is necessary or appropriate to carry out the provisions of this title.
>
> [T]he exceptions to the automatic stay of § 362(a) which are set forth in § 362(b) are simply exceptions to the stay which protect the estate automatically at the commencement of the case and are not limitations upon the jurisdiction of the bankruptcy court or upon its power to enjoin. That power is generally based upon § 105 of the Code. The court will have ample power to enjoin actions excepted from the automatic stay which might interfere in the rehabilitative process whether in a liquidation or in a reorganization case.

[I]t is necessary to mark out the circumstances under which the power or jurisdiction may be exercised. In *Otero Mills,* supra, the Court approved a ruling that "[t]o so enjoin a creditor's action against a third party, the court must find that failure to enjoin would effect [sic] the bankruptcy estate and would adversely or detrimentally influence and pressure the debtor through the third party." 25 B.R. at 1020. In *Johns-Manville,* the Court phrased somewhat fuller the circumstances when section 105 may support a stay:

> In the exercise of its authority under § 105, the Bankruptcy Court may use its injunctive authority to "protect the integrity of a bankrupt's estate and the Bankruptcy Court's custody thereof and to preserve to that Court the ability to exercise the authority delegated to it by Congress" [citing authority]. Pursuant to the exercise of that authority the Court may issue or extend stays to enjoin a variety of proceedings [including discovery against the debtor or its officers and employees] which will have an adverse impact on the Debtor's ability to formulate a Chapter 11 plan.

40 B.R. at 226.

(d)

Beyond these statutory powers under section 362 and section 105 to enjoin other actions whether against the debtor or third-parties and in whatsoever court, the bankruptcy court under its comprehensive jurisdiction as conferred by section 1334, 28 U.S.C., has the "inherent power of courts under their general equity powers and in the efficient management of the dockets to grant relief" to grant a stay. In exercising such power the court, however, must "weigh competing interests and maintain an even balance" and must justify the stay "by clear and convincing circumstances outweighing potential harm to the party against whom it is operative." *Williford* [v. Armstrong World Industries, Inc., 715 F.2d 124 (4th Cir. 1983)] * * *, *Metal Center,* and *Seybolt* [v. Bio-Energy of Lincoln, Inc., 38 B.R. 123 (D. Mass. 1984) (guarantor entitled to indemnity by the debtor)], discussed supra, are illustrative of situations in which courts have found sufficient grounds to grant a stay under this power.

(e)

There are thus four grounds on which the bankruptcy court may enjoin suits against the bankrupt or its assets and property. In some instances only one of these grounds may be relevant; in an involved and complex case, several or even all of the grounds may require consideration. The present case is such an involved and complex case. * * *

II.

The district court in this case applied the test for a grant of preliminary injunctive relief * * *. It found * * * that irreparable harm would be suffered by the debtor and by the defendants since any of these suits against these co-defendants, if successful, would reduce and diminish the insurance fund or pool represented in Aetna's policy in favor of Robins and thereby affect the property of the debtor to the detriment of the debtor's creditors as a whole. The likelihood of success by the debtor under these circumstances appeared indisputable. The hardships which would be suffered irreparably by the debtor and by its creditors generally in permitting these plaintiffs to secure as it were a preference in the distribution of the insurance pool herein to which all creditors were entitled, together with the unquestioned public interest in promoting a viable reorganization of the debtor can be said to outweigh any contrary hardship to the plaintiffs. Such * * * finding does not appear unreasonable here.

The appellants, however, suggest that the record is insufficient to support such findings by the district judge. We disagree. The record is not extensive but it includes every fact considered by the courts in the *Manville* cases to be necessary for their decision. The rights of Dr. Davis, Dr. Clark and the two Robins to indemnity and their status as additional insureds under Robins' insurance policy are undisputed on the record. That there are thousands of Dalkon Shield actions and claims pending is a fact established in the record and the limited fund available under Robins' insurance policy is recognized in the record. It seems incontestable that, if the suits are permitted to continue and discovery allowed, any effort at reorganization of the debtor will be frustrated, if not permanently thwarted. It is obvious from the record that if suits are permitted to proceed against indemnitees on claims on which the indemnitees are entitled to indemnity by Robins, either a binding judgment against the debtor will result or, as the court in *Metal Center* said, inconsistent judgments will result, calling for the exercise of the court's equitable powers. In our opinion, the record was thus more than adequate to support the district court's grant of injunctive relief. Certainly, the district court did not commit an abuse of discretion in granting the injunction herein. * * *

There are 5,000 suits pending against the debtor in this proceeding. There are perhaps an equal number not filed. * * *

In summary, we affirm the district court's order staying the suits of the plaintiffs against the debtor and all co-defendants, * * *.

F.T.L., Inc. v. Crestar Bank (In re F.T.L., Inc.)
United States Bankruptcy Court, Eastern District of Virginia, 1993
152 B.R. 61

DOUGLAS O. TICE, Jr., Bankruptcy Judge.

This adversary proceeding comes before the court on a complaint for injunctive relief filed by debtor and the principals of the debtor. Plaintiffs seek to temporarily enjoin Crestar Bank from foreclosing on the personal residence of Frank Lash, Jr., and Robyn Lash. * * *

Debtor ("FTL") operates a car wash under the trade name Car-Robics Brushless Auto Wash in Newport News, Virginia. On July 31, 1991, debtor filed a voluntary bankruptcy petition under chapter 11. Frank Lash, Jr., and Robyn Lash ("Lashes") are officers and directors of FTL, and together they hold 60 percent of the stock in FTL. Although Frank Lash, Jr., is the president of FTL, his sons Frank Lash, III, and Tom Lash oversee the day to day operations of the business. Frank Lash, Jr., is a pharmacist, and his primary occupation is operating a small pharmacy. However, the Lashes' pharmacy is of inconsequential value, and the Lashes' primary assets are their ownership interest in FTL and their personal residence in which they have substantial equity.

Crestar Bank is the primary secured creditor of FTL, holding secured debt of approximately $785,000.00. Frank Lash, Jr., and Robyn Lash personally guaranteed this debt. In January 1992 Crestar secured a judgment lien against the Lashes and subsequently perfected its lien against the Lashes' personal residence. A foreclosure sale on the residence was scheduled for January 28, 1993. Crestar also issued suggestions in garnishment on the Lashes' personal bank accounts.

Since the commencement of this case FTL has made monthly adequate protection payments to Crestar in the approximate amount of $11,000.00. This amount represents the monthly payments of principal and interest due prepetition. The evidence indicates that FTL is currently operating at a profit and that these adequate protection payments will likely continue throughout the bankruptcy case. All the assets of FTL are fully insured as is the Lashes' residence.

FTL filed its amended plan of reorganization in December 1992. The plan calls for the Lashes to contribute all the equity in their home to the reorganization. The Lashes are prepared to accomplish this through a home equity loan, and they have already obtained a $115,000.00 written loan commitment from First Fidelity Mortgage to be secured by a second deed of trust on their residence. In addition, FTL is conceivably 30-45 days away from a commitment on a SBA loan through NationsBank. However, this loan is conditioned upon the continued ownership and management of FTL by the Lash family and the personal guarantee of the Lashes. Frank Lash, III, and Tom Lash have been able to secure new financing commitments of approximately $41,000.00, and a personal friend of the Lashes, Don Sweeney, has expressed interest in investing up to $30,000.00 in FTL if a plan is eventually confirmed.

Discussion and Conclusions of Law

The plain language of 11 U.S.C. § 362 provides only for the automatic stay of judicial proceedings and enforcement of judgments against the debtor or the property of the estate. This court has previously held that in the absence of compelling unusual circumstances, guarantors of a debtor must file their own bankruptcy petition to receive the benefits of bankruptcy law. Nothing in § 362 suggests Congress intended to strip from creditors of a bankrupt debtor the protection they sought and received when they required a third party to guaranty the debt.[13] The very purpose of a guarantee is to assure a creditor that in the event the debtor defaults, the creditor will have someone to look to for reimbursement.

While the automatic stay provisions are generally said to be available only to the debtor and not to third party guarantors, the Fourth Circuit has held that in unusual circumstances the bankruptcy court can enjoin proceedings against non-debtor third parties pursuant to 11 U.S.C. § 105(a). Where the identity of the debtor and the third party are inexorably interwoven so that the debtor may be said to be the real party against whom the creditor is proceeding a bankruptcy court may exercise equitable jurisdiction to enjoin proceedings against non-debtor third parties. 11 U.S.C. § 105(a); A.H. Robins Co. v. Piccinin, 788 F.2d at 1004. For example, a situation may exist where proceeding against the third party would actually reduce or diminish property the debtor could otherwise make available to the creditors as a whole. A.H. Robins Co. v. Piccinin, 788 F.2d at 1008. Allowing such action would undermine two basic principles of chapter 11: to provide creditors with a compulsory and collective forum to sort out their relative entitlement to a debtor's assets and to provide the debtor with a realistic opportunity to formulate a plan of reorganization. See A.H. Robins Co. v. Piccinin, 788 F.2d at 998; see also Thomas H. Jackson, The Logic and Limits of Bankruptcy 4 (1986).

---

13. [Footnote 2 in original:] Congress knew how to extend the automatic stay to nonbankrupt parties when it intended to do so. Chapter 13, for example, contains a narrowly drawn provision to stay proceedings against a limited category of individual cosigners of consumer debts. See 11 U.S.C. § 1301(a); Credit Alliance Corp. v. Williams, 851 F.2d at 121.

However, before the court can grant injunctive relief the court must find:

1. The plaintiff is likely to succeed on the merits;
2. The plaintiff has shown that irreparable injury will result without such relief;
3. Issuing the injunction would not substantially harm other interested parties; and
4. The public interest is best served by preserving the status quo until the merits of the controversy can be fully considered.

I believe this four-part test is satisfied and that this case presents the kind of "unusual circumstances" set forth in *Robins* that warrant a *temporary* injunction against Crestar to cease collection activities against the Lashes.

First, the evidence establishes that the collection activities against the Lashes arise from FTL debt to Crestar, not direct personal obligations of the Lashes to Crestar. The evidence also establishes that FTL is currently operating at a profit with several promising avenues of new financing on the horizon. With a brief "respite from protracted litigation" the Lash family may be able to successfully reorganize this debtor. Accordingly, the court believes the debtor is "likely to succeed on the merits" by proposing a confirmable chapter 11 plan.

Second, the facts establish that proposing a confirmable plan will be virtually impossible without the active involvement of Frank Lash, Jr., in pursuing new financing arrangements. If Frank Lash, Jr., filed his own bankruptcy petition he probably would not be able to contribute the equity in his residence to the debtor's plan of reorganization as proposed, and his ability to secure new financing for the debtor would be foiled. Accordingly, the court must conclude that "irreparable harm will occur" to the debtor's realistic opportunity to reorganize if collection activities against the Lashes are allowed to continue.

Third, the evidence establishes that little or no harm will be caused to Crestar if it is *temporarily* enjoined from collection activities against the Lashes.[14] What Crestar seeks through foreclosure on the Lashes' residence is effectively being proposed under the plan of reorganization by the Lashes contributing all the equity in their home to the plan; as the primary secured creditor Crestar will be the beneficiary of these funds. The Lashes are not holding back any substantial asset that would otherwise be available to Crestar via the Lashes' guarantor liability. Moreover, since the commencement of this case Crestar has received and will continue to receive monthly adequate protection payments equivalent to the monthly payments of principal and interest due prepetition. Given its predominant secured creditor position it is unlikely that a plan can be confirmed over Crestar's objection. Accordingly, the court must find that issuing a temporary injunction "will not substantially harm" Crestar or any other interested party.

---

14. [Footnote 3 in original:] This injunction is *temporary* only, and issued to assist the debtor through a crucial point in the reorganization proceedings; the injunction will expire in 90 days or upon confirmation of a plan. The need for permanent injunctive relief in this case is remote because any confirmed plan would likely render unavailable the Lashes' main asset, the equity in their home. Moreover, this court is disinclined to permanently enjoin collection activities against a non-debtor because 11 U.S.C. § 524(e) arguably prevents what would in effect be granting a discharge to a non-debtor. See Peter M. Boyle, *Non-Debtor Liability in Chapter 11: Validity of Third-Party Discharge in Bankruptcy*, 61 FORDHAM L. REVIEW 421, 447 (1992). This type of extraordinary relief may be appropriate in rare circumstances like *A.H. Robins* but should not be liberally granted.

Fourth, the court believes the creditors as a whole are best served by giving this debtor an opportunity to propose a plan of reorganization. By seeking to foreclose on the Lashes' residence Crestar is attempting to opt-out of chapter 11's compulsory and collective forum of sorting out the creditors' relative entitlement to the debtor's assets. The creditors as a whole deserve the opportunity to evaluate and vote on a plan of reorganization in this case. Accordingly, the court concludes that the "public interest is best served by maintaining the status quo" and enjoining Crestar's collection activities against the Lashes for a period of 90 days or until the merits of the debtor's plan can be promptly and fully considered at a confirmation hearing.

Accordingly, the court will enjoin Crestar's collection activities against the Lashes for a period of 90 days. * * *

NOTES

1. In parts (a) and (b) of *Piccinin* the Fourth Circuit refers to cases in which "a bankruptcy court may properly stay proceedings against" nondebtors under section 362(a)(1), to situations that are "not such as to qualify for a stay under section 362(a)(1)," and to suits that "are to be stayed under section 362(a)(1)." Can the court be discussing the scope of the *automatic* stay?

2. Two years after it decided *Piccinin,* the Fourth Circuit held that suits against guarantors were not the kind of unusual cases in which an action against a nondebtor was precluded by the automatic stay. Credit Alliance Corp. v. Williams, 851 F.2d 119 (4th Cir. 1988) (cited in *FTL*). Thus the suggestion in *Piccinin* that ordinary guarantors would be protected by the automatic stay arising from the debtor's bankruptcy filing has not been accepted. What differences between the suits stayed in *Piccinin* and typical actions against guarantors would justify treating them differently? The rhetorical key seems to be whether or not "'there is such identity between the debtor and the third-party defendant that the debtor may be said to be the real party defendant and that a judgment against the third-party defendant will in effect be a judgment or finding against the debtor.'" Reliant Energy Servs., Inc. v. Enron Canada Corp., 349 F.3d 816 (5th Cir. 2003). Is the real issue whether a judgment against the nondebtor defendant would in effect convert a disputed claim against the debtor into an undisputed claim, thus depriving the debtor of the opportunity to present a defense?

3. What unusual circumstances justified the § 105(a) injunction in *F.T.L.*? The court implies that the Lashes had about $115,000 in "equity" in their home above the amount of the first mortgage; that figure apparently did not take into account Crestar Bank's $785,000 judgment lien. First Fidelity Mortgage planned to take a second mortgage on the Lashes' home and to lend them $115,000, which the Lashes then planned to contribute to the reorganization. If you were a loan officer for First Fidelity Mortgage, would the court's order give you sufficient "comfort" so that you would make the $115,000 loan? If the court's order does result in transfer of the $115,000 value of the Lashes' "equity" to the debtor corporation, do you agree with the court that little or no harm will result to Crestar Bank? (Note that the Virginia homestead exemption is only $5,000. See Va. Code § 34-4. The Lashes apparently could have freed from Crestar's judgment lien only $10,000—$5,000 each—of their $115,000 in "equity" using § 522(f). See In re Blevins, 53 B.R. 74 (Bankr. W.D. Va. 1985) (decided when homestead exemption was only $3,750).

4. If Crestar Bank sought to have the Lashes' shares of stock in *F.T.L.* seized and sold in order to satisfy its judgment against them, would that violate the automatic stay? Are the Lashes' shares of stock in *F.T.L.* property of the estate? What effect might a sale of the shares have on the chapter 11 case? See Advanced Ribbons & Office Prods., Inc. v. U.S. Interstate Distrib., Inc. (In re Advanced Ribbons & Office Prods., Inc.), 125 B.R. 259 (B.A.P. 9th Cir. 1991); cf. In re Marvel Entm't Group, Inc., 209 B.R. 832 (D. Del. 1997).

5. Net operating losses are important tax attributes of many distressed companies. Under the tax laws (as we discuss in Chapter Twelve of this text), a taxpayer that has lost money on business operations is entitled under certain circumstances to carry that loss (the net operating loss) forward to future years; thus the taxpayer can save income tax in future profitable years by offsetting income in those years with losses from past unprofitable years. That makes the business worth more now, because its value is based on the amount of net cash it can generate in the future above the amount of its ongoing expenses—and lower expenses for taxes will mean higher net cash flows in the future. The use of net operating losses to save taxes in future years may, however, be lost or severely limited if there is a change in ownership of the taxpayer's shares. Assuming *F.T.L.* has net operating losses that may save it taxes in the future, would a seizure and execution sale of the stock to pay Crestar's judgment violate the automatic stay? See Official Comm. Of Unsecured Creditors v. PSS Steamship Co. (In re Prudential Lines), 928 F.2d 565 (2d Cir. 1991); In re Phar-Mor, Inc., 152 B.R. 924 (Bankr. N.D. Ohio 1993). If not, should a seizure and sale be enjoined under § 105(a) to prevent damage to *F.T.L.*'s valuable tax attribute?

6. Although suits against guarantors are not stayed by the automatic stay, many courts have stayed them under § 105(a), as the court did in *F.T.L.* "The propriety of such temporary non-debtor stays in certain circumstances has gained widespread acceptance in the courts and, indeed, was implicitly sanctioned by the Supreme Court recently. * * * [T]he lower courts that have confronted the issue, for the most part, have correctly concluded that temporary non-debtor stays are within the core jurisdiction of bankruptcy judges." Brubaker, *Bankruptcy Injunctions And Complex Litigation: A Critical Reappraisal of Non-Debtor Releases in Chapter 11 Reorganizations*, 1997 U. ILL. L. REV. 959, 970, 1067 (citing Celotex Corp. v. Edwards, 514 U.S. 300, 115 S. Ct. 1493, 131 L. Ed. 2d 403 (1995)). Consider the following excerpt from an opinion by Judge Queenan in a case in which the debtor's principal, Roper, sought to enjoin a suit brought against him on his guaranty of the debtor's debts:

> We are unpersuaded that the defendants' lawsuit will so destroy Roper's incentive or so affect him psychologically that he will lose the desire or ability to lead the Debtor through reorganization. One could just as easily surmise that such pressure upon a debtor's principal will galvanize him into exerting his best efforts to bring about an early Chapter 11 plan for the payment of all creditors, including in particular the creditor hounding him on his personal guaranty. Furthermore, if one carries the Debtor's argument to its ultimate conclusion, it goes too far. If one suit on a guaranty is likely to hamper the Debtor's reorganization by diverting its principal's time and energy away from his duties, then all major proceedings against the principal, corporate-related or personal, are likely to do the same. If we accepted such reasoning, we would

enjoin such matters as divorce proceedings and other suits against corporate officers on personal matters with the same alacrity as the Debtor urges us to exercise in enjoining the suit on the notes here. Such an outcome "stretches beyond the purpose and intent of Chapter 11" and, indeed, of the Code itself. In any event, the Debtor has presented us with no evidence whatsoever that the effect of this law suit upon Roper will result in irreparable harm to the Debtor or its reorganizational process.

The Debtor is undaunted. It contends that regardless of lack of psychosis or loss of incentive, defense of the suit will consume Roper's time, attention and energy, all to the detriment of a reorganization in this Court. We fail to see how. No assertion has been made that Roper has any defense to the action. For all that appears, the case will be resolved through a default judgment or, at most, summary judgment. This situation is a far cry, for example, from what was before the court in Johns-Manville Corp. v. The Asbestos Litigation Group (In re Johns-Manville Corp.), 26 B.R. 420 (Bankr. S.D.N.Y. 1983), aff'd, 40 B.R. 219 (S.D.N.Y. 1984), where the debtor's officers, directors, and employees were faced with several suits against them and a multitude of discovery demands in numerous cases being prosecuted against other co-defendants. There the court understandably found that this massive potential drain upon the debtor's personnel was likely to frustrate its reorganizational efforts.

The Debtor does not attempt to link Roper's personal assets to a plan of reorganization by any indication that Roper will fund the plan. In Lahman Manufacturing Co. v. First National Bank of Aberdeen (In re Lahman Manufacturing Co.), 33 B.R. 681 (Bankr. S.D. 1983), the debtor was unable to finance its Chapter 11 reorganization on its own, and it anticipated using the unencumbered farm real estate of its principals as collateral. The court ruled that a bank's suit against the principals on their guaranty was a sufficient threat to a reorganization to justify injunctive relief; in order to protect the bank, it also enjoined the principals from mortgaging or conveying the property without further order of the court.

We do not believe, in any event, that the intention of a debtor's principal to devote personal assets to the reorganization should necessarily have the talismanic effect of shielding him from suit on his personal obligations. We agree with much of the analysis of Judge Hall in In re Larmar Estates, Inc., 5 B.R. 328 (Bankr. E.D.N.Y. 1980), who concluded that the debtor must go further and show that a plan calling for a 100% payment to the creditor is imminent, so that a temporary restraint against the creditor taking action will cause little damage to the creditor. Short of those circumstances, the act of a guarantor or accommodation maker transferring his assets to a debtor in order to facilitate partial payment to the creditor and avoid his own personal liability smacks of a fraudulent transfer. * * *

We are troubled, furthermore, by the public policy ramifications involved in the issuance of the requested injunction. The observations made by Judge Yacos in a similar case seem sound:

It has been a cardinal principle of bankruptcy law from the beginning that its effects do not normally benefit those who have not themselves 'come into' the bankruptcy court with their liabilities *and* all their assets. ... To violate this principle on the appealing facts of a particular case, where no specific necessity for doing so is set forth, is simply to invite a wholesale restructuring of the expectations of those involved in commercial transactions without any indication from Congress that such a profound change was intended.

In re Venture Properties, Inc., 37 B.R. 175, 177 (Bankr. D.N.H. 1984) (emphasis in opinion).

In summary, the Debtor has failed to carry its burden on all four of the requirements for the issuance of a preliminary injunction * * * . We disagree with those courts who have ruled that in the present context the requirement for likely success on the merits means merely that the Chapter 11 debtor must show it will probably be successful in its reorganizational efforts. We see no reason to depart from the more traditional requirement of likelihood of ultimate success in the litigation before the court. Whether or not a Chapter 11 debtor will probably be successful in reorganizing seems more relevant to the first requirement, that of irreparable injury if the injunction is not granted.

We therefore align ourselves with those courts who have refused to enjoin suit against the debtor's guarantor, even for a very short period of time, absent extraordinary circumstances. * * *

Apollo Molded Prods., Inc. v. Kleinman (In re Apollo Molded Prods., Inc.), 83 B.R. 189, 192-94 (Bankr. D. Mass. 1988).

7. In an increasingly common kind of case, the stay of a debtor corporation's bankruptcy "protects" third parties on an entirely different basis. A principal of the debtor has effectively robbed the corporation of value and thereby harmed both the debtor and the debtor's creditors. These creditors sue the principal. It is likely that the suit is enjoined by the stay of the debtor's bankruptcy case for reasons quite different from those given by the court in *FTL, Inc.* Why? It may help you to know that the debtor itself has an action against the principal, known as an "alter ego" action. This cause of action is property of the debtor that became property of the estate when the debtor filed bankruptcy. So, § 362(a) directly stays the creditors' individual claims. See Baillie Lumber Co. v. Thompson, 391 F.3d 1315 (11th Cir. 2004) (certifying question to Georgia S. Ct.), answer to certified question conformed to, 413 F.3d 1293 (11th Cir. 2005). Which provision of § 362(a) most directly applies to stop the creditors' actions against the principal?

Problem 3-2

Suppose that Chemco, an unsecured trade creditor, was one of only two suppliers of a flame retardant chemical that Foam Corporation used in manufacturing foam. When Foam Corporation filed its chapter 11 petition, Chemco ceased accepting orders (even cash on delivery orders and cash before delivery orders) from Foam Corporation. Chemco followed a firm policy of cutting off business with trade debtors who filed bankruptcy. The intent was to discourage bankruptcies and encourage payment of trade obligations. Foam Corporation thereby lost bargaining leverage in price negotiations with the other supplier of the flame retardant. Foam Corporation complained to the bankruptcy court that Chemco had violated the stay, and Foam Corporation asked the court for an order compelling Chemco to continue doing business with Foam Corporation. What should the court decide? See Elder-Beerman Stores Corp. v. Thomasville Furniture Indus., Inc. (In re Elder-Beerman Stores Corp.), 195 B.R. 1019 (Bankr. S.D. Ohio 1996); Sportfame of Ohio, Inc. v. Wilson Sporting Goods Co., (In re Sportfame of Ohio, Inc.) 40 B.R. 47 (Bankr. N.D. Ohio 1984). If the debt owed to Chemco is not large, would it be wiser for the debtor to ask the court to allow payment of the debt? Does the court have authority to permit such payment of a prepetition debt? See In re Eagle-Picher Indus., 124 B.R. 1021 (Bankr. S.D. Ohio 1991); In re Timberhouse Post and Beam, Ltd., 196 B.R. 547 (Bankr. D. Mont. 1996).

Would your answers change if Chemco were the only available source of the flame retardant? What if Chemco, with knowledge of the bankruptcy filing, sent a letter to Foam Corporation asking for immediate payment of the prepetition debt and stating that it would sell Foam Corporation flame retardant if and only the prepetition debt were paid off within 60 days?

Problem 3-3

You are an associate with the firm of Smith, Martinez & Johnson, the lawyers for Foam Corporation. Ed Johnson asked you to analyze several questions related to the automatic stay. Here are his questions:

1. Suppose Chemco [from Problem 3-2] had *contracted* to supply the flame retardant chemicals to Foam Corporation. What difference would the contract make? Would Chemco violate the stay by cancelling the contract because of Foam Corporation's bankruptcy? Remember the line from the *Piccinin* case that "even the right to cancel an insurance policy issued to the debtor has uniformly been held to be stayed under section 362(a)(3)." Are there other reasons why Chemco could not cancel the contract? See § 365(a),(b), (e)(1). Would finding a violation of the stay make a difference in the consequences of Chemco's cancellation? See Elder-Beerman Stores Corp. v. Thomasville Furniture Indus., Inc. (In re Elder-Beerman Stores Corp.), 195 B.R. 1019 (Bankr. S.D. Ohio 1996). Would Chemco violate the stay if it simply did not deliver chemicals under the contract and did not assert that the contract was cancelled? Compare id., and In re Megan-Racine Assocs., Inc., 203 B.R. 873 (Bankr. N.D.N.Y.), rev'd, 198 B.R. 650 (N.D.N.Y.), rev'd, 102 F.3d 671 (2d Cir. 1996), with Citizens Bank of Maryland v. Strumpf, 516 U.S. 16, 116 S. Ct. 286, 133 L. Ed. 2d 258 (1995) (reprinted below), and LDA Acquisition, LLC v. Flag Wharf, Inc. (In re Competrol Acquisition P'ship), 203 B.R. 914 (Bankr. D. Del. 1996).

2. Imperial Insurance Company leases four plants to Foam Corporation. Is Imperial in the same boat with Kick Credit and First Bank and stayed from repossessing the property from the debtor? Is it significant that, outside bankruptcy, a lessee in default loses its rights to the property, while a debtor in default under a mortgage or security agreement retains rights in the property? Is Foam Corporation's leasehold interest property of the estate that is protected by § 362(a)(3)? (What can you infer from § 541(b)(2)?) The debtor in possession can cure and assume an *unexpired* lease or other executory contract. See § 365(a) & (b). Does that affect your analysis?

3. Did Kick Credit violate the stay by refusing to make advances to Foam Corporation? Would it matter if Kick had committed to make advances and reneged when Foam Corporation filed bankruptcy? A contract for financial accommodation cannot be assumed. See § 365(c)(2). Nothing in the Bankruptcy Code, however, explicitly excuses the breach of such a contract. Assuming the loan agreement provides (as it undoubtedly will) that Kick Credit may cancel if Foam Corporation files a bankruptcy petition, may Kick Credit do so? See § 365(e)(2). Must Kick Credit still seek relief from the stay before cancelling the contract? Compare In re Computer Commc'ns, Inc., 824 F.2d 725 (9th Cir. 1987), with Watts v. Pa. Housing Fin. Co., 876 F.2d 1090 (3d Cir. 1989). What becomes of the lender liability action if, before the petition was filed, Kick breached its credit contract with Foam Corporation or was guilty of tortious conduct in dealing with Foam Corporation? Can other creditors sue Kick if state law allows them to recover for Kick's wrongs toward Foam Corporation?

4. Foam Corporation licensed More Foam, a North Carolina company, to use its trademark and patented water bed process. More Foam is considering selling this license to Feather-Float. The deal would not be structured as a sublicense, but as an outright transfer of all of More Foam's rights to Feather-Float. It is not certain that this sale would violate the license agreement between More Foam and Foam Corporation. Apart from this issue, would the sale violate the automatic stay? See the following case.

United States v. Inslaw
United States Court of Appeals, District of Columbia Circuit, 1991
932 F.2d 1467

Stephen F. Williams, Circuit Judge:

[*Inslaw contracted with the Department of Justice to provide prosecution management software known as PROMIS. Inslaw then developed an enhanced version of PROMIS. The Justice Department claimed it was entitled to the enhanced version under the contract; Inslaw disagreed but complied with the Justice Department's demand for a copy of the software code for the enhanced PROMIS. Pending determination of the dispute, Inslaw agreed (in contract Modification 12) to allow the Justice Department to use the enhanced PROMIS in 22 U.S. Attorneys' offices during the contract period. After Inslaw filed a chapter 11 petition, the Justice Department installed the enhanced PROMIS software in 23 additional U.S. Attorneys' offices. Inslaw filed a complaint in bankruptcy court seeking injunctive and declaratory relief and damages. Inslaw claimed it owned the enhanced PROMIS and that the installation in additional offices was an exercise of control over property of the estate in violation of the automatic stay. Inslaw also claimed the continued use of enhanced PROMIS at the original 22 offices violated the automatic stay because the original contract period had expired. After finding that the Justice Department had violated the automatic stay, the bankruptcy court enjoined expansion by the Justice Department of its use of PROMIS and awarded Inslaw almost $7 million in damages. The district court affirmed, but reduced the damages to slightly over $6 million.*]

* * *

The automatic stay protects "property of the estate". This estate is created by the filing of a petition and comprises property of the debtor "wherever located and by whomever held", including (among other things) "all legal or equitable interests of the debtor in property as of the commencement of the case." 11 U.S.C. § 541(a)(1) (1988). It is undisputed that this encompasses causes of action that belong to the debtor, as well as the debtor's intellectual property, such as interests in patents, trademarks and copyrights. * * * United States v. Whiting Pools, Inc., 462 U.S. 198, 204-05 & n. 9, 103 S. Ct. 2309, 2313 & n. 9, 76 L. Ed. 2d 515 (1983). The estate also includes property recoverable under the Code's "turnover" provisions, which allow the trustee to recover property that "was merely out of the possession of the debtor, yet remained 'property of the debtor.'" *Whiting Pools,* 462 U.S. at 204-09 & n. 11, 103 S. Ct. at 2313-16 & n. 11.

In its brief Inslaw refers rather vaguely to its interest in the enhanced PROMIS software as the "property of the estate" over which the Department supposedly exercised control. But for meaningful analysis, Inslaw's interests must be examined separately. One set of interests consists of (1) the computer tapes containing copies of the source and object codes that Inslaw sent to the Department * * * and (2) the copies of enhanced PROMIS that Inslaw installed on Department hardware * * * . As to these, Inslaw held no possessory interest when it filed for bankruptcy on February 7, 1985. Nor can it claim a possessory interest over them through the Code's turnover provisions, as could the debtor-in-possession in *Whiting Pools,* because, as Inslaw freely admits, the Department held possession of the copies under a claim of ownership (its view of the contract and Modification 12) and claimed the right to use enhanced PROMIS without further payment. It is settled law that the debtor cannot use the turnover provisions to liquidate contract disputes or otherwise demand assets whose title is in dispute. Indeed, Inslaw never sought possession of the copies under the turnover provisions.

The bankruptcy court instead identified the relevant property as Inslaw's intangible trade secret rights in the PROMIS enhancements. It then found that the Department's continuing use of these intangible enhancements was an "exercise of control" over property of the estate.

If the bankruptcy court's idea of the scope of "exercise of control" were correct, the sweep of § 362(a) would be extraordinary—with a concomitant expansion of the jurisdiction of the bankruptcy court. Whenever a party against whom the bankrupt holds a cause of action (or other intangible property right) acted in accord with his view of the dispute rather than that of the debtor-in-possession or bankruptcy trustee, he would risk a determination by a bankruptcy court that he had "exercised control" over intangible rights (property) of the estate.[15] In making that

---

15. [Footnote 2 in original:]   Under this view, it does not matter whether the Department has possession of the PROMIS enhancements under a claim of outright title, as they do, or under a more limited lease or license. In both situations, a party in possession of an asset in which the bankrupt has an interest would violate § 362(a) by any act inconsistent with the bankrupt's claims as determined by the bankruptcy court. As a result, a wide range of disputes, such as a bankrupt lessor's claims against a lessee, or a bankrupt co-owner's claims against other holders of concurrent property interests, would slide into bankruptcy court.

determination (one way or the other), the bankruptcy court would be exercising its "core" jurisdiction over the dispute, subject to review by an Article III court on fact issues only under the deferential "clearly erroneous" standard.

* * *

Even apart from constitutional concerns, Inslaw's view of § 362(a) would take it well beyond Congress's purpose. The object of the automatic stay provision is essentially to solve a collective action problem—to make sure that creditors do not destroy the bankrupt estate in their scramble for relief. Fulfillment of that purpose cannot require that every party who acts in resistance to the debtor's view of its rights violates § 362(a) if found in error by the bankruptcy court. Thus, someone defending a suit brought by the debtor does *not* risk violation of § 362(a)(3) by filing a motion to dismiss the suit, though his resistance may burden rights asserted by the bankrupt. Nor does the filing of a lis pendens violate the stay (at least where it does not create a lien), even though it alerts prospective buyers to a hazard and may thereby diminish the value of estate property. And the commencement and continuation of a cause of action against the debtor that arises post-petition, and so is not stayed by § 362(a)(1), does not violate § 362(a)(3). Since willful violations of the stay expose the offending party to liability for compensatory damages, costs, attorney's fees, and, in some circumstances, punitive damages, see 11 U.S.C. § 362(h) (1988), it is difficult to believe that Congress intended a violation whenever someone already in possession of property mistakenly refuses to capitulate to a bankrupt's assertion of rights in that property.[16]

* * *

[The court noted that a contrary ruling would allow debtors to make an end run around the limits on the turnover provisions. The court also noted that Inslaw retained whatever property rights it had in the enhanced PROMIS and could still seek recovery from the government in contract or tort, presumably in the district court or court of claims.]

As the bankruptcy court had no jurisdiction to hear the claims asserted under § 362(a), we reverse the district court and remand the case with directions to vacate all orders concerning the Department's alleged violations of the automatic stay and to dismiss Inslaw's complaint against the Department. So ordered.

NOTE

Compare *Inslaw* with 48th St. Steakhouse, Inc. v. Rockefeller Group, Inc. (In re 48th St. Steakhouse, Inc.), 835 F.2d 427 (2d Cir. 1987) (cited in footnote 3 in *Inslaw*). Debtor was the sublessee; the lessor sought to terminate the sublessor's lease for failure to pay rent. The effect would have been to terminate the debtor's sublease. The Second Circuit held that termination of the lease would violate § 362(a)(3). Also compare *Inslaw* with In re Colonial Realty Co., 122 B.R. 1 (Bankr. D. Conn. 1990). Debtor had a contract to manage a real estate complex, but had no ownership interest in the

---

16. [Footnote 3 in original.]   In adding the "exercise control" language to § 362(a)(3) in the 1984 Bankruptcy Amendments, see 98 Stat. at 371, Congress gave no explanation. One court has traced this language to the description of § 362(a)(3) found in the committee reports on the 1978 Bankruptcy Act, which refer to property of the estate as "property over which the estate has control or possession". See In re 48th Street Steakhouse, Inc., 61 B.R. 182, 187 & n. 10 (Bankr. S.D.N.Y. 1986), aff'd, 77 B.R. 409 (S.D.N.Y.), aff'd, 835 F.2d 427 (2d Cir. 1987); House Report at 341; Senate Report at 50.

complex. When the owner of the complex defaulted on its mortgage, the mortgagee obtained the appointment of a receiver to take over management of the complex. The debtor was thus unable to act as manager pursuant to its contract, and the bankruptcy court held that the mortgagee had violated § 362(a)(3) by interfering with the debtor's rights under the management contract. Is *Inslaw* consistent with *48th Street Steakhouse* and *Colonial Realty*? See also Checkers Drive-In Rests., Inc. v. Comm'r of Patents and Trademarks, 51 F.3d 1078 (D.C. Cir. 1995).

Problem 3-4

Very often, property of the estate is held by a third party. The stay still applies to prohibit the third party from exercising control over the property. Moreover, § 542(a) adds that "an entity * * * in possession, custody, or control * * * of property that the trustee may use, sell, or lease under section 363 * * * shall deliver to the trustee * * * such property or the value of such property * * *." Similarly, "an entity that owes a debt that is property of the estate and that is matured, payable on demand, or payable on order, shall pay such debt to, or on order of, the trustee, except to the extent that such debt may be offset under section 553 of this title against a claim against the debtor." Section 542(b). On the other hand, § 362(a)(7) explicitly prohibits setting off obligations owed the debtor.

1. Suppose that prior to the debtor's bankruptcy, a secured party had repossessed collateral that was equipment. The repossession perfectly complied with state law.

    a. Must the secured party return the property to the debtor in bankruptcy?

    b. In circumstances where the secured party must turn over the collateral, must the debtor pay the creditor's claim—or take the initiative to provide adequate protection of the creditor's lien—as a prerequisite to the turnover? Does the secured party violate § 362(a)(3) by refusing to turn over the property until it is satisfied that its lien is adequately protected? Must the secured party immediately seek relief from the automatic stay if it believes its lien is not adequately protected and is unwilling to turn over the property?

    Consider, in your analysis, the cases (and notes) immediately following this Problem, and the court's footnote 3 in *Inslaw*. Also compare Rutherford v. Auto Cash, Inc. (In re Rutherford), 329 B.R. 886 (Bankr. N.D. Ga. 2005), with In re Richardson, 135 B.R. 256 (Bankr. E.D. Tex. 1992).

2. Prior to Foam Corporation's bankruptcy, Kick Credit collected the debtor's receivables through a lock box and applied the collections against Foam Corporation's debt on its line of credit from Kick.

    a. Now that Foam Corporation has filed bankruptcy, must Kick turn over these collections to Foam Corporation, or can Kick continue to set off the collections against the debt Foam Corporation owes to it?

    b. Must the account debtors remit future payments directly to Foam Corporation rather than to the lock box that Kick controls?

    c. Does it matter how the deal with respect to the receivables is structured? For example, how would the situation be handled if Kick Credit had bought the receivables or if Foam Corporation had securitized the receivables and sold them to a special purpose vehicle or entity? See Plank, *The Security of Securitization and the Future of Security*, 25 CARDOZO L. REV. 1655 (2004); Janger, *The Death of Secured Lending*, 25 CARDOZO L. REV. 1759 (2004).

3. Every debtor corporation will have checking and other deposit accounts with
    a bank. Typically, the debtor is obligated to the bank on loans or other
    commitments. So, the debtor owes the bank for these commitments, and
    the bank owes the debtor any positive balance in the debtor's account. Can
    the debtor get access to its account balance without the bank reducing the
    balance to satisfy the obligations the debtor owes the bank? Consider the
    third case following this Problem.

United States v. Whiting Pools, Inc.
United States Supreme Court, 1983
462 U.S. 198, 103 S. Ct. 2309, 76 L. Ed. 2d 515

Justice BLACKMUN delivered the opinion of the Court.

Promptly after the Internal Revenue Service (IRS or Service) seized respondent's property to satisfy a tax lien, respondent filed a petition for reorganization under the Bankruptcy Reform Act of 1978 * * *. The issue before us is whether § 542(a) of that Code authorized the Bankruptcy Court to subject the IRS to a turnover order with respect to the seized property. * * *

* * *

* * * Most important, in the context of this case, § 541(a)(1) is intended to include in the estate any property made available to the estate by other provisions of the Bankruptcy Code. Several of these provisions bring into the estate property in which the debtor did not have a possessory interest at the time the bankruptcy proceedings commenced.

Section 542(a) is such a provision. It requires an entity (other than a custodian) holding any property of the debtor that the trustee can use under § 363 to turn that property over to the trustee. Given the broad scope of the reorganization estate, property of the debtor repossessed by a secured creditor falls within this rule, and therefore may be drawn into the estate. While there are explicit limitations on the reach of § 542(a), none requires that the debtor hold a possessory interest in the property at the commencement of the reorganization proceedings.

As does all bankruptcy law, § 542(a) modifies the procedural rights available to creditors to protect and satisfy their liens.[17] In effect, § 542(a) grants to the estate a possessory interest in certain property of the debtor that was not held by

---

17. [Footnote 14 in original:] One of the procedural rights the law of secured transactions grants a secured creditor to enforce its lien is the right to take possession of the secured property upon the debtor's default. Uniform Commercial Code § 9-503, 3A U.L.A. 211 (1981). [See U.C.C. § 9-609 (2000)–ed.] A creditor's possessory interest resulting from the exercise of this right is subject to certain restrictions on the creditor's use of the property. See § 9-504, 3A U.L.A. 256-257. [See U.C.C. § 9-610 (2000)–ed.] Here, we address the abrogation of the Service's possessory interest obtained pursuant to its tax lien, a secured interest. We do not decide whether any property of the debtor in which a third party holds a possessory interest independent of a creditor's remedies is subject to turnover under § 542(a). For example, if property is pledged to the secured creditor so that the creditor has possession prior to any default, 542(a) may not require turnover. See 4 L. King, Collier on Bankruptcy ¶ 541.08[9], p. 541-53 (15th ed. 1982).

the debtor at the commencement of reorganization proceedings.[18] The Bankruptcy Code provides secured creditors various rights, including the right to adequate protection, and these rights replace the protection afforded by possession.

This interpretation of § 542(a) is supported by the section's legislative history. * * * Moreover, this interpretation of § 542 in the reorganization context is consistent with judicial precedent predating the Bankruptcy Code. * * * Nothing in the legislative history evinces a congressional intent to depart from that practice. Any other interpretation of § 542(a) would deprive the bankruptcy estate of the assets and property essential to its rehabilitation effort and thereby would frustrate the congressional purpose behind the reorganization provisions.

We conclude that the reorganization estate includes property of the debtor that has been seized by a creditor prior to the filing of a petition for reorganization.

We see no reason why a different result should obtain when the IRS is the creditor. The Service is bound by § 542(a) to the same extent as any other secured creditor. The Bankruptcy Code expressly states that the term "entity," used in § 542(a), includes a governmental unit. § 101[(15)]. * * *

Of course, if a tax levy or seizure transfers to the IRS ownership of the property seized, § 542(a) may not apply. The enforcement provisions of the Internal Revenue Code of 1954 do grant to the Service powers to enforce its tax liens that are greater than those possessed by private secured creditors under state law. But those provisions do not transfer ownership of the property to the IRS.

The Service's interest in seized property is its lien on that property. The Internal Revenue Code's levy and seizure provisions are special procedural devices available to the IRS to protect and satisfy its liens and are analogous to the remedies available to private secured creditors. See Uniform Commercial Code § 9-503, 3A U.L.A. 211-212 (1981).[19] They are provisional remedies that do not determine the Service's rights to the seized property, but merely bring the property into the Service's legal custody. At no point does the Service's interest in the property exceed the value of the lien. The IRS is obligated to return to the debtor any surplus from a sale. Ownership of the property is transferred only when the property is sold to a bona fide purchaser at a tax sale. In fact, the tax sale provision itself refers to the debtor as the owner of the property after the seizure but prior to the sale. Until such a sale takes place, the property remains the debtor's and thus is subject to the turnover requirement of § 542(a).

When property seized prior to the filing of a petition is drawn into the Chapter 11 reorganization estate, the Service's tax lien is not dissolved; nor is its status as a secured creditor destroyed. The IRS, under § 363(e), remains entitled to

---

18. [Footnote 15 in original:] Indeed, if this were not the effect, § 542(a) would be largely superfluous in light of § 541(a)(1). Interests in the seized property that could have been exercised by the debtor—in this case, the rights to notice and the surplus from a tax sale—are already part of the estate by virtue of § 541(a)(1). No coercive power is needed for this inclusion. The fact that § 542(a) grants the trustee greater rights than those held by the debtor prior to the filing of the petition is consistent with other provisions of the Bankruptcy Code that address the scope of the estate. See, e.g., § 544 (trustee has rights of lien creditor); § 545 (trustee has power to avoid statutory liens); § 549 (trustee has power to avoid certain post-petition transactions).

19. [See U.C.C. § 9-609 (2000 revision)–ed.]

adequate protection for its interests, to other rights enjoyed by secured creditors, and to the specific privileges accorded tax collectors. Section 542(a) simply requires the Service to seek protection of its interest according to the congressionally established bankruptcy procedures, rather than by withholding the seized property from the debtor's efforts to reorganize.

The judgment of the Court of Appeals is affirmed.

It is so ordered.

Motors Acceptance Corp. v. Rozier (In re Rozier)
United States Court of Appeals, Eleventh Circuit, 2003
348 F.3d 1305, certified question answered, 597 S.E.2d 367 (Ga.),
answer to certified question conformed to, 376 F.3d 1323 (2004)

PER CURIAM:

CERTIFICATION FROM THE UNITED STATES COURT OF APPEALS FOR THE ELEVENTH CIRCUIT TO THE SUPREME COURT OF GEORGIA, PURSUANT TO O.C.G.A. § 15-2-9.

TO THE SUPREME COURT OF GEORGIA AND ITS HONORABLE JUSTICES:

Motors Acceptance Corporation ("Motors Acceptance") appeals the district court's affirmance of the bankruptcy court's grant of Derryl Franklin Rozier's ("Rozier") motion for contempt in a Chapter 13 bankruptcy proceeding. In affirming the bankruptcy court's order holding Motors Acceptance in contempt for failure to return to the debtor an automobile repossessed prior to the filing of the Chapter 13 petition, the district court construed Georgia law as providing that both legal title and right of redemption of a vehicle remain with a debtor after a creditor's repossession of that vehicle.

There appears to be no issues of fact. The parties agree that the case turns on state law. Having found no case law addressing this exact issue of Georgia law, we certify the following question of law to the Supreme Court of Georgia and postpone any further consideration of this appeal until we receive an answer from that court.

Rozier purchased an automobile in the State of Georgia, with financing which was assigned to Motors Acceptance. On August 8, 2002, Motors Acceptance repossessed the vehicle due to Rozier's failure to make installment payments as set forth in the sales contract. A few days later, on August 12, Rozier filed a petition under Chapter 13 of the United States Bankruptcy Code in the United States Bankruptcy Court for the Middle District of Georgia. Soon after filing his petition, Rozier requested that Motors Acceptance return possession of the vehicle back to him, which Motors Acceptance declined to do. He then filed a motion for contempt against Motors Acceptance for its refusal to return the vehicle. Although possession was relinquished under a Temporary Turnover Order, the parties reserved their right to pursue the issue. The bankruptcy court ultimately granted Rozier's motion for contempt, holding Motors Acceptance in willful contempt of the automatic stay under 11 U.S.C. § 362 by refusing to return the automobile.

The district court affirmed the bankruptcy court's contempt order, holding that because, under its interpretation of Georgia law, both the right of redemption and legal title of a vehicle remain with a debtor even after a creditor's repossession of that vehicle, Rozier's automobile should have been relinquished by Motors Acceptance to him as part of his Chapter 13 bankruptcy estate during the pendency of his bankruptcy petition.

Under the Bankruptcy Code, a court may order a third party to turn over to the debtor's bankruptcy estate property in its possession if, among other things, such property is considered "property of the estate." 11 U.S.C. §§ 541, 542. "Property of the estate" includes "all legal or equitable interests of the debtor in property as of the commencement of the case." Id. § 541(a)(1). See also Bell-Tel Fed. Credit Union v. Kalter, 292 F.3d 1350, 1351 (11th Cir. 2002).

The dispositive question on this appeal is whether a vehicle repossessed prior to the filing of a Chapter 13 bankruptcy petition is in fact the property of the debtor's bankruptcy estate. The answer to this question turns on whether, under Georgia law, legal ownership passes to a creditor at the time of repossession. See *Bell-Tel Fed. Credit Union*, 292 F.3d at 1353 (noting that "the nature and existence of the [debtor's] right to property is determined by looking at state law") (internal quotation and citation omitted).

If, as the district court held, both legal title and the right of redemption of a vehicle remain with a defaulted debtor even after his creditor's repossession of the vehicle, then the vehicle remains part of the debtor's bankruptcy estate under § 541(a)(1) of the Bankruptcy Code, and the district court properly affirmed the bankruptcy court's order holding Motors Acceptance in contempt for failure to relinquish the vehicle back to Rozier after he had filed his bankruptcy petition. If, as Motors Acceptance contends on appeal, Georgia law affords a debtor no right in a repossessed vehicle other than a right of redemption, then the district court erred by concluding that the repossessed vehicle was part of the bankruptcy estate and thus abused its discretion by finding Motors Acceptance in contempt for failure to relinquish the same.

To answer these questions, this Court now certifies the following question of Georgia law to the Supreme Court of Georgia:

DOES LEGAL TITLE, OR ANY OTHER OWNERSHIP INTEREST THAT WOULD GIVE A RIGHT OF POSSESSION, PASS TO THAT CREDITOR UNDER GEORGIA LAW UPON REPOSSESSION OF AN AUTOMOBILE SUBSEQUENT TO A DEBTOR'S DEFAULT ON AN AUTOMOBILE INSTALLMENT LOAN CONTRACT, OR DOES SUCH LEGAL TITLE OR OTHER OWNERSHIP INTEREST REMAIN IN THE DEBTOR?

We certify the above-styled question to the Supreme Court of Georgia. The phrasing used in this certified question should not restrict that court's consideration of the problems of state law posed by this case.
QUESTION CERTIFIED.

Motors Acceptance Corp. v. Rozier (In re Rozier)
United States Court of Appeals, Eleventh Circuit, 2004
376 F.3d 1323 (conforming to answer to certified question)

PER CURIAM:

Motors Acceptance Corporation, a creditor, appealed an order holding it in contempt for failure to return on demand to a Chapter 13 debtor his automobile that it had repossessed for the failure to make installment payments prior to the filing of his Chapter 13 Bankruptcy petition. Deciding that the validity of the contempt order turned on an undecided issue of Georgia state law, we certified the question to the Supreme Court of Georgia.

We have now received an answer to that Certified Question. Based upon the Georgia law therein establishing that ownership of a motor vehicle remains with the debtor after repossession by a creditor, without further proceedings, we affirm the decision that the vehicle should have been returned to the Chapter 13 bankruptcy debtor on demand.

* * *

The Supreme Court of Georgia has answered that "ownership of collateral does not pass to a creditor upon repossession, but remains with the debtor until the creditor complies with the disposition or retention procedures of the Georgia UCC." Motors Acceptance Corp. v. Rozier, 597 S.E.2d 367 (Ga. 2004).

Because legal title and the right of redemption of the vehicle remained with Derryl Franklin Rozier, a defaulted debtor, after creditor Motor Acceptance repossessed that vehicle, but had not yet complied with the disposition or retention procedures of the Georgia Uniform Commercial Code, the district court did not err by affirming the bankruptcy court's order holding Motors Acceptance in willful contempt of the automatic stay under 11 U.S.C. § 362 by refusing to return the vehicle.

AFFIRMED.

NOTES

1.   All states (including Georgia) adopted the 2000 version of U.C.C. Article 9 (though with some variation from the official text). After the debtor defaults and the secured creditor repossesses the collateral, the debtor has the right to redeem the collateral (by paying off the secured debt in full in one lump-sum payment, per U.C.C. § 9-623, before the secured creditor disposes of the collateral. But the debtor has other rights, as well, including:

– the right to receive any surplus, if the collateral is sold for more than the secured debt (including costs of sale and in some cases the secured creditor's attorney's fees), see U.C.C. § 9-615(d)(1);
– the right to have the secured party dispose of the collateral in a commercially reasonable way, see U.C.C. § 9-610(b); and
– the right, in most cases, to receive notice before any disposition, see U.C.C. §§ 9-611 to 9-613.

The debtor ordinarily also is liable for any deficiency if the collateral is sold for less than the amount of the secured debt. See U.C.C. § 9-615(d)(2). Thus as a matter of economics, the debtor has many of the incidents of ownership even after repossession, benefitting from a sale at a high price, and bearing the risk of a sale at a low price.

2.   In Bell-Tel. Fed. Credit Union v. Kalter, 292 F.3d 1350 (11th Cir. 2002), the Eleventh Circuit interpreted Florida law as providing for title to pass to the secured creditor on repossession, with the result that the debtor was not entitled to turnover of the repossessed vehicle. In an earlier case, the Eleventh Circuit reached the same conclusion, interpreting Alabama law. Charles R. Hall Motors, Inc. v. Lewis, 137 F.3d 1280 (11th Cir.1998). In each case the court found that state motor vehicle title laws provided for title to pass to the secured creditor on repossession.

3.   U.C.C. § 9-202 is entitled, "Title to Collateral Immaterial," and provides (with exceptions that do not apply to security interests in goods) that "the provisions of this article with regard to rights and obligations apply whether title to collateral is in the secured party or the debtor." Should it have mattered to the circuit court in *Rozier* whether the debtor retained title after repossession? Do the rights described in Note 1 immediately above constitute sufficient rights for a federal court to require turnover under the holding in *Whiting Pools* whether or not state law applies the label "title" to the rights retained by the debtor? See In re Sanders, 291 B.R. 97 (Bankr. E.D. Mich. 2003), aff'd. sub nom. In re Vaughn, No. 03-CV-70906-DT, 2006 WL 44261 (E.D. Mich. Jan. 6, 2006).

Also consider In re Nejberger, 934 F.2d 1300 (3d Cir. 1991), which held that a liquor license was property of the estate, because it was valuable and transferable. The Pennsylvania Supreme had held in various contexts that a liquor license was not "property," in reliance on a state statute that provided that such a license was only a "personal privilege" and that nothing in the statutory licensing scheme "shall constitute the license as property." Id. at 1302. But the label placed on the license by state law was not determinative:

> Although section 541 defines property of the estate, we must look to state law to determine if a property right exists and to stake out its dimensions. See Butner v. United States, 440 U.S. 48, 54-55, 99 S.Ct. 914, 917-18, 59 L.Ed.2d 136 (1979); In re Roach, 824 F.2d 1370, 1374 (3d Cir.1987) ("property interests are created and defined by state law"). The label, however, that state law affixes to a particular interest in certain contexts is not always dispositive. The principal question is whether the substance of the right or interest in question brings it within the scope of estate property under the Bankruptcy Act.

Id.

Citizens Bank of Maryland v. Strumpf
United States Supreme Court, 1995
516 U.S. 16, 116 S. Ct. 286, 133 L. Ed. 2d 258

Justice SCALIA delivered the opinion of the Court.

We must decide whether the creditor of a debtor in bankruptcy may, in order to protect its setoff rights, temporarily withhold payment of a debt that it owes to the debtor in bankruptcy without violating the automatic stay imposed by 11 U.S.C. § 362(a).

I

On January 25, 1991, when respondent filed for relief under Chapter 13 of the Bankruptcy Code, he had a checking account with petitioner, a bank conducting business in the State of Maryland. He also was in default on the remaining balance of a loan of $5,068.75 from the bank. Under 11 U.S.C. § 362(a), respondent's bankruptcy filing gave rise to an automatic stay of various types of activity by his creditors, including "the setoff of any debt owing to the debtor that arose before the commencement of the [bankruptcy case] against any claim against the debtor." 11 U.S.C. § 362(a)(7).

On October 2, 1991, petitioner placed what it termed an "administrative hold" on so much of respondent's account as it claimed was subject to setoff—that is, the bank refused to pay withdrawals from the account that would reduce the balance below the sum that it claimed was due on respondent's loan. Five days later, petitioner filed in the Bankruptcy Court, under § 362(d), a "Motion for Relief from Automatic Stay and for Setoff." Respondent then filed a motion to hold petitioner in contempt, claiming that petitioner's administrative hold violated the automatic stay established by § 362(a).

The Bankruptcy Court ruled on respondent's contempt motion first. It concluded that petitioner's "administrative hold" constituted a "setoff" in violation of § 362(a)(7) and sanctioned petitioner. Several weeks later, the Bankruptcy Court granted petitioner's motion for relief from the stay and authorized petitioner to set off respondent's remaining checking account balance against the unpaid loan. By that time, however, respondent had reduced the checking account balance to zero, so there was nothing to set off.

The District Court reversed the judgment that petitioner had violated the automatic stay, concluding that the administrative hold was not a violation of § 362(a). The Court of Appeals reversed. "[A]n administrative hold," it said, "is tantamount to the exercise of a right of setoff and thus violates the automatic stay of § 362(a)(7)." 37 F.3d 155, 158 (C.A.4 1994). We granted certiorari.

II

The right of setoff (also called "offset") allows entities that owe each other money to apply their mutual debts against each other, thereby avoiding "the absurdity of making A pay B when B owes A." Studley v. Boylston Nat. Bank, 229 U.S. 523, 528, 33 S. Ct. 806, 808, 57 L. Ed. 1313 (1913). Although no federal right of setoff is created by the Bankruptcy Code, 11 U.S.C. § 553(a) provides that, with certain exceptions, whatever right of setoff otherwise exists is preserved in bankruptcy. Here it is undisputed that, prior to the bankruptcy filing, petitioner had the right under Maryland law to set off the defaulted loan against the balance in the checking account. It is also undisputed that under § 362(a) respondent's bankruptcy filing stayed any exercise of that right by petitioner. The principal question for decision is whether petitioner's refusal to pay its debt to respondent upon the latter's demand constituted an exercise of the setoff right and hence violated the stay.

In our view, petitioner's action was not a setoff within the meaning of § 362(a)(7). Petitioner refused to pay its debt, not permanently and absolutely, but only while it sought relief under § 362(d) from the automatic stay. Whether that temporary refusal was otherwise wrongful is a separate matter—we do not consider, for example, respondent's contention that the portion of the account subjected to the "administrative hold" exceeded the amount properly subject to setoff. All that concerns us here is whether the refusal *was a setoff*. We think it was not, because—as evidenced by petitioner's "Motion for Relief from

Automatic Stay and for Setoff"—petitioner did not purport permanently to reduce respondent's account balance by the amount of the defaulted loan. A requirement of such an intent is implicit in the rule followed by a majority of jurisdictions addressing the question, that a setoff has not occurred until three steps have been taken: (i) a decision to effectuate a setoff, (ii) some action accomplishing the setoff, and (iii) a recording of the setoff. See, e.g., Baker v. National City Bank of Cleveland, 511 F.2d 1016, 1018 (C.A.6 1975) (Ohio law); Normand Josef Enterprises, Inc. v. Connecticut Nat. Bank, 230 Conn. 486, 504-505, 646 A.2d 1289, 1299 (1994). But even if state law were different, the question whether a setoff *under § 362(a)(7)* has occurred is a matter of federal law, and other provisions of the Bankruptcy Code would lead us to embrace the same requirement of an intent permanently to settle accounts.

Section 542(b) of the Code, which concerns turnover of property to the estate, requires a bankrupt's debtors to "pay" to the trustee (or on his order) any "debt that is property of the estate and that is matured, payable on demand, or payable on order ... *except to the extent that such debt may be offset under section 553 of this title against a claim against the debtor.*" 11 U.S.C. § 542(b) (emphasis added). Section 553(a), in turn, sets forth a general rule, with certain exceptions, that any right of setoff that a creditor possessed prior to the debtor's filing for bankruptcy is not affected by the Bankruptcy Code. It would be an odd construction of § 362(a)(7) that required a creditor with a right of setoff to do immediately that which § 542(b) specifically excuses it from doing as a general matter: pay a claim to which a defense of setoff applies.

Nor is our assessment of these provisions changed by the fact that § 553(a), in generally providing that nothing in the Bankruptcy Code affects creditors' prebankruptcy setoff rights, qualifies this rule with the phrase "[e]xcept as otherwise provided in this section and in sections 362 and 363." This undoubtedly refers to § 362(a)(7), but we think it is most naturally read as merely recognizing that provision's restriction upon *when* an *actual setoff* may be effected—which is to say, not during the automatic stay. When this perfectly reasonable reading is available, it would be foolish to take the § 553(a) "except" clause as indicating that § 362(a)(7) requires immediate payment of a debt subject to setoff. That would render § 553(a)'s general rule that the Bankruptcy Code does not affect the right of setoff meaningless, for by forcing the creditor to pay *its* debt immediately, it would divest the creditor of the very thing that supports the right of setoff. Furthermore, it would, as we have stated, eviscerate § 542(b)'s exception to the duty to pay debts. It is an elementary rule of construction that "the act cannot be held to destroy itself." Texas & Pacific R. Co. v. Abilene Cotton Oil Co., 204 U.S. 426, 446, 27 S. Ct. 350, 358, 51 L. Ed. 553 (1907).

Finally, we are unpersuaded by respondent's additional contentions that the administrative hold violated § 362(a)(3) and § 362(a)(6). Under these sections, a bankruptcy filing automatically stays "any act to obtain possession of property of the estate or of property from the estate or to exercise control over property of the estate," 11 U.S.C. § 362(a)(3), and "any act to collect, assess, or recover a claim against the debtor that arose before the commencement of the case under this title," 11 U.S.C. § 362(a)(6). Respondent's reliance on these provisions rests on the false premise that petitioner's administrative hold took something from respondent, or exercised dominion over property that belonged to respondent. That view of things might be arguable if a bank account consisted of money belonging to the depositor and held by the bank. In fact, however, it consists of nothing more or less than a promise to pay, from the bank to the depositor, see Bank of Marin v. England, 385 U.S. 99, 101, 87 S. Ct. 274, 276, 17 L. Ed. 2d 197 (1966); Keller v. Frederickstown Sav. Institution, 193 Md. 292, 296, 66 A.2d 924, 925 (1949); and petitioner's temporary refusal to pay was neither a taking of possession of respondent's property nor an exercising of control over it, but merely a refusal to perform its promise. In any event, we will not give §§ 362(a)(3) or (6) an interpretation that would proscribe what § 542(b)'s "except[ion]" and § 553(a)'s general rule were plainly intended to permit: the temporary refusal of a creditor to pay a debt that is subject to setoff against a debt owed by the bankrupt.

The judgment of the Court of Appeals for the Fourth Circuit is reversed.

It is so ordered.

NOTES

1. *Strumpf* was a chapter 13 case, but the holding is equally applicable to chapter 11 cases.

2. What is a bank account? Is it a box in the bank's vault where the bank keeps coins and currency deposited by the customer? One of your authors knows someone who, at age eight, deposited ten valuable silver dollars in a bank account; the person suffered great psychological injury when the silver dollars were not returned on request. Of course banks generally do not keep depositors' money in the form of coins or currency; instead, banks lend out their depositor's money. In fact, even though the balance in a checking account is considered by economists to be money and is often referred to as cash, a checking account is simply a kind of debt owed to the customer by the bank—a debt that the bank promises to pay back on demand as ordered by the customer. (A check is thus an order by the customer to the bank to pay a part of the debt to the holder of the check.) Under § 542(b) was Citizens Bank obligated to pay into the estate the debt represented by the bank account to Strumpf if Citizens Bank had a valid right of setoff equal to the balance of the account? Assume that the freeze caused Strumpf's checks to bounce; if Citizens Bank had no obligation to pay the amount of the debt into the estate, could Citizens Bank have had an obligation to pay checks drawn by Strumpf?

3. Suppose you have $10,000 in a checking account at Bank. Bank informs you that it will not honor any checks drawn on the account and that if you want your money you will have to sue. You are sure that the Bank is keeping your money from you, and you scream, "Give me my money!" Are you right that the bank is exercising control over your property, or is Justice Scalia right? Is the reasoning that Citizens Bank did not exercise control over property of the estate (because it simply failed to perform its promise to pay) necessary to the decision? See Jimenez v. Wells Fargo Bank (In re Jimenez), 335 B.R. 450 (Bankr. D.N.M. 2005). Hint: see the last sentence of *Strumpf* and consider whether all of the exceptions to the automatic stay are necessarily located in § 362(b). If another provision of the Bankruptcy Code expressly permits a creditor to take an action, is it likely that Congress intended the automatic stay to prohibit the creditor from taking the action? (For example, does a creditor violate § 362(a)(3) by filing a proof of claim as permitted

by § 501, because the filing of the claim is an act to obtain some payment on the debt out of the estate?) See also Holden v. United States (In re Holden), 236 B.R. 156 (Bankr. D. Vt. 1999) (construing *Strumpf*'s holding narrowly and finding that I.R.S. violated automatic stay by freezing tax refund).

4. Suppose Citizens Bank had frozen Strumpf's bank account but had not sought relief from the stay to set it off against the debt Strumpf owed to the bank. Would that have violated the automatic stay? See Town of Hempstead Employees Fed. Credit Union v. Wicks (In re Wicks), 215 B.R. 316 (E.D.N.Y. 1997); In re Cullen, 329 B.R. 52 (Bankr. N.D. Iowa 2005).

In re Holyoke Nursing Home, Inc.
United States Court of Appeals, First Circuit, 2004
372 F.3d 1

CYR, Senior Circuit Judge.

Chapter 11 debtor Holyoke Nursing Home, Inc. ("Holyoke") and its official unsecured creditors' committee challenge a bankruptcy court ruling which awarded summary judgment to the Health Care Financing Administration ("HCFA") on Holyoke's adversary proceeding complaint that HCFA's postpetition efforts to collect prepetition Medicaid overpayments to Holyoke either constituted preferential transfers or violated the automatic stay. We affirm the judgment.

I

BACKGROUND

In 1990, Holyoke became a participant in the Medicare Reimbursement Program pursuant to a Provider Agreement whereby HCFA periodically reimburses health care providers like Holyoke for the estimated costs of services they have provided to Medicare patients, 42 U.S.C. § 1395g(a), subject to an annual audit aimed at determining the reasonableness of the costs of those services, id. § 1395x(v)(1)(A). In the event HCFA determines that the costs of a provider's past reimbursement requests were either overstated or understated, HCFA is authorized by statute to make "necessary adjustments [to the provider's current reimbursement requests] on account of previously made overpayments or underpayments." Id. § 1395g(a); 42 C.F.R. §§ 405.1803(c), 405.371(a)(2), 405.373, 413.64(f).

In 2000, HCFA determined that it had overpaid Holyoke $373,639 for cost years 1997 and 1998, and proceeded to deduct a portion of the overpayment and interest—viz., $177,656.25—from Holyoke's pending reimbursement requests for cost-year 2000. In late 2000, Holyoke filed a voluntary chapter 11 petition, and thereupon commenced the instant adversary proceeding against HCFA, contending that HCFA's prepetition deductions ($99,965.97) constituted voidable preferential transfers, see 11 U.S.C. § 547(b), and that its postpetition deductions ($77,690.28) were effected in violation of the automatic stay, see id. § 362(a)(7).

In due course, the bankruptcy court entered summary judgment for HCFA, holding that the HCFA deductions from current reimbursement requests were in the nature of recoupment, and constituted neither voidable preferences nor violations of the automatic stay. The district court denied Holyoke's intermediate appeal in an unpublished opinion.

II

DISCUSSION

The lone issue on appeal—one of first impression in this circuit—is whether the HCFA deductions for a portion of the 1997-98 overpayments it made to Holyoke are more akin to a setoff, whose collection normally is barred by the automatic stay, see 11 U.S.C. § 362(a)(7) (staying "the setoff of any debt owing to the debtor that arose before the commencement of the [bankruptcy] case"), or to a recoupment, which normally is not barred. See United Structures of Am., Inc. v. G.R.G. Eng'g, S.E., 9 F.3d 996, 999-1000 (1st Cir. 1993); see also Malinowski v. N.Y. State Dep't of Labor (In re Malinowski), 156 F.3d 131, 133 (2d Cir. 1998). As the conclusions of law entered by the bankruptcy court rest upon its construction of the Medicare Act and the Bankruptcy Code, our review is de novo.

The pertinent distinction between a setoff and a recoupment is whether the debt owed the creditor (viz., HCFA) arose out of the "same transaction" as the debt the creditor owes the debtor. For example, if A were to buy a truck worth $1000 from B, but A finds that he must expend $100 to put the truck back into working condition, A might send B a check for only $900, rather than pay B $1000 and await a $100 refund from B. The $100 A recovers by deducting it from the amount he owes B constitutes a recoupment because the reciprocal obligations arose out of the same transaction, viz., the purchase-sale of the truck. Had B filed for bankruptcy protection, A could recoup the $100 prepetition debt from B without violating the automatic stay because "it would be *inequitable* for [B] to enjoy the benefits of that transaction without also meeting its obligations." Univ. Med. Ctr. v. Sullivan (In re Univ. Med. Ctr.), 973 F.2d 1065, 1081 (3d Cir. 1992) (emphasis added). Thus, in essence the recoupment doctrine constitutes an equitable exception to the Bankruptcy Code § 362(a)(7) prohibition against offsetting reciprocal debts.

However, were A to buy the same truck from B, but instead of sending a $1000 check to B, sends a $900 check (deducting the $100 B still owes him for a bicycle A sold B earlier), the $100 which A has deducted constitutes a setoff because the mutual obligations did not arise out of the same transaction, but from different transactions, viz., the sale of the bicycle and the sale of the truck. Upon the intervention of B's bankruptcy proceeding, Bankruptcy Code § 362(a)(7) would prohibit A from effecting such a deduction, and A's claim for $100 would be collectible (if at all) through the normal distributive mechanisms prescribed by the Bankruptcy Code.

Neither the Medicare statute, the Bankruptcy Code, nor their respective legislative histories expressly treats the issue before us, and other courts of appeals have split on the issue. Holyoke relies upon In re University Medical Center, 973 F.2d 1065 (3d Cir. 1992), which held that HCFA's deduction of these Medicare overpayments constituted a setoff, rather than a recoupment. The court there reasoned that since HCFA annually pays providers only for medical services provided in the current cost year, each annual payment constitutes a distinct and segregable "transaction," and that the offsets HCFA effected in order to recover overpayments HCFA had made in prior "cost years"—and which necessarily were paid for entirely *different* medical services—did not arise from the "same transaction" as the payments made to cover the provider's current cost-year expenditures. The Third Circuit is the only court of appeals which has adopted this rationale to date. In United States v. Consumer Health Services of America, Inc., 108 F.3d 390 (D.C. Cir. 1997), and In re TLC Hospitals, Inc., 224 F.3d 1008 (9th Cir. 2000), the District of Columbia Circuit and the Ninth Circuit have held that recoveries of these Medicare overpayments relating to previous cost years constitute transactions in the nature of recoupment. These courts note that subsection 1395g(a) does not compartmentalize HCFA's liability for provider services into a year-to-year determination, but that it expressly defines and modifies HCFA's liability for the provider's current cost-year services as the provider costs incurred in that year "with necessary adjustments on account of previously made overpayments or underpayments." See Consumer Health Servs., 108 F.3d at 394. Thus, "Congress rather clearly indicated that it wanted a provider's *stream of services* to be considered *one transaction* for purposes of any claim the government would have against the provider." Id. at 395 (emphasis added); see also TLC Hosps., 224 F.3d at 1012; In re Slater Health Ctr., Inc., 306 B.R. 20, 25 (D.R.I.2004). Moreover, the interpretation favored by the District of Columbia Circuit and the Ninth Circuit has been embraced by the overwhelming majority of district and bankruptcy courts nationwide which have ruled to date.

We likewise accept the majority view, and hold that the HCFA recovery of the $177,656.25 in overpayments previously made to Holyoke constituted a transaction in the nature of a recoupment, rather than a setoff. As such, it was neither a voidable preferential transfer nor a violation of the automatic stay. Both the Medicare statute and the provider agreement—by contemplating HCFA's payment of estimated costs, corrective audits, and retroactive adjustments or partial adjustments for overpayments and underpayments in determining HCFA's net liability for current cost-year services—strongly indicate that the contractual relationship between HCFA and Holyoke constitutes one, ongoing, integrated transaction.

Holyoke further contends that, even if HCFA's overpayment adjustments constitute recoupments, recoupment is an equitable doctrine, and therefore the case should be remanded to the bankruptcy court to determine the appropriate equitable balance to be struck as between itself and HCFA. Holyoke notes, for instance, that such recoupments for prepetition overpayments may either cut off or drastically reduce a bankrupt provider's most prominent cash flow, thereby diminishing the prospects for a successful chapter 11 reorganization, and jeopardizing the availability of healthcare to Medicare recipients. Holyoke argues, on the other hand, that HCFA will not be deprived of all recovery, but likely will be able to recover (albeit partially) on its overpayment claims under Holyoke's chapter 11 Plan.

We perceive no need for equitable balancing. First, the recoupment doctrine is equitable for the very reason that "it would be *inequitable* for [Holyoke] to enjoy the benefits of [the same] transaction without also meeting its obligations." *Univ. Med. Ctr.*, 973 F.2d at 1081 (emphasis added). Thus, HCFA was overcharged for the services provided by Holyoke in 1997 and 1998, and in equity, Holyoke should not be allowed to retain the windfall. Moreover, to allow these overpayments to become property of the Holyoke bankrupt estate would mean that its estate might apply a portion of those government-provided funds to satisfy Holyoke's other debts, thus violating the manifest congressional intent that HCFA expend such funds only to defray the costs of services provided to Medicare beneficiaries. Cf., e.g., In re Lan Tamers, Inc., 329 F.3d 204, 212 (1st Cir.) (noting that inclusion of government funds as "property of estate" would divert those funds to the other general creditors of the debtor, rather than to the purpose plainly intended by Congress), cert. denied, 540 U.S. 1047, 124 S. Ct. 808, 157 L. Ed. 2d 695 (2003).

Second, even assuming *arguendo* that further equitable balancing is permissible, the equitable powers of the bankruptcy court do not accord it "a roving commission to do equity," In re Ludlow Hosp. Soc'y, Inc., 124 F.3d 22, 27 (1st Cir. 1997) (citation omitted), nor "authorize courts to create substantive rights that are otherwise unavailable under the Code, or to expand the contractual obligations of parties." Id. (quoting Official, Unsecured Creditors' Comm. v. Stern (In re SPM Mfg. Corp.), 984 F.2d 1305, 1311 (1st Cir. 1993)). As we conclude that Congress contemplated that the Medicare provider agreements would constitute a single, ongoing, and integrated transaction, the equitable powers of the bankruptcy court do not entitle it to second-guess Congress's implicit policy choices. Both by statute and by contract, the HCFA has the unqualified right to recoup these overpayments *in full*, and to return the funds to the public fisc, where they can be used to fund other facilities providing care to Medicare beneficiaries. In our view, public policy would be ill-served by permitting insolvent providers—like Holyoke—a windfall at the expense of other Medicare providers which have managed their facilities prudently to avoid chapter 11. Accordingly, we conclude that a remand to the bankruptcy court for a balancing of the equities is not warranted.

AFFIRMED.

Problem 3-5

Not long before Foam Corporation filed its chapter 11 petition, a leak occurred from its main chemical waste storage tank. Two thousand gallons of toxins soaked the surrounding ground. The United States sued Foam Corporation in federal court to establish Foam Corporation's liability for the spill and also to effect a clean up of the mess. Is the suit stayed by Foam Corporation's bankruptcy? See the case and notes that follow immediately after this Problem. Does the stay prevent a money judgment for clean up costs? Execution to enforce such a judgment? An order directing Foam Corporation to clean up the mess? See §§ 362(b)(4), 362(a)(3). Could the bankruptcy court enjoin state or federal officials under § 105(a) from requiring Foam Corporation to clean up the spill? See Wilner Wood Prods. Co. v. Maine, 128 B.R. 1 (D. Me. 1991). Cf. Penn Terra Ltd. v. Dep't Of Envtl. Res., 733 F.2d 267 (3d Cir. 1984) (reprinted immediately below) (see additional excerpt in Note 3 after the case). If the debtor decides to pay for the clean up, or is required to do so, is the expense paid before the claims of other creditors? See §§ 507, 503, 506(c); Pennsylvania v. Conroy, 24 F.3d 568 (3d Cir. 1994). If the federal court orders Foam Corporation to clean up the toxins, and Foam Corporation fails to comply with the order, will the automatic stay prevent the court from holding Foam Corporation in criminal or civil contempt and fining Foam Corporation? See Seiko Epson Corp. v. Nu-Kote Int'l, Inc., 190 F.3d 1360 (Fed. Cir. 1999). Does the automatic stay prevent the court from requiring Foam Corporation to pay the civil or criminal fine? See Berg v. Good Samaritan Hosp. (In re Berg), 198 B.R. 557 (B.A.P. 9th Cir. 1996); In re Allison, 182 B.R. 881 (Bankr. N.D. Ala. 1995).

Before 1998, the Code dealt separately with (i) the commencement and continuation of governmental police or regulatory power actions and (ii) the enforcement of judgments obtained in such actions. Section 362(b)(4) excepted commencement and continuation of such actions from the provisions of § 362(a)(1). Section 362(b)(5) excepted the enforcement of judgments (other than money judgments) obtained in such actions from the provisions of § 362(a)(2). The 1998 amendments combined the old subparts (4) and (5) into subpart (4). The amendments also expanded § 362(b)(4) to include exceptions not just from the provisions of § 362(a)(1) and (2), but also from § 362(a)(3) and (6).[20] Thus it is now clear, for example, that police and regulatory actions are not stayed simply because they may involve an exercise of control over property of the estate (such as seizure of illegal drugs). The following case was decided under the pre-1998 version of § 362(b)(4)-(5).

Penn Terra Ltd. v. Department Of Environmental Resources
United States Court of Appeals, Third Circuit, 1984
733 F.2d 267

[*The debtor had operated its coal mines in violation of Pennsylvania's environmental protection laws. Through its Department of Environmental Resources (DER), the state frequently cited the debtor for these wrongs, and the debtor agreed in a consent order to do whatever was necessary to comply with the laws, including land reclamation. No changes were made in the debtor's operations. Instead, the debtor filed bankruptcy. Thereafter, the DER sued in state court, seeking an injunction ordering the debtor to comply with the consent order. The bankruptcy and district courts decided that this proceeding violated the automatic stay. It was not excepted by § 362(b)(5) because the proceeding aimed to force a clean up that would have required the debtor to spend money. It therefore was, in essence, an action to enforce a money judgment.*

The Third Circuit disagreed at two levels of analysis. First, the state-court proceeding did not involve, in form, enforcement of a money judgment.]

Garth, Circuit Judge. * * * In common understanding, a money judgment is an order entered by the court or by the clerk, after a verdict has been rendered for plaintiff, which adjudges that the defendant shall pay a [definite and certain] sum of money to the plaintiff. * * * The paradigm for * * * a proceeding [to enforce a money judgment] is when, having obtained a judgment for a sum certain, a plaintiff

---

20. The 1998 amendments also awkwardly inserted language to allow a chemical weapons treaty to be enforced against chapter 11 debtors who deal with chemicals, notwithstanding the automatic stay. As a result the new § 362(b)(4) is not easy to read. If you read it skipping the portion that begins with "or any organization" and that ends with "January 13, 1993," the non-chemical weapons portion will make sense. Could a court committed to wooden, literal interpretation of statutes conclude that the 1998 amendments narrowed the exception provided by § 362(b)(4) so that it only applies to chemical weapons matters? Can you find the drafting error that could lead to that interpretation? Also, note that there is now no § 362(b)(5).

attempts to seize property of the defendant in order to satisfy that judgment. It is this seizure of a defendant debtor's property, to satisfy the judgment obtained by a plaintiff creditor, which is proscribed by subsection 362(b)(5).

At least as a matter of form, it is clear to us that the proceeding initiated by DER in Commonwealth Court was not to enforce a money judgment. Indeed, it could not have resulted even in the mere entry of a money judgment. DER brought its action in equity to compel the performance of certain remedial acts by Penn Terra. It did not seek the payment of compensation to the Commonwealth's coffers, and the injunction actually issued by the Commonwealth Court did not direct such payment. This proceeding, therefore, could never have resulted in the adjudication of liability for a sum certain, an essential element of a money judgment. Since this action was in form and substance (see discussion infra), not one to obtain a money judgment, it follows that it could not be one *to enforce* the payment of such a judgment. * * *

[*The debtor responded, however, that in substance the proceeding involved the enforcement of a money judgment because obeying the injunction would cost money. The Third Circuit rejected this view and looked at the issue from a different perspective:*] * * * Were we to find that any order which requires the expenditure of money is a "money judgment," then the exception to section 362 for government police action, which should be construed broadly, would instead be narrowed into virtual nonexistence. Yet we cannot ignore the fundamental fact that, in contemporary times, almost everything costs something. An injunction which does not compel some expenditure or loss of monies may often be an effective nullity.

It appears that, in defining the scope of the exception to the automatic stay, the Bankruptcy Court in this case placed too much weight on the value of preserving the corpus of the debtor's funds and estate under its own exclusive control. Admittedly, that goal is normally central to the statutory scheme of the Bankruptcy Code. As noted at the beginning of this opinion, however, in some instances this policy is in inexorable conflict with other, no less salutary, governmental goals. We believe that the resolution of this conflict is contained in the statute itself. In enacting the exceptions to section 362, Congress recognized that in some circumstances, bankruptcy policy must yield to higher priorities. Indeed, if the policy of preservation of the estate is to be invariably paramount, then one could not have exceptions to the rule. Since Congress did provide for exceptions, however, we may assume that the goal of preserving the debtor's estate is not always the dominant goal.

We believe that the inquiry is more properly focused on the nature of the injuries which the challenged remedy is intended to redress—including whether plaintiff seeks compensation for past damages or prevention of future harm—in order to reach the ultimate conclusion as to whether these injuries are traditionally rectified by a money judgment and its enforcement. Here, the Commonwealth Court injunction was, neither in form nor substance, the type of remedy traditionally associated with the conventional money judgment. It was not intended to provide compensation for past injuries. It was not reducible to a sum certain. No monies were sought by the Commonwealth as a creditor or obligee.

The Commonwealth was not seeking a traditional form of damages in tort or contract, and the mere payment of money, without more, even if it could be estimated, could not satisfy the Commonwealth Court's direction to complete the back filling, to update erosion plans, to seal mine openings, to spread topsoil, and to implement plans for erosion and sedimentation control. Rather, the Commonwealth Court's injunction was meant to prevent future harm to, and to restore, the environment. Indeed, examining the state order, it is clear that erosion control, back filling, and reseeding were additionally meant to preserve the soil conditions from further deterioration (as well as to rectify a safety hazard). * * *

NOTES

1. According to Judge Garth in *Penn Terra*, the decisive issue is whether or not the remedy is intended to prevent future harm, not compensate for past wrongs. A key is whether the remedy that the government seeks is, in form or substance, a type of remedy traditionally associated with a conventional money judgment, in which case the government action is excepted from the stay under § 362(b)(4) only up to the point of entry of judgment.

2. Of course, if the government action is not to enforce its "police and regulatory power," then § 362(b)(4) does not apply at all to except the action from the automatic stay. Here is a typical description of the tests for whether an action is an enforcement of the police and regulatory power. Note that under this analysis to qualify for the exception the government's action must pass both tests:

    > To determine whether an action qualifies as a proceeding pursuant to a governmental unit's police or regulatory power, and therefore falls outside the ambit of the automatic stay, this court applies two tests: the pecuniary purpose test and the public policy test.
    > Under the pecuniary purpose test, reviewing courts focus on whether the governmental proceeding relates primarily to the protection of the government's pecuniary interest in the debtor's property, and not to matters of public safety. Those proceedings which relate primarily to matters of public safety are excepted from the stay. Under the public policy test, reviewing courts must distinguish between proceedings that adjudicate private rights and those that effectuate public policy. Those proceedings that effectuate a public policy are excepted from the stay.
    >   * * *

    > [W]hen the action incidentally serves public interests but more substantially adjudicates private rights, courts should regard the suit as outside the police power exception, particularly when a successful suit would result in a pecuniary advantage to certain private parties vis-a-vis other creditors of the estate, contrary to the Bankruptcy Code's priorities.

    Chao v. Hosp. Staffing Servs., Inc., 270 F.3d 374, 385-86, 390 (6th Cir. 2001). How do these tests fit together with the *Penn Terra* test for whether the government action is seeking to enforce a money judgment?

3. Compare the approach taken in *Chao* to the approach taken in a portion of the *Penn Terra* decision not reproduced above:

    > Proper respect, therefore, for the independent sovereignty of the several States requires that federal supremacy be invoked only where it is clear that Congress so intended. Statutes should therefore be

construed to avoid pre-emption, absent an unmistakable indication to the contrary. Where the traditional police power of the State is to "be deemed withdrawn by Congress in bankruptcy legislation, evidence of that withdrawal in fit language should be found within the act." In re Chicago Rapid Transit Co., 129 F.2d 1, 5 (7th Cir.), cert. denied, 317 U.S. 683, 63 S. Ct. 205, 87 L. Ed. 547 (1942).

Given the general rule that preemption is not favored, and the fact that, in restoring power to the States, Congress intentionally used such a broad term as "police and regulatory powers," we find that the exception to the automatic stay provision contained in subsection[ ] 362(b)[(4)] should itself be construed broadly, and no unnatural efforts be made to limit its scope. The police power of the several States embodies the main bulwark of protection by which they carry out their responsibilities to the People; its abrogation is therefore a serious matter. Congress should not be assumed, therefore, to have been miserly in its refund of that power to the States. Where important state law or general equitable principles protect some public interest, they should not be overridden by federal legislation unless they are inconsistent with explicit congressional intent such that the supremacy clause mandates their supersession. For the same policy reasons, the "exception to the exception" created by subsection 362(b)(5), rendering "enforcement of a money judgment" by a government unit susceptible to the automatic stay, should be construed narrowly so as to leave to the States so much of their police power as a fair reading of the statute allows.

There is another reason, specific to this case, why the automatic stay provision should, whenever possible, be read in favor of the States. Concededly, in some individual situations, the exercise of State power, even for the protection of the public health and safety, may run so contrary to the policy of the Bankruptcy Code that it should not be permitted. The statute provides for such exigencies, however. The bankruptcy court, in its discretion, may issue an appropriate injunction, even if the automatic stay is not operative. 11 U.S.C. § 105. Congress explicitly took note of this provision when it excepted government regulation from the automatic stay:

> Subsection (b) lists seven exceptions to the automatic stay. The effect of an exception is not to make the action immune from injunction.
>
> The court has ample other powers to stay actions not covered by the automatic stay. Section 105, of the proposed title 11, derived from the Bankruptcy Act § 2a(15), grants the power to issue orders necessary or appropriate to carry out the provisions of title 11. The district court and the bankruptcy court as its adjunct have all the traditional injunctive powers of a court of equity [statutory citations omitted]. Stays or injunctions issued under these other sections will not be automatic upon commencement of the case, but will be granted or issued under the usual rules for the issuance of injunctions. By excepting an act or action from the automatic stay, the bill simply requires that the trustee move the court into action, rather than requiring the stayed party to request relief from the stay. There are some actions, enumerated in the exceptions, that generally should not

> be stayed automatically upon commencement of the case, for reasons of either policy or practicality. Thus, the court will have to determine whether a particular action which may be harming the estate should be stayed.

S. Rep. No. 95-989 at 51, 1978 U.S. Code Cong. & Ad. News at 5787, 5837; H. Rep. No. 95-595 at 342, 1978 U.S. Code Cong. & Ad. News at 5963, 6298.

> Therefore, little harm is done to congressional purpose in allowing some latitude in favor of State regulatory powers when interpreting § 362(b), since if, in a particular case, that latitude results in an impermissible dilution of federal bankruptcy policy, then the bankruptcy court may always issue an injunction tailored to fit those circumstances. Such an injunction, however, would be based upon traditional equitable standards, and its propriety would also be reviewable on an abuse of discretion standard. The automatic stay, on the other hand, is not discretionary and must remain in effect unless and until the bankruptcy court later grants relief.

733 F.2d at 273-74.

4. Does the stay of § 362(a) apply in the following cases, or is the government action excepted from the stay by § 362(b)(4) up to the point of entry of judgment? Beyond that point?

   a. Environmental Protection Agency's (EPA's) enforcement of consent decree against chapter 11 debtor, in order to require debtor, as one of the parties who had hauled hazardous waste to site that had been subject of environmental clean-up action, to pay 13% of costs of monitoring groundwater at site following removal of waste and topsoil. See In re FV Steel and Wire Co., 324 B.R. 701 (Bankr. W.D. Wis. 2005).

   b. California Attorney General's action against chapter 11 debtor seeking divestiture of three electrical generating plants as part of the state's deregulation of its electrical generation industry. See Lockyer v. Mirant Corp., 398 F.3d 1098 (9th Cir. 2005).

   c. Department of Labor "hot goods" action under the Fair Labor Standards Act (FLSA) to prevent the dissemination, in interstate commerce, of business records that the debtor-employer had allegedly produced at competitive advantage by paying its employees a substandard wage. See Chao v. Hosp. Staffing Services, Inc., 270 F.3d 374 (6th Cir. 2001).

C. RELIEF FROM THE AUTOMATIC STAY

Relief from the stay under § 362(d) is primarily designed for and most often sought by secured creditors who want their collateral. Their security interests and liens survive the filing of the case and the stay, but the stay prevents them from realizing on their collateral. The secured creditors want the court to lift the stay as to their collateral, which permits them enforcement remedies under state law.

A secured creditor's usual routine is to file a motion for relief (i.e., a lift-stay motion) that first claims entitlement to relief under § 362(d)(2)—the debtor lacks equity in the property, which is not necessary to an effective reorganization. If both of these conditions are proved, the property is useless to the bankruptcy case. It would mean that there is no useable value and no use for the property itself. The secured creditor might as well take the property and enforce its lien or security interest. If either condition is not proved, however, there is no relief under § 362(d)(2). In the usual case, the debtor lacks any equity in the property. The fight concerns whether or not the property is needed for reorganization, and (because of language in *Timbers*) the issue most often narrows to whether or not reorganization is possible within a reasonable time. This issue becomes decisive because of the Supreme Court's reading of § 362(d)(2):

> What this requires is not merely a showing that if there is conceivably to be an effective reorganization, this property will be needed for it; but that the property is essential for an effective reorganization *that is in prospect*. This means, as many lower courts, including the en banc court in this case, have properly said, that there must be "a reasonable possibility of a successful reorganization within a reasonable time."

United Sav. Ass'n v. Timbers of Inwood Forest Assocs., 484 U.S. 365, 375-76, 108 S. Ct. 626, 633, 98 L. Ed. 2d 740, 751 (1988) (emphasis in original).

It is uncommon for a court to lift the stay on the basis of § 362(d)(2) during the early months of a bankruptcy case. Here is why:

> "The policy of the Code, as was that of the predecessor statutes, is to encourage reorganization * * *." Because of this, [d]eterminations that property is not necessary to an effective reorganization due to the lack of feasibility should not be favored in the early stages of a bankruptcy proceeding. "No one knows whether the debtor can survive until he has done what Chapter 11 affords him the occasion to do."
>
> Beyond this policy, "[a]t the beginning of the reorganization process, the court must work with less evidence than might be desirable * * *." These considerations require the court to resolve uncertainties about the debtor's future in favor of reorganization, if it is reasonably possible to do so.
>
> Just how far a debtor must go in order to demonstrate a reasonable possibility of a successful reorganization is, therefore, measured on a sliding scale. During the early stages of a proceeding, a less detailed showing may succeed. The same proof at a later time, however, may be insufficient.

Am. State Bank v. Grand Sports, Inc. (In re Grand Sports, Inc.), 86 B.R. 971, 974 (Bankr. N.D. Ind. 1988). To prevail under § 362(d)(2) during the early days of a case, the debtor is not required to present a plan. The debtor is obliged only to make some showing, albeit well-founded, that a reorganization is possible. Id. Courts tend to believe "the Debtor should at least have the opportunity to obtain confirmation of a plan proposed within the exclusive period." In re Cardinal Congregate I, 113 B.R. 371, 378 (Bankr. S.D. Ohio 1990). "[O]nly the debtor may file a plan until after 120 days after the date of the order for relief * * *." Section 1121(b).

If this issue is decided in favor of the debtor (as usually happens in the early stages of a case) so that relief under § 362(d)(2) is denied, the secured creditor commonly argues in the alternative for relief under § 362(d)(1)—for cause based on lack of adequate protection of its interest in the property. If the creditor is prevented from pulling its collateral out of the bankruptcy and enforcing its interest under state law, the value of its interest in the property must be ensured. It is this value that must be protected rather than the interest in the property itself, but the extent and worth of collateral determine the size and value of the interest. In the absence of adequate protection, relief must be granted under § 362(d)(1) even though the collateral is property that is necessary for reorganization. Conversely, if no reorganization is in prospect (and the debtor has no equity in the property), relief must be granted under § 362(d)(2) even though the creditor's interest is amply protected.

Consider the following problem in light of the two cases which follow it, *Timbers* and Orix Credit Alliance, Inc. v. Delta Resources, Inc. (In re Delta Resources, Inc.), 54 F.3d 722 (11th Cir. 1995).

Problem 3-6

When Foam Corporation filed bankruptcy, the value of Kick Credit's collateral—by one measure—just about equaled the amount of the debt owed to Kick Credit at that time. Under what circumstances will Kick Credit, or any other secured creditor, be entitled to relief from stay for lack of adequate protection of its property interest? Consider the following questions.

1. Even if the collateral's value was stable, Kick could still argue that its interest was threatened—not adequately protected. The argument is that Kick's interest , as defined by state law, includes the right to immediate foreclosure. Therefore, Kick should be compensated for losing the use of the foreclosure proceeds so long as the stay prevents Kick from enforcing its security interests. Absent such compensation, would Kick receive adequate protection that would "result in the realization by [Kick] of the indubitable equivalent of [Kick's] interest" in its collateral? Section 361(3). Does § 361 recognize that Kick has a general right to realize the "indubitable equivalent" of its interest, or does Kick only have that right if adequate protection is provided under 361(3)? Exactly what is the interest of the creditor that must be adequately protected?

2. What can threaten a secured creditor's interest other than depreciation in the value of the collateral? How is adequate protection provided to counter these threats?

3. Assume creditor M has a lien on some of the property of the estate to secure its claim. (Assume the property is not an apartment building, an office building, or other rental property.) M will have an allowed secured claim for the lesser of the amount of its allowed claim or the value of the property securing M's claim. Section 506(a). If M's allowed claim is greater than the value of the property securing the claim, then M will have a secured claim for the value of the property securing the claim, and an unsecured claim for the difference.

If M's allowed claim is less than the value of the property securing it, then M's entire allowed claim will be a secured claim, M will be oversecured, and M will be entitled to be allowed postpetition interest (and likely its reasonable attorneys' fees and other costs), up to the amount of the oversecurity or "equity cushion." See § 506(b). The value of the property securing M's claim is the value of the property minus the amount of any liens that are senior to M's lien (assuming there are no other liens with priority equal to the priority of M's lien).

Assume that, as of the petition date, M has a $70,000 second mortgage on real property worth $100,000. Assume E has a $60,000 first mortgage on the property, and Q has a $25,000 third mortgage. Then we get the following results. The value of the property securing E's first mortgage is $100,000, the value of the property securing M's second mortgage is $40,000 (the $100,000 value of the property minus the $60,000 senior lien), and the value of the property securing Q's third mortgage is zero. E would have a $60,000 secured claim, M would have a $40,000 secured claim and a $30,000 unsecured claim, and Q would have no secured claim but only a $25,000 unsecured claim. Note that of the three mortgagees, only E has a claim secured by more value than the amount of its claim; thus only E will be allowed interest under § 506(b).

What will happen to the amount of the E's secured claim as interest, fees, and costs accrues? What will happen, as a result, to the amount of value securing M's second mortgage and to the amount of M's secured claim? Do these questions suggest an additional threat to secured creditors' interests beyond those you might have given in answer to part 2 of this problem? How could M be given adequate protection against this threat? Note that under § 362(b)(18), which was added by the 1994 amendments, the automatic stay does not prevent property taxes that come due postpetition from becoming liens on property of the estate. Property tax liens have priority over mortgages and most other liens, even if the mortgages or other liens are recorded before the taxes come due. Does this create another threat to M's interest in the property?

4. Now assume that as of the petition date M has a $70,000 first mortgage on the property, assume the property is worth $80,000, and assume for the sake of simplicity that attorneys' fees and costs are negligible. M would be oversecured and would be entitled to be allowed up to $10,000 in postpetition interest out of its $10,000 equity cushion. The question then arises whether M is entitled to adequate protection of its $10,000 equity cushion so that M will be able to accrue the full $10,000 in interest if the case lasts long enough for that much interest to accrue. Does M have a protectable property interest in the full $80,000 of value that secures its claim, including the $10,000 equity cushion? Or does M only have a protectable property interest to the extent of the debt owed to M, which was $70,000 as of the petition date? (Note that a lien is not worth more than the amount—or present value—of the debt that it secures, no matter how great the value of the property securing the debt.)

Is M entitled to adequate protection of the $10,000 equity cushion against diminution caused by depreciation of the property, resulting from wear and tear or from a falling real estate market? Do the holdings of *Timbers* and *Orix* so require? Does their reasoning suggest M is so entitled? But see In re Lane, 108 B.R. 6 (Bankr. D. Mass. 1989) (stating that "there is no lack of adequate protection when the equity cushion above [the amount of the secured creditor's claim as of the petition date] is eroding through either a decline in collateral value or an increase in the claim due to the accrual of interest or expenses," but also finding that the value of the collateral, an office building, was not decreasing).

Is M entitled to adequate protection against diminution caused by accrual of property taxes? Against diminution caused by accrual of interest on M's own mortgage? Does accrual of interest on M's mortgage constitute a diminution of the equity cushion or merely its conversion into secured claim, to M's benefit? Is M entitled to have the equity cushion maintained indefinitely as interest accrues, so that M can accrue even more than $10,000 in interest? See id.; In re Senior Care Props., Inc., 137 B.R. 527 (Bankr. N.D. Fla. 1992).

Does § 506(b) actually provide for gradual "accrual" of interest, so that M's secured claim increases each day due to interest allowable under § 506(b)? Or does it provide that interest will be allowed at a particular time, perhaps near the end of the case when it is necessary to determine the amount of claims for purposes of distribution under a plan? If the former approach is correct, then what is the minimum amount of value that M is entitled to have protected at any particular time? If the latter approach is correct, would M's right to postpetition interest be limited to the right to be allowed postpetition interest out of whatever equity cushion, if any, happened to remain when the court finally determined the amount of the secured claim? Compare *Timbers* and *Orix* with In re Lane, 108 B.R. 6 (Bankr. D. Mass. 1989)

Does M have, at the beginning of the case, a contingent secured claim for the estimated postpetition interest, up to the amount of the equity cushion? If so, what is the amount of the noncontingent secured claim at any particular time, and how much value should be protected?

Suppose the property appreciates by $5,000 during the case. Should M be entitled to accrue $15,000 in interest? What date should be used for valuation? If M is entitled to interest under § 506(b), when should it be paid?

5. Does the existence of the $10,000 equity cushion give M a benefit beyond allowing M to accrue postpetition interest? What will happen to M if the real property drops in value by 15%, from $80,000 to $68,000? Do you see now how the equity cushion got its name? Assume that the real property is not depreciating due to wear and tear, that the debtor's reorganization will likely take 18 months, that M's mortgage carries a 6% per annum interest rate, and that normal fluctuations in the real estate market over that period could easily result in the real property appreciating or depreciating by 15%. Is M's property interest adequately protected by the $10,000 equity cushion? Many courts seem to apply a nearly mechanical test for lack of adequate protection: if the equity cushion is less than a certain percentage of the property's value, then the secured creditor's property interest is not adequately protected.

See, for example, the cases cited in In re Kost, 102 B.R. 829 (D. Wyo. 1989) (holding that adequate protection should not be determined by mechanical formula but stating that an equity cushion of 20% or more is uniformly held to provide adequate protection, that a cushion of 10% or less is uniformly held not to provide adequate protection, and that the cases split when the cushion is from 12% to 20%). But consider LNC Invs., Inc. v. First Fid. Bank, 1997 WL

528283 (S.D.N.Y. 1997) (holding that fact issue existed whether 50% equity cushion in aircraft collateral provided adequate protection), vacated on other grounds, 173 F.3d 454 (2nd Cir. 1999). Cf. Westchase I Assocs., L.P. v. Lincoln Nat'l Life Ins. Co. (In re Westchase I Assocs., L.P.), 126 B.R. 692 (W.D.N.C. 1991) (reversing bankruptcy court's finding of a lack of adequate protection, even though equity cushion was less than 2%, where real property collateral was appreciating slightly); In re Dunes Hotel Assocs., 188 B.R. 162, 174 (Bankr. D.S.C. 1995) ("The fact that the value of Aetna's collateral is not declining also requires a denial of stay relief.")

If M were undersecured (as in part 3 of this Problem) so that it had no equity cushion at all, would M be entitled for that reason alone to obtain relief from the stay? Would such a result be consistent with § 362(d)(2)? With the Supreme Court's decision in *Timbers*? If an undersecured creditor is not entitled to relief from stay simply because there is no equity cushion, how could the small size of an equity cushion entitle an oversecured creditor to relief from the stay? (A hint: What key finding was made in *Timbers*, which is reprinted following this Problem?)

6. Some courts have suggested that a prolonged postpetition failure to make mortgage payments is cause for relief from the stay, or at least can contribute to a finding of cause. See, e.g., In re James River Assocs., 148 B.R. 790 (E.D. Va. 1992) (affirming grant of relief from stay where, inter alia, debtor had failed to make payments for 7 months postpetition and equity cushion was small or nonexistent), vacated on other grounds and remanded, 156 B.R. 494 (E.D. Va. 1993); In re Morysville Body Works, Inc., 86 B.R. 51 (E.D. Pa. 1988) (noting that failure to make payments constitutes prima facie case for relief from stay and justifies relief from stay in absence of equity cushion, but is of minimal significance when there is a large equity cushion). Why do you suppose courts have made this suggestion? What might you conclude from a debtor's financial *inability* to make mortgage payments? Under *Orix* are debtors in possession permitted to make regular monthly mortgage payments without court approval even where the mortgagee is oversecured? Note that regular mortgage payments typically include interest. But see In re Family Health Food U.S.A. Inc., 223 B.R. 250 (Bankr. S.D. Fla. 1998) (holding that postpetition payments on secured debt were authorized by § 1108—and presumably § 363(c)(1)—as ordinary course payments made in operation of the business). Does any provision of the Code require regular mortgage payments to be made?

7. Suppose that the court defines Kick's interest (or M's interest) and orders the debtor to take certain steps to protect this interest, which the debtor then takes, such as maintaining casualty insurance on the property. The debtor does so, but the protection proves to be inadequate. For example, the equity cushion completely erodes, and the value of the property falls below the amount of the secured debt. What then? Is adequate protection a solid guarantee? See Ford Motor Credit Co. v. Dobbins, 35 F.3d 860 (4th Cir. 1994) (briefly noted in Chapter Nine below). What if the court had not ordered the debtor to take any steps because the equity cushion seemed ample and because the debtor already had casualty insurance? See LNC Invs., Inc. v. First Fid. Bank, 247 B.R. 38 (S.D.N.Y. 2000) (reprinted in Chapter Nine below).

United Savings Ass'n v. Timbers Of Inwood Forest Associates
United States Supreme Court, 1988
484 U.S. 365, 108 S. Ct. 626, 98 L. Ed. 2d 740

Justice SCALIA delivered the opinion of the Court.

Petitioner United Savings Association of Texas seeks review of an en banc decision of the United States Court of Appeals for the Fifth Circuit, holding that petitioner was not entitled to receive from respondent debtor, which is undergoing reorganization in bankruptcy, monthly payments for the use value of the loan collateral which the bankruptcy stay prevented it from possessing. In re Timbers of Inwood Forest Assocs., 808 F.2d 363 (1987). We granted certiorari to resolve a conflict in the Courts of Appeals regarding application of §§ 361 and 362(d)(1) of the Bankruptcy Code. * * *

On June 29, 1982, respondent Timbers of Inwood Forest Associates, Inc. executed a note in the principal amount of $4,100,000. Petitioner is the holder of the note as well as of a security interest created the same day in an apartment project owned by respondent in Houston, Texas. The security interest included an assignment of rents from the project. On March 4, 1985, respondent filed a voluntary petition under Chapter 11 of the Bankruptcy Code in the United States Bankruptcy Court for the Southern District of Texas.

On March 18, 1985, petitioner moved for relief from the automatic stay of enforcement of liens triggered by the petition, see 11 U.S.C. § 362(a), on the ground that there was lack of "adequate protection" of its interest within the meaning of 11 U.S.C. § 362(d)(1). At a hearing before the Bankruptcy Court, it was established that respondent owed petitioner $4,366,388.77, and evidence was presented that the value of the collateral was somewhere between $2,650,000 and $4,250,000. The collateral was appreciating in value, but only very slightly. It was therefore undisputed that petitioner was an undersecured creditor. Respondent had agreed to pay petitioner the postpetition rents from the apartment project (covered by the after-acquired property clause in the security agreement), minus operating expenses. Petitioner contended, however, that it was entitled to additional compensation. The Bankruptcy Court agreed and on April 19, 1985, it conditioned continuance of the stay on monthly payments by respondent, at the market rate of 12% per annum, on the estimated amount realizable on foreclosure, $4,250,000—commencing six months after the filing of the bankruptcy petition, to reflect the normal foreclosure delays. The court held that the postpetition rents could be applied to these payments. Respondent appealed to the District Court and petitioner cross-appealed on the amount of the adequate protection payments. The District Court affirmed but the Fifth Circuit en banc reversed. We granted certiorari to determine whether undersecured creditors are entitled to compensation under 11 U.S.C. § 362(d)(1) for the delay caused by the automatic stay in foreclosing on their collateral.

II

When a bankruptcy petition is filed, § 362(a) of the Bankruptcy Code provides an automatic stay of, among other things, actions taken to realize the value of collateral given by the debtor. The provision of the Code central to the decision of this case is § 362(d), which reads as follows:

On request of a party in interest and after notice and a hearing, the court shall grant relief from the stay provided under subsection (a) of this section, such as by terminating, annulling, modifying, or conditioning such stay—

(1) for cause, including the lack of adequate protection of an interest in property of such party in interest; or

(2) with respect to a stay of an act against property under subsection (a) of this section, if—

(A) the debtor does not have an equity in such property; and

(B) such property is not necessary to an effective reorganization.

The phrase "adequate protection" in paragraph (1) of the foregoing provision is given further content by § 361 of the Code, which reads in relevant part as follows:

When adequate protection is required under section 362 ... of this title of an interest of an entity in property, such adequate protection may be provided by—

(1) requiring the trustee to make a cash payment or periodic cash payments to such entity, to the extent that the stay under section 362 of this title ... results in a decrease in the value of such entity's interest in such property;

(2) providing to such entity an additional or replacement lien to the extent that such stay ... results in a decrease in the value of such entity's interest in such property; or

(3) granting such other relief ... as will result in the realization by such entity of the indubitable equivalent of such entity's interest in such property.

It is common ground that the "interest in property" referred to by § 362(d)(1) includes the right of a secured creditor to have the security applied in payment of the debt upon completion of the reorganization; and that that interest is not adequately protected if the security is depreciating during the term of the stay. Thus, it is agreed that if the apartment project in this case had been declining in value petitioner would have been entitled, under § 362(d)(1), to cash payments or additional security in the amount of the decline, as § 361 describes. The crux of the present dispute is that petitioner asserts, and respondent denies, that the phrase "interest in property" also includes the secured party's right (suspended by the stay) to take immediate possession of the defaulted security, and apply it in payment of the debt. If that right is embraced by the term, it is obviously not adequately protected unless the secured party is reimbursed for the use of the proceeds he is deprived of during the term of the stay.

The term "interest in property" certainly summons up such concepts as "fee ownership," "life estate," "co-ownership," and "security interest" more readily than it does the notion of "right to immediate foreclosure." Nonetheless, viewed in the isolated context of § 362(d)(1), the phrase could reasonably be given the meaning petitioner asserts. Statutory construction, however, is a holistic endeavor. A provision that may seem ambiguous in isolation is often clarified by the remainder of the statutory scheme—because the same terminology is used elsewhere in a context that makes its meaning clear, or because only one of the permissible meanings produces a substantive effect that is compatible with the rest of the law. That is the case here. Section 362(d)(1) is only one of a series of provisions in the Bankruptcy Code dealing with the rights of secured creditors. The language in those other provisions, and the substantive dispositions that they effect, persuade us that the "interest in property" protected by § 362(d)(1) does not include a secured party's right to immediate foreclosure.

Section 506 of the Code defines the amount of the secured creditor's allowed secured claim and the conditions of his receiving postpetition interest. In relevant part it reads as follows:

> (a) An allowed claim of a creditor secured by a lien on property in which the estate has an interest ... is a secured claim to the extent of the value of such creditor's interest in the estate's interest in such property, ... and is an unsecured claim to the extent that the value of such creditor's interest ... is less than the amount of such allowed claim ...
>
> (b) To the extent that an allowed secured claim is secured by property the value of which ... is greater than the amount of such claim, there shall be allowed to the holder of such claim, interest on such claim, and any reasonable fees, costs, or charges provided for under the agreement under which such claim arose.

In subsection (a) of this provision the creditor's "interest in property" obviously means his security interest without taking account of his right to immediate possession of the collateral on default. If the latter were included, the "value of such creditor's interest" would increase, and the proportions of the claim that are secured and unsecured would alter, as the stay continues—since the value of the entitlement to use the collateral from the date of bankruptcy would rise with the passage of time. No one suggests this was intended. The phrase "value of such creditor's interest" in § 506(a) means "the value of the collateral." H.R. Rep. No. 95-595, pp. 181, 356 (1977); see also S. Rep. No. 95-989, p. 68 (1978), U.S. Code Cong. & Admin. News 1978, pp. 5787, 5854, 6141, 6312. We think the phrase "value of such entity's interest" in § 361(1) and (2), when applied to secured creditors, means the same.

Even more important for our purposes than § 506's use of terminology is its substantive effect of denying undersecured creditors postpetition interest on their claims—just as it denies *over* secured creditors postpetition interest to the extent that such interest, when added to the principal amount of the claim, will exceed the value of the collateral. Section 506(b) provides that "*[t]o the extent that* an allowed secured claim is secured by property the value of which ... is greater than the amount of such claim, there shall be allowed to the holder of such claim, interest on such claim." (Emphasis added.) Since this provision permits postpetition interest to be paid only out of the "security cushion," the undersecured creditor, who has no such cushion, falls within the general rule disallowing postpetition interest. See 11 U.S.C. § 502(b)(2). If the Code had meant to give the undersecured creditor, who is thus denied interest on his *claim*, interest on the value of his *collateral*, surely this is where that disposition would have been set forth, and not obscured within the "adequate protection" provision of § 362(d)(1). Instead of the intricate phraseology set forth above, § 506(b) would simply have said that the secured creditor is entitled to interest "on his allowed claim, or on the value of the property securing his allowed claim, whichever is lesser." Petitioner's interpretation of § 362(d)(1) must be regarded as contradicting the carefully drawn disposition of § 506(b). * * *

Second, petitioner's interpretation of § 362(d)(1) is structurally inconsistent with 11 U.S.C. § 552. Section 552(a) states the general rule that a prepetition security interest does not reach property acquired by the estate or debtor postpetition. Section 552(b) sets forth an exception, allowing postpetition "proceeds, product, offspring, rents, or profits" of the collateral to be covered only if the security agreement expressly provides for an interest in such property, and the interest has been perfected under "applicable nonbankruptcy law." Section 552(b) therefore makes possession of a perfected security interest in postpetition rents or profits from collateral a condition of having them applied to satisfying the claim of the secured creditor ahead of the claims of unsecured creditors. Under petitioner's interpretation, however, the undersecured creditor who lacks such a perfected security interest in effect achieves the same result by demanding the "use value" of his collateral under § 362. It is true that § 506(b) gives the *over* secured creditor, despite lack of compliance with the conditions of § 552, a similar priority over unsecured creditors; but that does not compromise the principle of § 552, since the interest payments come only out of the "cushion" in which the oversecured creditor *does have* a perfected security interest.

Third, petitioner's interpretation of § 362(d)(1) makes nonsense of § 362(d)(2). On petitioner's theory, the undersecured creditor's inability to take immediate possession of his collateral is always "cause" for conditioning the stay (upon the payment of market rate interest) under § 362(d)(1), since there is, within the meaning of that paragraph, "lack of adequate protection of an interest in property." But § 362(d)(2) expressly provides a different standard for relief from a stay "of an act against property," which of course includes taking possession of collateral. It provides that the court shall grant relief "if ... (A) the debtor does not have an equity in such property [*i.e.*, the creditor is undersecured]; *and* (B) such property is not necessary to an effective reorganization." (Emphasis added.) By applying the "adequate protection of an interest in property" provision of § 362(d)(1) to the alleged "interest" in the earning power of collateral, petitioner creates the strange consequence that § 362 entitles the secured creditor to relief from the stay (1) if he is undersecured (and thus not eligible for interest under § 506(b)), *or* (2) if he is undersecured *and* his collateral "is not necessary to an effective reorganization." This renders § 362(d)(2) a practical nullity and a theoretical absurdity. If § 362(d)(1) is interpreted in this fashion, an undersecured creditor would seek relief under § 362(d)(2) only if its collateral was not depreciating (or it was being compensated for depreciation) and it was receiving market rate interest on its collateral, but nonetheless wanted to foreclose. Petitioner offers no reason why Congress would want to provide relief for such an obstreperous and thoroughly unharmed creditor.

Section 362(d)(2) also belies petitioner's contention that undersecured creditors will face inordinate and extortionate delay if they are denied compensation for interest lost during the stay as part of "adequate protection" under § 362(d)(1). Once the movant under § 362(d)(2) establishes that he is an undersecured creditor, it is the burden of the *debtor* to establish that the collateral at issue is "necessary to an effective reorganization." See § 362(g). What this requires is not merely a showing that if there is conceivably to be an effective reorganization, this property will be needed for it; but that the property is essential for an effective reorganization *that is in prospect*. This means, as many lower courts, including the en banc court in this case, have properly said, that there must be "a reasonable possibility of a successful reorganization within a reasonable time." 808 F.2d, at 370-371, and nn. 12-13, and cases cited therein. The cases are numerous in which § 362(d)(2) relief has been provided within less than a year from the filing of the bankruptcy petition. And while the bankruptcy courts demand less detailed showings during the four months in which the debtor is given the exclusive right to put together a plan, see 11 U.S.C. §§ 1121(b), (c)(2), even within that period lack of any realistic prospect of effective reorganization will require § 362(d)(2) relief.

III

A

Petitioner contends that denying it compensation under § 362(d)(1) is inconsistent with sections of the Code other than those just discussed. Petitioner principally relies on the phrase "indubitable equivalent" in § 361(3), which also appears in 11 U.S.C. § 1129(b)(2)(A)(iii). Petitioner contends that in the latter context, which sets forth the standards for confirming a reorganization plan, the phrase has developed a well-settled meaning connoting the right of a secured creditor to receive present value of his security—thus requiring interest if the claim is to be paid over time. It is true that under § 1129(b) a secured claimant has a right to receive under a plan the present value of his collateral. This entitlement arises, however, not from the phrase "indubitable equivalent" in § 1129(b)(2)(A)(iii), but from the provision of § 1129(b)(2)(A)(i)(II) that guarantees the secured creditor "deferred cash payments . . . of a value, *as of the effective date of the plan*, of at least the value of such [secured claimant's] interest in the estate's interest in such property." (Emphasis added.) Under this formulation, even though the undersecured creditor's "interest" is regarded (properly) as solely the value of the collateral, he must be rendered payments that assure him that value *as of the effective date of the plan*. In § 361(3), by contrast, the relief pending the stay need only be such "*as will result in the realization* . . . of the indubitable equivalent" of the collateral. (Emphasis added.) It is obvious (since §§ 361 and 362(d)(1) do not entitle the secured creditor to immediate payment of the principal of his collateral) that this "realization" is to "result" not at once, but only upon completion of the reorganization. It is *then* that he must be assured "realization . . . of the indubitable equivalent" of his collateral. To put the point differently: similarity of outcome between § 361(3) and § 1129 would be demanded only if the former read "such other relief . . . as will give such entity, *as of the date of the relief*, the indubitable equivalent of such entity's interest in such property." * * *

The reorganized debtor is supposed to stand on his own two feet. The debtor in process of reorganizing, by contrast, is given many temporary protections against the normal operation of the law.

Petitioner also contends that the Code embodies a principle that secured creditors do not bear the costs of reorganization. It derives this from the rule that general administrative expenses do not have priority over secured claims. See §§ 506(c); 507(a). But the general principle does not follow from the particular rule. That secured creditors do not bear one kind of reorganization cost hardly means that they bear none of them. The Code rule on administrative expenses merely continues pre-Code law. But it was also pre-Code law that undersecured creditors were not entitled to postpetition interest as compensation for the delay of reorganization. Congress could hardly have understood that the readoption of the rule on administrative expenses would work a change in the rule on postpetition interest, which it also readopted. * * *

B

Petitioner contends that its interpretation is supported by the legislative history of §§ 361 and 362(d)(1), relying almost entirely on statements that "[s]ecured creditors should not be deprived of the benefit of their bargain." H.R. Rep. No. 95-595, at 339; S. Rep. No. 95-989, at 53, U.S. Code Cong. & Admin. News 1978, pp. 5839, 6295. Such generalizations are inadequate to overcome the plain textual indication in §§ 506 and 362(d)(2) of the Code that Congress did not wish the undersecured creditor to receive interest on his collateral during the term of the stay. If it is at all relevant, the legislative history tends to subvert rather than support petitioner's thesis, since it contains not a hint that § 362(d)(1) entitles the undersecured creditor to postpetition interest. Such a major change in the existing rules would not likely have been made without specific provision in the text of the statute; it is most improbable that it would have been made without even any mention in the legislative history. * * *

The Fifth Circuit correctly held that the undersecured petitioner is not entitled to interest on its collateral during the stay to assure adequate protection under 11 U.S.C. § 362(d)(1). * * *

Orix Credit Alliance, Inc. v. Delta Resources, Inc.
(In re Delta Resources, Inc.)
United States Court of Appeals, Eleventh Circuit, 1995
54 F.3d 722

[*Orix Credit Alliance, Inc. ("Orix") held an Article 9 security interest in several pieces of heavy equipment owned by Delta Resources, Inc. ("Delta"). Delta filed a chapter 11 petition in late 1992; about a month later Orix moved for relief from the automatic stay. The parties agreed the equipment was worth $643,500 as of the time of the hearing. Apparently the debt owed to Orix was less than that amount, which would have made Orix an oversecured creditor except that another creditor (AmSouth Bank) also claimed a security interest in the equipment. If Orix's security interest was junior to AmSouth's security interest, then Orix would not have been oversecured, because the value of the collateral securing Orix's debt would have been $643,500 minus the amount needed to pay off AmSouth.*

The bankruptcy court denied Orix's motion, finding that Orix's security interest would be adequately protected if Delta paid Orix $9,972.41 per month to cover depreciation of the equipment. Orix claimed it was an oversecured creditor, and claimed that as an oversecured creditor its interest would not be adequately protected unless it also received payments of postpetition interest. The bankruptcy court refused to require payment of interest, deciding that even if Orix were oversecured, the allowance of postpetition interest was an issue that should be considered "at the time *of confirmation of the debtor's Chapter 11 plan." The district court reversed, holding that Orix was entitled to payment not only of the depreciation but also of $8,292.90 in postpetition interest each month "to maintain its equity cushion."*

After Delta appealed to the Eleventh Circuit, the bankruptcy court determined that Orix's security interest was in fact junior to AmSouth's security interest. The Eleventh Circuit took judicial notice of the bankruptcy court's ruling, but also noted that the ruling might be challenged on appeal. Thus the Court decided to address the question whether an oversecured creditor is entitled to payment of interest as part of adequate protection so as to maintain the equity cushion.]

PER CURIAM:
* * *

II. ANALYSIS
* * *

C. Adequate Protection

The question before us is not whether an oversecured creditor whose collateral is worth more than the amount of its debt in a Chapter 11 bankruptcy case may obtain postpetition interest as part of its claim. Indeed, it seems beyond peradventure that a creditor's right to recover postpetition interest on its oversecured claim pursuant to 11 U.S.C. § 506(b) is virtually "unqualified." United States v. Ron Pair Enters., Inc., 489 U.S. 235, 241, 109 S. Ct. 1026, 1030, 103 L. Ed. 2d 290, 298 (1989). Rather, the narrow legal issue presented for decision is whether Orix, purportedly an oversecured creditor, was entitled to receive periodic cash payments for accruing postpetition interest as part of adequate protection, pursuant to 11 U.S.C. § 362(d)(1), in order to preserve the value of its equity cushion. * * *

Here, the bankruptcy court did not make a factual finding as to Orix's status, but simply *assumed* that Orix was an oversecured creditor for purposes of determining the amount of adequate protection necessary to protect the creditor's interest. The district court, relying upon the Supreme Court's opinion in *Timbers*, reversed the bankruptcy court reasoning that

> [a]s an oversecured creditor, Credit Alliance is entitled to post-petition interest under 11 U.S.C. § 506(b). This section states that "to the extent that an allowed secured claim is secured by property the value of which ... is greater than the amount of such claim, there shall be allowed to the holder of such claim, interest on such claim, and any reasonable fees, costs, or charges provided for under the agreement under which the claim arose." As this interest accrues, it also becomes secured by the security interest held by the creditor in the property. Thus, the security cushion represented by the value of the property above the creditor's security interest in the property is depleted daily as the interest accrues. As used in the applicable bankruptcy provisions, the value of the creditor's interest means the value of the collateral. *The security or collateral cushion is an inherent part of the value of the collateral. Accordingly, the oversecured creditor has a valid property interest in this security cushion and has a right to adequate protection of this interest.*

(Emphasis added). And, not surprisingly, on appeal both parties rely on the Supreme Court's opinion in *Timbers* as support for their position.

The Supreme Court has determined that "[t]he phrase 'value of such creditor's interest' in § 506(a) means 'the value of the collateral.' ... We think the phrase 'value of such entity's interest' in § 361(1) and (2), when applied to secured creditors, means the same." *Timbers*, 484 U.S. at 372, 108 S. Ct. at 631, 98 L. Ed. 2d at 749. The enquiry before us turns on whether the "interest in property" to be protected by 11 U.S.C. § 362(d)(1) entitles an oversecured creditor to receive periodic postpetition interest payments to ensure against the diminution in value of its equity cushion as a part of adequate protection or whether it is designed only to protect against diminution in the value of the collateral, i.e.—depreciation.

Appellee Orix asserts that as interest accrues on its claim the interest by the terms of its contract also becomes secured by its security interest in Delta's assets. Therefore, Orix contends, an oversecured creditor's position erodes by the accrual of postpetition interest and ultimately the adequate protection becomes inadequate. That is, unless the interest is paid, Orix's debt becomes less and less oversecured and eventually becomes undersecured. While Orix is correct that the size of the equity cushion decreases as postpetition interest accrues, the increase in the size of its secured claim resulting from the accrual of that interest is entitled to adequate protection only to the extent that the value of the collateral at the time of filing exceeded the value of Orix's original secured claim.

To begin, "[u]pon the filing of a bankruptcy petition, § 362 of the Code imposes an automatic stay on actions by creditors to collect their claims from a debtor." United Sav. Ass'n of Texas v. Timbers of Inwood Forest Assocs., Ltd. (In re Timbers of Inwood Forest Assocs., Ltd.), 793 F.2d 1380, 1387 (5th Cir. 1986), on reh'g, 808 F.2d 363 (1987) (en banc court reinstates panel opinion), aff'd, 484 U.S. 365, 108 S. Ct. 626, 98 L. Ed. 2d 740 (1988). Yet a creditor is not without recourse to protect its interests. "Under § 362(d), a creditor may obtain relief from the [automatic] stay (1) 'for cause, including the lack of adequate protection' of the creditor's interest in the collateral." *Timbers*, 793 F.2d at 1387-88.

Ordinarily, creditors are not allowed a claim for interest accruing on their debts during bankruptcy proceedings. *Timbers*, 793 F.2d at 1385. Yet, *as an exception* to that rule, an oversecured creditor, but not an undersecured creditor having the same risk (indeed, it is possible for the undersecured creditor's risks to be much larger quantitatively), is entitled to receive postpetition interest as part of its claim at the time of confirmation of a plan or reorganization, that is, at or near the conclusion of the bankruptcy case. 11 U.S.C. § 506(b). Judge Randall of the Fifth Circuit explained the rationale for this exception.

> [T]he interest provisions of the Code and its predecessors, as interpreted by the Supreme Court for almost a century, are premised on the equitable principle that the unencumbered assets of a debtor's estate will not be used to benefit one class of creditors at the expense of another.... [Thus,] [a]llowing a claim for postpetition interest by an oversecured creditor, ... is not inconsistent with that equitable principle, *because only assets encumbered by the creditor's lien will be used to fund the payment of postpetition accrued interest.*

Timbers, 793 F.2d at 1387 (emphasis added).

Nevertheless, the Supreme Court has indicated that an oversecured creditor's allowed secured claim for postpetition interest, which is determined near the conclusion of the bankruptcy case, must be denied to the extent that, together with the principal amount of the claim, it exceeds the value of the collateral. Or put another way, the oversecured creditor's allowed secured claim for postpetition interest is limited to the amount that a creditor was oversecured at the time of filing. * * *

> Even more important for our purposes than § 506's use of terminology is its substantive effect of denying undersecured creditors postpetition interest on their claims—just as it denies oversecured creditors postpetition interest to the extent that such interest, when added to the principal amount of the claim, will exceed the value of the collateral. * * * If the Code had meant to give the under-secured creditor, who is thus denied interest on his *claim*, interest on the value of his *collateral*, surely this is where that disposition would have been set forth, and not obscured within the "adequate protection" provision of § 362(d)(1). Instead of the intricate phraseology set forth above, § 506(b) would simply have said that the secured creditor is entitled to interest "on his allowed claim, or on the value of the property securing his allowed claim, whichever is lesser."

Timbers, 484 U.S. at 372-73, 108 S. Ct. at 631, 98 L. Ed. 2d at 749. * * *

Ordinarily, the matter of adequate protection is determined at or near the inception of a bankruptcy case. By contrast, the determination of a creditor's secured status, pursuant to 11 U.S.C. § 506, comes at or near the conclusion of a bankruptcy case.

> Under [11 U.S.C.] § 506(c), the debtor may recover from property securing a creditor's allowed secured *claim* the reasonable and necessary costs and expenses of preserving or disposing of the property, to the extent of any benefit to the creditor. If, after reducing the amount of the allowed secured claim by the amount of that recovery, the creditor is oversecured, it is entitled to interest at the contract rate on its net allowed secured claim. § 506(b). *The timing of the payment of accrued interest to an oversecured creditor (at the conclusion of the proceeding) is doubtless based on the fact that it is not possible to compute the amount of the § 506(c) recovery (and, accordingly, the amount of the net allowed secured claim on which interest is computed) until the termination of the proceeding.*

Timbers, 793 F.2d at 1407 (emphasis added).

Similarly, we conclude that 11 U.S.C. § 506(b), providing for postpetition interest on oversecured claims, read in pari materia with 11 U.S.C. § 362(d)(1), concerning conditioning the automatic stay on adequate protection, and 11 U.S.C. § 502, regarding the allowance of claims, requires that the payment of accrued postpetition interest to an oversecured creditor await the completion of reorganization or confirmation of the bankruptcy case. The ratio decidendi enunciated by the Supreme Court in *Timbers* that an undersecured creditor is not entitled to receive postpetition interest on its collateral *during the stay* to assure adequate protection under 11 U.S.C. § 362(d)(1) applies equally well to an oversecured creditor. Such an interpretation of the Bankruptcy Code is consistent whether the secured creditor is undersecured or oversecured, otherwise "§ 506(b) would simply have said that the *secured* creditor [whether oversecured or undersecured] is entitled to interest 'on his allowed claim, or on the value of the property securing his allowed claim, whichever is lesser.' " *Timbers*, 484 U.S. at 372-73, 108 S. Ct. at 631, 98 L. Ed. 2d at 749 (emphasis added). Accordingly, viewing the allowance of postpetition interest to oversecured creditors as a limited exception only, we hold that an oversecured creditor's interest in property which must be adequately protected encompasses the decline in the value of the collateral only, rather than perpetuating the ratio of the collateral to the debt. The bankruptcy court accomplished that by allowing adequate protection in the amount of accruing depreciation. See In re Westchase I Assoc., 126 B.R. 692 (W.D.N.C. 1991); David G. Epstein et al., BANKRUPTCY § 3-27, at 142-43 (1993).

We think this rule results in the appropriate balance between the conflicting interests of the oversecured creditor on the one hand and the estate, as well as other creditors, secured and unsecured, on the other hand. As one commentator points out:

> [t]here is certainly no reason intrinsic to the phenomenon of credit that entitles over-secured creditors to interest out of their collateral before junior creditors, whether secured [perhaps by the identical collateral] or unsecured, receive any of their principal.

Niall L. O'Toole, *Adequate Protection and Postpetition Interest in Chapter 11 Proceedings*, 56 AM. BANK. L.J. 251, 253 (1982).

Here, even accepting the bankruptcy court's assumption that Orix was an oversecured creditor, although it never made such a factual finding, for the reasons stated above, Orix, as a matter of law, was not entitled to receive periodic payments for accruing postpetition interest as part of adequate protection for any period of time.[21]

III. CONCLUSION

The district court's order awarding Orix monthly postpetition interest in the amount of $8,292.90 is REVERSED and this case REMANDED to the district court for further proceedings not inconsistent herewith.

Problem 3-7

A partner in your firm has interrupted your research on an issue related to Foam Corporation's case to ask you to research § 362(d)(3). She suggests you review Condor One v. Archway Apartments, Ltd. (In re Archway Apartments, Ltd.), 206 B.R. 463 (Bankr. M.D. Tenn. 1997); In re Pensignorkay, Inc., 204 B.R. 676 (Bankr. E.D. Pa. 1997); NationsBank v. LDN Corp. (In re LDN Corp.), 191 B.R. 320 (Bankr. E.D. Va. 1996); Riggs Bank, N.A. v. Planet 10, L.C. (In re Planet 10, L.C.), 213 B.R. 478 (Bankr. E.D. Va. 1997) (chapter 7 case). She tells you to assume, as in part 3 of Problem 3-6, that M has a $70,000 second mortgage on a $100,000 piece of real property, that there is a $60,000 first mortgage on the property, and that there is a $25,000 third mortgage on it. In addition, assume

---

21. [Footnote 9 in original:] We express no opinion whether Orix may yet be entitled to postpetition interest on its claim, irrespective of the bankruptcy court's subsequent decision that Orix was not an oversecured creditor.

the real property—the only substantial asset of the debtor—is an apartment building containing five small studio apartments. Assume all of the debtor's gross income consists of rents from the tenants and of receipts from the coin-operated washing machines and dryers in the apartment building's laundry room. What must the debtor do to prevent the first mortgagee and M from obtaining relief from the stay under § 362(d)(3)? Does the third mortgagee have any rights under that section? If the debtor files a plan 85 days after the order for relief, and the court, 95 days after the order for relief, determines that the plan as filed does not have a reasonable possibility of being confirmed within a reasonable time, may the court keep the stay in effect if the debtor immediately begins paying interest to the first mortgagee and to M? May the court keep the stay in effect while the debtor drafts an amended plan, if the court believes an amended plan can be filed promptly and would have a reasonable possibility of being confirmed within a reasonable time? Suppose the debtor does not file a plan within 90 days after the order for relief, but instead makes an interest payment to M and to the first mortgagee 88 days after the order for relief. What will be the effect of a court determination 95 days after the order for relief that the amount of interest that was paid to M was slightly less than the amount that should have been paid? Can the court give the debtor an opportunity to make up the difference and keep the stay in effect? Can the first mortgagee take advantage of the underpayment to M? Can the third mortgagee?

Problem 3-8

Provide Foam Corporation with advice on the following questions that may arise during the case regarding motions for relief from stay:

1. Imperial Insurance Company is a lessor of substantial real estate to Foam Corporation. It is not a secured creditor. It is the owner of the property. Nevertheless, Imperial could lose value if Foam Corporation defaults and the bankruptcy prevents Imperial from retaking possession and disposing of the property. Is Imperial entitled to relief from the stay unless Foam Corporation provides adequate protection? Compare In re Ernst Home Ctr., Inc., 209 B.R. 955 (Bankr. W.D. Wash. 1997), with In re Sweetwater, 40 B.R. 733 (Bankr. D. Utah 1984), aff'd, 57 B.R. 743 (D. Utah 1985).

2. Many of Foam Corporation's trade creditors are totally unsecured, but each of them is entitled to share pro rata in any equity in property of the estate that remains after paying expenses and priority claims. Is this right an interest that is entitled to adequate protection? Cf. Grupo Mexicano de Desarollo, S.A. v. Alliance Bond Fund, Inc., 527 U.S. 308, 119 S. Ct. 1961, 144 L. Ed. 2d 319 (1999). Is there any other basis on which an unsecured creditor might seek relief from the stay? Is there any way other than relief from the stay that the creditor can seek its ultimate objective—to get at the debtor's property to satisfy the creditor's claim?

3. Suppose that some of Foam Corporation's creditors reached a workout agreement with Foam Corporation prior to bankruptcy. This very extensive agreement provided, as a major term, that if Foam Corporation ended up in bankruptcy, it would agree and consent to relief from the stay for any of the creditors who were parties to the agreement. After bankruptcy, a creditor who was a party to the agreement filed a lift-stay motion. The creditor cited the

> prepetition consent to relief in the workout agreement as "cause" for relief. Should relief be granted on this basis alone under § 362(d)(1)? Compare In re Atrium High Point Ltd. P'ship, 189 B.R. 599 (Bankr. M.D.N.C. 1995), with In re Pease, 195 B.R. 431 (Bankr. D. Neb. 1996). See Baxter, *Prepetition Waivers of the Automatic Stay: A Secured Lender's Guide*, 52 BUS. LAW 577 (1997); Adams & Baillie, *A Privatization Solution to the Legitimacy of Prepetition Waivers of the Automatic Stay*, 38 ARIZ. L. REV. 1 (1996); Bogart, *Games Lawyers Play: Waivers of the Automatic Stay in Bankruptcy and the Single Asset Loan Workout*, 43 UCLA L. REV. 1117 (1996).
>
> 4. Suppose Foam Corporation and Kick Credit agreed, after Foam Corporation's chapter 11 filing, that Foam Corporation would provide adequate protection of Kick Credit's lien on Foam Corporation's equipment by paying Kick Credit $40,000 cash per month to make up for depreciation. Suppose the agreement also provided that if Foam Corporation was more than ten days late with any such payment, then Kick Credit could immediately foreclose on its collateral. On ex parte application, the court entered an order approving the agreement. Is the agreement enforceable? Can creditors who did not receive notice of the ex parte application have the order set aside? See Tabb, *Emergency Preferential Orders in Bankruptcy Reorganizations*, 65 AM. BANKR. L.J. 75, 90, 113-14 (1991).

D. ARBITRATION AND THE AUTOMATIC STAY

ACandS, Inc. v. Travelers Casualty & Surety Co.
United States Court of Appeals, Third Circuit, 2006
435 F.3d 252, petition for cert. filed, 74 U.S.L.W. 3544
(U.S. Mar. 15, 2006) (No. 05-1191)

ALITO, Circuit Judge.
* * *

For decades, ACandS * * * was one of the nation's largest installers of asbestos insulation. Since the early 1970's, the company has been embroiled in asbestos litigation. On September 16, 2002, after selling many of its assets to Irex, ACandS filed for bankruptcy * * *. This appeal combines two related disputes arising out of the same set of insurance policies issued to ACandS between 1976 and 1979 by Travelers' predecessor, the Aetna Casualty & Surety Co.

[*The policies provided very limited coverage for products liability claims—apparently only $1 million total for each of the four annual policies—but very broad coverage for claims arising from ACandS's operations: $1 million per occurrence with no limit on the number of occurrences. The products liability coverage was quickly exhausted. The parties' 1988 Letter Agreement allocated 55% of each asbestos claim as a products liability claim (which therefore would not be paid by Travelers) and 45% as an operations claim (which would be paid by Travelers subject to the $1 million per occurrence limit). The Letter Agreement set up a demand, mediation, and arbitration process by which either party could try to have the allocation changed. Travelers eventually took the position that the use of asbestos in ACandS's operations was a single occurrence, which would limit Travelers' liability to $1 million for all operations claims under each policy.*

ACandS sought a declaratory judgment (in the "Number of Occurrences Action") that each asbestos claim was a separate occurrence. ACandS also sought an upward revision of the 45% allocation to products claims; an arbitration panel was formed to decide that issue. Travelers' position in the arbitration was that the allocation to operations should be reduced to 0%, because, according to Travelers, ACandS had stopped installing asbestos before the 1976 policy was issued. Therefore, Travelers argued, none of the asbestos claims arose from operations of ACandS during the 1976-79 period as opposed to its prior installation of products. Although ACandS then filed a chapter 11 petition, it took the position that the automatic stay did not prevent the arbitration from going forward (as is noted in the district court opinion reported at 2004 WL 2075117). When the arbitration panel then decided to reduce the operations allocation to 0%, ACandS argued that the award violated the automatic stay and should not be confirmed. The district court confirmed the award. The Number of Occurrences Action was dismissed as moot.]

* * * An arbitration award will be enforced if its form can be rationally derived from either the agreement between the parties or the parties' submissions to the arbitrators and the terms of the arbitral award are not completely irrational. Mut. Fire, Marine & Inland Ins. Co. v. Norad Reins. Co., 868 F.2d 52, 56 (3d Cir. 1989); see also Swift Indus., Inc. v. Botany Indus., Inc., 466 F.2d 1125, 1131 (3d Cir. 1972); Ludwig Honold Mfg. Co. v. Fletcher, 405 F.2d 1123, 1128 (3d Cir. 1969).

A long-standing exception to this general rule provides that courts may refuse to enforce arbitration awards that violate well-defined public policy as embodied by federal law. See Exxon Shipping Co. v. Exxon Seamen's Union, 11 F.3d 1189 (3d Cir. 1994) (vacating labor arbitration award that required the reinstatement of an able bodied seaman who was found to be highly intoxicated while on duty). We hold that the automatic stay provision of the Bankruptcy Code promotes a public policy sufficient to preclude enforcement of an award that violates its terms or interferes with its purposes. See In re Cavanaugh, 271 B.R. 414, 424 (Bankr. D. Mass. 2001) ("[T]he automatic stay is the single most important protection afforded to debtors by the Bankruptcy Code."); see also *Exxon Shipping*, 11 F.3d at 1193 n. 7 ("[A]n award may properly be vacated *either* because it 'violates a specific command of some law' *or* 'because of inconsistency with public policy.' ") (quoting *Honold*, 405 F.2d at 1128 n. 7) (emphasis supplied).

* * *

ACandS argues that, because the arbitration panel considered and accepted the argument that [the] operations [allocation] should be zero, the arbitration proceeding and award violated the automatic stay provision of 11 U.S.C. § 362. * * *

* * * The scope of the automatic stay is broad and covers all proceedings against a debtor, including arbitration. "Because the automatic stay serves the interests of both debtors and creditors, it may not be waived and its scope may not be limited by a debtor." Maritime Elec. Co. v. United Jersey Bank, 959 F.2d 1194, 1204 (3d Cir. 1992). Subsections 362(a)(1) and 362(a)(3) differ in that the stay of actions and proceedings provided for by § 362(a)(1) applies only to actions brought against the debtor—"the statute does not address actions brought by the debtor which would inure to the benefit of the bankruptcy estate." *St. Croix*, 682

F.2d at 448. Section 362(a)(3), on the other hand, applies to actions against third parties as well as actions against the debtor. See In re Krystal Cadillac Oldsmobile GMC Truck, Inc., 142 F.3d 631, 637 n. 11 (3d Cir. 1998).

ACandS argues that the arbitration panel's award violates both § 362(a)(1) and § 362(a)(3). We agree that the automatic stay applied to the arbitration and that the panel should have halted the arbitration once it became apparent that proceeding further could negatively impact the bankruptcy estate. We also hold that the arbitration award is invalid because it diminishes the property of the estate.

1.

With respect to the application of § 362(a)(1), the District Court held that the automatic stay did not apply because the arbitration was an action initiated by the debtor. While in the context of a trial it is simple to distinguish between claims and counter-claims that may support judicial relief, in the context of arbitration, especially in the absence of a joint statement of issues submitted, it is impossible to definitively classify the arguments presented. Travelers contends that its arguments in favor of a zero allocation of claims to the products coverage should be classified as a permissible defense. Defenses, as opposed to counter-claims, do not violate the automatic stay because the stay does not seek to prevent defendants sued by a debtor from defending their legal rights and "the defendant in the bankrupt's suit is not, by opposing that suit, seeking to take possession of it...." Martin-Trigona v. Champion Fed. Sav. & Loan Ass'n., 892 F.2d 575, 577 (7th Cir. 1989). In the trial context, a defendant's failure to formally plead a counter-claim prevents the court from granting affirmative relief on the basis of the defendant's arguments. See Fed. R. Civ. Pro. 8. By contrast, an arbitration award will be affirmed so long as its form can be rationally derived from either the agreement between the parties *or the parties' submissions to the arbitrators* and the terms of the arbitral award are not completely irrational. This procedural flexibility, which is essential to the utility of arbitration, allows Travelers to make a colorable argument that it respected the stay by merely defending its interests when there is no question that in the trial context it would have been required to file a counterclaim in order to obtain the result it seeks to uphold. See Maritime Elec. Co., 959 F.2d at 1204 ("[W]ithin one case, actions against a debtor will be suspended even though closely related claims asserted by the debtor may continue.") (emphasis omitted). Despite the importance of procedural informality, however, the panel's authority must yield when a dispute threatens the rights of third parties in violation of the laws of the United States. To avoid interfering with the broad purposes served by the automatic stay, it was necessary for the arbitration proceeding to halt as soon as the scope of the parties' submissions supported an award that could diminish ACandS's estate. By continuing beyond this point, the proceeding violated § 362(a)(1), and the panel's deliberations and the resulting award are therefore void.

2.

The District Court rejected ACandS's argument that the arbitration award itself, as distinct from the proceeding, violated § 362(a)(3) by stripping ACandS of a valuable property right. ACandS argues that the award's reallocation of claims under the Letter

Agreement to 0% operations and 100% products deprived the bankruptcy estate of property covered by the automatic stay by reducing the amount of insurance coverage available to the debtor. We agree with this argument because the contractual right secured by the Letter Agreement allocating 45% of the asbestos claims to operations was property of the bankruptcy estate. By effectively terminating ACandS's insurance coverage, the arbitration award had a clear adverse effect on that property interest.

The interests classified as "property of the estate" protected by § 362(a)(3) are defined by 11 U.S.C. § 541. It has long been the rule in this Circuit that insurance policies are considered part of the property of a bankruptcy estate. The fact that the Letter Agreement is not itself an insurance policy, and so the rights secured by that contract merely pertain to ACandS's right to coverage, does not exclude these contractual rights from the broad definition of property found in § 541. See Westmoreland Human Opportunities, Inc. v. Walsh, 246 F.3d 233, 242 (3d Cir. 2001) (definition of property "encompasses rights and interests arising from ordinary contractual relationships"). Furthermore, the contractual rights secured by the Letter Agreement and insurance policies are property of the estate regardless of the fact that all of the proceeds from any recovery will be exhausted in satisfaction of outstanding settlements.

For a claim to fall within the scope of § 362(a)(3), it must also be shown that the grant of affirmative relief to Travelers constitutes an act to obtain possession of ACandS's contractual right to a 45% allocation of claims to the operations coverage. Although it cannot accurately be said that Travelers obtained ACandS' rights under the policy, we nevertheless hold that the grant of affirmative relief was an act barred by the automatic stay. The possession or control language of Section 362(a)(3) has consistently been interpreted to prevent acts that diminish future recoveries from a debtor's insurance policies. See, e.g., A.H. Robins Co. v. Piccinin, 788 F.2d 994, 1001 (4th Cir. 1986) (noting that a debtor's insurance policy may well be the most important asset of the estate, and that "any action in which the judgment may diminish this 'important asset' is unquestionably subject to a stay under [11 U.S.C. 362(a)(3)]") (quoting In re Johns-Manville Corp., 40 B.R. at 229). In Matter of J & L Transport, Inc., 47 B.R. 51 (Bankr. W.D. Wis.), the court held that an insurer was barred by § 362(a)(3) from cancelling the debtor's policy so long as the debtor was not in monetary default. Similarly, because the grant of affirmative relief to Travelers had the effect of terminating ACandS's coverage, we hold that it violated the automatic stay.

3.

Travelers argues that even if the panel's award violates the automatic stay, equity precludes its application in this case. This argument fails because no equitable power to grant relief from an automatic stay rests with the District Court. To the extent that an equitable exception to the automatic stay exists, it rests solely in the Bankruptcy Courts. "Only the bankruptcy court with jurisdiction over a debtor's case has the authority to grant relief from the stay of judicial proceedings against the debtor." Maritime Elec. Co., 959 F.2d at 1204.

C.

The District Court dismissed the Number of Occurrences Action on the grounds that the enforceable arbitration award rendered it moot. The action was brought by ACandS in response to Travelers' stated intention to treat all operations claims as arising out of the same occurrence, and therefore subject to the $1 million per occurrence cap. The District Court addressed this issue in footnote 9:

> The complaint in this case deals with the "number of occurrences" under the insurance policies ACANDS has with Travelers. Since the Arbitration Panel has rendered this issue moot by ruling that there is zero remaining coverage under the products policies in this case, there is no reason for this court to decide the "number of occurrences" posed by ACANDS in this case.

As explained above, the panel's award violates the automatic stay and is therefore void ab initio. As a result, ACandS is still entitled to a 45% allocation of claims to the policies' operations coverage, and the dispute concerning whether the asbestos claims present multiple or single occurrences under those policies is justiciable. Accordingly, the Number of Occurrences Action should not have been held to be moot.

* * *

MBNA America Bank v. Hill
United States Court of Appeals, Second Circuit, 2006
436 F.3d 104

GIBSON, Circuit Judge.

MBNA America Bank, N.A. ("MBNA") appeals the district court's judgment affirming the bankruptcy court's order denying MBNA's motion to stay or dismiss an adversary proceeding brought by Kathleen Hill under 11 U.S.C. § 362[(k)]. Hill filed the adversary proceeding against MBNA on February 7, 2002, as a putative class action on behalf of herself and others similarly situated, alleging violations of section 362[(k)] of the Bankruptcy Code and unjust enrichment. MBNA moved to dismiss or stay the proceeding in favor of arbitration under the Federal Arbitration Act, claiming that an account agreement between MBNA and Hill mandated arbitration of the claims. We hold that the bankruptcy court did not have discretion to refuse to stay the proceeding pending arbitration, and we reverse the district court judgment.

On October 9, 2001, Hill filed a petition for relief under Chapter 7 of the Bankruptcy Code. In December 2001, the trustee appointed for Hill's bankruptcy estate filed a report concluding that "there is no property available for distribution from the estate over and above that exempted by law" and declaring that the estate had "been fully administered." The bankruptcy case was concluded in March 2003, when the bankruptcy court granted Hill a discharge.

Hill filed this adversary proceeding in February 2002, based on events that occurred shortly after she sought bankruptcy relief. Before filing for bankruptcy, Hill had authorized MBNA to withdraw monthly payments of $159.01 from her bank account to pay down the balance she owed MBNA on a consumer loan. MBNA made the first of these withdrawals days before Hill filed her bankruptcy petition. Hill included MBNA in the schedule of creditors she filed with the bankruptcy court, and the bankruptcy court mailed notices to all creditors on October 10, 2001. In addition, Hill's counsel sent MBNA notice of the bankruptcy filing on October 23, 2001. In spite of these notices, MBNA withdrew another $159.01 installment from Hill's bank account on November 5, 2001. Hill claimed that MBNA continued to attempt to collect monthly payments and argued that MBNA's actions constituted a willful violation of the automatic stay provision in section 362(a) of the Bankruptcy Code, and that MBNA was thereby unjustly enriched.

Hill styled her complaint as a class action, setting forth allegations specific to her situation and asserting that a class of persons exist who are similarly situated. She alleged common issues, including whether MBNA has engaged in conduct that violates automatic stays in bankruptcy, whether MBNA's conduct is willful, and whether MBNA should be required to make restitution. Hill requested class certification.

MBNA filed a motion seeking to stay or dismiss the adversary proceeding in favor of arbitration, based on an arbitration clause contained in an amendment to Hill's credit account agreement. Hill's original account agreement with MBNA included a provision that authorized MBNA to amend the agreement. In December 1999, MBNA amended the agreements of the class of account holders that included Hill, and notified all account holders of the amendment by mail. The amended agreements contained a mandatory arbitration provision. Hill's notice was not returned as undeliverable, and she did not exercise her opt-out right as set forth in the amendment. The arbitration amendment became effective February 1, 2000, and it provides:

> Any claim or dispute ("claim") by either you or us against the other … arising from or relating in any way to this Account Agreement or … your account (whether under a statute, in contract, tort, or otherwise and whether for money damages, penalties or declaratory or equitable relief) … shall be resolved by binding arbitration.

MBNA contends that this provision required the bankruptcy court to stay or dismiss Hill's claims pending arbitration.

In a thorough opinion and order, the bankruptcy court denied MBNA's motion, concluding that the bankruptcy court was the "most appropriate forum to adjudicate the matter." MBNA appealed the order to the district court. The district court affirmed in part and reversed in part, holding that the bankruptcy court did not abuse its discretion by refusing to dismiss or stay the adversary proceeding in favor of arbitration of the section 362 claim. The district court concluded that permitting arbitration of the alleged automatic stay violation would "seriously jeopardize the objectives of the Bankruptcy Code." The district court held that the bankruptcy court abused its discretion by denying arbitration of the unjust enrichment claim because it was "arbitrable and non-core." However, because Hill had stated that she would abandon the unjust enrichment claim if it were held to be arbitrable, the district court dismissed the claim, and Hill does not appeal that dismissal. MBNA appeals the district court's order denying arbitration of the alleged violation of the automatic stay.

* * *

The Federal Arbitration Act establishes a "federal policy favoring arbitration agreements," Moses H. Cone Mem'l Hosp. v. Mercury Constr. Corp., 460 U.S. 1, 24, 103 S. Ct. 927, 74 L. Ed. 2d 765 (1983), and mandates the enforcement of contractual arbitration provisions. The Act provides that written agreements to arbitrate "shall be valid, irrevocable, and enforceable, save upon such grounds as

exist at law or in equity for the revocation of any contract." 9 U.S.C. § 2. A court
has a duty to stay its proceedings if it is satisfied that the issue before it is
arbitrable, and "[t]his duty ... is not diminished when a party bound by an
agreement raises a claim founded on statutory rights." Shearson/Am. Express, Inc.
v. McMahon, 482 U.S. 220, 226, 107 S. Ct. 2332, 96 L. Ed. 2d 185 (1987).

However, as the Supreme Court acknowledged in *McMahon*, "[l]ike any
statutory directive, the Arbitration Act's mandate may be overridden by a contrary
congressional command." Id. The party opposing arbitration has the burden of
showing that Congress intended to preclude arbitration of the statutory rights at
issue. Congressional intent can be deduced from the statute's text or legislative
history, or from "an inherent conflict between arbitration and the statute's
underlying purposes." Id. at 227, 107 S. Ct. 2332.

Disputes that involve both the Bankruptcy Code and the Arbitration Act often
present conflicts of "near polar extremes: bankruptcy policy exerts an inexorable
pull towards centralization while arbitration policy advocates a decentralized
approach toward dispute resolution." In re U.S. Lines, Inc., 197 F.3d at 640 * * *.

In resolving these conflicts, courts distinguish between claims over which
bankruptcy judges have discretion to refuse arbitration and those that they must
send directly to arbitration. Bankruptcy courts generally do not have discretion to
refuse to compel arbitration of "non-core" bankruptcy matters, or matters that are
simply "related to" bankruptcy cases. As to these matters, the presumption in
favor of arbitration usually trumps the lesser interest of bankruptcy courts in
adjudicating non-core proceedings.

Bankruptcy courts are more likely to have discretion to refuse to compel
arbitration of core bankruptcy matters, which implicate "more pressing bankruptcy
concerns." However, even as to core proceedings, the bankruptcy court will not
have discretion to override an arbitration agreement unless it finds that the
proceedings are based on provisions of the Bankruptcy Code that "inherently
conflict" with the Arbitration Act or that arbitration of the claim would "necessarily
jeopardize" the objectives of the Bankruptcy Code. This determination requires a
particularized inquiry into the nature of the claim and the facts of the specific
bankruptcy. The objectives of the Bankruptcy Code relevant to this inquiry include
"the goal of centralized resolution of purely bankruptcy issues, the need to protect
creditors and reorganizing debtors from piecemeal litigation, and the undisputed
power of a bankruptcy court to enforce its own orders." If a severe conflict is found,
then the court can properly conclude that, with respect to the particular Code
provision involved, Congress intended to override the Arbitration Act's general
policy favoring the enforcement of arbitration agreements.

In this case, Hill's claim under § 362[(k)] of the Bankruptcy Code is properly
characterized as a "core" bankruptcy proceeding. Claims that clearly invoke
substantive rights created by federal bankruptcy law necessarily arise under Title
11 and are deemed core proceedings. So too are proceedings that, by their nature,
could arise only in the context of a bankruptcy case. Actions brought under 11
U.S.C. § 362[(k)] are therefore core proceedings because they derive directly from
the Bankruptcy Code and can be brought only in the context of a bankruptcy case.

In addressing the question of whether Hill's core proceeding should be arbitrated, both the bankruptcy court and the district court provided thoughtful analysis and addressed the relevant competing interests. The bankruptcy court recognized that "Code § 362[(k)] presents a conundrum in the context of a conflict between the jurisdiction of bankruptcy courts and arbitral fora." The bankruptcy court concluded that its court was the most appropriate forum for Hill's claim because a section 362[(k)] cause of action is strictly a product of the Bankruptcy Code. It is derived from the rights of a debtor, and recovery under it inures to the debtor rather than to the bankruptcy estate. Moreover, at the time of the bankruptcy court's ruling, Hill's bankruptcy case was open and she continued to require the protection of the automatic stay. Finally, the bankruptcy court noted that automatic stay provisions are the equivalent of an injunctive order of the bankruptcy court.

The district court held that the bankruptcy court did not abuse its discretion by denying MBNA's motion. The district court recognized it as a close case, but ultimately was persuaded by the fact that a ruling on Hill's claim did not require the bankruptcy court to address the terms of the agreement between Hill and MBNA. Instead, the court would decide whether MBNA violated the automatic stay provision. The district court also emphasized that to allow arbitration to go forward would seriously jeopardize the objectives of the Code in light of the fact that the automatic stay serves the same function as an injunction.

Although we reach the same conclusion as the lower courts that Hill's § 362[(k)] claim is a core proceeding, we hold that arbitration of her claim would not seriously jeopardize the objectives of the Bankruptcy Code because: (1) Hill's estate has now been fully administered and her debts have been discharged, so she no longer requires protection of the automatic stay and resolution of the claim would have no effect on her bankruptcy estate; (2) as a purported class action, Hill's claims lack the direct connection to her own bankruptcy case that would weigh in favor of refusing to compel arbitration; and (3) a stay is not so closely related to an injunction that the bankruptcy court is uniquely able to interpret and enforce its provisions.

* * *

Arbitration of Hill's automatic stay claim would not necessarily jeopardize or inherently conflict with the Bankruptcy Code. We hold that the bankruptcy court did not have discretion to deny the motion to stay or dismiss the proceeding in favor of arbitration. We reverse and remand, and direct the district court to remand to the bankruptcy court with directions to grant MBNA's motion to stay the proceeding in favor of arbitration.

NOTES

1. Is the holding in *ACandS*, that proceeding with the arbitration violated the automatic stay, consistent with the holding in *MBNA*, that arbitration had to be employed to determine whether the automatic stay had been violated?

2. For opinions in tension (at least) with *MBNA*, see Gruntz v. County of Los Angeles (In re Gruntz), 202 F.3d 1074 (9th Cir. 2000) (en banc) (holding that state court determination that automatic stay was not applicable was not res judicata and could be attacked collaterally in bankruptcy court); In re Cavanaugh, 271 B.R. 414, 426 (Bankr. D. Mass. 2001) ("In pursuing his

Complaint, the Debtor is seeking to redress an alleged abuse of the bankruptcy system. Arbitration is not a proper forum for adjudication of a dispute over whether the Defendants violated the fundamental protection of the automatic stay. Enforcement of the arbitration clause under these circumstances would be an abrogation of this Court's obligation to construe and enforce the injunction issuing under its authority and to determine the parties' rights and obligations under bankruptcy law.") (cited approvingly in *ACandS*); Grant v. Cole (In re Grant), 281 B.R. 721, 724 (Bankr. S.D. Ala. 2000) ("Debtor asserts that Conseco has violated this Court's automatic stay and discharge order. This Court entered those orders. This Court is a party to those orders and the Court is an entity offended if the orders are not obeyed. A party who has not agreed to arbitration of its claim cannot be forced to arbitrate. * * * This Court does not agree to arbitrate the claims. Therefore, the arbitration clause cannot require arbitration of the claims alleging violation of §§ 362 and 524 of the Code.").

3. If, on remand in *ACandS*, Travelers seeks relief from stay to proceed with the arbitration, should the bankruptcy court grant relief? May the bankruptcy court do so? Must the bankruptcy court do so?

4. In an opinion issued by the Third Circuit nine days before the *ACandS* opinion, the court held that the core/non-core status of a proceeding "does not affect whether the bankruptcy court had the discretion to deny arbitration." Mintze v. Am. Gen. Fin. Servs., Inc. (In re Mintze), 434 F.3d 222, 229 (3d Cir. 2006). But see Shubert v. Wellspring Media, Inc. (In Re Winstar Communications, Inc.), 335 B.R. 556, 562, 565 (Bankr. D. Del. 2005) (framing one of the issues as "whether the Court has discretion to deny the enforcement of the arbitration clause (i.e., whether the issue is core or non-core)" and stating that "[s]ince this matter is a core proceeding, the Court may decline to compel arbitration, but only if it finds that enforcement of the arbitration clause would conflict with the policies of the Bankruptcy Code, or where the dispute underlying the arbitration is based on rights created by the Bankruptcy Code."). According to *Mintze*, even in a core proceeding, the bankruptcy court would have discretion to deny arbitration only if the *McMahon* congressional-intent-to-preclude-arbitration test were met. Is that approach consistent with the approach in *MBNA*? Should it be applied even where the right or defense asserted by the trustee or debtor in possession is a creation of the Bankruptcy Code, such as a preference claim? Should the debtor's agreement to arbitrate apply to a claim or defense that never belonged to the debtor, and that is being asserted either by a trustee or by the debtor in its fiduciary role as debtor in possession?

5. Assume the holding in *Mintze* is correct, that the bankruptcy court should never reach the question whether it has discretion to deny arbitration unless it first finds that the *McMahon* congressional-intent-to-preclude-arbitration test is met. Should the bankruptcy court even get to the question whether the *McMahon* test is met if it does not find cause for relief from the automatic stay? For an opinion that says "no," see Safety Nat'l Cas. Corp. v. Kaiser Aluminum & Chem. Corp. (In re Kaiser Aluminum Corp.), 303 B.R. 299, 303-04 (D. Del. 2003) ("In this case, Kaiser has an interest in the scope of Safety's insurance obligations and there is evidence that Kaiser would be prejudiced if Safety was allowed to proceed with arbitration. Because Safety is not entitled to relief from the automatic stay to resolve its alleged dispute with Kaiser, the Court need not consider whether the arbitration of this dispute is required under the Federal Arbitration Act.").

6. The automatic stay and the § 502(b) claims allowance process work together; the stay prohibits actions on claims against the debtor from going forward in other forums, and § 502(b) allows the bankruptcy judge to adjudicate the claims centrally. If (1) a creditor has a claim related to a contract that includes an arbitration provision, (2) the debtor objects to the claim, and (3) the creditor moves for relief from stay and for an order that the claims allowance dispute be arbitrated, must the court permit arbitration to go forward? Does the combination of § 362(a) and § 502(b) commit the claims allowance process to the bankruptcy judge in a way that shows congressional intent to override enforcement of arbitration provisions, or at least intent to give the bankruptcy judge discretion to deny arbitration where enforcement of the arbitration provision would harm the prospects for reorganization?

E. CONSEQUENCES OF VIOLATING THE STAY

There are three major consequences of violating the stay. First, according to most courts, the conduct is void—it has no legal effect—as against the debtor and bankruptcy estate. Soares v. Brockton Credit Union (In re Soares), 107 F.3d 969 (1st Cir. 1997). In appropriate circumstances, however, the court can annul the stay retroactively, so as to let stand and give effect to the conduct *nunc pro tunc*. Id. (For this reason some courts are unwilling to say that actions taken in violation of the stay are void, but rather consider them to be voidable. See, e.g., Bronson v. United States, 46 F.3d 1573 (Fed. Cir. 1995).) Second, "[a]n individual injured by any willful violation of a stay provided by this section shall recover actual damages, including costs and attorneys' fees, and, in appropriate circumstances, may recover punitive damages." Section 362(k). Third, contempt sanctions may be imposed against one who violates the stay with notice of it, but not if the violator "acted without maliciousness and had a good faith argument and belief that its actions did not violate the stay." Maritime Asbestosis Legal Clinic v. LTV Steel Co. (In re Chateaugay Corp.), 920 F.2d 183 (2d Cir. 1990).

The automatic stay is "applicable to all entities." Section 362(a). The broad term "entities" includes not only persons (such as human beings, partnerships, and corporations), but also trusts, decedents' estates, the United States trustee, and, most importantly, governmental units. See § 101(15). Principles of sovereign immunity have, however, hindered the full application of the automatic stay and other bankruptcy provisions to governmental units.

In § 106 the United States to some degree waives its sovereign immunity from suit under the Bankruptcy Code. As noted in the following Problem, when the Supreme Court in 1992 interpreted § 106 narrowly, Congress amended § 106 to make the waiver more clear.

State sovereign immunity under the 11th Amendment and broader constitutional doctrines has created more of a problem. See Klee, Johnston & Winston, *State Defiance of Bankruptcy Law*, 52 VAND. L. REV. 1527 (1999). Section 106 purports to waive (to some degree) the immunity from suit of states and their instrumentalities and subdivisions. Under the 11th Amendment and related constitutional federalism doctrines, states (including their instrumentalities) often are immune from suit in federal court by private party plaintiffs. (States do not have such immunity where the United States is the plaintiff, nor do subdivisions of states, such as cities and counties, enjoy any immunity from suit in federal court.) Before 1996—at least from 1964 to 1996—it was thought that Congress had the power to abrogate state immunity from suit in federal court.

In 1996 the Supreme Court held otherwise, stating that "The Eleventh Amendment restricts the judicial power under Article III, and Article I cannot be used to circumvent the constitutional limitations placed upon federal jurisdiction." Seminole Tribe v. Florida, 517 U.S. 44, 72-73, 116 S. Ct. 1114, 1131-32, 134 L. Ed. 2d 252 (1996) (holding that legislation enacted pursuant to the Indian Commerce Clause could not abrogate state sovereign immunity).[22] The rationale of *Seminole Tribe* suggested that Congress could not abrogate state sovereign immunity by legislation enacted under its Art. I, § 8 power to establish bankruptcy laws.

The *Seminole Tribe* Court noted that state sovereign immunity would not prevent federal courts from issuing injunctions requiring state authorities to comply with federal law prospectively. Id. at 71 n. 14, 72 n. 16, 116 S. Ct. at 1131, nn. 14, 16. See Ex parte Young, 209 U.S. 123, 28 S. Ct. 441, 52 L. Ed. 714 (1908). That left open the possibility that § 105(a) injunctions could effectively protect debtors from actions of state officials, and even the possibility that the automatic stay might be enforceable against state officials as an Ex parte Young injunction. However, the reach of Ex parte Young may have been limited by later decisions, and in any event it does not permit suits against state officials which would have the effect of requiring state funds to be used to compensate for past violations of federal law. See Edelman v. Jordan, 415 U.S. 651, 94 S. Ct. 1347, 39 L. Ed. 2d 662 (1974).

State sovereign immunity does not protect states against suits instituted by the federal government. See Alden v. Maine, 527 U.S. 706, 119 S. Ct. 2240, 144 L. Ed. 2d 636 (1999). Thus Congress could authorize suit by the United States trustee to enforce bankruptcy law against the states. See Klee, Johnston & Winston, *State Defiance of Bankruptcy Law*, 52 VAND. L. REV. 1527, 1584-86,

---

22. In 1999, in a Fair Labor Standards Act case, the Court held that Congress, acting under its Article I powers, could not abrogate the sovereign immunity of states and their instrumentalities in their own *state* courts: "We hold that the powers delegated to Congress under Article I of the United States Constitution do not include the power to subject nonconsenting States to private suits for damages in state courts." Alden v. Maine, 527 U.S. 706, 119 S. Ct. 2240, 144 L. Ed. 2d 636 (1999).

In opinions handed down the same day, the Court (1) repudiated the doctrine of implied waiver of sovereign immunity and (2) placed obstacles in the way of Congress's use of the 14th Amendment to abrogate the sovereign immunity of states and their instrumentalities. See College Sav. Bank v. Florida Prepaid Postsecondary Educ. Expense Bd., 527 U.S. 666, 119 S. Ct. 2219, 144 L. Ed. 2d 605 (1999), and Florida Prepaid Postsecondary Educ. Expense Bd. v. College Sav. Bank, 527 U.S. 627, 119 S. Ct. 2199, 144 L. Ed. 2d 575 (1999).

supra. It is also possible that Congress could authorize a trustee for the case or the debtor in possession to sue states on behalf of the United States. See id. at 1586-89; cf. Vt. Agency of Natural Res. v. United States ex. rel. Stevens, 529 U.S. 765, 120 S. Ct. 1858, 146 L. Ed. 2d 836 (2000) (noting serious doubt whether Eleventh Amendment would prevent Congress from authorizing actions by qui tam relators against States).

In 2004, the Court held that an adversary proceeding filed in bankruptcy court by a debtor against a state instrumentality, seeking a determination that a student loan was dischargeable, was not barred by sovereign immunity, because the suit invoked the *in rem* jurisdiction of the bankruptcy court. Tenn. Student Assistance Corp. v. Hood, 541 U.S. 440, 124 S. Ct. 1905, 158 L .Ed. 2d 764 (2004) Then, in 2006, the Court considered whether the states, by ratifying the Constitution, had given up the right to assert sovereign immunity in actions under federal bankruptcy laws. If so, there would be no need for Congress to abrogate the states' sovereign immunity, and no need for any further consent by the states to federal jurisdiction over bankruptcy matters.

Central Virginia Community College v. Katz
United States Supreme Court, 2006
__ U.S. __, 126 S. Ct. 990, 163 L. Ed. 2d 945

Justice STEVENS delivered the opinion of the Court.

Article I, § 8, cl. 4, of the Constitution provides that Congress shall have the power to establish "uniform Laws on the subject of Bankruptcies throughout the United States." In Tennessee Student Assistance Corporation v. Hood, 541 U.S. 440, 124 S. Ct. 1905, 158 L. Ed. 2d 764 (2004), we granted certiorari to determine whether this Clause gives Congress the authority to abrogate States' immunity from private suits. Without reaching that question, we upheld the application of the Bankruptcy Code to proceedings initiated by a debtor against a state agency to determine the dischargeability of a student loan debt. In this case we consider whether a proceeding initiated by a bankruptcy trustee to set aside preferential transfers by the debtor to state agencies is barred by sovereign immunity. * * * we reject the sovereign immunity defense advanced by the state agencies.

Petitioners are Virginia institutions of higher education that are considered "arm[s] of the State" entitled to sovereign immunity. Wallace's Bookstores, Inc., did business with petitioners before it filed a petition for relief under chapter 11 * * *. Respondent, Bernard Katz, is the court-appointed liquidating supervisor of the bankrupt estate. He has commenced proceedings in the Bankruptcy Court pursuant to §§ 547(b) and 550(a) to avoid and recover alleged preferential transfers to each of the petitioners made by the debtor when it was insolvent. Petitioners' motions to dismiss those proceedings on the basis of sovereign immunity were denied by the Bankruptcy Court.

The denial was affirmed by the District Court and the Court of Appeals for the Sixth Circuit on the authority of the Sixth Circuit's prior determination that Congress has abrogated the States' sovereign immunity in bankruptcy proceedings. We granted certiorari to consider the question left open by our opinion in *Hood*: whether Congress' attempt to abrogate state sovereign immunity in 11 U.S.C. § 106(a)[23] is valid. As we shall explain, however, we are persuaded that the enactment of that provision was not necessary to authorize the Bankruptcy Court's jurisdiction over these preference avoidance proceedings.

Bankruptcy jurisdiction, at its core, is *in rem*. As we noted in *Hood*, it does not implicate States' sovereignty to nearly the same degree as other kinds of jurisdiction. * * *

We acknowledge that statements in both the majority and the dissenting opinions in Seminole Tribe of Fla. v. Florida, 517 U.S. 44, 116 S. Ct. 1114, 134 L. Ed. 2d 252 (1996), reflected an assumption that the holding in that case would apply to the Bankruptcy Clause. Careful study and reflection have convinced us, however, that that assumption was erroneous. * * *

Critical features of every bankruptcy proceeding are the exercise of exclusive jurisdiction over all of the debtor's property, the equitable distribution of that property among the debtor's creditors, and the ultimate discharge that gives the debtor a "fresh start" by releasing him, her, or it from further liability for old debts. "Under our longstanding precedent, States, whether or not they choose to participate in the proceeding, are bound by a bankruptcy court's discharge order no less than other creditors." *Hood*, 541 U.S., at 448, 124 S. Ct. 1905. Petitioners here, like the state agencies that were parties in *Hood*, have conceded as much.

The history of discharges in bankruptcy proceedings demonstrates that the state agencies' concessions, and *Hood*'s holding, are correct. The term "discharge" historically had a dual meaning; it referred to both release of debts and release of the debtor from prison. Indeed, the earliest English statutes governing bankruptcy and insolvency authorized discharges of persons, not debts. * * *

Common as imprisonment itself was, the American Colonies, and later the several States, had wildly divergent schemes for discharging debtors and their debts. Id. [Mann, REPUBLIC OF DEBTORS: BANKRUPTCY IN THE AGE OF AMERICAN INDEPENDENCE (2002)], at 79. * * *

* * *

The difficulties posed by this patchwork of insolvency and bankruptcy laws were peculiar to the American experience. In England, where there was only one sovereign, a single discharge could protect the debtor from his jailer and his creditors. As two cases—one litigated before the Constitutional Convention in Philadelphia and one

---

23. [Footnote 2 in original:] * * * The [current] version of § 106(a) is the product of revisions made in the wake of some of our precedents. The Bankruptcy Reform Act of 1978 contained a provision indicating only that "governmental unit [s]," defined to include States, were deemed to have "waived sovereign immunity" with respect to certain proceedings in bankruptcy and to be bound by a court's determinations under certain provisions of the Act "notwithstanding any assertion of sovereign immunity." This Court's decisions in Hoffman v. Connecticut Dept. of Income Maintenance, 492 U.S. 96, 109 S. Ct. 2818, 106 L. Ed. 2d 76 (1989), and United States v. Nordic Village, Inc., 503 U.S. 30, 112 S. Ct. 1011, 117 L. Ed. 2d 181 (1992), which held that Congress had failed to make sufficiently clear in the predecessor to § 106(a) its intent either to "abrogate" state sovereign immunity or to waive the Federal Government's immunity prompted Congress in 1994 to enact the text of § 106(a) now in force. See generally Gibson, *Congressional Response to Hoffman and Nordic Village: Amended Section 106 and Sovereign Immunity*, 69 Am. Bankr. L.J. 311 (1995).

litigated after it—demonstrate, however, the uncoordinated actions of multiple sovereigns, each laying claim to the debtor's body and effects according to different rules, rendered impossible so neat a solution on this side of the Atlantic.

* * *

These two cases illustrate the backdrop against which the Bankruptcy Clause was adopted. In both * * * the debtors argued that the earlier discharge should be given preclusive effect pursuant to the Full Faith and Credit Clause of the Articles of Confederation. That possibility was the subject of discussion at the Constitutional Convention when a proposal to encompass legislative Acts, and insolvency laws in particular, within the coverage of the Full Faith and Credit Clause of the Constitution was committed to the Committee of Detail together with a proposal " '[t]o establish uniform laws upon the subject of bankruptcies, and respecting the damages arising on the protest of foreign bills of exchange.' " See Nadelmann, *On the Origin of the Bankruptcy Clause*, 1 Am. J. Legal Hist. 215, 216-217, 219 (1957); see also Plank, *The Constitutional Limits of Bankruptcy*, 63 Tenn. L. Rev. 487, 527- 528 (1996). A few days after this proposal was taken under advisement, the Committee of Detail reported that it had recommended adding the power " '[t]o establish uniform laws upon the subject of bankruptcies' " to the Naturalization Clause of what later became Article I.

The Convention adopted the Committee's recommendation with very little debate two days later. * * * The absence of extensive debate over the text of the Bankruptcy Clause or its insertion indicates that there was general agreement on the importance of authorizing a uniform federal response * * *.

Bankruptcy jurisdiction, as understood today and at the time of the framing, is principally in rem jurisdiction. In bankruptcy, "the court's jurisdiction is premised on the debtor and his estate, and not on the creditors." *Hood*, 541 U.S., at 447, 124 S. Ct. 1905. As such, its exercise does not, in the usual case, interfere with state sovereignty even when States' interests are affected.

The text of Article I, § 8, cl. 4, of the Constitution, however, provides that Congress shall have the power to establish "uniform Laws on the subject of Bankruptcies throughout the United States." Although the interest in avoiding unjust imprisonment for debt and making federal discharges in bankruptcy enforceable in every State was a primary motivation for the adoption of that provision, its coverage encompasses the entire "subject of Bankruptcies." The power granted to Congress by that Clause is a unitary concept rather than an amalgam of discrete segments.

The Framers would have understood that laws "on the subject of Bankruptcies" included laws providing, in certain limited respects, for more than simple adjudications of rights in the res. The first bankruptcy statute, for example, gave bankruptcy commissioners appointed by the district court the power, inter alia, to imprison recalcitrant third parties in possession of the estate's assets. More generally, courts adjudicating disputes concerning bankrupts' estates historically have had the power to issue ancillary orders enforcing their in rem adjudications. * * *

* * * it is not necessary to decide whether actions to recover preferential transfers pursuant to § 550(a) are themselves properly characterized as in rem. Whatever the appropriate appellation, those who crafted the Bankruptcy Clause would have understood it to give Congress the power to authorize courts to avoid preferential transfers and to recover the transferred property. Petitioners do not dispute that that authority has been a core aspect of the administration of bankrupt estates since at least the 18th century. And it, like the authority to issue writs of habeas corpus releasing debtors from state prisons, see Part IV, infra, operates free and clear of the State's claim of sovereign immunity.

Insofar as orders ancillary to the bankruptcy courts' *in rem* jurisdiction, like orders directing turnover of preferential transfers, implicate States' sovereign immunity from suit, the States agreed in the plan of the Convention not to assert that immunity. So much is evidenced not only by the history of the Bankruptcy Clause, which shows that the Framers' primary goal was to prevent competing sovereigns' interference with the debtor's discharge, but also by legislation considered and enacted in the immediate wake of the Constitution's ratification.

* * * The Bankruptcy Act of 1800 was in many respects a copy of the English bankruptcy statute then in force. It was, like the English law, chiefly a measure designed to benefit creditors. * * *

The American legislation differed slightly from the English, however. That difference reflects both the uniqueness of a system involving multiple sovereigns and the concerns that lay at the core of the Bankruptcy Clause itself. The English statute gave a judge sitting on a court where the debtor had obtained his discharge the power to order a sheriff, "Bailiff or Officer, Gaoler or Keeper of any Prison" to release the "Bankrupt out of Custody" if he were arrested subsequent to the discharge. The American version of this provision was worded differently; it specifically granted federal courts the authority to issue writs of habeas corpus effective to release debtors from state prisons.

This grant of habeas power is remarkable not least because it would be another 67 years, after ratification of the Fourteenth Amendment, before the writ would be made generally available to state prisoners. Moreover, the provision of the 1800 Act granting that power was considered and adopted during a period when state sovereign immunity could hardly have been more prominent among the Nation's concerns. Chisholm v. Georgia, 2 Dall. 419, the case that had so "shock[ed]" the country in its lack of regard for state sovereign immunity, Principality of Monaco v. Mississippi, 292 U.S. 313, 325, 54 S. Ct. 745, 78 L. Ed. 1282 (1934), was decided in 1793. The ensuing five years that culminated in adoption of the Eleventh Amendment were rife with discussion of States' sovereignty and their amenability to suit. Yet there appears to be no record of any objection to the bankruptcy legislation or its grant of habeas power to federal courts based on an infringement of sovereign immunity.

This history strongly supports the view that the Bankruptcy Clause of Article I, the source of Congress' authority to effect this intrusion upon state sovereignty, simply did not contravene the norms this Court has understood the Eleventh Amendment to exemplify. * * * the Framers, in adopting the Bankruptcy Clause, plainly intended to give Congress the power to redress the rampant injustice resulting from States' refusal to respect one another's discharge orders. As demonstrated by the First Congress' immediate consideration and the Sixth Congress' enactment of a provision granting federal courts the authority to release debtors from state prisons, the power to enact bankruptcy legislation was understood to carry with it the power to subordinate state sovereignty, albeit within a limited sphere.

The ineluctable conclusion, then, is that States agreed in the plan of the Convention not to assert any sovereign immunity defense they might have had in proceedings brought pursuant to "Laws on the subject of Bankruptcies."[24] The scope of this consent was limited; the jurisdiction exercised in bankruptcy proceedings was chiefly in rem—a narrow jurisdiction that does not implicate state sovereignty to nearly the same degree as other kinds of jurisdiction. But while the principal focus of the bankruptcy proceedings is and was always the res, some exercises of bankruptcy courts' powers—issuance of writs of habeas corpus included—unquestionably involved more than mere adjudication of rights in a res. In ratifying the Bankruptcy Clause, the States acquiesced in a subordination of whatever sovereign immunity they might otherwise have asserted in proceedings necessary to effectuate the in rem jurisdiction of the bankruptcy courts.[25]

Neither our decision in *Hood*, which held that States could not assert sovereign immunity as a defense in adversary proceedings brought to adjudicate the dischargeability of student loans, nor the cases upon which it relied, rested on any statement Congress had made on the subject of state sovereign immunity. Nor does our decision today. The relevant question is not whether Congress has "abrogated" States' immunity in proceedings to recover preferential transfers. The question, rather, is whether Congress' determination that States should be amenable to such proceedings is within the scope of its power to enact "Laws on the subject of Bankruptcies." We think it beyond peradventure that it is.

Congress may, at its option, either treat States in the same way as other creditors insofar as concerns "Laws on the subject of Bankruptcies" or exempt them from operation of such laws. Its power to do so arises from the Bankruptcy Clause itself; the relevant "abrogation" is the one effected in the plan of the Convention, not by statute.

The judgment of the Court of Appeals for the Sixth Circuit is affirmed.

It is so ordered.

Justice THOMAS, with whom THE CHIEF JUSTICE, Justice SCALIA, and Justice KENNEDY join, dissenting.

Under our Constitution, the States are not subject to suit by private parties for monetary relief absent their consent or a valid congressional abrogation, and it is "settled doctrine" that nothing in Article I of the Constitution establishes those preconditions. Alden v. Maine, 527 U.S. 706, 748, 119 S. Ct. 2240, 144 L. Ed. 2d 636

---

24. [Footnote 14 in original:] One might object that the writ of habeas corpus was no infringement on state sovereignty, and would not have been understood as such, because that writ, being in the nature of an injunction against a state official, does not commence or constitute a suit against the State. See Ex parte Young, 209 U.S. 123, 159-160, 28 S. Ct. 441, 52 L. Ed. 714 (1908). While that objection would be supported by precedent today, it would not have been apparent to the Framers. The Ex parte Young doctrine was not finally settled until over a century after the Framing and the enactment of the first bankruptcy statute. Indeed, we have recently characterized the doctrine as an expedient "fiction" necessary to ensure the supremacy of federal law.

25. [Footnote 15 in original:] We do not mean to suggest that every law labeled a "bankruptcy" law could, consistent with the Bankruptcy Clause, properly impinge upon state sovereign immunity.

(1999). Yet the majority today casts aside these long-established principles to hold that the States are subject to suit by a rather unlikely class of individuals—bankruptcy trustees seeking recovery of preferential transfers for a bankrupt debtor's estate. This conclusion cannot be justified by the text, structure, or history of our Constitution. In addition, today's ruling is not only impossible to square with this Court's settled state sovereign immunity jurisprudence; it is also impossible to reach without overruling this Court's judgment in Hoffman v. Connecticut Dept. of Income Maintenance, 492 U.S. 96, 109 S. Ct. 2818, 106 L. Ed. 2d 76 (1989).

* * *

The majority finds a surrender of the States' immunity from suit in Article I of the Constitution, which authorizes Congress "[t]o establish ... uniform Laws on the subject of Bankruptcies throughout the United States." § 8, cl. 4. But nothing in the text of the Bankruptcy Clause suggests an abrogation or limitation of the States' sovereign immunity. Indeed, as this Court has noted on numerous occasions, "[t]he Eleventh Amendment restricts the judicial power under Article III, and Article I cannot be used to circumvent the constitutional limitations placed upon federal jurisdiction." *Seminole Tribe*, supra, at 72-73, 116 S. Ct. 1114. "[I]t is settled doctrine that neither substantive federal law nor attempted congressional abrogation under Article I bars a State from raising a constitutional defense of sovereign immunity in federal court." *Alden*, supra, at 748, 119 S. Ct. 2240. And we have specifically applied this "settled doctrine" to bar abrogation of state sovereign immunity under various clauses within § 8 of Article I.

It is difficult to discern an intention to abrogate state sovereign immunity through the Bankruptcy Clause when no such intention has been found in any of the other clauses in Article I. Indeed, our cases are replete with acknowledgments that there is nothing special about the Bankruptcy Clause in this regard. Today's decision thus cannot be reconciled with our established sovereign immunity jurisprudence, which the majority does not purport to overturn.

* * * Article I also empowers Congress to regulate interstate commerce and to protect copyrights and patents. These provisions, no less than the Bankruptcy Clause, were motivated by the Framers' desire for nationally uniform legislation. Thus, we have recognized that "[t]he need for uniformity in the construction of patent law is undoubtedly important." *Florida Prepaid*, 527 U.S., at 645, 119 S. Ct. 2199. Nonetheless, we have refused, in addressing patent law, to give the need for uniformity the weight the majority today assigns it in the context of bankruptcy, instead recognizing that this need "is a factor which belongs to the Article I patent-power calculus, rather than to any determination of whether a state plea of sovereign immunity deprives a patentee of property without due process of law." Ibid.

* * *

The majority also greatly exaggerates the depth of the Framers' fervor to enact a national bankruptcy regime. The idea of authorizing Congress to enact a nationally uniform bankruptcy law did not arise until late in the Constitutional Convention, which began in earnest on May 25, 1787. * * *

The majority's premise fares even worse in explaining the postratification period. The majority correctly notes that the practice of the early Congresses can provide valuable insight into the Framers' understanding of the Constitution. But early practice undermines, rather than supports, the majority's theory. "For over a century after the Constitution, ... the Bankruptcy Clause [authority] remained largely unexercised by Congress.... Thus, states were free to act in bankruptcy matters for all but 16 of the first 109 years after the Constitution was ratified." Tabb, *The History of the Bankruptcy Laws in the United States*, 3 Am. Bankr. Inst. L. Rev. 5, 13-14 (1995). And when Congress did act, it did so only in response to a major financial disaster, and it repealed the legislation in each instance shortly thereafter. It was not until 1898, well over a century after the adoption of the Bankruptcy Clause, that Congress adopted the first permanent national bankruptcy law.

The historical record thus refutes, rather than supports, the majority's premise that the Framers placed paramount importance on the enactment of a nationally uniform bankruptcy law. In reality, for most of the first century of our Nation's history, the country survived without such a law, relying instead on the laws of the several States.

Moreover, the majority identifies *no* historical evidence suggesting that the Framers or the early legislatures, even if they were anxious to establish a national bankruptcy law, contemplated that the States would subject themselves to private suit as creditors under that law. In fact, the historical record establishes that the Framers' held the opposite view. To the Framers, it was a particularly grave offense to a State's sovereignty to be hauled into court by a private citizen and forced to make payments on debts. Alexander Hamilton, the author of Federalist No. 81, followed his general discussion of state sovereign immunity by emphasizing that the Constitution would be especially solicitous of state sovereignty within the specific context of payment of state debts * * *.

* * *

The availability of habeas relief in bankruptcy between 1800 and 1803 does not support respondent's effort to obtain monetary relief in bankruptcy against state agencies today.[26] The habeas writ was well established by the time of the Framing, and consistent with then-prevailing notions of sovereignty. In Ex parte Young, 209 U.S. 123, 28 S. Ct. 441, 52 L. Ed. 714 (1908), this Court held that a petition for the writ is a suit against a state official, not a suit against a State, and thus does not offend the Eleventh Amendment:

> The right to so discharge has not been doubted by this court, and it has never been supposed there was any suit against the state by reason of serving the writ upon one of the officers of the state in whose custody the person was found. In some of the cases the writ has been refused as matter of discretion; but in others it has been granted, while the power has been fully recognized in all.

Id., at 168, 28 S. Ct. 441 (collecting cases).

This Court has reaffirmed *Young* repeatedly—including in *Seminole Tribe*. Although the majority observes that *Young* was not issued "until over a century after the Framing and the enactment of the first bankruptcy statute," this observation does nothing to reconcile the majority's analysis with *Young*, as the majority does not

---

26. [Footnote 5 in original:] This is particularly so given the absence of any known application of that law (let alone any test of its validity) during that time. The provision was enacted into law on April 4, 1800, ch. 19, 2 Stat. 19, and repealed on December 19, 1803 * * *.

purport to question the historical underpinnings of *Young*'s holding. The availability of federal habeas relief to debtors in state prisons thus has no bearing whatsoever on whether the Bankruptcy Clause authorizes suits against the States for money damages.

The majority's second observation—that the Framers were concerned that, under the Articles of Confederation, debtors were unable to obtain discharge orders issued by the court of one State that would be binding in the court of another State—implicates nothing more than the application of full faith and credit, as is apparent from the majority opinion itself. Accordingly, it has nothing to do with state sovereign immunity from suit.

* * * the majority describes at length two Pennsylvania court rulings issued under the Articles of Confederation. But as the majority's explanation makes clear, the problem demonstrated by these cases is the need for recognition of sister-state judgments by state courts, not disregard for state sovereign immunity against suit in federal courts. * * *

Accordingly, it is unsurprising that, when the issue of bankruptcy arose at the Constitutional Convention, it was also within the context of full faith and credit. As the majority correctly points out, the Framers "plainly intended to give Congress the power to redress the rampant injustice resulting from States' refusal to respect one another's discharge orders." But redress of that "rampant injustice" turned entirely on binding state courts to respect the discharge orders of their sister States under the Full Faith and Credit Clause, not on the authorization of private suits against the States.

* * *

In light of the weakness of its historical evidence that the States consented to be sued in bankruptcy proceedings, the majority's effort to recast respondent's action as *in rem* is understandable, but unconvincing.

It would be one thing if the majority simply wanted to overrule *Seminole Tribe* altogether. That would be wrong, but at least the terms of our disagreement would be transparent. The majority's action today, by contrast, is difficult to comprehend. Nothing in the text, structure, or history of the Constitution indicates that the Bankruptcy Clause, in contrast to all of the other provisions of Article I, manifests the States' consent to be sued by private citizens.

I respectfully dissent.

Problem 3-9

Foam Corporation was behind in paying federal taxes when it filed for bankruptcy. Despite its knowledge that Foam Corporation had filed for bankruptcy, the Internal Revenue Service garnished Foam Corporation's bank accounts and also garnished Kick Credit, which held the proceeds of Foam Corporation's accounts receivable. The bank turned over some of the funds in the accounts to the IRS, and Foam Corporation paid an additional amount to the IRS to have both garnishments lifted. Foam Corporation believed it had to act quickly—without complaining to or asking permission of the bankruptcy court—because the garnishments cut off Foam Corporation's access to cash and threatened an immediate end to business.

1. Did the garnishments violate the automatic stay?

2. Did the bank's payment to the IRS violate the stay or perhaps § 542(b))? If the bank did not know of Foam Corporation's bankruptcy filing at the time it paid the funds to the IRS, would the bank be liable for doing so? See § 542(c).

3. Did the bank and Foam Corporation violate § 549(a)?

4. To recover the funds from the United States will require imposing liability for money damages. Is the United States immune from being held liable for money damages under § 105(a) by way of an order holding the government in contempt, or under § 362(k) for violating the stay, or under § 550(a) for being the initial transferee of an illegal postpetition transfer that is avoidable under § 549(a)? See § 106(a). The sovereign is immune in the absence of an "unequivocally expressed" waiver of its immunity. United States v. Nordic Vill., Inc., 503 U.S. 30, 112 S. Ct. 1011, 117 L. Ed. 2d 181 (1992). *Nordic Village* held that § 106 as it existed before the 1994 amendments waived sovereign immunity for purposes of money damage claims only with respect to compulsory counterclaims to government claims and with respect to setoffs against government claims. Section 106 was amended in 1994 to overrule *Nordic Village* and another restrictive Supreme Court ruling. Does the new § 106(a) "unequivocally express" a waiver of immunity for purposes of recovering the funds from the federal government?

5. Suppose Foam Corporation had been behind in payment of state taxes rather than federal taxes. If the taxing authority in this Problem were a state authority (e.g., the California Franchise Tax Board) instead of the federal IRS, would § 106(a) allow Foam Corporation to recover the funds from the state? Would § 106(a) even be relevant, given the Supreme Court's decision in Central Virginia Community College v. Katz (reprinted above)? Despite *Katz*, would § 106(a)(3) and (a)(4) limit the relief that could be obtained against the state or the procedure by which any judgment could be enforced? If Foam Corporation sought return of the funds from the state taxing authorities in state court, would the state court be obligated to follow federal law and hold the state liable?

6. Is Foam Corporation eligible to use § 362(k) to recover damages from the bank or from the taxing authority? The terms of this section award damages only to an "*individual*" who is injured by a willful violation. Is the term "individual" defined in the Code? See § 101(41); Spookyworld, Inc. v. Town of Berlin (In re Spookyworld, Inc.), 346 F.3d 1 (1st Cir. 2003); Sosne v. Reinert & Duree, P.C. (In re Just Brakes Corp. Sys., Inc.), 108 F.3d 881 (8th Cir. 1997). Was the bank's action "willful"? If § 362(k) does not apply, does § 105(a) authorize the bankruptcy court order to award damages against the bank or taxing authority? May the bankruptcy court order payment of such damages as a civil contempt sanction, pursuant to § 105(a) or the court's inherent authority? Is the automatic stay an injunction (violation of which may lead to a contempt sanction) or a statutory prohibition? If it is a statutory prohibition, may the court find an implied civil right of action for violation of it, when the Code already provides an express (and limited) civil right of action under § 362(k)?

7. In any event, can Foam Corporation recover damages from the bank for violating § 549? If actions for these violations are time barred (see § 549(d)), can Foam Corporation nevertheless recover damages under § 362(k) if its terms are met?

8. Suppose the bank ignored the garnishment and paid the state taxing authorities nothing. May a state court hold the bank liable (assuming applicable nonbankruptcy law makes a garnishee personally liable for such failure)? May the bankruptcy court enjoin such a state court action?

Chapter 4

Finding The Cash To Continue Operations

A. INTRODUCTION

To continue operations, the debtor will need to use the property of the estate (and to sell or lease it, in the case of inventory). In particular, the debtor will need to use cash that is property of the estate in order to pay employees for postpetition work, to buy raw materials, and to meet the business's other cash needs.[1] In the rare case, a debtor will be able to continue operations simply by using, selling, or leasing property of the estate without the need for additional credit. For example, there may be substantial assets that are not needed for the reorganization and that can be sold to generate the needed cash. In most cases, however, debtors will need to obtain additional credit from lenders, suppliers, or lessors in order to continue their business operations during the restructuring process. This chapter focuses on (1) the decisions whether to continue operation of the business and whether to obtain credit in so doing and (2) legal issues involved in whether the debtor will be entitled to use property of the estate (especially cash in which secured creditors may have security interests), to sell property of the estate, and to obtain credit.

1. Continuation of the Operation of the Business

Most debtors in possession will desire to continue operation of the business. Operation of the business is essential to the maintenance of a going concern on which the plan of reorganization will be based. But often continuation of the operation of the business will mean that the enterprise will continue to incur losses, because entities whose operations are generating positive cash flow seldom file chapter 11 petitions. Accordingly, William Gruff, as the Chief Executive Officer of Foam Corporation, may desire to retrench business operations by closing down certain operations, liquidating others, and selling others as a going concern.

Section 1108 provides the general rule that the trustee may operate the debtor's business unless the court orders otherwise. Section 1107(a) makes clear that this power to operate the business applies to a debtor in possession as well. Thus, upon the commencement of its chapter 11 case, Foam Corporation will be

---

1. The estate will include cash generated postpetition by the business, such as cash received on sale of inventory or of surplus assets or cash received when customers pay off accounts owed to Foam Corporation. See § 541(a)(6) and (a)(7).

authorized to operate its business, but it is not required to do so. If cash is unavailable to pay laborers and credit is not forthcoming, a responsible chief executive officer will terminate operation of the business. Although it is good practice to inform the creditors' committee and the Office of the United States Trustee that operations will be suspended, a court order is not required. See, e.g., In re Curlew Valley Assocs., 14 B.R. 506 (Bankr. D. Utah 1981).

Sometimes management lacks the foresight to retrench operations of the business. In that event, creditors or the United States trustee may seek to obtain a court order to restrict operation of the business. Sections 1107(a) and 1108 empower the court to restrict the debtor in possession's operation of the business but do not provide a standard by which the court is to make that determination. In most circumstances, courts will defer to the business judgment of the debtor in possession. See Epstein, Nickles & White, BANKRUPTCY § 10-6, at 740-41. Even the continuation of substantial losses will not serve as a basis to terminate the operations early in the chapter 11 process in many cases. See § 1112(b)(1) (authorizing court to dismiss the chapter 11 case or convert it to chapter 7 because of continuing losses only if there is an "absence of a reasonable likelihood of rehabilitation"). But the debtor in possession is not given complete free rein. Section 959(b) of the Judicial Code requires a trustee or debtor in possession who conducts business to manage and operate the business in accordance with state law. 28 U.S.C. § 959(b). Thus, Foam Corporation will not be able to discharge toxic waste, fail to pay laborers their wages, or sell "hot goods" in interstate commerce in violation of non-bankruptcy law. See, e.g., Midlantic Nat'l Bank v. New Jersey Dep't of Envtl. Protection, 474 U.S. 494, 507 & 507 n.9, 106 S. Ct. 755, 88 L. Ed. 2d 859 (1986) ("[A] trustee may not abandon [polluted] property in contravention of a state statute or regulation that is reasonably designed to protect the public health or safety from [imminent and] identified hazards"); cf. Citicorp Indus. Credit, Inc. v. Brock, 483 U.S. 27, 107 S. Ct. 2694, 97 L. Ed. 2d 23 (1987) (Fair Labor Standards Act prevents foreclosing secured party from selling goods—called "hot goods"—produced in violation of minimum wage or overtime provisions); Brock v. Rusco Indus., Inc., 842 F.2d 270 (11th Cir. 1988) (holding that action filed by Secretary of Labor to restrain sale of "hot goods" in interstate commerce was within the police power exception to the automatic stay).

Because even a short cessation of business operations may irreparably damage prospects for reorganization, the debtor in possession often files motions for "first day orders" to keep the business going. See generally In re The Colad Group, Inc., 324 B.R. 208 (Bankr. W.D.N.Y. 2005) (reprinted near the end of this chapter). In the context of operating the business, the debtor in possession might want to obtain orders authorizing the following actions, among others:

1. Continuation of a common cash management system for members of the debtor's corporate "group," including possibly both debtor and non-debtor affiliates. See, e.g., In re Charter Behavorial Health Sys., LLC, 292 B.R. 36, 41 (Bankr. D. Del. 2003).

2. Payment of prepetition debts to "critical vendors," and payment of prepetition wages and health benefits to employees. See, e.g., In re Kmart Corp., 359 F.3d 866 (7th Cir.), cert. denied, 543 U.S. 986 and 995 (2004); In re CEI Roofing, Inc., 315 B.R. 50 (Bankr. N.D. Tex. 2004); In re Teligent, Inc., 306 B.R. 752 (Bankr. S.D.N.Y. 2004).

3. Establishment of a Management Retention or Bonus Incentive Program. See, e.g., In re Aerovox, Inc., 269 B.R. 74, 80 (Bankr. D. Mass. 2001). Note that § 503(c) severely limits the court's discretion in approving retention bonuses.

4. Honoring of prepetition deposits, prepetition sales incentive or discount programs, or warranties on products sold prepetition. See, e.g., Guarracino v. Hoffman, 246 B.R. 130, 133 (D. Mass. 2000).

5. Making adequate assurance payments to utilities within § 366(c) in amounts determined by the court to be sufficient. See, e.g., In re The Colad Group, Inc., 324 B.R. 208, 214 (Bankr. W.D.N.Y. 2005).

6. Obtaining emergency postpetition credit. See, e.g., In re Ames Dep't Stores, Inc., 115 B.R. 34, 36 (Bankr. S.D.N.Y. 1990).

The cases and materials in this chapter provide the foundation for our further consideration of "first day" orders at the end of the chapter.[2]

2. Supervising the Operation of the Business

Foam Corporation's operation of its business will not be free from supervision, as we discuss more fully in Chapter Six below. Section 1103(c)(2) empowers the creditors' committee to investigate the financial condition and operation of Foam Corporation's business. Often the creditors' committee will demand regular meetings with the debtor's management at which balance sheets, income statements, cash flow projections, and business plans are exchanged and discussed. The creditors' committee will be concerned with examining events that led to the business failure as well as focusing on solutions to redirect the business.

The United States trustee is also empowered to supervise the operations of the business. See 28 U.S.C. § 586(a)(3). Some regional offices have published lengthy regulations requiring the debtor in possession to submit

---

2.   Note that Problem 4-1 involves a "first day" emergency request for use of cash collateral that results in an agreement that Foam Corporation may use cash collateral pending a hearing to be held two weeks later. *Abbotts Dairies* (in section B.3 below) recounts an emergency motion for permission to turn the business operations over to a potential purchaser. Shapiro v. Saybrook Mfg. Co. (in section C.3 below) is an appeal from an order granting a postpetition lender extraordinary rights under an emergency financing order.

detailed financial statements on a regular basis for review by the United States trustee. Foam Corporation would be required to do this for its operations. (But it is unclear whether the United States trustee would have power to compel the production of information with respect to U Foam, Foam Corporation's non-debtor subsidiary. Cf. Peterson v. Scott (In re Scott), 172 F.3d 959, 968 (7th Cir. 1999) (debtor in possession has duty to disclose financial information regarding investments).)

Finally, the court itself may desire to supervise the operation of Foam Corporation's business. Initially, the Bankruptcy Reform Act of 1978 sought to separate the judicial from administrative functions. The administrative functions were to be left to the Office of the United States Trustee with the court to be strictly an arbiter of disputes. See H.R. Rep. No. 595, 95th Cong., 1st Sess. 89-91, 107 (1977). Indeed, § 1108 empowers the court to restrict the operation of the business only "on request of a party in interest".

Some courts were concerned that where creditors were inactive, the debtor in possession would operate its business without supervision. Accordingly, in 1986, Congress amended § 105(a) to permit the court to act "sua sponte" to restrict operation of the business in order to prevent an abuse of process. The Bankruptcy Reform Act of 1994 continued this trend by adding § 105(d) to permit the court to hold status conferences. From 1994 to 2005 some activist courts entered orders to show cause why the business should continue to be operated or held status conferences regarding that issue. Other courts, however, during that period were content to leave supervision of the business to the creditors' committee and the Office of the United States Trustee.

Coming full circle, under the Bankruptcy Abuse Prevention and Consumer Protection Act of 2005, Congress again amended § 105(d) to require courts to hold such status conferences as are necessary to further the expeditious and economical resolution of the case. Thus all courts are now charged with actively managing their cases through supervisory status conferences.

B. USE, SALE, OR LEASE OF PROPERTY OF THE ESTATE

At the inception of its chapter 11 case, Foam Corporation desired to continue to manufacture and sell foam products. It had chemicals on hand to manufacture new foam, and it also had finished product ready for distribution. Recall, however, that Kick Credit has a lien encumbering Foam Corporation's personal property.[3]

---

3. Section 552(a) provides that Kick Credit's lien will not encumber property acquired by Foam Corporation after the date of the filing of its chapter 11 case. Section 552(b)(1), an exception to § 552(a), validates Kick Credit's lien in proceeds of collateral if the lien would have encumbered proceeds under state law but permits Foam Corporation to take the proceeds free of Kick Credit's lien to the extent the court determines that the equities of the case require.

Section 363 provides the standards that determine whether Foam Corporation can continue to use cash and other property to operate its business with or without the consent of Kick Credit. The statute provides different rules depending on the answers to two questions. First, is the use of property in or out of the ordinary course of business? Second, is the property "cash collateral" or property other than cash collateral?

"Cash collateral" is defined in § 363(a) essentially to include cash and cash equivalents in which the estate and a secured creditor have an interest. While accounts receivable are not cash collateral, proceeds of accounts receivable upon collection will constitute cash collateral, even if collected after commencement of the chapter 11 case.[4] Rents and hotel revenues are also cash collateral, where a creditor holds a mortgage or deed of trust that extends to them. As a general proposition, if the business of the debtor is authorized to be operated, the debtor in possession may enter into transactions in the ordinary course of business without a court order and without the consent of any affected secured creditor. If, however, the debtor in possession desires to use, sell, or lease cash collateral in the ordinary course of business, § 363(c)(2) requires the debtor in possession to obtain the secured party's consent[5] or a court order authorizing the use of cash collateral. The cash collateral hearing will be scheduled in accordance with the needs of the debtor, often on short notice at a preliminary hearing under Rule 4001(b). The court should authorize the use of cash collateral without the consent of the secured party only if the court determines that the secured party's property interest is adequately protected in accordance with § 363(e). Whether the use is authorized by the secured creditor's consent or through a court order, the debtor in possession is required to segregate and account for cash collateral under § 363(c)(4).

The above principles only apply if the use of property is in the ordinary course of business. If the use, sale or lease of property occurs outside the ordinary course of business, different rules apply. Specifically, § 363(b)(1) requires a use, sale or lease out of the ordinary course of business to be done "after notice and a hearing". Rules 2002(a)(2) and 6004 govern the procedure with respect to a use, sale, or lease outside the ordinary course of business. Under the rules and § 102(1), notice of the proposed sale is given, and unless a party in interest requests a hearing, no court order is required. Sometimes, however, debtors want to obtain a court order to facilitate the issuance of title insurance or to satisfy the purchaser that the sale procedure has been approved by the court. Most courts will supply such an order, but a few will not.

---

4.   If the debtor has sold receivables as part of an asset-backed securitization, the receivables will not be property of the estate unless the court recharacterizes the sale as a financing transaction. See In re LTV Steel Co., 274 B.R. 278 (Bankr. N.D. Ohio 2001).

5.   The secured party's consent must be express, not implied. Freightliner Mkt. Dev. Corp. v. Silver Wheel Freightlines, 823 F.2d 362, 368 (9th Cir. 1987). Approval of an agreement providing adequate protection in exchange for consent must be obtained by motion under Rule 4001(d).

The standard with respect to use, sale, or lease of property outside the ordinary course of business applies to both cash and non-cash collateral. If Foam Corporation wanted to use the proceeds of Kick Credit's accounts receivable to purchase a piece of equipment outside the ordinary course of business, it would appear that neither court authorization nor Kick Credit's consent would be required. The burden would be on Kick Credit (after it received notice of the planned purchase) to request a hearing and raise an objection to the purchase under § 363(e). Thus Kick Credit would need to take the initiative to seek adequate protection of its interest in the proceeds. As a practical matter, however, Foam Corporation would probably seek to obtain a court order or an agreement with Kick Credit regarding the use of cash collateral. Bankruptcy Rule 4001(b) requires a motion to be filed to obtain authority to use cash collateral and does not distinguish whether the use is in or out of the ordinary course of business. Consider the following problem.

Problem 4-1

To simplify the analysis, assume, in lieu of inconsistent facts in Chapter Two, that Kick Credit is owed $6 million principal plus postpetition interest accruing at 12% fixed per annum secured by valid perfected security interests and deeds of trust encumbering *all* of Foam Corporation's assets (and proceeds) including the U Foam stock. Except for Kick Credit's deed of trust, the real estate is unencumbered. Assume the U Foam stock and all of the other assets set forth on the consolidated balance sheet in Chapter 2 are worth collectively $9 million valued as a going concern and $5 million on liquidation. Although Foam Corporation is losing $500,000 per month, the evidence shows that Foam Corporation expects to make a profit of $200,000 per month once the eastern operations are sold. Even though no offers have been received, experienced brokers will testify that the eastern operations should be sold within the next six months.

Concurrently with the filing of its chapter 11 petition, Foam Corporation filed an emergency motion for a preliminary hearing to obtain an order to use proceeds of existing and future accounts receivable and other cash collateral. The court set a hearing for 3:00 p.m. on the afternoon of the filing date and Kick Credit refused to consent to the use of its cash collateral. At the preliminary hearing, Foam Corporation offered Kick Credit a lien on future accounts receivable and inventory as adequate protection of Kick Credit's interest in cash collateral. On that basis Kick Credit agreed to let Foam Corporation use $150,000 in proceeds of existing accounts receivable pending a final hearing at 9:00 a.m. in two weeks. You (the bankruptcy judge) signed an order granting Kick Credit the lien that Foam Corporation offered. A $100,000 bi-weekly payroll is due to be paid next week and again the week following the scheduled final hearing. What facts and law would you need to know in order to rule on Foam Corporation's motion in two weeks?

1. Sale Free and Clear of Liens[6]

Where property of the estate is encumbered by a lien, the property can be sold either subject to or free and clear of the lien. Where property is sold "subject to" the lien, the purchaser of the property may lose the purchased collateral through foreclosure by the secured party if the debtor's obligation to the secured party is not timely paid. For example, if a purchaser desired to acquire one of the parcels of real property owned by Foam Corporation and the property were encumbered by a mortgage, the purchaser might be willing to acquire the property subject to the mortgage. In these circumstances, the purchaser would continue to service the mortgage even if the purchaser were not personally liable to the mortgagee.

In many circumstances, however, the purchaser is unwilling to acquire property "subject to" a lien. As a result, the debtor in possession may seek to sell the property free of the lien. This scenario can raise two issues. First, does the estate own the property subject to sale, and second, under what circumstances may the court order the property to be sold free and clear of liens? With respect to the ownership issue, several courts have noted that § 363(b) & (c) refer to sale of "property of the estate" and have refused to permit use of § 363 prior to determination of whether the property to be sold is property of the estate. See Connolly v. Nuthatch Hill Assocs. (In re Manning), 831 F.2d 205 (10th Cir. Colo. 1987); Warnick v. Yassian (In re Rodeo Canon Dev. Corp.), 362 F.3d 603, 610 (9th Cir. 2004) (holding that a "bankruptcy court may not allow the sale of property as 'property of the estate' without first determining whether the debtor in fact owned the property"), opinion withdrawn and superseded, 126 Fed. Appx. 353 (9th Cir. 2005) (apparently due to settlement of ownership dispute).[7] Moreover, a sale that would eliminate the secured creditor's lien obviously raises an issue of

---

6.   Section 363(f) actually permits sale free and clear of any "interest" in property. Although a "lien" is the most common form of property "interest" subject to a sale free and clear, some courts have applied § 363(f) to permit sales free and clear of other property interests. See Futuresource LLC v. Reuters Ltd., 312 F.3d 281 (7th Cir. 2002) (§ 363(f) sale free and clear of interests includes free and clear of a competitor's interest or intellectual property license in the property sold. Futuresource, a competitor of the debtor, sued Reuters to compel it to provide services that the debtor had provided under an intercompany service agreement. The Seventh Circuit held that purchase of the financial data at a bankruptcy auction under § 363(f) extinguished all interests in the assets acquired including Futuresource's intellectual property license.) We consider in Chapter Seven of this text the question whether real property may be sold free and clear of leasehold interests under § 363(f).

7.   But cf. In re Robotic Vision Sys., Inc., 322 B.R. 502 (Bankr. D.N.H. 2005) (noting that court "need not determine the outcome of the dispute, just whether one exists" in order to authorize sale of property under § 363(f)(4), citing Rodeo Canon for the proposition that "[t]he threshold determination as to the existence of a bona fide dispute necessarily requires a finding that the disputed property is or could become property of the bankruptcy estate," but refusing to permit sale of intellectual property that was not property of the estate because there was no bona fide dispute concerning ownership); Gorka v. Joseph (In re Atlantic Gulf Cmtys. Corp.), 326 B.R. 294 (Bankr. D. Del. 2005) (permitting trustee to "convey whatever interest the estate may have in the Disputed Property by quitclaim deed," thus "leaving any decision of who owns the Disputed Property to the Florida courts," on the theory that the litigation claim was property of the estate that could be sold).

adequate protection. Adequate protection probably will be provided by having the secured creditor's lien attach to the proceeds of sale. If adequate protection is not provided, the secured creditor will be able to block the sale under § 363(e).

Assuming the secured creditor's interest is adequately protected, the debtor still may not sell the property free of the creditor's lien unless one of the five subparts of § 363(f) authorizes the sale. Under § 363(f)(1), if applicable nonbankruptcy law permits the sale of property free and clear of the lien, then Foam Corporation will be able to sell the property in bankruptcy free and clear of liens to the same extent it could outside of bankruptcy. For example, in order to facilitate commerce, inventory usually may be sold in the ordinary course of business free and clear of the lien of an inventory financier. See U.C.C.§ 9-320(a). Of course, Foam Corporation's business would come to a quick halt if it could not sell foam, waterbeds, and children's pillows free of Kick Credit's security interest; no one would buy from Foam Corporation.

Foam Corporation also may be entitled to sell property free and clear of a lien if the secured creditor consents to the sale under § 363(f)(2). The consent may either occur as part of a bankruptcy pleading, or it conceivably could be based on a prepetition security agreement; for example, a mortgage on a large parcel of land under development may permit sale of individual lots free of the mortgage under certain conditions (such as the mortgagee receiving a certain amount from the sale).

Further, § 363(f)(3) authorizes a sale free and clear of liens if the price at which the property is to be sold is greater than the aggregate value of all liens encumbering the property. This standard appears to require the estate to have an equity in the property, e.g., In re Riverside Inv. P'ship, 674 F.2d 634, 640 (7th Cir. 1982), although some courts permit this provision to be used even when the value of the items to be sold do not exceed the secured debt. E.g., In re Collins, 180 B.R. 447, 451-52 (Bankr. E.D. Va. 1995); In re Oneida Lake Dev., Inc., 114 B.R. 352 (Bankr. N.D.N.Y. 1990); In re Beker Indus. Corp., 63 B.R. 474 (Bankr. S.D.N.Y. 1986); Seidle v. Modular Paving, Inc. (In re 18th Ave. Dev. Corp.), 14 B.R. 862 (Bankr. S.D. Fla. 1981); contra, e.g., In re Perroncello, 170 B.R. 189 (Bankr. D. Mass. 1994); Scherer v. Fed. Nat'l Mortgage Ass'n (In re Terrace Chalet Apts., Ltd.), 159 B.R. 821 (N.D. Ill. 1993).

Foam Corporation also would be entitled under § 363(f)(4) to sell property of the estate free and clear of a lien if the lien was in bona fide dispute. Perhaps Foam Corporation could contend that it had repaid the underlying debt or that the lien was subject to avoidance under the various trustee's avoiding powers.

Finally, § 363(f)(5) allows property to be sold free and clear of a lien if the secured creditor "could be compelled, in a legal or equitable proceeding, to accept a money satisfaction" of the lien. The content of this standard is unclear. One court has interpreted the standard to permit a sale free and clear of lien whenever a creditor can be compelled to receive money under a chapter 11 plan. Hunt Energy Co. v. United States (In re Hunt Energy Co.), 48 B.R. 472 (Bankr. N.D. Ohio 1985). Such a construction is questionable because it is so broad that it would render the other four parts of § 363(f) superfluous.

2. Sale of All or a Substantial Portion of Assets Outside of a Plan

In order to obtain needed cash, or to get rid of business operations that are losing money, the debtor in possession may need to sell a substantial portion of the property of the estate before confirming a plan of reorganization. The debtor may even want or need to sell its entire business operations before confirming a plan. A "white knight" may have made a particularly good offer, but one that will not remain open long enough for the debtor to confirm a plan providing for the sale. Alternatively, there may be insufficient cash to keep the debtor's business in operation long enough for it to be sold under a plan; if the business cannot be sold outside of a plan, there may be no choice but to liquidate.

Although § 363 authorizes the sale of property of the estate, courts are split whether the debtor in possession may sell all or a substantial portion of the assets of the estate during the case outside the context of a chapter 11 plan. Courts that restrict sales outside of a plan contend that creditors are entitled to receive a disclosure statement and to vote on a plan providing for the sale. See § 1123(a)(5)(D) and (b)(4). Other courts permit the debtor in possession to sell all assets under § 363, finding nothing that restricts the plain language of the statute. Yet other courts permit a sale of all assets outside of a plan only in an emergency. E.g., In re White Motor Credit Corp., 14 B.R. 584 (Bankr. N.D. Ohio 1981).

In Committee of Equity Sec. Holders v. Lionel Corp. (In re Lionel Corp.), 722 F.2d 1063 (2d Cir. 1983), the Court of Appeals for the Second Circuit held that the court may authorize a sale of significant assets outside of a plan when there is an articulated business purpose for the sale. An emergency is not required. But creditor pressure is not a sufficient reason to sell substantial assets—here the stock of a profitable subsidiary. The bankruptcy court should balance the interests of creditors, the debtor, and equity security holders in deciding whether to authorize the sale. Accord, Stephens Indus., Inc. v. McClung, 789 F.2d 386, 390 (6th Cir. 1986).

Where the sale of assets involves a significant restructuring of creditors' rights, the sale constitutes a "sub rosa" plan and cannot be authorized outside of a plan. Pension Benefit Guar. Corp. v. Braniff Airways, Inc. (In re Braniff Airways, Inc.), 700 F.2d 935 (5th Cir. 1983). Some courts have taken this interpretation to an extreme and prevented a debtor in possession from entering into significant sale or lease transactions even where creditors' distributional rights are not affected directly. E.g., Institutional Creditors v. Continental Air Lines, Inc. (In re Continental Air Lines, Inc.), 780 F.2d 1223 (5th Cir. 1986). A more recent decision of the Fifth Circuit approved a settlement that did not short circuit the chapter 11 plan process, even though it transferred substantial assets of the estate outside of a plan; the court concluded the settlement was not a sub rosa plan because it did not dispose of all of the claims against the debtor, did not dispose of virtually all of the debtor's assets, and did not restrict creditors' votes on any subsequent plan. See Official Comm. of Unsecured Creditors v. Cajun Elec. Power Coop., Inc. (In re Cajun Elec. Power Coop., Inc.), 119 F.3d 349, 355 (5th Cir. 1997).

3. Protecting the Purchaser in a Sale

Section 363(m) protects a purchaser of property from the estate. Unless an objector obtains a stay pending appeal, the reversal on appeal of the order authorizing the sale will not affect the validity of the sale to a good faith purchaser. Often there is no way to grant effective relief on appeal without affecting the validity of the sale; in such cases, any appeal must be dismissed as moot if no stay was obtained to prevent consummation of the sale. Some courts extend this protection to executory contracts or leases that are assumed under § 365 and assigned in sales under § 363. See, e.g., Cinicola v. Scharffenberger, 248 F.3d 110, 128 (3d Cir. 2001); L.R.S.C. Co. v. Rickel Home Ctrs., Inc. (In re Rickel Home Ctrs., Inc.), 209 F.3d 291, 302 (3d Cir. 2000); Krebs Chrysler-Plymouth v. Valley Motors, Inc., 141 F.3d 490, 499 (3d Cir. 1998). Orders authorizing sales of estate property (other than cash collateral) are automatically stayed for ten days, unless the court orders otherwise. See Rule 6004(g). Of course more time than that will be needed for the appeal, and in order to obtain a further stay the objecting party may have to post an expensive supersedeas bond in accordance with Rule 8005. Thus, there is a strong policy favoring the finality of bankruptcy sales.

Problem 4-2

Suppose that Foam Corporation proposes to sell the stock of U Foam under § 363. The sale is to be free of any liens that may be on the stock, such as Kick Credit's security interest, with any liens to attach to the proceeds of the sale. If you were the judge what questions would you want to have answered before deciding whether to approve the sale? Does the sale constitute a "sub rosa" plan?

What risk does the purchaser of the U Foam stock run if an appellate court determines that the sale should have been done as part of a plan? Suppose Foam Corporation had given a security interest in its U Foam stock to Global Bank to secure a prepetition loan, but Foam Corporation failed to give Global Bank notice of the proposed sale of the U Foam stock. If the court approves the sale free of liens, will Global Bank's security interest nonetheless be enforceable against the stock in the hands of the purchaser? See In re Edwards, 962 F.2d 641 (7th Cir. 1992); 3 Resnick & Sommer, COLLIER ON BANKRUPTCY ¶ 363.13, at 363-87 to -89. Could Global Bank move to set aside the sale on the basis that it had not been afforded due process? See Citicorp Mortgage, Inc. v. Brooks (In re Ex-Cel Concrete Co.), 178 B.R. 198, 203 (B.A.P. 9th Cir. 1995).

The protection afforded by § 363(m) is only available to the "good faith" purchaser or lessor. Is the determination that a purchaser is in "good faith" to be made at the bankruptcy hearing authorizing the sale or afterward if the order authorizing the sale is appealed? Consider the following case.

In re Abbotts Dairies, Inc.
United States Court of Appeals, Third Circuit, 1986
788 F.2d 143

SEITZ, Circuit Judge
The National Farmers' Organization, Inc. ("NFO") and Cumberland Farms Dairy, Inc. ("Cumberland") appeal from a final order of the district court, which dismissed as moot their appeals from an order of the bankruptcy court. This court has jurisdiction over their appeals by virtue of 28 U.S.C. §§ 158(d) and 1291.

I.

On August 10, 1984, Abbotts Dairies of Pennsylvania, Inc., Pennbrook Foods Company, Inc., The Pennbrook Corporation, Abbotts Realty Inc., and Abbotts Holding Company, Inc. (hereinafter referred to collectively as "Abbotts"), filed petitions for relief under Chapter 11 of the Bankruptcy Code (the "Code"), 11 U.S.C. §§ 1101-1174. On the same day, Abbotts filed motions for approval of two agreements it had entered into with ADC, Inc. ("ADC"): an "Interim Agreement Concerning Sale of Inventory and Lease of Certain Assets" (the "Interim Agreement"); and an "Asset Purchase and Lease Agreement" (the "Purchase Agreement").

The bankruptcy court held an emergency hearing that afternoon to consider Abbotts' motion for approval of the Interim Agreement, whereby ADC would effectively take over Abbotts' business. Notice of the hearing had been given only to the Philadelphia National Bank ("PNB") and Fairmont Pennsylvania Holdings, Inc. ("Fairmont"), Abbotts' two secured creditors, both of whom were represented at the hearing. Also present, almost by chance, was an attorney representing three of Abbotts' unsecured creditors, and Cream-O-Land Dairies, a prospective purchaser of the business.

In support of its motion, Abbotts' Chairman and Chief Executive Officer, Richard H. Gwinn, testified that PNB notified Abbotts in February of 1984 that it had defaulted on its loans, and that if Abbotts did not obtain financing from another lender, PNB would reduce Abbotts' line of credit at a rate of $100,000 per week. He also stated that unless the bankruptcy court approved the Interim Agreement, the company would have to cease operations when its current inventory was exhausted on August 11 (the next day), because it had no excess working capital with which to purchase any more milk. Finally, Mr. Gwinn opined that if Abbotts ceased operations, its trademarks and customer list would lose substantially all of their value, resulting in a loss of $3 to $4 million dollars to the estate.

On cross-examination by counsel representing one secured creditor, a prospective bidder, and three unsecured creditors, Mr. Gwinn testified that he had reached an informal agreement to act as a consultant to ADC during the pendency of the bankruptcy proceedings, at his current salary of $150,000 per year—provided that the bankruptcy court approved the Interim Agreement. He also testified that he had been offered a senior executive position with ADC for five years, once again at his current salary, and that he hoped that ADC would relieve him from personal liability on several of Abbotts' obligations—provided, once again, that the bankruptcy court approved ADC's purchase of Abbotts' assets.

At the conclusion of the hearing, the bankruptcy court entered an order approving the Interim Agreement. This order was supplemented by an order entered on August 17, 1984, which required ADC and its employees to hold themselves out as Abbotts' representative; to maintain, where possible and economically feasible, Abbotts' existing distribution system; to continue to distribute products under the Abbotts' trademarks and not act affirmatively to switch its customers to products sold under other trademarks; and to act reasonably so as not to prejudice the rights of Abbotts' creditors or diminish the value of its trademarks. These provisions represented concessions that Fairmont had extracted from Abbotts and ADC during the course of the hearing, which Fairmont hoped would preserve Abbotts' value as a going concern until the bankruptcy court could consider the Purchase Agreement and any other competing bids for Abbotts' assets.

Notice of the motion for approval of the Purchase Agreement was then sent to all interested parties. The notice summarized the Purchase Agreement, and set a deadline for objections to it, as well as for "higher or better" bids for Abbotts' assets. The notice did not, however, reveal that Mr. Gwinn was presently employed by ADC as a "consultant," nor did it indicate that he had been offered a permanent position with ADC, conditioned upon closing pursuant to the Purchase Agreement. Likewise, the notice did not indicate that an emergency hearing had been held on August 10, nor did it summarize the terms of the Interim Agreement that had been approved at that hearing; rather, the notice simply stated that "[ADC] previously purchased the inventories and has been in possession of certain operating equipment and facilities of [Abbotts] and have continued certain operations of Abbotts ... under an Interim Agreement pending approval by the Bankruptcy Court of the [Purchase] Agreement."

Three parties filed objections to the sale, only one of which—that filed by Fairmont—is at all pertinent to the present appeals. Fairmont asserted, *inter alia*, that the sale of Abbotts' assets should not be approved until a disclosure statement had been approved by the court and a plan of reorganization confirmed by Abbotts' creditors, because of a number of factors (including the Interim Agreement) that might chill the bidding for Abbotts' assets. Fairmont also objected to the lack of any appraisals of Abbott's assets, and argued that the "value" to be paid by ADC was insufficient.

    * * *

The bankruptcy court held a hearing on the Purchase Agreement on September 12. * * * Fairmont then sought to support its objections to the Purchase Agreement through the testimony of approximately ten witnesses who were present at the hearing. The bankruptcy court refused to hear this evidence; instead, it brought the auction to a close, and signed an order confirming the sale to ADC. In the order, the court found that "it appear[s] that the prices for the sale of the assets ... are fair and reasonable, that the sale and lease are in the best interest of the estate[ ] of [Abbotts] and [its] creditors, [and] that the assets will substantially diminish in value if not immediately sold." In re Abbotts Dairies, et al., No. 84-02623G, slip op. at 1 (Bankr. E.D. Pa. Sept. 12, 1984).

Fairmont, Cumberland, and NFO filed timely notices of appeal to the district court; Fairmont alone, however, sought a stay pending appeal. When the bankruptcy court initially enjoined the sale pending determination of Fairmont's motion for a stay, Fairmont, Abbotts, and ADC met and entered into a stipulation under which Fairmont withdrew its appeal and motion for a stay. The bankruptcy court then vacated its order enjoining the sale. With no stay in effect, ADC and Abbotts closed the sale pursuant to the terms of the Purchase Agreement; notice thereof was filed on September 14, 1984.

After it had closed the sale to ADC, Abbotts filed a motion to dismiss the Cumberland and NFO appeals as moot pursuant to 11 U.S.C. § 363(m). The district court, by order dated July 30, 1985, granted the motion. After reviewing the record in the bankruptcy court, the district court concluded that "[a]ppellants have not shown a lack of good faith on the part of ADC so as to justify their failure to seek a stay, and so the appeal is dismissed." In re Abbotts Dairies, et al., Civil Action No. 84-5118, slip op. at 2 n.1 (E.D. Pa. July 30, 1985).

II.

The Code provides that "[t]he trustee, after notice and a hearing, may use, sell, or lease, other than in the ordinary course of business, property of the estate." 11 U.S.C. § 363(b)(1). It also provides that

> [t]he reversal or modification on appeal of an authorization under subsection (b) ... of a sale or lease of property does *not* affect the validity of a sale or lease under such authorization to an entity that purchased or leased such property *in good faith,* whether or not such entity knew of the pendency of the appeal, *unless such ... sale or lease were stayed pending appeal.*

Id. § 363(m) (emphasis added). The latter provision reflects the salutary "'policy of not only affording finality to the judgment of the bankruptcy court, but particularly to give finality to those orders and judgments upon which third parties rely.'" Hoese Corp. v. Vetter Corp. (In re Vetter Corp.), 724 F.2d 52, 55 (7th Cir. 1983) (quoting 14 Collier on Bankruptcy 11-62.03 at 11-62-11 (14th ed. 1976)).

In the present case, neither NFO nor Cumberland sought to stay the bankruptcy court's September 12 order. They assert that a stay was not necessary, however, because the present record will not, as a matter of law, support a finding that ADC purchased "in good faith"; alternatively, they argue that we should remand the matter to permit them to develop a record on the controlling good faith issues. * * *

Unfortunately, neither the Bankruptcy Code nor the Bankruptcy Rules attempts to define "good faith." Courts applying section 363(m) (and its predecessor, Fed. R. Bankr. P. 805) have, therefore, turned to traditional equitable principles, holding that the phrase encompasses one who purchases in "good faith" and for "value." See, e.g., In re Bel Air Assocs., 706 F.2d 301, 305 (10th Cir. 1983); In re Rock Indus. Mach. Corp., 572 F.2d 1195, 1197 (7th Cir. 1978).

"The requirement that a purchaser act in good faith ... speaks to the integrity of his conduct in the course of the sale proceedings. Typically, the misconduct that would destroy a purchaser's good faith status at a judicial sale involves fraud, collusion between the purchaser and other bidders or the trustee, or an attempt to take grossly unfair advantage of other bidders." In re Rock Indus. Mach. Corp., 572 F.2d at 1198; see also Taylor v. Lake (In re Cada Invs.), 664 F.2d 1158, 1162 (9th Cir. 1981) ("Courts have generally appeared willing to set aside confirmed sales that were 'tinged with fraud, error or similar defects which would in equity affect the validity of any private transaction'").

In the present case, the bankruptcy court did *not* make an explicit finding of "good faith" as to ADC's behavior in the course of the sales proceedings. ADC and Abbotts argue, however, that the court implicitly made such a finding, in that "it simply would not have approved the sale to ADC if it had thought otherwise." Alternatively, they seek to rely upon the district court's conclusion that NFO and Cumberland "have not shown a lack of good faith on the part of ADC so as to justify their failure to seek a stay." In re Abbotts Dairies, et al., No. 84-5118, slip op. at 2 n.1. Under the circumstances, we find both of these arguments unpersuasive.

First, we reject the claim that the bankruptcy court made an "implicit" finding of good faith. The factual findings upon which ADC and Abbotts base this assertion go only to the need to act immediately so as to avoid any diminution in the value of Abbotts' trademarks and other assets. NFO's and Cumberland's assertion of collusion, on the other hand, concerns, *inter alia,* the claim that the "emergency" justifying the immediate sale of Abbotts was itself contrived or orchestrated by ADC and Abbotts. For example, they claim that—in exchange for a lucrative employment agreement for Mr. Gwinn, Abbotts' Chairman and Chief Executive Officer—Abbotts permitted ADC to manipulate the timing of Abbotts' bankruptcy so that the bankruptcy court had no choice but to approve the Interim Agreement on August 10, the terms of which were designed to preclude any truly competitive bidding for the assets on September 12. Surely, if NFO and Cumberland substantiated these claims, it would, as a matter of law, constitute "collusion between the purchaser and ... trustee [or in this case, the debtor-in-possession], or an attempt to take grossly unfair advantage of other bidders," sufficient to destroy ADC's "good faith status." In re Rock Indus. Mach. Corp., 572 F.2d at 1198.

We also reject the attempt to rely upon the district court's conclusion to the contrary, which was apparently premised upon the assumption that "[n]o objections to the sale on the basis of fraud, collusion or insufficient value were raised at the [September 12] hearing." In re Abbotts Dairies, et al., No. 84-5118, slip op. at 2 n.1. That assumption is not, however, borne out by the record.

For example, prior to the September 12 hearing, Fairmont filed a number of written objections to the proposed sale that were relevant to the issue of ADC's "good faith." These included, *inter alia,* claims that certain terms of the Interim Agreement had "chilled" the bidding for Abbotts and that insufficient value was being paid by ADC. Similarly, during his argument before the bankruptcy court, Cumberland's counsel questioned the assertion by Abbotts' counsel that an "emergency" existed that required the sale of Abbotts prior to the approval of a disclosure statement and confirmation of a plan of reorganization; he also argued that the Interim Agreement gave an undue advantage to ADC vis-a-vis other prospective bidders, which significantly depreciated the overall value of the company.

Finally, there is no indication in the district court's opinion that it reviewed the record of the August 10 "emergency" hearing in the bankruptcy court; we believe, however, that the court should have done so before it dismissed the appeals from the bankruptcy court. That hearing, and the circumstances surrounding approval of the Interim Agreement, was an integral part of the "sale" of Abbotts; as such, it must be considered in conjunction with the actual sale of the company at the September 12 hearing. The record from that hearing, moreover, indicates that counsel for a prospective bidder and three unsecured creditors filed a number of written objections going to ADC's "good faith." They included, for example, the claim that Interim Agreement so greatly diminished Abbotts' value as to "create a situation where all competitive bidding for [Abbotts'] business would be eliminated, leaving [ADC] to purchase [Abbotts] at an inadequate price, to the detriment of all interested parties."

Under these circumstances, then, the district court erred when it dismissed the present appeals as moot. Considering ADC's lucrative offer of employment to Mr. Gwinn, the timing of Abbotts' petitions in bankruptcy, and its motion for approval of the Interim Agreement, the situation was ripe for collusion and interested dealing between ADC and Abbotts. Cf. Wolverton v. Shell Oil Co., 442 F.2d 666, 669-70 (9th Cir. 1971) (affirming district court order setting aside private sale of an antitrust cause of action by the trustee to the bankrupt, because "a sale to the bankrupt, especially when it is of an asset such as a cause of action of unknown but potentially great value, as here, offers opportunities for skulduggery that make it suspect"). Thus, the district court should have remanded the matter to the bankruptcy court for a finding as to whether ADC purchased Abbotts' assets "in good faith," or whether ADC and Abbotts (through Mr. Gwinn) colluded in an attempt to take unfair advantage of prospective bidders like Cumberland; it should not have taken it upon itself to determine this question in the first instance. See, e.g., In re Bleaufontaine, Inc., 634 F.2d 1383, 1386 (5th Cir. 1981) (district court remanded appeals from an order approving the sale of the debtor's assets to bankruptcy court with directions to determine the good faith status of the purchaser). * * *

[I]n the absence of a finding of "good faith" behavior by ADC, we find Abbotts' and ADC's reliance upon the bankruptcy court's finding that the prices paid "are fair and reasonable" equally unavailing. Neither party introduced any evidence going to value, and the bankruptcy court refused to entertain the only proffer of such evidence—that is, Fairmont's proffer of evidence in support of its objection to the value to be paid by ADC. Instead, the bankruptcy court, like ADC, apparently believed that the "auction" it conducted adequately and conclusively established that value was paid.

Accordingly, if the bankruptcy court finds, on remand, that ADC did *not* purchase Abbotts' assets "in good faith," it will have to determine whether ADC indeed paid "value" for Abbotts. On the other hand, if it finds that ADC *did* act "in good faith," then its finding that the prices paid "are fair and reasonable" is not clearly erroneous, and is sufficient to establish that ADC paid "value" for Abbotts' assets. See Willemain v. Kivitz, 764 F.2d 1019, 1023 (4th Cir. 1985) ("[T]he bankruptcy court's express finding that the $100,000 price was 'not unreasonable,' a finding that is not clearly erroneous, demonstrates that Hampshire indeed gave value for the interest.").

In short, we hold that when a bankruptcy court authorizes a sale of assets pursuant to section 363(b)(1), it is required to make a finding with respect to the "good faith" of the purchaser. * * *

We think that such a requirement represents a proper exercise of our supervisory authority over both the district and bankruptcy courts. First, the bankruptcy court, given its greater familiarity with the parties and proceedings, represents the forum best able to make such a determination in the first instance. Second, it encourages finality of the bankruptcy court's judgments under section 363(b)(1), because it places prospective appellants on notice of the need to obtain a stay pending appeal; or face dismissal for mootness pursuant to section 363(m), should the district court affirm the bankruptcy court's finding of good faith. Finally, such a procedure ensures that section 363(b)(1) will not be employed to circumvent the creditor protections of Chapter 11, and, as such, it mirrors the requirement of section 1129 that the bankruptcy court independently scrutinize the debtor's reorganization plan and make a finding that it "has been proposed in good faith and not by any means forbidden by law." 11 U.S.C. § 1129(a)(3). * * *

V.

To conclude, the bankruptcy court should, upon remand of this matter from the district court, determine whether there was any impermissible collusion between ADC and Abbotts that would negate ADC's status as a purchaser "in good faith." If it finds such collusion, it should then determine whether ADC paid "value" for the assets purchased. If the court determines that ADC did not pay "value," it will then have to determine whether it has the power to undo the sale to ADC; implicit in this determination is the question whether, with respect to Cumberland, the sale has become moot under Article III. Finally, if the court determines that it has the power to undo the sale, it should, in an exercise of its equitable jurisdiction, determine whether to exercise that power, or whether another remedy should be pursued.

Accordingly, the district court's judgment will be reversed, and the matter remanded to the district court with instructions to remand it to the bankruptcy court for proceedings consistent with this opinion.

NOTES

1. Note that Rule 6004(g) was not adopted until 1999. Thus, in *Abbotts Dairies* there was no automatic ten day stay of the order confirming sale of the assets. Under the version of Rules 7062 and 9014 in effect at the time, orders authorizing use, sale or lease of assets of the estate were explicitly excepted from application of the ten day automatic stay that otherwise would have applied under Rule 7062. With the 1999 amendment of Rule 9014, Rule 7062 no longer applies to contested matters, such as motions for authorization to sell assets of the estate. See the Advisory Committee Notes to the 1999 Amendments.

2. The Court of Appeals in *Abbott's Dairies* required the bankruptcy court to make a finding of the purchaser's "good faith" in order for the purchaser to obtain the protections of § 363(m). Accord In re Thomas, 287 B.R. 782 (B.A.P. 9th Cir. 2002) (remanding where the bankruptcy court did not make a good faith determination); In re Wieboldt Stores, Inc., 92 B.R. 309, 313 (N.D. Ill. 1988) (remanding for specific finding where objector raised issue in bankruptcy court

and where district court could not determine from record on appeal whether purchaser acted in good faith). But see Gilchrist v. Westcott (In re Gilchrist), 891 F.2d 559, 561 (5th Cir. 1990) (precluding the objector from raising the purchaser's good faith for the first time on appeal); Official Comm. of Sr. Unsecured Creditors v. First RepublicBank Corp., 106 B.R. 938 (N.D. Tex. 1989) (stating that law is unclear whether bankruptcy court must make specific good faith finding, but holding that in any event objector failed to put good faith of purchaser into issue in the bankruptcy court). Note that a bankruptcy appellate panel decision specifically disagreed with the approach taken by the district court in *First Republic Bank*, which put the burden of proof on the party contesting good faith. T.C. Investors v. Joseph (In re M Capital Corp.), 290 B.R. 743, 749 n. 5 (B.A.P. 9th Cir. 2003). What evidence should a purchaser offer to prove its good faith? As long as the sale price is fair, when would a purchaser not be in good faith? What can or should an objecting party do if it discovers evidence of bad faith only after the bankruptcy court has made a finding of good faith and the matter is on appeal?

3.   Certain entities are prohibited by law from purchasing property from a bankruptcy estate. For example, under § 154 of the Criminal Code (Title 18, U.S.C.), a trustee or officer of the court who directly or indirectly purchases property of the estate has committed a federal crime. Is William Gruff, as an officer of Foam Corporation, an officer of the court? According to most courts, Gruff's status as an insider is not sufficient to disqualify him as a purchaser. See, e.g., In re Filtercorp, Inc., 163 F.3d 570 (9th Cir. 1998); In re Condere Corp., 228 B.R. 615 (Bankr. S.D. Miss. 1998); In re Bakalis, 220 B.R. 525 (Bankr. E.D.N.Y. 1998). Some courts would preclude an insider like Gruff from purchasing property in a bankruptcy sale on the theory that it would violate the insider's fiduciary duty to creditors if the insider were on both sides of the transaction. Cf. In re Grodel Mfg., Inc., 33 B.R. 693 (Bankr. D. Conn. 1983) (former chapter 11 trustee precluded from purchasing assets from estate). Purchasers precluded by law from purchasing property would not be in good faith. What result if the purchaser employs an officer of the debtor and the debtor's attorney? See Southwest Prods., Inc. v. Durkin (In re Southwest Prods., Inc.), 144 B.R. 100, 103-04 (B.A.P. 9th Cir. 1992) (allowing sale in "good faith"); cf. In re Allied Gaming Mgmt., Inc., 209 B.R. 201 (Bankr. W.D. La. 1997) (holding that fiduciaries, such as debtor in possession's accountant and general manager, are prohibited from purchasing assets); In re Bidermann Indus., U.S.A., Inc., 203 B.R. 547 (Bankr. S.D.N.Y. 1997) (holding that sales to fiduciaries are subject to heightened scrutiny); but see Fulton State Bank v. Schipper (In re Schipper), 933 F.2d 513 (7th Cir. 1991) (permitting debtor in possession to sell property to his parents who in turn resold at a profit).

4.   Occasionally, bidders will conspire to minimize the value offered at a bankruptcy sale. The successful bidder will acquire the property at a low price, and then proceed to resell it at a premium. The premium is then split among all of the original bidders who conspired to depress the price at the bankruptcy sale. Section 363(n) permits a trustee or debtor in possession to avoid a sale if the sale price was controlled by an agreement among the potential bidders. The debtor in possession may also recover damages, costs, attorney's fees, and expenses from a conspirator. In addition, the court may impose punitive damages in favor of the estate. See also U.S. v. Seville Indus. Mach. Corp., 696 F. Supp. 986 (D.N.J. 1988) (refusing to dismiss criminal indictment, and holding that bid rigging is a per se violation of federal antitrust law).

5. Prudent potential buyers of assets will not bid on them without performing "due diligence" (a careful and expensive investigation of the assets and, in some cases, of the debtor more generally). In addition, buyers who are seeking acquisitions can focus their attention only on a limited number of potential deals. Thus, unless the potential buyer believes that there is a good chance that (1) the buyer will in the end want to acquire the assets and (2) the buyer will be successful in acquiring them, it may decide not to invest the time and attention needed to prepare to bid on the assets. Instead, it may simply decide to look elsewhere.

The problem is particularly acute in bankruptcy. Appropriate notice must be given of a proposed sale under § 363(b); assuming a party in interest requests a hearing, the sales agreement does not become binding on the estate until and unless the court holds a hearing and approves the agreement. See §§ 102(1), 363(b). The delay in closing the sale provides an opportunity for other potential buyers to submit higher bids. Even if no higher bid is made by the time of the hearing, the court may insist that there be an auction process or other opportunity for higher bids to be made before authorizing the sale.

The result may be that a debtor in possession with assets for sale has difficulty attracting interest. In such a case, the debtor in possession may wish to offer incentives to encourage a potential buyer to make an initial bid and to enter into a tentative agreement. (The agreement will be subject to higher bids and to eventual court approval; the initial bidder then would often be called a "stalking horse" bidder.) Once the initial bid and tentative agreement are in place, other potential purchasers may look more seriously at the assets and may think it likely that the assets are worth at least as much as the amount of the initial bid. Thus the initial bid may prompt others to submit higher bids, with a resulting benefit to the estate.

Stalking horse bidders can negotiate in advance for court authorization to have their due diligence expenses paid by the estate (and the debtor in possession can negotiate for an expense cap and confidentiality agreement). There are several other kinds of protections that a stalking horse bidder may bargain to have included in the tentative purchase agreement:

    a.   A break up fee (ordinarily ranging from 1-3% of the price) so that the stalking horse bidder will be paid something if, for any reason that is not the fault of the stalking horse bidder, it does not acquire the assets.

    b.   A topping fee provision, under which the stalking horse bidder would receive a percentage of the incremental value to the estate if another party acquires the assets at the sale.

    c.   Overbid protection, so that the court will only consider overbids at a large first overbid and minimum increments thereafter.

    d.   A "no shop" clause so that the debtor in possession does not take the first bid and actively shop it to get better offers.

    e.   An agreement that the debtor in possession will not cooperate with any other bidder except to the extent required by law.

    f.   A requirement that all bids be presented in a uniform format.

See generally Calpine Corp. v. O'Brien Envtl. Energy, Inc. (In re O'Brien Envtl. Energy, Inc.), 181 F.3d 527 (3d Cir. 1999) (dealing with proposed sale pursuant to proposed plan of reorganization rather than sale under § 363); In re Women First Healthcare, Inc., 332 B.R. 115 (Bankr. D. Del. 2005); In re APP Plus, Inc., 223 B.R. 870 (Bankr. E.D.N.Y. 1998); Houser, Carvell & Smith, *Section 363 Issues—Acquiring Troubled Companies and Assets*, in CHAPTER 11 BUSINESS REORGANIZATIONS 253 (Annual Advanced ALI-ABA Course of

Study, No. SK092, 2005), available at SK092 ALI-ABA 253 (Westlaw) (citing cases not only involving § 363 sales but also sales pursuant to plans of reorganization); Markell, *The Case Against Breakup Fees in Bankruptcy*, 66 AM. BANKR. L.J. 349 (1992). Note that the estate will not be bound to pay amounts agreed to by the debtor in possession in the absence of court approval. See *Calpine Corp.*

Do these protections for the stalking horse bidder help or hurt the bidding process? Increase or reduce competition? Maximize the price received? What standard will the court use to determine whether to approve such protections? Business judgment? Best interest of the estate? What if officers of the debtor in possession stand to benefit personally from the sale by getting employment contracts or indemnities on personal guarantees?

C. OBTAINING CREDIT TO RUN THE BUSINESS

At the inception of a chapter 11 case, the debtor will frequently find itself without sufficient cash resources to operate the business even if it may use cash collateral and other property of the estate. As noted above, the debtor in possession may not operate the business in violation of nonbankruptcy law by refusing to pay wages and the like. Therefore, in order to achieve rehabilitation, it will be necessary for the debtor in possession to obtain credit during the chapter 11 case. Section 364 provides the standards under which credit may be obtained.

The Bankruptcy Code provides four different rules that govern the obtaining of credit during a chapter 11 case. The rules vary depending upon whether the credit is obtained in or out of the ordinary course of business and whether the credit is obtained on a priority, superpriority, or secured basis.

1. Obtaining Unsecured Credit in the Ordinary Course of Business

The easiest way for the debtor in possession to minimize the amount of cash necessary to run the business is to maintain or obtain unsecured trade credit repayable in the ordinary course of business. Without trade credit, the debtor in possession's cash needs will increase substantially.

It is not unusual for vendors to place a debtor in possession on cash terms, requiring cash on delivery or cash before delivery. Occasionally, however, where the cash flow of the debtor is particularly strong, or competition is intense, suppliers are willing to extend credit to the debtor in possession on an unsecured basis in the ordinary course of business.

Section 364(a) allows the trustee or debtor in possession to obtain credit in the ordinary course of business without a court order or a hearing. Credit so obtained is an administrative expense entitled to priority under §§ 503(b) and 507(a)(2). The holder of the administrative expense claim is entitled to be repaid in full in cash on the effective date of any confirmed chapter 11 plan, unless the holder agrees to other treatment. See § 1129(a)(9)(A).

While the administrative expense priority is significant, it is not without risk. If most or all of the estate's property is subject to liens, then there may be little unencumbered asset value that could be used to pay administrative expense claims in a liquidation. In addition, the priority is subordinate under § 364(c) to lenders who make postpetition loans and receive superpriority status, subordinate under § 507(b) to secured creditors who have been offered adequate protection that later proves to be inadequate, and subordinate under § 726(b) to administrative expense claimants in a superseding chapter 7 case. The trade creditor contemplating the extension of postpetition credit must consider the likelihood that the above-described claims will arise during the case and whether the estate contains sufficient assets to repay these claims. In some cases, trade creditors have required creditors providing a secured postpetition financing facility to subordinate to or share the postpetition lien with postpetition trade claims.

The vendor extending trade credit must be particularly sure that the credit is extended in the ordinary course of business. In order for a supplier to take advantage of the priority under § 364(a), the extension of trade credit must be done while the business is authorized to be operated and the credit must be extended in the ordinary course of business. The Bankruptcy Code does not define "ordinary course of business". Typically courts examine the "horizontal" and "vertical" dimensions of a debtor's business to determine whether the postpetition transaction arises in the ordinary course of business. See, e.g., Med. Malpractice Ins. Ass'n v. Hirsch (In re Lavigne), 114 F.3d 379, 384 (2d Cir. 1997). The horizontal analysis is an external industry-wide comparison of the debtor's business and other similar businesses to determine whether the transaction is ordinary for this type of business. Id. at 385. The vertical dimension examines the reasonable expectations of parties in interest who have dealt with this debtor. See, e.g., id. at 384-85; Martino v. First Nat'l Bank (In re Garofalo's Finer Foods, Inc.), 186 B.R. 414, 425 (N.D. Ill. 1995); In re Leslie Fay Co., 168 B.R. 294, 304 (Bankr. S.D.N.Y. 1994). If either dimension of the test is not satisfied, the disputed transaction is not in the ordinary course of business. See In re Crystal Apparel, Inc., 220 B.R. 816, 831 (Bankr. S.D.N.Y. 1998) (citing cases).

If the court finds that the creditor has extended credit outside the ordinary course of business without court approval, it is possible that the creditor's claim will be treated as an unsecured prepetition debt. See Sapir v. CPQ Colorchrome Corp. (In re Photo Promotion Assocs.), 87 B.R. 835 (Bankr. S.D.N.Y. 1988), aff'd, 881 F.2d 6 (2d Cir. 1989); Bezanson v. Indian Head Nat'l Bank (In re J.L. Graphics, Inc.), 62 B.R. 750 (Bankr. D.N.H. 1986), aff'd sub nom. New Hampshire Business Dev. Corp. v. Cross Baking Co. (In re Cross Baking Co.), 818 F.2d 1027 (1st Cir. 1987); In re Cascade Oil Co., 51 B.R. 877 (Bankr. D. Kan. 1985). See generally In re Jartran, Inc., 732 F.2d 584, 591 n.7 (7th Cir. 1984) (assuming that contract creditor that was denied administrative expense priority would have prepetition nonpriority claim).

Some courts, however, will struggle (as the court did in *Sapir*) to grant the creditor an administrative expense on the basis that the estate otherwise would be unjustly enriched. See also In re Am. Cooler Co., 125 F.2d 496 (2d Cir. 1942) (authorizing retroactive approval of unauthorized loans on equitable grounds under unusual circumstances, where creditors have not been harmed and borrowing would have been approved if application had been made in advance). Other courts question whether the bankruptcy judge retains the power to accord retroactive equitable relief. See In re Garofalo's Finer Foods, Inc., 186 B.R. 414, 431 n.10 (N.D. Ill. 1995). And some courts will disallow the creditor's claim entirely. See In re Ockerlund Constr. Co., 308 B.R. 325 (Bankr. N.D. Ill. 2004); In re Alfalia Land Dev. Corp., 40 B.R. 1, 5 (Bankr. M.D. Fla. 1984). The wiser course is to seek court approval whenever the vendor is in doubt whether the extension of credit is in the ordinary course of business.

2. Extension of Unsecured Credit Outside the Ordinary Course of Business

Section 364(b) permits the debtor in possession "after notice and a hearing" to obtain credit outside the ordinary course of business. The credit is entitled to priority as an administrative expense. Bankruptcy Rule 4001(c) requires a motion to obtain credit out of the ordinary course of business to be served on the creditors' committee (or if no committee has been appointed on the twenty largest creditors) not less than fifteen days before the hearing and on such other entities as the court may direct. The motion must be accompanied by a copy of the agreement governing the extension of credit. If necessary, the court can authorize an emergency extension of credit to the extent necessary to avoid irreparable harm during the fifteen days before the hearing.

The importance of proper notice and service cannot be overemphasized. Where the notice is incomplete or inaccurate, some courts have voided the order authorizing the extension of credit. Credit Alliance Corp. v. Dunning-Ray Ins. Agency, Inc. (In re Blumer), 66 B.R. 109 (B.A.P. 9th Cir. 1986), aff'd, 826 F.2d 1069 (9th Cir. 1987) (lending without notice to unsecured creditors is void). Although emergency borrowings may be made on short notice or an *ex parte* basis, this relief will not be available where the debtor has created the emergency by postponing the request to obtain credit until the last minute. E.g., In re Sullivan Ford Sales, 2 B.R. 350 (Bankr. D. Me. 1980).

Problem 4-3

Suppose that you represent a trade creditor who desires to extend trade credit to Foam Corporation. Examining Foam Corporation's balance sheet and cash flows, would you counsel the creditor to extend credit in the ordinary course of business? Would obtaining administrative expense priority following a court order under § 364(b) grant you sufficient comfort? What concessions, if any, would you demand from Kick Credit?

> Suppose that you represented an equipment lessor who was approached by Foam Corporation to enter into a lease of equipment following the filing of Foam Corporation's chapter 11 petition. What facts would you want to determine before deciding whether the transaction is in or outside the ordinary course of business? Why would you take the risk of being wrong?
>
> Suppose that you represent Foam Corporation. If you are uncertain whether a proposed credit transaction is inside or outside the ordinary course of business, do you have an obligation to err in favor of seeking a court order? What are the consequences to Foam Corporation if it enters into a transaction outside the ordinary course of business without court approval?

3. Obtaining Superpriority or Secured Credit Under Section 364(c)

Section 364(c) permits a debtor in possession "after notice and a hearing" to obtain secured credit or credit entitled to a superpriority administrative expense under certain circumstances. First, the debtor in possession must demonstrate that unsecured financing under § 364(a) and (b) is unavailable. There is no duty to seek credit from every possible lender, but some effort is required. Bray v. Shenandoah Fed. Sav. and Loan Ass'n (In re Snowshoe Co.), 789 F.2d 1085, 1088 (4th Cir. 1986). The debtor in possession should offer evidence in the record to prove this point delineating the efforts made by the debtor in possession to obtain credit on an unsecured basis. E.g., In re Ames Dep't Stores, Inc., 115 B.R. 34, 37 (Bankr. S.D.N.Y. 1990); In re Crouse Group, Inc., 71 B.R. 544, 550 (Bankr. E.D. Pa. 1987).

If the debtor in possession is unable to obtain unsecured financing under § 364(a) and (b), § 364(c) authorizes the debtor in possession to obtain credit on three additional bases or a combination of those bases. First, the postpetition credit may be granted priority over "any or all" administrative expenses. This is known as the § 364(c) superpriority administrative expense. The order granting superpriority status should specify to which administrative expenses the superpriority will be senior. Typically, the creditor will want the superpriority to come ahead of all administrative expenses, including administrative expenses awarded under § 507(b) to creditors whose adequate protection proves to be inadequate after the fact. Even if the order granting the superpriority specifies that the superpriority will come ahead of all administrative expenses, some courts may refuse to grant the superpriority seniority over chapter 7 administrative expenses incurred when the reorganization later fails and the case is converted to a chapter 7 liquidation. Cf. In re California Devices, Inc., 126 B.R. 82 (Bankr. N.D. Cal. 1991) (refusing to grant § 507(b) claims priority over chapter 7 administrative expenses). Some courts have even required that loan agreements providing for superpriority permit a reasonable amount to be paid to counsel for the debtor and for the creditors' committee (and for a trustee if one is eventually appointed)—even if that might keep the superpriority lender from being repaid in full. See, e.g., In re Ames Dep't Stores, Inc., 115 B.R. 34, 38-41 (Bankr.

S.D.N.Y. 1990) (approving superpriority loan agree-ment only after it was amended to provide a $5 million "carveout" for counsel fees, so that the adversary system would be preserved).

Under § 364(c)(2), a lender may extend postpetition credit secured by a lien on property of the estate that is unencumbered. Under § 364(c)(3), a lender may extend credit secured by a junior lien on property of the estate that already is encumbered. These two methods permit the debtor in possession to obtain postpetition secured credit only if unsecured financing is unavailable under § 364(a) and (b). The lender will want to make sure that the order authorizing the extension of credit specifies that perfection of the secured status is not required during the pendency of the bankruptcy case. As a matter of prudence, however, if the secured credit is to continue past the effective date of a confirmed plan (or in the event of a dismissal) the lender should consider perfecting the liens under applicable nonbankruptcy law (by recording a mortgage if the collateral is real property or filing a financing statement if it is personal property). From the lender's perspective, the borrowing order should authorize the perfection and should permit the costs of perfection to be added to the loan. The postpetition lending agreement also should specify events of default entitling the lender to terminate the agreement and pursue remedies.

Problem 4-4

> If you were the judge presiding over Foam Corporation's chapter 11 case, would you approve a postpetition credit agreement that made the appointment or election of a chapter 11 or chapter 7 trustee an event of default? Would you permit the borrowing agreement to provide for an event of default upon the filing of suit against the postpetition lender? Would you permit the order approving the postpetition credit extension to conclude that the lender had valid, perfected and enforceable prepetition debts and liens? Would you permit the borrowing order to waive the estate's rights against the collateral under §§ 506(c) and 552(b)? Compare In re Ames Dep't Stores, Inc., 115 B.R. 34, 38 (Bankr. S.D.N.Y. 1990) with In re FCX, Inc., 54 B.R. 833 (Bankr. E.D.N.C. 1985); also consider In re The Colad Group, Inc., 324 B.R. 208 (Bankr. W.D.N.Y. 2005) (reprinted below). Would you permit the borrowing order to include a provision requiring that the lender be paid postpetition interest on a current basis on the lender's prepetition oversecured debt? See Orix Credit Alliance, Inc. v. Delta Res., Inc., 54 F.3d 722 (11th Cir. 1995) (reprinted above in Chapter Three); New York Life Ins. Co. v. Revco D.S., Inc. (In re Revco D.S., Inc.), 901 F.2d 1359 (6th Cir. 1990).

Is it appropriate for a postpetition borrowing under § 364(c) to provide for the collateralization of prepetition credit extended by the lender? Frequently a lender will be willing to extend postpetition credit only if the lender's prepetition loan is secured by all assets that will serve as collateral for the postpetition loan. This is called "cross-collateralization". Lenders desire cross-collateralization when their prepetition loan may be undersecured. Lenders also desire cross-collateralization to avoid § 552, which otherwise permits the estate to use proceeds of their prepetition collateral when the equities of the case require. Finally, they want to avoid practical difficulties that arise when two overlapping sets of collateral secure the prepetition credit and the postpetition credit. (If the debtor is an appliance wholesaler who ends up with 5,000 televisions in its warehouse, there can be difficulties in determining which were purchased with money that is traceable to prepetition collateral and which were purchased with the postpetition loan money. If their purchase can be traced to prepetition collateral, then, within the limits the court can impose under § 552, the creditor can claim them as collateral for the prepetition loan.)

Although the Bankruptcy Code contains no specific prohibition of cross-collateralization, courts are split on the propriety of the device. For example, some courts interpret § 364(c) to permit the granting of a superpriority or a lien only with respect to credit that is extended postpetition after court approval. See, e.g., Shapiro v. Saybrook Mfg. Co., 963 F.2d 1490 (11th Cir. 1992) (reprinted immediately below); In re FCX, Inc., 54 B.R. 833, 841 (Bankr. E.D.N.C. 1985); In re Monach Circuit Indus., 41 B.R. 859, 862 (Bankr. E.D. Pa. 1984). Other courts, however, permit cross-collateralization where it is in the best interests of creditors, the financing is made on the best terms possible, no alternative financing is available, and absent the financing the business will be irreparably harmed. E.g., In re Babcox & Wilcox Co., 250 F.3d 955 (5th Cir. 2001); In re Vanguard Diversified, Inc., 31 B.R. 364, 366 (Bankr. E.D.N.Y. 1983); In re General Oil Distribs., 20 B.R. 873 (Bankr. E.D.N.Y. 1982). Read *Shapiro* and then consider the problem that follows.

Shapiro v. Saybrook Manufacturing Company
United States Court of Appeals, Eleventh Circuit, 1992
963 F.2d 1490

COX, Circuit Judge:

Seymour and Jeffrey Shapiro, unsecured creditors, objected to the bankruptcy court's authorization for the Chapter 11 debtors to "cross-collateralize" their pre-petition debt with unencumbered property from the bankruptcy estate. The bankruptcy court overruled the objection and also refused to grant a stay of its order pending appeal. The Shapiros appealed to the district court, which dismissed the case as moot under section 364(e) of the Bankruptcy Code because the Shapiros had failed to obtain a stay. We conclude that this appeal is not moot and that cross-collateralization is not authorized under the Bankruptcy Code. Accordingly, we reverse and remand.

I. Facts and Procedural History

Saybrook Manufacturing Co., Inc., and related companies, (the "debtors") initiated proceedings seeking relief under Chapter 11 of the Bankruptcy Code on December 22, 1988. On December 23, 1988, the debtors filed a motion for the use of cash collateral and for authorization to incur secured debt. The bankruptcy court entered an emergency financing order that same day. At the time the bankruptcy petition was filed, the debtors owed Manufacturers Hanover approximately $34 million. The value of the collateral for this debt, however, was less than $10 million. Pursuant to the order, Manufacturers Hanover agreed to lend the debtors an additional $3 million to facilitate their reorganization. In exchange, Manufacturers Hanover received a security interest in all of the debtors' property—both property owned prior to filing the bankruptcy petition and that which was acquired subsequently. This security interest not only protected the $3 million of post-petition credit but also secured Manufacturers Hanover's $34 million pre-petition debt.

This arrangement enhanced Manufacturers Hanover's position vis-a-vis other unsecured creditors, such as the Shapiros, in the event of liquidation. Because Manufacturers Hanover's pre-petition debt was undersecured by approximately $24 million, it originally would have shared in a pro rata distribution of the debtors' unencumbered assets along with the other unsecured creditors. Under the financing order, however, Manufacturers Hanover's pre-petition debt became fully secured by all of the debtors' assets. If the bankruptcy estate were liquidated, Manufacturers Hanover's entire debt—$34 million pre-petition and $3 million post-petition—would have to be paid in full before any funds could be distributed to the remaining unsecured creditors.

Securing pre-petition debt with pre- and post-petition collateral as part of a post-petition financing arrangement is known as cross-collateralization. The Second Circuit aptly defined cross-collateralization as follows:

> [I]n return for making new loans to a debtor in possession under Chapter XI, a financing institution obtains a security interest on all assets of the debtor, both those existing at the date of the order and those created in the course of the Chapter XI proceeding, not only for the new loans, the propriety of which is not contested, but [also] for existing indebtedness to it.

Otte v. Manufacturers Hanover Commercial Corp. (In re Texlon Corp.), 596 F.2d 1092, 1094 (2d Cir. 1979).

Because the Second Circuit was the first appellate court to describe this practice in In re Texlon, it is sometimes referred to as *Texlon*-type cross-collateralization. Another form of cross-collateralization involves securing post-petition debt with pre-petition collateral. See, e.g., In re Antico Manufacturing Co., 31 B.R. 103, 105 (Bankr. E.D.N.Y. 1983). This form of non-*Texlon*-type cross-collateralization is not at issue in this appeal. The Shapiros challenge only the cross-collateralization of the lenders' pre-petition debt, not the propriety of collateralizing the post-petition debt.

The Shapiros filed a number of objections to the bankruptcy court's order on January 13, 1989. After a hearing, the bankruptcy court overruled the objections. The Shapiros then filed a notice of appeal and a request for the bankruptcy court to stay its financing order pending appeal. The bankruptcy court denied the request for a stay on February 23, 1989.

The Shapiros subsequently moved the district court to stay the bankruptcy court's financing order pending appeal; the court denied the motion on March 7, 1989. On May 20, 1989, the district court dismissed the Shapiros' appeal as moot under 11 U.S.C. § 364(e) because the Shapiros had failed to obtain a stay of the financing order pending appeal, rejecting the argument that cross-collateralization is contrary to the Code. The Shapiros then appealed to this court.

    * * *

V. Discussion

A. Mootness

We begin by addressing the lenders' claim that this appeal is moot under section 364(e) of the Bankruptcy Code. Section 364(e) provides that:

> The reversal or modification on appeal of an authorization under this section to obtain credit or incur debt, or of a grant under this section of a priority or a lien, does not affect the validity of any debt so incurred, or any priority or lien so granted, to an entity that extended such credit in good faith, whether or not such entity knew of the pendency of the appeal, unless such authorization and the incurring of such debt, or the granting of such priority or lien, were stayed pending appeal.

11 U.S.C. § 364(e). The purpose of this provision is to encourage the extension of credit to debtors in bankruptcy by eliminating the risk that any lien securing the loan will be modified on appeal.

The lenders suggest that we assume cross-collateralization is authorized under section 364 and then conclude the Shapiros' appeal is moot under section 364(e). This is similar to the approach adopted by the Ninth Circuit in Burchinal v. Central Washington Bank (In re Adams Apple, Inc.), 829 F.2d 1484 (9th Cir. 1987). That court held that cross-collateralization was "authorized" under section 364 for the purposes of section 364(e) mootness but declined to decide whether cross-collateralization was illegal per se under the Bankruptcy Code. Id. at 1488 n. 6. See also Unsecured Creditors' Committee v. First National Bank & Trust Co. (In re Ellingsen MacLean Oil Co.), 834 F.2d 599 (6th Cir. 1987), cert. denied, 488 U.S. 817, 109 S. Ct. 55, 102 L. Ed. 2d 33 (1988).

We reject the reasoning of In re Adams Apple and In re Ellingsen because they "put the cart before the horse." By its own terms, section 364(e) is only applicable if the challenged lien or priority was authorized under section 364. See Charles J. Tabb, Lender Preference Clauses and the Destruction of Appealability and Finality: Resolving a Chapter 11 Dilemma, 50 Ohio St. L.J. 109, 116-35 (1989) (criticizing In re Adams Apple, In re Ellingsen, and the practice of shielding cross-collateralization from appellate review via mootness under section 364(e)); see also In re Ellingsen, 834 F.2d at 607 (Merritt, dissenting) (arguing that section 364(e) was not designed to prohibit creditors from challenging pre-petition matters and that "[l]enders should not be permitted to use their leverage in making emergency loans in order to insulate their prepetition claims from attack"). We cannot determine if this appeal is moot under section 364(e) until we decide the central issue in this appeal—whether cross-collateralization is authorized under section 364. Accordingly, we now turn to that question.

B. Cross-Collateralization and Section 364

Cross-collateralization is an extremely controversial form of Chapter 11 financing. Nevertheless, the practice has been approved by several bankruptcy courts. See, e.g., In re Vanguard Diversified, Inc., 31 B.R. 364 (Bankr. E.D.N.Y. 1983); In re Roblin Indus., Inc., 52 B.R. 241 (Bankr. W.D.N.Y. 1985); In re Beker Indus. Corp., 58 B.R. 725 (Bankr. S.D.N.Y. 1986). Contra In re Monach Circuit Indus., Inc., 41 B.R. 859 (Bankr. E.D. Pa. 1984). Even the courts that have allowed cross-collateralization, however, were generally reluctant to do so. See McLemore v. Citizens Bank (In re Tom McCormick Enterprises, Inc.), 26 B.R. 437, 439-40 (Bankr. M.D. Tenn. 1983).

In In re Vanguard, for example, the bankruptcy court noted that cross-collateralization is "a disfavored means of financing" that should only be used as a last resort. In re Vanguard, 31 B.R. at 366. In order to obtain a financing order including cross-collateralization, the court required the debtor to demonstrate (1) that its business operations would fail absent the proposed financing, (2) that it is unable to obtain alternative financing on acceptable terms, (3) that the proposed lender will not accept less preferential terms, and (4) that the proposed financing is in the general creditor body's best interest. Id. This four-part test has since been adopted by other bankruptcy courts which permit cross-collateralization. See, e.g., In re Roblin, 52 B.R. at 244-45.

The issue of whether the Bankruptcy Code authorizes cross-collateralization is a question of first impression in this court. Indeed, it is essentially a question of first impression before any court of appeals. Neither the lenders' brief nor our own research has produced a single appellate decision which either authorizes or prohibits the practice.

The lenders claim that the Sixth Circuit's decision in In re Ellingsen endorses cross-collateralization. Like In re Adams Apple, the issue in In re Ellingsen was whether section 364(e) rendered an appeal moot because the appellants failed to obtain a stay. Judge Wellford's opinion for the court notes that, while cross-collateralization is controversial, it appears to have been used and approved in the past. Therefore, "Congress would not have intended to exclude all cross-collateralization orders categorically from section 364(e)'s protection." In re Ellingsen, 834 F.2d at 602. The court concluded that the appeal was moot under section 364(e) because the bankruptcy court did not issue a stay of its cross-collateralization order. The court, however, did not hold that cross-collateralization itself was authorized under the Bankruptcy Code. In fact, Judge Nelson concurred separately to emphasize the limited scope of the court's decision, stating that he was uncertain as to whether section 364 permitted cross-collateralization. Id. at 606.

As noted above, the Ninth Circuit reached a similar conclusion in In re Adams Apple. In re Adams Apple held that the appeal was moot under section 364(e) but expressly declined to decide whether cross-collateralization was illegal per se under the Bankruptcy Code. In re Adams Apple, 829 F.2d at 1488 n.6. The Ninth Circuit reaffirmed this holding in Transamerica Commercial Finance Corp. v. Citibank (In re Sun Runner Marine, Inc.), 945 F.2d 1089 (9th Cir. 1991).

> The court in *Adams Apple* held only that where the bankruptcy court grants cross-collateralization under § 364, post-petition credit is extended to the debtor in reliance thereon, an appeal is taken, and no stay pending appeal is sought, § 364(e) renders the appeal moot because even reversal would not affect the post-petition lender's rights. The court explicitly declined to rule whether the Bankruptcy Code authorizes cross-collateralization.

> We also decline to rule whether cross-collateralization is appropriate in this case, or whether as a matter of law it is ever permissible.

Id. at 1094.

The Second Circuit expressed criticism of cross-collateralization in In re Texlon. The court, however, stopped short of prohibiting the practice altogether. At issue was the bankruptcy court's *ex parte* financing order granting the lender a security interest in the debtor's property to secure both pre-petition and post-petition debt. The court, in an exercise of judicial restraint, concluded that:

> In order to decide this case we are not obliged, however, to say that under no conceivable circumstances could "cross-collateralization" be authorized. Here it suffices to hold that ... a financing scheme so contrary to the spirit of the Bankruptcy Act should not have been granted by an *ex parte* order, where the bankruptcy court relies solely on representations by a debtor in possession that credit essential to the maintenance of operations is not otherwise obtainable.

In re Texlon, 596 F.2d at 1098. Although In re Texlon was decided under the earlier Bankruptcy Act, the court also considered whether cross-collateralization was authorized under the Bankruptcy Code. "To such limited extent as it is proper to consider the new Bankruptcy Act, which takes effect on October 1, 1979, in considering the validity of an order made in 1974, we see nothing in § 364(c) or in other provisions of that section that advances the case in favor of 'cross-collateralization.'" In re Texlon, 596 F.2d at 1098 (citations omitted).

Cross-collateralization is not specifically mentioned in the Bankruptcy Code. We conclude that cross-collateralization is inconsistent with bankruptcy law for two reasons. First, cross-collateralization is not authorized as a method of post-petition financing under section 364. Second, cross-collateralization is beyond the scope of the bankruptcy court's inherent equitable power because it is directly contrary to the fundamental priority scheme of the Bankruptcy Code. See generally Charles J. Tabb, *A Critical Reappraisal of Cross-Collateralization in Bankruptcy*, 60 S. Cal. L. Rev. 109 (1986).

Section 364 authorizes Chapter 11 debtors to obtain secured credit and incur secured debt as part of their reorganization. It provides, in relevant part, that:

> (c) If the trustee is unable to obtain unsecured credit allowable under section 503(b)(1) of this title as an administrative expense, the court, after notice and a hearing, *may authorize the obtaining of credit or the incurring of debt—*
>
> (1) with priority over any or all administrative expenses of the kind specified in section 503(b) or 507(b) of this title;
>
> (2) secured by a lien on property of the estate that is not otherwise subject to a lien; or
>
> (3) secured by a junior lien on property of the estate that is subject to a lien.
>
> (d) (1)The court, after notice and a hearing, *may authorize the obtaining of credit or incurring of debt* secured by a senior or equal lien on property of the estate that is subject to a lien only if—
>
> (A) the trustee is unable to obtain such credit otherwise; and
>
> (B) there is adequate protection of the interest of the holder of the lien on the property of the estate on which such senior or equal lien is proposed to be granted.
>
> (2) In any hearing under this subsection, the trustee has the burden of proof on the issue of adequate protection.

11 U.S.C. § 364(c) & (d) (emphasis added). By their express terms, sections 364(c) & (d) apply only to future—i.e., post-petition—extensions of credit. They do not authorize the granting of liens to secure pre-petition loans. * * *

Given that cross-collateralization is not authorized by section 364, we now turn to the lenders' argument that bankruptcy courts may permit the practice under their general equitable power. Bankruptcy courts are indeed courts of equity, see, e.g., Young v. Higbee Co., 324 U.S. 204, 65 S. Ct. 594, 89 L. Ed. 890 (1945); 11 U.S.C. § 105(a), and they have the power to adjust claims to avoid injustice or unfairness. Pepper v. Litton, 308 U.S. 295, 60 S.Ct. 238, 84 L.Ed. 281 (1939). This equitable power, however, is not unlimited.

> [T]he bankruptcy court has the ability to deviate from the rules of priority and distribution set forth in the Code in the interest of justice and equity. The Court cannot use this flexibility, however, merely to establish a ranking of priorities within priorities. Furthermore, absent the existence of some type of inequitable conduct on the part of the claimant, which results in injury to the creditors of the bankrupt or an unfair advantage to the claimant, the court cannot subordinate a claim to claims within the same class.

In re FCX, Inc., 60 B.R. 405, 409 (E.D.N.C. 1986) (citations omitted).

Section 507 of the Bankruptcy Code fixes the priority order of claims and expenses against the bankruptcy estate. 11 U.S.C. § 507. Creditors within a given class are to be treated equally, and bankruptcy courts may not create their own rules of superpriority within a single class. 3 Collier on Bankruptcy § 507.02[2] (15th ed. 1992). Cross-collateralization, however, does exactly that. See, e.g., In re FCX, 60 B.R. at 410. As a result of this practice, post-petition lenders' unsecured pre-petition claims are given priority over all other unsecured pre-petition claims. The Ninth Circuit recognized that "[t]here is no ... applicable provision in the Bankruptcy Code authorizing the debtor to pay certain pre-petition unsecured claims in full while others remain unpaid. To do so would impermissibly violate the priority scheme of the Bankruptcy Code." In re Sun Runner, 945 F.2d at 1094 (citations omitted). See also In re Tenney Village, 104 B.R. at 570 (holding that § 364 does not authorize bankruptcy courts to change the priorities set forth in § 507.)

The Second Circuit has noted that, if cross-collateralization were initiated by the bankrupt while insolvent and shortly before filing a petition, the arrangement "would have constituted a voidable preference." In re Texlon, 596 F.2d at 1097. The fundamental nature of this practice is not changed by the fact that it is sanctioned by the bankruptcy court. We disagree with the district court's conclusion that, while cross-collateralization may violate some policies of bankruptcy law, it is consistent with the general purpose of Chapter 11 to help businesses reorganize and become profitable. In re Saybrook, 127 B.R. at 499. Rehabilitation is certainly the primary purpose of Chapter 11. This end, however, does not justify the use of any means. Cross-collateralization is directly inconsistent with the priority scheme of the Bankruptcy Code. Accordingly, the practice may not be approved by the bankruptcy court under its equitable authority.

VI. Conclusion

Cross-collateralization is not authorized by section 364. Section 364(e), therefore, is not applicable and this appeal is not moot. Because *Texlon*-type cross-collateralization is not explicitly authorized by the Bankruptcy Code and is contrary to the basic priority structure of the Code, we hold that it is an impermissible means of obtaining post-petition financing. The judgment of the district court is REVERSED and the case is REMANDED for proceedings not inconsistent with this opinion.

REVERSED and REMANDED.

Problem 4-5

> Suppose Foam Corporation needs additional credit to pay trade creditors cash on delivery and to downsize its eastern operations and that Kick Credit is willing to extend such credit under § 364(c) only if its prepetition debt is cross-collateralized. Further suppose that no other source of postpetition financing is available on reasonable terms. Should the Bankruptcy Court approve an extension of credit by Kick Credit under § 364(c) that includes cross-collateralization? Would your answer change if Foam Corporation's business could survive by using the proceeds of Kick Credit's collateral under § 363(c) and (e)? See In re AMT Inv. Corp., 53 B.R. 274, 276 (Bankr. E.D. Va. 1985). What is the relationship between § 363 and § 364? Under which section is the secured creditor better off? Consider In re The Colad Group, Inc., 324 B.R. 208 (Bankr. W.D.N.Y. 2005) (reprinted below).

4. Obtaining Credit Secured by a Senior Lien Under Section 364(d)

If the debtor in possession is unable to obtain postpetition credit on any other basis, § 364(d) provides for the extension of credit secured by a lien that is senior or equal to existing liens that encumber property of the estate.[8] In order for the debtor in possession to prevail in availing itself of this extraordinary remedy, the court must determine that the interest of any other secured creditor with a lien encumbering the property is adequately protected, an issue on which the debtor in possession bears the burden of proof under § 364(d)(2).

The methods by which the debtor in possession may offer adequate protection are the same as those discussed in connection with the automatic stay above. The maintenance of an equity cushion[9] is a common form of

---

8. As is true when the debtor in possession obtains credit under § 364(b) or (c), the debtor in possession must comply with Bankruptcy Rule 4001(c) in moving to obtain credit under § 364(d). Notice must be given to all entities with liens encumbering the affected property as well as to the creditors' committee or the twenty largest creditors and other entities to which the court may require that notice be given. But the motion will be denied where there is no evidence that the debtor approached even one lending institution to obtain credit under § 364(b) or (c). In re Reading Tube Indus., 72 B.R. 329, 332 (Bankr. E.D. Pa. 1987).

9. Even if the estate has no equity, the property's value may provide adequate protection as long as (1) there is a value cushion to protect the primed senior lien and (2) holders of undersecured junior liens consent to the borrowing. Anchor Sav. Bank FSB v. Sky Valley, Inc., 99 B.R. 117, 122-23 (N.D. Ga. 1989).

adequate protection offered to those whose liens will be "primed" by the § 364(d) borrowing. E.g., In re Dunes Casino Hotel, 69 B.R. 784, 794-96 (Bankr. D.N.J. 1986). If the equity cushion is insufficient and the estate contains other assets that are unencumbered or have sufficient equity, a replacement lien may be offered as a form of adequate protection to the secured creditor whose lien is being primed. See, e.g., In re Phoenix Steel Corp., 39 B.R. 218 (D. Del. 1984).

It is critical to determine the method by which a creditor's collateral is valued for purposes of determining whether adequate protection exists. Use of reorganization or going concern value may yield an ample equity cushion whereas liquidation value would not. Some courts adopt an intermediate value when there is some probability that the debtor will avoid a forced liquidation, whether by rehabilitating its business or by selling its assets as a going concern to another entity. See In re Phoenix Steel Corp., supra, 39 B.R. at 226-27.

The classic instance to authorize a borrowing secured by a senior lien occurs in a real estate case with a half-built building when the construction lender is reluctant to supply additional financing to complete the building project. The court may determine that the completion of the building—made possible by a § 364(d) borrowing secured by a senior lien—will so greatly enhance the value of the collateral that the primed creditor's position will be improved. But the court must be cautious in reaching such a conclusion. See In re First S. Sav. Ass'n, 820 F.2d 700, 710-14 (5th Cir. 1987) (issuing limited mandamus to require stay pending appeal where evidence did not support § 364(d) borrowing).

Notice the leverage that § 364(d) gives the debtor in possession in negotiating with existing lenders. The threat of filing a motion under § 364(d) to obtain a "priming" loan can be used by the debtor in possession to encourage existing lenders to extend postpetition secured credit. A lender is in a far worse position holding a junior lien than a senior lien. If the debtor defaults under the senior credit facility, the junior lienor might find itself in the position of having to acquire the property at its own foreclosure sale subject to the new senior lien or losing its collateral entirely.

Problem 4-6

> Suppose Foam Corporation desires to obtain $1 million in postpetition financing from your client, Kick Credit. Foam Corporation indicates that if Kick Credit is unwilling to extend the financing, Chemical Savings will do so if it is granted a superpriority administrative expense under § 364(c) and secured by a senior lien under § 364(d). What advice do you give Kick Credit in determining whether to extend the credit requested by Foam Corporation?

Problem 4-7

> Foam Corporation desperately needs cash to continue its operations. Kick Credit, whose loans are accruing interest at prime plus 2% per annum (assuming they are oversecured), will not consent to the use of its cash collateral and will not advance new credit. Foam Corporation is unable to obtain credit on any basis

other than under § 364(c) & (d). William Gruff proposes to lend Foam Corporation $5 million for two years, bearing interest at 14% per annum, secured by a senior lien on all encumbered assets of the estate, a lien on all unencumbered assets of the estate and a superpriority administrative claim senior to all other administrative expenses. For this problem assume that all of the assets are worth $21.5 million on a going concern valuation and $7.5 million on liquidation, whereas Kick Credit's personal property collateral is worth $15 million on a going concern valuation and $6.1 million in liquidation. Assume further that the real property is unencumbered. Three million dollars of the new funds are to be used to fund continuing operations and $2 million to upgrade the plant and equipment in Foam Corporation's western operations. Gruff will testify that the $5 million loan will enable Foam Corporation to continue operating for six months to enable it to sell its eastern operations for $2 million. All parties agree that if such a sale occurs, Foam Corporation will then make $3 million in profit per year before interest and taxes and that the going concern value of its remaining assets will be $24 million. How do you rule on Foam Corporation's motion?

5. Protecting the Borrowing Pending Appeal

Just as § 363(m) protects purchasers or lessors of property from the estate from reversal on appeal, § 364(e) protects a lender from reversal on appeal of an authorization to obtain credit. In particular, the reversal or modification on appeal of a borrowing order will not affect the validity of the borrowing or any priority or liens so granted unless the borrowing order is stayed pending appeal, as long as the entity extended the credit in good faith.[10] As discussed more fully below, courts have applied the *Abbotts Dairies* approach—that a bankruptcy court finding of good faith is a prerequisite to protection of a purchaser under § 363(m)—to the analogous case in which a provider of postpetition financing seeks protection under § 364(e): a bankruptcy court finding of good faith ordinarily is essential. See, e.g., New York Life Ins. Co. v. Revco D.S., Inc. (In re Revco D.S., Inc.), 901 F.2d 1359 (6th Cir. 1990). Thus, if an appellant fails to obtain a stay pending appeal of a borrowing order, courts have dismissed the appeal as moot upon a showing that the creditor has extended credit in reliance on the order and in good faith. E.g., Boullioun Aircraft Holding Co. v. Smith Mgmt. (In re W. Pac. Airlines, Inc.), 181 F.3d 1191 (10th Cir. 1999) (noting that there was no contention that the credit was not extended in good faith). If, however, effective relief can be given without affecting the rights of the postpetition lender, the appeal can go forward even if no stay is obtained. Id.

---

10. There may be an exception to this rule if the borrowing order is obtained based on improper notice (or no notice at all). See Credit Alliance Corp. v. Dunning-Ray Ins. Agency (In re Blumer), 66 B.R. 109 (B.A.P. 9th Cir. 1986), aff'd, 826 F.2d 1069 (9th Cir. 1987); In re FCX, Inc., 54 B.R. 833, 838-39 (Bankr. E.D.N.C. 1985). However, in Owens-Corning Fiberglas Corp. v. Center Wholesale, Inc. (In re Center Wholesale, Inc.), 759 F.2d 1440 (9th Cir. 1985), the court stated that § 364(e) protected the postpetition lender's lien rights even though the court characterized the borrowing order as void, because of inadequate notice to a prepetition lienholder. The court suggested that on remand the prepetition lienholder should be given a § 507(b) superpriority to remedy the harm done to it. Cf. Problem 4-2, supra.

Rule 8005 permits an appellate court to condition the grant of a stay pending appeal on the posting of a supersedeas bond. E.g., Bleaufontaine, Inc. v. Roland Int'l (In re Bleaufontaine, Inc.), 634 F.2d 1383 (5th Cir. 1981). But an objector's willingness to post a bond may not lead to the issuance of a stay unless legal criteria to obtain a stay pertain. For example, most courts require the objecting party to meet requirements similar to those imposed to obtain an injunction under Federal Rule of Civil Procedure 65. In particular, the objector (the party seeking the stay) must be likely to prevail on the merits of the appeal, the objector must suffer irreparable harm unless the stay is granted, other parties must suffer no substantial harm if the stay is granted, and the public interest must not be harmed if the stay is granted. E.g., In re First S. Sav. Ass'n, 820 F.2d 700 (5th Cir. 1987); In re Baldwin United Corp., 45 B.R. 385, 386 (Bankr. S.D. Ohio 1984) (§ 363(m) case).

Given that the protection afforded by § 364(e) only applies if the lender is in "good faith," when must the lender prove that it is in good faith? How does the lender go about proving good faith? Consider your answers in light of the following decision.

In re EDC Holding Co.
United States Court of Appeals, Seventh Circuit, 1982
676 F.2d 945

POSNER, Circuit Judge.

Section 364 of the Bankruptcy Code empowers the bankruptcy judge to authorize the bankrupt to borrow money and give the lender priority over certain other creditors. Subsequent reversal, by the district court or the court of appeals, of the grant of priority does not affect the validity of the priority if it was granted "to an entity that extended such credit in good faith, whether or not such entity knew of the pendency of the appeal," unless the transaction was stayed pending appeal. 11 U.S.C. § 364(e). We are required in this case to interpret and apply the term "in good faith."

Before Wisconsin Steel (as we shall refer jointly to the affiliated corporations that are the bankrupts in this case) went bankrupt, the Chase Manhattan Bank had loaned it money secured by a lien on inventory and by a bank account that the company maintained with Chase. Wisconsin Steel defaulted, and Chase set off against these defaults the funds in the account. Wisconsin Steel was accustomed to paying its employees with checks drawn on this account. Chase's set-off caused those checks to bounce, which induced Wisconsin Steel to petition for protection under Chapter 11 of the Bankruptcy Code.

The union representing Wisconsin Steel's workers filed a complaint in the bankruptcy court seeking payment to its members of their unpaid wages. Chase was named as a defendant along with Wisconsin Steel. The union claimed that it had a lien on the same inventory on which Chase claimed a lien. Although the bankruptcy court authorized Chase to take possession of the inventory, the union, by picketing Wisconsin Steel, prevented Chase from doing so. Eventually a settlement was reached by which Chase agreed to lend Wisconsin Steel some $1.7 million in exchange for the union's dropping its suit and allowing the inventory to be removed. The agreement stated that Wisconsin Steel would pay out of the proceeds of the loan $77,000 to the union to reimburse it for attorneys' fees and other legal expenses incurred in its suit, and the rest (except for some small amounts for various taxes) to the company's employees in settlement of their claims. The agreement further provided that the entire loan was to receive the priority that 11 U.S.C. § 507(a)(3) gives wage claims.

Since the proposed loan involved the grant of a special priority to the lender, the bankruptcy judge's approval was required by section 364. He gave it, over the objection of the Official Creditors' Committee of WSC Sales Company, representing the general creditors of Wisconsin Steel, that the priority should not extend to the $77,000 earmarked for the union's lawyers. The Committee appealed to the district court from this part of the bankruptcy judge's order but the district court dismissed the appeal as moot. The Committee appeals that dismissal to this court.

The bankruptcy judge's order was never stayed. Therefore, if in lending Wisconsin Steel $77,000 to pay the union's legal expenses Chase was acting in good faith, its priority could not be affected by the validity of the order and the issue of validity is therefore moot as the district court held. See, e.g., In re Dutch Inn of Orlando, Ltd., 614 F.2d 504, 506 (5th Cir. 1980). But if Chase was not acting in good faith, the Committee was entitled to have the merits of its objection to the grant of priority adjudicated.

Section 364(e) is explicit that knowledge of the pendency of an appeal from a bankruptcy judge's order granting a lender special priority does not forfeit the protections that the statute gives to a lender who is in good faith, even though such knowledge implies the further knowledge that there are objections to the order. Therefore the mere fact that Chase knew the Committee objected to its receiving a special priority with regard to that portion of the loan that was to pay the union's legal expenses does not show bad faith. See In re Rock Indus. Mach. Corp., 572 F.2d 1195, 1199 (7th Cir. 1978), dealing with a parallel provision relating to purchasers in good faith of a bankrupt's property. These provisions seek to overcome people's natural reluctance to deal with a bankrupt firm whether as purchaser or lender by assuring them that so long as they are relying in good faith on a bankruptcy judge's approval of the transaction they need not worry about their priority merely because some creditor is objecting to the transaction and is trying to get the district court or the court of appeals to reverse the bankruptcy judge. The proper recourse for the objecting creditor is to get the transaction stayed pending appeal. See, e.g., In re Roberts Farms, Inc., 652 F.2d 793, 796-98 (9th Cir. 1981).

But all this presupposes good faith. See, e.g., Local Jt. Exec. Bd., AFL-CIO v. Hotel Circle, Inc., 419 F. Supp. 778, 783 (S.D. Cal. 1976), aff'd on other grounds, 613 F.2d 210 (9th Cir. 1980). And while it is clear as we have said that knowledge that there are objections to the transaction is not enough to constitute bad faith, we can find neither cases nor legislative history, pertaining either to good faith lenders to bankrupts or to good faith purchasers from bankrupts, that tell us what is enough. Chase argues that so long as the terms of the transaction are not misrepresented to the bankruptcy judge, as they were not here, the creditor may rely on the bankruptcy judge's order unless it is stayed, no matter how obviously erroneous the order is. But if this is what Congress intended, the words "in good faith" could have been deleted, as it would be perfectly clear even without them that an order obtained from a bankruptcy judge by fraud was ineffective to put the lender who procured the order ahead of other creditors. We assume the statute was intended to protect not the lender who seeks to take advantage of a lapse in oversight by the bankruptcy judge but the lender who believes his priority is valid but cannot be certain that it is, because of objections that might be upheld on appeal. If the lender *knows* his priority is invalid but proceeds anyway in the hope that a stay will not be sought or if sought will not be granted, we cannot see how he can be thought to be acting in good faith.

The loan agreement here stated that $77,000 of the proceeds would be used to pay the union for attorneys' fees and other legal expenses incurred in the prosecution of the union's action for the unpaid wages of its members. The agreement thus gave the union a claim against the bankrupt for $77,000 and simultaneously paid it in full, and Chase's priority meant that the burden would be borne by the bankrupt estate, in effect the general creditors, rather than by Chase itself.

Viewed realistically, as a claim by the union's attorneys for time and expenses incurred in prosecuting the union members' claims for unpaid wages, the union's claim not only was not entitled to priority over the claims of the general creditors but could not be paid out of the bankrupt's estate at all. Subject to exceptions that Chase does not claim the union's attorneys come within, the rule is that no allowance will be made to a creditor's attorney for proving his client's claim. * * *

Where it is evident from the loan agreement itself that the transaction has an intended effect that is improper under the Bankruptcy Code, the lender is not in good faith, and it is irrelevant what the improper purpose is. If the loan agreement had stated that Wisconsin Steel would use the proceeds to buy one-way airplane tickets to Brazil for its officers, we do not think Chase would be arguing to us that it had extended credit to the company in good faith and therefore had an untouchable priority. Of course in such a case the general creditors should be able to obtain a stay but we do not think their failure to do so would place Chase's priority beyond the power of judicial correction; otherwise the good faith requirement would be read out of the statute. The present case is less extreme but no different in principle. Just as Chase would not have been a purchaser in good faith if it had bought from Wisconsin Steel property to which it knew the company did not have good title, so it could not be a lender in good faith in extending credit in exchange for a priority that it knew the company could not properly give it since the transaction amounted to taking money out of the pockets of the general creditors to pay lawyers whose claims were not allowable under bankruptcy law at all.

But we must consider whether it may make a difference that the agreement to pay the lawyers was part of a settlement of the three-cornered litigation among the union, the bankrupt, and Chase. Normally if someone was willing to settle his suit against a bankrupt for $77,000, there would be no impropriety in a bank's lending money (and receiving a special priority) to finance the settlement and thereby enable the bankrupt to disentangle itself from potentially costly litigation, provided that the settlement was a reasonable one. But the origin of the litigation in this case has to be borne in mind. The union was trying to collect its members' wage claims. Those claims were valid creditors' claims but the cases * * * forbid the creditors' attorney to collect his fee from the bankrupt. * * * Wisconsin Steel could not grant Chase a special priority without showing that the proceeds of the loan would be used for a proper purpose. The stated purpose of $77,000 of those proceeds was improper. It is immaterial that the expenditure might, for all we know, have been justifiable on some other ground.

As all this must have been as obvious to Chase as it is to us—probably more so—we do not think that the context (settlement of litigation) in which the loan was made and the special priority received casts enough doubt on the forbidden nature of the transaction to rebut an inference of bad faith—that is, knowledge of improper purpose. Nor, finally, are we persuaded by Chase's argument that the priority it received on the $77,000 was a *sine qua non* of the entire loan transaction—a transaction beneficial to the bankrupt and hence to the general creditors of the bankrupt as well as to Chase—because the union would not have called off its pickets unless it was given its legal fees and unless the union did call off its pickets and thereby allowed Chase to remove the inventory on which it had a lien Chase would not have made the loan to cover the unpaid wage claims. Chase could have paid the union's legal fees out of its own pocket if that was what was required to get the inventory out. Instead it claims a right to force the company's general creditors to pay the union's legal expenses out of their pockets. That is an improper use of the bankrupt's estate, to which the general creditors are the residual claimants. The fact that Chase was a defendant in the suit by the union actually strengthens the inference of bad faith. Chase was not a disinterested lender but a settling litigant that saw an opportunity to reduce the cost of the settlement by putting the union's lawyers ahead of the general creditors of Wisconsin Steel. An extension of credit having such an ulterior purpose is not in good faith within the meaning of section 364(e).

The judgment of the district court is reversed, and the case is remanded with instructions to reverse the order of the bankruptcy judge approving the grant to Chase of a special priority with respect to the $77,000 that it loaned Wisconsin Steel to pay the union for its legal expenses.

NOTES

1. What could Chase, as lender in *EDC Holding Co.*, have done differently to protect its financing? Should the lending agreement and borrowing order have required the debtor in possession to use the proceeds only to pay postpetition debts? Should the borrowing order have required the proceeds to be used only to pay fee awards authorized by the bankruptcy court? If the bankruptcy court had mistakenly approved payment of the union's attorneys' fees in a separate order, would Chase have been protected under the borrowing order? Would it have mattered if the bankruptcy court order contained a finding that Chase was in good faith?

2. The courts of appeals appear to require the finding of good faith to be determined by the Bankruptcy Court at the hearing on the borrowing order. E.g., Kham & Nate's Shoes No. 2, Inc. v. First Bank of Whiting, 908 F.2d 1351, 1355 (7th Cir. 1990); New York Life Ins. Co. v. Revco D.S., Inc. (In re Revco D.S., Inc.), 901 F.2d 1359 (6th Cir. 1990). Note the similar issue discussed in Note 1 after *Abbott's Dairies*, above. Conclusory testimony of one witness might not be enough to establish good faith. See In re The Colad Group, Inc., 324 B.R. 208, 225 (Bankr. W.D.N.Y. 2005) (reprinted below).

3. If the order authorizing the borrowing provides for cross-collateralization, the lender is not presumed to have acted in bad faith. Indeed, if the lender extends credit based on the order and the appellant has not obtained a stay pending appeal, some appellate courts will dismiss the appeal as moot. Unsecured Creditors' Comm. v. First Nat'l Bank & Trust Co. (In re Ellingsen MacLean Oil Co.), 834 F.2d 599, 604 (6th Cir. 1987); Burchinal v. Central Washington Bank (In re Adams Apple, Inc.), 829 F.2d 1484, 1488 (9th Cir. 1987); but see Shapiro v. Saybrook Mfg. Co., 963 F.2d 1490 (11th Cir. 1992) (reprinted above). A different result can

obtain, however, where the order authorizing the borrowing requires all appeals to be final before the lending is authorized. See In re Brookfield Clothes, Inc., 31 B.R. 978, 981-82 (S.D.N.Y. 1983) (requirement of final order prior to consummation of sale negated mootness doctrine in § 363(m) context). It is also possible that an objector's failure to require the borrowing order to reference good faith of the lender waives the issue on appeal. See New York Life Ins. Co. v. Revco D.S., Inc. (In re Revco D.S., Inc.), 901 F.2d 1359 (6th Cir. 1990) (dictum). Finally, one court has held that the appeal is not moot if the lender has not yet loaned the entire agreed amount and would not be injured if future advances were not made; reversal of the order authorizing the lending cannot affect the rights of the lender with regard to amounts already loaned, but it can prevent the lender from making further disbursements under the reversed order. Resolution Trust Corp. v. Swedeland Dev. Group (In re Swedeland Dev. Group), 16 F.3d 552, 561-62 (3d Cir. 1994). Would *Swedeland* have been decided differently if the lender were making advances to complete construction of a housing development or shopping center?

D. REPRISE: FIRST DAY ORDERS

In Chapter Three we considered the court's power under § 105(a). In this Chapter we considered §§ 363 and 364. We are now ready to look again at "first day" orders. Consider Judge Bucki's approach in the first case below. Note also his treatment of the motion for final approval of a postpetition financing arrangement.[11] Consider, in the second case below, Judge Easterbrook's hard line approach to "critical vendors" orders. Does the addition of § 503(b)(9) (and perhaps the amendment of § 546(c)) by the 2005 BAPCA dilute the effect of his approach or affect his analysis? What about vendors of services (such as insurance)? Is Judge Easterbrook right that a supplier with a long-term contract violates the automatic stay by refusing to continue to deliver goods? See Citizens Bank of Maryland v. Strumpf, 516 U.S. 16, 116 S. Ct. 286, 133 L. Ed. 2d 258 (1995) (reprinted above). (In Chapter Seven of this text we return to similar "executory contract" issues under § 365.) If orders allowing payment of critical vendors are authorized under the Code, and if Kmart's breach entitled Fleming to cease deliveries, would Fleming's managers necessarily have been well-advised to continue to sell to Kmart without being paid for the goods delivered prepetition? Is Judge Easterbrook's management advice sound?

In re The Colad Group, Inc.
United States Bankruptcy Court, W.D.N.Y., 2005
324 B.R. 208

CARL L. BUCKI, Bankruptcy Judge.

This case provides an unusual opportunity to consider standards for the approval of first day motions in a case filed under chapter 11.

The Colad Group, Inc. ("Colad") is a specialty printer, whose primary business involves the production and sale of custom folders, binders and other stationery products. On the evening of Thursday, February 3, 2005, Colad electronically filed

---

11. The opinion does not discuss the severe limitations that § 503(c) places on retention bonuses payable to insiders, because that subsection had not yet been added to the Code. Similarly, the opinion does not discuss § 366(c) (added by the 2005 BAPCPA) or its conflict with § 366(b).

a petition for relief under chapter 11 of the Bankruptcy Code. The following day, debtor's counsel contacted the court to schedule an opportunity on an emergency basis to seek the court's approval of "first day orders." For this purpose, the court reserved time for both a conference and, if necessary, a hearing, on the afternoon of Tuesday, February 7. In attendance at those proceedings were counsel for the debtor; counsel from the Office of the United States Trustee; counsel for Continental Plants Group, LLC ("Continental"), the primary secured creditor in this case; and Daniel Williams, pro se.

Daniel Williams is the largest creditor in the chapter 7 bankruptcy case of William P. Brosnahan, Jr., an individual who at one time was affiliated with Colad. * * * [I]t suffices to note that Colad identifies the bankruptcy estate of Brosnahan as its largest unsecured creditor, and that Brosnahan's trustee has named Colad as a defendant in various adversary proceedings. For these reasons, this court directed that the Brosnahan trustee and its largest creditor receive notice of the conference and hearing relative to any first day motions in the Colad case. * * *

In bankruptcy practice, the phrase "first day motions" refers generally to any of a variety of requests made shortly after the filing of a chapter 11 petition, for prompt authorizations needed to facilitate the operation of the debtor's business. On February 7th, the debtor presented eight such motions * * *.

In attempting to justify the grant of many first day orders, debtors will urge reliance upon the so-called "Doctrine of Necessity." Based historically upon provisions of the Railway Labor Act, 45 U.S.C. § 151 et seq., the Doctrine of Necessity finds support from section 105(a) of the Bankruptcy Code, which authorizes the bankruptcy court to "issue any order, process, or judgment that is necessary or appropriate to carry out the provisions of this title." Nonetheless, section 105(a) does not create authority and rights that do not otherwise arise from the express provisions of the Bankruptcy Code. * * * Within this spirit, this court has discerned four principles that should apply to consideration of first day motions.

First, the requested relief should be limited to that which is minimally necessary to maintain the existence of the debtor, until such time as the debtor can effect appropriate notice to creditors and parties in interest. In particular, a first day order should avoid substantive rulings that irrevocably determine the rights of parties.

Second, first day orders must maintain a level of clarity and simplicity sufficient to allow reasonable confidence that an order will effect no unanticipated or untoward consequences.

Third, first day orders are not a device to change the procedural and substantive rights that the Bankruptcy Code and Rules have established. In particular, first day orders should provide no substitute for the procedural and substantive protections of the plan confirmation process.

Fourth, no first day order should violate or disregard the substantive rights of parties, in ways not expressly authorized by the Bankruptcy Code.
* * *

Payments to Employees and to Taxing Authorities

The debtor's first motion sought authority to pay pre-petition wages and benefits; its second motion sought to approve payment of pre-petition use and sales taxes. In papers filed with these motions, the debtor represented that nearly all of these wages, benefits and taxes would constitute priority claims; that the debtor had incurred these obligations in its ordinary course of operations; that the outstanding wages and benefits were pre-petition obligations that were not yet payable; that a disruption of wage and benefit payments could affect its ability to maintain its work force; and that the outstanding tax liabilities were ordinary obligations for use taxes and for sales taxes that the debtor had collected from its customers. In considering these two motions, the court was principally concerned for prejudice to the rights of other creditors. As against the interests of general unsecured creditors, the tax claims and nearly all of the employee claims held priority. No other priority claims appeared to be outstanding. Secured creditors might typically hold a superior interest in the cash that would be paid to the employees and taxing authorities, but here, the secured creditor consented to the debtor's proposed distribution. Based upon that consent and upon the various representations made on behalf of the debtor, the court granted both motions in substantial part. With respect to employee wages and benefits, however, the distribution could not exceed the priority limits of 11 U.S.C. § 507(a)[(4)] and [(5)], except for an amount that the court deemed to be de minimis and with restrictions on payments to an insider.

Post-petition Utility Services

Without prior notice to utilities, the debtor also moved for an order specifying adequate assurance of payment for post-petition utility services and to prohibit utilities from discontinuing, altering or refusing service. Concerned that a lack of notice had denied due process to the affected utilities, this court refused to consider such an ex parte application. Moreover, the motion sought extraordinary relief with respect to issues that Congress had already addressed in section 366 of the Bankruptcy Code. Section 366 protects a debtor's access to utility service during the first twenty days after the filing of a bankruptcy petition. Then, on "request of a party in interest and after notice and a hearing, the court may order reasonable modification of the amount of deposit or other security necessary to provide adequate assurance of payment." 11 U.S.C. § 366(b). By its first day motion, the debtor essentially sought to disregard the procedural requirements of section 366 for a notice and hearing. Nor was such special relief necessary, in light of the protection of utility access for twenty days. For these reasons, the court denied the debtor's motion, but without prejudice to a future application under section 366.

Key Employee Retention and Incentive Program

The debtor next moved for authority to implement a key employee retention and incentive program for non-insider personnel. Specifically, the debtor proposed to offer a bonus to key employees who would remain with the company through the completion of the anticipated sale of the debtor's operating assets. Contemplating a typical bonus equal to 133 percent of an individual's bi-weekly pay, the debtor estimated a total cost to the estate of less than $25,000. In support of its request, the debtor represented that it required the services of these key employees; that the debtor had no ability on the short term to replace these key employees; and that in light of the debtor's precarious financial condition, these employees might accept other employment unless they received sufficient financial incentive to remain with the company.

The retention and incentive program represents the type of operational decision for which this court will generally give reasonable deference to the sound discretion of management. In the present instance, to the satisfaction of this court, the debtor has demonstrated an immediate danger to its personnel requirements and hence, that it has an urgent need for the proposed program. The projected payments appear to be reasonable in amount. The court discerns nothing in the program that would violate any substantive rights of parties in interest. For these reasons, the court granted this first day motion to authorize a key employee retention and incentive program.

* * *

Debtor in Possession Financing Agreement

The most important of the first day motions was the application for authority to obtain post-petition financing. Like most debtors in chapter 11, Colad had pledged nearly all of its assets as collateral to secure a pre-petition credit facility. Among these assets were Colad's inventory, receivables, and the proceeds of its inventory and receivables, all of which [proceeds] are deemed to constitute "cash collateral," as defined by section 363(a) of the Bankruptcy Code. Pursuant to 11 U.S.C. § 363(c)(2), a debtor in possession may not use cash collateral unless either "(A) each entity that has an interest in such cash collateral consents; or (B) the court, after notice and a hearing, authorizes such use, sale, or lease in accordance with the provisions of this section." Hence, without either consent or court authorization, Colad would have had no access to most of the cash that would have been generated through its normal business operations. To satisfy its cash needs, Colad moved under 11 U.S.C. § 364 for emergency and final authority to obtain post-petition financing from Continental, the current holder of Colad's pre-petition loan facility.

Continental and Colad have proposed to link the post-petition financing facility to the debtor's pre-petition revolver loan. Under their agreement, proceeds of collateral would be applied first to the satisfaction of the balance due on the pre-petition loan. Meanwhile, Continental would fund the debtor's post-petition activities through new advances under the post-petition facility. Providing that post-petition advances would be secured by all assets of the debtor, the proposed facility would also create an obligation that would receive administrative and super priority status, as allowed under 11 U.S.C. § 364(c).

In a competitive and adversarial environment, one cannot fault a creditor for seeking an outcome that will maximize the return for itself. For this reason, this court has often approved the post-petition use of a revolving credit facility. From the lender's perspective, such an arrangement avoids the various legal problems of cross-collateralization. In a cross-collateralization arrangement, a lender advances new credit on condition that an enhanced set of collateral will secure both pre-petition and post-petition loans. Instead, the revolver arrangement permits a satisfaction of the pre-petition loan, so that an increasing percentage of the lender's total exposure will receive the security and benefits of the new post-petition credit facility. Although this court will approve a proper-post petition revolver facility, it will not allow a disregard of the procedural and substantive rights of other parties in interest.

Bankruptcy Rule 4001 imposes procedural rules for consideration of a motion for authority to obtain credit. Subdivision (c)(1) of this rule requires that the court treat such a motion as a contested matter under Rule 9014, and that notice of such a motion be served upon the members of the Official Committee of Unsecured Creditors, or if no committee has been appointed, then upon the twenty largest unsecured creditors. In a typical case, this requirement of notice presents practical challenges, in as much as most debtors have an immediate need for financing. For this reason, the following text of Bankruptcy Rule 4001(c)(2) attempts to find a balance that will accommodate both financial necessity and concerns for due process:

> The court may commence a final hearing on a motion for authority to obtain credit no earlier than 15 days after service of the motion. If the motion so requests, the court may conduct a hearing before such 15 day period expires, *but the court may authorize the obtaining of credit only to the extent necessary to avoid immediate and irreparable harm to the estate pending a final hearing.*

(emphasis added). Pursuant to this rule, therefore, the court may consider a first day motion to approve an emergency lending facility, but only if two conditions are satisfied. First, any emergency authorization must be limited only "to the extent necessary to avoid immediate and irreparable harm." Second, the authorization may be effective only until a final hearing on appropriate notice to creditors as required under Rule 4001(c)(1).

In support of its first day motion for authority to obtain post-petition financing, the debtor represented that it could not operate without a post-petition line of credit and that it had no ability to obtain such credit from any source other than Continental. Conceptually, this Court found that these representations were adequate to justify an appropriate form of emergency lending until the scheduled hearing for final approval. However, in the form that the debtor proposed, the emergency funding order was unacceptable for the following four reasons:

1.   The order failed to reflect any effort to limit the conditions of credit only to those which would be absolutely necessary to avoid immediate and irreparable harm. Rather, the proposed order would have approved an interim loan agreement with terms essentially identical to those contemplated for the final loan agreement. * * *

2.   The interim order was inappropriately complex, and thereby denied to the court a sufficient basis of confidence in the reasonableness of its terms. On an emergency basis, the debtor wanted the court to sign a twenty-six page order, which incorporated the terms of a loan agreement that filled 93 pages of single space text, including exhibits. This court appreciates the dollar value of the proposed lending facility, and accepts the need for a comprehensive agreement. For this reason, as hereafter discussed, the court has carefully examined the terms of the final loan agreement. A first day order is inherently different, however. Without benefit of opportunities for comment from creditors on notice, the court must view with skepticism the exigent submission of any such complex instrument.

3.   Based on its cursory review, the court discovered that the proposed order would change substantive and procedural rights, without allowing any reasonable opportunity for creditor objection. For example, the interim loan arrangement

included a grant of relief from the automatic stay in the event of default, limitations on the debtor's right to propose a plan of reorganization, and a waiver of various claims that the debtor might assert against Continental. Particularly troublesome were the provisions of section 11.6 of the Loan Agreement, which purported to require, as a condition for interim funding, the disavowal and waiver of various "rights and remedies provided under the Bankruptcy Code, the Federal Rules of Civil Procedure, and the Bankruptcy Rules." Furthermore, paragraphs 2.1 and 11.1 of the Loan Agreement seemingly attempted to grant administrative priority to the pre-petition claims of Continental. Later in this opinion, the court will discuss whether certain of these terms are appropriately included into an order that authorizes lending on a final basis. As part of a first day order, where unsecured creditors have had no opportunity to object, such terms are unacceptable.

4. As originally submitted, the first day lending order proposed to authorize a potential violation of state law and to waive the substantive rights of other creditors without prior notice to them. By its terms, the proposed loan agreement contemplated a post-petition advance of $500,000, for a term of approximately 90 day. In addition to interest at the rate of 4.5 percent over prime, Colad was to pay loan fees totaling in excess of $135,000. Based upon these facts, the court questioned whether the cost of borrowing would exceed New York State's criminal usury rate of 25 percent. Additionally, the debtor's proposed order would approve a loan that was conditioned upon a waiver of all marshaling obligations. Without deciding these issues, this court refused on an emergency basis to approve the loan charges or to consider a waiver of rights, where the affected creditors had yet to receive notice of the debtor's proposal.

At the hearing to consider the debtor's first day motions, the respective attorneys for Colad and Continental responded to the above concerns, by asserting that the proposed lending arrangement represented the best and only terms available to the debtor. In my view, this position seemed disingenuous. Continental had recently acquired its secured position, with the stated desire to effect a purchase of assets as a going concern under section 363 of the Bankruptcy Code. With this objective, Continental would be obviously disinclined to compel a distressed liquidation of its position. As holder of a first lien in the debtor's inventory and receivables, Continental was positioned to dictate terms. Consequently, the proposed loan did not represent terms negotiated in any form of open market. Although the reality of circumstances might compel acceptance of these terms after a final hearing, this court was unwilling to disregard the above mentioned concerns until at least after the twenty largest unsecured creditors had opportunity to object.

The resolution of the motion for interim financing confirmed the court's perception of disingenuousness with regard to the assertion that the debtor could obtain no better terms of lending. After this court refused to approve an order in the form that the debtor had first presented, the parties negotiated an arrangement that the court could accept on an interim basis. Ultimately, I signed a simpler order authorizing the debtor to borrow funds needed to pay necessary expenditures. With respect to these advances, the lender received a super-priority administrative expense claim secured by a lien on all of the debtor's assets. Without rejecting the possibility of eventual approval under the terms of a final lending order, the interim order deferred consideration of the various provisions which the court had found to be troublesome. In particular, the parties agreed that most of the proposed loan fees would be charged not in connection with the interim loan, but only if authorized under the terms of a final loan agreement.

The interim lending order authorized the debtor to borrow funds on an emergency basis, until such time as the court would decide the request to approve a final lending order. As required by Bankruptcy Rule 4001(c), the court also directed that the debtor give to the twenty largest creditors a fifteen day notice of the hearing to consider a final DIP lending facility. That hearing was initially scheduled for February 24, but on consent of all parties, was adjourned to March 8. A further hearing with respect to the terms of a possible order was then conducted on March 28, 2005.

Motion to Authorize a Final DIP Lending Facility

The debtor seeks authority to borrow funds under the terms of a final lending facility, whose present form incorporates changes designed to address some of the concerns that the court expressed to the parties at the hearing to approve interim lending. Appointed subsequent to the consideration of interim authorization, the Official Committee of Unsecured Creditors now supports the debtor's motion for final authority. However, Daniel Williams opposes the request. Primarily, he contends that the proposed facility entails excessive risk, particularly in light of the fact that the debtor's financial history indicates the improbability of a successful reorganization. The court might give greater consideration to this objection, if the debtor intended to reorganize as a going concern. In the present instance, however, the debtor has candidly indicated an intent to liquidate, most likely through a sale of assets under 11 U.S.C. § 363. Thus, the borrowing is designed only to maintain operations as a going concern for the short term, until a sale can be completed. Under these circumstances, the court is prepared to authorized borrowing under terms of an appropriate facility. However, the court cannot approve lending in the form that Colad and Continental have proposed.

* * * [T]his opinion will discuss five fatal defects that preclude approval of the proposed order in its current form.

1. The proposed order would sanction excessive and usurious interest.

The debtor seeks to borrow a maximum of $494,000.00 for a term of less than ninety days. On this loan, the debtor would pay interest at an annual rate of four and one-half percent over "the Chase Bank Rate." In addition, however, the debtor would pay a non-refundable loan commitment fee of $50,000, a closing fee of $50,000, collateral management fees of $10,000 at closing and $1,500 per month thereafter, and an unused line fee based on a formula that would be calculated each month. All of these various fees would be deducted from the amount that the debtor proposes to borrow. Thus, the debtor would actually receive operating funds of less than $381,000 dollars. Because the term of the loan is less than ninety days, the fees alone would represent charges equivalent to an interest rate in excess of 100 percent per annum.

New York law exempts corporate borrowings from the penalties of civil usury. N.Y. Gen. Oblig. L. § 5-521(1). However, pursuant to General Obligations Law § 5-521(3), this exemption does not extend to the prohibitions against criminal usury in Penal Law § 190.40. This latter section provides generally that a person or entity commits criminal usury in the second degree when it "knowingly charges, takes or receives any money or other property as interest on the loan or forbearance of any money or other property, at a rate exceeding twenty-five per centum per annum or the equivalent rate for a longer or shorter period." * * *

Subdivision (6)(b) of New York General Obligations Law § 5-501 states that the criminal usury statute shall not apply to any loan or forbearance in the amount of $2,500,000 or more. In its application for interim borrowing authority, Colad asked the court to approve an agreement that would allow a loan amount for "up to the maximum of $494,000." Now, in the application for final borrowing authority, Colad seeks to approve a restructured loan agreement. Although the restructured agreement also seeks a similar advance of new credit, it defines the "Post-Petition Loan Amount" as "up to the aggregate of $3,252,000.00, consisting of (a) the renewal of the pre-petition revolving line of credit and (b) the over-line facility in the amount of $494,000.00 ...." The issue for this court is whether such wordsmithery and linguistic legerdemain can transform the proposed post-petition loan into a transaction that is exempt from New York's usury prohibition.

This court believes that it must treat the post-petition advances as a separate loan that is subject to the prohibitions against criminal usury. Section 364 speaks only to court approval of post-petition indebtedness, and not to any ratification of pre-petition obligations. * * * Being less than $2,500,000, this new loan falls below any exemption to the applicable law of criminal usury.
　　　* * *

This court does not mean to suggest that in extending the proposed credit with court authorization, Continental would have met the scienter requirement of the Penal Law. Under no circumstance, however, will this court authorize acts that would otherwise be criminal under New York law. * * *

This court must also reject the proposed loan fees for a second independent reason. Even if the proposed transaction could overcome a usury defense, the fees serve as an inappropriate subterfuge to avoid the requirement for a commercially reasonable disposition of assets under U.C.C. § 9-610.

By its terms, the revised loan agreement contemplates a sale of the debtor's assets to Continental. Having recently acquired its secured position by assignment from the prior lender, Continental will make a credit bid for those assets. If it had elected to exercise the rights of a secured creditor under article 9 of the Uniform Commercial Code, Continental would have been required to fulfill the mandate of section 9-610(b). 4 James J. White & Robert S. Summers, UNIFORM COMMERCIAL CODE § 34-11 (5th ed. 2002). In relevant part, this section provides that "[e]very aspect of a disposition of collateral, including the method, manner, time, place, and other terms, must be commercially reasonable." Outside bankruptcy, the amount of Continental's credit bid would include only the balance due on its outstanding loan facilities, including any costs recoverable under the loan agreement. Now, Continental proposes to enhance the amount of that credit bid with loan fees totaling at least $113,000.00. Such an enhancement can only work to chill the prospects for competitive bidding. Any such chilling effect will jeopardize the possibility of a surplus that might inure to the benefit of unsecured creditors.

Interest and loan fees in any amount will necessarily reduce the surplus from the sale of secured assets. If proposed in isolation from the contemplated sale of assets, the loan might not be subject to the same criticism. But Continental acquired its current position in contemplation of an asset purchase. Now Continental proposes loan fees that can only serve to facilitate its desired acquisition, all to the possible detriment of any competing bid. These fees represent no "out of pocket" cost to the lender. In my view, such machinations would be commercially unreasonable outside bankruptcy. Investors may not use the bankruptcy process to obtain respectability for otherwise suspect efforts to influence a bidding process. Accordingly, the court will not approve the proposed loan fees in the present instance.

2. The debtor offers insufficient justification for a priming lien.

The debtor seeks an order which would give to Continental a priming lien over all other secured creditors. * * *

In the present instance, Continental seeks the benefit of a generalized priming as against the positions of all other secured creditors. However, the moving papers fail to identify any secured creditors whose liens would be primed. Under these circumstances, a priming lien of any kind would be inappropriate for two reasons. First, the notice requirement of section 364(d)(1) must necessarily inure to the benefit of superior lienors. Without an identification of those superior lienors, the court cannot possibly confirm the adequacy of notice. The debtor has satisfied the requirements of Bankruptcy Rule 4001, which mandates notice either to the twenty largest unsecured creditors or to a committee appointed under 11 U.S.C. § 1102. This notice, however, does not necessarily reach the holders of secured debt. Seeking to modify the rights of parties in absentia, the generalized priming lien cannot possibly satisfy the notice requirements of section 364(d)(1). Second, as required by section 364(d)(1)(B), in order to grant a priming lien, the court must make a finding of adequate protection of all senior or equal interests. With no identification of those interests, the court cannot begin to assess the adequacy of protection. * * *

3. The debtor proposes an impermissible modification of the rights of third parties.

Any extension of secured credit will usually impact the interests of other creditors. In bankruptcy, the court may authorize the debtor to exacerbate this impact in several narrowly defined ways. For example, under section 364(c) of the Bankruptcy Code, the court may grant priority over other administrative creditors. As noted earlier in this opinion, section 364(d) permits a priming lien in certain limited circumstances. Generally, however, the Bankruptcy Code gives to post-petition secured creditors only the same rights that a secured creditor could acquire outside bankruptcy. Unless the Bankruptcy Code expressly provides, this court has no power to diminish the rights of third parties as against a secured creditor.

Colad has asked the court to approve an order which provides that Continental "will not be subject to the equitable doctrine of 'marshaling' or any other similar doctrine with respect to any of the Collateral." Conversely, section 11.7 of the proposed loan agreement would preserve Continental's right to seek the equitable remedy of marshaling for its own benefit. These contrasting provisions obviously violate the maxim, that one who seeks equity must do equity. But more fundamentally, equitable principles like marshaling have potential application to every secured indebtedness. While the debtor may seek authority to waive its own rights, it cannot waive the marshaling rights of parties who have not consented and may not even have received notice of the debtor's motion. * * *

4. The debtor proposes an inappropriate modification of statutory rights and obligations in bankruptcy.

The debtor and its secured creditor do not constitute a legislature. Thus, they have no right to implement a private agreement that effectively changes the bankruptcy law with regard to the statutory rights of third parties. In three important respects, Colad and Continental have proposed terms that would impermissibly modify the laws and rules of bankruptcy.

First, the proposed order would prohibit any surcharge of collateral under section 506(c) of the Bankruptcy Code. This section provides that a trustee "may recover from property securing an allowed secured claim the reasonable, necessary costs and expenses of preserving, or disposing of, such property to the extent of any benefit to the holder of such claim." * * * This court can discern no basis to allow a secured creditor to ignore its application.

Second, to the detriment of any future trustee, the proposed order would change the procedural requirements for stay relief. Section 362(d) of the Bankruptcy Code provides that the court may grant relief from the automatic stay "[o]n request of a party in interest and after notice and a hearing." Instead, the proposed order would create a default procedure, whereby the stay would automatically lift upon a failure by any interested party to demand a hearing within five business days following notice of an event of default. To the extent that the debtor and creditors' committee consent, this court would approve such a procedure for purposes of notice to the consenting parties. However, the court will not sanction a waiver of the controlling standard for a hearing on notice to any trustee that may hereafter be appointed.

Third, the proposed order would repudiate the provisions of 11 U.S.C. § 546(a), which sets time limitations for commencement of an action to enforce the avoiding powers of sections 544, 545, 547, 548, and 553 of the Bankruptcy Code. Pursuant to section 546(a), unless a case is sooner closed or dismissed, the trustee may commence any avoidance action within the latter of 2 years after the entry of an order for relief, or one year after the appointment or election of a first trustee within the period of two years after entry of an order for relief. Instead, paragraph 26 of the proposed order would more severely limit the commencement of an avoidance action. For example, it would provide that upon conversion of the case to chapter 7, the trustee would be compelled to commence any avoidance action within the earlier of sixty days after appointment or thirty days after delivery of various documentation. Bankruptcy Rule 9006 allows an enlargement or reduction of many of the time limits in the Bankruptcy Rules. However, section 546(a) is a statute, not a rule. Consequently, this court lacks authority to approve the shorter time limits that Continental would impose.

5. The proposed order includes a finding of good faith that the parties have yet to establish on the record.

Section 364(e) of the Bankruptcy Code provides generally that a reversal or modification on appeal of an order authorizing secured debt "does not affect the validity of any debt so incurred, or any priority or lien so granted, to an entity that extended such credit in good faith ...." For this obvious reason, the debtor has proposed an order which includes a finding that Continental is extending credit in good faith. At the hearing on this motion, the debtor offered only one witness and his statements about good faith were conclusory. Moreover, the order's other defects cause uncertainty about intent, particularly with respect to any attempt to discourage competitive bidding. Any finding of good faith is more appropriately made with the benefit of testimony and argument after a reversal or modification on appeal. This is not to say that the debtor would not be able to establish good faith at a future hearing. At this time, however, the court simply lacks an adequate basis to reach any conclusion about Continental's good faith.

Conclusion

For the reasons stated above, this court will not approve the form of the debtor's proposed order. Nonetheless, the court would sign an appropriate order authorizing a post-petition loan that avoids the various defects identified herein. With hope that the parties will negotiate the necessary changes, I will continue the interim financing authorization until further order of the court.

So ordered.

In re Kmart Corporation
United States Court of Appeals, Seventh Circuit, 2004
359 F.3d 866

EASTERBROOK, Circuit Judge.

On the first day of its bankruptcy, Kmart sought permission to pay immediately, and in full, the pre-petition claims of all "critical vendors." * * * The theory behind the request is that some suppliers may be unwilling to do business with a customer that is behind in payment, and, if it cannot obtain the merchandise that its own customers have come to expect, a firm such as Kmart may be unable to carry on, injuring all of its creditors. Full payment to critical vendors thus could in principle make even the disfavored creditors better off: they may not be paid in full, but they will receive a greater portion of their claims than they would if the critical vendors cut off supplies and the business shut down. Putting the proposition in this way implies, however, that the debtor must *prove,* and not just allege, two things: that, but for immediate full payment, vendors *would* cease dealing; and that the business will gain enough from continued transactions with the favored vendors to provide some residual benefit to the remaining, disfavored creditors, or at least leave them no worse off.

Bankruptcy Judge Sonderby entered a critical-vendors order just as Kmart proposed it, without notifying any disfavored creditors, without receiving any pertinent evidence (the record contains only some sketchy representations by counsel plus unhelpful testimony by Kmart's CEO, who could not speak for the vendors), and without making any finding of fact that the disfavored creditors would gain or come out even. The bankruptcy court's order declared that the relief

Kmart requested—open-ended permission to pay any debt to any vendor it deemed "critical" in the exercise of unilateral discretion, provided that the vendor agreed to furnish goods on "customary trade terms" for the next two years—was "in the best interests of the Debtors, their estates and their creditors". * * *

Kmart used its authority to pay in full the pre-petition debts to 2,330 suppliers, which collectively received about $300 million. This came from the $2 billion in new credit (debtor-in-possession or DIP financing) that the bankruptcy judge authorized, granting the lenders super-priority in post-petition assets and revenues. Another 2,000 or so vendors were not deemed "critical" and were not paid. They and 43,000 additional unsecured creditors eventually received about 10¢ on the dollar, mostly in stock of the reorganized Kmart. * * *

* * * Section 105(a) allows a bankruptcy court to "issue any order, process, or judgment that is necessary or appropriate to carry out the provisions of" the Code. This does not create discretion to set aside the Code's rules about priority and distribution; the power conferred by § 105(a) is one to implement rather than override. Every circuit that has considered the question has held that this statute does not allow a bankruptcy judge to authorize full payment of any unsecured debt, unless all unsecured creditors in the class are paid in full. We agree with this view of § 105. * * *

A "doctrine of necessity" is just a fancy name for a power to depart from the Code. Although courts in the days before bankruptcy law was codified wielded power to reorder priorities and pay particular creditors in the name of "necessity"[,] today it is the Code rather than the norms of nineteenth century railroad reorganizations that must prevail. * * *

So does the Code contain any grant of authority for debtors to prefer some vendors over others? Many sections require equal treatment or specify the details of priority when assets are insufficient to satisfy all claims. E.g., 11 U.S.C. §§ 507, 1122(a), 1123(a)(4). Appellants rely on 11 U.S.C. §§ 363(b), 364(b), and 503 as sources of authority for unequal treatment. Section 364(b) * * * has nothing to say about how the [borrowed] money will be disbursed or about priorities among creditors. * * * Section 503, which deals with administrative expenses, likewise is irrelevant. Pre-filing debts are not administrative expenses; they are the antithesis of administrative expenses. * * *

That leaves § 363(b)(1): "The trustee [or debtor in possession], after notice and a hearing, may use, sell, or lease, other than in the ordinary course of business, property of the estate." This is more promising, for satisfaction of a pre-petition debt in order to keep "critical" supplies flowing is a use of property other than in the ordinary course of administering an estate in bankruptcy. * * * We need not decide whether § 363(b)(1) could support payment of some pre-petition debts, because *this* order was unsound no matter how one reads § 363(b)(1).

The foundation of a critical-vendors order is the belief that vendors not paid for prior deliveries will refuse to make new ones. * * *

Some supposedly critical vendors will continue to do business with the debtor because they must. They may, for example, have long term contracts, and the automatic stay prevents these vendors from walking away as long as the debtor pays for new deliveries. See 11 U.S.C. § 362. Fleming Companies, which received the largest critical-vendors payment because it sold Kmart between $70 million and $100 million of groceries and related goods weekly, was one of these. No matter how much Fleming would have liked to dump Kmart, it had no right to do so. It was unnecessary to compensate Fleming for continuing to make deliveries that it was legally required to make. Nor was Fleming likely to walk away even if it had a legal right to do so. Each new delivery produced a profit; as long as Kmart continued to pay for new product, why would any vendor drop the account? That would be a self-inflicted wound. To abjure new profits because of old debts would be to commit the sunk-cost fallacy; well-managed businesses are unlikely to do this. Firms that disdain current profits because of old losses are unlikely to stay in business. They might as well burn money or drop it into the ocean. Again Fleming illustrates the point. When Kmart stopped buying its products after the contract expired, Fleming collapsed (Kmart had accounted for more than 50% of its business) and filed its own bankruptcy petition. Fleming was hardly likely to have quit selling of its own volition, only to expire the sooner.

Doubtless many suppliers fear the prospect of throwing good money after bad. It therefore may be vital to assure them that a debtor will pay for new deliveries on a current basis. Providing that assurance need not, however, entail payment for pre-petition transactions. Kmart could have paid cash or its equivalent. (Kmart's CEO told the bankruptcy judge that COD arrangements were not part of Kmart's business plan, as if a litigant's druthers could override the rights of third parties.) Cash on the barrelhead was not the most convenient way, however. Kmart secured a $2 billion line of credit when it entered bankruptcy. Some of that credit could have been used to assure vendors that payment would be forthcoming for all post-petition transactions. The easiest way to do that would have been to put some of the $2 billion behind a standby letter of credit on which the bankruptcy judge could authorize unpaid vendors to draw. * * * If lenders are unwilling to issue such a letter of credit (or if they insist on a letter's short duration), that would be a compelling market signal that reorganization is a poor prospect and that the debtor should be liquidated post haste.

Yet the bankruptcy court did not explore the possibility of using a letter of credit to assure vendors of payment. The court did not find that any firm would have ceased doing business with Kmart if not paid for pre-petition deliveries, and the scant record would not have supported such a finding had one been made. The court did not find that discrimination among unsecured creditors was the only way to facilitate a reorganization. It did not find that the disfavored creditors were at least as well off as they would have been had the critical-vendors order not been entered. * * * Even if § 362(b)(1) allows critical-vendors orders in principle, preferential payments to a class of creditors are proper only if the record shows the prospect of benefit to the other creditors. This record does not, so the critical-vendors order cannot stand.

Affirmed.

PART III

TURNING THE BUSINESS AROUND

Chapter 5

Turning the Debtor Around —The Business Issues[1]

A. INTRODUCTION

Two critical aspects of the process of making a troubled business profitable again involve (1) solving the operational problems and (2) restructuring the debt and equity of the business. *Turnaround* is used to mean the process of solving the operational problems of a business. *Restructuring* is the process of developing a financial structure that will provide a basis for turnaround.

A turnaround involves improving the position of the business as a low-cost provider of increasingly differentiated products and services and nurturing a competent organization with industry-oriented technical expertise and a general sense of fair play in dealing with employees, creditors, suppliers, shareholders and customers. A restructuring involves reducing the business's debts—and therefore the periodic debt service payments that the business must make—so that the business's cash flow is sufficient not only to meet those payments but also to provide value to its owners.

Some troubled businesses have only operational problems. For such a business, a turnaround is sufficient without restructuring its debt and equity. It may be able to regain profitability by improving cost margins through reduction of manufacturing costs and elimination of unprofitable products. Other troubled businesses are operating very well, but are having difficulty making the high debt payments required by their over-leveraged capital structure. Such businesses may not need a turnaround, but only a restructuring of their debt and equity. Often this is accomplished by issuing stock or other equity interests to the creditors in exchange for cancellation of much of the debt.

---

1. Portions of this Chapter are adapted from Newton, BANKRUPTCY & INSOLVENCY ACCOUNTING: PRACTICE AND PROCEDURE (6th ed. 2000), with permission of John Wiley & Sons.

However, the majority of troubled businesses require attention to operating problems as well as changes to their financial structure. This chapter focuses on the turnaround process. The restructuring process is described in the several chapters that make up Part V of this book, including chapter 12 on determining the value of the business.

To effectively represent the debtor, a creditor, a shareholder, or a creditors' or equity holders' committee, the attorney must have some understanding of what caused the business to fail, of methods of detecting when a business is headed for trouble, and of what types of actions need to be taken to turn the business around. The attorney must also have some understanding of how the decision is made to reorganize or, on the other hand, to liquidate the business. In making or evaluating the decision as to what course of action to take, the parties involved must clearly understand the difference between solvency of a business and viability of a business.

B. CAUSES OF BUSINESS FAILURE

The causes of business failure are divisible into four categories: economic conditions (including characteristics of the economic system), inside underlying causes, outside influences, and fraud.

1. Economic Conditions

One factor often listed as the cause of business failures is a contraction of economic activity. For example the recessions (most of which were very mild) of 1948-49, 1953-54, 1957-58, 1960-1961, 1969-70, 1974-75, 1980, 1981-82, 1989-91, and 2000-01 all resulted in an increase in the number of business failures or the dollar amount of such failures. The number of bankruptcy petitions filed in 1992-1993 following the extended recession of 1991-92 almost reached the level of one million petitions. During the last half of 1993 the rate of petition filings began to decline, and the number of petitions filed during the year ending December 31, 1994, had dropped to less than 833,000. The rate of petition filings then began to increase again, reaching a new high of 1.4 million petitions in 1998. After declines in 1999 and 2000, total filings increased to almost 1.5 million in 2001, almost 1.58 million in 2002, and 1.66 million in 2003. After a slight decline in 2004, total filings reached approximately 2.0 million in 2005.

The increases during the 1990s and through 2005 were largely due to increased consumer filings. The surge of petitions in 2005, in particular, was due to consumer petitions that were filed prior to October 17, 2005, in order to avoid application of the 2005 BAPCPA, which is effective for most purposes with respect to cases filed on or after that date. Business petitions during this time period decreased, dropping to less than 2 percent of the total filings from 15 percent of the total filings in the 1980s. While the number of business filings remained rather low, the number of public company filings increased significantly during and after 2000, as did the total declared debt and asset values of the public company filings. The declared assets and the number of filings for public companies for years 2000-2004 were as follows:

Year	Number	Declared Assets (billions)
2000	176	$ 95
2001	257	258
2002	195	382
2003	143	97
2004	92	48

In periods of expansion the number of petitions filed will often decline; however, during the mid-1980s the number of petitions (both business and nonbusiness) increased even though the economy was not in recession. Problems in the agricultural, oil, and financial sectors contributed significantly to the large number of failures during this period. The large failures in the late 1990s and the first years of the new millennium were in the steel, energy, telecommunications, airline, and auto supplier sectors. Among the largest chapter 11 filings are the following:

Company	Declared Assets (billions)	Date Filed
WorldCom, Inc.	$103.9	7/21/2002
Enron Corp.	63.4	12/02/2001
Conseco	61.4	12/18/2002
Texaco	35.9	4/12/1987
Financial Corp. of America	33.6	9/09/1988
Global Crossing, Ltd.	30.2	1/28/2002
Pacific Gas & Electric	29.7	4/06/2001
Calpine Corp.	26.6	12/20/2005
United Airlines	25.2	12/09/2002
Adelphia Communications	21.5	6/25/2002
MCorp	20.2	3/31/1989
Mirant Corp.	19.4	7/14/2003

(Source: bankruptcydata.com)

The economic structure in the free enterprise system acts as a cause of failure for many businesses. One characteristic of the American economic system is freedom of enterprise, meaning the absolute right of individuals to engage in most businesses regardless of their personal qualifications. This permits the entry of people who lack experience and training in their chosen business and who are thus more susceptible to failure. Recall Ernestine Entrepreneur (from Problem 1-6). She apparently was well trained and qualified to run her PostHaste store, but not a frozen yogurt shop. Her lack of experience in making good-tasting frozen yogurt and in selecting a good location for such a business made it highly likely that the business would fail. Presumably it would be possible to have a government board screen out inexperienced entrepreneurs and prohibit them from opening businesses, but that has not ordinarily been our society's approach.

Analogous to intense competition is the challenge offered by business changes and improvements and by shifts in public demand. Companies that fail in the transition to modern methods of production and distribution, or that are unable to adapt to new consumer demands, must ultimately go out of business.

Business fluctuations are another characteristic of a free economic system. Adverse periods marked by maladjustment between production and consumption, significant unemployment, decline in sales, falling prices, and other disturbing factors will have some effect on the number of business failures, as was noted above. However, some suggest that a temporary lull in business activities is not a fundamental cause of business failures, although it may accelerate the movement of many weak businesses toward their inevitable failure.

The freedom of action characteristic of our society may result in actions by third persons that prove detrimental to a business firm. The demands of labor unions and organized actions by community and other special interest groups have in recent years contributed to the failure of some businesses. Recall that at least some of the losses from Foam Corporation's eastern foam plants are due to high unionized labor costs.

2. Internal Conditions

Internal causes of failure are those that could have been prevented by some action within the business, and often result from past mistakes or the failure of management to take action when it was needed. Management is primarily responsible for business difficulties resulting from internal factors.

a. Overextension of Credit

One inside cause of failure is the tendency of businesses to overextend credit to their customers and subsequently to become unable to collect from their account debtors in time to pay their own liabilities.

The obvious way to prevent such failures is for a business to investigate the creditworthiness of its customers more carefully, and possibly restrict sales made on account. Yet many businesses feel their sales volume would suffer as a result, perhaps causing more harm than the credit losses that would be avoided. However, one unusual, substantial default by a customer could cause serious financial trouble for the firm that might have been avoided by a more careful credit policy. Management's decision to grant credit too freely means risking the company's own financial stability. Unusual credit losses may so greatly weaken the firm's financial structure that it is no longer able to continue operation.

b. Inefficient Management

Businesses often fail because of management's lack of training, experience, ability, adaptation, or initiative. Indications of probable failure of an enterprise include management's inadequacy in any of the major functions of business, and lack of knowledge or experience in the particular line of business being pursued. Inefficient management has been found to be the cause of the majority of business failures. Refer to the previous example of Ernestine Entrepreneur's ill-fated foray into the frozen yogurt business.

A common situation involves managers who are experts in their particular fields, such as engineering, but lack simple tools necessary to control their finances or administer a going concern. In such cases it is often found that they fail to restrain salaries or benefits and are unable to maintain rapport with their accounting staff. Effective and efficient management is partially dependent upon adequate accounting records that will reveal inefficiencies and act as a guide in formulating policies. Several of the accounting and financial advisory firms actively involved in bankruptcy audits have estimated that at least 90 percent of the financially troubled businesses they examine have very inadequate accounting records. Although poor accounting information or records may not be the underlying cause of failure, their inadequacy does prevent the business from taking corrective action in many cases.

Inefficient management is often evidenced by its inability to avoid conditions that have resulted in the following:

Inadequate Sales This may be a result of poor location, an incompetent sales organization, poor promotion, or an inferior product or service.

Improper Pricing In relation to its costs the firm is charging too low a price, accepting either a loss on the item or very little profit. Improper pricing often results because there is no real understanding of the costs to make the products that are sold.

Inadequate Handling of Receivables and Payables Billings for product sold or services rendered should not be delayed. Every day that a bill is delayed in going out to the customer is a day that payment of the account receivable is likely to be delayed. Every dollar needed to run the business that does not come in from customers must be borrowed, often at a high interest rate. Delayed billing thus costs the business interest on the amount of the bill for the period of the delay; proper billing practices minimize interest costs. Proper handling of accounts payable may also reduce interest costs.

The business may be able to obtain a large discount for paying its accounts payable by a particular time. For example, if Foam Corporation buys chemicals from ChemCo on typical "2/10 net 30" terms, Foam Corporation will be entitled to a 2% discount if it pays for the goods within ten days of billing and, in any event, it is obligated to pay for the goods within thirty days. If Foam Corporation does not pay within ten days, it will be giving up a 2% discount in order to obtain an additional twenty days to pay. This is very expensive credit, amounting to more than 36% interest per year, even without compounding.

The failure to take large discounts and the failure to pay crucial creditors on time can create problems that could have been avoided with careful planning as to the timing of payment and selection of the creditor to be paid.

Excessive Overhead Expenses and Operating Costs, and Excessive Interest Charges on Long-Term Debt   All these act as fixed charges against revenue, rather than varying with the volume of goods produced. This means that the firm's break-even point is high: it must sell a relatively large volume of goods before it begins earning profit.

Overinvestment in Fixed Assets and Inventories   Both types of investment tie up cash or other funds so that they are no longer available to management for meeting other obligations; to the extent the money used to invest in fixed assets and large inventories is borrowed, interest will have to be paid.

As a company expands there is a need for greater investment in fixed assets. It becomes profitable for the company at the current production level to reduce labor costs by investing in additional equipment. If the company can continue to operate at this capacity, profits will continue; however, if production drops significantly the company is in a difficult position. Fixed assets are not used fully. As a result the level of production and sales may not generate enough cash to make the interest and principal payments on the debt that was incurred to purchase the fixed assets, or to replace the cash that was used and that is now needed for other purposes. If the reduction in production is not temporary, action must be taken very quickly to sell off excess fixed assets; it may be necessary to eliminate unprofitable divisions of the business and dispose of their assets. Under some conditions, it may be best to liquidate the entire business. The objective thus becomes to have the optimum level of investment and maximum utilization of the available capacity.

Carrying a large amount of inventories not only ties up capital unnecessarily; it also results in excessive storage costs, such as warehouse rent and insurance coverage, and the risk of spoilage or obsolescence. These types of costs add no value to the product being manufactured or held for sale. Under these conditions it becomes difficult for the business to compete with other firms (foreign and domestic) that use more efficient inventory practices and thus have lower costs.

Insufficient Working Capital, Including a Weak Cash Position   Working capital is the difference between the total current assets (mostly made up of cash and cash equivalents, inventory, and accounts receivable) and the total current liabilities (debts due within a year). Inadequate working capital is often the result of excessive current debt from acquisition of fixed assets through the use of short-term credit; overexpansion of the business without providing for adequate working capital; or deficient banking facilities, resulting in high cost of borrowing current funds.

As a business expands it may need to have increased production facilities (fixed assets) and increased inventories to serve the additional customers and volume of sales. It will also need to have more funds tied up in accounts receivables; as sales increase, its customers will owe it more and more for goods recently delivered on credit. If the business cannot finance the build up of fixed assets, inventories, and accounts receivable out of profits or other sources of cash, the business may borrow the money on a short term basis. This will result in high current liabilities and thus a low amount of working capital (the difference between current assets and current liabilities). With large debts due short term, any deviation from the projected sales and projected cash inflows may leave the business unable to pay its debts.

An unwise dividend policy may also use up funds that are needed for operating the business. Whatever its cause, a weak working capital position, if not corrected, will eventually cause a delay in the firm's payment of debt.

Unbalanced Capital Structure (Unfavorable Ratio of Debt to Equity) If the amount of bonds or similar long-term liabilities is relatively high, fixed charges against income will be large. Nevertheless, this is advantageous when the firm is earning a healthy profit and the residual (after interest charges) accrues to the owners. Lenders demand a lower rate of return than equity owners because they assume less risk. Thus, by borrowing much of the money needed to create or to buy an enterprise rather than raising the money by selling stock, the owners increase their return, if all goes well. This concept is called "leverage."

For example, suppose it will cost $1 million to assemble the assets and begin the operation of a business. Suppose the projected profits from operation of the business are $150,000 per year, 15% per year on the $1 million of assets. Suppose Owen Owner (the one who is planning to start the business) has $200,000 and thus needs to raise another $800,000 to start the business. Big Insurance Co. may be willing to lend the new business $800,000 at 10% annual interest. Eight other entrepreneurs may each be willing to contribute $100,000 to the new business in exchange for 10% ownership of the business for each. Note that Owen will make a higher return on his $200,000 if the business borrows the money from Big Insurance than if he sells equity interests to the other entrepreneurs, *assuming the projections are correct*. If the business borrows the money, it will pay Big Insurance $80,000 per year, leaving $70,000 for Owen to enjoy in earnings after interest payments. Thus, on his $200,000 investment, Owen will make $70,000 per year, for a 35% return per year. If the business had instead sold equity interests to the other entrepreneurs, Owen would have had a 20% ownership interest in a business with no debt, and he would have been entitled to 20% of the $150,000 in profits from operations each year, or $30,000. Thus he (along with the other entrepreneurs) would have made a 15% return on his investment. By causing the business to borrow the money from Big Insurance, Owen creates "leverage," and increases his return.

Suppose, however, that all does not go well; due to poor management, a recession, or some other reason the profits from operations are only $10,000 for the year. Now, after the business pays the $80,000 in interest to Big Insurance Co. (assuming it has the cash to pay it, which it may not have), the business will have lost $70,000 for the year, more than a third of its net worth. Owen will have lost a third of his investment, and the business will be only two years away from insolvency unless its performance improves. Note that if the business had been financed by selling equity interests to the other entrepreneurs, the business would still have made a profit (although not a large one), and so would Owen. Thus leverage provides greater returns to equityholders when things go well, but it increases their losses and may threaten the business with financial distress when things do not go as planned.

Many leveraged buyouts (LBOs) have ended in failure a few years after the buyouts were completed; often the causes of failure were insufficient working capital and unbalanced capital structure. In an LBO, much of the money used to buy the company is borrowed; often, in one way or another, the purchased company itself ends up being responsible for the debts incurred by the purchaser in purchasing it. The purchased company receives little or nothing of value as a result of being purchased, but its debts are greatly increased. After an LBO, companies thus often have very little capital and limited capacity to borrow for working capital needs. Thus, if sales decrease due to unfavorable economic conditions, if a competitor introduces a new product that competes favorably with the LBO company, or if other developments require extra working capital, the LBO company may end up in chapter 11, unable to fund its large debt payments. For example in the case of Revco (a Midwest retail drug store chain), the company's debt was increased from less than $700 million to over $1.5 billion in a leveraged buyout, leaving the company with very little equity. The book value of Revco's assets was almost doubled as a result of the leveraged buyout, because the buyout was treated as a purchase, which allowed the assets to be revalued on Revco's balance sheet. Even with the increased book value of the assets, total stockholders' equity after the leveraged buyout was less than $25 million. The leveraged buyout was completed at the end of 1986; a year and a half later, Revco filed a chapter 11 petition.

Inadequate Insurance Coverage   If a business is not adequately compensated for such losses as fire and theft, it might very well be forced to close its doors.

Inadequate Accounting Methods and Records Without adequate accounting methods and records, management will not have the information it needs to identify problem areas and take preventative action.

The existence of any one of these factors may be an indication of potential trouble due to management's inability or inefficiency.

c. Insufficient Capital

As previously mentioned, insufficient capital may be thought to be an inside cause of business failures. When business conditions are adverse and there is insufficient capital, the firm may be unable to pay operating costs and credit obligations as they mature. Many business that expand too rapidly end up with a shortage of capital for both operating purposes and expansion. Cash needed to fund operations is used instead to fund new store openings, causing existing operations to suffer.

3. Outside Influences

Government actions—for example, the enactment of new tax legislation, lowering or elimination of tariffs, wage and hour laws, court decisions, price regulations, and the like—occasionally result in the failure of some companies. As an example, several small manufacturers have been forced out of business because they were unable to meet the pollution standards established by the federal government.

The causes of trouble occasionally may be entirely beyond the control of the business. Some of these causes are known as "acts of God" and this category is found in all societies regardless of their particular economic system. Included are such things as fires, earthquakes, explosions, floods, tornadoes, and hurricanes, all of which may certainly cause the downfall of some businesses. Thus the limits within which a business must function prove to be an important determinant of its success. The challenge to management is to meet and adapt to changing conditions in such a manner as to survive adversity. A company cannot change the environment; but it might ultimately be able to use it to its benefit.

Outside influences that are blamed for business failure are often not the fundamental cause of the failure. Management of troubled entities may blame threatened or actual lawsuits, involuntary bankruptcy court petitions, levies, and setoffs by lending institutions; however, these actions are usually in response to management's failure to deal with the true causes of financial difficulty. For example, banks may set off money in their possession against past-due claims, but banks normally do not take such action unless a business is very weak financially. Thus, creditor actions such as set off, foreclosure, or eviction may be the precipitating cause of a bankruptcy petition but are typically not the underlying cause of the financial difficulty.

4. Fraud and Dishonesty

Occasionally businesses fail as the result of fraud and dishonesty. For example, the principal in the business may falsify financial statements so as to induce lenders and sellers to extend credit to the business, credit that the business in fact has no ability to repay. Or the principal may embezzle funds to the extent that the business is unable to repay its debts. Dun & Bradstreet has estimated that only three to five percent of the business failures in recent years were caused by fraud.[2] However, the number of bankruptcy filings involving fraud increased significantly in the last fifteen years, as evidenced by such large bankruptcies as WorldCom, Enron, and Adelphia Communications.

The underlying cause of fraud is a lack of values by those perpetrating the fraudulent acts. However, certain factors have contributed to the increase, including the desire of many credit grantors to maintain their sales volume at any cost, the neglect of creditors to investigate bankruptcy cases, and the belief of dishonest persons that they can take advantage of the benefits of the bankruptcy process without fear of prosecution.

C. STAGES OF FINANCIAL FAILURE

The general characteristics of firms that are failing include lower sales, slower growth in sales, poorer cash flow and net income positions, and large increases in debt levels. These factors combine to cause marked deterioration in the firm's solvency position. Unsuccessful firms also experience higher major operating costs, especially overhead costs that are higher than the average for similar successful firms. As the firm suffers losses, its asset size is reduced. Assets are not replaced as often as they were during more prosperous times, and this with the cumulative losses further reduces the prospects for profitable operations.

The course of financial failure may be divided into four distinct phases or stages: incubation, cash shortage, financial insolvency, and total insolvency.[3] The time period associated with each stage (and in some cases even the order) will differ depending on many factors.

1. Period of Incubation

A business does not suddenly or unexpectedly become insolvent. Any business concern having financial difficulty will pass through several transitional stages before it reaches the point where it is necessary to file a bankruptcy petition. An ailing business has been compared with an individual suffering at the start from a minor ailment, such as a common cold, which if not remedied, in due time could develop into a serious disease like pneumonia and result in death. During the period of incubation one or even a number of unfavorable conditions can be quietly developing without being recognizable immediately by outsiders or even by management. For example, a company whose major source of revenue came from steel fabrication work in connection with highway construction failed to take action two years previously, when it was obvious that interstate highway construction would be reduced in the company's market area. As a result the company was forced to file a bankruptcy petition. Some of the types of developments that may be occurring in the incubation period are listed below:

---

2.   Dun & Bradstreet, Inc., BUSINESS FAILURE RECORD 12 (1988 through 1994 editions).

3.   Helene M. A. Ramanauskas, *How Close to Bankruptcy Are You?*, 28 WOMAN CPA 3 (October 1966).

- Change in product demand.
- Continuing increase in overhead costs.
- Obsolete production methods (failure to modernize production facilities).
- Increase in competition.
- Incompetent managers in key positions.
- Acquisition of unprofitable subsidiaries.
- Overexpansion without adequate working capital.
- Incompetent credit and collection department.
- Lack of adequate banking facilities.

It is often in the incubation stage that an economic loss occurs, in that the return realized on assets falls below the firm's normal rate of return. It is at this stage of failure that management should give careful consideration to the cause. If the cause cannot be corrected, management must look for alternatives. It is best for the company if the problem is detected at this stage, for several reasons. First, replanning is much more effective if initiated at this time. Second, the actions required to correct the causes of failure are not nearly so drastic as those required at later stages. Third, the public confidence is less likely to be impaired if corrective action is taken at this stage.

It is possible that, under certain conditions, the economic loss may not occur until the enterprise is in the second stage, experiencing a shortage of cash.

2. Cash Shortage

The business for the first time is unable to meet its current obligations and is in urgent need of cash, although it might have a comfortable excess of physical assets over liabilities and a satisfactory earning record. The problem is that the assets are not sufficiently liquid and the necessary capital is tied up in receivables and inventories. The business's net worth and earning record probably may enable it to meet the urgent need for cash by borrowing the needed funds. However, if the managers do not correct the underlying problems, the business will proceed on to the next stage of financial failure.

3. Financial Insolvency

In this third stage, the business is unable to procure through customary channels the funds required to meet its maturing and overdue obligations. Management will have to resort to more drastic measures such as calling in a business or financial specialist, appointing a creditors' committee, or resorting to new financing techniques. However, there still exists, in some cases, a good possibility for survival and for future growth if substantial infusions of new money and financing can be obtained, and if the underlying causes of the financial difficulties are addressed.

4. Total Insolvency

At this point the business can no longer avoid the public confession of failure, and the management's attempts to secure additional funds by financing generally prove unsuccessful. Total liabilities typically exceed the value of the firm's assets. The business's only alternatives to immediate liquidation are to attempt an out of court workout or to file a chapter 11 petition. Unfortunately, businesses that wait this long to take one of those steps often have deteriorated past the point of no return and are unable to reorganize.

In addition to the stages listed above, broad situations that the management faces may be described as follows:

- Declining business — decreasing market share, operating and gross margins, market leadership, product quality, etc.
- Substantial or continuing losses — but survival not threatened.
- Danger of failure — the company may already be in chapter 11 or on the verge of filing.

The situation that the business is in will impact the nature, as well the speed, of actions that are needed to stabilize the business and begin the process of turning the business around. For example if the business is determined to be at the state of "danger of failure", unless immediate action is taken, liquidation may be the only alternative.

Problem 5-1

> Refer to the balance sheet, statement of operations, and statement of cash flows of Foam Corporation presented in Chapter Two. What are the causes of Foam Corporation's financial difficulty? In which stage of financial difficulty is Foam Corporation? Explain why Foam Corporation may have waited too long to take corrective action.

D. DETECTION OF FAILURE TENDENCIES

1. Introduction

Effective management cannot wait until the enterprise experiences total insolvency to take action, since at this final stage the remedies available are rather restricted. There are several tools that may be used to diagnose business failures, but they will not necessarily reveal the cause of failure. It is the cause that must be determined and corrected; it is not enough just to correct the symptoms. For example, a constantly inadequate cash position is an indication that financial problems are developing, but the problem is not solved by management's borrowing additional funds without determining the real cause for the shortage. However, if the cause of the shortage is ascertained and corrected, management can then raise the necessary cash and be reasonably certain that the future cash inflow will not be interrupted in such a manner as to create a similar problem.

External and internal methods may be used to detect failure tendencies. The most common sources of external data are trade reports and statistics and economic indicators published by the federal government and by private organizations.

2. Trend Analysis

Historical data　One of the most frequently used methods of examining data from within the firm is an analysis of the financial statements over a period of years so that trends may be noted. Using a certain period as base, a trend analysis of the important accounts is developed on a monthly or quarterly basis. The balance sheet trends will generally reveal the following failure tendencies:

- Weakened cash position
- Insufficient working capital
- Overinvestment in receivables or inventories
- Overexpansion in fixed assets
- Increasing bank loans and other current liabilities
- Excessive funded debt and fixed liabilities
- Undercapitalization
- Subordination of loans to banks and creditors

The operating account changes that may disclose additional tendencies are as follows:

- Declining sales
- Increasing operating costs and overhead
- Excessive interest and other fixed expenses
- Excessive dividends and withdrawals compared to earning records
- Declining net profits and lower return on invested capital
- Increased sales with reduced mark-ups

Actual versus forecast　An effective way to evaluate the performance of management is to compare actual results with managements' projections. Some aspects of the effectiveness of a corporation's management, based on publicly available information, can be evaluated by examining the plans described by the chief executive officer in management's letter accompanying the annual report, and comparing them with the actions that were subsequently taken. A trend may become evident, indicating that very few of management's plans were in fact implemented.

Among the comparisons that might be helpful are:

- Actual compared to standard cost per unit
- Actual compared to planned production costs
- Actual compared to planned fixed manufacturing costs
- Actual compared to budgeted gross margins[4]
- Actual compared to planned sales volume
- Actual compared to budgeted research and development costs

Comparisons over several years may reveal factors that will help identify the underlying cause of the company's financial problems.

4.　Gross margin is computed by subtracting the cost of the goods sold from the amount of sales.

Comparison with industry   A comparison of a company's operating results, financial condition, ratios, and other characteristics with those of companies of similar size in the same industry may indicate problem areas. Industry data are available from several sources including trade associations for the industry in which the debtor operates.

3. Analysis of Accounting Measures

In conjunction with the trend analysis, certain ratios or accounting measures are of benefit in indicating financial strength. The current ratio and other liquidity ratios are used to portray the firm's ability to meet current obligations. The current ratio is current assets divided by current liabilities. Current assets will be the sources of cash from which current liabilities will have to be paid. A current ratio of 2:1 is often considered good; a ratio of less than 1:1 would indicate a likely inability to pay current liabilities as they mature.

Efficiency in asset utilization is often determined by asset turnover (total assets divided by sales), inventory turnover (cost of goods sold divided by inventory), and accounts receivable turnover (credit sales divided by accounts receivable). The higher the turnover, the better the performance, since management will be able to operate with a relatively small commitment of funds.

The soundness of the relationship between borrowed funds and equity capital is set forth by certain equity ratios. The ratios of long-term liabilities to "total equity" (the sum of long-term liabilities and owners' equity), and of owners' equity to "total equity" assist in appraising the ability of the business to survive times of stress and meet both its short-term and long-term obligations. There must be an adequate balance of debt and equity. When the interest of outsiders is increased by incurring more debt, there is an advantage to the owners—leverage—in that they get the benefit of a return on assets (after the payment of interest on the debt) furnished by others. However, there is in this advantage an increased risk. By analyzing the equity structure and the interest expense, insight can be gained as to the relative size of the cushion of ownership funds creditors can rely on to absorb losses from the business. These losses may be the result of unprofitable operations or simply due to a decrease in the value of the assets owned by the business.

Profitability measures which relate net income to total assets, net assets, net sales, or owners' equity assist in appraising the adequacy of sales and operating profit. An analysis of the various measures and relationships for a given year may be of limited value, but when a comparison is made with prior years, trends can be observed that may be meaningful.

In a model designed by Professor Edward L. Altman,[5] five basic ratios are used in predicting corporate bankruptcy. The five ratios, X_1 through X_5, selected from an original list of twenty-two considered for the model, are as follows:

---

5.   Altman, *Corporate Bankruptcy and Its Implications for Commercial Loan Evaluation*, 53 J. COMM'L BANK LENDING 10–19 (December 1970).

1. X_1 = Working capital(current assets - current liabilities)/Total assets.
2. X_2 = Retained earnings/Total assets.
3. X_3 = Earnings before interest and taxes/Total assets.
4. X_4 = Market value of equity/Book value of total debt.
5. X_5 = Sales/Total assets.

The model may be defined as follows (the result is called the "Z-score"):

$$Z = 1.2X_1 + 1.4X_2 + 3.3X_3 + .6X_4 + 1.0X_5$$

The values for X_1, X_2, X_3, X_4, and X_5 are calculated from the five ratios listed above. Firms that have a Z-score greater than 2.99 clearly lie in the nonbankrupt sector, while a Z-score less than 1.81 indicates likely future bankruptcy. A Z-score between 1.81 and 2.99 falls in a gray area of less certain prediction value, because of susceptibility to error classification. Further analysis by Altman suggests that the Z-value that best discriminates between the firms headed for bankruptcy and other firms is 2.675; however, some analysts prefer to use the 1.81 and 2.99 scores as the classification criteria where users have the greatest confidence in the predictive value of the Z-score, expressing less certainty about Z-scores between 1.81 and 2.99.

The fourth ratio used in Altman's model is the relationship of market value of equity to the book value of total debt. It is difficult to determine the market value of the equity of privately held companies; thus this model is designed for publicly held companies. Market value of equity for a publicly held company can be determined from the price at which its shares are exchanged on public markets, such as the New York Stock Exchange. The market value per share can be multiplied by the number of outstanding shares to determine total market value of equity. The market value of the equity, according to Altman, appears to be a more effective predictor of bankruptcy than the commonly used book value of net worth taken from the financial statements.

To calculate the Z-score for privately held companies, book value may be used; however, Altman's research suggests that if book value of equity is substituted for market value the coefficients should be changed.[6] Altman revised the model for private firms to the following:

$$Z' = .717X_1 + .847X_2 + 3.107X_3 + .420X_4 + X_5$$

Also the Z' score indicating likelihood of bankruptcy now has a value of 1.23 (as compared to 1.81 under the public company formula), while the Z' score indicating no bankruptcy is 2.9 (as compared to 2.99 under the public company formula). Thus there is a larger gray area under the private company formula.

Based on the results of his research, Altman suggested that the bankruptcy prediction model is accurately forecasts failure up to two years prior to bankruptcy and that the accuracy diminishes substantially as the lead time increases.

---

6. See Altman, Corporate Distress Prediction Models in a Turbulent Economic and Basel II Environment (September 2002) (available at http://pages.stern.nyu.edu/~ealtman/Corp-Distress.pdf).

4. Analysis of Management

Certain characteristics giving evidence of inefficient and ineffective management also serve as warning signals of potential trouble. Those concerned with the firm's viability should be on the alert if it is known that management lacks training or experience in basic business methods, such as interpreting financial data, managing funds, scheduling production and shipping, coordinating departmental activities, and any other management functions. In a common situation, a manager may be an expert in a technical field, such as designing products, but have little managerial ability for directing the activities of the business.

Indications that management is ineffective and that trouble may result include the presence of any of the following: inefficient and inadequate information systems, disregard for operating and financial data which are supplied, lack of interest in maintaining an adequate sales volume, large fixed charges resulting from excessive overhead and operating expenses or large debt in the capital structure, or illogical pricing schemes. Other conditions pointing to inefficient management certainly are possible, and all such factors should alert those interested to the possibility of later trouble.

5. Other Factors

The following events may also indicate to the accountant that financial difficulties are imminent:

- Factoring or financing receivables, if they are normally handled on an open account basis. (This may indicate that the business is running short on cash and thus needs to receive cash for its accounts receivable more quickly than in the past.)
- Compromise of the amount of accounts receivable for the purpose of receiving advance collections.
- Substitution of notes for open accounts payable.
- Allowing certain key creditors to obtain security interests in the assets.
- Inability of the firm to make timely deposits of trust funds such as employee withholding taxes.
- Death or departure of key personal.
- Unfavorable purchase commitments.
- Lack of realization of material research and development costs.
- Change in accounting methods by client, primarily designed to improve the financial statements.

Problem 5-2

Part A:

Refer to the financial statements of Foam Corporation in Chapter 2. Determine the Z′ score for Foam Corporation. (Because Foam corporation is a privately held company, the second equation should be used.) Book value of the equity is the difference between the total assets and total liabilities as shown in the financial statements. Note that in determining the ratios for Foam Corporation, most of them are negative. For example the current liabilities exceed current assets resulting in a negative value for working capital. The book value of the equity is also negative since the total liabilities of $19.5 million are greater than the total assets of $14.9 million.

Part B:

Assume that a plan has been developed and that the reorganized Foam Corporation will emerge from chapter 11 with the following financial characteristics and projections for the next year.

- Total assets, $10 million
- Projected sales (for the first year), $20 million
- Projected net income (for the first year) before interest and taxes, $3 million
- Working capital, $2 million
- Retained earnings, $0
- Total liabilities, $6 million

If the reorganized Foam Corporation emerges from chapter 11 with the above debt/equity relationships and operates according to these projections, what conclusion would you reach regarding the ability of the reorganized company to survive?

E. STAGES IN THE TURNAROUND PROCESS

In order to effectively represent the chapter 11 debtor or creditors' committee, it is important that the attorney have some understanding of the process that a turnaround professional will utilize to turn the business around. The process can be summarized in six stages.

1. Management Change

Studies suggest that in most turnaround situations, top management is replaced, and that in most successful turnarounds, top management is generally replaced with outsiders rather than insiders. In situations where top management is not replaced, or where support for new management is deemed necessary, a turnaround professional may be retained.

2. Situation Analysis

Stage 2 often begins with the turnaround leader making a preliminary assessment of the viability of the business. The turnaround specialist must determine if the "bleeding" can be stopped and if there are parts of the business that can serve as the core for a successful restructuring. This stage involves an assessment of the strengths and weaknesses of the business and an identification of the opportunities and threats (or difficulties) faced by the business from the environment in which the debtor operates including its competitors.

3. Design and Selection of Turnaround Strategy

While it is often necessary for the debtor to modify its goals and long-term objectives as the turnaround progresses, the major focal point is often on developing an operational strategy. The operational strategy might involve the development of a strategy focusing on increasing revenue, reducing operating costs, reduction or redeployment of assets or repositioning the business so it can compete more effectively. Often it is a combination of two or more of these strategies that is adopted. However, studies suggest that companies that focus first on getting their costs in line and then focus on increasing revenue have a greater chance of successfully turning their business around.

4. Emergency Action

In this stage the turnaround professional takes the actions necessary to enable the organization to survive. The more serious the problem, the quicker and more decisive the action must be. Action may be in the form of employee layoffs; selling one or more profitable parts of the business to obtain cash necessary to survival of the remaining parts; or other steps necessary to obtain cash needed to implement the chosen turnaround strategy. While the action may be quick and decisive, it is important that the turnaround professional help the debtor protect and develop the resources that will be needed for future profitability and growth. For example, in downsizing, the debtor would not want to lay off the engineers responsible for the development of the line of products around which the business is restructuring.

5. Business Restructuring

The business must be restructured so that profitability is enhanced through more effective and efficient management of current operations. For example, the focus is on improving all aspects of the business and includes, among many other items, improving liquidity, improving sales and marketing productivity and effectiveness, establishing on-going profit improvement programs, making low cost products and rendering services at reduced costs through design, and developing reward and compensation systems that reinforce the turnaround efforts and that are based on increasing shareholder value.

6. Return-to-Normal

The objective in this stage is to institutionalize an emphasis on profitability, return on equity, and the enhancement of economic value added, to seek out opportunities for profitable growth, and to build the competitive strengths needed to exploit such opportunities.

F. FACTORS DETERMINING THE SUCCESS OF THE BUSINESS TURNAROUND

Several factors will determine the extent to which the business can be turned around and again operate profitably.

1. Extent to Which Early Action Was Taken

It is difficult for the owners or officers of a troubled business to admit that they are having financial and operating problems. As a result, decisions to call a meeting of creditors or to file a chapter 11 petition often are postponed until the last minute. This delay benefits no one, including the debtor. There are several reasons why it is advisable to take action as soon as it becomes obvious that some type of action is necessary to overcome the burden created by too much debt and inadequate cash flows from operations. First, the debtor at this stage has a considerable asset base. Creditors are not hostile and many of the key employees are still with the company. Key employees often leave when they see unhealthy conditions developing; early corrective action may encourage them to stay. In addition, prompt action may make it possible for the debtor to maintain some of the goodwill that was developed during successful operating periods. While the filing of a bankruptcy petition may be the last alternative the debtor might consider, the decision to file should not be delayed when it becomes obvious some type of relief is necessary. Thus, for the reorganization to be successful, it is helpful if the asset base for future operations has not been eroded too deeply, if the debtor has reasonable relationships with creditors, and if employees have some loyalty to the company.

2. Quality of Management

If the creditors are going to accept a plan that involves terms other than a cash settlement, they must have adequate confidence in the key executives who will be running the company. This confidence is often absent if there have been no changes in management. Thus, it may be necessary to replace existing top management in order to get the plan approved.

As we noted in Chapter Four, actions of the debtor once the petition is filed are monitored by the creditors' committee, the U.S. trustee's office and, possibly, the court. If the creditors or other interested parties believe that new management is necessary to correct the problems that caused the adverse financial condition, they may press for a change in management or the appointment or election of a trustee. In a large number of bankruptcies, old management is replaced. In the larger cases management may be replaced with individuals that specialize in taking over troubled companies. These specialists often eliminate the unprofitable aspects of the company's operations, reduce overhead and find additional financing as part of the turnaround process. Once the plan has been confirmed, turnaround specialists frequently move on to other troubled companies.

In other cases management may be replaced, not with turnaround specialists, but with individuals experienced in the industry represented by the debtor.

In small cases where the managers are also the stockholders, creditors are apt to be uncomfortable with existing management which may have created the problems in the first place. Creditors may want a trustee appointed unless management is willing to have workout or turnaround specialists exercise some type of control over operations. This could involve temporarily turning the management function over to the specialists, or having existing management work with the specialists in resolving financial problems and developing a plan.

3. Short Range Cash Budgets

The Bankruptcy Code gives the debtor the exclusive right to file a plan for 120 days (or longer if extensions, which are common, are granted). See Chapter Eleven below. During this time period, before the creditors will work with the debtor and not take other action (such as attempting to convert the case to chapter 7 or to have the chapter 11 case dismissed), they must have assurance that assets will not continue to dissipate during the plan development period. To impart such assurance, the debtor will often provide creditors with a cash budget covering a three to six month period following the petition filing. The debtor needs to convince the creditors that there will be a positive cash flow and that steps have been taken (and will be taken) to reduce overhead, including administrative expenses. If the debtor has failed to meet such budgets in the past, the creditors may have little confidence in the debtor's projections.

The creditors are subsequently interested in monthly comparisons between actual and projected cash flows. If the debtor meets the monthly cash projections, it will help convince the creditors' committee and other creditors that the debtor's operations are under control. The creditors are then able to place more confidence in the debtor and in the projections that serve as the basis for future payments included in the proposed plan.

It is critical that positive cash flows from operations be generated within a short time after the petition is filed. A negative cash flow means assets are continuing to dissipate (that is, the company is still "bleeding"). Even if the business has some prospect for future profitable operations, that prospect may not continue unless action is taken to stop the bleeding. Such action may be in the form of selling segments of the business or closing down plants. For example the elimination of a plant or division may result in cash from the collection of receivables being available to provide funds for the parts of the company that will be kept in operation and become part of the reorganized company. Closing the division or plant will eliminate many of the associated expenses, but for awhile the debtor will continue to collect accounts receivable earned by the division or plant before its closing. The result may be a substantial cash infusion as the accounts receivable from the closed division or plant are in effect liquidated. While this type of action can provide additional cash flow in the short run, the key to turning the business around is to generate positive cash flows from the operations that will continue.

Problem 5-3

On April 15, 2001, Foam Corporation filed a chapter 11 petition. The financial statements are the same as those presented in chapter 2 except that the cash has decreased to $185,000 and an additional $350,000 is owed to Kick Credit for loans extended during the workout attempt. To secure its $6 million pre-workout debt, Kick Credit has a security interest in Foam's cash of $185,000, receivables, inventory, and machinery and equipment. The $350,000 workout loan is secured by the same assets and by a first trust deed on the otherwise unencumbered real property on which Foam Corporation's Los Angeles plant is located. The contractual interest rate on Kick Credit's loans to Foam is 12% per annum.

Recall that in 1996, using a $3.2 million loan from Gruff, Foam Corporation unwisely expanded to the east; its four eastern plants are now losing money on a daily basis. During 2000, Foam Corporation lost $5 million even after taking into account a $1.5 million tax refund. During the same time Foam Corporation had a negative cash flow from operations of $3.9 million. The negative cash flow from operations was less than $5 million for two reasons. First, the $5 million loss took into account depreciation and other charges against income that did not require cash. Second, Foam effectively borrowed additional amounts from the trade creditors by not paying the creditors on a timely basis (often referred to as "stretching the payables"). Sale of surplus assets for $800,000 and the borrowing of $1 million more from Kick Credit during 2000 (making the total borrowed from Kick Credit $6 million) further cut the cash outflow for 2000, so that the net cash outflow was "only" $2.1 million.

The cushioning effect of those factors is no longer helping. Any tax refund will be offset against the withholding tax liability, Kick Credit is no longer lending the company funds, and the trade creditors will ship to Foam only on a cash-on-delivery basis. On the plus side, since Foam has filed chapter 11, it will not have to pay interest currently; interest will not even accrue except on oversecured claims. See § 506(b). In addition, Foam reduced its overhead expenses as part of the workout attempt and is continuing to take every possible step to cut overhead expenses. The best projections available indicate that the negative cash flow will thus be limited to about $230,000 per month.

Foam Corporation has decided to sell the eastern operations. It should take Foam Corporation about six months to sell the four eastern plants; if it can keep the plants operating until the sale, the plants will be worth much more—perhaps a million dollars more than if they are liquidated. On the other hand they contribute greatly to the cash flow problem, especially the two unionized plants at Camden and Philadelphia.

You have ascertained the following information regarding the **monthly** cash outflow and inflow with regard to the four eastern plants. The "cash outflow" column includes selling expense (but does not include any rent or mortgage payment and does not include each plant's share of general and administrative expenses). All cash inflows are from collections of accounts receivable, because all sales are on credit. The "Collection Accounts" column includes collections on accounts generated by sales of products manufactured at each plant. The average collection time for accounts receivable is two and a half months.

MONTHLY CASH FLOW INFORMATION BY PLANT

Plant	Cash Outflow	Collection Accounts	Payment Rent	Payment Mortgage
Camden	$300,000	$210,000		$7,000
Philadelphia	255,000	200,000		7,000
Cleveland	250,000	215,000	$10,000	
Detroit	240,000	210,000	10,000	

> The five western plants have enough cash flow from operations at the plant level to cover the general expense of running the business.
>
> 1. Foam Corporation wants to keep the eastern plants in operation while it tries to sell them. If the court will allow Foam Corporation to use cash collateral, will Foam Corporation be able to keep all of its operations going without additional financing? Will Foam Corporation be required to pay interest on a current basis to Kick Credit? Will it be obligated to pay the regular monthly payment on the mortgage to First Bank (which holds the first mortgage on the Camden and Philadelphia plants)? Current interest to First Bank? Monthly rent on the Cleveland and Detroit plants to Imperial Insurance?
>
> 2. Gruff and Simmons are prepared to lend Foam Corporation $1 million if the new loan is given superpriority administrative expense status under § 364(c)(1) and is secured by a priming lien on Kick Credit's collateral under § 364(d)(1). Assume Kick Credit's $6 million original loan and $350,000 workout loan are oversecured on a going concern basis (if the sale of the eastern plants is consummated) by $1.4 million total. Assume Foam cannot otherwise obtain financing and there are no assets on which Kick Credit could be given a replacement lien. Should the court approve the proposed loan?
>
> 3. Assume additional financing is not available from any source; thus Foam Corporation needs to make do with use of cash collateral. What steps could Foam take to permit it to survive on cash collateral alone? Consider (at least) (1) whether Foam Corporation should close down the Camden plant and/or (2) whether Foam Corporation should close down the Cleveland plant. Assume that a one-time cash outlay of $60,000 is needed to close a plant. Should the court permit Foam Corporation to use Kick Credit's cash collateral? Assume that the Los Angeles real estate (on which Kick Credit has a $350,000 mortgage to secure the workout loan) is probably worth $1 million (unless it has been seriously contaminated with toxic waste) and that Kick Credit's original $6 million loan is undersecured by $200,000.

4. Finding a Viable Part of the Business

Often companies that file a bankruptcy petition have expanded too quickly. They have moved into areas that are not as profitable as their original business. Thus, a question that must be asked at the start of the proceedings is, "Can this business be pruned back or adjusted to operate profitably again?" If it is determined that selected parts of the debtor's operations can provide a core for a profitable business, the decisions must be made as soon as possible to discontinue the unprofitable parts.

5. Development of a Viable Business Plan

Before an effective reorganization plan can be developed it is necessary for the debtor to prepare a business plan. Often companies do not have any type of business or strategic plan at the time they attempt to work out some form of arrangement with creditors out of court or in a chapter 11 proceeding. Up until the date the petition is filed the managers have devoted most of their time to day-to-day problems and have not analyzed the major financial problems faced by the business. They have failed to ask questions that are most important for the survival of the business such as:

1. What products are most profitable?
2. What are strengths and weaknesses of the company?
3. What areas should be expanded? liquidated?
4. In what areas does the real potential for this business lie?
5. What direction should this business take?

The greater the financial problems, the more time management devotes to day-to-day details. Thus, almost no time is spent on providing direction for the company. A properly developed business plan is critical to the development of a reorganization plan. In determining the viability of the business, consideration should be given to the following:

- Nature of the company's industry—is it a growth industry or one in decline?
- The company's position in the industry—is it an industry leader, regional leader, or a leader in a small aspect (product, component, etc.) in the industry?
- The quality of the company's management
- The cost structure of the company—does the company have the highest, lowest cost per unit, hour, etc.?
- The financial structure of the company—will the company emerge from chapter 11 with a financial structure that can be competitive?

These factors determine the viability of the business. Note that they do not relate to the current solvency or insolvency of the debtor. If the debtor can restructure its debt and there are viable aspects of the business, a plan may be developed that will in the long-run benefit all parties involved in the case.

6. Honesty of Debtor

The creditors are often willing to work with an honest debtor. A debtor that has dealt with the creditors in a reasonable and professional manner is going to find the creditors cooperative in most cases. In situations where the creditors have not received financial and other types of information that could be trusted and where the debtor has been involved in a large number of questionable transactions, the creditors are often less willing to work with the debtor. Often in such situations the only way progress toward a plan can take place is if new management is brought in to run the company.

Problem 5-4

Consider the information given in Chapter Two about Foam Corporation.
1. Explain the difference between the solvency or insolvency of Foam Corporation and the viability of the business.
2. Is Foam Corporation solvent?
3. Is Foam Corporation a viable business?
4. What additional information would you like to have before you make a decision as to whether or not you think Foam Corporation could be turned around?
5. What aspects of this business have future potential?
6. What needs to happen before this potential can be realized?

Chapter Six

Controlling and Supervising the Reorganization

In this chapter we consider how the course of the reorganization is controlled and supervised. In Chapter Two, Section D above we introduced the most important "players": the debtor in possession, the United States trustee, the creditors' committee, and the major secured creditors. Please reread that section now. We begin this chapter with a closer look at the debtor in possession. We consider the duties and rights of the debtor in possession and of those who act for it. We consider the circumstances under which the debtor in possession should be ousted by appointment or election of a trustee for the case. We also consider the circumstances under which those who act for the debtor in possession—typically the board of directors and the managers—may be replaced. We then look at the role of committees and of the United States trustee in supervising the debtor in possession and helping to control the course of the case. Although we do not further consider such motions in this Chapter, remember that a secured creditor has a powerful weapon—the motion for relief from stay—to supervise and check the actions of the debtor. The secured creditor may obtain relief from the stay where the secured creditor's collateral is at risk (see § 362(d)(1), discussed in Chapter Three above), where the debtor has no equity and there is no point in keeping the secured creditor from foreclosing because a successful reorganization is not in prospect (see § 362(d)(2)), or in a single asset real estate case if a confirmable plan is not promptly filed and interest payments are not made (see § 362(d)(3), also discussed above in Chapter Three).

Motions for relief from stay and motions for dismissal or conversion of the case to a chapter 7 liquidation are the ultimate form of supervision—if successful they will end the reorganization attempt. Where the debtor and creditors cannot agree on a consensual plan of reorganization, the court often is faced with choosing one of two alternatives: confirming the debtor's plan in a cramdown or, failing that, ending the reorganization attempt by granting relief from the stay, dismissing the case, or converting it to chapter 7.[1] Thus we further consider motions for relief from stay—particularly under § 362(d)(2)—and motions to dismiss or convert the case in Chapter Fifteen, which deals with cramdown and its alternatives. (In that Chapter we also

---

1. The Code was amended in 2005 to require the court to appoint a trustee or examiner rather than dismiss or convert the case, where there are grounds for dismissal or convertion but where such appointment (apparently in lieu of dismissal or conversion) "is in the best interests of creditors and the estate." Section 1104(a)(3).

consider another strong form of creditor supervision of the reorganization, "creditors' plans"—plans of reorganization proposed by creditors rather than by the debtor.)

A. THE DEBTOR IN POSSESSION

The "debtor in possession" is simply the term that describes a debtor in a chapter 11 case in which no trustee is serving. See § 1101(1). Occasionally courts will say that the debtor in possession is a new entity, distinct from the debtor who filed the bankruptcy petition. It is true that a debtor in possession has rights and duties that the prepetition debtor did not have, but that does not make it a new entity.[2] "For our purposes, it is sensible to view the debtor-in-possession as the same 'entity' which existed before the filing of the bankruptcy petition, but empowered by virtue of the Bankruptcy Code to deal with its contracts and property in a manner it could not have employed absent the bankruptcy filing." NLRB. v. Bildisco & Bildisco, 465 U.S. 513, 528, 104 S. Ct. 1188, 1197, 79 L. Ed. 2d 482, 497 (1984). Unless the court orders otherwise, the debtor in possession has almost all of the rights and duties that a trustee would have if one were appointed, subject, however, to "such limitations or conditions as the court prescribes." Section 1107(a); see In re Lifeguard Industries, Inc., 37 B.R. 3 (Bankr. S.D. Ohio 1983) (reprinted below).

Key to those rights and duties is the role of the debtor in possession (or trustee) as "the representative of the estate." See §§ 323(a) and 1107(a). Thus, the debtor in possession is vested with the power under § 363 to use, sell, or lease the property of the estate; under § 364 to borrow money or obtain credit on behalf of the estate; under § 365 to assume or reject executory contracts and unexpired leases of the debtor on behalf of the estate; under § 502 to object to claims made against the estate; under § 506(c) to recover out of secured creditors' collateral the expenses incurred by the estate in preserving or disposing of the collateral, to the extent of any benefit to the secured creditors; under § 542 to recover possession of property of the estate from others; under §§ 544, 545, 547, 548, 549, 550, and 553 to use the avoiding powers to recover property for the estate; and under § 1108 to operate the business for the estate.

The concept of a debtor in possession may seem strange at first. The courts freely admit that some level of mismanagement leads or at least contributes to the financial distress of the debtor in most cases. See, e.g., In re Evans, 48 B.R. 46 (Bankr. W.D. Tex. 1985). Nevertheless, "[i]t is settled that appointment of

---

2. The *estate* may be a new entity for income tax purposes under Internal Revenue Code § 1398 (if the debtor is a natural person), or for purposes of the mutuality requirement for setoffs under § 553. Further, the debtor may have two different roles or capacities—one as representative of the estate and another simply as the debtor—without thereby being two entities. See, e.g., An-Tze Cheng v. K & S Diversified Invs., Inc. (In re An-Tze Cheng), 308 B.R. 448 (B.A.P. 9th Cir. 2004), aff'd in unpublished opinion, 2005 WL 3525643 (9th Cir. 2005).

a trustee should be the exception, rather than the rule," and grounds for appointment of a trustee to oust the debtor in possession must be shown by clear and convincing evidence. In re Sharon Steel Corp., 871 F.2d 1217, 1225-26 (3d Cir. 1989). Critics ask why the law would allow the same people who got the debtor into financial distress to continue to manage the business in chapter 11. There are several answers to that criticism.

First, in many cases the debtor changes managers before filing the chapter 11 petition. Often, especially when the debtor is a large, publicly held company, the board of directors replaces the management team shortly before the chapter 11 filing. In most companies, the board of directors does little hands-on management of the debtor; rather, the board of directors selects one or two top managers (the chief executive officer and perhaps the chief financial officer) who then assemble and run a management team. When the board determines that the debtor is in financial trouble, the board often will replace the management team with a new one, perhaps headed by a turnaround specialist. The new team will attempt to work out the financial problems outside of bankruptcy. If that fails and a chapter 11 petition is filed, the debtor in possession will not be run by the same management that created the problems, but by the new team that has been working to resolve the problems.

Second, consider what would happen if the managers of a troubled company all immediately lost their jobs when a chapter 11 petition was filed. The management team would be reluctant to recommend to the board of directors that a petition be filed until the debtor's business was on the very brink of collapse. Directors who played an active role in management and who derived a substantial salary from that role would be reluctant to authorize a filing as long as any hope remained for an out-of-court workout. Even more often than is now the case, the bankruptcy filing would be delayed so long that the business would be beyond saving. A rule requiring appointment of a trustee to dispossess the debtor's management would be counterproductive.

Third, in most cases when a chapter 11 petition is filed, the debtor is in a very precarious financial condition with a need for immediate corrective action. A trustee appointed to take over the business would not be familiar with it; by the time the trustee had learned the business and figured out what needed to be done, there might be no business left to reorganize. Even if the trustee could become familiar with the business quickly enough, the trustee and his or her management team would have to be compensated for the time spent doing so, and that added expense might make reorganization much more difficult.

Fourth, in theory, the debtor in possession is supervised by the United States trustee and by the unsecured creditors' committee. That supervision is supposed to prevent abuses by incompetent debtors in possession. The reality, unfortunately, falls short of the ideal. When the United States trustee system was merely a pilot program in a few districts, a court remarked:

> Frequently, there is virtually no supervision of the debtor's day-to-day operation. In districts which do not have the pilot U.S. trustee program, there typically will be no trustee or examiner to monitor the debtor's day-to-day operation or to scrutinize the debtor's dealings with creditors.
>
> Under the Bankruptcy Reform Act of 1978, the bankruptcy judge has reduced administrative responsibility for supervising cases. While the Court does retain some administrative responsibility, the burden of supervising the debtor's day-to-day affairs in chapter 11 cases falls upon the creditors' committee.
>
> A creditors' committee is appointed in every chapter 11 case, but most creditors' committees, at least in this district, are totally inactive and ineffective. Consequently, with no trustee, no direct court supervision, and with unconcerned creditors, the debtor may operate virtually unsupervised.

In re B & W Tractor Co., 38 B.R. 613, 614-15 (Bankr. E.D.N.C. 1984). The court noted that out of 250 pending chapter 11 cases in its district, less than 5% had active creditors' committees. Id. at 615 n.4. After the U.S. trustee system had been extended to all regions of the nation other than Alabama and North Carolina, a court observed that debtors in possession are not adequately supervised:

> The debtor-in-possession provisions of the Bankruptcy Code envision a trustworthy, carefully run business or individual who is responsible as a fiduciary and will use his/its best efforts to reorganize itself. Through the system of creditors' committees and the United States Trustee, each debtor-in-possession will be carefully monitored and motions to convert or to dismiss as to those who abuse the system or cannot reorganize will be promptly heard by the Court. There will be a group of competitively paid, highly qualified professionals who will assist the debtor-in-possession in reorganizing itself and in constantly analyzing its position. Unfortunately fact does not match the hopes of Congress. During the 12 months ending June 30, 1987, 1,917 Chapter 11 petitions were filed in the Central District of California. There were 12 judges available to handle these cases; and there were approximately 7 attorneys and 7 analysts in the United States Trustee's office. Besides these 1,917 Chapter 11 cases, there were 36,657 Chapter 7 cases, 2 Chapter 12 cases, and 10,705 Chapter 13 cases filed in that same period. Annual Report of the Director of the Administrative Office of the United States Courts, 1987. This overwhelming volume of cases virtually assures that the contemplated monitoring will not occur.

In re Pacific Forest Indus., 95 B.R. 740, 743-44 (Bankr. C.D. Cal.1989).

The United States Trustee system has more resources now, and more unsecured creditors understand the need for active participation in the case. In addition, as we noted in Chapter Two, bankruptcy judges now have more tools to supervise the reorganization, and a larger role in doing so. Section 105(d), added in 1994, gives bankruptcy judges explicit statutory authority to hold status conferences in each case. It also authorizes bankruptcy judges to set deadlines and issue orders at such conferences "to ensure that the case is handled expeditiously and economically." Id. Some judges have used these options to enhance supervision; others have not. In 2005, § 105(d) was amended to require bankruptcy judges to "hold such status conferences as are necessary to further the expeditious and economical resolution of the case."

1. Ordinary Course Transactions

The norm is for the debtor to remain in possession and to control the operation of the business. Under § 363(c) the debtor is entitled to enter into transactions in the ordinary course of business without notice and without a hearing, as long as they do not involve use of cash collateral. Creditors and the United States trustee may well be concerned that the debtor will enter into imprudent transactions, but they will have little ability to prevent such transactions if the debtor is not even required to give notice of them. See Med. Malpractice Ins. Ass'n v. Hirsch (In re Lavigne), 114 F.3d 379 (2d Cir. 1997) (involving attempt by debtor in possession—a despondent physician facing over 70 malpractice claims—to cancel malpractice insurance covering his past acts). That makes very important the issue whether a transaction is or is not an ordinary course transaction.

In re Roth American, Inc.
United States Court of Appeals, Third Circuit, 1992
975 F.2d 949

Sloviter, Chief Judge.
* * *

Roth American, Inc., was a manufacturer of toys and gym sets in Wilkes-Barre, Pennsylvania, employing over 200 persons who were represented by Teamsters Local 401. In 1985, the company and the Union entered into a collective bargaining agreement covering the period from November 1, 1985 until June 30, 1988.

On February 2, 1988, Roth American filed a voluntary petition for reorganization under Chapter 11 of the Bankruptcy Code. In the meantime, Roth American had negotiated with the Union to obtain a modification of the collective bargaining agreement that was embodied in a separate memorandum of agreement. The 1988 memorandum of agreement, which became effective on February 4, 1988,[3] extended the existing collective bargaining agreement until January 1, 1989 and provided for a reduction in wages of seventy cents per hour across the board. Of particular importance to this appeal, it also provided:

> The Employer will maintain the operations covered by the current Collective Bargaining Agreement in the Wilkes-Barre area for a minimum of two (2) years, commencing upon the effective date of this Memorandum of Agreement. This commitment also includes the representation that equipment necessary to the operations of those facilities will not be moved from the Wilkes-Barre area.

Neither party sought approval of the new agreement from the bankruptcy court, nor was there any hearing before the bankruptcy court at which creditors could object to the new agreement.

Despite the seventy cent wage concession provided in the 1988 memorandum agreement, the employer only paid the lower wage for a two-week period. It resumed paying the preexisting higher wage when it could no longer provide the health insurance coverage mandated by the memorandum agreement.

---

3.   [Footnote 1 in original:] The union concedes that the 1988 memorandum agreement did not become effective until after Roth American filed its bankruptcy petition.

Roth American continued its operations for several months following the bankruptcy petition. In April 1988, the company entered into a contract, approved by the bankruptcy court, whereby the Michael Fox Company would solicit bids for the company initially in its entirety and, if that were unsuccessful, in its various parts. On June 5, 1988, Roth American ceased all manufacturing activity and laid off all its employees. On August 17, 1988, the bankruptcy court approved, over the Union's objection, the piecemeal sale of Roth American pursuant to the best bids that were received.

The Union filed three proofs of claim in the bankruptcy proceeding on behalf of the Roth American employees it represented. One claim sought damages of approximately $6.5 million in future wages and benefits for breach of the provision in the February 1988 memorandum agreement to maintain operations in Wilkes-Barre for at least two years. * * *

The bankruptcy court granted the Union's claim for damages for breach of contract only to the extent of the reduction in wages the employees were paid during the two week period following the new agreement. The bankruptcy court reasoned that because the 1988 memorandum agreement "was not accepted or rejected under the terms of the United States Bankruptcy Code," it was not "a valid post-petition Collective Bargaining Agreement." Alternatively, the court reasoned that the 1985 Collective Bargaining Agreement did not "provide any guarantees of continued employment," and therefore could not give rise to a claim for future unearned wages. Accordingly, the court held that since "[t]he employees received all their post-petition wages in full except for a two week period in which they were paid less than the amount called for in the Collective Bargaining Agreement[, t]his is the only measure of damages available to the Union." * * *

The Union appealed the bankruptcy court's decision to the United States District Court for the Middle District of Pennsylvania, which affirmed the bankruptcy court's decision in all respects. The district court agreed with the bankruptcy court that the 1988 memorandum agreement was not valid, reasoning that the enactment of 11 U.S.C. § 1113 demonstrated that "post-petition activity with respect to collective bargaining agreements are not transactions in the ordinary course of business and require a modicum of Bankruptcy Court supervision." Alternatively, the court stated that even if the 1988 memorandum agreement were enforceable, the language in that agreement did not guarantee future employment and therefore could not give rise to a claim for future unearned wages and benefits.

* * *

On this appeal, the Union argues that the 1988 memorandum agreement was a transaction in the "ordinary course of business" within the meaning of 11 U.S.C. § 363(c) and that therefore a hearing before the bankruptcy court was not required for the agreement to be fully enforceable.

* * *

The validity of the Union's claim for breach of the 1988 memorandum agreement turns on whether notice to creditors and a hearing before the bankruptcy court were required for the 1988 memorandum agreement to be enforceable. Only if the agreement is enforceable, would we need to answer the extent to which the Union is entitled to damages for its breach.

Section 363(c)(1) of the Bankruptcy Code provides:

> If the business of the debtor is authorized to be operated under section ... 1108 ... of this title and unless the court orders otherwise, the trustee may enter into transactions ... *in the ordinary course of business,* without notice or a hearing, and may use property of the estate in the ordinary course of business without notice or a hearing.

11 U.S.C. § 363(c)(1) (1988) (emphasis added). In contrast, a notice and hearing are required before the trustee (or debtor-in-possession) may use property of the estate other than in the ordinary course of business. 11 U.S.C. § 363(b)(1).

The framework of section 363 is designed to allow a trustee (or debtor-in-possession) the flexibility to engage in ordinary transactions without unnecessary creditor and bankruptcy court oversight, while protecting creditors by giving them an opportunity to be heard when transactions are not ordinary. See United States ex rel. Harrison v. Estate of Deutscher (In re H & S Transp. Co.), 115 B.R. 592, 599 (M.D. Tenn.1990) ("Section 363 is designed to strike [a] balance, allowing a business to continue its daily operations without excessive court or creditor oversight and protecting secured creditors and others from dissipation of the estate's assets."). Creditors are not given the right to notice and a hearing when transactions are in the ordinary course of business "because their objections to such transactions are likely to relate to the bankrupt's chapter 11 status, not the particular transactions themselves." In re James A. Phillips, Inc., 29 B.R. 391, 394 (S.D.N.Y. 1983).

Neither the Bankruptcy Code nor its legislative history provides a frame-work for analyzing whether particular transactions are in the ordinary course of a debtor's business for the purpose of section 363. In prior cases, the courts have engaged in a two-step inquiry for determining whether a transaction is in "the ordinary course of business": a "horizontal dimension" test and a "vertical dimension" test. See Benjamin Weintraub & Alan N. Resnick, *The Meaning of "Ordinary Course of Business" Under the Bankruptcy Code—Vertical and Horizontal Analysis,* 19 UCC L.J. 364 (1987) [hereinafter Weintraub & Resnick].[4]

The inquiry deemed horizontal is whether, from an industry-wide perspective, the transaction is of the sort commonly undertaken by companies in that industry. Id. at 367. For example, "raising a crop would not be in the ordinary course of business for a widget manufacturer because that is not a widget manufacturer's ordinary business." In re Waterfront Cos., 56 B.R. 31, 35 (Bankr. D. Minn. 1985).

The inquiry deemed vertical (more appropriately characterized as the creditor's expectation test) analyzes the transactions "'from the vantage point of a hypothetical creditor and [the inquiry is] whether the transaction subjects a

---

4. [Footnote 4 in original:] This framework has been routinely applied by many courts. See, e.g., In re Dant & Russell, Inc., 853 F.2d 700, 704-06 (9th Cir. 1988) (applying vertical and horizontal framework to conclude debtor-in-possession's post-petition execution of leases was in ordinary course of business); Habinger, Inc. v. Metro. Cosmetic & Reconstructive Surgical Clinic, 124 B.R. 784, 786 (D. Minn. 1990) (applying framework to debtor's post-petition payments for furniture and equipment); United States ex rel. Harrison, 115 B.R. at 598-99 (applying framework to conclude trustee's use of funds to repair boats, institute maintenance program, and reinstate insurance was in ordinary course of business); In re Glosser Bros., 124 B.R. 664, 667-68 (Bankr. W.D. Pa. 1991) (applying framework to execution of licensing agreement to operate department in debtor's stores).

creditor to economic risk of a nature different from those he accepted when he decided to extend credit.'" Weintraub & Resnick, 19 UCC L.J. at 365 (quoting In re Johns-Manville Corp., 60 B.R. 612, 616 (Bankr. S.D.N.Y. 1986)). Under this test, "[t]he touchstone of 'ordinariness' is ... the interested parties' reasonable expectations of what transactions the debtor in possession is likely to enter in the course of its business." *James A. Phillips,* 29 B.R. at 394. The primary focus thus is on the debtor's pre-petition business practices and conduct, although a court must also "consider the changing circumstances inherent in the hypothetical creditor's expectations." Weintraub & Resnick, 19 UCC L.J. at 366.

In this case, satisfaction of the horizontal test is readily apparent—many manufacturing companies have routinely entered into extensions of collective bargaining agreements in order to secure the continued benefits of a unionized workforce. Accordingly, several courts have ruled that post-petition collective bargaining agreements were in the ordinary course of business. See In re DeLuca Distributing Co., 38 B.R. 588, 594 (Bankr. N.D. Ohio 1984) (new collective bargaining agreement in ordinary course of business because employees were covered by agreement prior to bankruptcy); see also In re Illinois-California Express, Inc., 72 B.R. 987, 991 (D. Colo. 1987) (post-petition renegotiation of labor agreement without prior court approval was valid because it was transaction in the ordinary course of business); In re IML Freight, Inc., 37 B.R. 556, 559 (Bankr. D. Utah 1984) (decision to enter into a post-petition collective bargaining agreement falls within debtor-in-possession's discretion to make decisions in the ordinary course of business). The National Labor Relations Board has also noted that a debtor may enter into valid collective bargaining agreements in the ordinary course of business. See Sealift Maritime, Inc., 265 N.L.R.B. 1219 (1982) (petition of rival union seeking to represent employees of Chapter 11 debtor denied because modification and extension of preexisting collective bargaining agreement with different union was valid without bankruptcy court approval as transaction in the ordinary course of business).

The particular provisions of post-petition collective bargaining agreements must also be examined with reference to the reasonable expectations of creditors. Roth American argues that even if post-petition collective bargaining agreements may be "ordinary course of business" transactions, the nature of the particular agreement here was extraordinary inasmuch as it purported to bind the debtor to maintain its existing operations in the Wilkes-Barre area for two years.

We find Roth American's argument persuasive. The 1988 memorandum agreement is fundamentally different from the previous collective bargaining agreements entered into between Roth American and the Teamsters insofar as it contains the provision purporting to bind Roth American to maintain its operations. As has been stated by the Supreme Court:

> Collective bargaining between employer and the representatives of a unit ... results in an accord as to terms which will govern hiring and work and pay in that unit. The result is not, however, a contract of employment except in *rare cases;* no one has a job by reason of it and *no obligation to any individual ordinarily comes into existence from it alone.*

J.I. Case Co. v. NLRB, 321 U.S. 332, 334-35, 64 S. Ct. 576, 579, 88 L. Ed. 762 (1944) (emphasis added); see also In re Continental Airlines Corp., 901 F.2d 1259, 1264 (5th Cir. 1990) ("ordinarily a collective bargaining agreement … neither obligates any employee to perform work *nor requires the employer to provide work*") (emphasis added).

In contrast, the 1988 memorandum agreement here sought to bind the hands of a Chapter 11 debtor to maintain its then existing operations for two years in the Wilkes-Barre area. Thus, while "changes between prepetition and postpetition business activity alone are not *per se* evidence of extraordinariness," *Johns-Manville,* 60 B.R. at 617, we conclude that the nature of the agreement here ventures beyond the domain of transactions that a hypothetical creditor would reasonably expect to be undertaken in the circumstances. See In re Century Brass Prods., 107 B.R. 8 (Bankr. D. Conn. 1989) (large post-petition severance pay agreements entered into between debtor and debtor's officer not in ordinary course of business because no comparable severance pay agreement had ever been entered into between the debtor and its officers in past); cf. In re Waterfront Cos., 56 B.R. at 35 ("Some transactions either by their size, nature or both are not within the day-to-day operations of a business and are therefore extraordinary."). Accordingly, we hold that the 1988 memorandum agreement was not a transaction in the ordinary course of business. It follows that the district court did not err in holding that notice and a hearing in the bankruptcy court on that agreement was required for it to be enforceable. * * *

We have concluded that the 1988 memorandum agreement entered into between Roth American and the Teamsters was not a transaction in the ordinary course of business within the meaning of section 363(c). Therefore, the Union's claim for breach of contract could be granted only for the two week period in which the wages paid to the employees were below the amount required by the 1985 collective bargaining agreement. * * * Therefore, we will affirm the order of the district court affirming the judgment of the bankruptcy court.

NOTES

1. The court states that "Creditors are not given the right to notice and a hearing when transactions are in the ordinary course of business 'because their objections to such transactions are likely to relate to the bankrupt's chapter 11 status, not to the particular transactions themselves.'" Would the debtor's "chapter 11 status" cause a reasonable creditor to be more concerned about the debtor's choices of transactions than if the debtor were a healthy, solvent corporation not in bankruptcy?

2. The court quotes from two bankruptcy opinions which use the terms "daily operations" and "day-to-day" operations to describe the transactions which are ordinary course. See also Med. Malpractice Ins. Ass'n v. Hirsch (In re Lavigne), 114 F.3d 379, 384 (2d Cir. 1997) (describing ordinary course transactions as those "that the debtor would likely enter in the course of its normal, daily business"). Do the horizontal and vertical approaches described by the court limit ordinary course transactions to such day-to-day or "daily" operations?

3. If the collective bargaining agreement had not contained a job security pro-vision, would it have been an ordinary course transaction? Should creditors have notice and an opportunity to seek a hearing before the debtor in possession enters into a collective bargaining agreement on behalf of the estate? Was the court justified in considering the job security provision only in its analysis of the vertical (creditors' expectation test) but not in its analysis of the horizontal test?

4. What are the consequences if a debtor in possession enters into a contract in the ordinary course of business? The normal consequence would be that the contract would be enforceable against the estate (and any obligations under it arising until confirmation of a plan or dismissal of the case would therefore be administrative expenses that would have to be paid ahead of the prepetition unsecured creditors' claims). See, e.g., In re DeLuca Distrib. Co., 38 B.R. 588 (Bankr. N.D. Ohio 1984); Flint Hills Foods, Inc. v. Von Der Ahe (In re Isis Foods, Inc.), 19 B.R. 329 (Bankr. W.D. Mo.), aff'd, 27 B.R. 156 (W.D. Mo.1982). The Ninth Circuit, however, in Burlington N. R.R. v. Dant & Russell, Inc. (In re Dant & Russell, Inc.), 853 F.2d 700 (9th Cir. 1988), took a very strict approach to § 503(b)(1)(A) and refused to grant full administrative expense recovery to the nondebtor party even though the debtor entered into the contract in the ordinary course of business. Cf. Nostas Assocs. v. Costich (In re Klein Sleep Prods., Inc.), 78 F.3d 18 (2d Cir. 1996) (dictum suggesting that postpetition ordinary course transactions create administrative expense priority claims only after court determines that transaction provided benefit to estate, just as prepetition executory contracts give rise to administrative expense priority claims only after court approval of assumption); Interface Group-Nevada, Inc. v. Trans World Airlines, Inc. (In re Trans World Airlines, Inc.), 145 F3d 124, 138 (3d Cir. 1998) (stating similar dictum). If recovery by the nondebtor party is limited to the benefit received by the estate, as in *Dant & Russell,* then the estate is protected to some extent against imprudent transactions on the part of the debtor in possession. Does such an approach improperly penalize the nondebtor party?

5. Transactions held to be ordinary course include:
    *   the hiring of a lobbyist, Comm. of Asbestos-Related Litigants v. Johns-Manville Corp. (In re Johns-Manville Corp.), 60 B.R. 612 (Bankr. S.D.N.Y. 1986);
    *   an agreement to pay a potential lender's legal fees for transactional work done on a loan sought by the debtor, even though the loan itself would have required court approval, In re Ohio Ferro-Alloys Corp., 96 B.R. 795 (Bankr. N.D. Ohio 1989);
    *   the closing of several stores by a large chain of department stores, In re Glosser Bros., Inc., 100 B.R. 268 (Bankr. W.D. Pa.1989); and
    *   the making of a one-year contract for an armored car company to transport cash from the debtor's convenience stores, even though the debtor was attempting to sell its assets quickly, where it was not clear that a sale would be accomplished within the year and where existence of the favorable contract might have been attractive to a purchaser, In re Git-N-Go, Inc., 322 B.R. 164 (Bankr. N.D. Okla. 2004).

6. "Normally the court will not scrutinize or entertain objections to ordinary course transactions nor will the court substitute its judgment of business risk for that of the debtor. However, allegations of self dealing by insiders may stimulate court intervention. * * * Even where the Code requires notice and a hearing to authorize a transaction, courts generally refrain from interfering in the debtor's exercise of business judgment. In *In re Simasko Production Company* [47 B.R. 444 (D. Colo. 1985)], the debtor, a company engaged in development and production of oil and gas, sought approval of an interim financing arrangement. A creditor objected that the proposed drilling program posed a bad economic risk. Without considering the degree of risk, the court approved the financing and stated that business judgments should be made in the board room and not in the courtroom." Epstein, Nickles & White, BANKRUPTCY § 10-6, at 740-41. If a debtor is insolvent or nearly insolvent, what is the effect of allowing its

managers (who are often its equity owners) to pursue a risky business strategy? Who bears the risk? Who stands to gain the most if the strategy is very successful? What difficulty does this create for the debtor's managers, who owe fiduciary duties of loyalty and care to creditors and to the equity owners? See LoPucki & Whitford, *Corporate Governance in the Bankruptcy Reorganization of Large, Publicly Held Companies,* 141 U. PA. L. REV. 669, 767-96 (1993).

7. Non-ordinary course transactions involving sale of all or a substantial part of a debtor's assets are discussed in Chapter Four, supra, section B.2.

Problem 6-1

After filing its chapter 11 petition, Foam Corporation entered into an agreement with its top managers, including William Gruff (Foam Corporation's chief executive officer, chairman of the board, and majority shareholder). The agreement provided for a ten percent increase in the managers' salaries and also stated (1) that as an inducement to the managers to remain with the company during the chapter 11 case, they would each receive a bonus equal to six months' pay if they stayed with the company for a year (or until confirmation of a plan, if confirmation were to occur in less than a year), and (2) that they would in addition receive six months' severance pay if their employment were terminated prior to confirmation of a plan. Is any part of the agreement enforceable if Foam Corporation does not give notice of it to creditors? If Foam Corporation does give notice, creditors object, and the court holds a hearing, what arguments should Foam Corporation and the objecting creditors make? See § 503(c) (added in 2005); Dai-Ichi Kangyo Bank, Ltd. v. Montgomery Ward Holding Corp. (In re Montgomery Ward Holding Corp.), 242 B.R. 147 (D. Del. 1999); In re Crystal Apparel, Inc., 220 B.R. 816 (Bankr. S.D.N.Y. 1998); In re Regensteiner Printing Co., 122 B.R. 323 (N.D. Ill. 1990); In re Media Cent. Inc., 115 B.R. 119 (Bankr. E.D. Tenn. 1990); U.S. Bankr. Ct. Rules C.D. Cal., L.B.R. 2014-1(a) (West 2005), available at http://www.cacb.uscourts.gov.

2. Appointment or Election of a Trustee for the Case

We have seen that the norm is for the debtor to remain in possession, and that the debtor has wide discretion in entering into ordinary course transactions—and even substantial discretion in entering into non-ordinary course transactions. The question remains whether debtors in possession can be trusted in the usual case to manage the debtor competently and to carry out their fiduciary duties. The debtor in possession and its managers owe fiduciary duties both to the shareholders and to the creditors. CFTC v. Weintraub, 471 U.S. 343, 355, 105 S. Ct. 1986, 1994, 85 L. Ed. 2d 372, 382 (1985); Wolf v. Weinstein, 372 U.S. 633, 649-50, 83 S. Ct. 969, 979-80, 10 L. Ed. 2d 33, 46-47 (1963).

Cases can readily be found in which debtors in possession did not live up to their obligations. See, e.g., In re Sharon Steel Corp., 871 F.2d 1217 (3d Cir. 1989) (management was at best careless, failed to pursue claims against related companies, had systematically siphoned off assets to related companies before filing for bankruptcy, and kept unsatisfactory records—and company suffered continuing losses); In re U.S. Communications of Westchester, Inc., 123 B.R. 491 (Bankr. S.D.N.Y. 1991) (debtor in possession failed to keep records or to do any real accounting and engaged in questionable dealings with related companies); In re V. Savino Oil & Heating Co., 99 B.R. 518 (Bankr. E.D.N.Y. 1989) (debtor in possession secretly diverted business to newly formed affiliate); In re Nautilus of New Mexico, Inc., 83 B.R. 784 (Bankr. D.N.M. 1988).

Thus there are cases in which management should be replaced after the chapter 11 case is commenced. Section 1104(a) governs the appointment of a trustee to oust the debtor from possession. It provides that the court "shall order the appointment of a trustee" if requested by a party in interest or by the United States trustee,[5] and if the standards in either § 1104(a)(1), (2), or (3) are met. If the court orders appointment of a trustee, then the United States trustee "after consultation with parties in interest" will appoint the trustee for the case under § 1104(d) (although the creditors may choose to elect a trustee under § 1104(b), as noted immediately below). Note that the United States trustee may not appoint himself or herself as trustee for the case, that the appointment is "subject to the court's approval," that the trustee for the case must be "one disinterested person," and that the trustee may be either an "individual" or a "corporation" (a term that may include LLCs). See §§ 1104(d), 322(a), and 101(9); Rule 2007.1(c).

If, within 30 days after the court orders appointment of a trustee, a creditor requests an election, the United States trustee "shall convene a meeting of creditors for the purpose of electing one disinterested person to serve as trustee in the case." Section 1104(b) (added in 1994). Section 1104(b) requires that the election follow the procedures in § 702(a)-(c) for electing a chapter 7 trustee. See, generally, 6 Resnick & Sommer, COLLIER ON BANKRUPTCY ¶ 702.01-.12 (discussing § 702 and Rule 2009). Only holders of allowable general unsecured claims may vote, and only if their claims are "undisputed, fixed, [and] liquidated." Section 702(a)(1). Neither insiders nor anyone else with an interest materially adverse to the interests of the other general unsecured creditors may vote. Id. Thus, in Foam Corporation's case, Gruff, an insider, could not vote his unsecured claim; arguably, a competitor of Foam Corporation could not vote if it had a claim, because of its possible interest in seeing Foam Corporation's reorganization fail.

Even though the request of a single creditor will force the United States trustee to convene a meeting for purposes of electing a trustee, it is possible that under § 702(b) no election will be held at the meeting unless creditors holding 20% in amount of the claims entitled to vote appear at the meeting (in person or by proxy) and request that the election actually be held. It appears that if an

---

5. In the case of a corporate debtor (such as Foam Corporation), the United States trustee must move for appointment of a trustee if members (plural) of the debtor's current board of directors, or the debtor's chief executive or chief financial officer, or past members of the board of directors who selected the CEO or CFO "participated in actual fraud, dishonesty, or criminal conduct in the management of the debtor or the debtor's public financial reporting." Section 1104(e). Noncorporate debtors with governing bodies (or CEOs or CFOs) are also covered by § 1104(e). All such debtors must consider carefully before filing a chapter 11 petition whether to replace directors or other governing board members, CEOs, and CFOs, so that they will not be faced with a United States trustee motion for appointment of a trustee. Note, however, that § 1104(e) does not require the court to grant the United States trustee's motion.

election is held, no trustee will be elected unless creditors holding at least 20% in amount of the claims eligible to vote actually do vote, and one person receives the votes of the holders of a majority in amount of the claims that are voted. See § 702(c). Presumably several rounds of balloting may occur if no one receives a majority on the first ballot. The United States trustee certifies the result of the election ("[i]f an eligible, disinterested trustee is elected"), and the court resolves any disputes over the election. Section 1104(b)(2).

Elections of trustees have been rare in practice. Note that only two cases involving attempted elections of chapter 11 trustees appear in the annotations to § 1104 in the U.S. Code Annotated.[6] Perhaps the threat of an election has encouraged the United States trustee to appoint suitable candidates.

The court will order appointment of a trustee under § 1104(a)(1) or (a)(2) only if the need for a trustee to take over administration of the estate has been established by clear and convincing evidence. See, e.g., Official Comm. of Asbestos Claimants v. G-I Holdings, Inc., 385 F.3d 313 (3d Cir. 2004) (opinion by then Circuit Court Judge Alito). The court will order appointment of a trustee under § 1104(a)(3) only if the alternative to doing so is dismissal of the case or conversion to chapter 7, either of which will immediately end the reorganization. Thus the United States trustee is not likely to wait thirty days to see whether a creditor requests an election; instead, the United States trustee is likely to appoint a trustee and seek court approval of the appointment as soon as possible after the court orders appointment of a trustee. If the creditors then elect a trustee, the elected trustee would displace the appointed trustee. See § 1104(b)(2)(B). If no trustee is elected, the appointed trustee would continue to serve.

Section 1104(a)(1) calls for the court to order appointment of a trustee for "cause," which specifically includes "fraud, dishonesty, incompetence, or gross mismanagement * * * by current management, either before or after the commencement of the case." If the court finds that current management has been dishonest in any way, must the court order the United States trustee to appoint a trustee for the case? Section 1104(a)(2) calls for the court to order appointment of a trustee when it is "in the interests of creditors, any equity security holders, and other interests of the estate." The vagueness of section 1104(a)(2) would seem to give the court substantial leeway in deciding whether a trustee should be appointed. Consider how the following case deals with the issue of the extent of the court's discretion to order or not order appointment of a trustee under § 1104(a)(1) and (a)(2). Note that short of ordering the appointment of a trustee, the court, under § 1104(c), can order the United States trustee to appoint an

---

6.   In re Aspen Marine Group, Inc., 189 B.R. 859, 861 (Bankr. S.D. Fla. 1995) (applying proxy rules of Rule 2006 to govern election); In re Williams, 277 B.R. 114 (Bankr. C.D. Cal. 2002) (holding that creditor who held a judgment and who sought to require election of chapter 11 trustee was not entitled to vote for trustee because (1) claim was possibly secured, (2) claim was disputed due to apparently nonfrivolous pending appeal, and (3) creditor had an interest materially adverse to other creditors due to potential preference action that trustee could bring against creditor—and thus creditor should not be able to influence selection of trustee).

examiner who will investigate the debtor's actions, and who may be given authority under § 1106(b) to take over some of the duties of the debtor in possession that the court orders the debtor in possession not to perform.[7]

Committee of Dalkon Shield Claimants v. A.H. Robins Co.
United States Court of Appeals, Fourth Circuit, 1987
828 F.2d 239

DONALD RUSSELL, CIRCUIT JUDGE:

This is an appeal by the Dalkon Shield Claimants' Committee from the district court's order denying the Committee's motion pursuant to 11 U.S.C. § 1104 (1987) for the appointment of a * * * trustee for A.H. Robins Company. The issue before us is whether the court was obligated to appoint a trustee to manage Robins after the court found Robins in civil contempt of its Order barring Robins from selectively paying off pre-petition debts without prior court approval.

On August 23, 1985 the district court entered a Consent Order providing in part that Robins could not pay pre-petition debts without prior court approval. Subsequently, and without court approval or knowledge, Robins made payments on pre-petition claims including: (a) payments under a benefit plan to present and past executives of Robins, (b) payments through its subsidiaries on certain pre-petition debts, (c) payments under executory contracts which had not been assumed and (d) payments to settle a pre-petition lawsuit brought by an employee of Robins. Moreover, Robins used certain of its subsidiaries to make prohibited charitable contributions and to make certain investments.

The Committee moved for the appointment of a trustee pursuant to Section § [sic] 1104(a) to protect creditors from further abuses by Robins. Following the hearing on the appellants' motion, the district court ruled that Robins was in civil contempt and that sanctions would be imposed at a later date. The court found that the debtor had not only "knowingly, unknowingly, or because of failure to comprehend the Court's order violated a court order, but also [had] taken certain actions prohibited by both the spirit and the letter of the bankruptcy laws." The court, however, declined to appoint a trustee to run Robins' business as requested by the Committee, deciding instead to appoint an examiner pursuant to Section 1104[(c)]. * * *

The court stated that although a finding of civil contempt was warranted because of Robins' abuses, civil contempt was not to be equated with cause for appointment of a trustee under Section 1104(a)(1). The court noted that a trustee is needed where fraud or mismanagement arise but stated that it did not find such problems in this case. Moreover, the court said:

---

7. In cases involving more than $5 million in certain forms of unsecured debt—including publicly held unsecured debentures—if a trustee is not appointed, then the court is required to order appointment of an examiner. Bankruptcy courts may resist the statutory command in cases where they do not think the cost of an examiner is justified. See In re Loral Space & Communications, Ltd., 313 B.R. 577 (Bankr. S.D.N.Y. 2004) (refusing to order appointment of an examiner), rev'd, No. 04 Civ. 8645RPP, 2004 WL 2979785 (S.D.N.Y. 2004) ("In light of the straightforward language and legislative history of 11 U.S.C. § 1104(c)(2), this Court holds that the Bankruptcy Court had no discretion to deny appointment of an examiner where, as here, the $5,000,000 debt threshold is met and shareholders of a public company have moved for appointment of an examiner.").

As stated in In Re General Oil Distributors, Inc., 42 Bankr. 402 (Bankr. 1984), although the word "shall" in Section 1104(a) circumscribes the Court's discretion, the concepts of incompetence, dishonesty, gross mismanagement and even fraud all cover a wide spectrum of conduct. While under 1104(a)(1) the Court is not directly called upon to weigh the cost and benefits of appointing a trustee, it nevertheless cannot ignore competing benefit and harm that such appointment may place upon the estate. Coupled with those concerns is the overriding philosophy of Chapter 11, which is to give the debtor a second chance. Consistent with such a philosophy is this court's finding that current management should be permitted to identify and correct its past mistakes.

The court stated that it found the present management capable and amenable to a fair and expeditious plan to compensate claimants. The court further stated that the appointment of a trustee was neither "necessary [n]or desirable" and might "impede" present reorganization efforts. The court cautioned however, that "should the Court ever reach a contra conclusion, and should the debtor give the Court cause, the Court will not hesitate to appoint a trustee." On appeal, the Committee contends that the district court erred in not appointing a trustee.

An initial question is whether the district court's order denying the Committee's request for the appointment of a trustee is appealable at this stage of the bankruptcy proceeding. For purposes of this appeal, we will deem the order immediately reviewable as a final decision under 28 U.S.C. § 1291. While the court's order is perhaps not "final" in the technical sense, considerations unique to bankruptcy appeals require that courts consider "finality in a more pragmatic and less technical way in bankruptcy cases than in other situations." In re Amatex Corp., 755 F.2d 1034, 1039 (3d Cir. 1985). Such considerations include the protracted nature of bankruptcy proceedings and the large number of parties interested in the proceedings. "To avoid the waste of time and resources that might result from reviewing discrete portions of the action only after a plan of reorganization is approved, courts have permitted appellate review of orders that in other contexts might be considered interlocutory." Id; see also In re Paolino, 60 B.R. 828 (Bankr. E.D. Pa. 1986) (district court, using the analysis in *Amatex,* treated as a final order for purposes of appeal pursuant to 28 U.S.C. § 158, the bankruptcy court's order appointing a trustee). Accordingly, we will address the appeal on the merits.

The Committee first argues that the district court found cause within the meaning of Section 1104(a)(1) and, therefore, was required to appoint a trustee. To support its assertion that the court found cause but then improperly declined to appoint a trustee, the Committee points to this statement by the district judge: "I do not conclude that once having found cause … this Court is required to appoint a trustee in accord with Section 1104(a)(1)." Robins, on the other hand, contends that the court did not find cause and points to the following language in the court's opinion:

Frankly, a Trustee is not, on the present record, in the Court's view necessary or desirable. Indeed, such appointment may or may not impede the present efforts. In my view, appointment of a trustee would not be to the benefit of anyone. However, should the Court ever reach a contra conclusion, and should the debtor give the Court cause, the Court will not hesitate to appoint a Trustee.

We find that a careful reading of the court's opinion reveals that the court did not find cause to appoint a trustee within the meaning of Section 1104(a)(1). The court noted specifically that it had not found fraud or mismanagement. Further, it stated that the concepts of incompetence and dishonesty cover a wide spectrum of conduct and that the court has broad discretion in applying such concepts to show cause. The court examined the entire situation, including the consequences of appointing a trustee, and determined that the debtor had not given the court cause to appoint a trustee. The Committee misconstrues the court's statement regarding its discretion, given * * * a finding of cause, to appoint a trustee. We believe that the court's statement can only be construed to be a general assertion by the court of its discretionary authority in the event, not present here, that it were to find cause.

The Committee, however, also argues that the facts of this case compel a finding of cause. It asserts that Robins' lack of candor and preferential treatment of certain pre-petition creditors were dishonest and otherwise constituted cause. Like the district court, we recognize that Robins' conduct was improper and warranted a civil contempt sanction. But a policy of flexibility pervades the bankruptcy code with the ultimate aim of protecting creditors. A determination of cause, therefore, is within the discretion of the court and due consideration must be given to the various interests involved in the bankruptcy proceeding. "[T]he concepts of incompetence, dishonesty, gross mismanagement and even fraud all cover a wide range of conduct.... Implicit in a finding of incompetence, dishonesty, etc., for purposes of section 1104(a)(1), is whether the conduct shown rises to a level sufficient to warrant the appointment of a trustee." *General Oil*, 42 B.R. at 409. Obviously, to require the appointment of a trustee, regardless of the consequences, in the event of an act of dishonesty by the debtor, however slight or immaterial, could frustrate the purpose of the Bankruptcy Act. Section 1104(a)(1), therefore, must be construed, if possible, to make it harmonious with the Act in its entirety. Such a construction requires that the courts be given discretionary authority to determine whether conduct rises to the level of "cause."

Given the court's discretion and the careful consideration that it gave to the interests involved, we find that the court did not err in declining to find cause. The court's decision not to appoint a trustee was also within its discretionary authority and it is clear that the court did not abuse this authority. Since we hold that the court did not abuse its discretion in determining that cause did not exist, we need not reach the question concerning the statutory consequences of a finding of cause.

Accordingly, the decision of the district court is hereby
AFFIRMED.

NOTES

1. Does the decision in *Committee of Dalkon Shield Claimants* effectively eliminate § 1104(a)(1)? Note that the House report on § 1104(a) stated: "The court may order appointment only if the protection afforded by a trustee is needed and the costs and expenses of a trustee would not be disproportionately higher than the value of the protection afforded." H. Rep. No. 595, 95th Cong. 1st Sess. 402 (1977). Section 1104(a) in the bill which the House report accompanied provided in relevant part that:

[T]he court may order the appointment of a trustee only if—
    (1) the protection afforded by a trustee is needed; and
    (2) the costs and expenses of a trustee would not be disproportionately higher than the value of the protection afforded.

H.R. 8200, 95th Cong., 1st Sess. § 101 (1977) (containing proposed new text of Title 11, including proposed 11 U.S.C. § 1104). How does the proposed § 1104(a) in the House bill differ from § 1104(a) as enacted by Congress? What can you infer from the differences? Does the legislative history support the court's decision? What does this tell you about use of legislative history?

2.   Consider this statement from Oklahoma Refining Co. v. Blaik (In re Oklahoma Refining Co.), 838 F.2d 1133 (10th Cir. 1988): "Once the court has found that cause exists under § 1104, it has no discretion but must appoint a trustee." Id. at 1136. Is the Tenth Circuit's statement consistent with the decision in *Committee of Dalkon Shield Claimants*?

3.   "The appointment of a trustee in a Chapter 11 case is an extraordinary remedy available to creditors of the debtor. A strong presumption exists that the debtor should maintain control of the estate. In order to overcome this presumption, the movant bears the burden of proving by clear and convincing evidence the necessity for the appointment of a trustee.

"In the case at bar the movant alleges incompetence and gross mismanagement of the bankruptcy estate as grounds for the appointment of a trustee. In every bankruptcy there exists a certain level of incompetence or mismanagement. As a result, the courts have required a finding of more than simple mismanagement or incompetence * * * ." In re Evans, 48 B.R. 46, 47 (Bankr. W.D. Tex. 1985).

4.   "The appointment of a trustee in a Chapter 11 case is not the usual procedure because 11 U.S.C. § 1108 contemplates that the debtor will continue to manage its property and operate its business. The court must weigh all of the factors and interests carefully because the appointment of a trustee is an extraordinary remedy which will cause additional expense to the estate * * * .

"Not only has CSSC [the corporation which warehoused and shipped the debtor's inventory of books under a contract] not established cause for the appointment of a Chapter 11 trustee, but it also appears that such an appointment would not be in the best interests of creditors. The secured creditors and the official committee of unsecured creditors vigorously oppose the appointment of a trustee. They note that the debtor's management is sufficiently knowledgeable and experienced in the marketing of the debtor's books. Moreover, they do not wish to burden this estate with the additional administrative expenses associated with the appointment of a trustee, especially since there are no unencumbered assets to pay for the additional expense. * * * CSSC would not agree to pay for the expenses entailed in the appointment of a trustee, notwithstanding that CSSC is the only party in interest who seeks such an appointment. A secured creditor who does not expressly consent to bear the administrative expenses of a trustee appointed for its benefit in a Chapter 11 case may be held to have impliedly consented to assume such charges when there are no free assets to pay the trustee and the trustee's counsel and where the secured creditor, nevertheless, moved for the appointment of a Chapter 11 trustee. In re Hotel Associates, Inc., 6 B.R. 108 (Bankr. E.D. Pa. 1980). In the instant case, no such consent may be inferred because CSSC's counsel expressly refused to consent to CSSC's assumption of these costs, which would then have to be borne by the estate and its creditors, all of whom oppose the appointment of a trustee.

"Generally, the courts have applied a cost-benefit analysis, weighing the expense and time associated with the appointment of a trustee against potential benefits to the estate. Committee of Dalkon Shield Claimants v. A.H. Robins Co., Inc., 828 F.2d 239 (4th Cir. 1987). A trustee would not benefit any interests in this case. Not only will the costs of a trustee burden this estate, but current management's experience and knowledge are essential to the debtor's future." In re Stein and Day, Inc., 87 B.R. 290, 294-95 (Bankr. S.D.N.Y. 1988).

5. In *Stein and Day* (quoted in the previous note), the creditors generally opposed the appointment of a trustee. How much weight should a court give to the views of creditors, whether in support of or in opposition to the appointment of a trustee? In particular, should the court order appointment of a trustee when the creditors seem to have lost confidence in the debtor? Consider the following case.

In re Cardinal Industries, Inc.
United States Bankruptcy Court, S.D. Ohio, 1990
109 B.R. 755

[Cardinal Industries, Inc. ("CII") was a real estate developer and a manufacturer of modular housing units. CII and its subsidiaries (collectively "Cardinal") used the modular units in their real estate developments, including apartments, motels, retirement villages, offices, and other kinds of developments. The projects were financed by borrowing from secured lenders who received first mortgages on the properties. Cardinal would set up limited partnerships (with itself as general partner) to own and develop the projects. (In some cases, Cardinal itself lent the partnerships additional funds on a second mortgage basis, thus creating the "receivables" discussed in the court's opinion.) The plan was then to "syndicate" the partnerships—the partnerships were supposed to sell limited partnership interests to investors, thus generating cash for Cardinal, including cash to pay off the second mortgages which were owed to Cardinal. Cardinal developed more than a thousand projects, which included 50,000 apartment units, 200 motels, and sixteen retirement villages. Unfortunately, changes in the tax laws in 1986 made real estate developments less attractive to investors, and thus Cardinal was unable to find many investors who wanted to buy partnership interests. Thus, about half of the partnerships were left "unsyndicated," with Cardinal as general partner and as owner of the unsold limited partnership interests. Cardinal thus faced financial difficulty. The problems were made worse because (1) Cardinal kept on manufacturing modular housing units even though the demand for them had dried up, (2) many of the real estate developments were not generating enough rent to cover payments on their first mortgages and other expenses, which meant that Cardinal as general partner had to inject additional funds into the partnerships, and (3) Cardinal used $11 million to make imprudent loans to some of the partnerships in an attempt to counteract the negative effect of the tax law changes on the investors and to keep the investors' loyalty. Cardinal finally became so short of cash that it instructed the unsyndicated partnerships not to pay their February, 1989 first mortgage payments, but instead to send the money to CII. The resulting defaults infuriated the first mortgage holders just as Cardinal was about to try to negotiate with them to restructure the partnerships' debts. CII also decided that syndicated partnerships which had cash and which owed CII money should go ahead and pay CII, but CII took the money (more than a million dollars) from the wrong partnerships. In addition, the partnerships had failed to segregate their tenants'

security deposits but had instead spent the money. CII and its subsidiary Cardinal Industries of Florida ("CIF") finally filed chapter 11 petitions. After the petitions were filed, CII and CIF financial records were found to be unreliable, and the debtors failed to provide accurate and timely financial information to the creditors' committees. The committees, supported by the United States trustee, moved for appointment of a trustee.]

BARBARA J. SELLERS, Bankruptcy Judge.

* * *

The Court believes that the Creditors' assertions are correct and that the Debtors' management not only failed to take timely and effective steps to prevent serious financial difficulties, but also authorized activities which aggravated and accelerated the consequences of existing problems. Although some attempts were made to diversify products and raise new capital, few meaningful successes occurred. Undoubtedly those pre-petition decisions in part drove CII and CIF into Chapter 11. Most Chapter 11 debtors have histories of past errors in judgment, however, so those mistakes alone should not be sufficient grounds to establish cause for the appointment of a trustee. * * *

From its bankruptcy filing through October 31, 1989, CII has sustained cash losses of approximately $1,600,000. That figure does not include at least $3,400,000 in unpaid professional fees and $565,000 in other payables. * * *

The Creditors are understandably disturbed by the Debtors' inabilities to stem their continuing losses even though significant post-petition cutbacks have occurred in personnel, personnel benefits, facilities and equipment lease obligations. Although personnel cuts appear generally to have been overdue, the decreases in accounting staff during the consolidation of the Debtors' accounting systems from a regional to a centralized system may have resulted in increased errors in financial data which may be more costly to correct.

It is not contested that losses have continued. The Debtors believe the problem is being rectified, however, although admittedly at a slower pace than is desired. They believe that break-even will be reached during the first quarter of 1990.

[T]he founder, primary shareholder and former president of CII and his spouse have personally guaranteed obligations of Cardinal or its affiliated partnerships in the face amount of $120,000,000 to $150,000,000. While there is no indication that those guarantees have influenced any workout or deeds in lieu process, unless releases of those guarantees are negotiated, the guarantors' interests will be served by retaining partnership properties until the guaranteed mortgage debts can be repaid, whether or not such retention results in repayment of receivables to Cardinal for the benefit of unsecured creditors of these estates. And while accurate records of partnership expenses, payables, and income could allow the Creditors to determine whether their concerns regarding conflicts are justified, without those records the potential conflicts further erode confidence. * * *

III. DISCUSSION

The appointment of a trustee in a Chapter 11 case is an extraordinary remedy. If the Creditors are to prevail, the right to such remedy must be shown by clear and convincing evidence.

* * *

A. Appointment of a Trustee for Cause Pursuant to 11 U.S.C. § 1104(a)(1)

The examples of cause enumerated in § 1104(a)(1) are not exhaustive; the Court may find that cause exists for a reason not specifically set forth in the statute. In re Ford, 36 B.R. 501 (Bankr. W.D. Ky. 1983).

Finding cause to order the appointment of a trustee would be simple had there been clear evidence of dishonesty or fraud on the part of the Debtors' management. Other than the highly contested allegations of possible perjury through representations contained in the CIF amended schedules, however, fraud or dishonesty was not part of the Creditors' case. Because determination of that credibility issue carries grave implications for the participants if the Court's assessment is in error and because resolution of that matter is not necessary to the ruling on the motions, the Court will not find that cause has been established for fraud or dishonesty.

The Court also will not base a finding that cause exists for the appointment of a trustee solely upon management's incompetence or gross mismanagement. Certainly some of the Debtors' prepetition actions were highly questionable and there were numerous examples of mismanagement by inadequate control over administrative and financial systems. However, the evidence of incompetence or gross mismanagement is not sufficient to support the appointment of a trustee premised upon those grounds alone.

The fundamental problem in these cases is that there has been a serious and general loss of confidence in the Debtors' management. The alleged loss of confidence does not appear to the Court to be a ploy, but follows good faith efforts by the Creditors to permit the Debtors to direct their own reorganizations. The confidence problem has not resulted from one specific problem, but came about because of many events which, when seen in combination, make it appear that the Debtors are not properly in control of their reorganizations and should no longer be permitted to direct the process. Factors leading to this loss of confidence include decisions after the Tax Reform Act to continue the construction of projects and to extend loans to existing partnerships to equalize the tax treatment of investors at a time when the Debtors' cash reserves were being depleted by ordinary operations. Those factors further include specific pre-petition actions such as directing the payment of February, 1989 mortgage payment monies to the general partner, erroneously repaying loans from monies held by partnerships which either did not owe Cardinal or did not have those funds, failing to properly segregate partnership funds, particularly security deposits * * * .

That loss of confidence increased greatly after the Debtors failed to respond timely or accurately to data requests, failed to keep accurate or complete financial records or corporate books, continued to lose cash, and unduly delayed marketing assets or providing appropriate documentation for assets sought to be sold. Further erosion resulted from the continued appearance of certain conflicts of interest and a lack of strong direction or objective assessment of future plans for specific segments of the businesses, including manufacturing, syndication, the motel chains, property management services and new products for direct sales.

Finally, just when operations appeared to be beginning to stabilize and momentum was developing in workout negotiations with secured lenders to the partnerships, the Debtors not only fired the legal counsel which had contributed significantly to those positive developments, but also paid a retainer to replacement counsel at a time when other professionals were not being paid on a current basis. Such action caused considerable turmoil and contributed to the suspension of valuable assistance by the Debtors' accountants.

Perhaps none of the facts cited above, standing alone, would rise to the level of cause for the appointment of a trustee. Collectively, however, those facts have caused loss of confidence in the Debtors' management of crisis proportions. That crisis of confidence is cause which requires this Court to order the appointment of an independent trustee pursuant to 11 U.S.C. § 1104(a)(1).

> B. Appointment of a Trustee in the Interests of Parties Pursuant to 11 U.S.C. § 1104(a)(2).

Even if cause is not established within the meaning of § 1104(a)(1), the Court may order the appointment of a trustee under § 1104(a)(2) if the interests of creditors and other interests of the estate would be served thereby. If appointment is ordered pursuant to the Court's general equitable powers under § 1104(a)(2), the cost of a trustee to the estate, when compared with the benefit sought to be derived, will be a significant aspect of that determination.

The Court believes the interests of all parties to these cases will be served by the presence of an independent trustee. The presence of a trustee will provide secured creditors of these Debtors and of the partnerships with an objective party to decide whether to keep, sell or abandon particular assets. Unsecured creditors will have a party who is sensitive to the fiduciary duties owed to all constituencies. The United States Trustee may be able to receive more accurate and timely financial reports. Potential purchasers of assets of Cardinal or its affiliated partnerships will have a disinterested and dispassionate party on the other side of the negotiating table. Limited partner investors in the syndicated partnerships will have a chance to voice their needs. And finally, if the right person is selected, the Court will have an objective and realistic party to determine whether there is an estate of sufficient value to justify the time and resources expended on these cases.

Secured lenders to the Cardinal partnerships are being asked to restructure their loans. The professionals appointed in these cases are being asked to continue to provide services and wait for payment of their administrative claims. Limited partner investors are being asked to continue the Debtors as managing general partners of the partnerships. And unsecured creditors are being asked to wait five to ten years for the Debtors to receive payments of receivables from the partnerships which will form the basis for any distribution of dividends. All these requests are premised upon the Debtors' representations that such delay will result in the realization of value for all parties.

The Debtors may be correct in their assertions. Or the Debtors may be wrong and the assumptions they have made about the value of those partnership properties may be in error. The justified loss of confidence by all parties in the accuracy or completeness of financial information generated by these Debtors means those requests are being made without providing parties the data which is necessary to determine whether the requested actions or forebearances are in their best interests. In seven months, even in cases of this magnitude, the Court believes basic reliable data should have been provided to answer these questions posed by interested parties. Although the evidence established that the Debtors have recognized serious deficiencies in their record keeping processes since 1985, those failures have not been properly addressed. Accordingly, the Court has no basis to conclude that such deficiencies will soon be corrected.

Moreover, it is inescapable that the Unsecured Creditors' Committees of CII and CIF have lost faith in the Debtors' intentions and abilities to reorganize their affairs. That loss of faith is supported by facts established by evidence. No matter how much this Court might wish events were otherwise so that the trauma and risk of a trustee might be avoided, that loss of confidence has occurred and is justified. And denial of the motions will not reestablish trust or confidence. Essentially, these cases are at a standstill and the present state of the Debtors' affairs prevents the cases from progressing. Continued inability to move forward will jeopardize whatever chance exists to realize the potential values of these estates.

Both Debtors are insolvent. Accordingly, what value exists belongs to creditors and the interests of CII's two shareholders are secondary to the concerns of creditors. Since the Creditors, which hold unsecured debts, are willing to risk the costs, uncertainties and dislocations occasioned by the appointment of a trustee, the Court will exercise its equitable powers to order that appointment.

The Court also finds that the cost of a trustee should not exceed the benefit provided. Given the change of counsel and the current position of these estates, substantial expenditure of estate funds would be required to familiarize new counsel with the cases. Further, if it is possible for the Debtors to regain the confidence of all parties, that effort could be difficult and possibly expensive. The costs and expenses of a trustee should not be higher than those alternative costs would be, and the value of the protection afforded should be greater. Accordingly, appointing a trustee should serve the financial interest of all parties to these cases.

* * * The United States Trustee is ordered to appoint a trustee in each of these cases. * * * In addition to the duties enumerated in 11 U.S.C. § 1106, such trustee shall report orally to the Court and interested parties at each biweekly status conference. Although the Court is assuming that the same person will serve in both cases, if the United States Trustee, in consultation with the parties, believes the same person cannot serve as trustee for both estates, that determination will be acceptable to the Court.

IT IS SO ORDERED.

NOTES

1. Did the court find that appointment of a trustee would be in the best interests of the two shareholders of CII? Is such a finding necessary for appointment of a trustee under § 1104(a)(2)?

2. Is there a danger in permitting creditor loss of confidence in the debtor to be considered cause for appointment of a trustee? See In re Marvel Entm't Group, Inc., 140 F.3d 463 (3d Cir. 1998).

3. Analyze each of the facts that led to the creditors' loss of confidence in the debtor. Why would each of those facts tend to cause a creditor (and indeed the court) to lose confidence in the debtor's ability to reorganize?

4. In deciding whether to approve the United States trustee's selection of a trustee for the case the court should consider (1) whether the United States trustee has consulted in good faith with the interested parties, (2) whether the

person chosen is disinterested, and (3) whether the selection was an abuse of the United States trustee's discretion. In re Capital Servs. & Invs., Inc., 90 B.R. 382 (Bankr. C.D. Ill. 1988).

5.   What are the important qualities of a trustee for a chapter 11 case? Legal acumen? Long government service? Must the United States trustee's consultation with the parties in interest concerning selection of the trustee be more than perfunctory? Five days after the court's decision ordering the appointment of a trustee in the Cardinal cases, the court was faced with deciding whether to approve the United States trustee's choice of a trustee. The court refused:

> The provisions of 11 U.S.C. § 1104(c), which govern this proceeding, require the United States Trustee to consult with parties in interest * * * . Such consultation must be in good faith. In re Capital Services & Investments, Inc., 90 B.R. 382 (Bankr. C.D. Ill.1988). Based upon the evidence and statements of counsel, however, the Court finds that the process employed in these cases was not adequate or appropriate and does not satisfy the requirements of the statute.

> The Court further finds that the experience and credentials of the proposed appointee, while impressive and commendable in the legal and government community, do not include specialized experience in the private sector with either the operation of real estate properties or manufacturing facilities, or the direction of accounting and financial systems. Such experiences are necessary for the trustee of these bankruptcy estates. Accordingly, the Court must find that the individual proposed is not a candidate which the Court will approve for the position of trustee for these two bankruptcy estates. See In re Ruffin, Inc., 10 B.R. 862 (Bankr. D.R.I. 1981).

> Based upon the foregoing the Court finds that the relief requested by the Application should be, and the same is, hereby denied. The United States Trustee is hereby ordered to select another candidate with the background and experience necessary to satisfy the criteria suggested in the Court's order of January 4, 1990.

In re Cardinal Indus., Inc., 113 B.R. 378, 379-80 (Bankr. S.D. Ohio 1990).

     The United States trustee selected another candidate who was approved by Judge Sellers, and Cardinal was successfully reorganized. The trustee received compensation of $2.1 million plus 50,000 shares of stock in the reorganized company. That came to substantially more than $450 an hour for his services. Nevertheless, the court found that it was less than the market value of his services, in light of the results obtained. In re Cardinal Indus., Inc., 151 B.R. 843, 847 (Bankr. S.D. Ohio 1993).

6.   The bankruptcy judge has authority to order sua sponte the appointment of a trustee. Fukutomi v. United States Trustee (In re Bibo, Inc.), 76 F.3d 256 (9th Cir. 1996). However, the bankruptcy judge cannot require that the United States trustee submit more than one name so that the judge can have a choice. In re Plaza de Diego Shopping Ctr., Inc., 911 F.2d 820 (1st Cir. 1990). Neither can the court order the United States trustee to select the trustee for a chapter 11 case from the panel of private chapter 7 trustees (from which chapter 7 interim trustees must be appointed under § 701(a)(1)). In re Lathrop Mobile Investors, 55 B.R. 766 (B.A.P. 9th Cir. 1985).

7.   What do you think motivated Congress in 1994 to add § 1104(b) to the Code, thus permitting creditors to elect a trustee? Why is there a 20% participation requirement?

8. What do you think motivated Congress to add § 1104(e) in 2005? Why was
    there no motion for an order that a trustee be appointed in Enron, WorldCom,
    Adelphia, and other mass fraud cases?

Problem 6-2

Assume that Gruff (Foam Corporation's majority shareholder and chief
executive officer) owns a 50% stake in PadCo, a manufacturer of carpet
padding. For several years Foam Corporation has sold foam to PadCo for its
padding and given PadCo the typical 30 days to pay for the foam. When Foam
Corporation filed its petition, PadCo owed Foam Corporation $75,000 for foam,
and none of the debt was overdue. It is now eight months after Foam
Corporation filed its petition. PadCo owes Foam Corporation $225,000. Of that
amount, $100,000 is owed for foam delivered more than 60 days ago. Do these
facts raise an issue whether a trustee should be appointed? See Oklahoma
Refining Co. v. Blaik (In re Oklahoma Refining Co.), 838 F.2d 1133 (10th Cir.
1988). May the court order appointment of a limited trustee to oversee Foam
Corporation's financial affairs and require the trustee to leave operation of the
business in Gruff's hands? Consider In re Nartron Corp., 330 B.R. 573 (Bankr.
W.D. Mich. 2005); In re Intercat, Inc., 247 B.R. 911 (Bankr. S.D. Ga. 2000).

May the court, over the objection of Foam Corporation's board, enter an order
transferring the right to exercise the powers of the debtor in possession to a
"responsible person" chosen by the court or by the United States trustee? See In
re Gaslight Club, Inc., 782 F.2d 767, 771 (7th Cir. 1986) ("Sections 105(a) and
1107(a) * * * provide adequate authority for the bankruptcy court to approve the
replacement of the person designated to perform the duties and exercise the
rights of the debtor in possession if the creditors' committee, the person presently
in control and the majority and controlling shareholder of the debtor agree to this
course of action.") (also relying in part on provisions of Delaware General
Corporation Law); In re Adelphia Communications Corp., 336 B.R. 610, 667
(Bankr. S.D.N.Y. 2006) (rejecting creditors' committee motion for appointment of
nonstatutory fiduciary to act for debtors in disputes between affiliated debtors,
stating that use of §§ 105(a) and 1107(a) to make such an appointment "may be
altogether forbidden," and stating that "[t]hough there is no case yet unequivocally
so holding in the section 1107(a) context, relevant caselaw * * * comes close,
displacing a debtor in possession with a nontrustee only where there was consent,
and suggesting that the presence of consent to it was the controlling factor"), aff'd,
__ B.R. __ (S.D.N.Y. Mar 30, 2006) (No. 06 Civ. 1445 (SAS) (text not yet available
on Westlaw); In re Suncruz Casinos, LLC, 298 B.R. 821, 832 (Bankr. S.D. Fla.
2003) ("The Bankruptcy Code expressly provides for appointment of a trustee
when a debtor's management is replaced. The Code does not contemplate
appointment of a 'Responsible Person' to perform the duties of a trustee.")
Compare In re Communication Options, 299 B.R. 481 (Bankr. S.D. Ohio 2003)
(relying on Gaslight and ordering appointment of responsible person even without
agreement of parties where appointment of trustee would be too disruptive at late
stage of case), with In re Nat'l Century Fin. Enters., Inc., 292 B.R. 850 (Bankr.
S.D. Ohio 2003) (discussing Gaslight and Lifeguard Indus., and refusing to order
appointment of current corporate president as person to exercise powers of
debtor in possession despite risk that new board might be elected by shareholders
and might remove president). May the court accomplish the same thing under
§ 1106(b) by ordering appointment of an examiner to take over the debtor in
possession's functions?

3. Corporate Governance in Chapter 11: Replacing Officers or the Board of Directors

If no trustee is appointed or elected, the debtor will remain in possession. That does not necessarily mean, however, that the debtor's managers will be retained. For the most part, the corporation law of the state of incorporation applies to the internal governance of a corporation in chapter 11. The board of directors' state law right to replace the chief executive officer and other members of the management team is usually honored in chapter 11. Similarly, the shareholders' state law right to meet and to elect the members of the board of directors is usually honored in chapter 11.[8]

The right of shareholders to elect new directors raises difficult issues regarding the fiduciary duties of loyalty and care owed by the debtor in possession and its managers to the estate, to the creditors, and to the shareholders (or other interest holders). See generally LaSalle Nat'l Bank v. Perelman, 82 F. Supp. 2d 279 (D. Del. 2000). Especially if the debtor is on the borderline of insolvency, the creditors and the shareholders may have very different views as to what risks the debtor in possession should take in operating the business. If, for example, Foam Corporation expands its waterbed production, it *may* substantially increase its future cash flows, thus increasing the reorganization value of the assets. On the other hand, if Foam Corporation spends the large sums needed to expand waterbed production, and the expansion is not a success, the estate will suffer a substantial loss. If Foam Corporation is on the borderline of insolvency, the shareholders will reap most of the benefit if the expansion is a success, but the creditors will bear most of the burden if it fails.

There is also a strong conflict between the interests of the creditors and shareholders with regard to the terms of the plan of reorganization. The debtor in possession, through its directors and managers, is charged to consult with the creditors, see § 1103(c)(1)-(3) and (d), and then formulate and file a proposed plan of reorganization. See § 1106(a)(5). If the debtor is insolvent on a going concern basis, then every dollar of value that the shareholders receive under the proposed plan of reorganization is a dollar that is lost to the creditors. Thus the shareholders and the creditors have adverse interests. As noted above, the debtor in possession and its managers owe fiduciary duties *both* to the shareholders and to the creditors. In negotiating with the creditors and in formulating a plan, the debtor in possession's managers will have to take negotiating positions on the amount of value which the shareholders should receive, and they must do so without violating their fiduciary duties of loyalty and care to either group. The conflict is especially severe during the often lengthy period when the debtor has the exclusive right to file a plan. See § 1121, which is discussed below in Chapter Eleven of this text.

---

8. For a discussion (and criticism) of the substantial academic literature arguing that control of chapter 11 debtors should be turned over to those claimants whose money is at stake (typically some group of creditors), see LoPucki, *The Myth of the Residual Owner: An Empirical Study*, 82 WASH. U.L.Q. 1341 (2004).

It may be argued, on the other hand, that in filing a plan the debtor need not act as a fiduciary for the creditors. Section 1121(a) states that "[t]he debtor may file a plan * * * at any time * * * ." By referring to the "debtor" rather than to "the debtor in possession," the section may permit the debtor to file a plan not in its capacity as debtor in possession, the capacity in which the debtor represents the estate and owes fiduciary duties to the creditors, but in its capacity simply as debtor. Even then, under state corporation law, the debtor and its managers will generally owe duties to creditors if the debtor is insolvent and may owe them duties if it is near insolvency. See Geyer v. Ingersoll Publ'ns Co., 621 A.2d 784 (Del. Ch. 1992); Prod. Res. Group, LLC v. NCT Group, Inc., 863 A.2d 772 (Del. Ch. 2004); Credit Lyonnais Bank Nederland, N.V. v. Pathe Commc'ns Corp., 1991 WL 277613, 17 Del. J. Corp. L. 1099 (Del. Ch. 1991); Fed. Deposit Ins. Corp. v. Sea Pines Co., 692 F.2d 973 (4th Cir. 1982); Lin, *Shift of Fiduciary Duty Upon Corporate Insolvency: Proper Scope of Directors' Duty to Creditors,* 46 VAND. L. REV. 1485 (1993); Miller, *Corporate Governance in Chapter 11: The Fiduciary Relationship Between Directors and Stockholders of Solvent and Insolvent Corporations,* 23 SETON HALL L. REV. 1467 (1993).

Commentators take widely differing positions on the rights and duties of the debtor's managers in these conflict situations. See, e.g., Sheinfeld & Pippitt, *Fiduciary Duties of Directors of a Corporation in the Vicinity of Insolvency and After Initiation of a Bankruptcy Case,* 60 BUS. LAW. 79, 92-95 (2004); Trost & Schwartz, *Fiduciary Duties of Directors in the Chapter 11 and Insolvency Contexts (With a Note on The Fiduciary Duties of Counsel For The Debtor-in-Possession),* in CHAPTER 11 BUSINESS REORGANIZATIONS, (Annual Advanced ALI-ABA Course of Study, No. SE71, 2000), available at SE71 ALI-ABA 265 (Westlaw); Bogart, *Unexpected Gifts of Chapter 11: The Breach of a Director's Duty of Loyalty Following Plan Confirmation And The Postconfirmation Jurisdiction Of Bankruptcy Courts,* 72 AM. BANKR. L.J. 303 (1998); Cuevas, *The Myth of Fiduciary Duties in Corporate Reorganization Cases,* 73 NOTRE DAME L. REV. 385 (1998); LoPucki & Whitford, *Corporate Governance in the Bankruptcy of Large Publicly Held Companies,* 141 U. PA. L. REV. 669, 767-96 (1993); Miller, supra, 23 SETON HALL L. REV. at 1485-97, 1513-15 (1993); LoPucki & Whitford, *Preemptive Cramdown,* 65 AM. BANKR. L.J. 625 (1991). For now, however, the point is that the shareholders may be unhappy with the positions taken by the directors. Shareholders may want the directors to take large risks in order to try to make large profits—perhaps larger risks than the directors think appropriate. Shareholders may want the directors to use their leverage in plan negotiations to obtain as much value as possible for the shareholders—perhaps more value than the directors think they fairly can seek for the shareholders. If so, or if for some other reason the shareholders are dissatisfied with the management, the shareholders may try to install a new board and a new management team. When should the court intervene to prevent that? Does the bankruptcy court have the power to intervene? Consider the following cases.

In re Lifeguard Industries, Inc.
United States Bankruptcy Court, S.D. Ohio, 1983
37 B.R. 3

Randall J. Newsome, Bankruptcy Judge.

This Chapter 11 case is before the Court pursuant to an Application for Approval of New Management, a Motion to Confirm Appointment of New Directors, and a Motion for Appointment of Committee of Equity Security Holders. * * *

[Lifeguard was an aluminum siding manufacturer founded in 1956 by Louis and Joseph Guttman. Louis died, and Joseph ran the company until 1974, when Joseph's son Fred became president, secretary, and chief operating officer. Joseph died in 1980, which left only two members on Lifeguard's board of directors: Joseph's widow Marion, and Shirley Onie, daughter of Joseph and Marion. Fred owned a slight majority of Lifeguard's shares, most of which he had acquired from Joseph. Joseph—and later Shirley as personal representative of Joseph's estate–had the right to vote those shares until Fred finished paying for them. Joseph's estate, Marion, and Shirley also owned shares. Under an April 16, 1975 agreement with Fred, Shirley would not have been entitled to vote any shares, but Fred was in default under the agreement.]

[Lifeguard suffered losses and cash flow difficulties in 1980 and 1981; Lifeguard's primary lender, BancOhio, cut its credit line in half; and in 1982 Lifeguard filed a chapter 11 petition. In 1983 Fred caused Lifeguard to file a proposed plan which would have left him and two key employees (Epstein and Wendell) as the only shareholders. Shirley and Marion defended their interests by hiring advisors (Sycalik and Hevener) and by having Marion resign from the board of directors. Her resignation triggered a requirement, apparently under the corporation's by-laws, that a shareholders' meeting be held to elect directors. They intended to elect Shirley, Sycalik, and Hevener to the board and then to install Shirley, Sycalik, and Hevener as the corporation's officers, ousting Fred from control. Debtor's counsel applied to the Bankruptcy Court for instructions. The court "ordered that the shareholders' meeting should be held, but that any changes in management personnel or operating procedures could not be instituted until such time as the newly-elected board of directors obtained approval of the Court."]

10. On August 1, 1983, Shirley Onie, through counsel, sent notice of a shareholder's meeting to be held at 9:00 A.M. August 8, 1983 at the offices of Wilke and Goering, counsel for Shirley Onie.

11. On August 4, 1983, Fred Guttman sent notice by telegram of a shareholder's meeting to be held August 8, 1983 at 8:30 A.M. at the office of Joel Moskowitz, corporate counsel. This action was in violation of Ohio Revised Code § 1701.41(A) requiring written notice of a shareholder's meeting not less than seven nor more than 60 days prior to the date of the meeting.

12. On August 8, 1983 at 8:30 A.M., * * * Shirley Onie, through counsel, presented a protest regarding lack of proper notice of the meeting. The meeting was then adjourned.

13. The second shareholder's meeting of August 8 commenced at 9:05 A.M. in the law offices of Robert Goering. * * * Shirley Onie called this meeting to order and purported to vote 13,450 shares in favor of a new board of directors to include herself, Gary Sycalik and John Hevener. The meeting was then adjourned.

14. At approximately 9:10 A.M., Fred Guttman and Joel Moskowitz arrived at Mr. Goering's office and conducted yet another shareholder's meeting. * * * Mr. Moskowitz proceeded to disqualify all shares except the 1,350 owned by Fred. * * *

As a result, only Fred Guttman's unimpaired 1,350 shares were allowed to vote and Fred thereby purportedly elected himself, Louis Epstein and James Wendell the new directors.

* * *

16. We have previously found that the April 16 agreements were in default and that Shirley Onie thus remained owner of her shares. Thus, it was error to disqualify her 1,450 shares.

* * *

19. The Court further finds that prior to this litigation and again during the course of the litigation, the corporation submitted disclosure statements, both of which state that while Fred Guttman owned 51% of the stock, the proxy given his father reduced his voting rights to less than a majority. Such disclosure statements also state that the 1975 agreements are in default.

These facts raise serious concerns as to the good faith of counsel for debtor in so vigorously pursuing this issue, and the benefit which the debtor derived from the fray. The Court also has doubts as to whose interests are being represented by counsel for the debtor—those of the debtor, or those of Fred Guttman. These concerns will be more fully addressed at a later time.

* * *

29. [T]his Court finds that Shirley Onie is authorized to exercise the voting rights in 13,050 of the 15,000 outstanding shares of stock in Lifeguard Industries, Inc.; that she properly exercised such voting rights during the second meeting of shareholders held on August 8, 1983; and that Shirley Onie, Gary Sycalik, and John Hevener, Jr. shall constitute the board of directors of Lifeguard until such time as new directors may be elected pursuant to Lifeguard's articles of incorporation and code of regulations.

30. The newly-elected directors propose to change the management structure of the company by installing Gary Sycalik as president, Hevener as secretary, and Onie as treasurer, with Louis A. Epstein to continue as vice-president of marketing and James G. Wendell III to continue as vice-president of manufacturing. Fred Guttman would be employed as operations manager. It is unclear what (if any) his responsibilities would be, but it is clear that Fred Guttman would decline to accept the position regardless of what his responsibilities might be.

The new board of directors has also proposed the hiring of four consultants to act as a crisis management team. While the board agrees that Sycalik will act as coordinator of this team, they do not agree on who will run the day-to-day operations as chief executive officer. * * *

Hevener expects to be paid a salary of approximately $50,000 as chief executive officer. Sycalik was less specific as to his expected remuneration. However, he estimates that the services of the consultants which the board proposes to retain will cost the corporation approximately $40,000.00 over a two- to four-month period.

The Court notes in passing that neither Onie nor Sycalik nor Hevener intends to invest any of their own personal assets to financially resuscitate Lifeguard.

31. The new members of the board have proposed that Epstein and Wendell remain in their present positions. Neither Hevener nor Sycalik has ever met Epstein or Wendell, nor have they determined whether Wendell and Epstein are willing to remain employed for the corporation under the new management team. Both Epstein and Wendell testified at the hearing, and both indicated a strong probability that they would leave if Fred Guttman were ousted from control. The parties generally concede, and the Court finds, that both Epstein and Wendell are exceptionally well-qualified for their positions.

* * *

From the evidence presented, the Court entertains serious misgivings as to whether Lifeguard could continue to operate if both Wendell and Epstein should abruptly resign from the company.

* * *

Onie, Sycalik and Hevener share certain characteristics in terms of their qualifications to operate Lifeguard. None of the three has any knowledge of the aluminum siding industry; nor do they have a source of financing to solve Lifeguard's pressing financial problems; nor do they have a working knowledge of the business; nor do they have a clear plan of action for operating the business and solving the problems which they believe exist; nor do they have a clear idea of how they will utilize the services of the consultants which will compose their crisis management team.

* * *

33. Onie, Sycalik and Hevener argue that Lifeguard is no longer a viable corporation, and that mismanagement by Fred Guttman is almost exclusively to blame for its demise. Among other things, they cite poor accounting procedures, inadequate financial controls, and unwise business decisions as justifications for immediately ousting Fred Guttman from control.

Based upon the evidence presented, the Court agrees with their contention that neither Fred Guttman nor Anita Gabor, company accounting manager, has an adequate grasp of the details of Lifeguard's financial condition, either past or present. Indeed, no intelligible explanation of the company's present financial condition has been presented to this Court. * * *

34. Notwithstanding his lack of knowledge regarding the company's finances and the confused state of Lifeguard's financial picture, the evidence establishes that Fred Guttman has made a concerted effort to turn the business around, and that these efforts have met with some success. As of 1980 the company operated fifteen regional warehouses, had 25 to 30 salesmen, 3 regional managers, and $11 million in yearly sales. The increased debt burden and decrease in sales caused by the rise in interest rates required that Guttman make some difficult decisions in 1980 and 1981. To cut down overhead and improve cash flow, the sales force was reduced dramatically, and 12 of the 15 warehouses were closed. However, the benefits from these actions were not quickly realized due to the expenses inherent in closing the warehouses. Other cost-saving measures were instituted, including the termination of the company's vice-president of finance, material specialist, and certain office personnel. Guttman cut his own salary from $115,000 per year to $85,000 per year.

The company incurred additional financial setbacks in the form of continuing theft losses (which are still being investigated) and the reduction of their line of credit by BancOhio. Because the company was forced to do business with their suppliers on a cash basis, and because the economy failed to improve, sales continued to decrease.

Primarily due to Guttman's efforts, however, the company has increased its highly profitable tolling operations, which consists of custom painting for other manufacturers. It has sought and obtained distributorship rights for vinyl siding, and has established new outlets for the sale of its aluminum siding. It is undisputed that the company will probably show a profit this year although the amount is subject to question due to the unreliability of its financial statements.

The suggestion has been made that the company should have phased out its aluminum siding business longer ago and switched to the production of vinyl siding, which is expected to hold 60% to 70% of the siding market by 1985. This suggestion was effectively rebutted by Guttman, who noted that * * * machinery for the production of vinyl siding would cost at least $1 million alone and the product change-over would require a two-year lag time. Furthermore, there are presently 21 manufacturers of vinyl siding in the U.S. and 6 in Canada. The competitors are large corporations, the technology involved is difficult, and the industry presently has a large excess capacity.

35. Based upon his testimony, as well as that of Wendell and Epstein, the Court finds that Fred Guttman has a good working knowledge of the aluminum siding industry, has performed capably as a manager of Lifeguard's business activities, and has made a significant personal and financial commitment to turning the company around. Based upon the above findings and all of the evidence presented in this case, the Court further finds that the best interests of creditors would not be served by allowing the new slate of officers to take over the day-to-day operations of the business, at least not at this critical time.

OPINION AND CONCLUSIONS OF LAW

* * * There is little question that shareholders of a corporate debtor-in-possession retain their state law rights to control a corporation, and that such rights cannot be lightly cast aside by this Court. In re Lionel Corporation, 30 B.R. 327, 10 B.C.D. 960 (Bkrtcy. S.D.N.Y. 1983); * * * .

However, it is equally apparent that the shareholders' right to control a Chapter 11 debtor-in-possession is not without limitations under the Bankruptcy Code. Section 1107(a) specifically provides that a debtor-in-possession shall have all (or almost all) of the rights, powers and duties of a trustee subject "*to such limitations or conditions as the court prescribes ....*" Section 1108 states that "unless the Court orders otherwise, the trustee may operate the debtor's business." At least two courts have interpreted the language of § 1108 as prohibiting a court from interfering with a trustee's business judgments in operating a debtor's business. In re Curlew Valley Associates, 8 B.C.D. 495, 14 B.R. 506 (Bkrtcy. D. Utah 1981); * * * . Those same two courts also noted *in dicta* that no similar restriction can be gleaned from the language and legislative history of § 1107(a).

This same conclusion was reached in In re Lyon & Reboli, Inc., 24 B.R. 152, 9 B.C.D. 916 (Bkrtcy. E.D.N.Y. 1982), wherein it was held that § 105 and § 1107(a) of the Code vest the Court with the authority to review the propriety of salaries paid to the debtor-in-possession's officers. Judge Parente's reasoning is worth repeating here:

At issue is not the wisdom or efficacy of a business decision, but the propriety of insiders bestowing upon themselves compensation which may be excessive and detrimental to the creditors. The corporations in question are closely held, and the actions of the officers are subject to little, if any, internal review. Prior to the confirmation of a negotiated plan which might fix the compensation of the officers, the court has an obligation, when application is made by a party in interest, to pass upon the propriety of the salaries of insiders where there is the potential for, and the prima facie appearance of, abuse.

24 B.R. 152, 9 B.C.D. at 917.

While the propriety of salaries is not at issue here, there have been allegations of, and certainly potential for, abuse of the corporation by insiders to the detriment of both the creditors and the equity security holders. Thus, the Court has an obligation to scrutinize the actions of the corporation when asked by a party in interest to do so.

We heartily concur in the view expressed in the above-cited decisions that business judgments should be left to the board room and not to this Court. It is not this Court's responsibility to determine whether Lifeguard should increase its tolling operations, change its product lines, increase its distributing activities, cut back its sales force, or manufacture vinyl siding. It is this Court's responsibility to protect creditors' interests from the actions of inexperienced, incapable, or foolhardy management, whether old or new.

It may well be that Shirley Onie's management team might ultimately usher in a new era of unprecedented prosperity at Lifeguard. But no concrete means or plan have been suggested for achieving this promised result. Indeed, the new management slate has demonstrated no real understanding of the immediate problems facing the business, or for that matter, the business itself. If they fail in their efforts, only the creditors lose. We do not believe that such unwilling gamblers should be required to take that risk.

Accordingly, the motion to confirm the appointment of new directors is GRANTED; the application for approval of new management is DENIED. Since Shirley Onie is now effectively in control of the board of directors of the corporation, the Court views an equity security holders committee as unnecessary, and accordingly her motion to appoint such a committee is DENIED.

The Court further ORDERS as follows:

1. Fred Guttman, James Wendell, III, and Louis Epstein shall continue as President, Vice-President of Manufacturing, and Vice-President of Marketing and Sales at their present salary levels. They shall have sole and exclusive authority and responsibility for the day-to-day operation of Lifeguard Industries, Inc. Such authority and responsibility shall continue until the confirmation of a plan of reorganization or the expiration of four months, whichever occurs first. At such time the board of directors may install new officers of their choosing pursuant to the corporate code of regulations.

2. The newly-elected board of directors may propose a plan of reorganization on behalf of Lifeguard, such plan to be submitted within the next 60 days. The expense of preparing such plan shall be reimbursed by the corporation, subject to the approval of the Court. It may negotiate for the sale of the business, seek out sources of financing, engage in future planning for the business, and take any

action pursuant to the terms of the Bankruptcy Code which it deems appropriate; the expenses for such activities and the retention of persons to engage in such activities shall be subject to the approval of the Court. * * *

NOTES

1. Did Fred Guttman violate his fiduciary duties of loyalty and care by causing Lifeguard to propose a plan which eliminated the interests of the shareholders other than Fred?

2. Why did the court believe it unnecessary to appoint a committee to represent stockholders? Is there a major stockholder whose interests will likely not be taken into account by the new board of directors?

3. What was the statutory authority, if any, for the court's refusal to allow the newly elected directors to replace the management team? What standard did the court apply to decide the issue of whether the management team could be replaced?

Manville Corporation v. Equity Security Holders Committee (In re Johns-Manville Corporation)
United States Court of Appeals, Second Circuit, 1986
801 F.2d 60

Mahoney, Circuit Judge:

This action, one segment in a long-running Chapter 11 reorganization proceeding, arose in consequence of the competing interests of creditors, stockholders, and the board of directors in the development of rehabilitation plans for appellee, the Manville Corporation ("Manville"), formerly Johns-Manville Corporation. Appellants are the Equity Security Holders Committee and individual members of that committee (collectively the "Equity Committee"), appointed by the bankruptcy court to represent the interests of stockholders in Manville's reorganization. The Securities and Exchange Commission, although technically an appellee, shares the interests of the Equity Committee in the matter at hand.[9] Manville is aligned for purposes of this appeal with the Committee of Asbestos Health Related Claimants and/or Creditors (the "Asbestos Health Committee"), which represents the interests of the victims of diseases resulting from exposure to asbestos who have presently existing claims in tort against Manville, and with the Legal Representative, who represents the interests of future claimants who have not yet manifested such diseases.

The instant conflict arises in part because each of the committees representing the various interests in Manville must depend upon the Manville board of directors to advance those interests in the bankruptcy court at this stage of the rehabilitation proceedings. As debtor, Manville had the exclusive right under the Bankruptcy Code to file rehabilitation plans for the first 120 days of reorganization, and the bankruptcy court in these proceedings has granted Manville several extensions prolonging its exclusive filing period. See 11 U.S.C. § 1121(b), (d) (1982 & Supp. III 1985). Therefore, although in theory each of the

---

9.   [Footnote 2 in original:] Although it has standing to be heard in the first instance, the Securities and Exchange Commission does not have standing to appeal. 11 U.S.C. § 1109(a) (1982). It may, however, participate in an appeal taken by a party in interest. H.R.Rep. No. 595, 95th Cong., 1st Sess. 404, reprinted in 1978 U.S.Code Cong. & Ad.News 5787, 5963, 6360.

committees may one day have the opportunity to submit a rehabilitation plan to the bankruptcy court if Manville's own proposals are rejected or if a trustee is appointed to replace the Manville board, see id. § 1121(c), Manville has for three or four years enjoyed the exclusive right, after negotiating with the committees, to file proposed plans. And although any of the committees may decline to accept a plan submitted to the bankruptcy court for confirmation, the power to formulate such plans in the first instance or at least to exercise a voice in their formulation is clearly a desideratum under the program laid down by the Bankruptcy Code, because the bankruptcy court may confirm a plan with or without the acquiescence of all classes of claims. If any impaired class rejects Manville's proposed plan, the court will nevertheless confirm it, upon Manville's request, so long as at least one impaired class has accepted the plan and so long as the court determines that the plan "does not discriminate unfairly" and is "fair and equitable" to each impaired class that has not accepted it. 11 U.S.C. § 1129(b)(1) (1982 & Supp. III 1985).

In order to channel negotiations toward acceptable plans, the various factions interested in Manville's rehabilitation have formed *ad hoc* alliances when the occasion has called for them. The challenge all the committees have faced is to fashion a plan that will preserve Manville's capacity to generate enough revenue to pay existing creditors, to cover its liabilities to present and future tort claimants where liability is certain though its precise extent is unknown, and to satisfy Manville's shareholders. The seemingly strange bedfellows in the instant litigation, Manville and the committees representing present and future tort claimants, have long struggled to devise a reorganization plan acceptable to each. Along the way they have at times been antagonists rather than allies. For example, the Asbestos Health Committee opposed Manville's first proposed plan, sanctioned by the Equity Committee and filed on November 21, 1983. Other disputes, such as the Asbestos Health Committee's initial refusal to represent future tort claimants, which led to litigation over the appointment of the Legal Representative, and the Asbestos Health Committee's motion to dismiss Manville's Chapter 11 petition, which the Equity Committee opposed, also diverted the energies of all parties from negotiations that might earlier have led to an acceptable plan.

To their credit, Manville and the Legal Representative finally came to terms in August of 1985, formulating a plan that would earmark billions of dollars for payment to present and future asbestosis victims as well as to others damaged by the asbestos products that Manville once manufactured and sold. They have now received the blessing of the Asbestos Health Committee and apparently of the other creditor committees. Having reconciled their differences, however, they encountered opposition from the Equity Committee immediately following their breakthrough, on the eve of their submission of the plan to the bankruptcy court for confirmation. Under protest, the Equity Committee had been cut out of the negotiations that led to their plan, and if the product of Manville's new understanding with the tort claimants and other creditors is confirmed, equity may be diluted by 90% or more. Displeased with that prospect, which the Equity Committee views as evidence of the Manville board's abdication of its responsibilities to the shareholders, the Equity Committee brought an action in Delaware state court seeking to compel Manville to hold a shareholders' meeting, pursuant to section 211(c) of Delaware's General Corporation Law.[10] The Equity Committee's avowed purpose was to replace Manville directors, so that new directors might reconsider submitting the proposed plan.

Manville countered with the instant action. At Manville's behest, the bankruptcy court issued an injunction prohibiting the Equity Committee from pursuing the Delaware action on the ground that the holding of a shareholders' meeting would obstruct Manville's reorganization. Denying the Equity Committee's motion for summary judgment, the bankruptcy court granted summary judgment to Manville *sua sponte*. The district court affirmed. * * *

Turning, then, to the decision to enjoin, we first encounter the well-settled rule that the right to compel a shareholders' meeting for the purpose of electing a new board subsists during reorganization proceedings. See In re Bush Terminal Co., 78 F.2d 662, 664 (2d Cir. 1935); In re Saxon Industries, 39 B.R. 49, 50 (Bankr. S.D.N.Y. 1984); In re Lionel Corp., 30 B.R. 327, 330 (Bankr. S.D.N.Y. 1983). As a consequence of the shareholders' right to govern their corporation, a prerogative ordinarily uncompromised by reorganization, "a bankruptcy court should not lightly employ its equitable power to block an election of a new board of directors." In re Potter Instrument Co., 593 F.2d 470, 475 (2d Cir. 1979). In accordance with this rule, the parties and the lower courts agree that the Equity Committee's right to call a meeting may be impaired only if the Equity Committee is guilty of "clear abuse" in attempting to call one. See In re J.P. Linahan, Inc., 111 F.2d 590, 592 (2d Cir. 1940). The Equity Committee's principal argument is that the "clear abuse" standard was not satisfied. In addition, however, the Equity Committee seems to argue that the district court's analysis was incomplete; i.e., the Equity Committee contends that in reviewing the bankruptcy court's decision to issue the injunction, the district court should have required, in addition to a showing of clear abuse, the usual showing of irreparable injury.

An examination of both lower court decisions will clarify the analysis that follows. The bankruptcy court found that "any shareholder meeting and ensuing proxy fight has the potential to derail the entire Manville reorganization with devastating consequences or at least to delay or halt plan negotiations." Reviewing the bankruptcy court's findings, the district court concluded that the Equity Committee intended either to "torpedo" the reorganization or to acquire a bargaining chip in aid of its negotiation power. In either case, the district court reasoned, the bankruptcy court did not err in concluding that the Equity Committee was guilty of clear abuse.

[W]e cannot agree that the Equity Committee's professed desire to arrogate more bargaining power in the negotiation of a plan—in contrast to some secret desire to destroy all prospects for reorganization—may in itself constitute clear abuse. The law of this circuit directs that the shareholders' natural wish to participate in this matter of corporate governance be respected. In In re Bush Terminal Co., 78 F.2d 662 (2d Cir. 1935), for example, this court reversed an order enjoining a shareholders' meeting to be called for the purpose of advancing a rehabilitation

---

10. [Footnote 4 in original:] Del.Code Ann. tit. 8, § 211(c) (1983) provides that upon "a failure to hold the annual meeting ... for a period of 13 months ... after its last annual meeting, the Court of Chancery may summarily order a meeting to be held upon the application of any stockholder or director."

plan more favorable to equity. Expressly upholding the right of a majority shareholder to try to replace board members for that purpose, the court reasoned:

> [T]he debtor is given the right to be heard on all questions. Obviously, the stockholders should have the right to be adequately represented in the conduct of the debtor's affairs, especially in such an important matter as the reorganization of the debtor. Such representation can be obtained only by having as directors persons of their choice …. [T]he debtor is given the power to propose a plan of reorganization. No reason is advanced why stockholders, if they feel that the present board of directors is not acting in their interest, or has caused an unsatisfactory plan to be filed on behalf of the debtor, should not cause a new board to be elected which will act in conformance with the stockholders' wishes.

Id. at 664.

The court in In re Bush Terminal Co. thus clearly intended to protect the right of stockholders to be heard in negotiations leading to a rehabilitation plan. As the court concluded, "If the right of stockholders to elect a board of directors should not be carefully guarded and protected, the statute giving the debtor a right to be heard or to propose a plan of reorganization could not truly be exercised, for the board of directors is the representative of the stockholders." Id. at 665. Under this analysis, the shareholders' mere intention to exercise bargaining power—whether by actually replacing the directors or by "bargaining away" their chip without replacing the board, as the district court suggests they may have wished to do—cannot without more constitute clear abuse. Unless the Equity Committee were to bargain in bad faith—e.g., to demonstrate a willingness to risk rehabilitation altogether in order to win a larger share for equity—its desire to negotiate for a larger share is protected. Moreover, if rehabilitation is placed at risk as a result of the other committees' intransigent unwillingness to negotiate with the Equity Committee, as opposed to their real inability, within some reasonable amount of time, to formulate any confirmable plan more satisfactory to equity, the Equity Committee should not alone bear the consequences of a stalemate by being deemed guilty of clear abuse.[11]

In re Lionel Corp., 30 B.R. 327 (Bankr.S.D.N.Y.1983), buttresses our conclusion that shareholders' desire for leverage is not a basis for denying them an election, so long as leverage means only the improvement of their bargaining position or the assurance of their participation in negotiations. In In re Lionel Corp. the bankruptcy court held that the record failed to demonstrate how reorganization would be impeded merely because the shareholders might be successful in their quest to cause the reorganization to "take an entirely different turn." Id. at 330. Surely if the Equity Committee is permitted to elect new directors in order to redirect or alter the course of a reorganization—and the

---

11. [Footnote 6 in original:] We note that if Manville were determined to be insolvent, so that the shareholders lacked equity in the corporation, denial of the right to call a meeting would likely be proper, because the shareholders would no longer be real parties in interest. Although the bankruptcy court discussed the possibility of Manville's insolvency in connection with its treatment of the Equity Committee's request for retention of special counsel and reimbursement of expenses, an issue that is not a subject of this appeal, the district court did not uphold the determination of clear abuse on that basis, and the parties have not briefed that issue.

district court here explicitly recognized that the committee is permitted to do that—the Equity Committee should be permitted, in the district court's words of disapproval, to "use the threat of a new board as a lever vis-a-vis other interested constituencies and vis-a-vis the current Manville board." The Equity Committee denies that there is evidence tending to show that it meant to use any "threat" as a "lever," but if there is any such evidence, it would suggest only that the Equity Committee might be willing to back away from replacing the directors if it were to find the board more responsive to its interests. For related reasons, we are not persuaded that the Equity Committee's failure to call for a meeting at an earlier stage in the negotiations places its desire for leverage in a different light. If dissatisfaction with the board's representation of shareholders is a legitimate ground for calling a meeting, the Equity Committee did not waive the right to call a meeting by waiting until it became dissatisfied.[12]

    * * *

[T]he determination whether the Equity Committee is guilty of clear abuse turns on whether rehabilitation will be seriously threatened, rather than merely delayed, if Manville's present plan is not submitted for confirmation now. See In re Bush Terminal Co., 78 F.2d 662 (2d Cir. 1935); In re J.P. Linahan, Inc., 111 F.2d 590 (2d Cir. 1940); In re Lionel Corp., 30 B.R. 327 (Bankr.S.D.N.Y.1983). Quite apart from its right to contest confirmation, the Equity Committee has the right to a fair hearing on the latter question and to a decision that recognizes its right to influence its own board.

We now reach the district court's alternative ground for affirming the grant of summary judgment. The bankruptcy court's finding that the proposed stockholders' meeting might jeopardize the reorganization process, "or at least … delay or halt plan negotiations," a finding reflected in the district court's view that the Equity Committee might have intended to "torpedo" the reorganization, poses an issue more difficult than the question of the stockholders' desire for a voice in negotiations. While delay to rehabilitation would not by itself provide a ground for overriding the shareholders' right to govern Manville—delay being a concomitant of the right to change boards—real jeopardy to reorganization prospects would provide such a ground.

In In re Potter Instrument Co., 593 F.2d 470 (2d Cir. 1979), this court upheld the bankruptcy court's refusal, upon a finding of clear abuse, to order a shareholders' meeting to be called for the purpose of electing new directors. We reasoned that "such an election might result in unsatisfactory management and

---

12. [Footnote 7 in original:] We do not suggest, of course, that an equity committee's delay in calling a shareholders' meeting may never contribute to a finding of clear abuse. As the Securities and Exchange Commission pointed out in its brief, an attempt to call a shareholders' meeting after a plan has been submitted to the bankruptcy court and after confirmation hearings have begun would usually be more disruptive to the proceedings than an earlier attempt would be. Such an attempt might also indicate bad faith and a willingness to risk jeopardy to rehabilitation. On the other hand, a rule that required a call before dissatisfaction had crystallized would only encourage preemptive efforts that might otherwise be avoided by negotiation. In this case, the Equity Committee apparently acted promptly upon learning of Manville's proposed plan and is certainly not accountable for any movement toward confirmation that may have occurred thereafter over its objections.

would probably jeopardize both [the debtor's] rehabilitation and the rights of creditors and stockholders—sounding the 'death knell' to the debtor as well as to appellant himself." Id. at 475. In In re Potter Instrument Co., however, the facts were distinct from those considered here, at least on the record before us. Potter, the appellant, had agreed in a consent decree with the Securities and Exchange Commission to limit his management in the debtor and not to vote against any action recommended by a majority of the board of directors. Id. at 474. Attempting to circumvent the agreement, Potter sought to elect new directors who would vote against a proposed plan that would cause the debtor to issue new stock to unsecured creditors and thereby dilute Potter's holdings. The bankruptcy court had found that approval of a plan could probably never be accomplished without issuance of the stock. In addition, the bankruptcy court had noted that it would not be likely to approve control of the debtor by Potter in light of the record before it. Id.

It thus appears that the Equity Committee might distinguish itself from the shareholder in In re Potter Instrument Co., given the opportunity for an evidentiary hearing. The Equity Committee persuasively calls into question whether the bankruptcy court had any basis for concluding here that an election would jeopardize the reorganization process, particularly since the bankruptcy court's articulated basis appears to have been colored by an unsubstantiated suspicion that the Equity Committee affirmatively wished to jeopardize reorganization.[13] Perhaps Potter was willing to embark on a suicide mission, "sounding the 'death knell' to ... himself" along with the debtor. But as the Equity Committee argues, the lower courts in this case pointed to no evidence to support any finding that it wished to "torpedo" the reorganization, which the Equity Committee contends would be an irrational goal from its perspective.

---

13.   [Footnote 9 in original:] In reviewing the bankruptcy court's decision, the district court characterized its findings as follows:

> [T]he dim prospects for a successful reorganization following the election of a new board led the bankruptcy court to question the Equity Committee's motivation in seeking a new election. By its own admission, the Equity Committee brought the Delaware action in order to derail the proposed plan. Either the appellants seek to destroy any prospect for a successful reorganization, or they wish to use the threat of a new board as a lever vis-a-vis other interested constituencies and vis-a-vis the current Manville board. Neither the interest in torpedoing the reorganization nor in acquiring a chip to be bargained away are legitimate. Judge Lifland, who was well aware of the dynamics of the Manville bankruptcy, had ample evidence from which to conclude that by either attempting to destroy the prospects for a successful reorganization or by merely attempting to strengthen its bargaining position without changing the current board, the Equity Committee was acting in a clearly abusive manner.

60 B.R. at 852 (footnotes omitted). The bankruptcy court decision itself did not define the Equity Committee's supposed ill motives quite so clearly. At one point, however, the bankruptcy court observed that "[s]ection 105(a) contemplates the court's use of injunctive relief in precisely those instances where parties are attempting to obstruct the reorganization." 52 B.R. at 889. The bankruptcy court then concluded that "[t]he *carefully timed* Delaware action will have an adverse impact on the Debtor's ability to coalesce with others to formulate an acceptable Chapter 11 plan resulting in irreparable harm and the impeding of the negotiation process." Id. at 890 (emphasis added).

* * * The only evidence the bankruptcy court cited * * * , apart from evidence that the Equity Committee meant to influence negotiations in its favor, was the affidavit of G. Earl Parker, a Manville director who might have been replaced if an election had been held. Parroting In re Potter Instrument Co., Parker's affidavit merely concluded that "[t]he consequences flowing from yet another stalemate would place in jeopardy the ability of the Debtors ever to confirm a plan of reorganization or to pay its [sic] just debts." * * *

The evidence contained in the Parker affidavit, consisting principally of the conclusion quoted above, is insufficient to support the determination of clear abuse underlying the grant of summary judgment. While we agree with the district court that it was proper for the bankruptcy court to consider the record as a whole in determining whether summary judgment was appropriate, without being told which portions of the bankruptcy court's accumulated knowledge it relied on for decision, we cannot agree that no material issues of fact remain to be determined.[14]

Moreover, as the Equity Committee argues, a finding of clear abuse must be supplemented by a finding of irreparable injury before an injunction may issue. The bankruptcy court seemed to assume that the two inquiries coalesce; after finding clear abuse, it concluded without further analysis that an injunction was necessary to prevent irreparable harm to the reorganization. * * *

Although the inquiries into clear abuse and irreparable injury will likely yield the same result in most if not all cases, an articulated analysis of irreparable injury would achieve a better focus and assist the reviewing court. In this connection, it is worth noting that In re Potter Instrument Co., the only authority for a finding of clear abuse in circumstances resembling Manville's, did not deal with injunctive relief at all. There the court merely declined to direct a shareholders' meeting. In any event, on this record any harm to the reorganization was speculative enough that the irreparable injury requirement was not satisfied.

* * *

Conclusion

Whether the Equity Committee's call for a shareholders' meeting constitutes clear abuse and whether such a meeting would cause irreparable harm to Manville's reorganization are triable issues of fact. The summary judgment award to Manville is therefore reversed. On remand, the court should undertake a more elaborate inquiry into clear abuse and irreparable harm. Rather than focusing on the Equity Committee's conceded desire to enhance its bargaining position, the court should analyze the real risks to rehabilitation posed by permitting the Equity Committee to

---

14. [Footnote 10 in original:] In Manville's view, the bankruptcy court did review the facts that led it to find "clear abuse," adverting in its opinion to the facts that Manville had been in bankruptcy for three years without any resolution; that Manville and committee representatives had engaged in extensive but fruitless negotiations; that Manville did not reach agreement with any other constituency until August 1985; that "[w]ithin two weeks of the announcement of the Principal Elements Agreement, the Equity Committee filed its motion ... for the purpose of instituting the Delaware Action" ; and that "no shareholder or director has at any time sought to compel the calling of a shareholder's meeting for the years 1983, 1984 or 1985." We do not think that this bare recitation of the events culminating in Manville's plan and the Equity Committee's discontent, when added to the bankruptcy court's stated basis for decision, constitutes a showing that the Equity Committee committed clear abuse.

call a meeting of shareholders for the purpose of compelling reconsideration of Manville's presently proposed plan. We emphasize, however, that given its greater knowledge about this complex and perhaps fragile reorganization, the bankruptcy court may exercise its legitimate injunctive powers to control the future course of rehabilitation pursuant to appropriate legal standards and evidentiary showings.

OAKES, Circuit Judge (dissenting): * * *

NOTES

1. What do you suppose the bankruptcy court's decision was after the trial on remand? See Manville Corp. v. Equity Sec. Holders Comm. (In re Johns-Manville Corp.), 66 B.R. 517 (Bankr. S.D.N.Y. 1986).

2. If the shareholders are permitted to elect new directors, may those directors single-mindedly pursue the interests of the shareholders to the detriment of the creditors or the estate? Does the court's opinion suggest that directors are entitled to favor the interests of shareholders over the interests of creditors?

3. In footnote 6 the court says that if Manville were determined to be insolvent then the court could enjoin a meeting of the shareholders. Why might that be so? Do you agree with the court? Are shareholders indeed entitled to nothing if the debtor is insolvent? If Manville were insolvent on a liquidation basis but not on a going concern basis, would the shareholders have had a sufficient interest in the company to be entitled to hold a shareholders' meeting? For a contrasting approach, consider Comm. of Equity Sec. Holders v. Lionel Corp. (In re Lionel Corp.), 722 F.2d 1063 (2d Cir. 1983). The debtor in *Lionel* was apparently insolvent. (Its debts exceeded its assets by $23 million, although it is not clear how the assets were valued. See id. at 1065.) Despite the insolvency, the Second Circuit held that the stockholders were entitled to a voice and that their interests were entitled to be given weight. Thus, an order permitting the debtor to sell a major asset was reversed, because the courts below failed to give sufficient weight to the interests of the stockholders in deciding whether to approve the sale. In fact the debtor agreed to sell the assets only because of pressure from large creditors. Pressure from the creditors "is not a sound business reason and insufficient as a matter of law because it ignores the equity interests required to be weighed and considered under Chapter 11." Id. at 1071. The Second Circuit held that the bankruptcy judge should "act to further the diverse interests of the debtor, creditors and equity holders, alike." Id. The court pointed out that "[i]n enacting the 1978 Code Congress * * * clearly indicated as one of its purposes that equity interests have a greater voice in reorganization plans * * * ." Id. Would it be consistent with the approach in *Lionel* for a court to prevent stockholders from replacing the directors of an insolvent debtor? For conflicting views of the rights of shareholders where the debtor is insolvent, see LoPucki & Whitford, *Corporate Governance in the Bankruptcy of Large Publicly Held Companies,* 141 U. PA. L. REV. 669, 769-71 (1993); Miller, *Corporate Governance in Chapter 11: The Fiduciary Relationship Between Directors and Stockholders of Solvent and Insolvent Corporations,* 23 SETON HALL L. REV. 1467, 1504-06 (1993); LoPucki & Whitford, *Preemptive Cramdown,* 65 AM. BANKR. L.J. 625 (1991).

4. The court holds that even a clear abuse by shareholders in seeking to hold a shareholders' meeting and to replace the board could not be enjoined unless it would cause "irreparable injury" to Manville. Irreparable injury is generally a requirement for issuance of a preliminary injunction, the ordinary purpose of which is to maintain the status quo during proceedings which ultimately

determine whether a permanent injunction should be issued. The standard for issuance of a permanent injunction is whether the legal remedy (typically an award of money damages) is inadequate. For example, a buyer of gas under a long term, fixed price supply contract would ultimately be entitled to a grant of specific performance (a kind of permanent injunction) if the buyer prevailed in a breach of contract action and if the evidence indicated that no other suppliers would enter into a similar long term supply contract. See, e.g., Laclede Gas Co. v. Amoco Oil Co., 522 F.2d 33 (8th Cir. 1975). Money damages would be an inadequate remedy because the buyer might not be able to buy sufficient gas in a future shortage situation and because the damages which the buyer would incur in buying gas in the future for more than the original contract price could not be determined in advance and included in the damage award. Nevertheless, there might be no irreparable harm during the pendency of the lawsuit that would justify the court in issuing a preliminary injunction requiring the seller to supply gas before judgment. If the buyer prevailed at trial, the court could award specific performance as to the future, and also award damages to make up for any extra amounts paid by the buyer for gas up to that time. Thus, there is irreparable harm only if a failure to grant a preliminary injunction pending trial will prevent the court from giving an adequate remedy should the plaintiff win at trial.

Here, however, the bankruptcy court entered the injunction against holding a shareholder's meeting after granting summary judgment—a final determination on the merits—in favor of Manville. On remand, the bankruptcy court again entered an injunction, this time after trial. In neither case was the injunction a preliminary injunction entered pending determination of whether Manville was entitled to a permanent injunction against shareholders holding a meeting. If it is proved that the shareholders or any other parties to the bankruptcy proceeding are abusing the bankruptcy process, does it make sense to require a finding that the abuse will cause irreparable harm before the court can act to stop the abuse? Suppose Gruff in our Foam Corporation case were embezzling small amounts of money each week from Foam Corporation. Would the court need to find that the amounts were so large that irreparable harm would occur before taking any action to stop the embezzlement? Further, if the abuse by shareholders does not cause irreparable harm, would there be any remedy at all for the abuse? Could the shareholders be held liable in damages for holding a shareholders' meeting absent an injunction against it? Is there statutory authority for holding a party liable for damages who seeks to "torpedo" a reorganization? It is not clear that the use of a preliminary injunction analysis in cases like Manville Corp. v. Equity Security Holders Committee makes sense.

Problem 6-3

Assume Foam Corporation's By-Laws require the board of directors to hold a shareholder's meeting within four weeks following an application of the holder or holders of 51% or more of its stock. Assume that when Gruff guaranteed Foam Corporation's obligations to Kick Credit, he also gave Kick Credit an irrevocable proxy to vote his shares of Foam Corporation. The proxy was to become effective if Foam Corporation filed a bankruptcy petition. After Foam Corporation filed its petition, Kick Credit applied to Foam Corporation's board, requesting that it call a shareholder's meeting, but the board refused to do so. Kick Credit then filed suit in California Superior Court (a trial court) to require Foam Corporation's board of directors to call a meeting of shareholders. Kick Credit's announced purpose is to replace the board of directors with directors who will then move, under § 1112(a), to convert the case to a chapter 7 liquidation case. Foam Corporation sought an injunction in bankruptcy court against the continuation of the suit and in the alternative an order precluding any new directors from converting the case to chapter 7 without cause, precluding them from removing Gruff as chief executive officer, precluding them from reducing Gruff's duties as chief executive officer, and precluding them from interfering with Gruff's day to day management of the business. You are the bankruptcy judge. How will you rule? Does Kick Credit's suit violate the automatic stay? Is it contrary to the policies of the bankruptcy laws? Would your answer be different if Kick Credit were solely a creditor of Gruff and sought to vote pledged stock of Foam Corporation? See In re Country Estates Nursing Home, Inc., 268 B.R. 316 (Bankr. D. Mass. 2001); Official Bondholders Comm. v. Chase Manhattan Bank (In re Marvel Entm't Group, Inc.), 209 B.R. 832, 838-40 (D. Del. 1997).

B. CREDITORS' AND EQUITY SECURITY HOLDERS' COMMITTEES

As we have seen, not all debtors in possession can be trusted to manage the business competently and honestly. Thus the unsecured creditors' committee and the United States trustee should keep a vigilant watch on the debtor in possession. The creditors' committee will also play a key role in the negotiation of the plan of reorganization. The creditors' committee's recommendation will carry great weight with the body of unsecured creditors. If the negotiations between the debtor and the creditors' committee produce a plan which the creditors' committee endorses, the unsecured creditors are likely to accept the plan when it comes time to vote on it. The same is true if there is an official equity security holders' committee; it will participate in negotiating a plan, and its recommendation will carry great weight with the shareholders or other equity security holders when they vote on the plan.[15] See generally Glassman & Schlerf, *Equity Committees: A Consequence of the "Zone of Insolvency"*, 24-1 Am. Bankr. Inst. J. 28, 52 (2006).

Under § 1103 the official committee or committees appointed by the U.S. trustee have a broad mandate to be involved in the case. See generally, Klee and Shaffer, *Creditors' Committees Under Chapter 11 of the Bankruptcy Code,* 44 S.C.L. REV. 995 (1993); Zipes & Lambert, *Creditors' Committee Formation Dynamics: Issues in the Real World,* 77 AM. BANKR. L.J. 229 (2003). The committees are entitled to consult with the debtor in possession concerning the administration of the case. They are entitled to investigate anything relevant to the case or to the formulation of a plan, including specifically the debtor's conduct and financial condition, the operation of the

---

15. If the debtor is a corporation, the equity securities are the shares of stock in the debtor corporation, and its shareholders are the equity security holders. See § 101(16) and (17). If the debtor is a limited partnership, the equity securities are the limited partnership interests, and the limited partners are the equity security holders. Id.

business, and the desirability of continuing it. The committees are entitled to participate in the formulation of a plan of reorganization, to determine whether to support or oppose any plan, to communicate recommendations to the creditors or equity security holders represented by each committee, and to solicit votes on the plan. The committees are entitled to request the appointment or election of a trustee or of an examiner, and to perform "such other services as are in the interest of those represented." Section 1103(c). The committees may select, with the court's approval, attorneys and other professionals to assist them in carrying out those functions. See § 1103(a). The reasonable fees of those professionals for actual and necessary services will be paid by the estate as a cost of administration. See §§ 330(a), 503(b)(2), 507(a)(2), and 1129(a)(9)(A). Expenses of committee members will likewise be reimbursed as administrative expenses. See § 503(b)(3)(F).[16]

Section 1102(b)(3) (added by the 2005 BAPCPA) requires the committee to "provide access to information for creditors" represented by the committee, to solicit their comments, and to provide additional information to them as required by the court. The court in the Refco case reluctantly granted a "comfort order" at the request of the creditors' committee, detailing the required disclosure, which, in the context of the large Refco case, included setting up a "Committee Website" on the Internet. In re Refco, 336 B.R. 187 (Bankr. S.D.N.Y. 2006) (including the order as Exhibit A to the opinion).

As a "party in interest" under § 1109(b), the committee has standing to raise and be heard on any issue in the case. Courts disagree whether § 1109(b) is a statutory grant of a right to intervene in adversary proceedings, such as actions brought to avoid preferences or fraudulent transfers.[17] Compare Term Loan Holder Comm. v. Ozer Group, LLC (In re Caldor Corp.), 303 F.3d 161 (2d Cir. 2002) (holding that it is), with Fuel Oil Supply & Terminaling v. Gulf Oil Corp., 762 F.2d 1283 (5th Cir. 1985) (holding that it is not, because courts are reluctant to find that a statute grants an unconditional right to intervene for purposes of Fed. R. Civ. P. 24, made applicable to adversary proceedings by Rule 7024, and because § 1109(b)'s reference to "a case under this chapter" appears to be a reference to the case commenced by filing of a bankruptcy petition rather than to an adversary proceeding, which is commenced by filing of a complaint). It seems that courts could allow parties in interest to be heard (by way of amicus briefs, for example) without having to allow intervention,

---

16. It is now clear that a *member* of a committee is not entitled ordinarily to hire professionals such as attorneys and accountants to represent the committee *member* at the estate's expense. See § 503(b)(4) (amended in 2005 and omitting reference to § 503(b)(3)(F)). To the extent that such professionals, who are not working for the committee but for a member of the committee, help the member to make a substantial contribution in the chapter 11 case, their reasonable compensation may be allowable as an administrative expense. See § 503(b)(3)(D) & (b)(4).

17. In Chapters Eight and Nine of this text we consider the related question whether parties in interest, such as creditors' committees, may bring motions or initiate adversary proceedings under Code provisions that give the trustee or debtor in possession the right to do so, such as § 506(c) and § 547(b).

which makes the intervening party a full party[18] in the proceeding or case. Even if the committee is entitled to intervene and thus become a party, that does not mean the committee can control the action[19] or proceed without limits as if it owned the claim.[20]

The United States trustee appoints, or at least attempts to appoint, an official unsecured creditors' committee in all chapter 11 cases (other than small business cases in which there is a showing of cause not to appoint a committee under § 1102(a)(3)). The committee ordinarily consists of the persons "willing to serve" who hold the seven largest unsecured claims. See § 1102(a) and (b)(1). If there was a prepetition creditors' committee that was fairly chosen and is representative of the kinds of unsecured claims in the case, then the United States trustee may appoint its members as the members of the official committee. See § 1102(b)(1) and Rule 2007(b). The court can order the appointment of additional committees of creditors or of equity security holders if that is "necessary to assure adequate representation of creditors or of equity security holders." Section 1102(a)(2). The United States trustee then will choose and appoint the members of those additional committees. The United States trustee also has the authority to appoint additional committees without court order. Id.

The norm is for only one creditors' committee to be appointed, even in fairly complex cases and even where the interests of the unsecured creditors may conflict. In re Sharon Steel Corp., 100 B.R. 767 (Bankr. W.D. Pa. 1989). Although there is some disagreement in the cases, one creditors' committee is also the norm where several related companies all file chapter 11 petitions. See, e.g., In re Enron Corp., 279 B.R. 671 (Bankr. S.D.N.Y. 2002), aff'd sub nom. Mirant Americas Energy Mktg., L.P. v. Official Comm. of Unsecured Creditors of Enron Corp., 2003 WL 22327118 (S.D.N.Y Oct. 10, 2003); In re Orfa Corp. of Philadelphia, 121 B.R. 294 (Bankr. E.D. Pa. 1990); but see Gill v. Sierra Pac. Constr., Inc. (In re Parkway Calabasas), 89 B.R. 832 (Bankr. C.D. Cal. 1988), aff'd, 949 F.2d 1058 (9th Cir. 1991).

---

18. See 7C Wright, Miller & Kane, FED. PRAC. & PROC. § 1920 (1986). But see Adelphia Commc'ns Corp. v. Rigas (In re Adelphia Commc'ns Corp.), 285 B.R. 848 (Bankr. S.D.N.Y. 2002) (holding that intervenor does not have the "same rights as those who actually own the causes of action," and quoting Kirkland v. N.Y. St. Dept. of Corr. Servs., 711 F.2d 1117, 1126 (2d Cir. 1983), as stating that "the sum of rights possessed by an intervenor * * * is not necessarily equivalent to that of a party in the case and depends upon the nature of the intervenor's interest").

19. See Smart World Technologies, LLC v. Juno Online Services, Inc. (In re Smart World Technologies, LLC), 423 F.3d 166 (2d Cir. 2005) (holding that even though committee had the right to intervene in debtor in possession's action against a third party, the committee did not have the right to settle the claim against the third party over the objection of the debtor in possession).

20. See Adelphia Commc'ns Corp. v. Rigas (In re Adelphia Commc'ns Corp.), 285 B.R. 848 (Bankr. S.D.N.Y. 2002) (discussing the rights of intervenors under § 1109(b)). Cf. Official Comm. of Unsecured Creditors of Sunbeam Corp. v. Morgan Stanley & Co., Inc. (In re Sunbeam Corp.), 287 B.R. 861, 862 (S.D.N.Y. 2003) (citing *Adelphia Commc'ns* and limiting rights of creditor who intervened in action brought, with court's permission, by creditors' committee, and who sought "not just intervention, but the right, in essence, to take ownership of the Committee's causes of action").

The concept of "adequate representation" recognizes that different unsecured creditors may have different interests yet be represented by a single committee:

> To the extent that there have been differences of view with respect to the issues relating to a plan of reorganization, such differences do not provide support for the appointment of a separate debentureholders' committee. It is universally recognized that intercreditor conflicts inhere in any committee:
>
> > [Union] members may be interested in a plan of reorganization which preserves both their jobs and their collective bargaining agreement, while other creditors may be interested in a liquidation, or a reorganization involving a merger with a [third party]. *Such conflicts of interests are not unusual in reorganizations.* Materialman creditors, for example, may sometimes prefer to forego full payment for past sales in hopes of preserving a customer, while lenders may prefer liquidation and prompt payment. (emphasis supplied)
>
> In re Altair Airlines, Inc., 727 F.2d 88, 90 (3rd Cir. 1984); accord In re Daig Corp., 17 B.R. 41, 43 (Bankr. D. Minn. 1981); In re Baldwin-United Corp., 45 B.R. 375, 376 (Bankr. S.D. Ohio 1983) (conflicts among creditors are inherent in all bankruptcy cases; in complex cases, they are inevitable). The legal principle to be distilled from these cases is clear: adequate representation exists through a single committee as long as the diverse interests of the various creditor groups are represented on and have participated in that committee. The Debenture Group has not asserted facts tending to show that diverse interests have produced an inability of the Official Committee to function in the performance of its fiduciary obligations to all unsecured creditors.

In re Sharon Steel Corp., 100 B.R. 767, 777-78 (Bankr. W.D. Pa. 1989); cf. In re Walnut Equip. Leasing Co., 213 B.R. 285 (Bankr. E.D. Pa. 1997) (noting inherent conflict between each creditor and committee due to committee's obligation to investigate claims).

Each committee member seemingly is invited to seek to protect whatever economic interests it may have by acting as a "voice" for those interests. See In re Altair Airlines, Inc., 727 F.2d 88, 90 (3d Cir. 1984). In doing so, it will also protect the similar economic interests of other creditors or equity security holders for whom it is providing "adequate representation." On the other hand, *each* committee member owes fiduciary duties of care and loyalty to the entire class represented by the committee, not just to that part of the class with economic interests similar to the interests of the committee member. In re Sharon Steel Corp., 100 B.R. 767, 779 (Bankr. W.D. Pa. 1989). It is not clear how this conflict should be resolved between the committee member's duty to represent adequately the interests of creditors or shareholders with similar economic interests and the committee member's fiduciary duty to the entire class represented by the committee. Perhaps each committee member is entitled to assert its own interest as long as it does so in an open and honest way without harming the overall interests of the entire group represented by the committee. Cf. ABF Capital Mgmt. v. Kidder Peabody & Co. (In re Granite

Partners, L.P.), 210 B.R. 508 (Bankr. S.D.N.Y. 1997) (holding that fiduciary duty is owed to entire class but not to any individual member of the class). If each member of the committee does so, then the committee members should be able to build on their common interests as holders of unsecured claims, work together, and compromise their differences so that the committee can be an effective force in the case. See Bussel, *Coalition-Building Through Bankruptcy Creditors' Committees*, 43 U.C.L.A. L. REV. 1547 (1996); In re Hills Stores, 137 B.R. 4 (Bankr. S.D.N.Y. 1992) (reprinted below).

As we have pointed out, official committees appointed by the U.S. trustee are entitled to retain counsel, accountants, and other professionals "with the court's approval," § 1103(a), and to have their reasonable fees paid out of the estate. Parties who wish to have the estate pay for an attorney who will represent their particular interests may seek appointment of an extra committee as a vehicle for obtaining that payment.[21] Consider the following case.

In re Hills Stores Co.
United States Bankruptcy Court, S.D. New York, 1992
137 B.R. 4

Tina L. Brozman, Bankruptcy Judge.

Almost a year ago, the United States Trustee appointed a single committee of unsecured creditors (the Committee) in this Chapter 11 reorganization for a very large retailer. No challenge to the U.S. Trustee's action has been voiced, let alone mounted, until now. Four subordinated bondholders ask for the appointment of either an official subordinated bondholders' subcommittee of the Committee or, in the alternative, for their own committee. * * *

I.

This case was commenced on February 4, 1991 when Hills Stores Co. and the other related debtors (collectively, Hills or the Debtor) filed voluntary chapter 11 petitions. * * * At the time of its bankruptcy, Hills operated 154 department stores in twelve states. Sales at the end of its last fiscal year, ending February 3, 1991, were $2.1 billion.

Eleven days after Hills sought refuge in chapter 11, the U.S. Trustee appointed a 15 member committee pursuant to Section 1102(a) of the Code. Its membership consisted of three banks, two holders of senior notes, five trade creditors, one factor and four representatives of the four separate tranches of subordinated debt, each tranche with different priorities from the other.

---

21. In some circumstances, however, the court may have discretion to order that the fees be paid from the recovery that otherwise would go to the creditors who are represented by the committee. See Official Comm. of Unsec. Creditors v. Farmland Indus., Inc. (In re Farmland Indus., Inc.), 397 F.3d 647 (8th Cir. 2005) (affirming bankruptcy court order that contingent success fee of financial advisor to trade creditors' committee be paid out of trade creditors' recovery rather than as a general administrative expense, where bondholders' committee's financial advisor was being paid out of bondholders' recovery, and holding that "the discretion to impose such a provision (or to refuse approval of an agreement that lacks such a provision) is clearly consistent with the bankruptcy court's statutory authority under § 328(a) to approve the employment of a professional 'on any reasonable terms and conditions of employment' ").

Given that the Committee is large, to aid in its smooth operation its constituencies formed three subcommittees all of which have subordinated bondholder representation. The Orders Subcommittee makes decisions on matters between $50,000 and $2 million that are not deemed policy issues and recommendations on matter in excess of $2 million or on questions of policy. Throughout the course of this case the decision and/or recommendation of the Orders Subcommittee almost always has been unanimously approved by the full Committee. The Plan Subcommittee was formed to discuss preliminary plan of reorganization proposals with the Debtor and report back to the full Committee. The Finance Subcommittee was formed to work closely with the accountants and investment advisors.

The Subordinated Bondholders urge today that similarly situated creditors are not adequately represented by the Committee. This is so they say because:

(i) they have economic interests that diverge dramatically from the senior and trade creditors who dominate the committee;

(ii) the Committee has failed to investigate possible preference claims and lender liability actions against senior creditors on the Committee;

(iii) the various subordinated bondholders are numerically underrepresented in relation to the size of their aggregate unsecured claim vis-a-vis other types of creditors;

(iv) the structure of a plan of reorganization will likely follow that in other retail cases, a structure which they find unpalatable;

* * *

The Debtor and the Committee oppose the motion, contending that the subordinated bondholders' arguments are factually unfounded and based on speculation; the conflicts advanced are not unusual; the timing of the motion so late into the case will jeopardize the anticipated emergence of the Debtor from bankruptcy this spring or summer at unnecessary additional cost; and, finally, the Court lacks jurisdiction to direct the existing Committee to form a subcommittee.

II.

Section 1102(a)(2) of the Bankruptcy Code provides that "[o]n request of a party in interest, the court may order the appointment of additional committees of creditors or equity holders if necessary to assure adequate representation of creditors or of equity security holders." Thus, the Committee must provide adequate representation for unsecured creditors, including the subordinated bondholders. As the statute affords no "bright-line" test for adequate representation, the court is armed with the discretion after examining the facts to determine if additional committees are warranted. In re Beker Industries Corp., 55 B.R. 945, 948 (Bankr. S.D.N.Y. 1985). Considerations such as the ability of the committee to function, the nature of the case and the standing and desires of the various constituencies assume significance. In re McLean Industries, Inc., 70 B.R. 852, 860 (Bankr. S.D.N.Y. 1987). While bankruptcy courts have generally been reluctant to appoint separate committees of unsecured creditors notwithstanding the diverse and sometimes conflicting interests of creditors, In re Public Service Co. of New Hampshire, 89 B.R. 1014, 1020 (Bankr. D.N.H. 1988), a case which is sufficiently large and complex may strongly indicate the need for additional committees representing different interests. *Beker*, supra at 949. The potential added cost is not sufficient in itself to deprive the creditors of the formation of an additional committee if one is otherwise appropriate. *McLean,* supra, at 860.

Turning to the different economic interests argument, the subordinated bondholders posit that they will potentially support a business plan and plan of reorganization that will maximize the company's long term equity value while the senior and trade creditors are likely to press for an early payout at the expense of the company's operations and enterprise value. The subordinated bondholders claim that as a result of a wave of major retail bankruptcies, a consistent pattern (which, ironically, they have described in two different fashions) has emerged in which the senior debt is reinstated with an adjusted maturity, principal balance and interest rate; the trade debt is paid with cash and possibly new equity; and the bulk of the new equity and new subordinated debt is given to the subordinated bondholders. The subordinated bondholders then baldly advance that this preordains the future if their motion is not granted. Not only is this rank speculation but it is at odds with the facts. Hills has proposed terms for a plan which are materially different from what the subordinated bondholders project.

Contrary to the bondholders' assertion, the presence of potential conflict may not always require separate committees in order for representation to be adequate. In re Sharon Steel Corp., 100 B.R. 767, 777 (W.D. Pa. 1989); *McLean,* supra at 861. Indeed, creditors' committees often contain creditors having a variety of viewpoints. Conflicts are not unusual in reorganization and in most cases can be expected among creditors who are acting to protect their separate business interests. Id. What the subordinated bondholders have painted is a picture reflecting no darker image than the ordinary fears, concerns, and conflicts that are inherent in the reorganization process. Were this a case where the creditors of separate debtors had vastly conflicting aims and entitlement and had shown themselves unable to function on a single committee, I might be more inclined to the subordinated bondholders' view, but here there is only one operating debtor engaged in a single business. Albeit that Hills has a complicated capital structure, these cases are not nearly so complex as those multi-debtor, multi-business cases where more than one committee may be appointed.

The contention that the Committee has failed to investigate possible preference claims and lender liability actions against senior creditors on the Committee borders on bad faith, for the Debtor is undertaking a preference analysis, as is its obligation, and until this motion was made the subordinated bondholders never gave voice to their theory that there may be a lender liability claim available to the creditors. * * *

I turn now to the subordinated bondholders' claim that they are numerically underrepresented in relation to the size of their unsecured claim. Nowhere does the Code mandate a committee must faithfully reproduce the exact complexion of the creditor body. What is required is adequate representation of various creditor types. The disparity between the bondholders' claims, which constitute 35% of the debtor's total liabilities, and their Committee representation, which is approximately 27%, does not establish such inadequate representation as to warrant the formation of a separate committee. Under any scenario the bondholders will never comprise a majority of a single committee representing all unsecured creditors. More importantly, the bondholders have put forth no tangible evidence whatsoever which would tend to substantiate their claim that, as a result of their alleged underrepresentation the Committee will be unable to negotiate successfully with the Debtor. Despite the fact that the bondholders do not have a majority voice on the Committee, there is not one group which by itself can control the decisions of the Committee without the aid of another. Moreover, the subordinated bondholders have neglected to mention a most salient fact in their papers—that they have one-third of the seats on all three of the Committee's subcommittees, and to a large extent it is those subcommittees which exercise the initial decision-making authority of the Committee. To make an argument respecting numerical representation without mentioning the subcommittee membership evidences a surprising lack of candor to the Court.

This motion confuses adequate representation on a Committee with the right to charge a debtor's estate for separate professionals. What the Code requires is that conflicting groups of creditors have a voice through adequate representation on a Committee. That voice exists here. The subordinated bondholders' argument that they are effectively rendered impotent to protect their interests without a majority voice in the Committee ignores the role of the Committee as a catalyst for negotiation and compromise between the parties in the reorganization process. The fact that the Bondholders may not be able to protect all their interests and achieve *all* their goals is not paramount, as the ultimate aim is to strike a proper balance between the parties such that an effective and viable reorganization of the debtor may be accomplished. As in most Chapter 11 cases, there will be common interests among various groups of unsecured creditors. The inclusion of such groups within one committee may facilitate the consensual resolution of the conflicting priorities among the holders of unsecured claims and thereby facilitate the negotiation of a consensual plan. 5 L. King, COLLIER ON BANKRUPTCY, ¶ 1102.02, 1102-26 (15th ed. 1991). The bondholders have not demonstrated that there exists conflict among the unsecured creditors which is so profound as to impede the Committee's ability to function. Their claim of a pattern of discrimination by the senior and trade creditors against them is devoid of factual support.

* * *

It is late in the day for the subordinated bondholders' motion. The proceedings have advanced to a point where the detailed business plan has been critiqued and plan negotiations are about to commence. The Debtor has represented that the plan in these cases can be confirmed during the spring or summer of this year. The subordinated bondholders could have moved for the requested relief six or more months ago when the complained of action or inaction of the Committee was alleged to have occurred, instead of at a time when the appointment of an additional committee or subcommittee would no doubt delay the confirmation process, result in additional expense for the estate and possibly cause the proliferation of other committees. Nevertheless, if I believed the delay and expense were justified by facts instead of speculation, I would not hesitate to order the appointment of an additional committee to assure adequate representation.

What the subordinated bondholders seek is the appointment of a new committee which may retain professionals or the appointment of a subcommittee which may retain professionals. As the composition, function and rights of each as proposed are the same, aside from the jurisdictional issue raised by the Committee, this is a distinction without a difference. While I may order the appointment of additional *committees* under § 1102(a)(2) of the Code, the statute no longer permits the addition or deletion of *members* of committees by the court except in circumstances not relevant here. Section 1102(c) was amended in 1986 as part of a nearly nationwide expansion of the U.S. Trustee program, not only to revise § 1102(a) by vesting the appointment power in U.S. Trustees, but also to delete former § 1102(c) which expressly enabled the court to add and subtract creditors from creditors committees. For this reason, and because the reasons advanced for the appointment of a subcommittee, which are identical to those for appointment of a separate Committee, are without merit, I will not add a subcommittee to the committee.

Finally, as the Debtor points out, if the subordinated bondholders believe that the cases would be advanced by their taking a more active role, they are not precluded from forming an unofficial committee, retaining counsel and a financial advisor and seeking reimbursement of their expenses to the extent that they make a substantial contribution to the case, as permitted and even envisioned by § 503(b) of the Code. In fact, it emerged in oral argument this morning that the subordinated bondholders have had counsel for one year. This is not then a dispute about adequate representation, but about adequate assurance of alternative compensation. * * *

NOTES

1. Why would the supposed numerical underrepresentation of the subordinated bondholders matter? Does a creditors' committee have power to bind creditors or otherwise to make decisions that will influence the case?

2. It is expected that different creditors on an unsecured creditors' committee may have different interests. Are there cases, however, in which the interests of a particular creditor are so adverse to the interests of unsecured creditors as a whole that the creditor should not be permitted to serve on the committee? Consider the following case.

3. Judge Brozman holds that the 1986 amendment to § 1102 gave the U.S. trustee sole authority to add or remove members of committees, leaving the court only with the authority to add new committees if needed. Between 1986 and 2005, courts split on this issue. Many courts held that they still had authority under § 105(a) to review the U.S. trustee's actions, at least for abuse of discretion, and to add or remove members of committees (or even to disband committees). See In re Mercury Fin. Co., 240 B.R. 270 (N.D. Ill. 1999). Congress clarified matters in 2005 by enacting § 1102(a)(4), which gives the court the power to order the U.S. trustee to change the membership of a creditors' or equity security holders' committee. (The next case was decided before the 1986 amendments, and thus does not consider that issue.)

In re Daig Corporation
United States Bankruptcy Court, D. Minnesota, 1981
17 B.R. 41

Kenneth G. Owens, Bankruptcy Judge.

This matter is before the Court on the motion of debtor under 11 U.S.C. Section 1102(c) * * * to remove from the [creditors'] committee as presently constituted * * * INCO Electro Energy Corp. (INCO), and to restore a representative of Lake Region Manufacturing Company originally appointed to the committee by the United States Trustee but subsequently removed by him.

* * * Subsequent to the United States Trustee's appointment of [Lake Region Manufacturing] to the committee on June 22, 1981, he discovered its representative and principal operating officer Joseph F. Fleischacker is the father of John J. Fleischacker, chairman of the debtor, and an insider as defined in the Bankruptcy Code. The debtor does not dispute that the personal relationship is such that the presence of Joseph F. Fleischacker as representative of Lake Region would be improper and not representative of the interests of general unsecured creditors. It does point out that Lake Region Manufacturing holds the largest claim of any supplying creditor, that its presence on the committee would aid the debtor in its dealings with that particular type of creditor, and suggests that it might be restored to the committee if represented thereon by some other individual, its legal counsel being suggested as a proper representative. I conclude however that the presence of any of its representatives on the board [sic] would be improper as imperiling the necessary confidentiality of communication and discussion among the proper members of the committee. Since the action of the United States Trustee was justified, it would be improper for the Court to substitute its judgment in that regard.

[A]s indicated in 11 U.S.C. Section 1102(b)(1) such committee shall " * * * ordinarily consist of the persons, willing to serve, that hold the seven largest claims against the debtor of the kinds represented on such committee * * * ". The only other statutory adjuration is that the membership of the committee must be "representative" of the kinds of claims represented by such committee * * * .

INCO Electro Energy Corporation (INCO) which claims no security holds the largest single claim against the debtor. It seems undisputed that the amount of the INCO claim is larger in amount than the claims of all other creditors, secured and unsecured combined. The claim or indebtedness arises by reason of debtor's purchase from INCO of a dominant approximate 77% shareholder interest in a third corporation Medcor, Inc. on whose behalf a separate Chapter 11 case has been instituted in this Court. At the present stage of proceedings, the claim would appear to be a general unsecured claim ordinarily entitled to representation as one of the seven largest under 11 U.S.C. Section 1102(b)(1).

The debtor contends that INCO should be removed because it "disputes" the claim and by reason of the nature of the claim. Debtor suggests that policy dictates the committee should be so constituted as to maximize economy in its dealings with the debtor and encourage its assistance to the debtor in its attempt to reorganize. The debtor points out that the INCO claim is so preponderant as to require debtor to negotiate separately with it concerning its claim and that the nature of the obligation which arose out of the stock purchase separates that creditor from the interests of unsecured creditors generally.

While there may be merit in the contention of debtor as a matter of strategy, its contention ignores a fundamental concept underlying the Code and those minimum statutory requirements found in Section 1102. The creditors' committee is not merely a conduit through whom the debtor speaks to and negotiates with creditors generally. On the contrary, it is purposely intended to represent the necessarily different interests and concerns of the creditors it represents. It must necessarily be adversarial in a sense, though its relation with the debtor may be supportive and friendly. There is simply no other entity established by the Code to guard those interests. The committee as the sum of its members is not intended to be merely an arbiter but a partisan which will aid, assist, and monitor the debtor pursuant to its own self-interest.

The fact the debtor disputes INCO's claim is insufficient to warrant the Court's interference with the Trustee's choice which meets the statutory criteria. Here the dispute is stated only in general terms except as suggesting that such creditor may be separately classifiable in the context of a plan. In the early stages of this proceeding, it is clearly premature to assume a separate classification would be suitable or that it will in the end result. It is neither self-evident nor, as would be required, clearly demonstrated that INCO is other than a general unsecured creditor of the class of creditors to be represented by the established committee. So far as appears INCO is a claimant without security in a monetary amount approximately as indicated. It has not been shown to be a non-creditor, nor a creditor of a sufficiently unique nature that it should not be represented by the committee, nor to have any characteristics in conflict with its otherwise right to membership on the committee.

So far as appears the interest of INCO as a creditor is aligned with the interests of other general unsecured claimants. If it be later found otherwise, it can be expected that the other members of the creditors' committee will take appropriate action either directly or through their chosen counsel.

I conclude that the United States Trustee acted in accordance with the Code and that the committee as now constituted is proper and "representative" of the class of creditors intended to be represented.

ACCORDINGLY, IT IS ORDERED that the motion of Daig Corporation so far as it seeks to restore Lake Region Manufacturing Company to the committee, and to deprive INCO Electro Energy Corp. of membership therein should be and the same hereby is overruled and denied.

Problem 6-4

In the case of Foam Corporation, assume that Kick Credit is owed $6 million and that Kick Credit's collateral is worth only $4 million. Recall that William Gruff (the chief executive officer of and majority shareholder in Foam Corporation) personally guaranteed the debts owed to Kick Credit and to the two largest trade creditors, Tina Chemical Company and Swenson Chemical Company. Recall also that Gruff lent Foam Corporation $3 million and thus holds one of the seven largest unsecured claims. Should Gruff be appointed to the unsecured creditors' committee? Should Kick Credit be appointed? Consider In re Fas Mart Convenience Stores, Inc., 265 B.R. 427 (Bankr. E.D. Va. 2001). Recall that during the workout attempt the trade creditors elected a committee to represent them and that the committee retained Tina Chemical's attorney, Pat Gray, to represent it. Should the United States trustee appoint the members of that prepetition committee to be the members of the official unsecured creditors' committee? See § 1102(b)(1) and Rule 2007(b). If Tina Chemical is appointed to the official committee, and if the official committee seeks court approval to retain Pat Gray as its attorney, should the court approve? See § 1103(b); In re Whitman, 101 B.R. 37 (Bankr. N.D. Ind. 1989). How would your analysis be affected if Tina Chemical had received a large payment from Foam Corporation two months before Foam Corporation filed its chapter 11 petition? See § 547(b); cf. United States Trustee v. First Jersey Sec., Inc. (In re First Jersey Sec., Inc.), 180 F.3d 504 (3d Cir. 1999). Should Foam Union International (the union that represents many of Foam Corporation's employees) be appointed to the committee? What if its national policy is to preserve jobs at all costs? See In re Barney's Inc., 197 B.R. 431 (Bankr. S.D.N.Y. 1996). What burdens or risks might make an eligible creditor choose not to serve on the committee? Consider Westmoreland Human Opportunities, Inc. v. Walsh, 327 B.R. 561 (W.D. Pa. 2005); Singerman & Robson, *Actions Against Former Committee Members: Alleged Breach of Fiduciary Duty for Support of a Plan and Ramifications*, 24 AM. BANKR. INST. J. 20 (April 2005).

In re Wang Laboratories, Inc.
United States Bankruptcy Court, D. Massachusetts, 1992
149 B.R. 1

WILLIAM C. HILLMAN, Bankruptcy Judge.

Morton Salkind ("Salkind") alleges that he is the holder of 1.6 million of the 165 million shares of debtor's Class B common stock presently outstanding. His counsel requested that the United States Trustee appoint an equity committee pursuant to 11 U.S.C. § 1102(a)(1) but that officer deemed the appointment inappropriate. The present motion followed.

[T]he Court granted the motion in a bench decision, entered an appropriate order, and indicated that this opinion would follow. * * *

The statute involves two inquiries. It must first be determined whether the appointment of a committee is necessary to assure adequate representation. If it is, then the Court must consider whether it should exercise its discretion and make the appointment.

There is no statutory test of "adequacy of representation" and it must be determined by the facts of the case. Most discussions start with the tripartite test of In re Johns-Manville Corp., 68 B.R. 155, 159 (S.D.N.Y. 1986): (1) the number of shareholders; (2) the complexity of the case; and (3) whether the cost of the additional committee significantly outweighs the concern for adequate representation.

The debtor certainly has a significant number of shareholders. Salkind alleges that there are approximately 49,000 holders of Class B shares and 2,000 holders of Class C. The Securities and Exchange Commission ("SEC") asserts that this represents only shareholders of record, and that the true number of beneficial owners of equity interests is probably nearer to 70,000 in the aggregate. * * * The Court finds that there are sufficient shareholders to satisfy that ground for the appointment of an equity committee. * * *

As to complexity, the Court considers the "weight of the evidence" to support a positive finding. This case, less than three months old, has already generated 15 binders of documents in the office of the clerk of the Court. * * *

The final element of the *Johns-Manville* equation requires a balancing of the cost of the additional committee against the value of the representation to be provided. It is in this area that the Court must consider the assertion of the United States Trustee that no committee should be appointed since the debtor is insolvent.

The Trustee's argument derives from Judge Abram's assertion that

> generally no equity committee should be appointed when it appears that a debtor is hopelessly insolvent because neither the debtor nor the creditors should have to bear the expense of negotiating over the terms of what is in essence a gift.

In re Emons Industries, Inc., 50 B.R. 692, 694 (Bankr. S.D.N.Y. 1985).

The Court agrees. The difficulty arises in applying that principle to the circumstances of the present case, and in particular to the meaning of "insolvency" within the *Emons* rule.

This is not a simple matter of statutory construction where the Court can rest with citation to the balance sheet test of 11 U.S.C. § 101(32). Each party has its own view of the relevant considerations.

The United States Trustee points to the debtor's financial disclosures as of September 30, 1992, which indicate a negative equity of more than 400 million dollars. Thus, he continues, there is no interest to be represented.

Salkind, on the other hand, contends that his shares have value, as they are still trading actively on the American Stock Exchange at a value in excess of zero.

The Official Creditors' Committee disputes this contention, pointing out that debtor's publicly traded debt securities, senior in right to the equity holders, are selling at a deep discount from face value, indicating that the market assigns a no value to the shares.

* * * In any event, the debtor remains in operation at present, albeit at a loss, and is not *hopelessly* insolvent, which is the *Emons* test.

Having determined that a committee is necessary to provide adequate protection to equity holders, the Court must next determine whether it should exercise its discretion to do so.

The Court's concern is that, as Judge Buschman noted, "the appointment of additional committees is closely followed by applications to retain attorneys and accountants." In re Beker Industries Corp., supra 55 B.R. at 949 (citations omitted). Where the debtor, despite its protestations, is *prima facie* insolvent according to the balance sheet test, and continues to accrue operating loses, it may be that it will prove inappropriate to compensate the professionals hired by the equity committee.

If Salkind individually hires professionals to assist him in obtaining adequate protection for his equity position, the estate will reimburse him for the expenses and fees only if his efforts make a substantial contribution to the case. 11 U.S.C. § 503(b)(3)(D), (b)(4). The result should not be otherwise if he works through an official committee of equity holders.

Subject to the Court's approval, the equity committee may retain professionals. 11 U.S.C. § 1103(a). However, § 503(b) is expressly inapplicable to the compensation of professionals hired by a committee appointed under § 1102. They are hired on "any reasonable terms," 11 U.S.C. § 328(a), and receive their compensation under 11 U.S.C. § 330, subject to the Court's *ex post facto* control under the last sentence of 11 U.S.C. § 328(a).

The prerequisites to payment under § 330 are (1) an exercise of discretion by the Court to award compensation for (2) actual, necessary services. There is no express requirement that the services make a substantial contribution to the case, but the Court finds that such a requirement is implicit in the requirement that payment be for services which are actual and necessary. Once again we return to the language of Judge Abram:

> If a plan is proposed and confirmed that provides nothing for shareholders, then it may well be that no fees and disbursements would be awarded to the [counsel for the equity committee] because in light of the outcome the amounts were not reasonable nor reflective of actual, necessary services.... The value of the services must be viewed with the benefit of hindsight. There can be no doubt that counsel which takes on representation of the equity committee of an allegedly hopelessly insolvent debtor takes a significant risk.

In re Emons Industries, Inc., supra 50 B.R. at 694.[22]

The Court believes that the above thoughts should provide distant early warning to professionals contemplating employment by the equity committee, and will be incorporated into any order approving employment.

NOTES

1. Do you agree with the court that the stockholders are receiving "in essence a gift," when a chapter 11 plan provides value to them, despite the debtor's insolvency? See discussion in Chapter One of this text at pages 28-29 & 33.

2. As Judge Hillman indicated in his footnote 7, the court in the Evans Products reorganization took a different approach to the compensation of equity committees' professionals. See In re Evans Products Co., 62 B.R. 579 (S.D. Fla.1986). In an earlier *Evans Products* opinion the district court had reversed the bankruptcy court's refusal to allow the official equity committee to hire accountants. In re Evans Products, 58 B.R. 572 (S.D. Fla.1985). The district court held that the rights and responsibilities of an official equity committee are no different from those of the unsecured creditors' committee, that Congress did not "limit the right of shareholders to participate in bankruptcy proceedings because they stand behind creditors in the distribution of the assets of an estate," and that "[s]tockholders are no less entitled than creditors to independent, zealous representation by professionals free of any compromising influences or loyalties." Id. at 575-76. The court cited Committee of Equity Security Holders v. Lionel Corp. (In re Lionel Corp.), 722 F.2d 1063, 1069 (2d Cir. 1983), which is discussed earlier in this chapter after the text of In re Johns-Manville Corp., 801 F.2d 60 (2d Cir. 1986).

3. How do Manville Corp. v. Equity Security Holders Committee and *Lionel* compare to *Wang Laboratories* and to the two *Evans Products* decisions?

4. In an opinion by Justice (then Circuit Judge) Alito, the Third Circuit held that the bankruptcy court could, in the interests of keeping costs down,

    (1) require an equity committee to rely on information developed by the debtor in possession, even though the committee wanted its own accountants to develop the information independently, and

---

22. [Footnote 7 in original:] The Court does not agree that the expenses of the committee are presumed to be expenses toward the betterment of the estate, nor that § 1102 committee expenses should be reimbursed unless shown to be frivolous. In re Evans Products Co., 62 B.R. 579 (S.D. Fla. 1986) will not be followed.

(2) place a monthly cap on the fees of the equity committee's accountants.

Comm. of Equity Sec. Holders of Federal-Mogul Corp. v. Official Comm. of Unsecured Creditors (In re Federal Mogul-Global, Inc.), 348 F.3d 390 (3d Cir. 2003) (remanding for explanation of factual basis for cap). One reason for the cap was the bankruptcy judge's view that the stockholders were probably not entitled to receive any value, and that perhaps an equity committee should not even have been appointed, because the debtors were probably insolvent.

5.   Whether creation of an equity committee is "necessary to assure adequate representation * * * of equity security holders" may depend on the degree to which the stockholders' interests are aligned with interests of those already represented by a committee. See In re Williams Commc'ns Group, Inc., 281 B.R 216 (Bankr. S.D.N.Y. 2002). For example, where stockholders' only hope of recovery depends on avoidance of transfers, and where avoidance would also benefit creditors, the official creditors' committee's incentive to advocate for avoidance of the transfers lessens the need for an equity committee. See In re Leap Wireless Int'l, Inc., 295 B.R. 135 (Bankr. S.D. Cal. 2003). Courts sometimes suggest that the creditors' committee thus provides representation to the stockholders, but that is a substantial overstatement.

6.   Some courts take what seems to be a stricter approach to whether an equity committee should be appointed than the approach taken in *Wang Laboratories*. Consider this excerpt from *Williams Communications*:

> The Movants, however, argue that the UST could not have made a determination, from the facts before it, that the Debtors were "hopelessly insolvent" within the context of the *Emons* decision. That is, it is not just a simple reference to the balance sheet. *Wang*, 149 B.R. at 3. Instead, the Movants argue that the true test of the value of a debtor's assets is by looking at its reorganization value as set forth in Consolidated Rock Products Co. v. Du Bois, 312 U.S. 510, 525-26, 61 S. Ct. 675, 85 L.Ed. 982 (1941). Thus, the Movants contend that reorganization value must be determined by the entity's future earnings potential, and not by the debtor's balance sheet or how the capital markets have valued the company's securities.

> Nowhere in the *Emons* decision, or other courts recognizing that decision, does it mandate a finding by the court that the debtor is hopelessly insolvent. Instead, the language is whether the debtor "appears to be hopelessly insolvent." *Emons*, 50 B.R. at 694. This Court has made a determination that WCG and CGA appear to be hopelessly insolvent based on many different factors. The Debtors' balance sheet and market value were two such factors, but so are the host of other indicia of the Debtors' financial health set forth above. Regardless of the method used, the result will "rarely, if ever, be without doubt or variation." L. King Collier on Bankruptcy ¶ 1129.06 [3] (15th Ed. Rev., 2001).

> Valuation is a proper issue for confirmation, and no determination for this motion is binding on a subsequent determination. In short, this Court has not made a valuation, nor is one necessary at this stage. Instead, it has reached a practical conclusion, based on a confluence of factors, that the Debtors appear to be hopelessly insolvent.

* * *

> The appointment of official equity committees should be the rare exception. Such committees should not be appointed unless equity holders establish that (i) there is a substantial likelihood that they will receive a meaningful distribution in the case under a strict application of the absolute priority rule, and (ii) they are unable to represent their interests in the bankruptcy case without an official committee. The second factor is critical because, in most cases, even those equity holders who do expect a distribution in the case can adequately represent their interest without an official committee and can seek compensation if they make a substantial contribution in the case.

281 B.R. at 221 & 223. Accord Exide Technologies v. State of Wisconsin Inv. Bd., No. 02-1572-SLR, 2002 WL 32332000 (D. Del. 2002); In re Leap Wireless Int'l, Inc., 295 B.R. 135 (Bankr. S.D. Cal. 2003); In re Northwestern Corp., No. 03-12872 (CGC), 2004 WL 1077913 (Bankr. D. Del. May 13, 2004).

What justification is there, if any, for the *Williams Communications* court's reference to the "absolute priority rule"?

The court in *Northwestern Corp.* seems to have held that a debtor was "hopelessly insolvent" even though it was not impossible that the stockholders could show that it was solvent:

> Let us assume the best outcome for the Movants—that the testimony of Mr. Harris (their expert) is sufficiently compelling to create a credible argument that a higher value may be appropriate and the testimony of Lazard Freres, Debtor's expert, is sufficiently suspect to put the Debtor's valuation in doubt. Does that justify the appointment of a committee? The Court thinks not. All that would do is put the issue of value in play, not tip the scale to the extent that the valuation battle should be funded by the estate. Remember that there is a $700 million shortfall that needs to be overcome before there is any value for equity. While not impossible, that is a steep hill to climb; indeed, the Court could eventually accept nearly 80% of the additional value urged by the Movants and equity would still be out of the money. This does not satisfy the "substantial likelihood that [equity] will receive a meaningful distribution" test set forth in In re Williams.

Id. at *2.

Problem 6-5

If Gruff and Marilyn Simmons (Gruff's sister and minority shareholder in Foam Corporation) request appointment of a shareholders' committee, should the court order appointment of such a committee? See In re Lifeguard Indus., 37 B.R. 3 (Bankr. S.D. Ohio 1983) (reprinted above), and In re Beker Indus., 55 B.R. 945 (Bankr. S.D.N.Y. 1985) (ordering appointment of debenture holders' committee and of shareholders' committee where debentures and stock were widely held and where many of the holders had small holdings). How is Foam Corporation's case different from the case of a large, publicly held company a majority of whose directors are "outside" directors?

Chapter Seven

Executory Contracts

A. A TEXTUAL NOTE ON EXECUTORY CONTRACTS AND UNEXPIRED LEASES

1. The Need To Take Advantage of the Debtor's Contracts and Leases

Consider Foam Corporation's contracts and leases. Four of Foam Corporation's plants are leased from Imperial Insurance Company; one more is leased from the Gruff Family Trust. Under the leases Foam Corporation has the right to possess and use the plants but also has obligations, primarily the obligation to pay rent. Foam Corporation has an employment contract with Gruff, under which Foam Corporation is entitled to Gruff's services as chief executive officer and chairman of the board but is obligated to pay him a substantial salary. Foam Corporation has a collective bargaining agreement with Foam Union International ("FUI") covering two of the plants, under which Foam Corporation has the right not to be struck (and various other rights) but is obligated to hire only union members, to pay them in accordance with the collective bargaining agreement, and to provide working conditions and benefits provided under the agreement. Of course Foam Corporation has fire and theft insurance, liability insurance, and workers' compensation insurance, all pursuant to contract. Finally, Foam Corporation has various contracts to sell its products to its customers and to buy raw materials from its suppliers.

If chapter 11 debtors such as Foam Corporation could not take advantage of their rights under prepetition contracts and leases, reorganization often would be difficult or impossible. A debtor that operates on leased premises could not continue in business. A debtor that relies on long term contracts with major customers or suppliers could lose much of its sales volume or lose the sources of supply needed to keep the business operating. The value of a favorable contract—for example, a long term lease of premises at a below market rental, or a contract to buy chemicals at a price below market—would be lost; that would reduce the value of the debtor's business, harm the debtor's creditors (who look to that value for repayment), and lessen the chances of a successful reorganization. The debtor needs the benefit of continued coverage under its insurance contracts, as well. The U.S. trustee may seek to convert the case to a chapter 7 liquidation for "cause" or seek appointment of a trustee for "cause" if the debtor fails to maintain insurance coverage—fire and theft insurance to protect the value of the assets that make up the estate, liability insurance to protect those who may be harmed by torts committed in the course of reorganizing the debtor, and workers' compensation insurance to protect employees who may be hurt on the job. See, e.g., United States Trustee, Central District of California, Notice of Requirements For Chapter 11 Debtors in Possession (2003), www.usdoj.gov/ust/r16/pdfdocs/ch11_ntc_req.pdf (last visited Feb. 18, 2006).

Section 365(a) therefore permits the debtor in possession to take the benefit of prepetition contracts and leases for the estate by assuming them. Section 365(e)(1) even protects the debtor in possession's right to assume such a contract or lease by prohibiting enforcement of a contractual provision (called an ipso facto clause) that would allow the nondebtor party to modify or cancel the contract or lease due to the bankruptcy filing or due to the debtor's financial condition.

2. The Executory Contract as a "Package" of Benefits and Burdens—the Assume/Reject Election and "Ride Through"

However, the debtor's executory contracts and unexpired leases consist not only of rights but also of obligations. Under nonbankrupcty law, Foam Corporation's right to continued insurance coverage under its fire insurance policy depends on Foam Corporation's timely payment of premiums. Similarly, under nonbankruptcy law Foam Corporation's rights to continued use and possession of the plants leased from Imperial Insurance and from the Gruff Family Trust depend on Foam Corporation's timely payment of rent. A debtor's executory contracts and unexpired leases are thus in a sense both assets and liabilities. The debtor's right to further performance from the other party under the contract (or to further possession of property under a lease) can be considered an asset. The debtor's obligation to continue its performance under the contract or lease can be considered a liability. See, e.g., Enter. Energy Corp. v. United States (In re Columbia Gas Sys. Inc.), 50 F.3d 233, 238 (3d Cir. 1995). That duality creates complications and raises a fundamental question.

Must the estate take on the debtor's obligations under a contract or lease in order to obtain the future benefits of the contract or lease? Put more simply, are the debtor's rights and obligations under an executory contract or unexpired lease a "package" that must be taken by the estate, if at all, as a unit? The answer, in brief, is "yes." See id. Although there is not a completely cohesive philosophy behind § 365, there is a basic concept that if an executory contract or lease is to be assumed it must be assumed with all (or almost all) of the contract's burdens; it must be assumed *cum onere* ("with burdens"). If the contract or lease is assumed under § 365(a), the estate then becomes entitled to the debtor's rights under the contract or lease, but also succeeds to the debtor's obligations; those obligations become obligations of the estate itself, and thus have an administrative priority. Thus, if the benefits of the contract exceed its burdens, the debtor in possession (or trustee) likely will seek court approval to assume the contract; if the burdens exceed the benefits, the debtor in possession (or trustee) likely will seek court approval to reject the contract. See *Columbia Gas*, 50 F.3d at 238. The rejection will constitute a breach, which, under § 365(g)(1), will be considered to have occurred immediately before the filing of the petition. The nondebtor party will then have a general unsecured claim for damages for breach of contract (unless the nondebtor party has a secured claim as a result of having taken a security deposit or lien to secure performance of the contract).

Suppose Foam Corporation contracted on April 1, 2006 to purchase 10,000 gallons of solvent for $3 per gallon from Old Supply Co. ("OSC"), payment due on delivery, which was to be on April 30, 2001. When Foam Corporation filed its chapter 11 petition on April 10, neither party to the contract had performed. If Foam Corporation needs the solvent, and if the market price of the solvent has risen to $3.50 per gallon by April 30, it will be in the estate's interest for Foam Corporation, as debtor in possession, to assume the contract and buy the chemicals; the estate will receive $35,000 worth of needed solvent for $30,000.

On the other hand, if the market price of solvent has fallen to $2.50 per gallon by April 30, it will not be in the estate's interest to assume the contract; paying $30,000 for $25,000 worth of solvent would harm the estate. Thus Foam Corporation, as debtor in possession, would reject the contract. If Foam Corporation, as debtor in possession, rejects the contract, OSC will have a prepetition claim for damages for breach of contract. See §§ 365(g)(1) and 502(g). If OSC's claim is for $5,000 in damages, and if general unsecured creditors receive value equal to 30% payment of their claims under Foam Corporation's chapter 11 plan, only $1,500 (30% of $5,000) of the value of the estate will have to go to OSC. Thus, if Foam Corporation rejects the contract rather than assuming it, Foam Corporation will save $3,500 of the estate's value—the $1,500 that will have to go to OSC on OSC's $5,000 prepetition claim is $3,500 less than the $5,000 the estate would have lost by paying $30,000 for $25,000 worth of solvent. The point is that if Foam Corporation assumes the contract, Foam Corporation's obligations under the contract will be obligations of the estate that must be honored in full out of the estate. Cf. § 365(g)(2) (providing that "rejection" of contract that has been assumed is not considered a *prepetition* breach). If Foam Corporation does not assume the contract but instead rejects it, Foam Corporation's obligation to pay damages will be treated like all the other unsecured prepetition obligations, which usually are not paid at 100 cents on the dollar. Rejection thus saves the estate $3,500.

The assume or reject election was created by the courts in the 19th and early 20th centuries, as Michael Andrew has shown. See Andrew, *Executory Contracts in Bankruptcy: Understanding Rejection*, 59 U. COLO. L. REV. 845, 855-66 (1988) (hereinafter "*Understanding Rejection*"); Andrew, *Executory Contracts Revisited: A Reply to Professor Westbrook,* 62 U. COLO. L. REV. 1, 4-7 (1991) (hereinafter "*Executory Contracts Revisited*"). The courts thought that executory contracts and leases had to be seen as a package; the law could not reasonably require the nondebtor party to perform its obligations and receive in return a mere general unsecured claim, which might be paid off at ten cents on the dollar. If the debtor's estate was to receive all the benefit of the nondebtor's postpetition performance, then the debtor's estate would have to be responsible for the debtor's obligations as a priority expense of administration. The courts therefore determined that the debtor's rights under contracts which the debtor had not yet performed could not automatically pass to the estate, because, the courts reasoned, if the rights automatically passed to the estate, then the burdens might automatically pass as well. As we have seen, the burdens of an executory contract sometimes outweigh the benefits, so that the estate may be better off without the "package." Thus the representative of the estate should be able to choose whether to take the debtor's rights under the contract and thus to subject the estate to its burdens.

The courts also were concerned that the nondebtor party (such as OSC) might not be treated fairly in the bankruptcy case. If the debtor had not breached at the time the debtor filed for bankruptcy, as in the Foam Corporation-OSC contract case, it might be thought that the nondebtor party had no claim against the debtor as of the time of the bankruptcy filing. Even if the debtor had breached, if the breach was not a "total breach" entitling the nondebtor party to damages for breach of the whole contract, the nondebtor party might be thought to have a claim only for damages for the partial breach. Then, as now, claims were generally determined as of the date of the bankruptcy filing. See § 502(b). If the nondebtor party had no claim as of that date, the nondebtor might not be permitted to share in any distribution from the bankruptcy estate, even if the nondebtor party suffered substantial damages from nonperformance of the contract.[1] Even if there already had been a partial breach, damages for that prepetition partial breach might be only a small part of the damages caused by a complete failure of the debtor to perform; the nondebtor party's right to share in the value of the estate could be limited unfairly if its claim were limited to damages for the partial breach.

The courts were able to deal with both of these concerns—ensuring that contract obligations did not automatically become administrative obligations of the estate and treating nondebtor parties fairly—by creating an assumption/rejection election for the trustee in bankruptcy. If the contract was a favorable one for the estate—for example, a contract to buy needed goods under which the amount still owing by the debtor was less than the market value of the goods still to be delivered by the nondebtor party—then the trustee could assume it on behalf of the estate. The debtor's obligations then would become obligations of the estate (with administrative priority), but the estate would have a net gain by taking the benefit of the debtor's valuable rights under the contract. If the contract was not favorable, the trustee could reject the contract, thereby refusing to take the debtor's rights into the estate.

---

1.   For example, if the market value of solvent dropped to $2.50 per gallon, and Foam Corporation as debtor in possession therefore decided not to take on the rights and burdens of the contract with OSC for the estate, OSC would suffer damages from Foam Corporation's nonperformance. At the time Foam Corporation filed its bankruptcy petition, however, Foam Corporation was not in breach, so it might be difficult to see how OSC could have a claim in Foam Corporation's bankruptcy case.

The courts considered the rejection to be a breach of the contract, and deemed the breach to be a prepetition breach, so that the nondebtor party's claim for breach of contract could be recognized in the bankruptcy case. If the nondebtor party had no lien, its claim would be only a general unsecured claim, not a priority administrative expense claim; such a claim is not more deserving of payment than the other unsecured creditors' claims. See Andrew, *Executory Contracts Revisited*, supra, 62 U. COLO. L. REV. at 4-7.

The courts also created a "ride through" doctrine for reorganization cases, under which executory contracts and unexpired leases would "ride through" the reorganization unaffected if the trustee neither assumed nor rejected them. After the reorganization, the debtor still would be bound by such contracts. See Andrew, *Understanding Rejection*, supra, 59 COLO. L. REV. at 879-81.

Section 365 codifies the assume or reject election created by the early cases. Section 365(a) gives the trustee or debtor in possession the right (subject to court approval) to assume or reject almost any executory contract or unexpired lease of the debtor. In addition, the "ride through" (or "pass through") doctrine may still be good law[2] even though it was not explicitly codified in § 365.[3] Several courts seemingly have ignored the "ride through"

---

2. See, e.g., NLRB. v. Bildisco & Bildisco, 465 U.S. 513, 546 n. 12, 104 S. Ct. 1188, 1206 n. 12, 79 L. Ed. 2d 482, 508 n. 12 (1984) (dictum in Justice Brennan's concurrence and dissent for four members of the Court); Stumpf v. McGee (In re O'Connor), 258 F.3d 392, 404 (5th Cir. 2001) ("There appears to be general agreement that the 'pass-through' theory continues to apply in Chapter 11 cases governed by the Code, at least where an *assumable* executory contract is neither assumed nor rejected, and the Reorganized Debtor continues to operate the debtor's pre-bankruptcy business.") (also holding that "pass through" applies to nonassumable contracts); Century Indem. Co. v. Nat'l Gypsum Co. Settlement Trust (In re Nat'l Gypsum Co.), 208 F.3d 498, 504 n.4 (5th Cir. 2000) (dictum); Phoenix Mut. Life Ins. Co. v. Greystone III Joint Venture (In re Greystone III Joint Venture), 995 F.2d 1274, 1281 (5th Cir. 1991) ("A debtor in Chapter 11 must either assume or reject its leases with third parties * * *. If the debtor does neither, the leases continue in effect * * *."); In re Hernandez, 287 B.R. 795 (Bankr. D. Ariz. 2002) (canvassing authorities, determining that contract would "ride through" chapter 11 case unaffected if neither assumed nor rejected, and refusing to require debtor to reject contract (which was unassumable under § 365(c)(1)), but granting relief from stay to allow nondebtor party to exercise whatever nonbankruptcy law rights it might have to terminate the contract); In re Cajun Elec. Power Co-op., Inc., 230 B.R. 715 (Bankr. M.D. La. 1999) (recognizing ride through doctrine but requiring liquidating plan to assume or reject contracts, because ride through would leave nondebtor party with no remedy); In re Parkwood Realty Corp., 157 B.R. 687 (Bankr. W.D. Wash. 1993) (holding that due process would not permit contract to be rejected without notice to nondebtor party by blanket reject-all-contracts language in plan, and that contract therefore bound the reorganized debtor); Andrew, *Understanding Rejection,* supra, 59 COLO. L. REV. at 879-80; Campbell & Hastie, *Executory Contracts: Retention Without Assumption in Chapter 11—"Ride-through" Revisited,* 19-Mar. AM. BANKR. INST. J. 33 (2000).

3.   "Ride through" does not, however, apply in chapter 7 cases. It could not reasonably be applied to chapter 7 cases involving corporations. After a chapter 7 liquidation, a debtor corporation will have no assets and may well cease to exist. Permitting the nondebtor party to retain its rights under the contract against a corporation with no assets (or against a nonexistent corporation) would provide no protection at all of the nondebtor party's rights. Section 365(d)(1) ensures, in chapter 7 cases, that executory contracts and unexpired leases of residential real property or of personal property are either assumed (thus elevating the nondebtor party's rights to administrative expense status) or rejected; it provides that in a chapter 7 case such contracts and leases are deemed rejected if not timely assumed. Section 365(d)(4)(A) similarly provides (in cases under all chapters) that unexpired leases of nonresidential real property are deemed rejected if not timely assumed. Thus a contract or lease cannot

doctrine and treated the rights of nondebtor parties to executory contracts as claims even though the contracts were neither assumed nor rejected.[4] Other courts have taken the position that the nondebtor party to an executory contract does not have a claim in the bankruptcy case until and unless the contract is rejected, a position that is consistent with the "ride through" doctrine.[5] If the contract is never rejected, and if no claim arises to be discharged under § 1141(d), then it would seem that the contractual obligation would ride through bankruptcy untouched. See 3 Resnick & Sommer, COLLIER ON BANKRUPTCY ¶ 365.04[2][d], at 365-33.

It might be thought that the broadened definition of "claim" in § 101(5)(A) would permit courts to find that a nondebtor party to an executory contract or lease has a contingent claim under the Bankruptcy Code for damages for total breach, even though a claim would not have existed under the bankruptcy laws as they existed when the courts created the ride through doctrine. (The claim would be contingent on the occurrence of a total

---

"ride through" a chapter 7 case. However, even if a contract or lease is rejected in a chapter 7 case, it may still possible for the debtor to obtain the benefit of the contract or lease after the case. Otherwise, chapter 7 debtors would lose their apartment leases and would lose the benefit of employment contracts, even if the debtors never breached the contracts or leases. The courts have not allowed landlords to evict tenants simply because the tenant files a chapter 7 case in which the tenant's apartment lease is deemed rejected under § 365(d)(1). See Andrew, *Executory Contracts Revisited,* supra, 62 U. COLO. L. REV. at 22 n. 108; cf. § 365(p) (added by 2005 BAPCPA).

As noted, § 365(d)(4)(A) prevents any "ride through" of a nonresidential real property lease where the debtor is the lessee, even in a chapter 11 case. Under that section, in a bankruptcy case under any chapter, a lease of *nonresidential real property* under which the debtor is the lessee is deemed rejected if it is not timely assumed.

Note that even in a successful chapter 11 case the original corporate debtor may not have valuable assets at the end of the case. The successful resolution of the case may involve a sale of the debtor's assets as a going concern to an acquirer, with all of the consideration paid by the acquirer—cash, debt instruments, or stock in the acquirer—being distributed to the creditors and stockholders of the debtor. In such cases where the original corporate debtor does not survive bankruptcy with valuable assets, the nondebtor party to an executory contract or unexpired lease is not helped by the doctrine of "ride through." For that reason and others, § 365(d)(2) permits the nondebtor party to seek an order setting a deadline by which the debtor in possession or trustee must either assume or reject the contract or lease.

4.   See Air Line Pilots Ass'n v. Shugrue (In re Ionosphere Clubs, Inc.), 22 F.3d 403 (2d Cir. 1994) (treating vacation pay earned prepetition by Eastern Airlines employees as nonadministrative claims even though collective bargaining agreement was neither assumed nor rejected); In re Roth American, Inc., 975 F.2d 949 (3d Cir. 1992) (treating vacation pay and severance pay earned prepetition as nonadministrative claims even though collective bargaining agreement was never rejected). But see United Steelworkers v. Unimet Corp. (In re Unimet Corp.), 842 F.2d 879 (6th Cir. 1988) (whether or not obligations under unrejected collective bargaining contract constituted administrative priority claims, debtor could not escape them because § 1113(f) prohibits alteration of provisions of collective bargaining agreement except pursuant to terms of § 1113).

5.   See United States v. Dewey Freight System, Inc., 31 F.3d 620 (8th Cir. 1994) (holding that nondebtor party "had *no claim at all* for post-petition nonperformance until the contracts were rejected"); Phoenix Mut. Life Ins. Co. v. Greystone III Joint Venture (In re Greystone III Joint Venture), 995 F.2d 1274 (5th Cir. 1991) (stating, perhaps in dictum, that nondebtor party to lease has no "provable" claim and is not a creditor if lease neither assumed nor rejected); Pub. Serv. Co. of N.H. v. N.H. Elec. Coop., Inc. (In re Pub. Serv. Co. of N.H.), 884 F.2d 11 (1st Cir. 1989) (stating that nondebtor party had no "provable" claim against bankruptcy estate for purposes of setoff where wholly executory contract had neither been assumed nor rejected).

breach.) That could mean that the rights of the nondebtor party would not "ride through" the bankruptcy if the contracts or leases were neither assumed nor rejected. Instead, the nondebtor party would have a debt (see §101(12)) that would be discharged under § 1141(d)(1)(A) when a plan is confirmed. Professor Andrew points out, however, that the ride through doctrine was created by the courts in the 1930s and applied in many cases after the 1930s, even though the 1938 amendments to the old Bankruptcy Act permitted contingent claims to be proven and estimated. Andrew, *Understanding Rejection*, supra, 59 U. COLO. L. REV. at 879-80 n. 142. It remains to be seen which argument will prevail—the argument based on Professor Andrew's historical point or the argument based on the broad definition of "claim."

Under § 365(g)(1), rejection of a contract that has not earlier been assumed constitutes a breach of the contract as of a time immediately before the filing of the bankruptcy petition. Under § 502(g), the nondebtor party will then be treated as having a prepetition claim (but not an administrative expense claim) for damages for the breach.

If, however, the debtor or trustee assumes the contract or lease, thus taking the benefits of the debtor's rights under the contract for the estate, the debtor's obligations become obligations of the estate. In fact, if there has been a prepetition or postpetition default, in order to assume the contract or lease the debtor usually must either cure the default or give adequate assurances that the default will be cured and usually also must compensate the nondebtor party for losses caused by the default. See § 365(b). Of course any payment or other expense of curing the default will come out the property of the estate. If the debtor or trustee later rejects or breaches the contract, the nondebtor party probably will be treated as having a postpetition administrative expense claim. See §365(g)(2); Nostas Assocs. v. Costich (In re Klein Sleep Prods., Inc.), 78 F.3d 18 (2d Cir. 1996); In re Food City, 94 B.R. 91 (Bankr. W.D. Tex. 1988); Samore v. Boswell (In re Multech Corp.), 47 B.R. 747 (Bankr. N.D. Iowa 1985). But see In re Johnston, Inc., 164 B.R. 551, 556 (Bankr. E.D. Tex. 1994) (refusing to follow *Multech* but stating that in so doing "the Court feels akin to the lone salmon swimming upstream against a raging current").

3. The Meaning of Executory

Thus, under § 365(a), the debtor in possession has the right to assume or reject most "executory" contracts and unexpired leases. Leases may be assumed or rejected without any need for a determination that they are "executory."[6] But,

---

6. Although there is no need to determine whether an unexpired lease is executory, there is often a need to determine whether a transaction that is in form a personal or real property lease is a true lease. Some "leases" are in fact disguised sales; if a "lease" is in fact a sale, then the "lessor's" retention of title is treated as retention only of a security interest to secure the payments owed by the "lessee." See U.C.C. §1-201(37) (providing guidance for whether a purported lease is actually a disguised security interest) (1999 Official Text) (guidance relocated to U.C.C. § 1-203 by 2001 Official Text); White & Summers,

with regard to a contract that is not a lease, it might seem that it would always be crucial to determine whether the contract is "executory." After all, under § 365(a) a contract other than a lease can be assumed or rejected only if it is executory. However, it does not always matter whether a contract is considered to be executory. For example, suppose the debtor contracts to pay a commission to a broker who finds a buyer for a parcel of real estate owned by the debtor. After the broker finds a buyer, suppose that the debtor files a chapter 11 petition, consummates the sale to the buyer, and seeks to reject the separate contract with the broker. It does not matter whether the contract with the broker is executory. If it is executory, the debtor will reject it, and the broker will have a general unsecured claim for the commission. If it is not executory, the debtor can neither assume it nor reject it, and the broker will simply have a general, unsecured claim for the commission. Byrd v. Gardinier, Inc. (In re Gardinier, Inc.), 831 F.2d 974, 975 n.2 (11th Cir. 1987).[7]

It is important to understand, then, that a contract does not bind the estate just because it is not executory and hence not subject to being rejected. Suppose the nondebtor party has performed all of its obligations under a contract, but the debtor has performed none of its obligations. (A good example would be a loan agreement under which the nondebtor party has lent the debtor money and the debtor has not yet begun to pay it back.) As we will see, the whole point of considering such a contract to be nonexecutory is to ensure that the debtor in possession cannot foolishly assume the contract and thereby make the estate liable on it as a priority expense of administration. If we were to give a debtor in possession an election to assume or reject such a contract, the debtor in possession's only appropriate course would be to reject it. Thus it may make little difference whether a contract is found to be executory and is rejected by the debtor in possession or is found to be nonexecutory. In neither case will the estate be bound by the contract. In both cases, the nondebtor party simply will have a claim in the bankruptcy case, a general unsecured claim (unless the claimant has a lien or has some other basis for seeking a priority, such as a third priority for unpaid prepetition wages under § 507(a)(4)).

Michael Andrew therefore argues that there is no reason to require that a contract be executory before permitting rejection, and Professor Jay Westbrook argues that there is no need at all to ask whether a contract is executory.[8] But in some cases it matters whether a contract is executory.

UNIFORM COMMERCIAL CODE §21-3 at 716-27 (5th ed. 2000); United Airlines, Inc. v. HSBC Bank USA, N.A., 416 F.3d 609 (2d Cir. 2005) (holding that purported real property lease was actually a secured loan). If the "lessor" is in fact simply a secured creditor, then the "lease" is just a secured debt, which is not an executory contract. See infra text accompanying footnote 13.

    7.   If the contract is executory, and the broker performs substantial postpetition work, the court may award the broker a fee under unjust enrichment principles even if the contract is rejected. See Goldin v. Putnam Lovell, Inc. (In re Monarch Capital Corp.), 163 B.R. 899 (Bankr. D. Mass. 1994).

    8.   See Westbrook, *A Functional Analysis of Executory Contracts*, 74 MINN. L. REV. 227, 282-83 (1989) (hereinafter "*Executory Contracts*"); Andrew, *Executory Contracts Revisited,* supra, 62 U. COLO. L. REV. at 8-9 (arguing that there should be no requirement of "executoriness" for

First, if a contract is executory but is neither assumed nor rejected, it may "ride through" the case and be binding on the reorganized debtor. If the debtor does not wish to be bound by a contract, the debtor must be sure, in its capacity as debtor in possession, to reject the contract if there is any possibility at all that the contract will be found to be executory.[9]

Second, if a contract is not executory because the nondebtor party has completely performed, then the nondebtor party will simply have a claim in bankruptcy for the value of whatever it is entitled to under the contract. In such a case there would be no justification for elevating the nondebtor party's claim to administrative expense status by way of an assumption of the contract; a determination that the contract is nonexecutory and thus nonassumable prevents that from happening. (Of course, if the contract is thus nonexecutory, the nondebtor party must be sure to file a claim in the bankruptcy case before any bar date—deadline for filing of claims—that may be set.)

Third, if a contract is not executory because the debtor has completely performed, then the estate has an asset—the right to performance from the nondebtor party. There then would be no need for the debtor in possession to elect whether to assume or reject the contract. Assumption of the contract should not be necessary for the estate to be entitled to the performance, and rejection ordinarily would be wasteful—the only effect of rejection would be to throw away an asset of the estate. A determination that the contract is nonexecutory would prevent the debtor in possession from throwing away that asset unless the standards are met for abandonment under § 554.

Fourth, as discussed above, many courts hold that rejection prevents the nondebtor party from obtaining the remedy of specific enforcement, as Professor Vern Countryman demonstrated was the law under the old Bankruptcy Act with regard to contracts for sale of real property.[10] If the contract is executory, and hence subject to being rejected, the debtor may be able to eliminate a right to specific performance that otherwise might survive the bankruptcy case.

---

rejection but that there should be such a requirement before assumption is permitted). Congress has not amended § 365 to implement their suggestion that any contract should be subject to being rejected. At least one court has implemented their suggestion judicially—ignoring the language of the statute—by holding that a debtor in possession may reject a contract without satisfying a "threshold requirement" that the contract be "executory." Cohen v. Drexel Burnham Lambert Group, Inc. (In re Drexel Burnham Lambert Group, Inc.), 138 B.R. 687 (Bankr. S.D.N.Y. 1992) (permitting rejection of employment contract). The court's analysis may be the functional equivalent of a holding that it did not matter whether the contract was executory, as in *Gardinier* and as explained in the preceding paragraph in the text, but it is nonetheless a troubling judicial amendment of the statute.

9.   In many cases that possibility can be handled by way of a provision in the plan of reorganization providing that all unassumed contracts are rejected. There is a possibility, however, that such a general provision may fail to meet the requirements of due process as to nondebtor contracting parties who do not know that their contracts are being rejected. See In re Parkwood Realty Corp., 157 B.R. 687 (Bankr. W.D. Wash. 1993); Continental Country Club, Inc. v. Burr (In re Continental Country Club, Inc.), 114 B.R. 763 (Bankr. M.D. Fla. 1990).

10.   Countryman, *Executory Contracts in Bankruptcy: Part I*, 57 MINN. L. REV. 439, 463-74 (1973) (hereinafter, "*Contracts in Bankruptcy*").

Fifth, and finally, some courts treat the debtor's ability to reject a contract under § 365(a) as a kind of avoiding power—contrary to the views of Professors Andrew and Westbrook—rather than simply as the right to decline to make the contract the estate's contract. See Lubrizol Enterprises, Inc. v. Richmond Metal Finishers, Inc. (In re Richmond Metal Finishers, Inc.), 756 F.2d 1043 (4th Cir. 1985) (reprinted below); Cameron v. Pfaff Plumbing and Heating, Inc., 966 F.2d 414 (8th Cir. 1992). If rejection constitutes an avoiding power, the debtor may have a greater ability to affect the nondebtor party's rights if the contract is found to be executory and thus subject to being rejected.

Thus it seems we need a definition of "executory." As Professor Countryman pointed out, what it means for a contract to be executory can best be understood by considering those cases in which it would make sense to give the debtor in possession the election to assume or reject the contract. If either the debtor or the nondebtor party has fully performed, there is no reason to allow such an election, and the contract should not be considered to be executory. If the contract has been fully performed by the debtor (or at least substantially performed, so that the debtor is entitled to a return performance under the doctrine of constructive conditions), the debtor in possession should not be permitted to reject the contract and thus throw away the benefit of the return performance that the debtor has already earned. Thus the estate simply has an asset, the right to the return performance. (In the unusual case in which the return performance would be of inconsequential value to the estate, the debtor in possession could abandon it under § 554(a), and thus there is no need for a determination of whether the debtor in possession should assume or reject the contract.) On the other hand, if the nondebtor party to the contract (e.g., the broker in *Gardinier*) already has fully performed (or at least substantially performed), the debtor in possession would earn nothing (or very little) by finishing its performance; the debtor in possession should not be allowed to assume a contract where the only result would be to put a burden on the estate and use up resources that should be shared with all the creditors.[11] Thus, the other party to such an executed (non-

---

11. The Countryman definition does not perfectly identify the cases in which assumption may be of benefit. For example, if the contract is one for the debtor to construct a building and the debtor has nearly finished performance, it may make more sense for the debtor to go ahead and finish even if the debtor already has substantially performed. Substantial performance, it is true, gives the debtor the right to be paid, but the nondebtor party is entitled to deduct (recoup) its damages from the payment. If those damages would exceed the cost to the debtor in possession of finishing the performance, it would make sense for the debtor in possession to assume the contract, finish it, and receive the contract price without deduction. In addition, if rejection of a contract bars the nondebtor party from seeking specific performance or has an avoiding power effect, a very broad definition of "executory contract" will benefit the estate.

Thus some courts have worked overtime finding enough duties owing on each side so that they can conclude that the contract is executory under the Countryman test. See, e.g., *Lubrizol*, 756 F.2d 1043 (4th Cir. 1985) (reprinted below). Other courts have drawn a more inclusive definition from the legislative history of § 365: "Though there is no precise definition of what contracts are executory, it generally includes contracts on which performance remains due to some extent on both sides." H.R.

executory) contract simply has a prepetition claim for the performance that the debtor owes. As a result, under Professor Countryman's definition—which is by far the most used definition[12]—a contract is executory only if the obligations "of both the bankrupt and the other party to the contract are so far unperformed that the failure of either to complete performance would constitute a material breach excusing performance of the other." Countryman, *Contracts in Bankruptcy*, supra, 57 MINN. L. REV. at 460. Put another way, for a contract to be executory, both parties must be capable of materially breaching.

Thus we can see that a loan agreement under which the nondebtor party already has made the entire loan to the debtor before the filing of the bankruptcy petition is not an executory contract.[13] The lender has performed; the debtor has already received the value it was to receive under the contract. It would make no sense for the Code to allow the debtor in possession to turn the claim of the lender into an administrative priority claim by assuming the contract. Thus a lender simply has a prepetition claim in the debtor's bankruptcy—a general unsecured claim if the lender does not have a lien, a secured claim if the lender has a lien that fully secures the claim, or both a secured and an unsecured claim if the lender is undersecured.

Rep. No. 595, 95th Cong., 1st Sess. 347 (1977); S. Rep. No. 989, 95th Cong., 2d Sess. 58 (1978); see In re Harms, 10 B.R. 817 (Bankr. D. Colo. 1981) (discussed in Epstein, Nickles & White, BANKRUPTCY §5-4 at 231 n.10). Some courts go further and decide the issue whether or not a contract is executory by deciding the issue whichever way will help reorganization; this is the so-called "functional" test. See, e.g., Sipes v. Gen. Dev. Corp. (In re Gen. Dev. Corp.), 177 B.R. 1000 (S.D. Fla. 1995) (applying the functional test to find a contract executory even where only one party had remaining duties), aff'd on basis of district court opinion, 84 F.3d 1364 (11th Cir. 1996); In re Booth, 19 B.R. 53 (Bankr. D. Utah 1982) (discussed in Epstein, Nickles & White, BANKRUPTCY §5-4 at 231-32). *Booth* involved a long term installment land sale contract under which the debtor was the vendee and the vendor had retained title. The court held that the contract was not an executory contract but rather was the equivalent of an executed sale with retention of a lien by the vendor, even though Utah law did not treat such contracts in that way. Thus the debtor could keep the land without having to assume the contract with all of its burdens, and the estate was "enlarged." The authors doubt that this is a principled approach; the use of such a result-oriented test designed to "enlarge" the estate at the expense of others does not instill confidence in the impartiality of justice.

12. See, e.g., Kater v. Craig (In re Craig), 144 F.3d. 593 (8th Cir. 1998); Enter. Energy Corp. v. U.S. (In re Columbia Gas Sys., Inc.), 50 F.3d 233 (3d Cir. 1995); Phoenix Exploration, Inc. v. Yaquinto (In re Murexco Petroleum, Inc.), 15 F.3d 60 (5th Cir. 1994); La Electronica, Inc. v. Capo-Roman (In re La Electronica, Inc.), 995 F.2d 320, 322 n.3 (1st Cir. 1993) (stating that most courts apply Countryman test but that a few apply "a more 'functional' approach"); Comm'l Union Ins. Co. v. Texscan Corp. (In re Texscan Corp.), 976 F.2d 1269 (9th Cir. 1992); Sharon Steel Corp. v. Nat'l Fuel Gas Distrib. Corp., 872 F.2d 36, 39 (3d Cir. 1989) (stating that courts have generally relied on the Countryman definition); Terrell v. Albaugh (In re Terrell), 892 F.2d 469, 471 n.2 (6th Cir. 1989) ("Congress apparently had in mind the definition of executory contracts set forth in Countryman, *Executory Contracts in Bankruptcy: Part I * * **.*"); In re Crippin, 877 F.2d 594, 596 (7th Cir. 1989) (calling Countryman definition a "common definition, which this court has cited with approval"); Lubrizol Enters., Inc. v. Richmond Metal Finishers, Inc., 756 F.2d 1043 (4th Cir. 1985).

13. If the lender has not yet made all of the promised loans at the time of the bankruptcy filing, the contract may be executory, but the debtor in possession cannot assume it, and thus cannot require the lender to make further loans. See § 365(c)(2), discussed later in this Chapter in Section F.

Remarkably, some courts have thought that the estate is bound to perform the debtor's obligations under a nonexecutory contract simply because such a contract is not subject to being rejected. See, e.g., Hays & Co. v. Merrill Lynch, 885 F.2d 1149 (3d Cir. 1989). If the debtor still has substantial unperformed obligations under the contract—obligations that supposedly are binding on the estate—but the contract is nonexecutory, then the nondebtor party must have fully (or at least substantially) performed. (If both parties owed substantial obligations, the contract would be executory rather than nonexecutory.) That, of course, is the precise situation in which the Countryman definition calls the contract nonexecutory so that the debtor in possession cannot assume the contract and bind the estate to perform; there is no reason to make the contract an obligation of the estate when the estate will receive little or nothing more from the nondebtor, who already has fully or at least substantially performed. There is therefore no reason to give the debtor in possession an election to assume or reject; the obligations simply are obligations of the debtor and cannot be made obligations of the estate. Thus the statements of courts in cases like *Hays & Co.* cannot be taken literally. The result would be disastrous for the estate and for the other creditors; and the result would be directly contrary to the whole reason why such contracts are considered nonexecutory.

Consider the loan agreement discussed two paragraphs above. There is absolutely no reason to say that the debt owed to the prepetition lender should be an obligation of the estate, which would make it an administrative priority claim that would have to be paid in full in cash on the effective date of the plan. Of course, the debt is an obligation of the debtor; that is sufficient to give the lender a claim in the case under § 502(b). The debt does not have to be an obligation of the estate in order to give the lender a claim in the case and in order for the lender to receive a distribution pursuant to the plan of reorganization. See, e.g., Mason v. Official Comm. of Unsecured Creditors (In re FBI Distrib. Corp.), 330 F.3d 36 (1st Cir. 2003):

> Mason asks us to grant administrative priority on the theory that nonexecutory contracts should be treated differently because they can be neither assumed nor rejected, and thus should be enforceable against the debtor's estate as an administrative expense.
>
> Mason misses the point. While the claim under the Retention Agreement is enforceable against the estate in the bankruptcy proceeding, it is a prepetition claim. * * * Under a nonexecutory contract, in which the nondebtor owes no future performance, the nondebtor provides no consideration "after the commencement of the case," and thus is not entitled to priority.

Id. at 48. In fact, *Hays and Co.* did not bind the estate to pay the claim of a nondebtor as an administrative claim or to perform substantial obligations owed by the debtor; rather, the court simply held that the estate was bound by the arbitration agreement in the contract with Merrill Lynch to the extent that the estate was suing Merrill Lynch on claims that had belonged to the debtor. The result can be explained without concluding that the estate was bound to perform obligations owed by the debtor under the nonexecutory contract. Instead, the estate took from the debtor no better rights against Merrill Lynch than the debtor had, and the debtor's rights were limited by the arbitration agreement.

4. Five Exceptions to the "Package" Approach

a. "Ipso Facto" Clauses

There are five exceptions to the principle that the estate must take the burdens of a contract as part of the "package" if the estate is to have the benefits of the contract. The first exception deals with what are called "ipso facto" clauses, clauses that would terminate or modify the debtor's rights under a contract or lease due to the insolvency or financial condition of the debtor, due to the commencement of the debtor's bankruptcy case, or due to the appointment of a trustee in bankruptcy (or of a receiver or other custodian prior to the bankruptcy). Section 365(e)(1) precludes such clauses from having any effect after commencement of the bankruptcy case with regard to assumable contracts; thus, for example, once the petition is filed the nondebtor party cannot take advantage of a contract provision permitting it to cancel the contract due to insolvency of the debtor. Section 365(b)(2) provides that when a debtor in possession assumes a contract or lease, the debtor in possession need not cure a breach of an ipso facto clause (or satisfy certain penalty provisions), need not compensate the nondebtor party for any damage caused by breach of an ipso facto clause, and need not provide assurances that an ipso facto clause will be complied with in the future.[14] Note that § 365(b)(2) deals

---

14. Note that § 365(e)(1)(A) prevents the nondebtor party from terminating or modifying the contract "after the commencement of the case" under any provision conditioned on insolvency or financial condition of the debtor "at any time before the closing of the case." Thus, if the contract was terminated *before the petition was filed* so that at the time the petition was filed the debtor had no right under the contract or under antiforfeiture provisions of nonbankruptcy law to reinstate the contract, then it is not revived by the bankruptcy filing. See Moody v. Amoco Oil Co., 734 F.2d 1200 (7th Cir. 1984) (reprinted below). Further, once the case is closed, a term permitting modification or termination of the contract based on the debtor's financial condition becomes once again enforceable, as the text of § 365(e)(1)(A) and its legislative history both indicate:

> This subsection does not limit the application of an ipso facto or bankruptcy clause if a new insolvency or receivership occurs after the bankruptcy case is closed. That is, the clause is not invalidated in toto, but merely made inapplicable during the case for the purposes of disposition of the executory contract or unexpired lease.

See H.R. Rep. No. 595, 95th Cong., 1st Sess. 348 (1977); S. Rep. No. 989, 95th Cong., 2d Sess. 59 (1978). Thus, if a contract or lease is important to the debtor, the debtor must be sure that its financial condition *after reorganization* is good enough that it will no longer be in violation of any ipso facto clause in the contract or lease.

Note also that it has been held that provisions in option contracts calling for the price to increase over time are not ipso facto clauses because they change the parties' rights based on passage of time, not based on insolvency, financial condition, filing of a bankruptcy petition, or anything else listed in § 365(e)(1). See Yates Dev., Inc. v. Old Kings Interchange, Inc. (In re Yates Dev., Inc.), 256 F.3d 1285 (11th Cir. 2001); cf. In re Margulis, 323 B.R. 130 (Bankr. S.D.N.Y. 2005) (allowing claim for full

not merely with contract provisions but also with "applicable law" that would have the same effect. Query whether § 365(b)(2) thus preempts the state law right of nondebtor parties to demand adequate assurances of performance under U.C.C. §2-609 and Restatement of Contracts (Second) § 251, where the nondebtor party's insecurity stems from the insolvency or financial condition of the debtor or from the filing of the bankruptcy case.

b. Penalty Provisions and Incurable Nonmonetary Defaults

The second exception deals with "penalty rates," other "penalty provisions," and the cure of nonmonetary defaults. In the Bankruptcy Reform Act of 1994, Congress added subsection (b)(2)(D) to § 365. See Pub. L. 103-394, §219 (1994). The new subsection exempted certain defaults from the cure, compensation, and assurance requirements of § 365(b)(1). The 2005 BAPCPA added one word to the subsection, so that it applies to a "penalty rate or penalty provision," rather than to a "penalty rate or provision." Thus the exemption is of

> a default that is a breach of a provision relating to
> * * *
> (D) the satisfaction of any penalty rate or *penalty* provision relating to a default arising from any failure by the debtor to perform nonmonetary obligations under the executory contract or unexpired lease.

Section 365(b)(2)(D) (emphasis added to word "penalty" that was added by the 2005 BAPCPA).

After addition of the provision by the 1994 amendments, it seemed clear that if, for example, a lease provided that rents were increased by 20% during any time that the lessee was in default on the lease, the lessee debtor in possession would not need to pay the extra 20%—the "penalty rate"— in order to cure the default and assume the lease. "[S]ection 365(b) is clarified to provide that when sought by a debtor, a lease can be cured at a nondefault rate (i.e., it would not need to pay penalty rates)." H.R. Rep. 835, 103d Cong., 2d Sess. 50 (1994). But in several ways the meaning of the 1994 statutory language—crafted in Congress's rush to finish business in the fall of 1994—was far from certain.

For example, should the part of the subsection beginning with "arising" have been read to modify both "penalty rate" and "provision"? That would greatly restrict the protection the subsection provided against penalty rates—it would not apply where the penalty rate arose from a failure to make timely payments. It did not seem that such limited protection was intended by Congress.

---

amount of $791,000 judgment where deadline passed during bankruptcy case without payment by debtor of $140,000 under prepetition agreement that allowed debtor to satisfy judgment for that amount). In addition, there is a question whether options are executory contracts. See In re A.J. Lane & Co., Inc., 107 B.R. 435 (Bankr. D. Mass. 1989), reprinted below, and notes following it.

Further, did the adjective "penalty" modify both "rate" and "provision"? If so, then the subsection would not require cure of "penalty" provisions dealing with nonmonetary defaults, but would require cure of non-penalty provisions dealing with such defaults. The 2005 BAPCPA answered that question by adding "penalty" before "provision," but meanwhile, in 1997, the Ninth Circuit had interpreted § 365(b)(2)(D) to excuse only cures of "contractual provision[s] relating to the satisfaction of a penalty rate or the payment of a penalty." Worthington v. General Motors Corp. (In re Claremont Acquisition Corp.), 113 F.3d 1029, 1034 (9th Cir. 1997). The court thought that any other interpretation would not make grammatical sense, and seemed to think that the term "satisfaction" referred to a monetary payment. Under that questionable interpretation, the debtor, who was in default because its auto dealership had been closed prepetition for more than seven consecutive business days, could not assume the dealership contract because (1) § 365(b)(2)(D) did not excuse the default from the general requirement that defaults be cured, and (2) it was impossible to cure the default because there was no way to go back in time and change the historical fact that the dealership had been closed for more than seven days.

Just as the Ninth Circuit discovered an extremely limiting interpretation, a court in another circuit could have discovered an extraordinarily broad interpretation under the 1994 language. The subsection could have been interpreted to effect a wholesale revision of the rights of nondebtor parties where the debtor's obligations under the contract or lease did not consist of payment of money but rather of provision of property or services—seemingly "nonmonetary obligations." Suppose Foam Corporation had a contract to sell foam to General Motors for car seats, with deliveries to be made monthly. If Foam Corporation had defaulted by delivering defective foam that fell apart when touched—and that was therefore rejected by General Motors— would Foam Corporation have had to cure the breach in order to assume the contract under the 1994 version of the statute? Would Foam Corporation's default have been " a breach of a * * * provision relating to a default arising from any failure by the debtor to perform nonmonetary obligations * * * " ? If § 365(b)(2)(D) permitted Foam Corporation to assume the contract without curing the default, without compensating General Motors for the breach, and without providing assurances that future deliveries would be of nondefective foam, then the 1994 version of § 365(b)(2)(D) would have profoundly changed the law.

By adding the word "penalty" before "provision," the 2005 BAPCPA ruled out that broad interpretation. Foam Corporation's failure to do anything about the defective foam would not be a failure to satisfy a "penalty" provision relating to Foam Corporation's default, however we might describe the default. Thus Foam Corporation would have to cure the breach (by making a replacement delivery of nondefective foam).

The 2005 BAPCPA also amended § 365(b) to provide some protection—though in extremely dense and difficult statutory language—for real property lessees against the kind of problem that arose in *Claremont Acquisition*. For example, a lease of a department store may state that the debtor lessee must keep the store open at least six days each week and may permit the lessor to cancel the lease if the store is closed for more than 72 hours. If the debtor's store closed for more than 72 hours either before the filing of the chapter 11 petition or after, there would be a default, like the one by the auto dealer in *Claremont Acquistion*, that arguably could not be cured without a time machine. As amended by the 2005 BAPCPA, § 365(b) would excuse the lessee from having to do the impossible; the lessee simply would have to pay the lessor for any "pecuniary loss" caused by the default[15] and would have to operate the premises after assumption of the lease "in accordance with [the] lease." Id.

The 2005 BAPCPA does not explicitly assist the debtor whose default does not concern a real property lease but some other kind of contract, such as the auto dealership agreement in *Claremont Acquisition*. It may still be possible, however, to characterize the cancellation of a contract for a "cessation of business" breach or similar breach as a kind of penalty. See Broude, *Executory Contracts and Unexpired Leases in Bankruptcy*, in COMMERCIAL REAL ESTATE DEFAULTS, WORKOUTS, AND REORGANIZATIONS 751 (Advanced Annual ALI-ABA Course of Study, No. SK054, 2005), available at SK054 ALI-ABA 751 (Westlaw). Perhaps the cancellation of the contract is the "satisfaction" that need not be given to the nondebtor party in such a case. See § 365(b)(2)(D). But see Epstein & Normand, *"Real-World" and "Academic" Questions about "Nonmonetary Obligations" under the 2005 Version of 365(b)*, 13 AM. BANKR. INST. L. REV. 617 (2005) (arguing, in discussion of their example #3, that § 365(b)(2)(D) does not help such a debtor, but also arguing that if the default is immaterial or waived then the debtor might be able to assume the contract despite the incurable default).

c. Provisions That Prohibit, Restrict, or Condition Assignment

The third exception deals with assignment of contracts and leases. The Code permits the debtor in possession to assign a contract or lease despite any provision in the contract or lease that would prohibit, restrict, or condition assignment;[16] such contractual provisions are unenforceable in bankruptcy. Section 365(f)(1). In many cases, long term real estate leases with rental rates

---

15. For example, the lease of a motion picture theater might provide for rental payments based on the lessee's gross ticket sales; temporary cessation of business then would cost the lessor its share of the ticket sales that were not made due to the cessation of business.

16. Students who were careful in their Contracts courses to distinguish between *assignment* of contractual rights and *delegation* of contractual duties should note that the Code uses "assign" and "assignment" in a broad sense—as the provisions of § 365(f)(2)(B) show—to include not only the assignment of rights but also the delegation of duties to the assignee. See U.C.C. § 2-210(5) for a similar usage.

below a fair market level are major assets of the estate. If the debtor does not need to use the leased premises because of retrenching of the debtor's operations, the debtor can realize substantial value from the leases by assigning the leases to others in exchange for a substantial payment. Many commercial leases contain (1) nonassignability provisions, (2) provisions permitting the lessor to raise the rent if there is an assignment, and (3) provisions requiring any consideration given to the lessee for the assignment to be passed on to the lessor. If the debtor in possession had to assume the burden of such provisions along with the rest of the provisions of the leases, the debtor would not be able to realize value from assigning the leases. Thus, § 365(f)(1) permits the debtor to assign leases and executory contracts notwithstanding any provisions that would prohibit, restrict, or condition the assignment. In some instances, debtors file chapter 11 petitions rather than entering into an out of court work-out arrangement specifically so that the value of such leases can be realized. That can be very important in providing the cash which the debtor needs.

The interrelation between § 365(f)(1) and § 365(c)—which § 365(f)(1) explicitly recognizes as an exception to its provisions—is complex. Section 365(f)(1) purports to allow assignment despite "applicable law" that would prohibit, restrict, or condition assignment. However, § 365(c) seems to prohibit assumption and assignment where applicable law—apart from any anti-assignment provision in the contract—would permit the nondebtor party to refuse to accept performance from or give performance to an assignee. We explore this interrelation later in this chapter in Section F.

d. Release from Liability on Assigned Contracts

The fourth exception also deals with assignment. Outside bankruptcy, the debtor could not escape liability on a contract (or lease) by assigning its rights and delegating its duties to another. If the assignee failed to perform, the debtor would be liable on the contract or lease. See Restatement of Contracts (Second) § 318(3). Inside bankruptcy, there is a different result; the reorganized debtor likely will not be liable for any future breach by the assignee.

Note that in order to assign the contract, the debtor in possession must first assume it. See § 365(f)(2)(A). That obligates the estate on the contract and generally would make any damages for breach of the contract administrative expenses. However, if the contract is then assigned, the estate and the debtor in possession (or trustee) are relieved from any liability for any breach of the contract that occurs after the assignment. See § 365(k).

Section 365(k) does not explicitly state that the reorganized debtor is also relieved of liability on the contract (in its own capacity as opposed to its representative capacity as debtor in possession). It could be argued that the reorganized debtor would be relieved from liability only if the nondebtor party had a claim that was discharged in the case. Many courts have asserted that the nondebtor party to an executory contract does not have a claim until and unless the contract is rejected. Thus the nondebtor party to the assigned contract may not have a claim; it would follow that the discharge would not, of itself, relieve the reorganized debtor from liability on the assigned contract.[17] The courts, however, have interpreted § 365(k) as if it provided for the reorganized debtor to be relieved of liability. See Am. Flint Glass Workers Union v. Anchor Resolution Corp., 197 F.3d 76, 80 (3d Cir. 1999) (observing that a novation "reliev[es] the original obligor from its duty to perform the novated obligations," and stating that assignment under § 365(k) "effect[s] a novation by operation of law whether or not the obligee consents to the substitution"); Wainer v. A.J. Equities, Ltd., 984 F.2d 679, 683-84 (5th Cir. 1993).

Note further that if the debtor in possession merely assumes the contract but does not also assign it, adequate assurance of future performance need not be given unless the debtor has defaulted on the contract. See § 365(b)(1)(C). The contract cannot be assigned, however, even if there has been no default, unless adequate assurance of future performance by the assignee is given. Section 365(f)(2)(B). That makes sense because an assignment in bankruptcy puts the nondebtor at risk; as we have seen, if the assignee breaches, the nondebtor party's only remedy is against the assignee. Outside bankruptcy, any assignment of a contract for sale of goods that involves a delegation of duties gives the other party (the "obligor") the right to demand assurances that the assignee will perform. See U.C.C. § 2-210(5). That is true even though an assignment outside of bankruptcy will not relieve the assignor of liability. There is even more reason to require assurances where the assignment is done in bankruptcy, since neither the estate, the debtor in possession, nor (it seems) the reorganized debtor will be liable if the assignee does not perform.

d. Restrictions on Use of Leased Premises

The fifth exception deals with provisions in leases that restrict use of the premises, and that could, as a practical matter, prevent assignment. For example, a provision in a lease to the Acme Ballet Studio that the premises could be used only for a ballet studio would make it very difficult for Acme to find anyone who would want to pay for an assignment of the premises, if the use limitation were enforceable. Recall that for the lease to be assigned, adequate assurance must be given that the assignee will perform the lease obligations. Under the general approach of § 365—that the burdens of an assumed contract or lease must be taken with the benefits—it would seem that the lease obligations would include any use limitation that is enforceable

---

17.   See the district court opinion reprinted as an appendix to the circuit court's one paragraph per curiam opinion in Wainer v. A.J. Equities, Ltd., 984 F.2d 679 (5th Cir. 1993) (affirming district court on basis of district court opinion) . The district court opinion noted that discharge would have no effect on the debtor's liability for an assigned contract, because the nondebtor party would not have a claim, but also noted that § 365(k) would relieve the debtor from liability. Id. at 683-84. The circuit court in *Wainer* affirmed the district court on the basis of the district court opinion (reprinted as an appendix to the circuit court's one paragraph per curiam opinion).

outside bankruptcy. Thus the assignee would have to give assurances that it would use the premises only for a ballet studio and would be bound to use the premises only for that purpose after the assignment.

However, that approach could be seen to conflict with § 365(f)(1), because the strict use limitation effectively prevents or at least severely restricts assignment. Even a less strict limitation on use may make it difficult for a debtor to realize the value of a lease by assigning it. Thus some courts have held that a use limitation is not enforceable against an assignee who takes an assignment in bankruptcy, unless the landlord shows that lack of enforcement would "jeopardize the economic position of the landlord and/or the landlord's other tenants." In re Joshua Slocum., Ltd., 99 B.R. 250 (Bankr. E.D.Pa. 1989), aff'd, 1989 WL 428204 (E.D. Pa. 1989), rev'd, 922 F.2d 1081 (3d Cir. 1990). The circuit court in *Joshua Slocum* held that the leased premises were in a shopping center, thus triggering the enhanced requirements of § 365(b)(3), and that a minimum sales provision was a material term of the lease that the bankruptcy court should not in any even have excised, but the circuit court suggested that otherwise the principles applied by the bankruptcy court were correct. See also In re U.L. Radio Corp., 19 B.R. 537, 544 (Bankr. S.D.N.Y. 1982) (invalidating use clause in electronics store lease that would have prevented assignee from converting premises to a small bistro, and holding that "[t]o prevent an assignment of an unexpired lease by demanding strict enforcement of a use clause, * * * a landlord or lessor must show that actual and substantial detriment would be incurred by him if the deviation in use was permitted") (cited approvingly for non-shopping center leases by circuit court in *Joshua Slocum*).

Where a lease of premises in a shopping center is to be assigned, § 365(b)(3) (as amended in 1984) requires assurance that "assignment of such lease is subject to all the provisions thereof, including (but not limited to) provisions such as a radius, location, use, or exclusivity provision * * *." The circuit court in *Joshua Slocum* nevertheless suggested that "Congress did not envision literal compliance with all lease provisions; insubstantial disruptions in, inter alia, tenant mix, and insubstantial breaches in other leases or agreements were contemplated and allowed." 922 F.2d at 1090.[18] For a more recent case taking a harder line, see Trak Auto Corp. v. West Town Center LLC (In re Trak Auto Corp.), 367 F.3d 237 (4th Cir. 2004) (reversing order approving assignment of lease in shopping center to assignee who would not use the premises for the use required in the lease: retail sale of auto parts and accessories).

5. The Need for Time To Decide Whether To Assume or Reject

Now consider a contract between Foam Corporation and New Supply Company ("NSC") for 72 monthly shipments of 25,000 gallons of chemicals, at $5

---

18. Note that footnote 3 of the circuit court's opinion—written in 1990 and dealing with a case in which the chapter 11 petition had been filed in 1988—contains the pre-1984 version of § 365(b)(3), which required assurance that an assignment of a shopping center lease would not result in certain provisions, including use provisions, being breached "substantially." The 1984 amendments eliminated any reference in § 365(b)(3) to substantial breach of such provisions.

per gallon, delivery to be made on the 8th of each month, beginning February 8, 2006, with payment for each shipment due 35 days after delivery. Suppose NSC delivered the first two shipments, on February 8 and March 8, but did not deliver the April 8 shipment, because Foam Corporation had not paid for the February 8 shipment by the March 15 due date. Assume Foam Corporation still had not paid for either shipment when it filed its chapter 11 petition on April 10, 2006. Suppose the market value of the chemicals is $6 per gallon and is likely to stay at least that high for the next 6 years. It would seem to make sense for Foam Corporation as debtor in possession to assume the contract on behalf of the estate. Each further delivery will save Foam Corporation $1 per gallon, for a savings of $25,000 per delivery, if the market value of the chemicals stays at $6 per gallon. To assume the contract Foam Corporation will have to cure the defaults (or provide adequate assurance that it will be cured promptly); that will cost the estate $250,000 ($5 per gallon for the 50,000 gallons delivered prepetition).[19] But it will save the estate (or the reorganized Foam Corporation) far more: $1 per gallon, times 25,000 gallons per shipment, times 70 shipments. That comes to $1.75 million.

However, once the contract is assumed, the estate will be obligated on the contract to pay for those 70 shipments. If the market value of the chemicals falls, the estate (and ultimately the reorganized Foam Corporation) could lose money performing the contract by paying more for the chemicals than they are worth. More importantly, the reorganization may fail; if the case is converted to a chapter 7 liquidation, the estate will not need the chemicals, may not be able to pay for them, and likely will not even be in existence for 71 more months. If meanwhile the market value of the chemicals has dropped, NSC may have a large damage claim that will have to be paid as an administrative expense.[20] Every dollar of administrative expense that must be paid in full reduces further the already meager amount that general unsecured creditors will likely receive.

For these reasons it may not be at all prudent for Foam Corporation to assume a six year chemical supply contract shortly after filing its chapter 11 petition. It may be many months after the commencement of the case before Foam Corporation can determine whether it is likely stay in business for six more years, so that assumption of the contract would be prudent. Thus, for executory contracts and for some leases, the Bankruptcy Code gives Foam

---

19. The final cost to the estate is less than $250,000, because if Foam Corporation were to reject the contract, NSC likely would receive some distribution under the plan on account of the $250,000 debt. For example, if general unsecured claim holders receive value under the plan equal to 20% of the amount of their claims, NSC would in any event receive 20% of $250,000, which is $50,000. In that case, the cost to the estate of assuming the contract is $250,000 minus $50,000, or $200,000. Note that if a shipment had been received within 20 days before the petition filing date, it would have been an administrative expense claim under § 503(b)(9); such claims must be paid in full in cash on the effective date of the debtor's plan. See § 1129(a)(9)(A). Here the second shipment was delivered 33 days before the petition date. NSC might, however, have reclamation rights under § 546(c). See Chapter Eight below.

20. Of course, if the market value of the chemicals does not fall, NSC will not have substantial damages, since it would save money by reason of Foam Corporation's breach—unless NSC is a lost volume seller and would have made a profit on the contract even with its below-market price.

Corporation up until the date of confirmation of the plan of reorganization to decide whether to assume the contract with NSC, unless the court orders Foam Corporation to decide sooner. See § 365(d)(2).

The Code gives debtors much less flexibility in dealing with most real property leases. Under § 365(d)(4), a lessee debtor in possession has 120 days from the date of the order for relief to assume or reject leases of nonresidential real property—such as the leases of five of Foam Corporation's factories. Failure to assume a nonresidential real property lease within the time allowed results in the lease being deemed rejected under § 365(d)(4), which provides that in such a case "the trustee [or debtor in possession] shall immediately surrender [the] nonresidential real property to the lessor." The 2005 BAPCPA doubled the period previously specified in the section, from 60 days to 120 days. But the 2005 BAPCPA also amended the section to eliminate the open-ended authority bankruptcy judges previously had to extend the 60 day period. Now § 365(d)(4) prohibits the court from extending the 120 day period by more than 90 days, absent consent of the lessor. The limitation to no more than a total of 210 days will create substantial difficulty for many debtors.

Because the decision to assume or reject may be put off for months or perhaps even years—except in the case of nonresidential real property leases—we must consider what rights and duties the debtor and nondebtor parties may have pending the decision to assume or reject. The contract with NSC will not be enforceable *against debtor in possession Foam Corporation* until and unless Foam Corporation assumes it for the estate. NLRB v. Bildisco & Bildisco, 465 U.S. 513, 531-32, 104 S. Ct. 1188, 1198-1200, 79 L. Ed. 2d 482, 489-99 (1984). If NSC delivers more chemicals under the contract, and if Foam Corporation accepts them, the estate and Foam Corporation (as debtor in possession) will be obligated to pay their reasonable value. Id.

The more interesting issue is whether the contract is enforceable by Foam Corporation against NSC while Foam Corporation is deciding whether to assume or reject it. Foam Corporation may have a pressing need for the chemicals, even though it may not yet be prudent for Foam Corporation to assume the contract. Foam Corporation has breached the contract, by failing to pay for the prepetition (February 8 and March 8, 2006) shipments. Should Foam Corporation nevertheless be able to demand that NSC continue performing while Foam Corporation waits to see whether assumption is prudent? Arguably, Foam Corporation cannot legally pay NSC for that shipment prior to assuming the contract. Thus, while Foam Corporation takes the necessary time to decide whether to assume or reject the contract, Foam Corporation is prevented by bankruptcy law from curing the breach (absent application of the doctrine of necessity discussed above at the end of Chapter Four). Even if the breach is a material breach that, outside bankruptcy, would entitle NSC to suspend its performance, should NSC be permitted to suspend performance when it is the law that prevents Foam Corporation from curing the breach? We consider those questions in the next section.

B. RIGHTS AND OBLIGATIONS PENDING ASSUMPTION OR REJECTION

We begin this section with a classic and much-cited case decided under the old Bankruptcy Act. As you read it, consider what the court's view was of the obligations of the parties pending assumption or rejection of a contract. Note also the court's view of the duties that a trustee (or debtor in possession) owes to the nondebtor parties to executory contracts. Note that the Supreme Court has refused several times to find, in the absence of clear statutory language or clear legislative history, that enactment of the Bankruptcy Code altered settled principles of bankruptcy law under the old Act. Thus the following case is of much more than historic interest. We especially invite the reader's attention to the footnotes numbered 10, 15, 20, and 34 in the original.

Hall v. Perry (In re Cochise College Park, Inc.)
United States Court of Appeals, Ninth Circuit, 1983
703 F.2d 1339

[*Cochise College Park, Inc. ("Cochise") bought several thousand acres of Arizona desert, ran a national advertising campaign, and entered into thousands of installment contracts to sell residential lots to purchasers. Each purchaser signed a promissory note as well as a land sale contract. Cochise promised to improve the property by building streets and extending water and electric service lines to the lots. Cochise also promised to convey title to the lots by warranty deed after all payments were made. Cochise gave deeds to some of the purchasers before they finished making payments and took back mortgages on the lots to secure the remaining payments. After five years of selling lots, Cochise still had not made the improvements. In mid-1972 Cochise filed a Chapter X reorganization petition (after an involuntary liquidation bankruptcy petition had been filed against it), and Perry was appointed trustee. Perry told the purchasers that they had to keep making payments or else he would foreclose on their interests in the lots. He told some of them that he was keeping their payments in a separate account. Later, he obtained ex parte orders permitting him to use the payments to pay administrative expenses, including his fee as trustee. On June 7, 1973, Cochise was "adjudicated a bankrupt." That was the old Act equivalent of a Bankruptcy Code § 1112(b) conversion to a chapter 7 liquidation case. (Under the old Act, debtors in reorganization were not considered to be "bankrupt;" an adjudication of bankruptcy was a determination that the reorganization attempt should end and that the debtor should be liquidated.) The purchasers (the "Baldrian class" sued Perry in bankruptcy court, alleging that he "did not have title to payments made on the * * * notes and also that he was personally liable for fraud, negligence, and conversion with respect to the collection of the note payments. The class sought return to it of all payments made on the promissory notes, together with interest." The bankruptcy court granted summary judgment in Perry's favor; the district court affirmed; and the Baldrian class appealed to the Ninth Circuit.*]

FLETCHER, Circuit Judge:

* * *

I. Nature of the Land Sale Contracts.

The legal nature of the contractual relations between the members of the Baldrian class and Cochise on the date of the bankruptcy filing is of crucial importance in this case. If the contract between Cochise and a lot purchaser upon which payments were made was a fully executed contract on that date, then all payments on that note vested in the trustee. If the contract was executory, however, other consequences follow. Whether the land sale contracts were executed or executory also affects the liability of the trustee for misconduct. * * *

Seeking to sustain the grant of summary judgment, Perry argues that all of the contracts upon which payments were made were, as a matter of law, fully executed, not executory on June 5, 1972. We disagree.

Perry first contends that in each case the contract upon which payments were made comprised only the promissory note signed by the Baldrian class member, pursuant to which the class member promised to pay specified sums at times certain. Perry argues that any obligations of Cochise to convey a deed to the lot or to construct roads for and to provide utility connections to the purchased lot were commitments by Cochise that were not part of that promissory note "contract." We reject that argument.

* * * A promissory note, standing alone, is not a contract at all, because, simply put, it embodies only one of the mutual promises necessary to create a contract. It evidences only one side of the bargain.

The existence of a promissory note on any given date, therefore, is not in and of itself proof that the payments on the note are in performance of an executed contract. Since payments on a promissory note are merely the performance of one side of the bargain, the note must be examined in conjunction with the *other* undertakings that, together with the promissory note, constitute the relevant contract of which the promissory note is but a part to determine what commitments remain to be performed by the parties. Each land sale contract did not, and by definition could not, consist solely of the promissory note.

Perry also argues that even if the contracts here between the members of the Baldrian class and Cochise encompassed both the promissory notes and various obligations of Cochise, in any event, the contracts with the purchasers were not "executory" contracts under the terms of the Act. We reject that argument.

An "executory" contract under the Act is one:

> under which the obligations of both the bankrupt and the other party to the contract are so far unperformed [at the moment of filing] that the failure of either to complete performance would constitute a material breach excusing the performance of the other.

In re Select-A-Seat Corp., 625 F.2d 290, 292 (9th Cir. 1980) (per curiam) (quoting from Jenson v. Continental Financial Corp., 591 F.2d 477, 481 (8th Cir. 1979).[21]

---

21. [Footnote 4 in original:] Although whether a given contract is "executory" under the Bankruptcy Act is an issue of federal law to be resolved under the *Select-a-Seat* test, see In re Alexander, 670 F.2d 885, 888 (9th Cir. 1982), the question of the legal consequences of one party's failure to perform its remaining obligations under a contract is an issue of state contract law. * * *

Under this standard, the answers to interrogatories and affidavits raise a material issue of fact as to whether some if not all of the contracts between Cochise and the purchasers constituted executory contracts upon June 5, 1972, the date of the filing. The record shows that some if not all of the land sale contracts encompassed both obligations of the purchaser to make various payments at times certain *and* obligations of Cochise to deliver the deed to the lot to the purchaser, to release the mortgage, if any, on that lot upon completion of payments on the promissory note, and to construct various improvements. Under these circumstances, the failure of Cochise to develop the land as promised or to convey a warranty deed to the purchaser could each constitute a material breach excusing performance by the land purchaser of his remaining obligations. Likewise, the failure of any given land purchaser to make payments on his promissory note could constitute a material breach excusing Cochise from completing its performances under the land sale contract.[22] Thus, in all likelihood, some if not all of the land sale contracts here were executory on June 5, 1972.

The mere fact that the promissory notes presented to Cochise under the land sale contracts could be assigned to third parties does not change this conclusion. Although a real estate lessee typically is free to assign his leasehold interest to a third party, the ability of a lessee to assign the leasehold interest (i.e., the right to receive the use of certain real estate for a time certain) has never been thought to transform an unexpired real estate lease, a typical example of an executory contract, from an executory into an executed contract.

Since some if not all of the land sale contracts were probably executory on June 5, 1972, it is probable that the ownership of the payments received by the trustee as well as the trustee's conduct must be evaluated under the principles governing executory—as opposed to executed—contracts. Since under bankruptcy law, transactions involving executory contracts give rise to different legal consequences from those involving executed contracts, granting summary judgment on those issues without deciding whether the contracts were or were not executory was improper.

II. Ownership of Payments.

* * *

A. Payments on Contracts That Were Non-Executory on June 5, 1972.

The trustee properly took title on behalf of the estate to all payments received on any land sale contract that was fully executed on June 5, 1972, regardless of whether payments were made before or after June 5, 1972.

Sections 70a(5), 186 of the Act provide that a reorganization or bankruptcy trustee is vested by operation of law as of the date of filing with title to all "property ... which prior to the filing of the petition [the bankrupt] could by any means have transferred, or which might have been levied upon and sold under judicial process against him, or otherwise seized, impounded, or sequestered." 11 U.S.C. §§ 110(a)(5), 586 (1976). Such property includes cash and the like

---

22. [Footnote 6 in original:] We find it inconceivable that, under the terms of these land sale contracts and Arizona law, the mere execution of a promissory note, without more, constituted sufficient performance of the purchaser's obligations under the land sale contract so that default on note payments would *not* constitute a material breach excusing Cochise from further performance of its obligations (including delivery of deed, release of mortgage, or construction of improvements).

possessed by the bankrupt on the date of filing, whether held by the bankrupt himself, or by an agent on the bankrupt's behalf. On June 5, 1972, the trustee was vested with title to all cash held by Cochise or * * * on Cochise's behalf.

Property passing to the trustee under section 70a(5) also includes executed contracts between the bankrupt and third parties and any proceeds or right to proceeds still due. E.g., Hudson v. Wylie, 242 F.2d 435, 447 (9th Cir. 1957) (contract right to collect money based on performance of services by bankrupt that were completed before filing); In re Hannan, 127 F.2d 894, 897 (7th Cir. 1942) (contract right to receive commissions for services of bankrupt rendered prior to filing); In re Duncan, 148 F. 464, 469 (D.S.C. 1906) (promissory note of bankrupt's employer based on services of bankrupt rendered prior to filing). On June 5, 1972, the trustee was vested with both executed land sale contracts, if any, and the right to further payments, if any.[23] * * *

B. Payments on Contracts That Were Executory on June 5, 1972

Payments received by Cochise, Perry or [their agent] on land sale contracts that were executory at the time of filing did not necessarily vest in the trustee as property of the estate. The ownership and treatment of each of those payments, and claims arising therefrom, vary according to the date upon which the particular payment was received.

1. Payments Received Before June 5, 1972.

Payments received by Cochise or by [its agent] before June 5, 1972 on land sale contracts that were executory on June 5, 1972 were property of the bankrupt. Title to those payments vested in the trustee as of the date of filing of the original petition.[24] Act §§ 70a(5), 186 (1976). Compare In re Superior Motor Truck Co., 275

---

23. [Footnote 9 in original:] These fully executed contracts, by definition, include only those contracts, if any, under which Cochise had so completely performed its obligations thereunder by June 5, 1972 that any failure by Cochise (or by the trustee) to complete performance would *not* constitute a material breach of the contract by Cochise excusing further performance by the purchaser. Despite their obligation to continue payments on the notes, these purchasers might have claims against the estate for minor breaches by Cochise of the land sale contracts.

24. [Footnote 10 in original:] Unlike cash and bank accounts, promissory notes that were in Cochise's possession as of June 5, 1972 (if part of executory contracts) did not pass to the trustee as property of the estate. The broad language of subsections a(5) and a(6) of § 70 of the Bankruptcy Act, 11 U.S.C. § 110, would seemingly indicate that the trustee is vested on the date of filing with all contract rights of the bankrupt (including the right to payment on such promissory notes). However, those provisions must be read in conjunction with § 70b, 11 U.S.C. § 110(b), and the case law that has developed thereunder that hold that title to executory contracts and rights to future performance thereunder passes to the trustee only upon the affirmative act of adoption of the executory contract. Since the trustee never affirmed any of the executory contracts, title to the promissory notes (i.e., the right to collect payments in the future) never passed to the trustee. See, e.g., In re Gravure Paper & Board Corp., 234 F.2d 928, 930-31 & n.4 (3d Cir. 1956).

Even assuming that Perry did take "title" to such notes on June 5, 1972, and that such "notes" were in fact negotiable instruments, however, any "title" he took was taken by operation of law under the Act and *not* for value. Thus, he is merely a holder and not a holder in due course. Ariz. Rev. Stat. §§ 44-2532(C)(2), -44-2208(20) (1967) (U.C.C. §§ 3-302(3)(b), 1-201(20)). As a holder, Perry took the notes subject to all defenses of the lot purchasers, including such defenses as breach of the underlying land sale contracts, fraud in the making of the contracts, and failure of consideration. Ariz. Rev. Stat. § 44-2536(2) (1967) (U.C.C. § 3-306(b)). Unlike his right under a promissory note that is part of an executed contract, his right to enforce a note that is part of an executory contract was not unlimited but rather was subject to the defenses of the maker (the lot purchaser). Cf. Smith v.

F. 623, 624 (N.D. Ga. 1921) (payments to seller received by seller prior to filing held by bankrupt seller as his property not "on any sort of trust, or as the property of the buyer," even though trucks not delivered prior to filing) with Gulf Petroleum, S.A. v. Collazo, 316 F.2d 257, 261 (1st Cir. 1963) (pre-filing payments to seller of land to be held *in escrow* by bankrupt seller until closing of sale must be returned to buyer, where trustee rejects executory land sale contract before closing).

While Perry has title to all pre-filing payments, appellants, of course, have claims against the estate arising from payments made prior to filing.[25] Since those payments are property of the estate, Perry had no duty to notify the payors before using those funds to pay administrative expenses or other claims against the estate.

2. Payments Received On or After June 5, 1972 and Before August 6, 1973.

Payments received on executory contracts on or after the date of filing but prior to August 6, 1973 became property of the estate yet give rise to administrative expense claims against the estate in the amount of those payments.

An executory contract of the bankrupt vests in the trustee, if at all, only if the trustee affirms the contract. Palmer v. Palmer, 104 F.2d 161, 163 (2d Cir.), cert. denied, 308 U.S. 590, 60 S. Ct. 120, 84 L. Ed. 494 (1939); 4A J. Moore & L. King, Collier on Bankruptcy P 70.43[2], at 524-25 (14th ed. 1978). Until rejection, however, the executory contract continues in effect and the non-bankrupt party to the executory contract is not a creditor with a provable claim against the bankrupt estate. See Mohonk Realty Corp. v. Wise Shoe Stores, Inc., 111 F.2d 287, 290 (2d Cir.), cert. denied, 311 U.S. 654, 61 S. Ct. 47, 85 L. Ed. 418 (1940).

Where a bankrupt is in reorganization under Chapter X, the trustee need not affirm or reject an executory contract until a reorganization plan is submitted. 6 J. Moore & L. King, Collier on Bankruptcy P 3.23[6], at 580 (14th ed. 1978); see In re American National Trust, 426 F.2d 1059, 1064 (7th Cir. 1970); *Mohonk Realty,* 111 F.2d at 290. * * *

Latourrette-Fical Co., 37 Ariz. 265, 269-70, 293 P. 973, 976 (1930) (holder takes promissory note furnished to seller of land subject to defenses of promisor-buyer, including counterclaim for recoupment for breach of seller's covenant to supply land with water). Even if the trustee did take "title" to the notes on June 5, 1972, the breach of the underlying land sale contracts on the same date, see infra discussion in Part II(B)(2), excused the purchasers from further performance (i.e., making payments) on the notes.

25. [Footnote 11 in original:] The executory contracts upon which pre-filing payments were made were breached by operation of law as of June 5, 1972, because Perry never affirmatively adopted those contracts. Bankruptcy Act §§ 70b, 63c, 11 U.S.C. §§ 110(b), 103(c) (1976); In re Gravure Paper & Board Corp., 234 F.2d 928, 930-31 (3d Cir. 1956); see infra discussion in Part II(B)(2). The non-bankrupt party to an executory contract that has been breached, as a general creditor of the estate, has a provable claim against the estate for damages arising from the breach. Id. The appropriate damages are those ordinarily available for breach of contract and would account for any consideration paid to the bankrupt (including pre-filing payments).

Appellants apparently did not request the bankruptcy court to grant equitable liens on the purchased lots to secure the refund of pre-filing payments from the estate for those purchasers who had not received a warranty deed by the date of filing. Thus, we do not consider whether an equitable lien could be extended to such a purchaser in the bankruptcy situation, giving him priority over unsecured creditors. Compare Countryman, *Executory Contracts in Bankruptcy*, 57 MINN. L. REV. 439, 471-72 & n. 124 (1973) (questioning validity of lien) with Lacy, *Land Sale Contracts in Bankruptcy,* 21 U.C.L.A. L. Rev. 477, 485-91 (1973) (advocating lien); Levy, *Bankruptcy and the Land Sale Contract,* 23 CASE W. RES. L. REV. 393, 403-05, 409 (1972) (same); and 11 U.S.C. § 365(j) (Supp. V 1981) (Bankruptcy Reform Act of 1978) (providing for lien).

The rejection of an executory contract, whether by law or by affirmative act of the trustee, constitutes "a breach of such contract ... as of the date of the filing of the petition initiating a proceeding under this title." Bankruptcy Act § 63c, 11 U.S.C. § 103(c) (1976).[26] The anticipatory breach gives rise to a claim provable against the bankrupt estate for damages arising from the breach. Bankruptcy Act § 63a(9), 11 U.S.C. § 103(a)(9) (1976).[27] The claim for damages is treated on a parity with other similar claims.

Where the trustee does not submit a plan of reorganization and does not explicitly affirm the contract either during the period of reorganization or within the 60 days after the termination of reorganization, a contract that is executory on the date of the original filing under the Act is deemed rejected by operation of law on * * * the date 60 days after the date of the adjudication of bankruptcy that terminates the reorganization period. Thus, in this case, all of the land sale contracts that were executory on June 5, 1972 were rejected by operation of law on August 6, 1973, effective June 5, 1972, and hence were breached by Cochise as of June 5, 1972. The lot purchasers whose contracts were executory on June 5, 1972 were therefore not obligated to make payments on the notes after June 5, 1972, the date of the breach of those contracts.[28] Nevertheless, some of the purchasers here did continue to make payments on the executory contracts after the date of the breach of the underlying contract but before the date upon which the rejection took place.

Payments on a rejected executory contract made after the rejection takes place are not property of the estate. See infra Part II(B)(3). Since title to such contracts does not vest in the trustee, the trustee has no right to enforce them. The Bankruptcy Act does not address, however, the status of payments that are made to the trustee after the effective date of rejection but before rejection has occurred by action of the trustee or by operation of law.

* * * In light of the policies underlying the treatment of executory contracts under the Act, we conclude that payments received by the trustee on an executory contract during the period between the date of filing and the date of rejection do become property of the estate. However, these payments give rise to claims against the estate of an administrative expense priority in the amount of the reasonable value of the consideration tendered to the trustee. In reaching this conclusion, we find support both in previous case law and in the policies underlying the Act.

This treatment of executory contracts is supported by the well-settled principles governing treatment of creditors of a bankrupt who confer benefit on the bankrupt estate after the date of filing of a bankruptcy petition. Where the

---

26. [Footnote 12 in original:] See Central Trust Co. v. Chicago Auditorium Ass'n, 240 U.S. 581, 592, 36 S. Ct. 412, 415, 60 L. Ed. 811 (1916).

27. [Footnote 13 in original:] E.g., Central Trust Co. v. Chicago Auditorium Ass'n, 240 U.S. 581, 587, 592-93, 36 S. Ct. 412, 413, 415, 60 L. Ed. 811 (1916) (rejection of livery service concession agreement gives rise to claim for damages in amount of damages arising from breach).

28. [Footnote 15 in original:] The land sale contracts did not impose any obligation on the purchasers to continue payments on the notes to Cochise (the payee), or, conversely, any right of Cochise to collect such payments, after material breach of the underlying contracts. Consequently, even assuming that Perry took "title" to the promissory notes that were part of the executory land sale contracts, which we doubt, Perry's mere taking of "title" to a particular note without affirmation of the underlying contract gave him no right to collect payments on the note. See supra note 10.

consideration supporting the claimant's right to payment is both supplied to and beneficial to the trustee in the operation of the bankrupt's post-filing business, the consideration becomes property of the estate but the right to payment is accorded first priority under section 64a(1) of the Bankruptcy Act.

This rule is commonly applied in the situation arising when the trustee of a bankrupt lessee continues in possession of the leasehold during the period between the effective date of rejection and the date of the actual act of rejection of the lease. During the period between initial filing under the Act and the rejection of the lease, the trustee is not required to pay or to set aside in trust the rent due under the lease nor to refrain from using the leasehold for the benefit of the estate. The lessor obtains, however, a claim with administrative expense priority in the amount of the reasonable value of the leasehold used during the interim period by the trustee for the benefit of the estate.[29] This special administrative expense priority maintains parity among all of the creditors of an estate who confer benefits on the estate after the date of filing. If a lessor, or for that matter any individual, who confers economic benefit on a bankrupt estate, were not given such a priority, it is likely he would refuse to confer such benefits and would thereby jeopardize the orderly reorganization or administration of the estate.

Moreover, the Act gives the trustee the power to affirm or reject executory contracts on the theory that the value of the consideration still owed to the estate under some executory contracts exceeds the cost of the remaining obligations owed under the contract to the other party. The theory is that advantageous contracts should be affirmed by the trustee as a means of enhancing the likelihood of successful reorganization, or, if the estate is in liquidation, as a means of increasing creditor dividends. The Act provides that any claim arising from the trustee's post-filing obligations under the contract has an administrative expense priority where the trustee ultimately affirms, yet does not specify how payments made to the estate during the period while the trustee is deciding whether to affirm or to reject are to be treated if the trustee subsequently decides to reject.

We think the claim for return of such payments must receive a like priority. If payments made after the initial filing but before rejection were not given an administrative priority, a party who owes the bankrupt payments under an executory contract would face the risk that his claim for post-petition payments would be treated as a mere unsecured claim if the executory contract were rejected. A party placed in that situation would often be well-advised to cease making payments, even though he could

---

29. [Footnote 17 in original:] A claim for goods or services conferred on an estate pursuant to a contract entered by the trustee after the date of filing is valued according to the terms of that contract. A claim for the trustee's post-filing use of a leasehold pursuant to a lease entered by the bankrupt prior to filing is valued not according to the terms of the lease but objectively under a "reasonable worth" standard. In re First Research Corp., 457 F.2d 331, 332 (5th Cir. 1972); S. & W. Holding Co. v. Kuriansky, 317 F.2d 666, 668 (2d Cir. 1963) (allowance for use and occupancy by trustee of leasehold is an expense of administration of estate and does not arise out of lease or have any relation to it). The reasonable worth of use and occupancy by the trustee is, however, ordinarily presumed to be equal to the contractual rental. [Note that the Bankruptcy Code changed the law in this regard. Section 365(d)(3) requires the trustee to pay rent according to the terms of the lease from the date of the order for relief up until the date of assumption or rejection; section 365(d)(10) requires the trustee to do the same for leases of nonconsumer personal property for the period starting 60 days after the order for relief and going up to the date of assumption or rejection, unless the court orders otherwise based on the equities of the case. These provisions are discussed later in this Chapter.–Ed.]

be sued for breach of contract,[30] because he might well recover little or nothing as an unsecured claimant if the trustee rejects. Providing an administrative expense priority for post-filing payments in the event of rejection encourages parties to continue performance of their executory contracts with the debtor during the interim period and thus furthers the statutory policy of encouraging the continued performance of executory contracts which may be beneficial to the estate until the trustee makes his decision.[31]

In this case, the trustee was entitled to use post-filing payments in the administration of the estate. The lot purchasers have claims provable against the estate of administrative expense priority on parity with any other administrative expense claims against the estate.[32]

3. Ownership of Payments Received After August 6, 1973.

Payments made on an executory contract after rejection are not property of the bankrupt estate. The underlying contracts having been rejected and thus breached, these payments remain the property of the payors. See In re Gravure Paper & Board Corp., 234 F.2d 928, 930, 932 (3d Cir. 1956) (once trustee rejects lease, he no longer has any "right, title or interest" in lease or its proceeds); Green v. Finnigan Realty Co., 70 F.2d 465, 466-67 (5th Cir. 1934) (once trustee rejects lease, trustee is trespasser and has no right to use or occupancy).

Where the trustee takes or retains possession of property that is not an asset of the estate, he is personally liable for damages arising from this illegal act, unless he acts both in good faith *and* with reasonable grounds for believing that his possession is proper. * * *

Any payments on executory contracts received by Perry after August 6, 1973, the date upon which rejection of all of the executory contracts took place, never

---

30. [Footnote 20 in original:] If the trustee chooses to affirm an executory contract within the prescribed time limit, the trustee may sue the other party for damages if the other party has meanwhile failed to perform. 4A J. Moore & L. King, Collier on Bankruptcy P 70.43, at 536 (14th ed. 1978).

31. [Footnote 21 in original:] We recognize that a party to an executory contract who is injured or fears injury by a delay on the affirmance/rejection decision may request a court order directing the trustee to affirm or reject the executory contract immediately. See generally Mohonk Realty Corp. v. Wise Shoe Stores, Inc., 111 F.2d 287, 290 (2d Cir.), cert. denied, 311 U.S. 654, 61 S. Ct. 47, 85 L. Ed. 418 (1940); 6 J. Moore & L. King, Collier on Bankruptcy P 3.23[6], at 583-86 (14th ed. 1978). However, we do not believe that the mere possibility of petitioning the court for such relief precludes special priority for claims based on payments that are made by a party who does not request relief.

Likewise, the requirement that a trustee may not assume an executory contract unless at the time of assumption the trustee cures the default, together with the fact that Cochise had apparently defaulted on the land sale contracts long before June 5, 1972, does not require that the purchasers be treated as unsecured general creditors as to post-filing payments. As unlikely as the trustee's assumption of the executory land sale contract may have been, each purchaser was entitled to believe that the trustee might cure the default and assume the contract, to continue making payments on the contract, and to expect to have a claim against the estate for those payments of administrative expense priority, regardless of whether the trustee did or did not eventually affirm the contract.

32. [Footnote 22 in original:] All administrative expense creditors must be treated with "absolute equality," unless, of course, some creditors, with full knowledge of the facts, have agreed to subordinate their claims. Thomas Corp. v. Nicholas, 221 F.2d 286, 289 (5th Cir. 1955). In this case, previous disbursements to other administrative expense creditors of the Cochise estate could possibly prevent the appellants from recovering that pro rata share of the assets of the estate that they would have received if all disbursements had been delayed until the trustee's final accounting. The trustee, not having given notice to the land purchasers, is therefore personally liable for the difference. * * *

became property of the estate. The trustee was therefore obligated either to return these monies immediately to the payors, or, at a minimum, to set the monies aside in trust for them. Charged with knowledge of the principles of bankruptcy law, the trustee could not reasonably have believed that he was entitled to use the payments in the administration of the estate. To the extent they have not been returned to the purchasers, these are monies (together with appropriate interest) for which the trustee is personally responsible.

III. Misconduct of the Trustee.

* * *

A. Liability for Failure to Reject Executory Contracts.

A bankruptcy or reorganization trustee is a fiduciary of each creditor of the estate, including anyone who is a party to an executory contract with the bankrupt. See Wolf v. Weinstein, 372 U.S. 633, 650, 83 S. Ct. 969, 979, 10 L. Ed. 2d 33 (1963); Ford Motor Credit Co. v. Weaver, 680 F.2d 451, 461 (6th Cir. 1982); Sherr v. Winkler, 552 F.2d 1367, 1374 (10th Cir. 1977); Moulded Products, Inc. v. Barry, 474 F.2d 220, 224 (8th Cir.), cert. denied, 412 U.S. 940, 93 S. Ct. 2779, 37 L. Ed. 2d 400 (1973). As such, he has a duty to treat all creditors fairly and to exercise that measure of care and diligence that an ordinarily prudent person under similar circumstances would exercise. Although a trustee is not liable in any manner for mistakes in judgment where discretion is allowed, he is subject to personal liability for not only intentional but also negligent violations of duties imposed upon him by law, see *Mosser,* 341 U.S. at 272, 274, 71 S. Ct. at 682, 683.[33]

While a debtor is in reorganization and for the first 60 days of a [liquidation] bankruptcy proceeding, the decision whether to affirm or reject an executory contract is within the discretion of the trustee. Thus, as long as the trustee remains undecided on whether to affirm or to reject an executory contract and the decision remains in his discretion, the trustee has no duty to creditors to tell them that he is entitled by law to reject that contract. Once the trustee has finally decided to reject an executory contract and therefore not to perform his obligations under that contract, the trustee then comes under a duty to take formal steps to reject it. To fail to do so and thereby permit the creditor to continue to perform after the date of decision to reject directly and unnecessarily injures the creditor[34] and is not consonant with conduct of an ordinarily prudent person serving in the capacity of trustee. Such failure therefore gives rise to a claim for damages for which the trustee is personally liable.

---

33. [Footnote 26 in original:] We reject the approach of the Tenth and Sixth Circuits which, in an apparent misreading of the seminal case of Mosser v. Darrow, 341 U.S. 267, 71 S. Ct. 680, 95 L. Ed. 927 (1951), have concluded that a bankruptcy or reorganization trustee may be held personally liable for damages only for injuries arising from intentional—as opposed to negligent—conduct. Sherr v. Winkler, 552 F.2d 1367, 1375 (10th Cir. 1977); see Ford Motor Credit Co. v. Weaver, 680 F.2d 451, 461-62 (6th Cir. 1982) (applying *Sherr* holding to debtor in possession case); see also United States v. Sapp, 641 F.2d 182, 184-85 (4th Cir. 1981) (dictum). * * *

34. [Footnote 28 in original:] The injury would be particularly pronounced and especially invidious where the assets of the estate are not sufficient to cover all administrative expense claims. In such circumstances, every dollar of payment made by the creditor (lot purchaser), while giving rise to a priority claim in that amount, will ultimately be only partially returned, yet will increase the pro-rata share available to other administrative expense creditors, including the trustee himself. See *Mosser,* 341 U.S. at 271, 71 S. Ct. at 682 (stressing importance of maintaining disinterestedness of trustee's administration of the estate).

The papers before the bankruptcy court do not disclose whether the trustee had or had not decided before August 6, 1973 to reject some if not all of the land sale contracts that were executory on June 5, 1972. Nevertheless, the bankruptcy court entered summary judgment for the trustee on appellant's claim of misconduct by the trustee on the ground that the trustee's conduct was authorized by federal statute. This was error.

If the trustee is found to have decided before August 6, 1973 to reject the executory land sale contracts, the trustee is personally liable to the Baldrian class for damages arising out of this violation of his fiduciary duty. Damages would consist of all payments made post-filing, after the trustee's decision to reject, less any amount received from the estate. * * *

B. Liability for Misrepresentations.

Appellants claim that the trustee is personally liable for damages arising from fraudulent and negligent misrepresentations communicated to Baldrian class members regarding the use and status of payments made on the land sale contracts. * * *

The record is devoid of any indication that any of the trustee's statements were "authorized *and* ordered by the Court." Nor should they have been, since no "congressionally authorized statute or controlling case precedent" of which we are aware affirmatively "demand[s]" a trustee to increase the size of an estate through fraudulent or negligent misrepresentations. Furthermore, our review of the answers to interrogatories and affidavits before the bankruptcy court convinces us that genuine issue of material fact remain concerning the trustee's liability under Arizona law for the allegedly fraudulent and negligent misrepresentations. These issues could not properly have been determined on summary judgment.[35]

* * * The summary judgment is reversed. The case is remanded.

---

35. [Footnote 34 in original:] Apparently conceding that the summary judgment cannot be sustained on the grounds set forth below, Perry argues that, since the appellants here had entered contracts with Cochise, the trustee cannot be held liable for payments which purchasers were obliged to make under those contracts, even if the payments were induced by misrepresentations. See Berry v. Robotka, 9 Ariz.App. 461, 468, 453 P.2d 972, 979 (1969). We disagree, since the *Berry* defense is properly applicable only where the person relying on the alleged misrepresentations was in fact obligated under the terms of the contract or by law to continue performance. *Arizona Title,* 14 Ariz.App. at 494, 484 P.2d at 647. The answers to interrogatories and affidavits show that the continuation of payments on the land sale contracts was not the only course of action open to some, if not all, of the members of the Baldrian class on June 5, 1972. As to those land sale contracts which were executory on June 5, 1972, by operation of law and as conceded by the trustee himself, each land sale contract was rejected by the trustee and thereby breached by the bankrupt as of that date. Hence, from June 5, 1972 onward, these Baldrian class members were not obligated by law to continue making payments, and against them the *Berry* defense is unavailable to Perry. Indeed, by failing to affirm those contracts, Perry in effect abandoned the *Berry* defense which would have otherwise shielded him from liability for his post-filing misrepresentations, assuming, that is, that such parties to executory contracts were in fact otherwise obligated to continue performance, which we doubt. The bankruptcy court was not justified in granting summary judgment for defendant based on that defense.

As to those lot purchasers, if any, whose land sale contracts had been wholly executed by Cochise on June 5, 1972, the bankruptcy court should have applied a similar analysis. The *Berry* defense is simply not available to a misrepresenting party where the party who is misled had valid defenses to further performance available at law or by contract, even where the misrepresenting party has performed all of his contractual obligations. If a party to an executed contract was not obligated by law to continue making payments on his contract at the time Perry made the alleged misrepresentation, e.g., because he had an available claim for rescission or because fraud inhered in the making of the contract, that misrepresentation is actionable if that purchaser relied on the intentional or negligent false statement or promise in making payments to Perry.

NOTES

1. Under the court's approach, on what theory would a nondebtor party effectively be obligated to perform under a contract with the debtor before the debtor in possession assumed the contract? If the debtor in possession eventually rejects the contract, can the nondebtor party be held liable for breaching it during the postpetition, prerejection period? In such a case, did the nondebtor party have any obligation to perform during that period?

2. Is it proper for the debtor in possession to decide that a contract should be rejected but to delay rejection of the contract so as to obtain additional performance from the nondebtor party? If the nondebtor party is paid for all postpetition benefits conferred on the estate, is there any harm in the debtor in possession delaying rejection so as to obtain additional performance from the nondebtor party? See the court's footnote 28 (as originally numbered) and the two paragraphs following it in the text of the court's opinion.

3. If the debtor has materially breached a contract before the petition is filed, is the nondebtor party obligated to continue to perform, according to the court? Note that the debtor in possession cannot legally expend estate assets to cure prepetition defaults except in connection with assumption of the contract. The debtor in possession's fiduciary duty to exercise due care and prudence precludes the debtor in possession from making a hasty decision to assume a contract; the debtor in possession must take the necessary time to determine whether it is in the best interest of the estate. Since the debtor in possession may then be precluded from curing prepetition defaults, does it make sense to "penalize" the estate for those prepetition defaults by allowing the nondebtor party to suspend its performance? Does it make sense to "penalize" the nondebtor party by forcing him or her to perform despite the material breach? If the debtor in possession eventually cures the defaults and assumes the contract, does the cure "relate back" to the time of the petition filing, so that the nondebtor parties are in breach for not having performed after that date?

4. "Regarding automobile dealer agreements, 'until the contract ... is rejected or validly terminated ... the Debtor is entitled to compel specific performance and require the [Creditor] to abide by the provisions of the [Agreement].' In re Chick Smith Ford, Inc., 46 B.R. 515, 519 (Bankr. M.D.Fla. 1985)." South Motor Chrysler-Plymouth, Inc. v. Chrysler Motor Corp. (In re South Motor Co.), 161 B.R. 532, 547 (Bankr. S.D.Fla. 1993) (deletions and bracketed language by the court). In another case a bankruptcy court enjoined the nondebtor parties to a massive airliner leasing contract from breaching it while the debtor airline decided whether to assume it; thus the nondebtor parties were ordered to deliver additional jet airplanes to the airline. Braniff, Inc. v. GPA Group PLC (In re Braniff, Inc.), 118 B.R. 819 (Bankr. M.D.Fla. 1990). (Whether the contract in *Braniff* should have been held to be a nonassumable financial accommodation contract under § 365(c)(2) is another question, discussed below in section F of this Chapter.) As *South Motor, Braniff,* and the next two principal cases illustrate, under the Bankruptcy Code courts have routinely ordered nondebtor parties to perform contracts during the postpetition, prerejection period. Did the court in *Cochise* seem to believe that it had power to order the purchasers to make payments pending the trustee's decision to assume or reject the contracts? Compare the reasoning in the next two cases with the reasoning in *Cochise.*

5.   As the court points out in its footnote number 11, if the debtor in possession rejects
     a land sale contract with a purchaser who is in possession of the land but who had
     not received title as of the petition date, the Code gives the purchaser a lien on the
     land for all the payments made by the purchaser. Section 365(j). Alternatively, the
     purchaser can remain in possession and eventually receive a deed. Section 365(i).
     If the purchaser elects to remain in possession, the purchaser must make all
     payments required by the contract (with a limited right of setoff for damages
     caused by nonperformance of the debtor's obligations after the rejection), and the
     trustee or debtor in possession is relieved from any obligations under the contract
     other than the obligation to deliver title.

Data-Link Systems, Inc. v. Whitcomb & Keller Mortgage Co.
(In re Whitcomb & Keller Mortgage Co.)
United States Court of Appeals, Seventh Circuit, 1983
715 F.2d 375

JAMESON, District Judge [sitting by designation]:

This is an appeal from an order of the district court affirming a decision of the
bankruptcy court allowing the debtor, Whitcomb & Keller Mortgage Co., Inc.,
Appellee, to reject an executory contract with Data-Link Systems, Inc., Appellant,
and classifying Data-Link as a general unsecured creditor in the Whitcomb &
Keller bankruptcy proceeding for the sum of $12,954.63. We affirm.

I. Factual and Procedural Background

Whitcomb & Keller, a mortgage banker whose business included servicing
mortgage accounts for investors, executed an executory contract with Data-Link,
whereby, for a fee, Data-Link was to provide computer services to update and
maintain Whitcomb & Keller's customer accounts. The contract provided that
upon termination of the contract, Data-Link would return all master files and other
occupational data relating to Whitcomb & Keller upon payment in full of any
outstanding balance.

On October 27, 1980, Whitcomb & Keller filed for relief under Chapter 11 of
the Bankruptcy Code, 11 U.S.C. § 1101 et seq. The bankruptcy court approved
Whitcomb & Keller as a debtor in possession. At the time Whitcomb & Keller
filed its bankruptcy petition, it owed Data-Link $12,954.63 for computer services
previously rendered. Data-Link's claim for that amount was listed in the
bankruptcy schedule as a general unsecured claim. Data-Link continued providing
computer services, and Whitcomb & Keller paid for all services provided during
the administration of the estate.

During the course of the bankruptcy, Whitcomb & Keller determined that it
should sell its mortgage servicing contract assets. On February 26, 1981, the
bankruptcy court found the bids of Milliken Mortgage Company and Unity
Savings Association to be the best for the sale of the assets. As the district court
found, on March 4, 1981, Data-Link discontinued computer services to Whitcomb
& Keller, paralyzing it, and precipitated the filing of an application for a
temporary restraining order and preliminary injunction. Over Data-Link's
objections, the bankruptcy court entered an order enjoining Data-Link from
terminating the computer services, and the services were resumed.

On March 5, 1981, Data-Link filed its answer which included a counterclaim requesting the bankruptcy court either (1) to declare that Whitcomb & Keller, by its application requesting the court to enforce the executory contract and by its continued receipt of the benefits of the executory contract, had assumed the executory contract, or (2) to require Whitcomb & Keller to decide whether to assume or reject the executory contract within a specified period of time before the confirmation of the plan. After a hearing on March 9, 1981, the bankruptcy court took the matter under advisement and continued the restraining order in effect.

On March 12, 1981, Unity Savings informed the bankruptcy court that Data-Link refused to give either Whitcomb & Keller or Unity Savings essential information stored in the master data base, thereby preventing Unity Savings from purchasing the servicing contract assets. Data-Link contended that the restraining order did not require it to provide Unity Savings with test tapes of information stored in the master data base but only to provide computer services to Whitcomb & Keller. Following a hearing on March 16, 1981, the bankruptcy court directed Data-Link to cooperate and turn over test tapes to expedite the sale of Whitcomb & Keller's mortgage servicing assets. The parties stipulated that any right, lien or other interest Data-Link might have would attach to proceeds of the sale of Whitcomb & Keller's assets. Whitcomb & Keller paid Data-Link in full for all charges relating to the preparation of the master data base.

On April 8, 1981, the bankruptcy court found that Whitcomb & Keller had not assumed the executory contract. The court found further that Whitcomb & Keller had remained current on its post-petition debts and that Data-Link was adequately protected, in that any right, lien or other interest that it might have would attach to the proceeds of the sale of Whitcomb & Keller's assets. Accordingly, the bankruptcy court denied Data-Link's request to require Whitcomb & Keller to assume or reject the executory contract prior to the confirmation of the plan.

Also on April 8, 1981, Whitcomb & Keller requested authority to reject the executory contract. Data-Link objected, and the matter was set for trial. On April 24 the court confirmed the second amended plan of reorganization. Data-Link filed a proof of claim on April 30, asserting priority for the pre-petition claim of $12,954.63.

On July 10, 1981, a trial was held in bankruptcy court on Whitcomb & Keller's request for authority to reject the executory contract. By order dated April 15, 1982, the court found that Whitcomb & Keller had not assumed the executory contract and that the language of the contract did not give rise to an equitable lien or warehouseman's lien on the information stored in Data-Link's computer. Accordingly, the bankruptcy court concluded that (1) Whitcomb & Keller was entitled to reject the executory contract, and (2) Data-Link's pre-petition debt of $12,954.63 incurred under the executory contract was an unsecured claim. On appeal the district court affirmed the decision of the bankruptcy court.

II. Contentions on Appeal

Data-Link contends that:

(1) neither the debtor in possession nor the bankruptcy court had authority to enforce the executory contract unless the contract was assumed by the debtor;

(2) because of the essential nature of the services provided under the contract, the bankruptcy court should have specified a period of time within which Whitcomb & Keller was required to decide whether to assume or reject the contract;

(3) Whitcomb & Keller continued receiving benefits from the executory contract and should have been required to assume its burdens; and

(4) Whitcomb & Keller's request for an order prohibiting Data-Link from terminating computer services and the bankruptcy court's restraining orders constituted an assumption by Whitcomb & Keller of the executory contract.

III. Authority to Enforce Executory Contract Pending Acceptance or Rejection

Acceptance and rejection of executory contracts are governed by Section 365 of the Bankruptcy Code. Title 11 U.S.C. § 365(d)(2) provides:

> In a case under Chapter 9, 11 or 13 of this title, the trustee may assume or reject an executory contract or unexpired lease of the debtor at any time before the confirmation of a plan, but the court, on request of any party to such contract or lease, may order the trustee to determine within a specified period of time whether to assume or reject such contract or lease.[36]

In In re American National Trust, 426 F.2d 1059, 1064 (7 Cir. 1970), this court held that a trustee in a reorganization proceeding "is entitled to a reasonable time to make a careful and informed evaluation as to possible burdens and benefits of an executory contract," quoting from 6 Collier on Bankruptcy (14th Ed.) 576-80.

The executory contract between Data-Link and Whitcomb & Keller was in effect on October 27, 1980, when Whitcomb & Keller filed its bankruptcy petition. The contract remained in effect until Whitcomb & Keller made its decision to assume or reject the contract. Before Whitcomb & Keller made its decision, however, Data-Link ceased providing essential computer services. Whitcomb & Keller then applied for the restraining order, as it had a right to do. Similarly, the bankruptcy court had the authority to preserve the status quo until Whitcomb & Keller made its decision.[37] The district court held that the bankruptcy court did not err in issuing the restraining order. We agree.

IV. Requiring Debtors in Possession to Assume or Reject Executory Contract

Data-Link contends that because of the essential nature of the service it provided under the contract, the bankruptcy court, pursuant to Section 365 of the Bankruptcy Code, 11 U.S.C. § 365(d)(2), should have specified a period of time within which Whitcomb & Keller was required to decide whether to assume or reject the executory

---

36. [Footnote 3 in original:] The policy behind § 365(d)(2) was summarized by the bankruptcy court in its April 8, 1981, order as follows:

> Since a debtor is in limbo until confirmation of a plan, it is understandably difficult to commit itself to assuming or rejecting a contract much before the time for confirmation of a plan. Thus, the code allows for the debtor to provide for assumption or rejection of the executory contracts in its plan. This procedure insures that the debtor is not in the precarious position of having assumed a contract relying on confirmation of a particular plan, only to find the plan to have been rejected.

37. [Footnote 4 in original:] The Bankruptcy Code provides a sufficient legal basis for a bankruptcy court to issue an injunction or restraining order in appropriate situations. Section 105(a) empowers a bankruptcy court to issue any order that is necessary or appropriate to carry out the provisions of the Code, 11 U.S.C. § 105(a) (1979).

contract. The parties had, of course, stipulated that the computer services were essential and that the information stored in the computer included information essential to the sale of Whitcomb & Keller's accounts. Data-Link argues that time for further inquiry into the benefits and burdens of the contract was not needed.

Data-Link interprets the purpose of § 365(d) too narrowly. It is not enough that the trustee or debtor in possession recognize that the services provided under the contract are essential. Rather, § 365(d) allows the trustee or debtor in possession a reasonable time within which to determine whether adoption or rejection of the executory contract would be beneficial to an effective reorganization.

The bankruptcy court addressed this issue in its order of April 8, 1981. After discussing the purpose of allowing the trustee a reasonable time to make its decision, the court noted that Data-Link was adequately protected because (1) Whitcomb & Keller had paid for all services received during the administration of its estate, and (2) the parties had stipulated that any right, lien or other interest that Data-Link might have would attach to the proceeds of the sale of Whitcomb & Keller's assets. Accordingly, the court exercised its discretion under § 365(d) in denying Data-Link's request to require Whitcomb & Keller "to assume or reject the contract forthwith." We find no abuse of the bankruptcy court's discretion.

V. Receipt of Benefits and Assumption of Burdens

Data-Link next contends that a finding that [Whitcomb &] Keller assumed the contract is necessary to avoid the inequitable result of allowing Whitcomb & Keller to derive the benefits of the contract without assuming its burdens.

In the first place, it may be noted that general principles governing contractual benefits and burdens do not always apply in the bankruptcy context. The purpose of the Bankruptcy Code is to "suspend the normal operation of rights and obligations between the debtor and his creditors." Fontainebleau Hotel Corp. v. Simon, 508 F.2d 1056, 1059 (5 Cir. 1975). Moreover, successful reorganization under Chapter 11 depends on relieving the debtor of burdensome contracts and pre-petition debts so that "additional cash flow thus freed is used to meet current operating expenses." H.R. Rep. No. 595, 95th Cong., 1st Sess. 221 (1977), reprinted in 1978 U.S. Code Cong. & Ad. News 5787, 5963, 6181. The post-petition services provided by Data- Link were operating expenses which Whitcomb & Keller paid in full. But merely providing such services did not alter Data-Link's position as a general unsecured creditor on its pre-petition claim. U.S. Financial, Inc. v. Pacific Telephone & Telegraph, 594 F.2d 1275, 1279 (9 Cir. 1979); In re Kassuba, 396 F. Supp. 324, 326 (N.D. Ill. 1975).

The cases upon which appellant relies are factually distinguishable. Here it is undisputed that Whitcomb & Keller paid in full for all services rendered during the administration of the estate, including the preparation of the data base tape. The only alleged breach of the executory contract relates to the indebtedness owed by Whitcomb & Keller when the petition was filed. Data-Link suffered no harm nor prejudice through the continued utilization of its computer services. Rather it presumably earned a profit from the continued use.[38] We agree with the district

---

38. [Footnote 5 in original:] As the district court noted, Whitcomb & Keller in effect "assumed the burdens as it received the benefits during the administration of the estate. If Whitcomb & Keller

court that Whitcomb & Keller's utilization of the computer services during the administration of the estate did not support a finding that Whitcomb & Keller assumed the contract or that Data-Link was entitled to a priority.

VI. Requirements for Assumption of Executory Contracts

Finally, Data-Link contends that Whitcomb & Keller's "application for the enforcement of this essential executory contract and the Bankruptcy Court's mandatory order thereon (that Data-Link must perform) constituted an assumption with Court approval."

Under § 365(a) the trustee or debtor in possession, *"subject to the court's approval,* may assume or reject any executory contract....." 11 U.S.C. § 365(a) (emphasis added). Interpreting similar language[39] in In re American National Trust, supra, 426 F.2d at 1064, this court declared: "'Assumption or adoption of the contract can only be effected through an express order of the judge.'" (quoting 6 Collier on Bankruptcy 576-80 (14th ed.)). No such order issued in the present case. Neither the bankruptcy court nor Whitcomb & Keller exhibited any intention of assuming the contract when the court enjoined Data-Link's termination of services.[40] We will not infer such intention. Instead, we find the order was directed solely toward maintaining the status quo—a permissible purpose well within the bankruptcy court's power, as we have noted.

VII. Conclusion

We find no abuse of the bankruptcy court's discretion. We agree with the bankruptcy court and the district court that (1) Whitcomb & Keller did not assume the executory contract; but rather (2) was entitled to and did reject the contract; and (3) Data-Link's pre-petition claim of $12,954.63 is an unsecured claim.

AFFIRMED.

In re Gunter Hotel Associates
United States Bankruptcy Court, W.D. Texas
96 B.R. 696 (1988)

LEIF M. CLARK, Bankruptcy Judge.

Gunter Hotel Associates ("Debtor") filed a motion on November 3, 1988 to reject a license agreement with Carlson Hospitality Group, Inc. ("Carlson"). A hearing was held on December 13, 1988 on this motion and on Carlson's motion

---

had continued to receive the services of Data-Link during the administration of the estate and not paid for them, the law clearly states that that indebtedness would be entitled to priority status. See, e.g., Matter of Steelship Corp., 576 F.2d 128, 132 (8 Cir. 1978). However, that is not the case here."

39. [Footnote 6 in original:] 11 U.S.C. § 516(1) (repealed 1979), provided: "upon the approval of a petition, the judge may ... (1) permit the rejection of executory contracts of the debtor....."

40. [Footnote 7 in original:] As the district court noted:

"The fact that Whitcomb & Keller utilized the computer services of Data-Link during the administration of its Chapter 11 estate and obtained an injunction from the Bankruptcy Court in order to do so does not support a finding that Whitcomb & Keller assumed the contract. Whitcomb & Keller was entitled to a reasonable time to decide whether to assume or reject the contract and the contract remained in effect until it was rejected. The injunction therefore was necessary in order to give Whitcomb & Keller the time needed to make its decision."

to compel rejection of the license agreement. The hearing was held contemporaneously with the hearing on confirmation of the debtor's plan. The decision on these pending motions affects the feasibility of the debtor's plan, and hence the confirmation decision hinges on their resolution.

I. FACTS

Prior to bankruptcy, Debtor entered into a license agreement (an executory contract under Section 365 of the Bankruptcy Code) with Carlson. Under the license, Debtor was allowed to operate its hotel, the Gunter, as a "Radisson Hotel" under the "Radisson" system. Carlson was required, among other things, to furnish the Radisson Reservation System to Debtor (including a listing in the "Saber" airline reservation system); to include Debtor in Carlson's directory and in its other promotional materials; to include Debtor in Carlson's national or regional group advertising and promotions; and to solicit group meetings, conventions, incentive, and travel agency business for Debtor through Carlson's national sales office. Through these services, Gunter has established a nation-wide presence.

The Debtor has fully exploited its license, developing a valuable business link with the American Automobile Association's travel arm, and placing advertising in travel publications throughout the country. The advertising of course includes the Radisson name and logo, along with Radisson's nationwide toll-free telephone number for reservations. Many of the publications are published only quarterly. Some are published only once a year.

The Debtor seeks an order permitting it to reject the license agreement, but wants to condition the terms of rejection so that the effect of rejection would be postponed for approximately sixty days after the effective date of confirmation of the plan. The Debtor also wants to have continued rights to referrals of calls made into the Radisson reservation system through 1989, so long as callers are asking for the Gunter. Debtor argues that these adjustments will enable it to enter into a new licensing agreement with another hotel chain, and will also preserve the value of goodwill it has built up in the Radisson name (to say nothing of the advertising that will continue to bear the Gunter/Radisson association for the next year or so).

The Debtor is unwilling to assume the license, primarily because of its concerns that another Carlson subsidiary is now operating another hotel in San Antonio in competition with the Gunter. If true, then Carlson would be in violation of its license. More important to the debtor's future, however, the Debtor suspects that future business would be channeled to the other hotel, threatening the Gunter's own future. In addition (though not affirmatively urged by the Debtor), the debtor may owe Carlson back license fees in the neighborhood of $150,000, which, if in fact due, would have to be repaid in full once the license agreement were assumed.

Carlson responds that rejection cannot be conditioned, that the license must be rejected *in toto*. Carlson further argues that an extension beyond confirmation violates this court's August 4, 1988 order which required assumption or rejection before the confirmation hearing. Carlson further asserts that if the license agreement is not rejected prior to confirmation, the License Agreement will survive confirmation as an enforceable and binding contract which the Debtor cannot then reject.

After careful consideration and for the reasons stated below, this Court denies both motions and extends the deadline to assume or reject for sixty days following the effective date of confirmation.

II. REJECTION—A BALANCING OF BURDENS AND BENEFITS

The rejection decision requires a balancing of the license agreement's burdens and benefits. The main concern is whether rejection will likely benefit the estate.

The testimony clearly demonstrates that rejection of the licensing agreement will likely benefit the estate *eventually.* Rejection will *not* benefit the estate if done prior to or upon confirmation of the plan, however. Hotel chains are presently negotiating with the Debtor, but these suitors are not able or willing to contract with the Debtor until *after* confirmation. The testimony also shows that 60 days is a reasonable time for a new licensing agreement to be negotiated and implemented, but that, without some lead time, the debtor will be left with no licensing agreement at all and no assurance that one will be available. For a hotel such as the Gunter, a national affiliation is all but essential, especially when it relies so heavily on good relations with travel agents and a national exposure. As expensive and chancy as the current license might be, it is still preferable to no license at all.

The debtor's proposal to "condition" rejection is inimical to the overwhelming case authority that a bankruptcy court is not free to re-write an executory contract upon either its assumption or its rejection. Leasing Service Corp. v. First Tennessee Bank, N.A., 826 F.2d 434, 437 (6th Cir. 1987); In re Auto Dealer Services, Inc., 65 B.R. 681, 684 (Bankr. M.D. Fla. 1986) ("debtor may not reject the undesirable aspects of the contract while claiming the benefits of the contract"); In re EES Lambert Associates, 62 B.R. 328, 336 (Bankr. N.D. Ill. 1986) ("a debtor cannot retain those aspects of the contract to his benefit while rejecting the burdensome aspects thereof"); Matter of Executive Technology Data Systems, 79 B.R. 276, 282 (Bankr. E.D. Mich. 1987) ("if a debtor elects to reject an executory contract, he rejects the benefits as well as the burdens"); In re Allain, 59 B.R. 107, 109 (Bankr. W.D. La. 1986); In re Silver, 26 B.R. 526, 529 (Bankr. E.D. Pa. 1983). If the motion to reject is approved, then the Debtor immediately loses all the benefits which have accrued under the license. In re Allain, supra; In re E.E.S. Lambert Associates, supra. Effective upon rejection, Carlson would be relieved of any further duty to perform its end of the license. The court cannot and should not, in the name of "equity," try to blunt that consequence. Indeed, far from being inequitable, it is that very result that the court is constrained to evaluate in deciding whether rejection should even be permitted.

Thus, the difficulty facing the court is that rejection is not appropriate *at this time* (though it appears it may be appropriate in the near future). Carlson insists that the assumption/rejection decision must nonetheless be made now, either by the Debtor or by operation of law. For support, Carlson points to the August 4, 1988 order.

III. JURISDICTION TO EXTEND DEADLINE FOR REJECTION OR ASSUMPTION BEYOND CONFIRMATION HEARING

This court's order of August 4, 1988 setting the confirmation date as the deadline for rejection or assumption is not the absolute obstacle that Carlson contends. Bankruptcy courts retain broad discretion in determining when a debtor can assume or reject an executory contract. See In re Monroe Well Service, Inc., 83 B.R. 317, 324

(Bankr. E.D. Pa. 1988) (bankruptcy court's authority under 365(d)(2) to shorten the time period for rejection/assumption of utility agreements). The Debtor should be given great latitude in deciding whether to reject an executory contract. Further, the Bankruptcy Rules allow such extensions. Rule 9006(b) reads:

> ... when an act is required ... to be done at or within a specified period *by* ... *court order,* the court for cause shown may at any time in its discretion (1) with or without motion or notice order the period enlarged if the request therefor is made before the expiration of the period originally prescribed.

Bankr. R. 9006(b) (1987) (emphasis added). Here, the "cause shown" is that the debtor's chances for a successful reorganization increase greatly if the rejection decision is extended past the confirmation hearing, but drop radically if rejection is compelled at this time.

There is, however, a second, more daunting hurdle for this court to clear. Bankruptcy Code Section 365(d)(2) allows a debtor to "assume or reject an executory contract ... at any time *before the confirmation of a plan* but the court, on the request of any party to such contract ... may order [the debtor] to determine within a specified period of time whether to assume or reject such contract." 11 U.S.C. § 365(d)(2) (emphasis added). Does this court retain post-confirmation jurisdiction to decide the rejection/assumption issue?

Fortunately, there is judicial precedent. In re J.M. Fields, Inc., 26 B.R. 852, 855 (S.D.N.Y. 1983) held that, pursuant to a retention of jurisdiction clause in the plan of reorganization, the court had jurisdiction to permit rejection of a lease after confirmation. The Debtor's Plan contains such a clause:

> The court shall retain jurisdiction of the reorganization case after the Confirmation Date until Consummation of Plan with respect ... to hear and determine ... any matter relating to this Plan.

Debtor's First Amended Plan of Reorganization, Article IX, Sect. 9.01.

This court may thus retain exclusive post-confirmation jurisdiction over all matters relating to the license agreement. This exercise of post-confirmation jurisdiction promotes the purpose of reorganization and confirmation, namely the return of the debtor to the marketplace, free of judicial control and scrutiny. Rejection is fundamental to the reorganization process and provides a mechanism through which severe financial burdens may be lifted while the debtor attempts reorganization. In In re Malden Mills, Inc., 35 B.R. 71 (Bankr. D. Mass. 1983), the court retained post-confirmation jurisdiction pursuant to a retention of jurisdiction provision to determine the debtor's pending motion to reject an executory contract. The court stressed that the "[p]olicy inherent in reorganizations makes it impossible and impractical to require all issues involving motions to reject executory contracts to be finally adjudicated prior to confirmation." Id. at 73 (citing In re J.M. Fields). The court warned that

> Requiring final determination prior to confirmation of all applications to reject ... [an executory contract], with subsequent appeals and possible imposition of stays, would postpone confirmation of a debtor's plan of arrangement, thus impeding the debtor's rehabilitation and return to the marketplace.

Id. at 857. The court thus concludes that it may extend the deadline imposed by August 4, 1988 order, and that Section 365(d)(2) does not bar such an extension.

IV. POST-CONFIRMATION/PRE-REJECTION STATUS OF THE LICENSING AGREEMENT

Carlson correctly argues that the license agreement survives confirmation if rejection is delayed beyond confirmation. In re Marrero, 7 B.R. 586 (D. Puerto Rico 1980) the district court found "as long as rejection is not ordered, [an executory] contract continues in existence." Id. at 588. (citations omitted). Thus, Carlson is obligated to perform its obligations under the license agreement until 60 days after the confirmation hearing. However, Carlson may not proceed with enforcement actions against Debtor in the interim. "In the Court's view, an executory contract under Chapter 11 is not enforceable against the debtor party, but is enforceable against the nondebtor party prior to the debtor's assumption or rejection of the contract." In re Feyline Presents, Inc., 81 B.R. 623, 626 (Bankr. D. Colo. 1988).

The Supreme Court's *Bildisco* decision mandates this outcome. *Bildisco* held that "from the filing of a petition in bankruptcy until formal acceptance," a collective bargaining contract is not an enforceable contract. N.L.R.B. v. Bildisco & Bildisco, 465 U.S. 513, 104 S. Ct. 1188, 1199, 1200, 79 L. Ed. 2d 482 (1984). Douglas W. Bordewieck's seminal article on executory contracts sheds light as to *Bildisco*'s ramifications. Bordewieck, *The Postpetition, Pre-Rejection, Pre-Assumption Status of an Executory Contract,* 59 AMERICAN BANKRUPTCY LAW JOURNAL 197 (Summer, 1985). Bordewieck notes that "the Court spoke in general terms; it did not limit its discussion to the particular executory contract." Id. at 199. The *Bildisco* analysis applies to all executory contracts, including the license agreement in this case. Until the court acts to approve acceptance of the license, Carlson cannot enforce the license against the post-confirmation estate.

Carlson's rights prior to court-ordered rejection or assumption are not Debtor's equivalent. Bordewieck correctly points out that:

> [D]uring the period from the date of filing until the date on which the DIP [debtor in possession] rejects or assumes an executory contract, the non-debtor is bound to perform while the DIP temporarily is not bound to perform ... [T]he non-debtor party to an executory contract cannot require the DIP to adhere to the terms of the contract, for that contract is "unenforceable" against the DIP unless and until it is assumed. Stated differently, the *Bildisco* Court concluded that the DIP is not in fact bound by the provisions of an executory contract unless the DIP subsequently assumes the contract.

Bordewieck, 59 AMER. BANKR. L.J. at 200.

Other courts have barred nondebtors' enforcement actions against debtors prior to assumption or rejection. "An executory contract is unenforceable against a Debtor-in-Possession who has not yet assumed the contract." In re Wilson, 69 B.R. 960, 965 (Bankr. N.D. Tex. 1987). "We hold that a formal assumption of an executory contract by a debtor is required to render an executory contract enforceable against a debtor." In re Metro Transp. Co., 87 B.R. 338, 339 (Bankr. E.D. Pa. 1988). "In the Court's view, an executory contract under Chapter 11 is not enforceable against the debtor party, but is enforceable against the nondebtor party prior to the debtor's assumption or rejection of the contract." In re Feyline Presents, Inc., 81 B.R. 623, 626 (Bankr. D. Colo. 1988). "[A]n unexpired lease, otherwise not assumed or rejected by the trustee, does not give rise to a provable claim against the debtor." In re O.P.M. Leasing Services, Inc., 79 B.R. 161, 164 (S.D.N.Y. 1987). "The analysis that the trustee [or debtor-in-possession] is vested with the contract but that the contract is unenforceable against him unless and until assumed is the better approach." In re T.H.W. Enterprises, Inc. 89 B.R. 351, 354 (Bankr. S.D.N.Y. 1988).

This court orders that the motion to reject be denied, but further extends the deadline for seeking rejection for 60 days past the effective date of confirmation. Carlson's motion to compel Debtor to reject the license prior to the confirmation hearing is therefore denied. This court is not ordering rejection at this time, but neither is it ordering assumption. Furthermore, the license agreement will not be "assumed" by operation of law, because assumption of an executory contract requires an express court order. There cannot be assumption by implication. In re A.H. Robins Co., Inc. 68 B.R. 705, 709 (Bankr. E.D. Va. 1986); In re Memorial Hospital of Iowa County, Inc., 82 B.R. 478, 483-484 (W.D. Wis. 1988); In re Marrero, 7 B.R. 586, 588 (D. Puerto Rico 1980); In Re Gamma Fishing Co. 70 B.R. 949, 952 (Bankr. S.D. Cal. 1987). *Gamma* concluded that the "requirement of court approval furthers the Bankruptcy Code's policy of maximizing the value of the estate for the benefit of all creditors, while preserving certain rights of parties to contract with the debtor." Id. at 952.

By thus immunizing the Debtor from enforcement actions until rejection of the executory contract, the Debtor should be able to consummate a new license agreement and proceed with its plan of reorganization. This protection is afforded the debtor, not by virtue of the automatic stay (which expires upon confirmation), but by virtue of Section 365(d)(2). "The rights of a party to an executory contract with the debtor are not 'stayed' by section 362; those rights are rendered temporarily unenforceable by section 365." Bordewieck, 59 AM. BANKR. L.J. at 214.

    * * *

In accordance with analysis above, this court

1. DENIES Debtor's Motion To Extend Effective Date of Rejection, and with it, Debtor's Motion to Reject the Licensing Agreement with Carlson.

2. DENIES Carlson's Motion to Compel Debtor to Assume or Reject The Licensing Agreement on or prior to confirmation.

3. ENLARGES *sua sponte* the court-ordered deadline for the Debtor to reject or assume the Carlson license.

4. RETAINS exclusive jurisdiction over all matters relating to the license agreement.

So ORDERED.

NOTES

1. Are the decisions in *Whitcomb & Keller* and in *Gunter Hotel* consistent with the decision in *Cochise*? Would it matter under *Cochise* that the contracts in *Whitcomb & Keller* and in *Gunter Hotel* were never assumed? Is the Bankruptcy Code different from the old Act in a way that would indicate an intent of Congress to change the law in this regard? Are unassumed contracts and/or leases property of the estate under the Code even though they were not under the old Act? Compare Chbat v. Tleel, (In re Tleel), 876 F.2d 769 (9th Cir. 1989), with Computer Commc'ns, Inc. v. Codex Corp. (In re Computer Commc'ns, Inc.), 824 F.2d 725 (9th Cir. 1987). What conclusion might you draw from § 541(b)(2)? Outside bankruptcy, would we say that a tenant has a property interest in continued possession of the leased premises? Outside bankruptcy, if Whitcomb & Keller had not breached the contract with Data-Link, would we say that Whitcomb & Keller

had a property right to continued service from Data-Link? Note the breadth of Bankruptcy Code § 541(a) as compared with the comparable old Act provision (§ 70a(5)) quoted in *Cochise*. Nevertheless, was it the relative narrowness of the old Act provision that caused the court in *Cochise* to say that the contracts were not property of the estate until assumed? Were the contracts in *Cochise* property that could have been transferred? If unassumed contracts are not property of the estate, how can the estate have any rights under them until they are assumed?

2. Would the nondebtor parties in *Whitcomb & Keller* and in *Gunter Hotel* have been obligated to perform outside of bankruptcy? Did the courts in those cases hold that the nondebtor parties (Data-Link and Carlson, respectively) were obligated to perform their contracts absent court order to do so? If so, on what theory or theories? Did the court order that was affirmed in *Whitcomb & Keller* simply enforce an existing obligation of Data-Link to perform, or did it create a duty to perform, because failure of Data-Link to continue to perform would have destroyed the value of the debtor in possession's power to assume the contract? Once the debtor in possession in *Whitcomb & Keller* decided to sell its "mortgage servicing contract assets," was there any realistic chance that it would assume the contract? Did it then have an immediate duty to reject the contract under the principles stated in *Cochise*?

3. There is authority that a nondebtor party need not perform postpetition if an *express* condition precedent to its performance obligations does not occur. See South Motor Chrysler-Plymouth, Inc. v. Chrysler Motor Corp. (In re South Motor Co.), 161 B.R. 532 (Bankr. S.D. Fla. 1993) (manufacturer not liable for failing to repurchase parts inventory of auto dealer where dealer failed to obtain release of liens, failed to provide necessary inventory of parts, and failed to ship parts to location required by contract, all of which were both promises and express conditions); John Gruss Co. v. Paragon Energy Corp. (In re John Gruss Co.), 22 B.R. 236 (Bankr. D. Kan. 1982) (providing of affidavits was express condition precedent to nondebtor party's duty to pay for goods). As shown by *Whitcomb & Keller* and *Gunter Hotel,* the courts have not seemed to give the same treatment to *constructive* conditions under the Bankruptcy Code. A majority of courts hold that, if the debtor in possession elects to receive the benefits of the contract, the nondebtor party is obligated to perform even if the debtor or the estate has committed a monetary default—even one that would constitute a material breach and thus the nonoccurrence of a constructive condition under nonbankruptcy law. Is that consistent with the concept behind the Countryman definition of the term "executory contract"?

4. Assuming (contrary to *Cochise*) that the debtor's rights under an executory contract are property of the estate before the contract is assumed, can the estate's rights be better than the debtor's were, so that the estate can enforce a contract, prior to assumption, despite a material breach that would have prevented the debtor from enforcing the contract outside bankruptcy? Consider Butner v. United States, 440 U.S. 48, 99 S. Ct. 914, 59 L. Ed.2d 136 (1979). Under *Bildisco*, if the debtor "elects" to receive the nondebtor party's postpetition performance, the nondebtor party is only entitled to the reasonable value of that performance. Can the Court have meant that the nondebtor party is required to perform the contract without receiving the agreed contract rate? See In re StarNet, Inc., 355 F.3d 634, 637 (7th Cir. 2004) ("[T]he fact remains that neither § 365(a) nor anything else in bankruptcy law entitles debtors to more or different services, at lower prices, than their contracts provide. * * * In the main, and here, bankruptcy law follows non-bankruptcy entitlements.") (citing *Butner*).

5. How is *Gunter Hotel* different from *Whitcomb & Keller*? Did the court in *Gunter Hotel* act to preserve the value of the debtor's right to assume the contract? Was it proper for the court in *Gunter Hotel* to retain jurisdiction to permit rejection of the contract after confirmation? The court recognized that

unrejected and unassumed contracts survive confirmation, but the court stated that Carlson could not enforce the contract pending the postconfirmation rejection. Is the court's analysis consistent with the "ride through" doctrine?

6. Consider again Judge Easterbrook's view, in In re Kmart, 359 F.3d 866 (7th Cir. 2004) (reprinted above in Chapter Four), that a supplier with a contract to provide goods to the debtor must continue to perform after the debtor files a chapter 11 petition:

> Some supposedly critical vendors will continue to do business with the debtor because they must. They may, for example, have long term contracts, and the automatic stay prevents these vendors from walking away as long as the debtor pays for new deliveries. See 11 U.S.C. § 362. Fleming Companies, which received the largest critical-vendors payment because it sold Kmart between $70 million and $100 million of groceries and related goods weekly, was one of these. No matter how much Fleming would have liked to dump Kmart, it had no right to do so. It was unnecessary to compensate Fleming for continuing to make deliveries that it was legally required to make. * * *

Id. at 873. As the full opinion shows, Kmart filed its chapter 11 petition at a time when it owed millions of dollars to Fleming for goods delivered to Kmart. (The opinion states that another "critical vendor" was paid $49 million for goods delivered prepetition, and the paragraph excerpted here states that Kmart was paid more than any other "critical vendor.") Is Judge Easterbrook right that Fleming would have been obligated to perform the contract despite a failure by Kmart to pay $50 million or more owed under the contract? Do you need to review the contract between Kmart and Fleming to answer that question? See http://law.pepperdine.edu/scarberry for a link to the contract. Does a nondebtor party who fails to perform a contract necessarily violate the automatic stay?

Problem 7-1

A few months before filing its chapter 11 petition, Foam Corporation entered into a contract to purchase a parcel of real property next to its Denver factory for $600,000 from HighSkies Developers. Foam Corporation planned to use the parcel for a new waterbed manufacturing facility. Under the contract, Foam Corporation was to pay HighSkies $100,000 on March 20 and the remaining $500,000 on May 20. HighSkies was also to deliver possession of the parcel and a deed to Foam Corporation on May 20. Foam Corporation failed to pay the $100,000 on March 20, and still had not paid the money when it filed its chapter 11 petition on April 10. HighSkies had taken no action to try to cancel the contract as of April 10.

It is now May 20. Foam Corporation has not yet sought court approval to assume or reject the contract. BlueSkies Jet Service Co. has offered Foam Corporation $700,000 for the parcel, which is its fair market value. (A recent decision to expand the Denver airport yet again had caused the value of industrially zoned property in the area to increase.) Is HighSkies obligated to deliver possession and a deed to Foam Corporation today (a) if Foam Corporation tenders payment of $500,000 or (b) if Foam Corporation tenders nothing, but assures HighSkies that it will be entitled to an administrative expense claim in the chapter 11 case for the value of the land if the contract ultimately is rejected? What effect, if any, does the law of constructive conditions have on your analysis? What effect if any, does the Fifth Amendment's "takings" clause have on your analysis? (Remember that courts prefer to construe a statute so as to avoid constitutional difficulties, if such a construction is reasonable.)

C. CURING DEFAULTS IN EXECUTORY CONTRACTS AND UNEXPIRED LEASES

If an executory contract or unexpired lease is in default, the debtor in possession may not assume the contract or lease without first, in most cases, curing the default or giving adequate assurances that the debtor will promptly cure the default. Section 365(b). Several questions are raised by this requirement that defaults be cured. Does § 365(b) create merely an obligation to cure defaults, or does it also create a right to cure defaults that goes beyond the right to cure that would exist outside of bankruptcy? Does § 365(b)(1) authorize the debtor in possession to cure defaults beyond the time during which the debtor could have cured them under nonbankruptcy law and beyond the time provided in § 108(b)? Does it authorize the debtor in possession to cure defaults which had already become incurable under nonbankruptcy law by the time the petition was filed? When does the automatic stay prevent the nondebtor party from terminating an executory contract so that defaults can no longer be cured? Consider the following case.

Moody v. Amoco Oil Company
United States Court of Appeals, Seventh Circuit, 1984
734 F.2d 1200

[*Gerald Moody and his wholly owned corporation ("debtors") operated three Amoco service stations ("the dealerships") and a wholesale petroleum sales business selling Amoco products ("the jobbership"). In late 1982 Amoco sent debtors a termination notice for the jobbership, because debtors were more than $230,000 behind in payments for Amoco products for their jobbership business. Amoco later withdrew the termination notice and extended the deadline for payment into 1983, but debtors still did not pay the $230,000. On February 1, 1983, Amoco gave debtors notice that the jobbership would terminate on May 6, 1983 unless the past due $230,000 was paid ("cured") within fifteen days.*

Meanwhile, on January 27, 1983, Amoco had learned that debtors' bank had dishonored several checks which debtors had given to Amoco to pay for petroleum products purchased by two of the dealerships. Debtors claimed the checks were dishonored because the bank had accelerated a loan owed to the bank and seized debtors' bank account to pay the loan (as a setoff). Amoco demanded that the dishonored checks be cured (paid) within five days. Debtors and Amoco then entered into a "standstill" agreement with regard to one of the dealerships. The bankruptcy court found that the agreement was simply that Amoco would not immediately pump all of the gasoline out of the dealership's tanks as it had the right to do; the debtors claimed the agreement excused them from an immediate duty to cure the dishonored checks.

Debtors did not cure the checks and did not pay the $230,000 owed on the jobbership account. On February 3, 1983, Amoco sent notices to the debtors stating that the two dealerships would terminate in ninety days. Debtors filed chapter 11 petitions on February 4, 1983. They received the notices of termination of the dealerships the next day.

Debtors commenced an adversary proceeding in bankruptcy court seeking, among other relief, a determination that they could assume the dealership and jobbership contracts. The bankruptcy court held that the debtors could not assume any of the contracts. The district court affirmed, and the debtors appealed. The seventh circuit held, inter alia, that the notices of termination of the dealerships complied with the requirements of the contracts and of the federal Petroleum Marketing Practices Act (PMPA). The court then held that the notices were effective pursuant to the terms of the contracts when mailed, not when received. The court then turned to the debtor's third argument, which was based on the fact that, even if the notices were effective when mailed, the dealerships would not actually terminate under the notices until nearly ninety days after the filing of the petitions.]

FLAUM, Circuit Judge.

* * * Debtors' third argument relates to the timeliness of effectiveness of termination of the dealership contracts. They argue that the terminations were not effective for ninety days from the date of notice, and they filed under chapter 11 before the ninety-day period expired. Thus, according to debtors, the contracts were still executory when they filed and could be assumed under section 365.

Amoco argues that the ninety-day waiting period before the effective date of the termination does not give debtors the right to assume the contracts. After the termination notices were sent, all that remained under the contracts was the passage of time until the terminations were complete. Amoco argues that when debtors filed, there was nothing left to assume under the contract except the remaining time—ninety days—before the contract was terminated completely.

Section 365 of the Code only gives a debtor the right to assume an executory contract. If a contract has been terminated pre-bankruptcy, there is nothing left for the debtor to assume. However, the termination must be complete and not subject to reversal, either under the terms of the contract or under state law. L. King, 2 Collier on Bankruptcy ¶ 365.03 (15th ed. 1979); see In re Fontainebleau Hotel Corp., 515 F.2d 913 (5th Cir. 1975).

As discussed above, here the dealership termination notices were effective prior to debtors' filing in bankruptcy. The contract gave debtors no right to cure once the termination notices were mailed. Amoco did not have to take any further action to terminate the contracts; termination was automatic at the end of ninety days. Wisconsin law also gives debtors no right to cure.[41]

The fact that the termination itself was not effective for ninety days does not affect the result. The filing of the chapter 11 petition cannot expand debtors' rights as against Amoco. Schokbeton Industries, Inc. v. Schokbeton Products Corp., 466 F.2d 171, 176-77 (5th Cir. 1972); see Kopelman v. Halvajian (In re Triangle Laboratories, Inc.), 663 F.2d 463, 467- 68 (3d Cir. 1981). When the termination notice was sent, debtors only had a right to ninety days' worth of dealership contracts. The filing of the petition does not expand that right. This

---

41. [Footnote 10 in original:] Any right to cure to prevent termination provided by the Wisconsin Fair Dealership Law, Wis. Stat. § 135.04 (1974 & Supp. 1983) has been preempted by the PMPA. See 15 U.S.C. § 2806 (1982).

conclusion is supported by a number of decisions in the bankruptcy courts. See, e.g., New Media Irjax v. D.C. Comics, 19 B.R. 199 (Bkrtcy. M.D. Fla. 1982); In re Benrus Watch Co., 13 B.R. 331 (Bkrtcy. S.D.N.Y. 1981); In re Beck, 5 B.R. 169 (Bkrtcy. D. Haw. 1980).

Similarly, section 541(a) provides that a debtor's estate consists of "all legal or equitable interests of the debtor in property as of the commencement of a case." Thus, whatever rights a debtor has in property at the commencement of the case continue in bankruptcy—no more, no less. Section 541 "is not intended to expand the debtor's rights against others more than they exist at the commencement of the case." H.R. Rep. No. 595, 95th Cong., 1st Sess., reprinted in 1978 U.S. Code Cong. & Ad. News 5787.

Section 362, which creates an automatic stay of certain creditor actions upon the filing of a petition in the bankruptcy court, does not help debtors here. The automatic stay does not toll the mere running of time under a contract, and thus it does not prevent automatic termination of the contract. See Johnson v. First National Bank of Montevideo, 719 F.2d 270, 273 (8th Cir. 1983), cert. denied, __ U.S. __, 104 S. Ct. 1015, 79 L. Ed. 2d 245 (1984). See also, e.g., In re Anne Cara Oil Co., 32 B.R. 643, 647-48 (Bkrtcy. D. Mass. 1983); In re Nashville White Trucks, 5 B.R. 112, 117 (Bkrtcy. M.D. Tenn. 1980). Section 362 does not give a debtor greater rights in a contract. Trigg v. United States, 630 F.2d 1370, 1372 (10th Cir. 1980). Thus, debtors cannot rely on section 362 to prevent termination of the contracts. * * *

E.

Debtors argue that even if the dealerships were terminated before they filed for bankruptcy, they can assume the contracts because the power to cure defaults under section 365 includes the power to revive an executory contract terminated pre-bankruptcy. Debtors cite DiPierro v. Taddeo, 685 F.2d 24 (2d Cir. 1982), for the proposition that a debtor may cure and revive a contract.

Taddeo, however, is distinguishable. In *Taddeo,* debtors had defaulted on their mortgage payments. The mortgage holder accelerated the mortgage and instituted foreclosure proceedings. Before the holder could obtain a final judgment of foreclosure and sale, debtors filed a petition for relief under chapter 13. Under applicable state law, debtors could have avoided foreclosure by paying off the full amount of the mortgage. Thus, the contract had not been fully terminated pre-bankruptcy, in contrast to the situation in this case. See In re Clark, 32 B.R. 711 (W.D. Wis. 1983).

Where a contract has been validly terminated pre-bankruptcy, the debtors' rights to continued performance under the contract have expired. The filing of a petition under chapter 11 cannot resuscitate those rights. See In re Triangle Laboratories, Inc., 663 F.2d at 467-68. Here, the dealership contracts were terminated and cannot be revived.

F.

Debtors argue that the jobbership contract is assumable because they filed for bankruptcy before the expiration of the fifteen-day cure period allowed by the jobbership termination notice. Thus, according to debtors, the contract was executory at the time of filing. Under section 365(d)(1), debtors may assume an executory agreement at any time before confirmation of the plan. Debtors contend that therefore the jobbership is still assumable.

Amoco argues that under section 108(b) of the Code, debtors had only sixty days from the date of filing to cure the default. Because debtors failed to cure within the sixty days, Amoco argues that debtors may no longer assume the contract.

The bankruptcy court held that section 108(b) controlled and thus, debtors would have had to cure the default within sixty days if they wanted to assume the contract. The district court did not separately address the issue.

Section 365 provides that the debtor may assume or reject an executory contract at any time before confirmation of the plan. 11 U.S.C. § 365(d)(2). If there has been a default under the contract, the debtor must cure the default at the time of the assumption. 11 U.S.C. § 365(b)(1)(A). This court has summarized the policy behind section 365 as follows:

> Since a debtor is in limbo until confirmation of a plan, it is understandably difficult to commit itself to assuming or rejecting a contract much before the time for confirmation of a plan.... This procedure insures that the debtor is not in the precarious position of having assumed a contract relying on confirmation of a particular plan, only to find the plan to have been rejected.

Data-Link Systems, Inc. v. Whitcomb & Keller Mortgage Co., 715 F.2d 375, 378 (7th Cir. 1983) (quoting unpublished bankruptcy order of April 8, 1981).

Section 108(b) provides in part that where an agreement fixes a time period in which the debtor may cure a default, the debtor may cure before the later of the expiration of the time period or sixty days after the filing of the petition. We hold, however, that section 108(b) does not apply to curing defaults in executory contracts. Section 365 specifically governs the time for curing defaults in executory contracts, and thus, it controls here. See In re McLouth Steel Corp., 20 B.R. 688 (Bkrtcy.E.D.Mich. 1982).[42] At the time debtors filed their petition, the time for cure had not expired. The contract was still executory. See In re Easthampton Sand & Gravel Co., 25 B.R. 193, 197 (Bkrtcy.E.D.N.Y. 1982). Under section 365(a), debtors may still elect to assume the contract. If debtors ultimately determine to assume it, they may cure the default at any time prior to the assumption, pursuant to section 365(b)(1)(A).

---

42. [Footnote 15 in original:] The bankruptcy court relied on In re Santa Fe Development and Mortgage Corp., 16 B.R. 165 (Bkrtcy. 9th Cir. 1981), for the proposition that § 108(b) applied in this case. *Santa Fe,* however, applied § 108(b) to permit the debtor to make a payment to extend an escrow. The analysis did not deal with curing a default under an executory contract.

In Johnson v. First National Bank of Montevideo, 719 F.2d 270 (8th Cir. 1983), cert. denied, __ U.S. __, 104 S. Ct. 1015, 79 L. Ed. 2d 245 (1984), the court held that § 108(b) rather than § 362 controlled the time of expiration of a statutory period of redemption of a mortgage. *Johnson* is distinguishable. Section 362 does not explicitly provide a time limit for statutory periods of redemption, and thus there is no express conflict between § 362 and § 108(b). In contrast, § 365 expressly provides a time limit for cure of defaults under executory contracts. We should not apply § 108(b) so as to cause an irreconcilable conflict between the two sections. Id. at 278 (citing Bank of Commonwealth v. Bevan, 13 B.R. 989 (E.D.Mich. 1981). We express no opinion as to whether the decision in *Johnson* is correct.

This holding is consistent with the policies underlying the different provisions and the Code in general. The purpose behind section 108(b) is to permit the debtor an extension of time for doing certain acts necessary to preserve his rights. It would be anomalous to apply it to restrict debtors' rights, as Amoco would have us do here. Applying section 108(b) here would force debtors to decide whether to cure long before they must decide whether to assume or reject the contract and long before they know whether any reorganization plan will be confirmed. Finally, the purpose behind chapter 11 is "to permit successful rehabilitation of debtors" and "to prevent a debtor from going into liquidation." NLRB v. Bildisco & Bildisco, __ U.S. __, 104 S. Ct. 1188, 1197, 79 L. Ed. 2d 482 (1984). Debtors must be permitted a certain amount of flexibility in determining whether to assume or to reject a contract. Specific provisions of the Code should be interpreted with this goal in mind. To interpret the Code so as to minimize flexibility and rush the debtor into what may be an improvident decision does not further the purposes of the reorganization provisions.

We emphasize that this holding does not leave the other party to the contract without remedy until the time for confirmation of the plan. A party who cannot afford the uncertainty during the pendency of the reorganization may request the bankruptcy court to order the debtor to decide whether to assume or reject the contract within a specified period. 11 U.S.C. § 365(d)(2). * * *

NOTES

1. The court in *Moody* suggests that the automatic stay would prohibit Amoco from taking any action postpetition to cancel the contracts. It is generally held that an attempt postpetition by the nondebtor party to terminate a contract is a violation of the automatic stay, because it constitutes an attempt to exercise control over property of the estate. See, e.g., Computer Commc'ns, Inc. v. Codex Corp. (In re Computer Commc'ns, Inc.), 824 F.2d 725 (9th Cir. 1987); In re Edwards Mobile Home Sales, Inc. v. Ohio Cas. Ins. Co. (In re Edwards Mobile Home Sales, Inc.), 119 B.R. 857 (Bankr. M.D. Fla. 1990); see Epstein, Nickles & White, BANKRUPTCY §3-14 at 99-100. Such a result would seem to depend on the contract rights becoming property of the estate before the contract is assumed.

   There is an alternative reason why a nondebtor party cannot cancel an executory contract once a bankruptcy petition is filed, assuming cancellation means the complete and final elimination of the contract. As *Moody* illustrates, Section 365 gives the trustee (or debtor in possession) the power to cure any defaults and to assume the contract. See § 365(a) and (b); Bordewieck, *The Postpetition, Pre-Rejection, Pre-Assumption Status of an Executory Contract*, 59 AM. BANKR. L.J. 197, 204-06 (1985). Nothing in the Bankruptcy Code gives the nondebtor party the right to eliminate the trustee's power to cure defaults and to assume the contract. Cancellation—a complete and final elimination of the contract—would by definition prevent the trustee from exercising that power; thus the nondebtor party cannot have the right to cancel the contract.

2. Is the court right when it says that the filing of bankruptcy "cannot expand debtors' rights as against Amoco"? See § 365(b)(2) and (e)(1) (invalidating ipso facto clauses in bankruptcy and providing that certain defaults need not be cured that could permit termination of a contract outside of bankruptcy); § 365(f)(1) (expanding debtor in possession's right to assign contracts beyond right debtor had outside of bankruptcy). Did the filing expand the debtors' rights with respect to the jobbership contract? If so, what provision of the Code is responsible for the expansion?

3. If the debtors had an expanded right to cure the default on the jobbership contract, why did they not have an expanded right to cure the default on the dealership contracts? Is the court right when it says that those contracts were validly terminated prepetition and therefore the debtors' rights could not be resuscitated? Were the dealership contracts still in effect at the time the petition was filed? Were the dealership contracts "executory" at the time the petition was filed? Is the problem that the default became incurable—the right to cure had terminated—before the petition was filed? Cf. § 365(b)(2)(D).

4. In In re RB Furniture, Inc., 141 B.R. 706 (Bankr. C.D. Cal. 1992), the debtor and its landlord had agreed prepetition to a modification of the real property lease because of the debtor's financial difficulties. Under the agreement, the debtor did not have to pay rent for one year, but the debtor was still obligated to make other payments, including paying all property taxes on the premises. Under the agreement, all of the abated rent would be due and payable on ten days' notice if the debtor defaulted on any of its remaining obligations and failed to cure the default within twenty days. Within that year the debtor filed a chapter 11 petition and then paid only a portion of the property taxes that came due. When the default was not cured within twenty days, the landlord sent a notice that the entire amount of the abated rent was due in ten days. The court had determined that the debtor in possession was not required under § 365(d)(3) to pay the entire property tax bill but only the prorated portion for the period of time after the filing of the chapter 11 petition. The debtor in possession paid only that prorated amount—thus less than the lease required—and also paid it late, because the court had given the debtor in possession an extension of time under § 365(d)(3) to pay the prorated taxes. The court held that the failure to pay the full amount of the property taxes on time was a default under the lease, which, pursuant to the terms of the lease, would make all of the abated rent up to that point due and payable on ten days' notice. Much of that seven months' rent would be for the time after the filing of the petition, and thus the debtor in possession would seem to have been obligated to pay it under § 365(d)(3). In the course of determining that the debtor was not required at that time to pay the amount of the abated rent under § 365(d)(3), the court reasoned that if the debtor decided to assume the lease and cured the default by paying the unpaid part of the property taxes, then that cure of the default would also eliminate all consequences of the default. Thus, if the debtor cured the default, it would be as if no default had ever occurred and the debtor would never have to pay the abated rent. How would that approach apply to the dealership contracts in *Moody*? Is the court right in saying that an eventual payment of the unpaid part of the property taxes would cure the failure to pay it on time? Was the default in paying taxes late incurable? If so, would it be impossible for the debtor in possession to satisfy § 365(b)(1) and thus impossible for the debtor in possession to assume the lease? How would § 365(b)(2)(D) (added in 1994 and amended by the 2005 BAPCPA) have affected the analysis if it had been part of the Code at the time *RB Furniture* was decided?

5. If a contract has already been terminated when the petition is filed, to what extent can the debtor in possession take advantage of nonbankruptcy antiforfeiture laws to reinstate the contract? See 3 Resnick & Sommer, COLLIER ON BANKRUPTCY ¶ 365.02[2], at 365-23; In re Burke, 76 F.Supp. 5 (S.D. Cal. 1948); City of Valdez v. Waterkist Corp. (In re Waterkist Corp.), 775 F.2d 1089 (9th Cir. 1985).

Problem 7-2

> Foam Corporation purchased vinyl for its waterbed production line from VinCo under a three year contract. The contract provided that VinCo would provide all of Foam Corporation's requirements for vinyl at fifty cents per square foot, if payment was made within twenty days of delivery, as required by their contract. The contract also provided that the price would be fifty-two cents per square foot for vinyl delivered at any time when any amount owed by Foam Corporation under the contract was more than ten days overdue. Because of late payments, Foam Corporation had been paying the fifty-two cent price on all vinyl for a year and a half at the time Foam Corporation filed its petition. If Foam Corporation cures the defaults and assumes the contract, will it be entitled to a refund of two cents per square foot for all of the vinyl purchased and paid for within the year and a half before the petition was filed? For all of the vinyl delivered prepetition but not paid for, what price must be paid to cure the default? What else must Foam Corporation do under § 365(b) to assume the contract with Vinco?

Problem 7-3

> Foam Corporation leases four of its plants from Imperial Insurance under long term leases. The Denver and Seattle plants were built and leased in 1992, the Philadelphia and Camden plants in 1996. In 1996 Foam Corporation and Imperial Insurance entered into a "master lease" which covers all four plants, and which superseded the 1992 "master lease," which had covered the Denver and Seattle plants. The 1996 master lease includes a cross-default clause, under which a failure to pay rent or other default as to any of the plants is a default as to the entire master lease and all of the plants. Foam Corporation owes two months' rent on each plant for the two months before the filing of the chapter 11 petition. Foam Corporation has made the postpetition rental payments on all four plants faithfully up until now. Foam Corporation has made a reasoned determination that it will not be able to turn around the financial situation at either of the Philadelphia or Camden plants, and thus it has closed them. On the other hand, the Denver and Seattle plants are now producing enough revenue to more than cover their respective operating expenses. Thus Foam Corporation has now filed a motion seeking to reject the leases on the Philadelphia and Camden plants and to assume the leases on the Denver and Seattle plants. Is Foam Corporation entitled to do so? If Foam Corporation is entitled to assume the lease with respect to two plants and reject it with respect to the other two, what must Foam Corporation do to assume the Denver and Seattle plants? See In re Adelphia Bus. Solutions, Inc., 322 B.R. 51 (Bankr. S.D.N.Y. 2005).

D. THE DECISION TO ASSUME OR REJECT: STANDARDS FOR COURT APPROVAL AND THE EFFECT OF THE DECISION

The decision of the debtor in possession to assume or reject an executory contract or lease is subject to the court's approval. Section 365(a). What standard should the court apply in deciding whether to approve the debtor in possession's decision to reject? to assume? Should the court take into account the hardship that rejection could cause to the nondebtor party or only consider what is best for the bankruptcy estate? Should the court determine for itself whether rejection or assumption will be in the best interests of the estate, or should the court defer to the debtor in possession's business judgment?

There is substantial controversy over the effect of rejection. What is the effect on an executory contract or unexpired lease (and on the parties) if the debtor in possession rejects it?

One effect of rejection is noncontroversial: it gives the nondebtor party a claim for breach, which ordinarily will be a prepetition, general unsecured claim. See § 502(g). What other effects, if any, flow from rejection? Does rejection constitute a rescission of the contract or in some other way cause it to cease to exist? Does rejection eliminate any right that the nondebtor party might have to specific enforcement of the contract or to other injunctive relief? Is rejection a kind of avoiding power that will allow the debtor in possession to retrieve property already transferred under the rejected contract?

Suppose, for example, that the debtor filed a petition in bankruptcy some time after entering into a contract to sell land but before either party had performed. Outside bankruptcy, buyers ordinarily can obtain specific performance of such contracts. But, as we noted above, the traditional understanding was that rejection of a contract for sale of land would cut off the buyer's right to specific enforcement. See Countryman, *Contracts in Bankruptcy*, supra, 57 MINN. L. REV. at 463-74.

In influential articles published from 1988 to 1991 (and already noted above), Professors Andrew and Westbrook argued that rejection of an executory contract (or unexpired lease) should not have such a dramatic effect of relieving the debtor and the estate's property of contract obligations. Professor Andrew argued that rejection is simply the refusal of the debtor in possession to take the benefits of the contract for the estate and to make the burdens of the contract administrative obligations of the estate. Professor Westbrook argued that rejection is simply the exercise of a power given to the debtor in possession to breach the debtor's prepetition contracts. Both of them concluded that rejection does not amount to a rescission, does not eliminate the contract, does not destroy property rights transferred under the contract before rejection, and should not eliminate the nondebtor party's right to seek specific performance of the contract. See Andrew, *Understanding Rejection*, supra, 59 U. COLO. L. REV. 845 ; Westbrook, *Executory Contracts*, supra, 74 MINN. L. REV. 227; Andrew, *Executory Contracts Revisited*, supra, 62 U. COLO. L. REV. 1.

They argued specifically that rejection should not eliminate any property interest created by the contract, because bankruptcy law takes as a given the property interests "created and defined by state law." Butner v. United States, 440 U.S. 48, 55, 99 S. Ct. 914, 918, 59 L. Ed. 2d 136, 141-42 (1979). Those property interests can be altered or eliminated by specific bankruptcy provisions—such as the avoiding powers in sections 544, 547, and 548, which we discuss below in Chapter Eight—but, Andrew and Westbrook argued, section 365 is not such a provision. Thus, a contract for purchase of land from the debtor should remain specifically enforceable to the extent that the buyer merely seeks to obtain title to the land, because the contract gave the buyer a property interest in the land.[43]

Because rejection should thus have only a limited effect, Professors Andrew and Westbrook argued that the question whether a contract is executory—and thus subject to rejection under section 365(a)—is less important than many courts think, perhaps of so little importance that no test of "executoriness" should be required for a contract to be subject to being rejected.

As noted above, Professor Countryman demonstrated that rejection traditionally had a more dramatic effect, including the cutting off of the nondebtor buyer's right to specific performance of a contract for sale of land. Under that approach it can be very important to determine whether a contract is executory and thus subject to rejection. (As Professor Countryman explained, the cases held that a contract for sale of land was executory—and hence could be rejected—unless the seller had conveyed title or the buyer had paid the full price. See Countryman, *Contracts in Bankruptcy*, supra, 57 MINN. L. REV. at 463-74.) Many courts follow that traditional understanding by holding that rejection frees property of the estate from claims for specific performance of executory contracts. See, e.g., Lubrizol Enterprises, Inc. v. Richmond Metal Finishers, Inc. (In re Richmond Metal Finishers, Inc.), 756 F.2d 1043 (4th Cir. 1985) (reprinted below); Benevides v. Alexander (In re Alexander), 670 F.2d 885 (9th Cir. 1982); In re Nickels Midway Pier, LLC, 332 B.R. 262 (Bankr. D.N.J. 2005); In re Balco Equities Ltd., 323 B.R. 85 (Bankr. S.D.N.Y. 2005); Butler v. Resident Care Innovation Corp., 241 B.R. 37 (D.R.I. 1999); In re A.J. Lane & Co., 107 B.R. 435 (Bankr. D. Mass. 1989) (reprinted below).

Other courts have begun to accept the Andrew/Westbrook analysis, or at least parts of it. At least four circuits have held specifically that rejection does not terminate the rejected contract or lease, a key part of the Andrew/Westbrook analysis. See Med. Malpractice Ins. Ass'n v. Hirsch (In re Lavigne),114 F.3d 379 (2d Cir. 1997); Eastover Bank for Savings v. Sowashee Venture (In re Austin Development Co.), 19 F.3d 1077 (5th Cir. 1994); Kopolow v. P.M. Holding Corp. (In re Modern Textile, Inc.), 900 F.2d 1184 (8th Cir. 1990); Leasing Service Corp. v. First Tennessee Bank, 826 F.2d 434 (6th Cir. 1987) (pre-dating initial Andrew article). The Andrew/Westbrook analysis is finding its way into district court and bankruptcy court decisions, sometimes leading to a result contrary to what the traditional understanding would yield. See, e.g., In re Bergt, 241 B.R. 17 (Bankr. D. Alaska 1999) (holding that real estate right of first refusal given by debtor was not an

---

43. However, if the contract was not recorded before the filing of the bankruptcy petition, the buyer's property interest could be avoided under section 544(a)(3), the "hypothetical bona fide purchaser of real property" avoiding power, which is discussed below in Chapter Eight. In addition, we discuss in Chapter Sixteen the possibility that the right to specific performance might be a claim which is dischargeable in bankruptcy, with the result that the discharge would terminate the right to specific performance.

executory contract, and also apparently holding in the alternative that rejection would not in any event eliminate nondebtor's property rights); In re Walnut Associates, 145 B.R. 489, 494 (Bankr. E.D. Pa. 1992) (agreeing with Andrew and Westbrook that rejection "does not invalidate, rejudicate, repeal, or avoid an executory contract," that rejection's only effect is that the contract is not assumed so that the nondebtor party does not have an administrative claim, and that rejection has no effect on any right to specific performance).

It is not as clear that under the traditional approach rejection freed the debtor from a specifically enforceable personal obligation, such as a covenant not to compete. Courts split on whether rejection precludes such specific enforcement. Some courts influenced by Andrew and Westbrook hold that rejection has no effect on the nondebtor party's right to seek specific performance or similar equitable relief. They typically analyze the issue in terms of the discharge: if the right to equitable relief constitutes a claim under section 101(5)(B), and if that claim is discharged (e.g., under section 1141(d)), then the right to specific performance is eliminated. See, e.g., Creator's Way Associated Labels, Inc. v. Mitchell (In re Mitchell), 249 B.R. 55 (Bankr. S.D.N.Y. 2000). Other courts hold that rejection eliminates equitable rights flowing from the contract. See, e.g., In re Cloyd, 238 B.R. 328 (Bankr. E.D. Mich. 1999). See discussion in Chapter Sixteen of this text below.

The Supreme Court has held that Congress, in enacting the Bankruptcy Code in 1978, should not be thought to have intended major changes in pre-Code bankruptcy law unless there is a clear basis in the text of the Code or in its legislative history for thinking that a major change was intended. See Midlantic National Bank v. New Jersey Department of Environmental Protection, 474 U.S. 494, 106 S. Ct. 755, 88 L. Ed. 2d 859 (1986); Kelly v. Robinson, 479 U.S. 36, 107 S. Ct. 353, 93 L. Ed. 2d 216 (1986). The Court may not have been completely consistent in applying that approach, see United States v. Ron Pair Enterprises, Inc., 489 U.S. 235, 249-54, 109 S. Ct. 1026, 1034-37, 103 L. Ed. 2d 290, 303-07 (1989) (dissent by Justice O'Connor). Nevertheless there is a serious question whether the courts should be reformulating executory contract law under the Code, absent clear justification in the text of the Code or in its legislative history. That serious question must be answered whether the courts change the traditional pre-Code understanding in a way that helps nondebtors or in a way that hurts nondebtors and facilitates reorganization.

Consider the following cases and materials. Congress legislatively overruled the holding of the following case as it applies specifically to intellectual property licenses. See § 365(n). The case remains, however, very important and controversial for its general approach to the effect of rejection and to the application of the Countryman test for "executoriness."

Lubrizol Enterprises, Inc. v. Richmond Metal Finishers, Inc.
(In re Richmond Metal Finishers, Inc.)
United States Court of Appeals, Fourth Circuit, 1985
756 F.2d 1043

James Dickson Phillips, Circuit Judge:

The question is whether Richmond Metal Finishers (RMF), a bankrupt debtor in possession, should have been allowed to reject as executory a technology licensing agreement with Lubrizol Enterprises (Lubrizol) as licensee. * * *

I

In July of 1982, RMF entered into the contract with Lubrizol that granted Lubrizol a nonexclusive license to utilize a metal coating process technology owned by RMF. RMF owed the following duties to Lubrizol under the agreement: (1) to notify Lubrizol of any patent infringement suit and to defend in such suit; (2) to notify Lubrizol of any other use or licensing of the process, and to reduce royalty payments if a lower royalty rate agreement was reached with another licensee; and (3) to indemnify Lubrizol for losses arising out of any misrepresentation or breach of warranty by RMF. Lubrizol owed RMF reciprocal duties of accounting for and paying royalties for use of the process and of cancelling certain existing indebtedness. The contract provided that Lubrizol would defer use of the process until May 1, 1983, and in fact, Lubrizol has never used the RMF technology.

RMF filed a petition for bankruptcy pursuant to Chapter 11 of the Bankruptcy Code on August 16, 1983. As part of its plan to emerge from bankruptcy, RMF sought, pursuant to § 365(a), to reject the contract with Lubrizol in order to facilitate sale or licensing of the technology unhindered by restrictive provisions in the Lubrizol agreement. On RMF's motion for approval of the rejection, the bankruptcy court properly interpreted § 365 as requiring it to undertake a two-step inquiry to determine the propriety of rejection: first, whether the contract is executory; next, if so, whether its rejection would be advantageous to the bankrupt.

Making that inquiry, the bankruptcy court determined that both tests were satisfied and approved the rejection. But, as indicated, the district court then reversed that determination on the basis that neither test was satisfied and disallowed the rejection. This appeal followed.

II

We conclude initially that, as the bankruptcy court ruled, the technology licensing agreement in this case was an executory contract, within contemplation of 11 U.S.C. § 365(a). Under that provision a contract is executory if performance is due to some extent on both sides. NLRB v. Bildisco and Bildisco, __ U.S. __, __, 104 S. Ct. 1188, 1194 n.6, 79 L. Ed. 2d 482 (1984). This court has recently adopted Professor Countryman's more specific test for determining whether a contract is "executory" in the required sense. By that test, a contract is executory if the "'obligations of both the bankrupt and the other party to the contract are so far unperformed that the failure of either to complete the performance would constitute a material breach excusing the performance of the other.'" Gloria Manufacturing Corp. v. International Ladies' Garment Workers' Union, 734 F.2d

1020, 1022 (4th Cir. 1984) (quoting Countryman, *Executory Contracts in Bankruptcy: Part I,* 57 MINN. L. REV. 439, 460 (1973). This issue is one of law that may be freely reviewed by successive courts.

Applying that test here, we conclude that the licensing agreement was at the critical time executory. RMF owed Lubrizol the continuing duties of notifying Lubrizol of further licensing of the process and of reducing Lubrizol's royalty rate to meet any more favorable rates granted to subsequent licensees. By their terms, RMF's obligations to give notice and to restrict its right to license its process at royalty rates it desired without lowering Lubrizol's royalty rate extended over the life of the agreement, and remained unperformed. Moreover, RMF owed Lubrizol additional contingent duties of notifying it of suits, defending suits and indemnifying it for certain losses.

The unperformed, continuing core obligations of notice and forbearance in licensing made the contract executory as to RMF. In Fenix Cattle Co. v. Silver (In re Select-A-Seat Corp.), 625 F.2d 290, 292 (9th Cir. 1980), the court found that an obligation of a debtor to refrain from selling software packages under an exclusive licensing agreement made a contract executory as to the debtor notwithstanding the continuing obligation was only one of forbearance. Although the license to Lubrizol was not exclusive, RMF owed the same type of unperformed continuing duty of forbearance arising out of the most favored licensee clause running in favor of Lubrizol. Breach of that duty would clearly constitute a material breach of the agreement.

Moreover, the contract was further executory as to RMF because of the contingent duties that RMF owed of giving notice of and defending infringement suits and of indemnifying Lubrizol for certain losses arising out of the use of the technology. Contingency of an obligation does not prevent its being executory under § 365. See In re Smith Jones, Inc., 26 B.R. 289, 292 (Bankr. D. Minn. 1982) (warranty obligations executory as to promisor); In re O.P.M. Leasing Services, Inc., 23 B.R. 104, 117 (Bankr. S.D.N.Y. 1982) (obligation to defend infringement suits makes contract executory as to promisor). Until the time has expired during which an event triggering a contingent duty may occur, the contingent obligation represents a continuing duty to stand ready to perform if the contingency occurs. A breach of that duty once it was triggered by the contingency (or presumably, by anticipatory repudiation) would have been material.

Because a contract is not executory within the meaning of § 365(a) unless it is executory as to both parties, it is also necessary to determine whether the licensing agreement was executory as to Lubrizol. See *Bildisco,* ___ U.S. at ___, 104 S. Ct. at 1194 n.6. We conclude that it was.

Lubrizol owed RMF the unperformed and continuing duty of accounting for and paying royalties for the life of the agreement. It is true that a contract is not executory as to a party simply because the party is obligated to make payments of money to the other party. Therefore, if Lubrizol had owed RMF nothing more than a duty to make fixed payments or cancel specified indebtedness under the agreement, the agreement would not be executory as to Lubrizol. However, the promise to account for and pay royalties required that Lubrizol deliver written quarterly sales reports and keep books of account subject to inspection by an independent Certified Public Accountant. This promise goes beyond a mere debt, or promise to pay money, and was at the critical time executory. See Fenix Cattle, 625 F.2d at 292. Additionally, subject to certain exceptions, Lubrizol was obligated to keep all license technology in confidence for a number of years.

Since the licensing agreement is executory as to each party, it is executory within the meaning of § 365(a), and the district court erred as a matter of law in reaching a contrary conclusion.[44]

III

There remains the question whether rejection of the executory contract would be advantageous to the bankrupt. See Borman's, Inc. v. Allied Supermarkets, Inc., 706 F.2d 187, 189 (6th Cir. 1983). Courts addressing that question must start with the proposition that the bankrupt's decision upon it is to be accorded the deference mandated by the sound business judgment rule as generally applied by courts to discretionary actions or decisions of corporate directors. See *Bildisco,* __ U.S. at __, 104 S. Ct. at 1195 (noting that the business judgment rule is the "traditional" test); Group of Institutional Investors v. Chicago, Milwaukee, St. Paul & Pacific Railroad, 318 U.S. 523, 550, 63 S. Ct. 727, 742, 87 L. Ed. 959 (1943) (applying business judgment rule to bankrupt's decision whether to affirm or reject lease); Control Data Corp. v. Zelman (In re Minges), 602 F.2d 38, 43 (2d Cir. 1979) (applying *Institutional Investors* outside of railroad reorganizations); Carey v. Mobil Oil Corp. (In re Tilco, Inc.), 558 F.2d 1369, 1372-73 (10th Cir. 1977) (applying *Institutional Investors* to rejection of gas contracts).

As generally formulated and applied in corporate litigation the rule is that courts should defer to—should not interfere with—decisions of corporate directors upon matters entrusted to their business judgment except upon a finding of bad faith or gross abuse of their "business discretion." See, e.g., Lewis v. Anderson, 615 F.2d 778, 782 (9th Cir. 1979); Polin v. Conductron Corp., 552 F.2d 797, 809 (8th Cir. 1977). Transposed to the bankruptcy context, the rule as applied to a bankrupt's decision to reject an executory contract because of perceived business advantage requires that the decision be accepted by courts unless it is shown that the bankrupt's decision was one taken in bad faith or in gross abuse of the bankrupt's retained business discretion.

In bankruptcy litigation the issue is of course first presented for judicial determination when a debtor, having decided that rejection will be beneficial within contemplation of § 365(a), moves for approval of the rejection. The issue thereby presented for first instance judicial determination by the bankruptcy court is whether the decision of the debtor that rejection will be advantageous is so manifestly unreasonable that it could not be based on sound business judgment, but only on bad faith, or whim or caprice. That issue is one of fact to be decided

---

44. [Footnote * in original:] We disagree with the district court's characterization of the transaction as effectively a completed sale of property. If an analogy is to be made, licensing agreements are more similar to leases than to sales of property because of the limited nature of the interest conveyed. Congress expressly made leases subject to rejection under § 365 in order to "preclude any uncertainty as to whether a lease is an executory contract" under § 365. 2 Collier on Bankruptcy ¶ 365.02 (L. King 15th ed. 1984).

as such by the bankruptcy court by the normal processes of fact adjudication. And the resulting fact determination by the bankruptcy court is perforce then reviewable up the line under the clearly erroneous standard. See *Minges,* 602 F.2d at 43; see generally 1 Collier on Bankruptcy ¶ 3.03(8)(b) (L. King 15th ed. 1984).

Here, the bankruptcy judge had before him evidence not rebutted by Lubrizol that the metal coating process subject to the licensing agreement is RMF's principal asset and that sale or licensing of the technology represented the primary potential source of funds by which RMF might emerge from bankruptcy. The testimony of RMF's president, also factually uncontested by Lubrizol, indicated that sale or further licensing of the technology would be facilitated by stripping Lubrizol of its rights in the process and that, correspondingly, continued obligation to Lubrizol under the agreement would hinder RMF's capability to sell or license the technology on more advantageous terms to other potential licensees. On the basis of this evidence the bankruptcy court determined that the debtor's decision to reject was based upon sound business judgment and approved it.

On appeal the district court simply found to the contrary that the debtor's decision to reject did not represent a sound business judgment. The district court's determination rested essentially on two grounds: that RMF's purely contingent obligations under the agreement were not sufficiently onerous that relief from them would constitute a substantial benefit to RMF; and that because rejection could not deprive Lubrizol of all its rights to the technology, rejection could not reasonably be found beneficial. We conclude that in both of these respects the district court's factual findings, at odds with those of the bankruptcy court, were clearly erroneous and cannot stand.

A

In finding that the debtor's contingent obligations were not sufficiently onerous that relief from them would be beneficial, the district court could only have been substituting its business judgment for that of the debtor. There is nothing in the record from which it could be concluded that the debtor's decision on that point could not have been reached by the exercise of sound (though possibly faulty) business judgment in the normal process of evaluating alternative courses of action. If that could not be concluded, then the business judgment rule required that the debtor's factual evaluation be accepted by the court, as it had been by the bankruptcy court.

B

On the second point, we can only conclude that the district court was under a misapprehension of controlling law in thinking that by rejecting the agreement the debtor could not deprive Lubrizol of all rights to the process. Under 11 U.S.C. § 365(g), Lubrizol would be entitled to treat rejection as a breach and seek a money damages remedy; however, it could not seek to retain its contract rights in the technology by specific performance even if that remedy would ordinarily be available upon breach of this type of contract. See In re Waldron, 36 B.R. 633, 642 n.4 (Bankr. S.D. Fla. 1984). Even though § 365(g) treats rejection as a breach, the legislative history of § 365(g) makes clear that the purpose of the provision is to provide only a damages remedy for the non-bankrupt party. H. Rep. No. 95-595,

95th Cong., 2d Sess. 349, reprinted in 1978 U.S. Code Cong. & Ad. News 5963, 6305. For the same reason, Lubrizol cannot rely on provisions within its agreement with RMF for continued use of the technology by Lubrizol upon breach by RMF. Here again, the statutory "breach" contemplated by § 365(g) controls, and provides only a money damages remedy for the non-bankrupt party. Allowing specific performance would obviously undercut the core purpose of rejection under § 365(a), and that consequence cannot therefore be read into congressional intent.

IV

Lubrizol strongly urges upon us policy concerns in support of the district court's refusal to defer to the debtor's decision to reject or, preliminarily, to treat the contract as executory for § 365(a) purposes. We understand the concerns, but think they cannot control decision here.

It cannot be gainsaid that allowing rejection of such contracts as executory imposes serious burdens upon contracting parties such as Lubrizol. Nor can it be doubted that allowing rejection in this and comparable cases could have a general chilling effect upon the willingness of such parties to contract at all with businesses in possible financial difficulty. But under bankruptcy law such equitable considerations may not be indulged by courts in respect of the type of contract here in issue. Congress has plainly provided for the rejection of executory contracts, notwithstanding the obvious adverse consequences for contracting parties thereby made inevitable. Awareness by Congress of those consequences is indeed specifically reflected in the special treatment accorded to union members under collective bargaining contracts, see Bildisco, __ U.S. at __, 104 S. Ct. at 1193-96, and to lessees of real property, see 11 U.S.C. § 365(h). But no comparable special treatment is provided for technology licensees such as Lubrizol. They share the general hazards created by § 365 for all business entities dealing with potential bankrupts in the respects at issue here.

The judgment of the district court is reversed and the case is remanded for entry of judgment in conformity with that entered by the bankruptcy court.

NOTES

1. Congress legislatively overruled *Lubrizol* by enacting § 365(n). It permits the licensee, despite rejection of the licensing contract by the trustee (or debtor in possession), to retain its rights in licensed intellectual property as they existed immediately before the bankruptcy case commenced and to enforce exclusivity provisions of the agreement (but not to specifically enforce any other rights). If the licensee elects to retain its rights, the trustee must perform any obligation under the contract to deliver to the licensee any intellectual property held by the trustee. This delivery obligation allows a computer program licensee to ensure access to the "source code" version of the program when necessary. Computer programs are often written by programmers in what is called "source code," a format in which it is relatively easy to locate and fix problems in the programs—to "debug" them. But programs are usually delivered to licensees in a form known as "object code," a form in which it is very difficult to debug the program. The computer must convert source code to object code in order to run the program. Thus a program distributed as object code runs more quickly than one distributed as source code. Licensors are reluctant to distribute source code to customers for an additional reason. Access to the source code makes it much easier not only to debug the

program but also to modify it or enhance in violation of the licensor's copyright. Under § 365(n), if the license agreement gives the licensee the right to obtain a copy of the source code for the program so that the licensee can debug the program, the trustee would be obligated to deliver a copy. However, since § 365(n) only permits the licensee to retain the intellectual property as it existed immediately before the commencement of the case, would the licensee have the right to debug the program and then keep and use it in its newly debugged form?

2. Do you agree that the contract in *Lubrizol* was executory? Did the court stretch the Countryman test to reach that result? Suppose Vendor contracted to sell land to Vendee on an installment payment plan and conveyed the land to Vendee before Vendee had made all the payments. Could the court's approach in *Lubrizol* lead to a finding that the land sale contract was executory after conveyance of title, because Vendor still had duties not to trespass on the land and not to demand larger monthly payments than those provided for in the contract? As Professor Countryman pointed out, the courts do not treat such contracts as executory. See Countryman, *Contracts in Bankruptcy,* supra, 57 MINN. L. REV. at 463-74.

3. A simple example will illustrate one kind of analysis the debtor could undertake in deciding whether to reject a contract. Suppose the contract is to construct a retaining wall for $7,000; the debtor has been paid $3,000 already, but has done little work, so that finishing the wall will cost the debtor $5,000 in time and materials. The debtor thus can obtain a benefit of $1,000 from rejecting the contract—the debtor will save the $5,000 that would otherwise be spent on finishing the wall, but will forgo the $4,000 that the debtor would have earned by finishing the wall. (We assume that the debtor in possession would be paid the $4,000 promptly if it finished the wall; in the real world there are delays, and the nondebtor party may claim that $4,000 is not owed because of real or alleged defects in the work.) Assume the debtor's assets are worth $100,000 on a going concern basis, that the claims against the debtor are all general unsecured claims, totaling $1,000,000 (not counting any claim by the other party to the retaining wall contract), and that the stockholders will not retain any interest in the reorganized debtor. Thus, each creditor will receive value in the reorganization equal to 10% of its claim.

The debtor should reject the contract as long as the benefit to be gotten from rejection is more than 10% of the amount of the claim that would result. If the claim that would result is less than $10,000, then the creditors will benefit from the rejection. There will be $1,000 more in value to be split among the creditors, but less than $10,000 more in claims. Instead of receiving value equal to 10% of their claims, they will receive slightly more. Of course, this simple analysis does not take into account the damage to the debtor's business reputation (or "goodwill") that may result from rejection of the contract. In a chapter 11 reorganization, as opposed to a chapter 7 liquidation, the preservation of goodwill is a legitimate concern.

4. Suppose the debtor and nondebtor parties are involved in a dispute. For example, suppose Foam Corporation and Fancy Furniture Co. ("FFC") had a contract under which Foam Corporation was to deliver large amounts of foam to FFC each month for five years at a price that guaranteed a substantial profit for Foam Corporation. Two years into the five year period, FFC claimed that much of the foam delivered under the contract had been defective. Customers were complaining that their expensive furniture cushions had become lumpy and had lost resiliency much sooner than expected. To settle the dispute FFC demanded that Foam Corporation pay FFC $200,000 and agree to release FFC

from any further obligation to buy foam under the contract. Then Foam Corporation filed its bankruptcy petition. Gruff believes the foam delivered under the contract has been high quality and that the problems resulted from FFC's improper furniture construction methods. Gruff would like to have Foam Corporation assume the profitable contract for the estate. But he is worried that FFC might succeed in convincing a trier of fact that the foam was defective. If Foam Corporation desires to assume the contract, what must it do about the allegations that it breached the contract in the past by delivering defective foam? Can the bankruptcy court resolve the dispute when it hears Foam Corporation's motion to assume the contract? Must the bankruptcy court do so? If the bankruptcy court lacks jurisdiction to resolve the dispute, or declines to resolve it, what risk will Foam Corporation take in assuming the contract for the estate? Does Foam Corporation need to know whether it is liable for delivering allegedly defective foam before it makes the final decision to assume the contract? See Orion Pictures Corp. v. Showtime, 4 F.3d 1095 (2d Cir. 1993).

5. How did the debtor in possession in *Lubrizol* come to the conclusion that the contract should be rejected? Did the debtor in possession (or the court) have the necessary information to do the analysis suggested in the preceding note? Would debtors in possession typically have the necessary information to make such a scientific decision? Does that help to explain the deference courts have shown to decisions of trustees and debtors in possession?

6. Assumption of an executory contract or lease by the estate can be detrimental to the creditors, as the court pointed out in In re Food City, 94 B.R. 91 (Bankr. W.D. Texas 1988):

> In May 1988, one of the company's key senior management officials left the company. The board of directors then took action to place the rest of management under contract. Employment contracts were executed in early June, just days before the bankruptcy filing. The contracts assured each employee severance pay of six months salary, plus an additional month of salary for each additional month the employee remained with the company, up to a total benefit of not more than one year's salary. The benefit was to be paid in the event the employee was laid off or in the event the company was sold [or liquidated in a chapter 7 proceeding], and the employee not retained. * * *
>
> The debtor now seeks to assume these employment contracts, arguing that they are essential to the morale of the management team that is in turn essential to the successful reorganization of the debtor. Unless the key employees are assured a "safety net" in the event reorganization proves unsuccessful, they will be unwilling, according to the debtor, to continue assuming the risk of the employment with Food City and will likely instead go elsewhere.
>
> NCNB and the Committee each argue that assumption is not in the estate's best interest, pointing out that this same management team presided over the company's slide into bankruptcy. They also note that none of these employees previously had contracts, yet continued to work for the company even during successive years of loss. The Committee is especially concerned about the administrative expense claim with priority over unsecured creditors that would arise if the contracts, once assumed, are breached. 11 U.S.C. § 365(g)(2). In a chapter 7 case

especially, the $ 279,000 liability that would accrue would virtually eliminate any recovery for the unsecured creditor body. Finally, both parties note the chilling effect the contracts would have on the company's being acquired by a third party once the contracts were assumed, because a new buyer would either have to keep existing management or buy them off by paying off their contracts.

* * * The decision to assume or reject requires a balancing of the contract's benefits and burdens. In the context of rejection, this balancing is usually couched in terms of the "business judgment" test, under which a trustee need not affirmatively prove that a contract is burdensome in order to justify its rejection. * * * When the issue is assumption, the focus usually turns to the estate's ability to cure outstanding defaults and assure future performance, so the business judgment test is seldom referenced. * * * The ultimate issue in either event is still essentially the same, however. When assuming, the trustee must decide what benefit is to be gained by staying with the contract versus the burden thereby assumed. * * * When rejecting, the trustee must balance the benefit foregone against the burden of which the estate is being relieved.

* * * Despite the intangible benefits which would no doubt accrue to the estate by assuming these contracts, the burden on the creditors is too great to overlook. If the debtor's plan in fact succeeds, then assumption of these contracts under that plan would seem the appropriate reward for their efforts. If the plan should fail, however, assumption of these contract would only confer undue leverage on management, working to undermine (or even override) the absolute priority rule. See 11 U.S.C. § 1129(b).

All that is currently before the court is a request for approval of assumption of these contracts at this state of the bankruptcy. A refusal of that request at this time does not prevent the debtor from again seeking that approval later in the proceedings. With this in mind, the court denies the debtor's request to approve assumption of the employment contracts *at this time,* without prejudice to the debtor's seeking such approval at a latter date, including as part of the debtor's plan of reorganization.

Id. at 92-95. Does it appear that the business judgment test applies to the decision to assume a contract, as it does to the decision to reject? Should the same test apply to both? Does it matter whether an insider is involved? See Westship, Inc. v. Trident Shipworks, Inc., 247 B.R. 856 (M.D. Fla. 2000).

7.   Outside bankruptcy, if RMF demanded that Lubrizol not use the licensed metal coating technology, would Lubrizol have needed to obtain a decree of specific performance in order to use the technology? Note that Lubrizol's license was nonexclusive. If, as is often the case, the license were exclusive, would Lubrizol have needed to obtain a decree of specific performance in order to protect its rights under the contract?

8.   The court in *Lubrizol* refused to treat the grant of the license as a completed sale of intellectual property. What result would have followed if the court had treated it as a completed sale of property? Consider the next principal case. What result followed from the court's conclusion that the license agreement was more like a lease than a completed transfer of property, with the debtor RMF playing a role similar to a lessor? How does the Code treat lessees when the debtor in possession rejects a lease under which the debtor was the

lessor? See § 365(h)(1). If such lessees are permitted to remain in possession of the leased premises, why did the court not permit Lubrizol to retain its right to use the metal coating technology?

9. Does Congress' enactment of § 365(h)(1) imply that absent the protection of § 365(h)(1) a tenant would lose its right to possession of the premises when a debtor in possession rejected a lease under which the debtor was the lessor? See 3 Resnick & Sommer, COLLIER ON BANKRUPTCY ¶ 365.10, at 365-88.3 (stating that § 365 retains the basic approach, developed by the courts and codified in the old Act, that rejection of a real property lease could not deprive the nondebtor tenant of its vested estate but would permit the estate to avoid the burden of further performance such as providing heat). What conclusion does the court in *Lubrizol* draw from the enactment of § 365(h)(1)? Has Congress acted to prevent the rejection of a contract or lease from divesting the nondebtor party of a property interest whenever it has seemed that the courts might reach that result? See § 365(h), 365(i), and 365(n); Andrew, *Executory Contracts Revisited,* supra, 62 U. COLO. L. REV. at 10-11. But consider that § 365(h) applies only to leases of real property, not personal property, and even then only if the term of the lease "has commenced" (apparently as of the date the petition was filed). Also consider that § 365(i) does not apply—and thus cannot protect the purchaser's nonbankruptcy right of specific performance—where the purchaser under a land sale contract is not in possession of the land. As noted in Section A of this Chapter, it seems to have been settled law under the old Bankruptcy Act that rejection could deprive the nondebtor purchaser of the right of specific performance of an executory contract (at least one for sale of land). Is the buyer's right to specific performance of a contract for sale by the debtor of land or of unique goods a property interest in the land or goods? Should it be preserved when the contract is rejected? Consider the next case.

In re A.J. Lane & Co., Inc.
United States Bankruptcy Court, D. Massachusetts, 1989
107 B.R. 435

JAMES F. QUEENAN, Jr., Bankruptcy Judge.

The Debtor Andrew J. Lane moves to reject, pursuant to 11 U.S.C. § 365, a repurchase option contained in his deed of property in Ontario, California which he now wishes to sell rather than develop. Opposed to the motion is the successor-in-interest to the original grantor. The motion was granted by order dated November 20, 1989, which the court issued while this opinion was in draft form in order to facilitate a pending sale.

The facts are undisputed. Andrew J. Lane ("the Debtor"), as well as the other affiliated debtors in these administratively consolidated Chapter 11 proceedings, is engaged in the construction, development and management of commercial and residential real estate. On November 16, 1987 he purchased from Southern Pacific Development Company ("Southern Pacific") 16 acres of commercially zoned land in Ontario, California for the purpose of erecting commercial property thereon. Because Southern Pacific retained property in the vicinity whose value it wished to have enhanced by development of the entire area, the purchase and sale agreement gave Southern Pacific the right to repurchase if the Debtor did not develop the property. The deed accordingly provided that the Debtor "shall, following the recordation of this deed, construct one or more buildings comprised of at least 200,000 square feet of floor area … to be completed on or before November 17, 1991 ….” The deed goes on to state that if the Debtor does not so construct by then, Southern Pacific would have the right during the 90-day period following November 17, 1991, to elect to repurchase the property for about $2.8 million, the same price the Debtor paid Southern Pacific, less any debt secured by encumbrances placed on the property during the Debtor's ownership. The deed further gives Southern Pacific the option to repurchase within 90 days after being notified by the Debtor during the first year of his intention not to build on the property. Southern Pacific also has approval rights over any construction plans.

In financial straits because of the depressed real estate market, the Debtor and his affiliates filed Chapter 11 petitions with the court on March 24, 1989. Many of their commercial and residential projects are only partially completed, and a number of those which have been completed contain units which are neither occupied nor under commitment for lease or purchase. Some, including the property in question, have not been developed at all. The Debtor and his affiliates are now in the process of negotiating the framework of a substantively consolidated Chapter 11 plan of reorganization. They expect to file a formal plan with the court within a month. The plan will involve the liquidation of a number of properties; only those whose development or management present the most feasible short-term income potential will be retained. The Debtor is under considerable pressure from mortgagees to complete this process soon in order to avoid foreclosure upon a number of properties.

Next to the property in question is an improved parcel which is also owned by the Debtor. Both properties are among those which the Debtor wishes to sell in order to obtain ready cash for the funding of a consolidated Chapter 11 plan. He has signed an agreement with one Jack M. Langson to sell both parcels for a gross price of $16.5 million, without allocation of a portion of the purchase price to either parcel. With a closing scheduled in a few weeks, the sale would net the Debtor about $3 million after payment of encumbrances. The purchaser refuses to complete the transaction if the undeveloped parcel remains subject to the option, which is now held by Santa Fe Pacific Realty Corporation (“Santa Fe”) as successor-in-interest to Southern Pacific. As successor, Santa Fe also holds title to the other property in the vicinity owned by Southern Pacific at the time of the original sale.

I. THE OPTION AS AN EXECUTORY CONTRACT
UNDER § 365 OF THE BANKRUPTCY CODE

Section 365 of the Bankruptcy Code (11 U.S.C. § 365) provides, with exceptions not relevant here, that “subject to the court's approval” a trustee in bankruptcy (or debtor in possession exercising the powers of a trustee pursuant to § 1107) “may assume or reject any executory contract or unexpired lease of the debtor.” Rejection generally constitutes a breach of the contract or lease. § 365(g).

The parties dispute whether the option is an “executory contract” within the meaning of the statute. The legislative history offers minimal guidance:

“Though there is no precise definition of what contracts are executory, it generally *includes* contracts on which performance remains due to some extent on both sides. A note is not usually an executory contract if the only performance that remains is repayment. Performance on one side of the contract would have been completed and the contract is no longer necessary." (Emphasis added). H.R. Rep. No. 95-595, 95th Cong., 1st Sess. 347, reprinted in 1978 U.S. CODE CONG. & ADMIN. NEWS 5787, 6303; S. Rep. No. 95-989, 95th Cong., 2d Sess. 58, reprinted in 1978 U.S. CODE CONG. & ADMIN. NEWS 5844.

Professor Countryman offers this definition: "a contract under which the obligation of both the bankrupt and the other party to the contract are so far unperformed that the failure of either to complete performance would constitute a material breach excusing the performance of the other." Countryman, *Executory Contracts in Bankruptcy: Part I,* 57 MINN. L. REV. 439, 460 (1973). He reasons that a contract which has been performed by the debtor falls outside the concept of an executory contract because assumption adds nothing to the debtor's claim to performance by the other party, and rejection makes no sense. Id. at 459. Where the other party has already performed, he sees similar logical difficulties; the estate already has the benefit of the contract, so that assumption is unnecessary, and rejection would neither add to nor detract from the creditor's claim. Id. at 451. Although there may be exceptions to this logic for unusual situations,[45] Countryman's test of practicality seems sound.

The option here meets these criteria. It is part of a larger contract, the initial purchase and sales agreement, under which there remains further and substantial performance by both Santa Fe and the Debtor should Santa Fe decide to exercise its rights. Santa Fe would have us believe that the option is executory only with respect to the Debtor's performance, and that it therefore falls outside the scope of § 365. But an option has unusual characteristics. It is a unilateral contract until exercised; upon exercise, it becomes a bilateral contract. W. Jaeger, Williston on Contracts § 61B (3d ed. 1963). It is the contingency of exercise which makes the option executory for our purposes. Upon exercise, substantial performance remains on both sides—conveyance of the property by the Debtor and payment of the purchase price by Santa Fe. A material breach would occur should either party refuse to complete the transaction after exercise.

Viewing this agreement as an executory contract subject to rejection is consistent with the Countryman test of practical logic. The present posture of the agreement is quite unlike, for example, a contract of sale where goods have been delivered to a debtor on credit; rejection under those circumstances cannot alter the estate's obligation to pay. Here rejection converts a contingent *in rem* obligation into a fixed monetary one so as to permit the Debtor to deal with the property in order immediately to benefit his reorganizational efforts. The pending sale of this property and the adjoining parcel will bring in far more funds than would exercise of the option. And those funds would be generated now, whereas under the option funds may be generated two years from now, and perhaps never.

The decisions favor regarding an option, or the analogous right of first refusal, as an executory contract within the meaning of § 365. The contingency of the option exercise does not make the agreement non-executory. The decision in Brown v. Snellen (In re Giesing), 96 B.R. 229 (Bankr. W.D.Mo. 1989) is distinguishable.

---

45. [Footnote 1 in original:]   For example, where the debtor is the seller of uncompleted goods being specially made for a buyer who has already paid in full, it may make sense for the bankruptcy estate to assume and complete the contract in order to reduce the buyer's potentially large damage claim.

That case involved an attempted rejection by the holder of an option to purchase, presumably on the erroneous theory that rejection would entitle him to a return of the separate consideration paid for the option. The court properly held that the option in those circumstances was not executory. Id. at 232. Because the holder was in effect renouncing his election to purchase, the contract never could ripen into a bilateral contract unperformed on both sides. Id. at 232. * * *

Santa Fe says that a contract must be assumed or rejected in its entirety, and that the requested rejection violates this rule because the Debtor wishes to retain the property. This is sophistry. The Debtor seeks to reject the entire *remaining* portion of the contract. That is all that can be rejected. Where there has been partial performance by the non-debtor party, rejection leaves that performance undisturbed. Rejection under § 365 is simply that; it is not rescission. All property which has become part of the bankruptcy estate under § 541 remains undisturbed by rejection under § 365. We presume, as urged by Santa Fe, that the option was a major part of its motivation in entering into the transaction. But that is true of all material unperformed aspects of any contract whose performance a debtor seeks to reject. It goes only to Santa Fe's damages, not to whether the contract is executory.

Santa Fe's reliance upon In re Texstone Venture, LTD., 54 B.R. 54 (Bankr. S.D.Tex. 1985) is misplaced. There a debtor had borrowed money, agreeing to repay the principal either in cash or through the lender's exercise of an option to acquire equity in the debtor. The court prohibited rejection of the lender's equity option because the loan agreement was not executory on both sides--the lender had fully performed through its advance of the funds. Id. at 56. Attempted rejection of the option in these circumstances was viewed by the court as much like attempted rejection of a matured obligation to pay money in a currency to be selected by the lender. The court did not apply a test of practicality to the rejection in order to ascertain whether rejection would benefit the estate.

Santa Fe also argues that the Debtor seeks to disturb a property interest, emphasizing that the option is contained in a deed. But this does not make the option a property interest. It is only a contract right--the right to purchase--whose remedy is normally specific performance. That the world is given notice of this right though its appearance in a recorded deed prevents any other buyer from claiming the equities of an innocent third party, but that is all.

Congress certainly knows how to protect property interests from termination through rejection. Rejection by a lessor of real estate, by a seller of timeshare realty interests, or by a licensor of intellectual property does not terminate the property interest of the other party unless that party elects to treat his interest as terminated. § 365(h) and (n). Similar protection is given a purchaser in possession under the debtor's executory contract to sell real property. He is entitled to remain in possession notwithstanding the debtor's rejection of the contract, provided that he continues to make payments under the contract, and he has the right to offset against the remaining purchase price any damages caused by the debtor's non-performance. § 365(i). Upon completion of the payments, the bankruptcy estate is required to deed him the property. Id. If the purchaser chooses to treat the contract as terminated, he has a lien on the property for recovery of that part of the price already paid. § 365(j). Purchasers in possession were granted these rights in response to dissatisfaction with the absence of clear statutory protection for a consumer purchaser under a so-called "land sale contract," which involves payments over a number of years while the buyer is in possession. A buyer in these circumstances was considered to have particularly strong equities militating against rejection, and some courts regarded the arrangement as the practical equivalent of a mortgage. * * *

Strikingly absent from § 365 is any protection for a buyer not in possession, much less for the holder of an option to purchase. Rejection of such contractual commitments therefore comes within the general sweep of § 365. This seems clear from the statute. Moreover, it is a rule of statutory construction that if Congress intends to change an established judicial doctrine, it should make that intent specific. Midlantic Nat'l Bank v. New Jersey Department of Environmental Protection, 474 U.S. 494, 501, 106 S. Ct. 755, 759, 88 L. Ed. 2d 859 (1986). It was well established under the prior Bankruptcy Act that the estate could reject a contract to sell real estate where the buyer was not in possession. The buyer's right to specific performance, and the doctrine of equitable ownership flowing therefrom, were considered subordinate to the estate's right of rejection. Gulf Petroleum, S.A. v. Collazo, 316 F.2d 257 (1st Cir. 1963); In re Philadelphia Penn. Worsted Co., 278 F.2d 661 (3d Cir. 1960); In re New York Investors Mutual Group, Inc., 143 F.Supp. 51 (S.D.N.Y. 1956). The doctrine of equitable ownership is a relic of the days when promises of contracting parties were considered independent of each other. W. Jaeger, Williston on Contracts § 927 (3d ed. 1963). As pointed out by Williston, it clouds analysis. Id. at § 929. Indeed, where the buyer has paid most or all of the purchase price, recognition of the doctrine and allowance of specific performance against a debtor in bankruptcy proceedings would be to prefer one creditor over others. National Bank of Kentucky v. Louisville Trust Co., 67 F.2d 97, 100 (6th Cir. 1933), cert. denied 291 U.S. 665, 54 S. Ct. 440, 78 L. Ed. 1056 (1934).

Thus the Debtor could reject its obligation to Santa Fe even if Santa Fe otherwise now had the right of specific performance through an election to purchase. This is confirmed by § 101(4)(B) which defines "claim" to include a "right to an equitable remedy for breach of performance if such breach gives rise to a right to payment, whether or not such right to an equitable remedy is reduced to judgment ...." The legislative history indicates that this definition "is intended to cause the liquidation or estimation of contingent rights of payment for which there may be an alternative equitable remedy with the result that the equitable remedy will be susceptible to being discharged in bankruptcy." 124 Cong.Rec.H. 11089 (Sept. 28, 1978). See also Ohio v. Kovacs, 469 U.S. 274, 279-81, 105 S. Ct. 705, 707-08, 83 L. Ed. 2d 649 (1985) ("claim" in bankruptcy includes a mandatory clean-up injunction in favor of the state under environmental laws, parties and court assuming that any breach of a private contract gives rise to a claim). Subordination of the right of specific performance to a debtor's rejection rights is also manifest in § 365(n), where the licensee of intellectual property is expressly denied specific performance. I must therefore respectfully disagree with the decision in In re Lewis, 94 B.R. 789, 795 (Bankr. D.Mass. 1988) holding that a contract for the sale of real estate is not executory because of the right of specific performance. Roxse Homes, Inc. v. Roxse Homes LTD. Partnership, 83 B.R. 185, 187 (D.Mass. 1988), relied upon by In re Lewis, is distinguishable in that it involved a state court judgment ordering specific performance, which the court regarded as terminating the executory aspect of the parties' purchase and sale agreement. * * *

These findings and conclusions are issued in support of the court's order of November 20, 1989 permitting rejection and declaring Santa Fe's claim to be unenforceable against the property or any buyer.

NOTES

1. Santa Fe had no duties under the option. Would the option be an executory contract under a strict application of the Countryman test? See Unsecured Creditors Comm. v. Southmark Corp. (In re Robert L. Helms Constr. & Dev. Co., Inc.), 139 F.3d 702 (9th Cir. 1998) (en banc). Why did the court conclude that it was executory? Did the court conclude (1) that rejection eliminated Santa Fe's right to specific performance, (2) that the discharge eliminated it, (3) that either ground was independently sufficient to eliminate it, or (4) that the effect of both were needed in order to eliminate it? Had the debtor received a discharge at the time of the court's decision? Was it certain that the debtor would receive a discharge?

2. Under the court's approach, what seems to be the rule for deciding which interests in property created pursuant to a contract are eliminated by rejection of the contract?

3. Should an option held *by the debtor* be considered an executory contract? Suppose it had been Santa Fe that had filed a chapter 11 petition, rather than A.J. Lane. Such an option could safely be taken into the estate without imposing any obligations on the estate, because no obligation could arise unless the debtor in possession chose to exercise the option. Thus the historical reasons for giving the debtor in possession an assume/reject election simply do not apply. Would it make sense to consider such an option to be simply an asset that passes into the estate like any other property? See Unsecured Cred. Comm. v. Southmark Corp. (In re Robert L. Helms Constr. & Dev. Co., Inc.), 139 F.3d 702 (9th Cir. 1998) (en banc). Then the debtor in possession would have the ability to use the option under § 363 by exercising it (after notice and a hearing, if, as seems likely, exercise of the option would not be in the ordinary course of business). The resulting contract would then be between the estate and the nondebtor party.

4. Consider the following point-counterpoint discussion between two hypothetical lawyers who have read Judge Queenan's opinion:

    Smith: Despite rejection of the option contract by the debtor in possession, Santa Fe's option should have been specifically enforceable once the automatic stay no longer applied. It was a property right that should have survived bankruptcy. Property "exists" when there is a sufficient relationship between (1) a person and (2) a tangible item or a right. The sufficiency of the relationship depends on whether the law recognizes and enforces features of the relationship such as (1) the ability to use the item or right, (2) the ability to exclude others from using the item or the right, and (3) the ability to transfer the relationship so that another person will have the relationship with the item or right. Santa Fe's option to purchase the land was certainly a sufficient relationship to the land for us to say that Santa Fe had a property interest in the land outside of bankruptcy. Santa Fe had the legally recognized ability (through a specific performance action) to obtain title to the land and thus possession and use of the land in perpetuity. By exercising its option, Santa Fe could prevent others from using or possessing the land; in fact, even if the debtor sold the land to someone who did not know of the option, Santa Fe still could obtain the land and exclude that person from using or possessing it, because Santa Fe's option was recorded. The law recognizes that options are transferrable, and thus Santa Fe could transfer its relationship to the land to another person. Santa Fe thus had a property interest under state law, as would any purchaser of a tangible item or a right under a specifically enforceable contract. For bankruptcy purposes, property interests are "created and defined by state law." Butner v. United States, 440 U.S. 48, 55, 99 S. Ct. 914, 918, 59 L. Ed. 2d 136, 141-42 (1979). Unless there is a specific provision of bankruptcy law that modifies or eliminates state law property rights, such as an avoiding power, the estate takes no better rights than the debtor had, and thus state law property rights are recognized in bankruptcy (although the automatic stay may postpone their enjoyment.) The history of the assume/reject election, as Professor Andrew has explained, does not support its use as an avoiding power. Further, the Fifth Amendment "takings" clause applies even in bankruptcy, as the Supreme Court held in invalidating a depression era bankruptcy law that infringed too seriously on the rights of mortgagees. See Louisville Joint Stock Land Bank v. Radford, 295 U.S. 555, 55 S. Ct. 854, 79 L. Ed. 1593 (1935). The courts should avoid an interpretation of a federal statute which raises constitutional difficulties; thus rejection should not have eliminated Santa Fe's right to specific performance.

Jones: As Professor Countryman demonstrated, it was settled law under the old Act that rejection of a contract—in particular of a contract under which the debtor was to sell real property—would prevent specific enforcement of it against property of the estate. Congress did nothing to change that when it enacted the Bankruptcy Code. The Supreme Court has held that Congress should not be thought to have intended major changes in pre-Code bankruptcy law unless there is a clear basis in the text of the Code or in its legislative history for thinking that a major change was intended. See Midlantic National Bank v. New Jersey Dept. of Environmental Protection, 474 U.S. 494, 106 S. Ct. 755, 88 L. Ed. 2d 859 (1986). Further, your definition of "property" is a modern innovation, hardly what the Founders had in mind in the Fifth Amendment, and *Radford* was a reactionary decision by the pre-New Deal Court. Anyone who has entered into a contract in the last forty years has been on notice that their so-called property right to specific performance would not be good in bankruptcy. Further, as Judge Queenan pointed out, equitable conversion—the doctrine under which land sale contract purchasers were considered to have equitable ownership of land even before taking possession—is an antiquated doctrine not much in favor these days ...

Smith: I'd say equitable conversion was in favor in the 1790's, if you want to talk about the Founders, and none of your "settled law" was from the Supreme Court. I don't think an unconstitutional taking becomes constitutional just because it has been going on for forty years, either. And I get tired of reading bankruptcy decisions in which courts define "property" expansively when it helps the debtor but narrowly when it would hurt the debtor …

Jones: and as I was about to say before you interrupted me, the discharge clearly was intended by Congress to eliminate rights to specific performance because the equitable remedy of specific performance is a dischargeable claim under § 101(5)(B).

Smith: I disagree. Under § 524(a)(1) and the *Bullard*[46] line of cases, the discharge has no effect on property interests; it only affects personal liability of the debtor. But let's go get lunch; the effect of the discharge can wait until Chapter Sixteen.

5. Suppose a tenant under a long term ground lease of raw land builds a building on the land—thus making the rental value of the land much greater than the rent payable under the ground lease—and then mortgages its newly valuable leasehold interest to secure a loan. The tenant then files a bankruptcy petition, and, as debtor in possession, fails to take any steps to assume the ground lease. Sixty days after the filing of the petition, the ground lease will be deemed rejected, and the tenant/debtor in possession will be obligated to surrender possession to the lessor. See § 365(d)(4). If rejection terminates the leasehold and therefore renders worthless the lender's mortgage lien on the leasehold, the lender will no longer have any collateral for its loan; the lessor will also be greatly enriched, because it will retake possession of the property complete with improvements, free of the tenant's lease and free of the lender's leasehold mortgage. Does rejection have that effect? See Eastover Bank for Sav. v. Sowashee Venture (In re Austin Dev. Co.), 19 F.3d 1077 (5th Cir. 1994).

6. As *Eastover Bank* illustrates, the Andrew/Westbrook approach is finding its way into the opinions. See, e.g., In re Printronics, Inc, 189 B.R. 995 (Bankr. N.D. Fla. 1995) (holding that even though franchise agreement was executory contract that could be rejected, noncompete clause in agreement would still bind debtor); In re Weinstock,1999 WL 1041406 (E.D. Pa.) (holding accounting partnership agreement provision, that former partner would pay partnership 1/3 of earnings from former partnership clients, survived rejection and was enforceable with respect to postpetition earnings); First Security Bank of Utah v. Gillman, 158 B.R. 498, 503-04 (D. Utah 1993) (discussing ideas of Andrew and Westbrook, adopting Andrew approach that rejection of executory contract precludes burdens of contract from being administrative obligations of the estate but does not otherwise affect rights of nondebtor party, and determining that the nondebtor party therefore gained nothing from a finding that the contract was nonexecutory); South Motor Chrysler-Plymouth v. Chrysler Motor Corporation (In re South Motor Company), 161 B.R. 532, 546 (Bankr. S.D. Fla. 1993) (discussing Westbrook and Andrew positions and agreeing with them that "rejection has absolutely no effect upon a contract's continued existence," that "[t]he contract is not otherwise cancelled, repudiated, or in any other fashion terminated," and that "rejection of an executory contract does not ipso facto terminate rights and obligations that arise from rejected contracts [*sic*]"); Chestnut Ridge Plaza Assocs. v. Fox Grocery Co. (In re

---

46. Long v. Bullard, 117 U.S. 917, 6 S. Ct. 917 (1886).

Chestnut Ridge Plaza Assocs.), 156 B.R. 477, 483 (Bankr. W.D. Pa. 1993) (citing Andrew for proposition adopted by court that "[r]ejection does not alter the substantive rights of the parties to the lease" but "is merely the decision of the bankruptcy estate not to become a party to the lease thereby avoiding any unfavorable consequences of a bad bargain made prepetition by the debtor"); Cohen v. Drexel Burnham Lambert Group, Inc. (In re Drexel Burnham Lambert Group, Inc.), 138 B.R. 687 (Bankr. S.D.N.Y. 1992) (permitting rejection of employment contract without regard to any requirement of executoriness); A.J. Lane & Co., Inc. v. BSC Group (In re A.J. Lane & Co., Inc.), 115 B.R. 738, 742-43 (D. Mass. 1990) (adopting approach that the scope of the discharge determines whether a nonexecutory contract could be specifically enforced, stating that "failure to perform even a fully executory (and unassumed) contract should be treated no differently from the estate's failure to undertake any of the debtor's other obligations," and adopting Andrew approach that rejection is simply formal decision by estate not to take on obligations of contract).

Problem 7-4

> Recall that in exchange for a one-time payment of $200,000 Foam Corporation granted a 20 year nonexclusive license to More Foam, a North Carolina corporation, to use Foam Corporation's waterbed patent and "Waveless" trademark to manufacture and market waterbeds for the North Carolina market. In the license agreement, More Foam promised not to misuse or sublicense the patent or trademark, and Foam Corporation promised to defend the patent and trademark if the validity of either were challenged. Foam Corporation also promised not to compete with More Foam in North Carolina. The covenant not to compete is contained in a separate document from the license agreement, and it was supported by separate consideration, a cash payment of $50,000, but it covers the same territory (North Carolina) and time period as the license. In the same document that contains the covenant not to compete, More Foam promised that it would not sell not sell products incorporating the patent or trademark unless the license is in force. Foam Corporation would now like to sell waterbeds in North Carolina, and would rather not have competition there from More Foam. Can rejection of one or both of these agreements give Foam Corporation what it seeks? Is there one contract or two? Does that make a difference? Are they (or is it) executory?

Problem 7-5

> Ten months before filing its chapter 11 petition, Foam Corporation obtained an important piece of equipment (a chemical mixing vat) from LeaseCo under a 60 month "lease." Under the lease, Foam Corporation can become the owner of the mixing vat by paying LeaseCo $1 at the end of the 60 months, provided that all of the monthly payments have been made. LeaseCo promptly made a precautionary Article 9 financing statement filing which described the agreement as a lease. The present value of the remaining payments under the lease is at least $30,000, but the vat is worth no more than $20,000. Foam Corporation wishes to keep the vat, and LeaseCo has moved for an order requiring Foam Corporation to assume or reject the lease within the next thirty days. Assume the court will be likely to grant the motion if the lease is subject to assumption or rejection under § 365. Is the agreement actually a lease or is it a sale agreement with the result that LeaseCo's purported retention of title amounts merely to retention of a security interest in the vat? See U.C.C. § 1-201(37). What difference will the answer to that question make in terms of how LeaseCo must be treated if Foam Corporation keeps the vat? Compare § 365(b) with § 1129(b)(2)(A).

E. TEXTUAL NOTE ON COLLECTIVE BARGAINING AGREEMENTS

The business judgment test does not apply to court approval of rejection of collective bargaining agreements. In NLRB. v. Bildisco & Bildisco, 465 U.S. 513, 104 S. Ct. 1188, 79 L. Ed. 2d 482 (1984), the Supreme Court held that a debtor employer was entitled to reject a collective bargaining agreement with a union only if (1) reasonable efforts to negotiate a modification of the collective bargaining agreement had failed, (2) that failure threatened to impede the reorganization, (3) the collective-bargaining agreement burdened the estate, and (4) the equities balanced in favor of rejection. The Court refused to apply the very strict standard applied by the Second Circuit in Brotherhood of Railway and Airline Clerks v. REA Express, Inc., 523 F.2d 164 (2d Cir. 1975) (rejection of collective bargaining agreement permitted only if debtor demonstrates that its reorganization will fail unless rejection is permitted). The Court also held that the debtor could unilaterally implement changes in the collective bargaining agreement before rejection of it.

The Supreme Court's decision created a political furor, which made possible quick passage of a bankruptcy amendments bill that had been stalled in Congress since 1979. Even the Supreme Court's decision in 1982 that the bankruptcy court system set up under the 1978 Bankruptcy Reform Act was unconstitutional[47] did not create enough pressure for Congress to pass a bankruptcy amendments bill, but *Bildisco* did. Congress acted quickly. Included in the amendments was the addition of § 1113 to the Code, which governs treatment of collective bargaining agreements in chapter 11 cases only. It overruled the latter part of the Court's holding; under § 1113(f) the debtor in possession may not unilaterally alter provisions of a collective bargaining agreement without complying with § 1113.

---

47.   Northern Pipeline Constr. Co. v. Marathon Pipe Line Co., 458 U.S. 50, 102 S. Ct. 2858, 73 L. Ed. 2d 598 (1982). In *Northern Pipeline* the Court held that the wide grant of jurisdiction given to bankruptcy judges under the Bankruptcy Reform Act of 1978 (which also enacted the Bankruptcy Code) was unconstitutional because the bankruptcy judges were not Article III federal judges with life tenure and protection against reduction in their salaries. Remarkably, the Supreme Court in effect permitted the continued exercise of unconstitutional jurisdiction by bankruptcy judges by staying the effectiveness of its order for several months. When Congress was unwilling to pass remedial legislation, the Supreme Court extended the stay for another two and one half months. See Northern Pipeline Constr. Co. v. Marathon Pipe Line Co., 459 U.S. 813, 103 S. Ct. 199, 74 L. Ed. 2d 160 (1982). Eventually the Judicial Conference issued (legislated?) an "Emergency Rule" under which matters beyond the constitutional authority of the bankruptcy judges were to be decided by the federal district judges, with the assistance of the bankruptcy judges, who would propose findings of fact and conclusions of law. Congress was unable to correct the situation because agreement could not be reached on whether bankruptcy judges should be made full Article III judges or whether they should continue to be non-Article III judges but with a reduced scope of jurisdiction. The decision in *Bildisco* created a political furor which forced Congress to act. Thus the jurisdictional problem was finally addressed by Congress in the Bankruptcy Amendments and Federal Judgeships Act of 1984, which did not make bankruptcy judges Article III judges. Instead, it divided matters into "core" proceedings and "non-core" proceedings. Bankruptcy judges have power to enter final judgments only in core proceedings. They have jurisdiction to hear non-core proceedings, but cannot enter judgments in them; instead, the bankruptcy judges must submit proposed findings of fact and conclusions of law to the district court, which enters final judgment after "reviewing de novo those matters to which any party has timely and specifically objected." 28 U.S.C. § 157(b) and (c); see Epstein, Nickles & White, BANKRUPTCY §§ 12-1 to 12-3 at pp. 856-67.

Section 1113(e) permits the debtor in possession to implement interim changes before rejection, but only with court approval, which will be given only if the changes are "essential to continuation of the debtor's business, or in order to avoid irreparable damage to the estate." Section 1113(e). To obtain interim relief, the debtor must show "that the short term survival of the debtor is threatened unless immediate changes to the collective bargaining agreement are authorized," and the court should not be influenced by any argument of the debtor that the relief is needed to enhance its long term prospects of reorganization. Shugrue v. Air Line Pilots Association (In re Ionosphere Clubs, Inc.), 139 B.R. 772 (S.D.N.Y. 1992). It is not clear, however, in the absence of interim relief, whether § 1113(e) and (f) forces the debtor in possession to *perform* under the terms of the collective bargaining agreement before rejection—especially with respect to obligations to pay prepetition debts. There is a split in the circuits over this issue. See Air Line Pilots Ass'n v. Shugrue (In re Ionosphere Clubs, Inc.), 22 F.3d 403 (2d Cir. 1994) (holding that pilots' claims for vacation pay earned prepetition were not entitled to administrative priority status even though they were owed under collective bargaining agreement that had not been rejected or modified); In re Unimet Corp., 842 F.2d 879 (6th Cir. 1988) (holding that prepetition obligations for retiree benefits were entitled to administrative priority status because debtor in possession could not unilaterally terminate or modify collective bargaining agreement); In re Certified Air Techs., Inc. 300 B.R. 355 (Bankr. C.D. Cal. 2003) (noting split between the 2d, 3d, and 4th Circuits on the one hand, and the 6th on the other).

It also has not been settled whether an application (or motion) to reject the collective bargaining agreement must be pending for interim relief to be granted under § 1113(e). See Shugrue v. Air Line Pilots Ass'n (In re Ionosphere Clubs, Inc.), 139 B.R. 772 (motion to reject must be pending, at least in absence of danger of immediate liquidation); In re United Press Int'l, 134 B.R. 507 (Bankr. S.D.N.Y. 1991) (motion need not be pending); Beckley Coal Mining Co. v. United Mine Workers of Am., 98 B.R. 690 (D. Del. 1988) (holding that motion to reject need not be pending, because the procedural steps that must be taken under § 1113(b) before a motion to reject can even be filed might prevent interim relief from being granted in the emergency situations for which it was designed).

Section 1113 also provided a new procedure for rejection of collective bargaining agreements and a new test for whether the court should approve rejection. Before filing a motion to reject a collective bargaining agreement, the debtor must make a proposal to the union which "provides for those necessary modifications in the employees [sic] benefits and protections that are necessary to permit the reorganization of the debtor and assures that all creditors, the debtor, and all of the affected parties are treated fairly and equitably." Section 1113(b)(1)(A). The debtor must also provide the union with the information needed to evaluate the proposal and meet and confer with the union in an attempt to reach agreement on modifications to the agreement. Section 1113(b)(1)(B) and (2). If no agreement is reached, the court "shall" approve rejection of the agreement only if the debtor has made the required proposal to the union, the union has refused to accept it "without good cause," and "the balance of the equities clearly favors rejection of such agreement." Section 1113(c).

The statute's lack of clarity, due to its being a political compromise, permitted the pro-labor members of Congress and the pro-business members to claim victory. However, it is not at all clear that a proposal to the union can on the one hand contain only those changes in the collective bargaining agreement that are "necessary," and on the other hand treat the creditors, the debtor, and all other affected parties fairly and equitably. If "necessary" means "necessary to permit reorganization," then, the debtor in possession might, for example, be limited to proposing only a small decrease in wages, just enough barely to allow the debtor to reorganize, even though it would result in the debtor's cash flows being so small that creditors would recover only a few cents on the dollar. A more equitable division of the burdens of reorganization might require the union members to take a somewhat larger pay cut so that the creditors would not lose so much. As would be expected, the courts have given different interpretations to the standard for rejection of collective bargaining agreements. Some courts stress the requirement that the proposal to the union be limited to "necessary" changes and conclude that the debtor's proposal to the union may only include the minimum changes needed to keep the reorganization from failing. See Wheeling-Pittsburgh Steel Corp. v. United Steelworkers, 791 F.2d 1074 (3d Cir. 1986). On the other hand the "goal to be served by modifying the collective bargaining agreement * * * is not simply a reorganization but a successful reorganization, i.e., one from which the debtor emerges as an economically viable operation." Sheet Metal Worker's Int'l Ass'n v. Mile Hi Metal Sys., Inc. (In re Mile Hi Metal Sys., Inc.), 899 F.2d 887, 893 (10th Cir. 1990). Thus most courts have held that modifications of the collective bargaining agreement may be "necessary" to the goal of a successful reorganization even if they go beyond the absolute minimum needed to avoid liquidation. See id.; Truck Drivers Local 807 v. Carey Transportation, Inc., 816 F.2d 82 (2d Cir. 1987). That approach seems more consistent with the requirement that the proposal treat all of the parties fairly and equitably than does the strict *Wheeling-Pittsburgh* approach.

Whichever way the rejection standard is interpreted, the process set up by § 1113 seems well designed to create pressure for compromise. If the debtor's proposal to the union contains greater changes than are "necessary," the court is not supposed to permit rejection, both because the debtor will have failed to make a proposal that fulfills the requirements of § 1113(b)(1) and because the union's refusal to accept it will not be "without good cause." Thus the debtor is under some pressure to make a reasonable proposal to the union. On the other hand, the union is under pressure to accept the debtor's proposal if it is reasonable. If the union refuses to accept it, the court finds that the refusal was "without good cause," and the court finds that the other requirements of § 1113(c) are met, the court will permit rejection of the collective bargaining agreement. The debtor will not then be limited to modifying the collective bargaining agreement only in "necessary" respects, but will be free to reduce wages and change other terms to whatever degree it chooses.

The debtor will still have an obligation under the labor laws to try to negotiate a new collective bargaining agreement with the union. Further, the employees will retain the right to strike, and thus, even if the agreement is rejected, the debtor will be well-advised to make only reasonable changes from the terms of the rejected agreement.

F. TEXTUAL NOTE ON CONTRACTS THAT CANNOT BE ASSUMED OR ASSIGNED: FINANCIAL ACCOMMODATION CONTRACTS AND CONTRACTS MADE NONDELEGABLE OR NONASSIGNABLE BY LAW

Note that under § 365(c)(2), a contract can neither be assumed nor assigned if it is a financial accommodation contract, or as the statute puts it, "a contract to make a loan or extend other debt financing or financial accommodations, to or for the benefit of the debtor." Suppose Global Bank has agreed to make a loan of $400,000 to Foam Corporation; do you understand why Congress did not think it would be fair to Global Bank to allow a debtor in possession like Foam Corporation to assume that contract in a chapter 11 case and force Global Bank to make the loan? Of course, we may assume that the loan agreement provides Global Bank need not lend the funds if Foam Corporation's financial condition worsens or if Foam Corporation files a bankruptcy petition. Section 365(e)(1) ordinarily would prevent such provisions from having any effect in the case, but § 365(e)(2)(B) makes an exception for financial accommodation contracts. Thus Global Bank can rely on its contract provisions to prevent Foam Corporation from assuming the contract, and, even if it forgot to put such provisions in the contract, under § 365(c)(2) Foam Corporation still cannot assume the contract, because it is a financial accommodation contract.

Beyond the clear cases, like contracts to make or to guarantee loans, there is a grey area of contracts under which credit is extended to the debtor but which are not primarily loan or credit agreements. For example, under the 72 month Foam Corporation/NSC contract discussed above in this Chapter, Section A.7., Foam Corporation has twenty days to pay for the chemicals after each monthly delivery. Is it a financial accommodation contract that therefore cannot be assumed? Courts are not in agreement. One view is expressed in Citizens and Southern National Bank v. Thomas B. Hamilton Co. (In re Thomas B. Hamilton Co.), 969 F.2d 1013 (11th Cir. 1992) (holding that merchant's credit card agreement with bank was not a financial accommodation contract even though merchant might end up owing bank money if merchant's customers refused to pay for purchases); accord In re United Airlines, Inc., 368 F.3d 720 (7th Cir. 2004). The Eleventh Circuit stated:

> The term "financial accommodations" is not defined in the statute; however, the legislative history of § 365 provides insight into Congress' intent in using this term:
>
>> Characterization of contracts to make a loan, or extend other debt financing or financial accommodations, is limited to the extension of cash or a line of credit and is not intended to embrace ordinary leases or contracts to provide goods or services with payments to be made over time.
>
> [124 Cong. Rec. H11089 (daily ed. September 28, 1978) (statement of Rep. Edwards); 124 Cong. Rec. S17406 (daily ed. October 6, 1978) (statement of Sen. DeConcini).]
>
> Consistent with this legislative history, the authors of COLLIER ON BANKRUPTCY have concluded that the term "financial accommodations" must be strictly construed * * *

The courts that have construed § 365(c)(2) consistently agree with this commentary. Citing the legislative history quoted above and this passage from Collier on Bankruptcy, these courts uniformly conclude that § 365(c)(2) does not apply to all contracts that involve the extension of credit; rather, it applies to "contracts to make loans and other traditional kinds of debt financing arrangements." Thus, courts define the term "financial accommodations" narrowly, as "the extension of money or credit to accommodate another." [In re Sun Runner Marine, Inc., 945 F.2d 1089 (9th Cir. 1991); In re Placid Oil Co., 72 B.R. 135, 139 (Bankr. N.D. Tex. 1987).] Courts also distinguish between contracts for which the extension of credit is the primary purpose, that is, a primary contractual obligation, and contracts in which the extension of credit is only incidental to or a part of a larger arrangement involving the debtor; the former constitute contracts to extend financial accommodations while the latter do not. For example, in In re Cole Brothers, Inc., the bankruptcy court held that a set of related contracts establishing the debtor as a dealer for John Deere companies were assumable by the trustee notwithstanding that several of the contracts were financing agreements; the court determined that these financing agreements were "necessary but still incidental to the overall arrangement." [In re Cole Brothers, Inc., 137 B.R. 647 (Bankr. W.D. Mich. 1992).] And in In re The Travel Shoppe [88 B.R. at 470], the bankruptcy court, holding that an agreement to provide blank airline tickets and clearinghouse services to a debtor travel agent did not constitute a contract to extend financial accommodations, reasoned:

> To interpret "financial accommodations" to include the … agreement simply because the debtor may not make deposits from sales on time would turn every contract where the debtor owed money into a contract for financial accommodations and would "allow the exception to swallow the rule." [Citations omitted.]

On the other hand, courts have held that loan commitments, guaranty and surety contracts, and other contracts the principle [*sic*] purpose of which is to extend financing to or guarantee the financial obligations of the debtor are contracts to extend financial accommodations within the meaning of § 365(c)(2).

969 F.2d at 1018-19.

In *Thomas B. Hamilton* the court cited the bankruptcy court decision in *Cole Brothers* to support its analysis. The *Cole Brothers* bankruptcy court decision was later reversed on the ground that the agreement of the manufacturer to extend credit was an integral part of the dealership agreement, and hence the entire agreement was a financial accommodation contract. John Deere Co. v. Cole Brothers, Inc. (In re Cole Brothers, Inc.), 154 B.R. 689 (W.D. Mich. 1992). By way of extreme contrast with that district court opinion, consider Braniff, Inc. v. GPA Group PLC (In re Braniff, Inc.), 118 B.R. 819 (Bankr. M.D. Fla. 1990). In *Braniff,* the court enjoined the nondebtor parties to a massive airliner leasing contract from breaching it while the debtor airline decided whether to assume it; thus the nondebtor parties were ordered to deliver additional jet aircraft to the airline, thus providing a great deal of capital financing for the airline.

Does § 365(c)(2) permit a financial accommodation contract to be assumed with the consent of the nondebtor party? Suppose that a lender lent the debtor, on an unsecured basis, $100,000 out of $300,000 that the lender had committed to lend. Before the rest of the money was lent, the borrower filed a chapter 11 petition. Note that if the debtor in possession assumed the contract in order to obtain the other $200,000 in loans, the $100,000 prepetition loan would become an administrative expense claim in the case. That explains why a lender might be willing to consent to assumption of the loan agreement, and why other holders of general unsecured claims might object. Because of this concern about promoting prepetition debt to administrative priority status, and because of a view that § 364, not § 365, should be used if the debtor in possession needs to borrow money, some courts refuse to allow financial accommodation contracts to be assumed even if the nondebtor party consents. See Transamerica Commercial Fin. Corp. v. Citibank (In re Sun Runner Marine, Inc.), 945 F.2d 1089 (9th Cir. 1991). There is authority to the contrary. See In re T.S. Indus., Inc., 117 B.R. 682 (Bankr. D. Utah 1990) (holding that a workout agreement that included extension of a line of credit and which by its terms was to be enforceable in planned chapter 11 case was assumable, despite § 365(c)(2)); In re Prime, Inc., 15 B.R. 216 (Bankr. W.D. Mo. 1981). There is even earlier *Ninth Circuit* authority not mentioned in *Sun Runner* to the effect that the nondebtor party to a financial accommodation contract may waive the protection of § 365(c)(2) or be estopped from raising it. See Gill v. Easebe Enterprises, Inc. (In re Easebe Enterprises, Inc.), 900 F.2d 1417 (9th Cir. 1990), overruled on other grounds, Unsecured Creditors Comm. v. Southmark (In re Robert L. Helms Constr. & Dev. Co.), 139 F.3d 702 (9th Cir. 1998) (en banc). Under the rules of the Ninth Circuit, an *en banc* decision was required to overrule *Easebe*. Thus *Easebe* was mandatory authority at the time the Ninth Circuit panel decided *Sun Runner*.

There is one other kind of contract that cannot be assigned, and that probably cannot be assumed either: those contracts encompassed by § 365(c)(1). Section 365(c)(1) prohibits the assignment—and apparently even the assumption—of contracts and leases if "applicable law" does not give the debtor or debtor in possession the right to delegate duties to anyone else or if "applicable law" does not give the debtor or debtor in possession the right to assign to anyone else the right to receive performance of the contract. Note that whether "applicable law" permits assignment or delegation is to be determined without regard to any provision in the contract that would prohibit or restrict assignment or delegation. Of course, there are many contracts that are nondelegable even without taking into account any provision in the contract that would prevent delegation. From your contracts course you know that the duty to perform a personal service contract cannot be delegated. For example, if the famous actress, Meryl Hepburn, had a contract with StarStruck Studios to star in a motion picture, she could not send her niece Nellie (who was trying to break into show business) to act in the film for her. StarStruck Studios has a substantial interest in having Meryl Hepburn personally give the performance. Thus, were Meryl Hepburn to file a chapter 11 petition, she would not be able to assign the contract to Nellie or to anyone else. There are, of course, more mundane (though no less important) personal service contracts. Your contract to work as an summer associate for a law firm is a personal service contract as well. The law firm picked you, and it has a substantial interest in having you do the work.

It is hardly surprising that bankruptcy law would respect StarStruck Studio's state law right not to have a replacement actor forced on it, and your law firm's right not to have a replacement summer associate forced on it. It is also not surprising that § 365(c)(1) permits the assignment of such a contract if the nondebtor party consents.

What is surprising is that § 365(c)(1) not only prohibits assignment of such contracts without the consent of the nondebtor party—*it also appears to prohibit assumption of such contracts, even by a debtor in possession, without consent of the nondebtor party.* Note that § 365(c)(1) provides that the "trustee may not assume or assign" a contract if applicable law permits the nondebtor party to refuse to accept performance from someone other than the debtor or debtor in possession. It would make sense to prohibit a trustee in bankruptcy from assuming Meryl Hepburn's contract with StarStruck and showing up to perform for her, but would it make sense to keep Meryl Hepburn as debtor in possession from assuming her own contract and performing? Yet she would seem to have no greater rights than a trustee would have to assume her contract. See § 1107(a).[48]

While the predicament of the occasional sports figure, actor, or other performing artist who files for bankruptcy would be interesting, the importance of § 365(c)(1) is greatly magnified because personal service contracts are not the only contracts which the law makes nondelegable: U.S. government contracts, which account for a large part of all business transactions, are nondelegable by statute. See 41 U.S.C. § 15. Courts have also held that nonexclusive patent licenses—so important in our economy—are nondelegable, absent the consent of the patent licensor. See Perlman v. Catapult Entertainment, Inc. (In re Catapult Entertainment, Inc.), 165 F.3d 747 (9th Cir. 1999).[49] For a comprehensive discussion of additional kinds of contracts affected (or potentially affected) by § 365(c)(1)—including partnership agreements, copyright licenses, trademark licenses, and franchise agreements—see Harner, Black & Goodman, *Debtors Beware: The Expanding Universe of Non-Assumable/Non-Assignable Contracts in Bankruptcy*, 13 AM. BANKR. INST. L. REV. 187 (2005).

A few courts have held that § 365(c)(1) applies only to personal service contracts, but the prevailing view is that it applies to any contract made nondelegable (in the absence of a contractual anti-delegation provision) by any statute or common law rule. See, e.g., In re West Electronics, Inc., 852 F.2d 79 (3d Cir. 1988) (applying § 365(c)(1) to contract with the federal government); In re Pioneer Ford Sales, Inc., 729 F.2d 27 (1st Cir. 1984) (applying § 365(c)(1) to automobile dealership's contract with auto manufacturer).

---

48. She could argue that StarStruck was obligated to consent to her assumption of the contract because a refusal to consent would be discrimination by an employer against a debtor in bankruptcy, discrimination that may be prohibited by § 525(b). It is also possible that the person whose consent is needed under § 365(c)(1) might owe a duty under state law not to withhold consent arbitrarily or in bad faith. See In re Schick, 235 B.R. 318 (Bankr. S.D.N.Y. 1999) (holding that a hearing was needed to determine whether general partner violated covenant of good faith and fair dealing by refusing to consent to assignment of full partnership by debtor limited partner to purchaser of debtor's partnership interest). Meryl Hepburn could also argue, as we will see, that the statute should not be read literally.

49. The Ninth Circuit in Catapult expressed no opinion on the application of § 365(c)(1) to *exclusive* patent licenses. Id. at 750 n.3. At least one court has held that exclusive patent licenses are within the scope of § 365(c)(1). See In re Hernandez, 287 B.R. 795, 798 (Bankr. D. Ariz. 2002).

Several circuits have held that § 365(c)(1) should be applied literally. If the contract is not delegable (or not assignable), then the debtor in possession cannot assume it. See *West Electronics*, 852 F.2d 79 (3d Cir. 1988); RCI Tech. Corp. v. Sunterra Corp. (In re Sunterra Corp.), 361 F.3d 267 (4th Cir. 2004); *Catapult Entertainment*, 165 F.3d 747 (9th Cir. 1999); City of Jamestown v. James Cable Partners, L.P. (In re James Cable Partners, L.P.), 27 F.3d 534 (11th Cir. 1994). This is called the "hypothetical test," because it is applied by asking whether the nondebtor party could refuse performance from a hypothetical person to whom the debtor might attempt to delegate performance.

The First Circuit and perhaps a majority of lower courts from the other circuits apply what is called the "actual test." They argue that Congress intended to allow nondelegable contracts to be assumed, as long as the debtor in possession is the actual person assuming it. See Institut Pasteur v. Cambridge Biotech Corp., 104 F.3d 489 (1st Cir. 1997); see, e.g., In re Fastrax, Inc., 129 B.R. 274 (Bankr. M.D. Fla. 1991).

In *Fastrax,* the debtor (Fastrax) had contracted with the Air Force to install a computer system complete with software at an Air Force facility. Fastrax subcontracted out the software portion of the job to a software company (Southwest). Fastrax failed to make required payments to Southwest and then filed a chapter 11 petition. Fastrax assumed its prime contract with the Air Force; the opinion does not say whether that was with the Air Force's consent or not. Fastrax then sought to assume the subcontract with Southwest. Although the subcontract was not a contract with the government and thus was not governed by 41 U.S.C. § 15, Southwest argued that the subcontract was a nonassignable personal services contract. Southwest then relied on *West Electronics* for the proposition that a contract that is nonassignable under applicable law cannot be assumed by a debtor. The court held that

> * * * even though § 365(c) speaks in the disjunctive and provides that a debtor may not assume or assign an unexpired executory contract without consent, a sensible construction of this section permits but one conclusion—that this section was designed solely to govern the debtor-in-possession's ability to assign a contract which it already assumed. In fact, § 365(c)(1)(A) was amended in 1984 by substituting the phrase "an entity other than the debtor or the debtor-in-possession" for the words "the trustee." 11 U.S.C. § 365(c)(1)(A) (Supp. II 1985). The legislative history for this change provides:
>
>> This amendment makes it clear that the prohibition against a trustee's power to assume an executory contract does not apply where it is the debtor that is in possession and the performance to be given or received under a personal service contract will be the same as if no petition had been filed because of the personal service nature of the contract.
>
> H.R. Rep. No. 1195, 96th Cong., 2d Sess. § 27(b) (1980). This comment clearly indicates that Congress did not intend § 365(c)(1) to preclude assumption of an otherwise nonassignable personal service contract if the performance to be given or received "will be the same as if no petition had been filed." Rather, § 365(c)(1)

provides that a debtor-in-possession can assume a personal service contract that is nonassignable under state law as long as its performance is going to be the same as if no petition had been filed. Therefore, the hypothetical test established in *West Electronics* is clearly not appropriate under § 365(c)(1).

129 B.R. at 277.

Note that the legislative history cited in *Fastrax* is a committee report dated four years before the amendment to § 365(c)(1) was made. Further, given the Supreme Court's emphasis on the "plain meaning" of statutory language, the Court might be unwilling to look to the legislative history. And there is a further problem; even if the 1984 amendment fixed the problem in § 365(c)(1), Congress did not amend § 365(e)(2). Under § 365(e)(2), the nondebtor party is permitted to utilize an ipso facto clause to terminate the contract if "applicable law excuses [the nondebtor party] from accepting performance from * * * the trustee." The government—or StarStruck Studios—is definitely not required to accept performance from a trustee. Thus it seems that even if a debtor in possession could assume a nondelegable contract despite § 365(c)(1), the nondebtor party could obtain relief from stay[50] and then cancel the contract under the ipso facto clause that is almost sure to be in the contract.

One further complication is the confusing relationship between § 365(c)(1) and § 365(f)(1). Section 365(f)(1) permits the trustee or debtor in possession to assign executory contracts (and unexpired leases) "notwithstanding" contractual provisions, and notwithstanding provisions in "applicable law," that would prohibit, restrict, or condition the assignment. However, § 365(f)(1) begins with "Except as provided in subsection (c)," and thus it seems that § 365(c) should contain one or more exceptions to the general rule in § 365(f)(1). Instead, when we look at § 365(c)(1), we see what appears to be a wholesale reversal of § 365(f)(1)'s invalidation of provisions in "applicable law" that would prohibit, restrict, or condition the assignment.

It is not easy to see what is left of § 365(f)(1)'s invalidation of "applicable law." It is true that § 365(c)(1) instructs us to ignore any provisions in the contract or lease that prohibit or restrict assignment of the contract in deciding whether "applicable law" gives the debtor or debtor in possession the right to delegate duties and assign rights. Perhaps that means that § 365(f)(1) only invalidates "applicable law" that simply makes contractual anti-assignment or anti-delegation provisions enforceable, as Justice Breyer suggested in an opinion written when he was a circuit court judge. See In re Pioneer Ford Sales, Inc., 729 F.2d 27 (1st Cir. 1984). Most courts, though, reconcile § 365(c)(1) and (f)(1) in a different way:

> Subsection (f)(1) states the broad rule—a law that, as a general matter, "prohibits, restricts, or conditions the assignment" of executory contracts is trumped by the provisions of subsection (f)(1). Subsection (c)(1), however, states a carefully crafted exception to the broad rule—where

---

50. Most of the cases have held that the nondebtor party must obtain relief from the stay before cancelling a contract, even if the contract cannot be assumed because of § 365(c)(1) or (c)(2) or because the nondebtor party has a right to cancel the contract under § 365(e)(2). See Epstein, Nickles & White, BANKRUPTCY § 3-14, at 99 n.43. Presumably if the court is convinced that the Code gives the nondebtor party the right to cancel the contract under § 365(e)(2), the court will find that to be cause for granting relief from the stay.

applicable law does not merely recite a general ban on assignment, but instead more specifically "excuses a party ... from accepting performance from or rendering performance to an entity" different from the one with which the party originally contracted, the applicable law prevails over subsection (f)(1). In other words, in determining whether an "applicable law" stands or falls under § 365(f)(1), a court must ask why the "applicable law" prohibits assignment. Only if the law prohibits assignment on the rationale that the identity of the contracting party is material to the agreement will subsection (c)(1) rescue it.

Catapult Entertainment, supra, 165 F.3d at 752.

As a result, businesses that rely on government contracts, on nonexclusive (and perhaps even exclusive) patent licenses, or on other agreements within the scope of § 365(c)(1) will have a very difficult time reorganizing unless the government (or other nondebtor party to the contract) supports the reorganization.[51] Note, however, that in certain circumstances § 525(a) will limit to some extent the actions that a government may take against a debtor. If the debtor has or seeks rights that amount to a "license" (or a "permit, charter, franchise, or other similar grant") then governmental entities are prohibited from taking certain actions against a debtor or its associates during or after the bankruptcy case "solely because" the debtor is or was in bankruptcy, or was insolvent before the grant of a discharge, or failed to pay a dischargeable debt. Section 525(a). The government may not "deny, revoke, suspend, or refuse to renew" the license, or "condition" the grant of the license, or "discriminate with respect to [the] grant" of the license, solely for such a reason. Id.

When § 525(a) applies, the results can be spectacular. In FCC v. NextWave Personal Communications, Inc. 537 U.S. 293, 123 S. Ct. 832, 154 L. Ed. 2d 863 (2003), the Court held that the FCC violated § 525(a) when it purported to cancel radio spectrum licenses—to be used for cellphone service and other radio-based communications services—purchased by NextWave at an FCC auction. When NextWave filed a chapter 11 petition and failed to make a required payment on the $4.74 billion price that it had agreed to pay, the FCC claimed that the licenses had been canceled automatically under the regulatory scheme governing such auctions. The FCC then auctioned them off again, this time for $16 billion. The Court's ruling invalidated the second auction and left the licenses in NextWave's hands in a multi-billion dollar win for a chapter 11 debtor. See Greenhouse, *Supreme Court Rules F.C.C. Took Licenses Away in Error*, N.Y. Times, Jan. 28, 2003, at C1.

---

51. Space limitations preclude consideration of two additional issues—each of which concerns the relationship between § 365 and § 363—beyond the brief mention in this footnote. First, what is the effect, if any of § 363(m) on the ability of appellate courts effectively to review orders approving assignment of executory contracts and leases? If the assignment is a kind of sale of property, then § 363(m) may protect the assignee who gives value in good faith against having its rights affected by any appeal. See, e.g., Weingarten Nostat, Inc. v. Serv. Merch. Co., 396 F.3d 737 (6th Cir. 2004). Second, may a debtor in possession who is a lessor sell real property free and clear of a nondebtor lessee's leasehold interest under § 363(f), even though that would eliminate the nondebtor lessee's rights under § 365(h)? Compare Precision Indus., Inc. v. Qualitech Steel SBQ, LLC (In re Qualitech Steel Corp.), 327 F.3d 537 (7th Cir. 2003), with In re Haskell L.P., 321 B.R. 1 (Bankr. D. Mass. 2005).

PART IV

DETERMINING CLAIMS BY AND AGAINST THE ESTATE

Chapter Eight

Avoiding Secured Claims (And Other Transfers and Obligations)

A. INTRODUCTION

Solvent, well-capitalized debtors may transfer property and incur obligations as they choose, assuming they have not entered into agreements with creditors limiting their rights. If General Electric chooses to pay a large dividend to its shareholders, contribute to charity, pay off a large debt before it is due, or acquire a small high-tech company for much more than anyone else thinks it is worth, that is General Electric's prerogative (subject to corporation law protection of shareholders against corporate waste). G.E.'s owners—its shareholders—can control what is done by electing directors whose approaches they like. As long as G.E. stays solvent and well-capitalized, what it does is none of its creditors' business, absent an agreement to the contrary by G.E. with one or more creditors.

But when an enterprise is insolvent or so poorly capitalized as to be in grave danger of financial distress, the creditors—not just the owners—have a stake in the enterprise's transfers of property and incurring of obligations:

- When such an enterprise transfers property without receiving a reasonable amount of value in return, the value available for payment of debts is diminished, which harms the creditors. The total "pie" is smaller.
- When such an enterprise incurs obligations without receiving a reasonable amount of value in return, creditors are harmed, because now they have a new competitor for whatever value may be available.

In effect, the creditors who gave a reasonable amount of value (and whom we may call the "legitimate" creditors) each are now likely to get a smaller slice of the "pie."

- When such an enterprise pays one creditor first, or gives one creditor a lien on the enterprise's property, the other creditors may be harmed. The creditor who was paid or who got a lien may get a larger slice of the "pie," with only smaller pieces left for the others.

The law recognizes the creditors' stake in various ways. State law tends to focus on ensuring that the size of the "pie" not be unfairly reduced and that only legitimate creditors share in it. State corporation law, for example, limits the payment of dividends where a corporation is in financial distress. See, e.g., Del. Stat. Ann., title 8, § 170. When a debtor is in financial difficulty, state fraudulent transfer law may allow creditors to avoid—to reverse—transfers of property and incurring of obligations for which the debtor receives less than a reasonable amount of value. The Bankruptcy Code allows the trustee or debtor in possession to use the rights that the unsecured creditors have under state fraudulent transfer law and also provides its own independent fraudulent transfer provision (which was modeled on the typical state law and adapted for use by the trustee or debtor in possession). See §§ 544(b) and 548. The trustee's or debtor in possession's rights under state fraudulent transfer law and under § 548 are the subject of the next section of this chapter.

State law is generally not very concerned with whether legitimate creditors are treated equally. Under state law, each creditor generally acts individually to seek repayment. The primary feature of the state law of creditors' rights is the race of diligence: creditors who manage to obtain payment get to keep the money even if others are not paid, and the creditor who first receives a lien on property belonging to the debtor is entitled to be paid out of that property ahead of other creditors. Thus it is not surprising that state law does not ensure each creditor an equal slice of the "pie," but rather focuses on making sure the size of the "pie" available to creditors as a whole is not unfairly reduced, and on making sure that those who seek slices have legitimate claims for which they gave a reasonable amount of value.[1]

---

1. A few states prohibit preferential payment of one creditor as opposed to another. See, e.g., Michael, *The Past and Future of Kentucky's Fraudulent Transfer and Preference Laws*, 86 Ky. L.J. 937 (1997-98). In addition, the Uniform Fraudulent Transfer Act provides for recovery by certain creditors of certain preferential payments made to insiders. UFTA § 5(b). To some extent, however, the Bankruptcy Code may preempt state preference laws because of, and in deference to, the Code's own provisions allowing the recovery of certain prepetition preferential transfers by the debtor. See Sherwood Partners, Inc., v. Lycos, Inc., 394 F.3d 1198 (9th Cir. 2005). For trenchant criticism of *Sherwood Partners*, see Brubaker, *The Preemptive Effect of the Bankruptcy Code for Preference Avoidance Under State-Law Assignments for the Benefit of Creditors*, 25 BANKR. L. LETTER No. 4, at 1 (April 2005), available at 25 No. 4 BLL 1 (Westlaw).

Equality of result is more naturally a concern in collective proceedings which deal with creditors as a group. Thus, where state law provides for a collective proceeding—for example, where a debtor makes a general assignment of assets for benefit of creditors[2]—state law does show a concern for equal treatment of creditors. Bankruptcy is a collective proceeding, and thus it is not surprising that equal treatment of similarly situated creditors is an important policy in bankruptcy law; bankruptcy law is concerned that equally situated creditors obtain equal slices of the "pie."

For example, in a chapter 7 liquidation, general unsecured claims must be treated equally by being paid on a strict pro rata basis; each holder of a general unsecured claim will be paid the same percentage of its allowed claim. See § 726(a)(2) & (b). Along the same lines, in chapter 11 any impaired class that is unfairly discriminated against by a plan of reorganization can block confirmation of the plan by rejecting it. See § 1129(b)(1).

If bankruptcy policy calls for similarly situated creditors to be treated equally, how do we determine whether two creditors are similarly situated? The Bankruptcy Code distinguishes among creditors' claims on various grounds. Those whose contributions are necessary for the bankruptcy process are given administrative priority over almost all other unsecured claims. See § 507(a)(2). Those who are for some reason particularly vulnerable to harm from discharge of debt are also given special priority. See § 507(a)(3)-(7). The public treasury must be protected, and thus most tax claims and certain other claims owed to governmental units are given priority next. See § 507(a)(8)-(9). But the most important bases for distinguishing among claims are state law dealing with liability and state law dealing with property interests.

Bankruptcy law for the most part takes as a given the rights to payment that parties have under nonbankruptcy law. Thus the existence and the amount of a claim is determined, in most cases, by the substantive nonbankruptcy law that governs the existence and extent of liability. See § 502(b), and particularly § 502(b)(1). A creditor, C1, whose right to payment under nonbankruptcy law is $20,000, has a claim twice as large as another creditor, C2, whose right to payment under nonbankruptcy law is $10,000. Bankruptcy law recognizes that difference and generally gives C1 twice as large a slice of the pie as C2, assuming their claims are otherwise similar. Bankruptcy typically distributes payments and other property on this kind of pro rata basis, recognizing that larger claims are entitled to larger distributions. (Another way of looking at this is to see that each dollar of C1's claim is similarly situated to each dollar of C2's claim, and thus C1 and C2 should be treated equally for each dollar of their claims; that will result in C1 receiving twice the distribution as C2.)

---

2.   See, e.g., Michael, supra note 1. An assignment for benefit of creditors is the transfer of all the debtor's nonexempt assets to a trustee (called the "assignee") who holds the assets in trust for the benefit of all the creditors. Under state law, the assignee must treat most unsecured creditors equally. See, e.g., Linton v. Schmidt (In re Linton), 88 Wis. 2d 183, 198, 277 N.W. 2d 136, 143 (1979).

Just as bankruptcy law typically respects state substantive law as to the existence and extent of liability, bankruptcy law also typically respects state substantive law governing property rights. Creditors who have interests in the debtor's property to secure their debts—that is, creditors who have liens—usually can maintain their interests in the property when it comes into the bankruptcy estate. The estate succeeds to the debtor's interests in the property subject to whatever other interests nonbankruptcy law recognizes in the property. Butner v. United States, 440 U.S. 48, 99 S. Ct. 914, 59 L. Ed. 2d 136 (1979). Thus, if there is a mortgage on a parcel of real property owned by the debtor, the estate does not take the property free of the mortgage but rather subject to it—at least, that is the initial situation when the petition is filed. The value available to the estate for payment of unsecured claims out of a particular item of property is reduced by the amount of the secured creditor's lien on that property.

Under state law, however, a creditor's debt or property interest may be valid as against the debtor but subject to a successful attack by a third party. We have already seen that obligations and property interests obtained for less than a reasonable amount of value may be attacked under state fraudulent transfer law. Under state law, persons who have received such fraudulent obligations or transfers are subject to losing them. As we have seen, such fraudulent obligations and transfers have the effect of reducing each legitimate creditor's slice of the "pie" or of shrinking the size of the "pie" itself. Thus, as we have seen, the trustee or the debtor in possession is entitled to use state fraudulent transfer law to avoid such obligations and transfers. See § 544(b).

Similarly, secret liens—even if obtained nonfraudulently for a reasonable amount of value—often may be attacked successfully under state law. State law usually requires the holder of a lien to provide notice to the public in some particular way—to "perfect" the lien—so that the lien will not be a secret. If the lienholder does not provide public notice (for example by recording its real property mortgage or filing a financing statement to perfect its Article 9 security interest), others may be misled into thinking the debtor owns the property free and clear. To return to our "pie" analogy:

- When an enterprise transfers a lien or other property interest to a transferee who fails to give appropriate public notice of the transfer, an illusion is created that the "pie" is larger than it really is. In effect the transferee has already obtained a slice of the pie, but the pie appears to be whole. Creditors thus may be misled into thinking that they will get larger slices than will in fact be available *if* the transferee is permitted to keep its secret slice.

As a result, state law often departs from the "first in time, first in right" principle and provides that as long as a lienholder's lien is unperfected, third parties may obtain interests that will be senior to the lien. Thus state law provides that a judicial lien obtained on personal property at a time when an Article 9 secured party has an unperfected security interest in the property will be senior to the Article 9 security interest, even though the Article 9 security interest was created first. See U.C.C. § 9-317(a)(2).[3] In most states a judicial lien obtained on real property will be senior to a mortgage that was created before the judicial lien, if the judicial lien creditor obtains its lien without notice of the mortgage and before the mortgage is recorded.

But the automatic stay prevents creditors from obtaining judicial liens once the bankruptcy petition is filed. Does this mean that holders of unperfected liens can relax once the debtor files a bankruptcy petition? Not at all. The stay prevents individual creditors from acting, but the Bankruptcy Code gives the trustee or debtor in possession as representative of the creditors the same ability to defeat unrecorded mortgages and unperfected security interests.

The Code does so by, once again, incorporating and adapting state law; the trustee or debtor in possession is given whatever rights a creditor would have, under state law, who obtained a judicial lien on the debtor's property at the moment of filing of the petition. See § 544(a)(1). Using that "judicial lien creditor" power, the trustee or debtor in possession can avoid unperfected Article 9 security interests[4] and, in most states, avoid unrecorded mortgages. So that unrecorded mortgages will be avoidable in all states, the Code even gives the trustee or debtor in possession the rights of a bona fide purchaser of real property from the debtor. (Bona fide purchasers take free of unrecorded mortgages in all states; thus in every state the trustee can avoid unrecorded mortgages using the "bona fide purchaser of real property" power.[5])

When the trustee or debtor in possession avoids a secured creditor's secret lien on an item of property, the secured creditor becomes unsecured. The formerly secured creditor is now situated similarly to other unsecured creditors, and will be treated equally with them. The value of the lien becomes available to the estate for the benefit of the unsecured creditors. See, e.g., § 551. Thus the illusion that the "pie" was larger than it actually was becomes a reality—the pie is enlarged to the size it appeared to be.

In that situation, the state law vulnerability of the secured creditor's lien leads to its avoidance, which furthers the bankruptcy policy of equality. But in some situations bankruptcy law allows the trustee or debtor in possession to

---

3.   Under U.C.C. § 9-317(a)(2), to have priority over the security interest the judicial lien must arise before the secured party perfects the security interest and before the secured party files a financing statement covering the collateral. (The financing statement may be "pre-filed;" that is, filed before the security interest is created. The financing statement cannot perfect the security interest until the security interest comes into existence—until it "attaches" in Article 9 terminology—but the financing statement can provide priority over judicial liens that come into existence between the time the financing statement is filed and the time the security interest attaches. If a financing statement has been pre-filed, the security interest will be perfected as soon as it attaches.)

4.   See supra footnote 3.

5.   If the holder of the unrecorded interest is in possession of the real property, so that under state law there cannot be a bona fide purchaser who would take free of the unrecorded interest, then the unrecorded interest cannot be avoided under § 544(a)(3). The trustee's knowledge or actual notice of the unrecorded interest would not prevent the interest from being avoided. See § 544(a) ("without regard to any knowledge of the trustee or of any creditor"). But constructive notice does prevent avoidance.

avoid a property interest even when it would not be vulnerable under state law. Most importantly, for our purposes, bankruptcy law often does not respect property interests obtained by creditors—or perfected by creditors—shortly before the bankruptcy filing. In determining whether creditors are similarly situated, and therefore should be treated equally, bankruptcy law looks back to a date before the bankruptcy filing—usually 90 days before—and strips from creditors the advantages they may have obtained over other creditors after that date. They lose whatever "preferences" they may have been able to obtain on pre-existing debts in the last-minute flurry of activity that often accompanies a decline into bankruptcy. See § 547. If the debtor paid them, the transfer of funds may be avoided, and they may have to return the funds to the estate. If the debtor gave them liens—or if they took liens by judicial process—to secure previously unsecured claims, the liens may be avoided, returning them to their previously unsecured status of equality with other unsecured claim holders.

This is the antithesis of the state law race of diligence. By looking back to a date before the bankruptcy filing and stripping creditors of advantages obtained during that time, § 547 advances the policy of equality. It also advances another policy that may be more fundamental. It strips from creditors the benefits they obtained from running the state law race of diligence, a race that generally accelerates the debtor's slide into bankruptcy.

Creditors who obtained payment or other property interests shortly before bankruptcy without taking part in that race may be permitted to retain what they received. For example, a creditor who receives payment of a debt in the ordinary course of business, without taking unusual or coercive steps to obtain payment (and therefore not as a result of running the race of diligence) may be permitted to retain the payment. See § 547(c)(2). Note that creditors who take unusual steps to squeeze payment from the debtor—thereby stripping the debtor of cash that it likely needs to stay in business—cannot shield the payment under the § 547(c)(2) ordinary course exception to avoidance.[6] Perhaps Congress thought it worthwhile to reward those who refrain from running the race of diligence, even though allowing them to keep their payments violates the policy of equality. Or perhaps Congress simply wanted to protect—from the disruption caused by disgorgement of preferences—those creditors whose reliance on the stability of routine payments is reasonable. In any event, § 547(c)(2) substantially undermines the policy of equality.

---

6.   Note also that a creditor may have obtained payment or a lien shortly before bankruptcy without violating either the policy of equality or the policy of discouraging action which may cause the debtor to slide into bankruptcy. For example, a finance company that, shortly before the bankruptcy filing, lends money to the debtor and simultaneously takes a lien to secure the loan, does not improve its position by taking the lien; its original position as a creditor is as a secured creditor—it never was equal to the unsecured creditors and need not be treated equally with them. Such a loan may in fact help a debtor to turn its business around, avoid the slide into bankruptcy, and pay the other creditors. Thus a transfer of a lien to secure a new loan is not subject to avoidance under § 547; it is not a preference because it was not made "for or on account of an antecedent debt owed by the debtor before such transfer was made." Section 547(b)(2).

With this background, we can turn to the law of fraudulent transfers and of fraudulently incurred obligations. Note the reliance on state property law, on state fraudulent transfer law, and on state law fraudulent transfer concepts. Consider whether state law provides sufficient protection for creditors, whether bankruptcy law ought to go further in some instances, and whether bankruptcy law has gone too far in those instances in which it has departed from state law concepts.

B. FRAUDULENT TRANSFERS

Rather than see their property seized by creditors, debtors sometimes transfer their property to friends or relatives for little or no consideration or with the understanding that the debtor shall continue to have the use and benefit of the property. Since Roman law, such attempts to defraud creditors have been ineffective. The source of modern fraudulent transfer law is the Statute of Elizabeth (more particularly the Statute of 13 Elizabeth, chapter 5, enacted by Parliament in 1570). This law condemned any conveyance of property made with the intent "to delay, hinder or defraud" creditors. As interpreted and applied, the Statute of Elizabeth, and its more modern counterparts, render fraudulent transfers voidable by creditors of the debtor.

American jurisdictions either recognized the Statute of Elizabeth as part of inherited law or enacted identical or very similar versions of it. In 1918, the National Conference of Commissioners on Uniform State Laws (NCCUSL) promulgated the Uniform Fraudulent Conveyance Act (UFCA). About half the states adopted the UFCA. In 1984, the NCCUSL promulgated a new model statute entitled the Uniform Fraudulent Transfer Act (UFTA), which has now been adopted by forty-three states and the District of Columbia. See http://www.nccusl.org/Update/uniformact_factsheets/uniformacts-fs-ufta.asp (last visited Apr. 15, 2006). For the most part, the two uniform laws are very similar.

Like the Statute of Elizabeth, both the UFCA and the UFTA condemn transfers of property that are *actually fraudulent*, meaning that the debtor makes the transfer with the actual, subjective intention of defrauding, hindering or delaying creditors. See UFCA § 7; UFTA § 4(a)(1). The two uniform statutes—and the Statute of Elizabeth as interpreted—go much further, however, and render certain transfers of a debtor's property ineffective against creditors without regard to the debtor's actual subjective intention. See UFCA §§ 4, 5, 6 & 8; UFTA §§ 4(a)(2) & 5. This latter class of conveyances, which are *constructively fraudulent*, describes circumstances under which the law deems that a transfer of the debtor's property is unfair to creditors and is ineffective as to them, irrespective of the debtor's intention in making the transfer, solely because of the circumstances that existed at the time of the transfer. Here, most clearly, the law of fraudulent transfers overrides contracts doctrine that an enforceable agreement does not require equivalency as long as the exchange is bargained for.

A version of the UFCA has long been part of the federal bankruptcy laws and presently appears as § 548 of the Bankruptcy Code. Like similar state laws,

§ 548 condemns, as a matter of federal law, transfers that the debtor made with actual intent to defraud creditors, § 548(a)(1)(A), and certain other transfers that are deemed to be constructively fraudulent, § 548(a)(1)(B).

A closely-related avoiding power is § 544(b), which allows a trustee (or debtor in possession) to invoke state fraudulent conveyance law to avoid a transfer. Section 544(b) is useful when the letter of the state law, or judicial interpretations of it, condemn a wider range of transfers than § 548. Section 544(b) is particularly useful when the allegedly fraudulent transfer or obligation was made or incurred more than two years before the filing of the bankruptcy petition, in which case § 548 is inapplicable. See § 548(a)(1) (but note also that transfers or obligations are considered made or incurred for purposes of § 548 when they are perfected against bona fide purchasers, § 548(d)). In such a case, if the statute of limitations on the state law fraudulent transfer claim had not expired as of the date of the bankruptcy petition filing, § 544(b) may be available to avoid the transfer or obligation.

The purpose of fraudulent conveyance law, whatever its form, is simple: it protects a debtor's unsecured creditors from reductions in the debtor's estate to which they look, generally, for their security. Fairness would seem to require no less. In addition, as a result of this protection, the creditors presumably "need not monitor debtors so closely, and the savings in monitoring costs make businesses more productive." Bonded Fin. Servs. v. European Am. Bank, 838 F.2d 890, 892 (7th Cir. 1988). The Seventh Circuit also helpfully noted the difference between fraudulent and preferential transfers:

> The fraudulent conveyance must be distinguished from a preferential transfer to a creditor, which does not diminish the total payoff for the group, but which may be undone to reduce the incentive individuals creditors have to rush to dismember the debtor before rival creditors can do so. The collective bankruptcy proceeding solves the common pool problem, which otherwise may produce a reduction in the value of the productive assets taken jointly.

Id. at 892 n.1.

1. Transfers Fraudulent Under Bankruptcy Law, Section 548

Section 548 of the Bankruptcy Code empowers the trustee to avoid a transfer of the debtor's property, or any obligation incurred by the debtor, that was fraudulently made or incurred on or within two years before the filing of the bankruptcy petition.[7] Section 548 itself, as a matter of federal law, defines in its subsections (a) and (b) when a transfer or obligation will be considered fraudulent. First, a transfer or obligation is avoidable where the debtor made the transfer or incurred the obligation with actual fraudulent intent—that is, where the debtor acted

---

7.   The 2005 BAPCPA changed the lookback period from one year to two years.

with actual intent to hinder, delay or defraud any entity to which the debtor was or became, on or after the date that such transfer was made or such obligation incurred, indebted * * *.

Section 548(a)(1)(A).[8]

Section 548 also describes five instances of constructive fraud, that is, five situations in which a transfer or obligation is deemed to have been fraudulently made or incurred irrespective of the debtor's intention. The first four such situations are when a transfer was made (or obligation incurred) for less than reasonably equivalent value, § 548(a)(1)(B)(i), and the debtor:

- (1) was or thereby became insolvent, § 548(a)(1)(B)(ii)(I); or
- (2) was engaged in business with an unreasonably small capital, § 548(a)(1)(B)(ii)(II); or
- (3) intended to incur debts that would be beyond the debtor's ability to pay, § 548(a)(1)(B)(ii)(III); or
- (4) made a nonordinary course transfer (or incurred a nonordinary course obligation) to an insider under an employment contract, § 548(a)(1)(B)(ii)(IV).

The fifth kind of constructively fraudulently transfer is any transfer of partnership property to a partner in the debtor if the debtor was or thereby became insolvent. Section 548(b).

Certain requirements are common to both actually fraudulent and constructively fraudulent transfers under § 548.

- First, a *transfer* must have occurred involving *property of the debtor*.
- Second, the transfer must have been made, directly or indirectly, by the debtor.
- Finally, the transfer must have occurred within the two-year period preceding bankruptcy.

Significantly, for purposes of § 548, a transfer that must be perfected under nonbankruptcy law in order to be valid against a bona fide purchaser is deemed not to have been made until the necessary steps for perfection have been taken. Section 548(d)(1). If those steps are not taken before the debtor's bankruptcy, the transfer is deemed to have occurred immediately before the date of the bankruptcy petition. Id. Suppose, for example, that the debtor transfers real property under circumstances that render the transfer fraudulent under § 548. State law provides that no conveyance of real estate is effective against a bona fide purchaser unless and until the conveyance is recorded. Therefore, for purposes of § 548, the timing of the transfer is not determined on the basis of when it was effective between the debtor and transferee. Rather, the timing is determined according to when the transfer was recorded. So, if the transfer was

---

8. In addition, for transfers made with actual fraudulent intent to self-settled trusts and the like, also known as DAPTs (debtor asset protection trusts), § 548(e) provides for a ten-year, rather than a two-year, lookback period.

actually made 28 months before the debtor's bankruptcy petition was filed, but was not recorded until 21 months before that date, the transfer is deemed to have occurred within the two-year period preceding bankruptcy and is therefore avoidable under § 548.

Each kind of fraud—actual and constructive—involves other peculiar requirements. We focus on constructive fraud, which by far is the more common basis for avoidance under § 548 in chapter 11 business reorganization cases. The most common variety of constructive fraud is described by § 548(a)(1)(B)(i) & (B)(ii)(I). Those provisions allow the debtor in possession to

> avoid any transfer of an interest of the debtor in property, or any obligation incurred by the debtor, that was made or incurred on or within two years before the date of the filing of the petition, if the debtor voluntarily or involuntarily * * * received *less than a reasonably equivalent value* in exchange for such transfer or obligation and was *insolvent* on the date that such transfer was made or such obligation was incurred, or became insolvent as a result of such transfer or obligation.

(Emphasis supplied.) The biggest issues often are insolvency and reasonably equivalent value. These issues can be very difficult. They are fact-intensive and turn, in large part, on business judgment and valuation, which are not exact sciences. Illustrating how judges and lawyers actually handle them is hard to do in short problems for the law school classroom, but the two issues—like twin peaks—are towering and foreboding.

Problem 8-1

1. Decide which of the following transactions might be constructively fraudulent under § 548. In each case, assume (unless otherwise noted) that the transaction occurred within two years of Foam Corporation's bankruptcy and that Foam Corporation was insolvent or became so as a result of the transaction.

   a. Foam Corporation gave Gruff a lake-front home, as a gift, in appreciation of Gruff's many years of faithful service.

   b. Foam Corporation sold Swenson Chemical a transferable patent and trademark license permitting Swenson to make Waveless waterbeds and to sell them using the Waveless trademark. The price was nominal compared to the $200,000 price that More Foam paid for its license and, probably, was substantially less than market value.

   c. First Bank foreclosed its mortgage on a parcel of Foam Corporation's real estate and sold the property at the foreclosure sale—which fully complied with local law—for a price that, by some expert accounts, is only about 65% of market value. The mortgage was created and recorded years before the bankruptcy. Only the foreclosure occurred within two years before the bankruptcy petition was filed. Compare BFP v. Resolution Trust Corp., 511 U.S. 531 (1994) (foreclosure sale) (reprinted immediately below) with In re Chase, 328 B.R. 675 (Bankr. D. Vt. 2005) (strict foreclosure).

   d. Foam Corporation made a free transfer of certain assets to U-Foam, its corporately-separate subsidiary. (Hint: If U-Foam is solvent, does this transfer reduce the value of Foam Corporation's assets? What if U-Foam is insolvent?)

e.   Foam Corporation became a surety for personal loans that Commerce Bank made to Gruff, and backed its commitment with liens on its property.

f.   Suppose that in June, 2003, Foam Corporation delivered a written continuing guaranty of any loans that Commerce Bank might make to Gruff within three years. In March, 2006, a month before Foam Corporation filed its chapter 11 petition, Gruff borrowed $100,000 from Commerce Bank. When was Foam Corporation's obligation to Commerce Bank with respect to that $100,000 loan incurred? Compare Rubin v. Mfrs. Hanover Trust Co., 661 F.2d 979 (2d Cir.1981) (holding that obligation was incurred when loan was made, not when guarantee was delivered), with UFTA § 6(5)(ii); see Daley & Appelbaum, *The Modernization of Massachusetts Fraudulent Conveyance Law: The Adoption of The Uniform Fraudulent Transfer Act*, 82 MASS. L. REV. 337 (1998). What difference does it make when Foam Corporation's obligation was incurred? Would it matter which view a court took if the guarantee were delivered in May, 2004?

g.   Tina Chemical and Swenson Chemical acquired Foam Corporation by purchasing all of Gruff's (and Simmons's) stock. The deal was complicated, ill-conceived and too costly. Commerce Bank funded the deal which involved refinancing the huge debt to Kick Credit. Gruff netted about one million dollars in cash (and Simmons about $100,000) which the new owners paid with the proceeds of a loan to them by Commerce Bank. This loan, like all of the other financing, was secured by all of Foam's property. Simmons (Bill Gruff's sister) took no active role in the transaction and did not know how risky it was for Foam Corporation.

h.   Foam Corp. gave Kick Credit additional collateral for additional advances.

i.   Foam Corporation gave Kick Credit additional collateral to secure preexisting, unsecured debt. (Alternatively or additionally, is this transaction a preference?)

j.   As noted in Chapter Two, as of early 2006 Gruff intended to expand Foam Corporation's nationwide waterbed sales from $1 million to $10 million per year. To do so, Foam Corporation would have had to invest $2 million for plant expansion, equipment upgrading, and advertising. Foam Corporation paid Charlene Consultant $20,000 on January 10, 2006 (three months before filing its chapter 11 petition) in exchange for Consultant's promise to provide a nationwide waterbed market survey by February 1, 2006. Such a survey would only be of use if Foam Corporation expanded its waterbed operations within six months of the date of the survey. As Gruff should have known well before January 10, 2006, it was unreasonable to think that Foam Corporation could expand its waterbed operations before mid-2007, even if it was successful in restructuring its debts. Consider the next two cases.

k.   Foam Corp. paid its bankruptcy lawyer, Ed Johnson, a $100,000 retainer.

l.   Gruff paid a $100,000 retainer to Johnny Shapiro, a famous defense lawyer, for services Gruff expected he would be needing in connection with a criminal fraud charge. Gruff filed his own petition in bankruptcy two months later.

m.   Three years before Gruff personally filed a bankruptcy petition, Gruff transferred ownership of the Richmond foam plant, which he previously owned personally, to the Gruff Family Trust, an irrevocable trust of which

> he is the trustee and his children are the beneficiaries. He did so by executing and delivering to himself a deed from himself in his individual capacity to himself as Trustee. The deed was not recorded until two and a half years later. See § 548(d)(1).
>
> 2. With respect to each transaction that is fraudulent, who is accountable for what? See §§ 550; 548(c); 546. With respect to Problem 1.g., be aware of the holding that consideration paid to shareholders for their stock in connection with a leveraged buy out, that is paid through a financial intermediary or financial institution, is exempt from the avoiding powers of a trustee under § 546(e) as "settlement payments" made "by or to a * * * stockbroker, financial institution, or securities clearing agency." Lowenschuss v. Resorts Int'l Inc. (In re Resorts Int'l Inc.), 181 F.3d 505, 514 (3d Cir. 1999); but see Munford v. Valuation Research Corp. (In re Munford, Inc.), 98 F.3d 604, 610 (11th Cir. 1996).

BFP v. Resolution Trust Corporation
United States Supreme Court, 1994
511 U.S. 531, 114 S. Ct. 1757, 128 L. Ed. 2d 556

Justice SCALIA delivered the opinion of the Court.

This case presents the question whether the consideration received from a noncollusive, real estate mortgage foreclosure sale conducted in conformance with applicable state law conclusively satisfies the Bankruptcy Code's requirement that transfers of property by insolvent debtors within one year[9] prior to the filing of a bankruptcy petition be in exchange for "a reasonably equivalent value." 11 U.S.C. § 548(a)[(1)(B)(i)].

I

Petitioner BFP is a partnership, formed by Wayne and Marlene Pedersen and Russell Barton in 1987, for the purpose of buying a home in Newport Beach, California, from Sheldon and Ann Foreman. Petitioner took title subject to a first deed of trust in favor of Imperial Savings Association (Imperial) to secure payment of a loan of $356,250 made to the Pedersens in connection with petitioner's acquisition of the home. Petitioner granted a second deed of trust to the Foremans as security for a $200,000 promissory note. Subsequently, Imperial, whose loan was not being serviced, entered a notice of default under the first deed of trust and scheduled a properly noticed foreclosure sale. The foreclosure proceedings were temporarily delayed by the filing of an involuntary bankruptcy petition on behalf of petitioner. After the dismissal of that petition in June 1989, Imperial's foreclosure proceeding was completed at a foreclosure sale on July 12, 1989. The home was purchased by respondent Paul Osborne for $433,000.

In October 1989, petitioner filed for bankruptcy under Chapter 11 of the Bankruptcy Code. Acting as a debtor in possession, petitioner filed a complaint in bankruptcy court seeking to set aside the conveyance of the home to respondent Osborne on the grounds that the foreclosure sale constituted a fraudulent transfer under § 548 of the Code. Petitioner alleged that the home was actually worth over $725,000 at the time of the sale to Osborne. * * *

---

9.   [As noted above, the one-year period was changed to two years by the 2005 BAPCPA.]

Section 548 of the Bankruptcy Code sets forth the powers of a trustee in bankruptcy (or, in a Chapter 11 case, a debtor in possession) to avoid fraudulent transfers. It permits to be set aside not only transfers infected by actual fraud but certain other transfers as well—so-called constructively fraudulent transfers. The constructive fraud provision at issue in this case applies to transfers by insolvent debtors. It permits avoidance if the trustee can establish (1) that the debtor had an interest in property; (2) that a transfer of that interest occurred within one year of the filing of the bankruptcy petition; (3) that the debtor was insolvent at the time of the transfer or became insolvent as a result thereof; and (4) that the debtor received "less than a reasonably equivalent value in exchange for such transfer." 11 U.S.C. § 548(a)[(1)(B)(i)]. It is the last of these four elements that presents the issue in the case before us.

Section 548 applies to any "transfer," which includes "foreclosure of the debtor's equity of redemption." 11 U.S.C. § 101(54) (1988 ed., Supp. IV). Of the three critical terms "reasonably equivalent value," only the last is defined: "value" means, for purposes of § 548, "property, or satisfaction or securing of a ... debt of the debtor," 11 U.S.C. § 548(d)(2)(A). The question presented here, therefore, is whether the amount of debt (to the first and second lien holders) satisfied at the foreclosure sale (viz., a total of $433,000) is "reasonably equivalent" to the worth of the real estate conveyed. The Courts of Appeals have divided on the meaning of those undefined terms. In Durrett v. Washington Nat. Ins. Co., 621 F.2d 201 (1980), the Fifth Circuit, interpreting a provision of the old Bankruptcy Act analogous to § 548(a)[(1)(B)(i)], held that a foreclosure sale that yielded 57% of the property's fair market value could be set aside, and indicated in dicta that any such sale for less than 70% of fair market value should be invalidated. This "Durrett rule" has continued to be applied by some courts under § 548 of the new Bankruptcy Code. In In re Bundles, 856 F.2d 815, 820 (1988), the Seventh Circuit rejected the Durrett rule in favor of a case-by-case, "all facts and circumstances" approach to the question of reasonably equivalent value, with a rebuttable presumption that the foreclosure sale price is sufficient to withstand attack under § 548(a)[(1)(B)]. In this case the Ninth Circuit, agreeing with the Sixth Circuit, see In re Winshall Settlor's Trust, 758 F.2d 1136, 1139 (CA6 1985), adopted the position * * * that the consideration received at a noncollusive, regularly conducted real estate foreclosure sale constitutes a reasonably equivalent value under § 548(a)[(1)(B)(i)]. * * *

In contrast to the approach adopted by the Ninth Circuit in the present case, both Durrett and Bundles refer to fair market value as the benchmark against which determination of reasonably equivalent value is to be measured. In the context of an otherwise lawful mortgage foreclosure sale of real estate,[10] such reference is in our opinion not consistent with the text of the Bankruptcy Code. The term "fair market value," though it is a well-established concept, does not appear in § 548. In contrast, § 522, dealing with a debtor's exemptions, specifically provides that, for purposes of that section, "'value' means fair market value as of the date of the filing of the petition." 11 U.S.C. § 522(a)(2). "Fair market value" also appears in the Code provision that defines the extent to which indebtedness with respect to an equity security is not forgiven for the

---

10. [Footnote 3 in original:] We emphasize that our opinion today covers only mortgage foreclosures of real estate. The considerations bearing upon other foreclosures and forced sales (to satisfy tax liens, for example) may be different.

purpose of determining whether the debtor's estate has realized taxable income. § 346(j)(7)(B). Section 548, on the other hand, seemingly goes out of its way to avoid that standard term. It might readily have said "received less than fair market value in exchange for such transfer or obligation," or perhaps "less than a reasonable equivalent of fair market value." Instead, it used the (as far as we are aware) entirely novel phrase "reasonably equivalent value." "[I]t is generally presumed that Congress acts intentionally and purposely when it includes particular language in one section of a statute but omits it in another," Chicago v. Environmental Defense Fund, 511 U.S. __, __, 114 S. Ct. 1588, 1593, __ L. Ed. 2d __ (1994) (internal quotation marks omitted), and that presumption is even stronger when the omission entails the replacement of standard legal terminology with a neologism. One must suspect the language means that fair market value cannot—or at least cannot always—be the benchmark.

That suspicion becomes a certitude when one considers that market value, as it is commonly understood, has no applicability in the forced-sale context; indeed, it is the very antithesis of forced-sale value. "The market value of ... a piece of property is the price which it might be expected to bring if offered for sale in a fair market; not the price which might be obtained on a sale at public auction or a sale forced by the necessities of the owner, but such a price as would be fixed by negotiation and mutual agreement, after ample time to find a purchaser, as between a vendor who is willing (but not compelled) to sell and a purchaser who desires to buy but is not compelled to take the particular ... piece of property." Black's Law Dictionary 971 (6th ed. 1990). In short, "fair market value" presumes market conditions that, by definition, simply do not obtain in the context of a forced sale.

Neither petitioner, petitioner's amici, nor any federal court adopting the *Durrett* or the *Bundles* analysis has come to grips with this glaring discrepancy between the factors relevant to an appraisal of a property's market value, on the one hand, and the strictures of the foreclosure process on the other. Market value cannot be the criterion of equivalence in the foreclosure-sale context. The language of § 548(a)[(1)(B)(i)] ("received less than a reasonably equivalent value in exchange") requires judicial inquiry into whether the foreclosed property was sold for a price that approximated its worth at the time of sale. An appraiser's reconstruction of "fair market value" could show what similar property would be worth if it did not have to be sold within the time and manner strictures of state-prescribed foreclosure. But property that *must* be sold within those strictures is simply *worth less*. No one would pay as much to own such property as he would pay to own real estate that could be sold at leisure and pursuant to normal marketing techniques. And it is no more realistic to ignore that characteristic of the property (the fact that state foreclosure law permits the mortgagee to sell it at forced sale) than it is to ignore other price-affecting characteristics (such as the fact that state zoning law permits the owner of the neighboring lot to open a gas station).[11]

---

11. [Footnote 5 in original:] We are baffled by the dissent's perception of a "patent" difference between zoning and foreclosure laws insofar as impact upon property value is concerned. The only distinction we perceive is that the former constitute permanent restrictions upon use of the subject property, while the latter apply for a brief period of time and restrict only the manner of its sale. This difference says nothing about how significantly the respective regimes affect the property's value when they are operative. The dissent characterizes foreclosure rules as "merely procedural," and asserts that this renders them, unlike "substantive" zoning regulations, irrelevant in bankruptcy. We are not sure we agree with the characterization. But in any event, the cases relied on for this distinction all address creditors' attempts

Absent a clear statutory requirement to the contrary, we must assume the validity of this state-law regulatory background and take due account of its effect. "The existence and force and function of established institutions of local government are always in the consciousness of lawmakers and, while their weight may vary, they may never be completely overlooked in the task of interpretation." Davies Warehouse Co. v. Bowles, 321 U.S. 144, 154, 64 S. Ct. 474, 480, 88 L. Ed. 635 (1944). Cf. Gregory v. Ashcroft, 501 U.S. 452, __, 111 S. Ct. 2395, 2399-2101, 115 L. Ed. 2d 410 (1991).

There is another artificially constructed criterion we might look to instead of "fair market price." One might judge there to be such a thing as a "reasonable" or "fair" forced-sale price. Such a conviction must lie behind the *Bundles* inquiry into whether the state foreclosure proceedings "were calculated ... to return to the debtor-mortgagor his equity in the property." 856 F.2d, at 824. And perhaps that is what the courts that follow the *Durrett* rule have in mind when they select 70% of fair market value as the outer limit of "reasonably equivalent value" for forecloseable property (we have no idea where else such an arbitrary percentage could have come from). The problem is that such judgments represent policy determinations which the Bankruptcy Code gives us no apparent authority to make. How closely the price received in a forced sale is likely to approximate fair market value depends upon the terms of the forced sale—how quickly it may be made, what sort of public notice must be given, etc. But the terms for foreclosure sale are not *standard*. They vary considerably from State to State, depending upon, among other things, how the particular State values the divergent interests of debtor and creditor. To specify a federal "reasonable" foreclosure-sale price is to extend federal bankruptcy law well beyond the traditional field of fraudulent transfers, into realms of policy where it has not ventured before. Some sense of history is needed to appreciate this.

The modern law of fraudulent transfers had its origin in the Statute of 13 Elizabeth, which invalidated "covinous and fraudulent" transfers designed "to delay, hinder or defraud creditors and others." 13 Eliz., ch. 5 (1570). English courts soon developed the doctrine of "badges of fraud": proof by a creditor of certain objective facts (for example, a transfer to a close relative, a secret transfer, a transfer of title without transfer of possession, or grossly inadequate consideration) would raise a rebuttable presumption of actual fraudulent intent. See Twyne's Case, 3 Coke Rep. 80b, 76 Eng. Rep. 809 (K.B. 1601); O. Bump, *Fraudulent Conveyances: A Treatise upon Conveyances Made by Debtors to Defraud Creditors* 31-60 (3d ed. 1882). Every American bankruptcy law has incorporated a fraudulent transfer provision; the 1898 Act specifically adopted the language of the Statute of 13 Elizabeth. Bankruptcy Act of July 1, 1898, ch. 541, § 67(e), 30 Stat. 564-565.

The history of foreclosure law also begins in England, where courts of chancery developed the "equity of redemption"—the equitable right of a borrower to buy back, or redeem, property conveyed as security by paying the secured debt on a later

---

to claim the benefit of state rules of law (whether procedural or substantive) as property rights, in a bankruptcy proceeding. See United Savings Assn. of Texas v. Timbers of Inwood Forest Associates, Ltd., 484 U.S. 365, 370-371, 108 S. Ct. 626, 629-630, 98 L. Ed. 2d 740 (1988); Owen v. Owen, 500 U.S. 305, 313, 111 S. Ct. 1833, 1837-1838, 114 L. Ed. 2d 350 (1991); United States v. Whiting Pools, Inc., 462 U.S. 198, 206-207, and nn. 14, 15, 103 S. Ct. 2309, 2314-2315, and nn. 14, 15, 76 L. Ed. 2d 515 (1983). None of them declares or even intimates that state laws, procedural or otherwise, are irrelevant to prebankruptcy valuation questions such as that presented by § 548(a)[(1)(B)(i)].

date than "law day," the original due date. The courts' continued expansion of the period of redemption left lenders in a quandary, since title to forfeited property could remain clouded for years after law day. To meet this problem, courts created the equitable remedy of foreclosure: after a certain date the borrower would be forever foreclosed from exercising his equity of redemption. This remedy was called strict foreclosure because the borrower's entire interest in the property was forfeited, regardless of any accumulated equity. See G. Glenn, 1 Mortgages 3-18, 358-362, 395-406 (1943); G. Osborne, Mortgages 144 (2d ed. 1970). The next major change took place in 19th century America, with the development of foreclosure by sale (with the surplus over the debt refunded to the debtor) as a means of avoiding the draconian consequences of strict foreclosure. Osborne, supra, at 661-663; Glenn, supra, at 460-462, 622. Since then, the States have created diverse networks of judicially and legislatively crafted rules governing the foreclosure process, to achieve what each of them considers the proper balance between the needs of lenders and borrowers. All States permit judicial foreclosure, conducted under direct judicial oversight; about half of the States also permit foreclosure by exercising a private power of sale provided in the mortgage documents. See Zinman, Houle, & Weiss, *Fraudulent Transfers According to Alden, Gross and Borowitz: A Tale of Two Circuits,* 39 Bus. Law. 977, 1004-1005 (1984). Foreclosure laws typically require notice to the defaulting borrower, a substantial lead time before the commencement of foreclosure proceedings, publication of a notice of sale, and strict adherence to prescribed bidding rules and auction procedures. Many States require that the auction be conducted by a government official, and some forbid the property to be sold for less than a specified fraction of a mandatory presale fair-market-value appraisal. See id., at 1002, 1004-1005; Osborne, supra, at 683, 733-735; G. Osborne, G. Nelson, & D. Whitman, *Real Estate Finance Law* 9, 446-447, 475-477 (1979). When these procedures have been followed, however, it is "black letter" law that mere inadequacy of the foreclosure sale price is no basis for setting the sale aside, though it may be set aside (*under state foreclosure law*, rather than fraudulent transfer law) if the price is so low as to "shock the conscience or raise a presumption of fraud or unfairness." Osborne, Nelson, & Whitman, supra, at 469.

Fraudulent transfer law and foreclosure law enjoyed over 400 years of peaceful coexistence in Anglo-American jurisprudence until the Fifth Circuit's unprecedented 1980 decision in *Durrett.* To our knowledge no prior decision had ever applied the "grossly inadequate price" badge of fraud under fraudulent transfer law to set aside a foreclosure sale. To say that the "reasonably equivalent value" language in the fraudulent transfer provision of the Bankruptcy Code requires a foreclosure sale to yield a certain minimum price beyond what state foreclosure law requires, is to say, in essence, that the Code has adopted *Durrett* or *Bundles.* Surely Congress has the power pursuant to its constitutional grant of authority over bankruptcy, U.S. Const., Art. I, § 8, cl. 4, to disrupt the ancient harmony that foreclosure law and fraudulent-conveyance law, those two pillars of debtor-creditor jurisprudence, have heretofore enjoyed. But absent clearer textual guidance than the phrase "reasonably equivalent value"—a phrase entirely compatible with pre-existing practice—we will not presume such a radical departure.

Federal statutes impinging upon important state interests "cannot … be construed without regard to the implications of our dual system of government.… [W]hen the Federal Government takes over … local radiations in the vast network of our national economic enterprise and thereby radically readjusts the balance of state and national authority, those charged with the duty of legislating [must be] reasonably explicit." F. Frankfurter, Some Reflections on the Reading of Statutes, 47 Colum. L. Rev. 527, 539-540 (1947), quoted in Kelly v. Robinson, 479 U.S. 36, 49-50 n. 11, 107 S. Ct. 353, 360-362 n. 11, 93 L. Ed. 2d 216 (1986). It is beyond question that an essential state interest is at issue here: we have said that "the general welfare of society is involved in the security of the titles to real estate" and the power to ensure that security "inheres in the very nature of [state] government." American Land Co. v. Zeiss, 219 U.S. 47, 60, 31 S. Ct. 200, 204, 55 L. Ed. 82 (1911). Nor is there any doubt that the interpretation urged by petitioner would have a profound effect upon that interest: the title of every piece of realty purchased at foreclosure would be under a federally created cloud. (Already, title insurers have reacted to the *Durrett* rule by including specially crafted exceptions from coverage in many policies issued for properties purchased at foreclosure sales. See, e.g., L. Cherkis & L. King, Collier Real Estate Transactions and the Bankruptcy Code 5-18 to 5-19 (1992).) To displace traditional State regulation in such a manner, the federal statutory purpose must be "clear and manifest," English v. General Electric Co., 496 U.S. 72, 79, 110 S. Ct. 2270, 2275, 110 L. Ed. 2d 65 (1990). Cf. Gregory v. Ashcroft, 501 U.S., at __, 111 S. Ct., at 2401 (1991). Otherwise, the Bankruptcy Code will be construed to adopt, rather than to displace, pre-existing state law. See *Kelly,* supra, 479 U.S., at 49, 107 S. Ct., at 360-361; Butner v. United States, 440 U.S. 48, 54-55, 99 S. Ct. 914, 917-918, 59 L. Ed. 2d 136 (1979); Vanston Bondholders Protective Comm. v. Green, 329 U.S. 156, 171, 67 S. Ct. 237, 244, 91 L. Ed. 162 (1946) (Frankfurter, J., concurring).

For the reasons described, we decline to read the phrase "reasonably equivalent value" in § 548(a)[(1)(B)(i)] to mean, in its application to mortgage foreclosure sales, either "fair market value" or "fair foreclosure price" (whether calculated as a percentage of fair market value or otherwise). We deem, as the law has always deemed, that a fair and proper price, or a "reasonably equivalent value," for foreclosed property, is the price in fact received at the foreclosure sale, so long as all the requirements of the State's foreclosure law have been complied with. * * *

A few words may be added in general response to the dissent. We have no quarrel with the dissent's assertion that where the "meaning of the Bankruptcy Code's text is itself clear," post, at 1775, its operation is unimpeded by contrary state law or prior practice. Nor do we contend that Congress must override historical state practice "expressly or not at all," Ibid. The Bankruptcy Code can of course override by implication when the implication is unambiguous. But where the intent to override is doubtful, our federal system demands deference to long established traditions of state regulation.

The dissent's insistence that here no doubt exists—that our reading of the statute is "in derogation of the *straightforward language* used by Congress," post, at 1767 (emphasis added)—does not withstand scrutiny. The problem is not that we disagree with the dissent's proffered "plain meaning" of § 548(a)[(1)(B)(i)] ("the bankruptcy court must compare the price received by the insolvent debtor and the worth of the item when sold and set aside the transfer if the former was substantially ('[un]reasonabl[y]') 'less than' the latter," post, at 1768-1769)—which indeed echoes our own framing of the question presented ("whether the amount of debt ... satisfied at the foreclosure sale ... is 'reasonably equivalent' to the worth of the real estate conveyed," supra, at 1760). There is no doubt that this provision directs an inquiry into the relationship of the value received by the debtor to the worth of the property transferred. The problem, however, as any "ordinary speaker of English would have no difficulty grasping," post, at 1768, is that this highly generalized reformulation of the "plain meaning" of "reasonably equivalent value" continues to leave unanswered the one question central to this case, wherein the ambiguity lies: *What is a foreclosed property worth?* Obviously, until that is determined, we cannot know whether the value received in exchange for foreclosed property is "reasonably equivalent." * * *

For the foregoing reasons, the judgment of the Court of Appeals for the Ninth Circuit is
Affirmed.

Justice SOUTER, with whom Justice BLACKMUN, Justice STEVENS, and Justice GINSBURG join, dissenting.
    * * *

NOTES

1. Does the Court hold that the price obtained in a properly conducted, noncollusive sale under any state law real property foreclosure procedure is reasonably equivalent value? See Sherman v. Rose (In re Rose), 223 B.R. 555, 559 (B.A.P. 10th Cir. 1998) (involving foreclosure of real property tax lien under Wyoming law which "mandated that the property be sold to a person selected in a random lottery for the amount of the outstanding taxes"); Balaber-Strauss v. Town of Harrison (In re Murphy), 331 B.R. 107, 115-19 (Bankr. S.D.N.Y. 2005).

2. Should the Court's reasoning apply to foreclosure of Article 9 security interests in personal property? See Case v. TBAC-Prince Gardner, Inc. (In re Prince Gardner, Inc.), 220 B.R. 63 (Bankr. E.D. Mo. 1998); Carter v. H & B Jewelry and Loan, 209 B.R. 732 (Bankr. D. Or. 1997).

Mellon Bank v. Official Committee of Unsecured Creditors (In re R.M.L., Inc.)
United States Court of Appeals, Third Circuit, 1996
92 F.3d 139

COWEN, Circuit Judge.

We confront in this case a difficult issue arising under 11 U.S.C. § 548(a)[(1)(B)], the provision of the Bankruptcy Code (the "Code") allowing for avoidance of constructively fraudulent transfers. The principal question we must decide is whether a commitment letter Mellon Bank issued in connection with a contemplated $53-million loan conferred "reasonably equivalent value" on Intershoe (the debtor) in exchange for $515,000 in commitment fees that Intershoe paid to Mellon Bank. This question is complicated by the fact that the loan, which could possibly have saved Intershoe from bankruptcy, ultimately failed to close. We also must decide whether Intershoe was insolvent when it transferred the commitment fees to Mellon Bank.

After finding that Intershoe was insolvent during the relevant period, the bankruptcy court, relying on a "totality of the circumstances" test, concluded that Intershoe had not received "reasonably equivalent value" in exchange for the $515,000 in fees it had paid to Mellon. The court found that the loan commitment was so conditional when issued that it conferred virtually no indirect economic benefit on Intershoe. It therefore ordered Mellon Bank to remit to the bankrupt estate all but $127,538.04 of the commitment fees, an amount representing Mellon Bank's out-of-pocket expenses. The district court summarily affirmed. Because the commitment letter was so conditional that the chances of the loan closing were minimal, we agree that Intershoe did not receive value that was reasonably equivalent to the fees it paid Mellon Bank. Accordingly, we, too, will affirm.

* * * Intershoe was a large-scale wholesale distributor of women's shoes. Through 1991, its primary secured lender was Signet Bank. In the spring of 1991, Intershoe was aware that its financing arrangement with Signet would terminate that fall. It therefore sought to recapitalize and refinance its operations. Intershoe wanted to attract a $15 million equity investment; it also wanted to replace Signet as its lender with a bank group that would extend a $53 million loan facility.

In March of 1991, Three Cities Research ("TCR") made an initial, nonbinding proposal to make a $15 million investment in Intershoe and began to conduct due diligence and negotiations toward that end. Hoping that the prospect of an equity infusion would entice potential lenders, Intershoe approached Mellon Bank, Bank of New York ("BNY") and Citicorp to discuss potential refinancing. Each bank made clear that an equity infusion would be a prerequisite to any refinancing. Representatives of Mellon and Intershoe first met in either February or March of 1991.

On June 13, 1991, Mellon issued a proposal letter documenting its interest in extending a $53 million revolving line of credit and a $100 million foreign exchange line of credit. The proposal was contingent upon TCR's injection of $15 million in cash. At first, Intershoe did not accept Mellon's offer. Instead, it explored the possibility of obtaining financing from BNY and Citicorp. After completing its due diligence, however, Citicorp declined to extend credit to Intershoe. Although BNY had made a proposal, it subsequently revised the proposal to require a large equity infusion. Intershoe therefore declined to endorse BNY's proposal and, instead, turned its attention back to Mellon Bank.

On August 9, 1991, Mellon Bank issued a second proposal letter that was similar to the first in that it was conditioned upon the injection of new capital funds of at least $15 million. The letter also stated that Intershoe would be required to pay: (1) a facility fee equivalent to 3/4 of one percent (.0075) of the committed facility (half upon issuance of the commitment letter, half at closing); (2) a collateral management fee of $10,000; (3) all of Mellon's out-of-pocket expenses, regardless of whether the financing occurred; and (4) a "good faith deposit" of $125,000 to be remitted with written approval of the proposal letter. A fifth provision in the letter was that Mellon would be permitted to spread $28 of the $53 million loan among a group of banks. The loan contemplated by Mellon was known as a highly leveraged transaction ("HLT"), an asset-based loan bearing greater risk than an ordinary loan that requires extraordinary due diligence and monitoring of the borrower's accounts receivable, inventory and business plan.

On August 12, 1991, Intershoe remitted to Mellon the $125,000 "good faith deposit" in accordance with the proposal letter. Because it had reached its borrowing limit with the Signet Group, Intershoe could not borrow additional sums. Between August and October of 1991, Intershoe failed to pay the majority of invoices from its suppliers. While accounts payable increased by $10 million, its debt to the Signet Group decreased by the same amount; Intershoe was using what funds it had to pay down its debt. As a result, the Signet group agreed to extend its loan facility from September 30 to November 29, 1991, which permitted Intershoe to continue its business operations.

In early October of 1991, Mellon Bank requested an additional good faith deposit from Intershoe of $125,000, although there was nothing to document this request. On October 8 or 9, 1991, Intershoe remitted the additional $125,000 to Mellon Bank by wire transfer. * * *

On November 7, 1991, Mellon issued a formal commitment letter (the "Letter") with terms that tracked the August 9 proposal letter. The Letter referred to the $250,000 in good faith deposits that Mellon had previously received and indicated that the entire amount would be retained even if the loan did not close. These deposits would cover Mellon's expense, time and effort in attempting to consummate the financing. The Letter also required the remittance of an additional $265,000, half of which represented a nonrefundable "facility fee" for Mellon's commitment, with the other half representing a nonrefundable agent's fee for Mellon's syndication of the loan. The Letter also contained several conditions: (1) Intershoe had to produce a draft audited financial statement indicating that it had a net worth of at least $6.5 million; (2) Intershoe was required to repay or retire Westinghouse's debt and stock warrants and retain Westinghouse as a creditor for subordinated debt of at least $5 million; (3) $28 million of the loan commitment had to be participated out to a group of banks;[12] and (4) Intershoe would be required to pay a separate collateral monitoring fee relating to administering the loan after closing. By its terms, the commitment was set to expire on November 29, 1991, the same day that Signet's loan facility was due to expire.

On November 7, 1991, Intershoe accepted Mellon's commitment and remitted the $265,000 fee as contemplated by the Letter. That day Mellon began a "takedown examination" to update Intershoe's financial information through the closing date. Eight days later Mellon received a draft financial statement confirming that Intershoe possessed a positive net worth of $6.5 million dollars. Mellon then scheduled a meeting for November 20, 1991, with Intershoe, the loan participants, TCR (the equity investor) and Peat Marwick to discuss further the financial statements.

On November 17, 1991, however, TCR advised Intershoe that it had decided not to make the $15 million equity investment and confirmed its withdrawal from the proposed refinancing. Intershoe informed Mellon of this development the next day, and the entire deal collapsed. Intershoe's trade creditors continued to extend credit even after the collapse of the Mellon financing.

---

12. [Footnote 1 in original:] Mellon already had sufficient commitments from different banks to fulfill this condition.

On November 15, 1991,[13] Peat Marwick issued to Intershoe an audited financial statement for the fiscal year ending August 31, 1991. This statement indicated that as of August 31, Intershoe's liabilities exceeded its assets by four million dollars. In accordance with Generally Accepted Accounting Principles ("GAAP") and Generally Accepted [should be Auditing] Accounting Standards ("GAAS"), the financial statement took into account events subsequent to the end of the fiscal year (e.g., the collapse of the Mellon financing) as evidence of Intershoe's financial condition. Several questionable items on Intershoe's balance sheet were corrected or adjusted, resulting in an even lower net worth. The financial statement also indicated that Intershoe would have difficulty continuing as a going concern. On December 11, 1991, Intershoe agreed to accept Peat Marwick's suggested changes to its financial statements. Intershoe's financial condition continued to decline, reaching a point where its liabilities exceeded assets by $14 million. Intershoe sought protection under Chapter Eleven of the Code on February 18, 1992.

* * * [T]he Committee filed an adversary proceeding against Mellon Bank seeking to recover, as constructively fraudulent transfers, the three payments that Intershoe had made to Mellon in connection with the financing commitment, which totaled $515,000. Under section 548(a)[(1)(B)] of the Code, the Committee bore the burden of establishing that: (1) the debtor had an interest in the property; (2) the transfer of the interest occurred within one year of the petition; (3) the debtor was insolvent at the time of the transfer or became insolvent as a result thereof; and (4) the debtor received "less than a reasonably equivalent value in exchange for such transfer." The first two elements were not disputed. * * *

As it did in the courts below, Mellon Bank urges reversal on two grounds. First, Mellon Bank asserts that the commitment letter conferred "reasonably equivalent value" on Intershoe, the measure of which is the fair market value of the services it rendered (i.e., the $515,000 in commitment fees Intershoe paid). Second, Mellon Bank claims that based upon Intershoe's own balance sheets *at the time of the disputed transfers*, Intershoe was not insolvent.

* * * The concept of reasonably equivalent value unfortunately has not been defined in the Code. As the Supreme Court noted in BFP v. Resolution Trust Corp., "[o]f the three critical terms 'reasonably equivalent value', only the last is defined: 'value' means, for purposes of § 548, 'property, or satisfaction or securing of a … debt of the debtor'…." 511 U.S. 531, __, 114 S. Ct. 1757, 1760, 128 L. Ed. 2d 556 (1994) (quoting 11 U.S.C. § 548(d)(2)(A)). Thus, "Congress left to the courts the obligation of marking the scope and meaning of [reasonably equivalent value]." In re Morris Communications NC, Inc., 914 F.2d 458, 466 (4th Cir. 1990).

The lack of a more precise definition has led to considerable difficulty. This definitional problem is exacerbated in cases where, as here, the debtor exchanges cash for intangibles, such as services or the opportunity to obtain economic value in the future, the value of which is difficult, if not impossible, to ascertain. Because such intangibles are technically not within § 548(d)(2)(A)'s definition of "value," courts have struggled to develop a workable test for reasonably equivalent value.

---

13. [The bankruptcy court's opinion gives a date of "approximately" November 15. The date must have been after November 17, because, as the court of appeals notes immediately below, the Peat Marwick opinion refers to the November 17 collapse of the Mellon financing. --Ed.]

In attempting to determine whether Mellon's commitment letter conferred any value on Intershoe, the bankruptcy court purported to apply a totality of the circumstances test. Drawn from other reasonably equivalent value cases, that test takes into account the fair market value of the item received by, or services performed for, the debtor; the existence of an arm's-length relationship between the debtor and the transferee; and the good faith of the transferee. These factors, however, have no bearing on whether any "value" was actually conferred on the debtor. At most, the fair market value and the arm's-length nature of the relationship are relevant to the price the debtor paid. But the price that the debtor paid, in and of itself, reveals nothing about whether the debtor received something of actual "value." A simple example illustrates our point:

> Within one year of filing for bankruptcy, D pays a window-washer $1,000 to clean the windows in an office building. The $1,000 constitutes the going rate for such a job, and the window-washer is unaware of D 's financial condition.

That the $1,000 D paid represents the fair market value of the window-washer's services and that the transaction was at arm's length say absolutely nothing about whether the debtor received "value;" "value" was conferred because D obtained a palpable benefit from the service performed—i.e., clean windows.

The bankruptcy court, therefore, conflated two inquiries that should remain separate and distinct: before determining whether the value was "reasonably equivalent" to what the debtor gave up, the court must make an express factual determination as to whether the debtor received any value at all. The bankruptcy court seemed to recognize this as it attempted to reconcile the totality of the circumstances test with our analysis in *Metro Communications, Inc.*, 945 F.2d at 635.

Metro Communications, Inc. involved a loan that Mellon Bank provided to the acquiror in a leveraged buy-out ("LBO"). As collateral for the LBO loan, Metro, the target of the LBO, gave Mellon Bank a security interest and guarantee in substantially all of its assets. With the LBO loan, Mellon also provided a credit facility to Metro, also secured by Metro's assets. Less than one year later, Metro sought protection under the Code. A committee of unsecured creditors brought an adversary proceeding alleging, inter alia, that the granting of the security interests were constructively fraudulent transfers under § 548(a)[(1)(B)] of the Code. The bankruptcy and district courts concluded that Metro had not received reasonably equivalent value in exchange for the security interests it provided to Mellon Bank.

In reversing, we observed that "[b]ecause Metro did not receive the proceeds of the acquisition loan, it did not receive any direct benefits from extending the guaranty and security interest collateralizing that guaranty." Id. at 646. Nevertheless, we stressed that

> indirect benefits may also be evaluated.... These indirect economic benefits must be measured and then compared to the obligations the bankrupt incurred .... *The touchstone is whether the transaction conferred realizable commercial value on the debtor* reasonably equivalent to the realizable commercial value of the assets transferred.

Id. at 646-47 (emphasis added) (citations omitted). We went on to discover two indirect benefits that conferred "value" on Metro. The first was Mellon Bank's extension of a credit facility to Metro: "[t]he ability to borrow money has considerable value in the commercial world. To quantify that value, however, is difficult. Quantification depends upon the business opportunities the additional credit makes available to the borrowing corporation and on other imponderables in the operation or expansion of its business." Id. at 647. The second indirect benefit created by Metro's granting of a security interest in its assets, which allowed the LBO to close, was a "legitimate and reasonable expectation that the affiliation of these two corporations ... would produce a strong synergy." Id. (emphasis added). Significantly, we found that the expected synergy created "value," even though an unforseen change in the law prevented it from becoming a reality.

In spite of the plain requirement that the debtor actually receive something of value, Mellon Bank continues to insist that the fair market value of services rendered is conclusively determinative of reasonably equivalent value. To support this contention it relies on the Supreme Court's recent decision in BFP v. Resolution Trust Corp., 511 U.S. at 531, 114 S. Ct. at 1757. BFP, of course, stands for no such proposition. The Court there held that the proceeds of a mortgage foreclosure sale conducted in accordance with state law constitute "reasonably equivalent value" as a matter of law, even where those proceeds are substantially below the fair market value of the real estate sold. The BFP Court noted in passing that "the 'reasonably equivalent value' criterion will continue to have independent meaning (ordinarily a meaning similar to fair market value) outside the foreclosure context." 511 U.S. at __, 114 S. Ct. at 1765.

The dictum in BFP does not help Mellon Bank, however, because in the real estate context there is no doubt that the debtor is receiving something of "value" (i.e., cash) in exchange for real property, which also has a measurable value. Thus, the real issue in BFP was not whether any value was exchanged, but rather whether the value obtained was "reasonably equivalent" to what was given up. Thus, BFP in no way alters the requirement that when the debtor transfers property—whether it be real estate or cash—it must receive something of "value" in return.

This is fully consistent with our decision in Metro Communications, Inc., 945 F.2d at 646, which noted that the fraudulent conveyance laws are intended to protect the debtor's creditors. Rejecting Mellon Bank's contention that the debtor had received "value" simply the bank had parted with value by loaning funds, we said that "[t]he purpose of the laws is estate preservation; thus, the question whether the debtor received reasonable value must be determined from the standpoint of the creditors." Id. Mellon Bank's assertion in this case that it has conferred value simply because the fees it charged Intershoe represent the fair market value of Mellon Bank's services similarly misses the mark.

In sum, in light of our decision in Metro Communications, Inc., the bankruptcy court committed legal error to the extent that it applied a totality of the circumstances test to the initial question whether the commitment letter at issue conferred any value on Intershoe. To determine whether this threshold requirement was satisfied, the court should have examined whether Intershoe received any benefit from the commitment letter, whether direct or indirect, without regard to the cost of Mellon Bank's services, the contractual and arm's-length nature of the relationship, and the good faith of the transferee.

Its application of the totality of the circumstances test notwithstanding, the bankruptcy court announced two conclusions essential to the resolution of the question whether Intershoe had received any value in exchange for the commitment fees it had remitted to Mellon Bank. The court first determined that Mellon Bank's commitment letter did not confer any tangible, indirect benefits on Intershoe. For instance, the court found that Signet's extension of its credit facility beyond the original expiration date and the trade suppliers' decision to extend credit to Intershoe were not the direct result of Mellon Bank's willingness to lend funds to Intershoe. The court then determined that the loan commitment failed to confer any significant *intangible* benefits on Intershoe. Specifically, the court determined that the commitment letter essentially offered only a very slim "chance" of obtaining a substantial economic benefit in the future because it contained numerous conditions that, in all likelihood, could not have been satisfied.

With this latter determination the bankruptcy court implicitly held that money spent on an investment bearing a certain degree of risk can generate cognizable value within the meaning of § 548(a)[(1)(B)] of the Code, even where the investment ultimately fails to generate a positive return. * * *

Relying on the following language from our decision in *Metro Communications, Inc.*, the Committee argues that where the debtor's financial condition either continues to deteriorate or fails to stabilize, money spent on a losing investment cannot confer "value" as a matter of law:

> The touchstone is whether the transaction conferred realizable commercial value on the debtor reasonably equivalent to the realizable commercial value of the assets transferred. *Thus, when the debtor is a going concern and its realizable going concern value after the transaction is equal to or exceeds its going concern value before the transaction, reasonably equivalent value has been received.*

945 F.2d at 647 (emphasis added). We disagree. * * * [W]e view the highlighted passage as providing an example of how a court can determine that a debtor received direct benefits and, thus, "value" from a transaction. Significantly, the court in *Metro Communications, Inc.* went on to discover several potential, intangible benefits that, although incapable of precise measurement, conferred value on Metro despite their failure to materialize. That should dispel any suggestion that *Metro Communications, Inc.* stands for the proposition that a debtor must receive a direct, tangible economic benefit in order to receive "value" for purposes of § 548(a)[(1)(B)] of the Code.

Furthermore, were we literally to apply the highlighted statement from Metro Communications, Inc. as the categorical test for value under § 548(a)[(1)(B)], we would announce a rule for this Circuit that only successful investments can confer value on a debtor. This would permit a court viewing the events with the benefit of hindsight to conclude that any transfer that did not bring in the actual, economic equivalent of what was given up fails to confer reasonably equivalent value as a matter of law. Such an unduly restrictive approach to reasonably equivalent value has been soundly rejected by other courts, *Chomakos*, 69 F.3d at 771 (gambling losses conferred value on debtor); *Fairchild Aircraft Corp.*, 6 F.3d at 1119 (money spent in failed attempt to keep commuter airline afloat conferred value on debtor), and with good reason. Presumably the creditors whom § 548 was designed to protect want a debtor to take *some* risks that could generate value and, thus, allow it to meet its obligations without resort to protection under the Bankruptcy Code:

> According to [appellant], the only value that can be considered is property actually received. Under this view the value of an investment—no matter how large and how probable the potential return—cannot be considered unless it actually pays off, and only to the extent that it does so ... . The narrow "realized property" approach to value advanced by [appellant] finds no approbation in the law.

Fairchild Aircraft Corp., 6 F.3d at 1126-27. Accordingly, we hold that money spent on investments that fail to stabilize or improve the debtor's condition (i.e., "losing" investments) can confer value within the meaning of § 548(a)[(1)(B)] of the Code.

The question, then, is how to determine whether an investment that failed to generate a positive return nevertheless conferred value on the debtor. We think our decision in *Metro Communications, Inc.* answers this question implicitly. We held there that the mere expectation that the fusion of two companies would produce a strong synergy (an expectation that turned out to be inaccurate in hindsight) would suffice to confer "value" so long as the expectation was *"legitimate and reasonable."* Id. at 647 (emphasis added). See id. ("The touchstone is whether the transaction conferred *realizable* commercial value on the debtor ... .") (emphasis added). Thus, so long as there is some chance that a contemplated investment will generate a positive return at the time of the disputed transfer, we will find that value has been conferred. Accord *Chomakos*, 69 F.3d at 771 (because legalized gambling provides fair chance for significant pay-off, $7,710 in gambling losses conferred value on debtor); *Fairchild Aircraft Corp.*, 6 F.3d at 1126 ($432,380.91 spent in failed attempt to keep commuter airline viable conferred value because "the likelihood that a sale would occur was also demonstrably high"); cf. *Morris Communications NC, Inc.*, 914 F.2d at 458 (shares in a corporation whose only asset was a licensing application pending before the FCC with a one in twenty-two chance of approval had value).

We think our analysis appropriately balances a creditor's interest in estate preservation against a debtor's legitimate, pre-bankruptcy efforts to take risks that, if successful, could generate significant value and, possibly, avoid the need for protection under the Code altogether. As we noted above, requiring that all investments yield a positive return in order to find that they conferred value on the debtor would be unduly restrictive. But so, too, would a rule insulating from § 548's coverage investments that, when made, have zero probability of success. The best solution, therefore, is to determine, based on the circumstances that existed at the time the investment was contemplated, whether there was any chance that the investment would generate a positive return. In this way creditors will be protected when an irresponsible debtor invests in a venture that is obviously doomed from the outset.

With these legal principles in mind, our review of the bankruptcy court's conclusion that Intershoe did not receive reasonably equivalent value proceeds in two, discrete steps: first, we determine whether the commitment letter conferred any value on Intershoe; second, we consider the bankruptcy court's finding that whatever value was conferred was not "reasonably equivalent" to the two transfers of lending fees totaling $390,000 is clearly erroneous.[14]

Although the bankruptcy court did not announce an explicit finding on the question whether Mellon Bank's commitment letter conferred any value on Intershoe, it is clear that the court implicitly answered that question in the affirmative. The bankruptcy court stated that "all parties should have known there was *a substantial probability that the loan would not close* [.]"[15] Put another way, the court concluded that by November 7, 1991, there was a slight chance that the loan *would* close. This finding is amply supported by the record and, hence, cannot be disturbed on appeal. First, although TCR had not formally committed to participate in the deal, there is no evidence in the record that TCR had made known its intention to withdraw before November 17, 1991. Thus, as of November 7, 1991, when the commitment letter was executed and the disputed fees remitted, there was at least some chance that the most important condition in the letter could be fulfilled. With respect to the other conditions in the letter, which pertained mainly to Intershoe's financial condition, record evidence reveals that, despite Intershoe's deteriorating condition, Mellon was willing to waive or modify many of these conditions. Since we review the transaction at the time the transfer was made, the bankruptcy's court's implicit determination that the letter provided Intershoe with at least *some* chance of receiving a future economic benefit and, therefore, "value" is not clearly erroneous.

We next consider the bankruptcy court's determination that whatever value was conferred by the letter, it was not "reasonably equivalent" to the $390,000 in lending fees Intershoe paid to Mellon Bank. We conclude that in assessing the reasonable equivalence issue, the bankruptcy court appropriately relied on the totality of the circumstances test.

---

14. [Footnote 5 in original:] The bankruptcy court allowed Mellon to retain the initial $125,000 good-faith deposit because, it concluded, Mellon Bank had conferred some "value" on Intershoe, as reflected by Mellon Bank's out-of pocket expenses. As for the second "good-faith deposit" of $125,000, which Intershoe remitted to Mellon Bank on October 8, 1991, * * * [s]ince we do not view as clearly erroneous the bankruptcy court's determination that Intershoe retained the right to a return of its deposit until November 7, 1991, when the commitment letter was executed, we agree that November 7 is the pertinent date of the transfer for purposes of the reasonably equivalent value (and insolvency) analysis.

15. [Footnote 6 in original:] Mellon Bank complains about various statements in the bankruptcy court's decision indicating that it (Mellon Bank) should have known that the loan might not close. We fully agree that what Mellon Bank knew or should have known is irrelevant in an action to avoid a constructively fraudulent transfer, although it certainly would be relevant in an action for actual fraud under § 548(a)(1)[(A)] of the Code. Nevertheless, since the bankruptcy court implicitly found that some value was conferred in addressing the reasonably equivalent value issue, its references to what Mellon Bank knew or should have known amount to harmless error.

In any event, we can well understand why the bankruptcy court alluded to what Mellon Bank "should have known." As a potential lender contemplating a large, high-risk loan, Mellon Bank was engaged in extensive due diligence. Mellon Bank thus had access to financial information about the debtor that few transferees who are the target of actions under § 548(a)[(1)(B)] of the Code ever have. Such access should have put Mellon Bank on notice that Intershoe could not have met many of the conditions in the commitment letter. The bankruptcy court's finding that Mellon Bank continued to believe the loan would close until TCR's last-minute withdrawal tends to suggest serious problems with Mellon Bank's due diligence review, that Intershoe was affirmatively misrepresenting its financial condition to Mellon Bank hoping that the loan would close, or both.

Mellon Bank insists that the court's findings that: (1) the fees Intershoe paid were in line with market rates; (2) Mellon Bank acted in good faith; and (3) for the most part, the parties dealt at arm's length, render clearly erroneous its conclusion that Intershoe did not receive value that was "reasonably equivalent." We disagree. As our discussion of "value" should have made clear, supra III.A.2.a, while the chance of receiving an economic benefit is sufficient to constitute "value," the size of the chance is directly correlated with the amount of "value" conferred. Thus, essential to a proper application of the totality of the circumstances test in this case is a comparison between the value that was conferred and fees Intershoe paid.

So understood, the bankruptcy court's conclusion that the chance of receiving value represented by the commitment letter was so small that it was not reasonably equivalent to the $390,000 in fees Intershoe paid in no way conflicts with the court's observation that the commitment fees were in line with market rates. The bankruptcy court concluded that while a debtor reasonably might pay $390,000 in fees for a *real* chance to obtain a $53 million credit facility, the commitment letter at issue *in this case* was so conditional that it provided Intershoe with little chance, if any, to obtain the loan it sought. Accordingly, as long as there is support in the record for the bankruptcy court's conclusion that the commitment letter was highly conditional (and, thus, of little "value"), we must affirm.

That the loan was highly conditional cannot seriously be disputed. The bankruptcy court concluded that "both transfers were made in exchange for a highly conditional loan commitment, and all parties should have known there was a substantial probability that the loan would not close." Significantly, the court found that "TCR had made no commitment to participate in the transaction and Intershoe's deteriorating financial condition was a deterrent to an equity investor." The court further stated that "there was a significant possibility that Intershoe could not meet one or more of the conditions of the commitment letter, including the TCR equity investment." Finally, the court noted that "Intershoe's financial survival was contingent upon the Mellon refinancing and the Mellon refinancing was contingent upon dozens of conditions, the least certain and most important of which was an equity infusion from TCR." Since all of these findings have ample support in the record, the bankruptcy court's conclusion that the commitment letter conferred minimal value—value that was not reasonably equivalent to the fees Intershoe paid—is not clearly erroneous.

     * * *

Mellon Bank next contends that the Committee failed to establish that Intershoe was "insolvent" on the dates of the disputed transfers. Section 101(32)(A) of the Code defines insolvency as a "financial condition such that the sum of such entity's debts is greater than all of such entity's property, at a fair valuation … ." For purposes of § 548, solvency is measured at the time the debtor transferred value, not at some later or earlier time. *Metro Communications, Inc.*, 945 F.2d at 648. This is known as the "balance sheet" test: "assets and liabilities are tallied *at fair valuation* to determine whether the corporation's debts exceed its assets." Id. (emphasis added).

Mellon Bank's principal argument is that the bankruptcy court inappropriately relied on an audited, year-end financial statement indicating that Intershoe had a net worth of negative $4 million as of August 31, 1991. That financial statement was prepared several months *after* the disputed transfers were made and, according to Mellon Bank, reflected "substantial adjustments" that were "precipitated by the collapse of the Mellon-TCR transaction... ." But for that unexpected collapse, Mellon Bank argues, several alleged "credits" Intershoe was carrying on its books rendered it solvent, at least on paper, at the time it remitted the disputed commitment fees to Mellon Bank. In short, Mellon bank accuses the bankruptcy court of relying on hindsight to conclude that Intershoe was insolvent in October through November of 1991. This argument need not detain us long.

The use of hindsight to evaluate a debtor's financial condition for purposes of the Code's "insolvency" element has been criticized by courts and commentators alike.

Hindsight, however, is not what prompted the bankruptcy court to ignore certain alleged "credits" and, thus, conclude that Intershoe was insolvent. On the contrary, and as Mellon Bank acknowledges, at least two alleged "credits," which together totaled $4.3 million,[16] depended for their validity on Intershoe's belief that the loan would close. As we have already discussed, the bankruptcy court found, as a matter of fact, that Intershoe knew or should have known that its deteriorating financial condition would preclude it from meeting one or more of the conditions in the commitment letter * * *. This conclusion is fatal to Mellon Bank's position. The bankruptcy court correctly determined that a debtor's creative accounting practices, which have the effect of grossly overstating its financial condition, cannot be the basis of a court's solvency analysis.

Furthermore, if a debtor's treatment of an item as an "asset" depends for its propriety on the occurrence of a contingent event, a court must take into consideration the likelihood of that event occurring from an objective standpoint. See, e.g., In re Xonics Photochemical, Inc., 841 F.2d 198 (7th Cir. 1988) ("the asset or liability must be reduced to its present, or expected, value before a determination can be made whether the firm's assets exceed its liabilities"). Far from "hindsight" or "*post-hoc*" analysis, a court looks at the circumstances as they appeared to the debtor and determines whether the debtor's belief that a future event would occur was reasonable. The less reasonable a debtor's belief, the more a court is justified in reducing the assets (or raising liabilities) to reflect the debtor's true financial condition at the time of the alleged transfers.

In this case, moreover, Daniel Coffey, a certified public accountant who served as the Committee's insolvency expert, revealed that in the course of performing an audit, accountants abide by a far more stringent rule. Mr. Coffey testified that "in reality, if an auditor didn't think there was a real 99 percent chance that this loan is going to close, they wouldn't leave [the 'credits'] on the balance sheet. Everybody would say let's sit and wait and see what happens." Since the bankruptcy court found that the probability of the loan closing was essentially zero, a finding we have already determined is amply supported by the record, the court

---

16. [Footnote 8 in original:] Those credits include a $3.668-million advance owed to Intershoe by IS International, a subsidiary, and $754,000 in "pre-paid financing fees" in connection with the Mellon Bank/TCR financing. Had the loan closed, Intershoe's subsidiary could have continued to operate as a going concern, which in turn would have enabled it to repay the $3.668-million advance from its parent. Similarly, had the loan closed, Intershoe would have been permitted to expense the financing fees gradually over the life of the loan.

properly discounted (to zero) the $4.3 million Intershoe had carried on its balance sheet as alleged "assets." Thus, by November of 1991, Intershoe's actual assets were $4.3 million lower than its balance sheet had reflected.

Apart from properly refusing to consider $4.3 million as assets, the bankruptcy court also reversed a $4.5 million "asset" that Intershoe had carried on its books as a credit due from factory suppliers related to defective merchandise * * *. Far from relying upon hindsight, the court concluded that this entry had no basis in fact when it was made. As Intershoe was unable to produce any documentation to support this alleged "credit," the bankruptcy court's decision to ignore the credit is amply supported by the record and, hence, not clearly erroneous.[17]

In sum, Intershoe was found to have a net worth of negative $4 million on August 31, 1991, and negative $8 million on November 15, 1991. The bankruptcy court properly refused to consider various items totaling $8.8 million that Intershoe had attempted to portray as assets. Since the transfers at issue here occurred on November 7, 1991,[18] the bankruptcy court's insolvency determination will be affirmed. * * *

NOTES

1. When a company incurs expenses today that will provide a benefit in the future (such as paying insurance premiums to buy insurance coverage that will last for the next twelve months), the amount of those expenses is treated as an asset. In effect the right to the future benefit—e.g., the future insurance coverage—is an asset that is valued at the amount paid for it. See the discussion of "prepaid expenses" as a kind of asset in part c.1.a. of Appendix A at the end of this text. As of November 7, 1991, R.M.L., Inc. had paid a substantial amount of money in exchange for the right to a future benefit, i.e., the chance of obtaining a valuable loan from Mellon Bank. Why did the court refuse to consider that right to be a future benefit as an asset of R.M.L., Inc. as of November 7? Consider the testimony cited by the Third Circuit near the end of its opinion—testimony that accountants would not allow the credits for the expenses associated with the contemplated loan to be listed as assets on the balance sheet unless there was a 99% chance that the loan would be made. Is that the proper standard for the court to use in determining R.M.L.'s solvency or insolvency? Did the court use that standard?

2. If the commitment letter issued by Mellon Bank on November 7 was worth very little, as the court concludes, why did R.M.L.'s managers pay hundreds of thousands of R.M.L.'s dollars for it? Does their willingness to have R.M.L. spend that much for it indicate that it was worth that much?

3. What about managers who are paid hundreds or thousands of the debtor's dollars? Are their salaries and bonuses worth it in terms of § 548? In theory, employment benefits have always been subject to avoidance under § 548, even

---

17. [Footnote 9 in original:] The bankruptcy court went on to find that $6.7 million in affiliate receivables, which were properly treated as assets under Generally Accepted Accounting Practices, were essentially worthless from a fair valuation approach since the affiliates were themselves insolvent and depended for their existence on Intershoe. This finding, which is supported by the record, further buttresses the bankruptcy court's conclusion that Intershoe was insolvent during the time of the disputed transfers. Similarly, Intershoe's own monthly financial statement showed an operational loss for September and October of 1991 of $4.2 million, which the bankruptcy court found was not simply attributable to seasonal fluctuations in Intershoe's business, but rather further evidence of Intershoe's deteriorating financial condition.

18. [Footnote 10 in original:] See supra n. 5 [footnote 10 in this text] .

without § 548(a)(1)(B)(ii)(IV) which Congress added in 2005. Does this new subsection make it easier or harder to avoid payments of salaries and the like that are unreasonably high in market terms?

2. Transfers Fraudulent Under State Law, Section 544(b)

Transfers that are fraudulent under state law, as opposed to the federal law of § 548, are avoidable through § 544(b). It empowers the trustee to

> avoid any transfer of an interest of the debtor in property or any obligation incurred by the debtor that is voidable under applicable law by a creditor holding an unsecured claim that is allowable under section 502 of this title or that is not allowable only under section 502(e) of this title.

This provision subrogates the trustee to the right of any unsecured creditor of the estate to void, under any "applicable law," a prepetition transfer of the debtor's property. This "applicable law," which essentially means any nonbankruptcy law, includes state fraudulent transfer law. Indeed, state fraudulent transfer law is, by far, the "applicable law" most often relied on by trustees under § 544(b).

For the most part, however, the content of the typical state fraudulent transfer law is very similar to the substance of § 548. State law, like § 548, condemns any transfer that is made with actual intent to defraud, hinder or delay creditors; and state law essentially mirrors § 548 with respect to transfers that are deemed constructively fraudulent. Nevertheless, state laws are somewhat unique in ways that permit the trustee under § 544(b) to avoid transactions that are beyond the reach of § 548.

Although the main tenets of § 548 and state fraudulent transfer laws are generally the same, the laws of some states go beyond the substance of § 548 and define as fraudulent a slightly wider range of transfers. Moreover, the trustee's avoidance power under § 544(b) is not defined solely in terms of state fraudulent transfer laws. Section 544(b) allows the trustee to avoid a transfer that is voidable by an unsecured creditor under *any* nonbankruptcy law, which includes nonbankruptcy federal law and state law other than fraudulent conveyance law. For example, § 544(b) empowers the trustee to enforce bulk sales laws such as U.C.C. Article 6[19] that protect unsecured creditors, and to use a state preference statute rather than § 547 to avoid a preferential transfer.[20]

Most importantly, the reach-back period of state fraudulent transfer laws is typically longer than the two-year period of § 548. Using § 548 the trustee can only avoid transfers that occurred within two years before the bankruptcy petition was filed. When the trustee relies on state fraudulent transfer law through § 544(b), § 548's two-year rule does not apply. Rather, the trustee gets the benefit of the state statute of limitations on voiding fraudulent conveyances, which may be six or ten

---

19. Note that forty-four states have repealed Article 6 in accordance with the view of the U.C.C.'s sponsors that bulk sales laws are no longer necessary. See Nat'l Conf. of Commissioners on Unif. State Laws, Why the States Should Repeal the Uniform Commercial Code Article 6, http://www.nccusl.org/Update/uniformact_why/uniformacts-why-ucca6.asp (last visited Apr. 15, 2006).

20. However, there is some questionable authority that some state preference statutes are preempted by the Bankruptcy Code. See footnote 1 above in this chapter.

years or even longer. The trustee also gets the benefit of any gloss on these state statutes that starts the limitations period running only from the time that the fraud is (or should have been) discovered. See In re Walden, 207 B.R. 1 (D. Colo. 1997).

Field v. United States
(In re Abatement Environmental Resources, Inc.)
United States Court of Appeals, Fourth Circuit, 2004
102 Fed.Appx. 272, 2004 WL 1326597 (unpublished)

GREGORY, Circuit Judge.

Abatement Environmental Resources, Inc. ("Abatement" or "Debtor") filed a petition under Chapter 11 of the Bankruptcy Code (which was later converted to a Chapter 7 action), reporting claims exceeding the assets of the estate. The bankruptcy trustee Scott D. Field (the "Trustee") instituted an adversary proceeding against the United States Internal Revenue Service ("IRS") to recover three alleged fraudulent conveyances. Abatement's owner and principal officer, Joseph Downey ("Downey"), authorized the three payments to be made from corporate accounts to the IRS to satisfy his individual income tax liabilities. On cross-motions for summary judgment, the bankruptcy court granted summary judgment for the Trustee, holding that the Trustee could recover the payments as fraudulent conveyances under Maryland law. The district court reversed, holding that the Trustee's state law fraudulent conveyance claim was barred by Maryland's "voluntary payment" doctrine which prevents recovery from taxing authorities for voluntarily paid taxes, absent a special statutory provision allowing a refund. The Trustee now appeals the district court's reversal.

We find that the Trustee failed to carry his burden of showing that Abatement received no consideration for the transfers to IRS, thus we conclude that the Debtor cannot advance his claim under the Maryland Uniform Fraudulent Conveyance Act ("MUFCA"). While it is clear that the IRS extended consideration to Downey, rather than to Abatement, by releasing him from his tax liability, it is not clear that Abatement's payment to IRS did not constitute a repayment of a salary, loan, bonus or antecedent debt due Downey. Therefore, we affirm the district court on alternative grounds and do not need to examine the applicability of the voluntary payment doctrine.

I.

* * *

For the purposes of this appeal, it is sufficient to recount the following facts: Downey is a fugitive who was the owner and principal officer of the Debtor. During 1997 and 1998, he drew three checks on Abatement's corporate checking accounts, totaling $212,000, to pay individual income tax liabilities to the IRS. In 1999, IRS refunded Downey $166,294 resulting from overpayments and withholding credits on his individual income taxes.

In October 1999, Abatement filed a voluntary petition under Chapter 11 of the Bankruptcy Code. Claims against the estate totaled approximately $4,000,000, exceeding the estate's assets and those available for distribution to creditors. In March 2000, the bankruptcy court converted the case into a Chapter 7 proceeding and appointed Field as trustee. In March 2001, Field filed this adversary proceeding against the United States to recover alleged fraudulent conveyances of the Debtor's assets in the amount of

$212,000, the total amount of funds Downey transferred to IRS from Abatement's accounts to pay his individual income tax liability. The Trustee brought this action pursuant to 11 U.S.C. §§ 548, 550, or Md. Code Ann. Com. Law §§ 15- 204, 15-205, 15-206, 15-207 and 11 U.S.C. § 544(b), requesting the bankruptcy court to order that these conveyances be avoided and to enter judgment against the United States.

On cross-motions for summary judgment, the bankruptcy court held that 11 U.S.C. § 548 was unavailable to the Trustee because that section only permits the avoidance of transfers made within one year prior to filing of the bankruptcy petition[21], and Downey's three checks fell outside the limitations period. The court held, however, that the Trustee could utilize 11 U.S.C. § 544(b)(1), which permits a trustee to avoid certain transfers of the debtor's property if the transfer is voidable under "applicable state law by a creditor holding an unsecured claim," to recover the disputed funds. The court held that under the "applicable state law," provisions of the MUFCA, Md. Code Ann., Com. Law §§ 15-204, 15-205, authorized the Trustee's recovery of fraudulent conveyances from the IRS.[22] Thus, after determining that IRS was an "initial transferee" under 11 U.S.C. § 550(a)(1) against whom the Trustee could recover, the bankruptcy court granted summary judgment for the Trustee on his § 15-204 claim, and ordered IRS to pay the Trustee $212,000.

On appeal, the district court reversed, holding that the MUFCA, in generally permitting the avoidance of fraudulent conveyances, did not supplant Maryland's "voluntary payment" doctrine.[23] The district court found that Maryland law provided no cause of action to recover a tax voluntarily paid, even if in error or under an illegal imposition, absent a special statutory provision allowing a refund. Accordingly, the district court held that the Trustee was barred from recovery against the IRS on his MUFCA claim. The Trustee now appeals.

II.

We review the judgment of a district court sitting in review of a bankruptcy court de novo, applying the same standards of review that were applied in the district court. Specifically, we review the bankruptcy court's factual findings for clear error, while we review questions of law de novo.

III.

This appeal presents an unusual question under Maryland fraudulent conveyance law, namely whether a bankruptcy trustee may recover tax payments made by a debtor, authorized by its principal officer, to satisfy tax liabilities of said officer. This attempt to use a state law fraudulent conveyance action as a tax recovery provision clearly does not conform to the origins or purposes of fraudulent conveyance doctrine. Thus, with that background in mind, we proceed to analyze the application of the MUFCA in this most peculiar context.

---

21. [The one-year period was changed to two years by the 2005 BAPCPA.–Ed.]

22. [Footnote 2 in original:] There is no sovereign immunity bar to the Trustee's claim because 11 U.S.C. § 106(a)(1) abrogates the United States' sovereign immunity for actions brought pursuant to 11 U.S.C. § 544(b)(1).

23. [Footnote 4 in original:] The doctrine is best summarized as the principle that once a taxpayer voluntarily pays a tax or other governmental charge, under mistake of law or an illegal imposition, no common law action lies for the recovery of that tax absent a special statutory provision sanctioning a refund. See Apostol v. Anne Arundel County, 288 Md. 667, 421 A.2d 582, 585 (Md. 1980).

Fraudulent conveyance law has its origins in the Statute of 13 Elizabeth, ch. 5 (1571). The purpose of the fraudulent conveyance doctrine is to prevent assets from being transferred away from a debtor in exchange for less than fair value, leaving a lack of funds to compensate the creditors. In the foundational fraudulent conveyance case, In re Twyne's Case, 3 Co. Rep. 806, 76 Eng. Rep. 809 (Star Chamber 1601), the Star Chamber examined the facts surrounding such transfers to determine whether they had "signs and marks" of a fraudulent or malicious intent, such as secret transfers, continued ownership or possession of property after its alleged transfer, self-serving representations in transfer documents that the transfer was not intended to defraud creditors, transfers of substantially all assets, or transfers made while action was pending against the transferor. In short, fraudulent conveyance law is aimed at preventing debtors from making collusive transfers to others—often friendly recipients—in an attempt to avoid their creditors. See *Fraudulent Conveyance Law & its Proper Domain*, Douglas G. Baird & Thomas H. Jackson, 38 VAND. L. REV. 829, 830 (1985) ("A debtor cannot manipulate his affairs in order to shortchange his creditors and pocket the difference. Those who collude with a debtor in these transactions are not protected either.").

In the United States, § 67(e) of the 1898 Bankruptcy Act directly copied much of the Statute of 13 Elizabeth. Most states followed suit, either recognizing 13 Elizabeth through common law, or expressly adopting or reenacting it. Maryland adopted the English statute, which remained in effect until 1920, when the MUFCA was adopted. * * *

Section 15-204 of the MUFCA, under which the bankruptcy court held the Trustee could recover, provides: "Every conveyance made and every obligation incurred by a person who is or will be rendered insolvent by it is fraudulent as to creditors without regard to his actual intent, if the conveyance is made or the obligation is incurred without fair consideration." Md. Code Ann., Com. Law §15-204. Such a fraudulent conveyance claim thus consists of two elements (1) whether fair consideration was present and (2) whether the transferor is or will be rendered insolvent. In this case, it is uncontested that IRS did not directly extend consideration to Abatement in exchange for the $212,000 in tax payments. However, it is entirely unclear whether Abatement received "fair consideration" from Downey, the principal, in exchange for having paid tax liabilities on his behalf.

The MUFCA defines "fair consideration" as follows:

> Fair consideration is given for property or an obligation, if:
> (1) In exchange for the property or obligation, as a fair equivalent for it and in good faith, property is conveyed or an antecedent debt is satisfied; or
> (2) The property or obligation is received in good faith to secure a present advance or antecedent debt in an amount not disproportionately small as compared to the value of the property or obligation obtained.

Md.Code Ann., Com. Law §15-203.

At oral argument, the court asked Appellant's counsel whether Abatement had received consideration from Downey in exchange for the $212,000 paid to the IRS—whether such consideration from Downey was in the form of monies owed in repayment of salary, bonus, loan or some other obligation for services rendered. Appellant's counsel repeatedly answered that it had made no proffer of a lack of consideration from Downey before the bankruptcy court or the district court, and further expressed that he was uncertain how Abatement's financial records reflected the three checks paid to IRS for Downey's benefit. Given the lack of such showings, we have no way to determine whether the principal's actions were indeed adverse to the corporation, or whether Debtor's transfer to IRS was made to satisfy an obligation to Downey and consideration flowed to Debtor from the third-party. See Harman v. First Am. Bank of Md. (In re Jeffrey Bigelow Design Group, Inc.), 956 F.2d 479, 485 (4th Cir. 1992) ("It is well settled that reasonably equivalent value can come from one other than the recipient of the payments, a rule which has become known as the indirect benefit rule.") (citing Rubin v. Mfrs. Hanover Trust Co., 661 F.2d 979 (2d Cir. 1981)).

As the Second Circuit recognized in *Rubin*, "[t]hree-sided transactions ... present special difficulties" in determining whether "fair consideration" is present, but "a debtor may sometimes receive 'fair' consideration even though the consideration given for his property or obligation goes initially to a third person." Id. at 991. The court further remarked "[i]f the consideration given to the third person has ultimately landed in the debtor's hands, or if the giving of the consideration to the third person *otherwise confers an economic benefit upon the debtor*, then the debtor's net worth has been preserved...." Id. (emphasis added); see also In re Jeffrey Bigelow, 956 F.2d at 485 ("[T]he focus is whether the net effect of the transaction has depleted the bankruptcy estate.").

Here, there is a distinct possibility that precisely such a situation occurred where Abatement received an economic benefit; i.e., Downey was owed monies by Abatement, Debtor made the transfer to IRS on Downey's behalf, and its net worth was not reduced because it simply satisfied an outstanding liability. See, e.g., Klein v. Tabatchnick, 610 F.2d 1043, 1047 (2d Cir. 1979) (holding a transaction's benefit to the debtor "need not be direct; it may come indirectly through benefit to a third person"); Williams v. Twin City Co., 251 F.2d 678, 681 (9th Cir. 1958) (analyzing "fair consideration" under the federal bankruptcy act and holding "[c]onsideration can run to a third party, so long as it is given in exchange for the promise sought to be enforced"); Barr & Creelman Mill & Plumbing Supply Co. v. Zoller, 109 F.2d 924, 926 (2d Cir. 1940) (good faith novation agreement may constitute consideration); Hofler v. Marion Lumber Co., 233 F. Supp. 540, 543 (D.S.C. 1964) (examining Uniform Fraudulent Conveyance Act and stating, "[c]onsideration, of course, may run to a third party"). In this case, we cannot conclude that Debtor received no consideration for its transfer to the IRS.

At oral argument, the Trustee's counsel contended, however, that the Trustee's failure to show an absence of consideration was of no moment because the IRS had the burden to show that Abatement received no [sic] consideration from Downey. In support of this proposition, Appellant's counsel cited Braunstein v. Walsh (In re Rowanoak Corp.), 344 F.3d 126 (1st Cir. 2003). We find *Rowanoak* contrary to the position that Appellant claims it represents.

While *Rowanoak* did not concern the unusual tax recovery theory the Trustee asserts in this case, it did involve a Chapter 7 trustee's action under Massachusetts fraudulent conveyance law.[24] In *Rowanoak*, two years prior to filing for bankruptcy,

---

24. [Footnote 6 in original:] The Massachusetts provision at issue in *Rowanoak* states: "A transfer made or obligation incurred by a debtor is fraudulent as to a creditor ... if the debtor made the transfer or incurred the obligation: ... without receiving a reasonably equivalent value in exchange for the transfer or obligation, and the debtor: (i) engaged or was about to engage in a business or a transaction for which

the debtor corporation, Rowanoak, made six payments from its bank account to the mother of its principal. The trustee, uncertain about the basis for the checks, filed a motion to compel Rowanoak to turn over its books and records to the trustee. In response, the principal filed an affidavit stating it did not have documents in its possession relevant to payments made by the debtor to the principal's mother. The trustee then commenced an adversary proceeding seeking to recover the six payments as fraudulent conveyances. In response, the principal's mother claimed that the checks represented payments on various pre-petition loans made by [her] to the company. Unlike the instant case, the bankruptcy court held an evidentiary hearing, and heard testimony from the principal, her mother and the trustee, and considered evidence of "canceled checks, check registers, and credit card statements." Id. at 129. After considering the evidence, the court concluded that all of the checks from the principal's mother had been made payable to the principal, not the corporation, and that Rowanoak's tax returns did not identify any outstanding loans to the principal's mother.

The First Circuit held that "the Trustee undisputably has the burden of proving the transfers were fraudulent, and this burden never shifts to [principal's mother]." Id. at 131. The court continued, "to meet his prima facie burden, *the Trustee had to present sufficient evidence to establish the negative proposition that [principal's mother] did not loan funds to Rowanoak.*" Id. at 132 (emphasis added). The court concluded that the trustee carried that burden by "present[ing] evidence that no documents, such as a promissory note, mortgage, or security interest supported [principal's mother's claim] that she had loaned money to Rowanoak." Id. Although *Rowanoak* does not feature the third-party complication at issue here—specifically, did the debtor pay transferee to satisfy an obligation to principal—it clearly rejects the proposition Appellant claims it represents, namely that the transferee, not the debtor, has the burden to show lack of consideration.[25] See also Oles Envelope Corp. v. Oles, 193 Md. 79, 65 A.2d 899, 903 (Md. 1949) ("Where a conveyance is valid on its face, the burden of proof is upon the party attacking the conveyance to show either (1) that it was not made upon a good consideration, or (2) that it was made with a fraudulent intent on the part of the grantor to hinder, delay or defraud his creditors ....") (citations omitted); Totten v. Brady, 54 Md. 170 (1880) ("The burden of proof is upon the complainants to show that the deeds in question were made without consideration....."); Colandrea v. Union Home Loan Corp. (In re Colandrea), 17 B.R. 568, 579 (Bankr. D. Md. 1982) (holding that trustee "proved that no consideration flowed to [debtor] in exchange for the mortgage," and only after trustee showed the absence of any consideration "Maryland law placed the burden of proof as to the solvency of the transferor upon the party claiming under the

---

the remaining assets of the debtor were unreasonably small in relation to the business or transaction; or (ii) intended to incur, or believed or reasonably should have believed that he would incur, debts beyond his ability to pay as they became due." Mass. Gen. Laws ch. 109A, § 5(a).

    25. [Footnote 7 in original:] During the bankruptcy court proceeding, although the IRS mistakenly argued that Downey, not Abatement, was the transferor, it correctly noted that the Trustee failed to carry his burden to "show that the debtor did not receive reasonably equivalent value in exchange for the money taken by Downey," and that "[t]he trustee has proffered no evidence whatsoever that the debtor received less than reasonably equivalent value in exchange for the transfers at issue in this case. The transfers to and by Downey, the president, C.E.O. and ultimate shareholder of the debtor, could have been payment of salary, repayment of a loan, or repayment of the debtor's expenses."

conveyance"); Gen. Elec. Credit Corp. v. Murphy (In re Duque Rodriguez), 895 F.2d 725, 726 n. 1 (11th Cir. 1990) (burden of proving "reasonably equivalent" value under fraudulent conveyance provision of 11 U.S.C. § 548(a)(2)(A) lies with the trustee challenging the transfer); *Rubin*, 661 F.2d. at 993 (stating that the trustee has the burden of proving the absence of "fair consideration") (citations omitted).[26] Because the Trustee has failed to carry his burden to show that Abatement received no fair consideration from Downey, or another source, as a result of its transfer to IRS, we conclude that he cannot satisfy the MUFCA.

Although it is clear that Abatement owed no money directly to IRS, the Trustee has offered no evidence to show that the company received no consideration from a third party, specifically Downey, for the transfer. Thus, to allow the Trustee to prevail merely upon a showing that Abatement received no consideration from the transferee would undercut the purposes of the fraudulent conveyance doctrine. In analyzing fraudulent conveyances, Professor Glenn wrote of whether a transfer was for value that "the test is whether, as a result of the transaction, the debtor's estate was unfairly diminished." 1 Gerrard Glenn, FRAUDULENT CONVEYANCES AND PREFERENCES § 275 (rev. ed. 1940); see also Westminster Sav. Bank, 39 A.2d at 863 ("The object of the statute was to aid in the suppression of fraud by protecting creditors from any conveyances by debtors to relatives or friends under the pretext of discharging a moral obligation."). Under the facts as presented by the Trustee, we cannot conclude that Abatement's estate was unfairly diminished by the transfer to IRS. See 3 NORTON BANKRUPTCY LAW & PRACTICE 2d § 58:2 (1997 & Supp. 2003) (recognizing that under federal fraudulent conveyance law, like Maryland law, "'[v]alue' includes the satisfaction of antecedent debt. Thus, a fraudulent conveyance can occur where the debtor transfers property for the benefit of a third party and receives no property or debt reduction in return."). If Abatement owed sums to Downey, the payment to IRS—i.e., satisfaction of an "antecedent debt" constituting fair consideration pursuant to Md. Code Ann., Com. Law § 15-203(a)—did not unfairly diminish the company's estate, rather it merely satisfied a preexisting obligation.

IV.

Because Trustee Field failed to establish that Abatement received no consideration from its principal Downey or another third-party source for its payment to IRS on behalf of Downey, Appellant cannot recover under the MUFCA. Accordingly, we do not need to examine the district court's conclusion that Maryland's "voluntary payment" doctrine serves as a bar to the MUFCA.

AFFIRMED.

NOTE

Do you agree with the court's footnote 2 that § 106(a)(1) eliminates the IRS's sovereign immunity? Outside bankruptcy, could a creditor have sued the IRS successfully under Maryland fraudulent conveyance law?

---

26. [Footnote 8 in original:] Despite the Trustee's error as to who bears the burden of establishing the absence of consideration, as *Colandrea* and other cases recognize, the Trustee is correct that the burden of showing solvency to defeat a fraudulent conveyance action lies with the transferee. See *Lacey*, 267 A.2d at 98 ("[T]he burden of proving the solvency of the debtor, that is, that he retained sufficient means to pay his debts after the voluntary conveyance, is on the transferee.") (internal quotation marks and citation omitted). Yet because the Trustee failed to present evidence on the consideration prong, examination of the solvency prong is unnecessary.

A disadvantage of § 544(b) is that the trustee's rights thereunder are entirely derivative of an actual unsecured creditor. Section 544(b) permits the trustee to attack a transfer only on the basis of laws that would allow a transfer to be voided by a present creditor of the estate holding an allowable, unsecured claim. Thus, when relying on § 544(b) to avoid a transfer under state law, the trustee must establish not only that the conditions of the state law have been satisfied; the trustee must also establish that at least one of the actual, unsecured creditors of the estate could have invoked the state law and voided the transfer for its own benefit as of the time of the bankruptcy petition. Unlike § 544(a) which independently gives the trustee the power of a hypothetical creditor, § 544(b) requires that an actual creditor have the power to void a transfer; and, where such power exists, § 544(b) then allows the trustee to step into the actual creditor's shoes and use the power derivatively for the benefit of the estate and all unsecured creditors. This subrogation does not depend on the creditor, before bankruptcy, having already sued or otherwise acted to void the transfer. All that is necessary is that the creditor have had a right, at the time of the debtor's bankruptcy, to void the transfer.

Because the trustee's power under § 544(b) is derivative, the trustee must satisfy the same conditions, and is subject to the same defenses, that the state law would impose on the actual creditor whose shoes the trustee wears. Note, however, that if the trustee succeeds in avoiding a transfer or obligation under § 544(b), the entire transfer or obligation is avoided even if that would not have been the result under state law. Under state law a creditor typically can avoid a fraudulent transfer only to the extent necessary for the creditor's claim to be paid in full. But if a transfer or obligation is avoided under § 544(b), the entire transfer or obligation will be avoided. Thus a trustee could use the rights of a creditor with a $100 claim to avoid a $1 million transfer in its entirety, even though under state law the creditor could only set aside $100 of it. See Moore v. Bay, 284 U.S. 4, 52 S. Ct. 3, 76 L. Ed. 133 (1931). Moore v. Bay also teaches us that any recovery under § 544(b) is for the benefit of the estate (and thus all the creditors), rather than for the specific benefit of the creditor whose rights were used by the trustee to avoid the transfer.

Necessarily, when the trustee can satisfy the conditions for exercising the derivative avoiding power of § 544(b), there are actual creditors who—outside of bankruptcy and under state law—could have avoided the transfer that the trustee targets under § 544(b) in a bankruptcy case. However, there are limits on the extent to which the trustee, on the basis of § 544(b), can divest actual creditors of their state-law claims.

TUG Liquidation, LLC v. Atwood (In re Buildnet, Inc.)
United States Bankruptcy Court, Middle District of North Carolina, 2004
2004 WL 1534296

CARRUTHERS, Bankruptcy J.

This matter came on before the Court for hearing on April 20, 2004 upon the Motions to Dismiss by Bayard M. Atwood; Keith T. Brown; Justin Hall-Tipping; Norvell E. Miller; Nathan P. Morton; William W. Neal, III; Joel Koblentz; Peter J.

Smith; Jack F. Kemp; Charles M. Cosby; Peter B. Drayson; Stephen L. Holcombe; Steven C. Thompson, Sr.; and Peter Abene, Sr. (collectively referred to as the "Defendants") pursuant to Fed.R.Civ.P. 12(b)(6) and the Defendants' Motion for Sanctions. After review of the Motions and consideration of the matters asserted therein, the Court makes the following findings of fact and conclusions of law pursuant to Rule 7052 of the Federal Rules of Bankruptcy Procedure.

This action, which involves the bankruptcy estate of BuildNet., Inc. and its subsidiaries, (collectively referred to as "BuildNet" or "Debtor"), comes before this Court after being transferred to this district from the Northern District of Georgia. The District Court for the Middle District of North Carolina subsequently transferred this action to this bankruptcy court. Section 1334(a) vests original and exclusive jurisdiction in the district court over all cases arising under the Bankruptcy Code. Section 1334(b) provides that the District Court shall have original but not exclusive jurisdiction over all civil proceedings "arising under title 11, or arising in or related to cases under title 11." The District Court has determined that subject matter jurisdiction is found under § 1334(b). However the extent to which the bankruptcy court, rather than the District Court can adjudicate the matter must be determined pursuant to 28 U.S.C. § 157. This court obtained jurisdiction by referral from the District Court under 28 U.S.C. § 157. This section allows the bankruptcy court to hear and determine all cases under Title 11 and all core proceedings arising under Title 11 or arising in a case under Title 11. Other proceedings that are otherwise related to Title 11 cases are considered non-core proceedings. In non-core proceedings, absent consent of the parties, the bankruptcy court has limited jurisdiction and cannot issue a final judgment. It can only submit proposed findings of fact and conclusions of law to the district court, which in turn, can enter a final judgment. Bankruptcy Rule 7008 requires that every complaint allege whether the action is core or non-core. TUG Liquidation, LLC ("TUG" or "Plaintiff") has not complied with this provision and shall have ten days from entry of this order to comply.

BuildNet filed a petition under Chapter 11 of the Bankruptcy Code on August 8, 2001 and BuildNet's estate is currently under administration by this Court. The present action arises out of a complaint filed on January 7, 2003 (the "Complaint") and subsequently amended on April 19, 2003 (the "Amended Complaint") by TUG, individually and as assignee of BuildNet, against the Defendants, all former officers and directors of BuildNet. For the purposes of these motions to dismiss, the Plaintiff's version of the facts set forth in the Complaint and Amended Complaint will be taken as true, and nothing herein shall constitute a finding of fact by this Court.

BACKGROUND

BuildNet, formed in 1996, was engaged in the business of the development and sale of software based on a concept of collaborative e-commerce solutions for the residential construction industry. BuildNet hoped to design and implement an internet-based marketplace, called the BuildNet Exchange, which could provide informational and procurement links between homebuilders, suppliers and manufacturers. In 1999, BuildNet raised over $35 million through a sale of Series B preferred stock for sustaining operations, developing the BuildNet Exchange, and acquisition activity for construction management software companies. Also that year, certain defendants authorized the issuance of a Private Placement

Memorandum (the "PPM") for the sale of Series C preferred stock. BuildNet raised approximately $107 million from the sale of Series C preferred stock. According to BuildNet's projections in the PPM, this amount should have been sufficient to carry BuildNet through its period of losses and well into profitability.

In late 1999, BuildNet approached TUG about acquiring its business. During negotiations, several defendants made presentations to TUG in which they focused on BuildNet's strong financial condition, success in raising money, its management team's experience and strength, and their expectations for an initial public offering (the "IPO"). BuildNet provided TUG with the PPM for TUG's due diligence and was told it contained the necessary financial and operational information. The Plaintiff alleges that the PPM contained material misrepresentations regarding BuildNet's business plan, including misrepresenting BuildNet's current burn rate, grossly underestimating anticipated losses, misrepresenting the capabilities of the BuildNet Exchange, and omitting the fact that BuildNet would be unable to pay its debts (including any due TUG) if the IPO was unsuccessful.

On January 18, 2000, BuildNet acquired TUG, which became The Unilink Group, LLC ("UniLink"), for $27 Million. In connection with this acquisition, BuildNet executed and delivered a $27 million promissory note ("Note") with a term of 24 months to TUG and a security agreement ("Security Agreement") granting TUG a security interest in the purchased assets. The Note was convertible in its entirety into common BuildNet stock.

In the Amended Complaint, TUG alleges that between the time that BuildNet purchased UniLink and the bankruptcy filing, the Defendants grossly mismanaged UniLink. TUG contends that the Defendants failed to devise a business plan to integrate UniLink's operations into BuildNet. BuildNet removed former top management, and instead, had more than four different people overseeing UniLink in the first four months after its acquisition, and provided no new direction. Senior officers arbitrarily changed UniLink's pricing plan and for several months, instructed UniLink's sales force not to make any sales because of the officers' inability to devise an effective pricing strategy. At the time of purchase, UniLink's workforce was comprised of over 75 employees and had an annual revenue run rate in excess of $4,500,000. At the time of the bankruptcy filing, UniLink had less then five employees and minimal revenue.

The purchase of UniLink was one of many acquisitions made by BuildNet in the year 2000. With no business plan for the integration of additional companies, some defendants authorized the purchase of additional companies, while others traveled extensively around the world investigating other opportunities. BuildNet acquired four companies in January 2000 alone. BuildNet lost $53 million during this same time period. In July 2000, the Board of Directors authorized seven additional acquisitions without any due diligence reports, final acquisition documents, integration plans or analysis of the impact on BuildNet. Despite huge losses, the Defendants made no effort to control spending. For example, BuildNet entered into a lease for the BuildNet Exchange at a cost of $350,000 per month, and directors of BuildNet continued to authorize that officers receive exorbitant salaries. Meanwhile, BuildNet's Chairman, Keith Brown, was busy writing a book, developing a new business venture called "SmartPlan," and starting three other companies: Interactive Marketplace Incubator, Interactive Marketplace Ventures and International MarketPlace Venture Management.

Finally, after a third quarter loss of an additional $34,086,756 in the fall of 2000, the officers and directors began to make some effort to reduce the work force, and yet, severance packages ranging from $50,000 to over $800,000 were paid out to resigning officers. For example Atwood, who served as the Chief Operating Officer and as a member of the Board of Directors, was paid the sum of $75,000 upon his resignation and the Board authorized a payment of $25,000 per month for a period of three years. In February 2001, while BuildNet was in dire financial straits, promissory notes previously executed by various executives in consideration for the purchase of stock were reduced to ten percent of the balance, and in July 2001, just prior to bankruptcy, some defendants authorized the repurchase of stock in consideration for the cancellation of promissory notes totaling $1,670,000.

After the bankruptcy filing, TUG filed an unsecured claim in the amount of approximately $30 million against BuildNet. TUG repurchased its former business, and is now the holder of an unsecured claim in the amount of $21 million. TUG also began to raise questions about the possibility of claims related to the mismanagement or irregularity in the affairs of the Debtors. TUG filed a motion for an order directing a Rule 2004 examination of certain documents in the Debtors' possession or control.

On December 6, 2001, the court appointed Holmes P. Harden (the "Examiner") as an examiner to investigate and file a Statement of Investigation concerning any fact ascertained pertaining to incompetence, misconduct, mismanagement or irregularity in the management of BuildNet, or pertaining to a cause of action available to the estates with respect to any present or former officer or director of BuildNet. The Examiner filed his Preliminary Report on April 9, 2002. The report identified the existence of several claims BuildNet might have against certain officers and directors. BuildNet's counsel and the Examiner pursued some claims as a result of the evidence discovered during the investigation; however, TUG disagreed with some of the findings in the Preliminary Report and believed that BuildNet may have additional claims. The parties eventually reached an agreement whereby BuildNet assigned to TUG those claims which neither BuildNet nor the Examiner wished to pursue in consideration for $15,000 and TUG agreed to withdraw its objection to the BuildNet's proposed plan of reorganization. This court entered an order ("Assignment Order") on September 4, 2002 authorizing BuildNet to assign and transfer its rights to pursue, settle or collect monies from those claims. In addition, on October 15, 2002, the parties entered into a contract for the transfer and assignment of such claims ("Assignment").

In the Amended Complaint, the Plaintiff asserts claims both on behalf of itself, individually, and on behalf of BuildNet, as assignee. Individually, TUG has asserted the following claims: (Count I) fraud; (Count II) negligent misrepresentation; (Count III) breach of fiduciary duty and constructive fraud; (Count VIII) corporate waste; (Count IX) deepening insolvency; and (Count X) unfair and deceptive acts. As assignee of BuildNet, TUG has asserted the following claims: (Count III) breach of fiduciary duty and constructive fraud; (Count IV) gross negligence; (Count V) breach of duty of loyalty; (Count VII) unlawful stock redemption pursuant to 8 Del. C. § 174(a); (Count VIII) corporate waste; and (Count IX) deepening insolvency.

DISCUSSION

* * *

(2) TUG'S individual claims

In its Amended Complaint, TUG individually has asserted a total of six claims against various defendants. The claims asserted by TUG individually fall into two general categories. First, some of the claims brought by TUG individually rest upon a basic premise that the Defendants breached a duty owed *directly* to TUG. These claims include those for fraud (Count I); negligent misrepresentation (Count II); and unfair and deceptive acts (Count X). These three claims are predicated upon actions by the Defendants directed specifically towards TUG and are personal to TUG. The other type of claim brought by TUG individually is that in which the alleged injuries were sustained by BuildNet and all of its creditors, including TUG. These are claims that are predicated upon fiduciary duties owed to BuildNet's creditors in general upon insolvency: corporate waste (Count VIII), and deepening insolvency (Count IX). Lastly, Count III, TUG's claim for breach of fiduciary duty and constructive fraud, appears to fall into both categories.

In Count I of the Amended Complaint, TUG brings a claim for fraud against defendants Abene, Atwood, Brown, Drayson, Holcombe, Morton and Thompson ("Count I Defendants"). To state a claim for fraud under North Carolina law, the plaintiff must allege (1) false representation or concealment of a material fact; (2) reasonably calculated to deceive; (3) made with intent to deceive; (4) which does in fact deceive; and (5) which results in damage to the plaintiff. Federal Rule of Civil Procedure 9(b) requires a plaintiff alleging fraud to plead with particularity such that "upon a liberal construction of the whole pleading, the charge of fraud might be supported by proof of the alleged constitutive facts." Carver v. Roberts, 78 N.C. App. 511, 513, 337 S.E.2d 126, 128 (1985) (quoting Manufacturing Co. v. Taylor, 230 N.C. 680, 686, 55 S.E.2d 311, 315 (1949)).

The Count I Defendants contend that the Complaint fails to adequately delineate the specific facts which would support the elements of this claim; however, the court finds that any deficiencies which may have existed with regard to the original Complaint have been corrected in the Amended Complaint. The Amended Complaint sets forth allegations of specific misrepresentations and omissions by specific defendants. TUG contends that the Count I Defendants were responsible for preparing the PPM, that they knew the PPM was provided to TUG for its due diligence and that these defendants knew or should have known that the PPM contained numerous material misrepresentations and omissions. TUG recites the specific statements in the PPM that were allegedly false and lists specific facts that were omitted from the PPM. TUG also sets forth with particularity various meetings at which specific Count I Defendants made allegedly false representations. TUG contends that all of these alleged misrepresentations and omissions were made with an intent to induce reliance, did in fact induce reliance, and resulted in damages of at least $27 million. The court finds that TUG has pled with sufficient particularity to state a claim for fraud, therefore, the Count I Defendants' motions to dismiss will denied.

In Count II, TUG asserts a claim for negligent misrepresentation against Abene, Atwood, Brown, Cosby, Drayson, Hall-Tipping, Holcombe, Miller, Morton, Neal, and Thompson ("Count II Defendants"). Negligent misrepresentation ["]occurs when (1) a party justifiably relies, (2) to his detriment, (3) on information prepared without reasonable care, (4) by one who owed the relying party a duty of care." Brinkman v. Barrett Kays & Assoc., P.A., 155 N.C. App. at 742, 575 S.E.2d 40, 43-44 (citing Simms v. Prudential Live Ins. Co. of America, 140 N.C. App. 529, 532, 537 S.E.2d 237, 240 (2000)).

In this case, TUG's claim for negligent misrepresentation is based upon the allegations set forth in support of its claim for fraud. In addition, TUG alleges that the Count II Defendants took no steps to monitor, manage or control the accuracy of information presented to TUG both verbally and in writing thereby causing damages to TUG by inducing reasonable reliance upon the information. These allegations are sufficient to withstand the Count II Defendants' Rule 12(b)(6) motion to dismiss.

Recently, TUG added a claim pursuant to N.C. Gen. Stat. § 75-16 for unfair and deceptive acts. To prevail on a claim for unfair and deceptive trade practices, a plaintiff must show: (1) an unfair or deceptive act or practice; (2) in or affecting commerce; (3) which proximately caused actual injury to plaintiffs. A trade practice is unfair if it is immoral, unethical, oppressive, unscrupulous, substantially injurious to consumers or if it offends established public policy. Marshall v. Miller, 302 N.C. 539, 548, 276 S.E.2d 397, 403 (1981). A trade practice is considered deceptive if it has the capacity or tendency to deceive. Id. In North Carolina, "[p]roof of fraud necessarily constitutes a violation of the prohibition against unfair and deceptive trade practices." Webb v. Triad Appraisal and Adjustment Service, Inc., 84 N.C. App. 446, 449, 352 S.E.2d 859, 862 (1987); Hunter v. Guardian Life Ins. Co. of America, 593 S.E.2d 595, 601 (N.C. App. Feb. 3, 2004). Because the Plaintiff has alleged facts which, if proven, could support a finding of fraud, it has also alleged facts which could support a finding of unfair and deceptive practices.

TUG alleges that because of the sale of the assets of TUG to BuildNet in exchange for a $27 million promissory note, TUG had a special relationship with the Debtor which might create a duty other than that owed to other creditors of the corporation. TUG contends that they were induced to sell their assets based on fraudulent, reckless, and negligent misrepresentations and the failure to disclose material facts during the acquisition negotiations. These claims are personal to TUG and are not claims that belong to the corporation.

TUG individually asserts two general claims related to fiduciary duties owed to the corporation's creditors: corporate waste (Count VIII), and deepening insolvency (Count IX). The Defendants contend that the Plaintiff does not have standing to pursue fiduciary duty related causes of action individually if those causes of action are common to all creditors.

A single creditor may not individually maintain a general action against a corporation's directors and officers if that creditor shares that injury common to all creditors and has personally been injured only in an indirect manner. In re Sunshine Precious Metals, Inc., 157 B.R. 159, 162 (Bankr. D. Idaho 1993); see also Delgado Oil Co., Inc., v. Torres, 785 F.2d 857, 861 (10th Cir. 1986) (liability of the corporation's fiduciary for violating a trust relationship applied to all creditors); Whirlpool Corp. v. CIT Group/Business Credit, Inc., 258 F. Supp.2d 1140, 1146 (D. Hawai'i 2003) (creditor may have a superior interest, but still does not have standing to pursue an action for injury suffered by all creditors); *PHP Liquidating,*

LLC, 291 B.R. 592, 599 (D. Del. 2003) (claim for violation of a statute prohibiting a corporation from purchasing its own shares when its capital is impaired was a general claim which only a trustee or debtor could bring); In re Stoll, 252 B.R. 492 (9th Cir. BAP 2000). An injury that is common to all creditors is properly brought through the debtor corporation. Upon the filing of a bankruptcy petition, general claims held by the debtor's creditors become property of the bankruptcy estate. See 11 U.S.C. § 541. Section 544(b) of the Bankruptcy Code grants only trustees or debtors-in-possession standing to pursue general claims held by the debtor's creditors. PHP Liquidating, LLC v. Robbins, 291 B.R. at 599.

In determining whether a claim is general to all creditors and derivative of an injury to the corporation, the court must examine whether the asserted cause of action involves an injury particular to one creditor, or whether it is a cause of action that might be asserted by any creditor. In re Sunshine Precious Metals, Inc., 157 B.R. at 162. Corporate waste and deepening insolvency are claims designed for the protection of creditors and shareholders in general because they are derivative of an injury to the corporation, and are not the result of a direct injury sustained by a single creditor. These are not claims that address injuries sustained by TUG individually, but rather, injuries suffered by BuildNet. Therefore, to the extent that TUG *individually* attempts to state a claim for either corporate waste (Count VIII) or deepening insolvency (Count IX), those claims must be dismissed. Typical derivative claims that can be brought on behalf of the corporation and, thus, are [§] 541 property rights of the debtor include claims for mismanagement, breach of fiduciary duty, and corporate waste. In re Granite Partners, L.P., 194. B.R. 318, 327-28 (Bankr. S.D.N.Y. 1996).

The only remaining claim brought by TUG individually is Count III, breach of fiduciary duty and constructive fraud, which is asserted against all Defendants. As stated in the Amended Complaint, this claim is brought by TUG individually *both* by virtue of its special relationship to BuildNet and as a creditor in general. To the extent that TUG individually seeks to bring this claim on behalf of all creditors, this claim must be dismissed for the reasons set forth above regarding the claims for corporate waste and deepening insolvency. However, in North Carolina, a creditor may bring a claim against a director of a corporation alleging that the director has committed constructive fraud by breaching his or her fiduciary duty owed directly to the creditor. Keener Lumber Co., Inc. v. Perry, 149 N.C. App. 19, 26-27, 560 S.E.2d 817, 823 (2002) (citing Lillian Knitting Mills Co. v. Earle, 233 N.C. 74, 62 S.E.2d 492 (1950)). If that claim is founded upon injuries particular or personal to the individual creditor, it is a claim that belongs to the creditor, not the corporation. Id. In Count III of the Amended Complaint, TUG has alleged that the Defendants were in a fiduciary relationship specifically with TUG, that the Defendants breached their fiduciary duty to TUG, and that TUG suffered an injury particular to itself. These allegations are sufficient to withstand the Defendants' motion to dismiss.

In sum, TUG may assert a claim for a specific injury to TUG which is distinct from the action that may be maintained by the Debtor. See In re Reliance Acceptance Group, Inc., 235 B.R. 548 (D. Del. 1999); and In re Van Dresser Corp., 128 F.3d 945, 949 (6th Cir. 1997). TUG has a personal claim if they have been injured and no other claimant or creditor has an interest in the cause.

(3) Claims brought by TUG as assignee of BuildNet

Immediately after this case was filed, the Bankruptcy Administrator sent out a notice requesting that unsecured creditors form a creditors' committee in the case. Due to lack of response, no committee was formed. TUG, as the holder of the largest unsecured claim in the case, wanted the Debtor-in-Possession to pursue various actions against the officers and directors of the company. With the consent of the Debtor-in-Possession, the Bankruptcy Administrator and TUG, it was agreed that inasmuch as there was no creditors' committee, the best course of action would be to appoint an Examiner to investigate facts pertaining to fraud, dishonesty, incompetence, misconduct, mismanagement or irregularity in the management of the affairs of the Debtors, or pertaining to the course of action available to the estates with respect to any present or former officer. Holmes Hardin was appointed Examiner and filed a preliminary report with his findings on April 9, 2002. TUG disagreed with some of the Examiner's findings and conclusions and filed a Motion to Compel Debtor-in-Possession to Dispose of Property of the Estate, or in the Alternative, for Authorization to Assert Claims on behalf of the Debtor. Notice of the Motion to compel the debtor to sell the remaining claims and causes of action to TUG for the sum of $15,000, subject to a higher bidder by another party, was transmitted to all creditors in the case. No higher offer was obtained and no party objected to the sale of these causes of action to TUG. An order approving the Agreement between TUG and the Debtor-in-Possession was memorialized by order of this court on September 4, 2002.

The Debtor-in-Possession and the Examiner elected to pursue certain causes of action in this case. However, the Debtor elected to sell other causes of action to TUG for the sum of $15,000. This court stated that it was not making any determination as to the merits of the claim or whether TUG could legally purchase the claims, in part because the claims had not been identified. It is clear that the bankruptcy code permits a debtor-in-possession the power to use, sell or lease property of the estate. 11 U.S.C. § 363.

The Defendants contend that the assignment of tort claims from BuildNet to TUG was invalid inasmuch as it violates North Carolina public policy. If the assignment is invalid, TUG lacks standing to bring any tort claims as assignee of BuildNet. Prior to addressing the assignability of these claims, the court must determine what state's law applies to this case, which is heard by this court pursuant to 28 U.S.C. § 1334. Claims that are based upon state law must apply choice of law rules of the forum state absent a compelling federal interest which dictates otherwise. Therefore, this court must look to North Carolina choice of law rules to determine which body of state law is controlling.

BuildNet was incorporated in North Carolina on October 24, 1996, and reincorporated in Delaware on March 28, 2000. Both North Carolina and Delaware follow the "internal affairs" doctrine under which the corporate law of the jurisdiction of the organization would govern the duties of the directors and the relationship between the directors, officers and shareholders. Under the "internal affairs" doctrine, the law of the jurisdiction of incorporation generally governs claims related to the internal affairs of a corporation. Therefore, this court would look to both North Carolina and Delaware law to determine whether the Amended Complaint alleges facts sufficient to state the alleged claims. However, the court need not make a determination as to the sufficiency of the facts alleged in the Amended Complaint unless it determines that TUG has standing to bring the Assigned Claims.

As assignee of BuildNet, TUG has asserted six claims including, a claim for breach of fiduciary duty and constructive fraud, gross negligence, breach of duty of loyalty, unlawful stock redemption pursuant to 8 Del. C. § 174(a), corporate waste, and deepening insolvency (together referred to herein as the "Assigned Claims"). TUG asserts that it has standing to pursue the Assigned Claims by virtue of the Assignment and Assignment Order. The Assignment itself is a contract between BuildNet and TUG, which may be distinguished from the underlying claims. While this court was unable to locate any North Carolina cases that specifically address the issue of choice of law for an assignment of claim, under general North Carolina choice of law rules, the validity and interpretation of a contract are presumed to be governed by the law of the state in which the contract was formed. In this case, the Assignment Order was issued by this court in the bankruptcy proceeding in North Carolina, and the Assignment bears the heading for the Middle District of North Carolina. In contrast, the assignability of a claim may be viewed in light of the nature of the claim being assigned, as defined by the jurisdiction that created it. Accordingly, at least one court has held that, "the assignability of the right or obligation being assigned is determined by looking to the law which would govern the underlying contract (or … tort) which enabled the right to come into existence." Conopco, Inc. v. McCreadie, 826 F.Supp. 855, 864 (D.N.J. 1993), aff'd 40 F.3d 1239 (3rd Cir. 1994).

In any case, North Carolina courts will not apply the law of a foreign state if it offends the public policy of the forum. Boudreau v. Baughman, 322 N.C. 331, 368 S.E.2d 849 (1988). Rather, courts will apply North Carolina law if the law of the other state offends North Carolina public policy. Clayton v. Burnett, 135 N.C. App. 746, 749, 522 S.E.2d 785, 787 (1999). Because the Defendants contend that the Assignment offends North Carolina public policy, this court must examine North Carolina law to determine the validity of the Assignment.

In North Carolina, an action arising out of a contract can generally be assigned; however, an assignment of a personal tort claim is void as against public policy because it promotes champerty. Horton v. New South Insurance Co., 122 N.C. App. 265, 268, 468 S.E.2d 856, 858 (1996). Champerty is a form of officious intermeddling in a lawsuit, whereby a stranger makes a bargain with a plaintiff to carry on a lawsuit at his or her own expense. Daimlerchrysler Corp. v. Kirkhart, 148 N.C. App. 572, 561 S.E.2d 276 (2002).

The classic example of a personal tort claim is the personal injury claim. North Carolina courts have consistently held that the assignment of a personal injury claim is against public policy. Tort claims such as unfair and deceptive trade practices, personal injury, bad faith refusal to settle, breach of fiduciary duty, and tortious breach of contract are personal to a plaintiff and cannot be assigned.

North Carolina has not defined the term "personal tort." In some jurisdictions, the case law makes a clear distinction between personal torts and property torts. If the tort is to the person, such as bodily injury, injury to reputation or for emotional distress, the claim cannot be assigned. In contrast, torts which involve damage to property are assignable. While no North Carolina case could be found regarding this distinction, there is case law stating that a tort claim arising from property damage can be assigned. However, more recent North Carolina case law appears more concerned about the distinction between an action arising out of contract and actions sounding in tort than whether the injury is to a person or property. See *Horton*, 122 N.C. App. at 268-69, 468 S.E.2d at 858 (allegations seeking damages based on tort, not merely on simple breach of contract, may not be assigned). Such cases have focused on the special relationship of trust and confidence between the parties in finding a tort "personal," rather than whether a person or property has been damaged. Id.

The Plaintiff argues that, inasmuch as the causes of action are § 541 property, "once they become part of the estate, the trustee and the bankruptcy court have the power to sell and assign the claims." The Plaintiff contends that such an assignment is property and federal law prevails over state law where there is a conflict. The court is required to review 11 U.S.C. § 541 (property of the estate), 11 U.S.C. § 363 (authorizing the sale of property), and the preemption doctrine.

Federal law, specifically 11 U.S.C. § 541, defines what types of property comprise the bankruptcy estate. Section 541 reads in pertinent part:

> (a) The commencement of a case under section 301, 302, or 303 of this title creates an estate. Such estate is comprised of all the following property, wherever located and by whomever held:
>> (1) Except as provided in subsections (b) and (c)(2) of this section, all legal or equitable interests of the debtor in property as of the commencement of the case.
>
> …
>
> (c)(1)Except as provided in paragraph (2) of this subsection, an interest of the debtor in property becomes property of the estate under subsection (a)(1), (a)(2), or (a)(5) of this section notwithstanding any provision in an agreement, transfer instrument, or applicable nonbankruptcy law—
>> (A) that restricts or conditions transfer of such interest by the debtor;

11 U.S.C. § 541.

Causes of action are clearly § 541 property whether or not they are transferable by the debtor. See In re Cottrell, 876 F.2d 540, 542-43 (6th Cir. 1989) (personal injury action was estate property notwithstanding that action was non-transferable under Kentucky law); Tignor v. Parkinson, 729 F.2d 977, 980-81 (4th Cir. 1984) (unliquidated personal injury claim was § 541 property notwithstanding that claim was nontransferable under Virginia law) (effectively overruled on other grounds by Va. Code. Ann. § 34-28.1); *Integrated Solutions*, 124 F.3d 487 (3rd Cir. 1997) (claims for unfair competition, breach of duty of loyalty, misappropriating confidential information, and interference with contractual relations were property of the estate notwithstanding New Jersey law prohibiting assignment of prejudgment tort claims).

While federal law determine the scope of the estate property, a debtor's interest in property is determined by state law. Butner v. United States, 440 U.S. 48, 55, 99 S. Ct. 914, 918, 59 L. Ed. 2d 136 (1979); In re Equipment Services Inc., 290 F.3d 739 (4th Cir. 2002) (Chapter 11 debtor's property interest at the time it files its bankruptcy petition are generally determined as a matter of state law); In re Scalon, 239 F.3d 1195 (11th Cir. 2001); In re O'Dowd, 233 F.3d 197 (3rd Cir. 2000); In re

Newpower, 233 F.3d 922 (6th Cir. 2000; In re Pettit, 217 F.3d 1072 (9th Cir. 2000). The tort based causes of action acquired by TUG are § 541 property. They continue to be § 541 property nonwithstanding any North Carolina case law that prohibits their transfer. However, the sale of these tort claims under § 363 does nothing to change the impact of North Carolina policy that prohibits the assignment of tort claims.

Nothing in § 363 authorizes a trustee or a debtor to sell property in violation of a state law transfer restriction. "[N]either § 363(b)(1) nor § 704(1) expressly authorizes the trustee to sell property in violation of state law transfer restrictions." *Integrated Solutions*, 124 F.3d at 493. See also In re Schauer, 835 F.2d 1222, 1225 (8th Cir. 1987) (trustee's power to transfer property of bankruptcy estate could be restricted by Minnesota property law); In re Bishop College, 151 B.R. 394, 398 (Bankr. D.N. Tex. 1993) (the bankruptcy estate receives assets "subject to any restrictions imposed by state law").

North Carolina prohibits the assignment of personal tort claims. The Debtor's ability to sell those claims under § 363 is not "an empowering statute in the sense that new rights or powers for dealing with the property of the estate are created." In re FCX. Inc., 853 F.2d 1149, 1155 (4th Cir. 1988). In *Butner*, the Supreme Court made it clear that state law governs absent a compelling conflict with federal law to warrant preempting state law. *Butner*, 440 U.S. at 55, 99 S. Ct. at 918. North Carolina has established valid public policy arguments to restrict the assignment of tort claims. There is not a competing federal interest that would warrant a different result.

In conclusion, Counts III, IV, V, VIII, and IX are all personal tort claims which constitute § 541 estate property. The extent of the debtor's interest in property is governed by North Carolina law and limitations on that interest imposed by state law are applicable in bankruptcy. The assignment of these personal tort claims was in violation of North Carolina public policy and TUG may not go forward with these claims.

As for the claim for unlawful stock redemption, the court finds that the assignment was valid. The Delaware Code prohibits a corporation from purchasing its own shares when its capital is impaired as follows:

> Every corporation may purchase, redeem, receive, take or otherwise acquire ... its own shares; provided, however, that no corporation shall ... [p]urchase or redeem its own shares of capital stock for cash or other property when the capital of the corporation is impaired or when such purchase or redemption would cause any impairment of the capital of the corporation.

8 Del. C. § 160(a) (2002). Section 174 provides for liability of directors of a corporation for unlawful payment of a dividend or unlawful stock redemption. 8 Del. C. § 174(c) (2002). Because TUG is seeking a statutory remedy against the Defendants for violations of Delaware corporate law, the court finds that the assignment of this claim does not violate North Carolina public policy. Furthermore, the court finds that the allegations contained within the Complaint are sufficient to state a claim. Therefore, the court will deny the Defendants' motion to dismiss this claim.

* * *

Based upon the foregoing, the Defendants' Motions to Dismiss TUG's individual claims for fraud, negligent misrepresentation, breach of fiduciary duty and constructive fraud, and unfair and deceptive acts are denied. The Defendants'

Motions to Dismiss TUG's claim as assignee for BuildNet for unlawful stock redemption is denied. The remaining claims will be dismissed. An Order will be entered consistent with this Memorandum Opinion.

ORDER

For the reasons set forth in the memorandum opinion entered contemporaneously herewith, it is ORDERED and ADJUDGED that the Motions to Dismiss by Bayard M. Atwood; Keith T. Brown; Justin Hall-Tipping; Norvell E. Miller; Nathan P. Morton; William W. Neal, III; Joel Koblentz; Peter J. Smith; Jack F. Kemp; Charles M. Cosby; Peter B. Drayson; Stephen L. Holcombe; Steven C. Thompson, Sr.; and Peter Abene, Sr. for counts IV, V, VIII, and IX are GRANTED. It is ORDERED that the Motions to Dismiss Counts I, II, VII, and X are DENIED. It is FURTHER ORDERED that the Motions to Dismiss TUG's individual claim in count III is DENIED, and the Motions to Dismiss TUG's claim as assignee of BuildNet in count III is GRANTED.

C. UNPERFECTED TRANSFERS

It is commonplace under state law that certain interests in property, especially unperfected encumbrances, are subordinate to the claims of subsequent judicial lien creditors or bona fide purchasers. This universal theme of state law underlies the avoiding powers of § 544(a), commonly known as the trustee's "strong arm" powers. Section 544(a) provides:

(a) The trustee shall have, as of the commencement of the case, and without regard to any knowledge of the trustee or of any creditor, the rights and powers of, or may avoid any transfer of property of the debtor or any obligation incurred by a debtor that is voidable by

(1) a creditor that extends credit to the debtor at the time of the commencement of the case, and that obtains, at such time and with respect to such credit, a judicial lien on all property on which a creditor on a simple contract could have obtained a judicial lien, whether or not such a creditor exists;

(2) a creditor that extends credit to the debtor at the time of the commencement of the case, and obtains, at such time and with respect to such credit, an execution against the debtor that is returned unsatisfied at such time, whether or not such a creditor exists; or

(3) a bona fide purchaser of real property, other than fixtures, from the debtor, against whom applicable law permits such transfer to be perfected, that obtains the status of a bona fide purchaser and has perfected such transfer at the time of the commencement of the case, whether or not such a purchaser exists.

Most important, this federal law effectively gives the trustee or debtor in possession, in its own right for the benefit of the estate, the status (technically, "rights and powers") of two classes of claimants of property who claim through the debtor as of the time of bankruptcy: (1) a lien creditor with a *judicial lien*[27] on *all*

---

27. A lien is any "charge against or interest in property to secure payment of a debt or performance of an obligation." Section 101(37). The Bankruptcy Code recognizes two primary classes of liens: liens that arises by contract and nonconsensual liens. Liens arising by contract, i.e., liens based

property that a contract creditor could subject to such a lien under state law, and (2) a bona fide *purchaser* of *real property* from the debtor to whom the transfer is made and perfected as of the time of bankruptcy.

WARNING! Be especially careful to note the wider reach of the lien claim: It can stretch to both personal and real property, but the trustee's claim as purchaser reaches only real property and not personalty. Less important, § 544(a)(2) also deems that the trustee is an unsecured creditor as of the filing of bankruptcy who on the same day caused execution to issue and suffered a nulla bona return.

So what? Most important, third parties' prepetition liens and interests in property that could be defeated (under state law) by a judicial lien creditor of the debtor, or by a purchaser of real estate from the debtor, are avoidable by the trustee (under § 544(a)) if at the time of bankruptcy the interests would be subordinate (under state law) to the claim of such a lien creditor or purchaser.[28] Less important, § 544(a) also allows the trustee to avoid any *obligation* of the debtor that is voidable under state law by a lien creditor or real estate purchaser.

Federal law and state law thus work in tandem: First, § 544(a) confers on the trustee the status of both a judicial lienor and real property bona fide purchaser who claim property through the debtor, and provides that the trustee enjoys their rights and powers with respect to the property. Second, the substance of these rights and powers, primarily the priority of these claims in relation to other interests in the property, is then determined by reference to state law. Third, if state law provides that the trustee's claim (as a judicial lien creditor or bona fide purchaser) is entitled to priority over a third party's interest in the property, the consequence is prescribed by federal law, § 544(a), which is that the trustee can entirely avoid the inferior,

---

on the parties' agreement, are referred to as "security interests," whether the collateral is real or personal property. Section 101(51).

The class of liens that are nonconsensual divides into several subsets, including judicial liens, statutory liens, and various other nonconsensual liens. A "statutory lien" is a lien "arising solely by force of statute on specified circumstances or conditions, or lien of distress for rent, whether or not statutory, but does not include security interest or judicial lien." Section 101(53). A "judicial lien" is any "lien obtained by judgment, levy, sequestration, or other legal or equitable process or proceeding." Section 101(36). Typically, judicial liens are authorized by statute. They are distinguished from statutory liens on the basis that a judicial lien does not arise, attach or otherwise become effective against property without or apart from some kind of judicial process. In contrast, a statutory lien is not only created by statute, but attaches to property automatically without and apart from judicial process.

These three categories of liens—security interests, statutory liens, and judicial liens—are mutually exclusive, and the only kind of lien rights the trustee acquires under § 544(a)(1) are those of a judicial lien holder—not the rights of a holder of a statutory lien or security interest. (If however, the trustee avoids a statutory lien or a security interest, the estate will then be entitled to the benefit of that lien or security interest; in that sense, the use of the § 544(a)(1) judicial lien creditor power may result in the trustee, as the estate's representative having the rights of a holder of a statutory lien or security interest .)

28. Please note that the trustee's power to defeat such interests does not depend on there being an actual bona fide purchaser or an actual judicial lien creditor in the case (the actual existence of which would only complicate matters). Rather, the trustee is given the rights and powers that a bona fide purchaser would have if one existed, and that a judicial lien creditor would have, if one existed. Thus the trustee's powers are often called the "hypothetical judicial lien creditor" power and the "hypothetical bona fide purchaser" power.

third-party interest. Any claim of the third-party survives, but only as an unsecured claim. The third party is divested completely of the interest in the property even though the result under state law would be less severe.

On the other hand, the trustee's powers under § 544(a) are limited to those of a judicial lien creditor or of a bona fide purchaser of real property. The third party's interest is not vulnerable under § 544(a) just because some other kind of claimant—such as the holder of a tax lien[29] or mechanics' lien—might be able to prevail over the third party. The third party's interest is safe from avoidance under § 544(a) even if the third party has failed to give public notice of the interest—that is, even if under some definition we might say the interest is unperfected—as long as state law gives such an unperfected claim priority over a judicial lien creditor and (in the case of real property) a bona fide purchaser.

Problem 8-2

> Kick Credit has a U.C.C. Article 9 security interest in Foam Corporation's personal property. Suppose that Kick Credit failed properly to perfect the interest. Its financing statement was incomplete or misfiled. Because of § 544(a)(1), Foam Corporation, as debtor in possession, can defeat any interest that a hypothetical judicial lien creditor could have defeated if the judicial lien creditor had obtained its judicial lien the very moment the case commenced. Because of state law—Uniform Commercial Code

---

29. For example, the trustee does not have the power to defeat an interest that the Internal Revenue Service could defeat as a tax lien holder if, hypothetically, the debtor owed taxes. See In re Knapp, 285 B.R. 176, 182-83 (Bankr. M.D.N.C. 2002). In addition, the IRS is not the kind of "creditor that extends credit" referenced in § 544(a)(2). See Schlossberg v. Barney, 380 F.3d 174 (4th Cir. 2004). In *Schlossberg*, the chapter 7 debtor owned her home in Maryland with her nondebtor spouse as tenants by the entirety. She was entitled to exempt the home (and thus the spouses could retain their $210,000 in equity in it) because (1) under § 522(b) (specifically now § 522(b)(3)(B)) property held in tenancy by the entirety is exempt in bankruptcy to the extent creditors cannot reach it under state law, (2) under Maryland law any property held in tenancy by the entirety can be reached only by creditors owed debts by both spouses, and (3) the creditors in the case were creditors only of the debtor, not of both the debtor and her spouse. The trustee nevertheless claimed that he could reach the home by using § 544(a)(2). The trustee correctly argued that the Internal Revenue Service could reach the property if either of the debtors owed taxes, as the Supreme Court held in United States v. Craft, 535 U.S. 274, 122 S. Ct. 1414, 152 L. Ed. 2d 437 (2002) (holding that federal tax lien could attach to one spouse's interest in property held in tenancy by the entirety, even though the tax debt was not a joint debt of both spouses). The trustee then noted that the IRS in some cases gives taxpayers extra time to pay taxes, and thus argued that the IRS could be the hypothetical "creditor that extends credit" in § 544(a)(2). The result, according to the trustee, would be that because the IRS could reach the home, then so could the trustee. The Fourth Circuit correctly rejected the trustee's argument, holding that a debtor's incurring of tax liability is not an extension of credit by the IRS within the meaning of § 544(a)(2), because it is not voluntary, even if the IRS does not insist on immediate payment. Further, the court held that Congress did not intend to allow the trustee under § 544(a)(2) to "invok[e] the 'sovereign prerogative' to attach property" that the IRS has as the federal tax collector and not as an ordinary creditor. The court also noted that the trustee's theory would allow trustees to eliminate all state law exemptions, because none of them are effective against the IRS's tax lien. The court might have reached the same result more easily by noting that under *Craft* the IRS reaches property held in tenancy by the entirety only as a result of attachment of the federal tax lien to the property, and nothing in § 544(a)(2) provides the trustee with the power to defeat an interest that could be defeated by the holder of a statutory lien. The court might also have noted that if § 544(a) could be used to attack exemptions, no homestead exemption could survive in bankruptcy, because a bona fide purchaser of a home always takes free of the homeowner's homestead exemption, and thus the trustee could defeat the homestead exemption under § 544(a)(3). That would be absurd in light of § 522(d)(1) & (p)(1).

Article 9—a judicial lien on the property enjoys priority over the bank's unperfected security interest. U.C.C. § 9-317(a). Therefore, because of federal law, § 544(a)(1), Foam Corporation can successfully avoid Kick Credit's security interest. To do so, Foam Corporation will file an adversary proceeding under Rule 7001. Foam Corporation's obligation to Kick Credit would remain, but Kick Credit's claim in bankruptcy would be entirely unsecured.

1. Could Kick Credit file a proper financing statement after bankruptcy, thereby perfect its security interest, and therefore avoid this avoidance? See §§ 362(a)(4); 362(b)(3); 546(b).

2. Suppose that on April 5, 2006, Computer Co. sold and delivered to Foam Corporation, on secured credit, a laptop computer for use by Gruff and other Foam Corporation executives. Gruff signed a security agreement and financing statement on behalf of Foam Corporation. Foam Corporation paid Computer Co. $200 down, and agreed to pay $100 more per month for 24 months. Computer Co. did not file the financing statement until April 13, 2006, three days after Foam Corporation filed its chapter 11 petition. Did Computer Co. violate the automatic stay by filing the financing statement? Is Computer Co.'s security interest avoidable because it was unperfected as of the petition filing date? See, in addition to the sections cited in part 1 of this Problem, U.C.C. § 9-317(e) (1999 Official Text containing twenty day filing period, as compared to ten day period in prior Official Text's § 9-301(2) and twenty or twenty-one day period adopted in many states' nonuniform versions of § 9-301(2) prior to 1999).

3. Does § 546(b) apply even where the "generally applicable law" does not have a time limit? That is, if a state law permits perfection of a lien to be accomplished within an indefinite period of time, perhaps even years after creation of the lien (with the effect that the lien has priority over other judicial liens created during the intervening period), will § 546(b) give effect to postpetition perfection? The answer is "yes," according to the court in Vanderbilt Mortgage and Fin., Inc. v. Griggs (In re Griggs), 965 F.2d 54 (6th Cir. 1992). However, note that § 546(b) by its terms applies only where the trustee seeks to use § 544, 545, or 549. Unperfected (and late perfected) liens often will be avoidable as preferences under § 547. It will not help the lienholder to defeat the trustee's § 544 powers if the trustee nevertheless prevails under § 547. See infra Problem 8-12.

4. More later on § 546(b). Let's get back to Foam Corporation's bankruptcy. First Bank is a real estate mortgagee. Suppose that its mortgage covering a parcel of Foam Corporation's land is unrecorded. State law provides that any unrecorded real estate conveyance is void against any purchaser of the property. It is a pure race statute. Can the debtor in possession avoid the mortgage under § 544(a)(1)? Under § 544(a)(3)?

5. U-Haul rented certain equipment to Foam Corporation. The lease was not recorded. Can the debtor in possession avoid U-Haul's ownership of the equipment using § 544(a)? See U.C.C. § 2A-307(1).

6. Suppose that Gruff owned land that was held in the name of Foam Corporation. Can the debtor in possession avoid Gruff's beneficial interest in the land using 544(a)? Why is it unlikely that the debtor in possession would attempt to avoid Gruff's interest even if the interest is avoidable?

7. Shortly before bankruptcy, Foam Corporation sold a small tract of land adjacent to its L.A. plant. The deed was never recorded. State law provides that any unrecorded real estate conveyance is void against any purchaser of the property without knowledge of the conveyance.

    a. The buyer argues against avoidance of the conveyance under § 544(a) because (1) Foam Corporation had actual knowledge of the conveyance, (2) Foam Corporation is the debtor in possession, and thus (3) the debtor in possession—as purchaser of the real estate—had knowledge of the conveyance. Is this argument sound? (The trustee shall have the status of a lien creditor or bona fide purchaser "*without regard to any knowledge of the trustee or of any creditor* * * *." Section 544(a) (emphasis added).)

    b. Add the fact that the buyer had taken notorious possession of the land before Foam Corporation filed bankruptcy.

    c. The buyer had not taken possession before Foam's bankruptcy. Indeed, the deal closed only a very short time before Foam filed its petition. The deed was not recorded because the bankruptcy happened so quickly after the closing and also because Foam Corporation failed to cooperate in the recordation process in breach of covenants in the sales contract.

Belisle v. Plunkett
United State Court of Appeals, Seventh Circuit, 1989
877 F.2d 512

[*Plunkett formed a set of partnerships to buy an expensive leasehold from W.O.F. Associates. Plunkett bought the leasehold using partnership funds, but he closed the deal and recorded the transfer in his own name. In Plunkett's bankruptcy the trustee and the partnerships fought over the leasehold. Local law gave the partnerships an equitable claim to the property—a constructive trust on it—because of Plunkett's fraud. The trustee argued that the partnerships' claim was avoided under § 544(a) because local law gives priority to a bona fide purchaser of the leasehold over an unrecorded claim such as that of the partnerships, and 544(a)(3) gives the trustee the status of a purchaser as of the commencement of the bankruptcy case.*]

Easterbrook, Circuit Judge.
* * *

Not so fast!, the partners rejoin. The estate can't contain the leasehold "as of the commencement of the case" because § 541(d) says that it does not contain property in which the debtor holds bare legal title:

> Property in which the debtor holds, as of the commencement of the case, only legal title and not an equitable interest, such as a mortgage secured by real property, or an interest in such a mortgage, sold by the debtor but as to which the debtor retains legal title to service or supervise the servicing of such mortgage or interest, becomes property of the estate under subsection (a) of this section only to the extent of the debtor's legal title to such property, but not to the extent of any equitable interest in such property that the debtor does not hold.

If this were not enough, the partners continue, § 544(a)(3) speaks of a "transfer", yet Plunkett did not transfer the Pan-Am leasehold, and there is therefore nothing for the Trustee to avoid. As the partners see things, §§ 541(d) and 544(a)(3) allow a trustee to recover property transferred out of the estate before the filing, but not to claim for the estate property held in a constructive trust. Several courts have perceived a "conflict" between § 541(d) and § 544(a)(3). E.g., In re General Coffee Corp., 828 F.2d 699, 704- 06 (11th Cir. 1987); In re Quality Holstein Leasing, 752 F.2d 1009, 1013-14 (5th Cir. 1985). The parties ask us to decide which statute prevails. We believe, however, that there is no conflict.

Section 544(a)(3) pulls into the debtor's estate property that ostensibly was there all along. Dealing with ostensible ownership is not, however, the statute's objective—at least not its only one—because the benefits are not limited to those who relied on the asset in extending credit. Section 544(a)(3) complements §§ 544(a)(1) and (2), which give the trustee the status of a judgment creditor vis-a-vis chattels in the debtor's possession. If one creditor had (or could get) a judgment effective against the chattels, the trustee secures the same advantage for all—which reduces any creditor's incentive to try to be first in line, a rush that may reduce the value of the debtor's assets. Sections 544(a)(1) and (2) follow state law, however, in giving the trustee no *greater* rights than the judgment creditor would have. If the debtor possesses a stolen diamond ring, the real owner's rights would trump those of a judgment creditor, and under the Code therefore would defeat the claims of all of the debtor's creditors. Whether or not we say that the debtor holds the ring in "constructive trust" for the owner is a detail. Under state law the owner's claims are paramount; the debtor could not defeat those rights by pledging or selling the ring, and the creditors in bankruptcy receive only what state law allows them. Butner v. United States, 440 U.S. 48, 99 S. Ct. 914, 59 L. Ed. 2d 136 (1979). Under most states' laws, however, the buyer in good faith of *real* property can obtain a position superior to that of the rightful owner, if the owner neglected to record his interest in the filing system. Section 544(a)(3) gives the trustee the same sort of position.

A bona fide purchaser from Plunkett would have taken ahead of the partners under local law. They neglected to record the partnerships' interest, though recording is easy. (The partners could, and in retrospect should, have refused to invest funds except through an escrow agent, who would have held the cash until good title had been recorded in the partnerships' names.) One of Plunkett's creditors, extending $100,000 against a collateral assignment of the leasehold, actually obtained a position superior to that of the partners. The Trustee claimed the same position for the estate (meaning the creditors collectively, including the partners).

Nothing in the text or function of § 544(a)(3) makes the force of this claim turn on whether Plunkett once owned the leasehold and then sold it to the partnerships (but failed to record their interest) or whether, instead, Plunkett acquired the leasehold through the partnerships. The sequence W.O.F. to Plunkett (perhaps with a bridge loan) to Pan-Am partnerships, with Plunkett retaining ostensible ownership, is identical in every respect to the sequence W.O.F. to Pan-Am partnerships to Plunkett, with Plunkett obtaining ostensible ownership. Identical from the perspective of Plunkett, of the partners, and of Plunkett's (other) creditors—and identical from the perspective of § 544(a)(3). Section 544(a)(3) allows the trustee to have a bona fide purchaser's rights or avoid a transfer, so a "transfer" by the debtor cannot be a necessary condition of the exercise of the strong-arm power. * * *

Section 541(d) does not have anything to say about the effects of § 544(a)(3). It forbids including property in the debtor's estate "under subsection (a) of this section" and does not address whether property may be included under some other part of the Code. The courts that have perceived a conflict between §§ 541(d) and 544(a)(3) did not discuss this limitation on the domain of § 541(d). * * *

Section 541(d) was designed, its text and history reveal, to deal with persons with title to property who had sold the equitable interests. E.g., S.Rep. 95-989, 95th Cong., 2d Sess. 83-84 (1978), U.S.Code Cong. & Admin.News 1978, 5787, 5869, 5870. This is a common arrangement in secondary mortgage markets: a person with many titles sells certificates representing shares in the pool of income generated by the notes. Section 541(d) ensures that the creditors of the service corporation stand in line behind the owners of the income stream. The bankruptcy court thought that because the legislative history speaks only of secondary mortgage markets, § 541(d) is limited to such cases. 89 B.R. at 782-83. Legislative history does not carry so much force. Mortgage markets may have been the impetus for § 541(d), but statutes often create rules that reach beyond the immediate concerns that spawned them. "It is not the law that a statute can have no effects which are not explicitly mentioned in its legislative history". Pittston Coal Group v. Sebben, __ U.S. __, 109 S. Ct. 414, 420-21, 102 L. Ed. 2d 408 (1988). Section 541(d)'s genesis helps us understand, however, that reading the law as limited to inclusions in the estate under § 541(a) makes legal as well as linguistic sense. * * *

[W]e believe that both the Fifth and Eleventh Circuits got off on the wrong foot by finding a "conflict" in need of resolution.

Section 544(a)(3) gives the Trustee the status of a bona fide purchaser for value. * * *

AFFIRMED [for the trustee].

NOTES

1. For the contrary view, that § 544(a)(3) can apply only to avoid interests that were transferred by the debtor, see Kull, *Restitution in Bankruptcy: Reclamation and Constructive Trust*, 72 AM. BANKR. L.J. 265, 296-99 (1998); In re Mills Concepts Corp., 123 B.R. 938 (Bankr. D. Mass. 1991).

2. The distinction made by the court in *Belisle* between real property and personal property is not entirely accurate. Under state law, a thief (or even an innocent converter who takes another's property by mistake) does not obtain title to personal property; neither does a trespasser ordinarily obtain title to real property. In either case, a bona fide purchaser from the wrongdoer does not obtain title, and thus the original owner still has legal title and has the right to recover the property. Where the wrongdoer (or innocent mistaken recipient of the property) obtains title, for example by fraudulently inducing the original owner to sell the property to the wrongdoer, then a purchaser from the wrongdoer does obtain title, and a bona fide purchaser without notice of the fraud will take the property—real or personal—free of the equitable right of the original owner to obtain a constructive trust or equitable lien on the property. See Dobbs, LAW OF REMEDIES: DAMAGES, EQUITY, RESTITUTION § 4.7(1), at 450-53 (one-volume abridgment, West Group Hornbook Series, 1993); Mullins v. Burtch (In re Paul J. Paradise & Assocs., Inc.), 249 B.R. 360 (D. Del. 2000).

Nevertheless, under state law, the interest of a person entitled to a constructive trust on property to which a wrongdoer (or innocently mistaken recipient) has obtained title is superior to judicial liens obtained by the creditors of the wrongdoer (or innocent mistaken recipient). Thus the holder of the constructive trust can retake the property free of such liens. See id., § 4.3(2), at 395-96. In fact, state law provides for constructive trusts, and for their cousins, equitable liens, in part for the purpose of providing priority over judicial liens obtained by the creditors of the person who wrongfully (or by mistake) obtained title to the property.

Consider § 544(a)(1) & (a)(3), and answer the following question: Under the approach taken in *Belisle*, would the trustee have prevailed if the property at issue were personal property rather than real property?

3.   In XL/Datacomp, Inc. v. Wilson (In re Omegas Group, Inc.), 16 F.3d 1443 (6th Cir. 1994), the Sixth Circuit disagreed with *Belisle* on a fundamental basis. The court decided in *Omegas Group* that a "constructive trust is fundamentally at odds with the general goals of the Bankruptcy Code" and, in effect, refused to recognize in bankruptcy a constructive trust recognized by state law. This decision is itself at odds with the broad principle that property rights in bankruptcy are generally determined and defined by state law. The Sixth Circuit recognized this principle but finessed it: "just because something is so under state law does not necessarily make it so under the Bankruptcy Code. As this court has previously noted, '[w]hile the nature and extent of the debtor's interest are determined by state law[,] once that determination is made, federal bankruptcy law dictates to what extent that interest is property of the estate.' Ultimately, 'state law must be applied in a manner consistent with federal bankruptcy law.'" Id. at 1450. This pronouncement is hugely bold and, if generally accepted, could very fundamentally affect the rights of creditors in bankruptcy. How so?

4.   Consider this reaction to *Omegas Group* by the court in Fibre Form Corp. v. Slamin (In re Nova Tool & Eng'g, Inc.), 228 B.R. 678, 681 (Bankr. N.D. Ind. 1998):

"While *Omegas* has not been universally adopted, the better reasoned decisions have followed it. Two of these courts, even as they embraced *Omegas*, have extensively analyzed that decision because they had questions concerning the basis for its analysis and were searching for the underlying rationale supporting its conclusion. See In re Dow Corning Corp., 192 B.R. 428 (Bankr. E.D. Mich. 1996); * * *. *Dow Corning*, on the other hand, did discern a basis for *Omegas*' rationale, which it found was 'solely bankruptcy policy.' *Dow Corning*, 192 B.R. at 440. Judge Spector concluded 'that Omegas found ... a conflict between the federal bankruptcy policy of ratable distribution and state property law on constructive trusts.' Id. at 441. Consequently, a federal interest required that state law interests should be analyzed differently in a bankruptcy proceeding, so that 'the bankruptcy policy of ratable distribution trumps state law on constructive trusts.' Id.

"This court agrees with the Sixth Circuit's approach to constructive trusts. We are not, however, willing to go so far as *Dow Corning* and conclude that the sole basis for that decision is bankruptcy policy. That would represent a dramatic departure from the often complex interplay of state and federal law traditionally associated with bankruptcy proceedings. The same rationale would allow the disregard of secured creditors' liens in the pursuit of the policy of 'ratable distribution', yet only a few have ever argued that this should be done. Admittedly, *Omegas* is consistent with the Bankruptcy Code's policy of a ratable distribution to creditors. Nonetheless, there is a more temperate explanation for its conclusion than the adherence to some overarching federal policy which justifies altering the outcome of legal proceedings. *Omegas* is also consistent with the equitable origin and purpose of constructive trusts. When viewed against that background, it stands for nothing more dramatic than the relatively unexceptional proposition that a court of equity, in considering whether to grant equitable relief, should consider the origin and purpose of the rule it is being asked to apply and the impact of its decision upon third parties."

5.   There are strong arguments that the right to a constructive trust is a kind of property under the general background law of property and of restitution. Several of your authors believe that if state law treats the right to a constructive trust as a property interest, then that right should be recognized in bankruptcy (subject to application of the avoiding powers), just as other state-law property interests are recognized. For trenchant and authoritative criticism of *Omegas Group* on this ground, see Kull, *Restitution in Bankruptcy: Reclamation and Constructive Trust*, 72 AM. BANKR. L.J. 265, 296-99 (1998). (Professor Andrew Kull is the Reporter for the ALI's Restatement (Third) of Restitution.) Also consider this criticism of *Omegas Group*, from Curtis Mfg. Co. v. Plasti-Clip Corp., 933 F. Supp. 94, 105-07 (D.N.H. 1995):

> *Omegas Group* involved a creditor who was allegedly defrauded of certain funds as part of a business transaction by a debtor who took the funds knowing full well that a petition for bankruptcy protection was imminent. The creditor's constructive trust argument, accepted by the bankruptcy court and affirmed by the district court, was ultimately reversed by the circuit panel, * * *. After conducting further research into the law of constructive trusts and their application under New Hampshire precedent, this court finds that it cannot adopt the conclusions of the *Omegas Group* panel. * * *

> 'Because the debtor does not own an equitable interest in property he holds in trust for another, that interest is not "property of the estate."' Begier v. IRS, 496 U.S. 53, 59, 110 S. Ct. 2258, 2263, 110 L. Ed. 2d 46 (1990).

> When property is acquired by the debtor through fraud or misrepresentation, said 'property becomes estate property because the debtor holds legal title, but ... all the estate has is legal title, if the traceable property would be subject to a constructive trust under non-bankruptcy law.' 1 Robert E. Ginsberg & Robert D. Martin, BANKRUPTCY: TEXT, STATUTES, RULES § 5.02[j], at 5-34 (1992). Pursuant to New Hampshire law,

> > A constructive trust will be imposed whenever necessary to satisfy the demand of justice since a constructive trust is merely 'the formula through which the conscience of equity finds expression.' Beatty v. Guggenheim Exploration Co., 225 N.Y. 380, 386, 122 N.E. 378, 380 (1919). The specific instances in which equity impresses a constructive trust are numberless, as numberless as the modes by which property may be obtained through bad faith and unconscientious acts. Cf. Leonard v. Philbrick, 106 N.H. 311, 313, 210 A.2d 819, 820 (1965)…. Among the numerous bases for a constructive trust is the existence of 'circumstances which render it unconscientious for the holder … to retain and enjoy the beneficial interest.…' 4 J. Pomeroy, EQUITY JURISPRUDENCE § 1053 (5th ed. 1941). 'It is probably correct to say that the present state of the law in New Hampshire is that a constructive trust will be imposed in any

situation where unjust enrichment is found, regardless of whether there is a confidential relationship between the parties.' 7 Charles A. DeGrandpre, NEW HAMPSHIRE PRACTICE: WILLS, TRUSTS AND GIFTS § 663, at 271 (1986).

Assuming, without deciding, that imposition of a constructive trust is appropriate, what remains for resolution, therefore, is the point in time when said constructive trust springs into operation. Curtis, quoting language from *Omegas Group*, supra, contends that 'a constructive trust … does not exist until a plaintiff obtains a judicial decision finding him to be entitled to a judgment "impressing" defendant's property or assets with a constructive trust.' *Omegas Group*, supra, 16 F.3d at 1451. However, the weight of authority indicates that '[a] constructive trust arises at the time of the occurrence of the events giving rise to the duty to reconvey the property.' In re Shepard, supra, 29 B.R. at 932; accord City Nat'l Bank v. General Coffee Corp. (In re General Coffee Corp.), 828 F.2d 699, 702 (11th Cir. 1987) ('constructive trust arises when the facts giving rise to the fraud occur'), cert. denied, 485 U.S. 1007, 108 S. Ct. 1470, 99 L. Ed. 2d 699 (1988); Capital Investors Co. v. Executors of Morrison's Estate, 800 F.2d 424, 427 n. 5 (4th Cir. 1986) (same) * * *. Indeed,

> It has been suggested that the constructive trust does not arise until the defrauded person brings a suit in equity and the court decrees specific restitution. The notion seems to be that a constructive trust is created by the court and that it therefore does not arise until the court creates it by its decree. The notion is in part fostered by the terminology employed. It is sometimes said that when there are sufficient grounds for imposing a constructive trust, the court 'constructs a trust.' The expression is, of course, absurd. The word 'constructive' is derived from the verb 'construe,' not from the verb 'construct.' … The court construes the circumstances in the sense that it explains or interprets them; it does not construct them. So in the case of a constructive trust, the court finds from the circumstances that some of the consequences which would follow from the creation of an express trust should also follow…. It would seem that there is no foundation whatever for the notion that a constructive trust does not arise until it is decreed by a court. It arises when the duty to make restitution arises, not when the duty is subsequently enforced.

5 Austin Wakeman Scott, THE LAW OF TRUSTS § 462.4, at 3420-21 (1967) (emphasis added) (footnote omitted).

The court therefore finds and rules that the facts as alleged sufficiently portray an instance where the imposition of a constructive trust would be warranted and said trust would relate back to the time of filing the application which ultimately resulted in the '078 patent. Curtis, as the owner of a misappropriated patent, would have taken only its legal title to the patent through the bankruptcy proceedings, and thus plaintiffs' equitable interest was neither encumbered, diminished, nor discharged upon confirmation of the plan. Accordingly, Curtis's motion in limine seeking to exclude evidence relating to ownership of the '078 patent must be and herewith is denied.

6.   In a recent opinion, the Second Circuit moved closer to the *Omegas* approach:

"The tension between constructive trust law and bankruptcy law is another reason to proceed with caution. The chief purposes of the bankruptcy laws are 'to secure a prompt and effectual administration and settlement of the estate of all bankrupts within a limited period,' Katchen v. Landy, 382 U.S. 323, 328-29, 86 S. Ct. 467, 15 L. Ed. 2d 391 (1966) (internal quotation marks and citation omitted), 'to place the property of the bankrupt, wherever found, under the control of the court, for equal distribution among the creditors,' MacArthur Co. v. Johns-Manville Corp., 837 F.2d 89, 91 (2d Cir. 1988) (internal quotation marks and citation omitted), and 'to protect the creditors from one another,' Young v. Higbee Co., 324 U.S. 204, 210, 65 S. Ct. 594, 89 L. Ed. 890 (1945). But by creating a separate allocation mechanism outside the scope of the bankruptcy system, 'the constructive trust doctrine can wreak ... havoc with the priority system ordained by the Bankruptcy Code.' In re Haber Oil Co., 12 F.3d 426, 436 (5th Cir. 1994); see also In re Omegas Group, Inc., 16 F.3d 1443, 1451 (6th Cir. 1994) ('A constructive trust is fundamentally at odds with the general goals of the Bankruptcy Code.') (internal quotation marks and citation omitted).

"In this Circuit, we have rejected the notion that bankruptcy law trumps state constructive trust law: '[W]hile the outer boundaries of the bankruptcy estate may be uncertain, "Congress plainly excluded property of others held by the debtor in trust at the time of the filing of the petition." ' In re Howard's Appliance Corp., 874 F.2d at 93 (quoting United States v. Whiting Pools, Inc., 462 U.S. 198, 205 n. 10, 103 S. Ct. 2309, 76 L. Ed. 2d 515 (1983)).

"While we do not depart from our holding in Howard's, we note that our obligation to apply New York constructive trust law does not diminish the need to 'act very cautiously' to minimize conflict with the goals of the Bankruptcy Code. In re N. Am. Coin & Currency, Ltd., 767 F.2d 1573, 1575 (9th Cir. 1985). In light of the fact that these goals can be compromised by the imposition of a constructive trust, 'bankruptcy courts are generally reluctant to impose constructive trusts without a substantial reason to do so.' In re Haber Oil Co., 12 F.3d at 436 (internal quotation marks and citations omitted). Bankruptcy courts in this Circuit are no exception. See, e.g., In re Braniff Int'l Airlines, Inc., 164 B.R. 820, 827 (Bankr. E.D.N.Y. 1994) (stating that the policy underlying the bankruptcy laws 'runs counter to that underlying the imposition of a constructive trust' and declining to impose a constructive trust); In re Universal Money Order Co., 470 F. Supp. 869, 879 (S.D.N.Y. 1977) (declining to impose a constructive trust after observing that '[t]he destructive effect of [a constructive trust], within the context of a uniform national bankruptcy law, is apparent'); In re Commodore Bus. Machs., Inc., 180 B.R. 72, 83 (Bankr. S.D.N.Y. 1995) ('[C]onstructive trusts are anathema to the equities of bankruptcy since they take from the estate, and thus directly from competing creditors, and not from the offending debtor.') (internal quotation marks and citation omitted); In re Vichele Tops, Inc., 62 B.R. 788, 792 (Bankr. E.D.N.Y. 1986) ('[T]his court would be reluctant to recognize the [constructive] trust because such action would work an injustice on all the creditors not a party to this proceeding. The general creditor body should not be prejudiced .... Law suits are proceedings which seek to balance right, duties, equities, and entitlements. While courts, in non-bankruptcy matters, consider primarily the interests of the parties before it, a court of bankruptcy has a broader scope. It must interpret its enabling legislation in the light of its purpose.') (internal quotation marks and citations omitted).

"Although we do not disturb the general rule that constructive trusts must be determined under state law, we believe it important to carefully note the difference between constructive trust claims arising in bankruptcy as opposed to those that do not, as the 'equities of bankruptcy are not the equities of the common law.' In re Omegas, 16 F.3d at 1452. In the typical non-bankruptcy case, a constructive trust claim is intended to prevent one who failed to meet an obligation or committed fraud or other misconduct from becoming unjustly enriched. The Chapter 7 context, however, is fundamentally different. The trustee marshals the assets of the estate under judicial supervision, for distribution according to federal law, under circumstances in which unsecured creditors receive fair but not full returns. While FCFC's estate may have been enriched, it was not unjustly enriched * * *.

Superintendent of Ins. v. Ochs (In re First Cent. Fin. Corp.), 377 F.3d 209, 217-18 (2d Cir. 2004).

D. PREFERENCES

1. Overview

Bankruptcy law avoids some transfers for its own reasons, even though the transfers are perfectly legitimate and unassailable under state law. The best example is § 547(b). It defines and condemns prepetition transfers that are *preferences*. In unofficial and general terms, a preference is "a transfer of the debtor's property on the eve of bankruptcy to satisfy an old debt." Orelup, *Avoidance of Preferential Transfers Under the Bankruptcy Reform Act of 1978*, 65 IOWA L. REV. 209 (1979). The official, technical definition appears in § 547(b) which describes a preference as:

- Any transfer of an interest of the debtor in property;
- To or for the benefit of a creditor;
- For or on account of an antecedent debt owed by the debtor before such transfer was made;
- Made while the debtor was insolvent;
- Made on or within 90 days before the date of the filing of the petition, or within one year of the filing if the creditor is an insider; and,
- That enables the creditor to receive more than the creditor would receive in a Chapter 7 distribution of the bankruptcy estate had the transfer not been made.

Bankruptcy law permits avoidance of preferences for two purposes: to discourage creditors "from racing to the courthouse to dismember the debtor during his slide into bankruptcy," and in order to "facilitate the prime bankruptcy policy of equality of distribution among creditors of the debtor. Any creditor that received a greater payment than others of his class is required to disgorge so that all may share equally." H.R. Rep. No. 595, 95th Cong., 1st Sess. 177-78 (1977).

The creditor's subjective innocence is no defense. "Congress considered equality of distribution so important that it specifically eliminated consideration of creditors' good faith or knowledge from preference actions * * * ." In re Southern Indus. Banking Corp., 92 B.R. 297, 301 (Bankr. E.D. Tenn. 1988). Moreover, "[a]ny wrongdoing on the part of the debtor is not imputed to the Trustee so as to inhibit his avoidance powers [with respect to preferences]." In re Lendvest Mortg., Inc., 123 B.R. 623, 624 (Bankr. N.D. Cal. 1991), unpublished reversal by bankrupty appellate panel on other grounds aff'd, 42 F.3d 1181 (9th Cir. 1994).

Preferential effect—§ 547(b)(5)—is the real harm of a preference. There is no preference without it. Preferential effect, however, is not sufficient in itself to establish that a transfer was a § 547 preference. Every element of § 547(b) must be satisfied, and preferential effect is only one of the elements.

Transfers will occur that are technically preferences under § 547(b) but that do not offend the purposes of the law or that involve competing policies that override those purposes. Congress did not give the courts an open-ended power to save all inoffensive preferences. Congress did identify, however, nine limited, discrete exceptions to § 547(b) which are collected in § 547(c). A transfer that matches any of these § 547(c) exceptions cannot be avoided by the trustee even though the transfer is a preference as defined by § 547(b).

The trustee or other person attacking a transfer as preferential has the burden of establishing that the transfer involved all six elements of a § 547(b) preference. Section 547(g). This burden of proof is met by a preponderance of the evidence. See Arrow Elecs., Inc. v. Justus (In re Kaypro), 218 F.3d 1070, 1073 (9th Cir. 2000); In re Harvard Mfg. Corp., 97 B.R. 879, 882 (Bankr. N.D. Ohio 1989).) (However, as noted below, there is a presumption under § 547(f) that the debtor was insolvent during the 90 days before the petition was filed.) The transferee who defends by invoking a § 547(c) exception has the burden of establishing that the transfer satisfied every requirement of the exception. Section 547(g). The defense's burden is preponderance, too. See United States Trustee v. First Jersey Sec., Inc. (In re First Jersey Sec., Inc.), 180 F.3d 504, 512 (3d Cir. 1999); In re Cook United, Inc., 117 B.R. 884, 887 (Bankr. N.D. Ohio 1990). The courts tend to read § 547(b) broadly, but construe § 547(c) narrowly. The effect is to err in favor of the bankruptcy estate.

2. The Elements of Preference—Section 547(b)

Consider the following Problems. (We have done the first few of them for you to illustrate the analysis; make sure you understand each step.)

Problem 8-3

Suppose that two months before filing bankruptcy, Foam Corporation paid $10,000 in cash to a trade creditor, Bateman Fabrics, which supplies custom-made coverings that are essential to Foam Corporation's operations. The $10,000 payment satisfied a one-year-old, unsecured debt in the same amount. This debt had accumulated before Bateman finally put Foam Corporation on a C.O.D. basis. When Bateman learned of Foam Corporation's bankruptcy, it considered itself to be very lucky to have been paid. The bankruptcy estate is very poor. If Foam Corporation's assets were liquidated, as would happen in a chapter 7 case, its unsecured creditors would be paid, from the bankruptcy estate, no more than four cents on the dollar. Bateman would be paid a little more than $400, considerably less than the $10,000 it was actually paid. The $10,000 prepetition payment to Bateman is unassailable under state law. In bankruptcy, however, the payment is an avoidable preference under § 547(b). All the elements of a preference are satisfied.

- Foam Corporation is the debtor because it is the person concerning whom the bankruptcy case has been commenced. Section 101(13). The $10,000 belonged to Foam Corporation before the money was paid to Bateman. This $10,000 payment was a transfer of the debtor's property; actually it was a transfer "of an interest of the debtor in property". Transfer includes "each mode, direct or indirect, absolute or conditional, voluntary or involuntary, of disposing of or parting with" either "property" or "an interest in property;" transfer also includes "the creation of a lien," "the retention of title as a security interest," and "the foreclosure of a debtor's equity of redemption." Section 101(54).

- The money was transferred to Bateman who was a creditor. The term "creditor" includes any "entity that has a claim against the debtor that arose at the time of or before the order for relief concerning the debtor." Section 101(10)(A). "Claim" includes any "right to payment." Section 101(5)(A).

- The transfer was made "for or on account of an antecedent debt owed by the debtor before such transfer was made." Here the debt was in fact overdue when Foam Corporation paid it, but that is NOT the point. The debt came into existence no later than the time the fabrics were delivered. Any payment after delivery would have been a payment on a debt already "owed by the debtor before such [payment] was made." It is not clear whether there is a separate requirement that the debt have been "antecedent" or whether the phrase "owed by the debtor before such transfer was made" was intended to explain what it is for a debt to be "antecedent." It is possible to argue that even a payment made at the time the fabrics were delivered would be a payment of a previously owed debt—because a contingent obligation to pay for the fabrics came into existence when Foam Corporation contracted to buy them, some time before delivery. A possible reply is to argue that a debt is not antecedent to a payment where the creditor earns the right to be paid the debt at the same time that the payment is made. Courts split on this issue. For example, leases typically require monthly lease payments to be made in advance—that is, on or before the start of the monthly period for which the rent is being paid. Is such a payment on account of an antecedent debt, because it is pursuant to a lease entered into before the payment was made, or is it not payment on an antecedent debt, because the consideration for the payment—the next month's occupancy of the premises—has not yet been given by the lessor? Compare AERFI Group, PLC v. Barstow (In re MarkAir, Inc.), 240 B.R. 581 (Bankr. D. Alaska 1999), with Child World, Inc. v. Serv. Merch. Co. (In re Child World, Inc.), 173 B.R. 473 (Bankr. S.D.N.Y. 1994).

- The transfer was made within 90 days before Foam Corp.'s bankruptcy petition.

- It was made when Foam Corporation was insolvent, inasmuch as Foam Corporation's liabilities exceeded its assets at the time of the transfer. The Bankruptcy Code uses this balance sheet test of insolvency. See § 101(32)(A) (sum of debts is greater than fair valuation of all nonexempt property). Also, for purposes of § 547, "the debtor is presumed to have been insolvent on and during the 90 days immediately preceding the date of the filing of the petition." Section 547(f). (This is a presumption affecting the burden of producing evidence; thus Bateman must introduce sufficient evidence to support a finding that Foam Corporation was solvent at the time of the transfer, or else the court will find that Foam Corporation was insolvent. If Bateman introduces sufficient evidence to support a finding of solvency, then the court will find that Foam Corporation was solvent—and thus that there was no preference—unless Foam Corporation carries its burden of proving by a preponderance of the evidence that it was insolvent when the payment was made. See Fed. R. Evid. 301; Akers v. Koubourlis (In re Koubourlis), 869 F.2d 1319 (9th Cir. 1989).)

- Finally, the transfer had a preferential effect, that is, the $10,000 payment enabled Bateman to receive more than this creditor would receive in a chapter 7 case had the transfer not been made. The $10,000 cash would have been included in the bankruptcy estate if the payment had not occurred, and the distribution to each general creditor would therefore have been slightly larger. Yet, none of the general creditors, including C, would have been paid in full. Thus, the $10,000 payment to Bateman, which fully satisfied its claim, enabled this creditor to get more than it would otherwise have received in a chapter 7 distribution of the bankruptcy estate.

  Note that preferential effect is always determined by hypothesizing a chapter 7 liquidation and estimating what would happen in such a case, even when the actual case is a chapter 11 or something else. Also note that § 547(b) does **not** say that a transfer is avoidable *to the extent* that it allows a creditor to receive more than it would receive in a liquidation had the transfer not been made. The section just says that the trustee may avoid "any transfer" that enables the creditor to receive more (and if it also meets the four other requirements). Thus Bateman has to return the entire $10,000, not just the extra amount that the transfer enabled Bateman to receive.

Occasionally courts allow creditors as a matter of administrative convenience to keep the part of the preferential payment that they would end up receiving anyway in a distribution in the case. Cf. Page v. Rogers, 211 U.S. 575, 29 S. Ct. 159, 53 L. Ed. 332 (1909). In chapter 11 cases creditors sometimes receive stock or promissory notes with no immediate cash paid on the effective date of the plan. Further, it would help Foam Corporation a lot to have some extra cash—the full $10,000—to use in operating the business. Thus in most cases the court will require a creditor like Bateman to return the preference and then to wait like everyone else to receive whatever is finally distributed.

When Bateman repays the preference to the estate, then Bateman will once again have a $10,000 claim, which will be considered to be a prepetition general unsecured claim. See § 502(h).

Problem 8-4

Suppose that instead of paying Bateman $10,000, Foam Corporation had paid Bateman $10. The analysis of each element is exactly the same, except for the last element. Did the transfer allow Bateman to receive more than it would have received if a transfer had not been made and Foam Corporation had been liquidated in a hypothetical chapter 7 case? Surprisingly, the answer is still yes. Note that if the transfer is not avoided, Bateman will have $10 in its pocket and a claim in the bankruptcy case for $9,990. If Bateman receives 4% payment on the $9,990 claim, it will receive $399.60 in the bankruptcy case; with the $10 in its pocket, Bateman will receive a total of $409.60 out of Foam Corporation's property. That is $9.60 more than Bateman would have received if the transfer of the $10 had not been made and Foam Corporation were liquidated in a chapter 7 case, because 4% of $10,000 is only $400. Bateman received payment of $10 of its claim in full; that allowed it to get more than if its entire $10,000 claim were paid off at 4 cents on the dollar. It is true that in the hypothetical chapter 7 case we assume the transfer had not been made and that the estate would therefore be $10 larger—but how much of that extra $10 would Bateman receive? Bateman would have to receive $9.60 of the ten extra dollars—96% of it—in order to get $409.60 in the hypothetical liquidation. The only way Bateman would receive 96% of the extra $10 would be if Bateman's $10,000 claim amounted to 96%

of the general unsecured claims, which is certainly not true in Foam Corporation's case. Thus the $10 payment enables Bateman to receive more than it would in a chapter 7 if the payment had not been made. Therefore the final element is satisfied, and the transfer is a preference. We are left with the following conclusion: *any payment to an unsecured creditor —no matter how small—enables the creditor to receive more than it would receive in a chapter 7 liquidation without the payment, unless the creditor would have received full payment in the liquidation anyway.* See McCord v. Venus Foods, Inc., (In re Lan Yik Foods Corp.), 185 B.R. 103 (Bankr. E.D.N.Y. 1995). Foam Corporation probably would not bother to try to recover a mere $10, but prior to the 2005 BAPCPA Foam Corporation could have. Now, however, § 547(c)(9) would provide Bateman with a defense, because Foam Corporation is a "debtor whose debts are "not primarily consumer debts" and "the aggregate value of all property that constitutes or is affected by [the $10 payment] is less than $5,000. Id.

Problem 8-5

Suppose that instead of paying its debt to Bateman, Foam Corporation gave Bateman (two months before filing bankruptcy) a perfected security interest in personal property, or a recorded mortgage on real property, as collateral for the $10,000 debt. (Assume in either case that the property's value is $5,000 or more, so that § 547(c)(9) does not apply.) It so happens that the property had escaped Kick Credit's and First Bank's encumbrances. Foam Corporation therefore had sufficient equity in the collateral to secure fully the debt to Bateman. As a general rule, the transfer cannot be attacked under state law, and bankruptcy generally respects state law property interests, including liens. On these facts, however, the transfer is a § 547(b) preference that is avoidable in Foam Corporation's bankruptcy. Generally, "the substitution of a secured loan for an unsecured loan during the preference period * * * results in a preference to the extent of the value of the collateral transferred." In re Continental Country Club, Inc., 108 B.R. 327, 330 (Bankr. M.D. Fla. 1989). All of the elements of a preference are again satisfied. The only difference is that Foam Corporation made a security transfer, rather than an absolute conveyance, of its property. Nevertheless, the creation of this security interest or mortgage, which gave Bateman a lien on the collateral, is a transfer of an interest in the debtor's property. The creation of the lien also had a preferential effect. As a general rule, a lien perfected before a debtor's bankruptcy is recognized in the bankruptcy case, which means that Bateman will likely receive full payment of its claim (if permitted to keep the lien). Had the transfer not occurred, Bateman would have been a general unsecured creditor, and its claim would not have been fully satisfied. Thus, the security transfer (if it stands) enables Bateman to receive more than it would have received in a hypothetical chapter 7 case. If the collateral had been worth less than the debt owed to Bateman, Bateman would still have ended up with part of its claim secured. Bateman will likely receive full payment of whatever part of its claim is secured. Receiving full payment of any part of its claim will allow it to receive more than if its entire claim were unsecured. (The analysis is essentially the same as in Problem 8-4 where part payment was seen to be payment of part of the claim in full.) Thus we reach another nearly universal conclusion: *the transfer of any lien to a previously unsecured creditor enables the creditor to receive more than it would have received without the lien in a chapter 7 liquidation, unless the creditor would have been paid in full in the liquidation without the lien.*

Problem 8-6

In the 90 days before filing its bankruptcy petition, Foam Corporation made several payments to First Bank on the mortgages it holds on three of the factory properties. First Bank's mortgages were and are oversecured. The payments were not preferences, because they did not enable First Bank to receive more than it would have received if the payments had not been made and if Foam Corporation's assets had been liquidated in a hypothetical chapter 7. If it is permitted to keep the mortgage payments and then receives value in the chapter 11 case equal to the remaining balances on the mortgages, First Bank will still get no more than full payment. Even had it not gotten the mortgage payments, First Bank still would have been paid in full in a chapter 7 liquidation. Thus the payments did not enable First Bank to receive "more." The payments are not preferences. Note that, similarly, if Foam Corporation had given First Bank extra collateral shortly before filing the bankruptcy petition, even that would not have allowed First Bank to be repaid more than in full. Thus we reach another general conclusion: *a payment to or transfer of an additional lien to a creditor who was already fully secured is not a preference.* See Comm. of Creditors v. Koch Oil Co. (In re Powerine Oil Co.), 59 F.3d 969 (9th Cir. 1995). Note, however, that the question is not whether the creditor was fully secured at the time of the transfer but rather whether the creditor still would have been fully secured in the bankruptcy if the transfer had not been made. See Hall v. Chrysler Credit Corp. (In re JKJ Chevrolet, Inc.), 412 F.3d 545 (4th Cir. 2005) (explaining that under the pre-1999 version of U.C.C. § 9-306(4), a secured creditor's rights to commingled cash proceeds was different in bankruptcy than out of bankruptcy).

Problem 8-7

Just before bankruptcy, Kick Credit's claim was $200,000 undersecured, on a liquidation basis. Suppose that Foam Corporation paid Kick Credit $500,000 to cover the deficiency and create a small equity cushion. Is this payment a preference under § 547(b)? (Note: In Problems 8-3, 8-4, and 8-5 the transfer was made to a totally unsecured creditor, and in Problem 8-6 the transfers were made to a fully secured creditor. Here, the creditor is partially secured—thus undersecured or "undercollateralized.") "Where payments are made to an undercollateralized secured creditor within the 90 day period prior to the filing of a bankruptcy petition, `[t]he Court must assume, in the absence of proof to the contrary, that the payments were credited towards the unsecured portion of the debt, since this course of action would comport with standard business practice. Consequently, one must conclude that [the creditor] received greater payment on its unsecured claim than other unsecured creditors and that the transaction satisfies the requirements of Section 547(b)(5).'" Matter of Remes Glass, Inc., 136 B.R. 132, 138 (Bankr. W.D. Mich. 1992). What if, in exchange for the $500,000 payment, Kick Credit released its lien on $500,000 worth of Foam Corporation's equipment, thus enabling Foam Corporation to sell the equipment to a third party for $500,000? Would § 547(b)(5) be satisfied?

Problem 8-8

Change the facts in Problems 8-3 to 8-7. Suppose in each case the transfer was made—either the cash was paid or the encumbrance was created and perfected— six months before Foam Corporation filed bankruptcy. Is any of the transfers a voidable preference under § 547(b)? Foam Corporation is seriously—but very legitimately—indebted to Gruff. If Foam Corporation reduces or secures the debt to him six months before bankruptcy, is the transfer to Gruff a preference under § 547(b)? See §§ 547(b)(4)(B); 101(31) (definition of "insider").

Problem 8-9

Again change the facts in Problems 8-3 to 8-7 so that the transfers are made by Gruff out of his property to pay or to secure Foam Corporation's debts. Assume Gruff acted as a surety for Foam Corporation, paying debts he had guaranteed or securing debts he had guaranteed so that the creditors involved would not press for payment. The transfers are not preferences in Foam Corporation's bankruptcy because they did not involve Foam Corporation's property. Now suppose one of Foam Corporation's larger creditors, at Foam Corporation's request, paid debts owed to some of Foam Corporation's smaller unsecured, trade creditors—in effect refinancing these debts. (Thus Foam Corporation would be liable to the larger creditor to repay the funds that were advanced to pay off the smaller creditors' debts.) Are the payments by the larger creditor preferences? Would it matter that the larger creditor was secured under a security agreement which provided that any future indebtedness that Foam Corporation might incur to the creditor would be secured by the collateral? Would it matter that the payments were funneled through Foam Corporation instead of being made directly by the larger creditor to the smaller creditors? What if all the funds were paid to one of the smaller creditors—CertCo—for disbursal to the other smaller creditors? If the payment is an avoidable preference, could CertCo be liable for the entire payment instead of just for its share? Consider the "earmarking" doctrine, under which a payment to a creditor made with funds borrowed from another creditor for that purpose may not be considered a preference. See Lyon v. Contech Constr. Prods., Inc. (In re Computrex, Inc.), 403 F.3d 807 (6th Cir. 2005); Growe v. AT & T Universal Card Servs. (In re Adams), 240 B.R. 807 (Bankr. D. Maine 1999); Yoppolo v. Greenwood Trust Co. (In re Spitler), 213 B.R. 995 (Bankr. N.D. Ohio 1997). Also consider the "mere conduit" theory, under which a recipient of funds whose role is merely to transfer the funds on to the intended recipient may be considered not to be an "initial transferee" under § 550(a)(1). See In re Presidential Airways, Inc., 228 B.R. 594 (Bankr. E.D. Va. 1999).

Problem 8-10

Revisit Problem 8-3. The issue here concerns exactly when the transfer was made. Suppose that the payment to Bateman was made by check. The check was delivered to Bateman 92 days before bankruptcy but was not paid by Foam Corporation's bank—the drawee-payor bank—until three days later. Was the payment within the 90-day preference period of § 547(b)(4)(A)? See Barnhill v. Johnson, 503 U.S. 393, 118 L. Ed. 2d 39, 112 S. Ct. 1386 (1992).

Problem 8-11

This timing issue is terribly important. It is especially important with respect to encumbrances that are not promptly perfected. If a transfer is not perfected within thirty days, then for purposes of § 547 it is deemed to have been made when it is perfected (or at the time of the bankruptcy filing if the interest was not perfected before then). See § 547(e). For example, suppose that in Problem 8-5, Foam Corporation signed the security agreement or mortgage, that created the encumbrance, outside the 90-day preference period, but:

a.   The security interest or mortgage was never perfected by filing or recording so that, under state law, the encumbrance was ineffective against third persons. When did the transfer occur? See § 547(e)(2)(C). Could this encumbrance have been avoided equally as well—more easily—under § 544(a)? Compare Problem 8-12.

b.   The security interest or mortgage was perfected sometime within the 90-day period. See § 547(e)(2)(A)-(B). When did the transfer occur? The answer

> depends on whether or not the "sometime" was within thirty days after the transfer was effective between the immediate parties. If perfection occurred within this thirty-day window, the transfer is deemed to have occurred when it became effective between the parties, thus, in this case, outside the 90-day preference period. If perfection occurred beyond the thirty day window, the transfer is deemed to have occurred at the time of perfection and thus, in this case, within the preference period. See Fidelity Fin. Servs. v. Fink, 522 U.S. 211, 118 S.Ct. 651, 139 L. Ed. 2d 571 (1998).

Problem 8-12

> Debtors purchased a mobile home from Clayton Homes ("Clayton") on credit, giving Clayton a purchase money security interest to secure the payments Debtors promised to make. Clayton assigned to Vanderbilt both the security interest and the right to the payments from Debtors. Vanderbilt filed a financing statement nine days after Debtors' purchase, but the Kentucky motor vehicle officials mistakenly issued a "clean" certificate of title to the Debtors (that is, a certificate that did not show Vanderbilt's lien and made it appear that the Debtors owned the mobile home free and clear). The result apparently was that Vanderbilt's security interest was vulnerable to judicial lien creditors and thus unperfected.
>
> Kentucky then enacted a statute allowing secured creditors to file applications to correct such mistakes by the motor vehicle officials. On application the motor vehicle officials would issue a new certificate of title showing the lien. The Kentucky statute provided that on issuance of the new certificate the security interest would be considered to have been perfected as of the date the original financing statement was filed.
>
> Shortly after Kentucky enacted that statute, Debtors filed a chapter 7 bankruptcy petition. Vanderbilt sought relief from the automatic stay so it could file an application under the Kentucky statute for issuance of a new certificate. The bankruptcy court denied the motion and avoided Vanderbilt's unperfected security interest under § 544(a)(1). The district court reversed, holding that Vanderbilt was entitled to apply for a new certificate perfecting its security interest and that § 546(b) would then protect Vanderbilt's lien from avoidance under § 544(a)(1). The Sixth Circuit affirmed the district court. Vanderbilt Mortgage and Fin., Inc. v. Griggs (In re Griggs), 965 F.2d 54 (6th Cir. 1992).
>
> The trustee in *Griggs* apparently did not attempt to avoid the security interest under § 547. Given Fidelity Fin. Servs. v. Fink, 522 U.S. 211, 118 S.Ct. 651, 139 L. Ed. 2d 571 (1998), was the security interest an avoidable preference?

The following case discusses § 547(b)(2). It also provides a bridge to the next section, dealing with the § 547(c) exceptions to avoidability.

United States Trustee v. First Jersey Securities, Inc.
(In re First Jersey Securities, Inc.)
United States Court of Appeals for the Third Circuit, 1999
180 F.3d 504

SCHWARTZ, Senior District Judge.

This appeal addresses the propriety of the appointment of counsel for a debtor in possession, where the debtor transferred restricted securities to its counsel in payment for pre-petition services on the eve of its filing for bankruptcy.

First Jersey Securities, Inc. (the "debtor" or "First Jersey") filed a voluntary petition for relief under Chapter 11 of the Bankruptcy Code on August 7, 1995. This action was prompted after the SEC prevailed in a securities fraud action against First Jersey * * * and obtained an order for [it] to disgorge $75 million in illegal proceeds. Obtaining that order left the SEC as the largest unsecured creditor of the debtor.

Concurrent with the filing of the petition, the debtor filed an application pursuant to § 327(a) of the Bankruptcy Code to retain RSW as its counsel. First Jersey owed the firm approximately $389,000 for legal services rendered prior to the filing for bankruptcy primarily for work performed in the securities fraud litigation. * * * [T]he Trustee, joined by the SEC three days later, objected to the appointment of RSW as counsel, arguing the firm was not "disinterested" as is required by the Bankruptcy Code. 11 U.S.C. § 327(a). The Trustee and the SEC (collectively referred to as "SEC") maintained the transfer of ITB restricted stock was a preferential payment, thereby disqualifying RSW from acting as counsel for the debtor because it held an interest adverse to the estate.* * *

The Bankruptcy Court approved the debtor's application to retain RSW * * *. The District Court filed a memorandum and order affirming the Bankruptcy Court's decision. * * *

In summary, § 327(a) mandates disqualification when there is an actual conflict of interest, allows for it when there is a potential conflict, and precludes it based solely on an appearance of conflict. In the situation where the debtor in possession seeks to retain counsel, as is the case here, the Code provides, "[A] person is not disqualified for employment under § 327 of this title by a debtor in possession solely because of such person's employment by representation of the debtor before the commencement of the case." 11 U.S.C. § 1107(b). Where there is an actual conflict of interest, however, disqualification is mandatory. A preferential transfer to RSW would constitute an *actual conflict of interest* between counsel and the debtor, and would require the firm's disqualification. * * *

The Bankruptcy Court reasoned that not only must the debt be antecedent, but also the payment of a debt must be past due, as a prerequisite for establishing a voidable preference under § 547(b)(2). RSW certified the transfer of the securities was in the ordinary course of business dealings between the two parties, and was deemed timely payment. It further represented the invoices submitted by the firm did not constitute a final bill of an amount owed to the firm. Rather, the firm would negotiate with the debtor over several months worth of invoices, and adjust the bill accordingly. An invoice was not finalized until after negotiations. With respect to the final bill with First Jersey, the debtor agreed to pay $250,000 for legal services rendered from January to July 1995 almost simultaneously with the conclusion of negotiations over the final bill. The parties agreed the $250,000 was in settlement of the invoices presented by RSW for legal work performed from January to May 1995 (which totaled $314,327), as well as for work performed in June and July 1995 for which RSW had not yet generated an invoice ($75,000). RSW thus argues the payment was made before the debt was actually past due. The Bankruptcy Court agreed, reasoning the debt was not due prior to the time the payment was made. The District Court concurred with this conclusion under the same legal reasoning.

[T]he Code defines a claim broadly. * * * In addition, as debt is defined as a liability on a claim, it is coextensive with the definition of a claim, and both are construed broadly. It follows "when a creditor has a claim against a debtor—even if the claim is unliquidated, unfixed, or contingent—the debtor has incurred a debt to the creditor." In re Energy Cooperative, Inc., 832 F.2d 997, 1001 (7th Cir.1987).

The SEC contends First Jersey incurred a debt to RSW when the law firm performed legal services on the debtor's behalf. We agree. Courts which have considered this issue have concluded, consistent with the statutory definitions, that an antecedent debt owed by the debtor occurs when a right to payment arises—even if the claim is not fixed, liquidated, or matured. The right to payment generally arises when the debtor obtains the goods or services.

Under this reasoning, RSW had a claim at the time it performed legal services for First Jersey. Its claim was "antecedent" for purposes of Section 547(b)(2). The payment of $250,000 from the sale of ITB stock was to settle the debt owed by First Jersey for past legal services rendered between January and July 1995. We agree with our sister circuits and other courts that legal claims arise when the legal services are performed, not when the bill itself is presented to the client. * * *

The Bankruptcy Court's reasoning that a debt is not owed until payment is past due is not found in the preference statute. Its absence is readily understandable. If the Bankruptcy Court's conclusions were permitted to stand, the preference provision of the Bankruptcy Code would be largely vitiated. The Bankruptcy Court's judicial gloss would allow creditors to retain a prepetition payment simply by asserting that the payment was "timely," as was done by RSW. * * * This approach would "leave to the creditor the discretion to determine the date the obligation was incurred, creating the possibility not only of inequality of treatment of similarly-situated creditors (depending on the vagaries of their billing practices), but also the opportunity for a particular creditor, who foresees that his debtor is approaching bankruptcy, to secure preferential treatment for himself by the timing of the bill." Matter of Emerald Oil Co., 695 F.2d 833, 837 (5th Cir.1983).

* * * We have no trouble concluding the stock transfer was a preference under Section 547 of the Bankruptcy Code. As such, RSW had an actual conflict with the debtor and was therefore disqualified from serving as counsel under § 327, unless payment to it was in the ordinary course of business. * * *

The purpose of Section 547(c)[(2)] is to leave undisturbed normal financial relations between a debtor and its creditors, even as a company approaches bankruptcy. * * *

A trustee may not avoid a preferential transfer to the extent such transfer was: "(A) in payment of a debt incurred by the debtor in the ordinary course of business or financial affairs of the debtor and transferee; (B) made in the ordinary course of business or financial affairs of the debtor and transferee; and (C) made according to ordinary business terms." 11 U.S.C. § 547(c)(2).[30] * * *

---

30.   [The 2005 BAPCPA rewrote § 547(c)(2), placing old subparagraph (A) into the introductory text of paragraph (c)(2), relettering subparagraphs (B) and (C) as (A) and (B), respectively, and providing that either new subparagraph (A) or new subparagraph (B) must be proved. That makes it easier for the recipient to establish a defense. Note that in this case RSW was unable to prove that the transfer was made in the ordinary course as between the parties and also unable to prove that it was made according to ordinary business terms. Thus the result in this case would be the same under the statute as amended by the 2005 BAPCPA as it was under the pre-BAPCPA statute.]

It is undisputed the transfer of stock satisfies § 547(c)(2)(A)—the debt was incurred for legal services provided by RSW to First Jersey in the normal course of business. The conflict arises as to the other two elements. The term "ordinary" is not defined in the bankruptcy statute. [T]he determination of what is "in the ordinary course of business" is subjective, calling for the Court to consider whether the transfer was ordinary as between the debtor and the creditor. Factors such as timing, the amount and manner in which a transaction was paid are considered relevant.

Employing these criteria, we conclude the payment was not made in the ordinary course of business. The timing of the payment to RSW is clearly suspect. The transfer of stock was made on the day the debtor filed its petition for bankruptcy. RSW did not show that the payment date fit a particular practice between the parties. Rather, all the record shows is that First Jersey made periodic payments during 1994 and 1995. These payments consisted of:

10/28/94	$300,000
12/07/94	$150,000
12/22/94	$150,000
02/10/95	$150,000
03/24/95	$150,000
05/31/95	$150,000

We merely note the payment of $250,000 on August 7, 1995 deviates from the pattern of $150,000 payments from December 1994 to May 1995. However, we are very troubled by the absence in the record of any explanation for why the payment was made on the eve of the debtor's filing for bankruptcy. As First Jersey's counsel in the securities litigation, RSW had to know of the debtor's precarious financial position when it accepted restricted securities in lieu of cash payment because RSW prepared the bankruptcy petition filed on the same day as the stock was transferred to it.

The RSW firm also failed to produce any evidence that the payment of legal bills by transfer of restricted stock was in the ordinary course of business between the parties. RSW did not assert it had ever before received payment in the form of restricted securities. The stock in question was unregistered, and could not be sold publicly. In fact, RSW needed to find a sophisticated buyer for the securities--and the shares were not sold until October 19, 1995. It defies reason that the Robinson firm would accept payment in an illiquid asset unless it knew the debtor was in serious financial difficulties and could not pay otherwise. The manner and timing of the payment in the currency of restricted ITB stock suggests the transfer was not made in the ordinary course of business between the parties.

Moreover, the payment was not made "according to ordinary business terms", as is required by § 547(c)(2)(C). This phrase has been interpreted as encompassing "the practices in which firms similar in some general way to the creditor in question engage." In re Molded Acoustical Products, Inc., 18 F.3d 217, 224 (3d Cir.1994). "Only dealings so idiosyncratic as to fall outside that broad range should be deemed extraordinary and therefore outside the scope of subsection C." Id. This Court emphasized, moreover, that "the more cemented [as measured by duration] the pre-insolvency relationship between the debtor and the creditor, the more the creditor will be allowed to vary its credit terms from the industry norm yet remain within the safe harbor of § 547(c)(2)." Id. at 225.

While this test is deferential, it is not non-existent. The general practice of law firms is to receive cash in return for services, not restricted securities. While law firms have begun to accept equity positions as payment from "start-up" companies with strong growth potential, the reasoning in these situations is the expectation by the law firm that the stock of the *client* will appreciate in value. In contrast, here the restricted stock is not of a client with growth potential, but of a *third party*. Moreover, the record reflects it was common practice for First Jersey to pay RSW only in cash. In fact, up until the day the Chapter 11 petition was filed, there is no evidence in the record that First Jersey ever transferred securities, much less restricted securities, to RSW as payment for legal services.

Accordingly, the preferential payment was a preference, creating an actual conflict of interest, and thus, disqualifying RSW as counsel for the debtor. * * *

3. The Exceptions—Section 547(c)

Problem 8-13

Foam Corporation was dealing with some suppliers before bankruptcy on a C.O.D. basis, paying for goods by check at the time of delivery. Is the payment by check a payment on an antecedent debt under 547(b)(2)? Consider Barnhill v. Johnson, 503 U.S. 393, 118 L. Ed. 2d 39, 112 S. Ct. 1386 (1992); *First Jersey Secs.*, supra; Child World, Inc. v. Serv. Merch. Co. (In re Child World, Inc.), 173 B.R. 473 (Bankr. S.D.N.Y. 1994). Further, some courts rule that the debt for the price of goods is incurred, for purposes of § 547(b), when the debtor acquires a property interest in the goods. When goods are sold C.O.D., the debtor may not get the goods themselves until payment is made; but the debtor commonly gets a property interest in them before then. Therefore, even when goods are sold C.O.D., the debt for the goods may antedate—if only for the briefest time—the debtor's payment for them, even if the debtor pays with money (dollar bills) rather than by check. Literally, the payment is for an antecedent debt. Is it possible that a C.O.D. payment can be a preference under § 547(b)? Is it saved by § 547(c)(1)? See Problem 8-3, supra; *Child World*, supra.

Problem 8-14

Foam Corporation borrowed $20,000 from Specific Electric Credit Corporation specifically to buy a new chemical mixing vat. The loan agreement provided that SECC would have a security interest in whatever vat Foam Corporation ended up buying. A week after getting the funds, Foam Corporation contracted to buy for $20,000 a particular vat that was in the seller's warehouse. Three days later the seller delivered it to Foam Corporation, which paid for it on delivery. Eighteen days later, SECC perfected its security interest in the vat by filing a financing statement. SECC's security interest attached to the vat and therefore became effective between SECC and Foam Corporation as soon as Foam Corporation obtained rights in the vat. Note that the time period in § 547(c)(3)(B) was increased from ten days to twenty by the 1994 bankruptcy amendments and from twenty days to thirty by the 2005 BAPCPA.

a. Suppose the vat was delivered to Foam Corporation 100 days before Foam Corporation filed its bankruptcy petition. Is the transfer of the security interest to SECC a preference? Is it an avoidable preference? See § 547(c)(3) and (e).

b. Suppose the vat was delivered to Foam Corporation five days before Foam Corporation filed its bankruptcy petition. Is SECC's security interest avoidable under § 544(a)? Is the transfer of the security interest to SECC a preference? Is it an avoidable preference? See §§ 362(b)(3), 544(a), 546(b), 547(c)(3) and (e); U.C.C. § 9-317(e).

c. Suppose the vat was delivered 70 days before Foam Corporation filed bankruptcy, and SECC did not file a financing statement until 22 days later. Can the security interest be saved under § 547(c)(1)? Compare Lindquist v. Dorholt (In re Dorholt), 224 F.3d 871 (8th Cir. 2000) (following decisions from the Seventh and Ninth Circuits and holding that § 547(c)(1) can be applied to save a transfer from avoidance even where the transfer was not timely perfected under § 547(e)), with In re Arnett, 731 F.2d 358 (6th Cir. 1984) (refusing to permit § 547(c)(1) to be used to frustrate apparent purpose of § 547(e) to require timely perfection). Does the rationale of the Supreme Court's decision in Fidelity Fin. Servs. v. Fink, 522 U.S. 211, 118 S. Ct. 651, 139 L. Ed. 2d 571 (1998), shed light on the relationship between subsections 547(c)(1) and (e)?

Problem 8-15

1. During the workout negotiations before Foam Corporation's bankruptcy, Kick Credit was asked to loan more money to Foam Corporation that would be secured by a lien on property that did not already secure the preexisting debt to Kick Credit. If Kick Credit had agreed, could the deal have been structured so as to avoid § 547(b) altogether? So that the lien would be excepted under (c)(3)? Under (c)(1)?

2. A year before Foam Corporation filed bankruptcy, the company made certain improvements to one of its plants. Foam Corporation failed to pay the general contractor and, as a result, several subcontractors were not paid. These subs therefore acquired statutory construction liens against the improved real property. During the 90-day preference period, Foam Corporation paid the general who, in turn, paid the subs. They then released their liens. Can the general's payments to the subs be attacked as preferences? Probably not. Was Foam Corporation's payment to the general a preference? Probably. Is this preference excepted by (c)(1)? On the issues of the larger meaning of "value" and whether or not (c)(1) counts indirect value, see, e.g., Jones Truck Lines, Inc. v. Cent. States, Se. & Sw. Areas Pension Fund (In re Jones Truck Lines, Inc.), 130 F.3d 323 (8th Cir. 1997).

3. Before bankruptcy, Foam Corporation dealt with many suppliers who extended short-term credit. They supplied good and services on invoice that required payment within 30 or 60 days. Certainly, Foam Corporation's payments of these debts during the 90-day preference were preferences within § 547(b). Also, before bankruptcy, Foam Corporation made interest and principal payments on debts owed to Kick Credit. Assuming Kick Credit was not fully secured on a liquidation basis, those payments were also preferences. The payments to the suppliers and to Kick Credit are not excepted by § 547(c)(1). Why not? They may be excepted by paragraph (c)(2). Can payments on long term debt, such as the debts owed to Kick Credit, be protected by paragraph (c)(2)? See Union Bank v. Wolas, 502 U.S. 151, 112 S. Ct. 527, 116 L. Ed. 2d 514 (1991). How often would Foam Corporation incur long term such as the debts owed to Kick Credit? Daily? Monthly? Every few years? Can such a major and infrequent transaction be

considered "ordinary course"? It is possible that paragraph (c)(2) excepts payments even if they are made late—beyond the 30 or 60 days required by the invoice, or beyond the payment dates specified in the loan agreement between Foam Corporation and Kick Credit. How is this possibility explained—or denied—in light of the requirements of "ordinary course" in paragraph (c)(2)? See Luper v. Columbia Gas of Ohio, Inc. (In re Carled, Inc.), 91 F.3d 811 (6th Cir. 1996).

Problem 8-16

1. Just before bankruptcy, Kick Credit's claim was undersecured by $200,000. Suppose that Foam Corporation robbed its cash account for this amount and paid it to Kick Credit within the 90-day preference period. Kick Credit argues that § 547(c) (1), (2), or (4) protects this payment which freed an equal amount on the revolving line of credit. Do you agree?

2. Suppose that two months before filing bankruptcy, Foam Corporation paid $10,000 in cash to a trade creditor, Bateman Fabrics, which supplies custom-made coverings that are essential to Foam Corporation's operations. The $10,000 payment satisfied a one-year-old, unsecured debt in the same amount. This debt had accumulated before Bateman finally put Foam Corporation on a C.O.D. basis.

    a. The $10,000 payment probably is not protected by (c)(2). Why not?

    b. Add a fact. After the payment was made, Bateman shipped $6,000 worth of goods to Foam Corporation. Immediate payment was expected but has never been made. Does (c)(4) except $6,000 of the $10,000 payment?

    c. Suppose in part b. that Foam Corporation paid the $6,000 price of the last shipment of goods after several weeks, but not until Bateman threatened to organize suppliers in a boycott against Foam Corporation. Is the $6,000 payment a preference under § 547(b)? Yes. Is it protected by (c)(1)? By (c)(2)? Probably not. Does (c)(4) apply to protect the $6,000 payment? Does (c)(4) apply to protect $6,000 of the $10,000 payment? See the next case.

In re Check Reporting Services, Inc.
United States Bankruptcy Court, Western District Michigan, 1992
140 B.R. 425

Jo Ann C. Stevenson, Bankruptcy Judge.

The motion presently before the Court calls into question the proper interpretation of 11 U.S.C. § 547(c)(4)(B), which limits the extent to which a creditor may assert the new value defense in a preference action. * * *

The factual backdrop against which this motion arises is stereotypical of a creditor dealing with a debtor on a running account basis during the preference period. It is also stereotypical of the plethora of preference cases initiated by the Trustee in the underlying bankruptcy. Water Doctor had an agreement with the Debtor, Check Reporting Services, Inc. ("CRS") under which CRS processed charge card payments, called "sales drafts," for Water Doctor. When customers made purchases using MasterCard or Visa, the merchants would send the sales drafts to CRS which would in turn forward them for processing through the appropriate banking channels. In CRS's case the sales drafts always flowed through

Comerica Bank-Detroit ("Comerica"). At some point CRS would receive payment for the sales drafts through the same channels and would forward the payment on to merchants such as Water Doctor, less its processing fee. It appears undisputed that certain identifiable payments were made by CRS to Water Doctor under this arrangement. These payments, and the transfers of "new value" which Water Doctor alleges it made to CRS in the form of sales drafts, were as follows during the preference period:

Date	Alleged Preference	New Value
11/1/88	$ 1,477.18	
11/1/88	$ 176.91	
11/10/88		$ 211.02
11/15/88	$ 934.04	
12/6/88		$ 2,006.24
12/9/88		$ 43.76
12/12/88	$ 211.02	
12/13/88	$ 1,142.90	
12/14/88		$ 1,252.55
12/20/88		$ 881.13
1/6/89	$ 2,006.24	
1/6/89		$ 1,142.90
1/10/89		$ 781.57

Although Water Doctor argues that none of the transfers from CRS were preferences, it has assumed that the transfers were preferences for the purposes of this motion. There is no such reciprocal assumption on the Trustee's part regarding the new value transfers asserted by Water Doctor. Water Doctor attached seven vouchers prepared by CRS which it asserts establish the amount of the new value transfers. During discovery Trustee admitted that these vouchers were routinely prepared by CRS the day following the electronic tender of sales drafts by the merchant, in this case Water Doctor. The Trustee has presented no affidavit or other evidence to rebut these proofs. The Trustee does however intimate that these transfers have not been established as fact * * *

At some point after the commencement of bankruptcy proceeding the MasterCard and Visa organizations began to put pressure on Comerica to resolve claims of merchants who had used CRS to process their sales drafts. Ultimately, Comerica purchased the claims of a number of merchants, including some of those held by Water Doctor. According to the documents attached to Water Doctor's motion, these consisted of the December 20, 1988 transfer in the amount of $881.13, the January 6, 1989 transfer in the amount of $1142.90, and the January 10, 1989 transfer in the amount of $781.57. * * *

The crux of this case is the proper interpretation of § 547(c)(4)(B)'s provision that a preference defendant may assert as a defense only that new value "on account of which new value the debtor did not make an otherwise unavoidable transfer to or for the benefit of such creditor". Although this provision has not changed since its enactment in 1978, the majority of courts subsequently construing it have failed to carefully read and properly apply its language. * * *

In the Matter of Bishop, 17 B.R. 180 (Bankr. N.D. Ga. 1982) is the focus of Water Doctor's argument regarding the proper interpretation of 11 U.S.C. § 547(c)(4)(B). Water Doctor contends that this case initially interpreted that section and is the linchpin for the majority line of decisions which followed. The transfers between the parties during the preference period in *Bishop* followed the same general pattern as those alleged in this case and are set forth below:

Date	Alleged Preference	New Value
9/27/79	$18,418.50	
10/3/79		$ 9,140.80
10/4/79		$19,300.00
11/21/79		$10,000.00
11/28/79	$ 1,828.16	
12/4/79	$19,800.00	

The court interpreted this then-new provision in the context of these transfers:

> For § 547(c)(4) to apply, three requirements must be met. First, the creditor must extend new value as defined in § 547(a)(2) as "money or ... new credit" after the challenged payment. The payment which is the subject of Count III of the Amended Complaint was made on September 27, 1979. Following that date, Trust Company made three further credit extensions to Bishop on October 3rd, October 4th, and November 21st. Therefore, "new value" as defined in § 547(c)(4)(B) was extended after the payment. Secondly, the new value must be unsecured. Section 547(c)(4)(A). *Finally, the new value must go unpaid. Section 547(c)(4)(B).*

17 B.R. at 183 (emphasis supplied). The language emphasized in the quote above was the extent of the court's analysis of the proper interpretation of § 547(c)(4)(B).

The complaint in the *Bishop* case set forth the September 27 transfer of $18,418.50 as a separate count. Therefore the court first applied the exception as paraphrased above to this transfer alone. It concluded that the total amount of new value given after this transfer was $38,440.80, the sum of the October 3, October 4 and November 21 transactions. It then attempted to apply § 547(c)(4)(B), but in doing so, it did not apply the statutory language. Instead, it applied its own term, "unpaid":

> Of this amount [the $38,440.80 in new value] $21,628.16 was repaid: $1,828.16 (October 3 note) on November 28, 1979 and $19,800 (October 4 note) on December 4, 1979. The extent to which this new value went unpaid is $16,812.64. To this extent the payment of September 27, 1979, if found preferential, may be offset.

Id.

The next issue the court addressed was whether the "net result rule" used under the Bankruptcy Act had any remaining vitality under the Code. Under the net result rule the total of new value given is subtracted from the total of the preference payments to determine the creditor's maximum exposure. The defendant argued that because the total alleged preferences exceeded the total new value given by the defendant during the preference period by $1,605.86, the trustee's recovery should be limited to this amount. The court rejected this argument based upon language in § 547(c)(4) requiring that the new value be given "after" the allegedly preferential transfer. Under the net result rule, new value could also apply to a preference given after the new value, contrary to the statutory language. That the net result rule leads to statutorily incorrect results can be simply illustrated by two hypotheticals, each setting forth two transfers during the preference period:

Hypothetical # 1

Date	Alleged Preference	New Value
9/1/92	$1,000.00	
10/1/92		$500.00

Hypothetical # 2

Date	Alleged Preference	New Value
9/1/92		$500.00
10/1/92	$1,000.00	

In both of these hypotheticals, the net result of the transfers between the parties is that the estate was diminished by $500.00, and under the net result rule the creditor's maximum preference exposure would therefore be $500.00. However, in Hypothetical # 2, the new value was given *before* the preferential transfer occurred, and therefore would not be considered for purposes of § 547(c)(4). Thus in Hypothetical # 1 the preference recovery would be $500.00, while in Hypothetical # 2 the preference recovery would be $1,000.00. As can be seen, the net result rule works under some but not all factual scenarios. This discrepancy with the language of the statute varies depending upon the number, size and order of the various transfers. Certainly, as a generally applicable principle, the net result rule does not comport with the statute. This was the holding of the *Bishop* court.

While the *Bishop* court's rejection of the net result rule was rooted in the statutory language, its application of § 547(c)(4)(B) was not. The error in its reasoning can be seen by examining the two transfers from the debtor which partially "paid" the defendant's new value. The statutory language consists of several layers of negatives, which are more easily understood if applied to these two transfers one layer at a time. The trustee argued that each of these two transfers were preferences as well as transfers which render previously given new value unavailable as a defense under § 547(c)(4)(B). Assuming that the transfers were preferential, they were "avoidable" under § 547(b). Necessarily, then, the two transfers would not be *unavoidable* under any provision of the Code, including §§ 547(c)(1), (2), (3), (4), (5), (6), or (7). Excepting § 547(c)(4) from this laundry list, these two transfers would not be *otherwise unavoidable* under §§ 547(c)(1), (2), (3), (5), (6), or (7) or any other provision of the Code. Since these two transfers would not be "otherwise unavoidable", the debtor *did not make* an otherwise unavoidable transfer to the creditor; rather, it made two otherwise avoidable transfers. And, since no otherwise unavoidable transfer existed, it follows that "on account of [the new value previously given by the creditor] the debtor did not make an otherwise unavoidable transfer to or for the benefit of such creditor". In the exact language of the statute even after these two "paying" transfers were made § 547(c)(4)(B) remained satisfied. Simply put, the two transfers could not reduce the level of new value credited against the previous preference because they were not "otherwise unavoidable."

Applying this interpretation to the transactions involved in *Bishop* leads to the following result:

Date	Alleged Preference	New Value	Preference Exposure
9/27/79	$18,418.50		$18,418.50
10/3/79		$ 9,140.80	$ 9,277.70
10/4/79		$19,300.00	$ 0.00
11/21/79		$10,000.00	$ 0.00
11/28/79	$ 1,828.16		$ 1,828.16
12/4/79	$19,800.00		$21,628.16

Contrary to that court's interpretation, the reduction of defendant's liability on the first transfer should not have been limited to $16,812.64, the amount of the new value transfers less the "paying" transfers of November 28 and December 4 as a matter of law. Instead, a question remained as to whether the November 28th and December 4th transactions were otherwise unavoidable. It is conceivable that the transfers were made in the ordinary course or that at that particular point in the preference period the debtor was not insolvent. It is even possible (though doubtful) that the trustee might stipulate that the transfers were not avoidable. In any of these circumstances, the transfers would reduce the amount of new value which the creditor could have asserted as an offset against the September 27, 1979 transfer. However, the court's application of § 547(c)(4) has been read in conjunction with its rejection of the net result rule to produce a bizarre result. Under the case law developing after *Bishop,* a transfer may both "pay" previous new value from the creditor, thus disqualifying that new value as a defense to an earlier preference, and be preferential in and of itself. This Court rejects the *Bishop* paraphrase of § 547(c)(4)(B) in favor of applying the test delineated in the statute.

The interpretation of § 547(c)(4)(B) adopted by this Court is not novel. In the Matter of Isis Foods, Inc., 39 B.R. 645 (Bankr. D.C. 1984) involved a fact pattern similar to the one before the Court in this case. There the court expressly rejected the "unpaid" test set forth in *Bishop* employing a straight-forward reading of the statute:

> In In re Bishop, supra, the bankruptcy court stated that it was "inclined to agree [with the argument that section 547(c)(4)] is clear and unequivocal on its face." We fully agree. We add that section 547(c)(4) does not contain any language that even suggests that the new value rule contained therein is somehow limited to unpaid invoices.
>
> That section contains only two exceptions to the set off of new value advanced after a payment: (1) when the new value is secured by an otherwise unavoidable security interest; and (2) when, on account of the new value given, the debtor makes an otherwise unavoidable transfer to or for the benefit of the creditor. Neither exception is applicable under the facts of this case. The dictum in the cases relied upon by the appellee to the effect that the new value must be "unsecured" and go "unpaid" is an inaccurate and confusing paraphrase of the clearly stated statutory purpose. *The confusion engendered by the gloss formerly placed on the judicially evolved net result rule should be avoided in cases involving the construction and application of the new subsequent advance rule provided in section 547(c)(4).*

39 B.R. at 643 (emphasis supplied). Unfortunately the court's admonition has gone unheeded. In its opinion the *Isis* court failed to state that the concern the *Bishop* court's use of the term "unpaid" was intended to address was more precisely dealt with by

§ 547(c)(4)(B), i.e., that a creditor should not be able to assert that a transfer was "new value" when the estate was otherwise depleted by the debtor's payment for the new value. While such a statement would appear to be unnecessary, evidently it was needed, given the superficiality with which subsequent courts have dealt with the issue.

In support of the *Bishop* rule the Trustee has stated that "[t]he great majority of courts addressing the issue have held that a subsequent advance of new value must remain unpaid to satisfy § 547(c)(4)." The Trustee cites numerous cases which the Trustee asserts do not rely upon the reasoning of *Bishop* but reach a similar conclusion. While a brief discussion of each of these cases is set forth in the appendix to this opinion, suffice it to say that of the thirteen cases cited by the Trustee in support of his interpretation of the statute, in five (including one authored by this judge) the ability of the trustee to use an avoidable transfer to disqualify a transfer from the creditor from serving as new value was not at issue. Several of the remaining cases simply conclude that the rule stated in *Isis* "seems contrary to common sense." In re Global Int'l Airways Corp., 80 B.R. 990 at 992, fn. 4. One of the cited cases may even be read to implicitly take a position contrary to that of the Trustee.

The cases that follow *Global* frequently cite its off-hand dismissal of *Isis* without any examination of the rationale behind the *Isis* decision. Had they made such an examination, these courts would have found that what was *seemingly* adverse to common sense was a refinement of the common sense rule the courts were striving to create. That is, (1) common sense would dictate that a creditor should not be able to assert a new value transfer as a defense to a preference if the transfer was paid for by the debtor because the estate was not made whole by the new value transfer. But, (2) by the same token, the trustee should not be able to assert the new value was paid if the trustee is asserting that the paying transaction was in fact a preference which the trustee can avoid. By doing so the trustee will be able to eliminate the effect of the payment for the new value when he recaptures the preferential transfer. The statutory language expresses both the exception in sentence (1) and the caveat to the exception in sentence (2). The shorthand "unpaid," however, as employed by *Bishop* and subsequent courts, glosses over the statutory language creating the caveat. Therefore, the refusal of the *Isis* court to adopt the "unpaid" language was not out of lack of recognition that new value for which the creditor was already compensated should not be considered in defense of a preference, but instead arose out of a precise reading of the statutory language embodying that policy.

Though in the minority, the *Isis* opinion is more firmly rooted in the statutory language than *Bishop* and its progeny. * * *

Problem 8-17

1. Determine the amount of the avoidable preference in the following five scenarios, working your way through each as though its facts were the end of the story and as though the debtor filed a bankruptcy petition the next day. (That is, in each scenario assume that all prior payments and extensions of new value, in prior scenarios, have been made and that none of the payments or extensions of new value in the later scenarios will be made.) Assume that the creditor is unsecured and that at all times the debtor is insolvent.

Scenario, Date	Item	Payment	New Value	Total Debt Outstanding
	Original antecedent debt			$10,000
1. 11/1	Payment	$3,500		$ 6,500
2. 11/4	New Value		$4,000	$10,500
3. 11/7	Payment	$3,000		$ 7,500
4. 11/8	New Value		$2,000	$ 9,500
5. 12/4	Payment	$4,000		$ 5,500

2. What is the effect, if any, of § 503(b)(9) on your answers? Section 547(c)(9)?

Problem 8-18

1. Apply § 547(c)(4)(B) as construed in *Check Reporting Services*, to determine the "preference exposure" at the end of these transfers between the insolvent debtor and an unsecured creditor (all of which take place during the 90-day preference period):

Transfer No., Date	Alleged Preference	New Value	Preference Exposure
1. 11/1	$1,477.18		
2. 11/1	$ 176.91		
3. 11/10		$ 211.02	
4. 11/15	$ 934.04		
5. 12/6		$2,006.24	
6. 12/9		$ 43.76	
7. 12/12	$ 211.02		
8. 12/13		$1,142.90	
9. 12/14		$1,252.55	
10. 12/20		$ 881.13	
11. 1/6	$2,006.24		
12. 1/6	$1,142.90		
13. 1/10		$ 781.57	

What date should be used for the date of payment by the debtor if a payment was made by check, the date of delivery of the check or the date on which the drawee-payor bank paid the check? See Barnhill v. Johnson, 503 U.S. 393, 118 L. Ed. 2d 39, 112 S. Ct. 1386 (1992); Jones v. Aristech Chem. Corp. (In re Golco Indus., Inc.), 157 B.R. 720 (N.D. Ga. 1993).

2. Suppose that long before the preference period, a supplier had demanded and Foam Corporation had supplied a stand-by letter of credit against which the supplier could draw if Foam Corporation failed to pay accrued indebtedness. During the 90-day preference period, Foam Corporation made several preferential payments from its cash account, but the supplier also continued to supply goods and services on credit. There is, therefore, subsequent new value that counts under § 547(c)(4). On the other hand, also during the preference

period the supplier made several draws against the letter of credit to reduce the overall indebtedness. How are these draws treated? They are not direct preferences. Are the draws nevertheless counted as payments toward the new value which therefore reduce the defense of paragraph (c)(4)? See In re Lease-A-Fleet, Inc., 141 B.R. 853 (Bankr. E.D. Pa. 1992).

4. Preferences and After-Acquired Property

Problem 8-19

During the 90-day preference period, Kick Credit's collateral changed. The inventory turned over; some of the accounts were collected and new accounts were generated; additional equipment was acquired. Kick Credit's security interest attached to the new inventory, accounts, and equipment because the security agreement covered such property whenever the debtor acquired it. Kick Credit's security interest was a "floating lien" as to these types of property.

1. Is the security interest a preference under § 547(b) to the extent that it attached to the new collateral during the preference period to secure a preexisting debt? The key issue is when the transfer is deemed to have been made. The security agreement was made and the financing statement was filed long before the preference period. The key to the answer is § 547(e)(3).

2. To some extent, the security interest may be protected in any event by § 547(c)(5). To what extent? See the next case.

In re Ebbler Furniture and Appliances, Inc.
United States Court of Appeals, Seventh Circuit, 1986
804 F.2d 87

[*Bank had a floating lien on Ebbler's inventory and accounts receivable. Ninety days before Ebbler's bankruptcy filing (1) Ebbler owed Bank about $204,000, (2) Ebbler's inventory had a value at cost of about $125,000 (after making a $15,000 adjustment due to accounting discrepancies), (3) Ebbler had $19,000 worth of accounts receivable, and (4) Ebbler had $43,000 cash, which was subject to Bank's security interest to the extent it was proceeds of inventory and accounts receivable. During the 90 days before filing the petition (1) Ebbler conducted a going out of business sale and paid off all but $50,000 of Bank's debt in cash, (2) Ebbler purchased about $171,000 in new inventory, and (3) Ebbler sold inventory that had cost Ebbler $214,000. When Ebbler then closed its business, Bank took possession of $50,000 of inventory (valued at cost) and sold that inventory for $50,000, thus paying off the rest of the debt. About a week later, Ebbler filed its petition. The bankruptcy court held that Bank had received a $60,000 avoidable preference. Bank was not undersecured at all as of the petition date, because the debt had been paid off. But 90 days before the petition date, Bank had been undersecured by $60,000, which can be computed by subtracting the $125,000 value of the inventory collateral (at cost) and the $19,000 in accounts receivable from the $204,000 debt owed at that time. The improvement in undersecurity was therefore $60,000, and under § 547(c)(5) that was the amount of preference that could be avoided. If the inventory were valued at a "going concern" value, which Bank argued should include a 60% markup over cost, Bank would have been considered oversecured as of 90 days before the petition date. Total* *collateral value would have been $219,000. Thus there would have been a zero undersecurity as of 90 days before the petition date, and there would have been no improvement in the Bank's nonexistent undersecurity.*]

FLAUM, Circuit Judge.

* * * We are asked to define the word "value" as used in 11 U.S.C. § 547(c)(5). We affirm the bankruptcy court and district court in their use of "cost" as the proper measurement in this case. However, we remand this case for further proceedings to determine the precise amount of the preference * * *.

[P]erhaps most important for purposes of this appeal, the bankruptcy court determined that the parties "were relying on the cost basis of the inventory in evaluating the security for the indebtedness." * * *

The issue presented is the interpretation of "value" as used in § 547(c)(5) of the Bankruptcy Code. Section 547(c)(5) applies to situations where a secured creditor does not have sufficient collateral to cover his outstanding debt. Subparagraph five (5) codifies the "improvement in position test" and overrules an earlier line of cases such as Grain Merchants of Indiana, Inc. v. Union Bank & Savings Co., 408 F.2d 209 (7th Cir.), cert. denied, 396 U.S. 827, 90 S. Ct. 75, 24 L. Ed. 2d 78 (1969). Section 547(c)(5) prevents a secured creditor from improving its position at the expense of an unsecured creditor during the 90 days prior to filing the bankruptcy petition.

The first step in applying section 547(c)(5) is to determine the amount of the loan outstanding 90 days prior to filing and the "value" of the collateral on that day. The difference between these figures is then computed. Next, the same determinations are made as of the date of filing the petition. A comparison is made, and, if there is a reduction during the 90 day period of the amount by which the initially existing debt exceeded the security, then a preference for section 547(c)(5) purposes exists. The effect of 547(c)(5) is to make the security interest voidable to the extent of the preference. Of course, if the creditor is fully secured 90 days before the filing of the petition, then that creditor will never be subject to a preference attack. * * *

The language of section 547(c)(5), the "value of all security interest for such debt," was purposely left without a precise definition. See generally H.R. No. 595, S. Rep. No. 989, 95th Cong., 2d Sess., reprinted in 1978 U.S. Code Cong. & Ad. News, 5787, 6176; N. Cohen, *"Value" Judgments: Account Receivable Financing and Voidable Preferences Under the New Bankruptcy Code,* 66 MINN. L. REV. 639, 653 (1982) (hereinafter "Cohen"); In re Beattie, 31 B.R. 703, 714 (W.D.N.C. 1983). Furthermore, it has been persuasively argued that the other Bankruptcy Code sections' definitions of "value" would not be useful for section 547(c)(5) purposes. Cohen, supra, at 651-654. Thus, the only legislative guidance is "that we are to determine value on case-by-case basis, taking into account the facts of each case and the competing interests in the case." Matter of Lackow Bros., Inc., 752 F.2d 1529, 1532 (11th Cir. 1985), citing H.R. Rep. No. 545, 95th Cong., 1st Sess. 356 (1977) reprinted in 1978 U.S. Code Cong. & Ad. News 5787, 6312.

The method used to value the collateral is crucial in determining whether or not the bank received a preference. The Bank urges that we adopt an "ongoing concern" value standard, which, in this case, would be cost plus a 60% mark-up. The Bank relies on *Lackow Bros.*, supra, as authority for the use of this definition of value. We find *Lackow*

Bros. readily distinguishable. There, the only evidence of value before the court was ongoing concern value. As the Eleventh Circuit stated: "The only evidence in the record of value for the ninetieth day prior to the filing of the bankruptcy is the ongoing concern value; therefore, this is the *only* standard of valuation that can be applied to determine if Creditor's position improved ...." *Lackow Bros.* at 1532.

Another view as to how value should be defined is proposed by Professor Cohen. He proposes an after-the-fact determination of value. In his article discussing accounts receivable, Cohen argues that the courts should look at the actual manner in which the collateral was liquidated, i.e. cost or ongoing concern. Whatever method is used to dispose of the collateral, Cohen argues, should be used to value the collateral 90 days before the filing of the bankruptcy petition. *Cohen,* supra, at 664. At least one circuit has found Cohen's reasoning useful, though not necessarily adopting it as a rigid rule. Matter of Missionary Baptist Foundation, 796 F.2d 752, 761-62 (5th Cir. 1986).

In *Missionary Baptist Foundation,* supra, the appellate court remanded to the district court for factual determinations as to whether or not the bank improved its position during the preference period. Id. at 761. The court noted, however, that merely remanding for factual findings may not be sufficient in light of the ambiguous meaning of "value" in section 547(c)(5). Id. at 761-62. The Fifth Circuit quoted with approval Cohen's admonition of an individualized approach in defining value and his hindsight solution of the problem. We follow the Fifth Circuit's lead and hold that under Section 547(c)(5) value should be defined on a case by case basis, with the factual determinations of the bankruptcy court controlling.

In the present case we affirm the bankruptcy court's use of cost as the method for valuing the collateral for 547(c)(5) purposes. The bankruptcy court found that the parties were using a cost basis for valuing the security. Furthermore, when the Bank removed inventory with a *cost* of approximately $50,000, about a week before the petition was filed, Ebbler was given credit for that amount—$50,000. We do not find the bankruptcy court's factual findings so clearly erroneous as to warrant reversal. In re Kimzey, 761 F.2d 421, 423 (7th Cir. 1985).

Using these factual findings the bankruptcy court applied cost as the legal definition of "value." We affirm the use of this definition as applied to these facts.

We remand to the bankruptcy court, however, for a determination as to the amount of the preference. The bankruptcy court found, weighing the conflicting evidence, that a preference of $60,000 existed. It is not clear why the bankruptcy court did not consider the $43,000 in cash * * *.

The bankruptcy court held that the Bank had a security interest in the inventory and accounts receivable. The bankruptcy court's opinion is silent as to whether or not this security agreement covered cash proceeds, and whether or not the $43,000 in actuality was cash proceeds of the inventory. It must also be determined if these interests were properly perfected. The only evidence in the record is Mr. Ebbler's testimony that all the proceeds from sales of inventory were deposited into an account at the Bank. The bank statement shows that on the 90th day prior to the bankruptcy the account contained $43,000. Depending on the court's findings on these issues an adjustment downward in the amount of the preference might be appropriate. * * *

EASTERBROOK, Circuit Judge, concurring.

This case involves the meaning of "value" under 11 U.S.C. § 547(c)(5). I join the court's opinion, which concludes that the statute does not require bankruptcy judges to use one universal definition. The history of condemnation litigation shows that a single definition of "value" is not within judicial grasp. Still, we need not leave bankruptcy judges and litigants adrift. Security interests must be appraised with some frequency in bankruptcy litigation. The greater the uncertainty in the legal rule, the harder it is to settle pending cases. "Anything goes" is not a durable rule. The parties cannot know their entitlements until bankruptcy, district, and appellate courts have spoken. One important function of appellate courts is to provide additional clarity, when that is reasonably possible. It is possible here. The bankruptcy judge did better than to avoid an abuse of discretion. He decided the case correctly.

"Value" is defined for a purpose, which sets limits on the admissible standards of appraisal even though it does not govern all cases. Section 547(c)(5) requires the court to find whether the secured creditor improved its position at the expense of other investors during the 90 days before the filing of the petition in bankruptcy. This calls for two appraisals, one on the day of filing and one 90 days earlier, using the same method each time, to see whether there was an improvement in position. The only standard that might plausibly be used in this case is wholesale cost of goods, because that is the only standard that could have been applied on both dates.

Wholesale cost is also the appropriate standard as a rule because wholesale and retail goods are different things. A furniture store, a supermarket, or the manufacturer of a product (the three situations are identical) uses raw materials purchased at wholesale to produce a new item. In the retailing business the difference between the wholesale price and the retail price is the "value added" of the business. It is the amount contributed by storing, inspecting, displaying, hawking, collecting for, delivering, and handling warranty claims on the goods. This difference covers the employees' wages, rent and utilities of the premises, interest on the cost of goods, bad debts, repairs, the value of entrepreneurial talent, and so on. The increment of price is attributable to this investment of time and other resources. The Bank does not have a security interest in these labors. It has an interest only in its merchandise and cash on hand. The value of its interest depends on what the Bank could do, outside of bankruptcy, to realize on its security. See Thomas H. Jackson, *Avoiding Powers in Bankruptcy,* 36 Stan. L. Rev. 725, 756-77 (1984). What it could do is seize and sell the inventory. It would get at most the wholesale price—maybe less because the Bank would sell the goods "as is" and would not offer the wholesaler's usual services to its customer. The Bank does not operate its own furniture store, and if it did it would still incur all the costs of retailing the goods, costs that would have to be subtracted from the retail price to determine the "value" of the inventory on the day the Bank seized it.

To give the Bank more than the wholesale value is to induce a spate of asset-grabbing among creditors, which could make all worse off. If the Bank gets the whole increment of value (from wholesale to retail) during the last 90 days, other creditors may respond by watching the debtor closely and propelling it into bankruptcy when it has a lower inventory (and therefore less "markup" for the Bank to seize). The premature filing may reduce the value of the enterprise. There are other defensive measures available to creditors. The principal function of § 547(c)(5) is to reduce the need of unsecured creditors to protect themselves against the last-minute moves of secured creditors. It would serve this function less well if goods subject to a security interest were appraised at their retail price.

Too, the Bank's security interest does not reach the "going concern" value of the debtor; it had security in the *goods,* not in the *firm.* To value the inventory in a way that reflects "going concern" value is to give the Bank something for which it did not contract. At all events, this wrinkle does not make a difference. If Ebbler had been sold as a going venture 90 days before the filing of the bankruptcy petition, the buyer of the business would have paid only wholesale price for Ebbler's inventory. If Ebbler had been at the peak of health, the buyer would have paid no more for inventory. A buyer would not have paid retail, because it would have had to invest the additional time and money necessary to obtain the retail price. So whether Ebbler is valued as a defunct business or as a going business sold to a hypothetical buyer on the critical date, wholesale is the right valuation, because it reflects the price that a willing buyer would pay after arms'-length negotiation. (The "going concern" value of Ebbler is reflected in its name, reputation, customer list, staff, and so on—things in which the Bank did not have a security interest.)

To put this differently, a willing buyer of a flourishing retail or manufacturing business will not pay more than the wholesale price for inventory of goods or parts on hand, because this buyer could purchase the same items on the market from the original sellers. Why pay Ebbler $500 for a sofa when you can get the same item for $200 from its manufacturer? Nothing would depend on whether Ebbler planned to stay in business. The court therefore properly does not allow the outcome of this case to turn on the fact that Ebbler chose a Chapter 7 liquidation rather than a Chapter 11 reorganization. Chapter titles are of little use in valuing assets under § 547(c)(5). A "liquidation" may be a sale of the business en bloc as an ongoing concern, and a "reorganization" may be a transition from one line of business to another.

The difference between the wholesale and retail prices of the inventory is the compensation that the other factors of production—the employees, landlords, utilities, etc.—obtain for their services. To appraise Ebbler's inventory at "retail" is to award to the Bank the entire value of the work done during the last 90 days by these other creditors of Ebbler. It is to allow the Bank to improve its position at their expense. Because a valuation at "retail" would produce exactly the consequence that § 547(c)(5) is designed to avert, the bankruptcy court wisely chose to appraise the goods at wholesale. The court leaves to another day the question whether retail price is ever an appropriate measure of value under § 547(c)(5). The observation that the bankruptcy court has leeway, however, does not imply that the court's discretion should be exercised without reference to the function of § 547(c)(5) and the limits of the security interest.

NOTES

1. Is Judge Easterbrook right that a buyer of the business would not pay Ebbler more for its inventory than what it would cost to buy the inventory from a manufacturer? Suppose Ebbler had gathered an attractive and balanced set of inventory items from numerous manufacturers. Would a buyer of the business who did not acquire the inventory have costs in gathering a new set of inventory beyond simply the amounts it would need to pay manufacturers? How much

time would it take a buyer of the business to gather its inventory from scratch? How much money would the owner of the business make while awaiting the delivery of the inventory? How much less would a buyer pay for the business as a going concern if the sale did not include the inventory?

2. Is a valuation for purposes of § 547(c)(5) governed by the last sentence of § 506(a)? If so, what is the "proposed disposition or use of the property"? Is it the use to which Ebbler proposed to put the collateral ninety days before the petition filing, or as of the petition filing date? Does the same proposed disposition apply to the valuation as of 90 days prepetition and as of the petition date? The question whether collateral should be valued at wholesale, retail, or at some other value arises in many contexts in bankruptcy. Interpreting § 506(a), the Supreme Court held that replacement value should be used for plan confirmation purposes where a debtor's chapter 13 plan called for the debtor to retain the collateral. See Assocs. Comm'l Corp. v. Rash, 520 U.S. 953, 117 S. Ct. 1879, 138 L. Ed. 2d 148 (1997) (reprinted below in Chapter Fifteen). Did Ebbler propose to keep the collateral? Is *Rash* relevant?

5. Section 547(c)(6) and Statutory Liens

Section 547(c)(6) provides a defense against avoidance of the fixing (but not the payment of) statutory liens as preferences. Recall from Problems 8-2 and 8-12 that the effect of § 546(b) is tempered because it does not protect transfers from avoidance as preferences under § 547(b). If statutory liens are protected from avoidance as preferences, is there anything to prevent a state from enacting statutes creating all sorts of statutory liens that could be perfected postpetition, thus skewing the distributional scheme of the Bankruptcy Code?

Problem 8-20

Suppose Foam Corporation owned a plant in Milwaukee, and that for several years the plant manager had shorted the pay of some of the workers (pocketing the difference). The underpayment was discovered at about the time Foam Corporation filed its petition. Most of the unpaid wages were not entitled to priority under § 507(a)(4), because they were for a period more than 180 days before the filing. A Wisconsin statute, Wis. Stat. § 109.09(2), provides that the Wisconsin Department of Workforce Development "shall have a lien upon all property of the employer, real or personal, located in this state for the full amount of any wage claim or wage deficiency," and that the Department may claim the lien by filing a verified lien claim form with the county circuit court clerk. The lien covers unpaid wages for work done within two years prior to the filing of the lien claim form. The statute provides that on proper filing of a lien claim form "[t]he lien shall take precedence over all other debts, judgments, decrees, liens or mortgages against the employer" (with a few exceptions, none of which are relevant). Two months after Foam Corporation filed its chapter 11 petition, the Department filed a verified lien claim form with the Milwaukee County Circuit Court Clerk, claiming a lien for $60,000 in unpaid wages.

Did the filing of the lien claim form in the local court violate the automatic stay? Does section 552(a) prevent the lien from arising? Is the lien avoidable as a preference? Is it avoidable under § 544(a)(1) or (with regard to the real property) under § 544(a)(3)? What about § 545? Consider In re AR Accessories Group, Inc., 345 F.3d 454 (7th Cir. 2003); cf. 229 Main St. Ltd. P'ship v. Mass. Dep't of Envtl. Prot. (In re 229 Main St. Ltd. P'ship), 262 F.3d 1 (1st Cir. 2001).

6. Indirect Preferences

Recall that Gruff guaranteed Foam Corporation's debt to Kick Credit (a secured creditor), and to Tina Chemical and Swenson Chemical (unsecured creditors). Suppose Foam Corporation paid $100,000 to Tina Chemical two months before filing bankruptcy. The transfer would certainly be a preference as to Tina Chemical; all the requirements of § 547(b) are met. Would it also be a preference *as to Gruff?* Note that a transfer "to or *for the benefit* of a creditor" can be a preference. Section 547(b)(1) (emphasis supplied). The transfer to Tina (the payment) seems to have benefitted Gruff; it reduces the debt that he guaranteed, and thus reduces his potential liability. But was the transfer made for the benefit of Gruff as a "creditor"? And are the other elements of § 547 satisfied as to Gruff?

Gruff's guarantee of the debts owed to Kick Credit, Tina Chemical, and Swenson Chemical makes Gruff a creditor of Foam Corporation. As we discuss in Chapter Nine, a guarantor (Gruff) has the right to be reimbursed by the principal debtor (Foam Corporation) for any payment the guarantor makes on the guaranteed debt. Thus Foam Corporation will owe Gruff reimbursement if Gruff pays any part of the debts he guaranteed. That obligation to pay Gruff is contingent on the occurrence of a future event—payment by Gruff on a guaranteed debt—but even a contingent right to payment is a "claim" under the definition in § 101(5)(A). Thus, even before Gruff pays anything on any of the debts he guaranteed, he has a contingent claim against Foam Corporation for reimbursement. That contingent claim arose before Foam Corporation filed for bankruptcy, and thus Gruff's guarantee of Foam Corporation's debts makes him a "creditor" of Foam Corporation under the definition in § 101(10)(A). The payment to Tina Chemical was indeed a transfer for the benefit of a creditor, Gruff.

The payment was also on account of an antecedent debt owed Gruff; Gruff's contingent claim—and the resulting debt under § 101(12)—came into being when he guaranteed the debt, long before the payment was made. Note also that the payment allows Gruff to receive more on his claim for reimbursement than he would likely receive in a hypothetical chapter 7 case if the payment had not been made. If Foam were in chapter 7, Tina Chemical could force Gruff to pay the entire $3 million owed by Foam to Tina. Gruff then would have had an allowable, noncontingent, general unsecured claim against Foam in the bankruptcy case for reimbursement of the $3 million. Gruff would have received perhaps four cents on the dollar for that claim, or $120,000. As a result, Gruff would lose $2,880,000. On the other hand, Foam's $200,000 payment to Tina enables Gruff to receive more than four cents on the dollar on his $3 million claim; as a result of the payment, Foam will owe Tina only $2.8 million, and that is all Tina could force Gruff to pay. In Foam's chapter 11 case, Gruff would probably receive four cents (or more) on the dollar for the $2.8 million claim, or $112,000. Gruff's loss on the guarantee would thus be only $2,688,000 (the $2.8 million he has to pay to Tina minus the $112,000 distribution in the bankruptcy case). As a result of Foam's payment to Tina, Gruff's loss on the guarantee is cut by $192,000. (There would have been a

$2,880,000 loss if the payment had not been made versus a $2,688,000 loss with the payment being made.) In effect the payment to Tina satisfied in full $200,000 of Gruff's contingent claim against Foam, by eliminating $200,000 of Gruff's liability to Tina. (Note that the difference between being paid in full on $200,000 and being paid at four cents on the dollar is exactly the same $192,000 that Gruff saves because of Foam's payment to Tina.)

Foam Corporation as debtor in possession—or a trustee if one is appointed or elected—would have no difficulty proving the other elements required by § 547(b), and thus the payment to Tina Chemical is a preference as to Gruff. It is called an "indirect preference" because the transfer was not made to Gruff but did benefit him indirectly.

However, Gruff did not receive the money, so how can he be forced to return it? The answer is that § 550(a)(1) permits the trustee or debtor in possession, when a transfer is avoided, to recover the value of the property from "the initial transferee of the transfer *or the entity for whose benefit such transfer was made.*" (Emphasis supplied.) Gruff was not the initial transferee—in fact he was not a transferee of the money at all. But he was the "entity" for whose benefit the transfer was made, because he benefitted from the transfer. Thus the trustee or debtor in possession may recover the value of the property transferred—$200,000—from Gruff. It may seem unlikely that the Foam as debtor in possession will sue Gruff to recover the indirect preference. After all, Gruff controls Foam, and there is an available deep pocket defendant if the creditors' committee presses Foam to avoid the payment—Tina Chemical.

But what if the payment to Tina had been made six months before Foam filed for bankruptcy? Would the payment be a preference as to Tina? It would not be, because Tina is not an insider and hence the preference period as to Tina is only 90 days. The payment would, however, still be a preference as to Gruff; he is an insider and hence the preference period as to him reaches back a full year before the bankruptcy filing. See § 547(b)(4)(B).

That led to the possibility of a surprising result under the Code as it stood before the 1994 amendments. Remember that under § 550(a)(1), the value of an avoidable preference can be recovered either from "the initial transferee of the transfer or the entity for whose benefit such transfer was made." The payment is avoidable as to Gruff, the entity for whose benefit the transfer was made. Section 550(a)(1) on its face would seem then to permit the value of the payment to be recovered either from Gruff or from the initial transferee—Tina Chemical! In fact, several circuits held that a noninsider like Tina which had an insider as guarantor could therefore be held liable for transfers made within the entire year before the bankruptcy filing, even though noninsiders ordinarily are subject only to a 90 day preference period. See Levit v. Ingersoll Rand Fin. Corp. (In re V.N. Deprizio Constr. Co.), 874 F.2d 1186 (7th Cir. 1989); Ray v. City Bank & Trust Co. (In re C-L Cartage Co.), 899 F.2d 1490 (6th Cir. 1990); Mfrs. Hanover Leasing Corp. v. Lowrey (In re Robinson Bros. Drilling, Inc.), 892 F.2d 850 (10th Cir. 1989).

The 1994 amendments inserted a new subsection (c) in § 550, which prevents the trustee or debtor in possession from recovering a preference from a noninsider where the transfer was made for the benefit of an insider between 90 days and one year before the bankruptcy filing. See In re Vaughn, 244 B.R. 631 (Bankr. W.D. Ky. 2000). The transfer is nevertheless recoverable from the insider (though the insider is often insolvent, too, making collection from the insider doubtful).[31]

Note that § 550(c) explicitly protects the noninsider only where the transfer was made for the benefit of the insider. What if 100 days before filing its petition Foam pays money to Gruff for him to pass along to Tina Chemical, and he does so. Is Gruff "the initial transferee" *as opposed to* "the entity for whose benefit the transfer was made"? If so—if those labels are considered to be mutually exclusive—550(c) would not protect Tina Chemical from liability. Perhaps Gruff should not be considered the immediate transferee at all, because of the "earmarking" doctrine or the "mere conduit" doctrine, see supra Problem 8-9; thus the transfer would be made to Tina for Gruff's benefit, and Tina would have the protection of 550(c). Whether or not Gruff is the initial transferee, it seems

---

31. Despite § 550(c), the transfer also arguably remained avoidable, though not recoverable, against the non-insider. The 2005 amendments to the Bankruptcy Code fixed this earlier oversight. See 11 U.S.C. § 547(j). The House Report explains:

Section 547 of the Bankruptcy Code authorizes a trustee to avoid a preferential payment made to a creditor by a debtor within 90 days of filing, whether the creditor is an insider or an outsider. To address the concern that a corporate insider (such as an officer or director who is a creditor of his or her own corporation) has an unfair advantage over outside creditors, section 547 also authorizes a trustee to avoid a preferential payment made to an insider creditor between 90 days and one year before filing. Several recent cases * * * allowed the trustee to ''reach-back'' and avoid a transfer to a noninsider creditor made within the 90-day to one-year time frame if an insider benefitted from the transfer in some way. This had the effect of discouraging lenders from obtaining loan guarantees, lest transfers to the lender be vulnerable to recapture by reason of the debtor's insider relationship with the loan guarantor. Section 202 of the Bankruptcy Reform Act of 1994 addressed the * * * problem by inserting a new section 550(c) into the Bankruptcy Code to prevent avoidance or recovery from a noninsider creditor during the 90-day to one-year period even though the transfer to the noninsider benefitted an insider creditor. The 1994 amendments, however, failed to make a corresponding amendment to section 547, which deals with the avoidance of preferential transfers. As a result, a trustee could still utilize section 547 to avoid a preferential lien given to a noninsider bank, more than 90 days but less than one year before bankruptcy, if the transfer benefitted an insider guarantor of the debtor's debt. Accordingly, section 1213 of the Act [11 U.S.C. 547(j)] makes a perfecting amendment to section 547 to provide that if the trustee avoids a transfer given by the debtor to a noninsider for the benefit of an insider creditor between 90 days and one year before filing, that avoidance is valid only with respect to the insider creditor. Thus both the previous amendment to section 550 and the perfecting amendment to section 547 protect the noninsider from the avoiding powers of the trustee exercised with respect to transfers made during the 90-day to one year pre-filing period. This provision is intended to apply to any case, including any adversary proceeding, that is pending or commenced on or after the date of enactment of this Act.

H.R. Rep. No. 109-31, pt. 1, at 143-44 (2005).

he is also a person for whose benefit the transfer was made; nothing in the statute indicates that a person or entity cannot be both. Thus Tina should still enjoy the protection of § 550(c) even if Gruff is the initial transferee.

Are there other situations, not remedied by the 1994 amendments, under which a transfer which is not preferential as to the immediate transferee nevertheless may be recovered from the immediate transferee because it is preferential as to another creditor? Consider the following Problem.

Problem 8-21

> First Bank had a $550,000 first mortgage on Foam Corporation's Fresno, California factory real property, which is worth $800,000. Suppose that, 80 days before filing its chapter 11 petition, Foam gave a second mortgage on the Fresno property to secure a new loan of $400,000 from Friendly Finance. (Friendly's appraiser made a serious error in valuing the property.) Pursuant to the loan agreement, Friendly disbursed $300,000 to Foam and $100,000 directly to CredCo to pay off a $100,000 unsecured debt Foam owed to CredCo. During the next 80 days, Foam made two regular monthly payments—including principal and interest—on the first mortgage. As to each transfer, which creditors, if any, received avoidable preferences or are liable under § 550? Would § 547(c)(9) provide a defense if each payment were less than $5,000?

7. Setoff And Its Relation to Preference

McCoid, *Setoff: Why Bankruptcy Priority?*
75 Va. L. Rev. 15 (1989)

INTRODUCTION

Between solvent parties, setoff makes perfect sense. If you owe me $10 and I owe you $7, it is certainly efficient for you simply to pay me $3; it also avoids the possibility of my default after you have paid what you owe me. Striking that balance affects no one else. If, however, one of us is insolvent and has other creditors, the sense of this solution is less obvious. It is hardly news that setoff, whether it takes place postbankruptcy or in the period immediately preceding bankruptcy, is preferential in effect. A creditor who owes money to his debtor receives, to the extent of the debtor's claim against him, 100 cents on the dollar from his claim against the debtor, while other creditors receive less. Those who created setoff thought that 'natural justice and equity' between the debtor and the indebted creditor required this result. It is now so long-settled that re-examination, especially perhaps by one who has expressed doubt about the utility of recapture of prebankruptcy preferences, may seem surprising. The inquiry is prompted by a latter-day rationalization of the right of setoff as the equivalent of security entitling the creditor to the same kind of priority given to 'secured creditors'—those holding judicial, consensual, and statutory liens.

Whether setoff should continue as an exception to the principle of creditor equality deserves a further look. Those who formulated the 'natural justice' justification conceived of setoff as pitting the interests of the creditor with setoff power against the interests of the debtor rather than against those of other creditors. This focus, though once understandable, became altogether misplaced with the advent of discharge. The newer, 'security,' explanation of setoff invites comparison of setoff with recognized types of secured claims. Although it appears that a creditor with a nonbankruptcy power of setoff is more like a statutory lienor than like a holder of a judicial or consensual lien, even the analogy to the statutory lien is unpersuasive. The relationship of mutual obligation between debtor and creditor by itself does not warrant giving that creditor priority over other creditors. This conclusion leads to speculation about the practical consequences of discarding the setoff advantage conferred by present law. Those consequences, to me, seem of little moment. I begin, however, with a comparison of the outcomes of preference, security, and setoff.

I. SETOFF AS A PREFERENCE

Suppose that a debtor has five unsecured creditors and owes each of them $20, his liabilities thus totalling $100. The debtor's assets, however, are only $40, so that in a bankruptcy liquidation each creditor would receive a dividend of $.40 per $1 of debt, or $8. If the debtor pays $10 to one creditor immediately before bankruptcy, leaving the debtor with only $30 in assets to pay $90 worth of remaining claims, without preference recapture that creditor would receive a total of $13.33 ($10 [the preferential payment] + 1/3 of $10 [the dividend on the balance of the debt]). The other creditors, however, would each receive only $6.66 (1/3 of a $20 claim). On the other hand, preference recapture under section 547 of the Bankruptcy Code allows the trustee to recover the $10 from the preferred creditor, thus enlarging the bankruptcy estate to $40, and to pay $8 to all unsecured creditors, including the preferred one. Bankruptcy law's provisions for recapture of transfers made on the eve of bankruptcy (within one year if the transfer is to an insider; within 90 days to others) on account of an antecedent debt while the debtor is insolvent are designed to assure equality among unsecured creditors.

If one of the five creditors is secured by collateral worth $10, he will recover that collateral or its value and be paid an additional $3.33 on his bankruptcy claim for the unsecured balance. Thus, the secured creditor, like the recipient of the unrecaptured preference, will receive a total of $13.33. The remaining creditors will each receive $6.66 (1/3 of a $20 claim). The benefit to the secured creditor is not recaptured as a preference in bankruptcy, so long as the security was not granted during the vulnerable period on account of an antecedent debt, because the security interest gives the secured creditor a claim on the collateral generally accepted as superior to the claims of unsecured creditors. Indeed, payment of a previously secured debt during the vulnerable period is not preferential because it does not lead to a greater recovery than would have been realized without it in an ensuing bankruptcy.

Finally, if one of the creditors owes the debtor $10, that obligation constitutes part of the debtor's $40 in assets, and under section 553 that creditor is entitled to balance his claim against his obligation. He may do this in the 90 days immediately preceding bankruptcy or, on obtaining relief from the automatic stay, after the petition is filed. Doing so will reduce the estate to $30, because he will not pay into the bankruptcy estate the $10 owed the debtor, but will reduce his claim to $10. He will receive $3.33 on that residual claim, while the other creditors will receive $6.66 each on their $20 claims. In effect, then, this creditor will have received $13.33 for his claim. This is setoff, the nonbankruptcy right to which is preserved in bankruptcy.

The lesson is clear. The ability to set off has the same effect as an unrecaptured preference and is as valuable to a creditor as a security interest in part of the debtor's estate. Absent a persuasive basis for distinguishing the creditor with setoff power from other unsecured creditors, it is at odds with the principle of creditor equality.

The Bankruptcy Code limits setoff. Section 553(a) only preserves rights of setoff of mutual debts that would exist outside bankruptcy. Moreover, it is confined to rights arising before commencement of the bankruptcy case. Subsection (a)(1) denies setoff if the creditor's claim against the debtor is disallowed. Subsection (a)(2) prohibits the creditor from acquiring the claim against the debtor from one other than the debtor after the bankruptcy petition is filed or within 90 days before filing if the debtor is then insolvent. This provision prevents an obligor of the debtor from trading in claims in order to gain a preference. Subsection (a)(3) forbids setoff if the creditor acquired his obligation to a then-insolvent debtor within 90 days before the petition was filed. If setoff were allowed in such a case, a creditor could in effect acquire security for an antecedent debt when the need for such security became acute. Finally, section 553(b) provides for recapture of so much of a setoff within the prebankruptcy preference period as reflects an improvement of position (that is, a decrease in the amount by which the debtor's obligation to the creditor exceeds the creditor's obligation to the debtor) during that period. There is no such limitation, however, on postbankruptcy setoff.

These limits obviously mitigate the preferential effect of setoff in bankruptcy, but they do not eliminate it. In the absence of one of the limiting conditions, setoff remains preferential in the fashion illustrated above. * * *

[So why is this preference unsound in bankruptcy?] In short, the nature and historical purposes of setoff and security are different. Setoff is really a process, a procedure for striking a balance between creditor and debtor. Its early appearance in bankruptcy and insolvency matters is not at odds with this proposition. As argued above, adoption of setoff in bankruptcy stems from the view, which became more troubling when discharge appeared, of the contest as between debtor and creditor rather than as between creditors. On the other hand, liens, whether judicial, consensual, or relational, are substantive rights that focus on the relationship between creditors and operate in order to establish priority. Moreover, the utility of the power of setoff as a security device is questionable. The unexercised power is defeated with some frequency by other, secured claims.

If the creditors with the power to set off have come, because of that power, to feel secure against the prospect of bankruptcy, it is only because the preferential effect of setoff has so long been indulged. It is true that setoff has a bankruptcy history of long standing. Thus it might be argued that it has acquired a security-priority purpose. That ought not to be the case unless there are practical reasons for the priority. Absent such reasons, creditors with setoff power should be subject to the principle of equality that underlies preference recapture and bankruptcy distribution. * * *

IV. THE REORGANIZATION COMPLICATION

The distinction drawn by my analysis between rights of creditors inter se and rights of a creditor vis-a-vis the debtor to condemn bankruptcy setoff faces one puzzle not posed by current law. In a reorganization the owners of equity are very commonly participants in the reorganized firm. Consequently, it is plausible for a creditor with a nonbankruptcy power of setoff against the debtor to argue that such power must be recognized in fixing that creditor's status in Chapter 11 in the event of the participation therein of equity. In other words, any reorganization in which the debtor participates is a three-sided matter implicating the rights of a creditor with nonbankruptcy setoff power against the debtor as well as against other creditors.

Consider a case in which Creditor A is owed $10 by the debtor and owes $7 to it. Imagine, as well, unsecured Creditor B to whom the debtor owes $10. Under present law it is clear that pursuant to section 506(a) A would have a secured claim of $7 (the value of his obligation to the debtor) and an unsecured claim of $3, while B would have an unsecured claim of $10. That result preserves A's setoff rights against the debtor. At the same time it overrides B's claim to a right to equal treatment with A. Suppose that A is not given secured status. How can A's priority against the debtor be preserved while at the same time maintaining parity between A and B? The two claims—to setoff power and parity—can only be reconciled if both A and B are paid in full before equity participates in the reorganized firm. Payment in full sets A equal to B since both receive their due and honors A's setoff claim by satisfying the debtor's obligation to A. Of course, payment of unsecured creditors in full before equity participates is exactly what the absolute priority rule embodied in Chapter 11 cram-down requires in the absence of creditor consent to different treatment. Thus the dilemma is apparent rather than real. Both A and B can be treated as unsecured creditors with $10 claims so long as the absolute priority rule governs.

A quite different question is whether this treatment is required if A and B do not insist on it. Unsecured creditors are usually put in a single class. A reorganization plan proposes treatment by classes and then each class votes whether to accept the proposal. If a class rejects the proposal, the plan can only be confirmed by cram-down. It might be useful, however, to classify A and B separately for this purpose. Then distinct proposals can be made to A and B. A could choose to accept a plan that did not confer on him absolute priority over the debtor, or B could accept a plan that did not provide for equality with A. Such choices are conceivable, if unlikely. Nothing in the statute stands in the way of separate classification, and indeed such divisions occur occasionally.

Would a more compelling reason for separate classification be the reorganizing firm's need to make use of A's obligation to the debtor while plan confirmation is pending? Suppose, for example, that A is a bank in which the debtor's operating funds are deposited. Should the debtor be allowed to use that deposit for current operations without some provision for 'adequate protection' of A's setoff power? My analysis of setoff inclines me to an affirmative answer to this question. A secured creditor is entitled to protection against dissipation of his collateral. A, however, is not entitled to secured creditor status. He is only entitled to be paid in full before the debtor receives anything, and chapter 11 fully protects that right. The argument that the debtor enjoys some immediate benefit, equivalent to long-term participation, simply by using the obligation-asset seems to me too tenuous to warrant special treatment of Creditor A.

CONCLUSION

I believe that this analysis shows that both the historical and contemporary justifications for setoff in bankruptcy are unsound. * * *

Problem 8-22

On December 31, Foam Corporation had $800,000 in its cash account at Commerce Bank. Suppose the balance in the account was the same on December 15, and that as of December 15 Foam owed the Bank $1 million on an "unsecured" demand note. Suppose that the debt to Bank had dropped to $600,000 when Foam filed bankruptcy 90 days later, on March 15, and that by this time the cash account had dropped to $500,000. Under state law, Commerce Bank could have set off the account at any time to satisfy the note. This state-law right of setoff survives bankruptcy. See § 553(a). The effect is to treat the account as collateral—like property in which the Bank has a security interest or lien. Indeed, the account is considered "cash collateral" for purposes of § 363.

1. Is the Bank entitled to the whole account despite Foam's bankruptcy? Can the Bank unilaterally act to set off the whole account or any part of the account after Foam's bankruptcy? See § 362(a)(7) & (d). How is the stay of setoff reconciled with § 553(a)?

2. Suppose instead that the Bank set off the account on March 13, two days before Foam's bankruptcy. Immediately before the setoff was accomplished, the cash account held $500,000, and the debt to Bank was $600,000.

    a. The setoff would not be avoidable under § 547. One reason is § 553(a) itself. Is another reason that the setoff is not a preference under § 547(b)?

    b. Is any part of the setoff avoidable under § 553(b)? Should the answer to Part 1 be reconsidered?

    c. During the 90-day period, Foam apparently made principal payments on the note totalling $400,000, in addition to paying interest. Are these payments avoidable preferences under § 547?

3. In truth (as Chapter Two shows), Foam was not indebted to Commerce Bank. Suppose Foam owed $200,000 to DistCo. Suppose that during the 90 days before Foam's bankruptcy, DistCo sold its claim to the Bank for $100,000. Suppose, also, that at the time of bankruptcy, the cash account contained $500,000. Is the Bank entitled to set off its $200,000 "previously-owned" claim (which it bought from DistCo) against the account? Should the answer to Part 1 be reconsidered?

4. Suppose that Foam had a prepetition breach of contract claim against Swenson, a large trade creditor. This contract claim is property of Foam's bankruptcy estate and can be collected by the debtor in possession. Swenson can reduce or eliminate this liability by setting off Foam's trade debt. to Swenson. Suppose, however, that a plan of reorganization is confirmed, which has the effect of discharging the trade debt. Section 1141. Suppose the breach of contract claim against Swenson survives. If there is a suit on this claim, can Swenson set off the trade debt? See In re De Laurentiis Entm't Group Inc., 963 F.2d 1269 (9th Cir. 1992) (allowing network's prepetition quantum meruit claim to be set off against prepetition debt network owed debtor, even after confirmation of debtor's plan discharging prepetition debts). How is this result explained, technically and theoretically? Must the creditor at least raise the issue of its setoff rights during the bankruptcy case in order to preserve them? See United States v. Munson, 248 B.R. 343 (C.D. Ill. 2000) (noting circuit split).

5. Suppose that the breach of contract claim against Swenson is a postpetition claim. It arose from a fresh deal that the parties made after Foam filed bankruptcy. Can Swenson set off the discharged trade debt owed by Foam against its new contract liability?

> 6. Remember recoupment from Chapter Three. Recoupment is like setoff but different. Recoupment is a netting of cross, reciprocal claims that arise from the same transaction. Setoff nets claims from different transactions. Sections 362, 547, and 553 do not apply to recoupment. Is it recoupment , setoff, or preferential transfer if—within the 90-day period—the United States applies a tax refund that its owes the debtor against a loan the debtor owes the United States? Does it matter whether the debt is for unpaid taxes or for an unpaid Small Business Administration loan? See United States v. Maxwell, 157 F.3d 1099 (7th Cir. 1998).

E. LIMITATIONS ON AVOIDING POWERS

Section 546 details several limitations on the trustee's avoiding powers under §§ 544, 545, 547, 548, and 553. The most important generally applicable limitation is § 546(a), a statute of limitations, which was amended substantially in 1994. The trustee cannot bring an avoidance action after the earlier of:

> (1) the later of –
> > (A) 2 years after the entry of the order for relief; or
> > (B) 1 year after the appointment or election of the first trustee under section 702 [or] 1104 * * * of this title if such appointment or such election occurs before the expiration of the period specified in subparagraph (A); or
>
> (2) the time the case is closed or dismissed.

Section 546(a) (as amended in 1994). The statute is tolled by commencing an action or proceeding within the limitation period, which requires filing of a complaint.

Typically, the debtor in possession will not bring avoidance actions until late in the case, if at all. The reason is not legal. The reason is practical and political. Much of the time, the debtor is working to get creditors to agree to a reorganization plan and will use the avoiding powers as leverage to cut deals and settle disputes. The debtor in possession in chapter 11 will often not begin a full-court press bringing actions to enforce avoiding powers until the end of the case and perhaps only if it appears that reorganization will fail.

As the running of the two-year limitations period nears, the pressure on the debtor in possession to file or settle avoidance claims may become severe. Note that the two-year limitations period may be extended if, before it expires, a trustee is elected or appointed under § 1104. The limitations period then would expire either two years after the order for relief or one year after election or appointment of the trustee, whichever is later. If it appears that the debtor in possession is not appropriately pursuing avoidance actions, pressure may thus build for appointment of a trustee (or for authorization to be given to someone else, such as the creditors' committee,[32] to file the actions quickly). The two-year

---

32. Compare Official Comm. of Unsecured Creditors of Cybergenics Corp. v. Chinery, 330 F.3d 548 (3d Cir. 2003), with United Phosphorus, Ltd. v. Fox (In re Fox), 305 B.R. 912 (B.A.P. 10th Cir. 2004). Cf. Hartford Underwriters Ins. Co. v. Union Planters Bank, 530 U.S. 1, 120 S. Ct. 1942, 147 L. Ed. 2d 1 (2000) (reprinted in Chapter Nine below).

period may similarly be extended if no trustee is elected or appointed in the chapter 11 case, but the case is converted to chapter 7—a not uncommon occurrence—and a trustee is elected or appointed under § 702 before expiration of the two-year period. Note that an interim trustee is always appointed in a chapter 7 case under § 701; if no trustee is elected under § 702(a)-(c) at the § 341 meeting of creditors, then the interim trustee become a non-interim trustee under § 702(d). Arguably the one-year extension[33] does not apply in a chapter 7 case if the two-year period expires before a trustee either (1) is elected under § 702(a)-(c) or (2) becomes a non-interim trustee under § 702(d) when the meeting of creditors ends without election of a trustee.[34]

The Ninth Circuit's decision in El Paso v. Am. W. Airlines, Inc. (In re Am. W. Airlines, Inc.), 217 F.3d 1161 (9th Cir. 2000), creates the possibility that lien avoidance actions in effect may not be subject to the § 546(a) statute of limitations. The court held that "§ 502(d) disallows the claims of creditors who have received avoidable transfers, unless the creditor relinquishes the transfer," id. at 1163, and that application of § 502(d) did not depend on whether an action to avoid the transfer had been filed before expiration of the § 546(a) statute of limitations. Thus the court affirmed the disallowance of the claim of the city of El Paso, which was based on a personal property tax lien that would have been avoidable under § 545 but for the expiration of the limitations period. The court does not say that the lien then is void under § 506(d), but that is the likely result even under the limited reach of § 506(d) as interpreted by the Supreme Court in Dewsnup v. Timm, 502 U.S. 410, 112 S. Ct. 773, 116 L. Ed. 2d 903 (1992).

Another piece of § 546 is less generally applicable but is nevertheless very, very important in most business bankruptcy cases. It is subsection 546(c), which to some extent prevents a trustee from avoiding a seller's right to reclaim goods.

The law does not ordinarily give a credit seller of goods a lien for the price of the goods. Unless the buyer grants the seller a U.C.C. Article 9 security interest, the seller is an unsecured creditor for the unpaid price of any delivered goods. Therefore, if the sale was on credit and the buyer fails to pay when the

---

33. Although we refer to it as a one-year extension, it does not extend the two-year period by a year; rather, as stated above, it extends the statute of limitations to a date one year after appointment or election of the first trustee for the case (assuming that is more than two years after the order for relief). If the trustee is appointed or elected near the end of the two-year period, the extension will amount to nearly an extra year.

34. See Ga.-Pac. Corp. v. Burtch (In re Allied Digital Techs. Corp.), __ B.R. __, No. 00-4020(CGC), 2006 WL 864827 (D. Del. Apr. 4, 2006) (holding that one-year period did not apply in chapter 7 case where interim trustee was appointed within the two-year period but did not become permanent trustee under § 702(d) until after two-year period expired). But see Singer v. Kimberly-Clark Corp. (In re Am. Pad & Paper Co.), 307 B.R. 459 (Bankr. D. Del. 2004) (holding that one year extension applies in chapter 7 case if interim trustee who is appointed under § 701 within the two year period becomes permanent trustee under§ 702(d), even though that occurs after expiration of two year period). Note that in chapter 11 cases the initial appointment of a trustee (who may or may not be ousted by an elected trustee) and the election of a trustee *both* occur under § 1104; thus any such election or appointment within the two-year period in a chapter 11 case will trigger the one year extension. See § 546(a)(1)(B) (referring to § 1104).

price is due, the seller cannot recover the goods or any other property of the buyer. The goods belong solely to the buyer. The seller's only remedy is to sue for the price, get a judgment, and enforce the judgment through execution.[35]

In a narrow, exceptional case, however, U.C.C. Article 2 gives an unpaid credit seller a kind of nonconsensual lien on the goods. It is technically a right to reclaim, i.e., to repossess, the goods even in the absence of a security interest in them. Section 2-702 describes this state-law right of reclamation:

> Where the seller discovers that the buyer has received goods on credit while insolvent he may reclaim the goods upon demand made within ten days after the receipt, but if misrepresentation of solvency has been made to the particular seller in writing within three months before delivery the ten day limitation does not apply.

U.C.C. § 2-702(2). The newest official version of section 2-702(2), which not all states have enacted, slightly changes the right:

> Where the seller discovers that the buyer has received goods on credit while insolvent the seller may reclaim the goods upon demand made within a reasonable time after the buyer's receipt of the goods. Except as provided in this subsection the seller may not base a right to reclaim goods on the buyer's fraudulent or innocent misrepresentation of solvency or of intent to pay.

2003 Approved Amendments to Uniform Commercial Code Article 2, section 2-702(2).

Article 2 also implicitly recognizes a right of reclamation in favor of a cash seller who was paid with a check that bounced. This right is inferred from sections 2-507 and 2-511. The newest version of 2-507 explicitly codifies this right but conditions the right to reclaim under these circumstances upon a demand made within a reasonable time after the seller discovers or should have discovered that payment failed.

A problem for the seller is the possible vulnerability of this right of reclamation to a trustee's avoiding powers if the buyer files bankruptcy. Arguably, the right is subject to avoidance under § 544(a)(1)-(2), 545, 547, or 549. However, § 546(c) (as amended by the 2005 BAPCPA) provides that a trustee's avoiding powers are subject to a seller's right to reclaim goods sold in the ordinary course of business to the debtor if:

- the debtor, while insolvent, received these goods not later than 45 days prior to the commencement of the case, and
- written demand for reclamation of the goods is made not later than 45 days after receipt of such goods by the debtor or not later than 20 days after the commencement of the case if the 45-day period expires after the commencement of the case.

---

35. In some cases the seller may be able to sue the buyer and immediately seek a prejudgment writ of attachment, under which the seller could obtain an attachment lien on property held by the buyer, including perhaps the very goods that were sold to the buyer. In any event, the seller does not have a lien simply because the buyer did not pay for the goods; instead, the seller must go to court to obtain a lien, just like any other unsecured creditor.

If the seller fails to satisfy the requirements of § 546(c), the seller the seller may still assert the rights set forth in § 503(b)(9) of the Bankruptcy Code. It gives the seller an administrative expense priority claim for the value of goods received by the debtor within 20 days prior to the commencement of the bankruptcy case if the debtor purchased the goods in the ordinary course of its business.

Before the 2005 amendments to the Bankruptcy Code, everybody agreed that § 546(c) did not create any right of reclamation. It merely recognized such a right to a limited extent in a bankruptcy case if any such right existed under Article 2 or other nonbankruptcy law. Thus a seller who tried to reclaim goods from the buyer's bankruptcy estate initially had to establish a right of reclamation under nonbankruptcy law, usually U.C.C. § 2-702. The substantive and procedural requirements of that law had to have been satisfied. If there was no right under nonbankruptcy law, there was no right in bankruptcy.

Because the 2005 amendments changed the language of § 546(c), people immediately began to question if this dependence on nonbankruptcy law still exists. Maybe § 546(c) now creates a bankruptcy right of reclamation or, at a minimum, frees the U.C.C. Article 2 right of reclamation from any state-law demand requirement.

In any event, the new language of § 546(c) does nothing about the problem that reclaiming sellers—at least those who sold goods on credit—have always experienced under state law and also under bankruptcy law: subordination of the right to other claims. The credit seller's right to reclaim—in and out of bankruptcy—is subject to the claims of a good faith purchaser of the goods, including the rights of a holder of a security interest in the goods.

In very many business bankruptcy cases, the debtor has lots of trade creditors who have sold lots of goods to the debtor on credit. Some or all of these creditors may lack a consensual lien on the goods to secure the prices owed them but may have rights to reclaim the goods they sold the debtor. However, in the typical case there is also a principal lender who has a security interest in all of the debtor's personal property, present and after-acquired. This security interest attached to the goods the debtor bought from the trade creditors and, even if they have rights to reclaim, their rights are typically inferior to the rights of the lender qua secured party.

Here is a recent case that illustrates this problem for reclaiming sellers. The case was decided under § 546(c) before the 2005 amendments, though the judge mentions the amended § 546(c) and muses about its effect. Consider whether the somewhat revised, new language of § 546(c) would affect the seller's right to reclaim against the debtor and also would affect the priority of the right against a competing security interest in the goods.

Davis v. Par Wholesale Auto, Inc. (In re Tucker)
United States Bankruptcy Court, District of Arizona, 2005
329 B.R. 291

OPINION RE PAR'S RECLAMATION RIGHTS

RANDOLPH J. HAINES, Bankruptcy Judge.

This case presents the issue of whether a reclaiming seller has priority over an unperfected secured creditor. The Court concludes that it does, because an unperfected secured creditor does not qualify as an "other good faith purchaser."

Procedural Background

This matter is before the Court on cross-motions for summary judgment filed by Par Wholesale Auto, Inc. ("Par") and DAVCO Enterprises dba DAVCO Motors & DAVCO Leasing, and C.T. Cook (collectively "DAVCO"). The issue is the ownership of three vehicles sold by Par to Harvest Car Company, which was a dba of the Debtor Edward Tucker (hereafter referred to as "Tucker" or "Harvest"). On June 23, 2005, the Court ruled in favor of Par and against DAVCO as to ownership of the three vehicles, indicating that a subsequent opinion would more fully explain the Court's analysis and rationale. This is that opinion.

Undisputed Material Facts

The parties are not in total agreement on all the facts, but there are sufficient undisputed material facts upon which the Court is able to enter summary judgment. These are:

Tucker inspected vehicles at Par's place of business in Texas and purchased the three vehicles from Par in April 2001. Tucker delivered a check for one of the vehicles and promised to pay the balance for all of the vehicles. The vehicles were transported from Texas to Arizona and delivered to Tucker at Harvest Car Company.

Tucker and DAVCO had a financing agreement whereby DAVCO or C.T. Cook provided floor financing to Tucker to allow Tucker to purchase vehicles and hold them for resale. Per the financing agreement and business dealings between DAVCO and Tucker, Tucker would sign the certificates of title and deliver them to DAVCO. DAVCO would then hold these "open" titles until Tucker sold the vehicles. At least for the vehicles at issue here, DAVCO did not immediately record its alleged interest in the vehicles with the Arizona Motor Vehicle Division, or otherwise indicate the transfer with any other vehicle titling agency, including the Texas Department of Transportation. Nor did DAVCO file a U.C.C.-1 financing statement to perfect its security interest pursuant to Article 9 of the Uniform Commercial Code ("U.C.C."). At all times until DAVCO obtained new titles in Arizona, DAVCO held Texas certificates of title that had been endorsed by the previous owners.

When the check tendered by Tucker to Par to pay for at least one of the vehicles failed to clear Tucker's bank, Par timely made demand for replacement funds or for return of all of the vehicles. Unable to make good on the purchase price, Tucker agreed to return the vehicles, and they were returned to Par on May 24, 2001. At the time the vehicles were returned to Par, DAVCO did not hold registered title to the vehicles and DAVCO's interest was not reflected in the records of either the Arizona Motor Vehicle Division or the Texas Department of Transportation.

Par applied for new certificates of title in Texas, and they were issued to Par in May 2001. DAVCO applied for and obtained certificates in Arizona in June 2001. Also in June, 2001 DAVCO terminated the financing agreement with Harvest Car Company and Tucker, and demanded return of the vehicles.

At no time did DAVCO ever have possession of the vehicles. The vehicles were held on Tucker's car lot until they were returned to Par in May 2001. DAVCO merely held the Texas certificates of title that had been executed by the previous owners, which DAVCO calls "open" titles. DAVCO held these open titles to secure payment for the monies advanced to Tucker and Harvest Car Company. The executed certificates of title show the transfer from Par to Tucker, but regarding the transfers from Tucker to DAVCO, on at least one of the certificates of title, C.T. Cook signed for both Tucker and DAVCO.

* * *

Sellers' Rights of Reclamation vs. Secured Creditors

Pursuant to A.R.S. § 47-2702 (U.C.C. § 2-702), a seller has a right to reclaim goods when the seller discovers that the buyer has received goods on credit while insolvent. The demand for reclamation must occur within ten days of the buyer's receipt of the goods sold.[36] Under Arizona law, there is no requirement that the demand for reclamation must be in writing, so an oral demand will suffice. A seller's reclamation rights are subordinate to the rights of subsequent buyers in the ordinary course, other good faith purchasers, or lien creditors. A.R.S. § 47-2702(C).

In the present case, Par sold one of the vehicles in exchange for a check tendered by Tucker and was therefore a cash seller on that vehicle. A check is a negotiable instrument and the seller who accepts a check for payment is a cash seller because the transaction is considered a cash sale under the U.C.C. The other two vehicles were sold on credit in exchange for two bank drafts, and Par was a credit seller for those

---

36. [Footnote 8 in original:] The Bankruptcy Code also recognizes the seller's right of reclamation. 11 U.S.C. § 546(c). The Bankruptcy Abuse Prevention and Consumer Protection Act ("BAPCPA")(2005) has amended that provision, effective for cases filed after October 17, 2005. The amended § 546(c) extends the time for making the reclamation demand to 45 days (or 20 days after the commencement of the bankruptcy case). Prior to this amendment, the provision had been understood as "recogniz[ing], in part, the validity of section 2-702 of the U.C.C ." H[.R.] Rep. No. 595 , 95th Cong., 1st Sess. 371-72 (1977); S. Rep. No. 989 , 95th Cong., 2d Sess. 86-87 (1978). But since the U.C.C. still requires a demand within 10 days, perhaps the amended § 546(c) creates its own reclamation right, rather than merely validating the right that exists under the U.C.C. This impression is supported by the fact that the amendment also strikes the reference to "any statutory or common law" right to reclaim, and instead simply states that the trustee's powers are subject to "the right of a seller" to reclaim. If the amended § 546(c) creates its own reclamation right, then the analysis made here by applying the U.C.C. provisions and definitions may not apply in a bankruptcy case filed after BAPCPA's effective date, and the issue may instead be whether the amended Bankruptcy Code provision—"subject to the prior rights of a holder of a security interest in such goods or the proceeds thereof"—applies equally to an unperfected security interest as to a perfected security interest. On the other hand, it may be a mistake to assume that the amended § 546(c) was intended to provide an entirely new and self-contained body of reclamation law, because it fails to recognize the rights of buyers in the ordinary course, other good faith purchasers and lien creditors, who were always protected under the U.C.C. Perhaps the intent was to incorporate and expand on the U.C.C. reclamation rights, rather than to supplant them entirely, in which case some U.C.C. analysis may continue to be relevant in interpreting and applying the new § 546(c).

two vehicles. But the U.C.C., as adopted by Arizona, abolished the common law distinction between cash and credit sellers, and both now have reclamation rights. The cash buyer who issues a check for payment receives conditional title as against the seller, and the buyer's right to retain or dispose of the goods is conditional upon his making the payment due. The rights of a cash seller are also bound by the insolvency requirement and ten-day limitation period for reclamation.[37]

As previously stated, Tucker issued a check for one of the vehicles, and intended to pay the balance of the purchase price for the remaining vehicles under two bank drafts. When the check was dishonored and returned to Par, Par immediately contacted Tucker to demand replacement funds or return of the vehicles. Tucker was unable to provide replacement funds and offered to return the vehicles to Par. Based on Tucker's inability to pay his debts in the ordinary course of business or pay the debts as they come due, Tucker was insolvent for purposes of the reclamation statute. Par also made the demand for reclamation within ten days of delivery, as required by the statute. Tucker purchased the vehicles on April 21, 2001 and upon notification of dishonor of the check tendered by Tucker, Par made the demand for return of the vehicles on April 28, 2001. Par met all of the requirements under the Arizona statute for the reclamation of the vehicles, and Par re-took possession of the vehicles in May 2001.

Par's reclamation rights are subject only to the rights of a buyer in the ordinary course, other good faith purchaser, or a lien creditor. A.R.S. § 47-2702(C). DAVCO's security interest in the vehicles will defeat Par's reclamation rights only if it renders DAVCO a buyer in the ordinary course, an other good faith purchaser, or a lien creditor.

A lien creditor is defined as someone who has acquired a lien by attachment, levy, or the like and does not include a consensual secured creditor. A.R.S. § 47-9102(52). DAVCO's consensual security interest does not qualify DAVCO as a lien creditor.

DAVCO is also not a buyer in the ordinary course * * * .

Having found that DAVCO is neither a lien creditor nor a buyer in the ordinary course, the court must also consider whether DAVCO would fall under the "other good faith purchaser" exception to Par's right to reclaim the goods. The Ninth Circuit's seminal 1979 holding in [Los Angeles Paper Bag Co. v.] Talcott[, 604 F.2d 38 (9th Cir. 1979),] established that a secured creditor has the status of a good faith purchaser under A.R.S. § 47-2403. The U.C.C. definition of "purchaser" is broad enough to include an Article 9 (Secured Transactions) secured party. The issue that *Talcott* did not resolve, however, is whether all secured creditors qualify for "other good faith purchaser" status, or only perfected secured creditors. The creditor in *Talcott* was in fact perfected, so the Ninth Circuit had no occasion there to determine whether its conclusion would also apply to unperfected secured creditors.

A long line of cases suggests that perfection is required to qualify for the good faith purchaser priority over reclaiming sellers, but in each case the creditor was in fact perfected so reliance on such status in those cases was, at best, dictum. This Court has found only one reported case that considers the relative rights of an

---

37. [The text of and official comments to the U.C.C. do not support this sentence of the court's opinion. See U.C.C. § 2-507, Official Comment 3 ("There is no specific time limit for a cash seller to exercise the right of reclamation. However, the right will be defeated by delay causing prejudice to the buyer, waiver, estoppel, or ratification of the buyer's right to retain possession.").–Ed.]

unperfected creditor and a reclaiming seller, Guy Martin Buick, Inc. v. Colo. Springs Nat'l Bank, 184 Colo. 166, 519 P.2d 354 (1974) (en banc). The Colorado Supreme Court there held that because a seller's reclamation right was not listed in U.C.C. § 9-301 [now §9-317] as having priority over an unperfected security interest, the unperfected security interest must have priority over the seller's reclamation right. And although the reclaiming seller argued that it should be regarded as holding a perfected security interest upon retaking possession (and by § 9-301's cross reference to §9-312 [now § 9-322], the first to perfect has priority), the court rejected this argument by concluding that a reclamation right is not a species of a security interest. Id. at 184 Colo. 174-75, 519 P.2d 359.

Guy Martin was decided in 1974, and its analysis is not applicable in the Ninth Circuit after the *Talcott* decision in 1979. *Talcott* makes clear that priority is not determined by whether the reclamation rights are recognized in then § 9-301, but rather by whether the secured creditor qualifies as an "other good faith purchaser." Moreover, *Talcott* relied on two other decisions, the Arizona Supreme Court's decision in GECC [v. Tidwell Industries, Inc., 115 Ariz. 362, 565 P.2d 868 (1977)] and the Fifth Circuit's decision in *Samuels*.[38] Both of those cases equated the reclamation right to an unperfected security interest. Therefore to the extent that *Talcott* implicitly adopts the reasoning of *GECC* and *Samuels*, the reclaiming seller in *Guy Martin* would have prevailed because he perfected by obtaining possession before the unperfected secured creditor perfected.

To prevail under *Talcott*, *GECC* and *Samuels*, the secured creditor must qualify as a "good faith purchaser." As *Samuels* correctly notes, a secured creditor expressly satisfies the U.C.C.'s definition of purchaser. To qualify as a "good faith" purchaser, the secured creditor must observe "reasonable commercial standards of fair dealing in the trade." This Court concludes that an inventory financer such as DAVCO fails to observe reasonable commercial standards of fair dealing when it fails to file a financing statement so that credit sellers can become aware of the risk to their reclamation rights and protect themselves by perfecting an inventory purchase money security interest, which requires notification to the conflicting inventory financer. An inventory financer who had an opportunity to perfect and failed to do so therefore fails to qualify as an "other good faith purchaser," and therefore is subordinate to the rights of a reclaiming seller.

Based on all of the foregoing, the Court finds and concludes that Par had a right to reclaim the three vehicles; Par timely and properly exercised its rights of reclamation; and DAVCO does not possess an interest in the vehicles that is superior to Par's reclamation rights under A.R.S. § 47-2702.

* * *

F. POSTPETITION TRANSFERS—MAINLY, AFTER-ACQUIRED COLLATERAL

Postpetition transfers of estate property are usually avoidable if they are not authorized by the Code or the bankruptcy court. See § 549(a). Significantly, § 363(c)(1) authorizes the debtor in possession in a chapter 11

---

38.   [Stowers v. Mahon (In re Samuels & Co.), 526 F.2d 1238 (5th Cir. 1976).–Ed.]

case to make postpetition transfers of estate property in the ordinary course of business. Any chance of reorganization depends on keeping the business going, and doing business requires spending property—buying and selling inventory, paying wages, and keeping the lights on and doors open for customers and to lure lenders and investors. Section 363(b) authorizes the debtor in possession, after notice and a hearing, to make nonordinary course transfers of estate property.

Other postpetition transfers are mostly stayed under § 362 and avoidable under § 549 in the interest of preserving and protecting the estate. Section 552 confirms and strengthens this protection to guard against postpetition transfers effected by consensual, floating liens which are especially common in business bankruptcies—transfers that would result from prepetition security interests reaching postpetition collateral due to after-acquired property clauses in the mortgage or security agreement. For example, suppose that debtor secures its financing bank with a perfected U.C.C. Article 9 security interest in all of the debtor's accounts receivable, inventory and equipment. The parties' security agreement describes these kinds of property as collateral, and also provides, by way of a so-called *after-acquired property clause*, that collateral will include such property the debtor later acquires.

Article 9 validates after acquired-property clauses (except for certain consumer applications of such clauses and except with regard to commercial tort claims). See U.C.C. § 9-204. Because of this clause the bank's security interest will float over the debtor's property, automatically attaching to any equipment and inventory the debtor acquires and to any accounts receivable that arise. Thus accounts receivable, inventory and equipment the debtor acquires after the security agreement is made will also become collateral for the bank. No new or amended security agreement is required. The bank need not provide the debtor with additional, new value. Any antecedent debt that the security agreement covers is sufficient value in itself to support a security interest in after-acquired collateral. See U.C.C. § 1-201(44)(b) (§ 1-204 in 2001 Official Text) & § 9-203(b).

Also, because of state law, the bank's Article 9 security interest will automatically attach to any identifiable proceeds that the debtor receives upon disposing of or collecting any property that is the bank's collateral. U.C.C. § 9-315(a)(2). A security interest in proceeds is not dependent upon the parties' affirmative agreement. It arises by operation of law, unless the agreement provides otherwise.

Suppose that the debtor files chapter 11 bankruptcy and continues to operate the business as a debtor in possession. The debtor sells inventory that was on hand when the petition was filed and acquires fresh inventory and equipment. Under the proceeds provision of Article 9, the bank's security interest would attach to the sale proceeds (whatever they are, including money and also accounts receivable owed by the debtor's customers). Under the after-acquired property provision of the security agreement (which Article 9 validates), the security interest would attach to the new inventory, the new equipment, and (redundantly) to the new accounts receivable. In other words, under state law the force and effect of prepetition, floating security interests would continue despite the debtor's bankruptcy.

Such floating security interests are nevertheless highly vulnerable in bankruptcy due to § 552. Section 552(a) cuts off application of after-acquired property clauses as of the petition date. Section 552(b)(1) permits a security interest to attach to postpetition proceeds, but subject to the court's authority to limit the security interest "based on the equities of the case."

A real estate mortgagee typically does not automatically obtain a lien on any proceeds of *sale* of the real estate, but very often a rents clause in the mortgage will give the mortgagee an interest in the rents arising from any *lease* of the real estate. Section 552(b)(2) permits the rents clause to operate postpetition, as an exception to § 552(a), which otherwise would prevent the rents clause from operating to give the mortgagee an interest in postpetition rents.

With that introduction we can now consider § 552 in more detail.

1. General Rule, Section 552(a)

The general rule of § 552 is that "a prepetition security interest does not reach property acquired by the estate or debtor postpetition." United Sav. Ass'n of Tex. v. Timbers of Inwood Forest Assocs., 484 U.S. 365, 374, 108 S. Ct. 626, 631, 98 L. Ed. 2d 740, 750 (1988). Thus floating security interests created before bankruptcy are sunk by bankruptcy. This general rule is embodied in § 552(a) which provides in full:

> Except as provided in subsection (b) of this section, property acquired by the estate or by the debtor after the commencement of the case is not subject to any lien resulting from any security agreement entered into by the debtor before the commencement of the case.

But for the exceptions in subsection (b), the rule would apply equally to security interests that float because of the parties' agreement (e.g., after-acquired property clauses and rents clauses) and to those that float as a result of law (e.g., proceeds). Security interests, whatever their source, simply would not attach to property acquired after the petition was filed. The bankruptcy filing would be an impassable barrier.

Note that § 552(a) is limited to liens resulting from *security agreements*. For purposes of bankruptcy, a "security agreement" is "an agreement that creates or provides for a security interest." A "security interest" is a "lien created by agreement." So § 552(a) applies only to consensual liens, not judicial or statutory liens. On the other hand, the meaning of security interest includes a consensual lien on any kind of property. Thus, the application of § 552(a) is not affected by the nature of the collateral, and it applies equally to both real and personal property. Consensual, floating liens on real property are relatively uncommon, however, compared to the everyday routine and widespread use of floating Article 9 security interests on personal property.

Floating nonconsensual liens are uncommon too, but they are possible. For example, in most states a judgment lien automatically attaches to after-acquired real estate. Section 552 would not prevent such a lien from reaching postpetition property. Yet, § 549(a) and the automatic stay of § 362 generally prevent the creation of liens postpetition without court approval.[39] These sections, therefore, will likely stop the postpetition spread of a prepetition involuntary lien.

If a prepetition, floating security interest could attach to postpetition property, it would cause a postpetition transfer. Section 549 deals with postpetition transfers. What does § 552 add to § 549? The answer is in the effect and coverage of § 552. Section 549 gives the trustee the power to avoid postpetition transfers, but the burden is on the trustee to take action. In contrast, § 552 declares outright, as a matter of preemptive federal law, that postpetition property is immune from floating security interests created prepetition. There is nothing to avoid when § 552 applies because, as a result of its application, no transfer occurred. In addition, while § 549 applies only to estate property, § 552 equally immunizes both property of the estate and property of the debtor.

2. Exception, Section 552(b)

Section 552(b) creates an exception to the general rule of subsection (a) which sinks a prepetition floating security interest. The exception allows and enforces such an interest that extends to proceeds, product, offspring, rents and profits of prepetition collateral, including hotel and motel lodging charges. Simply stated, "Section 552(b) provides that if a pre-petition security interest encumbers proceeds of pre-petition collateral, the post-petition proceeds of pre-petition collateral will be subject to the creditor's pre-petition security interest." McGoldrick v. Juice Farms, Inc. (In re Ludford Fruit Prods., Inc.), 99 B.R. 18, 25 (Bankr. C.D. Cal. 1989).

Section 552(b) is most often applied in practice to personal property secured transactions governed by U.C.C. Article 9, and real property mortgages governed by local real estate law. It can also apply to proceeds or the like resulting from non-Article 9 security interests in personal property as long as the conditions of § 552(b) are met.

Be aware that the law of many states provides that a mortgagee's claim to rents is not effective against third parties, or even against the debtor in some instances, simply because the mortgage includes a rents clause and is recorded. Some further "perfection," "activation," or "enforcement" steps must be taken after the debtor's default, such as taking possession of the land, impounding the rents, obtaining appointment of a receiver to collect them, judicially sequestering the rents, or similar action. Courts have had difficulty deciding how to treat the mortgagee's interest in rents where, as is usually the case, the mortgagee has not taken the required steps before the debtor files bankruptcy:

---

39. However, § 362(b)(18) allows local property tax liens to attach to real property during the bankruptcy case. Consider also Section D.5. of this chapter, supra, § 546(b), and § 547(c)(6).

Several competing lines of authority have developed concerning whether Section 546(b) provides a means for post-petition perfection of a recorded rent assignment. There does not appear to be a clear majority view among the cases. The various approaches taken by courts may be generally summarized as follows.

(1) Section 546(b) does not permit the post-petition perfection of a pre-petition rent assignment. See In re Multi-Group III Ltd. Partnership, 99 B.R. 5, 9-11 (Bankr. D. Ariz. 1989). Recognition of an interest in rents post-petition, pursuant to Section 552(b), is premised on the existence of a right to rents prior to commencement of the case. Treating rents as cash collateral under Section 363(a) when state law requirements have not been satisfied improperly grants automatic perfection effect under Section 552(b) and precludes operation of the automatic stay. See also In re Wynnewood House Assocs., 121 B.R. 716, 724-27 (Bankr. E.D. Pa. 1990).

(2) Post-petition notice under Section 546(b) may be used to perfect a pre-petition rent assignment. Although acts to obtain possession are stayed, notice under this provision amounts to a constructive equivalent of such act if it is shown that outside bankruptcy the creditor would have been entitled to such relief provided 'relation back' effect exists under applicable state law. The security interest is considered 'perfected' as of the pre-petition recording date [of the mortgage] for purposes of Section 544, but enforceable only with respect to rents after the filing of the notice. See e.g. Casbeer v. State Federal Sav. & Loan Ass'n (In re Casbeer), 793 F.2d 1436 (5th Cir. 1986); Virginia Beach Federal Sav. & Loan Ass'n v. Wood, 97 B.R. 71 (N.D. Okla. 1988), aff'd, 901 F.2d 849, 853 (10th Cir. 1990); Saline State Bank v. Mahloch, 834 F.2d 690, 695-96 (8th Cir. 1987); Home Sav. Ass'n of Kansas City v. Woodstock Assocs. I (In re Woodstock Assocs. I), 120 B.R. 436, 447-48 (Bankr. N.D. Ill. 1990); In re National Real Estate Ltd. Partnership—II, 104 B.R. 968 (Bankr. E.D. Wis. 1989).

(3) Section 546(b) is not relevant because once recorded, a security interest in rents is effective against and notice to all persons as to the existence of the interest, regardless of whether the creditor is presently entitled to receive the rents, and such right is similarly recognized pursuant to Section 552(b). See e.g. Vienna Park Properties v. United Postal Sav. Ass'n (In re Vienna Park Properties), 976 F.2d 106 (2nd Cir. 1992); Tucson Partners, supra, 129 B.R. 614, 620, 624-25; In re Park at Dash Point L.P., 121 B.R. 850 (Bankr. W.D. Wash. 1990); Rancourt, supra, 123 B.R. at 148-49.

In re Polo Club Apartments Assocs. Ltd. P'ship, 150 B.R. 840, 851-52 (Bankr. N.D. Ga. 1993).

In 1994 Congress amended § 552(b) in order to "provide[ ] that lenders may have valid security interests in postpetition rents for bankruptcy purposes notwithstanding their failure to have fully perfected their security interests under applicable State law." 140 Cong. Rec. H. 10,768 (daily ed. October 4, 1994) (floor statement of Judiciary Committee Chairman Brooks). The idea was to overturn the result reached by courts following the first approach noted in the quote from *Polo Clubs*, including specifically the decision in *Multi-Group III,* supra. The amendment turned the prior § 552(b) into subsection 552(b)(1) and deleted all references to rents from it. The amendment then added a subsection to deal with rents, 552(b)(2); it tracks exactly the prior language of § 552(b) as applied to rents, with three changes.

The first change added language with regard to hotel and motel revenues from use or occupancy of rooms or other public facilities. The new language validates mortgage clauses which create liens on such revenues. Courts had split on whether such revenues were "rents" under the prior language of § 552(b) and thus had split on whether mortgage liens on such revenues from postpetition operation of hotels and motels would be recognized.

The second change was to add the phrase "and notwithstanding section 546(b)." The idea seemed to be that § 546(b) stood in the way of mortgagees' postpetition rent interests being validated where the mortgagees had not taken possession of the land or taken any of the other steps required by state law to "perfect" or enforce the lien on the rents. In fact, cases like *Multi-Group III* had simply held that § 546(b) did not apply to rents clauses and thus could not assist the mortgagee. Presumably "and notwithstanding section 546(b)" was intended to mean that the lien is valid even if § 546(b) does not assist the mortgagee. Finding it to mean that would have been a stretch for courts inclined to seek and apply the plain meaning of statutory language, except for the third change made by the 1994 amendments.

The third change was to delete the reference to "applicable non-bankruptcy law." Section 552(b)(1) still looks to applicable nonbankruptcy law in determining whether a lien will be permitted to attach to postpetition property. But § 552(b)(2) does not. Thus state law requirements for "perfection" or "activation" of a rents clause need not be met. See In re Wrecclesham Grange, Inc., 221 B.R. 978 (Bankr. M.D. Fla. 1997); In re Fairview-Takoma Ltd. P'ship, 206 B.R. 792 (Bankr. D. Md. 1997).[40]

It is important to note that the court can limit the security interest in proceeds and rents (including hotel revenues). Section 552(b) validates such interests "except to any extent that the court, after notice and a hearing and based on the equities of the case, orders otherwise."

Problem 8-23

> 1. Kick Credit enjoys a security interest in Foam Corporation's inventory and receivables, present and after-acquired. After bankruptcy, Foam sells inventory that was Kick Credit's collateral before bankruptcy, and receivables result from the sale. Kick Credit's security interest does not extend to the receivables on the basis of the after-acquired property clause in the security agreement. The postpetition effectiveness of that clause was killed by § 552(a). Yet, because the receivables were acquired upon the disposition of

---

40. Rents clauses raise other difficult issues. For example, suppose the mortgagee is undersecured. If the debtor in possession has $20,000 in net rents (rents after payment of operating expenses) in its hands when the plan is to be confirmed, is the mortgagee's secured claim increased by that $20,000, or is the secured claim limited to the value of the real property? If net rents are paid to the mortgagee during the case, does that reduce the amount of the secured claim or simply constitute a payment out of the mortgagee's collateral? See Beal Bank v. Waters Edge Ltd. P'ship, 248 B.R. 668, 684-86 (D. Mass. 2000) (holding that the secured claim is increased by the amount of the rents and that rents paid over during the case should not be subtracted, but noting split between "addition" approach and "subtraction" approach").

Kick Credit's collateral, they are proceeds under state law, and Kick Credit's security interest would continue to some extent in these proceeds by operation of state law even in the absence of an after-acquired property clause. The state law security interest in the proceeds is valid and enforceable in the debtor's bankruptcy because of § 552(b), notwithstanding § 552(a) and § 549(a).

   a.   Is the result different if the receivables are generated by sales of inventory acquired after bankruptcy?

   b.   Is the result different if the receivables are paid and the proceeds are deposited in the debtor in possession's checking account?

   c.   Should it matter in applying § 552 that the inventory was produced using not only Kick Credit's collateral but also other chemicals and goods belonging to or paid for by the estate, and using labor paid for by the estate? If that occurs, the unsecured creditors' share of the estate is reduced to the extent that Kick Credit's security interest enlarges.

2.   In any event, do the account debtors (the people who owe the receivables) risk liability to the estate if they pay the accounts to anyone other than the estate? Is doing so a violation of the stay? Does Commerce Bank face the same risks if, after bankruptcy, it pays checks that Foam has drawn against Foam's cash account at the Bank? See §§ 362(a), 542(b)-(c).

3.   First Bank's recorded real estate mortgage on Foam's Philadelphia factory covers not only the land, buildings, and fixtures but also rents, profits and the like. Is the Bank entitled to any of Foam's accounts receivable that are generated before or after bankruptcy? Suppose Foam leases part of the mortgaged property to suppliers who store goods there. Is the Bank entitled to their pre- and postpetition rent payments?

4.   To the extent a secured party obtained a security interest under an after-acquired property clause before the bankruptcy filing, § 552(a) does not invalidate the security interest. Suppose Foam Corporation gave its patent attorneys a prepetition retainer that was not exhausted during the bankruptcy case, leaving Foam Corporation with a right to a refund of a portion of the retainer. That right would be classified as a general intangible under U.C.C. Article 9. Kick Credit's security agreement includes an after-acquired property clause, and it extends to general intangibles. Would § 552 prevent Kick Credit from claiming a security interest in the right to a refund of the unused portion of the retainer? See In re E-Z Serve Convenience Stores, Inc., 299 B.R. 126 (Bankr. M.D.N.C. 2003), aff'd, 318 B.R. 637 (M.D. N.C. 2004).

5.   Suppose Foam Corporation sold a piece of unneeded equipment to Acme Corporation in a nonordinary course sale without providing the "notice and a hearing" required by § 363(b). Kick Credit's perfected security interest in the equipment would survive the sale. See U.C.C. §§ 9-201(a) (stating that security interest is effective against purchasers of collateral except as otherwise provided in U.C.C.), 9-317(b) (providing that a buyer of goods who lacks knowledge of *unperfected* security interest takes free of it), 9-320(a) (providing that buyer of goods in *ordinary course of business* takes free of security interest created by seller). Will Kick Credit's security interest survive Foam Corporation's avoidance of the sale under § 549? See In re Crowell, 304 B.R. 255 (W.D.N.C. 2004).

Chapter Nine

Claims Against the Estate

A. INTRODUCTION

The term "claim" is defined very broadly in the Bankruptcy Code. A claim is a

> right to payment, whether or not such right is reduced to judgment, liquidated, unliquidated, fixed, contingent, matured, unmatured, disputed, undisputed, secured, or unsecured.

Section 101(5)(A). The term "claim" also includes various rights to equitable remedies; we discuss equitable remedies as claims in Chapter Sixteen. See § 101(5)(B). When it is determined that a particular claim will be recognized in a bankruptcy case, we say that the claim has been "allowed." See § 502. The term "debt" is defined to mean simply "liability on a claim." Section 101(12). Note that the definitions of "claim" and "debt" are not limited in time; a right to payment does not have to arise prepetition to be a "claim" or for the liability on it to be a "debt." Thus postpetition obligations such as the estate's obligation to pay wages for postpetition services are "claims" that give rise to "debts."[1] On the other hand, the term "creditor" includes only holders of claims that arose at the time of or before the order for relief,[2] which of course in a voluntary case is simply the time of filing of the petition. See §§ 101(10) and 301.

Under § 501(a), a creditor may file a proof of claim. The proof of claim is simply "a written statement setting forth a creditor's claim." Rule 3001(a). It should conform substantially to Official Form 10, and if the claim is based on a writing (such as a contract or judgment), a copy of the writing should be attached. Rule 3001(a) and (c). If the creditor claims a security interest in property of the estate, proof of perfection of the security interest (such as a copy of a financing statement stamped "filed" or a copy of a mortgage stamped "recorded") also should be attached. Rule 3001(d). (Claim forms are available from the clerk of the bankruptcy court, in many stationery stores, and on the web at various sites, including www.uscourts.gov/bankform.) Most claims in bankruptcy are allowable and will not be the subject of any dispute. Thus the Code provides that

---

1. Under § 503(b)(1) such a claim is entitled to allowance as an administrative expense, and thus will be a second priority claim under § 507(a)(2). (Administrative expense claims were § 507(a)(1) first priority claims prior to enactment of the 2005 BAPCPA, which elevated domestic support claims—none of which will be owed by a debtor that is a business entity—to first priority.) Note that under § 1129(a)(9)(A) the holder of a § 507(a)(2) claim is entitled to payment in full in cash on the effective date of the plan, unless the holder agrees to other treatment.

2. Holders of claims that are *treated* as having arisen before the order for relief—such as claims based on rejection of unassumed executory contracts—are also "creditors." See §§ 101(10)(B) and 502(g).

a claim for which a proof of claim has been filed is deemed allowed, unless a party in interest objects;[3] that saves the court the trouble of having to pass on the allowability of the vast majority of claims.

In fact, many creditors in chapter 11 cases need not even file a proof of claim. A proof of claim will be *deemed filed* if the claim is listed on the debtor's schedule of liabilities and is not listed as disputed, contingent, or unliquidated. See § 1111(a) and Rule 3003(b). Nonetheless—and even though filing a proof of claim can cause a creditor to lose its right to jury trial on counterclaims by the estate[4]—a creditor is probably best advised to go ahead and file a proof of claim before the bar date set by the court under Rule 3003(c)(3).[5] That may be simpler and cheaper than going to the courthouse to inspect the list of creditors to make sure that the claim is listed correctly and is not listed as disputed, contingent, or unliquidated, if the schedule of liabilities is not available online.[6]

---

3. Note that the Code does not set any deadline for objection to claims. In the absence of a court order setting a deadline, objections may be made years into the bankruptcy case. The absence of an objection at any particular point in the case is not, therefore, a sure indication that the claim ultimately will be allowed. There is some authority that objections must be made before plan confirmation, if the proof of claim is filed in time to allow such an objection. See Adair v. Sherman, 230 F.3d 890, 895 n.6 (7th Cir. 2000) (holding in analogous chapter 13 situation that failure to object to claim before confirmation of plan precluded issue of validity of claim being litigated in later Fair Debt Collection Practices litigation, and "respectfully choos[ing] not to follow those cases allowing post-confirmation objections to proofs of claims to be filed even though the proof of claim itself was filed sufficiently in advance of the confirmation hearing"). But see In re Hovis, 356 F.3d 820 (7th Cir. 2004) (arguing that claim preclusion applies only in a separate suit, as in *Adair*, not in the bankruptcy case itself, and noting that no "statute or rule require[s] objection to precede confirmation"); In re Shank, 315 B.R. 799 (Bankr. N.D. Ga. 2004). At least where the plan provides for continuing bankruptcy court jurisdiction to determine objections to claims, confirmation of the plan should not preclude postconfirmation objection to a claim, unless the plan itself allows the claim. See Hosp. and Univ. Prop. Damage Claimants v. Johns-Manville Corp. (In re Johns-Manville Corp.), 7 F.3d 32 (2d Cir. 1993).

4. See Granfinanciera, S.A. v. Nordberg, 492 U.S. 33, 57-58, 109 S. Ct. 2782, 2798-99, 106 L. Ed. 2d 26, 50-51 (1989).

5. In a chapter 11 case, the consequences are severe for a creditor whose claim is not deemed filed and who does not timely file a proof of claim. The claim is disallowed under § 502(b)(9), and under Rule 3003(c)(2) the creditor "shall not be treated as a creditor with respect to such claim for the purposes of voting and distribution." If the failure to file on time is due to excusable neglect, the court may permit a late-filed claim to have effect. See Rule 9006(b)(1). Where notice of the bar date is not clear, the Supreme Court has interpreted the standard for excusable neglect in Rule 9006(b)(1) rather leniently. See Pioneer Inv. Servs. Co. v. Brunswick Assocs. Ltd. P'ship, 507 U.S. 380, 113 S. Ct. 1489, 123 L. Ed. 2d 74 (1993). An administrative claimant should also file a request for allowance of administrative expense by the bar date set by the court. See § 503(a).

6. The court may require the debtor to notify creditors whose claims have been scheduled as disputed, contingent, or unliquidated so that they will know that they need to file proofs of claim. However, creditors cannot count on getting such notice. In addition, even if a scheduled claim is not scheduled as disputed, contingent, or unliquidated, the debtor may have put the wrong amount of claim in the schedule. To be sure the claim will be allowed in the right amount, the creditor must either confirm that it has been scheduled correctly or else file a proof of claim. Even if the amount is scheduled correctly, the debtor may later amend the schedules to alter the amount or status of the claim.

Filing a proof of claim also protects the creditor if the case is converted to chapter 7, as very often happens. In chapter 7 a proof of claim must be filed for the claim to be allowed, and only holders of allowed claims share in proceeds of liquidation of the estate's assets. See § 726(a) and Rule 3002(a). Creditors who do not file a proof of claim in the chapter 11 case may often forget to file one in the chapter 7 case before the passing of the new bar date, which will likely be 90 days after the conversion to chapter 7.[7] A proof of claim filed in the chapter 11 case is still effective after conversion to chapter 7. See Rule 1019(3).

Of course not all claims are undisputed. The mere filing of a bankruptcy petition does not eliminate disputes that may have existed over whether the debtor is liable to various entities and in what amounts. The automatic stay generally prevents those disputes from being resolved outside the bankruptcy process, but they still must be resolved to determine who is entitled to share in the value of the estate and in what amount. The resolution can be either by a determination on the merits, or, if that would cause undue delay, by estimation of the amount of the claim under § 502(c). For purposes of determining who is entitled to vote on the plan (and the size of the claim that can be voted), the court can determine the merits, estimate the claim under § 502(c), or temporarily allow the claim under Rule 3018 "in an amount which the court deems proper." If the court temporarily allows the claim for purposes of voting, then resolution of the dispute may occur after confirmation of the plan, either by a determination on the merits or by estimation.

The allowance or disallowance of a claim (other than a "personal injury tort or wrongful death" claim) is a kind of "core proceeding" under 28 U.S.C. § 157, which governs the bankruptcy judge's jurisdiction. That jurisdiction derives from the *district court's* bankruptcy jurisdiction. The district court has exclusive jurisdiction of cases under title 11(including chapter 11 cases), exclusive jurisdiction of property of the estate, and "original but not exclusive jurisdiction of all civil proceedings arising under title 11, or arising in or related to cases under title 11." 28 U.S.C. § 1334(a), (b), and (d). Under 28 U.S.C. § 157(a), the district court may refer to the *bankruptcy judges* for the district "any or all cases under title 11 and any or all proceedings arising under title 11 or arising in or related to a case under title 11." District courts have ample work and thus uniformly have adopted rules referring bankruptcy matters to the bankruptcy judges for their district, which "constitute a unit of the district court to be known as the bankruptcy court for that district." 28 U.S.C. § 151. To the extent such matters are referred to the bankruptcy court

---

7.   In cases that start out as chapter 7 cases the bar date is 90 days after the first date set for the meeting of creditors, which will be between 20 and 40 days after the order for relief. See Rules 2003(a), 3002(c). When a chapter 11 case is converted to chapter 7, it appears that the bar date is 90 days after the date of the conversion, assuming the case had not previously been converted from chapter 7 to chapter 11. See Rule 1019(2). Note that in chapter 7 a holder of a claim who has notice of the case but who does not file a proof of claim by the bar date will not be entitled to any distribution until and unless all the timely filed claims are paid in full. See § 726(a)(2)-(3) and (b).

by the district court, a bankruptcy judge may hear, determine, and enter final orders and judgments in *core proceedings* arising under title 11 or arising in a title 11 case. See 28 U.S.C. § 157(b)(1).[8] A bankruptcy judge may hear proceedings that are not core proceedings but that are otherwise related to a title 11 case, but in such a proceeding the bankruptcy judge does not enter a final order or judgment. Rather, the bankruptcy judge submits proposed findings of fact and conclusions of law to the district court, which considers them and enters final judgment after reviewing *de novo* any part of them to which specific objection is made. See 28 U.S.C. § 157(c)(1); Rule 9033.

The allowance or disallowance of claims by a bankruptcy judge is considered a purely equitable (as opposed to legal) proceeding. Thus there is no right to jury trial under the Seventh Amendment. See Langenkamp v. Culp, 498 U.S. 42, 44-45, 111 S. Ct. 330, 331, 112 L. E. 2d 343 (1990); Katchen v. Landy, 382 U.S. 323, 336-37, 86 S. Ct. 467, 476-77, 15 L. Ed. 2d 391 (1966).

However, in the particular instance of personal injury tort and wrongful death claims, there is a right to jury trial to liquidate the claims for purposes of distribution—although, as we discuss later in this chapter, the bankruptcy judge can determine the claim for purposes of voting on a chapter 11 plan. Under 28 U.S.C. § 157(b)(2)(B), core proceedings do not include the "liquidation or estimation of contingent or unliquidated personal injury tort or wrongful death claims against the estate for purposes of distribution." Further, 28 U.S.C. § 157(b)(5) requires the district court to order that personal injury tort and wrongful death claims be tried in district court. Finally, 28 U.S.C. § 1411(a) provides that neither the Judicial Code (title 28) nor the Bankruptcy Code (title 11) "affect any right to trial by jury that an individual has under applicable nonbankruptcy law with regard to a personal injury or wrongful death tort claim." Thus the final determination of personal injury and wrongful death claims is withdrawn from the equitable bankruptcy proceedings in which there would be no right to jury trial, and the claimant's right to jury trial is to be determined "under applicable nonbankruptcy law" as if there were neither bankruptcy courts (set up by title 28) nor a bankruptcy statute (contained in title 11). Applicable nonbankruptcy law includes the Seventh Amendment; thus the personal injury tort or wrongful death claimant has a right to jury trial. See King, *Jurisdiction and Procedure Under the Bankruptcy Amendments of 1984*, 38 VAND. L. REV. 675, 702-06 (1985).[9]

---

8.   Review of orders and judgments in core proceedings is by way of appeal to the district court or to a bankruptcy appellate panel made up of three bankruptcy judges (if all parties consent) or directly to the court of appeals for the circuit (on proper certification and with the authorization of the court of appeals). See 28 U.S.C. § 158(a)-(d). Final orders entered by district courts or bankruptcy appellate panels in such appeals are appealable to the court of appeals for the circuit. See 28 U.S.C. § 158(d)(1).

9.   There is conflicting authority whether a bankruptcy court has power to decide dispositive pretrial motions, such as motions for summary judgment, in personal injury and wrongful death cases. See Stranz v. Ice Cream Liquidation, Inc. (In re Ice Cream Liquidation, Inc.), 281 B.R. 154 (Bankr. D.

For claims other than personal injury or wrongful death claims, not only is there no right to jury trial, there is not even a right to a full-fledged trial by the bankruptcy judge. Claims are allowed or disallowed by way of what is essentially a motion procedure in the chapter 11 case rather than by way of a separate action. Rule 3007 does not require more than thirty days' notice of the hearing at which the claim will be allowed or disallowed; that contrasts sharply with the years of discovery and preparation time typical in many civil cases outside of bankruptcy. The parties have the right to take discovery, and thus the bankruptcy court often will give the parties more than 30 days to prepare for the hearing, but nonetheless the process is greatly compressed and accelerated compared to the ordinary civil case.

Even that compressed and accelerated process may take so long that reorganization of the debtor would be delayed by waiting for a final resolution of all claims issues. That may be the case if there are many disputed claims or if the claims are contingent on future events. Thus Congress gave the bankruptcy courts authority to *estimate* contingent and unliquidated prepetition claims to avoid undue delay. Section 502(c). A prepetition claim may be estimated for various purposes: to determine voting rights of the creditor, to determine the contents and feasibility of a plan (for example, the amount of value that must be set aside on account of claims that are unliquidated or disputed), and (except for personal injury tort and wrongful death claims) to determine the amount of the claim for purposes of making a distribution to the creditor under the plan. Each of those purposes raises issues, including issues concerning the methodology of estimation, which we consider later in this Chapter.[10] In addition, § 502(c) authorizes the bankruptcy court to estimate the dollar value of equitable rights that are determined to be claims.

B. FOAM CORPORATION'S CREDITORS

We can see how § 502 and related sections operate by considering several of Foam Corporation's creditors. We assume that Foam Corporation has just filed its chapter 11 petition.

Conn. 2002) (discussing cases and deciding to lift stay to allow litigation to proceed in state court); In re Dow Corning Corp., 215 B.R. 346 (Bankr. E.D. Mich. 1997) (discussing cases and holding that bankruptcy court had authority to decide motion for summary judgment), supplemented, 215 B.R. 526 (recommending that the district court withdraw the reference and decide the summary judgment motion because of district court's greater familiarity with issue of admissibility of scientific evidence). Nevertheless, any trial of such a case would not fall within the bankruptcy court's core jurisdiction.

10. As noted above in the text, the bankruptcy court cannot estimate personal injury tort or wrongful death claims *for purposes of determining the distribution to which the claimant is entitled.* See 28 U.S.C. § 157(b)(2)(B) and (b)(4). From the point of view of the debtor, that limitation on the bankruptcy court's authority to estimate claims causes great difficulty in cases involving mass torts, such as the A.H. Robins case and the various asbestos manufacturers' cases, which are discussed later in this chapter. Note that estimation of the amount of claims for purposes of permitting their holders to vote on a plan is not expressly prohibited. Later in this chapter we consider that point along with Rule 3018(a), which permits temporary allowance of claims for voting purposes.

1. TC (a typical prepetition unsecured trade creditor)

Consider a typical unsecured trade creditor, TC, who delivered goods to Foam Corporation five months before the petition date under a contract for sale of the goods. Suppose the contract called for payment of the $10,000 price one month after delivery and for 2% per month simple interest on late payments. What is TC's allowable claim?

The introductory language in § 502(b) requires the court to "determine the amount of such claim * * * as of the date of the filing of the petition" and to allow the claim in that amount except as provided in various subparts of 502. That means TC's claim will include interest only up to the date of the petition filing; postpetition interest will not accrue on the claim. As of the date of filing of the petition, TC had a right to payment of the $10,000 price plus four months of interest at 2% per month, which would be $200 per month. Thus TC's claim "as of the petition date" would seem to be $10,800.

On the other hand, 2% interest per month may exceed the permissible finance charge under state law. Under § 502(b)(1) the claim will not be allowable to the extent that it is unenforceable under any agreement or under applicable law. Thus the validity of claims generally is governed by nonbankruptcy law—typically state law. If under state law TC only could collect 1% interest per month despite the 2% figure in the contract, then TC's claim would be $10,400. If under state law TC could not collect any interest because the 2% was higher than the lawful rate, then TC's allowable claim would be simply the $10,000 principal amount.

TC did not obtain a lien to secure the debt, and thus TC's claim, whatever its amount, is an *unsecured* claim. In addition, because TC's claim does not qualify as a priority claim under § 507, we refer to it as a *general* unsecured claim.

2. First Bank (a real property secured creditor)

Now consider First Bank. Foam Corporation owes First Bank $700,000 for a prepetition loan that is secured by real estate mortgages on two of Foam Corporation's plants. As we have seen, the introductory language in § 502(b) requires the court to determine the amount of First Bank's claim "as of the date of the filing of the petition" and to allow the claim in that amount. Assuming that Foam Corporation has not missed any of its mortgage payments and that the petition is not filed on the day that the next payment is due, there will be nothing immediately due on the mortgage as of the petition date. Nevertheless First Bank's claim "as of the date of the filing of the petition" is not zero, because even an *unmatured* right to payment is a claim as claim is defined in § 101(5)(A). First Bank has a right to be paid the $700,000 in the future and thus has a $700,000 claim in Foam Corporation's bankruptcy. In a sense then, bankruptcy operates to accelerate debts that are due in the future; they are considered claims even though unmatured.

One could argue that First Bank has a claim not only for the $700,000 principal amount of the mortgage debt but also for all of the hundreds of thousands of dollars of interest that Foam Corporation had agreed to pay it over the future years of the mortgage. First Bank does have an unmatured right to be paid that interest in the future.[11] Whether or not the right to be paid interest in the future is a claim, First Bank does not have an *allowable* claim for that interest, at least not under § 502(b). Under § 502(b) the determination of the amount of the allowable claim is made "as of the date of the filing of the petition." Further, under § 502(b)(2), a claim is not allowable to the extent that it is for "unmatured interest." Interest that had not yet accrued as of the petition date would not be "matured" as of that date; thus postpetition interest is not an allowable part of a claim under § 502.[12] On the other hand, unpaid interest that had accrued as of the petition filing date will be part of the allowed claim.[13]

That is not, however, the end of the story. Under § 506(b), *postpetition* interest accrues as part of an *oversecured* creditor's allowable claim. Thus, if the value of the real estate securing First Bank's $700,000 claim is more than $700,000, postpetition interest on the claim will be allowed, even though it was unmatured as of the petition date. Interest stops accruing, though, once the claim equals the value of the collateral. Thus, for example, if the real estate is worth $780,000, First Bank could accrue up to $80,000 in postpetition interest on its $700,000 claim. The allowed claim of an

---

11. The right to the future interest is probably not only unmatured but also "contingent." A contingent right to payment is one that will not become enforceable until an event occurs. If Foam Corporation has the right to prepay the mortgage, First Bank would become entitled to future interest payments only if Foam Corporation did not prepay the loan. Thus the right to payment of the interest depends on the occurrence of an event: the failure of Foam Corporation to prepay the loan. However, a right to payment is still a claim even though it is contingent. Section 101(5)(A).

12. In addition, § 502(b)(2) disallows unmatured interest that is in the form of "original issue discount." Many kinds of debt instruments are issued to lenders in exchange for a loan of less than the instrument's face amount. For example, the lender may lend the borrower $700 in exchange for issuance of a five year note with no stated interest rate but with a face value of $1000. Interest on the $700 that was borrowed is not paid currently but rather will be due at the end of five years, when the borrower will be obligated to pay the lender $1000. The $300 profit represents five years of interest on the $700 loan and is called the "original issue discount." If the borrower files a bankruptcy petition one year after issuing such a bond, the borrower has had the use of the $700 for only one year—not five—and hence most of the $300 in original issue discount has not been earned; most of it will therefore be "unmatured interest" that will be disallowed under § 502(b)(2). The court will need to determine the contract interest rate (which is called the discount rate) to determine how much of the original issue discount was earned as of the petition date. Financial tables or a financial calculator allow us to determine that for an original loan of $700 to grow to $1000 due over five years, the interest rate must be about 7.4% per year, assuming it is compounded annually. Thus the lender's claim would be about $752, because one year's interest on $700, at 7.4%, is about $52.

13. Thus, if First Bank were owed $700,000 in principal, and $4,000 in unpaid interest had accrued at the time Foam Corporation filed its chapter 11 petition, First Bank's allowable claim under § 502(b) would be $704,000. However, we assume in our examples that First Bank's claim as of the petition date, including any accrued but unpaid interest, is $700,000.

undersecured creditor—or an unsecured creditor like TC—will not accrue postpetition interest under 506(b).[14]

If First Bank is undersecured—if the real estate collateral is worth less than the $700,000 amount of First Bank's allowed claim—§ 506(a) divides First Bank's claim into two claims. The allowed claim of First Bank is a secured claim only to the extent of the value of the collateral; the remainder, if any, of the allowed claim is an unsecured claim. See § 506(a).

Real estate lenders sometimes agree to lend "without recourse" or "on a nonrecourse basis," meaning that, if the debtor defaults, the lender agrees to look only to the property for payment by way of foreclosure and not to look to the debtor personally. In addition to cases in which loans are nonrecourse by agreement, there also are "antideficiency" statutes in some states, which in some cases make real estate mortgage loans nonrecourse by law. Outside bankruptcy, a lender who has lent without recourse will have no right to payment from the debtor other than the right to foreclose on the property. If the foreclosure sale does not bring enough money to pay off the debt—if there is a deficiency—the lender cannot collect the deficiency from the debtor.

In a case under a chapter other than chapter 11, the nonrecourse lender's claim would be disallowed under § 502(b)(1) to the extent the claim exceeds the value of the property, because to that extent the claim is not enforceable under the terms of the loan agreement or under applicable law. Thus, if First Bank lent on a nonrecourse basis (as we will assume for the remainder of this section), and if its $700,000 mortgage were secured by property with a value of only $500,000, under § 502(b)(1) $200,000 of First Bank's claim seemingly would be disallowed. First Bank would have a $500,000 allowed secured claim and no allowed unsecured claim.

That would be the result in a chapter 7 bankruptcy case, *but § 1111(b) leads to a different result in a chapter 11 case,* if the estate retains the collateral. Under § 1111(b), nonrecourse claims usually are treated as if there were recourse. Thus in Foam Corporation's chapter 11 case, First Bank would probably have not only a $500,000 secured claim but also a $200,000 unsecured claim.[15]

---

14. Note, however, that in a chapter 7 liquidation, if all allowed claims can be paid in full with money left over—if the debtor is solvent on a liquidation basis—then holders of unsecured claims are entitled to be paid interest out of the surplus. See § 726(a)(5). The best interests of creditors test will prevent a chapter 11 plan from being confirmed unless all dissenting unsecured creditors with claims in impaired classes receive at least as much value under the plan as they would receive in a chapter 7 liquidation. See § 1129(a)(7). If the liquidation value of the assets would permit payment of postpetition interest in a chapter 7 case, then the chapter 11 plan must give the creditors postpetition interest in order to satisfy the best interests of creditors test. We discuss this further below in Chapter Fourteen.

15. Note also that, whatever chapter the debtor files under, a nonrecourse lender is considered to have a "claim against the debtor" as that term is used in the Code—even though the debtor is not personally liable on the loan—because of the rule of construction contained in § 102(2). See Johnson v. Home State Bank, 501 U.S. 78, 111 S. Ct. 2150, 115 L. Ed. 2d 66 (1991). As a result, the nonrecourse lender is also a "creditor" as that term is defined in § 101(10).

Section 1111(b) is designed to soften the effect of bankruptcy on the bargain made by First Bank as a nonrecourse lender. First Bank bargained either to be paid in full or to have the opportunity to foreclose on the collateral; in exchange, First Bank was willing to lend on a nonrecourse basis. First Bank was willing even to risk that a future downturn in real estate values might make it undersecured. On Foam Corporation's default First Bank could foreclose, bid the entire amount of its debt at the foreclosure sale, and obtain the property if no one else was willing to bid more. First Bank then could hold the property until the real estate market recovered, and then sell it for a better price.

Because the chapter 11 process takes away what nonrecourse lenders like First Bank bargain for, Congress thought it would be too harsh to enforce the nonrecourse agreement in chapter 11 cases. First Bank will not be paid in full in the bankruptcy case and may never be permitted to foreclose. In fact, Foam Corporation can keep the property and cram down a plan over First Bank's objection by giving First Bank deferred payments with a present value equal to the court-determined value of the real estate (perhaps a very low value if the real estate market is depressed or if the court accepts a "low-ball" appraisal). See § 1129(b)(2)(A)(i). Thus First Bank gets neither full payment nor the right to foreclose. Congress thought it would not be fair to allow bankruptcy to upset the bargain in that way and then to hold the lender to its agreement that the loan would be nonrecourse. See Tampa Bay Associates, Ltd. v. DRW Worthington, Ltd. (In re Tampa Bay Associates, Ltd.), 864 F.2d 47 (5th Cir. 1989). Thus nonrecourse debts are treated as if they were recourse debts under § 1111(b).

There are two statutory exceptions, however, to the rule that nonrecourse claims are treated in chapter 11 cases as if there were recourse. Under the first exception, found in § 1111(b)(1)(A)(i), First Bank will not be treated as if it had recourse if it elects the application of § 1111(b)(2). As we discuss in Chapter Fifteen of this text, § 1111(b) entitles many undersecured creditors to elect to have their entire claims treated as secured. If First Bank made the election, then it would be treated as having a $700,000 secured claim and no unsecured claim, even though the real estate collateral is worth only $500,000. However, the election is not nearly as favorable for First Bank or other undersecured creditors as it may appear.

Under the second exception, found in § 1111(b)(1)(A)(ii), First Bank will not be treated as if it had recourse if the real estate on which it has the mortgage is sold during the case under § 363 or if the plan provides for sale of the real estate. In either case, First Bank will be entitled to bid the full amount of its debt at the sale—see, e.g., § 363(k). Thus First Bank either will be paid in full (out of the payment made by a bidder who bids more than the amount of the debt) or First Bank will be the high bidder and will end up owning the real estate. Either of those outcomes fully protects the bargain First Bank made, and thus it is appropriate to hold First Bank to its agreement that the loan would be nonrecourse. Section 1111(b)(1)(A)(ii) only deals expressly with cases in which the property is sold under § 363 or sold under the plan, not cases in which a secured creditor obtains relief from the stay and the property is sold at a foreclosure sale. However, the courts have extended the exception to such cases, because the nonrecourse lender who is permitted to foreclose has obtained all of what it bargained for. See *Tampa Bay Associates,* supra, 864 F.2d 47. Thus, if First Bank obtains relief from stay and forecloses, it will not be entitled to be treated as if it had recourse, and thus will not have an unsecured claim in the case (assuming the loan was nonrecourse).

3. William Gruff (insider, lender, employee, guarantor, lessor)

Now consider William Gruff. As you will recall, Gruff owns 90% of Foam Corporation's stock, is the chairman of its board of directors and is its chief executive officer. Gruff also is a creditor of Foam Corporation in at least three ways, and perhaps four.

a. Gruff as Lender

Gruff lent Foam Corporation $3.2 million (unsecured), which has not been repaid. Recall that Gruff agreed to subordinate $1 million of his loan to the trade creditors' claims as part of the work out attempt. Thus it will make sense to think of Gruff as having two claims. He has a general unsecured claim for $2.2 million, plus any unpaid interest on that amount as of the petition date; that claim is equal in priority with the other general unsecured claims. Gruff's has a second general unsecured claim for $1 million, plus any unpaid interest on that amount as of the petition date; this second claim is subordinate to some of the other general unsecured claims.

b. Gruff as Unpaid Employee

For several months before the chapter 11 filing, Gruff was not paid the salary to which he was entitled under his five year employment contract with Foam Corporation. Gruff will have an allowable claim for that compensation or at least for some of it, plus a claim for damages for rejection of his employment contract, assuming Foam Corporation rejects it, as creditors will demand.[16] Under § 502(b)(4), Gruff's claim as an insider for compensation

---

16. We assume Foam Corporation breached Gruff's employment contract by not paying him the salary that was due him. Gruff, of course, is the one who decided not to pay his own salary, but not because it was not owing; rather he did not pay it because cash was short and there was a need to placate creditors. In addition, we assume that the creditors and other parties in interest would successfully demand that he cause Foam Corporation to reject his employment contract and that Foam Corporation would comply. If the contract is rejected, Gruff will have a general unsecured claim for the unpaid prepetition compensation and also for damages sustained by reason of the rejection, which constitutes a total breach of the contract. See §§ 365(g)(1) and 502(g). Section 502(b)(7) would then place an upper limit on the total claim that could be allowed: no more than one year's salary plus unpaid prepetition compensation, and in no event more than the total compensation left to be paid under the contract. (Thus, for example, if Gruff claims that termination of his contract somehow causes him consequential damages to his future earning capacity, such damages could not be used to inflate the amount of his claim beyond the total unpaid compensation under the contract.)

for services is not allowable to the extent it exceeds the reasonable value of
the services. On the positive side, $10,000 of Gruff's allowable claim for
prepetition compensation probably will be considered a priority wage claim
under § 507(a)(4).[17] In a chapter 7 case, Gruff's priority claim would have to
be paid in full before any payment would be made on claims with lesser
priority, including general unsecured claims. See § 726(a) and (b). In chapter
11, Gruff's priority wage claim will have to be paid in full unless Gruff
agrees to other treatment.[18]

c. Gruff as Guarantor

Third, Gruff guaranteed several of Foam Corporation's obligations,
including, for example, the trade debt owed to Tina Chemical Company. A
guarantor has a contingent claim against the debtor; if the guarantor pays the
debt or any part of it, the guarantor has a right of reimbursement against the
debtor. Thus Gruff has a contingent claim for reimbursement against Foam
Corporation, a claim that will become fixed (noncontingent) if and to the
extent that Gruff pays the guaranteed debts. Even though Gruff's claim is not
yet fixed, he still has a claim, because the definition of claim includes
contingent rights to payment.

Gruff initially might feel grateful that the Code considers him to have a
claim; he may think that he will receive something on account of that claim
under the plan. Gruff likely will change his mind when he finds out how such
contingent claims are treated under the Code. His contingent claim will not
be allowable; under § 502(e)(1)(B), because Gruff is liable along with Foam
Corporation on the debts that he guaranteed, Gruff's claim for reimbursement
is not allowable to the extent it is contingent.

Even assuming the contract will be rejected, Gruff is still entitled to be paid the reasonable
value of his postpetition services as an administrative expense of the reorganization. Indeed, Foam
Corporation may have authority as debtor in possession simply to pay Gruff for his services during
the reorganization at the contract rate. See this chapter at footnote 27.

17.   A few courts would limit the priority to those who served the debtor in subservient roles.
See, e.g., In re Comtec Indus., Inc., 91 B.R. 344, 346 (Bankr. E.D. Pa. 1988) (relying on limitation
of priority under old Bankruptcy Act). Most courts will follow the plain language of the Code, which
includes no such limitation. See, e.g., In re Wang Laboratories, Inc., 164 B.R. 404, 408 (Bankr. D.
Mass. 1994) (rejecting *Comtec Industries* approach of reading into former § 507(a)(3)—now
§ 507(a)(4)—all the limitations of the old Act); In re Jade West Corp., 53 B.R. 16, 17 (Bankr. D. Or.
1985) (holding that any employee, regardless of capacity, could qualify for wage claim priority).

The dollar amount of the § 507(a)(4) wage claim priority is adjusted for inflation every three
years. See § 104. The figure will be adjusted again no later than March 1, 2007, presumably to a
figure higher than $10,000. Note also that such a claim will qualify for § 507(a)(4) priority only to
the extent the compensation is for work done within 180 days before the earlier of the petition filing
date or "the date of the cessation of the debtor's business."

18.   If the class of priority wage claims accepts the plan, Gruff can be forced to accept deferred
payment of the wages with interest. If the class does not accept, Gruff is entitled to full payment on
the effective date of the plan. See § 1129(a)(9)(B). Of course, Gruff, as the person in control of the
debtor, will presumably be in agreement with whatever plan is proposed by the debtor.

That prevents double-dipping; if Gruff could have an allowed claim and Tina Chemical also could have an allowed claim, the estate would pay out double value on account of the debt owed to Tina Chemical. It is not fair to the other creditors for the Tina Chemical debt to receive a double share out of the estate just because Gruff guaranteed the debt. (Note that contingent claims are not in general subject to being disallowed just because they are contingent; however, the kinds of contingent claims that are disallowed under § 502(e)(1)(B) are very common and important.) Thus Gruff will have an allowable claim that can share in the distribution of value in bankruptcy only to the extent that he turns his contingent claim into a noncontingent claim by paying something on the guaranteed debts.[19]

Suppose Gruff pays part of Foam Corporation's debt to Tina Chemical. Gruff then will have an allowable, noncontingent claim for reimbursement. (To the extent Gruff pays Tina Chemical, Tina Chemical's claim in the case is reduced, and thus there is not a double-dipping problem in allowing Gruff's noncontingent claim.) Gruff still may not receive anything on account of his allowed claim under the chapter 11 plan. Under § 509(c), Gruff's allowed, noncontingent claim for reimbursement is subordinated to Tina Chemical's claim—any distribution Gruff would receive on account of his claim for reimbursement will go to Tina Chemical until Tina Chemical is paid in full.

Gruff's payment of part or all of the debt owed to Tina Chemical will give Gruff not merely a noncontingent, allowable claim for reimbursement but also an alternative claim by way of subrogation to Tina Chemical's rights. See § 509(a). Thus, to the extent Gruff pays Tina Chemical, Gruff is entitled to assert Tina Chemical's rights in the bankruptcy case. Unfortunately for Gruff, under § 509(c) that claim by way of subrogation is subordinated to Tina Chemical's claim just as is Gruff's claim for reimbursement, until Tina Chemical is paid in full. Further, subrogation to Tina Chemical's rights does not give Gruff anything his claim for reimbursement would not give him. Tina Chemical's claim is a mere general unsecured claim just like Gruff's claim for reimbursement; thus Gruff gets no better rights by way of subrogation to Tina Chemical's rights than he gets by asserting his own claim for reimbursement. (Thus Gruff will have an unsecured claim for subrogation or for reimbursement, whichever he chooses to assert; he cannot "double-dip" by asserting both. See §§ 502(e)(1)(C) and 509(b)(1)(A).)

---

19. In the meantime, Gruff can file a proof of claim on Tina Chemical's behalf under § 501(b) and Rule 3005 to make sure that Tina Chemical will participate in Foam Corporation's chapter 11 distribution. To whatever extent Tina Chemical receives payment under the plan, the debt will be paid, and Gruff's liability on the guarantee will be reduced. (Of course Gruff, as the person in control of the debtor, can make sure that Tina Chemical's claim is properly listed on the schedules filed in the chapter 11 case. Thus Gruff does not actually have to file a claim on behalf of Tina Chemical to ensure that Tina Chemical participates in the chapter 11 distribution. Many guarantors and other kinds of co-debtors will not be in a position to make sure that debts are properly scheduled; hence § 501(b) and Rule 3005 are valuable tools.)

There is, however, a debt Gruff guaranteed that is at least in part secured. Gruff guaranteed Foam Corporation's obligations to Kick Credit, which are secured by an Article 9 security interest in all or almost all of Foam Corporation's personal property. Just as with the guarantee of the debt to Tina Chemical, Gruff has a contingent claim for reimbursement with respect to his guarantee of the debt to Kick Credit. Of course, under § 502(e)(1)(B), that claim will not be allowable until and unless Gruff pays something to Kick Credit on Foam Corporation's debt, so that Gruff has a noncontingent claim for reimbursement. More importantly, once Gruff does pay something to Kick Credit, Gruff will have the right to be *subrogated* to Kick Credit's rights, to the extent of Gruff's payment. See § 509(a). That means that to the extent Gruff pays the debt, Gruff will be permitted to assert the rights that Kick Credit could have asserted in the bankruptcy, including its rights as holder of a secured claim. Now we see the benefits of subrogation; Gruff's claim for reimbursement is a mere general unsecured claim, but his claim by way of subrogation is (at least in part) a secured claim.

Thus, for example, if Gruff pays off the entire debt owing to Kick Credit, Gruff will have an allowable claim by way of subrogation that is just the same as the allowable claim that Kick Credit had. Suppose Kick Credit's total claim is $6 million and the collateral securing the debt is worth $5 million; then, when Gruff pays off Kick Credit, Gruff will have a $5 million secured claim and a $1 million unsecured claim on account of the $6 million debt, just as Kick Credit had before it was paid off by Gruff. It must be noted, though, that if Gruff pays only part of the debt owing to Kick Credit, then, under § 509(c), Gruff's claim by way of subrogation is subordinated to Kick Credit's claim until and unless Kick Credit ultimately is paid in full. Thus Gruff's subrogation rights do not benefit Gruff until some combination of payments by Gruff and value received by Kick Credit under the chapter 11 plan result in full payment to Kick Credit.

d.   Gruff As Trustee of Lessor Gruff Family Trust

Fourth, and finally, the Gruff Family Trust (with Gruff as trustee) owns the Richmond, California plant and leases it to Foam Corporation. Gruff, as trustee of the trust, is entitled to be paid rent at the rate specified in the lease for the period from the filing of the petition up until Foam Corporation either assumes or rejects the lease. See § 365(d)(3). The trust probably has an unsecured claim for any unpaid rent for the period before the filing of the petition. (As we saw in Chapter Seven, some courts may say that the trust has no claim for that prepetition rent until Foam Corporation either assumes or rejects the lease.) On the other hand, if Foam Corporation assumes the lease, the trust is entitled to have any defaults in payment of rent cured under § 365(b), and the obligations under the lease will become administrative expenses. Because the lessor is an entity that exists for the benefit of insiders, the court may scrutinize the lease carefully before allowing Foam Corporation to assume it. If the court refuses to permit Foam Corporation to assume the lease, then it will be rejected automatically under § 365(d)(4) 120 days after the petition filing date (or at the end of any extension of that 120 day period, which may not exceed 90 days).

If the lease is rejected, the trust will have a general unsecured claim for the unpaid prepetition rent and also for damages for breach of the remainder of the lease, beginning with the date on which it was rejected. Section 502(b)(6) limits the allowable amount of lessors' claims when a lease is rejected, so that a huge claim for breach of a long term lease will not overwhelm the other claims in a case. If the lease had ten years remaining when Foam Corporation filed its chapter 11 petition, then the trust's allowed claim could not exceed an amount equal to one and one-half year's rent plus any unpaid rent due at the time the petition was filed. See § 502(b)(6) (placing cap on allowed claim equal to the *greater* of one year's rent or rent for 15% of the remaining period of the lease, plus unpaid rent due before the earlier of the petition date or the date on which possession was returned to lessor). If the trust has a security deposit, will the amount of the deposit count against the cap? See AMB Prop., L.P. v. Official Creditors (In re AB Liquidating Corp.), 416 F.3d 961 (9th Cir. 2005).

    e.   Gruff as Creditor—Other Issues

Creditors may seek to have Gruff's claims—whether as lender, employer, guarantor, or lessor (as trustee of the Gruff Family Trust)—*equitably subordinated* to all the other claims in the case. See § 510(c). The holder of a claim that has been equitably subordinated to other claims is not entitled to any distribution until those other claims have been paid in full. We discuss equitable subordination in Chapter Ten of this text. For now it is enough for the student to know that the case law generally does not support equitable subordination of claims of insiders unless the insiders have engaged in inequitable conduct that harms other creditors. Nevertheless, some bankruptcy courts are very reluctant to permit the claims of insiders such as Gruff to be treated on an equal basis with the claims of other creditors (or to be given priority under an applicable subsection of § 507(a) or under subrogation principles) even if the insiders have not engaged in inequitable conduct. Further, other creditors may refuse to support a plan under which Gruff's claims are treated as equal to or senior to their claims; after all, they will think, Gruff is responsible for Foam Corporation's financial distress and for their losses.

It is also important to see that all of Gruff's claims, including contingent claims for reimbursement that are disallowed under § 502(e)(1)(B), will be discharged by confirmation of a plan. See § 1141(d).[20] Thus Gruff will not be

---

20.   In the unlikely event that Foam Corporation reaffirms a debt to Gruff under § 524(c), the debt would not be discharged. Gruff is in control of Foam Corporation and would seem to be able to cause Foam Corporation to reaffirm the debts owed to him, but he must exercise control consistently with his fiduciary duty of loyalty to the estate and creditors. Unless there are very good reasons for a reaffirmation, any attempt by Gruff to cause Foam Corporation to reaffirm the debts to him would seem to violate that duty and would almost certainly lead to an order for appointment of a trustee or more drastic action by the court.

able to seek reimbursement from the reorganized Foam Corporation if, after confirmation of the plan, he is forced to pay debts that he guaranteed. Of course, Foam Corporation's discharge does not discharge Gruff from his liability as a guarantor to Tina Chemical, to Kick Credit, or to anyone else. See § 524(e). (The question whether Foam Corporation's *plan* may in some way release Gruff from liability on the guarantees is discussed below in Chapter Sixteen.) Thus Gruff runs the risk of getting nothing in Foam Corporation's bankruptcy case on account of his contingent claims for reimbursement while still having to pay the creditors whose debts he guaranteed.

4. Charlie Consumer (holder of a warranty on a Foam Corporation waterbed)

Now consider Charlie Consumer, the owner of a Foam Corporation "Waveless" waterbed purchased a year before the petition date. Assume the waterbed carried a manufacturer's five year limited warranty against defects in materials and workmanship and that the exclusive remedy under the warranty was that Foam Corporation would repair or replace the waterbed if it failed during the five year period due to a defect. Does Charlie have a claim? Initially, it does not appear that Charlie has any right to payment even if the waterbed is defective, but only a right to repair or replacement. However, as those students who have taken a U.C.C. or Sales course know, Charlie does have a contingent right to payment. If the waterbed failed due to a defect and if Foam Corporation refused to repair or replace it, the exclusive limited remedy would fail of its essential purpose under U.C.C. § 2-719(3); Charlie then would have a right to damages for breach of warranty. Thus Charlie has a contingent claim.

Note that Charlie's contingent claim is not affected by § 502(e)(1)(B) the way Gruff's contingent claims are affected. Charlie's claim is not for reimbursement or contribution with respect to a debt owed by both Charlie and Foam Corporation, and thus § 502(e)(1)(B) does not operate to disallow Charlie's contingent claim.

Foam Corporation *should* list Charlie and the thousands of other holders of contingent waterbed warranty claims in its list of creditors or schedule of liabilities. See Rule 1007(a)(1) and (b). (That will permit the court clerk to send notice of the bankruptcy filing to Charlie and the other warranty holders pursuant to Rule 2002(f), or to order Foam Corporation to send or publish notice.) Even assuming Foam Corporation complies with this onerous duty and lists Charlie in its schedules as the holder of a claim, she or someone acting for her still will have to file a proof of claim in order for her claim to be allowed. Foam Corporation will list her claim as contingent, and thus the listing of her claim will not be deemed to be a filing of a proof of claim. See § 1111(a).

If Charlie does file a proof of claim—or if Foam Corporation files a proof of claim for her under § 501(c)—her claim should be allowed, but in what amount? It is an unliquidated claim because its amount is neither fixed nor readily ascertainable. That would be true even if the waterbed had already failed as of the time of claims allowance, since there could be a dispute as to the reasonable cost of repairs and the amount of any resulting water damage to other property. Since the waterbed has not yet failed, Charlie's claim is also contingent, which creates a further problem in determining the amount of the claim; the waterbed may or may not fail at all during the warranty period, and thus there is no way of knowing what amount of damages if any ultimately will be suffered by Charlie. Congress provided the way out of this dilemma by authorizing the court to estimate unliquidated or contingent claims, where liquidating them or waiting to determine whether the contingency occurs would cause delay in the case. See § 502(c); Salsburg & Williams, *A Statistical Approach to Claims Estimation in Bankruptcy*, 32 WAKE FOREST L. REV. 1119 (1997). The court has wide discretion in choosing how to estimate the claim and can use whatever method is best suited to the circumstances. Bittner v. Borne Chemical Co., 691 F.2d 134 (3d Cir. 1982). In estimating the claim,

> the court is bound by the legal rules which may govern the ultimate value of the claim. For example, when the claim is based on an alleged breach of contract, the court must estimate its worth in accordance with accepted contract law. However, there are no other limitations on the court's authority to evaluate the claim save those general principles which should inform all decisions made pursuant to the Code.

Id. at 135-36.

Thus Foam Corporation's case does not need to await the expiration of all the waterbed warranties on waterbeds sold prepetition; the court can estimate those contingent claims and let the case proceed. The court could hear evidence on the likelihood of future failure of Waveless waterbeds and of the likely cost of repair and other damages that could flow from failure. The court then could estimate Charlie's claim (and the thousands of similar claims of other waterbed owners) as equal to the percentage chance of a failure during the warranty period times the average repair costs and other damages that failure would entail. A bankruptcy court set up just such a procedure in one chapter 11 case involving several hundred thousand contingent automobile rust-proofing warranty claims. In re Rusty Jones, Inc., 143 B.R. 499 (Bankr. N.D. Ill. 1992), rev'd on other grounds sub nom. Beatrice Co. v. Rusty Jones, Inc. (In re Rusty Jones, Inc.), 153 B.R. 535 (N.D. Ill. 1993).[21]

Of course, the expense of the estimation procedure, in which thousands of waterbed owners must be notified of the estimation hearing, may be substantial. That expense, together with the expense of printing and mailing disclosure

---

21. Although the court in *Rusty Jones* did not do so, it might make sense for the court to discount the contingent claims to present value. If, on average, waterbeds that turn out to be defective are expected to fail two years after the effective date of the plan, then perhaps the claims should be discounted by two years' worth of interest. On the other hand, repairs may cost more in two years due to inflation; discounting the claims by a market rate of interest—a rate that includes a component for inflation—therefore may not be proper.

statements to and soliciting ballots from those thousands of claim holders may nearly equal the cost of providing continuing warranty coverage. Further, if Foam Corporation does not continue to provide warranty coverage to prepetition purchasers of its waterbeds, the customer backlash and negative publicity may seriously damage Foam Corporation's ability to sell more waterbeds and damage the value of its Waveless waterbed patent and trademark.

Thus it may well make sense for Foam Corporation to file a proof of claim on behalf of the waterbed owners and to ask court permission to provide continuing waterbed warranty protection during the case. Cf. Still v. United Pipe and Supply Co. (In re W.L. Jackson Mfg. Co.), 50 B.R. 498 (Bankr. E.D. Tenn. 1985) (holding that prepetition offer by debtor manufacturer to reimburse retailer for water heater warranty claims paid by retailer was not revoked by filing of chapter 11 petition and that postpetition claims of retailer might have administrative priority). Perhaps the doctrine of necessity would permit the court to give Foam Corporation permission to provide continuing waterbed warranty protection. See Chapter Four of this text above. Perhaps Foam Corporation could reaffirm its warranty obligations under § 524(c)[22] or argue that the warranties are executory contracts that Foam Corporation may assume.[23] In addition, Foam Corporation's plan could classify the warranty holders' contingent claims separately and provide that their rights will be unaffected by the case. Foam Corporation might persuade the bankruptcy judge to grant a motion under Rule 3017(d) ordering that its disclosure statement need not be sent to holders of claims in such an unimpaired class.

A court sensitive to the costs of providing notice to the warranty holders might easily determine that, since the warranty holders' rights are completely preserved under these approaches, notice to the warranty holders is not necessary, or that notice can be given by publication in appropriate newspapers. See Rule 2002(*l*). Ordinarily, service by publication would be suspect under the Due Process clause where the addresses of the persons to be served are available and where the proceeding could result in deprivation of life, liberty or property. See Mullane v. Central Hanover Bank & Trust

---

22. However, courts have held that a reaffirmation under § 524(c) cannot be accomplished by unilateral act of the debtor; agreement of the creditor—in this case the warranty holders—seems to be required. See In re Turner, 156 F.3d 713 (7th Cir. 1998). Traditionally, reaffirmations could be unilateral and did not require mutual assent. See Restatement (Second) of Contracts §§ 17(2) & 83. Obtaining agreement of the warranty holders could be very expensive.

23. However, it is doubtful that the warranties can be considered executory contracts. There does not seem to be any performance remaining on Charlie's part that would benefit Foam Corporation or the estate. In order to be entitled to warranty coverage, Charlie will have to refrain from abusing or misusing the product, but that refraining provides no value to Foam Corporation or to the estate. Ordinarily, where the debtor has little or nothing to gain from further performance by the nondebtor party, there would be no point in allowing the debtor the option to assume the contract. Thus there is a strong argument that such warranties are not executory contracts. See In re GEC Indus., Inc., 107 B.R. 491 (Bankr. D. Del. 1989); Countryman, *Executory Contracts in Bankruptcy: Part I,* 57 MINN. L. REV. 439, 451 and 451 n.55 (1973); contra In re Smith Jones, Inc., 26 B.R. 289 (Bankr. D. Minn. 1982).

Co., 339 U.S. 306, 70 S. Ct. 652, 94 L. Ed. 865 (1950). Here Foam Corporation may have a file with the names and addresses of waterbed purchasers who have returned warranty registration cards. Nevertheless, notice by publication should suffice where giving actual notice would be unreasonably expensive and where the rights of the warranty holders are preserved. See Fogel v. Zell, 221 F.3d 955, 962-63 (7th Cir. 2000).

5. Vanessa Victim (alleged victim of toxic fumes)

Now consider Vanessa Victim. Vanessa was the owner of a mobile home that had Foam Corporation polyurethane foam insulation in its walls. Vanessa claims that the foam gave off fumes, which, she claims, eventually caused her to develop a serious respiratory disease. She also claims that the mobile home is now worth very little because the continuing problem with the fumes makes it unusable. Her attorney demanded $500,000 from Foam Corporation, which replied that it did not believe that any harmful fumes were given off by the foam insulation. Her attorney was about to file suit against Foam Corporation for her alleged personal injuries and for the diminution in value of the mobile home, when Foam Corporation filed its chapter 11 petition.

Vanessa's claims are unliquidated and disputed,[24] but nonetheless they are claims. Foam Corporation has an obligation to list Vanessa in its schedule of creditors, but her claims will be listed as unliquidated and disputed; hence the listing of the claims will not cause proofs of the claims to be deemed filed. See § 1111(a). Thus Vanessa will need to file a proof of each claim. To be entitled to vote or to receive a distribution in the chapter 11 case, she will have to obtain allowance of her claims over Foam Corporation's inevitable objections. (For purposes of voting, Vanessa can seek temporary allowance of her claim in an amount "which the court deems proper." Rule 3018(a).)

As discussed above, Vanessa will be entitled to jury trial of her personal injury claim in the district court, unless the court in its discretion abstains to allow a state court trial. Vanessa will not be entitled to jury trial of her property damage claim, which will be allowed or disallowed by the bankruptcy judge. The judge cannot estimate her personal injury claim (at least not for purposes of distribution) but if necessary can estimate her property damage claim (for any and all purposes).

If the court chooses to estimate her property damage claim, the court could estimate the likelihood that she would prevail at trial (say, 10%), estimate the amount of her damages (say, $10,000), and then multiply the two to get the

---

24. They are not contingent claims, because there is no future event that must occur or not occur for Vanessa to have a right to payment; Foam Corporation either has committed an actionable tort against her or it has not. Of course, as with any obligation, Vanessa could not force Foam Corporation to pay her anything without going to court, but that should not be seen as making her claims contingent. See Mazzeo v. U.S. (In re Mazzeo), 131 F.3d 295 (2d Cir. 1997). Some courts, however, take the questionable view that disputed claims are necessarily contingent on a court determination of liability. See, e.g., In re Baird, 228 B.R. 324 (Bankr. M.D. Fla. 1999).

estimated value of her claim (10% times $10,000 equals $1,000). On the other hand, the court would not have to use this probabilistic approach and would appear to have discretion to estimate her claim as being worthless (zero dollars) if the court concluded that she would not be likely to prevail at trial. See Bittner v. Borne Chem. Co., 691 F.2d 134 (3d Cir. 1982).[25]

C. ADMINISTRATIVE PRIORITY CLAIMS

In the previous section we considered only "creditors" of Foam Corporation, who, by definition, hold claims that arose before the order for relief or at the time of the order for relief, which in Foam Corporation's case, as in all voluntary cases, is the time of the filing of the petition. See §§ 101(10) and 301. Claims also arise after the order for relief. For example, employees who provide postpetition services have postpetition claims for their wages or salaries; vendors who sell goods to the debtor on credit after the filing of the petition also have postpetition claims.

Postpetition claims often qualify for administrative expense status under § 503(b), as will likely be true in the case of those examples. Claims entitled to administrative expense status include "the actual, necessary costs and expenses of preserving the estate, including wages, salaries, or commissions for services rendered after the commencement of the case." Section 503(b)(1)(A). Thus claims of employees for compensation for postpetition services will be administrative expenses. In addition, "the words 'preserving the estate' include the larger objective * * * of operating the debtor's business with a view to rehabilitating it." Reading Co. v. Brown, 391 U.S. 471, 475, 88 S. Ct. 1759, 1762, 20 L. Ed. 2d 751 (1968) (construing § 64a of the old Bankruptcy Act). For example, as we saw in Chapter Four, if the debtor in possession obtains unsecured credit or incurs unsecured debt in the ordinary course of business, that credit or debt will be an administrative expense. See § 364(a). Thus vendors who sell goods to the debtor on credit will obtain an administrative expense priority as long as the debtor's purchase is in the ordinary course of its business (or is authorized by the court).

Holders of administrative expense claims are permitted to request payment pursuant to § 503(a) and to seek allowance of their claims under § 503(b). Often there is no need to resort to the court at all, because the debtor will simply pay the claimant. The debtor in possession (or trustee, if one is appointed) is authorized to operate the business under § 1108 and to use the property of the estate in the ordinary course of business without notice or a hearing under § 363(c)(1). That authorization includes the right to use the estate's cash to pay ordinary course postpetition expenses of the business without any need to seek court approval. See, e.g., U.S. ex rel. Harrison v.

---

25. The court approved a zero valuation *for voting purposes.* That prevented holders of very doubtful claims from controlling the voting on the plan of reorganization. *For purposes of distribution* the claims were to be determined in pending litigation. Thus *Bittner* could be distinguished.

Estate of Deutscher (In re H & S Transp. Co.), 115 B.R. 592 (M.D. Tenn. 1990) (holding that trustee was authorized to pay for needed supplies and to pay employee salaries, insurance premiums, maintenance costs, and other costs without providing notice and a hearing).[26] There is even authority that prepetition officers and directors who continue to serve the debtor postpetition may be paid for their postpetition work without notice and a hearing, at least if their compensation is not increased. See In re All Seasons Indus., Inc., 121 B.R. 822 (Bankr. N.D. Ind. 1990).[27]

All courts agree, however, that attorneys and other professionals may not be paid by the debtor in possession or trustee for their work in connection with the reorganization of the debtor without approval of the court. As we saw in Chapter Two, the debtor's attorneys and other professionals are entitled to compensation from the estate for such services only if their employment is approved by the court under § 327. Sections 328 and 330 govern the award of compensation; § 331 permits professionals to seek interim compensation every 120 days (unless the court permits more frequent applications). Section 503(b)(2) provides that such awards of compensation are allowable administrative expenses without any further requirements.

Compensation for nonprofessional services are governed by § 503(b)(1)(A)(i). The section speaks generally to compensation for services rendered in connection with the business and gives administrative expense status to "the actual, necessary costs and expenses of preserving the estate including—wages, salaries, and commissions for services rendered *after the commencement of the case*." (Emphasis supplied.) Compensation for *prepetition* services and other prepetition costs and expenses is not specifically included as an administrative expense by § 503(b)(1)(A); in fact, it would seem to be excluded by the requirement that administrative priority expenses be necessary to preserve the estate. The estate does not come into existence until the petition is filed, and thus prepetition costs and expenses can hardly be said to be necessary to preserve the estate. See 2 Epstein, Nickles & White, BANKRUPTCY § 7-11 at 303. Thus it would seem that only postpetition claims can qualify. See In re Abercrombie, 139 F.3d 755 (9th Cir. 1998); In re Sunarhauserman, Inc., 126 F.3d 811 (6th Cir. 1997).[28] Even

---

26. Of course if the cash is cash collateral of a secured party, consent of the secured party or court authorization is needed before it may be spent in the ordinary course. See § 363(c)(2).

27. Local court rules in some districts, however, provide that no compensation may be paid to officers or directors without approval of the court or of the U.S. Trustee. See, e.g., Local Bankruptcy Rule 2014-1(1) of the Central District of California.

28. There are a few limited exceptions, contained in § 503(b)(3) and (b)(4), to the rule that only postpetition expenses can qualify for administrative priority. A creditor is entitled to administrative priority for actual and reasonable expenses incurred in filing an involuntary bankruptcy petition; reasonable compensation for the creditor's attorneys and other professionals will also have administrative status. Id. The same is true for a creditor and associated professionals who take action in connection with prosecution of a criminal offense relating to the business or property of the debtor. Id. When the role of a custodian (such as a receiver or assignee for benefit of creditors) is superseded by the filing of a bankruptcy case, so

postpetition claims can qualify as administrative expenses under § 503(b)(1)(A), it would seem, only to the extent that the incurring of the obligations was necessary to preserve the estate.

We are thus left with two questions. Did the claim arise postpetition? Was the incurring of liability on the claim necessary to preserve the estate? If the answer is yes to both, then the claim is entitled to administrative expense status. If not, then the claim is not entitled to administrative expense, at least not under § 503(b)(1)(A).

Turning to the second question first, there are conflicting lines of authority as to how we determine whether the incurring of a liability was necessary to preserve the estate. Should we say that the attempt to reorganize the debtor is undertaken for purposes of preserving the estate (in particular its going concern value) and hence any liability incurred in the course of the attempt to reorganize is necessarily a cost or expense of preserving the estate? That would be consistent with the Supreme Court's decision in Reading Co. v. Brown, 391 U.S. 471, 88 S. Ct. 1759, 20 L. Ed. 2d 751 (1968), in which liability for the negligent actions of the reorganizing debtor's agents was held to be an administrative expense. Or should we say that only those costs and expenses that directly benefit the estate are in fact necessary for its preservation? Several circuits have taken this narrow approach. See Microsoft Corp. v. DAK Indus. (In re DAK Indus.), 66 F.3d 1091 (9th Cir. 1995); NL Indus. v. GHR Energy Corp., 940 F.2d 957 (5th Cir. 1991); Employee Transfer Corp. v. Grigsby (In re White Motor Corp.), 831 F.2d 106 (6th Cir. 1987); Trustees of Amalg. Ins. Fund v. McFarlin's, Inc., 789 F.2d 98 (2d Cir. 1986); Cramer v. Mammoth Mart, Inc. (In re Mammoth Mart, Inc.), 536 F.2d 950 (1st Cir. 1976). Cf. Ford Motor Credit Co. v. Dobbins, 35 F.3d 860 (4th Cir. 1994) (discussed below); Pa. Dep't of Envtl. Resources v. Tri-State Clinical Lab., Inc., 178 F.3d 685 (3d Cir. 1999) (holding that criminal fine for improper disposal of blood was not an expense ordinarily incident to operating business and thus was not an administrative expense).

Consider, on the other hand, In re N.P. Mining Co., 963 F.2d 1449 (11th Cir. 1992), in which the court held that a civil fine for improper strip mining was an administrative expense, even though it did not benefit the estate. The court reached that result even though it did not think that *Reading* or cases involving toxic waste cleanup required it; the fine was noncompensatory, would not be used to benefit health or safety, and would not be used to bring any property of the debtor into compliance with the law. But under 28 U.S.C. § 959(b) the debtor in possession was obligated to comply with general laws. Thus civil penalties arising from operation of the business were obligations of the reorganizing company, and hence administrative expenses.

---

that the custodian is required under § 543 to turn over the assets to the bankruptcy trustee, the custodian's actual and reasonable expenses (including prepetition expenses) are entitled to administrative status, as is reasonable compensation for professionals who assisted the custodian. Id.

In addition, the First Circuit has held that damages from postpetition operation of a nuisance were administrative expenses, giving *Reading* a fairly broad reading:

> That courts have found some resilience in *Reading* even beyond the field of torts is well illustrated by Carter-Wallace, Inc. v. Davis-Edwards Pharmacal Corp., 443 F.2d 867, 874 (2nd Cir. 1971), in which the Second Circuit, in setting aside a temporary injunction in favor of a patentee against a debtor in a Chapter 11 proceeding, noted that the patentee, if the patent's validity was subsequently sustained, would have a first priority claim. Summarizing the facts in *Reading*, Judge Friendly wrote for the court, "Damages for infringing a patent in the course of sales made for profit would seem an a fortiori case for priority." Id. So, too, is this case an even stronger one for priority than was *Reading*. The debtor in this case *deliberately* continued a violation of law month after month presumably because it was more lucrative for the business to operate outside the zoning ordinance than within it. If fairness dictates that a tort claim based on negligence should be paid ahead of pre-reorganization claims, then, a fortiori, an intentional act which violates the law and damages others should be so treated.

In re Charlesbank Laundry, Inc., 755 F.2d 200, 203 (1st Cir. 1985); accord Cumberland Farms, Inc. v. Fla. Dep't of Envtl. Prot., 116 F.3d 16 (1st Cir. 1997) (holding that under *Reading*, fundamental fairness required that civil penalty with regard to operation of underground petroleum storage tanks be considered an administrative expense). Cf. Tex. Comptroller v. Megafoods Stores, Inc. (In re Megafoods Stores, Inc.), 163 F.3d 1063 (9th Cir. 1998) (holding that statutory interest on sales taxes not remitted when due would be given administrative priority because of benefit estate received by utilizing the funds); In re Good Taste, Inc., 317 B.R. 112 (Bankr. D. Alaska 2004) (holding that under *Reading* fundamental fairness required that award of attorneys' fees against trustee be given administrative expense priority, where statute trustee had invoked in § 544(b) action provided for fees to the prevailing party).

Returning now to the first question, in order to determine whether a claim is a postpetition claim, we must have some way of determining when claims are considered to arise. That is not as simple as it may appear. Courts have had great difficulty articulating a single standard for determining when claims arise.

Further, the question of when a claim will be considered to have arisen has great importance beyond the issue of whether the claim may be entitled to administrative expense priority. The discharge that a debtor is likely to receive on confirmation of a plan includes all claims *that arose before the date of confirmation*. Under § 1141(d)(1)(A), except to the extent the plan or the confirmation order provides otherwise, confirmation of a chapter 11 plan discharges the debtor from all "debts" that arose before the date of confirmation, that is, from all liability on claims that arose before that date.[29]

---

29. However, debtors who are individuals (natural persons, flesh and blood human beings, as opposed to corporations or partnerships) are not discharged from debts that would not be dischargeable in a chapter 7 case, such as debts for money obtained by fraud. See §§ 1141(d)(2) and

Thus postpetition debts are discharged along with prepetition debts owed to creditors. Any debt that arose before the date of confirmation—any liability on a claim arising before that date—is discharged, whether or not the holder of the claim sought to participate in the case by filing a proof of claim, whether or not the claim was allowed, and whether or not the holder of the claim accepted the plan. See § 1141(d)(1)(A). *However, claims that do not arise until after the confirmation date are not discharged.*

There are many situations in which preconfirmation conduct by the debtor—such as distribution of a defective product—injures a tort victim after the confirmation date or causes injuries that are manifested only after the confirmation date. Is the tort victim's claim a preconfirmation claim or a postconfirmation claim? If it is a preconfirmation claim, it will be discharged under § 1141(d) (subject to possible constitutional due process limitations) even though the victim may have had no real opportunity to participate in the chapter 11 case or to share in the value distributed by the plan. If it is a postconfirmation claim, the claim will not be discharged; the victim (and perhaps many other similarly situated victims) will be able to sue the reorganized debtor. The result will be that the value of the stock and debt distributed to creditors in the chapter 11 plan will be reduced. It may even be likely that the reorganized debtor would again face financial distress; that prospect would doom the chapter 11 case by preventing the court from making the required finding of feasibility under § 1129(a)(11).

Although it would seem that a tort claimant would be better off having a postconfirmation claim, the opposite may be true. If the debtor is a corporation, and if the prospect of postconfirmation suits leads to the debtor being liquidated instead of reorganized, tort victims whose claims arise after the liquidation will be hurt the most; they will not share in the proceeds of the liquidation and will be left with a worthless claim against a nonexistent debtor. Cf. Ohio v. Kovacs, 469 U.S. 274, 285, 105 S. Ct. 705, 710-11, 83 L. Ed. 2d 649, 659 (1985).

If the victim is injured (or the injury manifests itself) after the filing of the petition but before confirmation, there is also a key issue that turns on when the claim will be considered to have arisen. The automatic stay prohibits "any act to collect, assess, or recover a claim against the debtor that arose before the commencement of the case." Section 362(a)(6). If the tort victim's claim arose prepetition, the stay prohibits the filing of an action; if it arose postpetition, the automatic stay will not apply to the filing and prosecution of an action to judgment.

All of these issues come into stark relief in mass tort cases. The next section of this Chapter focuses on such cases and on the effect of these issues on Foam Corporation.

523(a)(2). On the other hand, if the chapter 11 plan is a liquidating plan and the debtor does not engage in business after consummation of the plan, the only kind of debtor that would need a discharge would be an individual, and thus under such circumstances only individuals obtain a discharge of any debts. See §§ 1141(d)(3) and 727(a)(1). The discharge and other consequences of plan confirmation are discussed further in Chapter Sixteen of this text.

D. CLAIMS ISSUES IN MASS TORT CASES

In re UNR Industries, Inc.
United States District Court, Northern District of Illinois, 1984
45 B.R. 322

WILLIAM T. HART, District Judge.

The Official Creditor's Committee of Asbestos-Related Plaintiffs ("Committee") and Joseph Newton, an individual asbestos claimant, have moved for an order allowing some 17,000 asbestos claims against UNR, the debtor in this case, to proceed to trial. * * *

[T]he subsection on which the Committee and Newton rely, is [28 U.S.C.] § 157(b)(5), which states

> The district court shall order that personal injury tort and wrongful death claims shall be tried in the district court in which the bankruptcy case is pending, or in the district court in the district in which the claim arose, as determined by the district court in which the bankruptcy case is pending.

* * * [T]he Act clearly requires that these asbestos claims be tried in district court rather than bankruptcy court.[30] UNR makes several arguments to avoid the plain meaning of § 157(b)(5) but none are persuasive. First, UNR argues that the trial § 157(b)(5) refers to is not a full-blown adversary proceeding but only a "summary hearing." No reason is given for reading the phrase "shall be tried" in this fashion and this Court can think of none. District courts do not conduct "summary hearings" and UNR points to no statute or rule that either authorizes this departure from normal practice or explains what procedures constitute a "summary hearing." * * *

UNR's remaining argument concerns the wisdom of liquidating the asbestos claims through trial. The parties are certainly free to agree to a dispute-resolution procedure that does not involve trial, and UNR may be correct that some such procedure would be best for all concerned. However, this Court is not free to disregard the command of § 157(b)(5) that any *judicial* proceeding take the form of trial in the district court. * * *

[T]he Committee argues § 157(b)(5) specifies that estimation of such claims are not core proceedings and therefore the bankruptcy court has no power to estimate those claims. Since those claims obviously *must* be estimated if the bankruptcy proceedings are to go forward, the Committee concludes that the trials mandated by § 157(b)(5) must have been meant to serve as the estimation method for those claims and therefore those trials should begin immediately.

In response, UNR points out that § 157(c)(1) allows the bankruptcy judge to in effect act as a magistrate for non-core proceedings. However, to conclude that § 157(c)(1) authorizes the bankruptcy judges to act as a magistrate with respect to these asbestos claims for all purposes would render § 157(b)(5) a nullity, which as already noted is a result to be avoided. Therefore, the Committee is correct that § 157(b)(5) must take effect at *some* point before final distribution of the asbestos claims.

---

30. [Footnote 3 in original:] A brief filed by Commercial Union Insurance Co. argues that to avoid violating constitutional limits on federal jurisdiction this Court must abstain, under [28 U.S.C.] § 1334(c)(1), in favor of the state courts in those asbestos claims that lack diversity. In view of this Court's disposition of these motions, however, that question need not be decided at this time.

In choosing the beginning of the estimation process as that point, however, the Committee has overlooked the express terms of § 157(b)(2)(B). That section does not exclude from the definition of core proceedings estimation of personal injury and wrongful death claims for *all* purposes, but only "for purposes of distribution." Estimation of such claims for other purposes, such as "confirming a plan" (§ 157(b)(2)(B)), apparently remains a core proceeding for the bankruptcy judge. It is therefore not necessary to order trials now so that these claims can be valued; the presently proceeding study by Towers, Perrin, Foster & Crosby can, in both the statutory and empirical senses, fulfill that function.

The Committee also offers several policy reasons why the trials should begin now. Estimating these asbestos claims would require at least a hearing, asserts the Committee, and therefore allowing the bankruptcy judge to estimate the claims will not be any more efficient than ordering district court trials. This contention both understates the time and expense of trials and overstates the time and expense of the estimation process. Even should Judge Toles decide the Towers study is insufficient to accurately estimate asbestos claims and that some sort of hearing is necessary, there is no reason to believe 17,000 hearings must be held to get an accurate enough picture of the debtor's liability to asbestos victims.

The Committee also argues that trials should begin now so that when distribution time comes these plaintiffs can collect their due immediately rather than waiting until a trial can be had and concluded. This Court is certainly sympathetic to the plight of asbestos victims, but is persuaded that ordering the parties to trial makes no sense until there is at least some indication of the debtor's financial health and some reason to believe that the time and expense of trials will not simply deplete the estate and leave these plaintiffs and the other creditors with empty judgments. The Committee's final argument is that it would be unfair to allow the bankruptcy court to estimate these claims for purposes of developing a plan because that court may undervalue the claims "so that the trials to which such plaintiffs are entitled would serve only as a measure of their pro-rata share of a pie which is much too small." Committee's Reply Brief at 22. Contrary to the Committee's implication, this Court has the utmost confidence in the bankruptcy court's ability to accurately estimate the asbestos claims. Moreover, in this regard the asbestos claimants stand in the same position as any creditor with an unliquidated claim. Though problems of accuracy in estimation may be greater when personal injury and wrongful death claims are involved, nothing in the Act indicates such claims are to be treated differently from other unliquidated claims for purposes other than distribution. * * *

NOTES

1. For what purposes may a bankruptcy court estimate personal injury and wrongful death claims according to the court? What is the effect on the claimants' rights of each kind of estimation?

2. Do you share the district court's confidence in the bankruptcy court's ability to estimate accurately the amount of the claims? Are the claimants denied an integral part of their right to jury trial if the plan of reorganization sets aside a fixed amount of money to pay personal injury and wrongful death claims based on the bankruptcy court's estimate of those claims? Or does the right to jury trial only give the plaintiff to the right to receive a judgment based on a jury verdict, not the right to collect it or to collect any particular percentage of it? Does an estimation that creates a cap on

the amount that can be distributed to tort claimants constitute a prohibited estimation for purposes of distribution? Consider the very different Manville and A.H. Robins experiences, as described in the following case and notes.

Kane v. Johns-Manville Corporation
United States Court of Appeals, Second Circuit, 1988
843 F.2d 636

JON O. NEWMAN, Circuit Judge:

This appeal challenges the lawfulness of the reorganization plan of the Johns-Manville Corporation ("Manville"), a debtor in one of the nation's most significant Chapter 11 bankruptcy proceedings. Lawrence Kane * * * and the group of 765 individuals he represents (collectively "Kane") are persons with asbestos-related disease who had filed personal injury suits against Manville prior to Manville's Chapter 11 petition. * * *

Background

Prior to its filing for reorganization in 1982, Manville was the world's largest miner of asbestos and a major manufacturer of insulating materials and other asbestos products. Beginning in the 1960's, scientific studies began to confirm that exposure to asbestos fibers over time could cause a variety of respiratory diseases, including certain forms of lung cancer. A significant characteristic of these asbestos-related diseases is their unusually long latency period. An individual might not become ill from an asbestos-related disease until as long as forty years after initial exposure. Hence, many asbestos victims remain unknown, most of whom were exposed in the 1950's and 1960's before the dangers of asbestos were widely recognized. These persons might not develop clinically observable symptoms until the 1990's or even later.

As a result of the studies linking respiratory disease with asbestos, Manville became the target in the 1960's and 1970's of a growing number of products liability lawsuits. By the early 1980's, Manville had been named in approximately 12,500 such suits brought on behalf of over 16,000 claimants. New suits were being filed at the rate of 425 per month. Epidemiological studies undertaken by Manville revealed that approximately 50,000 to 100,000 additional suits could be expected from persons who had already been exposed to Manville asbestos. On the basis of these studies and the costs Manville had already experienced in disposing of prior claims, Manville estimated its potential liability at approximately $2 billion. On August 26, 1982, Manville filed a voluntary petition in bankruptcy under Chapter 11. From the outset of the reorganization, all concerned recognized that the impetus for Manville's action was not a present inability to meet debts but rather the anticipation of massive personal injury liability in the future.

Because future asbestos-related liability was the *raison d'etre* of the Manville reorganization, an important question at the initial stages of the proceedings concerned the representation and treatment of what were termed "future asbestos health claimants" ("future claimants"). The future claimants were persons who had been exposed to Manville's asbestos prior to the August 1982 petition date but had not yet shown any signs of disease at that time. Since the future claimants were not yet ill at the time the Chapter 11 proceedings were commenced, none had filed claims against Manville, and their identities were unknown. An Asbestos Health

Committee was appointed to represent all personal injury claimants, but the Committee took the position that it represented the interests only of "present claimants," persons who, prior to the petition date, had been exposed to Manville asbestos and had already developed an asbestos-related disease. The Committee declined to represent the future claimants. Other parties in the proceedings, recognizing that an effective reorganization would have to account for the future asbestos victims as well as the present ones, moved the Bankruptcy Court to appoint a legal guardian for the future claimants. The Bankruptcy Court granted the motion, reasoning that regardless of whether the future claimants technically had "claims" cognizable in bankruptcy proceedings, see 11 U.S.C. § 101[(5)], they were at least "parties in interest" under section 1109(b) of the Code and were therefore entitled to a voice in the proceedings. The Court appointed a Legal Representative to participate on behalf of the future claimants. Additionally, the Court invited any person who had been exposed to Manville's asbestos but had not developed an illness to participate in the proceedings, and two such persons appeared.

The Second Amended Plan of Reorganization resulted from more than four years of negotiations among Manville, the Asbestos Health Committee, the Legal Representative, the Equity Security Holders' Committee, and other groups interested in the estate.[31] The cornerstone of the Plan is the Asbestos Health Trust (the "Trust"), a mechanism designed to satisfy the claims of all asbestos health victims, both present and future. The Trust is funded with the proceeds from Manville's settlements with its insurers; certain cash, receivables, and stock of the reorganized Manville Corporation; long term notes; and the right to receive up to 20% of Manville's yearly profits for as long as it takes to satisfy all health claims. According to the terms of the Trust, individuals with asbestos-related disease must first try to settle their claims by a mandatory exchange of settlement offers with Trust representatives. If a settlement cannot be reached, the claimant may elect mediation, binding arbitration, or traditional tort litigation. The claimant may collect from the Trust the full amount of whatever compensatory damages he is awarded. The only restriction on recovery is that the claimant may not obtain punitive damages.

The purpose of the Trust is to provide a means of satisfying Manville's ongoing personal injury liability while allowing Manville to maximize its value by continuing as an ongoing concern. To fulfill this purpose, the Plan seeks to ensure that health claims can be asserted only against the Trust and that Manville's operating entities will be protected from an onslaught of crippling lawsuits that could jeopardize the entire reorganization effort. To this end, the parties agreed that as a condition precedent to confirmation of the Plan, the Bankruptcy Court would issue an injunction channeling all asbestos-related personal injury claims to the Trust (the "Injunction"). The Injunction provides that

---

31. [Footnote 1 in original:] The Plan provides for nine classes of claims and interests: administrative expenses (Class 1), secured claims (Class 2), asbestos property damage claims (Class 3), present asbestos health claims (Class 4), employee and non-asbestos material claims (Class 5), other unsecured claims (Class 6), interests of preferred stockholders (Class 7), interests of common stockholders (Class 8), and interests of certain individual plaintiffs in pending lawsuits (Class 9). Future asbestos health claimants are not part of any class but are treated as "other asbestos obligations" under the Plan and are subject to the same claims handling facility as the present health claimants in Class 4.

asbestos health claimants may proceed only against the Trust to satisfy their claims and may not sue Manville, its other operating entities, and certain other specified parties, including Manville's insurers. Significantly, the Injunction applies to all health claimants, both present and future, regardless of whether they technically have dischargeable "claims" under the Code. The Injunction applies to any suit to recover "on or with respect to any Claim, Interest or Other Asbestos Obligation." "Claim" covers the present claimants, who are categorized as Class-4 unsecured creditors under the Plan and who have dischargeable "claims" within the meaning of 11 U.S.C. § 101[(5)]. The future claimants are subject to the Injunction under the rubric of "Other Asbestos Obligation," which is defined by the Plan as asbestos-related health liability caused by pre-petition exposure to Manville asbestos, regardless of when the individual develops clinically observable symptoms. Thus, while the future claimants are not given creditor status under the Plan, they are nevertheless treated identically to the present claimants by virtue of the Injunction, which channels all claims to the Trust.

The Plan was submitted to the Bankruptcy Court for voting in June of 1986. At that time relatively few present asbestos health claimants had appeared in the reorganization proceedings. Approximately 6,400 proofs of claims had been filed for personal injuries, which accounted for less than half of the more than 16,000 persons who had filed pre-petition personal injury suits against Manville. Moreover, Manville estimated that there were tens of thousands of additional present asbestos victims who had neither filed suits nor presented proofs of claims. Manville and the creditor constituencies agreed that as many present claimants as possible should be brought into the proceedings so that they could vote on the Plan. However, the parties were reluctant to embark on the standard Code procedure of establishing a bar date, soliciting proofs of claims, resolving all disputed claims on notice and hearing, and then weighting the votes by the amounts of the claims, as such a process could delay the reorganization for many years. To avoid this delay, the Bankruptcy Court adopted special voting procedures for Class 4. Manville was directed to undertake a comprehensive multi-media notice campaign to inform persons with present health claims of the pendency of the reorganization and their opportunity to participate. Potential health claimants who responded to the campaign were given a combined proof-of-claim-and-voting form in which each could present a medical diagnosis of his asbestos-related disease and vote to accept or reject the Plan. For voting purposes only, each claim was valued in the amount of one dollar. Claimants were informed that the proof-of-claim-and-voting form would be used only for voting and that to collect from the Trust, they would have to execute an additional proof of claim establishing the actual value of their damages.

The notice campaign produced a large number of present asbestos claimants. In all, 52,440 such claimants submitted proof-of-claim-and-voting forms. Of these, 50,275 or 95.8% approved the Plan, while 2,165 or 4.2% opposed it. In addition to these Class-4 claimants, all other classes of creditors also approved the Plan. Class 8, the common stockholders, opposed the Plan.

A confirmation hearing was held on December 16, 1986, at which Manville presented evidence regarding the feasibility and fairness of the Plan. Objections to confirmation were filed by several parties, including Kane. On December 18,

1986, the Bankruptcy Court issued a Determination of Confirmation Issues in which it rejected all objections to confirmation. * * * By order dated July 15, 1987, the District Court affirmed the Bankruptcy Court's confirmation order * * *.

Discussion

A. Standing

The Legal Representative of the future claimants challenges Kane's standing to bring this appeal. * * * It is clear that some of Kane's claims are based exclusively on the rights of third parties. He asserts five claims:

(1) The Injunction violates the Bankruptcy Code because it affects the rights of future asbestos victims who do not have "claims" within the meaning of 11 U.S.C. § 101[(5)].

(2) The Injunction violates due process because future claimants were given inadequate notice of the discharge of their rights.

(3) The special voting procedures for Class 4 violate due process because present claimants were given inadequate notice of the hearing at which the voting procedures were adopted.

(4) The Class-4 voting procedures violate the Code because persons were permitted to vote before their claims were "allowed" pursuant to 11 U.S.C. § 502 (1982 & Supp. IV 1986), claims were arbitrarily assigned a value of one dollar each for voting purposes, and creditors were denied the opportunity to object to claims.

(5) The Plan fails to meet the requirements of 11 U.S.C. § 1129(a) and (b) because it was not proposed in good faith, it is not in the best interests of all creditors, it is not feasible, and it is not fair and equitable with respect to dissenting classes.

Kane does not dispute that his challenges to the Injunction (claims (1) and (2)) assert the constitutional and statutory rights only of the future claimants. Additionally, we note that claim (3) regarding notice of the voting procedures asserts only third-party rights. * * *

Prudential concerns weigh heavily against permitting Kane to assert the rights of the future claimants in attacking the Plan. First, Kane's interest in these proceedings is potentially opposed to that of the future claimants. Both Kane and the future claimants wish to recover from the debtor for personal injuries. To the extent that Kane is successful in obtaining more of the debtor's assets to satisfy his own claims, less will be available for other parties, with the distinct risk that the future claimants will suffer. Thus, we cannot depend on Kane sincerely to advance the interests of the future claimants. Second, the third parties whose rights Kane seeks to assert are already represented in the proceedings. Though it is true, as Kane points out, that the future claimants themselves are not before the Court, they are ably represented by the appointed Legal Representative. * * * Certainly as between Kane and the Legal Representative, there is no question that the latter is the more reliable advocate of the future claimants' rights, and we may confidently leave that task entirely to him.[32] * * *

---

32. [Footnote 3 in original:] Since the appointment of the Legal Representative in this case, two other courts have determined in the context of asbestos-related bankruptcy proceedings that future claimants are "parties in interest" entitled to participate and that they can best be represented by their own appointed

For similar reasons, Kane may not assert the rights of present claimants who he contends were given inadequate notice of the June 1986 hearing at which the special Class-4 voting procedures were adopted. * * *

Kane argues that he ought to be permitted at least to challenge the Injunction because his claim is "inextricably bound up with" the rights of the future claimants. See Singleton v. Wulff, supra, 428 U.S. at 114, 96 S. Ct. at 2874. Kane reasons that his own recovery from the Trust depends upon Manville's financial stability, which in turn could be jeopardized by a future claimant's successful challenge to the Injunction. If future claimants are not bound by the Injunction, then, Kane predicts, they will sue Manville's operating entities directly, Manville will be unable to meet its funding commitments to the Trust, and Kane will lose his rights to compensation under the Plan. Kane therefore contends that he should be able to test the validity of the Injunction as to the future claimants now so as to avoid a successful challenge detrimental to him in the future.

* * * The flaw in Kane's analysis is that it assumes that an onslaught of future victims' suits could impair the Trust before Kane is paid. Such is not the case. Kane and the other present claimants are, by definition, currently afflicted with asbestos disease. They may all initiate claims against the Trust immediately after confirmation. Resolution and payment of these claims is expected to take approximately ten years. The bulk of the future victims, in contrast, are not presently afflicted with disease. Many of them will not become ill until well into the 1990's or later. While some of the last of the present claimants may overlap with the first of the future claimants in presenting their damage claims, the claims of these groups will be presented essentially consecutively. By the time enough future claimants develop asbestos-related disease, challenge the Injunction, and, if successful, collect damages directly from Manville to an extent sufficient to impair the long-term funding of the Trust, Kane will have had years to enforce his own claims. Kane's concern that he will be precluded from collecting from the Trust because of future claimants' suits against Manville is therefore too speculative a basis on which to grant third-party standing.

We have so far determined that Kane does not have standing to challenge the Injunction nor to assert the rights of other Class-4 members in challenging the notice of voting procedures. In contrast, Kane does have standing to assert his remaining claims regarding the validity of the voting procedures and compliance with the requirements of section 1129(a) and (b); these claims allege violations of Kane's own rights under the Code.

B. Voting Procedures

Consideration of Kane's challenge to the voting procedures requires a brief outline of pertinent provisions of the Bankruptcy Code. A plan of reorganization must either be accepted by each impaired class of claims or interests, 11 U.S.C. § 1129(a)(8) (1982 & Supp. IV 1986), or meet certain rigid requirements with respect to each non-accepting class, 11 U.S.C. § 1129(b) (so-called "cram down" provision). A class of creditors has accepted a plan under the Code "if such plan

---

guardian rather than by creditors already in the proceedings. See In re Amatex Corp., 755 F.2d 1034, 1041-44 (3d Cir. 1985); In re UNR Industries, Inc., 46 B.R. 671 (Bankr. N.D. Ill. 1985).

has been accepted by creditors ... that hold at least two-thirds in amount and more than one-half in number of the allowed claims of such class held by creditors ... that have accepted or rejected such plan." 11 U.S.C. § 1126(c) (1982). Claims are "allowed" in the amount filed unless they are objected to by a party in interest, including the debtor or another creditor. 11 U.S.C. § 502(a); Bankruptcy Rule 3001(f). If a party in interest wishes to object to a claim, notice of the objection must be mailed to the claimant at least thirty days prior to a hearing at which the bankruptcy court determines the validity of the claim and the amount allowed. 11 U.S.C. § 502(b); Bankruptcy Rule 3007. However, objections to claims need not be finally resolved before voting on a plan may occur. Bankruptcy Rule 3018(a) provides that "[n]otwithstanding objection to a claim or interest, the court after notice and hearing may temporarily allow the claim or interest in an amount which the court deems proper for the purpose of accepting or rejecting a plan." * * *

We need not decide whether the special Class-4 voting procedures violate the Code because, in view of the outcome of the vote, the alleged irregularities were at most harmless error. * * *

None of the procedures that Kane contends were required would have changed the outcome of the vote. With respect to denial of the opportunity to object to the Class-4 claims before they were voted, no substantial rights were impaired because Kane is unable to show that, had he been afforded a chance to object, any of the present health claims would have been excluded. The only objection Kane contends that he would have asserted is that the combined proof-of-claim-and-voting form approved by the Bankruptcy Court permitted a filing supported only by a written medical diagnosis of an asbestos-related condition without evidence that the claimant was exposed to Manville's product, as opposed to the product of some other company. However, it is clear from the record that this objection would have been unavailing. The combined proof-of-claim-and-voting form required anyone who had not already filed a lawsuit against Manville to submit a diagnosis of his disease *and* to represent that he had been exposed to Manville's product. Such a representation would have sufficed to warrant accepting the claim for voting purposes, especially in the absence of any particularized contrary evidence from Kane. In any event, since 95.8% of those Class-4 members who voted approved the Plan, the result would not have been different unless more than 90% of those who voted in favor had invalid claims, an improbable circumstance.[33]

Similarly, Kane was not prejudiced by the assignment of a one dollar value to each claim. If we make the reasonable assumption that the percentage of claims that are valid is the same for "yes" votes and "no" votes, then the "no" votes

---

33. [Footnote 6 in original:] With all votes weighted equally, the number of "yes" votes would have to be less than two thirds of the total Class-4 votes cast in order for the Plan to lack approval by holders of two thirds of the aggregate value of the claims of this class. 11 U.S.C. § 1126(c). Since 2,165 opposed the Plan, the total of valid votes would have to be less than 6,495 in order to prevent the "yes" votes from constituting two thirds of the total votes cast; if the total is at least 6,495, the "yes" votes would be at least 4,330 (6,495 – 2,165), which is two thirds of 6,495. In order to reduce the total vote from the 52,440 cast to less than 6,495, the "yes" votes would have to be reduced from the 50,275 cast to less than 4,330 (6,495 – 2,165). To accomplish this result would have required invalidation of at least 91.4% of the "yes" votes (50,275 – 4,330 = 45,945, which is 91.4% of 50,275).

would have to be at least ten times larger, on average, than the "yes" votes in order to change the result from what occurred with equal weighting of each vote.[34] Nothing in the record gives any indication that such a large variation in claims existed, much less that the "no" votes were the larger claims. * * *

C. Section 1129 Requirements

* * *

Subsection 1129(a)(11) requires that the plan is not likely to be followed by liquidation or the need for further financial reorganization. As the Bankruptcy Court correctly stated, the feasibility standard is whether the plan offers a reasonable assurance of success. Success need not be guaranteed. * * * The Bankruptcy Judge found that "the Debtor's reasonable and credible projections of future earnings have established that the reorganized corporation is unlikely to face future proceedings under this title." 68 B.R. at 635. With specific reference to the Trust, the Court found that "[t]he evidence submitted by the Debtor ... provides a reasonable estimation, based upon known present claimants and reasonable extrapolations from past experience and epidemiological data, of the number and amount of asbestos-related claims that the AH Trust will be required to satisfy. The Debtor has also established that the Trust will, in fact, meet this burden." Id.

Kane argues that the Bankruptcy Court's finding of feasibility was incorrect because the Trust is inadequately funded and will not be able to satisfy the claims against it. * * * He contends that accepting Manville's estimate of $26,000 as the average liquidation cost of present claimants' suits, the Trust will need $1.352 billion to pay the 52,000 present claimants who filed claims. Since the Trust, according to Kane, is funded through the first five years with only $1.104 billion, he argues that it will fall $248 million short of paying the present claimants. There are two major errors in Kane's analysis. First, his account of the Trust's short-term funding is incorrect because he omits the value of Manville stock, which Kane estimates to be worth from $80.8 million to $146.4 million and which Manville estimates to be worth from $323 million to $585 million. Second, and more importantly, Kane completely ignores the long-term funding of the Trust. Not all present asbestos claims must be paid immediately upon confirmation, and many will not be liquidated and presented for payment even within the first five years. More likely, payment of present health claims will be spread out over roughly a ten-year period. In years six through ten, the Trust will receive annual payments of $75 million as well as up to 20% of Manville's yearly profits. This additional funding will be more than sufficient to pay the few present claimants who might not recover from the Trust's assets accumulated over the first five

---

34. [Footnote 7 in original:] The aggregate value of the "no" votes would have to exceed one third of the aggregate value of all Class-4 claims in order to prevent this class from approving the Plan. 11 U.S.C. § 1126(c). Since 2,165 votes opposed the Plan and 50,275 favored it, the multiple by which the average value of each "no" vote would have to exceed the average value of each "yes" vote in order to change the result can be derived from the formula, $2{,}165 \, (p)(x) = 1/3 \, (2{,}165 \, (p) + 50{,}275(p))$, where "p" equals the percentage of valid claims. In this equation, $x = 11.6$. Because we have assumed that the percentage of claims that are valid is the same for "yes" votes and "no" votes (i.e., "p" is the same throughout the equation), the multiple "x" is unaffected by the actual percentage of the claims that are valid.

years. Moreover, since the $75 million annual payments continue through year 27 and the 20% profit-sharing continues for as long as necessary to pay all claims, the Trust will also be adequate to pay the claims of the future asbestos victims. The Bankruptcy Court's finding that the Plan offers reasonable assurance of success in this regard is not clearly erroneous. * * *

The order of the District Court affirming the Bankruptcy Court's confirmation order is affirmed.

MINER, Circuit Judge, concurring:

Since the bankruptcy judge was empowered to estimate the claims of the Class-4 creditors, and did not abuse his discretion in doing so, I perceive no need to apply a harmless error analysis or to employ mathematical calculations to sustain the voting procedures adopted. * * *

In any event, the assignment of a value of $1.00 per claim is merely the temporary allowance contemplated by Rule 3018(a), with the right reserved to each claimant to seek actual damages from the Asbestos Health Trust. Although the Rule calls for objections to the claims, followed by notice and hearing, before temporary allowances for voting purposes are made, there was substantial compliance with this requirement here. * * *

NOTE

1. If future asbestos health claimants do not have "claims" until their injuries are manifested, will the discharge under § 1141(d)(1)(A) protect the reorganized Manville from being sued by them in the future? Section 1141(a) provides a list of categories of entities who are bound by a confirmed plan. Do future asbestos health claimants fall within any of those categories? The channeling injunction entered by the bankruptcy judge prohibited all asbestos health claimants, including future claimants, from seeking satisfaction of their claims from the reorganized Manville. It is therefore the functional equivalent of a discharge. Did the bankruptcy judge have authority to broaden the effect of the discharge in that way? Could Manville have been reorganized if the future asbestos health claimants were free to sue the reorganized Manville? See Epstein, Nickles & White, BANKRUPTCY § 11-8 at 90-93. Does § 105(a) provide the needed authority? Since the channeling injunction is an equitable remedy, is it subject to modification after confirmation the same as any other injunction?

2. The Bankruptcy Reform Act of 1994 added subsections (g) and (h) to § 524. The new subsections authorize plans to take the approach taken in the Manville case (and in the UNR case). Subsection (g) is modeled on the Manville plan. It provides the court in a bankruptcy case involving asbestos claims explicit authority to enter a channeling injunction like the one entered in Manville, an injunction that will be "valid and enforceable against all entities that it addresses," and that can protect the reorganized debtor and various third parties from liability on "claims" and "demands." Those who do not have claims at the time a plan is confirmed but who may be injured in the future as a result of asbestos exposure have "demands," under the terminology of the new subsections. See § 524(g)(5).

     Section 524(h) attempts to validate the Manville and UNR injunctions. As the next note indicates, the Manville injunction has been held specifically to qualify for validation under § 524(h).

3. Events in the Manville case subsequent to confirmation of its plan are
    sobering. The plan contemplated payment of 100% of the amount of all
    asbestos health claims as they were resolved. In December, 1994, eight years
    after confirmation of the plan, District Judge Weinstein approved a settlement
    under which asbestos victims will not be paid 100% of their claims, but will
    receive 10% of an arbitrary settlement value. Here is the story:

    > Following nearly two years of appeals, the confirmation order became
    > final on October 28, 1988. The Plan was executed and delivered on
    > November 28, 1988.
    >
    > Upon starting operations it was known to the Trust and others that
    > the Plan was grossly inadequate. Within a year-and-a-half of start-up,
    > the Trust was without liquid assets. Internal memoranda and meetings
    > of the Trust's personnel with selected plaintiffs' counsel made it clear
    > that the shortfall was recognized almost at once. Nevertheless,
    > settlements and payments went on with no allowance made for the
    > looming crisis.

    Findley v. Blinken (In re Joint Eastern and Southern District Asbestos Litig.),
    129 B.R. 710, 754 (E.D.N.Y. and S.D.N.Y. 1991), vacated, 982 F.2d 721 (2d
    Cir. 1992), modified on rehearing, 993 F.2d 7 (2d Cir. 1993).

    > Circumstances quickly outstripped projections concerning the number of
    > claims, the rate at which they were filed and their average value. The
    > confluence of these factors meant that the Trust began incurring liabilities
    > in excess of, and at a far greater rate than, the cash flow to the Trust.
    > Moreover, rather than containing disincentives for trial, in fact the practical
    > effect of certain provisions of the Plan was to encourage costly and
    > wasteful litigation. First, plaintiffs could accelerate the processing of their
    > claim if they obtained a trial date. The Trust would negotiate and settle
    > cases set for trial in an effort to lessen trial exposure and litigation defense
    > costs. Yet this avenue provided a vehicle for late-filing claimants to move
    > ahead of [others waiting in the first in, first out, processing queue].
    > Second, the provision permitting codefendants to implead the Trust in any
    > ongoing litigation increased exponentially the number of cases
    > simultaneously docketed for trial. * * *
    >
    > To the extent that cases were settled through the Claims
    > Resolution Facility, plaintiffs' attorneys exercised considerable and
    > effective influence over the Trust's settlement and payout practice.
    > The Trust began settling pre-petition claims in groups organized by
    > plaintiffs' counsel. * * *
    >
    > * * * [G]roup settlements were common and could involve
    > hundreds of claims with an aggregate settlement value ranging in the
    > millions of dollars. Not infrequently these claims were settled relying
    > on varying levels of information supplied by plaintiffs' counsel subject
    > to a random audit after settlement. For example, [over a two day
    > period] Trust personnel met with counsel from one plaintiff firm to
    > discuss settlement of 880 cases. After setting aside certain
    > extraordinary cases the parties proceeded to discuss and settle 835
    > cases in the course of an afternoon [for $31.5 million, with the total for
    > all that firms' cases apparently exceeding $50 million] * * *. No limit on
    > fees based on economies of scale was negotiated to reduce the
    > Trust's payment.

    129 B.R. at 755-56.

During the second year of the Trust's administration the number of claims filed with the Trust nearly doubled; by March 31, 1990 the Trust had received 143,000 claims. Thus, within its first two years of operation the Trust faced almost 50% more claims than the highest projection [100,000] made at the time of confirmation for the total number of claims to be filed during the entire life of the Trust. By February 5, 1991 the number of claims * * * had soared to over 170,000 and claims continue to flood in.

Beyond the number of claims asserted * * * the average liquidated value of each claim amounted to $42,128. This represented nearly a 40% increase over the original projection of $25,000 per claim.

129 B.R. at 758. Meanwhile, the Trust had begun to offer settlements to be paid over a period of time rather than in a lump sum, to try to stave off disaster.

In July, 1990, Judge Weinstein ordered a partial stay of payments by the Trust and suggested that a non-opt-out class action might be appropriate to achieve a global resolution. See Findley v. Blinken (In re Joint Eastern and Southern District Asbestos Litigation), 982 F.2d 721, 727 (2d Cir. 1992), modified on rehearing, 993 F.2d 7 (2d Cir. 1993). A special master appointed to look into the matter concluded that the trust was "deeply insolvent," that its assets were worth "between $2.1 and $2.7 billion, that current and future claims were estimated at $6.5 billion, and that the Trust currently lacked the cash to pay the then liquidated total of $448.5 million in claims." Id. Negotiations led to a proposal for a revised Trust Distribution Process, under which there would be caps on payments to all asbestos health claimants, with "Level One" claimants—the most severely harmed—being entitled to larger amounts and earlier processing of claims than "Level Two" claimants. Jury awards in excess of the caps would be paid only out of a fund that was unlikely to contain any money. Id. at 730.

In November, 1990, five asbestos health plaintiffs filed a class action in district court and bankruptcy court against the Trustees. Simultaneously, the plaintiffs and the Trust stipulated to settlement of the class action; the proposed settlement consisted of adoption of the revised Trust Distribution Process. Id. at 728. The courts stayed all other actions against the Trust, certified a mandatory, non-opt-out class under Fed. R. Civ. P. 23(b)(1)(B), and then approved the settlement. Id. at 729.

On appeal, the Second Circuit vacated the judgment approving the settlement. The court held, with some reluctance, that a mandatory, non-opt-out class action could be used to adjust the rights of the claimants—instead of a new bankruptcy filing—even though ordinarily such class actions should not be used in place of a bankruptcy filing. The court held, however, that several subclasses had to be set up because there were conflicting interests among the class members, including the conflict between Level One class members and Level Two class members who would be treated differently under the revised Trust Distribution Process. Id. at 739-45.

In July, 1994 the parties to the class action reached a settlement. As of that time, the Trust had received more than 200,000 claims, expected to receive another 300,000, and had settled 30,000 claims for more than $1 billion total. The Trust's remaining assets were thought to be worth only about $2 billion. See Adams, *Parties Reach Settlement in Manville Trust Cases,* 212 N.Y.L.J. 1 (July 28, 1994). Judge Weinstein approved the settlement, with amendments, by orders entered in December, 1994 and January, 1995. See Findley v. Falise (In re Joint E. & S. Dist. Asbestos Litig.) (In re Johns-Manville Corp.), 878 F. Supp. 473

(E.D.N.Y. & S.D.N.Y.), aff'd, 100 F.3d 944 2d Cir.), and aff'd, 100 F.3d 945 (2d Cir.), and aff'd in part and vacated in unrelated part, 78 F.3d 764 (2d Cir. 1996). The terms of the settlement thus were embodied in a court order.

The settlement reaffirmed the channeling injunction, permanently prohibiting asbestos claimants from suing the reorganized Manville. That was necessary to protect the value of the Trust's assets, which consisted largely of Manville stock. In addition, Judge Weinstein ruled that the channeling injunction satisfied the requirements of § 524(h). Thus Judge Weinstein concluded that

> The effect of compliance with [§ 524(h)] and the continued injunction is to enhance substantially the value of the corpus. Assets of the Trust in Manville stock may now be monetized free and clear of any possible asbestos claims against Manville * * *. Without such a guarantee the Corporation might have the cloud of future claims hanging over it, possibly reducing the value of the Corporation to potential purchasers of it or its stock and thus the amount available to the claimants.

878 F. Supp. at 572-73.   The settlement and orders also included a permanent injunction against claimants suing the Trust in state or federal court, except for the mostly hollow right to sue noted below.

The settlement provided for a Trust Distribution Process (TDP) under which the Trust offers claimants 10% of the settlement value of their claims, with that value being set at standardized Scheduled Values ranging from $12,000 to $200,000, depending on the severity of the claimant's disease category, as determined based on standardized Categorization Criteria. If the Trust and the claimant disagree on the claimant's disease category (or disagree whether the claimant has an asbestos related disease at all), then the claimant can seek further consideration of the claim by the Trust, and eventually obtain arbitration of the appropriate settlement amount, with a possible result above or below the relevant Scheduled Value. Only in rare cases can the value be set above standardized Maximum Values for each disease category (which range from $30,000 to $500,000).

A claimant dissatisfied with payment of 10% of the settlement amount set in the arbitration can return to the tort system and seek a judgment against the Trust. However, the Trust will initially pay only 10% of the lesser of (1) the judgment or (2) the Maximum Value for the claimant's disease category. (In the rare case in which the Trust offered, or an arbitrator awarded, more than the Maximum Value, the Trust will pay 10% of that offer or award). Any additional payment on the tort judgment will only be made if the Trust ends up being able to pay more than 50% of the settlement value of all the claims. The Trust is expected to be able to pay only 10%; the likelihood that the Trust could pay five times that much and have money left over is vanishingly small.

In April 1996 Manville issued additional common shares of stock to the trust in exchange for the trust giving up its yearly cash payment and profit sharing rights under the plan. The additional shares increased the Trust's 50% ownership of Manville stock to 79%. Manville changed its name to Schuller Corp. after selling off its only remaining non-building products business for over a billion dollars. The proceeds of the sale allowed Schuller Corp. to pay a $6 per common share dividend, which provided the trust with about $600 million in cash and left the trust with "$1.2 billion in cash and marketable securities and $2.3 billion in assets." Tejada, *Business Brief*, Wall St. J., March 29, 1996, at B4.

In 1997 Schuller changed its name back to Johns Manville Corporation with the approval of 99% of shareholders who voted. See http://jm.com/corporate/history.html; *News Notes*, THE BANKRUPTCY DATASOURCE, 1997 WL 278960

(May 15, 1997). The Trust's need to diversify its holdings and to raise money to pay claimants led Manville and the Trust to seek a buyer for the company. See, e.g., Templin, *Johns Manville To Explore a Sale*, WALL ST. J., Jan. 26, 1999, at C19. In June, 2000, an investment group agreed to buy Manville and take it private in a leveraged buyout. The Trust will receive about $1.5 billion cash and an 8.5% share of the privately held Manville's equity. Lipin & Scannell, *Deals & Deal Makers: Hicks Muse and Bear Stearns Join Forces To Buy Johns Manville for $2.4 Billion*, WALL ST. J., June 26, 2000, at C23.

4.   In the first edition of this book we predicted that "Because the Manville Trust will not pay all the asbestos health claimants in full, it seems certain that a large number of future asbestos health claimants will eventually consider challenging the injunction by bringing suit against the reorganized Manville." That has not happened. Congress' enactment of § 524(h) and the Second Circuit's affirmance of Judge Weinstein's order approving the class action settlement seem to have convinced claimants that any challenge would be futile. Based on a search of Manville's web site and on a Westlaw search of the EDGAR database of SEC filings, it appears that Manville's 1995 annual report is the last one in which Manville discusses any risk that the injunction might be challenged successfully in future legal proceedings. See www.jm.com; see, e.g., Filing 99566266, Item 3, Legal Proceedings (Westlaw) (Manville's March, 1999 10-K SEC filing, not discussing asbestos tort liability claims at all).

5.   For a recent case in which a court estimated future asbestos liabilities, see Owens Corning v. Credit Suisse First Boston, 322 B.R. 719 (D. Del. 2005) (estimating liability at $7 billion).

6.   In the A.H. Robins case, the confirmed plan set up a trust to pay claims of the thousands of women who had been injured by the Dalkon Shield intrauterine birth control device. Under the plan, American Home Products Corporation acquired A.H. Robins (by way of merger) and provided almost $2.475 billion to fund the trust. That figure was the district court's estimate of the amount needed to pay compensatory Dalkon Shield claims in full. The Dalkon Shield Claimants' Committee appealed, claiming that amount was too low; its expert testified that over $4 billion would be needed. The Fourth Circuit upheld the district court's estimation and affirmed the order confirming the plan. See Menard-Sanford v. Mabey (In re A.H. Robins Co.), 880 F.2d 694 (4th Cir. 1989).

     As it turns out, the Robins trust had slightly more than double the necessary funding to pay all compensatory claims in full. Minimal proof entitled claimants to a $725 payment. Most claimants (119,000) settled for that. Claimants could provide additional proof and seek higher settlement offers, and ultimately could choose arbitration or trial. Awards or judgments would be paid in full, but no punitive damages would be paid. In lieu of punitive damages, claimants who received more than the minimal $725 amount shared pro rata in any excess funds in the trust. See Bergstrom v. Dalkon Shield Claimants Trust (In re A.H. Robins Co.), 86 F.3d 364 (4th Cir. 1996). The trust was very well-managed, a high percentage of claims settled, and as of 1996 it was thought that there would be a 75% to 100% extra payment to those claimants. Id. The trust made several pro rata payments, and the final 4.5% payment on December 15, 1999 brought the total of the extra payments to slightly over 100%, for total compensation of slightly over 200%. See Cooper, *Dalkon Shield Trust to Pay $63.1 Million; Will Seek Court OK to Go Out of Business*, RICHMOND TIMES-DISPATCH, Dec. 15, 1999. The trust closed on April 30, 2000. See Cooper, *Dalkon Shield Trust Shuts Down After Paying Almost $3 Billion*, RICHMOND TIMES-DISPATCH, April 30, 2000, at A1.

7. As noted above, the need for the channeling injunction in cases like the A.H. Robins case and the asbestos cases arises in part from doubts whether future tort victims have claims, as defined in § 101(5)(A). Timing matters. (See *Piper*, immediately below.) The provisions of § 362(a)(1), (5), (6), and (7) prohibit debt collection activity only where the claim arises before commencement of the case. (The provisions of § 362(a)(3), (4), and (8) are not so limited, but may not give the needed protection.) Section 1141(a) binds creditors to the terms of the plan; but (with exceptions not relevant here) the term "creditor" does not include those whose claims arise after the filing of a voluntary petition in bankruptcy. Section 1141(d) discharges only claims that arise before the plan is confirmed.

If a person has already been exposed to the debtor's product, but has not yet developed any injury, does the person currently have a claim? The Third Circuit says "no," using a narrow and much-criticized approach that denies the existence of contingent tort claims, in seeming disregard of the broad language of § 101(5)(A).[35] Outside the Third Circuit, the answer is less clear. Consider the following case and problem.

In re Piper Aircraft Corporation
United States Bankruptcy Court, Southern District of Florida, 1994
162 B.R. 619, aff'd 168 B.R. 434 (S.D. Fla. 1994),
aff'd, 58 F.3d 1573 (11th Cir. 1995)

ROBERT A. MARK, Bankruptcy Judge.
* * *

Piper Aircraft Corporation ("Piper" or "Debtor") manufactures and distributes general aviation aircraft and spare parts throughout the United States and abroad. It began its manufacturing activities in 1937 and since that time has produced approximately 135,000 aircraft, of which approximately 50,000 to 60,000 are still operational in the United States. Over the years, Piper has been a defendant in several lawsuits based on its manufacture, design, sale, distribution and support of aircraft and parts. Although it has never acknowledged that its products are harmful or defective, Piper has suffered from the economic drain of escalating litigation costs in connection with defending these product liability claims. In large part because of this financial burden, on July 1, 1991, Piper filed a voluntary petition for relief under Chapter 11 of Title 11 of the United States Code.

With 50,000 to 60,000 Piper aircraft still in operation, accidents involving these aircraft undoubtedly will occur. Thus, additional though presently unidentifiable individuals will have similar product liability, property damage, or other claims as a result of incidents occurring after confirmation of the Debtor's Chapter 11 plan of reorganization, but arising out of or relating to aircraft or parts manufactured, sold, designed, or distributed by the Debtor prior to confirmation.

The Debtor's anticipated plan of reorganization contemplates finding a purchaser of substantially all of the Debtor's assets or obtaining investments from outside sources with the proceeds of such transactions serving to fund distributions to creditors. On April 8, 1993, the Debtor and Pilatus Aircraft Limited ("Pilatus") signed a letter of intent ("Letter of Intent") pursuant to which the Debtor agreed to

---

35. See In re M. Frenville Co., 744 F.2d 332 (3d Cir. 1984). For a sample of the cogent criticism of *Frenville*, see Grady v. A.H. Robins Co. (In re A.H. Robins Co.), 839 F.2d 198, 200-03 (4th Cir. 1988).

sell to Pilatus, and Pilatus agreed to purchase from the Debtor, substantially all of the Debtor's assets. The Letter of Intent required the Debtor to seek the appointment of a legal representative (the "Legal Representative") for future claimants to represent their interests in arranging a set-aside of monies generated by the sale to pay off future product liability claims. On May 19, 1993, the Court entered an order authorizing the appointment of David G. Epstein as Legal Representative of the "Future Claimants."[36] However, the Court specifically excluded from the appointment order any finding on whether the Future Claimants hold claims against the Debtor under § 101(5) of the Bankruptcy Code.

On July 12, 1993, the Legal Representative filed a proof of claim on behalf of the Future Claimants (the "Claim"). In the Claim, the Legal Representative asserts that the Debtor is indebted to the Future Claimants in the approximate amount of $100,000,000. The Claim purports to be based on statistical assumptions regarding the number of people who are likely to suffer personal injury or property damage after the confirmation of a reorganization plan, which is caused by Debtor's pre-confirmation manufacture, sale, design, distribution or support of aircraft and spare parts.

In conjunction with the Claim, the Legal Representative filed a motion requesting estimation of the Claim for voting purposes. At the July 26, 1993 preliminary hearing on this motion, the Debtor, the Official Committee of Unsecured Creditors (the "Committee") and the Legal Representative urged the Court to determine whether the Future Claimants hold "claims" as defined in § 101(5) of the Bankruptcy Code before conducting an evidentiary hearing on the estimation motion. * * *

* * * When Congress promulgated § 101(5), it intended to define "claim" more broadly than the term was defined under prior bankruptcy law.

Under the former Bankruptcy Act of 1898, a corporation could reorganize under Chapter X or Chapter XI.[37] Chapter XI defined claim very narrowly. Under Chapter XI, a claim had to be both "proved" and "allowed." Contingent obligations were theoretically "provable" under § 63 of the Bankruptcy Act. However, a contingent or unliquidated claim would not be "allowed" under § 57(d) of the Bankruptcy Act unless the claim could be estimated or liquidated. If the court believed a claim was not susceptible to liquidation or estimation, or that such liquidation or estimation would unduly delay the administration of the bankrupt's estate, the claim would be disallowed, and in turn be deemed unprovable under § 63(d) of the Act. Disallowed or unprovable claims were not subject to discharge.

---

36. [Footnote 1 in original:] The May 19 Order specifically defines "Future Claimants" to include:

> All persons, whether known or unknown, born or unborn, who may, after the date of confirmation of Piper's chapter 11 plan of reorganization, assert a claim or claims for personal injury, property damage, wrongful death, damages, contribution and/or indemnification, based in whole or in part upon events occurring or arising after the Confirmation Date, including claims based on the law of product liability, against Piper or its successor arising out of or relating to aircraft or parts manufactured and sold, designed, distributed or supported by Piper prior to the Confirmation Date.

37. [Footnote 5 in original: While Chapter X defined claim broadly, most corporations elected to file under Chapter XI to avoid a clause in Chapter X that provided for the automatic removal of management and the appointment of a Trustee upon the filing of a petition.

As a result of this narrow definition, Chapter XI of the Bankruptcy Act prevented a debtor from treating under its plan certain contingent claims that were not "provable," including contingent tort claims. Thus, the Act allowed such claims to be asserted against the reorganized debtor and caused two potential results which contravened established bankruptcy policy: first, it allowed similarly situated creditors to be treated differently; and second, it often led to the failure of the reorganization process.

In enacting the current Bankruptcy Code, Congress intentionally eliminated the "provability" requirement to broaden the range of claims that could be dealt with in bankruptcy and thereby avoid the inequities occurring under the Bankruptcy Act. The legislative history of § 101(5) reflects the intent of Congress in revising the definition of "claim," providing:

> By this broadest possible definition, and by the use of the term throughout title 11, especially in subchapter I of Chapter 5, the bill contemplates that all legal obligations of the debtor, no matter how remote or contingent, will be able to be dealt with in the bankruptcy case. It permits the broadest possible relief in the Bankruptcy Court.[38]

Based upon the statutory language and legislative history, virtually all courts agree that the definition of claim is expansive. The question is, how far can the concept of "claim" be expanded? In referring to the legislative history, one court has observed, "That language surely points us in a direction, but provides little indication of how far we should travel," In re Chateaugay Corp., 944 F.2d 997, 1003 (2d Cir. 1991). * * *

The issue before the Court is defining the extent to which a "contingent," "unmatured," and "unliquidated" potential right to payment is a claim under § 101(5). Several theories have emerged in the relevant case law. Under the most narrow interpretation, there is no claim for bankruptcy purposes until a claim has accrued under state law. Most notable among cases adopting this approach is the Third Circuit's decision in In re M. Frenville Co., 744 F.2d 332 (3d Cir. 1984), cert. denied, 469 U.S. 1160, 105 S. Ct. 911, 83 L. Ed. 2d 925 (1985). * * *

The problem with the *Frenville* decision and its progeny is that exclusive reliance on the accrual of a state law cause of action ignores the intent of Congress to define claim broadly in bankruptcy cases. * * *

Recognizing the shortcomings of the standard espoused in *Frenville*, several courts, including those addressing mass tort issues, devised a theory commonly referred to as the "Conduct Test." Under this test, a right to payment arises when the conduct giving rise to the alleged liability occurred. The leading Circuit Court of Appeals case describing and adopting the Conduct Test is Grady v. A.H. Robins Co. (In re A.H. Robins Co.), 839 F.2d 198 (4th Cir. 1988). * * *

Essentially the same test was applied in the asbestos case of In re Waterman S.S. Corp., 141 B.R. 552 (Bankr. S.D.N.Y. 1992), vacated on other grounds, 157 B.R. 220 (S.D.N.Y. 1993). In *Waterman*, former employees of the debtor sought a declaratory judgment holding that their asbestosis claims, which were manifested post-confirmation,

---

38. [Footnote 6 in original:] H.R. Rep. No. 595, 95th Cong., 2d Sess. 309, reprinted in 1978 U.S. Code Cong. & Ad. News 5963, 6266; see also, S. Rep. No. 989, 95th Cong., 2d Sess. 21-22, reprinted in 1978 U.S. Code Cong. & Ad. News 5787, 5807-08.

were not discharged by the confirmation order. In reaching his decision, Bankruptcy Judge Conrad bifurcated the analysis into two issues: first, whether the individuals held claims, and second, if they did hold claims, whether these claims were dischargeable.

In answering the first question, Judge Conrad followed the lead of the Johns-Manville asbestosis cases and reasoned that, in determining whether or not a claim exists, "the focus should be on the time when the acts giving rise to the alleged liability were performed," In re Johns-Manville Corp., 57 B.R. 680, 690 (Bankr. S.D.N.Y. 1986). Since the asbestos was manufactured prepetition, and since the individuals suffering injuries were exposed prepetition, the former employees held "claims" under § 101(5). However, because the debtor failed to include this known class of creditors in its schedules and failed to provide adequate notice to this known class, Judge Conrad held that the claimants did not have notice sufficient to meet due process requirements for discharging their claims.[39]

At least one case has used a similar application of the Conduct Test outside the mass tort context. In In re Edge, 60 B.R. 690 (Bankr. M.D. Tenn. 1986), the debtor was a dentist. After the debtor filed his Chapter 7 petition, a former patient sought a declaration that a "claim" based on negligent treatment received prior to the debtor's filing, but discovered afterwards, was a postpetition claim and thus not subject to the § 362 automatic stay. The court, applying a broad interpretation of claim as guided by the legislative history, concluded that the claim arose at the time of the debtor's prepetition misconduct and thus was subject to the automatic stay. Id. at 705. As in *Waterman* and *A.H. Robins*, the claimant had already been exposed to or had contact with the cause of injury (in Edge, the dentist's negligent treatment; in *Waterman* and *A.H. Robins*, known defective and dangerous products), but simply had not manifested injury as of the commencement of the case.

The Legal Representative urges a similar application of the Conduct Test in this case, with the relevant conduct being Piper's prepetition manufacture, design, sale and distribution of allegedly defective aircraft. However, unlike the asbestos and Dalkon Shield cases, the Legal Representative cannot pinpoint which aircraft or parts are defective or, more significantly, who will be exposed to the defective product in the future. In effect, under the Conduct Test, everyone in the world would hold a claim against Piper simply by virtue of their potential future exposure to any plane in the existing fleet. The conduct of Piper purporting to support the existence of prepetition "claims" is readily distinguishable from the conduct of the asbestos and Dalkon Shield manufacturers.[40] Thus, the Court

---

39. [Footnote 8 in original:]   On appeal, the District Court found that known potential claimants were entitled to actual personal notice; that potential claimants who could not be personally identified were entitled to reasonable notice by publication; and that potential future claims of individuals who had not manifested any detectable signs of disease when notice of the bar date was given were not discharged in the bankruptcy case. *Waterman*, 157 B.R. at 222 (S.D.N.Y. 1993).

40. [Footnote 9 in original:]   There is also no "great wrong" to be redressed in this case which mandates that present provisions be made for potential future claimants. In the asbestos and Dalkon Shield cases, manufacturers had produced and distributed products known to be harmful from well-documented and overwhelmingly accepted scientific evidence, and a defined group of individuals were exposed to these harmful products and could be expected to manifest injuries as a result. Here, although Piper has been involved in product liability litigation related to its

rejects application of a Conduct Test that would give rise to "claims" simply because the design and manufacture of products occurred prepetition. * * *

Recognizing that the Conduct Test may define a § 101(5) claim too broadly in some situations, several courts have recognized "claims" only for those individuals with some type of prepetition relationship with the Debtor. In In re Pettibone Corp., 90 B.R. 918 (Bankr. N.D. Ill. 1988), the debtor was sued for injuries sustained by the operator of a forklift designed and manufactured by the debtor before it filed its bankruptcy case. The claimant's employer purchased the forklift postpetition and therefore the claimant had no prepetition contact with the debtor or the forklift. The accident and the resulting injuries all occurred postpetition. The *Pettibone* court found that the facts before it were distinguishable from the asbestos and other mass tort cases where the injuries sustained could be tied to some type of prebankruptcy privity, contact, impact or hidden harm. Because the operator's injury occurred postpetition without any prepetition relationship or exposure to tie the claimant to the debtor, the court held there was no "claim" as of the petition date.

The Second Circuit suggested a similar analysis in In re Chateaugay Corp., 944 F.2d 997 (2d Cir. 1991). The issue in that case was whether the Environmental Protection Agency ("EPA") had a * * * claim for environmental cleanup costs which would not be incurred until after confirmation * * * . The court tied the concept of "claim" to the prepetition relationship between debtor and claimant, finding that the relationship between environmental regulating agencies and the parties subject to regulation makes those contingent obligations based on prepetition conduct "claims" under the Code's definition. Thus, even though the EPA could not identify all of the sites or the full extent of the removal costs, the future environmental response costs for sites contaminated prior to filing of the bankruptcy petition were prepetition claims under the Bankruptcy Code.

The finding in *Chateaugay* of a sufficient relationship is a narrow one, and that court expressly excluded several other scenarios from its holding. The court noted,

> We need not decide how the definition of "claim" applies to tort victims injured by pre-petition conduct, especially as applied to the difficult case of pre-petition conduct that has not yet resulted in detectable injury, much less the extreme case of pre-petition conduct that has not yet resulted in any tortious consequence to a victim.

Id. at 1004. In concluding that the degree of relationship between the debtor and the EPA was sufficient, the court found it "far closer than that between future tort claimants totally unaware of injury and a tortfeasor." Id. at 1005.[41]

---

manufacture, design, sale and distribution of aircraft and parts, and has expended considerable funds in such litigation, only a very small percentage of Piper aircraft will be involved in crashes, and only a fraction of those crashes are likely to result from prepetition manufacturing or design defects.

41. [Footnote 12 in original:] At least one court has found that even the test applied in *Chateaugay* was too broad. See In re Jensen, 995 F.2d 925 (9th Cir. 1993). In *Jensen*, the Ninth Circuit found that there must not only be a relationship between the claimant and the debtor, but that their prepetition interaction must be such that the claim is within the "fair contemplation" of the parties at the time of the bankruptcy.

Indeed, the *Chateaugay* court noted that defining claims to include any ultimate right to payment arising out of prepetition conduct by the debtor would yield questionable results. In pursuing this discussion, the court presented a hypothetical example of a company in bankruptcy which estimates that one out of the ten thousand bridges it built prepetition eventually will fail, causing the death of ten individuals. The court explored the problems inherent in attempting to recognize these "claims" pursuant to the Conduct Test:

> Is there a "claim" on behalf of the 10 people who will be killed when they drive across the one bridge that will fail someday in the future? If the only test is whether the ultimate right to payment will arise out of the debtor's pre-petition conduct, the future victims have a "claim." Yet it must be obvious that enormous practical and perhaps constitutional problems would arise from recognition of such a claim. The potential victims are not only unidentified, but there is no way to identify them. Sheer fortuity will determine who will be on that one bridge when it crashes.

Chateaugay, 944 F.2d at 1003.

The problem posed by this hypothetical has become reality here. We know that some planes in the existing fleet of Piper aircraft will crash, and we know that there may be injuries, deaths and property damage as a result. We also know that under theories of negligence and products liability, Piper, if it remains in existence, would be liable for some of these damages. Even so, there is no way to identify who the victims will be or to identify any particular prepetition contact, exposure, impact, privity or other relationship between Piper and these potential claimants that will give rise to these future damages. * * *

The Conduct Test and the Relationship Test are not mutually exclusive theories. Requiring that there be some prepetition relationship between the Debtor and claimant would not change the analysis or results of the Conduct Test cases. In fact, such a requirement appears to be implicit in those decisions. In the asbestos cases, the future claimants were individuals who were known to have had prepetition exposure to the dangerous product. See, e.g., *Waterman*, 141 B.R. at 556 (claims arose "at the moment the asbestos claimants came into contact with the asbestos"). Likewise, in *A.H. Robins*, the court determined that the claim arose when the claimant was inserted with a Dalkon Shield. And in *Edge*, the court noted that the Bankruptcy Code recognizes a claim for the victim of prepetition misconduct "at the earliest point in the relationship between victim and wrongdoer." *Edge*, 60 B.R. at 699. Thus, the Conduct Test cases presume not only that there was prepetition conduct, but also that there was some prepetition relationship between the debtor's conduct and the claimant.

The theories advanced by prior cases exploring the outer limits of the concept of claim, when thus reconciled, lead to the conclusion that in order for a future claimant to have a "claim" under § 101(5), there must be some prepetition relationship, such as contact, exposure, impact, or privity, between the debtor's prepetition conduct and the claimant. This is not to suggest that any and every prepetition relationship will give rise to a claim.[42] Rather, a prepetition relationship connecting the conduct to the claimant is a threshold requirement.

---

42. [Footnote 13 in original:] Thus, the Court makes no finding that the relationship between Piper and prepetition owners of Piper aircraft would give rise to "claims" even for this relatively small and identifiable subclass of Future Claimants.

In the instant case, the Claim advanced by the Legal Representative on behalf of the Future Claimants fails to fulfill this minimum requirement: the conduct upon which the claim is based, in its entirety, is merely the prepetition design, manufacture and sale of aircraft, without any discernible connection between that conduct and the Legal Representative's constituency. There is no prepetition exposure to a specific identifiable defective product or any other prepetition relationship between the Debtor and the broadly defined class of Future Claimants. Since there is no way to connect the future claims to some prepetition relationship, there is also no way to identify a discrete class of individuals who will have claims arising out of prepetition conduct. In short, the Claim in this case fails even the broadest test for recognition of a "claim."

* * * The Legal Representative and Pilatus argue that tying the issue of "claim" solely to whether the Debtor's conduct occurred prepetition would foster two primary policies of the Bankruptcy Code: (1) the effective reorganization of the Debtor, and (2) the equal treatment of similarly situated creditors. The Court disagrees. * * *

First, unlike the Dalkon Shield and asbestos cases, the Debtor in this case does not believe that recognition of these future interests in the plan is necessary for its reorganization. Indeed, both the Debtor and the Committee conclude that allowing the Claim will hinder, not promote reorganization. Second, as revealed by the *Waterman* case, a determination that the Future Claimants hold "claims" would not necessarily mean that the claims are dischargeable. If they are not dischargeable, calling them "claims" would not in any way facilitate Piper's reorganization. Here, significant and possibly insurmountable due process problems exist in providing notice to this vast class of Future Claimants sufficient to allow the discharge of their claims, regardless of the appointment of, and diligent efforts by, the Legal Representative. In sum, the Court cannot and does not find that recognizing the Future Claimants' "claims" will aid in an effective reorganization.[43]

Pilatus and the Legal Representative also argue that all individuals injured from Piper aircraft manufactured before confirmation should be treated equally, regardless of whether their injuries occur pre-confirmation or post-confirmation. * * * Should crash victim Jones be able to share in plan distributions if his plane crashes pre-confirmation, while crash victim Smith receives nothing under the plan if his plane crashes post-confirmation?

The Court concludes that the answer is yes, their treatment can and should be different. In bankruptcy, as in life, timing matters.[44] There is a major distinction

---

43. [Footnote 15 in original:] The Legal Representative argues, correctly, that a plan could provide for the Future Claimants by setting aside some portion of the plan distributions for their benefit. However, the Legal Representative also has steadfastly asserted that Future Claimants must be found to have "claims" to be treated under a plan in the instant case. Compare, Matter of Johns-Manville Corp., 68 B.R. 618, 628 (Bankr. S.D.N.Y. 1986), aff'd in part, rev'd in part, 78 B.R. 407 (S.D.N.Y. 1987), aff'd sub nom. Kane v. Johns-Manville Corp., 843 F.2d 636 (2d Cir. 1988), in which the plan provided for future asbestosis victims without determining that they had claims. The theoretical ability to provide a fund for the Future Claimants does not help resolve the independent and threshold issue of whether or not they have "claims".

44. [Footnote 16 in original:] The simple truth that timing matters is evident in numerous provisions of the Bankruptcy Code, including the avoidance provisions in § 547 and § 548. Creditor Jones, paid in full 91 days before the petition, may keep his money while creditor Smith, paid the very next day, will have to disgorge the entire amount and share in any distributions to unsecured creditors. * * * Similarly, the Code does not permit or contemplate the indefinite, unlimited forward reach urged by the Legal Representative, even though it might foster the theoretical goal of equitable distribution.

between Jones and Smith. Jones can be identified presently; Smith cannot. Only future events, impossible to predict at the time of confirmation of a plan, will determine who the future claimants will be, and whether Smith in fact will be one of them. Were Smith and his fellow claimants presently ascertainable and identifiable, the answer might be different; but in the instant case it is impossible to determine who ultimately will belong to the class of creditors, and whether any prepetition relationship to the Debtor gives rise to their potential future causes of action. * * *

In determining that the Future Claimants do not hold claims under the Bankruptcy Code, the Court is not determining whether any or all of the future victims may have a non-bankruptcy future remedy. The nature of the reorganization plan eventually confirmed in the case may affect the result as will, in the event of a sale of Piper's assets, application of successor liability laws which may vary among the states. The ruling simply means that the future claims are not bankruptcy "claims" that will be administered in this case.[45]

* * * [T]he Claim filed by the Legal Representative is disallowed.

NOTE

Note that the court did not have before it the question whether crash victims injured in crashes postpetition but preconfirmation would be considered to have claims or what the nature of any such claims might be. The court's Jones/Smith hypothetical suggests that if an accident occurs during the case, so that we can identify a claimant who allegedly was injured by a particular allegedly defective Piper aircraft, then that claimant should be considered to have a claim. In Piper Aircraft Corp. v. Calabro (In re Piper Aircraft Corp.), 169 B.R. 766 (Bankr. S.D. Fla. 1994), the court held that such persons do have claims, and that the claims are prepetition claims. The court stated its test this way:

> [A]n individual has a [prepetition] § 101(5) claim against a debtor manufacturer if (i) events occurring before confirmation create a "relationship" between the claimant and the debtor's product; and (ii) the basis for liability is the debtor's prepetition conduct in designing, manufacturing and selling the allegedly defective or dangerous product. This test still focuses on the Debtor's prepetition conduct. That conduct only gives rise to a "claim" to be administered in the case if there is a relationship established before confirmation between an identifiable claimant or group of claimants and that prepetition conduct.

Id. at 775; accord, Epstein v. Official Comm. Of Unsec. Cred. (In re Piper Aircraft Corp.), 58 F.3d 1573 (11th Cir. 1995). The court noted, however, that if Calabro prevailed on a theory that the debtor in possession violated a postpetition duty to warn of newly discovered dangers, then the claim would have administrative expense priority, because the debtor in possession would be the tortfeasor.

Problem 9-1

Assume that seven persons (the "Tort Claimants") who were seriously burned in automobile accidents sued Foam Corporation. The Tort Claimants alleged that the foam in the seat cushions—foam manufactured by Foam Corporation—was defective because it allegedly caught fire too easily, thus contributing to the seriousness of their burns. They also alleged that the foam gave off a toxic gas

---

45. [Footnote 17 in original:] Since postpetition, pre-confirmation claims are not within the defined group of Future Claimants, this decision does not determine the nature or treatment of such claims.

as it burned, which caused them to become disoriented and to have difficulty in extricating themselves from the burning automobiles. That, too, allegedly contributed to the seriousness of their burns. One of the Tort Claimants—a Mr. Peterson—obtained a prepetition judgment against Foam Corporation (after a jury trial) for $2 million in compensatory damages. The judgment was on appeal when Foam Corporation filed its chapter 11 petition. At that time the other Tort Claimants' suits had not yet gone to trial. Is Foam Corporation's appeal stayed by § 362? Must the court allow Peterson's claim in the amount of $2 million? After Foam Corporation's plan is confirmed, thousands of automobiles on the roads will have cushions made of foam sold before plan confirmation by Foam Corporation. There will certainly be fiery accidents involving some of those automobiles, and some of those who are burned will blame Foam Corporation. Is there any way to use the chapter 11 process to protect the reorganized Foam Corporation from suits by those persons?

E. ADDITIONAL ISSUES INVOLVING SECURED CREDITORS

In this section we discuss three additional issues regarding rights of secured creditors. First, to what extent does postpetition interest on oversecured claims depend on agreement of the parties? Section 506(b) states that "there shall be allowed to the holder" of an oversecured claim "interest on such claim, and any reasonable fees, costs, or charges *provided for under the agreement under which such claim arose.*" (Emphasis supplied.) Must there be an agreement in order for interest to be allowed, or are even nonconsensual lienholders, such as governmental units with tax liens, entitled to interest if they are oversecured? If there is an agreement that states an interest rate, will the claim accrue interest at that rate even if it is higher than the present market rate? Does the agreement control if it provides for an increase in the interest rate on default—for a "default interest rate"?

Second, what happens when a court determines that a secured creditor's interest in property is adequately protected, but that finding turns out to be incorrect? If a real property mortgagee is denied relief from the automatic stay because the court believes the value of the property will not decrease (and that the mortgagee's interest is therefore supposedly adequately protected), what remedy does the mortgagee have if the value in fact decreases with a resulting loss to the mortgagee? If the court permits the debtor to use a secured party's cash collateral to buy new inventory and pay business expenses, because the court believes the security interest is adequately protected, what remedy does the secured party have if the debtor's business continues to lose money so that the value of the cash collateral is diminished? Does § 507(b) automatically give these secured creditors superpriority administrative expense claims to make up for the loss caused by the failure of the supposedly adequate protection?

Third, when is the trustee or debtor in possession entitled under § 506(c) to some of the value of a secured party's collateral because of costs and expenses that the trustee or debtor in possession claims were incurred to preserve that property? For example, if the reorganization of the debtor preserves the value of the secured party's collateral in the sense that it is worth more as part of a going concern than if it were liquidated, will that justify "surcharging" the collateral for the ordinary administrative expenses, such as the debtor's attorneys' fees?

1. Interest on Oversecured Claims

United States v. Ron Pair Enterprises, Inc.
United States Supreme Court, 1989
489 U.S. 235, 109 S. Ct. 1026, 103 L. Ed. 2d 290

JUSTICE BLACKMUN delivered the opinion of the Court.

In this case we must decide the narrow statutory issue whether § 506(b) of the Bankruptcy Code of 1978, 11 U.S.C. § 506(b) (1982 ed., Supp. IV), entitles a creditor to receive postpetition interest on a nonconsensual oversecured claim allowed in a bankruptcy proceeding. We conclude that it does, and we therefore reverse the judgment of the Court of Appeals.

I

Respondent Ron Pair Enterprises, Inc., filed a petition for reorganization under Chapter 11 of the Bankruptcy Code on May 1, 1984, in the United States Bankruptcy Court for the Eastern District of Michigan. The Government filed timely proof of a prepetition claim of $52,277.93, comprised of assessments for unpaid withholding and Social Security taxes, penalties, and prepetition interest. The claim was perfected through a tax lien on property owned by respondent. Respondent's First Amended Plan of Reorganization, filed October 1, 1985, provided for full payment of the prepetition claim, but did not provide for postpetition interest on that claim. The Government filed a timely objection, claiming that § 506(b) allowed recovery of postpetition interest, since the property securing the claim had a value greater than the amount of the principal debt. At the Bankruptcy Court hearing, the parties stipulated that the claim was oversecured, but the court subsequently overruled the Government's objection. * * *

II

Section 506, enacted as part of the extensive 1978 revision of the bankruptcy laws, governs the definition and treatment of secured claims, i.e., claims by creditors against the estate that are secured by a lien on property in which the estate has an interest. * * * Subsection (b) is concerned specifically with oversecured claims, that is, any claim that is for an amount less than the value of the property securing it. Thus, if a $50,000 claim were secured by a lien on property having a value of $75,000, the claim would be oversecured, provided the trustee's costs of preserving or disposing of the property were less than $25,000. Section 506(b) allows a holder of an oversecured claim to recover, in addition to the prepetition amount of the claim, "interest on such claim, and any reasonable fees, costs, or charges provided for under the agreement under which such claim arose."

The question before us today arises because there are two types of secured claims: (1) voluntary (or consensual) secured claims, each created by agreement between the debtor and the creditor and called a "security interest" by the Code,

11 U.S.C. § 101(45) (1982 ed., Supp.IV), and (2) involuntary secured claims, such as a judicial or statutory lien, see 11 U.S.C. §§ 101(32) and (47) (1982 ed., Supp.IV), which are fixed by operation of law and do not require the consent of the debtor. The claim against respondent's estate was of this latter kind. Prior to the passage of the 1978 Code, some Courts of Appeals drew a distinction between the two types for purposes of determining postpetition interest. The question we must answer is whether the 1978 Code recognizes and enforces this distinction, or whether Congress intended that all oversecured claims be treated the same way for purposes of postpetition interest.

III

Initially, it is worth recalling that Congress worked on the formulation of the Code for nearly a decade. It was intended to modernize the bankruptcy laws, see H.R. Rep. No. 95-595, p. 3 (1977) U.S. Code Cong. & Admin. News 1978 pp. 5787, 5963, 5964 (Report), and as a result made significant changes in both the substantive and procedural laws of bankruptcy. In particular, Congress intended "significant changes from current law in ... the treatment of secured creditors and secured claims." Report, at 180. In such a substantial overhaul of the system, it is not appropriate or realistic to expect Congress to have explained with particularity each step it took. Rather, as long as the statutory scheme is coherent and consistent, there generally is no need for a court to inquire beyond the plain language of the statute.

A

The task of resolving the dispute over the meaning of § 506(b) begins where all such inquiries must begin: with the language of the statute itself. In this case it is also where the inquiry should end, for where, as here, the statute's language is plain, "the sole function of the courts is to enforce it according to its terms." Caminetti v. United States, 242 U.S. 470, 485, 37 S. Ct. 192, 194, 61 L. Ed. 442 (1917). The language before us expresses Congress' intent—that postpetition interest be available—with sufficient precision so that reference to legislative history and to pre-Code practice is hardly necessary.

The relevant phrase in § 506(b) is: "[T]here shall be allowed to the holder of such claim, interest on such claim, and any reasonable fees, costs, or charges provided for under the agreement under which such claim arose." "Such claim" refers to an oversecured claim. The natural reading of the phrase entitles the holder of an oversecured claim to postpetition interest and, in addition, gives one having a secured claim created pursuant to an agreement the right to reasonable fees, costs, and charges provided for in that agreement. Recovery of postpetition interest is unqualified. Recovery of fees, costs, and charges, however, is allowed only if they are reasonable and provided for in the agreement under which the claim arose. Therefore, in the absence of an agreement, postpetition interest is the only added recovery available.

This reading is also mandated by the grammatical structure of the statute. The phrase "interest on such claim" is set aside by commas, and separated from the reference to fees, costs, and charges by the conjunctive words "and any." As a result, the phrase "interest on such claim" stands independent of the language that follows. "[I]nterest on such claim" is not part of the list made up of "fees, costs, or charges," nor is it joined to the following clause so that the final "provided for under the agreement" modifies it as well. The language and punctuation Congress used cannot be read in any other way.[46] By the plain language of the statute, the two types of recovery are distinct.

B

The plain meaning of legislation should be conclusive, except in the "rare cases [in which] the literal application of a statute will produce a result demonstrably at odds with the intentions of its drafters." Griffin v. Oceanic Contractors, Inc., 458 U.S. 564, 571, 102 S. Ct. 3245, 3250, 73 L. Ed. 2d 973 (1982). In such cases, the intention of the drafters, rather than the strict language, controls. Ibid. It is clear that allowing postpetition interest on nonconsensual oversecured liens does not contravene the intent of the framers of the Code. * * *

C

Respondent urges that pre-Code practice drew a distinction between consensual and nonconsensual liens for the purpose of determining entitlement to postpetition interest, and that Congress' failure to repudiate that distinction requires us to enforce it. It is respondent's view, as it was the view of the Court of Appeals, that Midlantic National Bank v. New Jersey Dept. of Environmental Protection, 474 U.S. 494, 106 S. Ct. 755, 88 L. Ed. 2d 859 (1986), and Kelly v. Robinson, 479 U.S. 36, 107 S. Ct. 353, 93 L. Ed. 2d 216 (1986), so require. We disagree.

In *Midlantic* we held that § 554(a) of the Code, 11 U.S.C. § 554(a), which provides that "the trustee may abandon any property of the estate that is burdensome to the estate," does not give a trustee the authority to violate state health and safety laws by abandoning property containing hazardous wastes. 474 U.S., at 507, 106 S. Ct., at 762. In reaching that conclusion, we noted that according to pre-Code doctrine the trustee's authority to dispose of property could be limited in order "to protect legitimate state or federal interests." Id., at 500, 106 S. Ct., at 759. But we did not rest solely, or even primarily, on a presumption of continuity with pre-Code practice. Rather, we concluded that a contrary result would render abandonment doctrine inconsistent with other provisions of the Code itself, which embody the principle that "the trustee is not to have *carte blanche* to ignore nonbankruptcy law." Id., at 502, 106 S. Ct. at 760. We also recognized that the outcome sought would be not only a departure from pre-Code practice, but also "an extraordinary exemption from nonbankruptcy law," id., at 501, 106 S. Ct., at 759, requiring some clearer expression of congressional intent. We relied as well on Congress' repeated emphasis in environmental legislation

---

46. [Footnote 4 in original:] The United States Court of Appeals for the Fourth Circuit pointed out in *Best Repair Co.* that, had Congress intended to limit postpetition interest to consensual liens, § 506(b) could have said: "there shall be allowed to the holder of such claim, as provided for under the agreement under which such claim arose, interest on such claim and any reasonable fees, costs or charges." 789 F.2d, at 1082, n. 2. A less clear way of stating this, closer to the actual language, would be: "there shall be allowed to the holder of such claim, interest on such claim and reasonable fees, costs, and charges provided for under the agreement under which such claim arose." Ibid.

"on its 'goal of protecting the environment against toxic pollution.'" Id., at 505, 106 S. Ct., at 762, quoting Chemical Manufacturers Assn. v. Natural Resources Defense Council, Inc., 470 U.S. 116, 143, 105 S. Ct. 1102, 1117, 84 L. Ed. 2d 90 (1985). To put it simply, we looked to pre-Code practice for interpretive assistance, because it appeared that a literal application of the statute would be "demonstrably at odds with the intentions of its drafters." Griffin v. Oceanic Contractors, Inc., 458 U.S., at 571, 102 S. Ct., at 3250.

A similar issue presented itself in Kelly v. Robinson, supra, where we held that a restitution obligation, imposed as part of a state criminal sentence, was not dischargeable in bankruptcy. * * * In *Kelly*, as in *Midlantic*, pre-Code practice was significant because it reflected policy considerations of great longevity and importance.

Kelly and *Midlantic* make clear that, in an appropriate case, a court must determine whether Congress has expressed an intent to change the interpretation of a judicially created concept in enacting the Code. But *Midlantic* and *Kelly* suggest that there are limits to what may constitute an appropriate case. Both decisions concerned statutory language which, at least to some degree, was open to interpretation. Each involved a situation where bankruptcy law, under the proposed interpretation, was in clear conflict with state or federal laws of great importance. In the present case, in contrast, the language in question is clearer than the language at issue in *Midlantic* and *Kelly*: as written it directs that postpetition interest be paid on all oversecured claims. In addition, this natural interpretation of the statutory language does not conflict with any significant state or federal interest, nor with any other aspect of the Code. Although the payment of postpetition interest is arguably somewhat in tension with the desirability of paying all creditors as uniformly as practicable, Congress expressly chose to create that alleged tension. There is no reason to suspect that Congress did not mean what the language of the statute says.

D

But even if we saw the need to turn to pre-Code practice in this case, it would be of little assistance. The practice of denying postpetition interest to the holders of nonconsensual liens, while allowing it to holders of consensual liens, was an exception to an exception, recognized by only a few courts and often dependent on particular circumstances. It was certainly not the type of "rule" that we assume Congress was aware of when enacting the Code; nor was it of such significance that Congress would have taken steps other than enacting statutory language to the contrary.

There was, indeed, a pre-Code rule that the running of interest ceased when a bankruptcy petition was filed. Two exceptions to this rule had been recognized under pre-Code practice. * * * A third exception was of more doubtful provenance: an exception for oversecured claims. At least one Court of Appeals refused to apply this exception, and there was some uncertainty among courts which did recognize it as to whether this Court ever had done so.

What is at issue in this case is not the oversecured claim exception *per se,* but an exception to that exception. Several Courts of Appeals refused to apply the oversecured claim exception to an oversecured federal tax claim. * * *

More importantly * * * [n]one of the cases cited by the Court of Appeals states that the doctrine does anything more than provide a bankruptcy court with guidance in the exercise of its equitable powers. As such, there is no reason to think that Congress, in enacting a contrary standard, would have felt the need expressly to repudiate it. * * * Whether or not Congress took notice of the pre-Code standard, it acted with sufficient clarity in enacting the statute.

The judgment of the Court of Appeals is reversed.

It is so ordered.

JUSTICE O'CONNOR, with whom JUSTICE BRENNAN, JUSTICE MARSHALL, and JUSTICE STEVENS join, dissenting.
* * *

The relevant portion of § 506(b) provides that "there shall be allowed to the holder of [an oversecured] claim, interest on such claim, and any reasonable fees, costs, or charges provided for under the agreement under which such claim arose." The Court concludes that the only natural reading of § 506(b) is that recovery of postpetition interest is "unqualified." As Justice Frankfurter remarked some time ago, however: "The notion that because the words of a statute are plain, its meaning is also plain, is merely pernicious oversimplification." United States v. Monia, 317 U.S. 424, 431, 63 S. Ct. 409, 412, 87 L. Ed. 376 (1943) (dissenting opinion).

Although "the use of the comma is exceedingly arbitrary and indefinite," United States v. Palmer, 3 Wheat. 610, 638, 4 L. Ed. 471 (1818) (separate opinion of Johnson, J.), the Court is able to read § 506(b) the way that it does only because of the comma following the phrase "interest on such claim." Without this "capricious" bit of punctuation, In re Newbury Café, Inc., 841 F.2d 20, 22 (CA1 1988), cert. pending, No. 87-1784, the relevant portion of § 506(b) would read as follows: "there shall be allowed to the holder of [an oversecured] claim, interest on such claim and any reasonable fees, costs, or charges provided for under the agreement under which such claim arose." The phrase "interest on such claim" would be qualified by the phrase "provided for under the agreement under which such claim arose," and nonconsensual liens would not accrue postpetition interest. * * *

The Court's reliance on the comma is misplaced. "[P]unctuation is not decisive of the construction of a statute." Costanzo v. Tillinghast, 287 U.S. 341, 344, 53 S. Ct. 152, 153, 77 L. Ed. 350 (1932). * * *

Even if I believed that the language of § 506(b) were clearer than it is, I would disagree with the Court's conclusion, for *Midlantic* counsels against inferring congressional intent to change pre-Code bankruptcy law. At issue in *Midlantic* was § 554(a) of the Code, 11 U.S.C. § 554(a), which provided that "[a]fter notice and a hearing, the trustee may abandon any property of the estate that is burdensome to the estate or that is of inconsequential value to the estate." Despite this unequivocal language, the Court held that § 554(a) does not authorize a trustee to abandon hazardous property in contravention of a state statute or regulation reasonably designed to protect the public health or safety. Relying on only three pre-Code cases (one did not deal with state laws and in another the relevant language was arguably dicta), the Court concluded that under pre-Code bankruptcy law there were restrictions on a trustee's power to abandon property. 474 U.S., at 500-501, 106 S. Ct., at 759-760. The Court stated that the "normal rule of statutory construction is that if Congress intends for legislation to change the interpretation of a judicially created concept, it makes that intent specific," and noted that it had "followed this rule with particular care in construing the scope of bankruptcy codifications." Id., at 501, 106 S. Ct., at 759 (citations omitted). Given the pre-Code law and Congress' goal of protecting the environment, the Court was "unwilling to assume that by enactment of § 554(a), Congress implicitly overturned longstanding restrictions on the common law abandonment power." Id., at 506, 106 S. Ct., at 762.

The Court characterizes *Midlantic* as involving "a situation where bankruptcy law, under the proposed interpretation, was in clear conflict with state or federal laws of great importance." Though I agree with that characterization, I think there is more to *Midlantic* than conflict with state or federal laws. Contrary to the Court's intimation, *Midlantic* did not "concer[n] statutory language which ... was open to interpretation." The language of § 554(a) is "absolute in its terms," 474 U.S., at 509, 106 S. Ct., at 763 (REHNQUIST, J., dissenting), and the Court in *Midlantic* did not attempt to argue otherwise. Nonetheless, the Court concluded that such clear language was insufficient to demonstrate specific congressional intent to change pre-Code law. The rule of *Midlantic* is that bankruptcy statutes will not be deemed to have changed pre-Code law unless there is some indication that Congress thought that it was effecting such a change.

* * * Prior to the 1978 enactment of the Code, this Court, as well as every Court of Appeals to address the question, had refused to allow postpetition interest on nonconsensual liens such as the tax lien involved in this case. In order to deflect this line of cases, the Court refers to the practice "of denying postpetition interest to the holders of nonconsensual liens, while allowing it to holders of consensual liens," as "an exception to an exception." Regardless of how it is labeled, the practice was more widespread and more well established than the practice in *Midlantic*, and was certainly one that Congress "[would have been] aware of when enacting the Code." * * *

For the reasons set forth above, I respectfully dissent.

NOTES

1. Does the Court's method of statutory interpretation require that § 362(b)(4) be interpreted to provide an exception from the automatic stay only for police and regulatory proceedings dealing with chemical weapons matters? See Chapter Three of this text, above, footnote 20.

2. Does the Court's interpretation of § 506(b) make irrelevant the interest rate provided for in the oversecured creditor's agreement? In other words, should a court set the interest rate under § 506(b) without reference to the contractually agreed-upon interest rate, especially without regard to a higher rate of interest that the contract may provide for during periods when the loan is in default? Consider the following case.

Matter of Terry Limited Partnership
United States Court of Appeals, Seventh Circuit, 1994
27 F.3d 241

[Terry Limited Partnership ("Terry"), gave first, second, and third mortgages on its principal asset, an office building, to three creditors. Terry defaulted on the second and third mortgages. When Terry failed in its chapter 11 reorganization efforts, the court ordered the building sold. The third mortgagee, Invex Holdings, bought the building at the foreclosure sale for slightly over $4 million, apparently less than the total due on the three mortgages. The first mortgagee was paid in full

from the proceeds. A dispute arose over the amount of the claim of the second mortgagee (Equitable Life Insurance Company). Equitable's second mortgage carried a contractual interest rate of 14¼% per annum absent default, but 17¼% during any time when the second mortgage was in default. Invex Holdings, as third mortgagee, would receive back anything left out of the $4 million after payment of the first and second mortgages. If interest on the second mortgage during the chapter 11 case were calculated at the higher default rate, Invex would receive back little or none of the $4 million. The question then was what interest rate was applicable under § 506(b) in favor of Equitable, an oversecured creditor.]

BAUER, Circuit Judge.

* * * The bankruptcy court ordered that Equitable be awarded postdefault interest at the higher contract rate. On appeal, the district court affirmed. * * *

Crucial to the outcome of this case is the significance of the contract default rate. Section 506 of the Bankruptcy Code provides that a holder of an oversecured claim is entitled to "interest on such claim, and any reasonable fees, costs, or charges provided for under the agreement under which such claim arose." 11 U.S.C. § 506(b). The Supreme Court, in United States v. Ron Pair Enters., Inc., 489 U.S. 235, 242 (1989), held that while an award of "fees, costs, or charges" is dictated by the loan agreement, the award of interest is not. The Court did not elaborate, however, as to how the interest rate in the agreement should be treated.

Bankruptcy courts have construed *Ron Pair* to require analyzing default rates based on the facts and equities specific to each case. This does not render the contracted-for default rate irrelevant. "[D]espite its equity pedigree, [bankruptcy] is a procedure for enforcing pre-bankruptcy entitlements under specified terms and conditions rather than a flight of redistributive fancy." In re Lapiana, 909 F.2d 221, 223 (7th Cir. 1990). Creditors have a right to bargained-for post-petition interest and "bankruptcy judges are not empowered to dissolve rights in the name of equity." Id. at 224. What emerges from the post-*Ron Pair* decisions is a presumption in favor of the contract rate subject to rebuttal based upon equitable considerations. In re Courtland Estates Corp., 144 B.R. 5, 9 (Bankr. D. Mass. 1992); In re Hollstrom, 133 B.R. 535, 539 (Bankr. D. Colo. 1991); DWS Invs., 121 B.R. at 849 (Bankr. C.D. Cal. 1990).

Courts have found the presumption to be sufficiently rebutted in cases where the contract rate was significantly higher than the predefault rate without any justification offered for the spread. Id. For example, in *Consolidated Properties*, 152 B.R. at 458, the court refused to award interest based on a contract default rate which was thirty-six percent higher than the predefault rate where the contract already provided that the creditor would be entitled to late fees stemming from the debtor's default. A higher default rate of interest would have in effect enabled the creditor to recover twice for the same losses. In *Hollstrom* and in *DWS Investments*, contract default rates of thirty-six percent and twenty-five percent respectively were rejected because no evidence was presented to show that these rates were common in the market at the time of the transactions.

Conversely, in *Courtland Estates*, the creditor submitted evidence showing that the contract rate of eighteen percent was within the range of default rates charged at the relevant time. After considering the equities of the case, the court awarded the creditor postdefault interest based on the contract rate.

In the proceedings below, the bankruptcy judge heard extensive testimony about the purpose of a default rate of interest. Specifically, the evidence established that a default rate is commonly included in mortgage transactions to cover the additional but unforeseeable costs and risks associated with a defaulting borrower. Further, Schefmeyer, Invex Holdings's own expert witness, testified that given interest rates at the time of this transaction, a mortgage such as Equitable's with a predefault interest rate of 14¼ percent and a default rate of 17¼ percent was not unreasonable.

The record and the caselaw support the bankruptcy judge's conclusion that Equitable's contract default rate was reasonable. In cases where courts refused to award interest based on the contractual default rates, it was because those rates could not be justified by demonstrated need or by prevailing industry practice. Here, Schefmeyer's testimony confirmed that default rates customarily ranged between 2½ percent and 4½ percent over the predefault rate. And while Invex Holdings's mortgage was inherently riskier than Equitable's mortgage, the fact that their own mortgage note was payable at a rate of 17¼ percent does undermine to some degree the claim that Equitable's default rate was patently unreasonable.

Invex Holdings contends that the decision of the bankruptcy court should be reversed because awarding Equitable the default rate of interest would provide Equitable with double recovery. Because the bankruptcy court permitted Equitable to recover the costs and charges associated with the default as provided for in the promissory note, Invex Holdings argues that the award of default interest was inequitable.

As discussed earlier, a creditor is entitled to an award of "fees, costs, or charges," if the loan agreement provides for such an award and to the extent such an award is reasonable. 11 U.S.C. § 506(b). Equitable's note entitled it to receive appraisal fees and attorneys' fees. This provision fails, however, to compensate Equitable for the unforeseeable costs associated with Terry's default. As Schefmeyer's testimony bears out, a default situation requires a creditor to actively monitor the collateral to ensure that its value is preserved. The costs incurred in performing this task vary from case to case and simply cannot be provided for beforehand. Inclusion of a default rate of interest is designed to address this difficulty. *Consolidated Properties,* 152 B.R. at 457. Recognizing the distinction between the foreseeable and unforeseeable costs of a default, the bankruptcy court correctly determined that the default rate was designed to compensate for losses suffered in addition to those provided for in the agreement. * * *

By extending financing to Terry, Invex Holdings placed itself in a position subordinate to that of Roosevelt and Equitable and in doing so, knowingly took the risk that it would get nothing in the event of a default. Denying Equitable postdefault interest at the contract rate would be tantamount to transferring Invex Holdings's risk to Equitable after the fact. There is nothing equitable about such a redistribution. The decisions of the bankruptcy court and the district court awarding Equitable postdefault interest at the rate provided for in its agreement are
AFFIRMED.

NOTE

Some courts apply this "equitable considerations" approach to determining the interest rate allowable under § 506(b), including in cases where a default interest rate is sought. Other courts treat the extra interest payable under a default interest clause as a "fee" and thus allow it, under the language of § 506(b) only if it is reasonable. Yet other courts treat the absence of any explicit "reasonableness" limitation on interest in § 506(b) as a signal that any agreed-upon interest rate is allowable if it would be permitted by nonbankruptcy law. For a discussion of these approaches, see Hepner v. PWP Golden Eagle Tree, LLC (In re K&J Properties, Inc.), 338 B.R. 450 (Bankr. D. Colo. 2005) (allowing 36% default interest rate).

2. When Adequate Protection Fails

LNC Investments, Inc. v. First Fidelity Bank

United States District Court, Southern District of New York, 2000
247 B.R. 38, adhered to on denial of
reconsideration, 2000 WL 461612 (S.D.N.Y. 2000)

HAIGHT, Senior District Judge.

This case, in which plaintiffs, holders of bonds issued by a trust administered by defendants, allege claims under the Trust Indenture Act ("TIA"), 15 U.S.C. § 77aaa et seq., and state law, is now before this Court on remand for a new trial following the Court of Appeals' reversal of a judgment dismissing the complaint following a jury verdict in defendants' favor on the issue of liability in a bifurcated trial. The Court of Appeals held that this Court's charge erroneously required the jury to decide a question of law arising out of the United States Bankruptcy Code ("the Code"), specifically, whether on a proper construction of the Code a secured creditor's claim is entitled to "superpriority" status if the creditor files a motion with the bankruptcy court for an order lifting the stay of proceedings against the debtor or, in the alternative, for an order of adequate protection, the bankruptcy court denies any relief, and the creditor's collateral subsequently proves inadequate to cover its claim. * * *

[P]laintiffs owned bonds that were issued by an equipment trust ("the Trust") created as part of a secured financing for Eastern Airlines ("Eastern"). The defendants were the indenture trustees. * * * I will refer to plaintiffs as "the Bondholders" and defendants as "the Trustees."

On November 15, 1986, Eastern entered into a sale/leaseback transaction covering 110 of its used aircraft. That transaction created the Trust. Eastern sold the aircraft to the Trust, which leased them back to Eastern. To raise the funds to purchase the aircraft, the Trust issued three series of equipment trust certificates ("Bonds"). These are the Bonds that the Bondholders bought. The three series of Bonds, whose interest rates and maturity dates differed, had a total principal value of $500,000,000. The Trust indenture obligated Eastern to make lease payments to the Trust in amounts sufficient to pay the principal and the interest due on the Bonds. Title to the aircraft was held in trust as collateral for the Bonds.

On March 9, 1989, while still possessing and making use of the collateral aircraft to conduct its business, Eastern filed a voluntary petition in the Bankruptcy Court for this District seeking protection under Chapter 11 of the Code. As of the date of the petition, there were 104 aircraft in the "collateral pool," with an appraised principal value of $681,800,000. The aggregate value of the outstanding Bonds was $453,765,000. Accordingly the Bondholders were at that time oversecured to the extent of the difference between those amounts, namely, $228,035,000, an amount referred to in bankruptcy parlance as an "equity cushion."

Over the course of the ensuing months, as the result of factors I need not describe, the market value of the aircraft decreased significantly. "As of November 9, 1990," the Court of Appeals observed, "the appraised value of the 67 aircraft remaining in the collateral pool, together with the funds set aside in a 'cash collateral account' from the sales and leases of aircraft formerly in the collateral pool, totaled somewhere between $475,443,000 and $589,679,000." 173 F.3d at 458.

The aggregate value of the outstanding Bonds at that time is not stated in the prior opinions, but the Trustees were sufficiently alarmed by the eroding collateral to file a motion in the Bankruptcy Court (Lifland, J.) on November 14, 1990, for adequate protection under § 363(e) of the Code). That section requires a bankruptcy court to prohibit or condition a bankrupt party's use, sale or lease of property serving as collateral if such action is "necessary to provide adequate protection" of the secured creditor's interest in the collateral. Alternatively, the Trustees moved pursuant to § 362(d) of the Code for an order lifting the automatic stay of proceedings against Eastern imposed by § 362(a), which had been in effect since filing of the Chapter 11 petition and prevented the Trustees' foreclosing on the collateral. That application for relief, which * * * I will occasionally refer to as "the Lift Stay/Adequate Protection Motion" or "the Motion," was pending undetermined before Bankruptcy Judge Lifland when, on January 18, 1991, Eastern ceased all operations and stipulated to the return of the remaining collateral (aircraft and cash) to the Trustee.

The Bondholders claim that these unhappy events left them in the unenviable position of general unsecured claimants against Eastern for unpaid principal amounts, and, because the value of the assets in the Eastern estate was not enough to pay even all the administrative claims, the second and third Bondholders will receive nothing. Confronted with that substantial economic loss, the Bondholders brought this action against the Trustees for breach of their duty to discharge their fiduciary responsibilities in a prudent manner. The Bondholders' principal criticism of the Trustees is that they waited too long before making a Lift Stay/Adequate Protection Motion.

Even if one assumes an imprudent delay by the Trustees in making the Motion (which for all practical purposes might not have been made at all), the Trustees are not liable to the Bondholders unless the Bondholders can show that failure to make the Motion caused them damage. The Bondholders undertake to make that showing by contending that if the Trustees had made the Motion and the bankruptcy court denied it, the Bondholders' claims would have qualified for "superpriority" status under § 507(b) of the Code.[47] Whether the Bondholders are right (the Trustees say they are not) is central to the Bondholders' effort to

---

47. [Footnote 3 in original:] If a Lift Stay/Adequate Protection Motion had been made by the Trustees, granted by the bankruptcy court, and the stay lifted or adequate security provided in response to that court's order, presumably the instant action would not have been filed. If the bankruptcy court had made an order for adequate protection and the mandated protection ultimately proved inadequate, it is common ground that the Bondholders' claims would have qualified for "superpriority" status under § 507(b) of the Bankruptcy Code, whose provisions lie at the heart of the case and are quoted and discussed in text. What the parties dispute, and this opinion addresses, is the legal consequence within the § 507(b) context of a bankruptcy court's denial of such a motion.

demonstrate that they were damaged by the Trustees' inaction. It is also the question of law identified by the Court of Appeals to be decided by this Court on remand and in advance of the second trial.

"Superpriority" is not a word that appears in the Code. It has been fashioned by courts and commentators to describe the enhanced status conferred upon a secured claim in the distribution of a bankrupt estate if the claim qualifies for § 507(b) treatment. A secured claim meeting § 507(b)'s prerequisites takes on the enviable nature of an administrative claim under § 507(a)(1), the highest priority the Code recognizes; moreover, § 507(b) provides that a qualifying secured claim "shall have priority over every other claim" allowable under § 507(a)(1). Hence the entirely appropriate adjective "super priority": in the privileged world of administrative claims, the § 507(b)-anointed secured claim is primus inter pares. * * *

The Trustees contend that a bankruptcy court's denial of a motion for relief from stay or, in the alternative, for adequate protection on account of a pre-existing equity cushion does not entitle a secured creditor to a superpriority claim under § 507(b). They say that it is only when such a motion for adequate protection is granted and the additional protection conferred subsequently proves inadequate that a superpriority claim may become available.

The Bondholders contend that an order denying such a motion on the ground that the secured creditor was adequately protected by a pre-existing equity cushion triggers a superpriority administrative claim under § 507(b) if that equity cushion subsequently proves inadequate.

The parties agree that nowhere in the "opaque, inconsistent case law" generated by § 507(b) can one find a decision squarely in point. * * * Nor is there any legislative history which squarely addresses the issue. * * *

[T]he filing of a bankruptcy petition * * * automatically stays the secured creditor's power to foreclose upon the collateral. Thus the Code's automatic stay confers a considerable boon upon the debtor. The stay is also regarded as a source of "creditor protection," since without it creditors would race each other to achieve preferment through litigation, and "[b]ankruptcy is designed to provide an orderly procedure under which all creditors are treated equally." Historical and Statutory Notes following 11 U.S.C. § 361 (1993) (hereinafter "Notes") at 3. However, the secured creditor has no interest in that grand design. Its specific purpose in bargaining for an interest in the debtor's property was to avoid being treated equally with "all creditors." What does the Code do for a secured creditor, frozen in place as was the Trust, unable to avail itself of the security for which it had bargained? * * *

Section 507 of the Code, captioned "Priorities," deals comprehensively with the priorities of all claims against the bankrupt estate. Section 507(b) is the subsection dealing specifically with secured claims. It provides:

> If the trustee, under section 362, 363, or 364 of this title, provides adequate protection of the interest of a holder of a claim secured by a lien on property of the debtor and if, notwithstanding such protection, such creditor has a claim allowable under subsection (a)(1) of this section arising from the stay of action against such property under section 362 of this title, from the use, sale or lease of such property under section 363 of this title, or from the

granting of a lien under section 364(d) of this title, then such creditor's claim under such subsection shall have priority over every other claim allowable under such subsection.[48]

Section 507(b)'s reference to "a claim allowable under subsection (a)(1) of this section" is, by further cross-reference, an administrative expense allowed under section 503(b). See 11 U.S.C. § 507(a)(1). The relevant part of § 503(b) allows as administrative expenses "the actual, necessary costs and expenses of preserving the estate."

Section 507(b) reflects Congress's concern that, to the extent the section is applicable to a given case, a secured creditor have "adequate protection" for its claim. "The concept of adequate protection is derived from the fifth amendment protection of property interests as enunciated by the Supreme Court." Notes at 3 (citing Wright v. Union Central Life Ins. Co., 311 U.S. 273, 61 S. Ct. 196, 85 L. Ed. 184 (1940) and Louisville Joint Stock Land Bank v. Radford, 295 U.S. 555, 55 S. Ct. 854, 79 L. Ed. 1593 (1935)).

Section 507(b) also references §§ 362, 363 and 364 of the Code. The subsection is triggered if the debtor-in-possession "under section 362, 363, or 364 of this title" provides "adequate protection" to a secured creditor. As noted, § 362(a) stays creditors' proceedings against the debtor and its property. Section 363(b)(1) authorizes a bankruptcy trustee to "use, sell, or lease, other than in the ordinary course of business, property of the estate." Section 364(a) and (c) empower a trustee operating the business of the debtor to obtain unsecured or secured credit and incur unsecured or secured debt in the ordinary course of the business.

But each of these sections contains provisions under which secured creditors may invoke their interests. Thus § 362(d)(1) directs the bankruptcy court to grant relief from the stay to a party in interest "for cause, including the lack of adequate protection of an interest in property of such party in interest ..." Section 363(e) provides that on application "of an entity that has an interest in property used, sold or leased, by the trustee," the bankruptcy court "shall prohibit or condition such use, sale or lease as is necessary to provide adequate protection of such interest." Section 364(d)(1)(B) provides that the bankruptcy court may "authorize the obtaining of credit or the incurring of debt secured by a senior or equal lien on property of the estate that is subject to a lien only if ... there is adequate protection of the interest of the holder of the lien on the property of the estate on which such senior or equal lien is proposed to be granted." * * *

To the extent that this statutory scheme of adequate protection for secured creditors applies to the circumstances of a given case, its purpose is summarized by the Historical and Statutory Notes following § 361 at 8-9:

---

48. [Footnote 5 in original:] One clarifying note should be sounded. The "trustee" referred to in § 507(b)'s opening phrase is not the sort of Trustee that the defendants are. The statutory reference is to a trustee appointed by the bankruptcy court to preside over the insolvent debtor's estate. In the case at bar, Eastern filed a voluntary petition under Chapter 11, which permitted Eastern to continue as a debtor-in-possession. Since a debtor-in-possession "shall have all the rights ... and shall perform all the functions ... of a trustee serving in a case under this subchapter," 11 U.S.C. § 1107(a), the opening phrase in § 507(b) should be read for the purposes of this case as: "If the debtor-in-possession, under section 362, 363, or 364 of this title, provides adequate protection ..." * * *

Adequate protection of an interest of an entity in property is intended to protect a creditor's allowed secured claim. To the extent the protection proves to be inadequate after the fact, the creditor is entitled to a first priority administrative expense under section 503(b).

The careful reader will note in the last quoted sentence a veiled reference to § 507(b). That subsection, added by the 1984 Acts, is summarized by the Notes following § 507(b) at 844:

Subsection (b) provides that to the extent adequate protection of the interest of a holder of a claim proves to be inadequate, then the creditor's claim is given priority over every other allowable claim entitled to distribution under section 507(a).

The Trustees contend principally that the plain language of § 507(b) precludes conferring superpriority status upon the claim of a secured creditor if that creditor makes a Lift Stay/Adequate Protection Motion and the bankruptcy court denies it entirely, which is to say, the court refuses to lift the stay (so the collateral remains immune to suit and unavailable to the creditor), and also refuses to make an order of adequate protection, having concluded that the existing collateral adequately protects the creditor. Section 507(b) is not triggered by such circumstances, the Trustees argue, even if the court was wrong, and protection the court viewed as adequate ultimately proves to be so inadequate that the secured creditor recovers nothing on its claim.

That proposition necessarily follows, the Trustees say, from § 507(b)'s introductory phrases: "If the [debtor-in-possession], under section 362, 363, or 364 of this title, provides adequate protection ..." The verb "provides," cast in the present tense, is consistent only with protection provided after filing of the Chapter 11 petition, a temporal concept reinforced by the requirement that the protection covered by § 507(b) must be provided by "the debtor-in-possession," a status which a debtor attains only after a petition is filed. Thus, in the case at bar, Eastern became a debtor of the Trust and, derivatively, the Bondholders in 1986, upon completion of the financing arrangement which created the equity cushion. Eastern did not become a "debtor-in-possession" until 1989, when it filed its voluntary Chapter 11 petition.

Moreover, § 507(b) specifies that the debtor-in-possession provide adequate protection "under section 362, 363, or 364" of the Bankruptcy Code. "Under," in this context, may be read as synonymous with "pursuant to"; and the various mechanisms available to secured creditors for obtaining adequate protection pursuant to [or under] §§ 362, 363 and 364, further implemented by the remedies of § 361, can only come into effect upon the filing of a bankruptcy petition.

The Bondholders respond that this literal reading of § 507(b) thwarts the Code's relevant purpose, which is to protect secured creditors. They cite, among other cases, Holy Trinity Church v. United States, 143 U.S. 457, 460, 12 S. Ct. 511, 36 L. Ed. 226 (1892) ("If a literal construction of the words of a statute be absurd, the act must be so construed as to avoid the absurdity. The court must restrain the words. The object designed to be reached by the act must limit and control the literal import of the terms and phrases employed.") (citation omitted). In the case at bar, the Bondholders argue that with respect to a secured creditor's ultimate loss, there is no principled difference between a bankruptcy court's ordering additional protection which later proves to be inadequate, and the court's denying that relief based upon the equally erroneous conclusion that the pre-existing protection is adequate. In both instances, the bankruptcy's court's error and the adverse consequences to the secured creditor are precisely the same.[49]

Each party makes the point that if Congress intended § 507(b) to mean what the other party says it means, Congress would have used language saying so explicitly. Both parties correctly argue that Congress could have expressed itself more clearly, but the arguments cancel each other out, and I am left to deal with the Delphic aspects of the words Congress actually used. * * *

While the Bondholders' reading of the subsection is permissible, it requires considerable stretching of the language. The Trust's equity cushion came into being as part of the original financing transaction, when everyone's hopes were high and Eastern's horizon free of the gathering clouds of bankruptcy. It is a stretch to read § 507(b)'s reference to a "debtor-in-possession" as including an entity that became a "debtor" by means of the underlying transaction, at a time when becoming a "debtor-in-possession" was the last thing anyone wanted.

It is equally a stretch to read § 507(b)'s use of the present tense verb "provides" as including a bankruptcy court's order denying an adequate protection motion on the ground that in the past, that is to say prepetition, a debtor had provided collateral ostensibly sufficient to secure the claim of the moving creditor.

Of course, the court's order occurs postpetition, but that does not carry the Bondholders far enough. They must argue that for purposes of qualifying for superpriority status under § 507(b), a court's order denying adequate protection is the functional equivalent of a debtor-in-possession's providing that protection in response to a court order granting it. The semantic obstacles to that interpretation are apparent.

Accordingly there is considerable force to the Trustees' "plain meaning" argument, which if accepted would dispose of the issue, even if one sympathized with the Bondholders' plight, condemned the Trustees' sloth, and discerned no principled difference for superpriority purposes between orders granting and denying adequate protection.

Nevertheless, § 507(b) is less than precise, and as I have said, I think that the Bondholders' interpretation is permissible. But the subsection's language inclines sufficiently in favor of the Trustees to cast upon the Bondholders the burden of demonstrating that, given the objectives of the Bankruptcy Code, the Trustees' interpretation of § 507(b) leads to an absurd result. The Bondholders do not make that showing.

---

49. [Footnote 6 in original:] The parties' differences arise out [of] the first prerequisite to § 507(b) superpriority status, found in the subsection's introductory phrases. There are other prerequisites. Section 507(b) requires that a secured creditor's claim be "allowable under subsection (a)(1) of this section" and "arising from" conduct covered by §§ 362, 363, or 364(d). The Bondholders' claims satisfy these conditions. Section 507(a)(1) cross-references § 503(b), which provides that administrative expenses include the "actual, necessary costs and expenses of preserving the estate." The use of collateral to keep a business operating qualifies as an administrative expense. One cannot imagine a more "essential aspect" of an airline's efforts to reorganize than the use of its aircraft. Moreover, the Bondholders' claims arise from the automatic stay imposed by § 362(a)(1), which prevented the Trustee from foreclosing on the collateralized aircraft.

While the Bondholders rely upon general legislative statements that § 507(b) is intended for the protection of secured creditors, some of which I have quoted supra, such statements cannot trump plain indications of congressional purpose derived from the statute. Nor can the Code be regarded as expressing the intent of Congress that secured creditors receive total, 100% ironclad protection; see *Timbers* at 379-80, 108 S. Ct. 626 ("That secured creditors do not bear one kind of reorganization cost hardly means that they bear none of them.").

I think it plain that the Bankruptcy Code has a number of particular objectives * * *. The desires and purposes of debtors and creditors are inherently in conflict, as are the desires and purposes of creditors inter se (secured versus unsecured). The Bankruptcy Code necessarily embodies compromises between competing economic interests.

In the context of a Chapter 11 reorganization, a primary objective of the Code is the rehabilitation of the debtor. Congress's purpose in enacting Chapter 11 was "to establish a preference for reorganizations, where they are legally feasible and economically practical." In re Baker & Drake, Inc., 35 F.3d 1348, 1354 (9th Cir. 1994). "The object of Chapter 11 of the Code is to permit a potentially viable debtor to restructure and emerge from bankruptcy protection." In re Kings Terrace Nursing Home and Health Related Facility, 184 B.R. 200, 203 (S.D.N.Y. 1995). For obvious reasons, Congress prefers the successful reorganization of a corporate debtor to liquidation, dismemberment and death under Chapter 7.

Since a reorganization must be "economically practical" to succeed, it is at once apparent that a superpriority claim is the natural enemy of a reorganization. The superpriority claim is preferred even among administrative expenses, and must accordingly be a matter of concern to those whose postpetition dealings with a debtor-in-possession may be essential to the debtor's economic survival. Thus the overhanging, intimidating presence of a multi-million dollar superpriority claim may chill the willingness of others to do business with a debtor-in-possession, dooming that resolution preferred by Congress, a successful reorganization, and leading to liquidation.

These practical concerns resound in the case at bar because the Bondholders argue for the broadest conceivable superpriority for an oversecured creditor sitting on an equity cushion when a bankruptcy petition is filed. The Bondholders say that all a secured creditor need do to achieve superpriority status is to make a Lift Stay/Adequate Protection Motion. Superpriority is then guaranteed, whether the bankruptcy court grants relief or denies it. Opening to the jury at the first trial, counsel for the Bondholders likened their situation to that of the assureds under an insurance policy:

> Super priority is like an insurance policy. It's designed so that if the unexpected happens, you get protected. But, just like an insurance policy, you have got to pay a premium. You have got to do something. You have got to sign up for it.
>
> Well, the way you sign up for a super priority claim is very simple. It doesn't cost you money. All it requires is you raise your hand and ask. You go into bankruptcy court and you make a motion. You say to the judge, I'm not protected, please protect me. And once you start that process rolling, the please-protect-me process, if things go wrong, you get the super priority....

> And even if he denies your adequate protection motion, you get your priority claim if it turns out you are not going to get paid in full, because implicit in that denial is a determination by the judge that, I'm denying it because you are adequately protected. If he wasn't making that implicit determination, he has got to grant your motion.

Trial Tr. 139-141.

The analogy to an insurance policy is not entirely apt, since if the equity cushion disappears and the security proves to be inadequate, the superpriority- brandishing secured creditor is paid not by an insurance company but by the debtor, to the derogation of other creditors and, quite possibly, to the debtor's hope for rehabilitation.

I do not doubt that Congress could enact a statute so favorable to oversecured creditors, but I do not think that it has done so in the present Code. I think that the Code protects secured creditors up to a point, but not beyond, and the point of demarcation is reached when granting superpriority status would imperil other identifiable objectives of the Code, which include a preference for economically feasible reorganizations.

The limited nature of the benefit conferred upon secured creditors by § 507(b) is inherent in its reference to a debtor-in-possession who "under section 362, 363, or 364 of this title, provides adequate protection." That language conjures up the image of a debtor providing additional protection to a secured creditor in obedience to the bankruptcy court's order granting a motion brought by the creditor under one of the three designated sections. It is one thing to say that if this court-ordered, debtor-provided protection proves to be inadequate, then under § 507(b) the secured creditor "has superpriority for a claim in the amount that the debtor's use of the collateral during the time of the stay diminished the value of the collateral, but only to the extent such diminution is in excess of the adequate protection received." In re Blackwood Associates, L.P., 153 F.3d 61, 69 (2d Cir. 1998). It is quite another to say that the court's denial of any adequate protection entitles the creditor to a superpriority claim for the full diminution in the value of the collateral.

I do not think that the statutory scheme tips so far in favor of secured creditors. Although no court has explicitly said so, that is the view of a leading commentator. See 4 Lawrence P. King, et al., COLLIER ON BANKRUPTCY ¶ 507.12(1)(c)(ii) (15th ed. rev. 1999) at 507-90-91 * * *.

I reach that conclusion in the case at bar. I do so because (a) the Trustees' interpretation of § 507(b) conforms more closely to the language of that subsection and its interconnection with other provisions of the Bankruptcy Code, and (b) the Bondholders have failed to demonstrate that the Code's statutory scheme and objectives render the Trustees' interpretation an absurdity.

The Bondholders argue with considerable force that it is anomalous for the granting and denial of an adequate protection motion to have such disparate consequences, when the bankruptcy court's error in assessing adequacy and the consequent prejudice to the secured creditor are the same. However, in view of the language Congress used and the manner in which the Code's sections cross-reference each other, that is an anomaly that the Congress must remedy.

For the foregoing reasons, the Court answers the question presented in the negative, and will so instruct the jury.

It is SO ORDERED.

NOTES

1. In a later appeal, the Second Circuit declined to decide whether Judge Haight's interpretation of § 507(b) was correct. See LNC Invs., Inc. v. Nat'l Westminster Bank, 308 F.3d 169 (2d Cir. 2002).

2. Eastern Air Lines' general unsecured creditors did receive a small distribution, as noted above in Chapter One, footnote 21. It may also be helpful to know that "the market value of [Eastern Air Lines'] aircraft decreased significantly as a result of various factors, including the Iraqi invasion of Kuwait in August 1990, which caused fuel prices to rise." LNC Invs., Inc. v. First Fid. Bank, 173 F.3d 454, 458 (2d Cir. 1999).

3. If Judge Haight's interpretation of § 507(b) is correct, is a secured creditor's property interest adequately protected by the existence of an equity cushion? Is a secured creditor's property interest entitled to adequate protection in addition to the equity cushion regardless of the cushion's size? Is a debtor in possession permitted to offer superpriority administrative expense status as part of adequate protection? See § 361(3).

4. Suppose the Trustees had sought relief from the stay or sought adequate protection early in the case, but had asked only for a court order requiring Eastern Air Lines to maintain casualty insurance on the airplanes. If the court had granted such an order, would the bondholders have been entitled to a § 507(b) superpriority when the airplanes declined in value not due to an accident but due to market conditions?

5. Suppose (a) early in the case the Trustees had sought relief from the stay or had sought to condition use of the airplanes on provision of adequate protection, (b) Eastern Air Lines had offered, as adequate protection, to monitor the value of the airplanes and to inform the Trustees if their value dropped more than 5%, (c) the court so ordered, and (d) the value of the airplanes dropped so as to reduce the value of the bondholders' liens. Would the bondholders have been entitled to a § 507(b) superpriority for the amount of the loss? Would your answer depend on whether Eastern Air Lines breached its promise to inform the Trustees of the decline in value? What if Eastern Air Lines gave proper notice of the decline in value, but the decline occurred so rapidly that the value of the bondholders' liens was reduced before the Trustees could obtain relief from the stay?

6. Should it matter, in the various hypothetical cases posed in Notes 4 and 5 immediately above, whether the court order for adequate protection was entered as the result of a motion by the Trustees or, on the other hand, as the result of a stipulation entered into by Eastern Air Lines and the Trustees under Rule 4001(d)? Suppose Eastern Air Lines and the Trustees entered into such a stipulation but did not obtain a court order approving it?

7. The court mentions the Fifth Amendment. Does the court's interpretation of section 507(b) raise a Fifth Amendment "takings" issue—whether the bondholders' property interests were taken by the bankruptcy process without just compensation? Should a court interpret a statute so as to raise a constitutional question if another reasonable interpretation is available? See, e.g., Jones v. U.S., 529 U.S. 848, 857, 120 S. Ct. 1904,1911, 146 L. Ed. 2d 902 (2000) (relying on "the guiding principle that 'where a statute is susceptible of two constructions, by one of which grave and doubtful constitutional questions arise and by the other of which such questions are avoided, the Court's duty is to adopt the latter'").

8.   In footnote 49 above (originally the court's footnote 6), the court states that use
     of the airplanes during the case was of benefit to the estate, and thus the
     requirement of § 503(b)(1) that the expense be a necessary cost of preserving
     the estate was satisfied. Must a secured creditor who suffers loss due to failure
     of adequate protection prove that the estate received a benefit from use of the
     collateral in order to qualify for a § 507(b) superpriority?

     Suppose (i) a secured party receives court-ordered adequate protection of
     its interest in the collateral, (ii) the debtor in possession does not use the
     secured creditor's collateral during the case, other than to hold on to it in case
     it is needed, (iii) the debtor in possession eventually decides the collateral is not
     needed and thus agrees to relief from the stay to allow the secured creditor to
     foreclose its lien, and (iv) the collateral's value has dropped during the case
     despite the provision of what the court thought would be adequate protection,
     causing the secured creditor to suffer loss. Must the secured creditor show that
     the estate received an actual benefit from the availability of the collateral during
     the case, or is it sufficient that the estate had the potential to benefit from the
     availability of the collateral? See Ford Motor Credit Co. v. Dobbins, 35 F.3d 860
     (4th Cir. 1994) (denying superpriority because secured creditor's collateral which
     was held available for use was not actually used by debtor in possession and
     thus did not provide an "actual benefit" to the estate).

     Is the Fourth Circuit's requirement in *Dobbins* of an "actual benefit" unduly
     restrictive? Is it consistent with Reading Co. v. Brown, 391 U.S. 471, 88 S. Ct.
     1759, 20 L. Ed. 2d 751 (1968) (construing § 64a of the old Bankruptcy Act to
     require priority administrative expense status for property damage claims where
     reorganizing debtor's agent negligently caused a fire that spread to surrounding
     buildings)? Does it unnecessarily raise a 5th Amendment takings issue that could
     be avoided by a holding that the availability of collateral to the estate is a
     sufficient benefit to satisfy § 503(b)(1)?

3.   Surcharging Collateral Under Section 506(c)

In re Westwood Plaza Apartments, Ltd.
United States Bankruptcy Court, Eastern District of Texas, 1993
154 B.R. 916

HOUSTON ABEL, Chief Judge.

Before the Court is the Final Application for Allowance of Compensation and
Reimbursement of Expenses of Johnson, Bromberg & Leeds and Baskin &
Novakov, P.C. The Department of Housing and Urban Development ("HUD")
filed an objection to both Applications. HUD argued that the requested fees and
expenses should be denied because * * * the assets [from] which payment would
come * * * constitute HUD's cash collateral. * * * [T]he Court found that the fees
and expenses incurred by both firms were reasonable and necessary. Accordingly,
the Court approved the amount of compensation and reimbursement of expenses
sought in both fee applications.

However, the Court took under advisement the issue as to whether the rents
collected by the Debtor are cash collateral of HUD, and if so, may the Debtor use
the cash collateral to pay the fees and expenses that are approved. After reviewing
the arguments and the relevant case law, the Court is of the opinion the rents are
HUD's cash collateral and that the Debtor may not use the cash collateral to pay
the approved fees and expenses.

* * * [T]he Debtor asserts that even if this Court held that all the rents collected after the default are HUD's cash collateral, the Debtor may still use the money to pay the approved fees and expenses because HUD has benefitted from the services provided.[50] The basis of this argument is that HUD is receiving more under the approved Plan of Reorganization ("Plan") than it would receive under liquidation in Chapter 7. * * * HUD has a total allowed claim of $6,100,000.00 against property valued at $3,000,000.00. Because the original loan between the Debtor and HUD is non-recourse, if HUD were to foreclose its interest in the property, HUD would receive just the value of the property. HUD would not receive any money for its unsecured claim as it is in the Plan.

The general rule in bankruptcy is that administrative expenses are charged against the estate and not against secured creditors. The debtor must look to unencumbered assets of the estate to pay administrative expenses. However, § 506(c) provides an exception to this general rule. To charge a secured creditor with the administrative expenses under § 506(c), there must be a showing that the fees and expenses were: (1) necessary, (2) reasonable, and (3) incurred primarily for the benefit of the secured creditor resulting in a quantifiable direct benefit to the secured creditor. In re Senior-G & A Operating Co., Inc., 957 F.2d 1290, 1298-99 (5th Cir. 1992). Section 506(c) is to be interpreted narrowly with the burden of proving its elements on the Debtor. In re P.C., Ltd., 929 F.2d 203, 205 (5th Cir. 1991).

Because the Court has previously found that the fees and expenses were reasonable and necessary, the Court must now determine whether the fees and expenses *directly* benefitted HUD rather than the Debtor or other creditors. In re Flagstaff Foodservice Corporation, 739 F.2d 73, 75 (2d Cir. 1984); accord Brookfield Production Credit Association v. Borron, 738 F.2d 951, 952 (8th Cir. 1984), aff'g, 36 B.R. 445 (E.D. Mo. 1983). The Court agrees with the Debtor that HUD has received some benefit from the Plan— no matter how much HUD may disagree. HUD is receiving a return on its allowed unsecured claim that it would not have received in liquidation. However, the benefit that HUD has received is only incidental. The services were incurred directly, and primarily, to assist the Debtor to reorganize and maintain ownership of the apartment complex. *EES Lambert Associates,* 62 B.R. at 342; *Flagstaff Foodservice Corporation,* 739 F.2d at 76. The Debtor did not hire its attorneys to fashion a Plan that was best for HUD. The Plan was fashioned to help the Debtor reorganize and still meet the requirements of the Bankruptcy Code. To allow the Debtor to use HUD's cash collateral to pay the Debtor's attorneys would in essence be having HUD pay its own attorneys along with the attorneys it was opposing.[51] This clearly would not be fair and equitable to HUD and would go beyond the equitable intent of § 506(c).

---

50. [Footnote 7 in original:] Debtor relies upon 11 U.S.C. § 506(c) * * * .

51. [Footnote 9 in original:] Just because a creditor is getting more under a plan of reorganization than it would receive in liquidation does not establish that the creditor has received a direct benefit from the services. As part of receiving court approval of a plan, a debtor is required to establish that creditors are receiving as much as they would if the debtor were liquidated under Chapter 7. 11 U.S.C. § 1129. Therefore, to accept the Debtor's argument would mean that every debtor should be allowed to use encumbered assets to pay administrative expenses if the debtor was successful in getting its plan of reorganization approved.

Further, even if HUD received some incidental direct benefit, the Debtor has failed to meet its burden of establishing which fees and expenses were incurred primarily for, and directly benefitted, HUD. The Debtor seeks to use HUD's cash collateral to pay *all* the approved fees and expenses. It is clear from an overview of the billing statements that many of the fees and expenses have nothing to do with HUD. Therefore, the Debtor failed to sustain its burden. * * *

As a final argument, the Debtor seeks to avoid the restrictions of the Regulatory Agreement by requesting this Court to use its equitable powers. The Debtor asserts that the Regulatory Agreement is not binding upon the Court and that the Court should look to the provisions of the Bankruptcy Code regarding the use of cash collateral to pay administrative expenses.

As has been noted by other courts that have addressed this very argument, debtors * * * similar to the one before this Court are not without options. By denying Debtor's use of HUD's cash collateral, the Court is in no way preventing the Debtor from paying its counsel nor precluding the Debtor from exercising its rights under the Bankruptcy Code. The Debtor is still free to pay with funds which are not HUD's cash collateral.

Further, the Court can not ignore the historical precedent of other courts in their protection of the aims and objectives of the National Housing Act when interpreting and enforcing Regulatory Agreements. * * *

* * * HUD's interest in the rents were [*sic*] perfected the instant the Debtor defaulted on its loan documents. HUD had no affirmative duty to act to perfect its interest in the rents. Additionally, the Debtor has failed to meet its burden that it may use HUD's cash collateral pursuant to § 506(c). * * *

Accordingly, the Debtor is prohibited from using any monies which constitute HUD's cash collateral to pay the approved fees and expenses.[52] * * *

In re Lunan Family Restaurants Ltd. Partnership
United States Bankruptcy Court, Northern District of Illinois, 1996
192 B.R. 173

JACK B. SCHMETTERER, Bankruptcy Judge.

[*Debtor, a limited partnership, borrowed $13.5 million from Bank of America Illinois ("Bank") so that debtor could buy 31 Chicago area Wags restaurants and convert them to Shoney's restaurants. The debtor purchased some of the restaurant premises in fee simple and leased other restaurant premises from Marriott. To secure the $13.5 million loan (the "LFR credit"), Debtor gave Bank mortgages on its fee simple properties, leasehold mortgages on its leased restaurants, and security interests in its equipment and accounts receivable.*]

* * * The "Shoney's concept" did not take hold in the Chicago area. By late summer 1993, the Debtor was in default under the LFR Credit and in default under numerous Leases with Marriott for failure to pay rent and accrued real estate taxes. Marriott threatened to terminate the Leases. * * *

---

52. [Footnote 11 in original:] To the extent that the pre-petition retainer paid by the Debtor to its attorneys are from funds that are HUD's cash collateral, the attorneys are ordered to return the money to the estate.

[T]he Bank supported Debtor's selling of restaurants while Debtor was in default under the LFR Credit because that program was consistent with the Bank's belief that the best way to maximize the satisfaction of the Bank's debt was from liquidation of the Leases and Fee Properties on a going concern basis. The Bank did not seek to foreclose on the Leases or Fee Properties.

In October of 1994, the Debtor remained in default under the LFR Credit and the Leases. Marriott again threatened to terminate the Leases and take possession of the related restaurants. Marriott asserted that the Leases would be terminated on October 25, 1994, if taxes and rent were not paid. Notwithstanding ten months of defaults and threats of Lease terminations by Marriott, the Bank did not commence foreclosure actions with respect to Leases or Fee Properties. Instead * * * officers of the Bank met in October of 1994 with representatives of the Debtor and discussed with Debtor the filing of a Chapter 11 petition. Shortly thereafter, on October 25, 1994 (the "Petition Date"), the Debtor filed a voluntary petition under Chapter 11 of the Bankruptcy Code and continued to operate its business and manage its property as a debtor-in-possession. * * *

The Debtor presented alternative Chapter 11 plans to the Bank for consideration, but the Bank rejected any plans that involved a long term payout. The Bank has not presented its own plan and has not suggested on this record any modifications to Debtor's proposals.

On January 18, 1995, the Debtor obtained entry of an order authorizing employment of Site Location Specialists to continue its efforts begun pre-bankruptcy to market the Leases and Fee Properties for sale while business operations continued. Within five months of the Petition Date, eight Leases and Fee Properties were sold on a going concern basis. One other Lease was rejected and business operations at two of the other premises were closed. Within ten months from the petition date, the Debtor was able to sell a total of nineteen leased and fee restaurants, and it no longer operates at three premises. The Debtor is also actively marketing its remaining Leases and Fee Properties for sale, except for the lease of the restaurant known as Elm-Gurnee, which was rejected.

The Bank has not tried to convert this case to a Chapter 7 proceeding and has consented six separate times to use of cash collateral. The Bank also supported the extension of the Debtor's exclusivity period pursuant to 11 U.S.C. § 1121 to allow the Debtor more time to operate and liquidate the Leases and Fee Properties on a going concern basis.

The sale of nineteen Leases and Fee Properties generated over $11 million in gross proceeds, including $1,771,606.69 from sale of Leases, from which the Bank has received over $8.2 million in payments. In receiving such payments, the Bank remained subject to the possibility of § 506(c) surcharge, although it never agreed thereto.

In the course of Debtor's operations, the Debtor has incurred * * * costs and expenses which have not been paid from sales proceeds of the Leases and Fee Properties and which the Debtor lacks funds to pay * * *.

* * * The Debtor asks that it be reimbursed for all the foregoing expenses through a surcharge on the Bank's distribution from this estate, under § 506(c). * * *

Costs of administering a bankruptcy estate must generally be borne by the estate and its general creditors, and such expenses will not ordinarily be charged against collateral of secured creditors. Section 506(c) of the Bankruptcy Code sets forth a limited exception to this general rule to be applied to expenses incurred primarily for benefit of the secured creditor.

* * * A three-part test must be satisfied for expenses to be charged against a secured creditor's collateral. It must be shown that (1) the expenditure was necessary, (2) the amounts were reasonable, and (3) the secured creditor was the party primarily benefitted by the expenditure. The burden of proof is on any proponent of § 506(c) treatment, who must show by a preponderance of evidence that these elements are satisfied. Section 506(c) is based in equity and is the proper vehicle for making the Bank pay for benefit it reaped, if the requirements are met.
* * *

Primary Benefit

The utilities and wage-related expenses for the Fee Properties and leased restaurants which were sold produced an actual quantifiable benefit incurred primarily for benefit of the Bank. The requirement of a benefit to the secured creditor is the most important factor in applying § 506(c). Such a benefit must be shown in a quantitative rather than qualitative sense, and the expense must have been incurred primarily for the benefit of the secured creditor. These standards are satisfied in the instant case. Most expenses submitted by Claimants directly and primarily benefitted the Bank.

Costs expended while keeping the Debtor running as a going concern may be charged to the secured creditor where maintaining the going-concern value actually and specifically benefitted the secured creditor. United States v. Boatmen's First National Bank of Kansas City, 5 F.3d 1157, 1160 (8th Cir. 1993); In re AFCO Enterprises, 35 B.R. 512, 515 (Bankr. D. Utah 1983) (preservation of going concern value of a business can, under some circumstances, constitute benefit to secured creditor).

The Bank certainly received benefit of the increased price obtained from sale of the Fee Properties, and also from $1,771,606.69 it received through sale of leases by the Debtor. On the eve of bankruptcy, the Bank itself valued the leases as worth little to it, if anything, because there were no funds to cure delinquencies thereunder, and it valued the other restaurants ("Fee Properties") at much less than they were ultimately sold for. Had most of the asserted expenses not been paid or incurred by the Debtor, all the restaurants would have shut down and the Bank would have received nothing on the leases and a much lower price on sale of the Fee Properties.

The leases were certainly valueless unless someone put up the funds needed to cure obligations thereunder. Debtor's operations post-petition paid $495,000 to do just that. This was bread cast upon the waters which came back in the end as $1,771,606.69 to the Bank's benefit from sale of the leases alone. The Bank thereby received direct benefit from the funds paid from ongoing operations to satisfy rent owed to Marriott and to pay other lease and operating expenses. Its benefit came from the $1,771,606.69 received by it from sale of leases, an amount it would not have received had those restaurants not been kept open.

The evidence also demonstrated that the Bank benefitted by the Fee Properties being kept operational after the bankruptcy filing. Sales of the Fee Properties were expedited and the sale prices greatly enhanced by keeping the restaurants in operation. It is clear that much of the $6,415,400 produced from sale of fee simple restaurants was the result of good marketing, which only was possible because the lights were on and employees were working to keep the restaurants functioning.

Mr. Melaniphy, who was hired by Debtor to facilitate sale of the restaurants, convincingly testified to the significant price difference between a restaurant sold in operating condition, "lights on", and a restaurant that is sold while closed. Mr. Melaniphy testified that selling restaurant properties in a "lights on" condition allows prospective purchasers to witness the operation of a restaurant, inspect the quality of the equipment under working conditions, and analyze the patrons in terms of number and demographics. Closed restaurants do not allow prospective purchasers the opportunity to assess these conditions, which generally lowers their bids in the face of greater uncertainties. Closed restaurants are generally perceived to be available at "fire sale" prices and the owners to be in dire need of funds. Claimants proved that they were able to obtain higher prices for all the sold restaurants because they were sold as going concerns.

After Debtor filed for bankruptcy, the Bank had two general courses of action to choose: either foreclose or allow Debtor to keep the restaurants going to derive the benefit ultimately achieved. If it foreclosed, the Bank would have been faced with foreclosing costs and most of the operating costs involved here if it then sought to realize going concern value. Here the Bank saved all these costs and was directly benefitted because Debtor incurred most charges claimed here by keeping the restaurants open. * * *

In this bankruptcy proceeding, the Bank will be the only party, other than administrative creditors, that will receive distribution from the bankruptcy estate. * * * Where estate distribution is made only to one secured creditor in bankruptcy, the increased priced realized from selling the debtor as a going concern directly benefits that creditor. Equitable Gas Co. v. Equibank N.A. (In re McKeesport Steel Castings Company), 799 F.2d 91, 94 (3d Cir. 1986).

Necessary "Preservation" Expenses

Necessary costs are those which are unavoidably incurred in the preservation or disposal of the secured property. Here the utilities, wage-related taxes and withholdings, and health insurance claims incurred were necessary for the disposition of all fee simple and leased restaurants that were sold. * * *

In its pleadings and at trial the Bank has not argued that expenses for utilities were not necessary for preserving or disposing of the restaurants. It does argue that wage-related expenses such as payroll taxes and withholdings and health insurance claims are not proper § 506(c) expenses since, unlike utilities, they are not necessary to preserve the physical collateral such as the building and equipment. Utilities, the Bank argues, should be the only expense considered for allowance here since they are more like what Congress intended § 506(c) surcharges to be, viewed as directly necessary in maintaining or preserving the collateral.

In this case, distinguishing between labor costs and utilities is unrealistic. The leased restaurants could not have been sold without the employees that kept working during the bankruptcy process. Workers were needed as much as utilities, and their employment directly benefitted the Bank. The expenses of hiring workers include their payroll, related payroll taxes, and their health insurance benefits. The Debtor could not have kept the workers employed without such expenses and obligations. The taxes resulting from the payroll, including withholding and unemployment taxes, both state and federal, were directly related to the necessity of having employees working, as did health insurance claims. It is unrealistic to argue that, while gas, electricity, and water used in the interim period might be § 506(c) expenses, costs associated with employment are not. Without people on the job, there would have been no benefit to the Bank; and without the Debtor undertaking the obligations involved in this discussion, they would not have been on the job. * * *

Expenses Not Allowed

Claimants have also asked for § 506(c) treatment of other obligations that Debtor incurred in the ordinary course of operating the restaurants. Among those are obligations to its accountant for partnership tax services and for unspecified "Other DIP Payables." Unlike utilities and employment expenses, however, these obligations were not shown to be directly related to benefit received by the Bank. Claimants have not demonstrated a direct and immediate relationship between the $15,000 requested for "Other DIP Payables" and benefit to the Bank. Nor did the Bank receive a direct benefit from tax services afforded to Debtor, since this expense is incidental to any bankruptcy estate. Even though such expenses may have been a natural consequence of running the business, that does not mean that incurring them gave a direct and quantifiable benefit to the Bank.

* * * Claimants did not demonstrate that rent charges for Debtor's general office were necessary to keep the restaurants operating.

For failure to meet the required standards, the Bank is not to be surcharged for these and other miscellaneous expenses not allowed.

Expenses required to keep the Gurnee property operating are also not allowed under § 506(c). Claimants argue that, even though the Gurnee lease was not sold, the Bank was still benefitted by $2,000 per week in net cash flow from the Gurnee restaurant. These funds were allegedly used to pay expenses incurred at other restaurants that were sold. While there was some general testimony that excess cash in that amount was diverted regularly to other restaurants that were not as profitable as Gurnee, no accounting evidence was submitted to identify and specify any such cash flow as excess over expenses, or that such cash flow was used to pay particular expenses of direct benefit to the Bank. On this record, Claimants have not established by a preponderance of the evidence that excess cash flow from Gurnee was diverted in some specific amounts to other restaurants to pay for expenses of a nature otherwise here allowed under § 506(c). Since the Gurnee property was not sold for benefit of the Bank, Claimants are not to be reimbursed for any expenses incurred for it.* * *

Lack of Consent

The only exception to the requirement of a direct benefit applies when the secured creditor consents to or directly causes the costs to be incurred. Where the secured creditor expressly or by its actions consents to services and payment for those services out of collateral, it cannot avoid making such payment on the grounds that it received no actual benefit. Such consent will not be easily implied in the absence of express consent. In this case, clearly there was no express consent. Claimants argue, however, that the Bank impliedly consented to the expenditures when it approved the Cash Collateral Order, and failed to move for dismissal, conversion or a modification of the automatic stay to allow foreclosure. This argument is faulty as a matter of law, and also contrary to the evidence.

It is well-settled that creditor cooperation in the reorganization effort, including support for a cash collateral order, is not the same as consent to finance the costs of the reorganization case, and that failure to move for a modification of the automatic stay or for adequate protection does not constitute consent to § 506(c) charges. The policy underlying this rule is evident, since charging secured lenders with such costs merely because they did not close down the debtor would discourage creditors from providing financing and would be contrary to purposes of Chapter 11.

Here, the Debtor operated the restaurants in accordance with budgets approved by the Bank pursuant to the original consented Cash Collateral Order which was extended from time to time thereafter by agreement. The Cash Collateral Order expressly provided that the Bank was not consenting to imposition of any 11 U.S.C. § 506(c) surcharges against its distribution. Indeed, the Bank expressly conditioned its approval of the Cash Collateral Order on the fact that its approval of the Order was not to be construed as consent to § 506(c) charges. Thus, the Bank's actions in agreeing to that Order and its continued effectiveness could not and did not here constitute implied consent to § 506(c) payment of any expenses. Under all the circumstances established here by evidence, it is found that the Bank clearly did not consent thereto either expressly or impliedly.

CONCLUSION

Claimants proved by a preponderance of evidence that the utilities, payroll, withholding and unemployment taxes, and health insurance claims that the Debtor paid or incurred in order to keep the restaurants operating until their sale were reasonable and necessary expenses and were expended for primary benefit of the Bank. However, other claimed surcharges for expenses are disallowed.

The following table summarizes the allowed and disallowed claims and the final calculation of § 506(c) allowance:

Table 3
Calculation of expenses disallowed by the Court under § 506(c)

Categorical Expenses Rejected by the Court	$ 86,897.67
Portion of other Expenses Allocated to Elm-Gurnee Store and disallowed	$ 47,982.55
Total § 506(c) Expenses Disallowed	$ 134,880.22

Calculation of Net § 506(c) Expenses Allowed by the Court

Total Expenses Sought by the Debtor under § 506(c)	$ 451,691.55
Less Total Expenses Disallowed	$(134,880.22)
Total Net § 506(c) Expenses Allowed	$ 316,811.33

The Bank's distribution from sale of the fee simple restaurants and leased restaurants is to be surcharged in the amount of $316,811.33. An order and judgment effectuating this ruling is separately entered this date.

Hartford Underwriters Ins. Co. v. Union Planters Bank
United States Supreme Court, 2000
530 U.S. 1, 120 S. Ct. 1942, 147 L. Ed. 2d 1

Justice SCALIA delivered the opinion of the Court.

In this case, we consider whether 11 U.S.C. § 506(c) allows an administrative claimant of a bankruptcy estate to seek payment of its claim from property encumbered by a secured creditor's lien.

I

This case arises out of the bankruptcy proceedings of Hen House Interstate, Inc., which at one time owned or operated several restaurants and service stations, as well as an outdoor-advertising firm. On September 5, 1991, Hen House filed a voluntary petition under Chapter 11 of the Bankruptcy Code in the United States Bankruptcy Court for the Eastern District of Missouri. As a Chapter 11 debtor-in-possession, Hen House retained possession of its assets and continued operating its business.

Respondent had been Hen House's primary lender. At the time the Chapter 11 petition was filed, it held a security interest in essentially all of Hen House's real and personal property, securing an indebtedness of over $4 million. After the Chapter 11 proceedings were commenced, it agreed to lend Hen House an additional $300,000 to help finance the reorganization. The Bankruptcy Court entered a financing order approving the loan agreement and authorizing Hen House to use loan proceeds and cash collateral to pay expenses, including workers' compensation expenses.

During the attempted reorganization, Hen House obtained workers' compensation insurance from petitioner Hartford Underwriters (which was unaware of the bankruptcy proceedings). Although the policy required monthly premium payments, Hen House repeatedly failed to make them; Hartford continued to provide insurance nonetheless. The reorganization ultimately failed, and on January 20, 1993, the Bankruptcy Court converted the case to a liquidation proceeding under Chapter 7 and appointed a trustee. At the time of the conversion, Hen House owed Hartford more than $50,000 in unpaid premiums. Hartford learned of Hen House's bankruptcy proceedings after the conversion, in March 1993.

Recognizing that the estate lacked unencumbered funds to pay the premiums, Hartford attempted to charge the premiums to respondent, the secured creditor, by filing with the Bankruptcy Court an "Application for Allowance of Administrative Expense, Pursuant to 11 U.S.C. § 503 and Charge Against Collateral, Pursuant to 11 U.S.C. § 506(c)." The Bankruptcy Court ruled in favor of Hartford, and the District Court and an Eighth Circuit panel affirmed.

The Eighth Circuit subsequently granted en banc review, however, and reversed, concluding that § 506(c) could not be invoked by an administrative claimant. We granted certiorari.

II

Petitioner's effort to recover the unpaid premiums involves two provisions, 11 U.S.C. §§ 503(b) and 506(c). Section 503(b) provides that "the actual, necessary costs and expenses of preserving the estate, including wages, salaries, or commissions for services rendered after the commencement of the case" are treated as administrative expenses, which are, as a rule, entitled to priority over prepetition unsecured claims, see §§ 507(a)(1), 726(a)(1), 1129(a)(9)(A). Respondent does not dispute that the cost of the workers' compensation insurance Hen House purchased from petitioner is an administrative expense within the meaning of this provision. Administrative expenses, however, do not have priority over secured claims, see §§ 506, 725-726, 1129(b)(2)(A); United Sav. Assn. of Tex. v. Timbers of Inwood Forest Associates, Ltd., 484 U.S. 365, 378-379, 108 S. Ct. 626, 98 L. Ed. 2d 740 (1988), and because respondent held a security interest in essentially all of the estate's assets, there were no unencumbered funds available to pay even administrative claimants.

Petitioner therefore looked to § 506(c), which constitutes an important exception to the rule that secured claims are superior to administrative claims. That section provides as follows:

"The trustee may recover from property securing an allowed secured claim the reasonable, necessary costs and expenses of preserving, or disposing of, such property to the extent of any benefit to the holder of such claim." § 506(c).

Petitioner argued that this provision entitled it to recover from the property subject to respondent's security interest the unpaid premiums owed by Hen House, since its furnishing of workers' compensation insurance benefitted respondent by allowing continued operation of Hen House's business, thereby preserving the value of respondent's collateral; or alternatively, that such benefit could be presumed from respondent's consent to the postpetition financing order. Although it was contested below whether, under either theory, the workers' compensation insurance constituted a "benefit to the holder" within the meaning of § 506(c), that issue is not before us here; we assume for purposes of this decision that it did, and consider only whether petitioner—an administrative claimant—is a proper party to seek recovery under § 506(c).

In answering this question, we begin with the understanding that Congress "says in a statute what it means and means in a statute what it says there," Connecticut Nat. Bank v. Germain, 503 U.S. 249, 254, 112 S. Ct. 1146, 117 L. Ed. 2d 391 (1992). As we have previously noted in construing another provision of § 506, when "the statute's language is plain, 'the sole function of the courts'"—at least where the disposition required by the text is not absurd—"'is to enforce it according to its terms.'" United States v. Ron Pair Enterprises, Inc., 489 U.S. 235, 241, 109 S. Ct. 1026, 103 L. Ed. 2d 290 (1989) (quoting Caminetti v. United States, 242 U.S. 470, 485, 37 S. Ct. 192, 61 L. Ed. 442 (1917)). Here, the statute appears quite plain in specifying who may use § 506(c)—"[t]he trustee." It is true, however, as petitioner notes, that all this actually "says" is that the trustee may seek recovery under the section, not that others may not. The question thus becomes whether it is a proper inference that the trustee is the only party empowered to invoke the provision.[53] We have little difficulty answering yes.

Several contextual features here support the conclusion that exclusivity is intended. First, a situation in which a statute authorizes specific action and designates a particular party empowered to take it is surely among the least appropriate in which to presume nonexclusivity. "Where a statute … names the parties granted [the] right to invoke its provisions, … such parties only may act." 2A N. Singer, Sutherland on Statutory Construction § 47.23, p. 217 (5th ed.1992) (internal quotation marks omitted); see also Federal Election Comm'n v. National Conservative Political Action Comm., 470 U.S. 480, 486, 105 S. Ct. 1459, 84 L. Ed. 2d 455 (1985). Second, the fact that the sole party named—the trustee—has a unique role in bankruptcy proceedings makes it entirely plausible that Congress would provide a power to him and not to others. Indeed, had no particular parties been specified—had § 506(c) read simply "[t]here may be recovered from property securing an allowed secured claim the reasonable, necessary costs and expenses, etc."—the trustee is the most obvious party who would have been thought empowered to use the provision. It is thus far more sensible to view the provision as answering the question "Who may use the provision?" with "only the trustee" than to view it as simply answering the question "May the trustee use the provision?" with "yes."

Nor can it be argued that the point of the provision was simply to establish that certain costs may be recovered from collateral, and not to say anything about who may recover them. Had that been Congress's intention, it could easily have used the formulation just suggested. Similarly, had Congress intended the provision to be broadly available, it could simply have said so, as it did in describing the parties who could act under other sections of the Code. Section 502(a), for example, provides that a claim is allowed unless "a party in interest" objects, and § 503(b)(4) allows "an entity" to file a request for payment of an administrative expense. The broad phrasing of these sections, when contrasted with the use of "the trustee" in § 506(c), supports the conclusion that entities other than the trustee are not entitled to use § 506(c).

Petitioner's primary argument from the text of § 506(c) is that "what matters is that section 506(c) does not say that 'only' a trustee may enforce its provisions." To bolster this argument, petitioner cites other provisions of the Bankruptcy Code that do use "only" or other expressly restrictive language in specifying the parties at issue. See, e.g., § 109(a) ("[O]nly a person that resides or has a domicile, a place of business, or property in the United States, or a municipality, may be a debtor under this title"); § 707(b) (providing that a case may be dismissed for substantial abuse by "the court, on its own motion or on a motion by the United States trustee, but not at the request or suggestion of any party in interest"). Petitioner argues that in the absence of such restrictive language, no party in interest is excluded. This theory—that the expression

---

53. [Footnote 3 in original:] Debtors-in-possession may also use the section, as they are expressly given the rights and powers of a trustee by 11 U.S.C. § 1107.

of one thing indicates the inclusion of others unless exclusion is made explicit—is contrary to common sense and common usage. Many provisions of the Bankruptcy Code that do not contain an express exclusion cannot sensibly be read to extend to all parties in interest. See, e.g., § 363(b)(1) (providing that "[t]he trustee, after notice and a hearing, may use, sell, or lease ... property of the estate"); § 364(a) (providing that "the trustee" may incur debt on behalf of the bankruptcy estate); § 554(a) (giving "the trustee" power to abandon property of the bankruptcy estate).

Petitioner further argues that § 1109 evidences the right of a nontrustee to recover under § 506(c). We are not persuaded. That section, which provides that a "party in interest" "may raise and may appear and be heard on any issue in a case under [Chapter 11]," is by its terms inapplicable here, since petitioner's attempt to use § 506(c) came after the bankruptcy proceeding was converted from Chapter 11 to Chapter 7. In any event, we do not read § 1109(b)'s general provision of a right to be heard as broadly allowing a creditor to pursue substantive remedies that other Code provisions make available only to other specific parties. Cf. 7 L. King, COLLIER ON BANKRUPTCY ¶ 1109.05 (15th rev. ed.1999) ("In general, section 1109 does not bestow any right to usurp the trustee's role as representative of the estate with respect to the initiation of certain types of litigation that belong exclusively to the estate").

III

Because we believe that by far the most natural reading of § 506(c) is that it extends only to the trustee, petitioner's burden of persuading us that the section must be read to allow its use by other parties is "'exceptionally heavy.'" Patterson v. Shumate, 504 U.S. 753, 760, 112 S. Ct. 2242, 119 L. Ed. 2d 519 (1992) (quoting Union Bank v. Wolas, 502 U.S. 151, 156, 112 S. Ct. 527, 116 L. Ed. 2d 514 (1991)). To support its proffered reading, petitioner advances arguments based on pre-Code practice and policy considerations. We address these arguments in turn.

A

Section 506(c)'s provision for the charge of certain administrative expenses against lienholders continues a practice that existed under the Bankruptcy Act of 1898, see, e.g., In re Tyne, 257 F.2d 310, 312 (C.A.7 1958); 4 COLLIER ON BANKRUPTCY, supra, ¶ 506.05 [1]. It was not to be found in the text of the Act, but traced its origin to early cases establishing an equitable principle that where a court has custody of property, costs of administering and preserving the property are a dominant charge. It was the norm that recovery of costs from a secured creditor would be sought by the trustee, see, e.g., Textile Banking Co. v. Widener, 265 F.2d 446, 453-454 (C.A.4 1959); *Tyne*, supra, at 312. Petitioner cites a number of lower court cases, however, in which—without meaningful discussion of the point—parties other than the trustee were permitted to pursue such charges under the Act, sometimes simultaneously with the trustee's pursuit of his own expenses, but sometimes independently. Petitioner also relies on early decisions of this Court allowing individual claimants to seek recovery from secured assets, see Louisville, E. & St. L.R. Co. v. Wilson, 138 U.S. 501, 506, 11 S. Ct. 405, 34 L. Ed. 1023 (1891); Burnham v. Bowen, 111 U.S. 776, 779, 783, 4 S. Ct. 675, 28 L. Ed. 596 (1884); New York Dock Co. v. Poznan, 274 U.S. 117, 121, 47 S. Ct.

482, 71 L. Ed. 955 (1927). *Wilson* and *Burnham* involved equity receiverships, and were not only pre-Code, but predate the Bankruptcy Act of 1898 that the Code replaced; while *New York Dock* was a case arising in admiralty.

It is questionable whether these precedents establish a bankruptcy practice sufficiently widespread and well recognized to justify the conclusion of implicit adoption by the Code. We have no confidence that the allowance of recovery from collateral by nontrustees is "the type of 'rule' that ... Congress was aware of when enacting the Code." United States v. Ron Pair Enterprises, Inc., 489 U.S., at 246, 109 S. Ct. 1026. Cf. Dewsnup v. Timm, 502 U.S. 410, 418, 112 S. Ct. 773, 116 L. Ed. 2d 903 (1992) (relying on "clearly established" pre-Code practice); Kelly v. Robinson, 479 U.S. 36, 46, 107 S. Ct. 353, 93 L. Ed. 2d 216 (1986) (giving weight to pre-Code practice that was "widely accepted" and "established"). In any event, while pre-Code practice "informs our understanding of the language of the Code," id., at 44, 107 S. Ct. 353, it cannot overcome that language. It is a tool of construction, not an extratextual supplement. We have applied it to the construction of provisions which were "subject to interpretation," id., at 50, 107 S. Ct. 353, or contained "ambiguity in the text," *Dewsnup*, supra, at 417, 112 S. Ct. 773. "[W]here the meaning of the Bankruptcy Code's text is itself clear ... its operation is unimpeded by contrary ... prior practice," BFP v. Resolution Trust Corporation, 511 U.S. 531, 546, 114 S. Ct. 1757, 128 L. Ed. 2d 556 (1994) (internal quotation marks omitted). See, e.g., Pennsylvania Dept. of Public Welfare v. Davenport, 495 U.S. 552, 563, 110 S. Ct. 2126, 109 L. Ed. 2d 588 (1990); United States v. Ron Pair Enterprises, Inc., supra, at 245-246, 109 S. Ct. 1026.

In this case, we think the language of the Code leaves no room for clarification by pre-Code practice. If § 506(c) provided only that certain costs and expenses could be recovered from property securing a secured claim, without specifying any particular party by whom the recovery could be pursued, the case would be akin to those in which we used prior practice to fill in the details of a pre-Code concept that the Code had adopted without elaboration. See, e.g., United States v. Noland, 517 U.S. 535, 539, 116 S. Ct. 1524, 134 L. Ed. 2d 748 (1996) (looking to pre-Code practice in interpreting Code's reference to "principles of equitable subordination"); Midlantic Nat. Bank v. New Jersey Dept. of Environmental Protection, 474 U.S. 494, 501, 106 S. Ct. 755, 88 L. Ed. 2d 859 (1986) (codification of trustee's abandonment power held to incorporate established exceptions). Here, however, it is not the unelaborated concept but only a specifically narrowed one that has been adopted: a rule allowing the charge of costs to secured assets *by the trustee*. Pre-Code practice cannot transform § 506(c)'s reference to "the trustee" to "the trustee and other parties in interest."

B

Finally, petitioner argues that its reading is necessary as a matter of policy, since in some cases the trustee may lack an incentive to pursue payment. Section 506(c) must be open to nontrustees, petitioner asserts, lest secured creditors enjoy the benefit of services without paying for them. Moreover, ensuring that administrative claimants are compensated may also serve purposes beyond the avoidance of unjust enrichment. To the extent that there are circumstances in which the trustee will not use the section although an individual creditor would,[54] allowing suits by nontrustees could encourage the provision of postpetition services to debtors on more favorable terms, which would in turn further bankruptcy's goals.

Although these concerns may be valid, it is far from clear that the policy implications favor petitioner's position. The class of cases in which § 506(c) would lie dormant without nontrustee use is limited by the fact that the trustee is obliged to seek recovery under the section whenever his fiduciary duties so require. And limiting § 506(c) to the trustee does not leave those who provide goods or services that benefit secured interests without other means of protecting themselves as against other creditors: They may insist on cash payment, or contract directly with the secured creditor, and may be able to obtain superpriority under § 364(c)(1) or a security interest under §§ 364(c)(2), (3) or § 364(d). And of course postpetition creditors can avoid unnecessary losses simply by paying attention to the status of their accounts, a protection which, by all appearances, petitioner neglected here.

On the other side of the ledger, petitioner's reading would itself lead to results that seem undesirable as a matter of policy. In particular, expanding the number of parties who could use § 506(c) would create the possibility of multiple administrative claimants seeking recovery under the section. Each such claim would require inquiry into the necessity of the services at issue and the degree of benefit to the secured creditor. Allowing recovery to be sought at the behest of parties other than the trustee could therefore impair the ability of the bankruptcy court to coordinate proceedings, as well as the ability of the trustee to manage the estate. Indeed, if administrative claimants were free to seek recovery on their own, they could proceed even where the trustee himself planned to do so.[55] Further, where unencumbered assets were scarce, creditors might attempt to use § 506(c) even

---

54. [Footnote 4 in original:] The frequency with which such circumstances arise may depend in part on who ultimately receives the recovery obtained by a trustee under § 506(c). Petitioner argues that it goes to the party who provided the services that benefited collateral (assuming that party has not already been compensated by the estate). Respondent argues that this reading, like a reading that allows creditors themselves to use § 506(c), upsets the Code's priority scheme by giving administrative claimants who benefit collateral an effective priority over others—allowing, for example, a Chapter 11 administrative creditor (like petitioner) to obtain payment via § 506(c) while Chapter 7 administrative creditors remain unpaid, despite § 726(b)'s provision that Chapter 7 administrative claims have priority over Chapter 11 administrative claims. Thus, respondent asserts that a trustee's recovery under § 506(c) simply goes into the estate to be distributed according to the Code's priority provisions. Since this case does not involve a trustee's recovery under § 506(c), we do not address this question, or the related question whether the trustee may use the provision prior to paying the expenses for which reimbursement is sought, see In re K & L Lakeland, Inc., 128 F.3d 203, 207, 212 (C.A.4 1997).

55. [Footnote 5 in original:] We do not address whether a bankruptcy court can allow other interested parties to act in the trustee's stead in pursuing recovery under § 506(c). Amici American Insurance Association and National Union Fire Insurance Co. draw our attention to the practice of some courts of allowing creditors or creditors' committees a derivative right to bring avoidance actions when the trustee refuses to do so, even though the applicable Code provisions, see 11 U.S.C. §§ 544, 545, 547(b), 548(a), 549(a), mention only the trustee. Whatever the validity of that practice, it has no analogous application here, since petitioner did not ask the trustee to pursue payment under § 506(c) and did not seek permission from the Bankruptcy Court to take such action in the trustee's stead. Petitioner asserted an independent right to use § 506(c), which is what we reject today.

though their claim to have benefitted the secured creditor was quite weak. The possibility of being targeted for such claims by various administrative claimants could make secured creditors less willing to provide postpetition financing.

In any event, we do not sit to assess the relative merits of different approaches to various bankruptcy problems. It suffices that the natural reading of the text produces the result we announce. Achieving a better policy outcome—if what petitioner urges is that—is a task for Congress, not the courts. Kawaauhau v. Geiger, 523 U.S. 57, 64, 118 S. Ct. 974, 140 L. Ed. 2d 90 (1998); *Noland*, 517 U.S., at 541-542, n. 3, 116 S. Ct. 1524; *Wolas*, 502 U.S., at 162, 112 S. Ct. 527.

* * * We conclude that 11 U.S.C. § 506(c) does not provide an administrative claimant an independent right to use the section to seek payment of its claim. The judgment of the Eighth Circuit is affirmed.

It is so ordered.

NOTES

1. Consider the Court's footnote 4 (footnote 54 in this chapter). In earlier cases the standing issue masked the more important substantive issue: who is entitled to the § 506(c) surcharge? If an administrative claimant, AC, provided, on unsecured credit, the goods or services that the estate used to preserve the secured creditor's collateral, is that administrative claimant more deserving of recovery from the surcharge than any other administrative claimant? Would requiring the surcharge to be paid to AC amount to giving AC a statutory lien on the § 506(c) recovery? Does the Code provide for such a lien? On the other hand, would allowing all administrative expense claimants to share the surcharge improperly permit some of the value of the secured creditor's collateral to be used to pay general administrative expenses—those administrative expenses that conferred no benefit on the secured creditor? See Debbie Reynolds Hotel & Casino v. Calstar Corp. (In re Debbie Reynolds Resorts, Inc.), 255 F.3d 1061 (9th Cir. 2001).

2. Consider the Court's footnote 5. If a provision of the Code gives the trustee (or debtor in possession) the right to bring an action, may the bankruptcy court authorize another party to bring the action? The issue arises most often in the context of the avoiding powers. Compare Official Comm. of Unsecured Creditors of Cybergenics Corp. v. Chinery, 330 F.3d 548 (3d Cir. 2003), and Adelphia Commc'ns Corp. v. Bank of Am., N.A. (In re Adelphia Commc'ns Corp.), 330 B.R. 364 (Bankr. S.D.N.Y. 2005), with United Phosphorus, Ltd. v. Fox (In re Fox), 305 B.R. 912 (B.A.P. 10th Cir. 2004).

Chapter Ten

Dealing With Creditor Misconduct

A debtor often has no defenses to its creditors' claims, especially when the creditor is a lender or other financer. The size of the claims may be doubted but not liability. The debtor "defends" indirectly by asserting its own claims of recoupment and counterclaims.

These defensive claims are based on breach of reciprocal or collateral duties that the lender owes the debtor. They offset the debtor's obligations instead of denying them, but the effect is the same. The offsetting liability of the lender reduces the debtor's obligations, and can even give the debtor a net recovery against the lender to the extent that the debtor's damages exceed the lender's claim. This widely-based, diverse accountability of creditors is commonly lumped under the very general heading of "lender liability," "which encompasses theories of liability based upon an aggregation of traditional contract theories, tort theories, and federal statutes." Gott & Townsley, *Note, Lender Liability: A Survey of Theories, Thoughts and Trends*, 28 WASHBURN L.J. 238, 239 (1988). In Part A of this Chapter, we consider a creditor's liability to the debtor or other creditors based on modern notions of lender liability under state law.

Bankruptcy law, too, separately penalizes creditor misconduct that is based on inequitable conduct that harms the debtor or other creditors. The principal "remedy" is subordinating a creditor's claim under § 510(c) in order to "see that injustice or unfairness is not done in the administration of the bankrupt estate." Pepper v. Litton, 308 U.S. 295, 308 (1939). In Part B of this chapter, we consider whether misconduct (or other circumstances) may cause a creditor's claim to be equitably subordinated in the bankruptcy case under § 510(c). If a creditor has control (or obtains control) of the debtor's operations, and uses that control to benefit itself at the expense of other creditors, will that creditor's claim be subordinated to the claims of the other creditors? When else may equitable subordination be appropriate?

Finally, in Part C we consider issues of supposed misconduct in the trading of claims in a bankruptcy case. Holders of claims may not want to wait for whatever they may receive in the bankruptcy case; instead they may want to sell their claims for immediate cash. To what extent should the court police the trading in claims? Should the court ensure that sellers of claims have sufficient information so that they are not taken advantage of? What if a purchaser of claims would receive 60 cents on the dollar for claims for which it paid only 10 cents on the dollar? Should the court act to strip the "windfall" from the purchaser? Should the court allow the proponents or opponents of a plan to purchase claims for purposes of voting them for or against the plan?

A. LENDER LIABILITY IN BANKRUPTCY UNDER NONBANKRUPTCY LAW

Limor v. Buerger (In re Del-Met Corp.)
United States Bankruptcy Court, Middle District of Tennessee, 2005
322 B.R. 781

Keith M. Lundin, Bankruptcy Judge.

Ten remaining Defendants move to dismiss the First Amended Complaint filed by the Trustee in these consolidated adversary proceedings. The motions will be granted in part and denied in part as explained below.

THE PARTIES

The Plaintiff, Susan R. Limor, is the trustee for two Chapter 7 debtors, Del-Met Corporation ("DMC") and Del-Met of Tennessee, Inc. ("DMT").

Defendant Michael Buerger ("Buerger") is the 100 percent owner and only director of DMC and DMT. Buerger also owned 100 percent of Defendant Del-Met Winchester, Inc. ("DMW"). Collectively, Debtors DMC and DMT and Defendant DMW are sometimes called the "Del-Met companies."

Defendants General Motors Corporation ("GM"), Johnson Controls, Inc. ("JCI") and Lear Corporation ("Lear") were customers of the Del-Met companies. The Plaintiff refers to these three Defendants as the "Controlling Customers."

Defendants Bank One, N.A. ("Bank One") and GMAC Commercial Finance LLC (successor by merger to GMAC Business Credit, LLC) ("GMAC") provided financing to the Del-Met companies.

Defendant BBK, Ltd. ("BBK") provided management to the Debtors.

Defendant Conway MacKenzie & Dunleavy ("CMD") is a consulting firm that provided financial and accounting services to the Debtors.

Defendant Carson Fischer, PLC ("CF") provided legal services to the Debtors.

PRIOR PROCEEDINGS

DMC and DMT filed Chapter 7 cases on November 28, 2001. Susan Limor was appointed Chapter 7 trustee. Two years after the petitions, on November 28, 2003, the trustee filed this adversary proceeding styled: "Trustee's Complaint for the Avoidance and Return of Preferential Payments and Fraudulent Transfers, Equitable Subordination, and Damages, Together With Objections and Counterclaims to Creditor-Defendants' Claims" ("original Complaint").

After a pretrial conference on April 19, 2004 and a skirmish with respect to the scope of discovery, the Trustee filed a First Amended Complaint on June 1, 2004. Motions to dismiss were filed by all Defendants that challenge the sufficiency of the original Complaint and the First Amended Complaint. * * *

Four days before oral argument on Defendants' Motions to dismiss, the Trustee filed an "Expedited Motion for Leave to Supplement Trustee's First Amended Complaint." Citing Rule 15(d) of the Federal Rules of Civil Procedure, the Plaintiff sought to add to the First Amended Complaint "events which occurred after the date that the plaintiff's complaint was filed." The supplemental material offered by the Plaintiff was a discovery response from Defendant Buerger listing "payments made by Del-Met companies" to Buerger between December 2000 and January 2004. Defendant Buerger objected to Plaintiff's expedited motion to supplement the First Amended Complaint.

FACTS

These facts are as alleged in the Plaintiff's First Amended Complaint and do not constitute findings by the court.

Prior to 2000, the Del-Met companies—DMC, DMT and DMW—were a highly profitable supplier of parts to the automotive industry. Buerger owned the stock of all three entities.

In 1999, DMC, DMT and DMW had over 500 employees and total sales of $71,583,567. As of December 31, 1999, Del-Met had collectable accounts receivable of $18,507,556. Assets of Del-Met at the end of 1999 included machinery and equipment valued at $20,274,791, buildings and improvements totaling $2,649,438 and patents and trademarks valued at $122,989. In 1999, Del-Met distributed over $3,200,000 to Buerger. At December 31, 1999, DMC had retained earnings of $7,259,320. In contrast, at that same date, DMW had retained earnings of negative $711,844.

For several years before 2000, Bank One was Del-Met's lead lender. Bank One had a security interest in all of DMC's and DMT's machinery, equipment and accounts receivable. As of December 31, 1999, Del-Met owed Bank One $12,818,622—approximately $5,000,000 less than the collectible accounts receivable owed to Del-Met at that time. The debts of Del-Met to Bank One were personally guaranteed by Buerger.

GM, JCI and Lear were Del-Met's three largest customers. Del-Met was a direct supplier of automotive parts to GM and sold parts to JCI and Lear who then sold products fabricated from those parts to GM and other automobile companies.

In 1999, Del-Met had a contract with GM to manufacture and supply the center console for the Cadillac Escalade at a fixed price. A sharp increase in the price of leather rendered this contract unprofitable. In 1999 and 2000, Del-Met expanded sales to JCI and Lear including undertaking tooling management programs at the request of JCI and Lear.

By early 2000, Del-Met's cash position was negatively impacted by: (1) inability to properly manage the cash requirements of the tooling programs; (2) assumption of a major loss contract from Lear; (3) the sharp increase in the price of leather to fulfill the Escalade contract with GM; and (4) operating losses in the traditional production of wheel covers due to capacity constraints and quality problems.

In 2000, Del-Met informed GM that it had stopped production of the center console for the hot-selling Cadillac Escalade due to the prohibitive cost of leather. Del-Met asked GM to allow a price increase under the Escalade contract to cover the increased cost of raw materials. GM refused to adjust the contract price and threatened to stop payments on nearly $20,000,000 in accounts receivable and to assert an offset for Del-Met's nonperformance of the Escalade contract. Similar problems arose under the contracts with JCI and Lear.

By September 2000, the Controlling Customers' refusal to pay accounts receivable rendered DMC and DMT unable to pay their liabilities as they became due.

In late 2000, the Controlling Customers "brought in" BBK to "take over" the operations of Del-Met and brought in CMD to take over the accounting functions of Del-Met. In his cross-claim against GM, JCI and Lear, Defendant Buerger describes this "take over" by the Controlling Customers more forcefully:

> In early 2001, the Customers assumed control of all aspects of the operations of DMC and DMT. The customers engaged BBK, Limited ("BBK"), to manage the operations of DMC and DMT on a day-to-day basis. Individual representatives of BBK entered the premises of DMC and DMT for varying periods of time and assumed and performed all key management functions. In many cases, existing personnel of DMC and DMT were excluded, in whole or in part, from further participation in their historical duties. From this point forward, Michael Buerger was effectively precluded from further participation in the operations or management of DMC or DMT.

(Michael Buerger's Cross Claim Against Defs. General Motors Corp., Johnson Controls, Inc., and Lear Corp. ¶ 8.)

Although paid by Del-Met, BBK and CMD managed and operated Del-Met for the benefit of the Controlling Customers without regard to the impact on DMC, DMT or their creditors. BBK was only interested in funding materials and labor to fulfill the Del-Met contracts with GM, JCI and Lear. BBK refused to pay other "nonessential" debts. BBK and CMD managed and operated the Del-Met entities to fulfill unprofitable contracts with GM and JCI. On the Escalade contract alone, Del-Met was losing over $500,000 a month. BBK and CMD "used DMC and DMT for the financial benefit of the Controlling Customers … drastically increas[ing] the amount of debt incurred by DMC and DMT…. BBK and CMD … mismanaged DMC and DMT for the financial benefit of the Controlling Customers." (First Am. Compl. ¶ 20.)

In furtherance of this scheme, beginning in mid-2000 and continuing into 2001, the Controlling Customers made direct payments to Del-Met's tooling vendors to gain control of "hostaged" tools and made direct payments to Del-Met's critical material suppliers to maintain production of parts needed by the Controlling Customers.

In early 2001, the Controlling Customers approached Bank One—Del-Met's lender—about restructuring Bank One's debt and collateral position. As "bargaining leverage," GM asserted that it would stop paying its accounts receivable and would exercise $6,500,000 in offsets against the bank's collateral if Bank One did not renegotiate its loan and collateral position.

On April 10, 2001, the Controlling Customers, Bank One, Del-Met and Buerger entered into an "Accommodation Agreement." As described by the Plaintiff, this agreement:

> provided that Bank One would forbear on its loan default claims through July 31, 2001 to enable GM, JCI and Lear to meet Del-Met's future working capital needs outside of bankruptcy, and so GM, JCI and Lear could attempt to find buyers for Del-Met's facilities to continue their production of parts…. GM, JCI and Lear agreed to up-front payments to Bank One of approximately $6,000,000 and defendant GMAC … was to provide funding and … working capital loans to Del-Met…. Bank One 'sold' its lien position in Del-Met's collateral to the Controlling Customers.

(First Am. Compl. ¶¶ 24 & 25.) The Controlling Customers required Del-Met to pay $750,000 in fees to Defendants CF and CMD in connection with this agreement.

Between January of 2000 and November 28, 2001 (when DMC and DMT filed bankruptcy), DMC's and DMT's secured debt to Bank One and GMAC was reduced by $6.9 million—from $12.8 million to $5.9 million. During that same time, DMC's and DMT's unsecured debt increased by $22 million—from $21.3 million to $43.3 million.

In addition to the Accommodation Agreement, the Controlling Customers and Buerger carried out a plan to shift the assets and business operations of DMC and DMT to DMW. Although DMW had little or no value at the end of 1999, by the time DMC and DMT filed bankruptcy in November 2001, the Controlling Customers had transferred a substantial portion of DMC's assets to DMW. In March of 2003—despite protests from the bankruptcy trustee for DMC and DMT—the assets of DMW were sold to Zanini Auto Grup, S.A. for over $5,200,000. This sale of assets assured GM of continued production of the center console for the "still hot-selling Cadillac Escalade."

DISCUSSION

* * *

IV. Choice of Law with Respect to State Law Causes of Action

Following oral argument, the parties were invited to brief what law applied to the state law causes of action. (Order Amending Pretrial Order, Aug. 18, 2004.) By Stipulation filed August 27, 2004, Plaintiff and the remaining Defendants agreed that Tennessee law would govern the state law claims in Counts 5, 8, 9, 10, 13 and 14.

The court accepts the parties' choice of law stipulation with respect to Count 8 (unjust enrichment), Count 9 (contract) and Count 14 (accounting). Alter ego or single business enterprise liability arises from fraudulent use of corporate form, thus the parties' stipulation of Tennessee law for Count 13 also seems correct. Discussed in more detail below, to the extent Counts 5 and 10 allege torts that are not based on breach of the statutory duties of corporate officers and directors, the parties' stipulation of Tennessee law is sound. However, Counts 5 and 10 also allege breach of fiduciary duties imposed on corporate officers and directors. In matters of corporate governance, the parties' stipulation of Tennessee law collides with firmly established doctrine favoring the law of the states of incorporation— New York for DMC; Delaware for DMT.

Claims that involve the internal affairs of a corporation should be resolved in accordance with the law of the state of incorporation. "The internal affairs doctrine is a conflict of laws principle which recognizes that only one State should have the authority to regulate a corporation's internal affairs—matters peculiar to the relationships among or between the corporation and its current officers, directors, and shareholders—because otherwise a corporation could be faced with conflicting demands." Edgar v. MITE Corp., 457 U.S. 624, 645, 102 S. Ct. 2629, 2642, 73 L. Ed. 2d 269 (1982) (citing Restatement (Second) of Conflict of Laws § 302, Comment b, at 307-08 (1971)).

Tennessee has codified the internal affairs doctrine: Tennessee corporation statutes "do not authorize this state to regulate the organization or the internal affairs of a foreign corporation authorized to transact business in this state." Tenn. Code Ann. § 48-25-105(c) (West 2004). Put another way, even accepting the parties' stipulation, Tennessee law would direct us back to the states of incorporation to determine the fiduciary duties of corporate actors for purposes of Counts 5 and 10.

V. Motions to Dismiss

* * *

D. Count 4

Count 4 seeks equitable subordination under § 510(c)(1) of the claims of Defendants Buerger, DMW, GM, JCI, Lear, Bank One and GMAC. * * *

E. Count 5 and Count 10

Counts 5 and 10 of the First Amended Complaint allege causes of action for breach of fiduciary duties and aiding and abetting breach of fiduciary duties against Buerger, GM, JCI, Lear, BBK and CMD. With respect to Buerger, the source of fiduciary duties to the debtors is that Buerger was the "100% owner and sole director of DMC and DMT." The other Defendants named in Count 5 are described as "control persons" that, after September 2000, "exerted sufficient influence and control over the affairs of Del-Met so as to constitute 'insiders' within the meaning of § 101(31) of the Bankruptcy Code, thereby owing those entities fiduciary duties."

The Bankruptcy Code does not impose "fiduciary duties" simply because an entity is an insider under § 101(31). Fiduciary duties are imposed, if at all, by other state or federal law, not by § 101(31).

The Plaintiff cites no particular source of law for the assertion that Defendants (other than Buerger) owed fiduciary duties to the debtors.

Plaintiff's assertion of a "deepening insolvency" claim against the Defendants named in Counts 5 and 10 further obscures the source of fiduciary duties. In her brief, the trustee states, "Plaintiff has asserted a 'deepening insolvency' claim, not as an independent tort, but as part of the defendants' breach of fiduciary duties." (Plaint. Amended Resp. at 27.) At oral argument, counsel for the trustee reiterated that deepening insolvency was alleged as a breach of fiduciary duty by the Defendants, not as an independent tort.

Stopping there, the tough question would remain: What is the source of law for the fiduciary duties that the Defendants are alleged to have breached by deepening the insolvency of the debtors? But the Plaintiff didn't stop with its disclaimer of an "independent tort" of deepening insolvency. Instead, the Trustee states in her brief on these Motions to dismiss:

> While the issue of duty is a question of law, there are no Tennessee cases which have specifically accepted or rejected that duty. Like the courts in *Lafferty*, 267 F.3d at 349-52, and In re Exide Technologies, Inc., 299 B.R. 732, 750-52 (Bankr. D. Del. 2003), and for the reasons articulated by those courts, this court should likewise acknowledge the viability of the deepening insolvency theory under Tennessee law.

In Official Committee of Unsecured Creditors v. R.F. Lafferty & Co., 267 F.3d 340 (3d Cir. 2001), and Official Committee of Unsecured Creditors v. Credit Suisse First Boston, (In re Exide Technologies, Inc.), 299 B.R. 732 (Bankr. D. Del. 2003), the Third Circuit and the Delaware bankruptcy court—applying Pennsylvania and Delaware law—recognized tort actions for "deepening insolvency" against Defendants who were not all in fiduciary relationships with the debtor corporations by virtue of officer or director status. Here, the Plaintiff eschews reliance on any independent tort of deepening insolvency; invites the court to find that Tennessee would recognize such an action; and then uses deepening insolvency as a breach of fiduciary duty by Defendants not alleged to have fiduciary duties to the debtors under any identified legal theory other than deepening insolvency itself.

These circular positions by the trustee speak volumes to the lack of definition of the developing theory of deepening insolvency. See generally Jo Ann J. Brighton, *Deepening Insolvency*, 23-3 AM. BANKR. INST. J. 34 (2004); Paul Rubin, *New Liability Under "Deepening Insolvency,"* 23-3 AM. BANKR. INST. J. 50 (2004); Allen Michel & Israel Shaked, *Deepening Insolvency: Plaintiff vs. Defendant*, 21-5 AM. BANKR. INST. J. 32 (2002).

> [S]ince the theory of deepening insolvency is not well defined or universally embraced by all courts, and with few written opinions concerning the topic, creativity in the use of the theory abounds. The theory has expanded beyond the realm of officers and directors and has been successfully raised against insolvency professionals, such as accountants, investment brokers and lawyers .... Secured lenders may also be liable for deepening the insolvency of a company based on their agreement to continue to lend.

Deepening Insolvency, 23-3 AM. BANKR. INST. J. at 34.

Whether characterized as a separate tort or as an example of a breach of fiduciary duty, the Trustee's deepening insolvency claim is cognizable only if the Defendants owed duties to the debtor corporations under nonbankruptcy law by virtue of their domination and control such that the run up of debt, the performance of unprofitable contracts, the selective payment of vendors and other allegations in the complaint are actionable breaches.

This returns us to the question of choice of law: To the law of what state do we look to determine whether a duty arose in the Defendants with respect to the deepening insolvency of these debtors? The parties stipulated that Tennessee law applies to Count 5 and to Count 10. This suggests that the parties conceive of deepening insolvency as a tort independent of issues of corporate governance. This is not obvious.

Buerger was an officer, director and sole shareholder of both debtor corporations. As explained above, his fiduciary duties to the debtors arose under New York corporation law with respect to DMC and under Delaware corporation law for DMT. To the extent the deepening insolvency action alleged in Counts 5 and 10 is based on a breach of duty arising from Buerger's fiduciary duties as a corporate officer or director, that cause of action is governed by New York or Delaware law, not Tennessee law. Different analysis applies to the extent the deepening insolvency claims are based on duties arising outside of corporate governance.

The Defendants (other than Buerger) named in Counts 5 and 10 are customers of the debtors and agents of those customers alleged to have taken over the management and control of the debtors far in excess of the ordinary influence of customers on a supplier. Several of these Defendants are alleged to have advanced money on behalf of the debtors and to have acquired lien positions in the debtors' assets in furtherance of their control and use of the debtors. The theoretical foundation for Plaintiff's claims that these facts give rise to breachable duties roots less in corporate law than in general tort notions of a duty arising from a special relationship created by a course of dealings that includes unequal bargaining power, over-reaching and abuse of the less equal party.

The trustee's citations to *Lafferty* and *Exide* support the view that the deepening insolvency alleged with respect to defendants other than Buerger is a creature of tort law. In *Lafferty*, the Third Circuit reviewed Pennsylvania tort law to conclude that deepening insolvency was a sound legal theory. *Lafferty*, 267 F.3d at 349-50. The bankruptcy court in *Exide* finds an independent tort of deepening insolvency under Delaware law. These courts did not find deepening insolvency in corporation law but instead found breachable duties arising from domination and control of the corporate debtors by the defendants.

Although the issue is not free from doubt, for purposes of this adversary proceeding, the claims of deepening insolvency in Counts 5 and 10 against Defendants other than Buerger will be treated as tort claims. Tennessee law—the "situs" of the alleged events—will be consulted to determine whether these claims are viable.

Count 5 states that Buerger owed fiduciary duties to DMC and DMT based on his 100% ownership of the debtor corporations and his position as sole director. In contrast, Count 10 more generally states that Buerger owed fiduciary duties to DMC and DMT based on all the allegations in the First Amended Complaint. The cause of action against Buerger in Count 10 is thus more like the torts alleged against other Defendants in Counts 5 and 10. To the extent Count 10 alleges that deepening insolvency is a breach by Buerger of fiduciary duties arising independently of his positions in the corporate governance of the debtors, the cause of action would be measured under Tennessee law.

Fiduciary Duties

Under Delaware, New York and Tennessee law it is textbook that officers and directors owe fiduciary duties to the corporation. See, e.g., Del. Code Ann. tit. 8, §§ 141 & 142; N.Y. Bus. Corp. §§ 701, 713, 715, 717 & 720; Tenn. Code Ann. § 48-18-203, 48-18-301 & 48-18-403. Defendant Buerger owed the Debtors fiduciary duties under New York and Delaware law of good faith, loyalty and due care, and was charged with an unyielding fiduciary duty to protect the interests of the corporation.

Plaintiff alleges that Buerger breached fiduciary duties in many ways including self-dealing in the assets of the debtor corporations, the fraudulent conveyance of corporate assets and opportunities, abdicating responsibility for the finances, management and operations of the corporations, unauthorized payments and transfers to himself and others that injured the corporations and disregard of the separate identities of the corporations. These allegations are sufficient to state causes of action against Buerger for breach of fiduciary duties under New York and Delaware law.

New York and Delaware have well developed case law that addresses fiduciary relationships more broadly—involving majority or controlling shareholders, lenders and other parties exercising control of a corporation. Under Delaware law, it is well established that a party need not be a director or officer in order to owe fiduciary duties to a corporation. A fiduciary duty may arise from the exercise of control with respect to the corporation. "It is only when a person affirmatively undertakes to dictate the destiny of the corporation that he assumes such a fiduciary duty.'" Harriman v. E.I. DuPont De Nemours & Co., 372 F. Supp. 101, 105-06 (D. Del. 1974) (citing Allied Chemical & Dye Corp. v. Steel & Tube Co., 120 A. 486 (Del. Ch. 1923)).

Tennessee corporation law does not list "control persons" or "insiders" as individuals that owe fiduciary duties to a corporation. See, e.g., Tenn. Code Ann. §§ 48-18-203; 48-18-301; 48-18-403; 35-2-102 (defining fiduciary under the Uniform Fiduciaries Act); Nelson v. Martin, 958 S.W.2d 643 (Tenn. 1997), overruled on other grounds, Trau-Med. of Am., Inc. v. Allstate Ins. Co., 71 S.W.3d 691 (Tenn. 2002). Plaintiff's citation to McLemore v. Olson (In re B & L Laboratories, Inc.), 62 B.R. 494 (Bankr. M.D. Tenn. 1986), is not helpful: *B & L* analyzed fiduciary duties owed by defendants who were corporate officers or directors or general partners—relationships recognized by nonbankruptcy law to generate fiduciary duties. There is no claim that any Defendant named in Counts 5 or 10 other than Buerger was an officer, director or partner of the Debtors.

Tennessee courts have long recognized a common law fiduciary relationship between majority or controlling shareholders of a corporation and minority shareholders. See, e.g., Mike v. Po Group, Inc., 937 S.W.2d 790, 793 (Tenn. 1996); Nelms v. Weaver, 681 S.W.2d 547, 549 (Tenn. 1984); Dale v. Thomas H. Temple Co., 186 Tenn. 69, 208 S.W.2d 344, 352 (1948). Tennessee courts acknowledge that the fiduciary duties of majority or controlling shareholders are not based on the Tennessee corporation statutes but arises from more general tort law notions of duty attendant to the exercise of dominion or control. In *Po Group*, the Tennessee Supreme Court looked to tort law, and rejected Tennessee corporation law, for the statute of limitations with respect to an action against majority shareholders for breach of fiduciary duties. The Tennessee Supreme Court stated: "Other jurisdictions which have considered the limitations period applicable to actions by minority shareholders against majority shareholders alleging breach of fiduciary duty have held that such actions are governed by the statute of limitations for tortious injury to property.... There is a 'growing common law trend to declare that a breach of fiduciary duty is a tort.' " Mike v. Po Group, 937 S.W.2d at 795 (citations omitted).

In Intertherm, Inc. v. Olympic Homes Systems, Inc., 569 S.W.2d 467 (Tenn. Ct. App. 1978), the Court of Appeals of Tennessee explained that a shareholder becomes a fiduciary to a Tennessee corporation—and is subject to the special rule of scrutiny of transactions with the corporation—by exercising dominion or control over the affairs of the corporation:

> [C]ourts will closely scrutinize the transactions of a majority, dominant, or controlling shareholder with is corporation .... [T]he reason for applying the rule to a shareholder is the same as the reason for applying it to an officer or

> director, that is, that he occupies a fiduciary position with regard to the
> corporation .... Unless it is shown that a shareholder owns a majority of the
> stock or that he otherwise controls or dominates a corporation, however, a
> shareholder cannot be said to be a fiduciary and the reason for closely
> scrutinizing his transactions with the corporation disappears.... [C]ourts
> should apply the rule of close scrutiny ... when the shareholder owns a
> majority of stock, or is shown to dominate or control the corporation to a
> significant degree in some other way.

Intertherm, Inc. v. Olympic Homes Systems, Inc., 569 S.W.2d at 471- 73. Accord
Johns v. Caldwell, 601 S.W.2d 37 (Tenn. Ct. App. 1980) (control and domination
other than by way of majority stock ownership is one source of fiduciary duties
among shareholders); Security Bank & Trust Co. v. Nelms, 1986 WL 7813, at *4
(Tenn. Ct. App. July 14, 1986) (Shareholder did not occupy a fiduciary
relationship with corporation because shareholder "did not own a majority of the
stock ... it cannot be said that he 'otherwise controls or dominates' the
[corporation]."). See also Anderson v. Wilder, No. E2003- 00460-COA-R3CV,
2003 WL 22768666 (Tenn. Ct. App. Nov.21, 2003) (Controlling members of a
Tennessee LLC owe fiduciary duties to minority members notwithstanding that
Tennessee LLC statute only creates fiduciary duties of members to the LLC.).

Looking beyond the immediate corporate family, the Court of Appeals of
Tennessee has acknowledged the possibility that breachable duties can arise in the
context of a lending relationship when special facts or circumstances are present.
For example, in Oak Ridge Precision Industries, Inc. v. First Tennessee Bank
N.A., 835 S.W.2d 25 (Tenn. Ct. App. 1992), the court of appeals rejected a
borrower's claim for breach of fiduciary duties by a lender but had this to say
about the cause of action under Tennessee law:

> Although fiduciary relationships may arise whenever confidence is reposed
> by one party in another who exercises dominion and influence, the dealings
> between a lender and a borrower are not inherently fiduciary absent special
> facts and circumstances.

Id. at 30. See also Lipman v. First Nat'l Bank of Boston, No. 01A01- 9803-CH-
00139, 1999 WL 51875 (Tenn. Ct. App. Feb.5, 1999) (Court found insufficient
proof to support action by a limited partner against bank alleging civil conspiracy
and inducing breach of fiduciary duties through control of the general partner in
a business partnership.).

In Scott v. East Tennessee Production Credit Association of Greeneville, C.A.
No. 1106, 1987 WL 17244, at *4 (Tenn. Ct. App. Sept. 23, 1987), the Court of
Appeals of Tennessee cites its earlier unpublished opinion in Conley v. C.A.
Rawls, for the proposition that in the "extreme fact situation ... a fiduciary duty
existed" between a lender and a borrower. The courts of many states on various
theories of contract and tort have recognized that breachable duties to a
corporation can arise in a lender that exercises unreasonable or excessive control
over its borrower.

No Tennessee Supreme Court decision has been found directly embracing or
rejecting the possibility that Tennessee law would recognize fiduciary duties in a party
other than a shareholder, officer or director that exercises dominion or control over a

corporation. But the Tennessee cases cited above demonstrate that, on unusual facts, the exercise of domination or control in the context of a business relationship by a party not otherwise a fiduciary can give rise to fiduciary duties under Tennessee law.

The Plaintiff in this adversary proceeding has alleged special facts and extreme circumstances in the seizure of management and control of the debtors by the Controlling Customers, BBK and CMD. The imposition of the Accommodation Agreement, manipulation of the debt structure of the Debtors, operation of the Debtors by strangers to the corporate governance structure for the benefit of the Controlling Customers are extreme facts that this court believes would support a cause of action for breach of fiduciary duties under Tennessee law.

Deepening Insolvency

Deepening insolvency was first recognized as a theory for recovery in actions for breach of fiduciary duty alleging that officers or directors deepened the insolvency of the corporation and reduced or eliminated any return for creditors. See generally *Deepening Insolvency*, 23-4 AM. BANKR. INST. J. at 34 & n. 2 (citing Smith v. Arthur Andersen, 175 F.Supp.2d 1180 (D. Ariz. 2001)). Its origin has been traced to Bloor v. Dansker (In re Investors Funding Corp. of New York Securities Litigation), 523 F.Supp. 533 (S.D.N.Y. 1980). Kittay v. Atlantic Bank of New York (In re Global Serv. Group LLC), 316 B.R. 451, 456 (Bankr. S.D.N.Y. 2004).

"[T]he deepening insolvency theory of liability holds that there are times when a defendant's conduct, either fraudulently or even negligently, prolongs the life of a corporation, thereby increasing the corporation's debt and exposure to creditors." *Deepening Insolvency*, 23-4 AM. BANKR. INST. J. at 34. The action has morphed, both in form—from a breach of statutory duty claim to a form of common law tort liability—and in scope—now reaching lawyers, accountants, bankers and other financial and insolvency professionals. See Id. at 34. (citing cases). As recounted by the bankruptcy court in In re Global Service Group LLC:

> Since Investors Funding, several courts have accepted the theory that an insolvent corporation suffers a distinct and compensable injury when it continues to operate and incur more debt. Some have treated "deepening insolvency" as an independent cause of action. Other courts have viewed it as a theory of damages, often raised in response to the defense that increased debt injured the creditors, but did not harm (and actually helped) the corporation. Finally, some courts have rejected the theory outright, or raised serious questions about its viability.
>
> ....
>
> The distinction between "deepening insolvency" as a tort or damage theory may be one unnecessary to make. Prolonging an insolvent corporation's life, without more, will not result in liability under either approach. Instead, one seeking to recover for "deepening insolvency" must show that the defendant prolonged the company's life in breach of a separate duty, or committed an actionable tort that contributed to the continued operation of a corporation and its increased debt.

In re Global Serv. Group, LLC, 316 B.R. at 456-59.

No Tennessee decision has been found addressing deepening insolvency. This court must determine, as did the Third Circuit in *Lafferty* (looking to Pennsylvania law), whether the Tennessee Supreme Court would recognize deepening insolvency as an actionable breach of duty.

In *Lafferty* the court considered three factors: (1) soundness of the theory, (2) growing acceptance of the theory among courts and (3) the remedial theme in Pennsylvania law. The Third Circuit's reasoning deserves extended quotation:

> First and foremost, the theory is essentially sound.... Even when a corporation is insolvent, its corporate property may have value. The fraudulent and concealed incurrence of debt can damage that value in several ways. For example, to the extent that bankruptcy is not already a certainty, the incurrence of debt can force an insolvent corporation into bankruptcy, thus inflicting legal and administrative costs on the corporation. See Richard A. Brealey & Stewart C. Myers, *Principles of Corporate Finance* 487 (5th ed. 1996) ("[B]y issuing risky debt,[a corporation] give[s] lawyers and the court system a claim on the firm if it defaults."). When brought on by unwieldy debt, bankruptcy also creates operational limitations which hurt a corporation's ability to run its business in a profitable manner. See id. at 488-89. Aside from causing actual bankruptcy, deepening insolvency can undermine a corporation's relationships with its customers, suppliers, and employees. The very threat of bankruptcy, brought about through fraudulent debt, can shake the confidence of parties dealing with the corporation, calling into question its ability to perform, thereby damaging the corporation's assets, the value of which often depends on the performance of other parties. See Michael S. Knoll, *Taxing Prometheus: How the Corporate Interest Deduction Discourages Innovation and Risk-Taking*, 38 VILL. L. REV. 1461, 1479-80 (1993). In addition, prolonging an insolvent corporation's life through bad debt may simply cause the dissipation of corporate assets.

These harms can be averted, and the value within an insolvent corporation salvaged, if the corporation is dissolved in a timely manner, rather than kept afloat with spurious debt. As the Seventh Circuit explained in Schacht v. Brown:

> [C]ases [that oppose "deepening insolvency"] rest[ ] upon a seriously flawed assumption, i.e., that the fraudulent prolongation of a corporation's life beyond insolvency is automatically to be considered a benefit to the corporation's interests. This premise collides with common sense, for the corporate body is ineluctably damaged by the deepening of its insolvency, through increased exposure to creditor liability. Indeed, in most cases, it would be crucial that the insolvency of the corporation be disclosed, so that shareholders may exercise their right to dissolve the corporation in order to cut their losses. Thus, acceptance of a rule which would bar a corporation from recovering damages due to the hiding of information concerning its insolvency would create perverse incentives for wrong-doing officers and directors to conceal the true financial condition of the corporation from the corporate body as long as possible.

711 F.2d 1343, 1350 (7th Cir.1983) (citations omitted) (emphasis added).

Growing acceptance of the deepening insolvency theory confirms its soundness. In recent years, a number of federal courts have held that "deepening insolvency" may give rise to a cognizable injury to corporate debtors.

Lafferty, 267 F.3d at 349-51. Finally, the court noted, "one of the most venerable principles of Pennsylvania jurisprudence, and in most common law jurisdictions for that matter is that, where there is an injury, the law provides a remedy." Id. at 351.

The analysis in *Lafferty* is sound. As to the third factor, the Tennessee Supreme Court has adopted the same jurisprudential principle as the Pennsylvania high court: where there is a tortious injury, the law will provide a remedy. See, e.g., McFarlane v. Moore, 1 Tenn. 174 (1805) ("By the principles of the common law, there can be no injury without a correspondent remedy."). This court concludes that if presented with compelling facts, the Tennessee Supreme Court would recognize deepening insolvency as an actionable breach of duty to a corporation.

Against this backdrop, Plaintiff's deepening insolvency claims survive these Motions to dismiss. As to Defendants named in Counts 5 and 10 other than Buerger, Plaintiff alleges they deepened the insolvency of the debtors by taking over the finances, management and operations of the debtors for the purpose of supplying GM, Lear and JCI with products and services that were prohibitively unprofitable for the Debtors. Management was inserted from outside in the form of BBK and CMD. Creditors were paid selectively and enormous debts were incurred solely for the benefit of the Controlling Customers. Corporate assets were dissipated without regard to the interests of the corporations. The viability of DMC and DMT was utterly destroyed by the Defendants. The corporations' abilities to provide products and services to customers other than the Controlling Customers was destroyed. The corporations' debts were profoundly inflated without regard to the best interests of the corporations. Defendants' domination and control of the debtors gave rise to duties; deepening the insolvency of the debtors for the benefit of the Controlling Customers was an actionable breach.

The courts of both New York and Delaware have recognized that deepening insolvency can be a breach of the fiduciary duties owed to a corporation by its officers and directors. For all the reasons stated above, the First Amended Complaint alleges a cause of action against Buerger for deepening the insolvency of the debtors.

Aiding and Abetting a Breach of Fiduciary Duty

Counts 5 and 10 allege that GM, JCI, Lear, BBK and CMD aided and abetted Buerger's breach of fiduciary duties owed to DMC and DMT.

New York, Delaware and Tennessee each recognize an action for aiding and abetting a breach of fiduciary duty.

Aiding and abetting breach of fiduciary duties requires "a showing that there (1) existed a fiduciary relationship, (2) was a breach of the fiduciary's duty, (3) was a knowing participation in the breach by a defendant who is not a fiduciary and (4) that damages are proximately caused by the breach." Jo Ann J. Brighton, *Secured Creditors Beware: The Latest Tool in the Creditor's Committee Toolbox Aiding and Abetting in the Breach of a Fiduciary Duty*, 23-10 AM. BANKR. INST. J. 36 & n. 8 (2004).

As demonstrated above, Buerger owed fiduciary duties to the debtor corporations under Delaware and New York law. The First Amended Complaint alleges facts sufficient to constitute a cause of action against Buerger for multiple breaches of those duties, including the claim that Buerger deepened the insolvency of the Debtors.

The First Amended Complaint alleges that the Controlling Customers directly participated with Buerger in some of the conduct that would constitute a breach of duty by Buerger. For example, the Controlling Customers engineered the Accommodation Agreement to which Buerger was a party and which is alleged to be an instrument by which GM, JCI and Lear solidified their control of the Debtors—control that Buerger was duty bound to maintain by virtue of his corporate offices. The Controlling Customers are alleged to have participated with Buerger in the looting of assets from DMC and DMT and the fraudulent transfers of assets and business opportunities to DMW and ultimately to Zanini. The Controlling Customers are alleged to have participated with Buerger in deepening the insolvency of the Debtors by fraudulently expanding the debts of the Debtors, selectively paying venders and prolonging the lives of the Debtors for the benefit of the Controlling Customers, leaving corporate shells without assets, business opportunities or any ability to carry out corporate goals or to repay creditors.

BBK and CMD are alleged to have taken over the management and operations of the Debtor—responsibilities that were Buerger's by statute. BBK and CMD then managed and operated the Debtors for the benefit of the Controlling Customers and at great damage to the debtor corporations. Tremendous losses were generated for the Debtors by BBK and CMD through selective payment of suppliers and the performance of highly unprofitable contracts for the benefit of the Controlling Customers. It is alleged that BBK and CMD were paid by the Debtors for their mismanagement of the Debtors—on Buerger's watch as sole director of both corporations.

All the elements of aiding and abetting breach of fiduciary duty are stated with respect to the Defendants named in Counts 5 and 10.

Standing and In Pari Delicto

Standing

Some Defendants challenge the trustee's standing to bring actions for breach of fiduciary duty and aiding and abetting breach of fiduciary duty on the ground that these actions belong to creditors and cannot be pursued by the trustee on behalf of the corporations. Defendants also challenging standing with respect to Counts 5 and 10 on the basis of the defense of in pari delicto.

In pari delicto is a defense to an action in tort, not a basis upon which to challenge standing to sue.

Actions for breach of fiduciary duties and for aiding and abetting breach of fiduciary duties—in contrast to an action to disregard corporate identity—accrue to the corporation itself because fiduciary duties are owed to the corporation and it is the corporation that suffers injury when fiduciary duties are breached. See, e.g., Pepper v. Litton, 308 U.S. 295, 307, 60 S. Ct. 238, 84 L. Ed. 281 (1939) ("While normally that fiduciary obligation is enforceable directly by the corporation, or through a stockholder's derivative action, it is, in the event of bankruptcy of the corporation, enforceable by the trustee.") * * *.

The trustee has standing to maintain the actions in Counts 5 and 10.

In Pari Delicto

Defendants move to dismiss Counts 5 and 10 on the basis of in pari delicto.

In pari delicto is an equitable defense that "'refers to the plaintiff's participation in the same wrongdoing as the defendant.'" In re Dublin Sec., Inc., 133 F.3d at 380 (quoting Bubis v. Blanton, 885 F.2d 317, 321 n. 1 (6th Cir. 1989)). The phrase "in pari delicto" is part of a longer expression "In pari delicto potior est conditio defendentis,' which means that where the wrong of both parties is equal, the position of the defendant is the stronger." Theye v. Bates, 166 Ind. App. 652, 337 N.E.2d 837, 844 (1975). "This principle prevents a plaintiff from recovering damages arising from a wrongdoing for which the plaintiff bears substantial responsibility." DeNune v. Consolidated Capital of N. Am., Inc., 288 F. Supp. 2d 844, 851 (N.D. Ohio 2003) (citation omitted).

Citing *Dublin Securities*, the Defendants argue that Buerger was the sole director of the Debtors and his participation in the acts complained of in Counts 5 and 10 bars the trustee's recovery on behalf of the debtor corporations. In *Dublin Securities*, the Sixth Circuit allowed the defense of in pari delicto on a motion to dismiss a bankruptcy trustee's complaint against lawyers who counseled the Debtor in devising and carrying out fraudulent stock offerings. The Sixth Circuit acknowledged that in pari delicto is an "equitable defense." The trustee insisted that the defense of in pari delicto required a fact-finding inquiry and could not be resolved on a motion to dismiss. The Sixth Circuit found that the defense could be resolved without trial because the trustee conceded that "the debtors' own actions were instrumental in perpetrating the fraud ... [and] that the debtors intentionally defrauded their investors." *Dublin Sec.*, 133 F.3d at 380.

Dublin Securities was distinguished by an Ohio district court in *DeNune*. The plaintiff in *DeNune* was the receiver for TPSS Acquisition Corp., a wholly owned subsidiary of defendant, Consolidated Capital of North America. The other defendants were officers and directors of Consolidated. The receiver alleged that the parent corporation (Consolidated) and its officers and directors looted assets from TPSS. The defendants asserted that the receiver was barred by in pari delicto from bringing any action based on the alleged looting of TPSS, because any conduct of the defendants could be imputed to TPSS as the wholly owned subsidiary of Consolidated. Rejecting the defendants' interpretation of the doctrine, the *DeNune* court explained:

> [The receiver] has alleged a one-way transfer of funds: from TPSS to Consolidated and the related defendants. TPSS and its creditors are the victims of the alleged fraud, not its perpetrators or beneficiaries.... [As] explained in a closely analogous case, wherein an appointed receiver sued to recover looted corporate assets:
>
>> "The appointment of the receiver removed the wrongdoer from the scene .... Put differently, the defense of in pari delicto loses its sting when the person who is in parti delicto is eliminated. Now that the corporation[ ] ... [is] controlled by a receiver whose only object is to maximize the value of the corporation[ ] for the benefit of [its] investors and creditors, we cannot see an objection to the receiver's bringing suit to recover corporate assets unlawfully dissipated by [a principal of the corporation]."

DeNune, 288 F. Supp. 2d at 851 (quoting Scholes v. Lehmann, 56 F.3d 750, 754-55 (7th Cir.1995)). The *DeNune* court distinguished *Dublin Securities* on the ground that the trustee in *Dublin Securities* "specifically admitted the corporation's complicity/instrumentality in the fraud perpetrated by the defendant law firms." Id. at 851 n. 2.

"[T]he equitable context in which the in pari delicto defense is asserted is crucial." Baker O'Neal Holdings, Inc. v. Ernst & Young LLP, No. 1:03-CV-0132-DFH, 2004 WL 771230 (S.D.Ind. Mar.24, 2004). As the Second Circuit recognized in Kalb, Voorhis & Co. v. American Financial Corp., 8 F.3d 130 (2d Cir. 1993), and observed later in Committee of Unsecured Creditors of Color Tile, Inc. v. Coopers & Lybrand, LLP, 322 F.3d 147 (2d Cir. 2003), "where the parties do not stand on equal terms and one party controls the other, the in pari delicto doctrine does not apply."

In *Dublin Securities*, the plaintiff's admissions "establishe[d] conclusively that the debtors were at least as culpable as the defendants [.]" *Dublin Sec.*, 133 F.3d at 380. Here, as in *DeNune*, no similar conclusion is conceded or evident from the pleadings. To the contrary, it is alleged that Defendants GM, Lear, JCI, BBK and CMD usurped control and management of the Debtors for the benefit of the Controlling Customers, causing great injury to the Debtors. Buerger alleges in his cross-claim that the Controlling Customers took over, put their agents in charge of management and operations of the Debtors and pushed out the existing officers and managers. If proven, these allegations will place this case among those in which "delicto" is present, but not "in pari." See Kalb, Voorhis & Co. v. American Fin. Corp., 8 F.3d at 133 ("Because Appellant alleges that AFC dominated and controlled Circle K, the in pari delicto doctrine would not bar Circle K from asserting an alter ego claim[.]") * * *.

The Defendants will have ample opportunity to present their equitable defense of in pari delicto. On these Motions to dismiss, it cannot be said that the allegations of the Complaint establish the defense as a matter of law.
    * * *

G. Count 7

Count 7 of the First Amended Complaint alleges that Defendant Carson Fischer was the law firm for the Debtors and DMW from 1999 to 2001, and represented them during the takeover by the Controlling Customers, in connection with the Accommodation Agreement and during the transfer of assets from the Debtors to DMW. Plaintiff asserts that CF had a duty to "protect the separate interests of DMC and DMT" and that it breached that duty. Further, Plaintiff alleges that CF had a conflict of interest in its representation of DMC and DMT and its representation of Defendants Buerger and DMW, and that the interests of the Defendants were preferred.

CF's Motion to dismiss challenges the timeliness of Plaintiff's action, asserting that professional negligence actions have a one year statute of limitations under Tennessee law. See Tenn. Code Ann. §28-3-104.

The parties stipulated that Tennessee law controls the "state law counts" for purposes of these Motions to dismiss. In their stipulation, the parties listed many counts of the First Amended Complaint that involved state law. Incomprehensively, Count 7 was not among them. In their briefs, Plaintiff and CF discuss the Tennessee statute of limitations on actions against attorneys. Plaintiff filed a Supplemental Brief arguing the contradictory position that "Michigan has the most significant contacts" with respect to the legal malpractice claim in Count 7.

Generally, "a malpractice claim against a firm's lawyer is determined by the law of the state where the services are performed, for that state's law supplies the standard of performance and that is where the client normally would suffer injury." In re Bridgestone/Firestone, Inc., 288 F.3d 1012, 1018 (7th Cir. 2002). Under state or federal choice of law principles, courts look at the "significance of the relationship of a state with the occurrence and the parties." Among the factors to consider are: (1) the place where the injury occurred; (2) the place where the conduct causing the injury occurred; (3) the domicile, residence or place of business of the parties; and (4) the place where the relationship, if any, between the parties is centered.

The injuries to the debtors alleged in the First Amended Complaint seem to have occurred in Tennessee. The debtors, though incorporated elsewhere, are certainly most connected to Tennessee. No facts are alleged in the First Amended Complaint connecting the events in this lawsuit to Michigan. Consistent with the other stipulations of the parties, Tennessee law will be applied to CF's Motion to dismiss Count 7.

Plaintiff refers to Count 7 as claims for legal malpractice and an action for breach of fiduciary duties. Defendant sees Count 7 as a professional malpractice action only. This difference in characterization determines whether the one-year limitation on malpractice actions applies (Tenn. Code Ann. §28-3-104) or the three-year limitation applicable to breach of fiduciary duty[1] (Tenn. Code Ann. §28-3-105), or both.

As explained by the Tennessee Supreme Court, to determine which statute of limitations applies, courts should determine "the nature of the cause of action alleged.... The gravamen of a complaint and the injury alleged.... To ascertain the gravamen of the action, the Court must look at the basis for which damages are sought." Mike v. Po Group, Inc., 937 S.W.2d 790, 793 (Tenn. 1996). This analysis is not easily applied to Count 7. As one commentator explains:

> Three distinct causes of action are potentially available to clients for misbehavior by their lawyers: (1) breach of fiduciary duty; (2) breach of contract; and (3) the tort of malpractice. The courts, however, are not in agreement on the exact nature of and parameters for these causes of action. Many refuse to recognize the distinctions and dichotomies between and among the actions, and conclude that regardless of how the cause is characterized it is essentially a tort action for malpractice.
>
> ....
>
> Commentators suggest that the tort of breach of fiduciary duty, while involving a wrong distinct and independent from professional negligence, still constitutes legal malpractice. What this generalization overlooks is that legal malpractice is

---

1. [Footnote 22 in original:] As detailed above, breach of fiduciary duty has been identified as a common law tort, with a three year limitation period under Tennessee law. The Tennessee Supreme Court observed that "[t]here is a growing common law trend to declare 'that a breach of fiduciary duty is a tort.'" Mike v. Po Group, Inc., 937 S.W.2d 790, 795 (Tenn.1996) (citations omitted) (In an action for breach of fiduciary duty, "the applicable limitations period is three years as provided in Tenn. Code Ann. §28-3-105."). Michigan case law has also characterized a claim for breach of fiduciary duty as a common law tort and applied the three year, residual tort statute of limitations. See, e.g., Borock v. Comerica Bank-Detroit, 938 F.Supp. 428 (E.D. Mich.1996) (citing Mich. Comp. Laws §600.5805).

professional negligence. Like all negligence, professional negligence is failure to perform. Breach of fiduciary duty is not failure to perform. Breach of fiduciary duty is failure to adhere to the authority granted by the client. An attorney-client relationship imposes a fiduciary duty on the lawyer to represent the client with undivided loyalty. Failing to give undivided loyalty does not necessarily mean that the attorney performed legal services negligently. Instead, failure to give undivided loyalty to the client means that the attorney performed the legal service outside the scope of the authority (fiduciary duty) granted by the client.

Ray Ryden Anderson & Walter W. Steele, Jr., *Fiduciary Duty, Tort and Contract: A Primer on the Legal Malpractice Puzzle*, 47 SMU L. REV. 235, 235 & n. 4 (1994) (internal citations omitted).

Some state courts recognize breach of fiduciary duty as a tort distinct from professional negligence or malpractice. Other state courts hold that "[m]alpractice by any other name still constitutes malpractice.... [M]isconduct may consist either of negligence or of the breach of the contract of employment. It makes no difference whether the professional misconduct is found in tort or contract, it still constitutes malpractice." Muir v. Hadler Real Estate Mgmt. Co., 4 Ohio App. 3d 89, 446 N.E.2d 820, 822 (Ohio Ct. App. 1982) (cited in Omlin v. Kaufman & Cumberland Co. L.P.A., Case Nos. 00-04003 & 00-4142, 2001 WL 493387 (6th Cir. May 1, 2001)).

No Tennessee case is offered by the parties either accepting or rejecting separate causes of action against a lawyer for malpractice and breach of fiduciary duty in connection with client representation. In an unreported decision, the Tennessee Court of Appeals observed as much:

> [T]he duty alleged to have been breached in the case before us is one imposed and established by the Code of Professional Responsibility. The duty to maintain client confidences and secrets and not to use them after the termination of the attorney-client relationship is part of the ethical rules that govern attorney conduct. The Tennessee Supreme Court has the exclusive power to regulate the conduct of lawyers in the State of Tennessee. Our Supreme Court has not determined that a cause of action for breach of fiduciary duty lies against an attorney when the only allegation is a breach of the Code of Professional Responsibility. Because we have found that [plaintiff's] complaints do not provide a sufficient factual basis for its allegations that [defendant] used client confidences or secrets, we need not determine whether [plaintiff] could bring a cause of action for breach of fiduciary duty, separate from a malpractice action, against an attorney.

Image Outdoor Advertising, Inc. v. CSX Transp., Inc., Case No. M2000-03207-COA-R3CV, 2003 WL 21338700, at *10-11 (Tenn. Ct. App. June 10, 2003) (internal citations omitted).

This court need not resolve whether the Tennessee Supreme Court would allow separate actions against an attorney for malpractice and breach of fiduciary duties because Plaintiff has not pleaded misconduct by CF other than traditional malpractice. Count 7 redundantly recites that CF had "conflict[s] of interest" and failed to "protect the separate interests of DMC and DMT." (First Am. Compl. ¶57.) That CF was the debtors' lawyer in connection with the Accommodation Agreement and the transfers of assets to DMW (First Am. Compl. ¶55) is a third restatement of the allegation that CF breached its duty to represent the debtors' interests—not the conflicting interests of DMW or the Controlling Customers. CF is not named among the "Control Persons" in paragraph 45 of the First Amended Complaint and is not named anywhere else in the Complaint with respect to any misconduct outside the attorney/client relationship.

Conflicts of interest are specifically addressed by the Code of Professional Responsibility and are appropriately characterized as a cause of action for attorney malpractice.

Under Tennessee law, the statute of limitations for "actions and suits against attorneys … for malpractice, whether the actions are grounded or based in contract or tort" is one year. Tenn. Code Ann. § 28-3-104. "In legal malpractice actions, the one-year statute of limitations starts to run when the client suffers a legally cognizable injury resulting from an attorney's negligence or other wrongdoing, and the client knows or should know the facts sufficient to give notice of that injury." Cherry v. Williams, 36 S.W.3d 78 (Tenn.Ct.App.2000). "Because negligence without injury is not actionable, the legal malpractice statute of limitations does not begin to run until an attorney's negligence has actually injured the client. And there is no injury until there is the loss of a right, remedy, or interest or the imposition of a liability. Before that time, any injury is only prospective and uncertain. There is no legally cognizable injury where there exists only the mere possibility of harm." Id. at 84 (internal quotations and citations omitted).

Debtors' Chapter 7 cases were filed on November 28, 2001. Section 108(a) of the Bankruptcy Code extends the state law limitation period under certain circumstances:

> If applicable nonbankruptcy law, an order entered in a nonbankruptcy proceeding, or an agreement fixes a period within which the debtor may commence an action, and such period has not expired before the date of the filing of the petition, the trustee may commence such action only *before the later of*—(1) the end of such period, including any suspension of such period occurring on or after the commencement of the case; or (2) two years after the order for relief.

11 U.S.C. § 108(a) (emphasis added).

Plaintiff filed her original Complaint on November 28, 2003, two years after the order for relief. Any malpractice action against CF that was viable at the petition was timely commenced with the filing of the original Complaint. See Limor v. Weinstein & Sutton (In re SMEC, Inc.), 160 B.R. 86 (M.D.Tenn.1993) (section 108(a) preserves malpractice action that could have been commenced on the petition date).

In the year prior to the petition, Plaintiff has alleged that CF was debtors' counsel and that in late 2000 when the Controlling Customers "brought in" BBK to "take over" the operations of Del-Met and brought in CMD to take over the accounting functions of Del-Met; in early 2001 when the Controlling Customers approached Bank One—Del-Met's lender—about restructuring Del-Met's debt; during the transfers of assets to DMW; and, in April 2001 when the Controlling Customers, Bank One, Del-Met and Buerger entered into the "Accommodation Agreement"—an agreement that Plaintiff contends sealed the fate of the Debtors. Some or all of these allegations fall within the limitation period for malpractice actions under Tennessee law. Count 7 states a claim against CF.

H. Count 8

In Count 8, Plaintiff asserts that GM, Lear and JCI were unjustly enriched at the expense of the Debtors. Defendants move to dismiss on the ground that the existence of a contract precludes this unjust enrichment claim. Plaintiff responds that because "the valid contract defense to an unjust enrichment claim is an affirmative defense under Rule 8(c) ... it is too early to tell whether any valid contracts exist[.]" (Pl. Resp. at 28-9.)

"Actions brought upon theories of unjust enrichment, quasi contract, contracts implied in law, and quantum meruit are essentially the same. Courts frequently employ the various terminology interchangeably to describe that class of implied obligations where, on the basis of justice and equity, the law will impose a contractual relationship between the parties, regardless of their assent thereto." Paschall's, Inc. v. Dozier, 219 Tenn. 45, 407 S.W.2d 150, 154 (1966). The law imposes a contract when there is proof (1) that no enforceable contract exists between the parties, and (2) the defendant will be unjustly enriched absent a court-created obligation.

There was a contract (or contracts) between the Debtor corporation(s) and the Defendants named in Count 8. Whether that contract encompassed the conduct for which a remedy may lie in unjust enrichment is a factual issue yet to be developed in this adversary proceeding. The First Amended Complaint alleges actions by the Controlling Customers that broadly exceed the boundaries of any contract so far described. The Controlling Customers are alleged to have unjustly enriched themselves by seizing the management and operations of the debtors—facts not consistent with the ordinary contractual relationship between a supplier and its customer. Whether these Defendants will prove an existing, enforceable contract sufficient in scope to preclude recovery for unjust enrichment remains to be seen. Dismissal of Count 8 under Rule 12(b)(6) is premature.

* * *

K. Count 12

Count 12 names Defendants GM, JCI, Lear and GMAC, and seeks recharacterization from debt to equity of loans by these Defendants to Del-Met. Without limitation, Plaintiff identifies a loan of $251,927 from Lear to Del-Met on April 9, 2001, a loan of $255,216 from JCI to Del-Met on April 10, 2001, and a loan of $242,857 from GM to Del-Met on April 10, 2001. (First Am. Compl. ¶ 63.)

Plaintiff asserts that GM, JCI, Lear and GMAC "knew or should have known that Del-Met was insolvent at the time that additional sums were lent to Del-Met [.]" (First Am. Compl. ¶64.) Plaintiff states that these loans were repaid in May 2003 (post petition) by DMW—a nondebtor—upon the sale of Del-Met's assets to Zanini. Plaintiff asks that these loans be recharacterized from debt to equity, and that a constructive trust be impose on any loan repayments by DMW to these Defendants.

The timing of the loans described in Count 12 coincides with the Accommodation Agreement, dated April 10, 2001. Under the Accommodation Agreement, Del-Met was required to pay CF and CMD $750,000. The three loans in Count 12 total exactly $750,000. The Accommodation Agreement gave the Controlling Customers a lien on the debtors' assets.

The Plaintiff alleges in paragraphs 24, 25 and 26 that the Accommodation Agreement "solidified the Controlling Customers' control over the affairs of Del-Met." It is alleged that only the Controlling Customers benefited from the Accommodation Agreement. It certainly looks like the debtors paid for the Accommodation Agreement with money loaned by the Controlling Customers and then repaid by DMW from the sale of Del-Met's assets to Zanini. These transactions are evidence of domination, control and manipulation of the debtors by the Controlling Customers. As noted in Count 1 above, incurring $750,000 of debt for the benefit of the Controlling Customers, CF and CMD during the year before bankruptcy could be a fraudulent transfer. As explained in Count 6, payment of the $750,000 to CF and CMD may be preferential as to GM, JCI, Lear and CMD.

The Sixth Circuit has held that "[r]echaracterization is appropriate where the circumstances show that a debt transaction was 'actually [an] equity contribution [ ] ab initio.'" Bayer Corp. v. MascoTech, Inc. (In re AutoStyle Plastics, Inc.), 269 F.3d 726, 748 (6th Cir. 2001) (quoting In re Cold Harbor Assocs., 204 B.R. 904, 915 (Bankr. E.D. Va. 1997)). The Sixth Circuit states eleven factors relevant to recharacterization: (1) the names given to the instruments, if any, evidencing the indebtedness; (2) the presence or absence of a fixed maturity date and schedule of payments; (3) the presence or absence of a fixed rate of interest and interest payments; (4) the source of repayments; (5) the adequacy or inadequacy of capitalization; (6) the identity of interest between the creditor and the stockholder; (7) the security, if any, for the advances; (8) the corporation's ability to obtain financing from outside lending institutions; (9) the extent to which the advances were subordinated to the claims of outside creditors; (10) the extent to which the advances were used to acquire capital assets; and (11) the presence or absence of a sinking fund to provide repayments. Roth Steel Tube Co. v. Commissioner, 800 F.2d 625, 630 (6th Cir.1986). See also In re AutoStyle Plastics, Inc., 269 F.3d at 750 n. 12 ("We believe that the *Roth Steel* factors provide a general framework for assessing recharacterization claims that is also appropriate in the bankruptcy context. We note, however, that there is some disagreement as to whether tax court recharacterization factors are appropriate for use in bankruptcy cases.").

Plaintiff's recharacterization claim fails because there is no debt remaining to recharacterize. Plaintiff admits that the only debts identified in Count 12 were repaid from the postpetition proceeds of the sale of assets to Zanini.

Recognizing this defect in her recharacterization action, Plaintiff asks for relief consistent with the absence of debt—imposition of a constructive trust on debt payments by DMW.

"A constructive trust may [ ] be imposed against one who, by fraud, actual or constructive, by duress or abuse of confidence, by commission of wrong, or by any form of unconscionable conduct, artifice, concealment or questionable means, has obtained an interest in property which he ought not in equity or in good conscience retain." Intersparex Leddin KG v. Al-Haddad, 852 S.W.2d 245, 249 (Tenn. Ct. App. 1992) (citation omitted). Tennessee courts have imposed constructive trusts in four types of cases: (1) Where a person procures the legal title to property in violation of some duty, express or implied, to the true owner; (2) where the title to property is obtained by fraud, duress or other inequitable means; (3) where a person makes use of some relation of influence or confidence to obtain the legal title upon more advantageous terms than could otherwise have been obtained; and (4) where a person acquires property with notice that another is entitled to its benefits. Myers v. Myers, 891 S.W.2d 216, 219 (Tenn. Ct. App. 1994) (citations omitted). Most importantly, "constructive trust is merely a remedy used by courts to enforce substantive rights; it is not itself a substantive right." Rider ex rel. Rider v. Rider, No. M2002-00556-COA-R3CV, 2003 WL 22345475 (Tenn. Ct. App. Oct.15, 2003) (citing Howell Petroleum Corp. v. Samson Res. Co., 903 F.2d 778, 780 (10th Cir.1990)).

The constructive trust claim in Count 12 is an alternative remedy to recover assets sold by DMW to Zanini post petition which Plaintiff asserts were misappropriated or fraudulently conveyed from these bankruptcy estates. Also, mentioned above, imposition of a constructive trust may be an available remedy if stay violations are found under Count 11. But Count 12 does not state an independent cause of action for constructive trust.

* * *

CONCLUSION

For the reasons stated, the Defendants' Motions to dismiss will be granted in part and denied in part by separate order.

B. RECHARACTERIZATION AND EQUITABLE SUBORDINATION UNDER BANKRUPTCY LAW

Under state law and in bankruptcy, a creditor's claim against a debtor for debt trumps an investor's claim of an equity interest. Increasingly, bankruptcy courts are exercising their presumed equitable power to examine a creditor's claim and to recharacterize it as equity. The practical effect is to subordinate a creditor's claim.

Separately and differently, § 510(c) allows the bankruptcy court, under equitable principles, to subordinate claims and interests:

> [A]fter notice and a hearing, the court may—
>> (1) under principles of equitable subordination, subordinate for purposes of distribution all or part of an allowed claim to all or part of another allowed claim or all or part of an allowed interest to all or part of another allowed interest; or
>> (2) order that any lien securing such a subordinated claim be transferred to the estate.

11 U.S.C. § 510(c).

Klee & Mervis, *Recharacterization in Bankruptcy*
in CHAPTER 11 BUSINESS REORGANIZATIONS 211, 213-19
(Annual Advanced ALI-ABA Course of Study, No. SK092, 2005)

"Recharacterization" refers to an equitable power exercised by bankruptcy courts to look beyond a given label and instead characterize a purported claim or transaction according to its true economic nature. The Bankruptcy Code does not expressly grant any such power, but many courts have nonetheless found an implied power to recharacterize based on their general powers as courts of equity. * * *

I. Recharacterization of Debt as Equity.

A. Introduction.

"Recharacterization" is commonly understood to refer to a bankruptcy court's equitable power to look through a transaction labeled as a loan and instead characterize it based on its economic substance as an equity contribution.

Recharacterization might arise in the following scenario: Corporation is grossly undercapitalized. It must raise $6 million in order to meet payroll and other immediate and critical working capital needs. Unfortunately, Corporation cannot locate any lender willing to extend financing. Among other things, Corporation can barely service its current debt, it has no unencumbered assets to offer as security for an additional loan, and it does not have sufficient cash flow to service interest or principal on any additional loan. Two Investors sit on Corporation's board of directors, each of which have already invested millions of dollars in equity in Corporation at its inception and in subsequent financing rounds. Investors agree that they will each loan $3 million to Corporation in exchange for notes bearing interest at 10 percent. The notes are negatively amortized: they do not require any payment of principal or interest during their term but must be satisfied in their entirety by a balloon payment at maturity after three years. The loan proceeds are used immediately to fund Corporation's working capital needs. However, Corporation's financial condition continues to deteriorate; it cannot service its other debt; and it eventually files for bankruptcy relief. Investors file proofs of claim on account of their notes. At this point, Corporation's other unsecured creditors request that the bankruptcy court recharacterize the purported financing notes as equity contributions. They argue that the amounts advanced by Investors, although cast in the form of loans, were actually equity infusions.

Presented with such a request, under the majority view, the bankruptcy court is "not required to accept the label of 'debt' or 'equity' placed by the debtor upon a particular transaction, but must inquire into the actual nature of the transaction to determine how best to characterize it."[2] In other words, the court is required to scrutinize the transaction "according to an objective test of economic reality to determine its true economic nature."[3] If the transaction, although "cast in the form of a loan[,]" nevertheless has the "substance and character of an equity contribution[,]"[4] then the court may recharacterize the transaction as an equity contribution. This outcome, of course, has enormous consequences for the unsecured creditors as well as for the Investors in our above hypothetical. It is the difference between a party standing first in line as a creditor with claims against the debtor, perhaps secured by estate property, versus taking last as an equity holder.

---

2.   [Footnote 1 in original:] In re Cold Harbor Assocs., 204 B.R. 904, 915 (Bankr. E.D. Va. 1997).

3.   [Footnote 2 in original:] Cohen v. KB Mezzanine Fund II, L.P. (In re Submicron Sys. Corp.), 291 B.R. 314, 323 (Bankr. D. Del. 2003) (citations omitted)[, aff'd, 432 F.3d 448 (3d Cir. 2006)].

4.   [Footnote 3 in original:] Aquino v. Black (In re AtlanticRancher, Inc.), 279 B.R. 411, 437 (Bankr. D. Mass. 2002).

B. Authority to Recharacterize.

As a threshold proposition, jurisdictions do not agree uniformly whether bankruptcy courts have the power to recharacterize debt into equity. The vast majority of jurisdictions have held that bankruptcy courts may recharacterize debt as equity:

> Bankruptcy courts that have applied a recharacterization analysis have stated that their power to do so stems from the authority vested in the bankruptcy courts to use their equitable powers to test the validity of debts. The source of the court's general equitable powers is § 105 of the Code, which states that bankruptcy judges have the authority to "issue any order, process or judgment that is necessary or appropriate to carry out the provisions" of the Code.

Bayer Corp. v. Mascotech, Inc. (In re Autostyle Plastics, Inc.), 269 F.3d 726, 749 (6th Cir. 2001). These jurisdictions include the Fifth, Sixth, and Tenth Circuits, as well as numerous lower courts in these and other jurisdictions.

On the other hand, a minority of courts have taken the position that the Bankruptcy Code does not permit the recharacterization of debt to equity. In In re Pacific Express, Inc., [69 B.R. 112 (B.A.P. 9th Cir. 1986),] the Bankruptcy Appellate Panel for the Ninth Circuit reasoned that Bankruptcy Code section 502 authorizes a court to determine the "amount" of a claim, and section 157(b)(2)(B) of the Judicial Code authorizes a court to determine the "allowance or disallowance" of a claim, but that no provision authorizes a court to decide the character of a claim. The panel next examined Bankruptcy Code section 510(c), which authorizes the equitable subordination of claims under certain circumstances. It is well-settled that, although bankruptcy courts have broad authority to work equity under section 105(a), they may not do so in a manner inconsistent with the Bankruptcy Code. Stated another way, section 105(a) "supplements the courts' specifically enumerated bankruptcy powers by authorizing orders necessary or appropriate to carry out provisions of the Bankruptcy Code. However, section 105(a) has a limited scope. It does not create rights that would otherwise be unavailable under the Bankruptcy Code."[5] The panel found that recharacterization was inconsistent with the Bankruptcy Code. It therefore concluded that recharacterization was not a permissible exercise of a bankruptcy court's equitable power.

The Supreme Court's 1999 decision in Grupo Mexicano De Desarrollo v. Alliance Bond Fund [527 U.S. 308, 119 S. Ct. 1961 (1999)] may affect the debate over the authority of bankruptcy courts to recharacterize debt as equity. In *Grupo Mexicano*, the Supreme Court held that a preliminary injunction may not issue to preserve assets to which a party did not yet have a legal claim. The Supreme Court recognized that "equity is flexible; but in the federal system, at least, that flexibility is confined within the broad boundaries of traditional equitable relief. To accord a type of relief that has never been available before ... is to invoke a default rule ... not of flexibility but of omnipotence." [Id. at 322.] *Grupo Mexicano* may lend support to the minority position that recharacterization is not a legitimate exercise of a bankruptcy courts' general equitable powers under

5. [Footnote 11 in original:] In re WCI Cable, Inc., 282 B.R. 457, 468 (Bankr. D. Or. 2002) (quoting United States v. Pepperman, 976 F.2d 123, 131 (3d Cir. 1992)).

Bankruptcy Code section 105(a). Recharacterization is neither authorized by statute nor a traditional equitable power. Just as in *Grupo Mexicano*, it may be that to permit bankruptcy courts to recharacterize claims under section 105 would be to adopt a rule not of flexibility, but of omnipotence.

On the other hand, several relatively recent opinions have held that the holding in *Grupo Mexicano* may not be as comprehensive as may have first appeared. In Rubin v. Pringle (In re Focus Media, Inc.), [387 F.3d 1077 (9th Cir. 2004)] the Ninth Circuit Court of Appeals held that *Grupo Mexicano* appeared to except from its general rule the following two situations: where the plaintiff pleads for (i) equitable relief, and not just legal damages, in instances where a preliminary injunction is a reasonable measure to preserve the status quo; and (ii) avoidance of preference or fraudulent transfer claims, which are designed to prevent such conduct as "debtors' trying to avoid paying their debts, or seeking to favor some creditors over others."[6]

C. Recharacterization versus Equitable Subordination.

As described above, the propriety of recharacterization largely depends on whether recharacterization is distinct from Bankruptcy Code section 510(c)'s power to equitably subordinate claims.

Certainly, the effect of both recharacterization and equitable subordination is similar in that "in both cases, the claim is subordinated below that of other creditors."[7] However, there are important differences. Courts adhering to the majority view have held that a claim for equitable subordination under section 510(c) requires a showing of the following three elements: (i) the claimant has engaged in some type of inequitable conduct, (ii) the misconduct resulted in injury to the creditors or conferred an unfair advantage to the claimant, and (iii) equitable subordination of the claim would not be inconsistent with the provisions of the Bankruptcy Code. Where a plaintiff establishes these elements, the court may subordinate the claim to others claims but not to equity interests. Thus, "[i]n an equitable subordination analysis, the court is reviewing whether a legitimate creditor engaged in inequitable conduct, in which case the *remedy* is subordination of the creditor's claim to that of another creditor *only to the extent necessary* to offset injury or damage suffered by the creditor in whose favor the equitable doctrine may be effective."[8] On the other hand, where a claim is recharacterized, "the advance is not a claim to begin with, and the creditor is not a legitimate one [and therefore] equitable subordination never comes into play."[9] Accordingly, a court may recharacterize debt as equity "regardless of satisfaction of the other requirements of equitable subordination."[10]

---

6.   [Footnote 17 in original:] *Grupo Mexicano*, 527 U.S. at 322.

7.   [Footnote 18 in original:] In re Autostyle Plastics, Inc., 269 F.3d at 748.

8.   [Footnote 21 in original:] Id. [at 749] (emphasis in original) (quoting [and adding emphasis to quote from] In re W.T. Grant Co., 4 B.R. 53, 74 (Bankr. S.D.N.Y. 1980)).

9.   [Footnote 22 in original:] [Id.] (quoting In re Georgetown Bldg. Assocs. v. PWA, 240 B.R. 124, 137 (Bankr. D.D.C. 1999)).

10.   [Footnote 23 in original:] [Id.] (quoting In re Hyperion Enters., 158 B.R. 555, 561 (D.R.I. 1993)) (internal quotations omitted).

Notwithstanding the above, courts adhering to the minority view have held that recharacterization requires, as one element, some manner of inequitable conduct. For example, the bankruptcy court in In re SubMicron Sys. Corp. held that in order to recharacterize a loan as an equity contribution "there must be evidence of [] inequitable conduct. This is because any other analysis would discourage loans from insiders to companies facing financial difficulty and that would be unfortunate because it is the shareholders who are most likely to have the motivation to salvage a floundering company." [In re SubMicron Sys. Corp., 291 B.R. at 325 (quoting In re Octagon Roofing, 157 B.R. 852, 858 (N.D. Ill. 1993).]

D. Analysis.

Jurisdictions that have allowed bankruptcy courts to recharacterize debt as equity have adopted similar, although varying, multi-factor tests. These factors are "not exclusive, and no one factor is predominant, nor are the factors to be given rigidly equal weight."[11]

The overriding principle governing this determination is "whether the transaction bears the earmarks of an arm's length negotiation. The more such an exchange appears to reflect the characteristics of an arm's length negotiation, the more likely such a transaction is to be treated as debt."[12] A second key factor is whether the corporation is undercapitalized at the time the funds are advanced. "When a corporation is undercapitalized, a court is more skeptical of purported loans made to it because they may in reality be infusions of capital."[13] On the other hand, recharacterization may not be appropriate where a party is "acting as a lender of last resort and not as an investor."[14]

Courts have adopted three sets of factors in determining whether to recharacterize debt as equity. The Court of Appeals for the Sixth Circuit and lower courts in the First, Third, and Eighth Circuits have adopted the so-called "*Roth Steel*" [Roth Steel Tube Co. v. Comm'r of Internal Revenue, 800 F.2d 625, 630 (6th Cir. 1986)] set of 11 factors, as follows:

1. the names given to the instruments, if any.
2. the presence or absence of a fixed maturity date and schedule of payments.
3. the presence or absence of a fixed rate of interest and interest payments.
4. the source of repayments.
5. the adequacy or inadequacy of capitalization.
6. the identity of interest between the creditor and the stockholder.
7. the security, if any, for the advances.
8. the corporation's ability to obtain financing from outside lending institutions.
9. the extent to which the advances were subordinated to the claims of outside creditors.
10. the extent to which the advances were used to acquire capital assets.
11. the presence or absence of a sinking fund to provide repayments.

---

11. [Footnote 27 in original:] In re Cold Harbor Assocs., 204 B.R. at 915.
12. [Footnote 28 in original:] [Id.] (citing Pepper v. Litton, 308 U.S. 295 (1939)).
13. [Footnote 29 in original:] In re Submicron Sys. Corp., 291 B.R. at 325 (quoting In re Autostyle Plastics, Inc., 269 F.3d at 746-47) (noting that "undercapitalization alone is insufficient to justify the subordination of insider claims; there must be evidence of other inequitable conduct.").
14. [Footnote 30 in original:] In re AtlanticRancher, Inc., 279 B.R. at 438.

The Fifth, Tenth, and Eleventh Circuits, as well as lower courts in the Second Circuit, have adopted the following 13 factor test, largely identical to the *Roth Steel* factors:

1.   the names given to the certificates evidencing indebtedness.
2.   the presence or absence of a fixed maturity date.
3.   the source of payments.
4.   the right to enforce payment of principal and interest.
5.   participation in management flowing as a result.
6.   the status of the contribution in relation to regular corporate creditors.
7.   the intent of the parties.
8.   "thin" or inadequate capitalization.
9.   identity of interest between creditor and stockholder.
10. the source of interest payments.
11. the ability of the corporation to obtain loans from outside lending institutions.
12. the extent to which the advance was used to acquire capital assets.
13. failure of the debtor to repay on the due date or seek postponement.

Finally, lower courts in the Third Circuit also have adopted the following seven factor test, which incorporates various factors from the preceding tests:

1.   the name given to the instrument.
2.   the intent of the parties.
3.   the presence of a fixed maturity date.
4.   the right to enforce payment of principal and interest.
5.   the presence or absence of voting rights.
6.   the status of the contribution in relation to regular corporate contributors.
7.   the certainty of payment in the event of the corporation's insolvency or liquidation.

There is some disagreement whether the tax court's recharacterization factors, such as those borrowed from *Roth Steel* and Estate of Mixon, are suitable for use in the bankruptcy context. Some courts note that there are distinct policy considerations in tax cases that necessitate a different set of recharacterization factors in bankruptcy cases. However, no court "has identified what those different policy considerations are, let alone why those differences should preclude a bankruptcy court that is determining whether recharacterization is appropriate from relying on the factors that tax courts employ in conducting the same type of analysis. These factors serve their purpose; they enable the finder of fact to assess the true nature of a transaction." [Moglia v. Quantum Indus. Partners, LDC (In re Outboard Marine Corp.), No. 02C1594, 2003 WL 21697357, at *5 (N.D. Ill. July 22, 2003).]

Problem 10-1

1.   Foam owes millions of dollars to Gruff, who is an insider.

a.   Will Gruff's claim be subordinated under § 510(c) because he is an insider? How should Gruff's attorney respond to an argument that fairness requires subordinating all insiders' claims in chapter 11 cases?

b.   Suppose that as Foam's financial troubles worsened, Gruff caused the company to secure the debts that were owed him even though other unsecured claims were left unsecured and new unsecured debts were incurred. Can Gruff realize on this collateral ahead of unsecured creditors, or will his secured claim be subordinated to their claims or put on par with them? Are there other means that could possibly undo this secured claim? See § 547; § 544(b); Uniform Fraudulent Transfer Act § 5(b).

2. Equitable subordination under § 510(c) is not limited to insiders' claims, but generally the threshold for subordination is higher when the creditor is not an insider.

   a. Suppose that as Foam's financial troubles worsened, certain important suppliers insisted on security for the unsecured debts that Foam owed them. These creditors used their importance to Foam as leverage—threatening to cut off supplies—so that Foam was practically forced to give them collateral. Can these secured creditors realize on their collateral ahead of unsecured creditors, or will the court reduce the rank of the secured creditors' claims?

   b. Is the outcome more certain if the secured creditors reneged on the deal and discontinued their dealings with Foam after the company had provided them with collateral for preexisting debts? Is the outcome absolutely certain?

Bunch v. J.M. Capital Finance, Ltd.
(In re Hoffinger Industries, Inc.)
United States Bankruptcy Court, Eastern District of Arkansas, 2005
327 B.R. 389

Richard Taylor, Bankruptcy Judge.

The debtor, Hoffinger Industries, Inc., manufactures aboveground swimming pools and accessories. Its principal manufacturing plant is located in West Helena, Arkansas, and it has facilities in Rancho Cucamonga, California, and offices in Mississippi. The debtor filed its chapter 11 petition on September 13, 2001, in reaction to a personal injury judgment of approximately $13,500,000 in favor of Leesa Bunch [Bunch] rendered August 23, 2001, in Glenn County Superior Court, California. Bunch suffered her injuries in August 1993. The initial notice of litigation to the debtor and the retailer involved occurred in November 1998.

This Court denied confirmation of the debtor's proposed plan of reorganization in its Opinion dated February 24, 2005, and subsequent Judgment and Order dated March 3, 2005. Throughout this bankruptcy proceeding, the debtor has consistently refused to acknowledge that it has lost the Bunch litigation, both at the trial court and appellate levels. In the plan, Bunch's claim was simply not addressed as required by the code.

In conjunction with objecting to the debtor's plan, Bunch initiated this adversary proceeding questioning the claims filed by J.M. Capital Finance, LTD [JM Capital] and Arrowhead Insurance Co. [Arrowhead]. Bunch asserts that these two claims should be disallowed, reconsidered under 11 U.S.C. § 502(j), equitably subordinated under § 510, or reclassified. In addition to contesting Bunch's assertions, Arrowhead filed its request to have post-petition product liability insurance premiums due from the debtor treated as an administrative claim. By agreement of the parties, the adversary complaint and the administrative claim application were tried together the week of May 2, 2005. The debtor appeared and participated through its counsel and president.

For the reasons stated below, the Court disallows and recharacterizes/reclassifies the JM Capital claim as equity. Also, in the event that it is determined that JM Capital has a claim, the claim is subordinated to the claims of all other creditors of this debtor under the principles of equitable subordination. The administrative application filed by Arrowhead is granted in part, and denied in part.

* * *

MARTIN HOFFINGER AND THE HOFFINGER FAMILY
[AND THEIR COMPANIES AND THE TRANSACTIONS[15]]

* * *

[Martin Hoffinger, is the founder of the debtor, Hoffinger Industries, Inc. (HII), and is the patriarch of the Hoffinger family." Although Martin Hoffinger has divested his ownership interest in the debtor over the years, he has been and remains a director and its CEO. Martin Hoffinger and his family are integral to the transactions described below."

The family owns several other firms, including Clinton Pool Company (CPC) and Chief Enterprises, Ltd. (Chief). Chief, in turns, owns another player in this bankruptcy proceeding, Arrowhead, which is debtor's product liability insurance carrier. Arrowhead's sole customer and source of income is Hoffinger Industries and conducts no other business activities. Arrowhead wholly owns JM Capital, which is the secured claimant in the bankruptcy proceeding.

In the fall, 1993, the debtor borrowed $8,250,000 from CPC, which was an interactive corporation controlled by Hoffinger family members. The purpose of the loan was to enable Hoffinger Industries to pay its shareholders (the Hoffinger family) interest on their accumulated equity. CPC funded the loan by the Hoffinger family loaning CPC the money the family received from the Hoffinger Industries distribution. CPC took as collateral real and personal property constituting most, if not all, of the debtor's assets.

"The principal reason for all this was to pay interest to stockholders on accumulated earnings. A secondary effect was to collateralize this relationship and thus create a preferred secured creditor on debt that moments before had been stockholder equity. This effectively rendered the debtor judgment-proof from collection efforts by any unrelated third party, an expectation the debtor had given the status of the Fleck ... litigation, which was still extant at the June 1993 fiscal year end effective date. No real distribution occurred. The distribution funded the loan; the loan funded the distribution."

Thereafter, the debtor purportedly paid CPC interest on the loan until the JM Capital transaction in August 1999. At this time, the debtor incurred $10,000,000 debt to JM Capital. This money was used to pay the $8.250,000 debt to CPC, with

---

15. [This and related parts of the court's opinion are incredibly, thoroughly detailed and evidence great care and attention by Judge Taylor. The casebook authors have carefully abstracted and summarized these parts of the opinion so students can focus on the very key facts and Judge Taylor's equally thorough legal analysis of the recharacterization and subordination issues, which is reprinted here without substantial editing by the authors.—Ed.]

the $1.750 balance distributed as equity to the debtor's shareholders. Specially, the loan agreement between JM Capital and the debtor called for the transfer of $5,000,000 in cash directly to the debtor. Simultaneously, JM Capital was to execute five $1,000,000 notes in favor of the debtor. The debtor was then required, in satisfying its debt to CPC, to pay cash and securities to CPC and assign to CPC the five $1,000,000 notes. So, JM Capital would have been making payments on these notes to CPC. "[T]here is no credible evidence that the five $1,000,000 promissory notes were ever drafted, executed, or assigned."

The financing for JM Capital's $10,000,000 loan to the debtor came from Arrowhead, the debtor's products liability insurer, which was owned by Chief which was owned by the Hoffinger family. JM Capital was a wholly-owned subsidiary of Arrowhead. JM Capital was formed in the Cayman Islands in June or July, 1999; its principal activity was to provide financing to the debtor; and JM Capital had no other purpose or business activity. Its sole source of financing was Arrowhead. The debtor was Arrowhead's only customer and was its sole source of income, and from 1988 through 2002 the debtor paid Arrowhead premiums of about $20,000,000.

The loan from JM Capital created mortgages on property located in Arkansas and California and security interests in all of the debtor's personal property. Indeed, JM Capital got liens on all of the debtor's assets. Interestingly, the liens that the debtor gave JM Capital do not appear to have been fully perfected. However, from the beginning of the bankruptcy case, the debtor treated JM Capital's claim as fully secured and planned to pay the claim in full, even though—if the claim was to some extent unsecured—it would have been in the debtor's interest to treat the claim as such and propose a more limited payout. "The only valid resulting inference is that the secondary purpose of this transaction, like the earlier CPC loan, was to judgment-proof the debtor.

Testifying about the Arrowhead-JM Capital loan to the debtor, Martin Hoffinger testified:

Q. Who is a Director of Arrowhead?
A. I am.
Q. You are?
A. Yes.
Q. Who has control over whether Arrowhead pays money out on a claim or not?
A. I probably do.
Q. Anyone else?
A. We have—Terry Burke is Manager of the Britannia Insurance Management Company, and they are the managers of that account.
Q. Okay. What family members own Chief, which is the holding company for Arrowhead, which owns JM.?
A. To the best of my knowledge, my wife and four daughters.
Q. Okay. You're not an owner?
A. No, I'm not.
Q. And JM Capital loaned $10 million to Hoffinger Industries and refinanced the CPC note in about 1999?
A. That's correct.

Q. And this was to avoid people who have judgments from coming in and taking the assets of the company; correct?

A. It was just good business.

Q. Does good business include protecting your assets from judgment creditors?

A. Whatever is good business is what we practice.

Q. Could you please answer my questions, sir?

A. Please rephrase your question.

Q. Does good business include protecting your assets from judgment creditors?

A. Yes.

Compounding the inference of a real intent to judgment proof the debtor, there was a "total lack of any credible witness .... having the ability to explain even remotely how either the CPC or JM Capital transactions actually occurred. This extends to the reasons for the transactions, the movement of money, the execution of documents, the existence of documents, the release or not of collateral, the taking or perfection of collateral, the continuation of perfection, and whose money was used when and directed to whom. In a normal, typical, arm's length transaction, all of these factors are clear and susceptible to easy reconstruction in a court of law. Accounting is accounting and math is math. When math, accounting, and financial transactions are married, clarity—not confusion, dissimulation, or obfuscation—is the result. This lack of clarity permeates both the CPC and the JM Capital transactions."

"Once the debtor filed its chapter 11 petition and Arrowhead's income stream ceased, JM Capital was no longer able to make payments to CPC. Three $1,000,000 notes have become due and owing from JM Capital to CPC. Despite this fact, CPC has never made a demand or pursued collection from JM Capital, or made a claim against the debtor. Again, in a normal transaction it would be rare for the initial lender to accept third party notes (or, as in this case, non-existent third party notes) in full satisfaction of a debt, or without some recourse against the original maker, in this instance the debtor. Conversely, if the initial lender took the notes without recourse, the reasonable expectation is that someone on behalf of either CPC, JM Capital, or the debtor could explain the underlying logic, reason, or consideration. No one could in this instance.

*"Further, a setoff question presents itself. Specifically, Arrowhead claims it is owed approximately $5,000,000 in premiums from the debtor. The five $1,000,000 notes technically should be from JM Capital as maker to the debtor as lender/payee. JM Capital is Arrowhead's wholly-owned subsidiary and its sole source of funding, with Arrowhead's sole source of funding being the debtor. This stream was to continue, according to the debtor, as long as the JM Capital debt remained outstanding. * * * Were this a true arm's length transaction, Arrowhead and JM Capital would simply assert a setoff of the outstanding obligations due under the balance of the five $1,000,000 promissory notes. This would result in an offset of $3,000,000, which it would simply refuse to pay to the debtor, or its alleged assignee, CPC. Neither Arrowhead or JM Capital has attempted to do so.*

"Further, no documents or credible testimony exist that would explain the relationship between JM Capital and CPC regarding the balance of the note obligations. JM Capital has missed three of the $1,000,000 payments, but CPC has not sued or even made demand on either JM Capital or the debtor. The debtor has made some of its interest payments to JM Capital post-petition by signing new promissory notes rolling the interest into the principle and paying interest accordingly. According to its auditor, its CFO, and its president, the debtor is absolutely confident that CPC is paid in full as per its confirmation letter. That should not prevent JM Capital from asserting its right of setoff and leaving CPC apparently, but inexplicable, without recourse rights. Simply put, no one in this transaction seems to be operating in their own best interest. Also, no one seems capable of explaining either how the transaction actually took place or the parties' post-default actions, or lack thereof. Nor have they, with the exception of accounting entries, historically treated these as real debt obligations. Rather, each seems to be acting in a manner consistent with a unitary identity of interest; that is, paying the debtor's shareholders interest on their equity, with the secondary benefit of tying up the debtor's assets as collateral."]

CASH COLLATERAL HEARING

On April 5, 2002, JM Capital filed its proof of claim in the amount of $10,557,808. No supporting documents are attached to the proof of claim. JM Capital asserts that it has a fully secured claim. The debtor has consistently treated JM Capital as fully secured during the course of this bankruptcy. This non-critical favoritism began as early as the debtor's initial post-petition efforts to obtain financing.

On October 10, 2001, shortly after the September 13, 2001, petition filing date, the debtor filed its Motion for Authority to Use Cash Collateral and Incur Secured Debt [the Cash Collateral Motion]. The Cash Collateral Motion envisioned a $10,000,000 line of credit from C.M.A. Corporation [CMA] with JM Capital agreeing to subordinate its August 4, 1999, $10,000,000 loan contingent upon adequate protection payments and a superpriority administrative expense claim. The Cash Collateral Motion discloses that there may be infirmities in JM Capital's perfection of its collateral, including a potential preference action. Throughout, the debtor has never taken any action to dispute or otherwise question JM Capital's fully secured status. In addition to seeking superpriority status for JM Capital, the Cash Collateral Motion sought replacement liens and cross collateralization of prepetition indebtedness by those liens, as such would "preserve[ ] the collateral position of JM."

The Cash Collateral Motion does not contain any representations reflecting the ownership of JM Capital. Nor does it disclose JM Capital's relationship to Arrowhead or the absence of certain promissory notes essential to the credit relationship between the debtor, CPC, and JM Capital. In fact, the proposed cash collateral loan agreement involving CMA, JM Capital, and the debtor has the debtor waiving every claim, cause of action, or defense it might have against JM

Capital.[16] This is especially egregious given the unwinding of the realities of the JM Capital transaction discussed in this opinion. It is almost impossible to fathom any valid or appropriate reason for the debtor to treat JM Capital as some disinterested arm's length third party insisting on a superpriority status in return for subordinating its already subordinated, and inadequately documented and perfected, debt.

The debtor's complicity, if not leadership, in this regard has been consistent throughout this bankruptcy proceeding, beginning with the Cash Collateral Motion, continuing through its first proposed plan, and now with its position at the trial of this matter. As is evident from the facts, the debtor and JM Capital—under the direction of Martin Hoffinger—have acted with a unity of purpose inconsistent with the fiduciary duties of a debtor-in-possession, including its duty to act in good faith and in the debtor's best interest for the benefit of the estate and its creditors.

As a result of the cash collateral hearing, the debtor obtained the requested post-petition financing, but the Court ordered that payments to Arrowhead and JM Capital should be held in abeyance. In the interim, Bunch filed this adversary proceeding attacking the validity of the JM Capital and Arrowhead claims.

RECHARACTERIZATION / RECLASSIFICATION[17]

Some courts will not recharacterize a loan from debt to equity; instead, these courts consider recharacterization as part of the court's equitable subordination powers under § 510(c). See, e.g., Unsecured Creditors' Comms. of Pacific Express, Inc. v. Pioneer Commercial Funding Corp. (In re Pacific Express, Inc.), 69 B.R. 112, 115 (9th Cir. BAP 1986). The basis for that reasoning relates to the results obtained if a loan is recharacterized; specifically, the recharacterization has the effect of subordinating the loan because capital contributions would be repaid only after all other corporate obligations have been met. The *Pacific Express* court believed that where a specific provision of the code governs the determination made, in this case subordination, the court could not use its equitable powers to make the same determination. To do so would be using its equitable powers in a manner inconsistent with the provisions contained in the code. Id. However, this line of reasoning does not take into account the purpose of recharacterization, which is to determine the existence of a debt, not to decide whether the debt should be subordinated. If there is no debt, equitable subordination is not an issue, although de facto subordination is a consequence.

---

16. [Footnote 12 in original:] The proposed waiver provision, section 3.15, was amended in the final agreement and was the subject of this Court's order denying JM Capital's motion for summary judgment, which order is still valid and incorporated by reference. The Court notes that the following language did not survive and was not incorporated in the final loan agreement approved by the Court:

Provided however, the right of a Creditor's committee or other party in interest to object to the pre-petition claims of JM or bring suit ex rel, the DIP on any claim waived pursuant to this paragraph shall be preserved for a period of sixty (60) days following the entry of an order of the United States Bankruptcy Court approving this Agreement.

Defs.' Ex. 1, Cash Collateral Mot. Ex. 1 § 3.15.

17. [Footnote 13 in original:] These terms are frequently used interchangeably; here, the Court will use the term recharacterization.

The power of bankruptcy courts to recharacterize a loan from debt to equity comes from the courts' general equitable powers contained in § 105(a), which states that the court "may issue any order, process, or judgment that is necessary or appropriate to carry out the provisions of this title." According to the Supreme Court, "[i]n the exercise of its equitable jurisdiction the bankruptcy court has the power to sift the circumstances surrounding any claim to see that injustice or unfairness is not done in administration of the bankrupt estate." Pepper v. Litton, 308 U.S. 295, 307-08, 60 S. Ct. 238, 84 L. Ed. 281 (1939). According to the *Pepper* Court, "a bankruptcy court has full power to inquire into the validity of any claim asserted against the estate and to disallow it if it is ascertained to be without lawful existence." Id. at 305, 60 S. Ct. 238. The determination of whether a transaction is debt or equity falls within the powers granted to this Court by § 105(a).

In determining whether a debt should be recharacterized as an equity contribution, courts generally review the following factors:

> (1) the names given to the instruments, if any, evidencing the indebtedness; (2) the presence or absence of a fixed maturity date and schedule of payments; (3) the presence or absence of a fixed rate of interest and interest payments; (4) the source of repayments; (5) the adequacy or inadequacy of capitalization; (6) the identity of interest between the creditor and the stockholder; (7) the security, if any, for the advances; (8) the corporation's ability to obtain financing from outside lending institutions; (9) the extent to which the advances were subordinated to the claims of outside creditors; (10) the extent to which the advances were used to acquire capital assets; and (11) the presence or absence of a sinking fund to provide repayments.

Roth Steel Tube Co. v. Commissioner of Internal Revenue, 800 F.2d 625, 630 (6th Cir. 1986). In addition to the above factors, some courts also consider (1) the right to enforce payment of principal and interest; (2) participation in management flowing as a result of the transaction; (3) the intent of the parties; and (4) the failure of the debtor to repay the obligation on the due date or to seek postponement. See, e.g., In re Cold Harbor Assocs., 204 B.R. 904, 915 (Bankr. E.D. Va. 1997). The factors are applied to a particular case and transaction keeping in mind the specific circumstances surrounding the case. The list is not exclusive and no one factor is controlling or decisive. *Roth Steel Tube Co.*, 800 F.2d at 630. Of primary concern is whether the transaction "carries the earmarks of an arm's length bargain." *Pepper*, 308 U.S. at 306-07, 60 S. Ct. 238; *Cold Harbor Assocs.*, 204 B.R. at 915. The more characteristics of an arm's length transaction that are present, the more likely the transaction would be treated as debt instead of an equity contribution. *Cold Harbor Assocs.*, 204 B.R. at 915.

JM Capital's claim must be recharacterized as equity in its entirety. Any liens or security interests it has or asserts in the debtor's case are hereby set aside. A number of factors compel this result.

The principal purpose of the JM Capital transaction in 1999 was to perpetuate the CPC transaction, which was never a true arm's length credit transaction. Rather, both the CPC transaction and the JM Capital transaction were designed to pay interest on shareholder equity. The secondary purpose was to fully encumber all of the debtor's assets to the detriment of its unsecured creditors, including potential tort judgment creditors. The Court draws no conclusion as to the appropriateness in an accounting context of structuring transactions of this nature to pay interest on equity. The Court does conclude that the principles of recharacterization require that this relationship be accurately defined for purposes of plan confirmation and commensurate distribution in a chapter 11 reorganization.

The debtor's CFO, the debtor's outside auditor, and Martin Hoffinger each acknowledged that the purpose of the CPC and JM Capital transactions was to pay interest on shareholder equity. This return was significant over the years. Generally, in closely held subchapter S corporations, the shareholders expect the corporation to distribute enough money to address the tax consequences of undistributed earnings. In this instance, commencing in late 1993, through their ownership of CPC and JM Capital outlined above, the debtor's shareholders received interest payments of well over $500,000 a year. Not all the years can be precisely quantified from the debtor's books and records. However, distributions of $497,438 in 1995, $808,791 in 1997, $741,904 in 1998, $742,500 in 1999, $878,400 in 2000, and $797,671 in 2001 serve to illustrate the point. Additionally, the shareholders received an additional $6,750,000 in 1999 through the JM Capital transaction, $1,750,000 in an additional distribution, and the $5,000,000 that was transferred to CPC, an entity owned by eleven Hoffinger family members who were also each shareholders of the debtor.

As previously discussed, the original CPC transaction involved little more than check kiting, the effect of which was to benefit the debtor's shareholders with substantial interest payments, including an additional $6,750,000 being transferred to the shareholders in 1999. This, and judgment-proofing the debtor, was the purpose of the CPC and JM Capital transactions. Therefore, if not recharacterized, the net effect of the JM Capital transaction would be to perpetuate a nonexistent loan that has netted the debtor's shareholders well over $12,000,000[18] in the eight years before the debtor filed its bankruptcy case—November 1993 to September 2001. Additionally, to let the debt stand as is would net the debtor's shareholders an additional $12,000,000 in the form of accrued principal and interest to be paid under a confirmed plan of reorganization, all from this nonexistent original credit and to the detriment of all other creditors of this debtor.

The JM Capital transaction was not for any traditional legitimate business purpose. Ab initio, Martin Hoffinger on behalf of the debtor simply could not explain why the debtor, in effect, funded its own borrowing in the original CPC transaction, other than to offer that it was simply structured to pay interest on equity. Likewise, no one offered a credible explanation as to why the JM Capital transaction took place in 1999. The only explanation given was because the CPC loan was coming due, which is simply incorrect. The CPC loan was not scheduled to mature until October 2003.

The JM Capital transaction was poorly, inaccurately, and incompletely documented. Neither the note or loan agreement adequately defined the interest rate. It is clear that the appropriate collateral documents were not properly perfected. Regardless, the debtor has made no effort to treat JM Capital as anything other than

---

18. [Footnote 14 in original:] This figure results from taking the known interest payments discussed above, the unknown interest payments in the unquantified years estimated to be at least $500,000 annually, and the additional $6,750,000 in 1999.

a fully secured creditor. The credit transactions, both initially with CPC and then later with JM Capital, had no purpose in assisting the debtor in its operations. The debtor had no credit need for signing either note. No capital improvements resulted from the credit, and the credit was not incurred for operational or typical line of credit purposes. The JM Capital note was an interest only note with no reductions in principal until maturity for a 10 year period which, when viewed collectively with the CPC transaction, created an interest only loan for 16 years.

Only one of the five $1,000,000 promissory notes called for in the JM Capital transaction even exists. The other four notes do not exist, nor was any assignment document ever executed. There is no explanation why in 1999 CPC accepted these nonexistent notes in full satisfaction of the debt without recourse to the debtor. Further, it appears CPC has taken no steps to effect collection against JM Capital. Sadly, JM Capital's sole source of funds for its obligations to CPC appears to be the excessive premiums the debtor paid and was to pay to Arrowhead. Martin Hoffinger, in his correspondence and memos, acknowledges these premiums are well in excess of Arrowhead's concomitant insurance obligations back to the debtor.

Even though the transaction involved a loan agreement and promissory note, the transaction failed to include the interest rate and was incompletely documented. Although there was a fixed maturity date, there were no scheduled payments reducing principal. The CPC and JM Capital transactions taken together reflect at least 16 years of deferred payment on principal. As previously stated, the interest rate is unclear from the documents. Four of the incremental $1,000,000 promissory notes were never drafted, executed, delivered, or assigned. The source of repayment is the debtor's excessive premiums to an insurance company wholly controlled by members of the Hoffinger family, each one a stockholder of the debtor. Only Hoffinger family members, each one a stockholder of the debtor, benefited from these transactions. This debt, with its commensurate collateral, judgment-proofed the debtor to the detriment of its unsecured creditors. It is apparent that the debtor could have obtained outside financing, or utilized its occasionally enviable cash position, if, in fact, it truly wanted to distribute earnings. While the JM Capital credit was subordinated to outside secured creditors, the collateralization acted to the detriment of outside unsecured creditors. No capital assets were purchased with the credit extended and the debtor, using excessive premiums to Arrowhead, created a fund outside the reach of its creditors from which to effect repayment. Further, none of the parties acted in their own best interest or sought to enforce the obligations of the respective parties. Instead, each acted with a complete identity of interest as directed by Martin Hoffinger.

This simply is not debt. The debtor funded (or, more accurately, kited) its own loan from CPC. Then, through excessive premiums to Arrowhead, the debtor funded JM Capital's ability to pay CPC, all to the benefit of the debtor's shareholders, and those of Arrowhead/Chief, CPC, and JM Capital, inclusively one and the same. If not recharacterized, then the same shareholders would enjoy both the benefits of receiving interest on equity and the inconsistent benefit of having that equity treated as debt, thus enjoying an additional windfall. The ever compliant debtor, in its initial plan of reorganization, proposed to treat JM Capital as fully collateralized perfected debt, thus awarding JM Capital priority and full payment. The same proposed plan intended to pay unsecured creditors 30% on the dollar, with Bunch, for no discernible reason, receiving less. The purpose of the JM Capital transaction was not to incur debt necessary to the debtor's operations; its purpose was to pay interest on equity and to judgment-proof the debtor. If it was equity before filing, then surely it is equity now. The alleged debt is recharacterized accordingly.

RECONSIDERATION OF CLAIM

Under § 502(j), the court can reconsider an allowed or disallowed claim for cause, and then either allow or disallow the claim according to the equities of the case. "Cause" is not clearly defined in the code. Accordingly, several courts equate a motion for reconsideration of claim with a motion for relief from judgment under Federal Rule of Bankruptcy Procedure 9024, which incorporates Federal Rule of Civil Procedure 60. In re Gomez, 250 B.R. 397, 400 (Bankr. M.D. Fla. 1999); see also Kirwan v. Vanderwerf (In re Kirwan), 164 F.3d 1175, 1177 (8th Cir. 1999) ("This rule [60(b)] may be liberally construed to do substantial justice to allow parties to air meritorious claims in the absence of fault or prejudice."). Rule 60(b) permits a court to take into account mistake, inadvertence, surprise, excusable neglect, newly discovered evidence, fraud, a void or satisfied judgment, or any other reason justifying relief. According to the Fifth Circuit Court of Appeals, however, the standards listed in Rule 60(b) are only applicable when a claim was actually litigated. Gomez, 250 B.R. at 400. In cases where the claim was not actually litigated, a court should consider the following factors to determine whether sufficient cause was shown: "(1) the extent and reasonableness of the delay, (2) the prejudice to any party in interest, (3) the effect on efficient court administration, and (4) the moving party's good faith." Id. (citing In re Bernard, 189 B.R. 1017, 1022 (Bankr. N.D. Ga. 1996) and other cases).

The standards enumerated by the Gomez court are similar to those the Eighth Circuit Court of Appeals considers appropriate when a bankruptcy court exercises its discretion and reconsiders a claim under § 502(j). Specifically, a bankruptcy court may consider "whether delay would prejudice the debtors or other creditors, the reason for the delay and its length and impact on efficient court administration, whether the creditors acted in good faith, whether clients should be penalized for counsel's mistake or neglect, and whether claimants have a meritorious claim." Kirwan, 164 F.3d at 1177-78.

JM Capital attempted to interpose defenses based on Federal Rule of Bankruptcy Procedure 9024 in its motion for summary judgment. This Court has already concluded that the principles of res judicata or collateral estoppel do not conclusively prevent the Court from considering the issues raised in this adversary proceeding. However, to the extent that any argument exists that the defendants' proofs of claim have been previously litigated and considered, the Court specifically finds that their claims may be reconsidered pursuant to § 502(j) and Federal Rule of Bankruptcy Procedure 9024. Further, applying the standards set forth by the Eighth Circuit to the facts of this case, the Court finds that cause exists to reconsider the claims of JM Capital and, later in this opinion, Arrowhead Insurance.

JM Capital's proof of claim is hereby disallowed. First, the claim has been recharacterized as equity. Second, as is evident from the above discussion, the facts clearly demonstrate that JM Capital's claim does not, and should not, represent fully collateralized secured debt. JM Capital and the debtor have acted in concert, delicately ignoring realities known exclusively by them; specifically, that the JM Capital debt was funded by the debtor and its real purpose was not debt, but to pay interest on equity, with the secondary benefit of judgment-proofing the debtor. Bunch has indeed acted in good faith; JM Capital has not. In this case, no distributions have been made and, thus, no party has been prejudiced. The Court finds that JM Capital does not have a meritorious claim as a secured creditor.

EQUITABLE SUBORDINATION

Standing

Courts generally disagree whether individual creditors have standing to pursue equitable subordination claims against other creditors. The Eighth Circuit Court of Appeals briefly touched upon this issue in a 1985 decision, Vreugdenhil v. Hoekstra, 773 F.2d 213 (8th Cir.1985). In discussing standing to bring particular actions against an estate, the Eighth Circuit held that certain actions could be brought only by the trustee of the estate. In *Vreugdenhil*, the debtors filed a voluntary chapter 11 petition in January 1983. In October 1984, the case was converted to a case under chapter 7. Shortly after the conversion, the debtors initiated a collateral action in district court stating eight causes of action: (1-2) two claims to determine the nature, validity, extent, and priority of liens; (3) a request to use property of the estate in the ordinary course of its business; (4) a request to avoid or subordinate certain security interests; (5) a claim for contempt for violations of the automatic stay; and (6-8) three tort claims based on allegations of property damage. Id. at 214. The Eighth Circuit found that the district court properly dismissed the debtor's suit because each of the causes of action involved property of the estate in bankruptcy and the debtor's trustee-like authority as debtors-in-possession ended when the case was converted to chapter 7. According to the Eighth Circuit, "a debtor may not prosecute on his own a cause of action belonging to the estate unless that cause of action has been abandoned by the trustee." Id. at 215. Citing to 11 U.S.C. §§ 363, 544-550, and 774, the court stated that "with certain exceptions not applicable here, it is the trustee who is empowered under the Code to avoid or subordinate security interests and liens, and to use, sell, or lease property of the estate in the ordinary course of business." Id.

In the code provisions cited by the Eighth Circuit, §§ 363, 544-550, and 774, the trustee is the specific entity holding the avoidance powers allowed under the code. According to the Supreme Court, "Congress 'says in a statute what it means and means in a statute what it says there.'" Hartford Underwriters Ins. Co. v. Union Planters Bank, 530 U.S. 1, 120 S. Ct. 1942, 147 L. Ed. 2d 1 (2000) (quoting Connecticut Nat'l Bank v. Germain, 503 U.S. 249, 254, 112 S. Ct. 1146, 117 L. Ed. 2d 391 (1992)). The Court listed three contextual features in support of its conclusion of exclusivity:

(1) when a statute authorizes specific action and names the party empowered to take that action, it is not appropriate to presume nonexclusivity; (2) because the trustee plays a unique role in bankruptcy proceedings, it is plausible that Congress provided a power to him and not to others; and (3) had Congress intended the code provision to be broadly available, it could have said so.

Rice v. United States d/b/a Internal Revenue Serv. (In re Odom Antennas, Inc.), 258 B.R. 376, 384 (Bankr. E.D. Ark. 2001) (citing *Hartford Underwriters Ins. Co.*, 530 U.S. 1, 120 S.Ct. 1942).

Notably absent from the code provisions cited by the Eighth Circuit is § 510(c) dealing with equitable subordination. Section 510(c) provides that, "after notice and a hearing, the court may ... under principles of equitable subordination, subordinate for purposes of distribution all or part of an allowed claim to all or part of another allowed claim or all or part of an allowed interest to all or part of an allowed interest." There is no specific provision in the statute that states that an equitable subordination claim must be brought by the trustee. In fact, the statute is silent in this regard. Utilizing the contextual features recognized by the Supreme Court, it is apparent that Congress intended for § 510(c) to be broadly available. Had the trustee been the only party with authority to use this section, Congress could have so stated, as it has in many instances.

In their objection to the standing of Bunch to bring the equitable subordination action, JM Capital and Arrowhead ask the Court to follow the reasoning contained in Variable-Parameter Fixture Dev. Corp. v. Comerica Bank, Calif. (In re Morpheus Lights, Inc.), 228 B.R. 449 (Bankr. N.D. Cal. 1998). *Morpheus* introduced a mechanical standard by which courts can determine standing in an equitable subordination case. First, the court must determine the holder of the claim. If only the creditor holds the claim—in other words, has a "particularized injury"—then it has standing to pursue its claim. If, on the other hand, the injury is general, then the estate holds the claim and only a representative of the estate is the proper party to bring the claim. Id. at 453. According to the *Morpheus* court, "[s]uch an analysis is necessary to promote the orderly and equitable administration of the bankruptcy estate by preventing individual creditors from pursuing separate actions to the detriment of other creditors and of the estate as a whole." Id. To determine whether a claim is property of the estate or of an individual creditor, the court must first determine whether the claim is a general claim or a particular claim. A claim is general if there is no particular injury arising from the claim, and any creditor of the debtor could bring the claim. Id. If it is a general claim, then, according to *Morpheus*, only the trustee, or debtor in possession, is the proper person to bring the claim. If the Court were to follow the reasoning in *Morpheus*, it would first have to determine if Bunch has standing by virtue of a particularized harm to bring an equitable subordination claim. If successful, Bunch, as well as other unsecured creditors, would receive an increased distribution from the estate. Conversely, in the absence of equitable subordination, Bunch and other unsecured creditors are each suffering harm in the form of a reduced distribution. Under a *Morpheus* analysis, Bunch would probably lack standing.

However, this Court recognizes that there will always be at least one or more other creditors the alleged generalized harm has not harmed, and the cure will not benefit; specifically, the creditor(s) against whom the action is brought. In this case it is Arrowhead, an unsecured creditor, and JM Capital, a secured creditor. Because of this, the Court questions whether there can ever be a "general" equitable subordination claim that only belongs to the trustee or debtor-in-possession. The specific wording of § 510(c) recognizes this in the "all or part of another allowed claim" language. It would be absurd to permit the estate alone to seek to reorder priorities among specific creditors on all or part of their debt; that concept alone defines particularized harm to specific creditors.

This is perhaps especially so in this instance where the debtor, for now obvious reasons, has shown no interest in contesting JM Capital's proof of claim. Bunch has a particularized injury and may share that injury with other creditors of this estate, but she does not share it with all creditors of this estate. It is simply not logical to suggest that if many are harmed, then no more than one of the harmed may pursue the action. Certainly the debtor could have brought an equitable subordination suit, and as such, its claim is property of the estate. However, the claims of other parties belong to them and are not property of the estate. This bankruptcy case was filed as a result of the Bunch verdict. Many of the debtor's actions, alone and in concert with JM Capital, appear to be directed specifically at Bunch in an effort to minimize her distribution. The code permits her to address this harm, and she has done so.

Additionally, as discussed above, it is not logical to put such restrictions on § 510(c) in contravention of the plain language of the statute. Recognizing that the remedy contained in § 510(c) is broadly available under the code, the Court finds that Bunch has standing to pursue an equitable subordination claim against JM Capital and Arrowhead.

In re Mobile Steel Co.

The doctrine of equitable subordination is recognized in the code. As stated above, § 510(c) provides that, "after notice and a hearing, the court may ... under principles of equitable subordination, subordinate for purposes of distribution all or part of an allowed claim to all or part of another allowed claim or all or part of an allowed interest to all or part of an allowed interest." Application of the doctrine is at the discretion of the court. It is a three-part test that requires the following: " '(i) The claimant must have engaged in some type of inequitable conduct. (ii) The misconduct must have resulted in injury to the creditors of the bankrupt or conferred an unfair advantage on the claimant. (iii) Equitable subordination of the claim must not be inconsistent with the provisions of the Bankruptcy [Code].' " Bergquist v. Anderson-Greenwood Aviation Corp. (In re Bellanca Aircraft Corp.), 850 F.2d 1275, 1282 (8th Cir.1988).

The *Mobile Steel* court also recognized three principles a court must keep in mind when determining whether the conditions for equitable subordination have been met. First, "inequitable conduct directed against the bankrupt or its creditors may be sufficient to warrant subordination of a claim irrespective of whether it was related to the acquisition or assertion of that claim." *Mobile Steel*, 563 F.2d at 700. Second, "a claim or claims should be subordinated only to the extent necessary to offset the harm which the bankrupt and its creditors suffered on account of the inequitable conduct." Id. at 701. And third, the objecting party must come forward with enough evidence to " 'overcome the claimant's prima facie case and thus compel him to actually prove the validity and honesty of his claim.' " Id. (quoting 3A J. Moore & L. King, Collier on Bankruptcy, ¶63.06, at 1785 (14th ed.1976)). The purpose of equitable subordination is to "undo or offset any inequity in the claim position of a creditor that will produce injustice or unfairness to other creditors in terms of the bankruptcy results." Bostian v. Schapiro (In re Kansas City Journal-Post Co.), 144 F.2d 791, 800 (8th Cir. 1944). This is a power that must be "measuredly and not blankly exercised.... It should not operate to take away anything punitively to which one creditor is justly entitled ... and bestow it upon others, who in the relative situation have no fair right to it." Id. at 800-01. The Supreme Court recognizes this limited exercise of a court's power to equitably subordinate a claim as appearing in the third prong of the *Mobile Steel* factors. It stated that although a bankruptcy court is a court of equity, " 'it is not free to adjust the legally valid claim of an innocent party who asserts the claim in good faith merely because the court perceives that the result is inequitable.' " *Noland*, 517 U.S. at 539, 116 S.Ct. 1524.

In order to determine whether equitable subordination is appropriate, the court must first determine whether the creditor engaged in some sort of inequitable conduct. Without a showing of inequitable conduct, the remaining two prongs of the test are not applicable and the court cannot subordinate the claim. In re Lifschultz Fast Freight, 132 F.3d 339, 344 (7th Cir.1997); *Bellanca Aircraft Corp.*, 850 F.2d at 1282-83; Farmers Bank of Clinton v. Julian, 383 F.2d 314, 323 (8th Cir. 1967) (" 'fraud or unfairness' (unfairness is equated with inequity) is essential for a decision to subordinate"). The amount of inequitable conduct depends on the status of the claimant. If the claimant is an insider of the debtor, its conduct is closely scrutinized and the only proof required is that it breached a fiduciary duty or engaged in conduct that is somehow unfair to other creditors. Id. at 1282 n. 13. Typically, inequitable conduct falls into one of the following categories: (1) fraud, illegality, or breach of fiduciary duties; (2) undercapitalization; or (3) the creditor's use of the debtor as a mere instrumentality or alter ego. *Lifschultz Fast Freight*, 132 F.3d at 344-45.

As stated above, this Court has already determined that JM Capital's claim must be recharacterized as equity. Alternatively, it is clear that the necessary grounds exist to equitably subordinate JM Capital's claim to the claims of all other secured and unsecured creditors of this debtor.

The first element, that requiring "inequitable conduct," is met. While the debtor and JM Capital are separate entities, each are controlled by Martin Hoffinger. Again, this Court renders no decision on the tax or accounting appropriateness of paying shareholders interest on their equity, nor does this Court pierce the corporate veils. However, it is clear that the primary purpose of the 1999 JM Capital transaction, as discussed above, was not to incur typical debt necessary for the debtor's operations, but to pay interest on equity. It also had the intended secondary benefit of judgment-proofing the debtor by encumbering its assets to the ultimate benefit of members of the Hoffinger family.[19] Martin Hoffinger knew this. He, the CEO of the debtor, and also JM Capital's Rule 30(b)(6) witness and representative at trial, knew these facts and that there were perfection issues with the JM Capital credit. Martin Hoffinger also knew that, with one exception, the notes from JM Capital to the debtor did not exist and had not been assigned to CPC. The pleadings, the cash collateral motions, the use of excess premiums to Arrowhead to fund the credit, the payment to CPC based on essentially a non-existent debt, the transcript of the cash collateral hearing, the proposed plan treatment, the JM Capital proof of claim, and the waiver attempts in the cash collateral agreement and the plan, all point to a deliberate effort to ignore these known facts and, after having paid the stockholders millions over the eight years before the petition was filed, treat this as an arm's length fully secured debt. This would result in the debtor paying JM Capital several more millions, all ultimately to the benefit of Hoffinger family member stockholders, while paying its creditors, including Bunch, a minimal percentage figure.

The bankruptcy court is a court of equity possessing the inherent power to " 'prevent the consummation of a course of conduct by a claimant which would be fraudulent or otherwise inequitable by subordinating his claim to the ethically superior claims asserted by other creditors.' " Limerick v. Limerick (In re Answerfone, Inc.), 48 B.R. 24, 27 (Bankr. E.D. Ark. 1985) (quoting *Mobile Steel*, 563 F.2d at 699) (emphasis added). Martin Hoffinger used entities he controlled to pay interest on equity. It was never debt, and is fairly recharacterized as equity. It would be inequitable, viz unfair, to allow Mr. Hoffinger and his family to reap the benefits of that interest, as well as some actual cash distributions against accumulated earnings, and then in turn use the same vehicle to assert that this was always intended to be true debt that should be paid before the claims of third parties—persons who have actually extended credit or are valid judgment creditors of this debtor.

All three elements of equitable subordination are met. The conduct of JM Capital, controlled and acting at the direction of Martin Hoffinger, with the complicity of the debtor, another entity controlled by Mr. Hoffinger, is inequitable. Again, the Court makes no finding of the initial appropriateness of the interest paying vehicle structured by Martin Hoffinger. But the continuation of this fiction in the course of this bankruptcy proceeding cannot be countenanced by this Court. As suggested by the court in *Mobile Steel*, this Court may consider the inequitable conduct directed against the debtor or its creditors, "irrespective of whether it was related to the acquisition or assertion of that claim." *Mobile Steel*, 563 F.2d at 700. As stated by the Eighth Circuit in *Kansas City Journal-Post Co.*, and cited with approval by the *Mobile Steel* court:

> [I]n dealing with creditors' claims in a bankruptcy proceeding, the "subject matter in litigation" … goes beyond the legal foundation and legal structure of the individual claim. For claim and distribution purposes, a bankruptcy proceeding is an integrated proceeding, and the

---

19. [Footnote 15 in original:] See Pls.' Ex. 77, post-petition letter dated October 3, 2001, from Michael Monchick, member of the debtor's board of directors, to another director ("Why weren't all assets protected? A good question. People responsible did not do their job.").

"subject matter in litigation" in its practical aspect is the right of creditors to share in the bankruptcy assets themselves, not merely legally but in equitable relation to each other—for the assertion of a claim in bankruptcy is, of course, not an attempt to recover a judgment against the debtor but to obtain a distributive share in the immediate assets of the proceeding. The inequity which will entitle a bankruptcy court to regulate the distribution to a creditor, by subordination or other equitable means, need not therefore be specifically related to the creditor's claim, either in its origin or in its acquisition, but it may equally arise out of any unfair act on the part of the creditor, which affects the bankruptcy results to other creditors and so makes it inequitable that he should assert a parity with them in the distribution of the estate ....

Kansas City Journal-Post Co., 144 F.2d at 803-04.

These continuing actions have injured other creditors of the debtor and conferred an unfair advantage on JM Capital. Subordination in this instance is consistent with the provisions of the bankruptcy code. Accordingly, if recharacterization is inapplicable, then the claim of JM Capital must be and is hereby subordinated to the claims of all other secured and unsecured creditors. Any lien or security interest it may claim is hereby set aside.

    * * *

CONCLUSION

JM Capital's claim is disallowed as a secured claim and recharacterized or reclassified as equity. Any liens or security interests it may claim are set aside. To the extent that it has any claim, secured or unsecured, that claim is subordinated to the claims of all other creditors.

Arrowhead's stop loss insurance premiums that accrued post-petition are approved as an administrative expense. Arrowhead is awarded an administrative expense according to the formula outlined above; any excess expense remains a general unsecured claim. Any issues regarding the approximate $811,000 pre-petition payment to Arrowhead are reserved.

IT IS SO ORDERED.

NOTE

What does it mean, exactly, to subordinate a secured claim? When a secured claim is subordinated under § 510(c), is the security interest or lien avoided as happens when a transfer is found to be a preference under § 547 or fraudulent transfer under § 548? Here's an answer from the First Circuit, in Max Sugarman Funeral Home, Inc. v. A.D.B. Investors, 926 F.2d 1248 (1st Cir. 1991):

At the close of the equitable subordination analysis in its first opinion, the bankruptcy court *set aside* the 1981 transfers under Bankruptcy Code § 510(c) so as to relegate ADB's distributive rights against the debtor estates to a position inferior to the distributive position of post-1977 debenture claimants. Since Bankruptcy Code § 510(c) may not be employed to avoid a *transfer*, however, the use of principles of equitable subordination to avoid either the 1981 transfers or the 1982 transfers would exceed the powers conferred upon the bankruptcy courts by Bankruptcy Code § 510(c), which provides as follows:

> (c) Notwithstanding subsections (a) and (b) of this section, after notice and hearing, the court may—
>> (1) under principles of equitable subordination, *subordinate for purposes of distribution* all or part of an *allowed claim* to all or part of *another allowed claim* or all or part of an allowed interest to all or part of another allowed interest; or
>> (2) *order* that *any lien securing such a subordinated claim be transferred to the estate.*

11 U.S.C. § 510(c) (emphasis added). Subsection 510(c)(1) *only* empowers the bankruptcy court to "subordinate for purposes of distribution . . . an allowed claim . . . to another allowed claim . . . ." Although a secured claim, as well as an unsecured claim, may be filed and "allowed," see Bankruptcy Code §§ 101(4), 501, 502, and an allowed secured claim may then be equitably subordinated, under subsection 510(c)(1), to any other allowed claim, secured or unsecured, neither the "lien securing such a subordinated claim," nor the transfer which gave rise to the lien, can be *avoided* through recourse to subsection 510(c)(1).

Although subsection 510(c)(2) permits the bankruptcy court to "order that any lien securing *such a subordinated claim* [i.e., an allowed claim subordinated under subsection 510(c)(1)] be transferred to the estate," neither subsection 510(c)(1) nor (2) empowers *avoidance* of the lien or invalidation of the transfer which gave rise to the lien.

Bankruptcy Code § 510(c) is not an avoidance device for setting aside *liens* or *transfers.*

Id. at 1253-54 n. 10. So what? Is the practical effect the same as avoiding the creditor's lien or security interest?

A Digression to Explain and Distinguish
Contractual Subordination

Equitable subordination under § 510(c) is rare. Contractual subordination under § 510(a), which involves no creditor misconduct, is common. Creditors agree among themselves, with or without the debtor's participation, to reorder the statutory priority of their claims against the debtor or liens or other interests in the debtor's property. The common law, real estate finance law, and U.C.C. Article 9 authorize and respect contractual subordination outside of bankruptcy. The Bankruptcy Code honors these agreements in the debtor's bankruptcy case: "A subordination agreement is enforceable in a case under this title to the same extent that such agreement is enforceable under applicable nonbankruptcy law." 11 U.S.C. § 510(a).

In re Plymouth House Health Care Center
United States Bankruptcy Court, Eastern District of Pennsylvania, 2005
2005 WL 2589201

* * *

The plan administrator relies heavily upon In re Smith, 77 B.R. 624 (Bankr. N.D. Ohio 1987) for his contention concerning the effect of a subordination agreement. In Smith, Farmers Citizens Bank entered into a subordination agreement in favor of the FmHA. The loan made by the bank was secured, but the loan made by the FmHA was unsecured. Id., at 627 ("In the present case, the Bank is a secured creditor and FmHA is an unsecured creditor.")

The bank and the FmHA were each claiming entitlement to the proceeds of the bank's collateral. The *Smith* bankruptcy court applied the subordination agreement in the following manner:

> Although there has not been a great deal of litigation in this area, it appears that a subordination agreement between a secured creditor and an unsecured creditor may be given effect in the following manner. Under nonbankruptcy law, a subordination agreement may not adversely affect the rights of a creditor who is not a party to the agreement.... Thus, under § 510(a) the subordination of a secured claim may not impair the rights of the other creditors. Essentially, this is accomplished by the exchange of priorities between the parties to the agreement. The amount to be paid to the party subordinating its claim (the Bank) is determined without reference to the subordination agreement. That amount is then paid to the beneficiary of the subordination agreement (FmHA) to the extent of its valid interest through the subordination agreement, with any remaining balance going to the subordinating creditor (the Bank). The subordinating creditor then receives a claim with the same priority enjoyed by the beneficiary of the agreement, to the extent of the amount paid to the beneficiary.

Id. at 627 (citations omitted).

Other courts, however, have described the effect of a subordination agreement in different terms. For example, in In re Lunan Family Restaurants, 194 B.R. 429, 444 (Bankr. N.D. Ill. 1996), the court quoted approvingly the following explanation:

> "By executing a lien subordination agreement, the subordinating party agrees to demote the priority of its lien to that of another secured creditor, thereby delaying its recourse to the identified collateral until the other party's secured claim has been satisfied."

(quoting In re Lantana Motel, 124 B.R. 252, 256 (Bankr. S.D. Ohio 1990)); see also In re Bank of New England Corp., 364 F.3d at 361 ("[S]ubordination alters the normal priority of the junior creditor's claim so that it becomes eligible to receive a distribution only after the claims of the senior creditor have been satisfied."); In re Tri-Union Development Corp., 314 B.R. 611, 627 (Bankr. S.D. Tex. 2004) ("Subordination is the ordering of priority of debts between creditors."); In re Curtis Center L.P., 192 B.R. 648, 659 (Bankr. E.D. Pa. 1996) (the subordination agreement rendered the subordinating creditor's claim unsecured, because the value of the collateral was less than the amount due the new senior lienholder).

This difference in approach may be explained by observing that "subordination agreements may be generally classified as being one of two types: debt subordinations or property interest subordinations." In re Lantana Motel, 124 B.R. at 255.

> In a debt subordination, the agreement provides that the subordinated creditor's right to payment and collection will be subordinate to the rights of another claimant. If the debt subordination is "complete," the subordinated creditor is barred from receiving payments until the superior debt is paid in full.
>   * * *

Debt subordination should be contrasted to property interest subordination. In a property interest subordination, the agreement affects only the relative rights of parties in particular real or personal property. Property interest subordination does not concern any rights the parties may have to receive payments.

The most common type of property interest subordination is lien subordination. By executing a lien subordination agreement, the subordinating party agrees to demote the priority of its lien to that of another secured creditor, thereby delaying its recourse to the identified collateral until the other party's secured claim has been satisfied.

Id., at 255-56; accord In re Environmental Aspecs, Inc., 235 B.R. 378, 396 n. 6 (E.D.N.C.1999):

The *Lantana* court explained the difference between a debt subordination and a property interest subordination. In the former, the agreement "provides that the subordinated creditor's right to payment and collection will be subordinate to the rights of another claimant ... [and] the subordinated creditor is barred from receiving payments until the superior debt is paid in full." Id. at 255-256. In a property interest subordination, "the subordinating party agrees to demote the priority of its lien to that of another secured creditor, thereby delaying its recourse to the identified collateral until the other party's secured claim has been satisfied." Id. at 256. A property interest subordination does not limit the subordinated party's right to receive payments. Id. Although EAI of NC's agreements with both AAL (1996) and SouthTrust (1997) in this case essentially constituted restructuring of prior obligations and thus required regular payments by the debtors to the creditors, the subordination agreement at issue in this case is in the nature of a property interest subordination.

With the distinction between the two types of subordination agreements in mind, the differing constructions of *Smith* and *Lunan* become understandable. Smith was describing the effect of a "debt subordination"; Lunan was explaining the effect of a "property interest subordination."

Contractual Subordination
2 Steinberg, BANKRUPTCY LITIGATION § 10:44
(1989 & Supp. 2005)

Contractual commitments to subordinate are enforceable under most circumstances in most states. To the extent they are enforceable under applicable state law, such agreements should be enforced in bankruptcy cases. Subordination agreements often contain provisions prohibiting payments to the subordinated creditor until the senior creditor is paid in full and requiring the subordinated creditor to deliver any payments which that creditor may receive from the debtor to the senior creditor.

If the contractual subordination involves secured creditors, the impact of the agreement is fairly simple and straightforward. The subordinated creditor's lien on the collateral becomes junior to the senior creditor's lien on the collateral. Both creditors will be dealt with in the same manner as they would have been dealt with had the subordinated creditor always held a subordinate lien. There is little, if any, effect on other creditors.

A subordination agreement between two unsecured creditors has far more complicated effects. A subordination agreement between two unsecured creditors subordinates one unsecured creditor to another unsecured creditor, even though both creditors are entitled to equal priority with all other unsecured creditors.

For example, assume the debtor has three unsecured creditors: A, B, and C. Assume A agrees to advance money to the debtor only if B subordinates B's claim to A's claim. B agrees to subordinate B's claim to A's claim, but does not subordinate B's claim to C's claim. C has not agreed to subordinate C's claim to A's claim. Therefore, B's claim is subordinate to A's claim, but equal with C's claim, and A's claim is senior to B's claim, but is also equal with C's claim.

Assume that each creditor holds a claim for $200. The debtor files a bankruptcy proceeding and has only $300 available for distribution to creditors. In this illustration, C is entitled to $1 for every $1 received by A, B is entitled to $1 for every $1 distributed to C, but A is entitled to have no distribution made to B until A is fully satisfied. The result should be as follows: A receives payment in full ($200), B receives nothing, and C receives $100. This is calculated as follows. First, assume each creditor would receive an equal pro rata distribution ($300 in assets, divided by $600 in claims, multiplied by a $200 claim). Second, B's dividend would be paid to A, based on B's subordination of B's claim to A's claim, until A is satisfied in full. Therefore, A would receive A's $100 and B's $100. B would receive nothing, and C would receive C's $100.[20]

This type of circular priority is common when there is a contractual subordination involving unsecured creditors. Therefore, contractual subordinations among unsecured creditors often result in complicated patterns of distribution. A judicially created equitable doctrine known as the "Rule of Explicitness" recognizes that parties may use subordination agreements to consent to the payment of postpetition interest to senior creditors from funds that would otherwise go to the subordinated creditors; however, the Rule of Explicitness mandates that a senior creditor's claim for postetition interest will not be allowed unless the subordination agreement explicitly alerted the subordinated creditors to the enhanced risk.

Addressing an issue of apparent first impression in the circuit, the First Circuit Court of Appeals has held [HSBC Bank USA v. Branch (In re Bank of New England Corp.), 364 F.3d 355 (1st Cir. 2004) (reprinted below)] that the Rule of Explicitness was not part of the relevant state's general contract law outside of the bankruptcy context and, therefore, could not be applied in construing the subordination agreements in the case before it. In so holding, the court reasoned that while a federal court must defer when the highest court of a state interprets the state's general contract law, no such deference is due to a state court's importation of a bankruptcy-specific rule into its own jurisprudence. Reasoning that the subordination agreement provisions in 11 U.S.C.A. § 510(a) are nothing more than a codification of prior bankruptcy law practice under the 1898 Act and that the Rule

---

20.   [For a similar example from the legislative history of the Bankruptcy Reform Act of 1978, see section A.3. of Chapter Fifteen below.–Ed.]

of Explicitness should be regarded as part of the federal common law rather than state law, a commentator has contended that the Rule of Explicitness should have survived enactment of the Bankruptcy Code undisturbed; according to this commentator, such a major change in the existing rules would not likely have been made without specific provision in the text of the statute, and it is most improbable that it would have been made without even any mention in the legislative history.

HSBC Bank USA v. Branch (In re Bank of New England Corp.)
United States Court of Appeals, First Circuit, 2004
364 F.3d 355

SELYA, Circuit Judge.

This is a case that straddles a crossroads formed by the intersection of federal and state law. It requires us to decide an issue of first impression in this circuit regarding the enforceability in bankruptcy of agreements that allow the subordination of certain indebtedness. Our decision partially contradicts the decision of the only other court of appeals to have grappled with this same set of questions, see Chem. Bank v. First Trust of N.Y. (In re Southeast Banking Corp.), 156 F.3d 1114 (11th Cir.1998), and to that extent creates a circuit split.

The precise dispute between the parties focuses on the priority (if any) that attaches to payment of post-petition interest on indebtedness that benefits from the contractual subordination of other indebtedness. As the question has been framed by the litigants and the lower courts, the answer depends on whether the subordination provisions at issue comply with the Rule of Explicitness. So phrased, the question assumes the continued vitality of that rule. Because we doubt the accuracy of that assumption, we step back to the beginning and inquire into the basis for believing that the Rule of Explicitness remains alive and well.

That step places us at the head of a long and winding path. After traveling it, we conclude that the enactment of section 510(a) of the Bankruptcy Reform Act of 1978, Pub.L. No. 95-598, 92 Stat. 2549, 2586 (codified at 11 U.S.C. § 510(a)), extinguished the Rule of Explicitness in its classic form. We further conclude that states are not free to adopt rules of contract interpretation that apply only in bankruptcy. For purposes of this case, then, the Rule of Explicitness is a dead letter.

Faced with this reality, we proceed to analyze the effect of the subordination provisions under New York's generally applicable principles of contract law—principles that do not embody any canon that operates in the same manner as the Rule of Explicitness. That analysis reveals an ambiguity in the language of the subordination provisions. The resolution of this ambiguity requires an inquiry into the parties' intent. That inquiry is fact-based and the bankruptcy court has not made the necessary findings. Consequently, we vacate the judgment below and remand for further proceedings.

I. BACKGROUND

The underlying facts are largely undisputed. In its halcyon days, the Bank of New England (BONE) issued six separate series of debt instruments. Clearly worded choice of law provisions tie the construction and interpretation of these instruments to the law of New York. Three of these offerings (the Senior Debt) are entitled to the benefit of contractual subordination provisions. They include

(i) a series of debentures bearing interest at 7.625% per annum, due in 1998, in the aggregate principal amount of $25,000,000; (ii) a series of debentures bearing interest at 8.85% per annum, due in 1999, in the aggregate principal amount of $20,000,000; and (iii) a series of notes bearing interest at a rate of 9.5% per annum, due in 1996, in the aggregate principal amount of $150,000,000. HSBC Bank USA and JPMorgan Chase Bank, appellants here, serve as Indenture Trustees for the Senior Debt. The remaining three offerings (the Junior Debt) are subordinated to the Senior Debt. They include (i) a series of floating rate debentures, due in 1996, in the aggregate principal amount of $75,000,000; (ii) a series of debentures bearing interest at 8.75% per annum, due in 1999, in the aggregate principal amount of $200,000,000; and (iii) a series of debentures bearing interest at 9.875% per annum, due in 1999, in the aggregate principal amount of $250,000,000. Each trust indenture referable to Junior Debt contains a subordination provision that is substantially similar to the following:

> [E]ach Holder likewise covenants and agrees by his acceptance thereof, that the obligations of the Company to make any payment on account of the principal of and interest on each and all of the Notes shall be subordinate and junior, to the extent and in the manner hereinafter set forth, in right of payment to the Company's obligations to the holders of Senior indebtedness of the Company.

Each of these indentures also specifies that:

> The Company agrees that upon … any payment or distribution of assets of the Company of any kind or character, whether in cash, property or securities, to creditors upon any dissolution or winding up or total or partial liquidation or reorganization of the Company, whether voluntary or involuntary or in bankruptcy, insolvency, receivership, conservatorship or other proceedings, all principal (and premium, if any), sinking fund payments and interest due or to become due upon all Senior Indebtedness of the Company shall first be paid in full, or payment thereof provided for in money or money's worth in accordance with its terms, before any payment is made on account of the principal of or interest on the indebtedness evidenced by the [Junior] Notes due and owing at the time.…

On January 7, 1991, BONE filed a voluntary petition for bankruptcy. At that time, much of the Senior and Junior Debt was still outstanding. Everyone agrees that, in bankruptcy, the holders of the Senior Debt are contractually entitled to priority. Withal, the parties fiercely dispute whether that priority extends to the payment of post-petition interest.

Since filing for bankruptcy, BONE, under the careful stewardship of its Chapter 7 trustee, has made three distributions to creditors. Through these distributions, the bankruptcy estate has paid the holders of the Senior Debt the full amount of all unpaid principal and pre-petition interest, together with all approved fees and expenses incurred through the date of the last distribution (October 26, 1999). The trustee then created an ample reserve for future fees and expenses and, at that point, concluded that he had satisfied the obligations owed to the holders of the Senior Debt. When, thereafter, the trustee determined that there existed sufficient unencumbered funds, he sought permission to make a distribution in the amount of $11,000,000 to the holders of the Junior Debt. The appellants objected on the ground that the trustee had not yet paid post-petition interest on the Senior Debt.

The bankruptcy court overruled this objection and authorized the proposed distribution. In re Bank of New Engl. Corp., 269 B.R. 82, 86 (Bankr. D. Mass. 2001). The court based its decision on the Rule of Explicitness, holding that New York law recognized the rule and that the language of the subordination provisions failed to satisfy it. Id. at 85-86. The district court affirmed. The court's analysis differed somewhat from that of the bankruptcy court, but it too deemed the Rule of Explicitness controlling. This appeal ensued.

II. DISCUSSION

We cede no special deference to the district court's initial review of the bankruptcy court's decision. Rather, we look directly to the bankruptcy court's decision, examining that court's findings of fact for clear error and its conclusions of law de novo. Id. Insofar as the bankruptcy court's decision hinges on an interpretation of the Bankruptcy Code, it presents a question of law (and, thus, engenders de novo review).

As the litigants and the lower courts have framed the issue, the pivotal question is whether the language of the subordination provisions satisfies the Rule of Explicitness. We do not agree that this is the correct question. Thus, we retreat to first principles.

Subordination agreements are essentially inter-creditor arrangements. 4 Lawrence P. King et al., COLLIER ON BANKRUPTCY ¶ 510.03[2], at 510-7 (15th rev. ed. 2003). They are designed to operate in a wide range of contingencies, one of which is insolvency. As a hedge against the ravages of a future bankruptcy, subordination agreements typically provide that one creditor will subordinate its claim against the debtor (the putative bankrupt) in favor of the claim of another creditor. This subordination alters the normal priority of the junior creditor's claim so that it becomes eligible to receive a distribution only after the claims of the senior creditor have been satisfied. Id. at ¶ 510.01, at 510-3.

Prior to 1978, the Bankruptcy Act contained no specific mention of subordination agreements. Enforcing such agreements was necessary to prevent junior creditors from receiving windfalls after having explicitly agreed to accept less lucrative payment arrangements. Equity dictated enforcement because "[e]quality among creditors who have lawfully bargained for different treatment is not equity but its opposite." Chem. Bank N.Y. Trust Co. v. Kheel, 369 F.2d 845, 848 (2d Cir. 1966).

Defining the outer limits of this equitable rule, especially with respect to post-petition interest, posed a thorny problem. Generally, the accrual of interest on an unsecured or undersecured claim stops upon the debtor's filing of a bankruptcy petition. See, e.g., Nicholas v. United States, 384 U.S. 678, 682, 86 S. Ct. 1674, 16 L. Ed. 2d 853 (1966); Sexton v. Dreyfus, 219 U.S. 339, 344, 31 S. Ct. 256, 55 L. Ed. 244 (1911); see also 11 U.S.C. § 502(b)(2); Bankruptcy Act of 1898, § 63(a). Yet, subordination agreements sometimes contain language that prioritizes (or, at least, arguably prioritizes) the payment of post-petition interest on senior indebtedness over any recovery on junior indebtedness. From the outset, courts have been uncomfortable with enforcing this type of prioritization for fear that cases would arise "where a senior creditor may potentially recover more under a subordination agreement than its allowable claim against the estate." 4 COLLIER ON BANKRUPTCY, supra ¶ 510.03[3], at 510-8.

To ease this discomfiture, judges fashioned an equitable doctrine to deal with (and, essentially, limit) the prioritization of post-petition interest payments. In its simplest form, this equitable doctrine, called the Rule of Explicitness, required that a subordination agreement show clearly "that the general rule that interest stops on the date of the filing of the petition is to be suspended." *Time Sales*, 491 F.2d at 844. Over time, this evolved into a requirement that only unequivocal language could overcome the generic bar on recovery of post-petition interest.

That was the state of the law when Congress enacted the Bankruptcy Code in 1978. Unlike the earlier Bankruptcy Act, the Code deals explicitly with subordination agreements. Section 510(a) provides that a subordination agreement is enforceable in bankruptcy to the same extent as under "applicable nonbankruptcy law." This statutory provision supplants the judge-made doctrine through which the courts previously had dealt with such agreements. Because equitable powers possessed by bankruptcy courts "must and can only be exercised within the confines of the Bankruptcy Code," Norwest Bank Worthington v. Ahlers, 485 U.S. 197, 206, 108 S. Ct. 963, 99 L. Ed. 2d 169 (1988), the enactment of section 510(a) means that the enforcement of subordination provisions is no longer a matter committed to the bankruptcy courts' notions of what may (or may not) be equitable.

That Congress cabined the bankruptcy courts' equitable powers while providing an alternate means for preserving the viability of subordination agreements does not resolve the further question of whether the Rule of Explicitness, through some other medium, survived the enactment of section 510(a). To answer that query, we begin, as always, with the text of the relevant statute. We are mindful, of course, that the language of an unambiguous statute normally determines its meaning.

In terms, section 510(a) provides that a "subordination agreement is enforceable in a [bankruptcy] case ... to the same extent that such agreement is enforceable under applicable nonbankruptcy law." It is clear beyond peradventure that the phrase "applicable nonbankruptcy law" can refer to either federal or state law. Since the construction of private contracts is usually a matter committed to state law, the presumption is that state law will furnish the proper benchmark. That presumption is especially robust here because we can find no federal statute that might guide us in interpreting subordination agreements.

Of course, it might be possible to argue for the use of federal common law in this context. But resort to a federal common law of contract enforcement ordinarily is justified only when required by a distinct national policy or interest. The interpretation and enforcement of financial arrangements between private parties does not fill that bill.

To be sure, there is an important federal interest in the uniform application of the bankruptcy law—but that interest will not suffice in this instance to justify resort to federal common law. By requiring that the enforceability of subordination agreements be subject to applicable nonbankruptcy law, Congress determined that such agreements should be interpreted using non-uniform principles. It is not our province to second-guess this determination. To cinch matters, the Supreme Court has instructed us that in the absence of specific statutory provisions to the contrary, property interests should not be analyzed differently as a result of a party's involvement in a bankruptcy case. *Butner v. United States*, 440 U.S. 48, 55, 99 S. Ct. 914, 59 L. Ed. 2d 136 (1979). We take this to mean that bankruptcy courts should only modify the usual state-law compendium of rights and remedies if and to the extent that such modifications are specifically authorized or directed by the Bankruptcy Code.

For these reasons, we conclude that the applicable nonbankruptcy law referred to in section 510(a) is state law (and, particularly, state contract law). It follows inexorably that if the Rule of Explicitness retains any vitality, it does so only as part and parcel of state law.

This brings us to the parameters of the authority delegated by section 510(a). One thing seems very clear: in keeping with the principle that bankruptcy is an area of distinct federal competence, Congress has conferred on the federal courts the power to apply any and all generally applicable state rules of contract interpretation in construing subordination agreements. But section 510(a) does not vest in the states any power to make bankruptcy-specific rules: the statute's clear directive for the use of applicable nonbankruptcy law leaves no room for state legislatures or state courts to create special rules pertaining strictly and solely to bankruptcy matters.

Formulation of the bankruptcy law requires Congress carefully to balance competing considerations. That effort is manifest here. On the one hand, bankruptcy highly values equitable distribution that is in line with the priorities embodied in the Code itself. On the other hand, equity typically operates to enforce voluntarily bargained-for positions (some of which may contradict the Code's normal priorities). Section 510(a) encapsulates Congress's reconciliation of this conflict. A state's creation of a bankruptcy-only rule of enforcement would outstrip the authority that Congress conferred (and, thus, upset the equilibrium that section 510(a) was designed to achieve). We conclude, therefore, that such a course is not open to the states.

If the Rule of Explicitness is an interpretive principle unique to bankruptcy, it offends this principle. A contrary holding—one that allowed a state to adopt a bankruptcy-only Rule of Explicitness—would require certain contractual provisions (those arguably entitling senior noteholders to the payment of interest becoming due at future dates) to achieve a heightened degree of clarity only if the effort to enforce them arose in bankruptcy rather than in some other context. Such a holding would go well beyond the intended reach of section 510(a).

The short of it is that the enforceability of subordination agreements in bankruptcy must be judged by reference to generally applicable state contract law. As it pertains here, this holding limits our consideration to the general principles of New York contract law. If—and only if—the Rule of Explicitness is such a general principle can it be given effect in this case.

The New York courts do not appear to have developed any rules of interpretation that apply specifically to subordination agreements. Moreover, reported decisions from the New York state courts reveal only a single mention of the Rule of Explicitness. Although we are in something of an epistemological quandary—it is always difficult to prove a negative—the near-total absence of authority is compelling proof that the Rule of Explicitness is not part of New York's general contract law.

* * *

Let us be perfectly clear. If a state, as part of its general contract law, enunciates an interpretive principle that applies to subordination agreements generally (e.g., "construe all subordination provisions strictly and enforce them only if the intent to subordinate is, on a particular set of facts, super-clear"), that principle would be enforceable under section 510(a). In that event, rejecting the prioritization of post-petition interest in the absence of explicit language would be consistent with the general law of the state. Such a situation would not pose the same problem as does a state rule that applies only in bankruptcy.

* * *

We now proceed to apply New York's general principles of contract enforcement to the facts at hand. This exercise will allow us to ascertain the effect of the provisions at issue upon the post-petition interest priority claimed by the appellants. Typically, the first step is to determine whether the challenged provisions are subordination agreements within the meaning of section 510(a). 4 COLLIER ON BANKRUPTCY, supra ¶ 510.03[2], at 510-7. That step is a formality here: these are subordination clauses, pure and simple.

We next must determine the meaning and effect of the subordination provisions. Initially, we ask whether the provisions are ambiguous with respect to the relative priority of the payment of post-petition interest on the Senior Debt. This is a question of New York law. The New York Court of Appeals has provided us with clear, if conventional, guidelines:

Contracts are not to be interpreted by giving a strict and rigid meaning to general words or expressions without regard to the surrounding circumstances or the apparent purpose which the parties sought to accomplish. The court should examine the entire contract and consider the relation of the parties and the circumstances under which it was executed. Particular words should be considered, not as if isolated from the context, but in the light of the obligation as a whole and the intention of the parties as manifested thereby. Form should not prevail over substance, and a sensible meaning of words should be sought.

William C. Atwater & Co. v. Panama R. Co., 246 N.Y. 519, 159 N.E. 418, 419 (1927) (citations and internal quotation marks omitted).

We take it as a given that a contract is ambiguous when its provisions are susceptible of two or more reasonable interpretations. That is the case here. Although each word, taken in isolation, may have a reasonably definite meaning, we must examine these words collectively. When we do, ambiguity surfaces.

The pertinent language requires full payment of "interest due or to become due" upon the occurrence of a number of events (including bankruptcy, insolvency, receivership, conservatorship, or "other proceedings"). The meaning of "interest due or to become due" seems obvious in the context of, say, a municipal bond: upon the occurrence of a triggering event, interest that has been earned but is not yet due to be paid becomes entitled to a priority.[21] Thus, the

---

21. [Footnote 4 in original:] We provide an example. If interest accruing on a bond is paid every six months (e.g., February 1 and August 1) and a triggering event occurs on May 1, the contractual language provides that all interest earned from February 1 through May 1 is entitled to prioritization (even though that interest is not yet due).

application of this group of words in the context of most triggering events is fairly straightforward. But bankruptcy—an event specifically referenced in the subordination provisions—alters the equation. Bankruptcy provides a special system of legal rules that occupies the field upon the filing of a petition. One byproduct of this special set of rules is that all interest is considered due as of the filing date. See 11 U.S.C. §§ 101(5)(a), 502(b). Conversely, interest that normally would accrue after that date is generally not recoverable at all (at least, not recoverable from the debtor). See id. § 502(b)(2).

These special rules cloud the meaning of the phrase "interest due or to become due." On the one hand, those words reasonably can be interpreted to apply only to triggering events outside of the bankruptcy context (where they have an unambiguous meaning). On the other hand, those words reasonably can be interpreted—as the appellants exhort—to apply to all triggering events, including bankruptcy. In that context, however, the words have no clear meaning and a court faces further ambiguity in trying to determine their contours. After all, in most cases the phrase "due or to become due" simply refers to unmatured interest. At the time of a bankruptcy filing, however, there is no unmatured interest, so the clause may be interpreted either to carry the same "nonbankruptcy" meaning throughout or to take on a bankruptcy-specific meaning (which would cover post-petition interest). Because each of these interpretations seems plausible, we believe that the subordination provisions—as they apply in bankruptcy—are ambiguous.

In fine, we find the words "due or to become due" lacking in certitude as to whether they actually provide for the payment of post-petition interest on the Senior Debt prior to any payment referable to the Junior Debt. New York law requires that this amphiboly be resolved through a contextual examination of the parties' intent, taking full account of the surrounding facts and circumstances. Discerning this intent ordinarily requires the adjudication of factual questions. A trial can be avoided only if the parties' intent is made manifest within the four corners of the contract itself.

In the case at bar, it is impossible to glean the parties' intent from the language and structure of the instruments alone. These documents evidence complex commercial transactions, and the matter is further complicated because the beneficiaries of the subordination provisions—the holders of the Senior Debt—are not parties to the agreements containing the subordination provisions (those agreements are directly appurtenant to the Junior Debt). Given these realities, we are persuaded that resolution of the intent question cannot be accomplished by the simple expedient of examining the relevant paperwork, but, rather, requires differential factfinding. Because the bankruptcy court has not yet developed a record with this inquiry in mind, we remand for factfinding on the parties' intent vis-à-vis post-petition interest.

III. CONCLUSION

We need go no further. We hold that the Rule of Explicitness has no application in the context of bankruptcy where, as here, the state has not adopted the rule as one of general applicability. Consequently, we turn to generic principles of state law to interpret the contractual provisions at issue. Applying those principles, we find the subordination provisions ambiguous as to whether they provide for the priority payment of post-petition interest. This finding necessitates an examination into the intent of the parties—an inquiry which, in the circumstances of this case, entails questions of fact that must in the first instance be addressed by the bankruptcy court. We therefore vacate the decision of the district court and remand with instructions that the district court vacate the judgment of the bankruptcy court and remand the matter to that tribunal for further proceedings consistent with this opinion.

Vacated and remanded. All parties shall bear their own costs.

Klee, *Adjusting Chapter 11: Fine Tuning the Plan Process*
69 AM. BANKR. L.J. 551, 561, 569 (1995)

There is uncertainty under current law whether a plan of reorganization can override a contractual subordination provision and permit a majority within a class to compel a minority within the class to waive subordination rights. The legislative history supports the concept of majority rule. Section 510(a) of the Code, which makes subordination agreements enforceable in bankruptcy to the same extent such agreements are enforceable outside of bankruptcy, and § 1129(a)(1) of the Code, which requires the plan to conform to the provisions of Title 11, appear, however, to require enforcement of the subordination agreement outside the context of cramdown.

Congress [should] specifically amend § 1123(b) of the Code in order to permit a plan to override § 510(a), if the affected senior class votes to accept the plan. Also, § 1129(b), by virtue of its reference to § 510(a) in cramdown, appears to have the anomalous result of overriding § 510(a) and eliminating the enforcement of subordination agreements in cases in which the class rejects the plan. The Commission should recommend to Congress that the reference to § 510(a) in § 1129(b)(1) of the Bankruptcy Code be deleted.

* * *

[In short,] § 510(a) should, as a general proposition, be retained to the extent it provides for the enforceability of subordination agreements in bankruptcy cases. However, the reference to § 510(a) should be removed from § 1129(b)(1) of the Bankruptcy Code because the subordination agreement should be enforced when the senior class is impaired and votes to reject the plan. Instead, the Code should be amended to allow any plan to override § 510(a) by vote of the senior class; and all classes of equal rank in Chapter 11 should be subjected to the unfair discrimination test, even in the context of a consensual plan.

C. TRADING CLAIMS

1. Overview

The reorganization process is not static. Many things can change during the course of a chapter 11 reorganization case, including the identity of the creditors. We conclude this chapter by analyzing the motivations and mechanics of trading claims during a chapter 11 reorganization case and the consequences that may follow.

Claims may be acquired for different reasons. Purchasers may desire to acquire claims for the simple purpose of profiting from a subsequent sale of the claim or through a distribution received in the reorganization case. Claims may also be acquired by those involved in the reorganization process to gain a sufficiently large position to be able to block confirmation of a consensual plan of reorganization. Sometimes, claims are acquired in sufficient quantities to enable the purchaser to control the reorganization process or the reorganized company.

Claims are also sold for different reasons. Obviously, a seller may need cash and willingly will transfer the claim in exchange for cash. On the other hand, a claimholder may sell a claim to avoid deterioration in value such as where the holder expects the underlying value of the debtor's business to decline. Timing considerations may also induce a creditor to sell a claim to book a profit or loss within a particular earnings period or to incur or avoid certain tax consequences.

Different kinds of claims and interests can be acquired during the bankruptcy case. Some debtors have issued notes or debentures that are publicly traded. These instruments may be secured or unsecured. In addition, debtors may have private debt[22] such as bank debt, privately placed debentures, amounts owed to vendors and purveyors of goods and services (known as "trade" claims), and involuntary claims such as tort claims, tax claims, environmental claims, and the like. The preferred and common stock interests of a corporate debtor or the limited partnership interests of a debtor that is a limited partnership may be traded as well.

Claims and interests can be acquired in different contexts. Often times, claims are acquired in the context of an out-of-court restructuring. Sometimes, claims are traded as part of a pre-packaged chapter 11 strategy in which the acquired claims are voted in accordance with § 1126(b) before the chapter 11 petition is filed. Although numerous issues arise in the out of court restructuring process, most of the controversy in the claims trading area involves trading during the chapter 11 reorganization case. That is the primary focus of this subchapter.

It is important to evaluate the status of the purchaser and seller of claims that are traded during a chapter 11 case. One or both of the parties may be an insider of the debtor, such as an officer or director, or a member of a creditors' committee. The purchaser could be an ordinary creditor with no special relationship to the debtor or it could be a member of a prepetition creditors' group. The purchaser could be an outsider with no other connection to the debtor or it could be an acquirer that desires to take control of the debtor. The status of the purchaser and seller has taken on much importance in the case law.

---

22. We define "private debt" to mean debt that is not listed for trading on a securities exchange or with respect to which bid and ask quotations in a public trading market are not recorded on a regular basis.

2. Nonbankruptcy Law Can Affect Trading in Claims or Interests

Before examining the impact of bankruptcy law on trading claims during a chapter 11 reorganization case, it is necessary to canvas briefly the nonbankruptcy law that may apply. The most comprehensive body of law that regulates trading of certain claims is the securities laws. The term "security" is defined extensively in the Securities Act of 1933 and Securities Exchange Act of 1934.[23] Although the definitions are somewhat different, they essentially include stocks, bonds, debentures, certificates of deposit, puts, calls, options, warrants, investment contracts, and other "traditional" securities. The definition does not include any note which has a maturity at the time of issuance not exceeding nine months. Case law has interpreted the statute to exclude commercial or consumer notes from the definition of "security" as contrasted with investment notes which are included within the definition. E.g., Reves v. Ernst & Young, 494 U.S. 56, 110 S. Ct. 945, 108 L. Ed. 2d 47 (1990). In evaluating whether a note is a commercial or consumer note on the one hand or an investment note on the other hand, the Court has adopted a four point test that considers (1) the motivation of the transaction; (2) whether there is common trading for speculation or investment; (3) the reasonable expectation of the investing public; and (4) the presence of another regulatory scheme that reduces the risk of investment. Id. at 66-67, 110 S. Ct. at 951-52, 108 L. Ed. 2d at 60-61.

If the claim traded is a security within the definition of § 3(a)(10) of the Securities Exchange Act, then the purchase and sale of the claim will be subject to Rule 10b-5. 17 C.F.R. § 240. 10b-5 (1990). The anti-fraud provisions of Rule 10b-5 make it unlawful for any person to make any untrue statement of a material fact or to omit to state a material fact in order to make the statements made not misleading or to otherwise participate in fraud in connection with the purchase or sale of any security. As a matter of practice, the rule is restricted to regulate purchases and sales by persons who have a duty to protect, and to not benefit from, confidential, inside information such as officers, directors, or employees of the debtor or professionals or advisors of the debtor company who receive confidential information in the course of rendering services to the company. E.g., SEC v. Texas Gulf Sulphur Co., 401 F.2d 833 (2d Cir. 1968) (en banc). Thus, a buyer or seller of a claim has

---

23. 15 U.S.C. §§ 77a(1), 78c(a)(10). The states have adopted definitions of "security" that are different than (and sometimes inconsistent with) these federal definitions. In the bankruptcy context, generally it would appear that bonds, debentures, and investment notes are securities, whereas trade claims are not. See Fortgang & Mayer, *Trading Claims and Taking Control of Corporations in Chapter 11,* 12 CARDOZO L. REV. 1, 47-50 (1990). The situation might change, however, if it becomes clear as a result of the plan process that the traded claims will be convertible into debt or equity securities of the reorganized company. The interface between the federal Bankruptcy Code and the federal and state securities laws is quite complex, particularly with respect to tender offers and other offers to purchase securities of a debtor during a chapter 11 reorganization case or under a plan.

engaged in a violation if he trades for his own account or that of another in breach of a duty of confidence or loyalty owed by him (or the person from whom he bought the securities) to a third party while he has material, non-public information. To do so would violate the undivided duty of loyalty that he has to the debtor not to use confidential information (or to misuse a property interest of the debtor) for his own benefit.

It is possible that the tender offer provisions of sections 13(e), 14(d) and 14(e) of the Securities Exchange Act apply to a tender offer in a reorganization case. 15 U.S.C. §§ 78m(e), 78n(d)-(e).[24] By its terms, section 14(d) applies to tender offers for "any equity security which is registered pursuant to section 12" of the Securities Exchange Act. Thus, these sections might apply to a tender for registered equity securities, at least outside the context of a plan. Although it would not appear that these sections should apply to a tender for claims, a different conclusion may be reached where a plan of reorganization has been filed that provides for claims to be converted into stock of the reorganized company and the stock is being traded on a "when, if and as issued" basis. See SEC v. Tex. Int'l Co., 498 F. Supp. 1231, 1241 (N.D. Ill. 1980) (holding that 14(d) applied); but see Lipper v. Tex. Int'l Co., Fed. Sec. L. Rep. (CCH) ¶ 96,837 (W.D. Okla. Apr. 6, 1979) (holding, with respect to same offer as in SEC v. Texas Int'l, that 14(d) did not apply). Apparently, the provisions of the Williams Act contained in sections 13(e) and 14(d) of the Securities Exchange Act "do not apply to tender offers and exchange offers made pursuant to a plan." Fortgang & Mayer, *Trading Claims and Taking Control of Corporations in Chapter 11*, 12 CARDOZO L. REV. 1, 83 (1990).

Even if the information requirements and procedural provisions of the Williams Act do not apply to a tender offer, the acquirer may still be required to comply with the unlawful tender offer practices provisions of section 14(e) of the Securities Exchange Act. 15 U.S.C. § 78n(e). Section 14(e) of the Securities Exchange Act appears to be inapplicable, however, to the information standard to be applied to solicitations made in the context of a plan of reorganization. See section 1125(d), 11 U.S.C. § 1125(d). Indeed, in the context of a plan of reorganization the tender offer itself has been viewed as an improper avoidance of the plan process prescribed by the Bankruptcy Code. See In re Allegheny International, Inc., 118 B.R. 282, 295 (Bankr. W.D. Pa. 1990).

Aside from the federal securities laws, federal criminal laws may also apply to restrict claims trading in chapter 11 cases. The federal mail and wire fraud laws prohibit schemes to defraud by means of false, fraudulent pretenses,

---

24. If the tender offer is coupled with a proxy contest,, sections 14(a)-(b) would appear to apply. But cf. Pub. Serv. Co. v. Consol. Utils. and Commc'ns, Inc., 846 F.2d 803, 808-09 (1st Cir. 1988) (applying Bankruptcy Code rather than § 14(a) even to solicitations made before approval of the disclosure statement).

representations, or promises in a manner similar to Rule 10b-5. 18 U.S.C. §§ 1341, 1343. Unlike Rule 10b-5, however, there is no requirement that the transaction involve the purchase or sale of a security. These statutes, therefore, should apply to fraudulent purchases and sales of securities or trade claims where the purchaser or seller has breached a duty of confidence owing to the company by trading claims based on such information.

Some transactions will involve purchasers or sellers that are fiduciaries of the debtor. Irrespective of securities laws, these fiduciaries may be culpable for breaching a duty of loyalty under state corporate law, trust law, or equity. It is fundamental, for example, that a director of a corporation must not appropriate a corporate opportunity by engaging in self-dealing to the detriment of the corporation. It is important to ask which of the characters in the chapter 11 case owes a fiduciary duty and to identify the nature of the duty and to whom the duty is owed.

3. Trading Claims During a Reorganization Case

The Federal Rules of Bankruptcy Procedure and the Bankruptcy Code provide guidance with respect to trading claims during a chapter 11 reorganization case. Effective August 1, 1991, Bankruptcy Rule 3001(e) was amended to provide in part as follows:

(e) **TRANSFERRED CLAIM.**

(1) *Transfer of Claim Other Than for Security Before Proof Filed.* If a claim has been transferred other than for security before proof of the claim has been filed, the proof of claim may be filed only by the transferee or an indenture trustee.

(2) *Transfer of Claim Other Than for Security After Proof Filed.* If a claim other than one based on a publicly traded note, bond, or debenture has been transferred other than for security after the proof of claim has been filed, evidence of the transfer shall be filed by the transferee. The clerk shall immediately notify the alleged transferor by mail of the filing of the evidence of transfer and that objection thereto, if any, must be filed within 20 days of the mailing of the notice or within any additional time allowed by the court. If the alleged transferor files a timely objection and the court finds, after notice and a hearing, that the claim has been transferred other than for security, it shall enter an order substituting the transferee for the transferor. If a timely objection is not filed by the alleged transferor, the transferee shall be substituted for the transferor.
    * * *

The Advisory Committee note accompanying the amended rule is illuminating.

Subdivision (e) is amended to limit the court's role to the adjudication of disputes regarding transfers of claims. If a claim has been transferred prior to the filing of a proof of claim, there is no need to state the consideration for the transfer or to submit other evidence of the transfer. If a claim has been transferred other than for security after a proof of claim has been filed, the transferee is substituted for the transferor in the absence of a timely objection by the alleged transferor. In that event, the clerk should note the transfer without the need for court approval. If a timely objection is filed, the court's role is to determine whether a transfer has been made that is enforceable under nonbankruptcy law. This rule is not intended either to encourage or discourage postpetition transfers of claims or to affect any remedies otherwise available under nonbankruptcy law to a transferor or transferee such as for misrepresentation in connection with the transfer of a claim. * * *

As the Advisory Committee note makes clear, the purpose of the amended rule is to take the court out of the process of regulating claims trading unless the transferor raises a dispute. In the absence of an objection by the transferor, the transfer of the claim will take place through a minis-terial action of the bankruptcy court clerk without the need for court approval.

Under the former rule, there was no bankruptcy regulation of the transfer of a bond or debenture. Under the current rule, there is no regulation if the claim transferred is a publicly traded bond or debenture.[25] The requirement that a bond or debenture be "publicly traded" is new and represents an expansion of the scope of the rule to cover privately traded bonds and debentures. In this respect, it appears that the amended rule may be overbroad since other mechanisms exist to regulate trading by qualified institutional investors of unregistered securities. See SEC Rule 144A, 17 C.F.R. § 230. 144A. As a matter of policy, it is doubtful that the bankruptcy court should play a role in regulating the trading of claims when another recognized clearing mechanism exists.

Nevertheless, Federal Rule of Bankruptcy Procedure 3001(e) represents a dramatic shift in favor of the free market by comparison with its predecessor. Under former Bankruptcy Rule 3001(e), only unconditional transfers were permitted. If a transfer was conditional so that the transferor retained vestiges of ownership or power to control the claims, the transferee would not be substituted for the transferor. In re Ionosphere Clubs, Inc., 119 B.R. 440, 444 (Bankr. S.D.N.Y. 1990). The rule also required the transferee to state the consideration for the transfer of the claim. This enabled the bankruptcy court to determine if the claim was being acquired at a substantial discount and provided an impetus for many courts to regulate the claims trading process.[26] Some courts reasoned that if the filing of the reorganization

---

25. It is unclear what the rule means by "publicly traded". The phrase might relate to the existence of a public market for a class of claims, or it could require that a particular claim be traded publicly in the transaction in question. While trades on a securities exchange are certainly public, other transactions that are consummated off an exchange might or might not be labeled "public".

26. If the transfer involved a claim with respect to which a proof of claim was filed or if the claim was scheduled other than as disputed, contingent, or unliquidated so that a proof of claim was deemed filed under § 1111(a), former Bankruptcy Rule 3001(e)(2) required the bankruptcy court to enter an

case created a market within which claims could be traded, then it was incumbent upon the debtor or transferor to provide adequate information so that the market could function efficiently. Consider the following case.

In Re Revere Copper and Brass, Inc.
United States Bankruptcy Court, S.D.N.Y., 1985
58 B.R. 1

ABRAM, Bankruptcy Judge

This court has been presented by the Bankruptcy Clerk with twenty-eight proposed orders approving the subrogation of Phoenix Capital Corp. ("Phoenix") as assignee-claimant to the rights of twenty-eight different assignor-claimants. In each case the Clerk's Office sent a standard form notice under date of February 13, 1985 to the assignor-claimant that the assignment and request for subrogation had been filed by Phoenix and advised that the court would enter an order of subrogation unless an objection was entered by the assignor-claimant on or before March 5, 1985. See [former] Bankruptcy Rule 3001(e)(2). No objections have been filed.

Attached to each of the assignment of claim instruments is an original letter, identical in content, on Phoenix's letterhead, the body of which reads as follows:

"Dear Sir:

"SUBJECT: Sale of your claim against Revere Copper and Brass Incorporated, Bankruptcy Case No. 82B 12073 (PA)

"Phoenix Capital Corporation is prepared to pay immediate cash for your claim against the bankrupt Revere Copper and Brass Incorporated.

"The schedule of accounts payable filed with the U.S. Bankruptcy Court for the Southern District of New York, indicates that your company has a claim in the amount of [$_____]. Our offer is to pay twenty percent (20%) of the face amount of any valid, uncontested and unpaid claim.

"If you wish to accept this offer, please acknowledge your acceptance in the space provided below and return one copy to me for my further handling. A check will be issued to your company at once. Claims will be purchased on a first offered, first bought basis."

Nineteen of the letters were sent on six dates between November 5 and 29, 1984. The balance of nine letters were sent on December 6, 1984. In six cases, Phoenix tendered payment to the assignor-claimant and the payment check was cashed prior to November 29, 1984. In five other cases, Phoenix's checks were dated November 29, 1984 and were cashed between December 4 and December 11, 1984. In the balance of seventeen cases, Phoenix's checks were dated between December 3, 1984 and January 15, 1985. The claims assigned range in amount from $1,000 to $8,161.94. Fourteen, or one-half, of the assigned claims are between $1,000 and $2,000 in amount.

---

order substituting the transferee for the original claimant or otherwise entering such order as may be appropriate. Coupled with § 105(a) this provided an impetus for some bankruptcy courts to regulate the claims trading process. E.g., In re Allegheny Int'l, Inc., 100 B.R. 241, 243-44 (Bankr. W.D .Pa. 1988) (debtor required to inform potential assignor of claim of debtor's estimate of value of claim).

On November 30, 1984, *The Wall Street Journal* published an article . . . based on an announcement by Revere Copper and Brass, Inc. ("Revere"), the debtor in this Chapter 11 reorganization, outlining the details of a plan of reorganization. To date, Revere has not filed a formal plan of reorganization nor, obviously, has any disclosure statement been approved. As it relates to general unsecured creditors whose claims total $45.4 million, Revere's announcement states that such creditors would have three options, one, 65% cash, two, 60% cash plus 10% of their claim in Revere common stock or three, 39% cash, 46% in notes and 15% of the claim value in Revere common stock.

Revere has been in Chapter 11 since October 27, 1982. Although negotiations for a reorganization plan are being seriously pursued and the outline of a plan has been agreed upon, it is uncertain when a plan will be filed and when thereafter confirmation will occur. Confirmation could not occur earlier than summer 1985 since the plan has not yet been filed and the disclosure statement is as yet unapproved. However, no assurance exists that confirmation would occur as early as summer 1985 and it could occur many months later.

Phoenix has no relationship to Revere known to the court other than as the assignee of claims. Phoenix is not a member of the Creditors' Committee or the Equity Securityholders' Committee.

The assignor-creditors may indeed prefer the certainty of the 20% cash in hand offered by Phoenix today over the possibility of 65% cash at an uncertain time in the future under Revere's announced plan of reorganization. However, the court is concerned that the assignor-creditors have not been plainly advised of their options. [Former] Bankruptcy Rule 3001(e)(2) contemplates that the court will enter the order of substitution only after a hearing on notice and further permits the court to enter such an order as is appropriate. The Advisory Committee Note to this [former] rule states in relevant part:

> "The interests of sound administration are served by requiring the post-petition transferee to file with the proof of claim a statement of the transferor acknowledging the transfer and the consideration for the transfer. Such a disclosure will assist that court in dealing with evils that may arise out of post-bankruptcy traffic in claims against an estate. Monroe v. Scofield, 135 F.2d 725 (10th Cir. 1943); In re Philadelphia & Western Rv., 64 F. Supp. 738 (E.D. Pa. 1946); cf. In re Latham Lithographic Corp., 107 F.2d 749 (2d Cir. 1939)."

One of the evils attendant upon a solicitation of assignment of claims for a cash payment such as is being made by Phoenix is that solicited creditors may be unaware of their rights and options and fall prey to the belief that bankruptcy inevitably will result in their receiving the proverbial 10 cents on the dollar or worse. Creditors may not be aware of the difference between a straight bankruptcy case under Chapter 7 and a reorganization case under Chapter 11 of the Bankruptcy Code. Bankruptcy Code § 1125 prohibits solicitation of acceptances or rejections of a filed plan unless the solicitation is accompanied or preceded by a disclosure statement. The disclosure statement must contain adequate information which means information of a kind and in sufficient detail to enable a hypothetical reasonable investor typical of holders of claims to make an informed judgment about the plan. Code § 1125(a)(1). The assignor-claimant[s] have not been shown to [have] been given sufficient information by Phoenix that they might make an informed judgment about the offer made to them. That much is required.

The court has determined that it will not approve the assignments until the assignor-creditors have been given until May 1, a period of approximately 30 days, in which to revoke their assignment to Phoenix. The revocation must be made by tendering to Phoenix a check in the amount paid with an indication of a desire to revoke. A copy of the revocation must be filed with the court not later than May 1, 1985. If any revocations are received by that date, the court will decline to approve those assignments but will approve Phoenix's subrogation under any assignments that are not revoked.

Phoenix is advised that as to any claims assigned to it that the court will in the future decline to approve the assignments unless it appears that the claim-ants have been advised at the time of solicitation and again at the time a check in payment of Phoenix's offer is tendered of the pertinent terms of Revere's announced or any subsequently filed plan and the procedural status of the Chapter 11 case and plan, so that the solicited creditor may know where along the plan filing-disclosure statement hearing-confirmation line the case stands.

It is so ordered.

* * *

NOTES

1. How would Judge Abram decide *Revere Copper and Brass* if the present version of Bankruptcy Rule 3001(e)(2) applied instead of the former version? Wouldn't the court remain concerned "that the assignor-creditors have not been plainly advised of their options"? The "evil" still exists "that solicited creditors may be unaware of their rights and options and fall prey to the belief that bankruptcy inevitably will result in their receiving the proverbial 10 cents on the dollar or worse." Could Judge Abram use § 105(a) to require the transferee to disclose adequate information? See In re Lynn, 285 B.R. 858, 862 (Bankr. S.D.N.Y. 2002). How could Phoenix, as an outsider, acquire such information? Could Judge Abram compel the debtor to disseminate adequate information to the public outside the context of a disclosure statement? Alternatively, could Judge Abram enter an order under § 105(a) enjoining the acquisition of claims until after the dissemination of a disclosure statement? To the extent § 105(a) provides the predicate to regulate trading in claims, the amendment to Bankruptcy Rule 3001(e) cannot properly alter the court's ability to exercise jurisdiction over the matter. See 28 U.S.C. § 2075 and Fed. R. Bankr. P. 9030.

2. Would the court be able to regulate or prevent a transfer that was conditional? Recall that under the former rule, the transfer had to be unconditional in order to be approved. See In re Ionosphere Clubs, Inc., 119 B.R. 440, 444 (Bankr. S.D.N.Y. 1990). If a transferee can obtain part of a claim or can "rent" a claim for purposes of voting, the potential for abuse exists with respect to voting and distribution in a chapter 11 case. Although Bankruptcy Rule 3001(e) no longer requires disclosure of these arrangements, Bankruptcy Rule 2019 may dictate a contrary result. In particular, if the transferee represents more than one creditor and fails to disclose the terms of the conditional transfer, the court may be authorized to "grant appropriate relief". See Bankruptcy Rule 2019(b)(2). Moreover, cases interpreting Bankruptcy Rule 3017(e) require that the

beneficial holder actually vote the claim. See, e.g., In re St. Therese Care Center, Inc., 1991 WL 217669 (Bankr. D. Minn. 1991); In re Southland Corp., 124 B.R. 211 (Bankr. N.D. Tex. 1991).

3. The remedy imposed by Judge Abram on Phoenix Capital Corp. in *Revere Copper and Brass* was to require future claimants to be advised at the time of solicitation of the terms of the announced plan of reorganization and to delay approval of the transfer of claims until the transferors were given a 30 day right to revoke the assignments. What other remedies could the court have fashioned? Is there a legal basis for the court to disallow any votes that Phoenix Capital Corp. might cast with respect to the acquired claims? Is there a legal basis to restrict or deny distribution to Phoenix Capital Corp. based on such claims?

4. Phoenix Capital Corp. was an arbitrageur looking to make a profit with respect to the claims it acquired. Would it have mattered whether Phoenix Capital Corp. was an acquirer trying to seize control of Revere Copper and Brass? Would it have mattered if Phoenix Capital Corp. were a member of the creditors' committee in the Revere Copper and Brass, Inc. chapter 11 case? Would it have mattered if Phoenix Capital Corp. were the proponent of a competing plan of reorganization?

5. If Phoenix Capital Corp. successfully acquired claims from 28 creditors, how many votes would it have for purposes of satisfying the numerosity requirement of a majority in number of allowed *claims* under § 1126(c)? See Figter Ltd. v. Teachers Ins. & Annuity Ass'n (In re Figter, Ltd.), 118 F.3d 635, 640 (9th Cir. 1997) (holding that creditor gets one vote for each claim acquired) (reprinted in Chapter Thirteen below); In re Gilbert, 104 B.R. 206 (Bankr. W.D. Mo. 1989) (single creditor holding two claims given two votes); accord, Concord Square Apartments, Ltd. v. Ottawa Props., Inc. (In re Concord Square Apartments, Ltd.), 174 B.R. 71 (Bankr. S.D. Ohio 1994). Cf. In re Messengill, 113 F. 366 (E.D.N.C. 1902) (creditor who purchased several claims treated as one *creditor* holding several *claims*). But see Neely, *Investing in Troubled Companies and Trading in Claims and Interests in Chapter 11 Cases—A Brave New World,* in FUNDAMENTALS OF CHAPTER 11 BUSINESS REORGANIZATIONS 109, 165-69 (Annual Advanced ALI-ABA Course of Study, No. C836, 1993), available at C836 ALI-ABA 109 (Westlaw) (hereinafter Neely, *supra, Brave New World*).

In addition to the Bankruptcy Rules, the Bankruptcy Code contains some provisions that apply to trading claims.[27] Although no direct provision of the Bankruptcy Code appears to regulate trading in claims, some provisions apply

---

27. The problems raised by trading claims are not new. Under the former Bankruptcy Act, express statutory provisions gave the court power to make sure that fiduciaries would not profit from their positions in trading claims. See sections 212 and 249 of the Bankruptcy Act, 11 U.S.C. §§ 612, 649 (repealed 1979). These sections gave the court the power to limit the allowance of claims against the estate to the amount paid for the claims and to deny compensation or reimbursement of expenses to insiders or members of creditors' committees. The sections did not, however, give courts the power to impose penalties or sanctions with respect to trading by fiduciaries. See In re Cont'l Inv. Corp., 637 F.2d 8, 11 (1st Cir. 1980). Although sections 212 and 249 of the Bankruptcy Act were not carried over into the Bankruptcy Code, the law interpreting those sections may remain authoritative if it has not been expressly or implicitly contradicted. See Midlantic Nat'l Bank v. N.J. Dept. of Envtl. Protection, 474 U.S. 494, 106 S. Ct. 755, 88 L. Ed. 2d 859 (1986).

indirectly. Section 1145(b)(1)(A) disqualifies entities that purchase a claim with a view to distribution of securities received under a plan from the exemption granted by § 1145(a) from section 5 of the Securities Act of 1933, 15 U.S.C. § 77(e) (1990). Thus these purchasers will not be allowed to rely on any exemption in reselling securities issued under the plan except for ordinary trading transactions.[28] 11 U.S.C. § 1145(a)-(b).

Section 502(j) permits the court to reconsider the allowance or disallowance of a claim for cause based on the equities of the case. This section is the successor to section 57k of the Bankruptcy Act which was the statutory underpinning of the landmark case Pepper v. Litton, 308 U.S. 295, 60 S. Ct. 238, 84 L. Ed. 281 (1939). Pepper v. Litton stands for the proposition that a bankruptcy court may use its inherent equity powers to disallow a claim. Id. at 305, 60 S. Ct. at 244-45, 84 L. Ed. at 288. To the extent a bankruptcy court is apprised of inequitable conduct with respect to the transfer of a claim, § 502(j) remains available to support the extraordinary remedy of equitable disallowance.[29]

Section 1126(e) provides the most direct statutory authority for regulating trading in claims. That section permits the court to "designate any entity whose acceptance or rejection of such plan was not in good faith, or was not solicited or procured in good faith or in accordance with the provisions of this title." The effect of designation is to disallow the entity's vote under § 1126(c)-(d). Generally, creditors are free to trade in claims and their votes will not be limited. See *Figter, Ltd.*, 118 F.3d at 639; In re Gladstone Glen, 739 F.2d 1233, 1237 (7th Cir. 1984) (chapter XII case). But if the creditor desires to acquire the debtor and purchases the claims in bad faith to block a competing plan, the purchaser's votes can be designated and disallowed as being cast in bad faith. See In re Allegheny Int'l, Inc., 118 B.R. 282, 289-90 (Bankr. W.D. Pa. 1990). Accord In re P-R Holding Corp., 147 F.2d 895 (2d Cir. 1945) (acquirer's vote disallowed

---

28. Neither the Bankruptcy Code nor the Securities Act of 1933 defines "ordinary trading transactions". SEC no action letters construe ordinary trading transactions by the absence of three factors:

(a) (i) concerted action, by recipients of securities distributed under a plan of reorganization, in connection with the sale of such securities, or (ii) concerted action by distributors on behalf of one or more such recipients in connection with such sales, or (iii) both;

(b) informational documents concerning the offering of the securities prepared or used to assist in the resale of such securities other than the Disclosure Statement and any supplements thereto and documents filed with the Commission by the issuer pursuant to the Exchange Act; or

(c) special compensation to brokers and dealers in connection with the sale of such securities designed as a special incentive to resell such securities, other than the compensation that would be paid pursuant to arm's-length negotiations between a seller and a broker or dealer, each acting unilaterally, and not greater than the compensation that would be paid for a routine similar-sized sale of a similar issuer. E.g., UNR Industries, Inc., SEC No-Action Letter (July 11, 1989).

29. Following the enactment of § 510(c) which permits a claim to be equitably subordinated below other claims but not below classes of interests, there is some doubt whether the remedy of equitable disallowance retains vitality.

on purchased claims but court confirmed plan and refused to reinstate negative votes of transferor).[30] If the claim is purchased or voted with the intention of influencing future litigation, the court might designate the creditor who voted the claim in bad faith. Compare Zantek GBV Fund IV, LLC v. Vesper, 19 Fed. Appx. 238 (6th Cir. 2001) (affirming designation of creditor who purchased claim with ulterior purpose of gaining advantage in future negotiations with trustee to limit his own liability) with In re Lehigh Valley Prof'l Sports Club, Inc., No. 00-11296DWS, 2001 WL 1188246 (Bankr. E.D. Pa. Sept. 7, 2001) (finding no bad faith even though purchaser acquired claims to propose competing plan so that it would not be sued).

As a general rule, the price paid for a claim does not affect voting or distribution. Lorraine Castle Apartments Bldg. Corp. v. Machiewich (In re Lorraine Castle Apartments Bldg. Corp.), 149 F.2d 55, 58 (7th Cir. 1945); Dressel Assocs., Inc. v. Beaver Valley Builder's Supply, Inc. (In re Beaver Valley Builder's Supply, Inc.), 177 B.R. 507 (Bankr. W.D. Pa. 1995). A non-fiduciary creditor may purchase a claim to vote against the plan in good faith. E.g., *Figter, Ltd.*, 118 F.3d at 639; In re Pine Hill Collieries Co., 46 F. Supp. 669, 671 (E.D. Pa. 1942); Concord Square Apartments, Ltd. v. Ottawa Props., Inc. (In re Concord Square Apartments, Ltd.), 174 B.R. 71 (Bankr. S.D. Ohio 1994); In re Pleasant Hill Partners, 163 B.R. 388 (Bankr. N.D. Ga. 1994) Cf. In re Dune Deck Owners Corp., 175 B.R. 839 (Bankr. S.D.N.Y. 1995) (holding that evidentiary hearing was needed to determine whether to disallow voting of unsecured claims by mortgagee who may have had legitimate purpose of voting against plan to benefit its interests as secured creditor or may have had illegitimate ulterior motive of profiting from transaction with another party); In re Applegate Prop., Ltd., 133 B.R. 827 (Bankr. W.D. Tex. 1991) (disallowing votes cast against creditor's plan by insider which had purchased claims, and stating in dictum that if creditor/plan proponent had purchased the claims to vote them in favor of the plan, those votes would also have been disallowed). Creditors can also purchase claims to support confirmation. In re Gilbert, 104 B.R. 206 (Bankr. W.D. Mo. 1989) (creditor permitted to purchase control of class to protect its claims). But insiders, acquirers, or plan proponents may not do so without risk.

In addition to the express remedy of disallowance of votes by "designation", bankruptcy courts have long adopted special rules with respect to claims purchased by insiders with a fiduciary duty of loyalty.[31]

---

30. Indeed the power of the bankruptcy court to disallow the vote of a creditor whose acceptance is not in good faith inheres in the power of the bankruptcy court and is not dependent on any statutory provision. Am. United Mut. Life Ins. Co. v. City of Avon Park, 311 U.S. 138, 61 S. Ct. 157, 85 L. Ed. 91 (1940) (city fiscal agent failed to disclose self-interest in soliciting acceptances so votes disallowed).

31. While officers and directors of the debtors are fiduciaries to the company, members of a creditors' committee are fiduciaries to those they represent. See, e.g. Woods v. City Nat'l Bank & Trust Co., 312 U.S. 262, 268-69, 61 S. Ct. 493, 497, 85 L. Ed. 820, 826 (1941); Official Unsecured

Thus, as a general proposition, an insider with material non-public information and a duty of loyalty who purchases a claim postpetition at less than face value can only recover based on the amount paid for the claim. E.g., In re UVAS Farming Corp., 91 B.R. 575, 577 (Bankr. D.N.M. 1988); Citicorp Venture Capital, Ltd. v. Comm. of Creditors Holding Unsecured Claims (In re Papercraft Corp.), 160 F.3d 982, 987-92 & 987 n.3 (3d Cir. 1998) (leaving open whether per se rule applies, but finding that inequitable conduct warrants equitable subordination to require at least a disgorgement of profits).[32] A few courts, however, have refused to adopt a per se rule to limit the allowed dollar amount of claims purchased by a fiduciary as long as there is no breach of fiduciary duty or bad faith in the trading of the claims. In re Northern Bldg. Supply, No. 97-12487, 2003 WL 22945631 (Bankr. N.D. Cal. Feb. 13, 2003) (holding that there is nothing inherently wrong with partners buying up creditors' claims at a discount without disclosure); Dressel Assocs., Inc. v. Beaver Valley Builder's Supply, Inc. (In re Beaver Valley Builder's Supply, Inc.), 177 B.R. 507, 514 (Bankr. W.D. Pa. 1995) (holding that purchaser's claim would not be reduced to amount paid even if purchaser were an insider, because debtor did not have funds to purchase claims at a discount and because "[a]n insider of a corporation may seize a business opportunity * * * when the corporation is

---

Creditors' Comm. v. Stern (In re SPM Mfg. Corp.), 984 F.2d 1305, 1315 (1st Cir. 1993); In re First Republicbank Corp., 95 B.R. 58, 61 (Bankr. N.D. Tex. 1988). Persons who serve on creditors' committees are considered to be temporary insiders. See Dirks v. SEC, 463 U.S. 646, 655 n. 14, 103 S. Ct. 3255, 3262 n. 14, 77 L. Ed. 2d 911, 922 n. 14 (1983). It may be possible for a committee member who is in the regular business of trading securities to do so without breach of duty if it employs a proper information blocking device and files evidence of the device with the bankruptcy court. In re Federated Dep't Stores, Inc., Bankr. No. 1-90-00130, 1991 WL 79143 (Bankr. S.D. Ohio March 7, 1991). Cf. In re Midland United Co., 64 F. Supp. 399, 417 (D. Del. 1946), aff'd, 159 F.2d 340 (3d Cir. 1947) (committee members not disqualified from receiving compensation when customers of brokerages in which members were partners traded securities of debtor). The case authority prohibiting trading in claims by creditors' committee members consists of pre-Code cases in which courts used their statutory authority to deny compensation for services rendered by creditors' committee members who traded in claims. See Neely, supra, *Brave New World,* at 185-89 (suggesting that trading by committee members should be permissible under certain circumstances but noting that case authority is not sympathetic to that viewpoint).

32. On remand the bankruptcy judge ordered Citicorp Venture Capital not only to disgorge profits but to pay damages including interest, professional fees, and expenses for the four-month delay it caused while it purchased claims and diverted the debtor's management from promptly confirming the debtor's plan. See Committee of Creditors Holding Unsecured Claims v. Citicorp Venture Capital, Ltd. (In re Papercraft Corp.), 2000 WL 1435066 (Bankr. W.D. Pa. Sept. 21, 2000), aff'd, CitiCorp Venture Capital, Ltd. v. Comm. of Creditors Holding Unsecured Claims, 323 F.3d 228, 235 (3d Cir. 2003) (affirming bankruptcy court's subordination of claims secretly purchased by CVC, an insider and fiduciary of the debtor, where "CVC's conduct delayed the plan process by at least four months, and … CVC's intent was to benefit itself over and above other creditors to whom it owed a fiduciary duty not to self-deal.").

incapable of taking advantage of that opportunity for itself"); In re Apex Oil Co., 92 B.R. 847 (Bankr. E.D. Mo. 1988) (insider permitted to purchase secured party's claims and contribute them to estate as part of purchase price even though competing bidder locked out). Cf. EEE Comm'l Corp. v. Holmes (In re ASI Reactivation, Inc.), 934 F.2d 1315, 1321 (4th Cir. 1991) (equitable subordination case stating that "[t]here is nothing in the bankruptcy act which *per se* forbids a principal from obtaining and asserting rights as a lien creditor."). And even a person with a close relationship with the debtor or with an insider is permitted to purchase claims and enforce them for their full value, as long as the purchaser does not have material non-public information:

> [C]ourts have been reluctant to extend fiduciary standards to others, even though they have significant business relationships with the debtor. Thus, in In re Pine Hill Collieries Co., 46 F. Supp. 669 (E.D. Pa. 1942), the court approved the trading activities of the company that managed the debtor's mining operations and was also a creditor. And, in In re Philadelphia & Western Ry., 64 F. Supp. 738 (E.D. Pa. 1946), the court did not limit the claims purchased by an officer of the company that had a management contract with respect to the debtor's business. Similarly, persons with business or social ties to fiduciaries have not been subjected to scrutiny under fiduciary standards if they have not traded on confidential information. See, e.g., Manufacturers Trust Co. v. Becker, 338 U.S. 304, 70 S. Ct. 127 (1949) (office associate of a director was not treated as a fiduciary); Moulded Prods., Inc. v. Barry, 474 F.2d 220 (8th Cir. 1973) (close friend of trustee for whom trustee negotiated assignment of claim was not treated as a fiduciary); In re Automotive Equip. Mfg. Co., 106 F. Supp. 699 (D. Neb. 1952), appeal dismissed, 202 F.2d 955 (8th Cir. 1953) (by stipulation) (client of trustee's accountant, who was assisted by accountant to acquire claims with the trustee's encouragement, was not a fiduciary and claims were not limited); In re Gilbert, 104 B.R. 206 (Bankr. W.D. Mo. 1989) (votes on purchased claims by business partner of the debtor were not cast in bad faith). Further, relatives of fiduciaries are not necessarily treated as fiduciaries. Compare Manufacturers Trust Co. v. Becker, 338 U.S. 304, 70 S. Ct. 127, 94 L. Ed. 107 (1949) (acquisitions by director's wife and mother were treated as purchased by a fiduciary) with In re Philadelphia & W. Ry., 64 F. Supp. 738 (E.D. Pa. 1946) (father of an officer of the debtor was not a fiduciary).

Neely, supra, *Brave New World,* 184-85.

A person who seeks standing to file a plan of reorganization as a party in interest under § 1121(c) can purchase a claim and obtain standing. In re Rook Broadcasting, Inc., 154 B.R. 970 (Bankr. D. Idaho 1993); In re First Humanics Corp., 124 B.R. 87 (Bankr. W.D. Mo. 1991). If the person, however, gets access to inside information and then purchases claims in order to cause its plan to be confirmed or to block a competing plan, it risks sanctions including but not limited to disallowance of its votes. See In re Allegheny Int'l, Inc., 118 B.R. 282 (Bankr. W.D. Pa. 1990).

Thus far we have focused on the purchase of claims by a fiduciary. What happens if the fiduciary is a seller rather than a purchaser? The principle remains the same that a fiduciary should not profit because of the misuse of material non-public information or a breach of the duty of loyalty. One court fashioned a remedy to deduct trading profits from claims that were sold against distributions on claims retained by the insider. In re Philadelphia & W. Ry., 64 F. Supp. 738, 741 (E.D. Pa. 1946). What effect, if any, will the purchase from the insider have on the acquirer?[33] Unless the acquirer is a bona fide purchaser for value, the acquirer who knowingly purchases a claim from a fiduciary can be held jointly and severally liable for the profits of the transferor. In re Los Angeles Lumber Prods. Co., 46 F. Supp. 77, 92-94 (S.D. Cal. 1941). But cf., In re Latham Lithographic Corp., 107 F.2d 749, 750 (2d Cir. 1939) (purchaser of claim has right to vote to elect trustee, even if assignor did not, as long as assignment in good faith and not a subterfuge). Since the filing of bankruptcy seemingly constitutes a default and causes acceleration of the debt, the purchaser of a negotiable instrument with notice of the bankruptcy case will not be a holder in due course, although the purchaser could have the rights of a holder in due course if the seller was a holder in due course. See UCC §§ 3-203(b), 3-302(a)(2), 3-304(b). The status of the seller is difficult, if not impossible, to determine in the context of a market purchase.[34]

Two additional issues will concern those who wish to buy or sell claims. First, several debtors in possession—Ames Department Stores and Pan Am—obtained orders prohibiting or limiting trading in claims because of the effect that trading might have on the debtors' net operating loss tax attributes. See Fortgang & Mayer, *Developments in Trading Claims: Participations and Disputed Claims,* 15 CARDOZO L. REV. 733, 756-59 (1993) (hereinafter Fortgang & Mayer, *Developments*). We discuss net operating losses below in Chapter Twelve; for now it is enough to know that a debtor with past losses can in some circumstances use those past losses to offset future profits and thus save on income taxes. If there is too great a change in the ownership of the debtor, the debtor's ability to use its past net operating losses to save on future taxes may be limited or eliminated. The Second Circuit, in Official Comm. of Unsecured Creditors v. PSS S.S. Co. (In re Prudential Lines, Inc.), 928 F.2d 565 (2d Cir. 1991), held that the debtor's net operating losses were property of the estate and that actions taken that would prevent the use of the

---

33. Whether or not the acquisition is from a fiduciary, the acquirer will be precluded from objecting to the discharge of an individual debtor. Young v. Beugen (In re Beugen), 99 B.R. 961 (B.A.P. 9th Cir. 1989), aff'd, 930 F.2d 26 (9th Cir. 1991).

34. Although the matter is not free from doubt, the Resolution Trust Corporation and Federal Deposit Insurance Corporation may be holders in due course of claims that they hold against a bankrupt company. Compare FDIC v. Meo, 505 F.2d 790 (9th Cir. 1974) with Langley v. FDIC, 484 U.S. 86, 108 S. Ct. 396, 98 L. Ed. 2d 340 (1987) and Dendinger v. First Nat'l Corp., 16 F.3d 99 (5th Cir. 1994) (following prior Fifth Circuit decision and quoting it for the proposition that "the *Langley* Court destroyed the 'wholly innocent borrower' exception to the *D'Oench, Duhme* doctrine").

net operating losses were therefore prohibited by the automatic stay. Debtors in possession have used *Prudential Lines* to argue that the bankruptcy court can prohibit or limit trading in claims to protect net operating losses. Fortgang & Mayer, *Developments,* supra, at 756-59.

Second, some debtors in possession have attempted to discriminate against claims purchasers in their plans of reorganization. Id. at 763. As we discuss in Chapter Fifteen (dealing with cramdown), there is some authority that the claims of trade creditors with whom the debtor needs to continue to do business can be separately classified and treated more favorably than other general unsecured claims without the discrimination being considered to be "unfair discrimination" under § 1129(b). To the extent that plans are permitted to discriminate against purchasers of trade claims just because the debtor does not need a relationship with the purchaser, trading in trade claims will certainly be chilled, with the result that trade creditors who wish to sell their claims for cash either will be unable to do so or will receive a lower price. Such discrimination also violates the long-established principle that "a claim in the hands of a buyer is no different than a claim in the hands of a seller." Id. at 759.

The controversial process of trading in claims should become more defined as case law develops. In the meantime, parties involved in the process proceed at their peril.[35] For more information on this developing area of the law see Groshong, *Trading Claims in Bankruptcy: Debtor Issues*, 10 AM. BANKR. INST. L. REV. 625 (2002); Drain & Schwartz, *Are Bankruptcy Claims Subject to the Federal Securities Laws?*, 10 AM. BANKR. INST. L. REV. 569 (2002); Novikoff, *Update on Recent Developments in Trading Claims and Taking Control of Corporations in Chapter 11*, in CHAPTER 11 BUSINESS REORGANIZATIONS 197 (Annual Advanced ALI-ABA Course of Study, No. SE71, 2000), available at SE71 ALI-ABA 197 (Westlaw); Donegan, Note & Comment, *Covering The "Security Blanket": Regulating Bankruptcy Claims And Claim-Participations Trading Under the Federal Securities Laws*, 14 BANKR. DEV. J. 381 (1998); Tung, *Confirmation and Claims Trading*, 90 Nw. U.L. REV. 1684 (1996); Neely, supra, *Brave New World*; Fortgang & Mayer, *Developments,* supra; Logan, Note, *Claims Trading: The Need for Further Amending Federal Rule of Bankruptcy Procedure 3001(e)(2)*, 2 AM. BANKR. INST. L. REV. 495 (1994); Whitaker, Note, *Regulating Claims Trading in Chapter 11 Bankruptcies: A Proposal for Mandatory Disclosure*, 3 CORNELL J.L. & PUB. POL'Y 303 (1994).

---

35. To discover how perilous the process can be, see In re Allegheny Int'l, Inc., 118 B.R. 282 (Bankr. W.D. Pa. 1990).

PART V

RESTRUCTURING THE DEBTS AND DIVIDING THE ENTERPRISE'S VALUE

Chapter Eleven

Proposing a Plan of Reorganization — Exclusivity, Classification, and Impairment

A. INTRODUCTION

As we will see, the debtor typically has the first opportunity to file a plan of reorganization. Before filing a plan, the debtor typically will negotiate its terms with the creditors and other interested parties, so that the plan has a good chance of being confirmed. To understand this process, we must understand the basic elements of a plan of reorganization.

Consider the following summary of a simple plan of reorganization for Acme, Inc., a fictitious corporation. Assume the following facts. Acme owns real property on which its factory is located. First Bank holds the first mortgage on the real property and is fully secured. The contractual interest rate on the first mortgage is 6%, slightly less than the 6.5% interest rate that we assume is the present fair market rate for first mortgages of this kind. Second Finance Company ("SFC") holds a second mortgage (with a contractual interest rate of 11% and eight years of payments remaining) and is only partially secured. Other creditors also hold unsecured claims. Acme owes no priority claims other than administrative claims and tax claims. All of the stock in Acme is common stock.

SUMMARY OF PLAN OF REORGANIZATION FOR ACME, INC.
PROPOSED BY DEBTOR, ACME, INC.

I. Classification of Claims and Interests:
    A. Class 1 consists of the secured claim of First Bank, which is the first mortgage on Acme's factory property.
    B. Class 2 consists of the secured claim of Second Finance Company ("SFC"), which is the second mortgage on Acme's factory property.
    C. Class 3 consists of all unsecured claims (including SFC's deficiency claim if any) other than claims that are in Class 4.

D.   Class 4 consists of all general unsecured claims that are allowed in the amount of $200 or less. Any holder of an unsecured claim that is allowed in an amount greater than $200 and who agrees that the claim will be treated (for all bankruptcy related and nonbankruptcy related purposes) as having been in the amount of $200 as of the date of the order for relief, may elect to have its reduced, $200 claim included in Class 4.

E.   Class 5 consists of the interests of the common stockholders of Acme.

II.   Treatment of Classes

A.   Class 1 is unimpaired. The legal, equitable, and contractual rights of the holder of the claim in Class 1 will be unaltered.

B.   The holder of the claim in Class 2 will receive payment of the value of its interest in the factory property (the value of the property minus the principal amount of First Bank's mortgage) together with 10% interest per annum in 120 equal monthly payments. The holder will retain its lien on Acme's factory property only to secure the payments provided for in this Plan with respect to Class 2.

C.   The holders of the claims in Class 3 will receive 5% of the amount of their claims in cash on the effective date; promissory notes in an amount equal to 25% of the amount of their claims, which shall be payable in five equal annual installments of principal and interest, at a rate of 12% per annum simple interest; and one share of common stock in the reorganized Acme for each $100 of claim.

D.   Class 4 is unimpaired. The legal, equitable, and contractual rights of holders of claims in Class 4 are unaltered by this plan. Confirmation of this plan does not constitute a determination of whether the rights of holders of claims in Class 4 may have been altered in some manner by the federal bankruptcy laws other than by confirmation of this plan. Acme intends to pay each holder of a claim in Class 4 cash on the effective date of the plan equal to the allowed amount of the holder's claim. Acme intends to tender payment to each holder by means of a check that will not be marked "payment in full" and that will not in any other way constitute an offer of an accord. Any additional rights that any holder of a claim in Class 4 may have (such as the possible right to interest on the Class 4 claim) will therefore, because of applicable nonbankruptcy law and not because of the terms of this plan, be unaffected by the holder's obtaining of payment of the check.

E.   The holders of the interests in Class 5 will receive one share of common stock in the reorganized Acme for each five shares of stock currently held. All existing shares of stock in Acme will be cancelled.

III.   Treatment of Unclassified Claims

A.   Holders of allowed administrative expense claims (§ 507(a)(2)) will receive payment in cash in full on the effective date of the plan (or as soon as the claims are allowed, if the claims are not allowed until after the effective date), unless they agree to other treatment. Holders of administrative priority claims for goods sold and services rendered postpetition (other than professional services rendered in connection with this case) will be paid in the ordinary course, according to the terms agreed upon when the claims were incurred.

B.   Holders of priority tax claims (§ 507(a)(8)) will be paid in full (with interest from the effective date of the plan at the rate determined by applicable nonbankruptcy law) by equal payments made at least semiannually over a period ending five years from the date of the filing of the petition in this case.

IV. Means for Implementation of Plan
  A. The assets of Acme's metal fabrication division will be sold to Metalmatic Corp. for a cash payment pursuant to the asset sales agreement executed by Acme and Metalmatic Corp.
  B. Acme will retain the remainder of its assets for use in its business, other than the cash that is to be paid to holders of administrative expense claims and claims in Classes 3 and 4.
  C. On the effective date of the plan, Acme will issue promissory notes and shares of its common stock pursuant to the terms of this plan to holders of the claims in Class 3 and to holders of the interests in Class 5.

V. Effective Date: The effective date of this plan shall be the first business day on which no stay of implementation of this plan is in effect and that is at least eleven days after entry of the order of confirmation of this plan.

Note that Acme's plan includes three basic elements that are required by § 1123. First, it designates classes of claims and interests. See § 1123(a)(1). As required by § 1122(a), only claims that are substantially similar are placed together in the same class.[1] Note that the secured claims are each placed in a separate class because they are not substantially similar. Although the collateral for the two claims is the same, they have different priority; First Bank's first mortgage is senior to SFC's second mortgage. Later in this chapter, and again in Chapter Fifteen, we will explore several very important classification issues.

Second, the plan specifies how each class will be treated and identifies any classes that are not impaired. See § 1123(a)(2) and (3). Each claim or interest in a particular class is treated the same as every other claim or interest in the same class, as required by § 1123(a)(4). Thus each unsecured creditor with a claim in Class 3 will receive the same amount of cash, debt, and stock for each $100 of claim. (Creditors with larger claims thus receive more value.) In addition, the plan provides the treatment required by the Code for claims that are not eligible to be placed in classes—administrative expense claims and priority tax claims. See §§ 1123(a)(1), 1129(a)(9)(A) & (C).[2]

---

1.   The plan classifies SFC's unsecured claim (which it has as an undersecured creditor) together with other unsecured claims. Recall that, even if SFC's debt is "nonrecourse"—meaning that SFC would be entitled outside of chapter 11 only to foreclose on its collateral if Acme defaulted, and not entitled to seek payment of any deficiency from Acme—SFC likely will have an unsecured claim for the amount by which it is undersecured, unless SFC makes the election permitted by § 1111(b). See §§ 506(a)(1) and 1111(b), and the discussion supra in Chapter Nine. If SFC's debt would be nonrecourse outside of chapter 11, then there is an argument that its unsecured claim is not substantially similar to the other unsecured claims and must therefore be classified separately. We discuss that argument in Chapter Fifteen. We also discuss in Chapter Fifteen the very important question whether the debtor has discretion to classify an undersecured creditor's unsecured claim separately from other unsecured claims, even if they are all considered to be substantially similar. Note that § 1122(a) does not explicitly require that all substantially similar claims be put in one class, but simply that no claims be put together unless they are substantially similar.

2.   Section 1123(a)(1) requires that the plan designate classes of claims and interests other than the priority claims specified in § 507(a)(2), (a)(3), and (a)(8). The Code does not expressly prohibit placing those priority claims in classes, but doing so has no effect. Each holder of a § 507(a)(2), (a)(3), or (a)(8) priority

Impairment, defined in § 1124, is a key concept that will be explored later in this chapter. Important consequences flow from the decision of the plan drafter to impair or not to impair a class.

Holders of allowed claims or interests in impaired classes are permitted to vote on the plan. Section 1126(a) and (f). The plan can be confirmed consensually under § 1129(a) only if all impaired classes accept the plan by the required majorities. See §§ 1126(c) & (d), 1129(a)(8). Holders of claims or interests in unimpaired classes do not get to vote on the plan; they and their unimpaired classes are conclusively deemed to have accepted the plan. See § 1126(f). Thus, by leaving Class 4 unimpaired, Acme can avoid the expense of soliciting votes from the holders of the small claims in that class and avoid the worry that they might not accept the plan.

Holders of claims or interests in unimpaired classes are not eligible for protection under the "fair and equitable" standard of § 1129(b). Thus, as we will see, by leaving First Bank unimpaired Acme can avoid the possibility that it might have to raise the interest rate on First Bank's mortgage.

Almost all plans will impair at least one class of claims. Assuming the plan does so, then the plan cannot be confirmed consensually or in a cramdown unless at least one impaired class of claims accepts the plan, not counting acceptances of insiders. Thus the debtor must try to make sure that the plan creates and impairs at least one class of claims that will accept the plan without the aid of insiders' acceptances. See § 1129(a)(10), (b)(1).

Third, the plan provides adequate means for implementing its terms. See § 1123(a)(5). One division of Acme will be sold off under the plan to raise cash needed to implement the plan. That cash and some of the cash saved up by Acme during the case will be used to make the cash payments that the plan requires to be made on its effective date. Acme will use the rest of its assets to run its business; that will allow it to implement the plan by generating the cash needed to make future payments on the promissory notes given out under the plan.

---

claim is entitled to a certain kind of treatment under the plan regardless of whether other holders of such claims support the plan or try to vote for it. See § 1129(a)(9)(A), (C). Thus a vote by members of a class of such priority claimants cannot have any effect on the rights of the dissenting members of the class. There is therefore no point in creating such classes, except possibly for ease of reference to the claims. Plans sometimes do place such claims into classes, and some courts tolerate the creation of such classes as a harmless exercise; others do not. Certainly such a class should not be considered to be a class for purposes of determining whether the confirmation requirements of § 1129 have been met. See Travelers Ins. Co. v. Bryson Properties, XVIII (In re Bryson Properties, XVIII), 961 F.2d 496, 501 n. 8 (4th Cir. 1992); In re Union Meeting Partners, 165 B.R. 553, 568-69 (Bankr. E.D. Pa. 1994), aff'd, 52 F.3d 317 (3d Cir. 1995) (unpublished table opinion); In re Perdido Motel Group, Inc., 101 B.R. 289, 293-94 (Bankr. N.D. Ala. 1989). The 2005 BAPCPA added § 1129(a)(9)(D) to the Code; it requires that holders of secured tax claims that would have been § 507(a)((8) priority tax claims if they were unsecured are entitled to the same priority treatment under a plan that § 507(a)(8) claims must receive. There is a question whether a class consisting of one or more such secured tax claims should be considered to be a class for purposes of the confirmation requirements of § 1129; note that, just as with a supposed class of § 507(a)(8) unsecured priority tax claims, a vote by members of such a secured tax claim class cannot have any effect on the treatment that the plan must provide for holders of claims in the class.

It has been argued that § 1123(a)(5) preempts nonbankruptcy laws that would limit the provisions of a plan concerning plan implementation. Section § 1123(a) begins with the phrase, "Notwithstanding any otherwise applicable nonbankruptcy law." Note that § 1142(a) (concerning plan implementation) begins with a very similar phrase but seemingly is more limited: "Notwithstanding any otherwise applicable nonbankruptcy law, rule, or regulation *relating to financial condition* * * *." Id. (emphasis supplied). Those phrases were added to §§ 1123(a) and 1142(a) by the same act in 1984. The Ninth Circuit held in 2003 that the preemptive effect of § 1123(a)(5) is limited to laws "relating to financial condition," arguing that the phrases in §§ 1123(a)(5) and 1142(a) should be read together, and that the legislative history did not support an expansive reading of the phrase in § 1123(a)(5). Pac. Gas & Elec. Co. v. California ex rel. Cal. Dept. of Toxic Substances Control, 350 F.3d 932 (9th Cir. 2003) (reversing district court's reversal of bankruptcy court order disapproving disclosure statement for plan that relied on express preemption by § 1123(a)(5) of California public utilities laws). The United States argued as an amicus that the plan proponents' broad interpretation of § 1123(a)(5) could lead to preemption of federal environmental laws and should be rejected. Id. at 937.

Although the Code does not require it expressly, the plan sets an effective date. An effective date must be set so that the court can make the finding required by the best interests of creditors test in § 1129(a)(7), which refers to "value, as of the effective date of the plan" (and, if a cramdown is needed, the findings required by § 1129(b)(2), which also refers to the effective date). The effective date set by the plan respects the command of Rule 3020(e), which provides for a ten day stay of the order confirming the plan (unless the court orders otherwise). Note that, if the plan is confirmed, objecting parties will have that same ten day period in which to file a notice of appeal. See Rule 8002(a). If there is no further stay of implementation of the plan, the plan goes into effect on the eleventh day after entry of the order of confirmation (or on the next business day if the eleventh day is not a business day). That gives an objecting party the required opportunity to file a notice of appeal and to seek a further stay, but not a day more. If, as is likely, no further stay is granted, the effective date provision in the plan will cause the plan to go quickly into effect even though an appeal is pending. The plan then will likely be implemented irreversibly before the appeal can be heard, which will result in dismissal of the appeal as moot. See text following footnote 11 in Chapter Sixteen below.

B. EXCLUSIVITY AND THE FILING OF PLANS

In an out of court workout, the debtor typically proposes terms; the creditors then typically try to negotiate changes in the debtor's proposal. They cannot force the debtor to agree to any particular terms. If the creditors demand too much, the debtor simply can refuse to agree. The creditors then can use their state law rights to force a piecemeal liquidation of the debtor's assets, but they cannot not force the debtor to agree to a reorganization.

By the same token, outside of bankruptcy each individual creditor can decide whether to be bound by a proposed workout agreement. The debtor cannot reorganize in a workout without the support of almost all creditors; thus the creditors can keep a workout from succeeding unless the terms are acceptable to them. Indeed, even if the vast majority of creditors agree on terms for a workout, the dissenting creditors will not be bound by it and can insist on payment in full. See supra Chapter One, sections B and C, and Chapter Two, section B.

Who then should be in control of the reorganization process in chapter 11? Who should be permitted to propose plans on which creditors and interest holders will vote? One approach would be to give the debtor a permanent exclusive right to file plans; creditors could then reject the debtor's proposals and thus force eventual liquidation but could not force a plan of reorganization on the debtor. That approach, the one taken under the old Bankruptcy Act's chapter XI, would force the creditors to agree to the debtor's plan or else face the loss of the going concern value of the business. Another approach would be to give every party in interest an equal right to file a plan. That approach, much like the approach taken under the old Bankruptcy Act's chapter X, would take away from the debtor the right to control the direction of the reorganization. The prospect of losing control would cause debtors to put off filing petitions—probably for so long that their businesses would typically be too depleted to be reorganized by the time they filed bankruptcy petitions.

When it enacted the Bankruptcy Code, Congress decided to take a middle approach, giving the debtor the exclusive right to file a plan for a limited period of time—a period of time designed to give the debtor a fair opportunity to propose and confirm a plan of reorganization. Thus § 1121(a) permits the debtor to file a plan at any time. Parties other than the debtor cannot file a plan unless a trustee is appointed, or unless the debtor fails to file a plan within 120 days after the order for relief, or unless the debtor fails to obtain acceptances of its plan from all impaired classes within 180 days after the order for relief. Section 1121(b), (c). The 120 day and 180 day "exclusivity periods" can be reduced or extended by the court "for cause." See § 1121(d) (limiting extensions to approximately 14 additional months as amended in 2005). Once the relevant periods expire, the debtor has lost exclusivity, and any party in interest can file a plan. See § 1121(c). (A different scheme applies if the debtor is a "small business debtor" as defined in § 101(51D), so that the case is a "small business case" as defined in § 101(51C). See § 1121(e); Interim Rule 1020.)

The 120 day exclusivity period is designed to give the debtor the time that is needed to prepare for filing a plan. Initially, the debtor's managers will be spending all of their time stabilizing the business, obtaining the cash needed to keep the business afloat, and beginning to take the steps needed to turn the business around. Then the debtor must determine what its economic future is likely to hold; the debtor cannot negotiate seriously with creditors about the terms of the plan until it has some idea of the cash flows that it will likely have in the future out of which payments to creditors can be made. Once the debtor has a sense of what the financial future is likely to bring, the debtor can begin to negotiate with creditors to determine what they would be willing to accept in the debt restructuring. Only after those negotiations will the typical debtor be ready to draft and file a realistic plan that has a reasonable chance of being confirmed.

The 180 day period is designed to give the debtor the time that is needed to obtain acceptances of its plan from all the impaired classes. In the typical case, neither acceptances nor rejections can be solicited until a disclosure statement has been approved and distributed to the creditors and interest holders, so that they can cast informed votes. (Disclosure, solicitation, and voting are the subject of Chapter Thirteen of this book.) Even though the debtor will have negotiated with creditors before filing its plan, further negotiations often occur after it is filed; they often result in amendments to the plan. That may require that an amended disclosure statement be prepared, approved, and distributed; if parties have already voted, they may need to be given an opportunity to change their votes. Assuming the debtor files its initial plan near the end of the 120 day period, the 180 period will give the debtor roughly sixty days to do all of this and to obtain acceptances from all the impaired classes. Congress may have been overly optimistic in thinking that this could usually be accomplished in sixty days after the filing of a plan, but that is the statutory framework.

The 120 and 180 day exclusivity periods also give the creditors time to cool off and to decide that it is better after all for the debtor's business not to be liquidated. Many creditors will see the chapter 11 filing as a betrayal of trust by the debtor. They also will likely believe that the debtor's business loses money each day it stays in operation—money that could have been used to pay them something on their debts. Thus if creditors could file plans immediately, they would be likely to file plans calling for the liquidation of the debtor. The exclusivity periods give the debtor a chance to convince the creditors that rehabilitation of the business rather than liquidation is in their best interest.

Part of that persuasion will likely come from the continued business that the debtor likely will do with its trade creditors. During the exclusivity periods the debtor likely will continue to buy goods and services—very likely on a cash on delivery basis—from many of the trade creditors. They may see that it is better to help the debtor to rehabilitate its business and save a customer than to act out of anger. They may also see that the debtor is taking effective steps to turn its business around so that it will have a substantial positive cash flow from operations. That may convince them that continuation of the debtor's business will not use up assets but rather will generate cash that can be used to pay debts. The creditors may come to the conclusion that more value will be available to pay debts if the business continues than if it is liquidated.

The exclusivity periods also give the debtor negotiating leverage. The creditors have an incentive to accept a reasonable plan proposed by the debtor; the alternative is to face the delay involved in waiting until the exclusivity periods (and any extensions of them) expire, so that creditors can file their own plans. On the other hand, Congress did not intend to allow the debtor to threaten undue delay in order to coerce creditors into accepting an unfair plan. In creating one unified business reorganization chapter to replace the several different chapters under the old Bankruptcy Act, Congress tried to strike a balance between the lack of debtor control under the old Act's chapter X and the lack of creditor control under the old Act's chapter XI:

> Under chapter X * * * any party in interest, including the trustee, creditors, and the debtor, may propose a plan. This feature has been heavily disfavored by debtors when choosing a reorganization chapter, because they lose control over the future of the enterprise.
>
> By contrast, chapter XI gives the debtor the exclusive right to propose a plan. Creditors are excluded. The exclusive right gives the debtor undue bargaining leverage, because by delay he can force a settlement out of otherwise unwilling creditors * * * . The debtor is in full control, often to the unfair disadvantage of creditors.
>
> Proposed chapter 11 recognizes the need for the debtor to remain in control to some degree, or else debtors will avoid the reorganization provisions in the bill until it would be too late for them to be an effective remedy. At the same time, the bill recognizes the legitimate interests of creditors, whose money is in the enterprise as much as the debtor's, to have a say in the future of the company. The bill gives the debtor an exclusive right to propose a plan for 120 days.

H.R. Rep. No. 595, 95th Cong. 1st Sess. 231-32 (1977) (footnotes omitted).

Use the following problems to test your understanding of the mechanics of the exclusivity periods.

Problem 11-1

Foam Corporation filed its chapter 11 petition on April 10, 2006. If Foam Corporation does not file a plan and does not seek any extension of exclusivity, when may Kick Credit file a plan? If Foam Corporation files a plan on August 4, 2006 but does not obtain the acceptance of every impaired class, when may Kick Credit file a plan?

Would it matter if Foam Corporation obtained approval of its disclosure statement on October 3, 2006? The pre-December 1, 1996 version of Rule 3016(a) would have prohibited Kick from filing a plan after approval of Foam Corporation's disclosure statement, until and unless Kick obtained the court's approval to file one, or until the court denied confirmation of Foam Corporation's plan. The Bankruptcy Rules must be consistent with the Bankruptcy Code, see 28 U.S.C. § 2075, and thus it was held that courts were required to give approval under Rule 3016(a) for filing of "good faith, nonfrivolous competing plan[s,]" where exclusivity had terminated under § 1121, at least absent "a compelling reason" not to give approval. In re Landmark Park Plaza Ltd. Partnership, 167 B.R. 752 (Bankr. D. Conn. 1994). That version of Rule 3016(a) was abrogated effective December 1, 1996. But if Kick Credit files a plan after the court approves Foam Corporation's disclosure statement, could Kick Credit have practical difficulties obtaining an opportunity to have its proposed plan confirmed? Consider this excerpt from the Committee Note, prepared by the Committee on Rules of Practice and Procedure of the Judicial Conference of the United States, which accompanied the Committee's proposal to abrogate the prior version of Rule 3016(a):

Section 1121(c) gives a party in interest the right to file a chapter 11 plan after expiration of the period when only the debtor may file a plan. Under § 1121(d), the exclusive period in which only the debtor may file a plan may be extended, but only if a party in interest so requests and the court, after notice and a hearing, finds cause for an extension. Subdivision (a) [of Rule 3016] is abrogated because it could have the effect of extending the debtor's exclusive period for filing a plan without satisfying the requirements of § 1121(d). The abrogation of subdivision (a) does not affect the court's discretion with respect to the scheduling of hearings on the approval of disclosure statements when more than one plan has been filed.

Problem 11-2

Suppose that as of the petition filing date Debtor (a manufacturer of skates) owed $1 million to Bank for a loan, $800,000 to various trade creditors for goods and services, and an unknown amount—but probably at least $500,000—to Victor Victim, who had been injured in a fall when a defective skate manufactured by Debtor failed. How can we determine whether Debtor's case is a "small business case"? See § 101(51C), (51D); Interim Rule 1020. How might Debtor, the creditors, or the United States trustee influence that determination? What if the case has an active creditors' committee at the beginning that becomes inactive 300 days into the case? Can a debtor change status during the case? Compare the provisions of § 1121(e) with the exclusivity provisions that would apply if Debtor's case were not a small business case. Which seem more favorable to Debtor? Are there potential benefits to Debtor if its case is considered to be a small business case? See §§ 1102(a)(3), 1125(f). Suppose Debtor's case is a small business case, that Debtor files a plan 175 days after the order for relief, and that a creditor then files a plan 185 days after the order for relief. Should the court schedule hearings so that both plans can be considered by creditors together? Or should the court "fast track" the debtor's plan so that it will be considered first? See § 1129(e). Note that once one plan is confirmed, generally no other plan can proceed to confirmation. See § 1129(c).

The key issue with regard to exclusivity is under what circumstances courts should grant extensions of exclusivity so as to maintain the balance struck by Congress. That balance can be threatened if the 120 day and 180 day periods (applicable in cases that are not small business cases) do not give the debtor enough time to put together and obtain acceptances of a realistic plan. The balance can also be threatened (in the opposite way) if a court too readily grants extensions of the exclusivity periods. That would permit the debtor to take longer than is necessary to put together a plan, thus harming the creditors who are waiting for payment and whose claims are not accruing postpetition interest. It would also permit the debtor to use the threat of delay to force creditors to accept an unfair plan.

The legislative history discusses reasons for extending or reducing the 120 and 180 day periods, although the House and Senate Reports may be at cross purposes. The House Report states:

> In most cases, 120 days will give the debtor adequate time to negotiate a settlement, without unduly delaying creditors. The court is given the power, though, to increase or reduce the 120-day period depending on the circumstances of the case. For example, if an unusually large company were to seek reorganization under chapter 11, the court would probably need to extend the time in order to allow the debtor to reach an agreement. If, on the other hand, a debtor delayed in arriving at an agreement, the court could shorten the period and permit creditors to formulate and propose a reorganization plan.

H.R. Rep. No. 595, 95th Cong. 1st Sess. 232 (footnotes omitted). The House Report also states that cause for an increase or a reduction in the exclusivity periods "might include an unusually large or unusually small case, delay by the debtor, or recalcitrance among creditors." Id. at 406. The Senate Report states:

> Since, the debtor has an exclusive privilege for 6 months during which others may not file a plan, the granted extension should be based on a showing of some promise of probable success. An extension should not be employed as a tactical device to put pressure on parties in interest to yield to a plan they consider unsatisfactory.

S. Rep. No. 95-989, 95th Cong., 2d Sess. 118 (1978) (referring to 180 day period after the order for relief—approximately six months—during which debtor has exclusivity if debtor files a plan within 120 days after the order for relief).[3]

How will a court determine whether a case is so large and complex that more than 120 days is needed to propose a realistic plan? Should an extension be granted simply because of size and complexity without a showing of probable success? What is "success"? Is confirmation of a plan in a cramdown "success," so that a debtor may be entitled to prevent creditors from filing plans even if there is no hope of success in negotiations? If the debtor seeks an extension of exclusivity because negotiations toward a plan have made slow progress, how will a court determine whether there is "recalcitrance among the creditors" or whether, on the other hand, the debtor is seeking to use delay to coerce creditors into accepting a "plan they consider unsatisfactory"? Can creditors be considered recalcitrant for not agreeing to a plan they consider unsatisfactory? If actions taken by creditors—such as filing motions to dismiss and motions for relief from stay—prevent the debtor from focusing its attention on negotiation of a plan, is there cause for an extension of exclusivity? If there are large disputed claims in the case—either claims against the debtor or claims that the debtor is asserting against others—should the debtor be granted an extension on the ground that those disputes must be resolved before a realistic plan can be proposed?

---

3.   The joint explanatory statement of the House and Senate floor managers—printed beginning at 124 Cong. Rec. 32,398 (Rep. Edwards) and 124 Cong. Rec. 33,998 (Sen. DeConcini)—says that § 1121 as agreed to by the Conference Committee was derived from the House version of § 1121. See 124 Cong. Rec. S17,419 (daily ed. Oct. 6, 1978). While that might suggest that the House Report is more authoritative, the House and Senate versions of § 1121 were nearly identical, and the only possibly substantive difference between them was resolved in favor of the Senate version.

In deciding whether to extend exclusivity, courts often consider a lengthy list of factors:

> Fortunately, courts have distilled certain factors to consider when tasked with deciding whether to on the one hand, extend, or on the other, terminate, a debtor's statutory period of exclusivity. While not all courts agree on the precise formulation, most rely on the same factors. For the purposes here, we will use the factors as stated by the court in In re Express One Int'l, Inc., 194 B.R. 98, 100 (Bankr. E.D. Tex. 1996), with the exception that the seventh factor, being essentially the same as the second, will not be addressed. That court listed the following nine factors:
> 1. the size and complexity of the case;
> 2. the necessity of sufficient time to permit the debtor to negotiate a plan of reorganization and prepare adequate information;
> 3. the existence of good faith progress toward reorganization;
> 4. the fact that the debtor is paying its bills as they become due;
> 5. whether the debtor has demonstrated reasonable prospects for filing a viable plan;
> 6. whether the debtor has made progress in negotiations with its creditors;
> 7. the amount of time which has elapsed in the case;
> 8. whether the debtor is seeking an extension of exclusivity in order to pressure creditors to submit to the debtor's reorganization demands; and
> 9. whether an unresolved contingency exists.

In re Dow Corning Corp., 208 B.R. 661, 664-65 (Bankr. E.D. Mich. 1997). In affirming an order extending exclusivity, the Ninth Circuit Bankruptcy Appellate Panel observed that the case was close because

> [A]ffirmative answers to a number of the inquiries listed in *Dow Corning* and *Express One* do not necessarily favor extending exclusivity. Professors Epstein, Nickles, and White have cogently debunked the propositions that complex cases require extended exclusivity, negotiations are facilitated by extended exclusivity, and pending litigation warrants extended exclusivity. EPSTEIN ET AL., § 11-15.
> There is truth in their observation, backed by examples from prominent cases, that a likely consequence of the denial of an extension of exclusivity is "not that creditor plans will be proposed and approved, but that the threat of such plans will cause the debtor to come forward more quickly than he might otherwise." Id. (footnote omitted). For example, in the *Public Service Co. of New Hampshire* case, which still qualifies as one of the all-time largest and most complex chapter 11 cases and which (as here) required independent negotiations with governmental entities, the debtor was permitted one seven-month exclusivity extension. A second extension was denied in the face of apparent deadlock, after which a consensual plan was achieved. EPSTEIN ET AL., § 11-15.
> Even if a competing plan were to be filed, the court would retain control over scheduling confirmation. It is, for example, common for competing plans to be placed on the same schedule so that they can be considered in tandem.
> We also agree with the *Dow Corning* court that a transcendent consideration is whether adjustment of exclusivity will facilitate moving the case forward toward a fair and equitable resolution.

The key question to us, then, is whether the first extension of exclusivity functioned to facilitate movement towards a fair and equitable resolution of the case, taking into account all the divergent interests involved.

Official Comm. of Unsecured Creditors v. Henry Mayo Newhall Mem'l Hosp. (In re Henry Mayo Newhall Mem'l Hosp.), 282 B.R. 444, 452-53 (B.A.P. 9th Cir. 2002).

In re Newark Airport/Hotel Limited Partnership
United States Bankruptcy Court, District of New Jersey, 1993
156 B.R. 444, aff'd, 155 B.R. 93 (D.N.J. 1993)

[FGH, the holder of the mortgage on debtor's hotel property, sought relief from the automatic stay so that it could foreclose on the hotel. At the same time, the debtor sought an extension of the exclusivity periods. The following excerpt includes not only the court's discussion of the motion for an extension of exclusivity but also the discussion of FGH's argument that it was entitled to relief from the stay under § 362(d)(2). In discussing that argument the court discusses the likelihood that debtor will be able to reorganize successfully—a factor that is also relevant to debtor's motion for extension of exclusivity.]

WILLIAM F. TUOHEY, Bankruptcy Judge.

* * * FGH argues initially that relief from the automatic stay is appropriate because the debtor has no equity in the Hotel and the Hotel is not necessary to an effective reorganization that is in prospect.

With regard to whether the debtor has any equity in the Hotel, it has been stipulated that FGH's debt exceeds the value of the Hotel and that the debtor has no equity. Thus, FGH is an undersecured creditor and the first requirement of § 362(d)(2) is deemed satisfied.

Whether or not the Hotel is necessary for an effective reorganization requires a more in depth analysis of the factual situation of the debtor. In this regard, the burden is on the debtor to demonstrate that the property is necessary for its reorganization efforts. 11 U.S.C. § 362(g)(2). As the United States Supreme Court stated, such a showing must demonstrate that: 1) the property is essential for an effective reorganization that is in prospect; and 2) there is "a reasonable possibility of a successful reorganization within a reasonable time." United Savings Assoc. v. Timbers of Inwood Forest Assoc., 484 U.S. 365, 376, 108 S.Ct. 626, 633, 98 L.Ed.2d 740 (1988). While the debtor need not prove that the plan will actually be confirmed, the proof cannot be entirely speculative and there must be some evidence that the plan is achievable.

In the instant case, the debtor filed its petition on July 7, 1992 and, at the time the within motions were filed, the case was not even four (4) months old. Given the early stage in the proceedings, the debtor has provided ample evidence to support a finding that there is a reasonable possibility of a successful reorganization within a reasonable period of time. In particular, the debtor has indicated that, to the extent necessary to fund a plan, it has a source of funding available from its limited partners.[4] Moreover, as the record shows, the Hotel is an ongoing business with over one hundred (100) employees and has ongoing contractual agreements with several airlines to provide guaranteed rooms. In addition, the Hotel has a number of contractual commitments for private parties in its restaurant and catering facilities. Finally, the debtor has been generating sufficient revenues to pay its expenses and to pay FGH pursuant to the consent cash collateral order entered by this court on October 20, 1992.

As the United States Supreme Court stated in *Timbers,* "the bankruptcy courts demand less detailed showings during the four months in which the debtor is given the exclusive right to put together a plan." *Timbers,* 484 U.S. at 376, 108 S. Ct. at 633. Had FGH allowed the debtor more time to develop its reorganization efforts before bringing the within motion, the debtor would have been required to make a stronger showing. See In re Marion Street Partnership, 108 B.R. at 225. Nevertheless, at this early stage in the proceedings, the debtor has met its burden imposed by § 362(g)(2). * * *

Extension of Debtor's Exclusivity Period Pursuant to § 1121(d)

The court's authority to grant the debtor's request for an extension of its exclusivity period is found in § 1121(d) * * * . Since the debtor seeks the extension, the burden is on it to demonstrate the existence of good cause. As the legislative history to § 1121(d) indicates, the legislature intended that the granting of an extension would be based "on a showing of some promise of probable success [for reorganization]." 11 U.S.C.A. § 1121(d) (Historical and Revision Notes, S. Rept. No. 95-989). Further, "[a]n extension should not be employed as a tactical measure to put pressure on parties in interest to yield to a plan they consider unsatisfactory." Id.

The court notes that FGH's principal argument in opposition to the debtor's request is that the debtor does not offer any justification in its motion papers for preventing creditors from the opportunity to propose their own plan. FGH furthers states that it would like the opportunity to propose its own plan, and, in a case like this with a simple capital structure and where the debtor is clearly insolvent, there is no just reason to delay that happening. The court disagrees.

The purpose of the debtor's exclusivity period is to make a chapter 11 filing attractive enough to encourage ailing businesses to seek reorganization without unduly delaying creditors. If the chapter 11 provisions did not enable the debtor to remain in control for at least some period of time, debtors would likely avoid the provisions of chapter 11 reorganization until it would no longer be an effective remedy.

As its basis for relief, the debtor offers a number of factors that it believes lend credence to its request for an extension. While the court is not apt to accept all of the debtor's reasons for an extension as warranted, it does find merit with some, including: 1) a delay in the formation of an Official Creditor's Committee; 2) a lack of opportunity for the debtor to obtain its own appraiser of the Hotel in order to begin the process of negotiation with FGH on a consensual plan; 3) the pendency of

---

4.   [Footnote 7 in original:] The court notes that FGH's only argument with respect to the debtor's ability to reorganize is that the debtor will be unable to identify a third-party investor or buyer in a reasonable period.

accounts receivable claims of the debtor against Eastern Airlines and Continental Airlines; and 4) the pending appeal of the state court foreclosure proceeding and the debtor's counterclaim against FGH in the Appellate Division of the Superior Court of New Jersey. Finally, the court also notes that the debtor has obviously spent a considerable amount of time defending the within motions and the cash collateral dispute, all which arose very early in the administration of the case. Thus, although the traditional grounds for granting an extension—the large size of the debtor and the concomitant difficulty in formulating a plan of reorganization—may not have been established here, the court is nevertheless satisfied that the above facts, taken in conjunction with the overall intent of chapter 11 discussed above, warrant granting the debtor's request. Moreover, this is the debtor's first request for an extension of the exclusivity period, which has been made early in the case. This fact supports the argument that the debtor is not seeking an extension merely to pressure its creditors.

Therefore, after considering all the evidence, and keeping in mind the limitations imposed on the court's discretion by virtue of the legislative history of § 1121(d), the court nevertheless concludes that the debtor is entitled to an additional period of exclusivity and will grant the extension requested to March 26, 1993. The time in which to solicit and obtain acceptances for such a plan will correspondingly be extended to May, 26, 1993. In granting this extension, the court is mindful of the fact that FGH is the largest creditor of the debtor and the sole secured creditor, leaving aside any tax liens. The court recognizes that the debtor's unreasonable delay in filing a plan of reorganization could ultimately have an effect on the value of FGH's claim. Therefore, if the debtor fails to submit its plan by March 26, 1993 or receive the court's confirmation of said plan by May 26, 1993, FGH will be free to move for relief from the automatic stay. * * *

In re All Seasons Industries
United States Bankruptcy Court, N.D. Indiana, 1990
121 B.R. 1002

ROBERT E. GRANT, Bankruptcy Judge.

This matter is before the court to consider debtor's motion for an extension of the exclusive time that it has to file a proposed Chapter 11 plan, pursuant to 11 U.S.C. § 1121. Although the motion has the support of the unsecured creditors committee, two secured creditors, Summit Bank and Peru Trust Company, object.

Section 1121 of the Bankruptcy Code gives the debtor the exclusive right to file a plan during the first 120 days after the order for relief. 11 U.S.C. § 1121(b). This 120 day period may be increased or reduced "for cause." 11 U.S.C. 1121(d). The party seeking a change in this statutory time period bears the burden of proving that the requisite cause exists. Whether or not it has done so is a question committed to the sound discretion of the bankruptcy judge.

In passing upon a request for a change in the debtor's exclusivity period, the court needs to consider more than just the articulated cause presented to it. It must also consider the history and purpose of § 1121 and the competing interests which Congress sought to balance when it enacted these time tables.

The limited exclusivity period, which is a feature of Chapter 11 proceedings under the Bankruptcy Code contrasts with the procedure under Chapter XI of the Bankruptcy Act which gave the debtor the exclusive right, throughout the Chapter XI proceedings, to propose a plan. The House Report accompanying H.R. 8200 noted that '[t]he exclusive right [under old Chapter XI] gives the debtor undue bargaining leverage, because by delay he can force a settlement out of otherwise unwilling creditors'.... Additionally, Sec. 1121 represents a congressional acknowledgement that creditors, whose money is invested in the enterprise no less than the debtor's, have a right to a say in the future of the enterprise ... [W]e think that any bankruptcy court involved in an assessment of whether 'cause' exists should be mindful of the legislative goal behind Sec. 1121. The bankruptcy court must avoid reinstituting the imbalance between the debtor and its creditors that characterized proceedings under the old Chapter XI. Section 1121 was designed, and should be faithfully interpreted, to limit the delay that makes creditors the hostages of Chapter 11 debtors.

In re Washington-St. Tammany Electric Co-op, Inc., 97 B.R. 852 (Bankr. E.D. La. 1989) (quoting In re Timbers of Inwood Forest Assoc., Ltd., 808 F.2d 363, 372 (5th Cir. 1987) (en banc) (aff'd 484 U.S. 365, 108 S. Ct. 626, 98 L. Ed. 2d 740 (1988)) (citations omitted). As a result, a request to either extend or reduce the period of exclusivity is a serious matter. Such a motion should "be granted neither routinely nor cavalierly." *McLean Industries, Inc.,* 87 B.R. at 834.

The debtor advances three primary arguments in support of its motion for an extension. The first involves pending litigation, before the District Court, in which debtor seeks to recover substantial sums from Ashland Chemical. This matter was originally scheduled to be tried to a jury in April of 1990 but has recently been continued to July of this year. Debtor contends that the successful prosecution of the litigation will have a substantial impact upon the course and, perhaps, the need for this reorganization and that a proper plan cannot be formulated without knowing the outcome. Debtor's second reason involves the seasonality of its business building boats. Debtor believes that the additional time requested will allow it to generate a more accurate, and perhaps more favorable, prediction of its business operations. Debtor's third reason is premised upon the substantial amount of litigation that it has had to undertake, particularly with Summit Bank, during the early stages of this reorganization. This litigation supposedly has been of sufficient volume and consequence that it has distracted the debtor in possession from the primary goal of this proceeding—the formulation, proposal, and confirmation of a plan of reorganization.

Having considered the debtor's arguments for an extension of the period of exclusivity, the court finds that, when these arguments are considered against the background of the Congressional policy behind § 1121 and the other aspects of this case, cause does not exist for an extension of time.

In reaching this conclusion the court notes that its decision does not sound a death knell for debtor's reorganization. "Denying such a motion only affords creditors their right to file the plan; there is no negative effect upon the debtor's co-existing right to file its plan." *Parker Street,* 31 B.R. at 207. The debtor remains free to take as long as it wishes or feels appropriate to develop and propose its own plan. "The risk is, of course, that while it is developing its plan, another party in interest will file a plan. However, that is as Congress intended." *Tony Downs,* 34 B.R. at 408. Even if, as appears likely in this case, another party would file a plan, that plan will be subject to the same procedures and standards governing confirmation that would apply to any plan debtor might wish to propose. "[T]he debtors and other creditors can object to confirmation on any number of grounds. Filing such a plan does not guarantee confirmation." *Southwest Oil Co.,* 84 B.R. at 454.

The need to conclude the District Court litigation does not appear to be critical to the debtor's efforts to propose a plan. The debtor should be able to "propose its plan taking into consideration the possible results of that action." *Parker Street,* 31 B.R. at 208. Conversely, if a resolution of that litigation is crucial to any plan, no one, neither debtor nor creditor, will be able to propose such a plan until the verdict comes in. Id. While the court can understand that it might be more convenient to know the results of the litigation, it does not seem that this Chapter 11 proceeding must be placed in limbo until that time.

Beyond the convenience that would flow from a judgment, one way or the other, in the District Court litigation, there is another consideration which must also be weighed in the balance. The court does not feel that the entry of judgment on the jury's verdict will end that litigation. The dollars involved are substantial. As a result, it would seem that regardless of the jury's decision, the result could, in all likelihood, be appealed creating additional delays and continuing any uncertainty.

Shortly after this case was filed the debtor made bright predictions about its future, which were shared with the court at a trial on debtor's motion for use of cash collateral. Although that motion was granted, these predictions do not appear to have been fulfilled, at least not as completely as debtor had hoped. The second major premise for the requested extension appears to be the debtor's belief that additional time will provide the opportunity for these predictions to yet come true. Consequently, if given more time, the debtor believes it will be able to present better financial information to its creditors in connection with a plan and disclosure statement. "Better" in this sense means not only more accurate but also more profitable. In other words the debtor hopes that during an extended period of exclusivity its financial situation will improve.

While the court can and does appreciate the need to present creditors with accurate and reliable information concerning a debtor's historical and projected operations, the court does not feel that the basis for debtor's request rises to the level of cause required by § 1121. Debtor has been operating under the protection of Chapter 11 since November of 1989 and over these months should have developed an accurate record of its income and expenses. The fact that its post-petition track record may not be as successful as it would like should not be used to justify an extension of the exclusivity period, based upon the hope that additional time will allow the debtor's financial fortunes to improve.

Debtor's post-petition litigation in this court does not weigh heavily in favor of extending the period of exclusivity. Indeed, "[t]he ordinary Chapter 11 debtor is expected to bring with it litigation, or the potential for it." *Southwest Oil Co.,* 84 B.R. at 452. Litigation with creditors is not unusual. In this particular instance, debtor's post-petition litigation has been nothing "more than predictable creditor litigation, symptomatic of any business difficulty in its advanced stages." Id. at 453. It is not the type of litigation which justifies extending the period of exclusivity.

In enacting § 1121(d), Congress contemplated that one of the most common causes for an extension of the exclusivity period would be the size and complexity of the case. This case is neither large nor unique. There is nothing unusual about the nature of the debtor's business or the financial problems which resulted in the need to seek relief under Chapter 11. The number of creditors that debtor brought with it to this court and the claims they have against the debtor and its assets are not particularly extraordinary. Consequently, the size, nature, and complexity of the case do not seem to call for an extension of time.

One of the most important reasons for extending the debtor's period of exclusivity is to give the Chapter 11 process of negotiation and compromise an opportunity to be fulfilled, so that a consensual plan can be proposed and confirmed without opposition. In this instance, it does not appear that the objecting creditors are "recalcitrant" or refuse to discuss the possibilities of reorganization with the debtor in good faith. Instead, it appears that the debtor and its primary opponents have a good faith difference of opinion about the future prospects of debtor's business. As a result, it does not seem that they have been able to find or will be able to find a common ground upon which to structure a mutually satisfactory plan. Further, it does not seem that an extension of the period of exclusivity will change this state of affairs. Rather, it would seem that such an extension would have the result of continuing to hold creditors hostage to the Chapter 11 process and pressuring them into accepting a plan they believe to be unsatisfactory. While the court does not believe that debtor filed its motion with this purpose in mind, it does appear that this will be or may be one of the unintended consequences of granting the request.

One of the reasons that the debtor and its major secured creditors have not been able to find common ground upon which to build a plan of reorganization is that these creditors have lost faith in the capability and perhaps the integrity of debtor's management. In extreme cases, such a loss of faith may constitute cause for the appointment of a trustee. While the court makes no finding as to whether or not this loss of faith is justified (indeed the nature of the hearing and the evidence presented do not permit the court to determine this question) for the purposes of the present motion, it is only necessary to realize that a loss of confidence exists. This is a factor the court should and must consider in its determination.

Having considered debtor's motion and the support it has received from the unsecured creditors committee and having carefully balanced all of counsels' arguments, both in favor of and against the motion, in light of the Congressional purpose behind § 1121, the court is persuaded that debtor's motion for an extension of the exclusive time within which it may file a Chapter 11 plan should be denied. An order doing so will be entered.

NOTES

1. Do the courts in *Newark Airport/Hotel* and *All Seasons* take different approaches to the question whether to extend exclusivity or do the differences in the facts explain the different outcomes?

2. Exclusivity brings with it responsibility. If the debtor does not use the exclusivity period well so as to make progress toward a successful reorganization, then undersecured creditors are likely to be successful in obtaining relief from the automatic stay under § 362(d)(2).

3.   According to the court in *Newark Airport/Hotel,* the fact that the debtor was seeking its first extension of exclusivity supported a conclusion that the debtor was not seeking an extension "merely to pressure its creditors." However, the *All Seasons Industries* court is not the only one to refuse to grant a first motion for extension of exclusivity. Consider In re General Bearing Corp., 136 B.R. 361 (Bankr. S.D.N.Y. 1992). The debtor had been unable to negotiate a restructuring acceptable to one of its two secured creditors, whose liens fully encumbered the estate's assets. The debtor's cash flows apparently were insufficient to provide the payments to that secured creditor that would be needed in a cramdown. The case was not complex, and there had not been a great deal of litigation that would have kept the debtor from making progress toward a successful reorganization. The court denied the first motion for an extension, stating that "In these circumstances, the secured claimants should not continue as hostages in this Chapter 11 case." Id. at 367.

     On the other hand, some courts are more open than the *All Seasons Industries* court to the argument that the debtor may need more time to propose a plan where there has been substantial litigation during the case. See In re Sletteland, 260 B.R. 657 (Bankr. S.D.N.Y. 2001).

4.   The Supreme Court's decision in *Timbers*, discussed in *Newark Airport/Hotel* and reprinted in this text in Chapter Three, seems to have had a substantial effect not only on motions for relief from stay but also on motions for extension of exclusivity. The Court's concern that creditors not be mired in a reorganization attempt that is likely to fail seems to have made courts less willing to grant extensions of exclusivity, particularly in single asset real estate cases, which tend to be simple cases in which jobs are not at stake and going concern value will not be lost in a liquidation. (The work that must be done to run and maintain an office building or apartment building does not depend on whether the debtor remains the owner or whether there is a new owner as the result of a foreclosure sale. Further, the tenants will not be turned out just because of a foreclosure sale, and thus a "liquidation" at a foreclosure sale does not change the nature of the building as a "going concern.") As shown by *All Seasons*, the en banc Fifth Circuit opinion in *Timbers*, which the Supreme Court affirmed, has also had an effect. There now seem to be fewer cases in which bankruptcy courts grant extension after extension almost as a matter of course. Cf. Gaines v. Perkins (In re Perkins), 71 B.R. 294 (W.D. Tenn. 1987) (affirming orders that gave the debtor exclusivity for more than 800 days).

5.   As amended in 2005, § 1121(d) prohibits extensions of the 120 day and 180 day periods to more than 18 months and 20 months respectively.

6.   There are few appellate decisions regarding extension of exclusivity. Before the 1994 amendments, many courts took the position that orders extending or reducing exclusivity periods were interlocutory orders appealable only with leave of the court to which the appeal was taken. See, e.g., Rosin v. RCN Anlagenivestitionen Frodsgesellschaft II (In re RCN Anlagenivestitionen Frodsgesellschaft II), 118 B.R. 460 (W.D. Mich. 1990). The Bankruptcy Reform Act of 1994 amended 28 U.S.C. § 158(a) to make such orders immediately appealable as of right to the district court or bankruptcy appellate panel, thus guaranteeing one—but only one—level of appeal. (As amended in 2005, 28 U.S.C. § 158(d) allows that appeal to be taken directly to the court of appeals upon the proper certification, but the circuit court need not hear the direct appeal unless it so chooses.) The House Judiciary Committee Chairman (in his section-by-section analysis of the 1994 bill in its final form) stated that

Exclusivity is intended to promote an environment in which the debtor's business may be rehabilitated and a consensual plan may be negotiated. However, undue extension can result in excessively prolonged and costly delay, to the detriment of the creditors.* * * The Committee intends that the district court carefully consider the circumstances of each case so appealed with a view to encouraging a fair and equitable resolution of the bankruptcy.

140 Cong. Rec. H10764 (daily ed. Oct. 4, 1994) (remarks of Chairman Brooks). The Chairman and his committee may have had in mind cases like *Perkins*, cited in the previous note. Even with the amendment, it remains doubtful whether in many cases there can be an effective appeal of an order extending exclusivity. Appeals often take so long to decide that the appeal is likely to be mooted by the expiration of the extended exclusivity period before the appeal of the extension order can be decided.

In light of those concerns, is an appellate court obligated to expedite review of an order extending (or reducing) exclusivity? And when would the appeal be mooted? Suppose (1) a party appeals an order granting an extension of exclusivity, (2) before that extended exclusivity period expired the debtor filed a motion for another extension of exclusivity, (3) by the time the appeal is heard, the time period covered by the appealed order has passed, but (4) the bankruptcy court has not yet decided the motion for a further extension of exclusivity, with the result that exclusivity effectively has been conditionally extended (in the sense that if the bankruptcy court grants the requested further extension of exclusivity, any plans filed by other parties in the meantime will be stricken). Is the appeal of the extension order moot because the time period it covered has already passed?

When the Committee requested an expedited briefing schedule, we promptly granted the request even though it was not made immediately upon filing the appeal. Although the parties tried to talk about the respective merits of their positions in their motion papers regarding the briefing schedule, we ruled—and now reiterate—that the probable merits, or lack thereof, are irrelevant to the question of whether to fix an expedited schedule for the appeal.

In sum, the fact that Congress has prescribed an appeal of right from § 1121 exclusivity adjustments requires us to take steps to assure that there is, in fact, substantive and meaningful appellate review. The ephemeral nature of exclusivity adjustments that are easily mooted by time and tide compels the conclusion that we must fix expedited schedules for timely, substantive appellate review regardless of whether we think the appellant is likely to succeed on the merits.
        * * *

This appeal would be moot if events have occurred that make it either impossible or inequitable for the appellate court to fashion effective relief. An unqualified expiration of exclusivity probably would be an event that renders it impossible to fashion effective relief.

We are not, however, faced with events that make it impossible to fashion effective relief because there was not an unqualified termination of exclusivity on June 28, 2002 [when the period covered by the appealed order ended]. Rather, there was then pending an as-yet undecided motion for a second extension of exclusivity.

The fact that a subsequent extension of exclusivity is pending in bankruptcy court enables us to fashion effective relief in this appeal from the order on the first extension. Reversal of one extension would necessarily be fatal to all subsequent extensions because § 1121(d) forbids retroactive requests: "On request of a party in interest made within the respective periods specified in subsection (c) of this section ...." 11 U.S.C. § 1121(d). A subsequent request that is made during an extension that does not survive appeal is not made "within" a qualifying exclusivity period. As a reversal would alter the status quo in favor of appellant, we are thus able to fashion effective relief.

This conclusion obviates the concern expressed by a prominent commentator that clever debtors might evade review by the tactic of a series of short-duration extensions that would expire before review could be completed. Klee, 69 AM. BANKR. L.J. at 553 ("It remains to be seen whether the mootness doctrine will undercut review of exclusivity orders."). An appeal of a short-duration extension is not mooted by expiration in the presence of subsequent extensions.

Thus, this appeal cannot become moot unless and until the subsequent request for extension is finally denied. As that has not yet occurred, the appeal is not moot.

Official Comm. of Unsecured Creditors v. Henry Mayo Newhall Mem'l Hosp. (In re Henry Mayo Newhall Mem'l Hosp.), 282 B.R. 444, 450 (B.A.P. 9th Cir. 2002). The court in *Henry Mayo* also held that the a de novo standard of appellate review applies to whether there is cause under § 1121(d) for an extension (or presumably for a reduction) in the exclusivity period, because "[t]he stated Congressional intention that the appellate court 'carefully consider the circumstances of each case' is not consonant with review for abuse of discretion." Id. at 451. Contra Bunch v. Hoffinger Indus., Inc. (In re Hoffinger Indus., Inc.), 292 B.R. 639, 642 (B.A.P. 8th Cir. 2003) ("We review the bankruptcy court's decision to extend the debtor's exclusivity periods for abuse of discretion.").

Problem 11-3

Foam Corporation had negotiated diligently with the unsecured creditors' committee and had tried to negotiate with Kick Credit (the major secured creditor) and with Imperial Insurance Company (lessor of four of Foam Corporation's plants). Neither Kick Credit nor Imperial were willing to negotiate seriously. Foam Corporation moved for "extension of its period of exclusivity for filing of a plan." The court granted the motion, entering an order "extending the debtor's period of exclusivity to and including October 17, 2006," a date 190 days after the petition was filed.

By the beginning of October it became clear that Foam Corporation and the committee were not going to be able to reach agreement on a plan, even though both were convinced that the debtor's business should continue. Tina Chemical, a member of the committee, had concluded that the debtor's proposals were nearly acceptable, but a majority of the committee members disagreed. Kick Credit continued to take the position that negotiations were pointless and that the only solution was a liquidation. Imperial was similarly unwilling to negotiate any concession on any of the leases; it insisted that the debtor should sell its operations at the four leased plants to a buyer Imperial had located. Gruff thought Foam Corporation needed to keep at least two of the leased plants (Denver and Seattle). Ben Ture, an investor who had purchased several small trade claims, wanted to propose a plan under which he would take control of Foam Corporation and radically change its business direction. Despite his record of past business failures, he was a very persuasive conversationalist who had convinced a number of small trade creditors that his ideas made sense. All of the financial professionals involved in the case thought that implementing his proposal would lead to quick financial ruin.

Foam Corporation filed its plan on October 3, 2006. On October 11 it filed a motion for a further extension of exclusivity. The same day Tina Chemical filed a motion asking that it be permitted to file a plan. A hearing on those motions was scheduled for October 16 pursuant to an order shortening time. The committee, Kick Credit, and Ben all opposed Foam Corporation's motion; all of them argued that they had plans they wished to file and that there was not sufficient cause for an extension. Kick Credit also argued that § 1121(d) permits extensions only if the motion for extension is brought within the original 120 or 180 day period; thus multiple extensions are not permitted. Foam Corporation filed a notice of nonopposition to Tina Chemical's motion, stating that the filing of a plan by Tina Chemical—one that would be fairly similar to the debtor's plan—might cause other creditors to move toward the debtor's position and might help to break the logjam.

Then, on October 13, the parties received notice through the mail that Imperial also had filed something on October 11—a proposed plan. Imperial did so without leave of court. Its plan called for the debtor's operations at the four leased plants to be sold to the buyer it had located, for the rest of the debtor's assets to be liquidated, and for the proceeds to be divided among the creditors in accordance with their relative priorities.

At the hearing on October 16, Foam Corporation moved to have Imperial's plan stricken. Imperial argued that exclusivity had terminated no later than midnight of Tuesday, October 10 (after the Columbus Day weekend), because the debtor had never obtained an extension of the 180 day exclusivity period for obtaining acceptances. Imperial also argued that since the period had expired before the debtor filed its motion on October 11, the court was without power to extend exclusivity.

You are the judge. You have a memorandum prepared by your former law clerk in 1995 on this general subject; it discusses the cases noted in the rest of this paragraph. You may need to do additional research.

Will you hold that the 180 day period was extended along with the 120 day period and thus strike Imperial's plan, or will you find that exclusivity terminated no later than midnight of October 10? See In re Judd, 173 B.R. 941 (Bankr. D. Kan. 1994).

Will you extend the 180 day exclusivity period even if you find that it expired before the motion was brought? Compare In re Sills, 1992 WL 247102 (Bankr. E.D. Ark.) (if exclusivity period expires before motion to extend it is brought, court has no authority to extend it), with In re Crescent Mfg. Co., 122 B.R. 979 (Bankr. N.D. Ohio 1990) (finding excusable neglect under Rule 9006(b)(1) and granting extension of exclusivity even though motion brought one day after exclusivity expired).

Is Kick Credit correct in arguing that § 1121(d) permits extensions to be granted only on motions brought within the original *unextended* exclusivity periods and thus prohibits multiple extensions? Compare Gaines v. Perkins (In re Perkins), 71 B.R. 294 (W.D. Tenn. 1987), with In re Westgate General Partnership, 55 B.R. 562 (Bankr. E.D. Pa. 1985).

Did Imperial have standing to file a plan, assuming Foam Corporation had not rejected any of the leases and was current on its lease payments to Imperial? Does Ben have standing? See In re First Humanics Corp., 124 B.R. 87 (Bankr. W.D. Mo. 1991).

Can you extend exclusivity *selectively* in any of the following ways:

⇨ permitting only Tina Chemical to file a plan in addition to the debtor?

> ⇨ permitting only Tina Chemical and the committee to file plans in addition to the debtor?
>
> ⇨ permitting any party in interest but Ben to file a plan?
>
> See In re Public Serv. Co. of New Hampshire, 88 B.R. 521 (Bankr. D.N.H. 1988); In re Texaco Inc., 76 B.R. 322 (Bankr. S.D.N.Y. 1987); In re United Press Int'l, Inc., 60 B.R. 265 (Bankr. D.D.C. 1986).
>
> Suppose later in the case the court is unable to grant further extensions due to the prohibitions of § 1121(d)(2) (added in 2005). May the court nevertheless prohibit some of the parties in interest—such as Ben—from filing a proposed plan? What can Ben do if the court refuses to schedule a hearing to approve the disclosure statement on Ben's plan?

C. CLASSIFICATION OF CLAIMS AND INTERESTS

Under § 1123(a)(1), the plan must designate classes of claims and interests. Thus, within certain constraints, the debtor (or whoever files a plan) controls how the claims and interests are classified.

How that control is exercised may determine whether the plan can be confirmed, because the holders of claims and interests vote to accept or reject the plan by class. For example, if most general unsecured creditors support the debtor's plan, then the debtor may draft the plan so that all general unsecured creditors are placed in one class. The plan supporters may then be able to outvote the plan opponents so that the class accepts the plan.[5] As a result, the debtor may be able to confirm the plan consensually under § 1129(a) and avoid the need for a § 1129(b) cramdown.

On the other hand, if too many general unsecured creditors oppose the plan, a single class made up of all general unsecured claims would reject the plan. In such a case, there is no way to divide up the general unsecured claims into classes all of which will accept the plan; thus consensual confirmation will not be possible. See § 1129(a)(8) (requiring acceptance by all impaired classes for consensual confirmation under § 1129(a)). Instead of trying to create classes in a way that would lead to all of the classes accepting the plan, the debtor will need to change its goal. The debtor must be sure that the plan creates *at least one* impaired class of claims that will accept the plan (not counting acceptances of insiders); otherwise the plan will not be confirmable even in a § 1129(b) cramdown. See § 1129(a)(10) and (b)(1). For example, even if most general unsecured creditors oppose the plan, there may be a group of trade creditors who rely heavily on the debtor's business and who may not be able to survive if the debtor's reorganization fails. If that group's claims can be placed in a separate class, that class will likely accept the plan, thus satisfying the confirmation requirement that at least one impaired class accept the plan.

---

5.   A class of claims accepts a plan if, out of the claims in the class that are voted, two thirds in dollar amount and more than half in number are voted in favor of the plan. A class of interests accepts the plan if, out of the interests that are voted, two thirds in amount accept. See § 1126(c) and (d), and Chapter Thirteen below.

So far we have assumed that classification has no effect on whether a particular creditor will support or oppose the plan. This static approach is not entirely correct. A careful use of the power to create classes can in fact help the debtor gain support from creditors. This follows from two facts: (1) different creditors may be willing to accept different kinds of treatment, and (2) all claims or interests placed in the same class must be treated the same (unless the holder of a particular claim or interest agrees to a less favorable treatment). See § 1123(a)(4).

One group of creditors may be interested primarily in getting as much immediate cash as possible and may be willing to accept less total value in order to get it. Another group of creditors (for example, investors who have bought claims against the debtor) may be more interested in the total value they will receive and less interested in its form; they may be willing to take most of their value in the form of stock in the reorganized debtor and long term promissory notes. Yet another group may have a special reason for wanting the reorganization to succeed—for example, a few trade creditors who are relying for their future viability on having the reorganized debtor as a customer; they may be willing to take less value than other creditors if that is necessary for the reorganization to succeed.

If the claims of all of these creditors had to be placed in one class and thus had to be treated the same, the class might not accept the plan. If the debtor can feasibly offer the creditors as a whole only 50% repayment, 15% in immediate cash, 20% in the form of promissory notes, and 15% in the form of stock, then it may be that neither the first nor the second group will support the plan. The first group may complain that a 15% cash payment is insufficient. The second group may complain that 50% is too low a total amount. The third group will support the plan but probably will outvoted by the other two groups. The result would be that the class would reject the plan.

Consider, however, what could happen if the debtor created a separate class for each group so that it could treat them differently. Assume the first and second groups each hold $4 million in claims, and the third group holds $2 million, for a total of $10 million in claims. As noted above, the debtor can pay 15% of that amount in cash ($1.5 million), 20% in notes ($2 million worth), and 15% in stock ($1.5 million worth). The debtor's plan could propose to give the first group simply $1.2 million in cash. Even though that is only a 30% payment—not the 50% total that a one-class plan would give—it is twice as much cash, and it might be enough to get the first group's support. The plan could give the third group most of the remaining available cash, say $200,000 (a 10% cash payment on the group's claims), three quarters of the notes that it would get under the one-class plan, and the same amount of stock that it would get under the one-class plan. That would be $300,000 in promissory notes (15% of the group's claims) and $300,000 in stock (15% of the group's claims), in addition to 10% in cash. The third group would thus receive a total value equal to only 40% of the group's claims—instead of the 50% that a one-class plan would provide—but that might be enough to cause the group to support the plan;

the group needs the debtor to survive. Then the debtor could offer the second group much more total value than it could get under a one-class plan: $100,000 in cash, $1.6 million in promissory notes, and $1.2 million in stock, for a total value of $2.9 million, which is 72.5% of the amount of the group's claims. That would likely induce the second group to support the plan.

Thus, if the debtor is permitted to draft its plan so as to create several classes of general unsecured claims, the chances of confirming a plan may be greatly increased. All three classes may accept the plan, which would likely permit consensual confirmation under § 1129(a).[6] If one of the classes does not accept, then the chances that a § 1129(b) cramdown can occur are increased if the debtor can place the friendly creditors—the third group—in a separate class; they can provide the needed acceptance by an impaired class of creditors (not counting acceptances of insiders). See § 1129(a)(10).[7]

Does the debtor have the discretion to create separate classes of general unsecured claims? How much discretion does the debtor have in creating classes? Section 1122 provides a partial answer. Section 1122(b) permits the plan to create a separate administrative convenience class of small unsecured claims. Section 1122(a) prohibits the plan from placing two claims or interests in the same class unless they are substantially similar, and seems to characterize § 1122(b) as an exception to its rule. However, § 1122(a) does not

---

6.   It would be possible to try to do the same thing with a plan that put all the unsecured creditors into one class. The plan could set forth the three different kinds of treatment and let each holder of an unsecured claim decide which to take. Each creditor therefore could choose to take 30% (all in cash), or to take 40% (10% in cash, 15% in notes and 15% in stock), or to take 72.5% (2.5% in cash, 40% in notes, and 30% in stock). Each creditor would thus be treated equally by being given an equal choice. Presumably this would result in at least as high a level of creditor support for the plan as there would be under a three class plan. There is, however, a "common pool" problem. There would not be enough value to go around if some of the creditors in the first and third groups decided to take the 72.5% option. In fact, it would cease to be a 72.5% option if many of them took it. Too much debt and stock would be issued. The reorganized debtor might be unable to handle the extra debt. The value of the notes would be less because of the higher risk. The value of the stock would be less because there would be less net worth (due to the extra debt), and the lesser amount of net worth would be divided up among more shares. The prospect of this would probably cause the creditors in the second group to vote against the plan, because they would not be receiving the 67.5% that they wanted. Even if the trade creditors in the third group decided not to go for the 67.5% option, they might well choose the 30% all cash option. If many of them chose that, the debtor might not have enough cash to make the payments that the plan would require.

Thus, if the creditors are allowed to choose individually, the plan may fail. Of course, if the claims are placed in separate classes and the creditors are not allowed to choose among the three treatments, some of the creditors may be unhappy, may feel that they have been discriminated against, and may desire to have their claims in a different class. However, if their class accepts the plan, the dissenting creditors are not entitled to demand that there be no unfair discrimination; the "no unfair discrimination" requirement only applies in favor of classes that do not accept the plan. See § 1129(b)(1), and compare § 1322(b)(1). The dissenters' objection—if their class accepts the plan—can only be an objection to the classification. See § 1129(a)(1).

7.   Note, however, that if a class does not accept the plan, then the plan cannot be confirmed—cannot be crammed down— if it unfairly discriminates against that class. See § 1129(b)(1). Unfair discrimination is discussed in Chapter Fifteen of this text.

explicitly require that all substantially similar claims be placed in the same class. Does it implicitly require that by characterizing § 1122(b) as an exception to its rule? Or does it characterize § 1122(b) as an exception because § 1122(b) allows dissimilar claims to be classified together? Section 1122(a) also does not define "substantially similar." What does that term mean? Consider the following materials.

Teamsters National Freight Industry Negotiating Committee v. U.S. Truck Company (In re U.S. Truck Company)

United States Court of Appeals, Sixth Circuit, 1986
800 F.2d 581

CORNELIA G. KENNEDY, Circuit Judge.

* * *

Underlying this appeal is the Teamsters Committee's claim that U.S. Truck is liable to its employees for rejecting a collective bargaining agreement between the local union and U.S. Truck. After filing its petition for relief under Chapter 11 of the Bankruptcy Code on June 11, 1982, U.S. Truck, a trucking company primarily engaged in intrastate shipping of parts and supplies for the automotive industry, sought to reject the collective bargaining agreement. U.S. Truck rejected the agreement with the approval of then-Bankruptcy-Judge Woods, in December 1982. Judge Woods found that rejection of the agreement was "absolutely necessary to save the debtor from collapse." Memorandum Opinion and Order, December 6, 1982, at page 8. New agreements have been negotiated to the satisfaction of each participating local union. Such agreements have been implemented over the lone dissent of the Teamsters Joint Area Rider Committee. Under the most recently mentioned agreement in the record (due to have expired in March 1985), U.S. Truck was able to record monthly profits in the range of $125,000 to $250,000. These new agreements achieved such results by reducing wages and requiring employees to buy their own trucking equipment, which the employees then leased to the company.

The parties agreed to an estimate of the size of the Teamsters Committee claim against U.S. Truck * * *.

Section 1129 contains two means by which a reorganization plan can be confirmed. The first way is to meet all eleven of the requirements of subsection (a), including (a)(8), which requires all impaired classes of claims or interests to accept the plan. The other way is to meet the requirements of subsection (b), which, first, incorporates all of the requirements of subsection (a), except for that contained in subsection (a)(8), and, second, imposes two additional requirements. Confirmation under subsection (b) is commonly referred to as a "cram down" because it permits a reorganization plan to go into effect over the objections of one or more impaired classes of creditors. In this case, U.S. Truck sought approval of its plan under this "cram down" provision.

The Teamsters Committee's first objection is that the plan does not meet the requirement that at least one class of impaired claims accept the plan, see 11 U.S.C. § 1129(a)(10), because U.S. Truck impermissibly gerrymandered the classes in order to neutralize the Teamsters Committee's dissenting vote. The reorganization plan contains twelve classes. The plan purports to impair five of these classes—Class VI (the unsecured claim of Manufacturer's National Bank of Detroit based on a mortgage); Class VII (the secured claim of John Graham, Trustee of Transportation Services, Inc., based on a loan); Class IX (the Teamsters Committee's claim based on rejection of the collective bargaining agreement); Class XI (all secured [*sic*, probably "unsecured"] claims in excess of $200.00 including those arising from the rejection of executory contracts); and Class XII (the equity interest of the stockholder of the debtor). As noted above, section 1129(a)(10), as incorporated into subsection (b)(1), requires at least one of these classes of impaired claims to approve the reorganization plan before it can be confirmed. The parties agree that approval by Class XII would not count because acceptance must be determined without including the acceptance of the plan by any insider.[8] See 11 U.S.C. § 1129(a)(10). The Code's definition of "insider" clearly includes [the sole stockholder] McKinlay Transport, Inc. See 11 U.S.C. § 101(28)(B)(iii), (30). Thus, compliance with subsection (a)(10) depends on whether either of the other three classes that approved the plan—Class VI, Class VII, or Class XI—was a properly constructed impaired class. The Teamsters Committee argues that Classes VI and VII were not truly impaired classes and that Class XI should have included Class IX, and hence was an improperly constructed class.[9] Because we find that Class XI was a properly constructed class of impaired claims, we hold that the plan complies with subsection (a)(10).[10]

The issue raised by the Teamsters Committee's challenge is under what circumstances does the Bankruptcy Code permit a debtor to keep a creditor out of a class of impaired claims that are of a similar legal nature and are against the same property as those of the "isolated" creditor. The District Court held that the Code permits such action here because of the following circumstances: (1) the employees represented by the Teamsters Committee have a unique continued interest in the ongoing business of the debtor; (2) the mechanics of the Teamsters Committee's claim differ substantially from those of the Class XI claims; and (3) the Teamsters Committee's claim is likely to become part of the agenda of future collective bargaining sessions between the union and the reorganized company. See 47 B.R. at 939-40. Thus, according to the court, the interests of the Teamsters Committee are substantially dissimilar from those of the creditors in Class XI. We must decide whether the Code permits separate classification under such circumstances.

Congress has sent mixed signals on the issue that we must decide. Our starting point is 11 U.S.C. § 1122.

---

8. [Note that Class XII is a class of interests, not a class of claims; thus acceptance by Class XII could not satisfy the requirement of § 1129(a)(10) that at least one impaired class of *claims* accept the plan, even if the holders of the interests were not insiders. Ed.]

9. [Footnote 6 in original:] Had the debtor included the Teamsters Committee's claim in Class XI, the Committee's vote to reject the plan would have swung the results of the Class XI vote from an acceptance to a rejection. See 11 U.S.C. § 1126(c) (setting forth the requirement that creditors holding at least two-thirds in amount of allowed claims of a class accept).

10. [Footnote 7 in original:] For this reason, we need not decide the challenge to the status of Class VI and Class VII.

§ 1122. Classification of claims or interests

(a) Except as provided in subsection (b) of this section, a plan may place a claim or an interest in a particular class only if such claim or interest is substantially similar to the other claims or interests of such class.

(b) A plan may designate a separate class of claims consisting only of every unsecured claim that is less than or reduced to an amount that the court approves as reasonable and necessary for administrative convenience.

The statute, by its express language, only addresses the problem of dissimilar claims being included in the same class. It does not address the correlative problem—the one we face here—of similar claims being put in different classes. Some courts have seized upon this omission, and have held that the Code does not require a debtor to put similar claims in the same class. * * *

Further evidence that Congress intentionally failed to impose a requirement that similar claims be classified together is found by examining the "classification" sections of the former Bankruptcy Act. The applicable former provisions were 11 U.S.C., sections 597 (from former Chapter X) and 751 (from former Chapter XI).

§ 597. Classification of creditors and stockholders

For the purposes of the plan and its acceptance, the judge shall fix the division of creditors and stockholders into classes according to the nature of their respective claims and stock. For the purposes of such classification, the judge shall, if necessary, upon the application of the trustee, the debtor, any creditor, or an indenture trustee, fix a hearing upon notice to the holders of secured claims, the debtor, the trustee, and such other persons as the judge may designate, to determine summarily the value of the security and classify as unsecured the amount in excess of such value.

§ 751. Classification of creditors

For the purposes of the arrangement and its acceptance, the court may fix the division of creditors into classes and, in the event of controversy, the court shall after hearing upon notice summarily determine such controversy.

Section 597 was interpreted to require all creditors of equal rank with claims against the same property to be placed in the same class. Congress' switch to less restrictive language in section 1122 of the Code seems to warrant a conclusion that Congress no longer intended to impose the now-omitted requirement that similar claims be classified together. However, the legislative history indicates that Congress may not have intended to change the prior rule. The Notes of the Senate Committee on the Judiciary state:

This section [1122] codifies current case law surrounding the classification of claims and equity securities. It requires classification based on the nature of the claims or interests classified, and permits inclusion of claims or interests in a particular class only if the claim or interest being included is substantially similar to the other claims or interests of the class.

S. Rep. No. 989, 95th Cong., 2d Sess. 118, reprinted in 1978 U.S. Code Cong. & Ad. News 5787, 5904.

It is difficult to follow Congress' instruction to apply the old case law to the new Code provision. The old case law comes from two different sources. Chapter X of the old Act was designed for thorough financial reorganizations of large corporations. It imposed a very formal and rigid structure to protect the investing public. Chapter XI was designed for small nonpublic businesses, did not permit the adjustment of a secured debt or of equity, and thus contained few investor-protection measures. The idea behind Chapter 11 of the Code was to combine the speed and flexibility of Chapter XI with some of the protection and remedial tools of Chapter X. Thus, Congress has incorporated, for purposes of interpreting section 1122, the case law from two provisions with different language, that were adopted for different purposes, and that have been interpreted to mean different things.

In this case, U.S. Truck is using its classification powers to segregate dissenting (impaired) creditors from assenting (impaired) creditors (by putting the dissenters into a class or classes by themselves) and, thus, it is assured that at least one class of impaired creditors will vote for the plan and make it eligible for cram down consideration by the court. We agree with the Teamsters Committee that there must be some limit on a debtor's power to classify creditors in such a manner. The potential for abuse would be significant otherwise. Unless there is some requirement of keeping similar claims together, nothing would stand in the way of a debtor seeking out a few impaired creditors (or even one such creditor) who will vote for the plan and placing them in their own class.[11]

We are unaware of any cases that deal with this problem as it arises in this case. As we noted above, the legislative history of the Code provides little assistance in determining what limits there are to segregating similar claims. Nevertheless, we do find one common theme in the prior case law that Congress incorporated into section 1122. In those pre-Code cases, the lower courts were given broad discretion to determine proper classification according to the factual circumstances of each individual case. We also find some guidance in two cases that considered the need to adjust the classification of creditors to account for differing postures and interests.

In First Nat'l Bank of Herkimer v. Poland Union, 109 F.2d 54 (2d Cir.), cert. denied, 309 U.S. 682, 60 S.Ct. 723, 84 L.Ed. 1026 (1940), two of the largest accepting creditors of a reorganization plan were also shareholders who stood to profit from a provision in the plan releasing their disputed liability to the debtor. The Second Circuit affirmed the lower court's denial of confirmation, because it concluded that a lower court lacks the power to do what the plan required it to do—restrain suits against shareholders. The court also noted, "In such circumstances, it may be doubtful whether [the shareholders/creditors] should be permitted to vote in the same class with other creditors not so intimately connected with the enterprise." Id., 109 F.2d at 55.

In American United Mut. Life Ins. Co. v. City of Avon Park, 311 U.S. 138, 61 S.Ct. 157, 85 L.Ed. 91 (1940), the city's fiscal agent—who administered the reorganization—held claims on which he would enjoy significant profit from the plan. The Court refused confirmation because it was not clear that when the agent solicited the necessary votes from bondholders he had disclosed his interest. The Court noted that where investigation discloses "unfair dealing, a breach of fiduciary

---

11. [Footnote 8 in original:] We need not speculate in this case whether the purpose of separate classification was to line up the votes in favor of the plan. The debtor admitted that to the District Court.

obligations, profiting from a trust, special benefits for the reorganizers, or the need for the protection of investors against an inside few, or of one class of investors from the encroachments of another, the court has ample power to adjust the remedy to meet the need." Id., 311 U.S. at 146, 61 S.Ct. at 162. One remedy the Court mentioned was "the separate classification of claimants." Id. (citing *Poland Union*).

We find that the rationale of these two cases applies here. The District Court noted three important ways in which the interests of the Teamsters Committee differ substantially from those of the other impaired creditors. Because of these differences, the Teamsters Committee has a different stake in the future viability of the reorganized company and has alternative means at its disposal for protecting its claim. The Teamsters Committee's claim is connected with the collective bargaining process. In the words of the Committee's counsel, the union employees have a "virtually unique interest." See 47 B.R. at 939. These differences put the Teamsters Committee's claim in a different posture than the Class XI claims. The Teamsters Committee may choose to reject the plan not because the plan is less than optimal to it as a creditor, but because the Teamsters Committee has a noncreditor interest— e.g., rejection will benefit its members in the ongoing employment relationship. Although the Teamsters Committee certainly is not intimately connected with the debtor, to allow the Committee to vote with the other impaired creditors would be to allow it to prevent a court from considering confirmation of a plan that a significant group of creditors with similar interests have accepted. Permitting separate classification of the Teamsters Committee's claim does not automatically result in adoption of the plan. The Teamsters Committee is still protected by the provisions of [section 1129] (a) and (b), particularly the requirements of subsection (b) that the plan not discriminate unfairly and that it be fair and equitable with respect to the Teamsters Committee's claim. In fact, the Teamsters Committee invokes those requirements, but as we note in the following sections, the plan does not violate them. * * *

In re Bloomingdale Partners
United States Bankruptcy Court, N.D. Illinois, 1994
170 B.R. 984

RONALD BARLIANT, Bankruptcy Judge.
     * * *

The Debtor is a limited partnership organized under Illinois law. Its primary asset is an apartment building * * * .

The Debtor failed in its first attempt to confirm a plan of reorganization. * * * The Debtor subsequently filed a new plan, captioned "Third Plan of Reorganization" (the "Third Plan").

After the first confirmation hearing, creditors John and Jean Zarlenga filed a motion, pursuant to § 502(c)(1), for an order allowing and assigning a value to their contingent and unliquidated claim for the purpose of voting on the Debtor's Third Plan. The Zarlengas' claim is based upon a state common law private nuisance theory; the Zarlengas assert that the noise emanating from the air-conditioning units attached to the Debtor's apartment building interfered with their interest in the quiet enjoyment of their adjoining land and that they are entitled to damages. The Debtor strenuously objected to the Zarlengas' claim. After a lengthy hearing, this Court overruled the Debtor's objection and estimated and allowed the Zarlengas' claim in the amount of $40,000.

The Third Plan classifies all unsecured claims together so that the Zarlengas' claim is in the same class, Class 5, as the other unsecured claims. Three days before the close of voting, the Debtor filed its "Modified Third Plan of Reorganization" (the "Modified Third Plan"). This plan retains the Zarlengas' claim in Class 5, but it places all of the other unsecured claims in a separate class, Class 6.

Hancock [which held the mortgage on the apartment building and whose secured claim was the only claim in Class 3] and the Zarlengas voted against the Debtor's plan. The two unsecured creditors in Class 6 who were entitled to vote cast their ballots in favor of the plan.[12] Consequently, if the Zarlengas' claim is classified separately from the other unsecured claims (as the Modified Third Plan provides), then that plan may be confirmed if the cramdown standards contained in § 1129(b) are met. However, if the Zarlengas' claim is classified together with the other unsecured claims (as the Third Plan provides), then the Zarlengas in effect have veto power over the plan because without their acceptance, no impaired class entitled to vote will have accepted the plan. See §§ 1126(c) (providing that a particular class accepts a plan only if at least two-thirds in amount of the claims in that class vote in favor of the plan) and 1129(a)(10) (providing that a plan may be confirmed only if at least one impaired class accepts the plan).

In support of its motion to strike the Modified Third Plan and to dismiss the case, Hancock argues that the revised classification scheme established in the Modified Third Plan is improper because "the Debtor attempts to artificially classify the Law Firm Claims separately from the Zarlenga Claim for the purpose of gerrymandering an assenting impaired class of unsecured creditors in violation of [the Bankruptcy Code]."

The Court agrees with Hancock that the classification scheme set forth in the Modified Third Plan is improper, but its conclusion is not based upon an "artificial classification" nor a so-called "gerrymandering" theory. Instead, the Court applies the "restrictive classification" standard and concludes that its factual finding of "substantial similarity" between the Zarlengas' claim and the other unsecured claims compels its decision to strike the Modified Third Plan, to deny confirmation of the Third Plan, and to dismiss the case.

* * * The Code's primary provisions regarding classification are set forth in § 1122. "Unfortunately, the Code does not expressly address the question [of classification of 'substantially similar' claims]." *Route 37,* 987 F.2d at 158.

Subsection (a) of § 1122 addresses only claims that are *not* "substantially similar"; it prohibits their placement in the same class. Subsection (a) is silent as to the classification of claims that *are* "substantially similar."

---

12. [Footnote 5 in original:] These two unsecured creditors, Holleb & Coff ($8,307.36 claim) and Katten, Muchin & Zavis ($6,490.00 claim), are law firms whose claims are based upon pre-petition work that they performed for the Debtor. All of the other unsecured claims are held by "insiders," see § 101(31)(C) (defining "insider" when the debtor is a partnership), whose votes are not considered for the purpose of * * * § 1129(a)(10) (providing that the acceptance of a class is "determined without including any acceptance of the plan by any insider"). * * *

Subsection (b) merely provides that a plan may separately classify one or more unsecured claims from the other unsecured claims under certain circumstances for administrative convenience. The Code contains no provision regarding the classification of "substantially similar" claims—either authorizing or prohibiting their separate classification.

Some courts, however, have discerned a restriction on the separate classification of "substantially similar" claims in the interplay between the two subsections of § 1122. Their reasoning is that if the plan proponent possesses the discretion to classify "substantially similar" claims separately, then § 1122(b), which permits a plan proponent to carve out a separate class of *de minimis* unsecured claims for administrative convenience, is superfluous—the plan proponent could create this administrative convenience class even without § 1122(b). Since one section of the Code should not be interpreted in such a way as to render another section superfluous, the "wholly permissive" view of classification must be incorrect. See, e.g., *Greystone*, 995 F.2d at 1278 .

This logic is flawed. Subsection (b) of § 1122 is not superfluous because it expressly authorizes the joint classification of claims that are not "substantially similar," notwithstanding the general prohibition on such joint classification contained in § 1122(a), provided only that the amounts of the claims are less than a certain amount. The first words of § 1122(a) are "Except as provided in subsection (b) of this section …." Subsection (b) is explicitly an exception to the prohibition contained in subsection (a) against classifying claims that are not "substantially similar" in the same class.

Consequently, the plain language of the Code provides no express guidance concerning any restrictions on the separate classification of "substantially similar" claims. * * *

Although the term "restrictive classification" may be new, the mandatory joint classification of "substantially similar" claims is not a new concept under the Bankruptcy Code. Ten years ago the First Circuit stated:

> The general rule regarding classification is that "'all creditors of equal rank with claims against the same property should be placed in the same class.'"
> Separate classifications for unsecured creditors are only justified "where the legal character of their claims is such as to accord them a status different from the other unsecured creditors …."

Granada Wines, Inc. v. New England Teamsters & Trucking Indus. Pension Fund, 748 F.2d 42, 46 (1st Cir.1984) (quoting In re Los Angeles Land & Invs., Ltd., 282 F. Supp. 448, 453 (D. Haw. 1968), aff'd, 447 F.2d 1366 (9th Cir. 1971), which was quoting Scherk v. Newton, 152 F.2d 747, 751 (10th Cir. 1945)). Indeed, it appears that most courts applied the "restrictive classification" standard (although not by that name) in the years immediately after the Code was enacted. See Peter E. Meltzer, *Disenfranchising the Dissenting Creditor Through Artificial Classification or Artificial Impairment,* 66 Am. Bankr. L.J. 281, 290-96 (1992) [hereinafter Meltzer] (discussing "the early cases … that prohibited artificial classification").

After about 1985, however, "[f]or reasons not entirely clear, … courts suddenly began examining the literal terms of § 1122(a) more closely, and noticing that this section does not technically prohibit artificial classification." Id. at 290. A convenient way to illustrate the logic supporting the "restrictive classification" standard is to examine the shortcomings of the alternate approaches to the classification issue taken by some courts after 1985.

a. "Flexible Classification" Standard

Several courts have interpreted the absence in the Code of an explicit prohibition on the separate classification of "substantially similar" claims as an implicit authorization for such separate classification. See, e.g., In re ZRM-Oklahoma Partnership, 156 B.R. 67, 71 (Bankr. W.D. Okla. 1993) ("Congress plainly fashioned a broad classification scheme, subject only to limitations contained elsewhere in the Code."). See generally In re AG Consultants Grain Div., Inc., 77 B.R. 665, 671 n. 15 (Bankr. N.D. Ind. 1987).

ZRM is representative of the most permissive view of "flexible classification." That court employed what it denominated "The Correct Method of Statutory Interpretation," to conclude that a plan proponent possesses absolute flexibility to classify "substantially similar" claims together or separately, as it sees fit, subject only to "other explicit protection mechanisms in the Code which Congress agreed to in sections 1111, 1123, and 1129."

AG Consultants, another opinion adopting "flexible classification," took a slightly narrower approach by imposing some meager restrictions on a plan proponent's right to establish separate classes of "substantially similar" claims. That court granted the plan proponent the flexibility to classify "substantially similar" unsecured claims in separate classes "if [the classes as established in the plan] are in the best interest of creditors; foster reorganization efforts (ensure success); do not violate the absolute priority rule; and, do not uselessly increase the number of classes." *AG Consultants,* 77 B.R. at 674 (brackets added; parentheses in original).

Other courts and commentators have raised a fundamental objection to the application of the "flexible classification" standard: "Flexible classification" renders § 1129(a)(10), the Code provision requiring the assent of at least one impaired class, a mere ministerial requirement.

Section 1129(a)(10) requires that if any class is impaired under the plan, at least one impaired class must accept the plan. As pointed out by several Circuit Courts of Appeals, § 1129(a)(10) is in direct conflict with the "flexible classification" standard. The Third Circuit stated:

> Nevertheless, it seems clear that the Code was not meant to allow a debtor complete freedom to place substantially similar claims in separate classes. The critical confirmation requirements set out in Section 1129(a)(8) (acceptance by all impaired classes) and Section 1129(a)(10) (acceptance by at least one impaired class in the event of "cram down") would be seriously undermined if a debtor could gerrymander classes. A debtor could then construct a classification scheme designed to secure approval by an arbitrarily designed class of impaired claims even though the overwhelming sentiment of the impaired creditors was that the proposed reorganization of the debtor would not serve any legitimate purpose. This would lead to abuse of creditors and would foster reorganizations that do not serve any broader public interest.

Route 37, 987 F.2d at 158. Seven years earlier, the Sixth Circuit declared:

[T]here must be some limit on a debtor's power to classify creditors in such a manner. The potential for abuse would be significant otherwise. Unless there is some requirement of keeping similar claims together, nothing would stand in the way of a debtor seeking out a few impaired creditors (or even one such creditor) who will vote for the plan and placing them in their own class.

U.S. Truck, 800 F.2d at 586.

* * *

In other words, the "flexible classification" standard is flawed because it would permit the plan proponent to carve out a separate class for one friendly creditor who the plan proponent knows will vote for the plan.[13] Permitting this action would circumvent the requirement, set forth in § 1129(a)(10), of an assenting impaired class, rendering it, at best, a mere ministerial requirement. * * *

b. "Gerrymandering" and "Reasonableness" Standards

The recent trend, at least among the Circuit Courts of Appeal that have faced the issue of the propriety of a classification scheme in a Chapter 11 plan, is for the court to conduct an implicit two-pronged analysis. First, the court determines whether a particular claim is "substantially similar" to other claims in a different class under the plan. If not, the analysis ends; under § 1122(a), the claim is required to be classified separately from the other claims. See *Woodbrook,* 19 F.3d at 319.

On the other hand, if the claim is found to be "substantially similar" to claims in another class, then the court next determines whether it is nevertheless appropriate for this claim to be classified separately. In the course of this analysis, courts have employed various non-Code-based tests, including "gerrymandering," e.g., *Greystone,* 995 F.2d at 1279, and "reasonableness," e.g., *Jersey City Medical Center,* 817 F.2d at 1061.

(1) "Gerrymandering"

* * * In the context of the classification of claims in a Chapter 11 plan of reorganization, to "gerrymander" is to create classes of claims in an artificial way with the purpose of ensuring that the plan will be confirmed. Perhaps the most influential case banning the practice of "gerrymandering" is *Greystone,* which states that "one clear rule ... emerges from otherwise muddled caselaw on § 1122 claims classification: thou shalt not classify similar claims differently in order to gerrymander an affirmative vote on a reorganization plan." *Greystone,* 995 F.2d at 1279.

Greystone's "one clear rule" prohibiting "gerrymandering" has been soundly criticized on two grounds. First, at least some of the authorities cited in that opinion do not support the "one clear rule":

---

13. [Footnote 13 in original:] Indeed, the case at bar reflects precisely this risk. The two law firms who are the only non-insider unsecured creditors (other than the Zarlengas) are undoubtedly friendly creditors. Although this Court has previously held that the impairment of the class containing their claims is not "artificial impairment" such that their votes should not be counted, this is a different issue than whether their claims may be classified separately from the Zarlengas' claim. It is not inconsistent with the purposes of § 1129(a)(10) for the Court to consider the votes of creditors who support the plan even though their support may be based upon their non-economic relationships with the debtor, but it would be inconsistent to classify pro-debtor creditors separately from other creditors solely because of those relationships.

For its "one clear rule" prohibiting gerrymandering of similar claims the [Fifth Circuit] cited three Circuit Court decisions, none of which found impermissible gerrymandering for an acceptance, and one of which *approved* it. The separate classification in In re *U.S. Truck Co.,* [800 F.2d 581 (6th Cir.1986)], was approved on the basis that employee creditors had different interests in the debtor's survival than trade creditors, a rationale that is indistinguishable from the "gerrymandering" at issue in *Greystone.* * * * The cases hardly provide a "clear rule" on what constitutes inappropriate efforts to "gerrymander an affirmative vote," and the holding of *U.S. Truck* is inescapably to the contrary. * * *

Haines [*Greystone Becomes Tombstone,* NORTON BANKR. L. ADVISOR, Jan. 1992], at 3 (emphasis in original).

Second, and more significantly, it is difficult or impossible for a court to apply the "gerrymandering" standard in the context of a Chapter 11 classification scheme because "gerrymandering" focuses upon the plan proponent's state of mind. See *Greystone,* 995 F.2d at 1279 ("[I]f [the debtor's] proffered 'reasons' for separately classifying the [undersecured creditor's] deficiency claim simply mask the intent to gerrymander the voting process, that classification scheme should not have been approved."). "The 'one clear rule' is not easy to apply since it is not about 'classifying similar claims'; it is about the debtor's purpose." *Woodbrook,* 19 F.3d at 318.

Every plan proponent creates its classification scheme with the goal of maximizing the probability that its plan will be confirmed. The characterization of a plan proponent's efforts as "gerrymandering" is pejorative and falsely conclusive. In other words, every plan proponent "gerrymanders" to some extent; an examination of the plan proponent's intent is neither helpful nor feasible. Instead, the question remains: How far may the plan proponent go in drawing its class boundaries?

(2) "Reasonableness"

Similarly, opinions that employ a "reasonableness" standard to a plan proponent's classification scheme are not particularly illuminating or easy to apply. See, e.g., *Jersey City Medical Center,* 817 F.2d at 1061 ("[T]he authorities recognize that the classification of claims or interests must be reasonable .... We immediately note the reasonableness of distinguishing the claims of physicians, medical malpractice victims, employee benefit plan participants, and trade creditors.").

This "standard" raises more questions than it answers: How is a court to determine whether a classification scheme in a Chapter 11 plan is reasonable? What aspects of a given classification scheme cause it to be reasonable or unreasonable? The best way to answer these questions is to look to the Code itself.

c. "Restrictive Classification" Standard

As discussed at length in part III.A.1. above, the Code provides a test, "substantial similarity," to determine when a claim cannot be placed in a particular class; § 1122(a) provides that claims that are not "substantially similar" must be classified separately. It is logical to apply this Code-based test in a correlative manner to fill the void left by the amorphous "reasonableness" and "gerrymandering" standards. That is, the "restrictive classification" standard is not remarkably different from the "gerrymandering" and "reasonableness" standards that many courts have been applying; "restrictive classification" merely looks to the Code for a test to establish the bounds of "reasonableness." Under the "restrictive classification" standard it is reasonable for the plan proponent to classify claims separately only if these claims are not "substantially similar."

This Court, therefore, concludes that "restrictive classification" is the appropriate method for evaluating the classification of claims in a Chapter 11 plan. Instead of conducting a two-part analysis, the Court will determine, as a single finding of fact, whether the particular claim is "substantially similar" to the other claims in the class at issue.

If it is not "substantially similar," then, as under the two-pronged analysis, this claim must be classified separately pursuant to the plain language of § 1122(a). However, if this claim is "substantially similar" to other claims, then it must be classified together with these other claims. This analysis preserves the viability of § 1129(a)(10) without requiring an examination of a plan proponent's subjective motives.

The plan proponent has broad discretion in classifying claims. If the plan proponent can articulate differences among the claims—that is, if the plan proponent can demonstrate the lack of "substantial similarity"—then separate classification is proper. Cf. *Boston Post Road,* 21 F.3d at 483 (disapproving a "restrictive classification" standard, but nevertheless holding that "the [plan proponent] must adduce credible proof of a legitimate reason for separate classification of similar claims."). The differences may relate to legal rights or bankruptcy priorities; or business reasons relevant to the success of the reorganized debtor, see, e.g., *Lumber Exchange,* 968 F.2d at 649 ("There is some authority for the proposition that a plan may classify trade creditors separately from, and treat them more generously than, other creditors if doing so is necessary to a debtor's ongoing business."); but see *Hanson,* 828 F.2d at 1313 ("Although there is some case authority for this distinction, ... the interests of trade creditors are not sufficiently 'unique' to warrant separate classification in this case." (citation omitted)).

As an example, it might be vital to a debtor to be able to treat customers' warranty claims differently than trade creditor claims, even though they are all general unsecured claims. In this instance, a court may reasonably find that warranty claims are not "substantially similar" to trade debt. The significant aspect of the "restrictive classification" analysis is that the inquiry focuses objectively upon the claims themselves, not upon the plan proponent's subjective intent.

* * *

The Court finds that the Zarlengas' claim is "substantially similar" to the unsecured claims in Class 6 of the Debtor's Modified Third Plan. They are all unsecured claims with the same bankruptcy priority. Although the Zarlengas' claim is based upon a state common law private nuisance theory—that is, it is a tort claim—the Zarlengas' claim has the same non-bankruptcy legal status as the contract-based claims contained in Class 6. For the purposes of this bankruptcy case, the dispute regarding the Zarlengas' claim has been resolved, and their claim is liquidated in the amount of $40,000. Outside of bankruptcy, the Zarlengas and the contract claimants may look to the partnership, then to the general partners, to satisfy their claims. None of these claims entitles its holder to receive punitive damages. Outside of bankruptcy, all of these claims share the same priority and "race to the courthouse" pressures; none is subject to equitable subordination. And finally, the Debtor has not articulated any business or economic difference among these claims.

The Debtor only asserts that the Zarlengas' claim is not "substantially similar" to the claims in Class 6 of the Modified Third Plan because the Zarlengas have a different motivation; the Zarlengas' attorney stated on the record that the Zarlengas will vote against any plan proposed by the Debtor because they do not agree with the Debtor's proposed solution to the noise problem that gave rise to their $40,000 pre-petition claim. Accordingly, the Debtor argues, the Zarlengas' claim should not be classified with the Class 6 claims, whose holders all favor the Debtor's reorganization.

The Court is not persuaded by the Debtor's argument. Different creditors will always have different motivations. The relevant issue is the similarity among the characteristics of the claims, not the motives of the holders of the claims. The way in which the holder of a particular claim is likely to vote is not a legitimate factor for a court to take into account when evaluating the issue of "substantial similarity." See *Route 37*, 987 F.2d at 161 ("Absent bad faith or illegality (see 11 U.S.C. § 1126(e) (1988)), the Code is not concerned with a claim holder's reason for voting one way or the other, and undoubtedly most claim holders vote in accordance with their overall economic interests as they see them.").

* * * Under the "restrictive classification" standard adopted by the Court, the Zarlengas' claim cannot be separately classified. The Debtor's Modified Third Plan violates this standard; therefore, the Modified Third Plan is stricken. Under the classification scheme set forth in the Debtor's Third Plan, no impaired class has accepted the plan, so confirmation is denied. Finally, the case is dismissed because it is apparent to the Court that, without the support of either Hancock or the Zarlengas, the Debtor is unable to effectuate a plan of reorganization. * * *

NOTES

1. Would the *U.S. Truck* Court affirm the decision in *Bloomingdale Partners* (with respect to classification issues) if the case were somehow brought before it on appeal? Is exclusion of the Zarlengas' claim from the class of other general unsecured creditors analogous to the exclusion of the Union's claim in *U.S. Truck*? How would the *Bloomingdale Partners* court have resolved the issue in *U.S. Truck*?

2. Is the determination of "substantial similarity" a factual determination, or is it in reality an exercise of discretion by the bankruptcy court?

3. Many of the classification cases deal with whether the unsecured deficiency claim of an undersecured, nonrecourse, secured creditor in a single asset real estate case may be classified separately from other unsecured claims. That issue is discussed in Chapter Fifteen of this text, because it requires an understanding of § 1111(b) and because the cases that raise it also raise a key cramdown issue: whether there is a new value "exception" (or "corollary") to the absolute priority rule.

Problem 11-4

Assume that the general unsecured claims in Foam Corporation's case consist of Gruff's $3.2 million claim based on the loan he made to Foam Corporation, $1 million of which is subordinated to the trade debts; trade debts owing to Tina Chemical and Swenson Chemical of $3 million and $2 million respectively, both of which were guaranteed by Gruff; trade debts owing to thirty-seven other suppliers and totaling $3 million; $30,000 in nonpriority unpaid salary owed to Deborah Bell (an officer of Foam Corporation); and Imperial Insurance Company's $400,000 claim arising from Foam Corporation's rejection of the leases on the Detroit and Cleveland plants. Foam Corporation rejected those leases—for which the monthly rentals were higher than fair market rentals—but plans to assume the leases on the Denver and Seattle plants—for which the monthly rentals are well below the fair market level. Imperial has been severely strained financially as a result of the rejection of the Detroit and Cleveland leases. Imperial has stated that its prime goal is to prevent the debtor from reorganizing, in hopes that it can get back the Denver and Seattle properties and lease them to someone else at a fair market rate. (Imperial believes that a restrictive use provision in the leases would make it difficult for the debtor or a trustee to assign them to someone else.) Foam Corporation is the largest customer of three of the trade creditors (TC1, TC2, and TC3, who hold a total of $1 million in general unsecured claims); all three would face financial ruin if Foam Corporation ceased to buy from them. They are willing to take all their value in the form of stock to keep Foam Corporation in business; they are also willing to take a lesser percentage than other trade creditors—but not less than 40%. One other trade creditor (TC4) is one of only two suppliers worldwide of a fire retardant chemical additive for foam that Foam Corporation must have to continue in business; TC4 has stated that it will not sell to Foam Corporation after the chapter 11 case is over unless the plan provides it with at least 70% cash payment of its $200,000 claim and 10% in promissory notes. Assume all of the other trade creditors—except Swenson Chemical and Tina Chemical—will support Foam Corporation's plan as long as it provides at least a 10% payment in cash and 35% in promissory notes. Swenson Chemical is outraged that the court enjoined it under § 105 from seeking to collect its debt from Gruff personally and will oppose any plan other than its own. Swenson believes Gruff has substantial assets that it will be able to reach once the injunction is lifted. Tina Chemical has not sought to enforce Gruff's guarantee thus far and thinks Gruff has little in assets other than his Foam Corporation stock, but has thus far refused to say what it would find acceptable by way of treatment in a plan. None of the trade creditors would support a plan under which Gruff got to keep anything more than a token amount of value on account of the subordinated part of his claim. Bell will support any plan Foam Corporation files.

You are an associate with the firm of Smith, Martinez & Johnson, the attorneys for debtor in possession Foam Corporation. Johnson has asked you to consider whether a plan could permissibly (1) place all of the general unsecured claims in one class, (2) place Tina's and Swenson's claims together in a class by themselves, (3) place the claims of TC1, TC2, and TC3 together in a class by themselves, (4) place the claim of TC4 in a class by itself, (5) place Imperial's claim in a class by itself, (6) place Swenson's and Imperial's claims together in a class by themselves, or (7) divide Gruff's claim into a subordinated $1 million claim placed in its own class (subordinate to the trade debt) and a $2.2 million unsubordinated claim, placed in a class together with Imperial's $400,000 claim and Bell's $30,000 claim. He asked you if you understood why Foam Corporation might or might not want to use one or more of those classifications in its plan.

Problem 11-5

Assume the same facts as in the preceding Problem. Johnson asked you to outline how you thought Foam Corporation's plan should handle the general unsecured claims—how it should classify them and how it should treat the class or classes of general unsecured claims. He suggested that you build on possibility (7) from the preceding paragraph and simply provide $900,000 worth of stock for the class that includes Gruff's $2.2 million unsubordinated claim, Imperial's claim, and Bell's claim; he suggested you give the class of Gruff's subordinated claim $1, so little that you can ignore it. Johnson reminded you that for an impaired class of claims to accept a plan, two thirds in amount and more than half in number of the claims that are voted must accept the plan. Johnson told you to assume that all the claims will be voted and said he wanted a plan that would be accepted by all the classes. He told you that the Foam Corporation plan can give the general unsecured creditors as a whole $820,000 cash, $2.4 million in promissory notes (at a market interest rate), and $1.3 million worth of common stock. He told you that Gruff is willing to take all of his value in the form of stock. He said to assume, for purposes of your outline, that Tina Chemical will accept the plan if it receives 10% payment in cash and 35% in the form of promissory notes, just like most of the other trade creditors. He asked whether you thought Imperial would like the plan, and whether Imperial could block its confirmation assuming Imperial would be paid 25% of its $400,000 claim in a liquidation.

D. IMPAIRMENT OF CLASSES

The purpose of a plan of reorganization is to restructure the debtor's debts, not to leave the creditors' rights unaltered. It should come as no surprise then that § 1123(b)(1) permits the plan to "impair" almost any class of claims or interests. Section 1123(a)(5) explicitly permits the plan to extend due dates, change interest rates, and change other terms of debt instruments; to cancel or modify the terms of the agreements (known as indentures) that protect certain creditors (usually holders of publicly issued debt); and to modify any lien. Note that § 1123(b)(5), added by the 1994 Bankruptcy Reform Act, specifically authorizes the plan to modify the rights of holders of secured and unsecured claims, or to leave their rights unaffected.[14]

In fact, the plan can include any "appropriate" provisions that are not inconsistent with the Code. Section 1123(b)(6). That includes provisions that alter the rights of creditors in ways not specifically mentioned in § 1123. For example, the

---

14. However, § 1123(b)(5) protects from modification the rights of holders of secured claims that are secured only by a mortgage on real property that is the debtor's principal residence. Apparently that protection extends to an undersecured mortgagee's rights with respect to the entire home mortgage debt, including the unsecured claim portion that the undersecured mortgagee has under § 506(a), not simply to the secured claim portion (at least as long as the mortgagee is not completely "underwater"). See Nobelman v. American Sav. Bank, 508 U.S. 324, 113 S. Ct. 2106, 124 L. Ed. 2d 228 (1992) (construing identical language in § 1322(b)(2), holding that a chapter 13 plan could not strip down the lien of an undersecured home mortgagee to the value of the home, and holding that the plan could not modify the rights of the mortgagee with respect to the unsecured claim portion). Entrepreneurs often grant mortgages on their homes to secure business debt. Thus chapter 11 cases sometimes involve home mortgages given by a sole proprietor or major shareholder who who seeks chapter 11 protection. Cf. Toibb v. Radloff, 501 U.S. 157, 111 S. Ct. 2197, 115 L. Ed.2d 145 (1991) (holding, in a case in which debtor owned stock in a business, that debtor need not operate a business to be eligible to be a debtor in chapter 11).

plan may of course provide less than full payment of unsecured claims. There is, however, a limit on how much less: any creditor who does not accept the plan and whose claim is in an impaired class must receive at least as much value as a liquidation would provide. See § 1129(a)(7) (known as the best interests of creditors test), which is discussed in Chapter Fourteen of this text. Further protections apply under § 1129(b) if the impaired class does not accept the plan—the "fair and equitable" standard and the "no unfair discrimination" standard, which are discussed in detail in the Chapter on cramdown, Chapter Fifteen of this text. In particular, if an impaired class of unsecured claims does not accept the plan, then holders of claims in that class must receive property of a value equal to the full allowed amount of their claims or else no holder of any claim or interest in a junior class can receive or keep any property on account of the holder's claim or interest. See § 1129(b)(2)(B) (fair and equitable requirement). "Any property" includes stock in the debtor. Thus in a cramdown, if such a class dissents, and if holders of claims in the class do not receive property with a value equal to the amount of their claims, then the stockholders of the debtor will not be able to keep any of their stock.[15] If the debtor's managers are also its owners—as in most cases of small and medium sized companies—then the debtor will have this extra incentive to try to make sure that all impaired classes of unsecured claims accept the plan.

Even though the Code places firm limits on how little value the plan can give to unsecured creditors, it places almost no limit on the form of that value. Provisions requiring general unsecured creditors to take promissory notes or voting stock in the reorganized company (or even payment in kind in the form of goods) are "not inconsistent with the applicable provisions" of the Code, and hence they are permissible. See § 1123(b)(6). In fact, the provisions of § 1129 that codify the best interests of creditors test and the fair and equitable standard (as it applies to unsecured creditors) specifically use the broad term "property" to refer to what the unsecured creditors are entitled to receive. See § 1129(a)(7) and 1129(b)(2)(B). When Congress meant to require that money be given to creditors, it used the term "cash" or "cash payments." See § 1129(a)(9) (dealing with priority claims); § 1129(b)(2)(A)(i)(II) (dealing with secured claims).

Thus we see that debtor (or any other plan proponent) has broad discretion as to how general unsecured creditors may be treated in the plan. Of course if the debtor does not exercise that discretion with a keen appreciation for the desires of the creditors, it will be hard to get all the impaired classes of claims to accept the plan, which is necessary for a consensual confirmation.

The debtor has less discretion with regard to how to treat holders of secured claims. Each secured claim will typically be in its own class; thus if a holder of a secured claim rejects the plan, the holder's class will also reject it, thus triggering application of the fair and equitable standard with regard to that

---

15. We will discuss in Chapter Fifteen whether they may be able to contribute new value to the debtor and thus buy stock in the reorganized company. If they can do so, they may continue to own all or part of the company even after a cramdown.

class. As applied to classes of secured claims that do not accept the plan, that standard usually requires the plan to provide (1) that the holder of the claim retain its lien on the collateral for the amount of the allowed secured claim[16] and (2) that the holder receive *cash payments* over time that total at least the allowed amount of the secured claim and have a present value as of the effective date at least equal to the lesser of the amount of the allowed secured claim and the value of the collateral. See § 1129(b)(2)(A)(i).[17]

We will consider those requirements in detail in Chapter Fifteen. For now, it is important to see that the debtor cannot require a secured creditor to take stock in the reorganized debtor as payment on its secured claim. The result is that in most chapter 11 cases secured creditors are entitled to demand the lion's share of the debt that the debtor can afford to give out. That follows because there is a limit to how much debt can be given out to the creditors if the reorganized debtor is not to be overloaded once again with debts. If there are substantial secured claims in a chapter 11 case, much of that debt may have to be given to the secured creditors, unless they can be convinced to take *voluntarily* some of their value in the form of the debtor's stock.[18] The result is that unsecured creditors may have no choice but to accept most of their value in the form of stock, if there is to be a reorganization.

Note also how Acme's plan (set out at the beginning of this Chapter) impairs the class that contains Second Finance Company's secured claim, Class 2. The plan reduces SFC's interest rate from the contractual rate of 11% to a rate of 10%; it also increases the time for paying off the mortgage from eight years to ten. Section 1123(a)(5)(H) explicitly permits both of those changes in SFC's rights.

---

16. Instead of providing for the lien to remain on the collateral, the plan may provide for sale of the collateral free of the lien with the lien attaching to the proceeds of the sale. See § 1129(b)(2)(A)(ii).

17. If the creditor is undersecured and makes the § 1111(b)(2) election to have its entire claim treated as secured, then the present value of the payments need only equal the value of the collateral, not the entire amount of the secured claim. See § 1129(b)(2)(A)(i)(II). Nevertheless, the creditor is entitled to receive a total number of dollars equal to the amount of its allowed secured claim, which will be the entire amount of the debt if the 1111(b)(2) election is made. The 1111(b)(2) election is treated at length in Chapter Fifteen of this text.

18. The plan does not need to provide for monetary payments to the secured creditor if, instead of providing fair and equitable treatment under § 1129(b)(2)(A)(i), the plan provides fair and equitable treatment under § 1129(b)(2)(A)(iii), by giving the secured creditor the "indubitable equivalent" of its secured claim. A plan cannot provide the indubitable equivalent of the secured creditor's claim by giving the secured creditor stock (or other form of ownership interest) *in the reorganized debtor.* See Metropolitan Life Ins. Co. v. San Felipe @ Voss, Ltd., (In re San Felipe @ Voss, Ltd.), 115 B.R. 526 (S.D. Tex. 1990); In re TM Monroe Manor Assocs. Ltd., 140 B.R. 298 (Bankr. N.D. Ga. 1991) (holding that plan did not provide the indubitable equivalent by providing for conversion of secured debt into limited partnership interest). However, as the court in *San Felipe @ Voss* held, the plan may provide the indubitable equivalent of the secured creditor's claim if it gives the secured creditor stock in another company, assuming the stock has sufficient value and has a "history of stability and liquidity." In *San Felipe @ Voss,* the court held that the plan provided a secured creditor with the "indubitable equivalent" of its secured claim by giving it shares of stock in a third party. The shares were restricted stock that could not be sold until six months after receipt, but they were listed on the London International Stock exchange and had a worth substantially more than the amount of the secured claim, thus providing a cushion against a drop in value during the six months. In Chapter Fifteen below we discuss *San Felipe @ Voss* and how a plan can provide the "indubitable equivalent" of a secured claim.

The plan also reduces the principal amount of the mortgage to the amount of SFC's secured claim as determined under § 506(a). Unless SFC makes the § 1111(b)(2) election, that seems to be permitted by § 1123(a)(5)(E), (b)(1), and (b)(6). Whether the plan's treatment of SFC's claim satisfies the fair and equitable standard will depend on whether 10% is an appropriate market interest rate, on whether SFC makes the "1111(b) election," and, if SFC does make that election, on whether the total number of dollars to be paid over the ten years of the plan is at least equal to the total mortgage debt. See Chapter Fifteen.

We have seen how the plan may impair classes of claims and interests. Is there any reason why the debtor (or other plan proponent) might want to leave certain classes unimpaired? Consider Acme's plan, which appears at the beginning of this Chapter. Why does the plan leave Class 1 unimpaired? See §§ 1126(f), 1129(a)(7) and 1129(b)(2)(A). Why does the plan leave Class 4 unimpaired? See §§ 1125(b), 1126(f), 1129(b)(2)(B), and Rule 3017(d).

How then can a class be left unimpaired? Section 1124, as amended by the Bankruptcy Reform Act of 1994 (and by the 2005 BAPCPA), gives the drafter of a plan only two ways to leave a class unimpaired. The plan must, "with respect to each claim or interest of such class" either (1) "leave unaltered the legal, equitable, and contractual rights to which such claim or interest entitles the holder," or (2) leave such rights unaltered except for curing defaults, reinstating maturity dates (in case claims have been accelerated), and compensating the holders for reasonable reliance on whatever nonbankruptcy rights they may have had to accelerate their debts. See § 1124(1)-(2). In the following problems we explore what is required to "cure" a default, and what kinds of compensation the holder of a claim may be entitled to under § 1124(2)(C). As a basic matter, however, a cure will require at least that any missed payments of money be made up. Compensation for reasonable reliance on acceleration rights should at least include compensation for costs a creditor may have incurred in attempting to collect an accelerated debt, including costs of attempts to foreclose on collateral. The required payments may not be made over time under the plan; they must be made on or before the effective date of the plan. See In re Jones, 32 B.R. 951 (Bankr. D. Utah 1983).

Note, however, that debtors are not required to cure defaults "of a kind specified in section 365(b)(2) * * * or of a kind that section 365(b)(2) expressly does not require to be cured." The 1994 Act added a subsection (D) to § 365(b)(2), which was slightly amended by the 2005 BAPCPA, as described in Chapter Seven above. Section 365(b)(2) now includes not just defaults under ipso facto clauses—clauses that provide for a default based on the filing of a bankruptcy case, the appointment of a receiver, the making of an assignment for benefit of creditors, or the insolvency or other financial condition of the debtor—but also defaults arising from a breach of an obligation to pay a "penalty rate" (also known as a default rate) of interest where the penalty rate became payable due to a nonmonetary default. See § 365(b)(2)(D). Many loan agreements provide, as we saw in Chapter Nine, for a higher rate of interest, a penalty or default rate, if the loan is in default. Some defaults that trigger such higher rates are nonmonetary, such as, for example, the failure to retain in office a particular chief financial officer whom the creditor trusted and whose departure from the debtor's business was therefore made an agreed event of default.

Further, for loan agreements entered into after the 1994 Act's enactment date, Oct. 22, 1994, § 1123(d) provides that the requirements for curing defaults are to be determined "in accordance with the agreement and with applicable nonbankruptcy law." Although § 1123(d) expressly overrides §§ 506(b), 1129(a)(7), and 1129(b), it does not expressly override § 1124. Thus at least one of your authors believes a plan may be able to cure defaults at a non-default rate of interest while leaving a class unimpaired.[19] Another author disagrees strongly and believes that the *Entz-White* court's analysis was seriously flawed even before the 1994 amendments.[20]

Before passage of the Bankruptcy Reform Act of 1994, there was a third way that a plan could leave a class of claims unimpaired; it could provide for payment of the full allowed amount of the claims in the class in cash on the effective date. See former § 1124(3) (deleted by Pub. L. No. 103-394, § 213(d) (1994)). Do you see why former § 1124(3) might have caused unsecured or undersecured creditors to be denied postpetition interest on their claims even if the debtor were solvent on a liquidation basis? Consider whether the allowed amount of the claims would include postpetition interest and see §§ 502(b)(2), 726(a)(5) and 1129(a)(7). See In re New Valley Corp., 168 B.R. 73 (Bankr. D.N.J. 1994). *New Valley* reached a result that the drafters of the 1994 Act sought to preclude by deleting § 1124(3). See 140 Cong. Rec. H10768 (daily ed. Oct. 4, 1994) (section-by-section analysis of 1994 Act, placed in record by House Judiciary Committee Chairman Brooks).

There is a question whether the rights that must be left unaltered for a class to be unimpaired are the full nonbankruptcy rights that the holder of the claim or interest had, or only those rights as modified by provisions of the Bankruptcy Code. Arguably, if the *plan* does not affect the rights of holders of claims or interests in a class, then the *plan* leaves those rights unaltered, and the class might be thought to be unimpaired. Such an approach was accepted by the Third Circuit in a case

---

19. See Florida Partners Corp. v. Southeast Co., (In re Southeast Co.), 868 F.2d 335 (9th Cir. 1989) (cited in Problem 11-6 below); Great Western Bank & Trust v. Entz-White Lumber and Supply, Inc. (In re Entz-White Lumber and Supply, Inc.), 850 F.2d 1338 (9th Cir. 1988) (holding that cure under the Bankruptcy Code eliminates all consequences of the default, including obligation to pay default interest); cf. MW Post Portfolio Fund Ltd. v. Norwest Bank Minn., N.A. (In re Onco Inv. Co.), 316 B.R. 163 (Bankr. D. Del. 2004) (holding that (1) "cure and reinstatement * * * roll[s] back the clock to the time before the default existed * * * for all purposes and as to all parties," (2) debtor therefore did not owe $11 million amount, including default interest, that depended on existence of default, and (3) holders of subordinated debt therefore were not required to disgorge $11 million to senior lender out of payments they were to receive under the plan).

20. See Southland Corp. v. Toronto-Dominion (In re Southland Corp.), 160 F.3d 1054, 1059 n.6 (5th Cir. 1998) ("not[ing] that Congress, in bankruptcy amendments enacted in 1994, arguably rejected the Entz-White denial of contractual default interest rates"); In re 139-141 Owners Corp., 313 B.R. 364 (S.D.N.Y. 2004) (affirming award of default interest and holding that § 1124(2) does not provide a basis for denial of default interest).

involving the § 502(b)(6) cap on the allowable claim of real property lessors, which apparently (as interpreted by the Third Circuit) reduced the lessor's claim from over $4 million to perhaps as little as $100,000. See Solow v. PPI Enters. (U.S.), Inc. (In re PPI Enters. (U.S.), Inc.), 324 F.3d 197 (3d Cir. 2003). The court held that if the lessor's rights were maintained with respect to the amount of the capped claim—the $100,000 or so remaining after application of § 502(b)(6)—then the plan would not impair the class containing that claim.

The court reasoned that the rights that had to be left unaltered were the rights to which the lessor's "claim" entitled it, and that the lessor's claim (as capped by § 502(b)(6)) was not a $4 million claim but only a $100,000 (or so) claim. Thus only the lessor's rights with respect to the $100,000 claim had to be left unaltered. This argument is somewhat similar to arguments rejected by the Supreme Court in the *Nobelman* decision cited in footnote 14 of this chapter above. For several additional reasons it is not at all clear (to at least one of your authors) that such an approach is consistent with the language of § 1124, or with Congress's intent in amending § 1124 in 1994.

Section 1124 requires that contractual rights be left unaltered. Arguably, the lessor did not have severable contractual rights with respect to any $100,000 claim that could be left unaltered. In addition, part of the court's reasoning is seriously overstated. The court reasoned that "[t]o hold that [§ 502(b)(6)'s] mere application in a bankruptcy proceeding causes impairment would nullify its meaning." 324 F.3d at 205. That is simply not true; the lessor's claim still would be limited, and the only result would be that the lessor would have an opportunity to vote on the plan and to receive the same protections that holders of other claims in impaired classes receive. A plan that paid the capped claim on the plan's effective date in full in cash with postpetition interest—the kind of plan apparently at issue in *PPI Enterprises*—would more than satisfy the fair and equitable requirement with respect to the class containing the capped claim. The § 1141(d) discharge would eliminate any personal liability of the reorganized debtor for the disallowed part of the lessor's claim. Sections 506(d), 545(3), and 1141(c) would provide multiple avenues for eliminating any lien the lessor might have for the disallowed part of its claim.

An even stronger reason to question the analysis in *PPI Enterprises* is that it arguably would allow the *New Valley* approach to unimpairment to be resurrected, despite Congress's intent to bury it permanently by way of the 1994 amendments. Note that provisions of the Code, not of the plan, cause an unsecured claim to be allowed in an amount that does not include postpetition interest. See § 502, providing for the amount of the claim to be determined as of the petition filing date, and in particular § 502(b)(2), disallowing "unmatured interest" (meaning interest not earned as of the petition date). If a class is unimpaired when the plan leaves unaltered the rights of holders of claims as limited by § 502(b)(6), it would seem that a plan similarly could leave unaltered the rights of holders of claims as the claims are limited by § 502's denial of postpetition interest. Under that approach, cash payment in full of the allowed claim, without postpetition interest, would leave unaltered the rights of the holders of the claims, and result in the class being considered unimpaired. As a result, just as under the *New Valley* decision, the best interests test of § 1129(a)(7) would not apply. Then, just as in *New Valley*, postpetition interest would not have to be paid even by a debtor that was solvent on a liquidation basis.

Is it possible—after the 1994 amendment to § 1124—to provide in the plan for cash payment of claims in a class and thereby leave the class unimpaired? Suppose a plan provides for payment of the claims in a class in full in cash on the effective date of the plan, including postpetition interest (and any fees or costs to which any creditor with a claim in the class would have been entitled under nonbankruptcy law). If a creditor receives everything under the plan that it would be entitled to receive outside bankruptcy, the plan would seem not to alter the creditor's rights but rather to honor them. Cf. *PPI Enterprises*, 324 F.3d at 206-07 (agreeing with analysis of bankruptcy court below and of bankruptcy court in In re Rocha, 179 B.R. 305, 307 n.1 (Bankr. M.D. Fla. 1995) that payment of the amount of the allowed claims in a class in full in cash with postpetition interest would render the class unimpaired). Of course the court in *PPI Enterprises* did not require that the claim holder receive everything it would have been entitled to receive under nonbankruptcy law, but rather just the allowed claim—an amount drastically reduced by § 502(b)(6)—plus postpetition interest on the allowed claim. At least one of your authors would insist that the payment be of the full amount owed under nonbankruptcy law, including not only postpetition interest through the effective date[21] but also any fees or costs to which the claim holder would be entitled under nonbankruptcy law.

Finally, we need to make two points very clearly. First, impairment is a term that is applied to classes, not to claims. Even where a class contains only one claim, it is important to use the terminology correctly: the class, not the claim, is impaired or unimpaired.

Second, a plan does not leave a class unimpaired just because it calls for full payment, over time, of the claims in the class, even if postpetition and postconfirmation interest is included. If the plan calls for payments to be made over time on the schedule provided for in the contract between the debtor and the creditor, then the class may be unimpaired. Otherwise, the class is impaired if

---

21. Nonbankruptcy law does not in all cases call for payment of interest on amounts owed. Arguably, if a claim on which nonbankruptcy law does not require payment of interest is placed in a class with a claim on which nonbankruptcy law does require payment of interest, § 1123(a)(4) requires that the plan equally provide interest for both or for neither. In such a case, if interest were provided for neither, then the rights of the holder of at least one claim in the class arguably would be altered, thus making the class an impaired class. See § 1124 (providing that the "*class*" is impaired unless the plan leaves rights unaltered "with respect to *each claim* or interest of such class") (emphasis added). (Note that impairment is an attribute of classes, not of claims.) If none of the claims in the class entitled its holder to interest under nonbankruptcy law, it is possible that a plan calling for full payment of the claims in cash on the effective date without interest would leave the class unimpaired, but, if the debtor is solvent on a liquidation basis, such a result could clash with the purpose of the 1994 amendment to § 1124 by allowing the plan to give the creditors in a supposedly unimpaired class less than they would receive in a chapter 7 case.

payments are to be made over time, even if the payments have a present value equal to 100% of the claims in the class. See In re G.L. Bryan Invs., Inc., __ B.R. __, 2006 WL 92514 (Bankr. D. Colo. Mar. 3, 2006). In addition, as noted above, a class is impaired even if the plan calls for full payment of the claims in cash on the effective date, if the payment does not include postpetition interest.

Problem 11-6

Foam Corporation owed First Bank $550,000 (as of the date of its petition) secured by a real estate mortgage on the Fresno, California, plant. The contractual interest rate on the debt is 7%. (Assume that is substantially below the present fair market interest rate for a similar loan). Under the contractual schedule, the mortgage was to have been fully paid off about fourteen and one half years after the date of the petition, in the latter part of the year 2020. The mortgage includes provisions stating that Foam Corporation will be in default if (1) Foam Corporation fails to pay any payment when due, (2) if Foam Corporation files a bankruptcy petition, (3) if Foam Corporation's ratio of current assets to current liabilities (its "current ratio") falls below two, or (4) if Foam Corporation's net worth falls below $500,000. In the event of default, the mortgage provided that First Bank was entitled to charge a default interest rate of 11% interest on the entire balance owing, including the entire amount of any unpaid installments. Thus the mortgage would permit First Bank to charge 11% interest on the interest portion of the payments that Foam Corporation missed. Assume California law is not clear whether a mortgage may enforceably provide that interest will be paid on unpaid interest in this way. First Bank was also entitled on default to accelerate the debt and, if the entire amount was not paid immediately, to foreclose on the plant. Of course for months before its filing, Foam Corporation's current ratio was far below two and its net worth was negative. Two months before Foam Corporation filed its petition, after Foam Corporation had failed to make two payments to First Bank, First Bank delivered a notice of acceleration to Foam Corporation and began taking steps toward foreclosure. By the time Foam Corporation filed its chapter 11 petition, it had missed four monthly payments of $5,040 each to First Bank. Pursuant to an adequate protection order, Foam Corporation has made all the postpetition monthly payments in the regular $5,040 amount; the order stated that acceptance of such payments would be without prejudice to any rights First Bank otherwise might as a result of the default. Consider §§ 365(b), 1123(d) (effective only for loan agreements entered into after Oct. 22, 1994), 1124.

If the Fresno real property is worth $800,000, what should Foam Corporation's plan provide with respect to the class that contains First Bank's Fresno mortgage secured claim? What will the plan have to provide to leave the class unimpaired? In order to reinstate the mortgage, which of the defaults will have to be cured? What will have to be done to cure the defaults? Will First Bank be entitled to be paid interest at an 11% rate from the time of the first default up until the time that the defaults are cured? Will First Bank be entitled to be paid postpetition interest on the overdue installment payments, including interest on the unpaid interest from those missed payments? In addition to the Code sections noted above and the cases cited in footnotes 19 and 20 above in this chapter, see Rake v. Wade, 508 U.S. 464, 113 S. Ct. 2187, 124 L. Ed. 2d 424 (1993) (holding that oversecured mortgagee was entitled to interest on arrearages, including interest on unpaid interest, where defaulted home mortgage was cured and reinstated under § 1322(b)(5)); United States Trust Co. v. LTV Steel Co. (In re Chateaugay Corp.), 150 B.R. 529 (Bankr. S.D.N.Y.1993), aff'd, 170 B.R. 551 (S.D.N.Y. 1994); In re Arlington Village Partners, Ltd., 66 B.R. 308 (Bankr. S.D. Ohio 1986). House Judiciary Committee Chairman Brooks' section-by-section analysis of the Bankruptcy Reform Act of 1994 states, with respect to section 305 of the 1994 Act (adding § 1123(d)), that "This section will have the effect of overruling * * * Rake v. Wade, * * * [which] had the effect of giving secured creditors interest on interest payments * * * even where applicable law prohibits such interest and even when it was * * * not contemplated in the original transaction." 140 Cong. Rec. H10770 (daily ed. Oct. 4, 1994). Would it also have the effect of requiring payment of interest at the default rate to accomplish the cure? What will happen if immediately after confirmation of the plan (or sometime later), Foam Corporation's current ratio is below two or its net worth is below $500,000?

If Foam Corporation were solvent on both liquidation and reorganization bases, and if the Fresno real property were worth only $400,000, would Foam Corporation benefit from reinstating the mortgage under § 1124(2)? Would Foam Corporation benefit even if First Bank were completely unsecured?

At what point would Foam Corporation lose the right to cure defaults and reinstate the First Bank mortgage? If First Bank accelerated the debt before Foam Corporation filed its chapter 11 petition? Only if First Bank held a foreclosure sale before the petition was filed? Only if First Bank sold the property at a foreclosure sale and Foam Corporation's redemption rights under state law expired before the petition was filed? Only when such rights expire as provided under state law (as perhaps extended by § 108(b)? See In re 210 Roebling, LLC, 336 B.R. 172 (Bankr. E.D.N.Y. 2005). Cf. § 1322(c)(1).

Problem 11-7

After the court denied Foam Corporation's request for extension of exclusivity, the Unsecured Creditors' Committee filed a plan that, among other things, would allow Gruff and Simmons to keep their stock but would also cause 900 new shares of stock in Foam Corporation to be issued to creditors. At present, Gruff and Simmons hold all 100 shares of Foam Corporation stock; Gruff holds 90 shares, and Simmons holds 10. Is the class of interest holders impaired or unimpaired by the Creditors' Committee's plan? Would it affect your analysis if there were 900 shares that had been authorized and that were held as treasury stock by Foam Corporation as of the date of the filing of its petition? What if the plan did not call for issuance of new shares but did provide for a sale of a substantial part of Foam Corporation's assets, a sale that, under the relevant state corporation law, would require approval of shareholders?

**Connecticut General Life Insurance
Company v. Hotel Associates of Tucson
(In re Hotel Associates of Tucson)**
Ninth Circuit Bankruptcy Appellate Panel, 1994
165 B.R. 470

MEYERS, Bankruptcy Judge:
* * *

Hotel Associates of Tucson ("the Debtor") filed a voluntary Chapter 11 petition on February 28, 1992. The Debtor is an Arizona limited partnership whose sole asset is a 204-room hotel (the "Hotel") in Tucson, Arizona. The general partners of the Debtor are Lawrence Smira, Robert Ewing, Gary Wieser, Saliterman/Goldstein Investments (collectively, the "Paragon Group"), the Paragon Hotel Corporation and C.R.H.C. of Tucson, Inc. ("CRHC"). * * *

Connecticut General is the Debtor's largest and only non-governmental secured creditor. It holds a secured lien against the Hotel in the sum of $8,597,300 as of the petition date. Connecticut General's claim is evidenced, *inter alia,* by a promissory note dated December 5, 1981, in the original sum of $7,500,000 and a deed of trust and security agreement executed on the same date. The note provides for monthly installments of principal and interest calculated at the rate of 14 percent per annum, together with additional interest equal to 20 percent of the "gross annual room revenues" of the Hotel in excess of $3,100,000. The note further provides for payment of interest at a specified default rate following a default by the Debtor.

The Debtor defaulted on its obligation to Connecticut General in the summer of 1991. Since that time the Debtor has not made any payments of principal or interest to Connecticut General.

Both the Paragon Group and CRHC filed plans of reorganization. The Paragon Plan contains eight classes of claims and interests. It purports to capitalize all outstanding principal and non-default rate interest on Connecticut General's claim as of the effective date of the Paragon Plan and to pay such claim over a seven-year period, with interest at the prime rate plus 1½ percent, based on a 25 year amortization schedule. It is undisputed that Connecticut General's claim is impaired under the Paragon Plan. Connecticut General voted to reject the Paragon Plan.

The Paragon Plan pays all other creditors in full. It pays all of the Class 6 general unsecured claims in cash, but delays payment for a period of 30 days, with interest paid on such claims at the prime rate.

The CRHC Plan also impairs Connecticut General's claim and proposes to pay all other creditors in full. It proposes to repay the Connecticut General loan at a base interest rate of 10 percent and offers Connecticut General a 40 percent participation in net cash flow and in the net proceeds of any sale or refinancing of the Hotel. The CRHC Plan proposes to remove the Paragon Group as the managing general partner of the Debtor, to install an affiliate of CRHC to operate the Hotel and to reduce the Paragon Group's aggregate ownership share in the Debtor from 45 percent to 22.5 percent. Connecticut General voted to accept the CRHC Plan.

Both plans propose to utilize all available cash of the estate as of the effective date. The Paragon Plan proposes to pay all creditors other than Connecticut General, implement a capital improvement plan and distribute all of the excess cash to the Debtor's general and limited partners. The CRHC Plan proposes to use the cash to pay all creditors, implement a capital improvement plan and reinstate the claim of Connecticut General.

On November 13, 1992, the bankruptcy court entered an order confirming the Paragon Plan and denying confirmation of the CRHC Plan. * * *

On the merits, Connecticut General asserts that the Paragon Plan should not have been confirmed because no properly impaired class accepted it. Under Bankruptcy Code ("Code") Section 1129(a)(10), a plan cannot be confirmed unless at least one "impaired class" accepts the plan, excluding acceptance by any insider. Connecticut General contends that the only reason the Paragon Plan paid the Class 6 general unsecured creditors 30 days after the effective date was to create an artificially impaired class which would vote for the plan. Connecticut General maintains that the Debtor had sufficient cash on the effective date to pay Class 6 claims at that time. It cites several cases holding that an alteration intended only to create an impaired class to vote for a plan so that a debtor can effectuate a cramdown will not be allowed. In re Windsor on the River Associates, Ltd., 7 F.3d 127, 132 (8th Cir. 1993); * * *.

Although it appears that the 30-day wait was employed solely to create a slightly impaired class to vote on the plan, a recent Ninth Circuit Court of Appeals case found a similar action permissible. In *L & J Anaheim Associates,* supra, 995 F.2d at 943, a secured creditor's rights and remedies under the Uniform Commercial Code were abrogated by that creditor's plan purporting to sell the creditor's collateral at public auction. The court in *L & J Anaheim Associates* noted that the plain language of Section 1124 states that a creditor's claim is "impaired" unless its rights are left "unaltered" by the plan. The court interpreted the language in Section 1124 as Congress's way of defining impairment in the broadest possible terms. The court found no suggestion that only alterations of a particular kind or degree can constitute impairment. The court concluded that the narrow question that arises is whether a creditor's legal, equitable or contractual rights were changed by the plan. If so, its claim is considered impaired.

The court then looked at the appellant's argument that the general rule defining impairment should not be used abusively, as where the plan proponent enhances its own position, then attempts to use this fact to show impairment and so cram down the rest of the creditors. The Court of Appeals held that abuses on the part of a plan proponent ought not affect the application of Congress's definition of impairment. Rather, such abuses should be addressed by the bankruptcy court by denying confirmation on the ground that the plan has not been proposed in good faith. The Court of Appeals concluded that the bankruptcy court's finding that the plan was proposed in good faith was not clearly erroneous. In sum, *L & J Anaheim Associates* holds that a plan proponent's motivations will not be questioned in determining whether a class is impaired under Section 1129(a)(10), but will be examined in deciding whether a plan was proposed in bad faith.

This Ninth Circuit case is binding on the Panel, while cases such as *Windsor on the River Associates,* supra, have persuasive authority only. Aside from our duty to follow Ninth Circuit precedent, we find the reasoning in *L & J Anaheim Associates* more convincing than that in the Eighth Circuit case of *Windsor on the River Associates*. The Eighth Circuit held that a claim is not impaired if the alteration of rights arises solely from the plan proponent's exercise of discretion. The court determined that two classes in the debtor's plan were not impaired, because the plan could have provided for these classes in full on the effective date if it had paid $100,000 less to the secured creditor.

We do not believe it is the bankruptcy court's role to ask whether alternative payment structures could produce a different scenario in regard to impairment of classes. Denying confirmation on the basis that another type of plan would produce different results would impede desired flexibility for plan proponents and create additional complications in the already complex process of plan confirmation. Moreover, nowhere does the Code require a plan proponent to use all efforts to create unimpaired classes. Such a requirement should not be imposed by judicial fiat.

The Paragon Plan provided that payment to the Class 6 general unsecured creditors would be delayed for 30 days. Therefore, based on *L & J Anaheim Associates,* the class was impaired. The ability of the Debtor to pay that class on the effective date does not alter that analysis. However, the necessity for the delay in payment may be considered in determining if Paragon proposed its plan in good faith.

* * *

Connecticut General argues that the Paragon Plan was proposed in a bad faith attempt to artificially impair the Class 6 claims and to benefit the Debtor's general and limited partners. * * *

The court did not make any findings regarding good faith. The only finding remotely addressing the issue is in the November 13, 1992 order confirming the plan, in which the court stated: "IT IS FURTHER ORDERED that all the objections to the Paragon plan are overruled, the Paragon plan satisfies the requirements of section 1129, and the First Amended Plan of Reorganization Proposed By the Paragon Group on Behalf of the Debtor, Hotel Associates of Tucson, dated July 27, 1992 and filed July 28, 1992, is CONFIRMED."

This is an insufficient substitute for findings of fact in resolving the contested issue of good faith. Therefore we will remand this matter to the bankruptcy court for findings on whether the plan was proposed in good faith. On remand the court should recognize that the act of impairment in an attempt to gerrymander a voting class of creditors is indicative of bad faith.

* * *

NOTES

1. In L & J Anaheim Assocs. v. Kawasaki Leasing Int'l, Inc. (In re L & J Anaheim Assocs.), 995 F.2d 940 (9th Cir. 1993), cited in *Hotel Assocs. of Tucson*, the debtor's exclusivity period expired. A secured creditor then filed a plan under which the assets of the estate—including the creditor's collateral, a hotel—would be auctioned off in a court supervised auction. The Ninth Circuit held that the secured creditor's rights would be altered under the plan, because it would be unable to exercise the state law remedies it would otherwise have on default. Even though the right to have a court supervised auction was arguably superior to any rights the secured creditor would have had under state law, the Ninth Circuit held that the secured creditor's alteration of its own rights by way of its plan was sufficient to impair the class made up of the secured creditor's secured claim. (The Ninth Circuit also found no basis to reverse the bankruptcy court's finding that the secured creditor had proposed the plan in good faith.) Since the secured creditor's class was impaired, the secured creditor's vote in favor of its plan caused there to be one impaired class that had accepted the plan. The plan could therefore be confirmed in a cramdown. Is the decision sound? Should the court have held that the secured creditor became an "insider" by filing a plan, at least with respect to its own plan? See §§ 101(31) and 102(3). What difference would such a holding have made?

2. At the time the court decided *Hotel Ass'n of Tucson*, § 1124(3) had not yet been deleted from the Code. Under § 1124 as amended in 1994, would Class 6 (consisting of the claims of the general unsecured creditors) have been an impaired class even if the plan had provided for payment of the full amount of the allowed claims in cash on the effective date of the plan? If so, would the debtor's plan be open to a charge of bad faith impairment if the case were decided today? What would the debtor's plan have to provide in order to leave Class 6 unimpaired under the amended Code? Consider how the Acme plan at pp. 588-89 above treats its Class 4. Is that class unimpaired as the Acme plan states? Would a failure to provide for postpetition interest or otherwise to leave a convenience class unimpaired show a lack of good faith on the part of the plan's proponent?

Chapter Twelve

Determining The Enterprise's Value

Valuation is central to much of bankruptcy. In particular, a determination of the going concern value that the reorganized debtor's business will have is central to the negotiation and confirmation of a chapter 11 plan. The negotiations occur in the shadow of a potential cramdown; the power of the debtor in possession to seek cramdown is one of its strongest negotiating levers. Usually it is very hard for a party to judge whether the debtor could succeed in a cramdown against a dissenting unsecured claim class without some idea of what the reorganized enterprise's going concern value will be. See Chapter Fifteen. Furthermore, without some idea of what the reorganized enterprise will be worth, the parties will not know the size of the pie they are dividing up as they negotiate a plan, nor, in most cases, will the parties know the value of the particular slice that each will receive under the plan. Very often the plan will distribute stock (or other ownership interests) to creditors; without some idea of what the reorganized enterprise will be worth, they will have no idea what the stock will be worth. Thus, the determination of the going concern value of the entity that will emerge from bankruptcy is usually an important part of the process of developing a plan.

Valuation techniques are discussed in this chapter, along with the tax issues that can have a great effect on valuation. There is also a brief discussion of a particular problem that sometimes arises in determining the enterprise's value, where the debtor and another entity have assets or liabilities that are so intertwined and commingled that it is difficult to separate them. In such cases it can be extremely difficult to determine the value of the debtor's assets and to determine who is entitled to share in that value. Therefore courts sometimes pool the assets and liabilities of intertwined entities, in what is called a substantive consolidation.

There are also two appendices at the end of this casebook that relate to this chapter. Appendix B discusses the manner in which an appropriate discount rate—a "weighted average cost of capital"—is determined for present value calculations. Appendix C discusses the concept of present value. At the end of Appendix C are two tables (Tables C-1 and C-2)that provide the present value factors needed to calculate present value.

A. DETERMINATION OF ENTERPRISE VALUE

Determining the value of a chapter 11 debtor is an important part of the process of developing a plan. Before creditors or shareholders can make an informed decision about a proposed plan, they must have some indication as to the value of the entity that will emerge from chapter 11. For example, if the proposed plan suggests that the unsecured creditors are to receive notes in an amount equal to 30 percent of their claims and also are to receive 40% of the common stock of the emerging entity, the creditors must have some indication of the value of the emerging entity to know how to vote on the plan. Statement of Position 90-7, *Financial Reporting by Entities in Reorganization under the Bankruptcy Code*, issued by the American Institute of Certified Public Accountants, indicates that a disclosure statement cannot contain adequate information unless the reorganization value of the entity that will emerge from chapter 11 is disclosed.[1]

Several terms are used to describe the value of a chapter 11 debtor, including going concern value, liquidation value, enterprise value and reorganization value. The term "going concern" value is a general term used to describe the basic underlying assumption regarding the continued existence of the business. A value based on the assumption that the business will continue in existence is referred to as "going concern value," and a value based on the assumption that the business will not survive as a going concern is referred to as "liquidation value." A chapter 11 disclosure statement generally contains values based on both assumptions. If the plan provides for the business to continue, then a "going concern value" will be included. Additionally, because of the § 1129(a)(7) confirmation requirement that the plan must be in the best interest of creditors, liquidation values must be presented to show that creditors will receive at least as much under the chapter 11 plan as would be received in a chapter 7 liquidation.

The focus of the appraiser is on determining "enterprise value," representing the value of the invested capital. The invested capital consists of the value of the funded debt (generally interest bearing debt such as notes and bonds) plus the value of the equity of the business (whether it is represented by just common stock or by both preferred stock and common stock). Funded debt generally does not include current liabilities such as

---

1.   Statement of Position 90-7 does not require inclusion of reorganization value if the plan is a simple extension or composition of debts, where there is less than a fifty percent change in control of the ownership interests of the chapter 11 entity. While § 1125(d) provides that "[w]hether a disclosure statement * * * contains adequate information is not governed by any otherwise applicable nonbankruptcy law, rule, or regulation,"and § 1125(b) permits the court to approve a disclosure statement that does not include a valuation of the debtor, it is difficult to argue that reorganization value is not a part of the adequate information required by § 1125, where there is more than a fifty percent change in control of the entity. How else will creditors be able to judge the value of the equity interests that they are to receive under the plan?

accounts payable and accrued expenses, but it would include the current portion of long-term debt that is a part of the funded debt. The goal is to determine the value that is available to be given out under the plan in the form of funded debt and stock. Enterprise value may be determined by using several methods as described below.

The term "reorganization value" generally is used to refer to the value of all of the assets, which must equal the total of liabilities (all liabilities, including those that are not part of the funded debt) plus stockholders' equity. Because current liabilities are not part of the funded debt, reorganization value will be larger than enterprise value by the amount of those current liabilities. For companies that qualify for fresh start reporting under SOP 90-7, the balance sheet must be revised to include the enterprise value. The details of how the balance sheet is adjusted to show enterprise value, even though enterprise value is less than total asset value, are beyond the scope of this text.

The Supreme Court concluded in Consolidated Rock Products Co. v. Du Bois, 312 U.S. 510, 61 S. Ct. 675, 85 L. Ed. 982 (1941), that value is based on an estimate of future activity. The Court stated that:

> Findings as to the earning capacity of an enterprise are essential to a determination of the feasibility as well as the fairness of a plan of reorganization. Whether or not the earnings may reasonably be expected to meet the interest and dividend requirements of the new securities is a sine qua non to a determination of the integrity and practicability of the new capital structure. It is also essential for satisfaction of the absolute priority rule * * *.
>
> As Mr. Justice Holmes said * * * "the commercial value of property consists in the expectation of income from it." * * * The criterion of earning capacity is the essential one if the enterprise is to be freed from the heavy hand of past errors, miscalculations or disaster, and if the allocation of securities among the various claimants is to be fair and equitable. Since its application requires a prediction as to what will occur in the future, an estimate, as distinguished from mathematical certitude, is all that can be made. But that estimate must be based on an informed judgment which embraces all facts relevant to future earning capacity and hence to present worth, including, of course, the nature and condition of the properties, the past earnings recorded and all circumstances which indicate whether or not that record is a reliable criterion of future performance. A sum of values based on physical factors and assigned to separate units of the property without regard to the earning capacity of the whole enterprise is plainly inadequate.

Id. at 525-26, 61 S. Ct. at 685.

Generally, there are three approaches (or kinds of approaches) used to determine enterprise value: an income approach based on discounted cash flows; market multiple (or capitalization) approaches; and the asset approach. The choice of which approach to use in a particular situation will depend upon several factors including the nature of the company and its operations, as well as the economic, financial and operational risks. Often an estimate of value is determined by using more than one approach.

The most common method used to determine value under the Bankruptcy Code has been based on discounted cash flows. See, e.g., In re Lafayette Hotel P'ship, 227 B.R. 445 (S.D.N.Y. 1998), aff'd, 198 F.3d 234 (2d Cir. 1999); In re 203 N. LaSalle St. Ltd. P'ship, 190 B.R. 567 (Bankr. N.D. Ill. 1995), aff'd sub nom. Bank of Am., Ill. v. 203 N. LaSalle St. P'ship, 195 B.R. 692 (N.D. Ill. 1996), aff'd sub nom. In re 203 N. LaSalle St. Ltd. P'ship, 126 F.3d 955 (7th Cir. 1997), rev'd on other grounds sub nom. Bank of Am. Nat'l Trust & Sav. Ass'n v. 203 N. LaSalle St. P'ship, 526 U.S. 434, 119 S. Ct. 1411, 143 L. Ed. 2d 607 (1999); In re Cellular Info. Sys., Inc., 171 B.R. 926 (Bankr. S.D.N.Y. 1994); In re Consul Rest. Corp., 146 B.R. 979 (Bankr. D. Minn. 1992); In re VIP Motor Lodge, Inc., 133 B.R. 41 (Bankr. D. Del. 1991); In re Southmark Storage Assocs. Ltd. P'ship, 130 B.R. 9 (Bankr. D. Conn. 1991).

Other courts have approved use of a combination of methods in determining enterprise value. In avoiding power proceedings, where it is often necessary to determine the solvency of the debtor at a particular point in time, many courts have used the asset approach to valuation.

One of the most discussed valuation opinions is In re Exide Technologies, 303 B.R. 48, (Bankr. D. Del. 2003), in which the court compared two expert valuations introduced in the case—one by Arthur Newman of the Blackstone Group and the other by William Derrough of Jefferies & Co.—and detailed the various approaches to the valuation process. Throughout this chapter, reference will be made to this case, focusing on the court's discussion and the exhibits presented by the experts. It should be realized that this is one bankruptcy court's decision and that other courts have taken a different view of the valuation process. As excerpts later in the chapter show, the court in *Exide* placed more emphasis on the pure theory of valuations and less on the judgment and experience of the expert from Blackstone. Also as you will see, the court gave very little weight to the amount of the prior bids received for the company. (Blackstone had attempted to market the company and had received three comparable bids, but decided not to pursue a sale to any of the bidders.) Other courts have given more emphasis to potential transactions that might be more representative of market value.

Here are the initial comments of the court in *Exide*, describing the valuations submitted by Newman (for the debtor) and Derrough (for the creditors' committee). These comments are presented at the beginning of this discussion to introduce you to the issues that were involved; please reread them again after you have finished the enterprise value section (Section A) of this chapter. Note that further excerpts from the court's opinion in *Exide*, and several of the exhibits presented by the experts in that case, are included at different points in this chapter.

In re Exide Technologies
United States Bankruptcy Court, District of Delaware, 2003
303 B.R. 48

KEVIN J. CAREY, Bankruptcy Judge.

The Debtor asks that this Court confirm its Fourth Amended Joint Plan of Reorganization Under Chapter 11 of the Bankruptcy Code (the "Plan"). Objections to the Plan have been filed by various parties, including, the Official Committee of Unsecured Creditors, Smith Management, LLC, HSBC Bank USA as Indenture Trustee, Enersys, Inc., and others. * * *
* * *

2. The Debtor's Enterprise Valuation.

The Debtor and the Creditors Committee each offered their own expert to testify about the Debtor's enterprise value. The Debtor presented the expert testimony and valuation analysis of Arthur B. Newman ("Newman"), a senior managing director and founding partner of the Restructuring and Reorganization Group of The Blackstone Group, L.P. ("Blackstone"), who has over 38 years of experience in the merger and acquisitions market for restructuring companies. The Creditors Committee presented the expert testimony and analysis of William Q. Derrough ("Derrough"), a managing director and co-head of the Recapitalization and Restructuring Group of Jefferies & Company, Inc. ("Jefferies"), who also was qualified as an expert based upon his experience in numerous restructuring, financings, and merger and acquisition transactions.[2]

Both experts used the same three methods to determine the Debtor's value: (i) comparable company analysis; (ii) comparable transaction analysis; and (iii) discounted cash flow. However, the end results of their valuations were far from similar. Newman, the Debtor's expert, set the Debtor's value in a range between $950 million and $1.050 billion, while Derrough, the Creditors Committee's expert, set the value in a range between $1.478 billion and $1.711 billion.[3] It becomes necessary, therefore, to delve deeper in the parties' respective approaches to valuation, so that the court may make its own determination.

The Debtor argues that its expert used a "market-based approach" to valuation that determines value on a going concern basis by analyzing the price that could be realized for a debtor's assets in a realistic framework, assuming a willing seller

---

2.   [Footnote 22 in original:] Initially, the Creditors Committee also designated as an expert in valuation Masroor Siddiqui of Jefferies. Mr. Siddiqui was deposed, but was not called to testify at trial, the expert designation having been "withdrawn" by the Creditors Committee. The Debtor, largely through its cross-examination of Derrough, highlighted conflicts between the views of the Jefferies brethren, to which I give little weight, the exercise having proved primarily that the Creditors' Committee was perhaps mistaken in its initial designation of Mr. Siddiqui.

3.   [Footnote 23 in original:] The parties also disagree about the "hurdle" amount, i.e., the amount that the Debtor must be worth to enable it to pay all secured, administrative and priority claims and have some value left to distribute to the unsecured creditors. The Creditors Committee used a hurdle amount of $1.190 billion based upon Exhibit C to the Debtor's Disclosure Statement. At the confirmation hearing, the Debtor argued that its expert had "updated" the hurdle amount and set it at $1.285 billion.

and a willing buyer. Travelers Int'l AG v. Transworld Airlines, Inc. (In re Transworld Airlines, Inc.), 134 F.3d 188, 193-94 (3d Cir. 1998). The Debtor claims that Newman's application of the valuation methods in this case "reflects the manner in which he believes real world purchasers will view the Company." The Debtor also argues that Newman's value is confirmed by the "private equity process" conducted by the Debtor during the chapter 11 case, during which offers were solicited from potential purchasers, including private equity firms and one strategic buyer. The Debtor claims that the process fixed the total enterprise value of the Debtor in a range of $782 million and $950 million.[4]

The Creditors Committee, on the other hand, argues that the most accurate way to determine the enterprise value of a debtor corporation is by the straight-forward application of the three standard valuation methodologies. To support its position, the Creditors Committee presented expert testimony of Professor Edith Hotchkiss ("Hotchkiss"), a professor of finance at Boston College who, in addition to teaching the topic of how to value companies, has performed research and written articles specifically related to valuation of companies in bankruptcy.[5] Hotchkiss agreed with the Creditors Committee's argument in favor of objective application of the valuation methods, and opined that although determining the "inputs" for the methods of valuation tends to involve some subjectivity (e.g., choosing the comparable companies or transactions), the mechanics of the calculating value [sic] based upon standard methods should not. Hotchkiss noted that, in this case, the input information chosen by the experts was not significantly different; what caused the variance was that Newman made a subjective determination to reduce further the multiples determined from the input information prior to applying the valuation formula.

The Creditors Committee argues, too, that Hotchkiss' research also supports its argument that the Debtor has undervalued the company. In her research, Hotchkiss compared the value of chapter 11 debtor companies prior to confirmation, which she

---

4.   [Footnote 24 in original:] The "private equity process" was conducted by Newman's employer, Blackstone, for the purpose of raising $2 to $3 million in cash in exchange for some percentage investment in the reorganized Exide. Blackstone approached approximately 75 equity firms, 35 of which signed confidentiality agreements and received the offering memorandum and financial information, and seven of which submitted expressions of interest in March 2003. Three participants then performed extensive due diligence and submitted second round bids in late June 2003. Blackstone informed the participating parties the Debtor was unlikely to consider seriously offers in which the enterprise value of the Debtor was considered to be under $900 million. However, the enterprise value was set by the highest second round bid at approximately $950 million, with the other two bids under $900 million. A subsequent round of telephone calls to the lower bidders did not generate any interest in continuing the process to attempt to increase the bids. At this point, the private equity process was terminated, partially due to the fact that only one party seemed interested in bidding more than $900 million, and partially due to the fact that the Prepetition Lenders' Steering Committee had expressed a willingness to convert the entire bank debt, including the domestic and European debt, to equity. Newman testified that he did not believe that a subsequent auction would have generated a higher offer.

5.   [Footnote 25 in original:] See Stuart C. Gilson, Edith S. Hotchkiss & Richard S. Ruback, *Valuation of Bankruptcy Firms*, 13-1 REV. OF FIN. STUD. 43 (2000).

determined by applying the valuation methods to the cash flows in the Debtor's disclosure statements, to the market price of the debtor companies after exiting chapter 11. Her research showed that, in some cases, the debtors' disclosure statement cash flows were significantly overvaluing or undervaluing the debtors and, from those findings, she extrapolated certain factors that tended to predict when debtors were being overvalued or undervalued. She noted that plans providing management and/or senior creditors with the majority of stock or options in the reorganized company (as in the Debtor's Plan) is a strong indicator that the company is being undervalued, resulting in a windfall for management and the senior creditors.[6]

A determination of the Debtor's value directly impacts the issues of whether the proposed plan is "fair and equitable," as required by 11 U.S.C. § 1129(b). Section 1129(b)(2) sets forth the "absolute priority rule," applicable to unsecured creditors, which provides that a plan may be confirmed despite rejection by a class of unsecured creditors if the plan does not offer a junior claimant any property before each unsecured claims [sic] receives full satisfaction of its allowed claim. 11 U.S.C. § 1129(b)(2)(B)(ii); *Genesis Health Ventures*, 266 B.R at 612. Courts have decided that "a corollary of the absolute priority rule is that a senior class cannot receive more than full compensation for its claims." Id. citing In re MCorp Financial, Inc., 137 B.R. 219, 225 (Bankr. S.D. Tex. 1992). The Creditors Committee argues that the Debtor's expert has undervalued the company and that the Plan will result in paying the Prepetition Lenders more than 100% of their claims to the detriment of the unsecured creditors. The Debtor, on the other hand, argues that the Creditors Committee's expert has overvalued the company and that the Plan is fair and equitable in its treatment of unsecured creditors. * * *

1. Income Approach—Discounted Cash Flows

The economic value of an entity is the sum of the value of its funded debts and its equity.[7] This value is often called corporate[8] or enterprise value. One approach used to estimate enterprise value is to discount the cash flows by a discount rate equal to the "cost of capital." The cost of capital is the rate

---

6. [Footnote 26 in original:] The Creditors Committee also relies upon the testimony of John Craig, President and CEO of Enersys, Inc. ("Enersys"), to support its argument that the Debtor's enterprise value has been significantly undervalued. Mr. Craig testified that he sent a letter to Craig Mulhauser of Exide on August 28, 2003 expressing his interest on behalf of Enersys to acquire Exide's transportation division for $950 million. However, I can afford little weight to this. First, the August 28, 2003 letter itself states that it is a "nonbinding" "expression of interest." Second, Mr. Craig admitted that he had not determined whether Enersys's interest included taking on the environmental liabilities, pension liabilities and an allocation of shared services with the industrial division. Third, the Debtor and Enersys are embroiled in a vigorously contested dispute about whether the Debtor may reject a valuable intellectual property license now used by Enersys. While Enersys's interest in acquiring Exide's transportation business may be genuine, the timing of the "expression of interest"—after the Debtor filed its Disclosure Statement and Enersys was aware that the Debtor's valuation was in dispute—may be considered suspect.

7. See Chapter One, above, text at footnote 39.

8. Rappaport, CREATING SHAREHOLDER VALUE 50-51 (1986).

of return investors expect from the company; it is discussed in Appendix B at the end of the book. Because plans generally provide for issuance of both debt and equity to creditors (and in some cases equity to interest holders), the cost of capital is a blend—actually a weighted average—of the rate of interest the debtor will have to pay for borrowing funds on emergence from chapter 11 and the rate of return investors would demand on stock in the reorganized company. (Stock is riskier than debt, and thus investors demand a higher expected return on stock.)

Technically, as Appendix B explains, the cost of capital is the required return that must be earned on new investments by the company for the value of the company to remain unchanged. Suppose the company is considering investing some of its funds in a project that will earn a 10 percent return per year. If the company's cost of capital is 15 percent, then an investment in the project will cause the company's value to decline, because the company will not be earning the rate of return expected by investors.

Under the discounted cash flow approach, the enterprise's value is equal to the sum of three components:[9]

a) The present value of free cash flows during the period in which cash flows are forecast.
b) The residual or terminal value representing the present value of the business attributable to the period beyond the forecast period.
c) The value of assets not be needed for operations by the reorganized entity, typically consisting of excess working capital and assets to be liquidated under the plan.

a.   Free Cash Flow During Projection Period

Cash flow from operations is the difference between the net cash inflows and outflows from operating activities. In practice EBITDA—earnings before interest, taxes, depreciation, and amortization—is used in cash flow projections. An enterprise's earnings for a specific period of time are generally determined by subtracting the enterprise's expenses for that period from its revenues for the same period. (See Foam Corporation's Statement of Operations in Chapter Two of this text, and chief financial officer Bell's explanation of the Statement of Operations in Appendix A at the end of the book.) For financial statement purposes, expenses normally include items that do not require cash payments, such as depreciation and amortization. By definition, when computing earnings before interest, taxes, depreciation, and amortization (EBITDA), noncash expenses such as depreciation and amortization are not subtracted from revenues. By excluding noncash

---

9.   Id. at 51.

expenses, EBITDA comes closer to representing cash flows from operations than do the earnings or net income from operations figures to be found on an income statement or statement of operations.

To determine free cash flows, EBITDA is reduced by taxes that must be paid[10]—which changes it into EBIDA—and also reduced by capital expenditures that must be made (e.g., to replace worn out equipment or to provide for business growth). It is then either reduced further by the amount of additional needed investments in working capital or increased by the amount of any reduction in working capital.[11] If EBIDA can be projected for future years, and if capital expenditures and increased investments in working capital can be projected and subtracted from EBIDA for the same years, the result will be an estimate of the free cash flows for those future years.[12]

The projection period will often be between four and ten years, with five years being the most common time period used. In the Exide case, the experts used a four and one-half year projection period. Exhibit 12-1 shows the free cash flows for Exide as estimated by the Blackstone Group based on the debtor's latest business plan.[13]

---

10.   Taxes are based on net income. Noncash items such as depreciation and amortization are taken into account in determination of net income. However, the tax impact of interest is not considered in this discounted cash flow analysis.

As shown in Exhibit 12-1 below, net operating income after depreciation, amortization, and taxes, but before interest, may also be used as a starting point (instead of EBITDA) in calculating cash flow from operations. Noncash items such as depreciation and amortization would be added back, and the resulting figure then would be reduced by additional working capital needs and additional capital expenditures to arrive at a figure for cash flow from operations.

11.   If the reorganized enterprise's business grows, typically it will need to have more working capital—more inventory on hand and higher levels of accounts receivable. Building up inventory requires an investment of cash. Higher levels of accounts receivable indicate that at any given time the business has manufactured and shipped even more products than before without yet being paid for them. This also requires an investment of cash to manufacture and ship the extra products for which the enterprise has not been paid. On the other hand, if the enterprise scales back its operations in its turnaround, it likely will reduce its inventory and accounts receivable, thus generating extra cash as some of the inventory and accounts receivable are in effect liquidated. See Problem 5-3 above.

12.   Interest expense is not subtracted from EBITDA here in determining the amount of free cash flows that will provide value to the creditors (and perhaps the interest holders) of the chapter 11 debtor. The value of the reorganized enterprise will include not only the value of its shares of stock, but also the value of its funded debt, as noted above in this chapter and also in Chapter One. Much of the value of the funded debt is provided by the interest payments that will be made on the funded debt. Thus the value of the cash that is to be used to pay interest is part of the enterprise value.

It might be thought that the amount of the free cash flows used in determining enterprise value should be increased due to the tax savings caused by deductibility of interest payments. However, the impact of interest deductibility has already been considered in the weighted average cost of capital where the cost of debt is reduced by the income tax benefit. See Appendix B. To consider the deductibility of interest on debt here as well would result in double counting of the impact of taxes.

13.   The cash flows as determined by Jefferies & Co. were very similar because Jefferies also relied on projections prepared by the debtor. However, Jefferies did not have access to the latest business plan and thus used projections made in an earlier business plan.

Exhibit 12-1: Exide Free Cash Flow ($ in millions)

	6 Months Ended March 31, 2004	Fiscal Year Ended March 31,			
		2005	2006	2007	2008
Net Revenue	**$1,248.5**	**$2,428.0**	**$2,530.0**	**$2,643.2**	**$2,768.4**
Operating Income[1]	84.0	162.2	194.0	208.5	222.0
Plus: Depreciation & Amortization	43.5	78.7	74.5	74.5	74.5
Less: Cash Taxes[2]	(11.6)	(41.1)	(56.0)	(60.9)	(65.5)
Less: Capital Expenditures	(30.8)	(60.0)	(60.0)	(60.0)	(60.0)
Less: Existing Liability/ Legacy Cost[3]	(20.5)	(20.7)	(13.1)	(13.1)	(13.1)
Less: Changes in Working Capital[4]	11.0	9.9	(8.7)	(18.5)	(24.1)
Less: Cash Restructuring/ Severance Costs	(21.7)	(45.3)	(13.5)	(0.8)	(0.8)
Less: Pensions	2.4	(25.9)	(18.2)	(20.3)	(3.2)
Free Cash Flow[*]	**$56.4**	**$57.9**	**$99.0**	**$109.3**	**$129.8**

(1)   Excludes Chapter 11 Related expenses, including KERP, Alix Partners and other restructuring professional fees.

(2)   Assumed to be 38% of EBIT in North America, 25% of EBIT in Europe / ROW [rest of world].

(3)   Includes cash legal and environmental costs, as well as Daramic penalty payments.

(4)   Includes changes in inventory, accounts receivable, accounts payable, employee medical and warranty accruals.

[*   Totals do not add up exactly due to rounding.]

Source: Blackstone Exhibits, In Re Exide Technologies, 303 B.R. 48 (Bankr. D. Del. 2003).

After projected free cash flows for a projection period have been estimated, they are discounted to present value. This provides the value today of each year's free cash flows for the projection period. Adding those values together yields the present value of all the free cash flows expected during the projection period. Problem 12-1 illustrates the calculation of the value of the projection period cash flows. We have done it for you—study it carefully.

Problem 12-1: Product Company

It is now late 2006. The Product Company is in the process of developing a chapter 11 plan. As part of the analysis, you are trying to determine the value of the Company using the discounted cash flow approach. You have determined the following information.

1.   The cost of capital for other companies similar to Product is around 12%.

2.   The net income figures shown on the five-year projections below were determined by subtracting projected expected expenses from projected revenues. Depreciation expense does not require the outlay of any cash; it is simply a way to account for cash spent in the past to purchase productive assets. For example, if three years ago Product Company purchased for $500,000 a plastic injection molding machine for making small plastic parts, and if the machine has a useful life of ten years, then Product Company will consider a part of that $500,000 to be an expense during each of the ten years in which the machine will be useful. If Product uses the simplest way of determining depreciation expense, it will consider one tenth of the $500,000 to be an expense during each of the ten years. That means that for each of the five years of the projection period, the "Cost of Goods Sold" will include a $50,000 expense item for depreciation on the machine. Similarly, if Product had purchased office furniture and a computer for use by its managers and salespeople, depreciation on those items would be included in "Selling and Administrative Expenses." Since depreciation expense does not require an outlay of cash, it is added back in to the net income to determine the cash flows that will be available to pay to creditors and shareholders. Depreciation expense during each of the projection period years will equal about $1 million.

3.   Depreciation expense does not use up cash, but actual purchases of new equipment to replace worn out equipment or to expand production capacity do use cash. Thus the planned expenditures for new equipment and other planned capital expenditures are subtracted in order to determine cash flows. In addition, if the plans call for adding to working capital—for increasing inventory levels and increasing levels of account receivables—the investment in that additional working capital will use up cash; thus that investment must be subtracted as well. As the sales increase during the projection period, Product Company probably will need to have larger inventories in order to serve its customers. Increased sales will also generate increased accounts receivable; as time goes on, there will be a larger and larger amount of goods that Product Company has paid to produce and deliver but which Product Company's customers have not yet paid for. Thus the increase in accounts receivable requires an increased investment of cash in producing and delivering products on credit. In some cases, this increased investment in inventory and accounts receivable may be paid for in whole or in part by the reorganized debtor obtaining additional trade credit from its suppliers. However, Product Company does not anticipate that its suppliers will extend it additional credit; thus the entire amount of the planned increases in inventories and accounts receivable each year is subtracted below in determining cash flows.

4.   Equipment that will not be needed for the reorganization can be sold for approximately $300,000.

5.   A net operating loss of approximately $13,000,000 will survive the reorganization of this company and be usable to offset future income so as to save on income taxes.

6. The five-year cash projections are as follows:

PRODUCT COMPANY
Projected Statement of Operations
For Years Ending December 31
(in thousands)

	2007	2008	2009	2010	2011
Sales	$35,000	$40,250	$46,287	$53,230	$61,215
Cost of goods sold	(22,750)	(26,162)	(30,087)	(34,600)	(39,790)
Gross profit	12,250	14,088	16,200	18,630	21,425
Selling & Admin. expenses	(8,950)	(9,843)	(10,869)	(12,049)	(13,407)
EBIT (Earnings before interest and taxes	3,300	4,245	5,331	6,581	8,018
Depreciation & Amort. expense (no cash outlay needed, add back)	+1,000	+1,000	+1,000	+1,000	+1,000
EBITDA	4,300	5,245	6,331	7,581	9,018
Taxes (40% of EBIT)	0	0	0	(2,632)	(3,207)
EBIDA	4,300	5,245	6,331	4,949	5,811
Additional investment for working capital and capital expenditures	(1,300)	(1,745)	(1,831)	(1,949)	(2,011)
Free cash flows	3,000	3,500	4,500	3,000	3,800
Present value factor at 12%	x .893	x .797	x .712	x .636	x .567
Present value amount	$2,679 +	$2,790 +	$3,204 +	$1,908 +	$2,155

= Total present value of five years of cash flows = $12,736

For Product Company, the present value of the five years of free cash flows is equal to $12,736,000 as shown above. The present value of these cash flows would be the value of the company as of today assuming that it would cease operations at the end of five years and that nothing could be realized from the liquidation of the assets at that time. However, if the Company has life after 5 years, a terminal value must be added to the present value of the cash inflows for the projection period (which is five years in this example). In part b below we calculate the terminal value.

Note that the projected amount of income taxes is subtracted from the net income from operations. No taxes are included for the first 3 years because of the net operating loss carryover of $13 million. After the third year it is assumed that taxes must be paid at the rate of 40 percent of earnings before interest and taxes (EBIT). Taxes will actually be paid, not on EBIT, but on EBT (earnings before taxes). However, as noted in Appendix B, the tax effect of the interest expense is considered in determining the cost of debt and is not considered in the cash flow analysis.

Note that in 2007, the cash flow that is available after the additional investment for working capital and capital expenditures (equipment) is $3 million dollars. That $3 million value is discounted to the present because a dollar to be received at the end of the first year is worth less that it would be worth if received at the beginning of the year. (For simplicity, it is assumed that for each year the entire year's cash flows are received at the end of the year.) Since Products has a cost of capital (as defined in Appendix B) of 12 percent, the cash flow is discounted to the present using a rate of 12 percent. Table C-1 in Appendix C indicates that for 1 period at a rate of 12 percent the present value factor is .893. (That means that if an investor demanded a 12 percent per year rate of return, the investor would pay 89.3 cents today for each dollar expected to be returned in one year; in one year, the investor would then get back the 89.3 cents plus 12 percent of the 89.3 cents, which just equals one dollar.) For 2 periods (years, in this example) the factor is .797. Of course it is less than .893 because the same amount to be received after a longer time period will be worth less in present value today. The factors are less for each succeeding year.

b. Terminal Value

The terminal or residual value represents the additional value the reorganized enterprise will generate beyond the projection period. The terminal value depends, among other factors, on the assumptions made about operations during the projection period and on the assessment of the competitive position of the reorganized enterprise at the end of the projection period.

If the reorganized debtor plans to invest heavily in growing areas of its business, then its cash flows during the projection period may be low, because it is spending its cash on building the business. However, then the terminal value would be high, because those investments would be expected to pay off in the future in higher cash flows from the expanded areas of the business.

On the other hand, the reorganized debtor might plan to make little in the way of investments during the projection period in order to "grow" the business. If so, then the value of the cash flows available to be paid out during the projection period may be high, but the terminal value of the company after the projection period may be low.

For example, if the assumption is made that over the projection period the debtor will sell its highly technical, "growth" divisions and keep only the divisions that operate in very mature industries—divisions that will be declining over the next five years but that will generate a large amount of cash—the present value of the cash flows from operations during the projection period will be high and the terminal value will be low. On the other hand, if the assumption is made that cash from divisions in the mature industry will be used to fund research and development costs in the technical, "growth" divisions, the present value of cash flows from operations during the projection period will be low, but the terminal value will be high.

While several techniques are used to estimate the terminal value, two of the more common methods used are: (i) the perpetuity method, and (ii) the multiple of EBITDA method.

(i)   The Perpetuity Method

The perpetuity method—when applied without a "growth rate"— assumes that the reorganized debtor will not be able to enhance the value of its existing investors' investments beyond the projection period by raising money to invest in its operations. A company that is able to generate returns that are greater than the cost of capital will attract competitors that will eventually drive the returns down to the cost of capital. The perpetuity method assumes—again, when applied without a "growth rate"—that after the projection period the reorganized debtor will earn, on average, only the cost of capital on its new investments.[14] However, in many chapter 11 cases the assumption of zero growth is not appropriate. Both situations—those in which growth is anticipated and those in which it is not—are described below.

In a situation in which no growth in free cash flows is anticipated, the yearly cash flows after the projection period can be calculated very simply from the cash flow for the final year of the projection period (with appropriate adjustments discussed below). If, on the other hand, growth is anticipated in the free cash flows, the impact of such growth would be included in the cash flow projections from operations for the first year after the projection period.

Problem 12-2 shows the calculation of the terminal value component of the enterprise value for Product Company, first with a "no growth" assumption and second with an assumption that there will be growth in free cash flows. Note how the free cash flow for 2012 is determined in Problem 12-2. Under the "no growth" assumption, capital expenditure for 2012 was set at $1 million, which equals the yearly amount of depreciation for Product Company. Over the long run, to maintain operations at existing levels, the reorganized enterprise will need to make capital expenditures roughly equal to the depreciation expense. If it is anticipated that the cash required to replace assets will be greater than the depreciation charge of $1 million due to increase in equipment prices, then the capital expenditure would be estimated to be greater than $1 million. Since there has been no increase in the cash flows from operations, it is assumed that there will be no additional needs for working capital.

With a "no growth" assumption, the following equation is used to calculate the terminal value, as of the end of the projection period:

$$\text{Terminal Value} = \frac{\text{Free Cash Flow (for the year following the end of the projection period)}}{\text{Cost of capital}}$$

With such a "no growth" assumption, the terminal value for Product Company at the end of the five year projection period is determined by dividing the free cash flows for the sixth year, $4,811,000, by the cost of capital, 12%, as shown here:

---

14.   Rappaport, supra note 8, at 60-61. Cost of capital is defined in Appendix B at the end of this casebook as the return that must be earned by the company on its various projects in order for the value of the entity to remain unchanged.

$$\text{Terminal value} \quad = \quad \frac{\$4,811,000}{.12} \quad = \quad \$40,091,000$$

This terminal value is what an investor would pay for the enterprise once the projection period is over—five years in the future, in the case of Product Company. If those cash flows will be worth a certain amount in five years, they are worth less than that now, because of the time value of money. Thus we must discount the terminal value to present value. The present value of the terminal value is equal to the terminal value, $40,091,000, multiplied by the present value factor for five years into the future at the cost of capital rate of 12 percent, namely .567 (from Table C-1 at the end of the book). As Problem 12-2 shows, $40,091,000 times .567 equals $22,731,597; that amount—almost $23 million—is the present value of the terminal value under the "no growth" assumption.[15]

In many valuations in bankruptcy a growth rate is used; the rate may vary from two to five percent or even more in some situations. To illustrate the use of the growth rate, the second part of Problem 12-2 assumes (1) that EBITDA will grow enough for free cash flows to be $4,950,000 in the year following the end of the projection period (about 3% higher than the $4,811,000 "no growth" figure for that year), and (2) that free cash flows will grow 3% every year thereafter. The terminal value equation is modified by adding the growth factor as shown below (and by using the larger figure for the cash flow for the year following the end of the projection period):

$$\text{Terminal Value} \quad = \quad \frac{\text{Free Cash Flow (for the year following end of projection period)}}{\text{Cost of capital} - \text{Growth Rate}}$$

With the 3% growth assumption for Product Company, here is how the terminal value would be calculated in its case:

$$\text{Terminal value} \quad = \quad \frac{\$4,950,000}{.12 - .03} \quad = \quad \frac{\$4,950,000}{.09} \quad = \quad \$55,000,000$$

Again, just as in the "no growth" calculation, the terminal value must be reduced to present value. Multiplying the $55 million terminal value by the .567 present value factor (for five years at a 12% discount rate) yields a present value of the terminal value equal to $31,185,000. Note the use, in the second part of Problem 12-2, of the $55 million and $31,185,000 figures.

---

15. As footnote 44 in Chapter One states, the perpetuity calculation assumes the first payment is to be received one year from today. Here the first payment is not to be received until six years from the date of valuation. Thus the perpetuity calculation determines the value as of a date five years in the future, requiring that it be discounted by the five year present value factor. (As Problem 12-1 notes, to make the calculations simpler it is assumed that the cash flows come in all at once at the end of each year; the first cash flow that will come in after the projection period is thus assumed to come in six years from the valuation date.)

Problem 12-2: Product Company

PRODUCT COMPANY
Projected Statement of Free Cash Flows
For Years Ending December 31
($ in thousands)

	2007	2008	2009	2010	2011	2012
No Growth						
EBITDA	4,300	5,245	6,331	7,581	9,018	9,018
Taxes (40% of EBIT)	0	0	0	(2,632)	(3,207)	(3,207)
EBIDA	4,300	5,245	6,331	4,949	5,811	5,811
Additional investment for working capital and capital expenditures	(1,300)	(1,745)	(1,831)	(1,949)	(2,011)	(1,000)*
Free cash flows	3,000	3,500	4,500	3,000	3,800	4,811

Total present value of five years of cash flows (see Problem 12-1)   12,736
Terminal value ($40,091,000 x .567 p.v. factor for five years)   22,732
Total value of 5 year projection period cash flows and terminal value **$35,468**

	2007	2008	2009	2010	2011	2012
3% Growth						
EBITDA	4,300	5,245	6,331	7,581	9,018	9,350
Taxes (40% of EBIT)	0	0	0	(2,632)	(3,207)	(3,340)
EBIDA	4,300	5,245	6,331	4,949	5,811	6,010
Additional investment for working capital and capital expenditures	(1,300)	(1,745)	(1,831)	(1,949)	(2,011)	(1,060)**
Free cash flows	3,000	3,500	4,500	3,000	3,800	4,950

Total present value of five years of cash flows (see Problem 12-1)   12,736
Terminal value ($55,000,000 x .567 p.v. factor for five years)   31,185
Total value of 5 year projection period cash flows and terminal value **$43,921**

* Under the assumption of no growth in the years after the projection period, there should be no need to increase working capital. This "normalized" $1 million figure then would represent capital expenditures for 2012, which are assumed to be approximately the same as the amount of depreciation, as explained in the text. The much larger $2.011 million figure for 2011 includes some increase in working capital to support increased sales over 2010, and also a continuation of the large capital expenditures from 2008-10, perhaps due to a need for large capital expenditures required during that period to repair and replace plant and equipment due to deterioration prior to bankruptcy. Thus, free cash flow is substantially higher for 2012 than 2011 despite the "no growth" assumption, due to the high expenditures forecast for 2011.

** Under the assumption of 3% growth in free cash flows, some additional investment in working capital will likely be needed to support increased sales, and Product Company may also need to invest more in capital improvements than the $1 million depreciation amount that merely allows replacement of existing equipment as it wears out. Thus an additional $60,000 expenditure per year is forecast over the amount required under the "no growth" assumption. Note again that free cash flow is substantially higher for 2012 than 2011, due in this case both to the assumption of growth and to the high expenditures forecast for 2011.

(ii) The Multiple of EBITDA Approach

Another common way of determining the terminal value is to multiply EBITDA (earnings before interest, taxes, depreciation, and amortization) or EBITDAR (earnings before interest, taxes, depreciation, amortization, and restructuring costs) by an appropriate factor, called the EBITDA multiple. Generally, the first step to determine the EBITDA multiple is to calculate the EBITDA multiple for companies that are in the same specific industry and, if possible, of similar size to the chapter 11 entity. The EBITDA multiple for each of the comparable companies is calculated by using the following formula:

$$\text{EBITDA multiple} = \frac{\text{Interest bearing debt} + \text{market value of equity}}{\text{EBITDA}}$$

For example, the multiple for Company A, a competitor of Product Company (see Problem 12-1) is determined in the following manner based on the following data:

Interest bearing debt: $30,000,000
Number of common shares issued and outstanding: 10,000,000
Market price per share: $7.00   EBITDA: $20,000,000

The interest bearing debt is the company's long-term debt, plus the current portion of its long-term debt and other short-term interest bearing debt that may be a part of the permanent financing. For example, if a company used short-term financing, such as a line of credit, as permanent financing, that debt would be included in total interest bearing debt. The total value of the equity is determined by multiplying the number of shares issued and outstanding times the market value of a share of stock. The number of shares issued and outstanding can be taken from page 1 of the company's most recent 10-Q or 10-K SEC filing, which will generally be more current than the number of shares reported in the equity section of the balance sheet. The market value is generally the closing price of the stock on the date as of which the valuation is being determined. The value can be determined by looking up the closing price of the stock for Company A on the internet or in the business section of major newspapers (such as the Wall Street Journal) that report stock prices for the exchange (such as the New York Stock Exchange or the NASDAQ) where the stock is listed. For Company A the value of the equity is $7.00 (market price of the stock) times 10,000,000 (shares issued and outstanding), or $70,000,000.

EBITDA is generally equal to the net income from operations plus the depreciation, amortization and other charges that do not require cash. The EBITDA multiple for Company A is determined in the following manner.

$$\text{EBITDA multiple} = \frac{\text{Interest bearing debt} + \text{market value of equity}}{\text{EBITDA}}$$

$$\text{EBITDA multiple} = \frac{\$30,000,000 + \$70,000,000}{\$20,000,000} = 5$$

A multiple for other companies similar to Product Company would be calculated in a similar manner. Then the multiples for each of the companies would be summed and divided by the number of companies to determine the average EBITDA multiple. For illustration purposes, assume the average EBITDA multiple for the companies comparable to Product Company is 5. To determine the terminal value for Product Company, the EBITDA of $9,018,000 for year 5 is multiplied times the EBITDA multiple of 5 to get a figure of $45,090,000, which is the terminal value at the end of year 5 (2011). Multiplying that figure times the year 5 present value factor of .567 (see Problem 12-1) yields a present value of the terminal value of $25,566,030.

The terminal value based on the EBITDA multiple is greater than the $22,731,000 value obtained above using the perpetuity method with a no-growth assumption, but less than the $31,185,000 obtained using the perpetuity method with a 3% growth assumption.[16] Both the perpetuity method and the EBITDA method are used in determining the terminal value. Generally, the academic community believes the perpetuity method has greater valuation theory support than does the EBITDA method. However, in determining the value of businesses in chapter 11, appraisers rely on the EBITDA method for determining terminal value much more frequently than on the perpetuity method.[17] One experienced appraiser explained that he feels much more comfortable in court justifying an EBITDA multiple than trying to justify the "g" (growth per year) used in the perpetuity method.

c. Present Value of Nonoperating Assets

To determine the total value available to the parties in the bankruptcy case, one more factor must be included. If there are assets in the estate that will not be needed in the operations of the reorganized debtor ("nonoperating assets"), then those assets can be sold or in some other way turned into cash. Thus the present value of nonoperating assets is added to the value of the discounted cash flows for the projection period and the discounted terminal value to determine the total enterprise value of the entity that will emerge from chapter 11.

Included in the nonoperating assets would be proceeds to be realized on the disposal of assets in segments of the business that will be eliminated or curtailed, and excess working capital, such as the collections of receivables for plants or divisions that are eliminated. Note that in Chapter Five, when some of the east coast operations of Foam Corporation were eliminated, cash was received from the collection of accounts receivable that would otherwise have been needed to

---

16. Note that the EBITDA multiple was determined using data from companies similar to Product Company. Those similar companies presumably pay income tax on their income. If Product Company has a net operating loss carryforward sufficient to reduce its taxes even beyond the projection period, then the present value of those future tax benefits may be added to the terminal value as determined by the EBITDA multiple method. Such adjustment is beyond the scope of this text.

17. The appraiser who relies on the EBITDA method will nevertheless compute a terminal value under the perpetuity method for comparison purposes. Any significant difference would be analyzed.

fund the operations of those east coast plants. See Problem 5-3.In the case of Product Company, assume that equipment not needed by the reorganized company will be sold for $300,000, which then is added to the total value.

d. Total Enterprise Value

The enterprise value of the reorganized Products Company is summarized as follows:

Net present value of cash flow projections	$12,736,000
Present value of terminal based on EBITDA multiple	+25,566,000
Amount realized from the sale of equipment	+ 300,000
Total value of reorganized entity	$38,602,000

Based on the perpetuity method for determining the terminal value, with an assumption of a 3% growth rate, the enterprise value would be:[18]

Net present value of cash flow projections	$12,736,000
Present value of terminal based on perp. (3% growth)	+31,185,000
Amount realized from the sale of equipment	+ 300,000
Total value of reorganized entity	$44,221,000

In summary, calculating the value of a debtor in bankruptcy is difficult because of changes that will be made in the debtor's operations as a result of the reorganization proceedings. Yet, a plan usually cannot be developed properly unless the interested parties have some indication of the value of the business. The discounted cash flow model is one approach that can be used to help estimate the reorganization value of the entity that will emerge from bankruptcy. This approach is used by both debtors and creditors as they attempt to develop and evaluate the terms of the plan.

Often the appraiser will use a range of value rather than a discrete number as used in the above examples. For example, the value of Product Company may be determined to be between $39 and $44 million.

Bankruptcy courts have accepted this approach for the determination of reorganization values for the fair and equitable standard in a cramdown and for other purposes. The discounted cash flow approach was used both by the financial advisor for the debtor and the financial advisor for the creditors' committee in *Exide Technologies*, 303 B.R. 48, (Bankr. D. Del. 2003). The following pages present two exhibits (one from each expert in *Exide*) and a further excerpt from the court's opinion.

Exhibit 12-2 shows the discounted cash flow valuation by the expert for the debtor (Newman of The Blackstone Group). Blackstone used a weighted average cost of capital range of 15 to 17 percent and an EBITDA multiple range of 5x to 6x after adjustments were made. The discounted cash flow approach resulted in a valuation range between $1.02 billion and $1.25 billion.

---

18. If the terminal value were determined using the perpetuity method under a no-growth assumption, the total value would be $12,736,000 + $22,732,000 + $300,000, which equals $35,768,000.

Exhibit 12-3 includes the discounted cash flow valuation by the expert for the creditors' committee (Derrough of Jefferies & Company). Note that Jefferies determined the value based on two alternatives—(1) a 6.5x terminal value EBITDA multiple and a weighted average cost of capital of 11.5%, and (2) a 7.5x terminal value EBITDA multiple and a cost of capital of 10.5%. This analysis generated values between $1.6 and $1.8 billion.

Exhibit 12-2

Exide Technologies Valuation Analysis
DISCOUNTED CASH FLOW ("DCF")

- A DCF valuation is determined by calculating the present value of the Company's projection of free cash flows during the forecast period and adding to this the present value of the Company's terminal value.
- Free cash flow is defined as operating profit, plus depreciation and amortization, less unlevered cash taxes, less capital expenditures, and less (plus) changes in working capital. Also deducted from operating profit is the Company's required pension cash contributions and restructuring costs.
- Blackstone estimated the terminal value by applying a Market EBITDA Multiple to the FY 2008 EBITDA.
  - Cash taxes were forecast based upon the Company's five-year projections. Management's current assumption is that substantially all the Company's existing domestic NOL carry forwards will be utilized to shield cancellation of indebtedness income, while the Company will retain the benefit of certain foreign NOL carry forwards.[1] Based on the above, the Company has assumed cash tax rates of 38% and 25% in North America and Europe / ROW, respectively, for valuation purposes. There is a possibility that the basis in the Company's depreciable assets in North America will be reduced as a result of COD income, thereby increasing the effective tax rate.
  - Capital expenditures are as projected in the five-year projections and are bases on the level of capital needed to fund the business as well as to fund initiatives.
  - Pension cash needs of $149.2 million over the forecast period (including amounts expensed of $84.0 million).
  - One-time cash restructuring cost of $97.0 million related to head count reduction, plant closures and other initiative are included over the forecast period.
- Blackstone estimated the terminal value by applying a Market EBITDA Multiple to the FY 2008 EBITDA.
  - Blackstone used am EBITDA multiple range of 5.0x to 6.0x
- The annual cash flow and terminal value were discounted back to September 30, 2003 at an appropriate weighted average cost of capital ("WACC").
  - The WACC was determined using Blackstone's estimate of an appropriate pro forma capital structure. Free cash flows and the terminal values were discounted using a range of WACCs from 15% to 17%. See Appendix D for Blackstone's WACC analysis.

[1]Further, it has been assumed that there will be no tax liability resulting from the forgiveness of any existing indebtedness.

DISCOUNTED CASH FLOW TO SEPTEMBER 30, 2003 ($ in millions)

- While the Company is projected to generate significant improvements in EBITDA, its free cash flow is negatively affected by a number of considerable cash outflows, including:
  - One-time cash costs to fund restructuring initiative;
  - Cash required to fund its pension plans;
  - Large capital expenditures; and
  - Legacy restructuring expenses.
- Offsetting significant cash outflows are positive changes in working capital during the post-emergence period, which reflect an expected return to normalized credit terms.

	6 Months Ended March 31,	Fiscal Year Ended March 31,				
	2004	2005	2006	2007	2008
Free Cash Flow -Exhibit 12-1	$56.40	$57.90	$99.00	$109.30	$129.80

	Present Value of Terminal Value			Total Enterprise Value		
	Terminal EBITDA Multiple(1)			Terminal EBITDA Multiple(1)		
	5.0x	5.5x	6.0x	5.0x	5.5x	6.0x
PV of Cash						
WACC	**Flows**					
14.00%	$312.8	$822.0	$904.2	$986.5	$1,134.8	$1,217.0	$1,299.2
15.00%	305.5	790.4	869.2	948.4	1,095.9	1,174.9	1,254.0
16.00%	298.6	760.2	836.2	912.2	1,058.7	1,134.8	1,210.8
17.00%	291.9	731.4	804.5	877.6	1,023.2	1,096.4	1,169.5
18.00%	285.4	703.9	774.3	844.7	989.3	1,059.7	1,130.0

(1) Based on $296.5M of EBITDAR in FY 2008

Source: Blackstone Exhibits to *In Re Exide Technologies*, 303 B.R. 48 (Bankr. D. Del. 2003)

Exhibit 12-3 (p. 1)

VALUATION ANALYSIS
Discounted Cash Flow Analysis – Range of Value

- The following enterprise values were determined based on a Discounted Cash Flow Analysis

- See the Appendix [next two pages] for additional detail to the Discounted Cash Flow Analysis

Weighted Average Cost of Capital ("WACC")	Terminal EBITDA Multiple Projected Bankruptcy Exit Date 12/31/03		
	6.5x	7.0x	7.5x
12.0%	$ 1,556	$ 1,649	$ 1,743
11.5%	1,583	1,678	1,773
11.0%	1,611	1,708	1,805
10.5%	1,639	1,738	1,837
10.0%	1,668	1,769	1,870

Applying a discount rate range of 10.0% to 11.5% and a terminal multiple range of 6.5x to 7.5x, the Discounted Cash Flow Analysis suggests an Enterprise Value range of $1.6 to $1.8 billion

Source: Jefferies Exhibits to *In Re Exide Technologies*, 303 B.R. 48 (Bankr. D. Del. 2003).

DISCOUNTED CASH FLOW VALUATION ANALYSIS   Exhibit 12-3 (p. 2)

DCF analysis using a 6.5x terminal value EBITDA multiple and 11.5% WACC ($in millions)

	3 Months Ended March 31, 2004	Projected [1]				Terminal Value
		2005	2006	2007	2008	
Operating Income	$27.2	$170.0	$196.4	$214.4	$227.8	$302
Plus: Depreciation and Amortization	20.4	78.1	74.1	74.1	74.1	
Less: Cash Taxes[2]	(2.0)	(44.0)	(57.7)	(64.6)	(69.6)	
Less: Capital Expenditures	(14.1)	(60.0)	(60.0)	(60.0)	(60.0)	
Less: Existing Liability / Legacy Cost	(6.3)	(17.2)	(10.1)	(10.0)	(10.1)	
Less: Changes in Working Capital	53.3	16.6	(7.3)	(17.7)	(24.3)	
Less: Cash Restructuring / Severance Costs	26.1	(43.1)	(16.7)	(0.8)	(0.8)	
Less: Pension	(0.6)	(25.9)	(18.2)	(20.3)	(3.2)	
Less: Daramec Costs	(2.0)	(3.5)	(3.0)	(3.0)	(3.0)	
Free Cash Flow	$ 50	$ 71	$ 98	112	$ 131	
2008 Projected EBITDAR						4.25
Discount Period Convention	0.25	1.25	2.25	3.25	4.25	
Discount Rate / Factor 11.5%	0.9732	0.8728	0.7828	0.7020	0.6296	0.6296
Terminal Values EBITDDA[(3)] Multiple 6.5x						1,962
Present Values	$ 48	$ 62	$76	$79	$ 82	$1,235
Sum of Discrete Present Values	$ 348					
Present Value of Terminal Value	1,235					
Implied Enterprise Value	$ 1,583					

(1) Provided by the Company and its financial advisor.
(2) Assumed to be 38% of EBIT in North America and 25% of EBIT in Europe / ROW as per guidance from the Company and its financial advisor
[(3) Earnings before interest, taxes, depreciation, depletion, and amortization]

Source: Jefferies Exhibits to *In Re Exide Technologies*, 303 B.R. 48 (Bankr. D. Del. 2003).

DISCOUNTED CASH FLOW VALUATION ANALYSIS

Exhibit 12-3 (p. 3)

DCF analysis using a 7.5x terminal value EBITDA multiple and 10.5% WACC ($in millions)

	3 Months Ended March 31, 2004	Projected				Terminal Value
		2005	2006	2007	2008	
Operating Income	$ 27.2	$ 170.0	$ 196.4	$ 214.4	$ 227.8	$ 302
Plus: Depreciation and Amortization	20.4	78.1	74.1	74.1	74.1	
Less: Cash Taxes(2)	(2.0)	(44.0)	(57.7)	(64.6)	(69.6)	
Less: Capital Expenditures	(14.1)	(60.0)	(60.0)	(60.0)	(60.0)	
Less: Existing Liability / Legacy Cost	(6.3)	(17.2)	(10.1)	(10.0)	(10.1)	
Less: Changes in Working Capital	53.3	16.6	(7.3)	(17.7)	(24.3)	
Less: Cash Restructuring/Severance Costs	(26.1)	(43.1)	(16.7)	(0.8)	(0.8)	
Less: Pension	(0.6)	(25.9)	(18.2)	(20.3)	(3.2)	
Less: Daramec Costs	(2.0)	(3.5)	(3.0)	(3.0)	(3.0)	
Free Cash Flow	**50**	**71**	**98**	**112**	**131**	
2008 Projected EBITDAR						
Discount Period Convention	0.25	1.25	2.25	3.25	4.25	4.25
Discount Rate / Factor 10.5	0.9753	0.8827	0.7988	0.7229	0.6542	0.6542
Terminal Values EBITDDA Multiple 7.5x						2,264
Present Values	**$ 49**	**$ 63**	**$ 78**	**$ 81**	**$ 86**	**$1,481**

Sum of Discrete Present Values	$ 356
Present Value of Terminal Value	1,481
Implied Enterprise Value	**$1,837**

(1) Provided by the Company and its financial advisor.
(2) Assumed to be 38% of EBIT in North America and 25% of EBIT in Europe / ROW as per guidance from the Company and its financial advisor
Source: Jefferies Exhibits to *In Re Exide Technologies*, 303 B.R. 48 (Bankr. D. Del. 2003).

Here is a second excerpt from Judge Carey's opinion in *Exide Technologies*, this time dealing with discounted cash flow valuations:

In re Exide Technologies
United States Bankruptcy Court, District of Delaware, 2003
303 B.R. 48

* * *

The experts' valuations based on a discounted cash flow analysis differed greatly, with Newman [of The Blackstone Group] calculating value in a range between $ 1.023 and $ 1.254 billion and Derrough [of Jefferies & Company] calculating value in a range between $ 1.583 and 1.837 billion. Derrough applied the discounted cash flow analysis in a straight-forward manner, while Newman adjusted his formula based upon his "market-based approach" to valuation to account for the manner in which he believed prospective purchasers would view the Debtor.

The discounted cash flow ("DCF") analysis has been described as a "forward-looking" method that "measure[s] value by forecasting a firms' ability to generate cash." Pantaleo, supra. n. 29, [Pantaleo & Ridings, *Reorganization Value*, 51 BUS. LAW. 419 (1996)] at 427. DCF is calculated by adding together (i) the present value of the company's projected distributable cash flows (i.e., cash flows available to all investors) during the forecast period, and (ii) the present value of the company's terminal value (i.e., value of the firm at the end of the forecast period). In this case, the experts relied on the Debtor's projected cash flows for the fiscal years ending March 31, 2004 through March 31, 2008, as set forth in the Debtor's five-year business plans.[19] The DCF factors which the parties dispute are (1) the discount rate; and (2) the multiple used to calculate terminal value. See, generally, 7 COLLIER ON BANKRUPTCY ¶ 1129.06[2][a][ii] (15th ed. rev. 2003).

Newman used a discount rate in the range of 15% to 17%, while Derrough used a discount rate in the range of 10.5% and 11.5%. Both experts relied on a weighted average cost of capital (the "WACC") to determine the discount rate, which is based upon a combined rate of the cost of debt capital and the cost of equity capital. In determining the cost of equity, Derrough used the generally accepted method known as the capital asset pricing model or "CAPM."[20] Newman, however, chose not to use

---

19. [Footnote 31 in original:] Again, it appears that Newman used the Debtor's most recent business plan prepared in October 2003, while Derrough used the older business plan provided by the Debtor in its Disclosure Statement.

20. [Footnote 32 in original:] CAPM is a formula that was developed to calculate the cost of equity capital. Pantaleo, supra n. 29, at 433 n. 52. "While there are other models to determine equity, CAPM is probably the most widely used." Id. The CAPM formula is:

Cost of Equity $= R(f) + (Beta \times [R(m) - R(f)])$

Where: R(f) = risk free rate
Beta = beta of the target's equity security
R(m) = expected return on a market portfolio consisting of a large number of diversified stocks

Id. "This formula, in essence, provides that a firm's cost of equity is equal to the sum of the risk-free rate of return plus a risk premium (i.e., a return above the risk free rate). The risk premium for the firm is calculated by multiplying the risk premium that the equity market generally must pay to attract

CAPM because he noted that CAPM can be inaccurate when applied to company that is not publicly traded. However, in such cases, comparable companies are used to determine the "beta" for a CAPM valuation (see Tr. 10/25/03, pp. 212-13 (Derrough)), but Newman felt that comparable companies are inappropriate in this instance because the Debtor is emerging from chapter 11 and will face substantial risk in executing its five-year projected business plan.

Therefore, Newman determined cost of equity based upon information showing the rate of return on equity that a prospective purchase would demand. Based upon the private equity process (and, the Debtor argues, supported by the testimony of John Craig of Enersys, Inc), Newman used a cost of equity between 20% and 30%; while the standard CAPM method employed by Derrough resulted in a cost of equity between 13.6% and 14.6%.[21]

Furthermore, in calculating WACC, Newman determined the cost of debt at 7.5%, while Derrough's calculation resulted in a cost of debt at 5.9%. The Debtor's own five-year plan assumes a cost of debt at 6.2%.

Discounted cash flow analysis has been used to determine valuation in many chapter 11 cases. See, e.g., In re Zenith Elecs. Corp., 241 B.R. 92, 103-05 (Bankr. D. Del. 1999); and In re Cellular Information Systems, Inc., 171 B.R. 926, 930-37 (Bankr. S.D.N.Y. 1994). Newman's numerous subjective adjustments to the analysis stray too far from the generally accepted method of determining the discount rate. Therefore, I will rely on Derrough's more straight forward determination of the discount rate.

Newman determined the terminal value in his discounted cash flow analysis by using the same adjusted EBITDA multiple as used in his comparable company analysis (i.e., 5.0x to 6.0x). Derrough, however, used the actual multiple which he derived from his comparable company analysis. Again, Newman's terminal value multiple was adjusted, causing his calculation to depart from the standard discounted cash flow methodology.

The Debtor argues that in the final determination of enterprise value, Derrough accorded too much weight to his DCF analysis. Derrough elected to attribute 60% of his total valuation to his DCF analysis. The Debtor argues that a DCF analysis is dependent on a company's ability to meet long-range projections, in this case the Debtor's FY 2008 projections. Because the long-range projections are the most speculative and uncertain, and because testimony of the Debtor's officers showed that the Debtor's past and current performance has not met the projections in its business plans, the Debtor argues that Derrough's strong reliance on his DCF is misplaced.

---

investors by the firm's 'beta,' which ... reflects the risk associated with an equity investment in the firm relative to the risk of an investment in the equity market as a whole." Id. at 433-34. "For companies that are not publicly traded—including most Chapter 11 debtors—the only way to measure beta is by reference to comparable companies." Id. at 435. [See Appendix B at the end of this casebook for a discussion of cost of capital.—Ed.]

21. [Footnote 33 in original:] The Creditors Committee points out that the Derrough's only departure from the "textbook" CAPM calculation was to include a risk premium of 1-2% to increase the cost of equity. This actually reduced his opinion of the Debtor's enterprise value.

Courts often rely upon DCF analyses in valuing reorganizing debtors. I conclude that it is appropriate to consider DCF when determining such value and no less weight should be accorded to DCF because it relies upon projections. When other helpful valuation analyses are available, as in this case, each method should be weighed and then all methods should be considered together. * * *

Problem 12-3: Foam Corporation

On April 10, 2006, Foam Corporation filed a chapter 11 petition. Eight months later, Foam Corporation is developing a plan of reorganization and has asked you to determine the value of Foam Corporation using the discounted cash flow approach. Please do so. You have determined the following information:

1. The cost of capital for other companies similar to Foam Corporation is 16 percent, and their average EBITDA multiple is 4.
2. A projection period of five years will be used.
3. Sales are expected to grow at an annual rate of 10 percent per year during the next five years.
4. The gross profit percentage is 33 1/3 percent.
5. Depreciation expense for each year will be $1 million. (The depreciation expense is already included in the various expenses set forth in the net income projections below. For example, depreciation on factory equipment makes up part of the "Cost of goods sold.")
5. The cash that will need to be invested in additional working capital and for capital expenditures will equal $1 million for the first year. (The needed investment can be funded out of Foam's revenues; no new cash infusion will be needed to enable Foam Corporation to do business.) During each of the other years in the projection period, the cash needed for such purposes will equal $1 million plus an amount equal to 10 percent of the increase in sales beyond the previous year's sales.
6. A net operating loss of approximately $4.5 million will survive the reorganization.
7. Listed below are the net income projections for 2007-2011.
8. Assets not needed for operations of the reorganized Foam Corporation can be liquidated for $500,000.

	2007	2008	2009	2010	2011
Sales	$30,000	$33,000	$36,300	$39,930	$43,923
Cost of goods sold	(20,000)	(22,000)	(24,200)	(26,620)	(29,282)
Gross profit	$10,000	$11,000	$12,100	$13,310	$14,641
Selling expenses	(3,000)	(3,300)	(3,630)	(3,993)	(4,392)
General and admin. expenses	(5,000)	(5,200)	(5,400)	(5,700)	(6,000)
Total selling and general admin. expenses	(8,000)	(8,500)	(9,030)	(9,693)	(10,392)
Net income before taxes (EBIT)	$2,000	$2,500	$3,070	$3,617	$4,249
Taxes - 40 percent	0	0	(1,228)	(1,447)	(1,700)
Net income after taxes (EBI)	$2,000	$ 2,500	$ 1,842	$ 2,170	$ 2,549

2. Market Multiple Approaches

The market approach is based on the concept that a prudent buyer would pay no more for an asset than it would cost to acquire a substitute asset with the same utility. This approach utilizes real-world transactions in the marketplace to derive a value or range of values for the subject asset. Just as with the income approach, the market approach is applicable whether the asset being valued is tangible or intangible, and it can be used to value a single asset or a business entity. The extent of market transactional data will vary depending on the asset being valued.

In the case of an investment or holding company, the market values of the securities on hand may be used to determine the reorganization value. This approach was used in Central States Electric Corp. v. Austrian, 183 F.2d 879, 884 (4th Cir. 1950), even though the appellants argued that going concern values should be used to include matters such as increases in the value of securities held, increases in dividends, and "restoration of 'leverage' through the borrowing of money and the earnings of skilled management in the purchase and sale of securities." It should be noted that the securities held by the debtor in that case did not represent a controlling interest in any company.

"The rationale for the market value approach is logical. The investment company has no fixed assets oriented toward a particular function as would an industrial business; moreover, a specialized service is rendered only in the sense that the company offers diversification of investment and management of assets." Id. The situation, however, is altered when the debtor's only assets consist of stock representing total control of other businesses. Under such circumstances, it is apparent that the debtor's financial outlook is completely dependent upon the financial success or failure of the wholly owned businesses. Accordingly, the debtor's valuation is based on the future earnings of those entities. See In re Equity Funding Corp. of Am., 391 F. Supp. 768 (C.D. Cal. 1975); cf. In re Mahoney, 251 B.R. 748 (Bankr. S.D. Fla. 2000) (relying on going concern valuation of business to value 45% stock interest in business, with appropriate reductions because interest was not controlling interest and because shares were not publicly traded and thus could be hard to sell).

The two most commonly used approaches to value are the guideline publicly traded company method (comparable company analysis), and the comparable merger and acquisition transactions (M&A) method. A third method used is the historical internal transactions method.

    a.   Guideline Publicly Trade Company

The guideline publicly traded company method (also referred to as the comparable company analysis) determines the current trading multiples for financial measures such as revenue, EBITDA (or EBITDAR[22]), EBIT (or EBITR[23]), and FCF,[24] of comparable public companies and then applies the multiples so determined to the company being valued.

Assuming EBITDA is to be used, then the two factors needed to estimate the enterprise value using this method are the subject company's EBITDA and the appropriate multiple. The subject company's EBITDA is then multiplied by the multiple, to obtain the subject company's enterprise value.

A key question that has to be answered is what EBITDA number should be used? In general, where a company is not in bankruptcy, EBITDA should be determined based on the current annual earnings of the subject company. However, because of the current problems being dealt with in the bankruptcy case, the use of current earnings may not provide a reasonable enterprise valuation. An EBITDA figure based on the earnings projected for the first or second year after reorganization may be more appropriate. One possibility is to base the determination on the earnings that are currently being generated without considering the reorganization costs (EBITDAR). However, this number must be adjusted for any changes in the nature of the operations that may be provided for in the chapter 11 plan.

In the Exide Technologies case, Blackstone used the historical EBITDAR, while Jefferies used an EBITDAR based on a period that included six months of future projected operations. The bankruptcy court noted that

> The experts significantly differed on their choice of the data to use for the Debtor's EBITDAR. Newman [Blackstone] used the EBITDAR for the twelve months ending June 30, 2003, ($179.4 million) as set forth in the Debtor's revised five-year plan prepared in October 2003. Newman explained that using the "historical" EBITDAR is appropriate in this case since it is the latest date for which actual EBITDAR is available for both the Debtor and the comparable companies. Derrough [Jefferies], however, used the EBITDAR based on projected earnings for the trailing twelve months ending December 31, 2003 ($196 million). Derrough's figure is based upon the Debtor's business plan that was prepared in December 2002 because he did not have access to the revised October 2003 business plan.
>
> Hotchkiss testified that a comparable company analysis for companies emerging from chapter 11 should use the first year's projected EBITDAR because the historical EBITDAR does not reflect any of the benefits from the debtor's restructuring, which results in understating value. Derrough's use of the December 31, 2003 figure uses half historical and half projected EBITDAR, so it is an arguably more conservative approach than that suggested by Hotchkiss.

---

22. EBITDAR is earnings before interest taxes, depreciation, amortization, and restructuring charges.
23. EBITR is earnings before interest, taxes, and restructuring charges.
24. FCF is free cash flows.

In determining the Debtor's value for purposes of deciding whether the Debtor's Plan is fair and equitable, it is appropriate to include the benefit of the Debtor's restructuring. Part of the purpose of this exercise is to determine whether the Debtor's intent to give common stock to the Prepetition Lenders results in paying the Prepetition Lender[s] more than 100% of the value of their claims. This requires a forward-looking valuation and I conclude that it is appropriate to use projected, rather than historic, EBITDAR.[*] Because the Debtor has revised its projections, the most appropriate EBITDAR to use would be for the trailing twelve months ending December 31, 2003 as set forth in the October 2003 business plan ($188.2 million).

Based on the foregoing comparable company analyses, Newman determined that the Debtor's enterprise value was a range between $897 million to $1.076 billion, while Derrough determined that the Debtor's enterprise value was $1.515 billion.[**] However, because I find that it is appropriate to calculate value based upon the EBITDAR for the trailing twelve months ending December 31, 2003 ($188.2 million), and the appropriate multiple is between 7.2 (the multiple calculated by Newman before subjectively reducing it) and 7.7x (Derrough's multiple), the comparable company value should be in the range between $1.355 billion (using 7.2x) and $1.449 billion (using 7.7x).

---

*　　[Footnote 29 in original:] See also Peter V. Pantaleo and Barry W. Ridings, *Reorganization Value*, 51 BUS. LAW. 419, 437 (1996)("[V]aluations based on comparable company analysis are 'backward looking' in that they generally rely on historical information about earnings or cash flow in order to determine value. If history is not a reliable guide to future performance—and, arguably, in many reorganizations, it is not—then relying on past earnings to determine value is problematic as a matter of economic theory"). While applying a current market multiple against several years of forecasted EBITDA can result in overvaluation (see id. at 426), use of the trailing twelve months ending December 31, 2003 in the revised projections does not reach so far into the future so as to detract from its reliability.

**　　[Footnote 30 in original:] Derrough's comparable company analysis provided a range between $ 1.427 billion and 1.537 billion. However, his valuation range was based upon analysis of the Debtor's EBITDAR (7.7x), EBITR (earnings before interest, taxes and restructuring charges) (12.8x), and FCF (free cash flow, which was defined as EBITDAR minus capital expenditures) (11.6x). Because Newman's report used only EBITDAR and because Derrough's EBITDAR value falls in the middle of his comparable company analysis, I have compared only the experts' EBITDAR analysis.

Exide Technologies, 303 B.R. at 61-62.

As with the forecast of future expected earnings, the determination of the multiple is best done on a case-by-case basis, and any factors that appear relevant to a specific company's risk evaluation may be utilized to determine the multiple. Thus, when determining the appropriate multiple, courts have considered the cyclical nature of the industry, the number and character of the debtor's customers, the possible uncertainties in management, expenses and operations, the age and condition of the debtor's plant and equipment, and the rate of technological progress in the industry.

Courts have also displayed a tendency to utilize in their calculations figures obtained from other companies within the industry, provided these companies are similar in nature to the debtor corporation. See, e.g., In re Greate Bay Hotel & Casino, Inc., 251 B.R. 213, 229 n.17 (Bankr. D.N.J. 2000). However, where the debtor has been compared to other concerns substantially differing in character, the courts have rejected the rate of capitalization so determined. For example, in In re Muskegon Motor Specialties, 366 F.2d 522 (6th Cir. 1966), the expert witness had calculated the capitalization rate[25] by using the price earnings ratio of thirty-six selected auto parts manufacturers listed on the stock exchange. Since the debtor was an unlisted company with no real market for its shares—and its sales varied from four times as great to only one-hundredth as great as the sales of the companies whose capitalization rates had been computed—the court concluded that a comparison between such entities would yield little beneficial information.

Assuming several appropriately similar companies can be found, the multiple for each of them will be determined, and then those figures may be averaged by adding them all together and dividing by the number of similar companies used. Weights may also be used, giving greater consideration to certain companies that are more in line with the subject company. However, the financial advisor performing the valuation will often decide to remove from the sample the companies' multiples that are outliers and that thus have limited meaning. For example, an otherwise comparable company that is incurring substantial losses and that has a very low EBITDA[26] may have a very high EBITDA multiple.

The comparable company multiples used by Blackstone in the Exide case are presented in Exhibit 12-4 below (following Problem 12-5). Blackstone assigned a value between $897 million and $1.076 billion. Jefferies assigned a value, on the other hand, between $1.4 and $1.5 billion. The bankruptcy judge in *Exide Technologies* made the following comments related to the guideline publicly traded company (comparable company analysis) approach:

> The key components of a comparable company analysis are the Debtor's EBITDA (i.e., earnings before interest, taxes, depreciation and amortization) and the selection of an appropriate multiple to apply to the EBITDA to arrive at enterprise value. The appropriate multiple is determined by comparing the enterprise value of comparable publicly traded companies to their trailing

---

25. The multiple is the reciprocal of the capitalization rate; for example, if the capitalization rate is 20%, the multiple is one divided by .20, which equals 5.

26. A company with negative earnings may nevertheless have a positive EBITDA, because interest, depreciation, and amortization expenses are added back to earnings to calculate EBITDA.

twelve months EBITDA.[*] A subjective assessment is required to select the comparable companies and, here, the parties argue about which comparable companies are more appropriate to use.

However, as pointed out by the Creditors Committee, regardless of the comparables used, both experts arrived at similar EBITDA multiples, with Newman [Blackstone] at 7.x and Derrough [Jefferies] at 7.7x. However, Newman then reduced his multiple to a range between 5.0x and 6.0x, because he determined that his comparable for the Debtor's industrial division (C&D Technologies) should be given less weight. The Debtor also argues that Newman's reduced multiple is more in line with the implied EBITDA multiples that can be derived from the Debtor's private equity process.

---

*   [Footnote 27 in original:] Exide is held publicly, but was delisted by the New York Stock Exchange sometime around February 2002.

303 B.R. at 61.

The capitalization multiples for EBITDAR were illustrated previously in this chapter. Multiples of EBIT, EBI and revenue are determined in a similar approach. For example, the EBIT multiple is calculated in the following manner:

$$\text{EBIT Multiple} \; = \; \frac{\text{Interest bearing debt} + \text{market value of equity}}{\text{Net income before interest and taxes (EBIT)}}$$

To determine the enterprise value of the chapter 11 debtor, we take the multiple determined through the analysis of similar companies and multiply it times the projected current earnings (EBIT) as described above.

Carefully consider Problem 12-4, which has been answered for the reader, and then try Problem 12-5.

Problem 12-4: Product Company

> You have determined the following information for Product Company (from Problem 12-1). Six companies in the same industry as Product Company and whose stock is traded over-the-counter each had EBIT (earnings before interest and taxes)multiples very close to 7. The multiple was determined for each company by adding the total market value of its equity and the total present value of its debts (which just equaled the face value of the debts in each case because in each case the debts carried a fair market rate of interest). Then, for each company, that total was divided by the company's EBIT. Next it is necessary to estimate the EBIT of Product Company that should be multiplied times the EBIT multiple. Generally, the EBIT should be based on values not including any of the reorganization costs and should take into consideration the changes provided for in the plan. For purposes of this exercise, assume the projections for 2007 do not include any restructuring charges and do take into consideration changes made by the plan. The projection for EBIT was $3.3 million for 2007.
>
> The value would consist of the following components, in millions:

1.	Earnings capitalization ($3.3 million times multiple of 7)	$ 23.1
2.	Value of net operating loss (computed below)	4.1
3.	Value of nonoperating assets	0.3
	Total value	$27.5

The company has a net operating loss carryforward of approximately $13 million that will allow the company to avoid paying income tax for the first three years. The EBIT multiple was calculated from companies that did not have any net operating loss carryforwards. Product Company has extra value because it will not be required to pay any taxes during the first three years of operations. Using a discount rate of 12 percent, the value of the net operating loss was determined to be approximately $4 million in the following manner:

Year	EBIT	Tax Rate	Tax Savings	Present Value Factor	Pres. Value of Savings
2007	$3,300	40%	1,320	.893	$1,179
2008	4,245	40%	1,698	.797	1,353
2009	5,331	40%	2,132	.712	1,518
Total present value of savings					$4,050

The amount to be realized from the disposal of equipment is also included in the total value as item 3 above: $300,000, or $0.3 million.

Under the discounted cash flow approach the value was determined to be approximately $38 million, and under the EBIT multiple approach the value was estimated to be approximately $27.5 million. It might be concluded that this company has a value of about $28 million to $38 million. Alternatively, the appraiser may assign weights to the two approaches (for example, 65% to discounted cash flow and 35% to EBIT multiple) to determine the value.

On the other hand, some valuation experts prefer the discounted cash flow approach and would conclude that the value is approximately $38 million, as indicated by the discounted cash flow approach.

Generally appraisers develop a range for the value rather than a discrete number, using various approaches including "sensitivity analysis" (discussion of which is beyond the scope of this text).

Problem 12-5: Foam Corporation

Refer to Problem 12-3. You have decided to estimate the value of Foam Corporation using the guideline publicly traded company method and to use an earnings before interest and taxes (EBIT) multiple in your analysis. By examining several publicly traded companies, you have determined that a reasonable EBIT multiple to use in determining the value of Foam Corporation is 7. Estimate the value of Foam Corporation.

Exhibit 12-4

Exide Technologies
B. Comparable Company Analysis
SUMMARY ($ in millions, except per share amounts)

Company	Stock Price (10/10/03)	Equity Value	Total Enterprise Value (TEV)	TEV/ LTM EBITDA	Business
Description					
Automotive Comparables					
Johnson Controls Inc.	$103.10	$9,353.2	$11,805.0	7.0x	Supplies seating systems Interiors systems and batteries to the automotive industry. Also provides building control systems.
Delphi Automotive Systems	9.03	5,059.5	6,958.5	4.0x	Supplies Batteries to the automotive industry.
Industrial Comparables					
C&D Technologies	20.47	526.8	550.7	10.5x	North American producer integrated network power reserve system.

Source: Blackstone Exhibits to *In Re Exide Technologies*, 303 B.R. 48 (Bankr. D. Del. 2003)

Exhibit 12-4 (cont.)

Exide Technologies
B. Comparable Company Analysis (cont.)

Company	Ticker	Stock Closing Price (10/10/03)	Equity Market Value	Total Enterprise Value	TEV/ LTM Revenue	TEV/ LTM EBITDA	TEV/ LTM EBIT	Stock Price/ LTM EPS
Johnson Controls Inc.	JCI	$103.10	$9,353.2	$11,805.0	0.5x	7.0x	10.3x	16.3x
Delphi Automotive System	DPH	9.03	5,059.5	6,958.5	0.3x	4.0x	9.4x	13.1x
C&D Technologies	CHP	20.47	526.8	550.7	1.7x	10.5x	18.6x	31.5x

LTM OPERATING PERFORMANCE
($ in millions, except per share amount)

| | | | LTM | | | | % of | |
Company	Revenue	EBITDA	EBITDA Margin	EBIT	EBIT Margin	CapEx	Revenue	EPS
Johnson Controls Inc.	$21,864.5	$1,680.8	7.7%	$1,145.9	5.2%	$699.9	3.2%	$6.34
Delphi Automotive System	27,693.0	1,751.0	6.3%	741.0	2.7%	1,036.0	3.7%	0.69
C&D Technologies	326.1	52.5	16.1%	29.6	9.1%	5.4	1.7%	0.65
Exide Technologies	2,390.7	179.6	7.5%	74.3	3.1%	49.4	2.1%	NM

Source: Blackstone Exhibits to *In Re Exide Technologies*, 303 B.R. 48 (Bankr. D. Del. 2003)

b. Mergers and Acquisitions Comparable Transactions

In the mergers and acquisition (M&A) comparable transactions approach, the focus is on the consideration paid in recent transactions occurring in the subject company's industry or in related industries. This approach has the advantage of being based on the price that was paid for a company between a willing buyer and a willing seller. The disadvantages are that it may be difficult to find recent and similar transactions data that is relevant to the subject company and that the terms of such transactions my make it difficult to actually determine the price that was paid. Once the price for a comparable transaction has been determined, the appraiser must then determine the EBITDA or earnings of the acquired comparable company to develop a multiple to use to value the subject company. There often are published data that will indicate one or more multiples resulting from the transaction; however, before such data is used the appraiser must ascertain that the underlying financial data supports the published multiple.

In analyzing the values of recent transactions the appraiser must make a distinction between an investment purchase and a strategic purchase. Frequently strategic buyers are willing to pay a premium for a company that can be integrated into their operations.

Once the multiple to be used has been determined, it is then multiplied times the appropriate EBITDA or earnings of the subject company to determine the enterprise value.

Exhibit 12-5 contains an example of the M&A comparable transaction approach used by Jefferies in the Exide case.

In its *Exide Technologies* opinion the court made the following comment regarding the M & A comparable transaction approach:

> The comparable transaction analysis is similar to the comparable company analysis in that an EBITDA multiple is determined from recent merger and acquisition transactions in the automotive and industrial battery industries and that multiple is then applied to the appropriate trailing twelve months of the Debtor. Newman calculated multiples for two transactions that took place in 2002 (6.0x and 7.2x) and set his multiple in a range of 5.5x to 6.0x, after adjusting the comparable transaction multiples, due to his knowledge of the companies involved in the 2002 transactions and his opinion that a similar strategic acquisition was not likely for the Debtor because of antitrust concerns. Derrough, on the other hand, looked at more than a dozen merger and acquisition transactions occurring between May 1998 and November 2002 to derive an EBITDA multiple of 7.0x. However, Derrough's "comparable transactions" for 1998 and 1999 probably are not useful in this matter since the experts agreed that the market had changed considerably since 2000.

Exhibit 12-5

VALUATION ANALYSIS
Comparable M&A Transaction Analysis ($ in millions)

- The following multiples were chosen for comparison based on the TTM period prior to the announcement of each of the selected transactions

- Enterprise values are calculated using median multiples applies to Exide's projected results for the TTM period ended December 31, 2003. Blended multiples are calculated based on revenue assuming a 66% allocation for the transportation segment, and a 34% allocation for the industrial segment

- See the Appendix for additional detail to the comparable M&A Transaction Analysis

| | Implied Ent. Valuation Using Multiples of: | | | |
	Revenue	EBITDAR	EBITR[1]	FCF[2]
Transportation Segment Multiple	0.8x	6.9x	9.7x	11.0x
Industrial Segment Multiple	0.5x	7.2x	10.0x	11.6x
Blended Multiple	0.7x	7.0x	9.8x	11.2x
TTM 12/31/03 Metric	$ 2,323	$ 196	$ 112	$ 133
Implied Enterprise Value- As of 12/31/2003	**$ 1,609.6**	**$ 1,371.8**	**$ 1,094.5**	**$ 1,487.7**

[1] EBITR is defined as earnings before interest, taxes, and restructuring charges.
[2] Free cash flow is defined as EBITDAR minus capital expenditures.

Applying EBITDAR, EBITR, and FCF multiples as of the Projected Bankruptcy Exit Date, the Comparable M&A Transaction Analysis suggests an enterprise value range of $1.1 billion to $1.5 billion.

Source: Jefferies Exhibits to *In Re Exide Technologies*, 303 B.R. 48 (Bankr. D. Del. 2003)

Therefore, for the reasons discussed above regarding the comparable company analysis, a straightforward application of the multiple derived from Newman's comparable transactions before his adjustment should be applied here. The Committee argues that a proper weighting of the multiples derived from Newman's 2002 transactions would result in a multiple of approximately 6.4x.

As in the comparable company analysis, Newman then applied his multiple to the Debtor's revised latest twelve months ending June 30, 2003 ($179.4 million), while Derrough applied his multiple to the Debtor's trailing twelve months ending December 31, 2003 ($196 million) as set forth in the December 2002 five-year plan. Also, for the reasons discussed in the comparable company analysis above, I have concluded that the trailing twelve months ending December 31, 2003, as updated in October 2003 plan, should be used ($ 188.2 million). Applying the 6.4x EBITDA multiple to the trailing twelve months ending December 31, 2003 results in a valuation of $ 1.204 billion.

303 B.R. at 62-63.

The bankruptcy court in *Exide Technologies* focused on the adjustments that Newman, Blackstone's expert, made based on his experience, and the court disallowed such judgments. In doing so the court failed to take into consideration allowances that often need to be made to the multiples to adjust for the specific company risks that were discussed above.

c.   The Historical Internal Transactions Method

If there has been an exchange of control of the subject company's ownership during a period reasonably close to the valuation date, it may provide a value for use in valuing the company. Multiples should be adjusted to account for any changes in industry, economic, or other relevant conditions.

Additionally any offer made after the completion of due diligence, made with a source of funding, and made on an arms length basis may provide the basis for a creditable valuation. In Blackstone's valuation of Exide, this approach was used. A summary of that valuation is described in Exhibit 12-6.

Exhibit 12-6

Exide Technologies
A. Summary of Private Equity Bids

OVERVIEW OF BIDS

- A summary of the three bids received is shown below. ($ in millions)

	Firm #1	Firm #2	Firm #3
Date Received	6/20/03	6/20/03	6/20/03
Transaction Summary:	▪ $950M bid based on FY03 EBITDA of $177M	▪ $875M bid based on 6.0x FY03 Adjusted EBITDA of $147M[1]	▪ $1.2B bid based on 6.8x FY03 EBITDA of $177M; "normalized" bid of $728M excluding assumed liabilities of $425M[2] (4.4x EBITDA)
	▪ Offer to purchase up to 100% of common equity	▪ DM Notes assumed rather than refinanced	
	▪ Banks have option to Receive pro rata share of common stock (up to 49%) or pro rata share of $500M in cash	▪ Banks' recovery to include $150-$200M cash, $141M seller note and $100-$150M equity	▪ Banks receive combination of cash, equity and notes (if exit facility of $500M is not attained) with total value of $396M

[1]Reduced by $30 million for cash environmental, pension and Daramic supply contract cost.
[2]Includes pension of $280 million, OPEB of $27 million, environmental liabilities of $78 million, Daramic commitments of $40 million

Source: Blackstone Exhibits to *In Re Exide Technologies*, 303 B.R. 48 (Bankr. D. Del. 2003)

3. Asset Approach

The third general approach to determining enterprise value is the asset approach. Book values of assets are restated, and unrecorded assets are booked, based on appraisal of individual assets or groups of assets to reflect current values, under the appropriate standard of value. For example liquidation values would be used in the case of a liquidation standard, and fair value or fair market value would be used in the case of a going concern assumption.

The asset approach tends to be most useful when there are significant tangible assets (such as holding companies, investment companies, and finance companies with short-term assets) and little in the way of intangible assets that cannot be identified and valued. It is particularly useful in determining liquidation value, which must be included in the disclosure statement. Section 1125(b) requires that the disclosure statement include adequate information to allow the creditors to make an informed decision about the plan. At a minimum the disclosure statement should include a description of the debtor's business, the debtor's prepetition history, the debtor's postpetition management (and management compensation), a description of the plan and how it will be executed, financial information, tax consequences of the plan, a *liquidation analysis,* litigation, and transactions with insiders.[27]

The purpose of the liquidation analysis is to provide information allowing the creditors to determine whether to accept or reject a plan and to provide information to help determine whether the best interest of creditors test is met. Section 1129(a)(7) requires that creditors or stockholders who do not vote in favor of the plan receive at least as much value under the plan as they would receive if the company liquidated under chapter 7.

A liquidation analysis may also be appropriate for use in determining solvency for recovery actions. Section 101(32)(A) defines insolvency as "financial condition such that the sum of such entity's debts is greater than all of such entity's property, at fair valuation." This standard of determining insolvency is referred to as the "Balance Sheet Test." The "fair valuation" of the entity's assets should be based on a going-concern premise of value, unless the entity is on its "death-bed" at the time of the preference or fraudulent transfer, in which case a liquidation premise is appropriate. See footnote 13 in Chapter One above.

When performing a solvency analysis and applying the Balance Sheet Test, the methodology that the analyst uses is the Asset Approach. While the liquidation analysis and the solvency analysis (Balance Sheet Test) may be presented in a similar form (i.e., the Asset Approach) the premise of value for the liquidation analysis is generally orderly liquidation value, and the premise

---

27. 1 Grant W. Newton, BANKRUPTCY AND INSOLVENCY ACCOUNTING 295 (6th ed., John Wiley & Sons, Inc., 2000).

of value in a solvency analysis (Balance Sheet Test) is typically going concern value, except in the rare "death-bed" situation as noted above.[28] Liquidation values are discussed in greater detail below, in section B of this chapter.

4. Summary

Calculating the value of a debtor in bankruptcy is difficult because of changes that will be made in the debtor's operations as a result of the reorganization proceedings. Yet, a plan usually cannot be developed properly unless the interested parties have some indication of the value of the business. As described earlier in this chapter, three major approaches are used—the income approach based on discounted cash flows, the market multiples approach, and the asset approach—to estimate the value of the entity that will emerge from bankruptcy. These approaches are used by both debtors and creditors as they attempt to develop the terms of the plan. Which approach is used will depend on various factors. Frequently more than one approach may be used, with various weights assigned to each. In the Exide case, both Blackstone and Jefferies used a combination of methods. The weights assigned were as follows:

	Blackstone	Jefferies
Discounted Cash Flow	33%	60%
Comparable Company Analysis	33%	27%
Comparable M&A	33%	13%

Blackstone also noted that the "theoretical" valuation it performed was supported by additional market data, the offers submitted by three potential investors.

The chapter 11 reorganization of Prime Motor Inns provides a further example of valuation methods and of how the valuations are presented in the disclosure statement. The reorganization value for Prime Motors Inns was determined based on several approaches, including a multiple of cash flows, discounted cash flows using two different projection periods, and appraisals. Here is the description of the valuation that appeared in the disclosure statement in the Prime Motors Inns case:

Excerpt from Prime Motors Inns Disclosure Statement

The Debtors have been advised by their investment bankers, Bear Stearns, with respect to the value of the Debtors. Bear Stearns has estimated a range of enterprise value for the Debtors of between $502 and $586 million. For purposes of the Plan, the Debtors selected the upper end of this range as the enterprise value of the Debtors as of the Effective Date. Based upon an assumed enterprise value of the Debtors of approximately $586 million (including aggregate federal tax refunds for tax years 1988 and 1989 of approximately $29 million) and assuming that: (a) the principal amount of debt to be Reinstated or issued under the Plan by Reorganized Prime is $264.6 million (excluding approximately $8.3 million of

---

28. Adapted from *Certified Distress Business Valuation*, Part 3, p. 5-2 (AIRA, 2005).

construction financing related to Nondebtor Affiliates); (b) Cash distributed under the Plan approximates $85.1 million; and (c) Allowed Offset Claims approximate $25.4 million (exclusive of $19.1 million in Allowed Offset Claims included in Cash distributed), the Debtors have estimated the aggregate value of Reorganized Prime's New Common Stock at approximately $210.8 million ($6.38888 per share of New Common Stock). Such value is based upon a number of assumptions, including a successful reorganization of the Debtors' businesses and finances in a timely manner, the completion of the restructuring of certain hotel management agreements and mortgage receivables, the restructuring of several leaseholds and mortgage loans, the renewed availability of debt and equity capital for the purchase and refinancing of hotel properties, no further decline in market conditions, and the achievement of the projections reflected in the Debtors' Business Plan. Although the Debtors recognize that, for among other reasons, including those described in "Risk Factors To Be Considered—Lack Of Established Market for the Reorganization Securities; Volatility," the New Common Stock is expected to initially trade at a level that does not correspond to the estimated enterprise value chosen by the Debtors, the Debtors believe that in a normalized trading market, the trading price of the New Common Stock would more closely approximate such value.

Bear Stearns' valuation does not represent a liquidation value for the Debtors or their assets. The valuation does not represent an appraisal of the Debtors' assets, although Bear Stearns did review estimates of investment value for certain assets prepared by an independent appraisal firm. Bear Stearns' valuation represents a hypothetical going concern valuation of Reorganized Prime as the continued owner and manager of its non-cash assets, assuming the accuracy of the key assumptions listed above, among others.

Bear Stearns undertook to value separately each of the Debtors' and their Nondebtor Affiliates' major business segments. A variety of methodologies and techniques was employed by Bear Stearns, depending on the asset or business segment being valued. For all valuations of assets relating to hotel properties managed by the Debtors and their Nondebtor Affiliates (see "Reorganized Prime—Business Plan of Reorganized Prime—Prime Properties"), Bear Stearns relied primarily upon management's property budgets for calendar year 1991 and the five-year cash flow projections derived by management from such budgets. In the case of owned and leased hotel properties, Bear Stearns used a discounted cash flow approach, including the discounting of estimated terminal values at the end of a ten-year holding period, derived by capitalizing projected cash flow before debt service for the year following sale. A range of holding company discounts was applied to the aggregate property valuation. The aggregate value of the Debtors' and their Nondebtor Affiliates' owned and leased hotels was also compared to the market capitalization of certain publicly-traded hotel owners and operators.

Bear Stearns valued the Debtors' and their Nondebtor Affiliates hotel management operations (see "Reorganized Prime—Business Plan of Reorganized Prime—Prime Management") based on a range of multiples of projected operating cash flow.

Prime's investment assets (see "Reorganized Prime—Business Plan of Reorganized Prime—Prime Investments" and "Exhibit VIII—Secured Note Collateral") fall into three basic categories: (I) receivables secured by hotel properties managed by the Debtors and their Nondebtor Affiliates; (2) receivables that are unsecured or secured by properties not managed by Prime; and (3) miscellaneous real estate assets held for sale. For the first category, Bear Stearns relied upon management's assumptions as to the outcome of restructurings of these receivables, projected cash flows which were in turn discounted at various rates depending on the nature of the receivables and their underlying collateral. The resultant calculated values were compared to the estimated value of the collateral, using the same basic methodology employed in valuing the Debtors' owned hotels. Other receivables and assets held for sale were valued based on a variety of techniques including the review of property data, marketing status, settlement negotiations, appraisals, and discussions with the Debtors.

The Bear Stearns valuation also assumes that the Plan becomes effective in accordance with its terms [and utilizes] estimates and other assumptions discussed in "Reorganized Prime—Projected Financial Information."

Although Bear Stearns conducted a review and analysis of the Debtors' businesses assets, liabilities and business plans[,] Bear Stearns assumed and relied on the accuracy and completeness of all the financial and other information furnished to it by the Debtors, other firms retained by the Debtors and publicly available information. In its analyses Bear Stearns made numerous assumptions with respect to industry performance, general business and economic conditions and other matters which the Debtors and Bear Stearns deem to be reasonable. Any assumptions employed therein are not necessarily indicative of actual outcomes which may be significantly more or less favorable than those set forth therein. Estimates of value do not purport to be appraisals or necessarily reflect the values which may be realized if assets are sold. Because such estimates are inherently subject to uncertainty neither the Debtors their Nondebtor Affiliates nor Bear Stearns nor any other person assumes responsibility for their accuracy. In addition Bear Stearns did not independently verify the Debtors' projections in connection with the foregoing valuation and no independent evaluations or appraisals of the Debtors' and their Nondebtor Affiliates' assets (other than those provided to Bear Stearns by the Debtors) were sought or obtained in connection therewith. Bear Stearns' valuations were developed solely for purposes of formulation of the Plan and the analysis of the implied relative recoveries to creditors and holders of equity interests thereunder.

Such valuations reflect computations of the estimated reorganization enterprise value of Reorganized Prime derived through the application of various valuation techniques and do not purport to reflect or constitute appraisals or estimates of the actual value that may be realized through the sale of any Reorganization Security to be issued pursuant to the Plan, which may be significantly different than the amounts set forth herein, which amounts are based on the estimated reorganization enterprise value used by the Debtors. The valuation of newly-issued securities is subject to uncertainties and contingencies, all of which are difficult to predict. Actual market prices of such securities at issuance will depend upon prevailing interest rates, market conditions, the conditions and prospects, financial and otherwise, of the Debtors, including the anticipated initial securities holdings of prepetition creditors some of which may prefer to liquidate their investment rather than hold it on a long-term basis, and other factors which generally influence the prices of securities. Actual market prices of such securities may be affected by the Debtors' history in their Reorganization Cases or by other factors not possible to predict. Such valuation also includes assumed recoveries by the Debtors on claims by the Debtors against certain third parties, including claims that the Debtors are in the process of, or expect to settle or restructure. The information available to the Debtors regarding the outcome of any such restructuring and the assets from which such recoveries may be obtained is limited and incomplete, and therefore, the actual amounts recovered may be materially different from those assumed. Many of the analytical assumptions upon which these valuations are based are beyond the Debtors' control and there will be variations between such assumptions and the actual facts. These variations may be material. See "Risk Factors to be Considered" for a discussion of various other factors which could materially affect the value of Reorganization Securities distributed pursuant to the Plan.

B. DETERMINATION OF LIQUIDATION VALUES

Liquidation values may have to be determined for several reasons. As discussed in Chapter Fourteen, in order to confirm a plan of reorganization the court ordinarily must determine that each creditor or interest holder who does not accept the plan will receive an amount not less than the amount that would be received if the debtor's assets were liquidated under chapter 7. Liquidation values do not necessarily mean the amount that would be obtained in a forced sale; often liquidation value will appropriately be considered to be the amount that could be obtained in an orderly liquidation. For example, in the case of Revco, which is presented below, a hypothetical liquidation over a period of nine months was used to estimate liquidation value.

Liquidation values usually will be much less than going concern values. For example, in situations where the business is liquidated, inventory in the garment industry is often worth no more than one-third of its cost and, in many situations, much less.

To determine the size of the payment that could be expected upon liquidation, the value of all assets remaining in the estate must be established. Several methods are used to determine the immediate market price for the assets. Another client in the same type of business may be able to supply information about the values of some of the assets, especially inventory. The values of the assets may be reasonably estimable through earlier experience with companies in the same industry. In order to determine the value of plant and equipment, the manufacturer or a used equipment dealer may be contacted. It is often necessary for the court or the creditors' committee to employ an auctioneer or appraiser to evaluate the assets. Most of the larger accounting firms, and some small firms as well, have individuals who specialize in determining values. The assets listed will include not only the property on hand but also whatever assets may be recovered such as those concealed by the debtor, voidable preferences, questionable transactions involving payments to creditors, returns of merchandise to vendors, sales of fixed assets and repayment of loans from owners.

In determining liquidation values certain outlays must be considered that would be necessary if the debtor's estate were liquidated under chapter 7. Examples include administration expense, priority claims, costs of avoiding certain transfers, and related costs associated with the recovery of assets for the benefit of the estate. The liquidation value of the business, therefore, is a projected evaluation of asset recoveries net of estimated expenses.

The following comments dealing with liquidation value were contained on page 58 of Revco's disclosure statement:

Excerpt from Revco Disclosure Statement

During 1990 the Revco Debtors sold approximately 700 stores in 18 states. The gross proceeds of the sales of those stores were approximately $182,000,000. Based on that experience, it is the Revco Debtors' opinion that a liquidation of the Revco Debtors' remaining stores and other assets under chapter 7 of the Bankruptcy Code would produce proceeds substantially less than the going-concern value of the Reorganized Companies.

The "liquidation value" of the Revco Debtors would consist primarily of the proceeds from a sale of the Revco Debtors' assets by a chapter 7 trustee and any recoveries by the Revco Debtors in the LBO Litigation. The proceeds from a chapter 7 liquidation that would be available to all holders of unsecured claims would be reduced by the costs and expenses of liquidation and litigation, postpetition debt secured by super priority liens and secured claims that did not lose their security in the LBO Litigation to the extent of the value of their collateral. Costs of liquidation under chapter 7 of the Bankruptcy Code would include the fees of a trustee and of counsel and other professionals (including financial advisors and accountants) retained by the trustee, asset disposition expenses, and claims arising from the operation of the Revco Debtors' business during the chapter 7 case. The liquidation itself could trigger certain priority claims such as claims for severance pay and could accelerate other priority payments that otherwise would be due in the ordinary course of business. Priority claims would be paid in full out of the liquidation proceeds before the balance would be made available to pay unsecured claims or to make any distributions in respect of interests.

A chapter 7 liquidation analysis is set forth in Exhibit C [not included] to this Disclosure Statement. This analysis is provided solely to disclose to holders of claims and interests the effects of a hypothetical chapter 7 liquidation of the Revco Debtors, subject to the assumptions set forth in the analysis. The analysis makes no allowance for the LBO Litigation or potential preference claims. In confirming the Revco Plan the Bankruptcy Court will decide whether the Revco Plan provides a greater recovery for creditors and interest holders than a liquidation of the Revco Debtors under chapter 7. In doing so, the Bankruptcy Court will make its own finding as to the liquidation value of the Revco Debtors.

———————————————

In the notes to the liquidation analysis, the Revco disclosure statement includes the following statement:

> In conjunction with developing the Plan included in the Disclosure Statement to which this is an exhibit, management has prepared a Liquidation Analysis (the "Analysis") which may be helpful to holders of claims and interests in reaching their determination of whether to accept or reject the Plan. The Analysis is based on the assumptions discussed below.
>
> The Analysis reflects the Revco Debtors' estimates of the proceeds they would realize if the Revco Debtors were to be liquidated in accordance with chapter 7 of the Bankruptcy Code. The Analysis is based on Revco's projected assets as of May 2, 1992. Underlying the Analysis are a number of estimates and assumptions that, although developed and considered reasonable by management, are inherently subject to significant economic and competitive uncertainties and contingencies beyond the control of Revco and its management and upon assumptions with respect to liquidation decisions which could be subject to change. Accordingly, there can be no assurance that the values reflected in the Analysis would be realized if the Revco Debtors were, in fact, to undergo such a liquidation.
>
> The issue of potential recoveries resulting from potential preference claims, fraudulent conveyance litigation, the Salomon Claims and the Dworkin Unwind Claims have not been addressed in the Analysis.
>
> The Analysis assumes a liquidation period of nine months during which a three phase approach to the liquidation will occur.
>
> Phase I will entail a two month detailed study and market analysis to determine which stores could be sold on a going concern basis to buyers willing to operate them. The stores to be sold intact would be identified based on performance, a review of the stores' regional market and the availability of competitive buyers.
>
> Phase II would entail a five month period in which the store sale program would take place. The proceeds to be realized on assets from the sale of these stores are based on the factors mentioned above and Revco's historical experience with its Downsizing Program. The Analysis assumes that the liquidation proceeds from stores not identified to be sold on a going concern basis will be realized in a going out of business ("G.O.B.") sale. At the beginning of Phase II, an eight week G.O.B. program would be instituted to sell inventories and shut down store operations of those stores not in the store sale program.

Phase III would entail a two month period after the completion of the store sale program and the G.O.B. program. This period would be needed for an orderly liquidation of all other assets.

The Analysis assumes that the stores in the store sale program will be operated on a breakeven cash flow basis during the liquidation period until they are sold. * * * However, management believes that cash flow could potentially be impaired due to: (i) an adverse impact on the customers' perceptions, (ii) disruptions in the employee base, (iii) a loss of vendor support and/or change in terms and promotional programs and (iv) an adverse effect on the relationship with third party carriers. If these and similar factors adversely affect interim operations, negative cash flows could reduce the net liquidation proceeds calculated in the Analysis.

Costs that have specifically identified to the liquidation of individual assets have been netted against their estimated gross liquidation value. All other costs associated with the liquidation are included in "Costs Associated with Liquidation" * * * . In preparing the Analysis, management has considered the potential recoveries resulting from turning virtually all operations over to a liquidation; however, based upon management's experience in its Downsizing Program and other factors, the approach described above was estimated to yield greater net proceeds to the estate.

Notice that in the case of Revco, an orderly liquidation was used as the basis for estimating the liquidation values. In an orderly liquidation some of the stores, plants, etc., may be sold at a value that is in excess of the amount that might be realized in a quick, forced liquidation. Liquidation in a chapter 7 case need not always be an orderly liquidation; § 704(1) requires the trustee to liquidate the property of the estate and close out the estate "as expeditiously as is compatible with the best interests of parties in interest." Consider the following analysis from In re Crowthers McCall Pattern, Inc., 120 B.R. 279 (Bankr. S.D.N.Y. 1990), in which the court determined that the hypothetical liquidation for purposes of the best interests of creditors test should be a hypothetical orderly liquidation:

Section 1129(a)(7)(A)(ii) speaks of a comparison between plan values on the effective date and those to be hypothetically received were the Debtor liquidated "on such date." An overly literal reading of these words would indicate that Congress intended comparison with a fire sale taking only one day. We strongly doubt that this is what Congress intended. Section 704, in setting forth the duties of a Chapter 7 trustee, contains no such intimation. Rather it permits a trustee with court approval to continue to operate a business for a limited time, 11 U.S.C. § 704(8), and speaks in terms of flexibility requiring a trustee to "collect and reduce to money the property of the estate … and close such estate as expeditiously as is compatible with the best interests of parties in interest." 11 U.S.C. § 704(1). As explained in a principal treatise:

The trustee may carry out the mandate of this provision by collecting accounts; by instituting necessary legal actions; by securing the necessary orders to compel the debtor or others to deliver over property belonging to the bankrupt estate; by selling the real and personal property of the estate; by carrying out or rejecting executory contracts entered into by the debtor prior to his adjudication, by proceeding to set aside fraudulent or preferential transfers or liens; or by submitting claims to arbitration or compromise. In short, it is the trustee's duty to both the debtor and the creditors to realize from the estate all that is possible for distribution among the creditors and to this end he may assert claims and collect assets even though, in many cases, the debtor would be estopped.

4 COLLIER ON BANKRUPTCY ¶ 704.01[3] (15th ed. 1989) (footnotes omitted).

Here, it would appear that an orderly liquidation, through retaining a small staff to ship out, as ordered, the inventory remaining at the Debtor's premises, to order, perhaps, the printing of additional copies of catalogues necessary to sell that inventory and to take care of the myriad of other tasks necessary to winding down the business would be the path a prudent trustee would take in satisfying his duty of maximizing a distribution to creditors.

The industry in which the Debtor operates is fairly oligarchic in nature. The Debtor has a 35.7% market share and only two principal competitors. This is not a case where a restaurant has closed and a trustee needs to immediately sell furniture in order to avoid an additional month's rent or where the supply of goods in established stores outstrips whatever demand may remain for the debtor's product. To be sure, the patterns are seasonal in nature because the garments that can be made from them are seasonal in nature. And to be sure, styles do change and some patterns are discarded in recognition of changing styles. But there is no indication that competition could step in immediately to service the demand for the Debtor's patterns evidenced by its market share or that those patterns cannot be liquidated in an orderly fashion rather than in a fire sale. It is with these notions in mind that the Debtor's assets are to be evaluated.

120 B.R. at 292-93.

C. PRESERVING VALUABLE TAX ATTRIBUTES

There are at least four major tax advantages of filing a chapter 11 petition:

• *Bankruptcy Court Determines the Tax* — Section 505 allows the bankruptcy court to determine the tax. The debtor may find that the bankruptcy court will hear the tax issues much faster than is the case outside of bankruptcy.

• *Deferred tax payments* — Priority tax claims may be paid over a period of five years from the date of the order for relief. See § 1129(a)(9)(C).[29]

---

29. See Chapter Fourteen of this text, section B.3.

• *Special rules for income from debt discharge* — In bankruptcy, income from debt discharge is not taxed as income (but valuable tax attributes may have to be reduced due to the discharge of debt).

• *Preservation of net operating loss ("NOL") carryovers* — In situations where the net operating loss carryover may be subject to reduction or elimination, a larger amount may be preserved under special rules relating to corporations in bankruptcy.

Rules regarding debt discharge and use of net operating losses are discussed in this section.

Income taxes that must be paid on future earnings directly affect the value of those earnings. A chapter 11 debtor generally will have suffered large losses before it files its chapter 11 petition. The tax laws may allow those losses—called net operating losses or "NOLs"—to be carried forward to future years and used to offset taxable income that the reorganized debtor will earn. If so, the "NOL carryover" will enable the reorganized debtor to pay less tax on its future income, and thus will increase the going concern value of the enterprise.

There are two important issues that determine whether the reorganized debtor will be able to use the debtor's NOLs. First, will the NOLs be lost or reduced because of the cancellation of debt that occurs in the chapter 11 case? Second, will the reorganized debtor's use of NOLs be limited because of the change of ownership of the debtor that may occur as a result of the reorganization?

Before we discuss those two issues, we must give you a **WARNING**. Tax issues in chapter 11 cases can be exceedingly complex. In this book we can do no more than alert you to a few of the issues and discuss general approaches to resolving them.

1. Reduction of Tax Attributes Due to Discharge of Debt

To understand the first issue, the student must see that cancellation of debt usually results in taxable income. A person who is released from liability on a debt without having to pay it has become economically better off, and the tax laws generally consider that the person has received income. Internal Revenue Code (IRC) § 61 lists discharge of debts as one of the items subject to tax, and Treas. Reg. § 1.61-12(a) provides that the discharge of indebtedness may, in whole or in part, result in the realization of income.

Of course, to the extent that debts are discharged because they are paid, there is no income from debt discharge. Thus, to determine the amount of income from debt discharge, we would subtract from the amount of the debt the value of anything received by the creditor in exchange for discharging the debt. In a chapter 11 case or a workout, that could include cash, promissory notes, stock or other ownership interests, and other kinds of property as well.

a. The Bankruptcy and Insolvency Exception

Even so, in many cases it would be very difficult to reorganize a financially troubled company if cancellation of debt were treated as income on which the debtor or the estate had to pay income tax. The debtor could use its NOLs to offset some of the income from debt discharge, but in many cases there would be a substantial tax and not enough cash to pay it. The only way to reorganize would be to sell the business, and then in many cases most of the funds generated from the sale would have to be paid to the IRS to pay the tax on the debt discharge income. Thus IRC § 108 provides that gain on debt discharge can be excluded from gross income if the discharge occurs in a bankruptcy case or if the discharge occurs when the taxpayer is insolvent.

If the discharge does not occur in a bankruptcy case, the amount of gain on debt discharge that can be excluded from income cannot exceed the amount by which the debtor is insolvent. Suppose that in an out-of-court workout the debt outstanding is $10 million, the fair market value of the debtor's assets is $7 million, and $4 million of indebtedness is discharged without being paid. Under IRC § 108, $3 million of the gain on debt discharge would be excluded from income—because the debtor was insolvent by $3 million—but $1 million would be taxable income. If, however, that $4 million had been discharged in a bankruptcy case, the entire $4 million could have been excluded from income. Thus, in deciding whether to reorganize in an out-of-court workout or in a chapter 11 case, the debtor needs to consider tax effects.

Although the amount of gain on debt discharge is not considered income in a bankruptcy case (or in an out-of-court workout, to the extent that the debtor is insolvent), IRC § 108(b) provides that the following "tax attributes" are to be reduced in the order listed by the amount of the gain on debt discharge (but see election to reduce basis below). In many situations the debtor does not avoid paying taxes, but defers the payment of taxes over an extended time period, which is of significant benefit to the taxpayer at a time when it is in financial difficulty. For example, by reducing the basis in property by the amount of income from debt discharge the taxpayer does not have to report the income for debt discharge in the current year, but in future years the taxpayer will have to pay more taxes than otherwise would have been paid because the depreciation expense will be less.

1. *Net operating losses*—any net operating loss for the taxable year of discharge and any net operating loss carryover to the year of discharge.
2. *Certain credit carryovers*—any carryover to or from the year of discharge of a credit under IRC § 38.
3. *Minimum tax credit carryovers*—any carryover under IRC § 53(b) of minimum tax credit (the excess of the sum of the minimum tax imposed for all prior taxable years following 1986 over the amount allowed as a minimum tax credit for those prior taxable years) as of the beginning of the taxable year immediately after the year of the discharge.

4. *Capital loss carryovers*—any capital loss for the taxable year of the discharge and any capital loss carryover to the year of discharge under IRC § 1212.

5. *Basis reduction*—the debtor's basis in property (reduced according to the provisions of IRC § 1017).

6. *Passive activity loss and credits carryovers*—any passive activity loss or credit carryover of the taxpayer under IRC § 469(b) from the taxable year of the discharge.

7. *Foreign tax credit carryovers*—any carryover to or from the taxable year of discharge of the credit allowed under IRC § 33.

Credit carryovers (from items 2, 3, 6 and 7 above) are reduced 33 1/3 cents for each dollar of debt canceled. All other reductions are dollar for dollar. Suppose the debtor had $3 million in net operating losses (NOLs) and $600,000 in IRC § 38 credit carryovers, and that the debtor had $4 million of gain from debt discharge in a chapter 11 case. First, the debtor would lose all of its $3 million in NOLs, which would account for $3 million of the gain from debt discharge. The remaining $1 million of gain from debt discharge would cause the § 38 credit carryovers to be reduced by $333,333; thus the debtor would end up with no NOL carryover and $266,667 in IRC § 38 credit carryovers. The remaining tax attributes (items 3 through 7) would be unaffected. (Tax literate students may want to know that reductions are made after the tax has been calculated for the year in which the discharge occurred. For net operating and capital losses, the reductions are made first from the losses for the taxable year and then from the loss carryovers in the order of the taxable years for which the losses arose. The reduction of tax credits is made in the order the carryovers are considered for the taxable year of the discharge. IRC § 108(b)(4).)

The key point here is that discharge of debts will cost the debtor some or all of its NOLs. If the debtor had built up a net operating loss of $10 million, but then in chapter 11 the debtor discharged $8 million of debts without paying them, the NOL carryover would be reduced to $2 million. That means that rather than being able to earn $10 million of income before having to pay tax, the reorganized debtor will be able to earn only $2 million of income before having to pay income tax. The result is a loss of millions of future dollars to the IRS.

Thus we see that even though the discharge of debt in bankruptcy is not income and the debtor need not pay tax on it, the discharge will likely result in higher taxes in the future.

b. Election to Reduce Basis First

NOLs are the first tax attribute in the list above, and thus they ordinarily are the first tax attribute to the reduced when there is discharge of debt. However, the debtor can elect under IRC § 108(b)(5) to reduce first its basis in depreciable property, such as equipment and buildings. The "basis" of property is what the debtor paid for it, with adjustments, such as a reduction by the amount of any depreciation taken for tax purposes. Depreciation is considered an expense for tax purposes, and thus depreciation expense reduces the debtor's income. Once an item's basis is down to zero, no more depreciation can be taken on it. Thus, if the debtor elects to reduce the basis of its depreciable property by the amount of the discharged debt, there will be less depreciation expense in the future for tax purposes; that means the debtor's income will be higher in the future, and thus the debtor's future taxes will be higher.

The debtor will need advice from a tax adviser whether to choose to elect to reduce basis first, or not to elect that, which will result in NOLs being reduced first. If the debtor elects to reduce basis first, the amount of the reduction cannot exceed the aggregate adjusted basis of depreciable property held by the taxpayer as of the beginning of the first taxable year subsequent to the taxable year of discharge. (This prevents the debtor from reducing the basis of property that was sold during the year of the discharge, as was allowed under prior law.) The amount of the discharged debt may be greater than the amount by which basis can be reduced; the excess will then result in reduction of NOLs.

c.   The Amount of the Gain on Discharge of Debt—Debt for Debt

If the debtor's plan discharges a $1000 debt for $650 cash paid on the effective date, the amount of the gain on discharge of debt is easy to calculate: the amount of the debt, $1000, minus the value of what is received for it, $650, equals $350. That is the amount by which NOL carryovers or depreciable basis of assets would need to be reduced on account of discharge of the $1000 debt. But what if the $1000 debt is discharged in exchange for a ten year debt instrument in the face amount of $800 which carries a stated interest rate of 5% per annum ($40 per year on the $800 face amount)?

One might think that the debtor gave $800 in value to discharge a $1000 debt and thus had a gain of $200. The tax laws are not so simple. Two different rules will apply to determine the amount of gain.

First, if either the discharged debt or the new debt is publicly traded, then the market value of the debt is used. For example, if the new debt is publicly traded for $550, then there would be $450 in gain on debt discharge. If the new debt is not publicly traded, but the old debt was a debenture that could have been sold in public trading for $550, then there still would be $450 in gain on debt discharge. (The assumption seems to be that the market accurately values how much the owner of the debenture will receive for it; if an investor is willing to pay $550 for the old debt, which will entitle the investor to get the new debt, the new debt must therefore be worth $550.)

Second, if neither the old nor the new debt are publicly traded, the new debt will be valued at its face amount, as long as the stated interest rate on it is at least equal to the "applicable federal rate" (the "AFR"), which is a low, essentially risk-free rate of interest determined by the Treasury Department. See, e.g., Rev. Rul. 2006-22, 2006 WL 678968 (also available at http://www.irs.gov/pub/irs-drop/rr-06-22.pdf) (stating short-, mid-, and long-term AFRs of 4.77%, 4.72%, and 4.79%, respectively, for April, 2006); see Pratt, *Shifting Biases: Troubled Company Debt Restructurings After the 1993 Tax Act*, 68 AM. BANKR. L. J. 23, 48 (1994) ("*Shifting Biases*"). If the stated interest rate on the new debt is less than the AFR, then the new debt is valued at less than face value, at an amount equal to "the present value of all payments to be made on the debt, discounted at the AFR." Id. at 49. Thus the value of the new debt is the amount that an investor would pay for it in order to make a return equal to the AFR. Assuming the 5% stated interest rate on the $800 debt instrument is not less than the AFR, the $800 debt instrument will be valued at $800 for tax purposes, and the gain on debt discharge will be only $200 rather than $450. Thus the amount of gain on debt discharge can be very different depending on whether (1) neither the new nor the old debt is publicly traded, or (2) one or both of them are publicly traded.

Note, however, that if the new or old debt is publicly traded, so that the debtor in the example is considered to have given only $550 to discharge the $1000 debt, the effect on the debtor is not all negative. The debtor will have a relatively large amount of gain from debt discharge, $450 rather than $200. That will cause the debtor's NOLs or other tax attributes to be reduced by $450 and will probably eventually cause the debtor to pay more in taxes. However, the debtor will get a tax benefit as well. Because the debtor will be considered to have issued an $800 debt in exchange for only $550, the debtor will be treated as having promised to pay much more than $40 per year in interest. The extra $250 that the debtor will have to repay beyond the $550 in value that the debtor got when it issued the $800 debt will be treated as an extra interest payment called "original issue discount." (Note that an investor would get much more than a 5% return on its money if it paid $550 for the $800 debt; the investor would be entitled to be paid the whole $800 when the debt came due, which would give it a profit of $250 beyond the amount of the stated interest on the debt.) Thus, over the ten year life of the promissory note, the debtor will be considered for tax purposes to have paid an extra $250 of interest, interest that may well be deductible for income tax purposes. That may save the debtor taxes. However, if the amount of interest is too great, some of it may be disallowed as a deduction under legislation that was designed to discourage issuance of junk bonds. See Pratt, *Shifting Biases*, supra, at 48.

d. The Amount of Gain on Discharge of Debt—Stock for Debt

Many of the chapter 11 plans of public companies (and other companies) provide for the issuance of stock to satisfy all or part of the unsecured debt. Tax attributes, beginning with net operating losses, will be reduced to the extent that the amount of debt discharged exceeds the value of the stock issued plus other consideration received.

2. Change of Ownership and the Availability of Net Operating Losses

IRC § 172 provides for the carryback and carryforward of net operating losses. Under this provision, a corporation is, in most cases, allowed to carry forward for up to twenty years net operating losses that were (1) sustained in a particular tax year and (2) not carried back to prior years. Taxpayers can elect not to carry losses back to the prior five years currently allowed. If the debtor paid substantial income taxes during the five previous tax years, the debtor likely will carry the losses back and obtain a tax refund from the IRS. In many chapter 11 cases, the debtor has not paid enough income tax during the five previous years to use up very much of the NOLs, and thus a substantial benefit can be obtained by carrying them forward to save taxes in future years.

The extent, however, to which the net operating loss may be preserved in bankruptcy and insolvency proceedings so that it can be carried forward depends on the manner in which the debt is restructured. The net operating loss, or at least part of it, is generally preserved where there is no change in ownership. As noted above the carryover may be reduced to the extent of the discharge of debt, but, if there is no change of ownership, whatever NOL remains can be used by the reorganized debtor. Unfortunately for debtors, IRC § 382 limits the use of NOLs where there has been a change of ownership.

a. IRC Section 382 Limitation

The "section 382 limitation" minimizes the effect of tax considerations on investors' decisions to acquire "loss corporations" (corporations that have NOL carryovers) by placing a limit on the use of NOL carryovers.

Net operating loss limitations are considered only when there is a change in ownership of the corporation holding the carryovers. IRC § 382(g) contains a complex definition of change in ownership; very much simplified, a change of ownership has occurred if there has been a more than 50 percent change in ownership of the value of the loss corporation's stock during the past three years. The section 382 limitation includes a formula that restricts the use of any pre-change-of-ownership net operating losses in a post-change-of-ownership taxable year. The amount that can be used per year after the change of ownership equals the fair market value of the loss company's equity multiplied by the "long-term tax-exempt rate" published by the Internal Revenue Service.

See, e.g., Rev. Rul. 2006-22, 2006 WL 678968 (also available at http://www.irs.gov/pub/irs-drop/rr-06-22.pdf) (stating, in Table 3, a rate of 4.26% for April, 2006). (Any usable NOLs within the section 382 limitation that are not used in a given year due to insufficient taxable income are added to the amount that can be usable for a following year.)

For example, suppose X Corporation has a net operating loss of $4 million. Then P purchases 70 percent of X Corporation's outstanding stock from stockholder Q for $700,000. A change of ownership has occurred since there was more than a 50 percent change in the ownership of the company. Suppose the long-term tax-exempt rate is six percent. Since 70% of X Corporation's stock sold for $700,000, the value of all of X Corporation's stock was about $1 million total ($700,000 divided by .70). Multiplying the $1 million value of the stock times the long-term tax-exempt rate of six percent results in a $60,000 maximum use per year of the net operating loss. That means X Corporation can only use $60,000 each year of its $4 million NOL carryover. An NOL for a particular year can only be carried forward twenty years. At $60,000 per year, in twenty years X Corporation can use only $1.2 million of its $4 million NOL carryover. X Corporation's NOLs may have been suffered several years in the past and thus may expire in substantially less than twenty years; thus X Corporation may be able to use even less than $1.2 million of the NOLs before they expire. The value of the NOLs may therefore be reduced dramatically by a change in ownership.

The key factor in determining the use of net operating losses is the fair market value of the loss corporation's equity. In the case of a taxable purchase of stock, this valuation will be relatively simple. However, in the situation where a change in control is the result of a reorganization in which the purchase price consists, in part or in whole, of stock of a corporation which is not publicly traded, this valuation will be much more difficult.

  b. Special Rules for Corporations in Bankruptcy: IRC Section 382(*l*)(5)

Under IRC § 382(*l*)(5), the section 382 limitation would not apply, if immediately prior to the ownership change the corporation was under the jurisdiction of a court in a federal bankruptcy proceeding (or similar case) and the historical creditors and shareholders of the loss corporation, after the change in ownership, own stock constituting 50 percent or more of the value of the loss corporation's equity. Those creditors who held their claim for at least 18 months before the filing of the bankruptcy petition or whose claim arose during the ordinary course of the loss corporation's trade or business are considered historical creditors. IRC § 382(*l*)(5)(B) indicates that net operating losses will be reduced by any interest deducted during the three previous complete taxable years and the partial year from the beginning of the taxable year to the change of ownership which occurs on confirmation of the plan.

It is very important to note that if there is another change of ownership (as defined in IRC § 382) within two years after the reorganization, then *all net operating loss carryovers remaining from the pre-reorganization period are eliminated.* Thus if too many of the parties who receive stock under the plan of reorganization sell their stock within two years of receiving it, there may be a disastrous tax consequence to the reorganized debtor. As a result, some plans include "lockup" provisions that limit transfer of shares during the two years following reorganization, in order to prevent a change of ownership from occurring during those two years. The inclusion of such a provision, however, may cause opposition by creditors who want to be able to liquidate the shares they receive in the reorganization and do not want to take the risk of holding the shares for two years.

c.   IRC Section 382(*l*)(6)

If the debtor elects not to have the bankruptcy exception under IRC § 382(*l*)(5) apply or if the debtor does not qualify for the bankruptcy exception, the regular IRC section 382 limitation will apply. However, under § 382(*l*)(6) the section 382 limitation is calculated based on the value of the equity of the corporation after the debt is discharged rather than before. In cases where a large part of the outstanding debt is exchanged for stock, the value of the equity of the reorganized corporation will be much larger than it was before reorganization; often it is negative before the reorganization. As a result of this increase in value, more of the value of the NOLs may be preserved under the section 382 limitation than by using the § 382(*l*)(5) exception. For example, if the total value of the reorganized debtor's stock is $10 million, and the long-term tax-exempt rate is 6%, then the reorganized debtor could use $600,000 of its NOL carryover each year.

D. SUBSTANTIVE CONSOLIDATION

Are creditors of a parent corporation typically entitled to look to the assets of a subsidiary corporation for repayment? Are creditors of a subsidiary entitled to look to the assets of the parent and to the assets of other subsidiaries? The answers, generally, are "no" and "no." However, beginning in the 1940s, courts developed a bankruptcy tool for pooling the assets and liabilities of related companies: substantive consolidation.

Courts do not have a uniform approach to substantive consolidation, though many courts would agree that "because substantive consolidation is extreme (it may affect profoundly creditors' rights and recoveries) and imprecise, this 'rough justice' remedy should be rare and, in any event, one of last resort after considering and rejecting other remedies." In re Owens Corning, 419 F.3d 195, 211 (2005) (reprinted immediately below). See generally Baird, *Substantive Consolidation Today*, 47 B.C. L. REV. 5 (2005) (discussing *Owens Corning*); 3 Epstein, Nickles & White, BANKRUPTCY §§ 11-40, 11-41. In addition, serious questions have been raised whether substantive consolidation is authorized by the Bankruptcy Code at all. See *Substantive Consolidation Today*, at 15-22; Wells Fargo Bank of Tex. N.A. v. Sommers (In re Amco, Inc.), __ F.3d __, 2006 WL 832678 (5th Cir. 2006).

An important practical point is that substantive consolidation is easy to accomplish if no one objects to it; it is much harder to accomplish if there is an objection. Another practical point is that substantive consolidation may save the family of debtor companies time, trouble, and money, potentially to the benefit of all parties. It permits the debtor companies to file one set of schedules rather than separate schedules for each company, and it makes it easier to ferret out the duplicate claims that creditors otherwise might file in each debtor's separate case.

Recall that Foam Corporation has a wholly-owned subsidiary, U Foam, which has done much better financially than Foam Corporation. In fact, if U Foam had not guaranteed Foam Corporation's debts, U Foam would be solvent. Suppose that U Foam's guarantees of Foam Corporation's debts can be attacked successfully as fraudulent obligations under § 548 or § 544(b). Foam Corporation and U Foam used centralized cash management, and may not have been careful to keep track of how much of the cash belonged to U Foam. Further, the corporate formalities of holding meetings of U Foam's board of directors and passing resolutions of the board to authorize important transactions may not have been followed. Should Foam Corporation and U Foam be substantively consolidated? What would be the effect on Foam Corporation's creditors? On U Foam's creditors? On any creditor of Foam Corporation which had been paid by U Foam pursuant to the guarantees? On U Foam's own creditors which may have received payment within ninety days before U Foam filed its chapter 11 petition?[30]

There are, broadly speaking, two approaches followed by the courts, one developed by the Second Circuit and another developed by the D.C. Circuit. The following recent circuit court opinion aligned the Third Circuit with the Second, but it explains both approaches.

---

30. If Foam Corporation filed a chapter 11 petition, but U Foam did not, could the bankruptcy court in Foam Corporation's case pull U Foams assets and liabilities into a common pool with Foam Corporation's by ordering substantive consolidation of a debtor and a non-debtor? Consider footnote 37 (footnote 13 in the original) in the following Third Circuit opinion. What would the petition filing date be for the non-debtor U Foam that was thus pulled into a bankruptcy case? What difference would that make for avoidance actions? See, e.g, § 547(b)(4). If two debtors who are substantively consolidated filed their petitions on different dates a similar issue may arise: whether the substantive consolidation should be approved *nunc pro tunc* so as to make the earlier petition filing date apply to both cases for purposes of avoidance actions. See Wells Fargo Bank of Tex. N.A. v. Sommers (In re Amco, Inc.), __ F.3d __, 2006 WL 832678 (5th Cir. 2006).

In re Owens Corning
United States Court of Appeals, Third Circuit, 2005
419 F.3d 195

AMBRO, Circuit Judge.

We consider under what circumstances a court exercising bankruptcy powers may substantively consolidate affiliated entities. Appellant Credit Suisse First Boston ("CSFB") is the agent for a syndicate of banks (collectively, the "Banks") that extended in 1997 a $2 billion unsecured loan to Owens Corning, a Delaware corporation ("OCD"), and certain of its subsidiaries. This credit was enhanced in part by guarantees made by other OCD subsidiaries. The District Court granted a motion to consolidate the assets and liabilities of the OCD borrowers[31] and guarantors in anticipation of a plan of reorganization.

* * * Though we reverse the ruling of the District Court, we do so aware that it acted on an issue with no opinion on point by our Court and differing rationales by other courts.

While this area of law is difficult and this case important, its outcome is easy with the facts before us. * * *

OCD and its subsidiaries (which include corporations and limited liability companies) comprise a multinational corporate group. Different entities within the group have different purposes. Some, for example, exist to limit liability concerns (such as those related to asbestos), others to gain tax benefits, and others have regulatory reasons for their formation.

Each subsidiary was a separate legal entity that observed governance formalities. Each had a specific reason to exist separately, each maintained its own business records, and intercompany transactions were regularly documented.[32]

---

31. [Footnote 2 in original:] For ease of reference, we refer hereinafter solely to OCD as the borrower.

32. [Footnote 3 in original:] For example, Owens-Corning Fiberglass Technology, Inc. ("OCFT") was created as an intellectual property holding company to which OCD assigned all of its domestic intellectual property. OCFT licensed this intellectual property back to OCD in return for royalty payments. OCFT also entered into licensing agreements with parties outside of the OCD family of companies. This structure served to shield OCD's intellectual property assets (valued at over $500 million) from liability. OCFT operated as an autonomous entity. It prepared its own accounting and financial records and paid its own expenses from its separate bank accounts. OCFT had its own employees working at its Summit, Illinois plant, which contained machinery and equipment for research and development.

IPM, Inc. ("IPM") was incorporated as a passive Delaware investment holding company by OCD to consolidate the investments of its foreign subsidiaries. IPM shielded the foreign subsidiaries' investments from OCD liability and likewise shielded OCD from the liability of those foreign subsidiaries. OCD transferred ownership of its foreign subsidiaries to IPM and entered into a revolving loan agreement under which IPM loaned dividends from those subsidiaries to OCD. OCD paid interest on this revolving loan. IPM, like OCFT, entered into agreements with parties unaffiliated with the OCD group and operated as an autonomous entity. IPM also prepared its own accounting and financial records and paid its own expenses from its separate bank accounts. IPM's officers oversaw all investment activity and maintained records of investment activity in IPM subsidiaries.

Both OCFT and IPM operated outside of OCD's business units. Neither company received administrative support from OCD and both paid payroll and business expenses from their own accounts. Although summaries of their accounting ledgers were entered into OCD's centralized cash management system, the underlying records were created and maintained by the subsidiaries, not OCD. OCFT and IPM even had their own company logos and trade names.

Although there may have been some "sloppy" bookkeeping, two of OCD's own officers testified that the financial statements of all the subsidiaries were accurate in all material respects. Further, through an examination of the subsidiaries' books, OCD's postpetition auditors (Ernst & Young) have eliminated most financial discrepancies, particularly with respect to the larger guarantor subsidiaries.

In 1997 OCD sought a loan to acquire Fibreboard Corporation. At this time OCD faced growing asbestos liability and a poor credit rating that hindered its ability to obtain financing. When CSFB was invited to submit a bid, it included subsidiary guarantees in the terms of its proposal. The guarantees gave the Banks direct claims against the guarantors for payment defaults. They were a "credit enhancement" without which the Banks would not have made the loan to OCD. All draft loan term sheets included subsidiary guarantees.

A $2 billion loan from the Banks to OCD closed in June 1997. The loan terms were set out primarily in a Credit Agreement. Among those terms were the guarantee provisions and requirements for guarantors, who were defined as "present or future Domestic Subsidiar[ies] ... having assets with an aggregate book value in excess of $30,000,000." Section 10.07 of the Agreement provided that the guarantees were "absolute and unconditional" * * *.

CSFB negotiated the Credit Agreement expressly to limit the ways in which OCD could deal with its subsidiaries. For example, it could not enter into transactions with a subsidiary that would result in losses to that subsidiary. Importantly, the Credit Agreement contained provisions designed to protect the separateness of OCD and its subsidiaries. The subsidiaries agreed explicitly to maintain themselves as separate entities. To further this agreement, they agreed to keep separate books and financial records in order to prepare separate financial statements. The Banks were given the right to visit each subsidiary and discuss business matters directly with that subsidiary's management. The subsidiaries also were prohibited from merging into OCD because both entities were required to survive a transaction under § 8.09(a)(ii)(A) of the Credit Agreement. This provision also prohibited guarantor subsidiaries from merging with other subsidiaries unless there would be no effect on the guarantees' value.

On October 5, 2000, facing mounting asbestos litigation, OCD and seventeen of its subsidiaries (collectively, the "Debtors") filed for reorganization under Chapter 11 of the Bankruptcy Code. Twenty-seven months later, the Debtors and certain unsecured creditor groups (collectively, the "Plan Proponents") proposed a reorganization plan (as

---

Integrex was formed by OCD as an asbestos liability management company. For OCD's asbestos liability, Integrex ultimately processed only settled asbestos claims. The company also provided professional services (such as litigation management and materials testing) to the public. It had its own trade name and trademarked logo, its own business unit and its own financial team for business planning, and began several startup businesses that ultimately failed.

* * * [I]n 1997 OCD acquired Fibreboard Corporation. Subsequently, OCD formed Exterior Systems, Inc. ("ESI") as a separate entity after several subsidiaries of Fibreboard merged in 1999 in order to shield itself from successor liability for Fibreboard's asbestos products. Although the directors and managers of ESI and OCD overlapped, ESI observed corporate formalities in electing its directors and appointing its officers. In addition, it filed its own tax returns and kept its own accounting records. ESI held substantial assets, including over $1 billion in property, 20 factories, and between 150 and 180 distribution centers.

amended, the "Plan") predicated on obtaining "substantive consolidation" of the Debtors along with three non-Debtor OCD subsidiaries. Typically this arrangement pools all assets and liabilities of the subsidiaries into their parent and treats all claims against the subsidiaries as transferred to the parent. In fact, however, the Plan Proponents sought a form of what is known as a "deemed consolidation," under which a consolidation is deemed to exist[33] for purposes of valuing and satisfying creditor claims, voting for or against the Plan, and making distributions for allowed claims under it. Yet "the Plan would not result in the merger of or the transfer or commingling of any assets of any of the Debtors or Non-Debtor Subsidiaries, ... [which] will continue to be owned by the respective Debtors or Non-Debtors." Plan § 6.1(a). Despite this, on the Plan's effective date "all guarantees of the Debtors of the obligations of any other Debtor will be deemed eliminated, so that any claim against any such Debtor and any guarantee thereof ... will be deemed to be one obligation of the Debtors with respect to the consolidated estate." Plan § 6.1(b). Put another way, "the Plan eliminates the separate obligations of the Subsidiary Debtors arising from the guarant[e]es of the 1997 Credit Agreement." Plan Disclosure Statement at A-9897.

The Banks objected to the proposed consolidation. * * * Judge Fullam * * * granted the consolidation motion in an order accompanied by a short opinion. In re Owens Corning, 316 B.R. 168 (Bankr. D. Del. 2004).

Judge Fullam concluded that there existed "substantial identity between ... OCD and its wholly-owned subsidiaries." He further determined that "there [was] simply no basis for a finding that, in extending credit, the Banks relied upon the separate credit of any of the subsidiary guarantors." In Judge Fullam's view, it was "also clear that substantive consolidation would greatly simplify and expedite the successful completion of this entire bankruptcy proceeding. More importantly, it would be exceedingly difficult to untangle the financial affairs of the various entities." As such, he held substantive consolidation should be permitted, as not only did it allow "obvious advantages ... [, but was] a virtual necessity." In any event, Judge Fullam wrote, "[t]he real issue is whether the Banks are entitled to participate, pari passu, with other unsecured creditors, or whether the Banks' claim is entitled to priority, in whole or in part, over the claims of other unsecured creditors." But this issue, he stated, "cannot now be determined."

* * *

III. Substantive Consolidation

Substantive consolidation, a construct of federal common law, emanates from equity. It "treats separate legal entities as if they were merged into a single survivor left with all the cumulative assets and liabilities (save for inter-entity liabilities, which are erased). The result is that claims of creditors against separate debtors morph to claims against the consolidated survivor." Genesis Health Ventures, Inc. v. Stapleton (In re Genesis Health Ventures, Inc.), 402 F.3d 416, 423 (3d Cir.2005). Consolidation restructures (and thus revalues) rights of creditors and for certain creditors this may result in significantly less recovery.

* * *

---

33. [Footnote 7 in original:] "[A]ll assets and liabilities of each Subsidiary Debtor ... *will be treated as though* they were merged into and with the assets and liabilities of OCD...." Plan § 6.1(b) (emphasis added).

The concept of substantively consolidating separate estates begins with a commonsense deduction. Corporate disregard[34] as a fault may lead to corporate disregard as a remedy.

Prior to substantive consolidation, other remedies for corporate disregard were (and remain) in place. For example, where a subsidiary is so dominated by its corporate parent as to be the parent's "alter ego," the "corporate veil" of the subsidiary can be ignored (or "pierced") under state law. Kors, supra, at 386-90. Or a court might mandate that the assets transferred to a corporate subsidiary be turned over to its parent's trustee in bankruptcy for wrongs such as fraudulent transfers, Kors, supra, at 391, in effect bringing back to the bankruptcy estate assets wrongfully conveyed to an affiliate. If a corporate parent is both a creditor of a subsidiary and so dominates the affairs of that entity as to prejudice unfairly its other creditors, a court may place payment priority to the parent below that of the other creditors, a remedy known as equitable subordination, which is now codified in § 510(c) of the Bankruptcy Code.

Adding to these remedies, the Supreme Court, little more than six decades ago, approved (at least indirectly and perhaps inadvertently) what became known as substantive consolidation. Sampsell v. Imperial Paper & Color Corp., 313 U.S. 215, 61 S. Ct. 904, 85 L. Ed. 1293 (1941). In *Sampsell* an individual in bankruptcy had transferred assets prepetition to a corporation he controlled. (Apparently these became the corporation's sole assets.) When the bankruptcy referee ordered that the transferred assets be turned over by the corporation to the individual debtor's trustee, a creditor of the non-debtor corporation sought distribution priority with respect to that entity's assets. In deciding that the creditor should not be accorded priority (thus affirming the bankruptcy referee), the Supreme Court turned a typical turnover/fraudulent transfer case into the forebear of today's substantive consolidation by terming the bankruptcy referee's order (marshaling the corporation's assets for the benefit of the debtor's estate) as "consolidating the estates." Id. at 219, 61 S. Ct. at 907.

Each of these remedies has subtle differences. "Piercing the corporate veil" makes shareholders liable for corporate wrongs. Equitable subordination places bad-acting creditors behind other creditors when distributions are made. Turnover and fraudulent transfer bring back to the transferor debtor assets improperly transferred to another (often an affiliate). Substantive consolidation goes in a direction different (and in most cases further) than any of these remedies; it is not limited to shareholders, it affects distribution to innocent creditors, and it mandates more than the return of specific assets to the predecessor owner. It brings all the assets of a group of entities into a single survivor. Indeed, it merges liabilities as well. "The result," to repeat, "is that claims of creditors against separate debtors morph to claims against the consolidated survivor." In re Genesis Health Ventures, 402 F.3d at 423. The bad news for certain creditors is that, instead of looking to assets of the subsidiary with whom they dealt, they now must share those assets with all creditors of all consolidated entities, raising the specter for some of a significant distribution diminution.

---

34. [Footnote 10 in original:] A term used by Mary Elisabeth Kors in her comprehensive and well-organized article entitled *Altered Egos: Deciphering Substantive Consolidation*, 59 U. Pitt. L.Rev. 381, 383 (1998) (hereinafter "Kors").

Though the concept of consolidating estates had Supreme Court approval, Courts of Appeal (with one exception [in 1942]) were slow to follow suit. * * * Little occurred thereafter for more than two decades, until the Second Circuit issued several decisions * * * that brought substantive consolidation as a remedy back into play * * *. Other Circuit Courts fell in line in acknowledging substantive consolidation as a possible remedy. * * *

Ultimately most courts slipstreamed behind two rationales—those of the Second Circuit in *Augie/Restivo*[35] and the D.C. Circuit in *Auto-Train*[36]. The former found that the competing "considerations are merely variants on two critical factors: (i) whether creditors dealt with the entities as a single economic unit and did not rely on their separate identity in extending credit, ... or (ii) whether the affairs of the debtors are so entangled that consolidation will benefit all creditors...." In re Augie/Restivo, 860 F.2d at 518 (internal quotation marks and citations omitted). *Auto-Train* touched many of the same analytical bases as the prior Second Circuit cases, but in the end chose as its overarching test the "substantial identity" of the entities and made allowance for consolidation in spite of creditor reliance on separateness when "the demonstrated benefits of consolidation 'heavily' outweigh the harm." In re Auto-Train, 810 F.2d at 276 (citation omitted).

Whatever the rationale, courts have permitted substantive consolidation as an equitable remedy in certain circumstances.[37] No court has held that substantive consolidation is not authorized,[38] though there appears nearly

---

35. [Union Sav. Bank v. Augie/Restivo Baking Co. (In re Augie/Restivo Baking Co.), 860 F.2d 515 (2d Cir. 1988)–Ed.]

36. [Drabkin v. Midland-Ross Corp. (In re Auto-Train Corp.), 810 F.2d 270 (D.C. Cir. 1987)–Ed.]

37. [Footnote 13 in original:] Indeed, they have not restricted the remedy to debtors, allowing the consolidation of debtors with non-debtors, see, e.g., In re Bonham, 229 F.3d at 765 * * *, and in some cases consolidation retroactively (known also as nunc pro tunc consolidation), see, e.g., In re Bonham, 229 F.3d at 769-71, * * *.

In addition, though we do not permit the consolidation sought in this case, no reason exists to limit it under the right circumstances to any particular form of entity. (Indeed, this case involves corporations and limited liability companies.) Accord 2 Collier on Bankruptcy ¶ 105.09[1] [c] (15th rev. ed.2005).

38. [Footnote 14 in original:] See In re Bonham, 229 F.3d at 765 (explaining that "the equitable power [of substantive consolidation] undoubtedly survived enactment of the Bankruptcy Code" and noting that "[n]o case has held to the contrary"); but see In re Fas Mart Convenience Stores, Inc., 320 B.R. 587, 594 n. 3 (Bankr. E.D. Va. 2004) (noting "there is persuasive academic argument that there is no authority in bankruptcy law for substantive consolidation") (citing Daniel B. Bogart, *Resisting the Expansion of Bankruptcy Court Power Under Section 105 of the Bankruptcy Code: The All Writs Act and an Admonition from Chief Justice Marshall*, 35 Ariz. St. L.J. 793, 810 (2003); J. Maxwell Tucker, *Grupo Mexicano and the Death of Substantive Consolidation*, 8 Am. Bankr. Inst. L. Rev. 427 (2000) (hereinafter "Tucker")). Since the Supreme Court's decision in Grupo Mexicano de Desarrollo, S.A. v. Alliance Bond Fund, Inc., 527 U.S. 308, 119 S. Ct. 1961, 144 L. Ed. 2d 319 (1999) (federal district courts lack the equitable power to enjoin prejudgment transfers of assets, as such an equitable remedy did not exist at the time federal courts were created under the Judiciary Act of 1789), some argue that substantive consolidation, judge-made law not expressly codified in the Bankruptcy Code adopted in the late 1970s, does not qualify as an available equitable remedy. See, e.g., Tucker, supra at 442-45. * * * Consolidating estates (indeed, consolidating debtor and non-debtor entities) traces to the Supreme Court's *Sampsell* decision in 1941. 313 U.S. at 219, 61 S. Ct. 907. What the Court has given as an equitable remedy remains until

unanimous consensus that it is a remedy to be used "sparingly." In re Augie/Restivo, 860 F.2d at 518.

* * * [W]e have commented on substantive consolidation only generally in *Nesbit*, 347 F.3d at 86-88, and In re Genesis Health Ventures, 402 F.3d at 423-24. The latter nonetheless left little doubt that, if presented with a choice of analytical avenues, we favor essentially that of *Augie/Restivo*. The *Auto-Train* approach (requiring "substantial identity" of entities to be consolidated, plus that consolidation is "necessary to avoid some harm or realize some benefit," 810 F.2d at 276) adopts, we presume, one of the *Augie/Restivo* touchstones for substantive consolidation while adding the low bar of avoiding some harm or discerning some benefit by consolidation. To us this fails to capture completely the few times substantive consolidation may be considered and then, when it does hit one chord, it allows a threshold not sufficiently egregious and too imprecise for easy measure. For example, we disagree that "[i]f a creditor makes [a showing of reliance on separateness], the court may order consolidation … if it determines that the demonstrated benefits of consolidation 'heavily' outweigh the harm." [*Auto-Train*, 810 F.2d] at 276 (citation omitted). If an objecting creditor relied on the separateness of the entities, consolidation cannot be justified vis-à-vis the claims of that creditor.[39]

In assessing whether to order substantive consolidation, courts consider many factors (some of which are noted in *Nesbit*, 347 F.3d at 86-88 nn. 7 & 9). They vary (with degrees of overlap) from court to court. Rather than endorsing any prefixed factors, in *Nesbit* we "adopt[ed] an intentionally open-ended, equitable inquiry … to determine when substantively to consolidate two entities." Id. at 87. While we mentioned that "in the bankruptcy context the inquiry focuses primarily on financial entanglement," id., this comment primarily related to the hopeless commingling test of substantive consolidation. But when creditors deal with entities as an indivisible, single party, "the line between operational and financial [factors] may be blurred." Id. at 88. We reiterate that belief here. Too often the factors in a checklist fail to separate the unimportant from the important, or even

---

it alone removes it or Congress declares it removed as an option. * * * In short, the Court's opinion in *Grupo Mexicano* acknowledged that bankruptcy courts do have the authority to deal with the problems presented by that case. One way to conceptualize this idea is to recognize that, had the company in *Grupo Mexicano* been in bankruptcy, the bankruptcy court would have had the authority to implement the remedy the district court lacked authority to order under general equity power outside the bankruptcy context. * * * As for the argument's second facet, it begins with a concession. Bankruptcy Code § 1123(a)(5)(C)'s very words allow for "consolidation of the debtor with one or more persons" pursuant to a plan "[n]otwithstanding any otherwise applicable non-bankruptcy law." Whether § 105(a) allows consolidation outside a plan is an issue we need not address—though that arguably is what the Plan Proponents propose by moving for a "deemed" consolidation—because, as we note below, consolidation, no matter how it is packaged, cannot pass muster in this case. * * *

39. [Footnote 16 in original:] This opens the question whether a court can order partial consolidation (such a consolidation order "could provide that … [a creditor relying on separateness] would receive a distribution equal to what [it] would have received absent consolidation and that the remainder of the assets and liabilities be consolidated.") Kors, supra, at 450-51. Because this theoretical issue is not before us—and in any event (i) facts bringing it to the fore are unlikely, id. at 451 ("If circumstances lead one party to rely on the single status of the one debtor, it is unlikely that other creditors are relying on the joint status of the two entities, especially as reliance must be reasonable."), and (ii) may present practical concerns depending on the facts of a particular case—we do not decide it in this case.

to set out a standard to make the attempt. Accord Br. of Law Professors[40] as Amici Curiae at 11-12. This often results in rote following of a form containing factors where courts tally up and spit out a score without an eye on the principles that give the rationale for substantive consolidation (and why, as a result, it should so seldom be in play). Id. ("Differing tests with a myriad of factors run the risk that courts will miss the forest for the trees. Running down factors as a check list can lead a court to lose sight of why we have substantive consolidation in the first instance ... and often [to] fail [to] identify a metric by which [it] can ... [assess] the relative importance among the factors. The ... [result is] resort to ad hoc balancing without a steady eye on the ... [principles] to be advanced....").

What, then, are those principles? We perceive them to be as follows.

(1) Limiting the cross-creep of liability by respecting entity separateness is a "fundamental ground rule[ ]." Kors, supra, at 410. As a result, the general expectation of state law and of the Bankruptcy Code, and thus of commercial markets, is that courts respect entity separateness absent compelling circumstances calling equity (and even then only possibly substantive consolidation) into play.

(2) The harms substantive consolidation addresses are nearly always those caused by debtors (and entities they control) who disregard separateness. Harms caused by creditors typically are remedied by provisions found in the Bankruptcy Code (e.g., fraudulent transfers, §§ 548 and 544(b)(1), and equitable subordination, § 510(c)).

(3) Mere benefit to the administration of the case (for example, allowing a court to simplify a case by avoiding other issues or to make postpetition accounting more convenient) is hardly a harm calling substantive consolidation into play.

(4) Indeed, because substantive consolidation is extreme (it may affect profoundly creditors' rights and recoveries) and imprecise, this "rough justice" remedy should be rare and, in any event, one of last resort after considering and rejecting other remedies (for example, the possibility of more precise remedies conferred by the Bankruptcy Code).

(5) While substantive consolidation may be used defensively to remedy the identifiable harms caused by entangled affairs, it may not be used offensively (for example, having a primary purpose to disadvantage tactically a group of creditors in the plan process or to alter creditor rights).

The upshot is this. In our Court what must be proven (absent consent) concerning the entities for whom substantive consolidation is sought is that (i) prepetition they disregarded separateness so significantly their creditors relied on

---

40. [Footnote 17 in original:] They are Robert K. Rasmussen of Vanderbilt Law School, Barry Adler of the NYU School of Law, Susan Block-Lieb of Fordham University School of Law, G. Marcus Cole of Stanford Law School, Marcel Kahan of the NYU School of Law, Ronald J. Mann of the University of Texas Law School, and David A. Skeel, Jr. of the University of Pennsylvania School of Law.

the breakdown of entity borders and treated them as one legal entity,[41] or (ii) postpetition their assets and liabilities are so scrambled that separating them is prohibitive and hurts all creditors.[42]

Proponents of substantive consolidation have the burden of showing one or the other rationale for consolidation. The second rationale needs no explanation. The first, however, is more nuanced. A prima facie case for it typically exists when, based on the parties' prepetition dealings, a proponent proves corporate disregard creating contractual expectations of creditors[43] that they were dealing with debtors as one indistinguishable entity. Kors, supra, at 417-18; Christopher W. Frost, *Organizational Form, Misappropriation Risk, and the Substantive Consolidation of Corporate Groups*, 44 Hastings L. J. 449, 457 (1993). Proponents who are creditors must also show that, in their prepetition course of dealing, they actually and reasonably relied on debtors' supposed unity. Kors, supra, at 418-19. Creditor opponents of consolidation can nonetheless defeat a prima facie showing under the first rationale if they can prove they are adversely affected and actually relied on debtors' separate existence.[44]

C. Application of Substantive Consolidation to Our Case

With the principles we perceive underlie use of substantive consolidation, the outcome of this appeal is apparent at the outset. Substantive consolidation fails to fit the facts of our case and, in any event, a "deemed" consolidation cuts against the grain of all the principles.

To begin, the Banks did the "deal world" equivalent of "Lending 101." They loaned $2 billion to OCD and enhanced the credit of that unsecured loan indirectly by subsidiary guarantees covering less than half the initial debt. What the Banks got in lending lingo was "structural seniority"—a direct claim against the guarantors (and thus against their assets levied on once a judgment is obtained) that other creditors of OCD did not have. This kind of lending occurs every business day. To undo this bargain is a demanding task.

---

41. [Footnote 19 in original:] This rationale is meant to protect in bankruptcy the prepetition expectations of those creditors. Accord Kors, supra, at 419. The usual scenario is that creditors have been misled by debtors' actions (regardless whether those actions were intentional or inadvertent) and thus perceived incorrectly (and relied on this perception) that multiple entities were one.

42. [Footnote 20 in original:] This rationale is at bottom one of practicality when the entities' assets and liabilities have been "hopelessly commingled." In re Gulfco Inv. Corp., 593 F.2d at 929. Without substantive consolidation all creditors will be worse off (as Humpty Dumpty cannot be reassembled or, even if so, the effort will threaten to reprise *Jarndyce and Jarndyce*, the fictional suit in Dickens' *Bleak House* where only the professionals profited). With substantive consolidation the lot of all creditors will be improved, as consolidation "advance[s] one of the primary goals of bankruptcy—enhancing the value of the assets available to creditors ...—often in a very material respect." Kors, supra, at 417 (citation omitted).

43. [Footnote 21 in original:] "[T]ort and statutory claimants, who, as involuntary creditors, by definition did not rely on anything in becoming creditors," Kors, supra, at 418, are excluded, leaving only those creditors who contract with an entity for whom consolidation is sought.

44. [Footnote 22 in original:] As noted already, supra n. 16, we do not decide here whether such a showing by an opposing creditor defeats totally the quest for consolidation or merely consolidation as to that creditor.

1. No Prepetition Disregard of Corporate Separateness

Despite the Plan Proponents' pleas to the contrary, there is no evidence of the prepetition disregard of the OCD entities' separateness. To the contrary, OCD (no less than CSFB) negotiated the 1997 lending transaction premised on the separateness of all OCD affiliates. Even today no allegation exists of bad faith by anyone concerning the loan. In this context, OCD and the other Plan Proponents cannot now ignore, or have us ignore, the very ground rules OCD put in place. Playing by these rules means that obtaining the guarantees of separate entities, made separate by OCD's choice of how to structure the affairs of its affiliate group of companies, entitles a lender, in bankruptcy or out, to look to any (or all) guarantor(s) for payment when the time comes. As such, the District Court's conclusions of "substantial identity" of OCD and its subsidiaries, and the Banks' reliance thereon, are incorrect. For example, testimony presented by both the Banks and the Debtors makes plain the parties' intention to treat the entities separately. CSFB presented testimony from attorneys and bankers involved in negotiating the Credit Agreement that reflected their assessment of the value of the guarantees as partially derived from the separateness of the entities. As OCD concedes, these representatives "testified that the guarant[e]es were ... intended to provide 'structural seniority' to the banks," and were thus fundamentally premised on an assumption of separateness.

In the face of this testimony, Plan Proponents nonetheless argue that the Banks intended to ignore the separateness of the entities. In support of this contention, they assert, inter alia, that because the Banks did not receive independent financial statements for each of the entities during the negotiating process, they must have intended to deal with them as a unified whole. Because the Banks were unaware of the separate financial makeup of the subsidiaries, the argument goes, they could not have relied on their separateness.[45]

This argument is overly simplistic. Assuming the Banks did not obtain separate financial statements for each subsidiary, they nonetheless obtained detailed information about each subsidiary guarantor from OCD, including information about that subsidiary's assets and debt. Moreover, the Banks knew a great deal about these subsidiaries. For example, they knew that each subsidiary

---

45. [Footnote 24 in original:] Debtors make a similar argument on the basis of the Banks' failure to exercise their right to monitor the entities independently. For much the same reasoning that follows in the text, we reject that argument as well.

We reject outright Debtors' claim that the Banks' alleged reliance on corporate separateness fails because they did not obtain a third-party legal opinion from counsel that substantive consolidation was unlikely to occur were OCD or the guarantors subject to bankruptcy. By custom and practice this type of counsel opinion is requested and given for newly formed entities whose "special purpose" is to obtain structured financing (i.e., where "a defined group of assets ... [are] structurally isolated, and thus serve as the basis of a financing...." Committee on Bankruptcy and Corporate Reorganization of The Association of the Bar of the City of New York, *Structured Financing Techniques*, 50 Bus. Law. 527, 529 (1995)). It is customarily not given (nor even requested) for entities in existence for any significant period of time or set up for other than a structured financing transaction. See Tribar Opinion Committee, *Opinions in the Bankruptcy Context: Rating Agency, Structured Financing, and Chapter 11 Transactions*, 46 Bus. Law, 717, 726 & n. 42 (1991).

guarantor had assets with a book value of at least $30 million as per the terms of the Credit Agreement, that the aggregate value of the guarantor subsidiaries was over $900 million and that those subsidiaries had little or no debt. Additionally, the Banks knew that Fibreboard's subsidiaries (including the entities that became part of ESI) had no asbestos liability, would be debt-free post-acquisition and had assets of approximately $700 million.

Even assuming the Plan Proponents could prove prepetition disregard of Debtors' corporate forms, we cannot conceive of a justification for imposing the rule that a creditor must obtain financial statements from a debtor in order to rely reasonably on the separateness of that debtor. Creditors are free to employ whatever metrics they believe appropriate in deciding whether to extend credit free of court oversight. We agree with the Banks that "the reliance inquiry is not an inquiry into lenders' internal credit metrics. Rather, it is about the fact that the credit decision was made in reliance on the existence of separate entities...." CSFB Opening Br. at 31 (emphasis in original).[46] Here there is no serious dispute as to that fact.

2. No Hopeless Commingling Exists Postpetition

There also is no meaningful evidence postpetition of hopeless commingling of Debtors' assets and liabilities. Indeed, there is no question which entity owns which principal assets and has which material liabilities. Likely for this reason little time is spent by the parties on this alternative test for substantive consolidation. It is similarly likely that the District Court followed suit.

The Court nonetheless erred in concluding that the commingling of assets will justify consolidation when "the affairs of the two companies are so entangled that consolidation *will be beneficial.*" In re Owens Corning, 316 B.R. at 171 (emphasis added). As we have explained, commingling justifies consolidation only when separately accounting for the assets and liabilities of the distinct entities will reduce the recovery of every creditor—that is, when every creditor will benefit from the consolidation. Moreover, the benefit to creditors should be from cost savings that make assets available rather than from the shifting of assets to benefit one group of creditors at the expense of another. Mere benefit to some creditors, or administrative benefit to the Court, falls far short. The District Court's test not only fails to adhere to the theoretical justification for "hopeless commingling" consolidation—that no creditor's rights will be impaired—but also suffers from the infirmity that it will almost always be met. That is, substantive consolidation will nearly always produce some benefit to some in the form of simplification and/or avoidance of costs. Among other things, following such a path misapprehends the degree of harm required to order substantive consolidation.

But no matter the legal test, a case for hopeless commingling cannot be made. Arguing nonetheless to the contrary, Debtors assert that "it would be practically impossible and prohibitively expensive in time and resources" to account for the voluntary bankruptcies of the separate entities OCD has created and maintained. In support of this contention, Debtors rely almost exclusively on the District Court's findings that

---

46. [Footnote 25 in original:] Further, a creditor's lack of diligence is relevant only insofar as it bears on the credibility of its assertion of reliance on separateness.

it would be exceedingly difficult to untangle the financial affairs of the various entities ... [and] there are ... many reasons for challenging the accuracy of the results achieved [in accounting efforts thus far]. For example, transfers of cash between subsidiaries and parent did not include any payment of interest; and calculations of royalties are subject to question.

In re Owens Corning, 316 B.R. at 171. Assuming arguendo that these findings are correct, they are simply not enough to establish that substantive consolidation is warranted.

Neither the impossibility of perfection in untangling the affairs of the entities nor the likelihood of some inaccuracies in efforts to do so is sufficient to justify consolidation. We find R 2 Investments, LDC v. World Access, Inc. (In re World Access, Inc.), 301 B.R. 217 (Bankr. N.D. Ill. 2003), instructive on this point. In *World Access* the Court noted that the controlling entity "had no uniform guidelines for the recording of intercompany interest charges" and that the debtors failed to "allocate overhead charges amongst themselves." Id. at 234. The Court held, however, that those accounting shortcomings were "merely imperfections in a sophisticated system of accounting records that were conscientiously maintained." Id. at 279. It ultimately concluded that "all the relevant accounting data ... still exist[ed]," that only a "reasonable review to make any necessary adjustments [was] required," and, thus, that substantive consolidation was not warranted. Id.

The record in our case compels the same conclusion. At its core, Debtors' argument amounts to the contention that because intercompany interest and royalty payments were not perfectly accounted for, untangling the finances of those entities is a hopeless endeavor. Yet imperfection in intercompany accounting is assuredly not atypical in large, complex company structures. For obvious reasons, we are loathe to entertain the argument that complex corporate families should have an expanded substantive consolidation option in bankruptcy. And we find no reason to doubt that "perfection is not the standard in the substantive consolidation context." Id. We are confident that a court could properly order and oversee an accounting process that would sufficiently account for the interest and royalty payments owed among the OCD group of companies for purposes of evaluating intercompany claims—dealing with inaccuracies and difficulties as they arise and not in hypothetical abstractions.

On the basis of the record before us, the Plan Proponents cannot fulfill their burden of demonstrating that Debtors' affairs are even tangled, let alone that the cost of untangling them is so high relative to their assets that the Banks, among other creditors, will benefit from a consolidation.[47]

3. Other Considerations Doom Consolidation as Well

Other considerations drawn from the principles we set out also counsel strongly against consolidation. First of all, holding out the possibility of later giving priority to the Banks on their claims does not cure an improvident grant of

---

47. [Footnote 26 in original:] For example, we simply cannot imagine that it would cost Debtors even 1% of the Banks' asserted $1.6 billion claim to account for the allegedly incalculable intercompany interest and royalty payments.

substantive consolidation. Among other things, the prerequisites for this last-resort remedy must still be met no matter the priority of the Banks' claims.

Secondly, substantive consolidation should be used defensively to remedy identifiable harms, not offensively to achieve advantage over one group in the plan negotiation process (for example, by deeming assets redistributed to negate plan voting rights), nor a "free pass" to spare Debtors or any other group from proving challenges, like fraudulent transfer claims, that are liberally brandished to scare yet are hard to show. If the Banks are so vulnerable to the fraudulent transfer challenges Debtors have teed up (but have not swung at for so long), then the game should be played to the finish in that arena.[48]

But perhaps the flaw most fatal to the Plan Proponents' proposal is that the consolidation sought was "deemed" (i.e., a pretend consolidation for all but the Banks). If Debtors' corporate and financial structure was such a sham before the filing of the motion to consolidate, then how is it that post the Plan's effective date this structure stays largely undisturbed, with the Debtors reaping all the liability-limiting, tax and regulatory benefits achieved by forming subsidiaries in the first place? In effect, the Plan Proponents seek to remake substantive consolidation not as a remedy, but rather a stratagem to "deem" separate resources reallocated to OCD to strip the Banks of rights under the Bankruptcy Code, favor other creditors, and yet trump possible Plan objections by the Banks. Such "deemed" schemes we deem not Hoyle.

IV. Conclusion

Substantive consolidation at its core is equity. Its exercise must lead to an equitable result. "Communizing" assets of affiliated companies to one survivor to feed all creditors of all companies may to some be equal (and hence equitable). But it is hardly so for those creditors who have lawfully bargained prepetition for unequal treatment by obtaining guarantees of separate entities. Accord Kheel, 369 F.2d at 848 (Friendly, J., concurring) ("Equality among creditors who have lawfully bargained for different treatment is not equity but its opposite...."). No principled, or even plausible, reason exists to undo OCD's and the Banks' arms-length negotiation and lending arrangement, especially when to do so punishes the very parties that conferred the prepetition benefit-a $2 billion loan unsecured by OCD and guaranteed by others only in part. To overturn this bargain, set in place by OCD's own pre-loan choices of organizational form, would cause chaos in the marketplace, as it would make this case the Banquo's ghost of bankruptcy.

With no meaningful evidence supporting either test to apply substantive consolidation, there is simply not the nearly "perfect storm" needed to invoke it. Even if there were, a "deemed" consolidation—"several zip (if not area) codes away from anything resembling substantive consolidation," In re Genesis Health Ventures, 402 F.3d at 424—fails even to qualify for consideration. Moreover, it is here a tactic used as a sword and not a shield.

We thus reverse and remand this case to the District Court.

---

48. [Footnote 27 in original:] The same sentiment applies to the argument of the bondholders that, subsequent to the 1997 loan to OCD, the Banks defrauded them in connection with a prospectus distributed with respect to a sale of OCD bonds underwritten by some of the Banks. If the bondholders have a valid claim, they need to prove it in the District Court and not use their allegations as means to gerrymander consolidation of estates.

Chapter Thirteen

Making Disclosure, Soliciting Votes, And Voting On The Plan

A. INTRODUCTION

Once a plan has been filed, the creditors and interest holders of Foam Corporation (or any other chapter 11 debtor) will need to decide whether to accept or reject it. To do that they will need information and advice. Supporters and opponents of the plan will want to provide that information and advice, in an attempt to sway the votes of the creditors and interest holders. Finally, the creditors and interest holders will vote. The entire decision-making process—from the dissemination of information to the solicitation of votes to the actual voting process—is the subject of this chapter.

1. The Need for Information and Advice on the Four Critical Questions

For most creditors and interest holders, the decision to accept or reject the Foam Corporation plan will depend on four questions. First, is the plan feasible? Second, how much value (if any) does the plan provide to the creditor or interest holder? Third, is the creditor or interest holder receiving his fair share of the available value? Fourth, is the form in which the value is given acceptable?

Creditors and interest holders may need the disclosure of substantial amounts of information to answer those questions. They may also need advice on how to vote from the debtor's management, from the creditors' committee, and from other parties who have the resources to digest and analyze the information. Thus the disclosure process and the solicitation process are both crucial.

Consider TC, a trade creditor of Foam Corporation who has a $10,000 general unsecured claim. Suppose that the Foam Corporation plan will provide TC with $2000 cash on the effective date of the plan, a five year interest-only $5000 note (with a balloon payment at the end of five years) at 10% interest, and ten shares of stock in the reorganized Foam Corporation (out of a total of 100,000 shares that will be outstanding). What will TC need to answer the four questions?

a.   The Feasibility of the Plan

Because the Foam Corporation plan calls for TC to receive a promissory note as part of his distribution, TC will be intensely interested in whether Foam Corporation will be able to make the payments called for under the note. TC is already suffering through one bankruptcy case and has no desire to go through another as a creditor of the reorganized debtor. TC will want and need information from which he can determine whether the reorganized Foam Corporation will succeed or fail.

The debtor's prospects for success or failure also matter greatly to TC because TC will receive stock in the debtor. That stock will likely be worth-less in the end if the reorganized debtor fails. Its value immediately after the reorganization will depend on the debtor's prospects for success or failure. Since TC (along with many other creditors) may wish to sell his stock immediately after the reorganization, whether the debtor *appears* likely to succeed may be as important to TC as whether the debtor ultimately does succeed.

As we have seen, there are financial tools (such as key financial ratios and the Altman formula) which help to predict whether a business will succeed or fail. So that these tools can be applied, there must be substantial and accurate disclosure of financial information concerning the debtor's assets, liabilities, and operations.

Foam Corporation will be unable to meet its obligations to TC and others under the notes unless its cash flows provide the cash to make the needed payments at the required times. Further, if cash is not available in the future to pay dividends or to reinvest in the debtor, the reorganized debtor's stock may be of little value. The plan proponent needs to disclose projections of future cash flows that show that enough cash will be available to meet the debtor's obligations and to give value to the stock. Of course, TC and the other creditors will want to know the assumptions that went into the cash flow projections, and the reasons for making the assumptions, so that they can determine for themselves whether the projections are realistic. For example, Foam Corporation's cash flow projections may be based on the assumption that sales will increase 25% every year for five years; TC needs to know that Foam Corporation is making that assumption and why Foam Corporation thinks it will do so well.

TC will also want to know who will be managing the reorganized Foam Corporation. Mismanagement is the number one cause of business failure; TC will want to assure himself that the management of the reorganized Foam Corporation will be competent.

Information about the debtor's industry and about its future outlook will also be needed. If the reorganized debtor will be competing in a very tough, competitive industry that as a whole will probably not be growing very much, then TC and the other creditors may be skeptical about the debtor's chances.

b. The Value To Be Received Under the Plan

The Foam Corporation plan will provide TC with $2000 cash on the effective date of the plan, a five year interest-only $5000 note at 10% interest, and ten shares of stock in the reorganized Foam Corporation. How can TC determine how much value he will receive under the plan if it is confirmed?

Cash to be paid immediately under the plan is worth its face amount; there is no difficulty in valuing it, so TC will receive $2000 in value from the cash payment. Shares of stock, bonds, or promissory notes are harder to value, because of the delay involved in receiving cash and because of the risks of the business.[1] Their value can be estimated, as we have seen in Chapter Twelve, if there is enough reliable information. Thus TC will need reliable information as to the debtor's prospects for success and as to the risks involved in order to estimate the value of the note and the stock. (Again that will include information about the persons who will manage the reorganized debtor, since mismanagement is the main cause of business failure.) More importantly, a small creditor like TC will need the assistance and advice of those with the sophistication and resources to do the actual valuation.

c. Whether that Value Is a Fair Share of the Available Value

Whether the amount which TC will receive under the plan is his fair share of the available value depends on how much value is available. It also depends on the relative priorities of the parties and on their negotiating leverage.

The available value in a reorganization should be no less than liquidation value; as a baseline, TC's fair share in the reorganization should not be less than what he would receive in a liquidation.[2] TC needs information about what he would receive in a liquidation to put a floor on the amount of value that could represent his fair share. Cf. § 1129(a)(7) (allowing a single dissenter to block confirmation if it will not receive at least what it would receive in a liquidation).

---

1. If the recipient can sell the stock, bonds, or notes, the recipient can receive immediate cash. However, the price that can be obtained for the stock, bonds, or notes will reflect the delay and the risks that the buyer will encounter in eventually getting cash payouts.

2. What a party would receive in a liquidation will depend on the liquidation value of the debtor, the amount of the claims, and the relative priorities of the parties in a liquidation. An example will show how the total liquidation value and the relative priorities matter. Assume administrative expenses already incurred in a chapter 11 case plus administrative expenses that would be involved in liquidating the assets total $800,000. Assume total liquidation value is $3 million. Assume the debtor owes $2 million to a bank, which has a valid lien on all the debtor's assets. Assume the debtor owes $1.5 million to an insurance company, which is unsecured, and $500,000 to subordinated debenture holders, who are unsecured and subordinated to the insurance company's debt. In a liquidation, the bank would receive its $2 million, the administrative expense claimants would receive their $800,000, and only $200,000 of value would remain to be split up among the general unsecured creditors. Since there would not be enough to pay the insurance company in full, it would receive the entire $200,000; the debenture holders would receive nothing. Of course, neither the preferred stockholders nor the common stockholders would receive anything in the liquidation; the preferred stockholders are junior to all the debt, and the common stockholders are junior to all the debt and to preferred stock. See § 726(a).

To the extent that reorganization value is greater than liquidation value, TC, the other creditors, and Gruff (Foam Corporation's sole existing stockholder) may have differing views of the fair way of dividing the excess. Each will be entitled to accept or reject the plan depending on his view of whether he is receiving his fair share. Of course this decision will require some idea of what the reorganization value is. We have seen that liquidation and reorganization values can be estimated, see Chapter Twelve above, but to do so the creditor or interest holder must have information about the business's assets, operations, and prospects. TC and the other small creditors will also need advice from someone with the experience, expertise, and resources to do the valuations and to consider what the creditor's fair share may be.

Chapter 11 initially leaves it up to negotiation to determine who gets the excess of reorganization value over liquidation value. This is on the theory that outside of bankruptcy no one has an absolute right to the reorganization value of a company that cannot pay its debts. The proposed plan is typically therefore the result of negotiations between the debtor and representatives of the creditors. Thus it will be especially important for TC to find out from his negotiating representatives (the creditors' committee) why they believe the division of value is fair. Recommendations from creditors' committees typically carry great weight with the body of creditors. Those recommendations can explain why, given the negotiating leverage that each group has under chapter 11, the plan gives out value fairly.

Ultimately, if negotiations are not successful, chapter 11 gives absolute priority to creditors over stockholders, and to senior creditors over subordinated creditors. See § 1129(b)(2)(B). This priority scheme for cramdown will heavily influence the parties in negotiating a consensual plan and in determining whether the amount they will receive under the proposed plan is their fair share. It provides leverage for the creditors in the Foam Corporation case in their negotiations with Gruff, the sole stockholder. Gruff cannot obtain cramdown of a plan unless the plan either (1) provides the creditors with value equal to the full amount of their claims, or (2) provides that Gruff will not receive or retain anything on account of his ownership of Foam Corporation's stock. If the debtor is insolvent even on a going concern basis (as is usual in chapter 11 cases), then there is not enough value available to give the creditors value equal to the full amount of their claims. Gruff's interest as a stockholder will therefore be eliminated under the plan unless he can obtain enough creditor support to confirm a consensual plan. In the negotiations, the creditors can insist that the plan give Gruff only a small amount of value and threaten to vote against the plan if it gives him more; they can point out that without creditor approval of the plan, Gruff will be unable to obtain confirmation of a plan that gives him anything for his stock.

Gruff may have some leverage of his own, even if a class of impaired unsecured claims dissents. The absolute priority rule which is part of the "fair and equitable" standard for cramdown would not permit Gruff to retain or to obtain any value *on account of his stock* if Foam Corporation is insolvent on a reorganization value basis, but there may be another way for Gruff to obtain some of the value of the reorganized Foam Corporation. Gruff may be able to obtain some or all of the stock of the reorganized debtor in exchange for a contribution of new money by Gruff. See Chapter Fifteen below.

Further, as sole stockholder and chairman of Foam Corporation's board of directors, Gruff probably will effectively control Foam Corporation's actions as debtor in possession. As we have seen, the debtor in possession initially has the exclusive right to file a plan. Unless exclusivity ends or is terminated by the court, creditors cannot file plans. That means Gruff can hold up the reorganization if the creditors will not agree to give him what he sees as his fair share of the value. Alternatively, he can cause the debtor to propose a plan under which he will receive some or all of the stock in the reorganized debtor in exchange for a contribution of new capital. If Gruff is not successful in obtaining confirmation of a plan, then eventually exclusivity will end; the creditors will then be able to file their own plans, but the cost of the delay to the creditors may be substantial. The cost of delay includes the time value of money and may include continued losses to the business while it is in chapter 11.

Even after exclusivity ends, Gruff can still make it expensive for the creditors to confirm a plan which does not give him what he believes is his fair share. If Gruff votes against the creditors' plan, the common stock class will have rejected the plan, so the plan can only be confirmed in a cramdown. See § 1129(a)(8). In the cramdown, the creditors will have the burden of showing that the plan gives Gruff value for his stock at least equal to the excess (if any) of the reorganization value of the debtor over the amount of the creditors' claims.[3] This will typically require that the creditors present expert valuation testimony at a lengthy and expensive hearing.

Finally, Gruff will have leverage if a successful reorganization requires his personal participation. In some chapter 11 cases (such as those in which the debtor is an athlete, an entertainer, a professional or a partnership of professionals), the business is worth very little as a going concern or may not be a going concern at all if the principal or principals leave. In such a case, if the creditors want a reorganization to succeed, they will have little choice but to provide enough value to entice the principal or principals to stay.

---

3. If the plan provides no value for Gruff on account of his stock, then the common stock class will be deemed to have rejected the plan, and Gruff does not even have to vote for a cramdown to be necessary. See §§ 1126(g) and 1129(a)(8). In the ensuing cramdown, the creditors will have the burden of showing that Foam Corporation is insolvent on a going concern basis—that the reorganization value of the debtor does not exceed the amount of the creditors' claims. If it is solvent on a going concern basis, so that the value of its assets exceeds the amount of its debts, then a plan which gives nothing to the stockholders must give more than 100% value to one or more classes of claims. As we note in Chapter Fifteen, such a plan would not be fair and equitable with respect to the dissenting class of stockholders' interests and therefore could not confirmed in a cramdown.

d. The Form of the Value

Finally there is the question whether the form of the value is acceptable. TC may not wish to receive too much of his value in the form of common stock, because common stock is the riskiest form of value. TC and the other creditors may be "risk averse" and may prefer to take most of their value in the form of cash and debt obligations (bonds or notes). On the other hand, if the reorganized debtor is much more successful than expected, the common stock will rise greatly in value; if TC takes only cash and debt obligations, TC will miss out on the benefits of the unexpected success. Further, if TC and the other creditors insist on taking too much in cash and debt obligations, the reorganized debtor may not be able to succeed. Foam Corporation may be hindered in its operations if it has too little remaining cash. It may default on its debt obligations if they are too large, requiring a further reorganization. These considerations will be taken into account in the negotiation of the plan. To cast an informed vote, the creditors and interest holders will need information and advice as to the proposed capital structure of the reorganized debtor, as to the amount of cash that can be paid immediately without hindering the debtor's operations, as to the amount, interest rates, and maturities of debts that the reorganized debtor can handle successfully, and as to the possible future value of the stock.

Under the Foam Corporation plan, TC will receive some immediate cash, so all is not lost for TC even if the reorganized Foam Corporation fails. The five year note will result in TC being repaid another 50% of its claim with interest if Foam Corporation is able to meet its obligations; however, the 10% interest rate may be a below market rate for loans to the reorganized debtor, resulting in the value of the note being less than $5000. If the reorganized Foam Corporation does very well, then TC will share in its good fortune by way of ownership of some of Foam Corporation's stock. Of course, TC would need a substantial amount of information to evaluate the value of the note and of the stock. Given the small amount of TC's claim, TC will probably not attempt any independent evaluation, but will rely on the advice of others as to the value of the note and the shares. As a trade creditor with some knowledge of the industry, TC may however have some sense of the likelihood of the reorganized Foam Corporation succeeding. That will affect TC's willingness to take some of its value in the form of the note and the shares.

2. Consequences of the Substitution of a Collective Right To Vote for the Individual Creditor's Right Not To Be Bound

In all of this the student (and the court!) should remember why there is a vote at all. There would be no voting by classes except for the way in which chapter 11 denies to creditors like TC their nonbankruptcy rights. Outside of bankruptcy, TC could decide whether to agree to the terms of a workout agreement; TC would only be bound if he agreed. Significant creditor dissent (and sometimes significant interest holder dissent) would doom the workout. Inside bankruptcy, a confirmed chapter 11 plan binds the creditors, including TC, to its terms, even if they oppose the plan.

In place of TC's individual right not to be bound, chapter 11 gives TC (and the other creditors and interest holders) the right to vote in classes on any proposed plan. Thus they exercise collective control over whether the plan can be confirmed.

Four consequences follow from this substitution of a collective right to vote for the individual creditor's right not to be bound. First, TC's right to vote and to have his vote count should be carefully protected. TC is being denied the autonomy given by nonbankruptcy law. Fairness demands careful protection of the lesser substitute, the right to vote on the plan. The court should not second-guess TC's reasons for voting to accept or reject the plan, unless there is strong evidence of impropriety. Protection of the right to vote also requires that TC receive sufficient information and advice from other parties to cast an informed vote; otherwise, as we have seen, the right to vote would be hollow.

Second, TC should not be bound by the vote of other creditors unless *their* votes are informed votes. That follows from the theory of class voting. Each class is to be made up of similar claims so that the class members will have similar economic interests. If TC's class votes to accept the plan then the likelihood is that the plan is in the economic interests of all the class members, even the dissenting members. That inference cannot be drawn, however, unless the voters have enough information and advice to draw sound conclusions about the plan. Informed voting is essential.

Third, TC and the other creditors should have the freedom to explain their reasons to the other creditors and influence their votes. Outside bankruptcy, a few dissenting creditors (or the holders of a substantial block of stock) who doubt the wisdom of a proposed workout agreement can block it; in chapter 11, they must be permitted to explain their reasons and solicit votes to reject the plan. They must be permitted to do so without undue fear of liability under federal securities laws or state law governing unintentional misrepresentations. Similarly, those who support a proposed plan, especially those who negotiated its terms, must be able to express their reasons and solicit votes for it without undue fear of liability.

On the other hand, some control over voting and the solicitation of votes may be justified to help ensure that the collective decision is reasoned and informed. Some creditors or interest holders may have ulterior motives for the positions they take; for example, a creditor may also be a competitor, who would rather see the reorganization fail. Emotions sometimes run high in bankruptcy cases; some creditors may prefer, out of spite, to see the debtor fail.

False or misleading statements made in the disclosure statement or in solicitation may cause harm to TC, to the other creditors or to interest holders. To the extent chapter 11 gives the makers of false or misleading statements protection from liability, it lessens the protection that TC and the others would have outside of chapter 11. Again the question arises: to what extent should nonbankruptcy rights be sacrificed by chapter 11 for the sake of facilitating a reorganization?

Fourth, the nonbankruptcy rights of the parties should influence the standards in chapter 11 for allocating voting power and for deciding how much support a plan must have from holders with claims or interests in a class before we will say that the class has accepted the plan. A small number of creditors—or even one with a large claim—can block reorganization outside of bankruptcy. Outside of bankruptcy, TC or any other creditor can choose not to be bound even if there is enough support for a workout to succeed. The allocation of voting power should take these dual sources of nonbankruptcy power into account: a creditor has power based on the size of its claim to influence whether a workout can be accomplished, and power regardless of the size of its claim to refuse to be bound by any workout agreement.

Further, some supermajority scheme should be required; a bare majority vote should not be sufficient to constitute acceptance of the plan by a class. A shift from near absolute autonomy to control by bare majority vote would be too great a decrease in TC's or any other creditor's rights.

On the other hand, if those who bother to participate in the process favor a plan, that should suffice. For example, if a two thirds vote in amount of claims is required, it should be two thirds of the amount of claims that are voted, rather than two thirds of all the claims. Just as many registered voters fail to vote, many holders of claims and interests will not think it worth their while to vote in a chapter 11 case. Their apathy should not prevent a reorganization if those who have bothered to participate accept the plan by the required majority.

3. The Balance Struck by Chapter 11

Chapter 11 attempts to balance all of these concerns by

1) requiring, in most cases, the creation and distribution of a court-approved "disclosure statement" that must contain "adequate information," see § 1125(a) and (c);

2) permitting prepetition solicitation of acceptances of a plan (typically where the debtor hopes to file a chapter 11 petition with the acceptances already in hand to permit quick confirmation of a prepackaged or prearranged plan of reorganization), but requiring that such prepetition solicitations "compl[y] with any applicable nonbankruptcy law, rule, or regulation governing the adequacy of disclosure," or, "if there is not any such law, rule or regulation," requiring prior disclosure to solicitees of "adequate information, as defined in section 1125(a)," see § 1126(b);

3) permitting postpetition solicitation of a creditor's or interest holder's vote only after the solicitee has received the plan (or a summary of it) and the disclosure statement, see § 1125(b), subject to an exception where the solicitee initially was solicited prepetition, see § 1125(g);[4]

4) providing "safe harbor" protection to good faith participants in the disclosure and solicitation process against liability under the federal and state securities laws and state common law, see § 1125(e);

5) permitting the court to "designate" creditors or interest holders whose votes should not be counted because they were cast in bad faith or were solicited improperly, see § 1126(e);

6) requiring (before a class of claims will be considered to have accepted the plan) acceptance by both a simple majority vote in number of claims and by a supermajority (2/3) vote in amount of claims, out of those creditors who bother to vote, see § 1126(c); and

7) requiring (before a class of interests will be considered to have accepted the plan) acceptance by a supermajority (2/3) vote—based on amount of ownership interests—of the interest holders who bother to vote, see § 1126(d).

The disclosure statement is the cornerstone of the disclosure, solicitation, and voting process, so we turn to it first.

B. THE DISCLOSURE STATEMENT

The function of the court-approved disclosure statement is to provide "adequate information" to creditors and interest holders so that they can "make an informed judgment about the plan." Section 1125(a) and (b). When a proposed plan is filed, a disclosure statement is supposed to be filed with it, or within a time fixed by the court. Rule 3016(b).[5] The court then holds a hearing on the disclosure statement. Section 1125(b); Rule 3017(a). If the court approves the disclosure statement, the statement will be mailed to all creditors and interest holders, along with the plan or a summary of the plan, a ballot, and a notice of the deadline for

---

4. Section 1125(g) (added by the 2005 BAPCPA) permits continued solicitation of a holder of a claim or interest after the filing of the petition without the need for bankruptcy court approval of a disclosure statement, *if the holder was solicited prepetition* (and if both solicitations comply with applicable nonbankruptcy law). This should assist debtors in expeditiously completing solicitations in prepackaged or prearranged cases where the need arises to file a petition before the solicitations are completed (or where an involuntary petition is filed while the debtor is soliciting acceptances of its plan). See Levin & Ranney-Marinelli, *The Creeping Repeal of Chapter 11: The Significant Business Provisions of the Bankruptcy Abuse Prevention and Consumer Protection Act of 2005*, 79 AM. BANKR. L.J. 603, 630-31 (2005).

Note also that in a small business case, postpetition solicitations may be based on a "conditionally approved disclosure statement * * * subject to final approval after notice and a hearing." Section 1125(f)(3); see Rule 3017.1.

5. If no postpetition solicitation is planned (other than under § 1125(g)), the plan proponent may file "evidence showing compliance with § 1126(b)" instead of a disclosure statement. See Rule 3016(b). In a small business case, "the court may determine that the plan itself provides adequate information and that a separate disclosure statement is not necessary." Section 1125(f)(1) (as amended by 2005 BAPCPA).

voting on the plan. Rule 3017(d). Except as permitted by § 1125(g), acceptances and rejections of the plan cannot be solicited legally postpetition from any creditor or interest holder until that person has received the disclosure statement.

What information do TC, the other creditors, and the interest holders need to make an informed decision?

In re Cardinal Congregate I
United States Bankruptcy Court, S.D. Ohio, 1990
121 B.R. 760

BARBARA J. SELLERS, Bankruptcy Judge. [*Debtor Cardinal Congregate I ("CCI") was a limited partnership which owned a retirement home. Cardinal Industries, Inc. ("CII") was the general partner of the debtor with a nine per cent partnership interest; the remaining 91 per cent ownership was apportioned among thirty-one individual limited partners. Part of the debtor's financing was raised in the form of a $3.5 million non-recourse loan from Cardinal Industries Mortgage Company ("CIMC"), secured by a mortgage on the retirement home. CIMC assigned its rights to six banks and a savings and loan association (the "Loan Participants"). The Loan Participants assigned their rights to James F. Kacsmar & Company ("Kacsmar") to service the loan for them. The debtor later filed a petition under Chapter 11 and ultimately filed the proposed plan and the disclosure statement at issue. The Loan Participants and Kacsmar opposed approval of the disclosure statement.*]
    * * *

The issues before the Court are whether the Disclosure Statement should be approved and whether it contains "adequate information" within the meaning of 11 U.S.C. § 1125.

The Objectors have raised numerous objections to the Disclosure Statement. Those objections may be generally classified as relating either to the confirmability of the debtor's Amended Plan of Reorganization or to the quantity and quality of information disclosed.

* * * The Objectors assert that the Amended Plan of Reorganization is not confirmable under the requirements of 11 U.S.C. § 1129 and that pursuit of Disclosure Statement approval is a waste of time and resources for all concerned. * * *

The Court believes that disapproval of the adequacy of a disclosure statement may sometimes be appropriate where it describes a plan of reorganization which is so fatally flawed that confirmation is impossible. In re Monroe Well Service, Inc., 80 B.R. 324 (Bankr.E.D.Pa.1987). However, "[s]uch action is discretionary and must be used carefully so as not to convert the disclosure statement hearing into a confirmation hearing, and to insure that due process concerns are protected." Monroe Well Service at 333 (footnote omitted). Where objections relating to confirmability of a plan of reorganization raise novel or unsettled issues of law, the Court will not look behind the disclosure statement to decide such issues at the hearing on the adequacy of the disclosure statement.

In this case, the Court finds that the Amended Plan of Reorganization is not so patently nonconfirmable as to bar consideration of the adequacy of the Disclosure Statement. The objections raised as to the confirmability of the Amended Plan of

Reorganization may or may not ultimately be found meritorious; however, the Court will not determine such objections and the related issues at this juncture. * * *

The Objectors also contend that approval of the Disclosure Statement must be denied because it fails to provide the quantity and quality of information required by 11 U.S.C. § 1125. Before addressing the specific objections advanced by the Objectors and making some additional findings and observations, the Court will first review the governing legal principles.

1. Governing Legal Principles.

The codal prerequisite to court approval of a disclosure statement is that it contain "adequate information." Specifically, 11 U.S.C. § 1125(b) provides:

> An acceptance or rejection of a plan may not be solicited after the commencement of the case under this title from a holder of a claim or interest with respect to such claim or interest, unless, at the time of or before such solicitation, there is transmitted to such holder the plan or a summary of the plan, and a written disclosure statement approved, after notice and a hearing, by the court as containing *adequate information*. The court may approve a disclosure statement without a valuation of the debtor or an appraisal of the debtor's assets (emphasis added).

Section 1125(a)(1) of the Bankruptcy Code defines "adequate information" in general terms to mean:

> ... information of a kind, and in sufficient detail, as far as is reasonably practicable in light of the nature and history of the debtor and the condition of the debtor's books and records, that would enable a hypothetical reasonable investor typical of holders of claims or interests of the relevant class to make an informed judgment about the plan, but adequate information need not include such information about any other possible or proposed plan.

Congress left vague the standard for evaluating what constitutes adequate information so as to permit a case-by-case determination based on the prevailing facts and circumstances. H. R. Rep. No. 595 at 225, 409 (1977); S. Rep. No. 989 at 121 (1978). While providing for judicial flexibility, Congress intended that the courts should consider as part of their determination the cost of preparing a more detailed disclosure statement, the nature and history of the debtor, the condition of the debtor's records, the need for expediency in the solicitation and confirmation process, and the necessity for protection of the reorganization constituencies. H. R. Rep. No. 595 at 409.

Numerous courts have prescribed a list of disclosures which typically should be included in a disclosure statement. In *Scioto Valley*, [In re Scioto Valley Mortgage Co., 88 B.R. 168 (Bankr.S.D.Ohio 1988)] the court adopted a 19-point nonexhaustive list of the types of information that may be required in a disclosure statement. That list of disclosures is as follows:

1. The circumstances that gave rise to the filing of the bankruptcy petition;
2. A complete description of the available assets and their value;
3. The anticipated future of the debtor;
4. The source of the information provided in the disclosure statement;

5. A disclaimer, which typically indicates that no statements or information concerning the debtor or its assets or securities are authorized, other than those set forth in the disclosure statement;

6. The condition and performance of the debtor while in Chapter 11;

7. Information regarding claims against the estate;

8. A liquidation analysis setting forth the estimated return that creditors would receive under Chapter 7;

9. The accounting and valuation methods used to produce the financial information in the disclosure statement;

10. Information regarding the future management of the debtor, including the amount of compensation to be paid to any insiders, directors, and/or officers of the debtor;

11. A summary of the plan of reorganization;

12. An estimate of all administrative expenses, including attorneys' fees and accountants' fees;

13. The collectibility of any accounts receivable;

14. Any financial information, valuations or pro forma projections that would be relevant to creditors' determinations of whether to accept or reject the plan;

15. Information relevant to the risks being taken by the creditors and interest holders;

16. The actual or projected value that can be obtained from avoidable transfers;

17. The existence, likelihood and possible success of non-bankruptcy litigation;

18. The tax consequences of the plan; and

19. The relationship of the debtor with affiliates.

This Court finds the *Scioto Valley* list to be a helpful guidepost in its analysis and adopts the list as well. The Court cautions, however, that the list is but a yardstick against which the adequacy of disclosure may be measured; the precise information required will be governed by the facts and circumstances presented in each case. As the *Scioto Valley* court noted, disclosure of the listed information may be insufficient or excessive in the context of any given case.

Generally, a disclosure statement must contain all pertinent information bearing on the success or failure of the proposals in the plan of reorganization. A disclosure statement should likewise contain all material information relating to the risks posed to creditors and equity interest holders under the proposed plan of reorganization. The disclosure statement, on the other hand, should not be burdened with "overly technical and extremely numerous additions," where such information would serve only to diminish the understanding of a typical creditor or interest holder. *Scioto Valley* at 171.

    2.   Evaluation of The Objections in Light of the Legal Requirements.

* * *

The Court finds that the Disclosure Statement lacks certain necessary information. First, the Disclosure Statement contains an inadequate discussion of the claims held by various affiliates of CII for loans made and services provided to the debtor. The Disclosure Statement should contain more detailed information regarding the nature of these claims and should specifically identify the holders of such claims. Additionally, a more complete discussion of the Amended Plan's proposed treatment of these claims is necessary.

Second, the Disclosure Statement must contain more information regarding the debtor's operations postpetition. It is not enough that the Disclosure Statement refers its reader to the monthly operating reports filed by the debtor with this Court; the Disclosure Statement should contain a detailed textual description of the debtor's postpetition performance. * * *

Third, the Disclosure Statement should include a discussion of the anticipated future of the debtor's business. Merely attaching pro forma income calculations to the Disclosure Statement is insufficient. A more detailed analysis of the projected income, expenses, and surplus funds available for satisfaction of claims and interest is appropriate. Further, the Disclosure Statement should clearly identify all assumptions made in calculating pro forma information and should set forth those facts supporting all estimates. Information regarding the accounting and valuation methods used in preparation of the Disclosure Statement's financial exhibits must also be included.

Fourth, both the Disclosure Statement and Amended Plan of Reorganization identify "Net Cash Flow" as a source of funds for the satisfaction of allowed claims and interests. However, the Court can find no definition of Net Cash Flow in either document. The Disclosure Statement must clearly state how Net Cash Flow is defined and calculated.

Fifth, the Disclosure Statement and Amended Plan of Reorganization discuss as a potential source of funds those proceeds that will be realized upon the contemplated sale or refinancing of the retirement facility. The Disclosure Statement should more fully explain the consequences of any such sale or refinancing upon all allowed claims and interests. Additionally, the Disclosure Statement should contain a discussion of any efforts to date, as well as intended future efforts, to bring about a sale or refinancing of the property.

Sixth, the Disclosure Statement should provide a more detailed estimation of allowable administrative expenses. This should include, without limitation, all estimated fees for attorneys and accountants.

Finally, an identification and discussion of all causes of action which the debtor may pursue under the Bankruptcy Code or other applicable law should be included in the Disclosure Statement. The debtor's intentions as to these causes of action must also be disclosed.

The information required by the Court is neither unreasonable nor voluminous. Where, as here, the satisfaction of claims and interests is dependent upon the debtor's ability to improve its financial performance or to consummate contemplated transactions, it is not overly demanding for the Court to require detailed disclosure of the facts and assumptions underlying the debtor's belief that it will accomplish its reorganization effort. * * *

Based upon the foregoing, approval of the Disclosure Statement, as proposed, is denied. The debtor is given twenty (20) days to file an amended disclosure statement which supplements the current statement to accommodate the Court's concerns. * * *

NOTES

1. The court in *Cardinal Congregate I* identified seven particular areas in which more disclosure was needed. Why would full disclosure in those areas be important for the creditors and interest holders (the general and limited partners)?

2. Item 19 in the *Scioto Valley* list of typically needed disclosures is "[t]he tax consequences of the plan." The 2005 BAPCPA amended § 1125(a)(1) to state explicitly that "adequate information" includes "a discussion of the potential material Federal tax consequences of the plan."

3. Is there a danger of too much disclosure? If the disclosure statement is extremely long and complex, will creditors like TC be able to make sense of it? The court in *Cardinal Congregate I* stated that "The disclosure statement, on the other hand, should not be burdened with 'overly technical and extremely numerous additions,' where such information would serve only to diminish the understanding of a typical creditor or interest holder." 121 B.R. at 765-66. Why would anyone be interested in demanding that such "overly technical" additions be made to a disclosure statement? Unfortunately, objections are sometimes raised to the disclosure statement not for purposes of ensuring that it contains adequate information, but in order to delay a vote on the plan and in order to put the plan proponent to the additional expense of drafting several amended versions of the disclosure statement. If the court determines that the purpose of the objections was delay or increased expense, the court can sanction the attorney who signed the objections for violating Rule 9011. The attorney's signature on the objections constitutes a certificate that the objections are not frivolous and are not "interposed for any improper purpose, such as to harass, to cause delay, or to increase the cost of litigation." Rule 9011 is arguably a strengthened version of Fed. R. Civ. P. 11, which refers to "unnecessary" delay and to "needless" increase in the cost of litigation. Further, there is authority that the filing of a complaint for an improper purpose does not violate Fed. R. Civ. P 11 unless the claim is also frivolous. Townsend v. Holman Consulting Corp., 929 F.2d 1358 (9th Cir. 1990) (en banc). Whatever the merits of the *Townsend* decision, the Ninth Circuit does not follow it with regard to Rule 9011; an improper purpose will suffice to permit sanctions to be imposed even if the action taken is not wholly frivolous. Marsch v. Marsch (In re Marsch), 36 F.3d 825 (9th Cir. 1994). Thus Rule 9011 may have a more serious bite than Fed. R. Civ. P. 11.

4. Consider the last sentence of § 1125(b). Does it permit the court to require inclusion of a full going concern valuation of the debtor in the disclosure statement? Does a creditor or interest holder have sufficient information to cast an informed vote without such a valuation? Note that a full, formal going concern valuation can be a very expensive matter. However, the parties to the plan negotiations very often come to a consensus on the approximate going concern value of the debtor. If a consensus has been reached on that value, then the valuation typically will be included in the disclosure statement. If a certified public accountant prepares financial projections for the disclosure statement or certifies financial projections made by the debtor's management and if the existing stockholders will end up owning less than 50 percent of the debtor's stock under the plan, then Statement of Position 90-7 (issued by the American Institute of Certified Public Accountants and discussed above in Chapter Twelve) will apply; it *requires* the plan proponent in most cases to disclosure the estimated reorganization value in the disclosure statement. S.O.P. 90-7 cannot bind the court,

but it reflects the view of the accounting profession and should carry great weight as to what information is needed by the parties. If the proposed disclosure statement does not include the reorganization value, then the proponent's accountants will have to note that as a deficiency in their certification of the financial projections and may even have to resign. Where accountants for a public company resign, they are required to inform the Securities and Exchange Commission of their resignation and of the reasons for it, so it will be a public event that may be embarrassing for the debtor.

Why would creditors need to know the approximate reorganization value of the debtor? Do the creditors have a greater need to know that value if they will be receiving stock under the plan rather than just cash and debt?

5. Courts uniformly require disclosure statements to include a liquidation analysis setting forth the estimated return to creditors and interest holders if the debtor is liquidated. Does this violate the last sentence of § 1125(b)? Why do creditors and interest holders need the liquidation analysis? In In re Crowthers McCall Pattern, Inc., 120 B.R. 279 (Bankr. S.D.N.Y. 1990), the court refused to confirm the proposed plan only because the disclosure statement had underestimated the liquidation value of the debtor. The subordinated debentureholders had voted to accept the plan. The underestimate had led them to believe they would receive nothing in a chapter 7 liquidation. However, the liquidation value was in fact high enough that there might be some payment to debentureholders in a chapter 7. The court found that all of the creditors would receive more value under the plan than in a liquidation. Thus the plan met the "best interests of creditors" standard contained in § 1129(a)(7). That did not change the fact that the erroneous disclosure statement might have affected the votes of the debentureholders. The court stated:

> Section 1129(a)(2) of the Code requires that the Court find compliance by the plan proponent with applicable provisions of the Code prior to confirming a plan. Although the Court determined, prior to transmission of the Disclosure Statement to creditors, that it contained "adequate information" * * * that issue can be revisited at the confirmation hearing. * * * If it appears that a disclosure statement is materially erroneous or inadequate, the Court simply cannot make the finding required by section 1129(a)(2). * * *
>
> In this case, it is apparent that the Liquidation Analysis contained in the Disclosure Statement is significantly in error. It is also clear that a hypothetical reasonable investor typical of a Debentureholder would view the possibility of a return under liquidation as significantly altering the total mix of information made available to him in the disclosure statement which predicted no return to Debentureholders in liquidation.
>
> It might be argued that the errors make no difference in light of the Court's finding of satisfaction of the best interests test. It might also be argued that the errors make no difference because the plan may be confirmable under section 1129(b) regardless of the vote of the Debentureholders because the plan seemingly tracks the absolute priority rule with respect to Debentureholders in that it provides for payment in full to them prior to a dividend to junior classes.
>
> The command of section 1129(a)(2) for compliance with the Code, however, does not admit inquiry as to whether a class would have approved a plan notwithstanding the error or whether approval by that class is required. Disclosure statements are required to contain liquidation analyses that enable creditors to make their own

judgment as to whether a plan is in their best interests and to vote and object to a plan if they so desire. The protections of creditors at confirmation and during the confirmation process are exceptionally strong. The confirmation process and the protections of creditors are not to be denigrated by a liquidation analysis such as that presented in this case.

Id. at 300-01. The court required the plan proponent to submit a corrected liquidation analysis and new ballots to the creditors for a new vote.

6.   The court in *McCall Pattern* also stated that the test for adequacy of the information in a disclosure statement "parallels the materiality standard adopted by the Supreme Court with respect to proxy solicitations under section 14(a) of the Securities Exchange Act of 1934." Id. at 300. Under that standard "[a]n omitted fact is material if there is a substantial likelihood that a reasonable [investor] would consider it important in deciding how to vote." TSC Indus., Inc. v. Northway, Inc., 426 U.S. 438, 449, 96 S. Ct. 2126, 2132, 48 L. Ed. 2d 757, 766 (1976). As a matter of common sense, if a disclosure statement omits available information that would likely be considered important by the typical member of a class, it would be hard to say that the disclosure statement met the § 1125 requirement that it contain enough information to "enable a hypothetical reasonable investor * * * to make an informed judgment about the plan."

However, the standards of disclosure under the securities laws do not apply to disclosure statements. See § 1125(d). But for §§ 1125(d) and 1145, the federal securities laws could require several forms of detailed disclosure. The soliciting of acceptances or rejections of a plan would be a kind of proxy solicitation, which could require delivery of a proxy statement to the person solicited.[6] If the plan calls for issuance of new stock or bonds to anyone, the debtor might be required to file a registration statement with the SEC and give a prospectus to those who will receive the new securities.[7] The debtor could also be required to disclose information about the "trust indenture" protections

---

6.   If the debtor's stock or bonds are listed on a national securities exchange, or if the debtor's assets exceed $5 million, or if there is a class of stock of the debtor owned by 500 persons or more, then a "proxy statement" requirement would apply. But for § 1125(d), section 14(a) of the Securities Exchange Act of 1934 would require delivery of a "proxy statement" to the owners of the stock or bonds before their proxies could be solicited in favor of or against the plan of reorganization.

7.   Unless there is an exception, section 5 of the Securities Act of 1933 requires the filing of a registration statement with the SEC before securities can be issued. Section 5 also requires that a prospectus be delivered to any buyer of the newly issued securities. Bankruptcy Code § 1145 exempts the issuance of securities under a chapter 11 plan in most cases from Securities Act section 5's registration requirements. It does not exempt the issuance of securities by an "underwriter," as that term is defined in Bankruptcy Code § 1145(b). Section 1145(b)(1)(D) would seem to strip the exemption of any real application, since it defines "underwriter" to include any "issuer" of securities; that would on its face seem to include the reorganizing debtor. However, the courts have interpreted § 1145(b)(1)(D) not to apply to the debtor or any successor of the debtor, so the debtor or its successor can issue securities as part of the plan (or debt securities under § 364(f)) without having to file a registration statement. See In re Standard Oil & Exploration, 136 B.R. 141 (Bankr. W.D. Mich.1992); In re Amarex Inc., 53 B.R. 12 (Bankr. W.D. Okla. 1985); In re Stanley Hotel, Inc., 13 B.R. 926 (Bankr. D. Colo. 1981); cf. Nextel Commc'ns, Inc., SEC No-Action Letter, 1999 WL 288755 (May 10, 1999).

given to recipients of debt securities.[8] Proxy statements, registration statements, and prospectuses all must be submitted to the SEC in advance for examination, and all require excruciating detail.

The chapter 11 disclosure statement is analogous to a proxy statement, registration statement, and prospectus rolled into one, but its sufficiency is not governed by section 14 of the 1934 Act, section 5 of the 1933 Act, or any other nonbankruptcy law. Section 1125(d). As the legislative history points out:

> The bill also permits the disclosure statement to be approved without the necessity for compliance with the very strict rules of Section 5 of the Securities Act of 1933, section 14 of the Securities Exchange Act of 1934, or relevant State securities laws. Without such a provision, the court would have no discretion in approving disclosure statements that go to public classes, but would be required in every case to require a full proxy statement or prospectus whenever public classes were solicitated [sic]. Such a statement requires certified audited financial statements and extensive information. The cost of developing a prospectus or proxy statement for a large company often runs well over $1 million. That cost would be nearly prohibitive in a bankruptcy reorganization. In addition, the information normally required under section 14 may simply be unavailable, because of the condition of the debtor. Finally, court supervision of the contents of the disclosure statement will protect the public investor from any serious inadequacies in the disclosure statement.
>
> The provision does not prohibit a section 14-type statement or a prospectus. In some cases it may indeed be appropriate to go to that length in disclosure. The courts will have to determine the need on a case-by-case basis. The section merely does not require it in every public case.

H. R. Rep. No. 595, 95th Cong., 1st Sess., 227-28 (1977). That $1 million cost in 1977 dollars would be substantially more today.

One commentator suggests that "The closer the case comes to a major reorganization of a widely held debtor, the closer will be the requirement of the disclosure statement to that of a non-bankruptcy prospectus." Cowans, COWANS BANKRUPTCY LAW AND PRACTICE, § 20.16 (1987). That suggestion was explicitly and forcefully rejected in the Texaco reorganization, one of the largest chapter 11 cases to date. Kirk v. Texaco Inc., 82 B.R. 678, 681-82 (S.D.N.Y. 1988).

The Securities and Exchange Commission (and its state counterparts) can appear and be heard on the question of the adequacy of the disclosure statement. Section 1125(d). However, they cannot appeal the order approving the disclosure statement. Id. Why are they denied the right to appeal?

7. An order approving a disclosure statement is not an appealable final order. It can, however, be reviewed on appeal from an order confirming a plan. See Everett v. Perez (In re Perez), 30 F.3d 1209 (9th Cir. 1994); cf. Adams v. First

---

8.　See Trust Indenture Act of 1939, sections 305-307, 15 U.S.C. §§ 77eee-77ggg. Section 1125(d) exempts the disclosure statement from the disclosure requirements of the Trust Indenture Act. It does not exempt the debtor from the Trust Indenture Act requirement of obtaining qualification from the SEC of debt securities to be issued under the plan. Unless an exemption applies, the debtor will have to seek such qualification and comply with the other substantive provisions of the Trust Indenture Act. Section 1145(d) exempts notes with maturities of one year or less from the provisions of the Trust Indenture Act, but it does not exempt longer term notes.

Fin. Dev. Corp. (In re First Fin. Dev. Corp.), 960 F.2d 23 (5th Cir. 1992) (holding that order sustaining certain objections to disclosure statement and overruling others was not final order). Interlocutory orders of bankruptcy judges are appealable to the district court if the district court grants leave to appeal. See 28 U.S.C. § 158(a)(3). (As amended in 2005, 28 U.S.C. § 158(d) allows that appeal to be taken directly to the court of appeals upon the proper certification, but the circuit court need not hear the direct appeal unless it so chooses.) Interlocutory decisions of district courts are appealable to the court of appeals by leave of the court of appeals. See 28 U.S.C. § 1292(b). The court's analysis in Abel v. Shugrue (In re Ionosphere Clubs, Inc.), 179 B.R. 24 (S.D.N.Y. 1995), suggests that leave to appeal orders approving disclosure statements will seldom be granted. See also In re WorldCom, Inc., 2003 WL 21498904 (S.D.N.Y. 2003) (holding that bankruptcy court order approving disclosure statement was interlocutory and refusing to grant leave to appeal it).

8. The court in *Cardinal Congregate I* refused to consider the confirmability of the plan at the disclosure hearing. Why is such a refusal usually right? In what cases should a court consider confirmability at the disclosure hearing? Should a court approve a disclosure statement which shows on its face that the plan fails to recognize the claim of a creditor who has a valid claim? See In re Beyond.com Corp., 289 B.R. 138, 140 (Bankr. N.D. Cal. 2003) ("Because the underlying plan is patently unconfirmable, the disclosure statement may not be approved."); In re Allied Gaming Management, Inc., 209 B.R. 201 (Bankr. W.D. La. 1997); In re Atlanta West VI, 91 B.R. 620, 622 (Bankr. N.D. Ga.1988) (sending of disclosure statement to creditors and soliciting of votes would be "wasteful and fruitless exercise" and would only serve to delay reorganization if the plan is unconfirmable on its face, but consideration of whether plan satisfies requirements of § 1129 is "generally addressed at confirmation"). Should the court approve a disclosure statement which shows that the interest rate which would be paid on a secured claim after confirmation would be less than the appropriate market rate, so that the undersecured creditor would not receive payments on account of its secured claim with a present value equal to the value of the collateral? See In re S.E.T. Income Properties, III, 83 B.R. 791 (Bankr. N.D. Okla.1988), and § 1129(b)(2)(A). Would your answer depend on who is raising the objection to the disclosure statement?

9. Section 1125(f) permits the court in a small business case to approve a disclosure statement conditionally, apparently without "notice and a hearing." The disclosure statement then can be used to solicit acceptances and rejections. Final approval is not given until parties have an opportunity to object to the disclosure statement. The hearing on final approval of the disclosure statement then can be combined with the hearing on confirmation of the plan. See id.

10. Section 105(d)(2)(B)(vi)—which is not explicitly limited to small business cases—also permits the court to order that the hearing on the disclosure statement and the hearing on confirmation be combined, *unless such an order would be inconsistent with another provision of the Bankruptcy Code or with an applicable Rule*. If it applies only to small business cases, § 105(d)(2)(B)(vi) would seem to add nothing to § 1125(f); thus a standard rule of statutory interpretation suggests that it should have some application to other cases. Where the plan proponent solicits acceptances of the plan postpetition in a case that is not a small business case, a combined disclosure statement and confirmation hearing would seem to be inconsistent with the § 1125(b)

requirement that no postpetition solicitation occur until a court-approved disclosure statement has been distributed.[9] If acceptances were solicited prepetition in accordance with applicable nonbankruptcy law disclosure requirements, and if no solicitation is done postpetition, then neither the Code nor the Rules appear to require that a disclosure statement be filed and approved. See §§ 1125(b), 1126(b); Rule 3016(b).[10] Thus no hearing to approve a disclosure statement (not even one combined with the hearing on plan confirmation) would be needed. That leaves little or no room for § 105(d)(2))(B)(vi) to apply in non-small business cases.[11]

Problem 13-1

The unsecured creditors' committee objected to the disclosure statement filed by Foam Corporation on the ground that it did not provide adequate information for general unsecured creditors to cast informed votes. The committee claimed the disclosure statement should have included certain negative information on the management skills of Gruff, who would continue to manage Foam Corporation under the plan. The court approved the disclosure statement, overruling the objection. Each class of claims and interests accepted the plan, but TC (an unsecured trade creditor) and a few others voted to reject it. At the confirmation hearing TC sought to raise the same objection to the disclosure statement that the committee had raised before. The bankruptcy court confirmed the plan, and TC appealed to the district court. Does TC have standing to raise the issue on appeal? Consider the following arguments:

Foam Corporation's counsel: TC does not have standing. TC voted against the plan, so TC was not misled into accepting the plan by the omission of the information about Gruff. Since TC's vote would not have changed had the information been included, TC was not harmed by its omission, and hence TC is not an "aggrieved party" with standing to raise the issue on appeal. See In re Sweetwater, 57 B.R. 354, 358 (D. Utah 1985) (secured creditor argued that disclosure statement was not adequate as result of modification of plan but, because it voted against plan, secured party was not an "aggrieved" party); In re Middle Plantation of Williamsburg, Inc., 47 B.R. 884, 891 (E.D. Va. 1984) ("Holders of impaired claims who have been induced to vote in favor of a plan are the only ones who may raise the issue of the adequacy of the Disclosure Statements."), aff'd without opinion, 755 F.2d 928 (4th Cir. 1985).

---

9. See In re Gerlinger, Inc., No. 03-39184 (Bankr. N.D. Ohio, Jan. 18, 2005), http://www.ohnb.uscourts.gov/judges/whipple.asp#UnpublishedOpinions (refusing to permit combined hearing on disclosure statement and confirmation in non-small business case).

10. Most courts do not require disclosure statements to be sent to holders of claims in unimpaired classes, because they do not vote on the plan (being deemed conclusively to have accepted it. See, e.g., In re Highway Truck Drivers & Helpers, 100 B.R. 209 (Bankr. E.D. Pa. 1989). But see In re Forrest Hills Assocs., 18 B.R. 104 (Bankr. D. Del. 1982) (noting that class might not be impaired even though plan says it is, and that holders of claims even in a truly impaired class may wish to solicit acceptances or rejections of plan and need information to do so). By analogy, if no votes are solicited postpetition, there would seem to be no need for a disclosure statement.

11. For an unusual non-small business case in which the court approved the disclosure statement and confirmed the plan at such a combined hearing, see In re Advanced Tissue Sciences, Inc., 02-09988 (Bankr. S.D. Cal, Mar. 20, 2003), http://advancedtissue.com/pdf/Final%20Order%20on%20Confirmation.pdf.

TC's counsel: TC does have standing. TC is bound by the acceptance of the class of which TC is a member. TC is entitled to have the members of that class cast informed votes if TC is to be bound by their votes. Otherwise, the plan might be accepted by TC's class even though it is not actually in the economic interests of the class members. TC was "aggrieved." See Everett v. Perez (In re Perez), 30 F.3d 1209 (9th Cir. 1994) (holding that creditor who voted against plan had standing because misinformation in disclosure statement deprived creditor of correct information which it could have used to try to convince other creditors to reject plan); In re Adana Mortg. Bankers Inc., 14 B.R. 29 (Bankr. N.D. Ga.1981) (creditors may object to disclosure statement only as to their class).

Which argument makes the most sense? Note that the secured creditor in *Sweetwater* was the only member of its class; is it therefore distinguishable? Note that *Adana* was not a decision on appeal. Can Foam Corporation effectively distinguish *Adana* on that basis by pointing out that (1) the aggrieved person requirement is an appellate requirement (see *Sweetwater*), and (2) the bankruptcy court in *Adana* had the independent duty to determine that all the requirements for confirmation were met even if no one with standing raised an objection (see *McCall Pattern*, 120 B.R. at 284, 284 n.5)? Is *Perez* distinguishable? Consider In re PWS Holding Corp., 228 F.3d 224 (3d Cir. 2000).

Problem 13-2

You are the bankruptcy judge in the case of Foam Corporation. Thirty days ago, Foam Corporation filed a plan and disclosure statement. That was one week after Foam Corporation's exclusivity period expired under § 1121(c)(2). The hearing on the disclosure statement will be held tomorrow. You must now prepare for the hearing. The plan contains the following terms:

1) administrative expense claimants will be paid in cash and in full on the effective date;
2) the holder of the claim in Class 1 (Kick Credit's secured claim) will be paid in cash and in full on the effective date, without any post-petition interest;
3) the holders of the claims in Class 2 (all general unsecured claims other than Gruff's) will be paid 40% of their claims in cash on the effective date in full satisfaction of their claims;
4) the holder of the claim in Class 3 (Gruff's $3.2 million claim) will receive all the stock of the reorganized Foam Corporation in full satisfaction of his claim;
5) the holders of the interests in Class 4 (the common stock owned by Gruff and his sister Simmons) will receive nothing on account of their interest and the existing common stock will be canceled;
6) the prepetition priority tax claims will be paid in full with 11% interest over the six year period from the date they were assessed.

Two weeks ago, Lonnie Latex (one of Foam Corporation's trade creditors) filed a competing plan with very different terms and an accompanying disclosure statement.

Foam Corporation's disclosure statement carefully explains the arrangement Foam Corporation reached with New Finance Co., a very reputable firm. New Finance Co. will take a security interest in all of Foam Corporation's assets and lend Foam Corporation the cash needed to effectuate the plan. Lonnie objected to Foam Corporation's disclosure statement because it does not mention Lonnie's plan, because it contains very little information about the postpetition operations of Foam Corporation, because it contains no information about the prospects for Foam Corporation in the future, and because it gives the liquidation value of one of Foam Corporation's plants as $100,000. Lonnie contends the liquidation value of the plant is $200,000. The Internal Revenue Service has objected to the failure to disclose how the 11% interest rate was determined for the prepetition priority tax claims.

You have decided to take oral testimony on the value of the plant, so you do not yet know if it was undervalued. You do need, however, to think through the question of why that would matter in this case, if it would matter at all. You also want to come to tentative conclusions on the other objections before the hearing begins.

Does the possible undervaluation matter? Why or why not? What are your tentative conclusions on the other objections? Is Foam Corporation's disclosure statement required to disclose the existence of Lonnie's plan? Is there any reason why holders of Class 2 claims like Lonnie would need to know about the postpetition operations of Foam Corporation or about its prospects for the future when they will receive only immediate cash under the plan? Is the IRS entitled to receive a disclosure statement containing information that would enable a typical priority tax claimant to make an informed decision about the plan?

C. SOLICITATION OF ACCEPTANCES AND REJECTIONS OF THE PLAN

Once the disclosure statement has been distributed, but not before, supporters of the plan may solicit acceptances and opponents may solicit rejections. There are cases, however, in which it is not clear whether a communication is a solicitation. Before a plan is filed, and of course before the disclosure statement is approved and distributed, the parties need to engage in negotiation. What if, in the negotiation of a plan, a party communicates to others that he supports or opposes the terms that have been suggested? Can that be considered a solicitation of a vote, which would violate § 1125(b) and make the party subject to sanctions? Would such a result chill negotiations?

Once a plan has been filed and the disclosure statement has been distributed, the parties may solicit votes. Can they solicit votes against the plan by suggesting that an alternative, unfiled plan would be better? Does that constitute impermissible *solicitation of an acceptance of the unfiled plan* before any disclosure statement has been distributed concerning the unfiled plan? Does it constitute impermissible *solicitation of a rejection of the filed plan* because it provides information beyond the information contained in the disclosure statement? Must a solicitor who wishes to provide information beyond the information in the disclosure statement obtain court approval of his solicitation materials?

Are all communications to be controlled by the court? Is the approach of the court in In re Portland Electric Power Co., 97 F. Supp. 903 (D. Ore. 1947), proper under the Bankruptcy Code? In *Portland Electric*, a bond trustee, without court approval, mailed the bondholders a letter which criticized the plan. Applying the old Bankruptcy Act, the court nearly held the bond trustee, its officers, and its counsel in criminal contempt. The court did not hold them in contempt primarily because they assured the court that they would do nothing more to obstruct the proceedings.

Consider the following materials.

Century Glove, Inc. v. First American Bank
United States Court of Appeals, Third Circuit, 1988
860 F.2d 94

Hunter, Circuit Judge.
* * *

I.

Century Glove filed its petition seeking reorganization in bankruptcy on November 14, 1985. On August 1, 1986, Century Glove filed its reorganization plan, along with a draft of the disclosure statement to be presented along with the plan. Arguing that Century Glove's largest claimed assets are speculative lawsuits (including one against FAB [First American Bank]), FAB presented a copy of an alternative plan to the unsecured creditors' committee. FAB advised that it would seek court approval to present its plan as soon as possible. [However, the court had extended exclusivity; thus FAB could not file its plan. FAB did not obtain permission to file its plan.] The committee ultimately rejected the plan in favor of that of the debtor. On December 2, 1986, the bankruptcy court approved Century Glove's disclosure statement. A copy of the plan, the statement, and a sample ballot were then sent to Century Glove's creditors entitled to vote on the plan's acceptance.

Between December 12 and December 17, 1986, an attorney for FAB, John M. Bloxom, telephoned attorneys representing several of Century Glove's creditors. Among these creditors were Latham Four Partnerships ("Latham Four") and Bankers Trust New York Corporation ("BTNY"). Bloxom sought to find out what these creditors thought of the proposed reorganization, and to convince them to vote against the plan. He said that, while there was no other plan approved for presentation, and thus no other plan "on the table," FAB had drafted a plan and had tried to file it. The creditors' attorneys then asked for a copy of the plan, which FAB provided. The copies were marked "draft" and covering letters stated that they were submitted to the creditors for their comments. The draft did not contain certain information necessary for a proper disclosure statement, such as who would manage Century Glove after reorganization.

With a copy of its draft plan, FAB also sent to Latham Four a copy of a letter written to the unsecured creditors' committee by its counsel. In the letter, dated August 26, 1986, counsel questioned the committee's endorsement of the Century Glove plan, arguing that the lawsuits which Century Glove claims as assets are too speculative. As stated, the committee endorsed the plan anyway. Upset with this decision, one of its members sent a copy of the letter to a former officer of Century Glove. The officer then sent a copy, unsolicited, to FAB. Uncertain whether the letter was protected by an attorney-client privilege, FAB asked the committee member whether he had disclosed the letter voluntarily. He said that he had, and furnished a second copy directly to FAB. FAB attached this letter to a motion before the bankruptcy court seeking to have the committee replaced. The bankruptcy court later held the letter a privileged communication.

BTNY had made a preliminary decision on September 12, 1986, to reject Century Glove's plan. It reaffirmed this decision on December 15, when it received a copy of the plan and disclosure. Counsel for BTNY spoke with Bloxom the next day, December 16, 1986, and Bloxom mailed a letter confirming the call, but by mistake Bloxom did not send a draft of the alternate plan until December 17. On that day, counsel for BTNY prepared its ballot rejecting Century Glove's plan, and informed Bloxom of its vote.

After receiving the several rejections, Century Glove petitioned the bankruptcy court to designate, or invalidate, the votes of FAB, Latham Four and BTNY. Century Glove argued that FAB had acted in bad faith in procuring these rejections.

II.

The bankruptcy court held that FAB had violated 11 U.S.C. § 1125(b), which allows solicitation of acceptance or rejections only after an approved disclosure statement has been provided the creditor. Though a statement had been filed and provided, the bankruptcy court stated that:

> solicitations . . . must be limited by the contents of the plan, the disclosure statement, and any other court-approved solicitation material. The solicitee may not be given information outside of these approved documents.

The bankruptcy court found that FAB violated the section by providing additional materials such as copies of its draft plan.

The bankruptcy court also concluded that FAB had violated "the spirit of § 1121(b), since FAB was apparently seeking approval of a plan which was not yet filed and which it could not file . . . ."[12] This "impropriety" was "heightened" by the absence from the FAB plan of such information as "who will manage the debtor." The bankruptcy court also found "improper" the disclosure by FAB of the August 26, 1986 letter to the creditors' committee. The court found that FAB's "machinations" in procuring a second copy of the letter showed that it was "obviously wary" that the letter might be privileged.

---

12. [Note 2 in original:] The parties do not dispute that 11 U.S.C. § 1121(b), which provides the debtor the exclusive right to file a plan for a limited period of time, applied at all times relevant to this action.

The bankruptcy court held invalid Latham Four's vote. It allowed the vote of BTNY, however, finding that the creditor had proved it had not relied on FAB's statements in deciding to reject Century Glove's plan. The court declined to bar FAB from participating further in the reorganization finding such a sanction "too harsh," but instead, ordered FAB to pay for "all costs incurred by [Century Glove] in prosecuting" its motions. [The bankruptcy court did not designate FAB's vote and thus apparently allowed it to count. See 81 B.R. at 277.] The amount of these damages was not specified. Both parties appealed the decision to the district court.

In a decision dated January 5, 1988, the district court affirmed the bankruptcy court rulings allowing BTNY's vote, but reversed the designation of Latham Four and the imposition of money sanctions against FAB. * * *

III.

[*The court of appeals considered whether it had jurisdiction to review the district court's orders. The court held that the district court's decision reversing the designation of the votes was not a final order; thus it was not appealable, and the court of appeals had no jurisdiction to review it. The court held that the district court's reversal of the imposition of money sanctions against FAB was an appealable final order.*]

IV.

* * * There is no question that, at the time of FAB's solicitations, the solicitees had received a summary of the plan and a court-approved statement disclosing adequate information. Also, the bankruptcy court's factual conclusion that FAB was seeking rejections of Century Glove's plan is not clearly erroneous, and so must be assumed. Century Glove argues that FAB also was required to get court approval before it could disclose additional materials in seeking rejections.

Century Glove's interpretation of the section cannot stand. Century Glove argues and the bankruptcy court assumed, that only approved statements may be communicated to creditors. The statute, however, never limits the facts which a creditor may receive, but only the *time* when a creditor may be solicited. Congress was concerned not that creditors' votes were based on misinformation, but that they were based on no information at all. See H. R. Rep. No. 595 at 225-25 (1977) (House Report). Rather than limiting the information available to a creditor, § 1125 seeks to guarantee a minimum amount of information to the creditor asked for its vote. See S. Rep. No. 989 at 121 (1978) ("A plan is necessarily predicated on knowledge of the assets and liabilities being dealt with and on factually supported expectations as to the future course of the business....") (Senate Report). The provision sets a floor, not a ceiling. Thus, we find that § 1125 does not on its face empower the bankruptcy court to require that all communications between creditors be approved by the court.

As the district court pointed out, allowing a bankruptcy court to regulate communications between creditors conflicts with the language of the statute. A creditor may receive information from sources other than the disclosure statement. Section 1125 itself defines "typical investor" of a particular class in part, as one having "such ability to obtain such information from sources other than the disclosure required by this section...." 11 U.S.C. § 1125(a)(2)(C). In enacting the bankruptcy code, Congress contemplated that the creditors would be in active negotiations with the debtor over the plan. See infra, part V. The necessity of "adequate information" was intended to help creditors in their negotiations. Allowing the bankruptcy court to regulate communications between creditors under the guise of "adequate information" undercuts the very purpose of the statutory requirement.

Lastly, Century Glove's reading of § 1125 creates procedural difficulties. Century provides this court no means to distinguish predictably between mere interpretations of the approved information, and additional information requiring separate approvals. Therefore, to be safe, the creditor must seek prior court approval for every communication with another creditor (or refrain from communication), whether soliciting a rejection or an acceptance. Congress can hardly have intended such a result. It would multiply hearings, hence expense and delay, at a time when efficiency is greatly needed. We also note that, as expressed in the House Report, Congress evidently contemplated a single hearing on the adequacy of the disclosure statement. See House Report, 1978 U.S.C.C.A.A.N. at 6186.

Century Glove argues that two additional instances show that FAB violated § 1125(b). First, it claims that FAB's draft plan contained material misrepresentations, mostly omissions. Second, it claims that FAB improperly disclosed to Latham Four a letter the bankruptcy court later found privileged. The bankruptcy court found both "improper" in support of its finding under § 1125(b), and Century Glove argues that the bankruptcy court's decision can be affirmed on these grounds. The problem with the argument is that it rests on an erroneous interpretation of the law. Once adequate information has been provided a creditor, § 1125(b) does not limit communication between creditors. It is not an antifraud device. Thus, the bankruptcy court erred in holding that FAB had violated § 1125(b) by communicating with other materials. The district court therefore properly reversed the bankruptcy court on this issue.

V.

Though FAB was not limited in its solicitation of rejections § 1125 did prevent FAB from soliciting acceptances of its own plan. The bankruptcy court held that, "since FAB was apparently seeking approval of a plan which was not yet filed," FAB violated § 1125. The court also found that FAB's actions violated the spirit of § 1121, which provides the debtor with a limited, exclusive right to present a plan. Reversing, the district court held that solicitations barred by § 1125(b) include only the "specific request for an official vote," and not discussions of and negotiations over a plan leading up to its presentation. Because Bloxom explained that he was sending the draft only for discussion purposes, the district court found that the transmittal "may only be fairly characterized as part of FAB's negotiations." We exercise plenary review over the proper interpretation of the legal term "solicitation."

We agree with the district court that "solicitation" must be read narrowly. A broad reading of § 1125 can seriously inhibit free creditor negotiations. All parties agree that FAB is not barred from honestly negotiating with other creditors about its unfiled plan. "Solicitations with respect to a plan do not involve mere requests for opinions." Senate Report, 1978 U.S.C.C.A.A.N. at 5907. The purpose of negotiations between creditors is to reach a compromise over the terms of a tentative plan. The purpose of compromise is to win acceptance for the plan. We find no principled, predictable difference between negotiation and solicitation of future acceptances. We therefore reject any definition of solicitation which might cause creditors to limit their negotiations.[13]

A narrow definition of "solicitation" does not offend the language or policy of 11 U.S.C. § 1121(b). The section provides only that the debtor temporarily has the exclusive right to *file* a plan (and thus have it voted on). It does not state that the debtor has a right to have its plan *considered* exclusively.[14] A right of exclusive consideration is not warranted in the policy of the section. Congress believed that debtors often delay confirmation of a plan, while creditors want quick confirmation. Therefore, unlimited exclusivity gave a debtor "undue bargaining leverage," because it could use the threat of delay to force unfair concessions. House Report, 1978 U.S.C.C.A.A.N. at 6191. On the other hand, Congress evidently felt that creditors might not seek the plan fairest to the debtor. Therefore, Congress allowed a *limited* period of exclusivity, giving the debtor "adequate time to negotiate a settlement, without unduly delaying creditors." Id. Section 1121 allows a debtor the threat of limited delay to offset the creditors' voting power of approval. FAB did nothing to reduce Century's threat of limited delay, and so did not offend the balance of bargaining powers created by § 1121 or the "spirit" of the law.

On the contrary, Century Glove's reading of § 1121(b) would in fact give the debtor powers not contemplated by Congress. The ability of a creditor to compare the debtor's proposals against other possibilities is a powerful tool by which to judge the reasonableness of the proposals. A broad exclusivity provision, holding that only the debtor's plan may be "on the table," takes this tool from creditors. Other creditors will not have comparisons with which to judge the proposals of the debtor's plan, to the benefit of the debtor proposing a reorganization plan. The history of § 1121 gives no indication that Congress intended to benefit the debtor in this way. The legislative history counsels a narrow reading of the section, one which FAB's actions do not violate.

We recognize that § 1125(b) bars the untimely solicitation of an "acceptance or rejection," indicating that the same definition applies to both. A narrow definition might allow a debtor to send materials seeking to prepare support for the plan, "for the consideration of the creditors," without adequate information approved by the court. Though such preparatory materials may undermine the purpose of adequate disclosure, the potential harm is limited in several ways. First, a creditor still must receive adequate information before casting a final vote,

---

13. [Note 9 in original:] Barring negotiations also would provide an unwarranted boon for the debtor: creditors wholly unable to be sure that an alternative plan can be agreed are more likely to vote for the debtor's proposal rather than risk unknown delay.

14. [Note 10 in original:] The bankruptcy court, perhaps recognizing this, found only that FAB violated the section's "spirit".

giving the creditor a chance to reconsider its preliminary decision. The harm is further limited by free and open negotiations between creditors. Last, because they are not "solicitations," pre-disclosure communications may still be subject to the stricter limitations of the securities laws. 11 U.S.C. § 1125(e). Where, as here, the creditors are counselled and already have received disclosure about the debtor's business, there seems little need for additional procedural formalities.

Therefore, we hold that a party does not solicit acceptances when it presents a draft plan for the consideration of another creditor, but does not request that creditor's vote. Applying this definition, FAB did not solicit acceptances of its plan. Century Glove does not dispute that FAB never asked for a vote, and clearly stated that the plan was not yet available for approval. Bloxom communicated with lawyers for the creditors, and there is no suggestion by Century that these lawyers did not understand the limitations. Also as Century argues, FAB never sent its plan to Hartford Insurance because Hartford firmly opposed Century's plan. Contrary to Century's conclusion, though, this fact argues that FAB sent copies of its plan because it was interested in obtaining rejections, not acceptances. (An opponent of Century's plan would be an ideal person to solicit for acceptances.) These undisputed facts require a finding that FAB did not "solicit" acceptances within the meaning of § 1125(b).

VI.

We hold that the district court correctly determined that Century Glove failed to show that FAB violated 11 U.S.C. § 1125 by soliciting acceptances or improperly soliciting rejections. We therefore will affirm the district court's order reversing the imposition of costs against FAB. We do not decide, however, whether the circumstances merit designation of the votes of any creditors.

NOTES

1. Under the Third Circuit's decision, what is a "solicitation" of acceptances or rejections? Does an oral expression of "hope" that a creditor will support the plan constitute a solicitation of an acceptance? See In re Gilbert, 104 B.R. 206 (Bankr. W.D. Mo.1989). If it is permissible to send a draft of a potential plan to the creditors, is it permissible to send a draft of a disclosure statement to all of the creditors in the case? See In re Rook Broadcasting, 154 B.R. 970 (Bankr. D. Idaho 1993). What about a letter—sent two weeks before the hearing on approval of disclosure statements for competing plans—telling creditors that they should support the debtor's plan and reject the other plan? See Duff v. U.S. Trustee (In re California Fidelity, Inc.), 198 B.R. 567 (B.A.P. 9th Cir. 1996).

2. The court in In re Snyder, 51 B.R. 432, 437 (Bankr. D. Utah 1985), stated that "meaningful creditor participation in Chapter 11 cases would cease to exist" if the definition of solicitation included exchanges of information, negotiations, or tentative arrangements which might lead to the development of a plan or of a disclosure statement. In Snyder, a trustee had been appointed. The debtor's counsel sent a letter to all of the creditors; the letter asked for their input on several potential alternative plans that the debtor was considering filing and invited them to a meeting with the debtor and the debtor's counsel to try to work out a solution. The court held that the letter was not a solicitation; only an official request for a vote would be considered to be a solicitation. However, the court found that debtor's

counsel had violated the rules of professional conduct by communicating directly with creditors who, debtor's counsel knew, were represented by lawyers. Such communications would only be permissible with the consent of the creditors' lawyers. The court also stated that neither the debtor's counsel nor the debtor were permitted to communicate with members of the creditors' committee except through the committee's counsel, without first obtaining permission from the committee's counsel for such communications. The court stated that disclosure statements and ballots could be sent directly to persons represented by counsel without violating the rules of professional conduct, because such communications were expressly authorized by the Bankruptcy Code.

3. The Third Circuit's opinion in *Century Glove* has been very influential, but many bankruptcy courts continue to impose restrictions on negotiation and solicitation that seem inconsistent with *Century Glove*. Even courts that seem to embrace *Century Glove* often retain such restrictions. One court attempted to synthesize the case law in the wake of *Century Glove*, noting that *Century Glove* is the key case, but reaching a conclusion contrary to a key component of *Century Glove*:

> Synthesizing the above case law, the current state of the law regarding § 1125(b) and solicitation of creditors after the court has approved the debtor's disclosure statement may be stated as follows. The ultimate objective in the balloting process is to ensure that the voting creditors receive "adequate information". Thus, creditors may engage in "free and open negotiations". Furthermore, debtors may distribute information not contained in the approved disclosure statement at their peril, as § 1125 contains no express provision which requires bankruptcy courts to become filters for all material used in solicitation of creditor votes. Thus, this Court holds that a party need not receive prior court approval of all material used to solicit another creditor's acceptance or rejection of the debtor's plan.

> This Court does not mean to imply from the above holding, however, that a party's post-disclosure statement solicitation efforts should go completely unchecked. That is, assuming that the debtor's exclusivity period has expired, soliciting parties need not obtain prior court approval of solicited materials only if: 1) the information provided is truthful and absent of any false or misleading statements or legal or factual mischaracterizations; 2) the information is presented in good faith; 3) the soliciting party *does not propose or suggest an alternative plan* which has yet to gain court approval or otherwise failed to travel through the appropriate legal channels, as dictated by the Bankruptcy Code. This Court believes that the third point has been the most problematic for courts and creditors alike, and therefore exhibits the greatest need for further clarification.

> The overriding goal in the voting phase of a confirmation process is to provide the holders and interests with as much relevant and meaningful information as possible. In furtherance of this goal, Chemical or other claim holders may solicit acceptances or rejections of the Debtor's Plan. However, this Court shall not allow a party to circumvent the system established by the Bankruptcy Code by proposing or suggesting an alternative plan which has neither gained court approval nor been subject to adequate disclosure. Since a party may ask what are the parameters of such solicitation, the following checklist may prove helpful:

A soliciting party may without prior court approval—

1) offer a narrative, evidence, conclusions, or opinions contrary to that enunciated in the plan or disclosure statement;

2) assert positions, evidence, conclusions, or opinions of relevant matters which are not contained in the plan or court-approved disclosure statement;

3) offer evidence or opinions of an alternative liquidation analysis, since the debtors have a liquidation analysis as part of their disclosure statement.

In sum, a soliciting party may react to and present contrary views regarding the court-approved disclosure statement, but *may not present or suggest an alternative plan which has not been subject to court scrutiny regarding adequacy of disclosure.*

In re Apex Oil Co., 111 B.R. 245, 249-50 (Bankr. E.D. Mo.1990) (emphasis added). Citing *Apex Oil*, a district court called *Century Glove* "the high-water mark for parties seeking to solicit rejections of another's plan by comparing it to an unfiled plan of their own." Colo. Mountain Express, Inc. v. Aspen Limousine Serv., Inc. (In re Aspen Limousine Serv., Inc.), 198 B.R. 341, 348 (D. Colo. 1996) (affirming order imposing sanctions on creditor who circulated a draft plan to induce other creditors to vote against the debtor's plan, and attempting to distinguish *Century Glove*, but coming close to limiting it to its facts). Not all courts will allow solicitors to contradict the disclosure statement. See In re Kellogg Square Partnership, 160 B.R. 336, 341 (Bankr. D. Minn.1993) ("[S]o long as such extrajudicial material and solicitation does not contradict the court-approved disclosure statement, or contain mischaracterizations or misstatements of material fact that might unfairly influence solicitees, a plan proponent or third party may transmit additional materials to creditors and other interested parties to induce their votes.").

4.   "A majority of courts have now adopted the narrow reading of "solicitation" proffered by *Century Glove*. See * * * In re Dow Corning Corp., 227 B.R. 111, 118 (Bankr. E.D. Mich. 1998) ('Solicitation, then, is the process of seeking votes for or against a plan.'); * * *.

"Other courts, however, have criticized such a narrow definition of 'solicitation' when a creditor's communication includes information not raised by an approved disclosure statement. * * *

"In reviewing the legislative history of § 1121, the Third Circuit, in *Century Glove*, seemed to focus solely on Congress' intention to limit a debtor's exclusivity period to prevent unreasonable delays in formulating a reorganization plan. * * * Employing its interpretation of legislative history, the court held that a plan opponent's submission of an unapproved disclosure statement and reorganization plan to a creditor did not reduce the debtor's threat of limited delay, and, therefore, did not violate the terms of § 1121.

"This Court believes that the *Century Glove* analysis fails to sufficiently recognize Congress' intention to allow the debtor a reasonable time to obtain confirmation of a plan without the threat of a competing plan. Therefore, whether a creditor's action during the exclusivity period violates § 1121(b) must be evaluated not only in terms of its effect on the ability of a debtor to delay reorganization, but also in terms of its interference with the debtor's efforts to propose and confirm a plan of reorganization. See Barbara E. Nelan, *Multiple Plans 'On The Table' During the Chapter 11 Exclusivity Period*, 6 BANKR. DEV.

J. 451, 476 (Fall, 1989); see also *Temple Retirement*, 80 B.R. at 369 (When a party in interest proposes an unapproved draft plan to other creditors, it is in effect 'solicit[ing] rejections by dangling an alternative plan before other creditors, suggesting in essence that, if the debtor's plan were scuttled, then a better alternative could then be proposed.').

"Based on Congress' policy goals as expressed in the Code's legislative history, this Court concludes that § 1121 provides the debtor with the exclusive right to propose a plan during its exclusivity period."

In re Clamp-All Corp., 233 B.R. 198, 205-08 (Bankr. D. Mass. 1999).

5. Some courts have permitted debtors in possession to enter into agreements with creditors that limit the creditors' voting discretion even before a disclosure statement has been approved and disseminated. See, e.g., In re Bush Indus., Inc., 315 B.R. 292 (Bankr. N.D.N.Y. 2004); In re Kellogg Square Partnership, 160 B.R. 336 (Bankr. D. Minn.1993) (holding that contract which called for creditor to cast ballot in favor of debtor's plan did not amount to solicitation because creditor could rescind the contract and reject the plan if the court-approved disclosure statement turned out to include material information not previously provided to the creditor; thus solicitation would not occur until transmission of disclosure statement and ballot to creditor); Trans World Airlines v. Texaco Inc. (In re Texaco Inc.), 81 B.R. 813, 815-16 (Bankr. S.D.N.Y. 1988) (holding that settlement agreement between Texaco and Pennzoil—the holder of a multi-billion dollar judgment against Texaco—did not violate § 1125(b) even though it required Texaco and Pennzoil to use best efforts to confirm plan which would pay $3 billion to Pennzoil and required Pennzoil not to "vote for, consent to, support or participate in the formulation of any other plan").

6. Courts sometimes permit plan opponents to include their views and the factual support for those views in the disclosure statement. See, e.g., Kirk v. Texaco Inc., 82 B.R. 678, 680-81 (S.D.N.Y. 1988). Courts sometimes permit plan opponents to include a separate letter in the disclosure statement and ballot package that is sent to creditors and interest holders. See, e.g., Central Transport, Inc. v. Roberto (In re Tucker Freight Lines), 62 B.R. 213, 216 n.1 (Bankr. W.D. Mich.1986). If the court does not expressly authorize the solicitation of a rejection in one of these ways, must a plan opponent obtain court approval of its own disclosure statement before soliciting rejections?

A nonbankruptcy analogy suggests that the plan opponent must do so, but the analogy does not hold. The securities laws generally require each group that solicits proxies in a proxy contest to have its own proxy statement. For example, if there is a proxy contest over a management proposal to merge the corporation with another corporation, there will be a management proxy statement used in connection with soliciting proxies in favor of the merger and an opponents' proxy statement used in connection with soliciting proxies against the merger.

The § 1125 disclosure statement is a substitute for the proxy statement, so, by analogy, must each group that solicits acceptances or rejections in a chapter 11 case have its own disclosure statement? On the contrary, § 1125 does not appear to contemplate more than one disclosure statement per proposed plan (at least in the ordinary case), and it appears to allow solicitation of acceptances and rejections of the plan after approval and dissemination of one disclosure statement. The analogy to proxy statements does not hold. As the court of appeals in *Century Glove* held, once one disclosure statement has been approved and disseminated, solicitation of acceptances *and* rejections is proper. See Glassman, *Solicitation of Plan Rejections Under the Bankruptcy Code*, 62 AM. BANKR. L.J. 261 (1988).

7. What risks are taken by a party who does not obtain court approval of a communication that is a solicitation? If the communication is misleading, some courts have enjoined the party from sending further unauthorized communications or required the party to pay for the sending of corrective materials. See In re Snyder, 51 B.R. 432, 437 n.8 (Bankr. D. Utah 1985); contra Transworld Airlines, Inc. v. Texaco Inc. (In re Texaco Inc.), 81 B.R. 813 (Bankr. S.D.N.Y. 1988) (exclusive relief afforded under Code is to have improperly solicited acceptances or rejections disregarded under § 1126(e)). Under the Third Circuit's approach in *Century Glove*, use of false or misleading communications does not violate § 1125(b), because § 1125(b) "is not an antifraud device." 860 F.2d at 101.

Liability for fraud, for securities law violations, or on other theories is, however, a possibility. Section 1125(e) provides a safe harbor defense for persons who solicit acceptances or rejections "in good faith and in compliance with the applicable provisions of" the Bankruptcy Code. However, the contours of the safe harbor defense are somewhat disputed, and there is little case authority construing it. See Jacobson v. AEG Capital Corp., 50 F.3d 1493 (9th Cir. 1995) (refusing to hold that § 1125(e) safe harbor protects plan proponent accused of violating Rule 10b-5 under forced sale doctrine by freezing out shareholders of debtor, but holding that forced sale doctrine is incompatible with law governing chapter 11 process); Kaufman v. Pub. Serv. Co. of N.H. (In re Pub. Serv. Co. of N.H.), 43 F.3d 763 (1st Cir. 1995) (questioning whether bankruptcy court finding of good faith could be given collateral estoppel effect in later securities fraud suit so as to bring parties within § 1125(e) safe harbor, but holding that bankruptcy court could enjoin collateral attack on disclosure statement in order to protect its judgment, at least in absence of evidence of secret fraud).

A key issue is whether § 1125(e) protects a person who in good faith solicits acceptances or rejections using information beyond what is contained in the court-approved disclosure statement. Consider the following legislative history to § 1125(e):

> The purpose of the provision is to protect creditors, creditors' committees, counsel for committees, and others involved in the case from potential liability under the securities laws for soliciting acceptances of a plan *by use of an approved disclosure statement.*
>
> * * * If a creditor or creditors' committee relies on an order of a Federal bankruptcy court that the disclosure statement contains adequate information, that is, states all material facts that should be stated under the circumstances, and meets any other applicable requirement of chapter 11, then that creditor or committee should not be held liable for soliciting acceptances based on a securities law theory that he failed to disclose adequately. Such liability would gut the effectiveness of the disclosure section, and require compliance with all securities laws in spite of the pendency of the reorganization case. As noted above, this would render the reorganization chapter far less valuable to distressed debtors than it would otherwise be.

H. R. Rep. No. 595, 95th Cong., 1st Sess., 229-30 (1977) (emphasis added). See Yell Forestry Products v. First State Bank, 853 F.2d 582 (8th Cir. 1988) (stating that the purpose of § 1125(e) is to protect creditors and others from potential liability under the security laws, when they solicit acceptance of a plan through the use of an approved disclosure statement); Cent. Transp., Inc. v. Roberto (In re Tucker Freight Lines, Inc.), 62 B.R. 213, 216 n.2 (Bankr. W.D. Mich., 1986) (noting that if the solicitation letter that allegedly contained false statements "were found to be an unauthorized disclosure statement then that might * * * be grounds for denial of the §1125(e) 'safe haven' of securities law immunity."). The SEC appears to read § 1125(e) narrowly to protect against liability "for any omission or misstatement *in the disclosure statement* if the solicitation was made in good faith. This leaves in effect the civil and criminal penalties of the federal securities laws for inadequacies that are beyond the limits of the 'safe harbor' provisions of Section 1125(e)." Puritan-Bennett Corp., SEC No-Action Letter, 1983 WL 28913 (Dec. 23, 1983) (emphasis added).

The language of § 1125(e) does not contain any limitation of its protection to those who merely use the disclosure statement in soliciting votes. There may not be sufficient ambiguity in the statute to permit reliance upon the legislative history to limit the scope of the protection. The SEC has no charter to construe the bankruptcy laws, so its view should not be entitled to deference. *Yell Forestry Products* involved a claim that material information was omitted from the disclosure statement, not a claim that false or misleading information beyond that in the disclosure statement was used. Statements in *Yell Forestry Products* and *Tucker Freight* on this issue are dicta.

8.   As noted above on pages 759-61, the debtor can solicit acceptances of a chapter 11 plan even before filing the chapter 11 petition. Section 1126(b) permits the use in a chapter 11 case of acceptances or rejections solicited before the bankruptcy petition is filed. Section 1125(b) does not prevent this; it requires that a court approved disclosure statement be disseminated before solicitation only if the solicitation occurs *after* the filing of the petition and only if § 1125(g) does not apply. Section 1125(g) permits continued postpetition solicitation without approval and distribution of a disclosure statement where the solicitees were solicited prepetition under § 1126(b) in compliance with "applicable nonbankruptcy law."

To obtain the prepetition acceptances, the debtor will need to negotiate with the creditors. Successful negotiations may eliminate the need for a chapter 11 filing; an out of court workout may be accomplished. If a chapter 11 filing is still needed,[15] the debtor can use the acceptances[16] (if enough have been obtained) to quickly confirm a chapter 11 plan without the need for further solicitations. This is called a prepackaged plan.

If the debtor chooses not to solicit acceptances prepetition—or not to solicit all the needed acceptances prepetition—it stil can be beneficial for the debtor to negotiate with creditors before filing. A chapter 11 filing may be avoided. If a chapter 11 filing is needed, the "prenegotiation" of plan terms will speed the process of confirming a plan.

---

15.   A chapter 11 filing may be needed for several reasons. There may be too much dissent for an out of court workout to succeed. The debtor may need to use the avoiding powers available in bankruptcy. The debtor may need to use § 365 to deal with executory contracts and leases. Chapter 11 may provide important tax benefits.

16.   Out of court workout acceptance forms often provide that the acceptance can be used as acceptance of a chapter 11 plan containing the same terms as the proposed workout agreement. Thus, if most but not all creditors agree to the workout, the debtor has the option of filing a chapter 11 petition and using the acceptances.

Whether the plan is prepackaged or prenegotiated, the length of time that the debtor spends in chapter 11 before confirmation may be shortened. The result may be lower administrative expenses and less damage to the debtor's reputation and business.

Often the debtor will want to negotiate the terms of a reorganization privately with the institutional lenders or other important creditors. Then, when the debtor announces to the rest of the creditors (and thus to the world) that a reorganization is necessary, that negative news can be balanced with the positive news that the terms of a reorganization have been worked out with the institutional lenders. If the other creditors then fall in line, a chapter 11 filing may not be needed. Even if one is needed, most of the debtor's creditors and customers will retain some confidence in the debtor's ability to reorganize. In such a case, the debtor has the option of asking the institutional creditors to give prepetition acceptances of the plan, which then can be used if a chapter 11 filing is needed. Of course the debtor would like to "nail down" the acceptances of the institutional lenders before filing the petition, if they will give their acceptances.

This sort of nailing down of the institutional lenders was effectively prohibited by Rule 3018(b) until its amendment in 1991. Section 1126(b) and Rule 3018(b) provide limitations on the use of acceptances and rejections solicited before the filing of the petition. If there is "applicable law" outside of bankruptcy governing disclosure to the creditors and interest holders, then the solicitor must have complied with it for the acceptances or rejections to be usable in chapter 11. Section 1126(b). The applicable law with regard to solicitation of bondholders and stockholders will often be section 14(a) of the 1934 Act and SEC Rule 14a-3, which require the delivery of very expensive, full-blown proxy statements. If there is no such applicable law, then the solicitor must have disclosed "adequate information" to the solicitees before soliciting their votes. Section 1126(b). With regard to institutional lenders, there often will be no "applicable law," and the required disclosure may be minimal due to the ability of the lenders to obtain information on their own. See § 1125(a)(2)(C).

The prior version of Rule 3018(b) effectively prevented prepetition solicitation of the institutional lenders by requiring solicitation of the stockholders and bondholders as well. It prohibited use of prepetition acceptances or rejections unless a copy of the plan was sent to *all or substantially all* the creditors and equity security holders who held claims in impaired classes. That required a breaching of the privacy in which debtors would prefer to negotiate with their institutional lenders. It also often required the creation of a full-blown proxy statement to be delivered along with the plan to bondholders and stockholders (assuming the sending of the plan would constitute a solicitation of them). The 1991 amendment to Rule 3018(b) adopts a class by class approach—acceptances or rejections obtained from holders of claims or equity securities *in a class* will not be usable in the chapter 11 unless the plan was transmitted to substantially all holders of claims or equity securities *in that class*. As long as the plan can permissibly classify the claims of the institutional creditors apart from the claims of other creditors, this will permit private prepetition solicitation of the institutional lenders.

For an interesting discussion of the difficulties involved in using prepetition acceptances in chapter 11, see In re Southland Corp., 124 B.R. 211 (Bankr. N.D. Tex.1991); Southland Corp. is the parent company of the Seven-Eleven convenience store chain. The court in *Southland* refused to permit use of prepetition acceptances by Southland's stockholders; the court held that prepetition acceptances by equity security holders must be made by the beneficial owners of the securities to be effective, rather than by the brokerages which had accepted for the stockholders (presumably on their instructions). Many stockholders have their stock held by brokerage houses in the brokerages' names; it is not clear that the debtor who wishes to solicit prepetition acceptances from its shareholders will be able to force the brokerages to reveal the identity of the stockholders and their holdings so that the debtor will know who to solicit and whose acceptances are needed. The holding in *Southland* thus makes the 1991 amendment of Rule 3018(b) even more important. Interestingly, although the court in *Southland* refused to permit use of the prepetition acceptances, a resolicitation resulted in confirmation of the plan with only an 18 day delay.

The record for speed in a prepackaged chapter 11 case now seems to be held by the Blue Bird Body Company, a bus manufacturer. See footnote 16 in Chapter One above. For an example of a prenegotiated chapter 11 case, and a description of the difference between prepackaged and prenegotiated cases, see United Artists Theatre Co. v. Walton, 315 F.3d 217, 224 n.5 (3d Cir. 2003).

Problem 13-3

It is now 110 days after Foam Corporation filed it chapter 11 petition. Negotiation of a plan of reorganization for Foam Corporation is nearly complete. After a few more details are ironed out, it appears that Foam Corporation will be able to file a plan which will be supported by Kick Credit and by the unsecured creditors' committee. Lonnie Latex opposes the plan that is being worked out and has drafted his own proposed plan. Yesterday, Lonnie sent his unfiled plan to all the major creditors with the following note:

> *I urge you not to support the debtors' plan. Instead I urge you to support the plan that is attached. The debtor's plan is not feasible, but my plan is. Let the members of your creditors' committee know what you think!*

Has Lonnie violated § 1125(b)?

D. VOTING ON THE PLAN

We have already considered several aspects of voting on the plan.[17] The mechanics of voting and some issues regarding protection of the right to vote still remain for discussion. The mechanics of voting are simple. When the disclosure statement is distributed, creditors and interest holders are sent a ballot and notice of the deadline for filing acceptances and rejections. Rule 3017(d). Appendix B near the end of this text contains an example of a form of ballot.

Protection of the right to vote is not so simple. Chapter 11 takes away the creditor's individual right to refuse to agree to a workout. Chapter 11 gives the creditor a lesser substitute: the right to vote on the plan. That lesser substitute should be carefully protected. Important questions concerning protection of the right to vote include: (1) When is a creditor entitled to change its vote? (2) When may the bankruptcy court "designate" votes so that they will not be counted?

Votes can be designated under § 1126(e) if they were "not solicited or procured in good faith or in accordance with the provisions of" the Bankruptcy Code. We discussed that basis for designation above, in connection with the Third Circuit's opinion in *Century Glove*. Here we are concerned with the other basis in § 1126(e) for designating acceptances or rejections: where the "acceptance or rejection of such plan was not in good faith." Recall that we considered in Chapter Ten above the circumstances under which the votes of a purchaser of claims should be designated. Here we consider the general issue of when a vote should be considered not to be cast in good faith and therefore should be designated.

---

17. In Chapter Nine we discussed the estimation and allowance of disputed claims for purposes of voting. In Chapter Ten we discussed "trading in claims" and whether a creditor who buys another claim will then have two claims to vote or only one. In Chapter Eleven we explored the concept of impairment and noted that only holders of claims or interests in impaired classes are entitled to vote. Also in Chapter Eleven, we discussed the creation of classes, and the limits on "gerrymandering" the classes. As we noted, classification is important because (1) the creditors and interest holders vote by class, (2) the plan proponent would like to create classes in such a way that the necessary majorities of holders of claims and interests in each class will accept the plan, so that the plan can be confirmed consensually under § 1129(a), but (3) the plan proponent must create at least one impaired class of claims the holders of which will accept the plan (not counting acceptances by insiders). We saw that a class of interests accepts the plan if it is accepted by interest holders holding two thirds in amount of the interests in the class that are voted. We saw that a class of claims accepts the plan if the plan is accepted by creditors holding two thirds in amount and more than half in number of the claims in the class that are voted. (The reasons for these majority and supermajority requirements are discussed in the introduction to this chapter.)

Figter Ltd. v. Teachers Ins. and Annuity Ass'n of America
(In re Figter Ltd.)
United States Court of Appeals, Ninth Circuit, 1997
118 F.3d 635

FERNANDEZ, Circuit Judge.

Figter Limited, a Chapter 11 debtor and owner of Skyline Terrace, an apartment complex, appeals from the district court's affirmance of the bankruptcy court's decision that Teachers Insurance and Annuity Association of America (Teachers), the holder of a $15,600,000 promissory note secured by a first deed of trust on Skyline Terrace, bought twenty-one unsecured claims in good faith and that it could vote each one separately. We affirm.

BACKGROUND

Figter filed a voluntary petition under Chapter 11 of the Bankruptcy Code. It owns Skyline Terrace, a 198-unit residential apartment complex located in Los Angeles. Teachers is a creditor. It holds a $15,600,000 promissory note executed by Figter. The note is secured by a first deed of trust on Skyline Terrace and by $1,400,000 of cash on hand. In fact, Teachers is Figter's only secured creditor and is the only member of Class 2 in a reorganization plan proposed by Figter. The plan contemplates full payment of Teachers' secured claim, but at a disputed rate of interest. Thus, under Figter's plan, Teachers' claim is not impaired.[18] The plan calls for the impairment of Class 3 unsecured claims by payment at only 80% of their face value.

Teachers has opposed Figter's reorganization plan from its inception because, among other things, that plan contemplates the conversion of Skyline Terrace Apartments into condominiums, with payment to and partial releases by Teachers as the units sell. That could easily result in a property that was part condominium and part rentals, if the plan ultimately fails in operation.

Teachers proposed a plan of its own, which provided for the transfer of Skyline Terrace and the cash collateral to Teachers in satisfaction of its secured claim, as well as a payment of Class 3 unsecured claims at 90%. Teachers' plan was premised on the assumption that its claim was partly unsecured. However, on May 31, 1994, before the purchases of other claims took place, the bankruptcy court determined that Skyline Terrace had a value of $19,300,000. Thus, Teachers' claim in the amount of $17,960,000 was fully secured. It did not thereafter pursue its plan. From October 27, 1994 until October 31, 1994, Teachers purchased twenty-one of the thirty-four unsecured claims in Class 3 at one hundred cents on the dollar, for a total purchase price of $14,588.62. Teachers had made the same offer to all of the Class 3 claim holders, but not all accepted it. The offer remained open. Teachers then filed notices of transfer of claims with the court, as is required under Bankruptcy Rule 3001(e)(2). Those notices were served on all affected parties, including Figter. No objections were filed by the unsecured creditors. The district court upheld the bankruptcy court's determination regarding Teachers' purchase of the unsecured claims. As a result, Figter's plan is unconfirmable because it is unable to meet the requirements of 11

---

18. [This is a slip of the Court's pen. Teachers' Class 2 is impaired. As the Court notes below, Figter is attempting to alter Teachers' rights considerably and to cram the plan down on Teachers.– Ed.]

U.S.C. § 1129(a)(10); there will not be an impaired, consenting class of claims. That will preclude a "cram down" of Teachers' secured claim under 11 U.S.C. § 1129(b). Figter has appealed in an attempt to avoid that result. * * *

Figter asserts that Teachers should be precluded from voting its purchased Class 3 claims because it did not buy them in good faith. Figter also asserts that even if the claims were purchased in good faith, Teachers cannot vote them separately, but is limited to one total vote as a Class 3 creditor. * * *

The Bankruptcy Code provides that "[o]n request of a party in interest, and after notice and a hearing, the court may designate any entity whose acceptance or rejection of [a] plan was not in good faith, or was not solicited or procured in good faith or in accordance with the provisions of this title." 11 U.S.C. § 1126(e). In this context, designate means disqualify from voting. The Bankruptcy Code does not further define the rather murky term "good faith." That job has been left to the courts.

The Supreme Court brought some clarity to this area when it decided Young v. Higbee Co., 324 U.S. 204, 65 S. Ct. 594, 89 L. Ed. 890 (1945). In *Young*, the Court was discussing the predecessor to § 1126(e) when it declared that if certain persons "had declined to accept [the] plan in bad faith, the court, under section 203 could have denied them the right to vote on the plan at all." Id. at 210-11, 65 S. Ct. at 598 (footnote omitted). It went on to explain that the provision was intended to apply to those "whose selfish purpose was to obstruct a fair and feasible reorganization in the hope that someone would pay them more than the ratable equivalent of their proportionate part of the bankrupt assets." Id. at 211, 65 S. Ct. at 598. In other words, the section was intended to apply to those who were not attempting to protect their own proper interests, but who were, instead, attempting to obtain some benefit to which they were not entitled. * * *

If a person seeks to secure some untoward advantage over other creditors for some ulterior motive, that will indicate bad faith. See In re Marin Town Ctr., 142 B.R. 374, 378-79 (N.D. Cal. 1992). But that does not mean that creditors are expected to approach reorganization plan votes with a high degree of altruism and with the desire to help the debtor and their fellow creditors. Far from it.

> If a selfish motive were sufficient to condemn reorganization policies of interested parties, very few, if any, would pass muster. On the other hand, pure malice, "strikes" and blackmail, and the purpose to destroy an enterprise in order to advance the interests of a competing business, all plainly constituting bad faith, are motives which may be accurately described as ulterior.

In re Pine Hill Collieries Co., 46 F. Supp. 669, 671 (E.D. Pa. 1942). That is to say, we do not condemn mere enlightened self interest, even if it appears selfish to those who do not benefit from it.

Thus, if Teachers acted out of enlightened self interest, it is not to be condemned simply because it frustrated Figter's desires. That is true, even if Teachers purchased Class 3 claims for the very purpose of blocking confirmation of Figter's proposed plan. See 255 Park Plaza Assocs. Ltd. Partnership v. Connecticut General Life Ins. Co. (In re 255 Park Plaza Assocs. Ltd. Partnership), 100 F.3d 1214, 1218-19 (6th Cir. 1996). That self interest can extend even further without being an ulterior motive. It has been held that a creditor commits no wrong when he votes against a plan of a debtor who has a lawsuit pending against the creditor, for that will not, by itself, show bad faith. See Federal Support Co., 859 F.2d at 20; * * *. It has also been held that no bad faith is shown when a creditor chooses to benefit his interest as a creditor as opposed to some unrelated interest. See In re Landing Assocs., Ltd., 157 B.R. 791, 803 (Bankr. W.D. Tex. 1993); In re Peter Thompson Assocs., Inc., 155 B.R. 20, 22 (Bankr. D.N.H. 1993). And the mere fact that a creditor has purchased additional claims for the purpose of protecting his own existing claim does not demonstrate bad faith or an ulterior motive. "As long as a creditor acts to preserve what he reasonably perceives as his fair share of the debtor's estate, bad faith will not be attributed to his purchase of claims to control a class vote." In re Gilbert, 104 B.R. 206, 217 (Bankr. W.D. Mo. 1989).

Courts, on the other hand, have been sensitive to situations where a company, which was not a preexisting creditor, has purchased a claim for the purpose of blocking an action against it. They have seen that as an indication of bad faith. See In re Keyworth, 47 B.R. 966, 971-72 (D. Colo. 1985). The same has been true where creditors were associated with a competing business and desired to destroy the debtor's business in order to further their own. See In re MacLeod Co., Inc., 63 B.R. 654, 655 (Bankr. S.D. Ohio 1986); see also In re Allegheny Int'l, Inc., 118 B.R. 282, 289 (Bankr. W.D. Pa. 1990). And when the debtor had claims against itself purchased by an insider or affiliate for the purpose of blocking a plan, or fostering one, that was seen as a badge of bad faith. See In re Holly Knoll Partnership, 167 B.R. 381, 389 (Bankr. E.D. Pa. 1994) (fostering); In re Applegate Property, Ltd., 133 B.R. 827, 834-35 (Bankr. W.D. Tex. 1991) (blocking). Figter would have us add that in a single asset bankruptcy, claim purchasing activities, like those of Teachers, are in bad faith. It cites no authority for that, and we see no basis for establishing that as a per se rule.

In short, the concept of good faith is a fluid one, and no single factor can be said to inexorably demand an ultimate result, nor must a single set of factors be considered. It is always necessary to keep in mind the difference between a creditor's self interest as a creditor and a motive which is ulterior to the purpose of protecting a creditor's interest. Prior cases can offer guidance, but, when all is said and done, the bankruptcy court must simply approach each good faith determination with a perspicacity derived from the data of its informed practical experience in dealing with bankrupts and their creditors.

Here, the bankruptcy court did exactly that. It decided that Teachers was not, for practical purposes, the proponent of an alternate plan when it sought to purchase the Class 3 claims. Nor, it found, did Teachers seek to purchase a small number of claims for the purpose of blocking Figter's plan, while injuring other creditors, even if it could do that in some circumstances. Rather, Teachers offered to purchase all Class 3 claims, and only some of those claimants' refusals to sell precluded it from doing so. Moreover, Teachers was a lender, not a competing apartment owner. It acted to protect its interests as Figter's major creditor. It reasonably feared that it could be left with a very complex lien situation, if Figter went forward with its plan. Instead of holding a lien covering the whole of the property, it could have wound up with separate fractured liens on various parts of the property, while other parts were owned by others. That could create a very undesirable mix of owners and renters and of debtors and nondebtors. Added to that was the actual use of cash, which was collateral for the debt owed to Teachers. It cannot be said that Teachers' concerns were irrational.

Based on all that was before it, the bankruptcy court decided that in this case Teachers was a creditor which acted in a good faith attempt to protect its interests and not with some ulterior motive. We cannot say that it erred in making that ultimate determination.

Figter's fallback position is that even if Teachers did act in good faith, it must be limited to one vote for its twenty-one claims. That assertion is answered by the language of the Bankruptcy Code, which provides that:

> A class of claims has accepted a plan if such plan has been accepted by creditors ... that hold at least two-thirds in amount and more than one-half in number of the allowed claims of such class held by creditors ... that have accepted or rejected such plan.

11 U.S.C. § 1126(c) (emphasis added). That language was interpreted in Gilbert, 104 B.R. at 211, where the court reasoned:

> The formula contained in Section 1126(c) speaks in terms of the number of claims, not the number of creditors, that actually vote for or against the plan.... Each claim arose out of a separate transaction, evidencing separate obligations for which separate proofs of claim were filed. Votes of acceptance ... are to be computed only on the basis of filed and allowed proofs of claim.... [The creditor] is entitled to one vote for each of his unsecured Class X claims.

* * * We agree. It would not make much sense to require a vote by creditors who held "more than one-half in number of the allowed claims" while at the same time limiting a creditor who held two or more of those claims to only one vote. If allowed claims are to be counted, they must be counted regardless of whose hands they happen to be in.

Figter seeks some succor from the Supreme Court's indication in Dewsnup v. Timm, 502 U.S. 410, 419-20, 112 S. Ct. 773, 779, 116 L. Ed. 2d 903 (1992), that ambiguous language in the Code should not be taken to effect a sea change in pre-Code practice. However, that does not help Figter's cause. In the first place, as we have indicated, the present language is not ambiguous. In the second place, the old law to which Figter refers relied upon a code section which required voting approval by a "majority in number of all creditors whose claims have been allowed." Bankruptcy Act of 1898, ch. 541, § 12, 30 Stat. 544, 549-50 (repealed 1938). It is pellucid that "a majority in number of all creditors" is not at all like "more than one-half in number" of all claims. The former focuses on claimants; the latter on claims. * * *

Of course, that is not to say that a creditor can get away with splitting one claim into many, but that is not what happened here. Teachers purchased a number of separately incurred and separately approved claims (each of which carried one vote) from different creditors. There simply is no reason to hold that those separate votes suddenly became one vote, a result which would be exactly the opposite of claim splitting. * * *

AFFIRMED.

In re Featherworks Corporation
United States Bankruptcy Court, E.D.N.Y., 1982
25 B.R. 634, affirmed 36 B.R. 460 (E.D.N.Y. 1984)

Cecelia H. Goetz, Bankruptcy Judge.

[*Arthur Puro's wife and daughter owned Windsor Trading Corporation ("Windsor"), which owned Puro International, Ltd., which owned Hudson Feather & Down Products, Inc. ("Hudson"), which owned the debtor, Featherworks Corporation ("Featherworks"). Arthur was the president and chief executive officer of Windsor and Hudson and controlled Featherworks, which was in the business of buying, selling, and processing feathers and down. Far West Garments, Inc. ("Far West") obtained a $387,000 judgment against Featherworks for breach of warranty. Featherworks filed its chapter 11 petition five days before the scheduled execution sale of Featherworks' business premises under Far West's judgment. Walter E. Heller & Co. ("Heller") had been financing Featherworks; its $5 million claim was secured by Featherworks' inventory and accounts receivable, which the parties thought was worth $4 million. When Heller obtained relief from the stay to collect the accounts and foreclose on the inventory, only $3.5 million was realized, leaving Heller with a $1.5 million unsecured claim. Featherworks' only major creditors were Heller, Far West, Hudson, Windsor (which provided financing for Featherworks after the chapter 11 petition was filed), and the attorneys who represented Featherworks in the breach of warranty action.*]

[*Featherworks filed a plan under which the unsecured creditors would each receive a pro rata share of a $40,000 lump sum contribution to be made by Windsor. Windsor would also contribute $21,000 cash to pay administrative claims (other than its own, which would be left unimpaired). Windsor would waive participation on its $4 million unsecured claim; as a result the other unsecured creditors (including Heller on its $1.5 million unsecured claim) would receive 1.3% of their claims in cash. For its secured claim, Heller would receive title to the accounts receivable and inventory, apparently not including the inventory financed by Hudson; this provision would confirm Heller's right to keep the $3.5 million it had realized from sale of the original inventory and collection of the accounts. The real estate mortgagees with trust deeds on Featherworks' business premises would be left unimpaired. Apparently Hudson would be left owning all the stock of the reorganized Featherworks.*]

[*The creditors then voted on the plan. Heller voted to reject the plan. No impaired class accepted the plan, not counting the votes of insiders such as Windsor and Hudson. Thus the plan could not be confirmed because § 1129(a)(10) was not satisfied. Arthur Puro then paid Heller $25,000, after which Heller sought to change its vote.*]

* * * Heller moved for an order pursuant to § 1126(a) of the Bankruptcy Code to allow it to change its ballot and to vote to accept the amended plan of reorganization. Subsequently, Far West cross-moved for an order disqualifying that acceptance in accordance with 11 U.S.C. § 1126(e) and notifying the United

States Attorney that an investigation should be had to determine whether a violation of 18 U.S.C. § 152 has taken place. The alleged violation consisted of the receipt by Heller of $25,000 from Windsor coincidentally with the attempted change in its vote. * * *

* * * [T]he plan lacks the necessary votes unless Heller's motion for leave to change its vote is allowed. * * * In support of its application for authority to change its vote, Heller has explained that it had been prepared to vote for the debtor's plan until sometime before March 30, 1982, when it took possession of and sold the debtor's remaining pre-petition inventory. It then discovered that the inventory was inferior in quality and weight to what it had been represented to be. Heller then decided both to reject the debtor's plan, and allegedly threatened to sue the debtor, Windsor, and [Arthur] Puro. Allegedly to avoid litigation, Puro paid Heller $25,000, receiving in return the assignment of certain accounts receivable and the exchange of general releases running to himself and Windsor. The attorneys for the parties drafted the necessary papers, and on May 19, 1982, the same date that the agreements were executed, Heller advised the debtor of its change of vote.

11 U.S.C. § 1126, which lays down the rules governing acceptance of a plan, authorizes disqualification of a vote for lack of good faith. Subsection (e) of that section provides:

> On request of a party in interest, and after notice and a hearing, the court may designate any entity whose acceptance or rejection of such plan was not in good faith, or was not solicited or procured in good faith or in accordance with the provisions of this title.

Relevant to giving content to this section is 18 U.S.C. § 152, which makes it a criminal offense punishable by a fine or imprisonment for not more than five years, or both, to give or receive money for taking or forbearing to take any act in connection with a proceeding under Title 11 when done fraudulently and willfully.

Although Heller stoutly maintains that the change in its vote was not influenced by the contemporaneous receipt of $25,000 from Windsor, the timing and the surrounding circumstances are at least suspect. Until Heller received the $25,000, it was voting against the plan; afterwards, it changed position. * * *

The bankruptcy laws extend extraordinary relief to insolvent debtors by permitting them to slough off their debts and continue in operation, provided their creditors agree to that course of action. The Code depends upon the self-interest of the creditors to act as a barrier against abuse of the bankruptcy laws. If a majority in number and amount of all creditors vote for a plan, there is good reason to believe that that plan is in the best interest of all creditors, since it would not receive such a vote otherwise. However, if any creditor receives some special consideration peculiar to him, his vote is no longer disinterested and unbiased and the Code's built-in controls are neutralized.

Bearing in mind all the circumstances, the Court will not permit Heller to change its vote on the plan from rejection to acceptance. The Court does not believe such acceptance to have been solicited, procured, or given in good faith when the total amount to be received by all unsecured creditors is only $40,000.

A change in vote by the debtor's major unsecured creditor, coincidental with the receipt from the same source as the $40,000 funding the plan of an additional $25,000 over and above what other creditors are receiving, will not be allowed.

The Court does not know enough with respect to what occurred to find, as Far West requests, that there are reasonable grounds for believing that there has been a violation of 18 U.S.C. § 152 and to refer the matter to the United States Attorney pursuant to 18 U.S.C. § 3057.

Whatever either Heller or Puro did was apparently done with the advice and knowledge of their respective attorneys, who are among the most respected lawyers appearing in this Court. It has long been recognized with respect to other types of violations of 18 U.S.C. § 152 that acting on the advice of counsel negates the presence of the necessary fraudulent intent. * * *

NOTES

1. The court in *Featherworks* does not cite it , but Rule 3018(a) provides that

    > For cause shown, the court after notice and hearing may permit a creditor or equity security holder to change or withdraw an acceptance or rejection.

    Why does the Rule require notice, hearing, and a showing of "cause"? Do the facts of *Featherworks* provide a reason? Should the court have decided the case on the basis of Rule 3018(a)? The most important situation in which a party may need to change a vote is in response to a modification of the plan; that situation is governed by § 1127(d) and Rule 3019. See In re Frontier Airlines, Inc., 93 B.R. 1014 (Bankr. D. Colo. 1988).

2. In affirming the bankruptcy court's decision in *Featherworks*, the district court included the following quote from the Supreme Court's decision in Young v. Higbee Co., 324 U.S. 204, 211 n. 10, 65 S. Ct. 594, 598 n. 10, 89 L. Ed. 890 (1945), to explain the genesis of the good faith requirement in the predecessor to § 1126(e):

    > A year before the House Committee on the Judiciary held its extensive hearings on the Chandler Act, a Circuit Court of Appeals held that a creditor could not be denied the privilege of voting on a reorganization plan under § 77B, although he bought the votes for the purpose of preventing confirmation unless certain demands of his should be met. Texas Hotel Corp. v. Waco Development Co., 87 F.2d 395 [5th Cir.1936]. The hearings make clear the purpose of the Committee to pass legislation which would bar creditors from a vote who were prompted by such a purpose. To this end they adopted the 'good faith' provisions of § 203. Its purpose was to prevent creditors from participating who 'by the use of obstructive tactics and hold-up techniques exact for themselves undue advantages from the other stockholders[/creditors] who are cooperating.' Bad faith was to be attributed to claimants who opposed a plan for a time until they were 'bought off'; those who 'refused to vote in favor of a plan unless . . . given some particular preferential advantage.' Hearings on Revision of the Bankruptcy Act before the Committee on the Judiciary of the House of Representatives, 75th Cong., 1st Sess., on H.R. 6439, Serial 9, pp. 180-82.

3. A court has noted that

> [t]he *Featherworks* court's phraseology * * * is a little unfortunate:

>> . . . if any creditor receives some special consideration peculiar to him, his vote is no longer disinterested and unbiased and the Code's built-in controls are neutralized.

> 25 B.R. at 641. This characterization does not jibe with the more accurate recognition earlier in the same paragraph:

>> The Code depends upon the self-interest of the creditors to act as a barrier against abuse of the bankruptcy laws.

> Id. In at least a general sense, the statutory framework for plan confirmation is a very Madisonian construct: it is premised on the assumption that debtors, creditors, and interestholders will all act in their own interest in their participation in a reorganization case. See In re Applegate Property, Ltd., 133 B.R. 827, 834 (Bankr. W.D. Tex. 1991) (". . . good faith voting and solicitation does not demand selfless disinterest . . ."). The Code attempts to channel that self-interest toward a substantive result that is least destructive of the options of all of the constituencies in a Chapter 11 case, through a process that minimizes disruption and conflict during the reordering of all parties' rights.

    In re Kellogg Square Partnership, 160 B.R. 336, 342 n. 8 (Bankr. D. Minn. 1993).

4. In Federal Support Co. v. Insinger Machine Co., 859 F.2d 17 (4th Cir.1988), cited by Judge Fernandez in *Figter*, the Fourth Circuit held that the vote of a creditor who was also a defendant in the debtor's antitrust suit should be counted:

> Federal Support contends that the pendency of the state court antitrust suit gave Insinger an ulterior motive.

> Federal Support offered some testimony that its former officers would be willing to put up the money to finance the prosecution of the antitrust claim provided the plan of reorganization were approved. Federal Support suggested that a trustee in bankruptcy might not be as willing to prosecute the antitrust claim.

> The contention is entirely speculative. The antitrust claim is the bankrupt's only asset. The claim is assigned great value, and, with some justification, it is alleged in the antitrust suit that the Birsch conspiracy caused the complete destruction of the business of Federal Support. * * *

> However Insinger must have thought that disapproval of the plan of reorganization coincided with its self-interest. It voted for disapproval of the plan.

> One's self-interest, however, does not provide an ulterior motive. Insinger was entitled to cast its vote in accordance with its perception of its self-interest, and nothing suggests that Insinger was motivated by any other interest or purpose. It may have thought that rejection of the reorganization plan would reduce the likelihood of a vigorous prosecution of the antitrust claim, although the reason for any such belief is difficult to perceive.

> No representative in the bankruptcy court has the financial resources to prosecute the antitrust claim. The claim itself is the only asset. Whether the bankruptcy proceeding is in reorganization or liquidation, the state court antitrust litigation can move forward only if

> Federal Support's former officers and stockholders provide the money. From all that appears, they have as much to gain from a successful prosecution of the antitrust claim whether the bankruptcy proceeding is in liquidation or reorganization. Either way, success in the antitrust litigation would provide funds for the payment of creditors, and any excess would go to Federal Support's former stockholders.
>
> There is nothing to gain from such speculation, however. It was for Insinger to decide its own self-interest. Without any other evidence, the pendency of the lawsuit itself is not enough to support an inference of a lack of good faith.

Id. at 19-20. What is the difference between acting out of an "ulterior motive" and acting out of "self-interest"? If Insinger admitted that it rejected the plan in order to hinder prosecution of the antitrust case, would the designation of its vote have been proper?

Suppose Insinger suggested to Federal Support "in confidence" that Insinger would accept the plan if Federal Support would dismiss Insinger from the antitrust suit. Should Insinger's acceptance be designated if Federal Support dismisses Insinger from the suit? Should Insinger's rejection of the plan be designated if Federal Support refuses to dismiss Insinger and Insinger then votes against the plan? See Texas Extrusion Corp. v. Lockheed Corp. (In re Texas Extrusion Corp.), 844 F.2d 1142, 1163 (5th Cir. 1988); see 18 U.S.C. § 152 (" * * * Whoever knowingly and fraudulently gives, offers, receives or attempts to obtain any money or property, remuneration, compensation, reward, advantage, or promise therefor, for acting or forbearing to act in any case under title 11 * * * [s]hall be fined not more that $5,000 or imprisoned not more than five years, or both."); cf. In re Landau Boat Co., 8 B.R. 432 (W.D. Mo. 1981).

5. Is there a danger that bankruptcy judges will designate votes in order to confirm a plan of reorganization in cases in which the judge thinks a creditor is acting unreasonably in rejecting the plan?

6. If creditors have a settled view that the debtor should be liquidated, and if they refuse to consider arguments in favor of reorganization, should their votes be designated as being cast in bad faith? Is failure to bargain over a reorganization evidence of bad faith? Cf. In re Fairfield Executive Assocs., 161 B.R. 595 (D.N.J. 1993) (holding that statement of undersecured creditor that it would not vote for any plan that did not provide for full payment did not constitute bad faith). An undersecured creditor seemingly is entitled to consider its entire economic interest in the case when it votes its secured claim and its unsecured claim. It is not required to act as if it only held an unsecured claim in deciding how to vote the unsecured claim, and it is seemingly entitled to vote its unsecured claim to block a plan so that it can seek relief from the stay under § 362(d)(2) and foreclose. See In re Marin Town Center, 142 B.R. 374 (N.D. Cal. 1992); In re Dune Deck Owners Corp., 175 B.R. 839 (Bankr. S.D.N.Y. 1995); In re Pleasant Hills Partners, 163 B.R. 388 (Bankr. N.D. Ga. 1994); Fairfield Executive Assocs.

7. Acme and BendCo operated the only machine shops in Central County. Acme filed a chapter 11 petition. BendCo then purchased the stock of Sheetmetal, Inc., one of several sheet metal suppliers in the area. Sheetmetal held one of the largest claims in Acme's chapter 11 case. Sheetmetal had expressed support for Acme's reorganization efforts, but after the purchase by BendCo Sheetmetal took the position that liquidation of Acme would be best. Sheetmetal voted to reject Acme's plan. Should Sheetmetal's vote be designated? Cf. In re MacLeod Co., 63 B.R. 654 (Bankr. S.D. Ohio 1986).

8.   Note that the court has authority to protect the integrity of the voting process from intimidation. See In re Greate Bay Hotel & Casino, Inc., 251 B.R. 213 (Bankr. D.N.J. 2000).

Problem 13-4

Foam Corporation is insolvent on a going concern basis but has filed a plan under which its majority stockholder (Gruff) will keep a substantial amount of the value of Foam Corporation. The plan impairs Kick Credit's secured claim, but Kick Credit has accepted the plan. Thus § 1129(a)(10) is satisfied. Gruff's unsecured claim is in the same class with the trade creditors. Gruff voted his $3.2 million claim to accept the plan. Trade creditors holding $4.3 million in claims and holding a majority in number of claims also have accepted. Trade creditors holding $3.7 million in claims have rejected the plan. Gruff's vote counts for purposes of §§ 1126 and 1129(a)(8), if his vote is not designated. See In re Gilbert, 104 B.R. 206 (Bankr. W.D. Mo. 1989). Thus, if his vote is not designated, cramdown will not be necessary for the plan to be confirmed. Should Gruff's vote be designated as a bad faith acceptance?

Consider the excerpt from *Federal Support* in note 2 above. Also note that the House bill (H.R. 8200) did not include a provision like § 1129(a)(10), but did include a provision (§ 1126(e) of the House version) permitting the court to designate the vote of an entity who had a conflict of interest, if the conflict was of such nature as to justify the designation. The House report states that this was to overrule in the bankruptcy context cases like Aladdin Hotel Corp. v. Bloom, 200 F.2d 627 (8th Cir. 1953). H. R. Rep. No. 595, 95th Cong., 1st Sess., 411 (1977). In *Aladdin Hotel* (a nonbankruptcy case) the majority stockholders in the hotel corporation also owned more than two thirds of the bonds which the hotel had issued. The bond indenture permitted modification of the bonds by agreement of the hotel and the holders of two thirds of the bonds. Without giving prior notice to the other bondholders, the stockholders agreed with their corporation to give the corporation ten extra years to pay off the bonds. The court of appeals refused to grant relief to the plaintiff, a minority bondholder who had purchased her bonds after the extension and with knowledge of it.

In the conference committee the conflict of interest provision included in H.R. 8200 was deleted, and § 1129(a)(10) was added. Does that history indicate that a conflict of interest is not a basis for designating votes under § 1126(e)? Could a vote be designated under § 105(a) on account of conflict of interest? See In re Dune Deck Owners Corp., 175 B.R. 839, 845 and 845 n.13 (Bankr. S.D.N.Y. 1995); In re Pleasant Hills Partners, 163 B.R. 388, 393 (Bankr. N.D. Ga. 1994). Do undersecured creditors who vote their unsecured claims so as to block a plan have interests that conflict with the interests of unsecured creditors? What conclusion might you draw from § 1111(b)(1) and Rule 3018(d) about whether that level of conflict is great enough to permit designation of votes?

Chapter Fourteen

Consensual Confirmation

A. INTRODUCTION

The successful chapter 11 reorganization case results in a confirmed plan. Plans of reorganization can be confirmed in two ways. Most plans are confirmed consensually under § 1129(a) of the Bankruptcy Code. By a consensual plan, we mean that every impaired class has voted to accept the plan of reorganization. That is the focus of this chapter. If an impaired class fails to accept the plan, the plan sometimes may be confirmed under § 1129(b) of the Bankruptcy Code on a non-consensual basis known as "cramdown." Non-consensual confirmation is the focus of the next chapter.

1. Objections To Confirmation

Section 1128 of the Bankruptcy Code requires the Court to conduct a confirmation hearing and gives any party in interest the right to file an objection to confirmation. In order to prevail, the objection to a consensual plan must show that the plan fails to meet one of the sixteen requirements of § 1129(a) of the Bankruptcy Code.

On its face, the statute appears to grant any party in interest the right to file an objection to confirmation. Section 1128(b). Section 1109(b) of the Bankruptcy Code specifies that a party in interest includes the debtor, the trustee, a creditors' committee, an equity security holders' committee, a creditor, an equity security holder, or any indenture trustee.

Despite the terms of the statute, courts have denied standing to certain parties who have asserted objections to confirmation. For example, some courts have held that a creditor holding a claim in a class that is not impaired lacks standing to object to confirmation. E.g., In re Wonder Corp. of Am., 70 B.R. 1018, 1022 (Bankr. D. Conn. 1987). But see In re Scott Cable Commc'ns, Inc, 232 B.R. 558, 564 n.4 (Bankr. D. Conn. 1999) ("[A]n unimpaired creditor may not have standing to object to its treatment under a plan * * * but it would nonetheless have standing to object to confirmation on other grounds, i.e., feasibility, §§ 1129(a)(11)."). Other courts have held that administrative claimants who will receive cash in full on the effective date of a plan lack standing to object to confirmation. E.g., In re Cheatham, 78 B.R. 104 (Bankr. E.D.N.C. 1987), aff'd, 91 B.R. 377 (E.D.N.C. 1988). One whose claim has been disallowed does not have standing to object to a plan of reorganization but may ask the court to suspend further proceedings on plan confirmation while it appeals the disallowance of its claim. In re Whatley, 155 B.R. 775 (Bankr. D. Colo. 1993), aff'd, 169 B.R. 698 (D. Colo. 1994).

Even a party who has standing to object to confirmation will not have standing to object to parts of the plan that only affect the rights of others. See, e.g., In re Andreuccetti, 975 F.2d 413 (7th Cir. 1992) (holding that debtors were "aggrieved parties" entitled to appeal confirmation of creditors' plan, stating that there was a separate issue whether debtors had standing to raise their objections in the bankruptcy court, and holding that they lacked standing to object to that plan's limitation on the rights of administrative expense claimants).[1] However, the debtor in possession owes fiduciary duties to all the creditors and interest holders. Thus, where another party files a plan that would violate the rights of one or more creditors or interest holders, the debtor in possession may have standing to assert their rights and object to the plan in order to protect them. See In re Union Meeting Partners, 165 B.R. 553 (Bankr. E.D. Pa. 1994), aff'd without opinion, 52 F.3d 317 (3d Cir. 1995).

In the main, despite the limits on standing, parties whose rights will be affected by confirmation of a plan of reorganization may file an objection to confirmation. For example, the participation by a member of a creditors' committee in negotiation of the plan of reorganization will not prevent the individual member from objecting to the plan and filing an objection to confirmation even if the committee has supported the plan. E.g., In re Ne. Dairy Coop. Fed'n, Inc., 73 B.R. 239 (Bankr. N.D.N.Y. 1987). A creditors' committee retains standing to object to a plan even if the class represented by the committee votes to accept the plan. In re Cent. Med. Ctr., Inc., 122 B.R. 568 (Bankr. E.D. Mo. 1990). A nondebtor joint obligor has standing to object to confirmation, even when he had settled creditors' claims against him, based on his claim for reimbursement from the debtor. In re Shoen, 193 B.R. 302 (Bankr. D. Ariz. 1996).

Objections to confirmation assist the court in determining whether the requirements of § 1129(a) have been met. Even if no objection to confirmation is filed, however, the better view is that the court has an independent duty to determine whether the plan meets the requirements of § 1129(a). E.g., In re Zaleha, 162 B.R. 309 (Bankr. D. Idaho 1993); In re Future Energy Corp., 83 B.R. 470, 481 (Bankr. S.D. Ohio 1988); In re White, 41 B.R. 227 (M.D.Tenn.1984). But see Seaport Auto. Warehouse, Inc. v. Rohnert Park Auto Parts, Inc. (In re Rohnert Park Auto Parts, Inc.), 113 B.R. 610, 614 (B.A.P. 9th Cir. 1990) (in the absence of objection, the court is not under a duty to insure that the plan satisfies every requirement of § 1129(a)); In re Richard Buick, Inc., 126 B.R. 840 (Bankr. E.D. Pa.1991) (in absence of timely objection, court had discretion whether to deny confirmation due to failure of plan to satisfy all elements of § 1129(a), but court exercised its discretion to deny confirmation because of "magnitude" of deficiency in plan which improperly classified secured claims together and improperly treated

---

1. For a further discussion of appellate standing, see Kane v. Johns-Manville Corp., 843 F.2d 636 (2d Cir.1988), reprinted above in Chapter Nine of this text.

them disparately). Thus even an objection by a party who lacks standing could lead a court to consider an issue. See In re Union Meeting Partners, 165 B.R. at 574.

2. The Confirmation Hearing

At the confirmation hearing, the plan proponent will have the burden of producing evidence in support of confirmation of the plan. The court need not take new evidence but may rely on evidence adduced at previous hearings in the case. Acequia, Inc. v. Clinton (In re Acequia, Inc.), 787 F.2d 1352 (9th Cir. 1986). Some courts will require live testimony while others will exercise their discretion to allow testimony on affidavits or declarations with witnesses present for cross-examination.[2] The proponent may also choose to supply the court and opposing parties with a confirmation hearing memorandum setting forth the proponent's contentions that the elements of § 1129(a) have been met and summarizing the testimony to be offered on direct examination at the confirmation hearing. It is important that the proponent make an evidentiary record in support of the plan in order to protect the record on any appeal from the confirmation order.[3] Of course the proponent need not offer evidence with respect to provisions that do not apply to it. For example, a corporate or partnership debtor need not offer evidence on paragraph 15 of § 1129(a) which applies only if the debtor is an individual.

---

2.   Federal Rule of Bankruptcy Procedure 9017 provides that the Federal Rules of Evidence and Federal Rule of Civil Procedure 43 apply in cases under the Bankruptcy Code. Federal Rule of Civil Procedure 43(a) specifies that in all trials, the testimony of witnesses shall be taken orally in open court unless otherwise provided by the rules. Rule 43(e) of the Federal Rules of Civil Procedure provides that when a motion is based on facts not appearing of record, the court may hear the matter on affidavits or on oral testimony. Federal Rule of Bankruptcy Procedure 3020(b)(1) specifies that an objection to confirmation is a contested matter under Federal Rule of Bankruptcy Procedure 9014. Federal Rule of Bankruptcy Procedure 9014 makes clear that a contested matter is governed by motion practice. Accordingly, the Bankruptcy Court has the discretion to take testimony on affidavits (or declarations) in lieu of oral testimony. Adair v. Sunset Bank (In re Adair), 965 F.2d 777 (9th Cir. 1992); see also Mills v. Gergely (In re Gergely), 110 F.3d 1448 (9th Cir. 1997).

3.   As we discuss in Chapter Sixteen of this text, in many cases it will be difficult to obtain effective appellate review of an order confirming a chapter 11 plan. The appeal will be dismissed as moot if the reorganization plan becomes so substantially consummated that effective relief is no longer available. E.g., In re Cont'l Airlines, 91 F.3d 553, 565 (3d Cir. 1996) (en banc); Manges v. Seattle-First Nat'l Bank (In re Manges), 29 F.3d 1034 (5th Cir. 1994). "Effective relief is impossible if funds have been disbursed to persons who are not parties to the appeal or if failure to obtain a stay has permitted such a comprehensive change as to render it inequitable to consider the merits of the appeal." Credit Alliance Corp. v. Dunning-Ray Ins. Agency Inc. (In re Blumer), 66 B.R. 109, 113 (B.A.P. 9th Cir. 1986), aff'd, 826 F.2d 1069 (9th Cir. 1987). Accordingly, the failure of an objector to obtain a stay pending appeal may bar the appellant from obtaining relief in many reorganization cases. E.g., Manges, 29 F.3d 1034. But see Bank of Am. v. 203 North LaSalle St. P'ship (In re 203 N. LaSalle St. P'ship), 126 F.3d 955, 961 (7th Cir. 1997) (refusing to dismiss appeal from order confirming substantially consummated plan as moot), reversed on other grounds, 526 U.S. 434, 119 S. Ct. 1411, 143 L. Ed. 2d 607 (1999); In re Andreuccetti, 975 F.2d 413 (7th Cir. 1992) (permitting appeal of aspects of confirmation order without a stay); Salomon v. Logan (In re Int'l Envtl. Dynamics, Inc.), 718 F.2d 322, 326 (9th Cir. 1983) (permitting appeal without stay).

B. THE REQUIREMENTS FOR CONSENSUAL CONFIRMATION

In order to confirm a plan consensually under § 1129(a) of the Bankruptcy Code, the bankruptcy judge must determine that each of the requirements in paragraphs 1-16 of § 1129(a) is met or does not apply in the pending case.[4]

1. Boiler Plate Requirements

Several of the sixteen requirements are routine or "boiler plate" provisions that seldom form the basis for an objection to confirmation. Nevertheless, many courts will require proof that the basic requirements have been met even in the absence of an objection. And in certain contexts, particularly single asset real estate cases, two of the boiler plate requirements have caused debtors serious difficulties.

Section 1129(a)(1)-(2) requires the plan and its proponent to have complied with the applicable provisions of title 11. Thus, the evidence should show that the plan contains the mandatory provisions required by § 1123(a) and that its permissive provisions are within the scope of § 1123(b). For example, a plan that fails to amend the debtor's corporate charter to prohibit the issuance of non-voting stock will violate § 1123(a)(6) and will not be confirmable. In re Perdido Motel Group, Inc., 101 B.R. 289 (Bankr. N.D. Ala. 1989). An objector might contend that the classification set forth in the plan violates § 1122, 1123(a)(1), or 1123(a)(4).[5] (We discuss classification issues above in Chapter

---

4.   In addition to meeting the sixteen requirements of § 1129(a), sometimes a plan must comply with the requirements of subsections (c) and (d) of § 1129. Section 1129(c) applies when more than one plan is presented to the court for confirmation. The statute permits the court to confirm only one plan. If both plans are confirmable, the court is to consider the preferences of creditors and equity security holders in determining which plan to confirm. The court is likely to give substantial weight to the preferences expressed, but is not bound by them. See, e.g., In re Schwarzmann, 203 B.R. 919 (Bankr. E.D. Va. 1995), aff'd, 103 F.3d 120 (4th Cir. 1996); In re Rolling Green Country Club, 26 B.R. 729, 735 (Bankr. D. Minn. 1982). For example, the court can confirm a creditors' liquidating plan in preference to a debtor's plan of reorganization that is contingent on future events. In re Holywell Corp., 54 B.R. 41 (Bankr. S.D. Fla. 1985), aff'd, 59 B.R. 340 (S.D. Fla.1986), affirmance by district court vacated and case remanded to district court for dismissal of appeal as moot, 838 F.2d 1547 (11th Cir. 1988); but cf. In re Schwarzmann, 203 B.R. at 925 (confirming debtor's reorganization plan in preference to creditor's liquidating plan). Under § 1129(d), a governmental unit such as the Securities Exchange Commission or the Internal Revenue Service may request the court to deny confirmation of a plan if the principal purpose of the plan is the avoidance of the application of section 5 of the Securities Act of 1933, 15 U.S.C. § 77e, or the avoidance of taxes. This determination will only be made on the request of the governmental agency. Moreover, if the debtor is an individual, section 1228(b) of the 2005 BAPCPA provides that the court may not confirm a plan of reorganization unless "requested tax documents have been filed with the court."

5.   Sometimes an objector will file a motion in advance of the confirmation hearing to determine the propriety of the classification under Rule 3013. While the proponent might desire to determine the propriety of classification by filing a motion under Rule 3013, it is seldom advisable to put the spotlight on classification. Rather, most proponents prefer to have the issue considered as part of the confirmation hearing when several other issues will be before the court and the momentum to confirm the plan will be at its maximum.

Eleven of this text and again below in Chapter Fifteen. Classification issues are particularly important in those single asset real estate cases in which an undersecured mortgagee has a large deficiency claim, as we will see in Chapter Fifteen.) An objector also might contend that § 1129(a)(1) is violated because the plan does not adhere to the subordination provisions of § 510 of the Bankruptcy Code. If the proponent solicits acceptances without having obtained a court-approved disclosure statement and complying with the requirements of § 1125, it is possible for the court to deny confirmation under § 1129(a)(2) on the basis that the proponent has violated title 11.

On its face, the statute would appear to require the court to deny confirmation under § 1129(a)(2) if the debtor uses cash collateral in violation of § 363 or makes postpetition transfers in violation of § 549. See In re Lapworth, 1998 WL 767456, *3 (Bankr. E.D. Pa. 1998) (denying confirmation under § 1129(a)(2) when debtor in possession made unauthorized payments of postpetition interest to unsecured creditor). Arguably, however, it is the debtor in possession who transgresses these provisions, not the debtor. Under § 1121, it is the debtor who proposes the plan. At least one court, however, has denied confirmation based upon the debtor in possession's refusal to pay administrative expenses when ordered to do so by the court. In re Midwestern Companies, 55 B.R. 856, 863 (Bankr. W.D. Mo. 1985). Another court denied confirmation because the debtor in possession had violated its duties by spending cash collateral without consent of the secured creditor and without court authorization. Cothran v. United States, 45 B.R. 836 (S.D. Ga. 1984).

Generally, however, compliance with the requirements of § 1129(a)(1)-(2) is not problematic. In fact, insubstantial violations of these provisions that constitute "harmless error" have been held by one court of appeals not to bar confirmation of the plan. Kane v. Johns-Manville Corp. (In re Johns-Manville Corp.), 843 F.2d 636, 648 (2d Cir. 1988) (reprinted above in Chapter Nine of this text). One court noted appropriately that a "slavish interpretation" of § 1129(a)(2) would lead to "draconian results not intended by Congress;" the court confirmed a plan of reorganization despite unauthorized use of cash collateral that occurred early in the case, where the money had been replaced. In re Landing Assocs., Ltd., 157 B.R. 791 (Bankr. W.D. Tex. 1993); accord, In re Greate Bay Hotel & Casino, Inc., 251 B.R. 213 (Bankr. D.N.J. 2000).

Under § 1129(a)(3), the court must determine whether the plan has been proposed in good faith and not by any means forbidden by law. If no objection to confirmation challenges the good faith proposal of the plan, the court need not take evidence on this point. Rule 3020(b)(2). Where a plan is proposed with a legitimate and honest purpose to reorganize and has a reasonable chance of success, the good faith standard is satisfied. In re Gen. Teamsters, Warehousemen & Helpers Union, 265 F.3d 869 (9th Cir. 2001); McCormick v. Banc One Leasing Corp. (In re McCormick), 49 F.3d 1524, (11th Cir. 1995); Brite v. Sun Country Dev., Inc. (In re Sun Country Dev., Inc.), 764 F.2d 406 (5th Cir. 1985). Accord, e.g., Hanson v. First Bank, 828 F.2d 1310 (8th Cir. 1987);

Connell v. Coastal Cable T.V., Inc. (In re Coastal Cable T.V., Inc.), 709 F.2d 762, 764 (1st Cir. 1983). The court is to determine good faith based on the totality of the circumstances. Fin. Sec. Assurance v. T-H New Orleans Ltd. P'ship (In re T-H New Orleans Ltd. P'ship), 116 F.3d 790, 802 (5th Cir. 1997). Courts disagree whether the plan proponent's prepetition conduct is relevant to the good faith determination. Compare, e.g., In re Seatco, 257 B.R. 469, 480 (Bankr. N.D. Tex. 2001) (prepetition conduct irrelevant) with, e.g., In re Natural Land Corp., 825 F.2d 296, 298 (11th Cir. 1987) (taint of prepetition conduct must extend to any subsequent reorganization plan).

Courts also disagree whether it is good faith for a solvent debtor to propose a chapter 11 plan solely to take advantage of a provision of the Bankruptcy Code. The Ninth Circuit has held that a solvent corporate debtor's use of § 1124(2) to cure a default and avoid paying postpetition interest at the default rate is not per se bad faith but may be justified based on the totality of the circumstances. Platinum Capital, Inc. v. Sylmar Plaza, L.P. (In re Sylmar Plaza, L.P.), 314 F.3d 1070, 1075 (9th Cir. 2002). The Third Circuit reached a different result where a solvent debtor confirmed a chapter 11 plan that rejected a real property lease, under which the debtor was the lessee, solely to take advantage of the damages cap in § 502(b)(6). See NMSBPCSLDHB, L.P. v. Integrated Telecom Express, Inc. (In re Integrated Telecom Express, Inc.), 384 F.3d 108, 112 (3d Cir. 2004) (staying confirmation order and dismissing chapter 11 case filed by a financially healthy debtor with no intention of reorganizing or liquidating as a going concern); the panel questionably distinguished, as cases that were used to maximize value for creditors, both *Sylmar Plaza* and Solow v. P.P.I. Enters. (U.S.), Inc. (In re P.P.I. Enters. (U.S.), Inc.), 324 F.3d 197, 211 (3d Cir. 2001), which had affirmed confirmation of a chapter 11 plan filed to take advantage of § 502(b)(6) and § 363(f) by a corporation that claimed to be insolvent based on insider debt.

An individual debtor's invocation of the 5th Amendment privilege in related nondischargeability litigation is not sufficient evidence of bad faith to merit denial of confirmation. *McCormick*, 49 F.3d 1524. A liquidating plan proposed by creditors may meet this standard even though it prevents rehabilitation of the debtor. Jasik v. Conrad (In re Jasik), 727 F.2d 1379 (5th Cir. 1984). So will a creditors' plan that proposes to take over the debtor corporation. In re Evans Prod. Co., 65 B.R. 31 (Bankr. S.D. Fla.), aff'd, 65 B.R. 870 (S.D. Fla. 1986). Some courts have refused to confirm plans proposed to avoid taxes or to delay the Internal Revenue Service as not being proposed in good faith. E.g., In re Nikron, Inc., 27 B.R. 773, 778 (Bankr. E.D. Mich. 1983); In re Maxim Indus., Inc., 22 B.R. 611 (Bankr. D. Mass. 1982). Application of the good faith standard in these cases seems to be at odds with § 1129(d) which requires the governmental unit to sustain the burden of proving that *the* principal purpose of the plan is the avoidance of taxes in order to defeat confirmation. See footnote 4 supra.

Section 1129(a)(4) requires that payments to be made in connection with the plan for services rendered in the chapter 11 case be disclosed and approved as reasonable by the court. Compliance with this section may be troublesome in the context of a creditors' plan where the proponent is paying its professionals and advisors from its own funds. Applied literally, the standard requires the disclosure and approval of fees paid by the creditors to their professionals and advisors. See, e.g., In re Hendrick, 45 B.R. 976, 985 (Bankr. M.D. La. 1985). This may give the debtor or objectors undue leverage in opposing a creditors' plan. The standard also appears to apply to payments made to management including so-called success fees or confirmation bonuses. Managers may be reluctant to have their compensation approved by the court, but compliance with the standard requires disclosure and approval of payments for services rendered in the chapter 11 case even if payments are to be made after confirmation. By the same token, § 1129(a)(4) does not provide an independent basis for a professional person to negotiate a compensation agreement that would violate the professional's duties of loyalty, disinterestedness, and disclosure. See United States v. Schilling (In re Big Rivers Elec. Corp.), 355 F.3d 415, 439 (6th Cir. 2004) (examiner incorrect in arguing that § 1129(a)(4) overrides other sections of the Bankruptcy Code).

Section 1129(a)(5) requires the identity of officers and directors to be disclosed and subject to court approval as consistent with the interests of creditors and shareholders and with public policy. Failure to disclose the identity of officers and directors can result in denial of confirmation of a plan of reorganization. In re M.S.M. & Assocs., 104 B.R. 312 (Bankr. D. Haw. 1989). In addition, future compensation arrangements to insiders must be disclosed, but there is no requirement for approval. Presumably, if the compensation arrangements relate to services rendered in the chapter 11 case, approval would be required under § 1129(a)(4).

Section 1129(a)(6) applies only in cases of public utilities or other regulated companies whose rates are subject to regulatory approval. The standard requires any rate changes that are subject to regulatory commission approval to be subject to such approval in order for the plan to be confirmed.

Section 1129(a)(13) requires the plan to provide for the continuation of all retiree medical, disability and death benefits as defined in § 1114. This section is really a mandatory plan provision that could have been placed in § 1123(a). It will only apply in cases where the debtor is obligated to pay these kinds of retiree benefits.[6]

---

6. Section 1114 sets forth a complex treatment of "retiree benefits". This section does not apply to pension benefits but rather applies to "medical, surgical, or hospital care benefits, or benefits in the event of sickness, accident, disability, or death". It is possible for a labor organization or Retiree Benefits Committee to agree to modify the retiree benefits in certain circumstances if the modification is necessary to permit the reorganization of the debtor and assures that all creditors, the debtor, and all of the affected parties are treated fairly and equitably. See § 1114(g)(3). If the retiree benefits are governed by a collective bargaining agreement, the provisions in § 1113 might also apply.

Section 1129(a)(14) concerns payment of domestic support obligations and is unlikely to apply if the debtor is not an individual. Section 1129(a)(15) contains confirmation standards similar to those in chapter 13 that apply when the debtor is an individual; we discuss it further in Chapter Sixteen below in connection with discharge of debts of individuals in chapter 11.

Section 1129(a)(16) requires all transfers of property of the plan to be made in accordance with any applicable provisions of nonbankruptcy law that govern the transfer of property by a corporation or trust that is not a "moneyed, business, or commercial corporation or trust." (Of course true trusts are not eligible to be debtors in bankruptcy,[7] though business trusts may be.[8]) If a nonprofit religious or charitable corporation is a chapter 11 debtor it may hold property that, under nonbankruptcy law, may not be transferred to a recipient other than another religious or charitable corporation. Section 1129(a)(16) prevents the plan from providing for sale of such property in violation of these nonbankruptcy restrictions on alienability. Further, to the extent that nonbankruptcy law requires particular procedures, such as prior notice to the state attorney general, before nonprofit corporations may transfer property, it appears that the plan must provide for those procedures to be followed.

This provision may be of particular importance in the important area of sale of distressed nonprofit hospitals and other health care providers to for-profit entities. See Peterman & Koenig, *Patient Care Ombudsman: Why So Much Opposition?*, 25-Mar. Am. Bankr. Inst. J. 22, 23 (2006); DeMarco & Valentine, *Health Care Hazards and Eleemosynary Elocutions: BAPCPA Changes the Sale of Nonprofit Health Care Assets*, 24-Oct. Am. Bankr. Inst. J. 16 (2005) (noting coordinated "triad of new statutory provisions," including § 1129(a)(16), § 363(d), and § 541(f)); Miller, *Chapter 11 and Business Bankruptcy Amendments*, in UNDERSTANDING THE RADICAL BANKRUPTCY CODE CHANGES 1, 16-17 (Comm'l Law League of Am., 2005), reprinted in The Bankruptcy Abuse Prevention and Consumer Protection Act (BAPCPA) Series: Business Issues (ABA 2005), available at http://www.abanet.org/cle/programs/nosearch/materials/t05buscm1.pdf. ("The impact of these changes will be significant in the health care arena where debtors are often non-profit corporations that seek to reorganize or liquidate through the sale of their assets to moneyed, commercial corporations. Under prior law, absent the attorney general of the applicable state objecting to such transfer and the court upholding such objection, the sales would be permitted. Now, such sales are explicitly prohibited absent compliance with applicable nonbankruptcy law."); Levin, *Sale of Nonprofit Hospitals in Bankruptcy*, 20-

---

7.   See §§ 101(15) (defining "entity" to include "trust"), 101(41) (defining "person" without including "trust"), 109 (providing that only a "person" may be a debtor, except that municipalities may be debtors under chapter 9).

8.   See §§ 101(9)(A)(v) (including "business trust" within definition of "corporation"), 101(41) (including "corporation" within definition of "person").

Jan. AM. BANKR. INST. J. 12 (Dec. 2001/Jan. 2002). See generally, with regard to conversion of nonprofit entities into for-profit entities in the context of a particular state, Buck & Jedrey, *Conversion from Nonprofit to For-Profit Status*, in 2 MASSACHUSETTS NONPROFIT ORGANIZATIONS, Supplement to Chapter 23 (Supp. 2004) (Westlaw cite: NPOII MA-CLE S-23-i).

2. Acceptance Requirements

In addition to the "boiler plate" provisions, the court must determine that the reorganization plan has been accepted by classes entitled to vote. In order to obtain consensual confirmation, the plan must comply with the provisions of § 1129(a)(8). The court must determine that each class of claims or interests either has voted to accept the plan or is not impaired under the plan.[9] In addition, if a class of claims is impaired under the plan, § 1129(a)(10) requires at least one class of claims to actually vote to accept the plan, excluding the acceptances by any insider. Acceptance by an impaired class of interests will not do. The court must exclude the acceptances of insiders and determine that the remaining votes in the class meet the acceptance requirements of § 1126(c).[10] The statute does not specify on what date the creditor must be an insider in order for the acceptance to be excluded. It makes sense, however, to exclude acceptances cast by creditors who are insiders on the date of the vote rather than on the date the debt arose. See In re Gilbert, 104 B.R. 206 (Bankr. W.D. Mo. 1989); cf. Mut. Life Ins. Co. v. Patrician St. Joseph Partners Ltd. P'ship (In re Patrician St. Joseph Partners Ltd. P'ship), 169 B.R. 669, 679 n.4 (D. Ariz. 1994) (acceptance by FDIC would not be excluded for purposes of § 1129(a)(10) even though claim was originally held by insider).

3. Treatment Of Priority Claims

Section 1129(a)(9) specifies the treatment that certain priority claims must receive under the plan.[11] The statute provides separate treatments for three different categories of priority claims. First, under § 1129(a)(9)(A),

---

9. Impairment is discussed above in Chapter Eleven of this text. The voting requirements for acceptance of a plan by a class are discussed above in Chapter Thirteen of this text. If an impaired class does not vote to accept the plan, then the plan can only be confirmed under the cramdown provisions of § 1129(b) as the requirements of § 1129(a)(8) will not have been met with respect to such class. Chapter Fifteen of this text deals with cramdown.

10. It appears that the court is required to count rejections of the plan by insiders. The term "insider" is illustrated in § 101(31) of the Bankruptcy Code to include entities in control of the debtor. Generally, insiders are inclined to accept a plan proposed by the debtor, but the opposite may be true in the case of a creditors' plan.

11. In 1990, Congress enacted a priority for allowed unsecured claims based on commitments by the debtor to certain United States governmental agencies to maintain the capital of an insured depository institution. See § 507(a)(9). No corresponding amendment was made to § 1129(a)(9) specifying the method of payment for these priority claims. Accordingly, it would appear that such claims are susceptible to classification and will not be required to be paid in cash as are other priority claims. See § 1123(a)(1). A similar analysis applies with respect to the priority created in the 2005 BAPCPA for allowed claims for death or personal injuries resulting from the unlawful operation of a motor vehicle or vessel while the debtor was intoxicated. Section 507(a)(10).

administrative expenses entitled to priority under § 507(a)(2) or involuntary gap claims entitled to priority under § 507(a)(3) are entitled to be paid in cash in full on the effective date of the plan unless the holder of a particular claim agrees to a different treatment. Since these claims are not classified, each holder of an administrative expense or involuntary gap claim can insist on payment in full or agree to a different treatment. For example, many plans propose to pay trade debt incurred after the date of the filing of the petition in the ordinary course of business following the effective date of the plan. It is possible that entities supplying trade credit to the estate have impliedly agreed to be repaid in accordance with ordinary business terms. Alternatively, the proponent might delay the effective date of the plan until a trade cycle is completed thereby permitting preconfirmation trade credit to be paid in the ordinary course. Where the administrative expense entitled to priority is a financial advisor's success fee based on a percentage recovered by general unsecured creditors, nothing prevents the court from calculating the amount that will be recovered by the unsecured creditors as long as the administrative expense is paid first. Official Comm. of Unsec. Creditors v. Farmland Indus., Inc. (In re Farmland Indus., Inc.), 397 F.3d 647, 652-53 (8th Cir. 2005). Section 1129(a)(12) requires expenses of the United States trustee and other fees and charges incurred under § 1930 of title 28 to be paid on the effective date of the plan. This requirement is surplusage because all such expenses are entitled to priority under § 507(a)(2) and are required to be paid in cash on the effective date under § 1129(a)(9)(A).

Section 1129(a)(9)(B) treats with employee wage and benefit priorities as defined in § 507(a)(4)-(5), priorities accorded to grain merchants and United States fishermen in § 507(a)(6), consumer deposit claims entitled to priority under § 507(a)(7), and family support claims entitled to priority under § 507(a)(1). These claims may be classified under a plan, and their holders are entitled to vote as a class to accept or reject the plan. See § 1123(a)(1). The court may confirm the plan if it provides each holder of a priority claim of these kinds with payment in cash in full on the effective date. If the class votes to accept the plan, however, the court may confirm the plan if it provides deferred cash payments that have a present value, as of the effective date of the plan, equal to the allowed amount of the priority claims. Thus, these priority claimants will receive payment in full on a present value basis, although the payments may be deferred if an appropriate interest rate is paid.[12]

---

12. Most of the case law on the appropriate rate of interest to be paid on priority claims involves priority tax claims and § 1129(a)(9)(C). Prior to the amendments made by the 2005 BAPCPA, it was not clear that a special interest rate was required to be paid on priority tax claims. The majority view required payment of a market rate of interest—the rate that a debtor would pay to a commercial lender for a loan of equivalent amount and duration considering the risk of default and any security. Thus, the bankruptcy judge would determine on a case by case basis the interest rate that the reorganized debtor would have to pay a creditor in order to obtain a loan on equivalent terms in the open market. See, e.g., United States v. Camino Real Landscape Maint. Contractors, Inc.

Holders of § 507(a)(8) priority tax claims are similarly entitled under § 1129(a)(9)(C) to be paid the full present value of their claims as of the effective date of the plan; either they must be paid in full, in cash, on the effective date, or, if they are given deferred cash payments, they must be paid interest. Section 511, added by the 2005 BAPCPA, requires use of the applicable nonbankruptcy interest rate for tax claims for the month in which the plan is confirmed. For federal tax claims, that would be the rate provided under 26 U.S.C. § 6621(b), 26 C.F.R. § 301.6621-1, and the applicable Revenue Ruling.[13] Holders of priority tax claims are entitled to be paid in regular installments, "in a manner not less favorable than the most favored nonpriority unsecured claim," (except for cash payments made to convenience classes under § 1122(b)), and over a period not exceeding five years from the date of the order for relief.[14] Section 1129(a)(9)(C). These eighth priority tax claims are not classified; thus their holders are not entitled to vote to accept or reject the plan. Many plan proponents take advantage of the provision that permits the deferral of payments on priority tax claims without the consent of the taxing agency (and without a vote of priority tax claimants). See, e.g., In re S. States Motor Inns, Inc., 709 F.2d 647 (11th Cir. 1983).

Occasionally, the principals of the debtor in possession will care which taxes are paid in what order under a confirmed plan of reorganization. The most obvious example arises when an officer or director of the debtor in possession is personally liable for taxes that the debtor in possession has refused to pay. Examples of such taxes can include unpaid sales taxes under certain state laws and nonpayment of trust fund taxes such as employee withholding taxes under § 6672 of the Internal Revenue Code. Although the Bankruptcy Code does not specify whether the plan may allocate tax payments to specific obligations owed by the debtor in possession, the United States Supreme Court has held that the bankruptcy judge has discretion to confirm a plan providing for payments to be allocated first to trust fund tax obligations where it is necessary to do so for the success of the plan. United States v. Energy Res. Co., 495 U.S. 545, 110 S. Ct. 2139, 109 L. Ed. 2d 580 (1990).

(In re Camino Real Landscape Maint. Contractors, Inc.), 818 F.2d 1503, 1508 (9th Cir. 1987); United States v. Neal Pharmacal Co., 789 F.2d 1283 (8th Cir. 1986). That pre-BAPCPA case law should remain applicable to the required interest rate under § 1129(a)(9)(B). As discussed below in the text, the BAPCPA added a provision to the Code that requires a particular interest rate to be paid on priority tax claims. See § 511. It remains to be seen whether the Supreme Court's decision in Till v. SCS Credit Corp., 541 U.S. 465, 124 S. Ct., 1951, 158 L. Ed. 2d 787 (2004) (reprinted below in Chapter Fifteen) will affect the analysis of the required interest rate under § 1129(a)(9)(B).

13. For the first quarter of 2006, the standard interest rate is 7%, though the rate on "large corporate underpayments" of tax is 9%. Rev. Rul. 2005-78, 2005-51 I.R.B. 1157.

14. The order for relief apparently refers to the original petition under § 301, 302, or 303, even if it was filed in a case under chapter 7 that was converted to chapter 11.

4. Financial Standards

In order to confirm a plan consensually under § 1129(a) of the Bankruptcy Code, the Court must find that the plan complies with two financial standards set forth in § 1129(a)(7) and (11). Section 1129(a)(11) is the so-called feasibility requirement. Unless the plan provides for liquidation of the debtor or further financial reorganization, in order to confirm the plan the court must find that confirmation of the plan "is not likely to be followed by the liquidation, or the need for further financial reorganization, of the debtor or any successor to the debtor under the plan". Section 1129(a)(11). Thus, the Court may confirm a liquidating plan or a plan that proposes to divest, split up, spinoff, or merge the debtor. See § 1123(a)(5)(B)-(D) & (b)(4).[15] If the plan proposes to reorganize the debtor, however, the proponent must show a reasonable likelihood of the debtor's survival; that is, the plan must have a reasonable probability of success. Kane v. Johns-Manville Corp. (In re Johns-Manville Corp.), 843 F.2d 636, 649 (2d Cir. 1988); Acequia, Inc. v. Clinton (In re Acequia, Inc.), 787 F.2d 1352 (9th Cir. 1986). One court explained:

> [T]he debtor need not establish at confirmation that all of the proposed payments to creditors will, in fact, be received. The debtor need only establish by a preponderance of the evidence that there is a reasonable probability that it can make the required payments pursuant to the terms of the Plan.

Mut. Life Ins. Co. v. Patrician St. Joseph Partners Ltd. P'ship (In re Patrician St. Joseph Partners Ltd. P'ship), 169 B.R. 669, 682 (D. Ariz. 1994).[16] The length of repayments proposed to be made under the plan determines the period over which feasibility must be found. The uncertainty of the debtor's ability to repay increases as the period over which payments are to be made increases. E.g., In re White, 36 B.R. 199 (Bankr. D. Kan. 1983). Thus a plan that requires a 68 year old debtor to work for another 30 years to repay creditors does not have a reasonable likelihood of success. See United States

---

15. But a plan provision that simply contains a "drop dead" provision allowing the secured lender to foreclose if the debtor fails to perform does not meet the feasibility standard, because the foreclosure of primary assets is not the same as liquidation; liquidation requires the end of a debtor's existence. Danny Thomas Props. II Ltd. P'ship v. Beal Bank, S.S.B. (In re Danny Thomas Props. II Ltd. P'ship), 241 F.3d 959, 962 (8th Cir. 2001).

16. There is some authority that, in a cramdown, compliance with the requirements of § 1129(b) must be shown by clear and convincing evidence. See In re Cellular Info. Sys., Inc., 171 B.R. 926, 937 (Bankr. S.D.N.Y. 1994) (describing split in authorities and holding that correct burden is preponderance of the evidence). The Fifth Circuit has held that even the cramdown requirements need be proved only by a preponderance of the evidence. Heartland Fed. Sav. & Loan v. Briscoe Enters., Ltd., II (In re Briscoe Enters., Ltd., II), 994 F.2d 1160, 1163-65 (5th Cir. 1993). The court in *Briscoe* suggested that there was an issue whether compliance with the requirements of § 1129(a) might need to be proved by clear and convincing evidence in a cramdown, but the court held that they need not be—a preponderance of the evidence is sufficient. Of course, compliance with § 1129(a)(8) need not be proven at all in a cramdown; failure to comply with (a)(8) is what makes cramdown necessary.

v. Haas (In re Haas) 162 F.3d 1087, 1090 (11th Cir. 1998). But a plan that requires a 60 year old man to work another six to eight years as a computer consultant may be feasible. See Computer Task Group, Inc. v. Brotby (In re Brotby), 303 B.R. 177, 192 (B.A.P. 9th Cir. 2003).

The purposes of the feasibility standard are to prevent financial cripples from re-entering the stream of commerce and to "prevent confirmation of visionary schemes which promise creditors and equity security holders more under a proposed plan than the debtor can possibly attain after confirmation." Pizza of Hawaii, Inc. v. Shakey's, Inc. (In re Pizza of Hawaii, Inc.), 761 F.2d 1374, 1382 (9th Cir. 1985) (quoting 5 King, COLLIER ON BANKRUPTCY ¶ 1129.02[11] (15th ed. 1984) (currently ¶ 1129.03[11]). Thus, courts will examine the debtor's capital structure, including the debtor's debt-equity ratio, in order make sure that the debtor is not undertaking an inordinate amount of debt. The court will also analyze future cash flow projections to determine whether the debtor will be able to meet debt service proposed under the plan as well as to have adequate working capital to run the business and to make capital improvements. If the debtor is litigating a large disputed claim, the plan must provide for the possibility that the debtor will lose the litigation. If the loss of litigation will impair the debtor's performance under the plan, then the court may not confirm the plan. *Pizza of Hawaii.*

Some plans propose to reorganize the debtor and pay creditors over a period of time. In the event the debtor is unable to pay creditors, a plan that provides for postconfirmation modification procedures would impermissibly provide for further financial reorganization in violation of § 1129(a)(11). In re Beyond.com Corp., 289 B.R. 138, 146 (Bankr. N.D. Cal. 2003). Suppose instead that the plan provides that if the debtor is unable to pay creditors, assets of the debtor will be liquidated in order to repay creditors at the conclusion of a specified period of time. Does a plan that adopts this hybrid approach to feasibility meet the requirements of § 1129(a)(11)? Consider the following case:

In re Nite Lite Inns
United States Bankruptcy Court, S.D. Cal., 1982
17 B.R. 367

HERBERT KATZ, Bankruptcy Judge.

Nite Lite Inns, a California corporation, filed for relief under Chapter 11 of the Code on December 7, 1979. The major assets of Nite Lite Inns were three hotels located in Ontario, San Diego and National City. The San Diego hotel consists of 156 rooms, 2 banquet rooms and a 14-unit recreational vehicle park. Cost overruns arising out of the construction of the San Diego hotel in 1979 were the major contributing factor to the filing of the reorganization proceeding herein.

On March 4, 1980, Grosvenor Square Restaurant filed a petition under Chapter 11 of the Code. The major asset of this debtor is a restaurant located immediately adjacent to the San Diego hotel.

Shortly thereafter, on June 6, 1980, J. Mark Grosvenor, Judson R. Grosvenor and Rachel J. Grosvenor filed individual petitions under Chapter 11 of the Code. The Grosvenors are the major stockholders and principals of the other related debtors. While each individual debtor had particular personal debts, the majority of their debts arose out of personal guarantees made to creditors of the other business estates. The above Chapter 11 cases were subsequently consolidated for administrative purposes.

* * *

On August 12, 1981, the debtors submitted their fourth amended plan of reorganization. This plan basically envisions a 100-percent payout, plus interest, over 36 months. At the end of 36 months the debtors intend to obtain new long-term financing or in the alternative sell the San Diego hotel. Numerous objections were filed in opposition to the plan and hearings were held on October 21, 29 and 30, November 5 and 24 and December 3, 1981, to deal with them. One by one almost every objection was either withdrawn or compromised through last-minute changes in the plan. After the ballots were tallied it became evident that only one class of creditors had failed to accept the plan. Because of Class 8's rejection of the plan the debtors requested that the court confirm or "cram down" the plan over their objection under 11 U.S.C. § 1129.

Class 8, a class consisting of an entity known as Burke Investors, vigorously opposes the use of cram down in this case. At the hearings on confirmation, Burke Investors objected to confirmation of the plan on the grounds that it is not feasible [11 U.S.C. § 1129(a)(11)], not fair and equitable [11 U.S.C. § 1129(b)(2)], not proposed in good faith [11 U.S.C. § 1129(a)(3)], provides for an improper classification [11 U.S.C. § 1129(a)(1)], does not provide this creditor with property of a value that is not less than the amount such holder would receive if the debtors were liquidated [11 U.S.C. § 1129(a)(7)(A)(ii)(b)(2)(B)(i)] [sic], and lastly that consolidation of the cases is not in the best interests of creditors. Burke Investors also moved to block the use of some $300,000 on deposit pending a final determination as to whether Burke Investors is entitled to such sums. This opinion is filed to deal with each of Burke Investors' objections and to determine whether the debtors' fourth amended plan should be confirmed.

* * *

Feasibility under 11 U.S.C. § 1129(a)(11)

The plan in this case anticipates that payments will be made out of current surplus operating revenues. In this regard the debtors presented testimony and a pro forma projection which would tend to show that the debtors could make the payments provided for in the plan. Burke Investors submitted expert testimony which tended to show that the debtors' expectations as to future operating revenues were not realistic in light of recent economic trends in the hotel industry. It was the expert's opinion that the debtors would not be able to meet the payment schedule under the plan.

Section 1129(a)(11) provides that a plan may be confirmed if:

"(11) Confirmation of the plan is not likely to be followed by the liquidation, or the need for further financial reorganization, of the debtor or any successor to the debtor under the plan, unless such liquidation or reorganization is proposed in the plan."

This section is a slight elaboration of the law that developed under the Act regarding the application of the word "feasible." S. Rep. No. 95-989, 95th Cong., 2d Sess. 126 (1978), U.S. Code Cong. & Admin. News 1978, p. 5787.

Had the plan merely provided for periodic payments with a possible refinancing at the end of 36 months, the court would have denied confirmation on this ground alone. However, the plan provides for a liquidation of the San Diego hotel in the event the debtors default in the payment scheme of the plan. It is undisputed that the value which would be realized upon a sale of the San Diego hotel is greater than all debts owed in the case. The plan also provides for the bankruptcy court to retain jurisdiction over the operation and enforcement of the plan.

Under these circumstances it appears that in the event the debtors defaulted on the payment schedule of the plan, a subsequent sale would provide the creditors with all sums promised to them. The liquidation provisions, therefore, bring the plan in compliance with 11 U.S.C. § 1129(a)(11) and render the plan feasible. See also H.R. Rep. No. 95-595, 95th Cong. 1st Sess. 412 (1977).

* * *

Confirmation of a Plan under 11 U.S.C. § 1129(b)

Section 1129(b)(1) provides:

"Notwithstanding section 510(a) of this title, if all of the applicable requirements of subsection (a) of this section other than paragraph (8) are met with respect to a plan, the court, on request of the proponent of the plan, shall confirm the plan notwithstanding the requirements of such paragraph if the plan does not discriminate unfairly, and is fair and equitable, with respect to each class of claims or interests that is impaired under, and has not accepted, the plan."

The ability to confirm a plan over the objection of creditors is commonly known as "cram down." Without "cram down" it is questionable whether many plans would be confirmed where there are disputes between creditors and the debtor. The presence of the "cram down" provision actually facilitates settlements in many cases, while at the same time allows for confirmation where a settlement cannot be reached. Having already determined that the plan meets the applicable requirements of 11 U.S.C. § 1129(a) and that the plan does not discriminate unfairly, the court must only determine whether the plan is fair and equitable.

Section 1129(b)(2)(B) provides that with respect to a class of unsecured claims the plan is fair and equitable if "the plan provides that each holder of a claim of such class receive or retain on account of such claim property of a value, as of the effective date of the plan, equal to the allowed amount of such claim ...."

Burke Investors claims that the plan is not fair and equitable in two respects. Initially it is submitted that even though Burke Investors is to be paid 100% of his claim, plus interest, the plan violates the "best interests of creditors" test found in 11 U.S.C. § 1129(a)(7)(A)(ii). Secondly, it is argued that the interest rate provided under the plan does not allow such class to receive on the effective date of the plan, a value equal to the amount of such claim.

Burke Investors does not claim that they would receive more than a 100-percent payment in a liquidation. However, they claim that payment in full over a period of time is not equivalent to receiving full payment now because of the current tax liabilities they will be required to pay as a result of their claim. Prior to the filing of the bankruptcy herein, Burke Investors attempted to effectuate a tax-free exchange through the use of funds obtained from the sale of a prior investment and a sale and lease back of the Nite Lite Inns San Diego. In Burke Investors v. Nite Lite Inns, 13 B.R. 900 (Bkrtcy. S.D. Cal. 1981), the court determined that the transaction was not a bona fide sale and lease back, but instead was merely an unsecured loan. Hence, the tax-free exchange also fell through. Burke Investors is now saddled with a current tax liability and is apparently without the financial ability to pay it. If the debtors were to liquidate, it is argued that Burke Investors will be able to meet their tax liability.

While it is true that if the plan is confirmed Burke Investors may have a significant tax problem, the provisions of 11 U.S.C. § 1129 do not require the court to look beyond a determination as to whether a creditor is to receive under the plan the value of his claim as of the effective date of the reorganization. The unfulfilled hopes of this financial transaction need not be satisfied in order to meet this test. By requiring no more, the Bankruptcy Code attempts to achieve a balance between the due-process rights of creditors and the needs of a society bent on rehabilitating debtors. It is doubtful whether any ordered system of bankruptcy would be operable under the level of scrutiny urged by Burke Investors.

* * *

Conclusion

In any bankruptcy case there are seldom any winners, just survivors. This case is no exception to the general rule. The debtors and several of their creditors have engaged in combat for the past two years. The climate of compromise which has recently prevailed in these proceedings has produced a plan which complies with the provisions of 11 U.S.C. § 1129. All classes have accepted the plan except Class 8. Upon the request of the debtors the court finds that the plan may be confirmed over the dissent of Class 8. The plan will therefore be confirmed.

* * *

NOTES

1. Although the court in *Nite Lite Inns* discussed the best interest of creditors test as if it were part of the fair and equitable standard applicable under § 1129(b) in a cramdown, it is not. The best interest of creditors test is of course found in § 1129(a), in particular in § 1129(a)(7), and thus it is a requirement both for consensual confirmation and for cramdown.

2. The bankruptcy judge in *Nite Lite Inns* confirmed the plan based on the determination that in the event the debtor was unable to repay creditors out of operating income, liquidation of the assets would almost certainly provide creditors with payments in full. Other courts have confirmed plans providing for a default option of liquidation even where liquidation might not result in creditors being paid in full. See Travelers Ins. Co. v. Pikes Peak Water Co. (In re Pikes Peak Water Co.), 779 F.2d 1456 (10th Cir.1985) (providing for liquidation three years after the effective date); Acequia, Inc. v. Clinton (In re Acequia, Inc.), 787 F.2d 1352 (9th Cir.1986) (providing for liquidation nine years after confirmation). Where payment of creditors is uncertain, is it appropriate to confirm a plan of reorganization where a liquidation might be the ultimate result?

3. As we have discussed, formulation of a consensual plan of reorganization usually results in negotiating the going concern value of the reorganized enterprise based on a capitalization of future earnings or discounting of future net cash flows. Junior ownership interests, such as common stock, general partnership, or limited partnership interests, are permitted to participate because creditors are receiving reorganization securities based on the premise that the enterprise will operate as a going concern. If liquidation is to ensue prior to the time creditors are paid under the terms of their reorganization securities, is it appropriate to confirm the plan premised on reorganization value rather than liquidation value?

4. How does the proponent prove a reasonable likelihood of the debtor's survival? What constitutes a "reasonable probability of success"? Does your answer differ where the reorganization value and liquidation value of the businesses are the same?

5. How does the feasibility standard relate to the interest to be paid on reorganization securities and the maturity date of reorganization securities? Compare the evidence on feasibility that would be offered in support of a plan that purports to pay creditors under a debt instrument over a thirty year period at an annual interest rate of ten percent with a plan that proposes to pay creditors over a five year period at an annual interest rate of nine percent. Is there a difference between long term debt and short term debt other than the increased interest rate on long term debt? What additional evidence, if any, must be proved if the reorganization securities require interest to be repaid at a variable rate?

Section 1129(a)(7) prescribes the financial standard that is applied to protect dissenting members of an accepting impaired class from an unfair plan. Recall that acceptance of an impaired class requires two-thirds in dollar amount and a majority in number of claims held by those voting (excluding votes designated under § 1126(e)). Thus, a substantial minority may vote against a plan and the class may nevertheless be found to accept the plan as a matter of law. In this event, the Bankruptcy Code requires dissenting creditors to receive at least as much as they would receive in a liquidation of the debtor; this standard is known as the best interest of creditors test.

Section 1129(a)(7)(A) of the Code codifies the best interest of creditors test. In particular, the statute requires each dissenting member of a class to "receive or retain under the plan on account of such claim or interest property of a value, as of the effective date of the plan, that is not less than the amount that such holder would so receive or retain if the debtor were liquidated under chapter 7" on the effective date of the plan. Thus, while the substantive provisions of chapter 7 do not apply directly in a chapter 11 case, they can be referenced indirectly by application of the best interest of creditors test. For example, if a debtor is solvent on a liquidation basis, an unsecured creditor will be entitled to receive postpetition interest on an unsecured claim under § 726(a)(5) of the Bankruptcy Code. See In re Dow Corning Corp., 237 B.R. 380 (Bankr. E.D. Mich. 1999) (awarding postpetition interest at the federal judgment rate under 28 U.S.C. § 1961(a)). Thus, a plan proposing to satisfy the creditor's unsecured claim in full without the payment of postpetition interest might not satisfy the best interest of creditors test. Notice, however, that the best interest of creditors test only applies to impaired classes.

The Bankruptcy Reform Act of 1994 deleted § 1124(3). Section 1124(3) provided that a class of unsecured claims would be unimpaired if holders of claims in the class received under the plan cash payment of the full allowed amount of their claims on the effective date of the plan. Thus, prior to the deletion of § 1124(3), if a plan proposed to pay an unsecured class of claims in cash in full on the effective date, the class would not be impaired and the best interest of creditors test would not apply. Thus holders of unsecured claims theoretically could have been denied postpetition interest even though the debtor was solvent on a liquidation basis. Some courts refused to confirm such plans on the basis that the courts had the inherent power to order the payment of postpetition interest when the debtor was solvent on a liquidation basis. See, e.g., In re Shaffer Furniture Co., 68 B.R. 827 (Bankr. E.D. Pa. 1987), abrogated on other grounds, In re Chiapetta, 159 B.R. 152 (Bankr. E.D. Pa. 1993). However, in In re New Valley Corp., 168 B.R. 73 (Bankr. D.N.J. 1994), the court held that such a plan could be confirmed unless the facts of the case—beyond the mere solvency of the debtor on a liquidation basis—showed that such a plan was not proposed in good faith. In response to *New Valley*, Congress deleted § 1124(3). Thus, even if a plan provides for full cash payment on the effective date of the allowed amount of the claims in a class, the class might be considered to be impaired, with the result that the best interest of creditors test will apply—and that will require that dissenting claimholders be given postpetition interest where the debtor is solvent on a liquidation basis. See Chapter Eleven of this text, Section D.

The best interest of creditors test is of particular importance where the debtor is a partnership whose general partners are solvent (or at least have substantial assets). In a chapter 7 case, the chapter 7 trustee would have the right to recover from the general partners whatever deficiency there was in the estate to pay the claims of the partnership's recourse creditors. If the general partners are solvent, then the trustee could recover enough to allow payment of claims in full—presumably with postpetition interest—in a chapter 7 case. Creditors should be entitled to the same recovery in a chapter 11 case under the best interest of creditors test even though § 723 does not apply directly. In re Union Meeting Partners, 165 B.R. 553 (Bankr. E.D. Pa. 1994), aff'd without opinion, 52 F.3d 317 (1995); In re Heron, Burchette, Ruckert & Rothwell, 148 B.R. 660 (Bankr. D.D.C. 1992); Bell Road Inv. Co. v. M. Long Arabians (In re M. Long Arabians), 103 B.R. 211, 216-17 (B.A.P. 9th Cir.1989); MBank Corpus Christi v. Seikel (In re I-37 Gulf Ltd. P'ship), 48 B.R. 647 (Bankr. S.D. Tex. 1985); but see In re Duval Manor Assocs., 191 B.R. 622 (Bankr. E.D. Pa. 1996) (holding that chapter 11 plan need not provide recovery that creditors would receive under § 723 where creditors retain right to seek payment from partners). Could this result be avoided if the chapter 11 plan provided that in addition to payments given to creditors under the plan they would retain whatever rights they had against general partners under nonbankruptcy law? See *Duval Manor Assocs.*, 191 B.R. 622; *Union Meeting Partners*, 165 B.R. 553; *Heron, Burchette*, 148 B.R. 660.

Sometimes the difference of treatment of a claim in chapter 11 and chapter 7 can distort the distributional effects under a plan of reorganization. For example, assume that a corporate debtor has assets that would liquidate for $10 million in chapter 7 and creditors' claims consist only of unsecured claims in the allowed amount of $20 million. On its face, a plan that proposes to pay unsecured creditors 50% of the allowed amount of their claims on the effective date would meet the best interest of creditors test. Assume, however, that of the $20 million in general unsecured claims, $4 million is a penalty claim (such as a tax penalty or a punitive damage award). Does the plan still meet the best interest of creditors test? See § 726(a)(4). If the plan does not meet the best interest of creditors test, how could the plan be modified so that it would meet the test? Note that some courts have equitably subordinated penalty claims in chapter 11 cases, even though § 726(a)(4) does not apply in chapter 11. See Chapter Ten, supra, Section B.

A similar problem exists when the debtor's estate involves a nonrecourse loan[17] that is secured by collateral with a value less than the allowed amount of the claim. Under § 1111(b)(1) of the Bankruptcy Code, as long as the estate retains property[18] that is collateral for the nonrecourse loan, and the creditor's class does not elect application of § 1111(b)(2), the nonrecourse creditor is given an allowed secured claim equal to the value of its interest in the collateral and an unsecured deficiency claim as a matter of bankruptcy law. Section 1111(b)(1)(A). Assume that the debtor's estate has assets that would liquidate for $10 million including real estate worth $6 million mortgaged on a nonrecourse basis to a secured creditor who was owed $7 million. Assume further that other creditors hold unsecured claims of $4 million against the estate. Does a plan that proposes to pay the secured creditor $6 million cash on the $6 million allowed secured claim and the unsecured creditors (including the $1 million deficiency claim) the remaining $4 million meet the best interest of creditors test? If not, can the deficiency claim be separately classified? Compare In re Woodbrook Assocs., 19 F.3d 312 (7th Cir. 1994); LW-SP2, L.P. v. Krisch Realty Assocs., L.P. (In re Krisch Realty Assocs., L.P.), 174 B.R. 914 (Bankr. W.D .Va. 1994); Principal Mut. Life Ins. Co. v. Baldwin Park Towne Ctr., Ltd. (In re Baldwin Park Towne Ctr., Ltd.), 171 B.R. 374 (Bankr. C.D. Cal. 1994); with, e.g., Barakat v. Life Ins. Co. (In re Barakat), 99 F.3d 1520, 1526 (9th Cir. 1996);

---

17. A nonrecourse loan is a loan that is secured by a lien encumbering property of the debtor which by terms of an agreement or applicable law entitles the creditor upon default to proceed only against the collateral. The creditor has no basis to proceed against the debtor *in personam* for any deficiency.

18. As drafted, the statute deprives the nonrecourse creditor of the deficiency claim if the class of which such claim is a part makes the § 1111(b)(2) election or if the collateral is "sold under section 363 of this title or is to be sold under the plan." Section 1111(b)(1)(A)(ii). Although the statute only removes the deficiency in the event of a sale under § 363 or under a plan, a similar result should follow no matter how the property leaves the estate as long as the creditor has a right to credit bid upon disposition. E.g., Tampa Bay Assocs., Ltd. v. DRW Worthington, Ltd. (In re Tampa Bay Assocs., Ltd.), 864 F.2d 47 (5th Cir. 1989); John Hancock Mut. Life Ins. Co. v. Cal. Hancock, Inc. (In re Cal. Hancock, Inc.), 88 B.R. 226, 230-31 (B.A.P. 9th Cir.1988); In re Woodridge N. Apts. Ltd., 71 B.R. 189 (Bankr. N.D.Cal. 1987).

Travelers Ins. Co. v. Bryson Props. (In re Bryson Props.), 961 F.2d 496 (4th Cir. 1992); In re Dean, 166 B.R. 949 (Bankr. D. N.M. 1994). The classification issue is discussed below in Chapter Fifteen of this text.

Notice that the best interest of creditors test requires the court to compare the present value of deferred payments creditors receive under a plan with what they would receive in a liquidation case. The statute uses the language "property of a value as of the effective date of the plan". The property to be distributed may constitute securities, cash, or property in kind. What is meant, however, by the effective date of the plan? Under § 1141(a) of the Bankruptcy Code, unless the plan or the order confirming the plan otherwise provides, the date on which the plan becomes binding between the debtors and creditors is the date of confirmation. The plan may specify a different effective date on which the plan will become effective between the parties and binding upon the debtor and creditors. For example, the plan might specify that it will become effective on the date on which the order confirming the plan becomes final or some other date specified in the plan. See In re Jones, 32 B.R. 951, 958 n.13 (Bankr. D. Utah 1983). The plan proponent is not free to specify an effective date that has no reasonable relationship to confirmation of the plan. In particular, the effective date should mean a date within a reasonable time, In re Rolling Green Country Club, 26 B.R. 729, 735 (Bankr. D. Minn. 1982), not a date many months in the future. In re Krueger, 66 B.R. 463 (Bankr. S.D. Fla. 1986). For example, courts have approved an effective date that is twenty business days following the date the confirmation order becomes final. In re Wonder Corp. of Am., 70 B.R. 1018, 1021 (Bankr. D. Conn. 1987),[19] but disapproved an effective date delayed for one

---

19. Could the effective date be the date the confirmation order is entered? The confirmation hearing is a contested matter by virtue of Federal Rule of Bankruptcy Procedure 3020(b)(1). Prior to December 1, 1999, it was unclear whether orders confirming plans were automatically stayed under Rule 7062. See In re Ewell, 958 F.2d 276, 278 (9th Cir. 1992) (questioning whether previous version of Rule 7062 applied to judicial sales); In re Whatley, 155 B.R. 775 (Bankr. D. Colo.1993) (orders disallowing claim, authorizing sale of property, and confirming plan were all self-executing, immediately effective orders on which parties could act despite stay), aff'd, 169 B.R. 698 (D. Colo. 1994), aff'd, 54 F.3d 788 (1995); Van Bossche v. Hartford Accident & Indem. Co. (In re Vanden Bossche), 125 B.R. 571 (N.D. Cal. 1991) (stay does not prevent recording of abstract of judgment). Under the amendment to Rule 3020(e), effective December 1, 1999, an order confirming a chapter 9 or chapter 11 plan is stayed automatically for 10 days from entry, unless the court orders otherwise. This amendment will give parties opposing confirmation the opportunity to seek a stay pending appeal. A corresponding amendment to Rule 3021 provides that distribution under a confirmed plan may be made after confirmation except as provided in Rule 3020(e). Presumably while the order is stayed, distribution may not be made. To avoid controversy in cases commenced before December 1, 1999, confirmation orders entered on or after December 1, 1999 should specify whether it is just and practicable for the order confirming plan to be stayed under the amended rule. If there is a year-end deadline or other emergency, parties might be able to persuade the court to abbreviate or eliminate the stay. In light of the mootness doctrine, however, it may be necessary to give an objecting party an opportunity to obtain a stay pending appeal as a matter of due process of law. Therefore, many plans define the effective date to be the first business day that is at least eleven calendar days after the date of entry of the confirmation order on which no stay pending appeal is in effect. For a more complete discussion of the mootness doctrine see note 3, supra.

year after confirmation when the only reason for delay is to enable the debtor to collect accounts receivable while the creditors bear all the risks of operations. In re Potomac Iron Works, Inc., 217 B.R. 170 (Bankr. D. Md. 1997).

Once the court has determined the "effective date", the court must discount deferred cash payments in order to determine the present value to be distributed to creditors as of the effective date of the plan. This is done through selecting an appropriate discount rate for the note or debt instrument given to the creditor determined in light of any security to collateralize the note, the length of time over which payments will be made, and the risk and uncertainty faced by the creditor in light of the credit-worthiness of the rehabilitated debtor.

Once the present value of deferred cash payments is computed, the court is required to consider what the creditor would receive or retain on account of the claim if the debtor were liquidated under chapter 7 on the effective date. Does the court consider what would actually happen if the debtor's case were converted to a case under chapter 7 and the estate were liquidated over a period of time? Or is the court to assume a hypothetical instantaneous chapter 7 liquidation and distribution on the effective date of the plan? As a matter of policy, the purpose of the best interest of creditors test is to insure that a creditor receives economic value under the chapter 11 plan that is at least as great as the value the creditor would receive in the chapter 7 liquidation case. Accordingly, the court probably should look to the actual effects of a chapter 7 liquidation (including allowance for administrative expenses) rather than assuming a hypothetical instantaneous liquidation. See Chapter Ten of this text; In re Crowthers McCall Pattern, Inc., 120 B.R. 279 (Bankr. S.D.N.Y. 1990). For example, if a creditor would receive $49 in cash on the effective date in full satisfaction of a $100 claim but would receive $50 in a chapter 7 liquidation case two years after the effective date, should the court find that the plan complies with the best interest of creditors test?

Notice that the best interest of creditors test applies to an impaired class of secured claims as well as to an impaired class of unsecured claims. In the normal case, the accepting secured creditor will hold an allowed secured claim in a class by itself because there will be no other substantially similar secured claim—none whose lien has the same priority and covers the same collateral. If the creditor votes to accept the plan, the requirements of § 1129(a)(7)(A)(i) will be met. Because each member of the class has voted to accept the plan, the usual best interest of creditors test will not apply. If, however, the creditor fails to vote or votes "no" then § 1129(a)(7)(A)(ii) will require the plan to provide the creditor present value equal to the value the creditor's interest in the collateral would have in a chapter 7 liquidation. Ordinarily, this requirement will add nothing to the fair and equitable requirement that will apply under § 1129(b)(2)(A) to the dissenting class, and which would require payment of at least that amount of present value. However, some courts hold that where no creditor holding a claim in a class bothers to vote, the class should be deemed to accept the plan. See, e.g., In

re Ruti-Sweetwater, Inc., 836 F.2d 1263 (10th Cir. 1988); but see In re Jim
Beck, Inc., 207 B.R. 1010 (Bankr. W.D. Va.), aff'd, 214 B.R. 305 (W.D. Va.
1997), aff'd without op., 162 F.3d 1155 (4th Cir. 1998); Bell Road Inv.
Co. v. M. Long Arabians (In re M. Long Arabians), 103 B.R. 211 (B.A.P. 9th
Cir. 1989). In such a case, the fair and equitable standard would not apply but
the creditor might still be entitled to the protection of the best interest of
creditors test. Further, if there is more than one secured claim in a class, such
as in the case of mortgage bonds or mechanics liens, the class may accept the
plan despite the dissent of one or more claimants—thus making the fair and
equitable standard inapplicable—and thus forcing dissenting secured
creditors to rely on the best interest of creditors test.

If an undersecured creditor with recourse against the debtor makes the
§ 1111(b)(2) election, a separate best interest of creditors test applies, under
§ 1129(a)(7)(B), although it is probably technically surplusage. If the election
is made, the creditor is given an allowed secured claim equal to the full
amount of the debt, even if the creditor's interest in the collateral is not worth
the amount of the debt. As a consequence, however, the creditor waives any
recourse deficiency claim. Because the only claim held by the electing
creditor is a secured claim, it is only with respect to that secured claim that
the creditor can insist on the protection of the best interest of creditors test.
Thus by making the election the creditor gives up the right to insist on
receiving the value it would have received in a chapter 7 liquidation on
account of its unsecured deficiency claim. Section 1129(a)(7)(B) reinforces
that result by providing that the electing creditor only need receive on account
of its secured claim present value equal to the value of its interest in the
collateral. That is just the same amount that the creditor is entitled to receive
under the ordinary best interest of creditors test in § 1129(a)(7)(A) on
account of its secured claim; thus the different standard is probably
technically surplusage. (However, it may be argued that the § 1129(a)(7)(B)
test does not refer to the value that would be obtained in a liquidation and
thus may entitle the secured creditor to present value equal to the going
concern value of its collateral; that could be a higher amount than the
liquidation value required by § 1129(a)(7)(A).)

Of course, a nonrecourse undersecured creditor would have no deficiency
claim in a chapter 7 case, and thus would obtain nothing on account of any
unsecured claim in chapter 7. Thus there is no need for a separate best
interest of creditors test when the class of which such a claim is a part elects
application of § 1111(b)(2).

If all of the requirements of § 1129(a) are met, the court may enter its
order confirming the plan. On the other hand, if an impaired class has
rejected the plan, the only circumstance under which the plan may be
confirmed is if it complies with the requirements of § 1129(b). That is the
subject of the next chapter.

Chapter Fifteen

Cramdown (And Creditors' Remedies Related To The Plan Process)

What happens when a debtor cannot confirm a plan consensually under § 1129(a), because one or more impaired classes have not accepted the plan proposed by the debtor (or because it is certain that one or more impaired classes will not accept a plan, if one is proposed by the debtor)? In this Chapter we consider four possible options instead of consensual confirmation of a plan: (1) nonconsensual confirmation under § 1129(b) in what is known as a cramdown, (2) confirmation (consensual or under a cramdown) of a competing plan filed by one or more creditors or other parties in interest, (3) grant of relief from stay to secured creditors (thus ending the attempted reorganization), and (4) termination of the chapter 11 reorganization under § 1112 by dismissal of the case or conversion of the case to chapter 7.

We suggest strongly that the student reread section E.4. of Chapter One at this time. We also encourage the student to read two articles by one of your authors that explain the rules for cramdown and provide many concrete examples of their application. Klee, *Cramdown II*, 64 AM. BANKR. L.J. 229 (1990); Klee, *All You Ever Wanted to Know About Cram Down Under the New Bankruptcy Code,* 53 AM. BANKR. L.J. 133, 156 (1979).

A. REQUIREMENTS FOR CRAMDOWN

If an impaired class does not accept the plan, the plan can still be confirmed under § 1129(b) in a cramdown, if four requirements are met—one procedural and three substantive requirements. The procedural requirement is that the proponent of the plan must request that the court confirm the plan in a cramdown. See § 1129(b)(1) ("the court, on request of the proponent of the plan, shall confirm the plan * * * if * * * "). We assume that the debtor (or whoever proposed the plan) makes such a request, and thus we move on to the three substantive requirements for cramdown.

1. Satisfaction of All Requirements for Consensual Confirmation Except Section 1129(a)(8), But Including the Key Requirement in Section 1129(a)(10)

The first substantive requirement is that all the requirements of § 1129(a) must be satisfied, except for § 1129(a)(8) (which requires acceptance by all impaired classes). See § 1129(b)(1). A key requirement of § 1129(a) that must be met for the plan to be eligible to be confirmed consensually or in a cramdown is the requirement of § 1129(a)(10)—if the plan impairs one or more classes of claims, then at least one impaired class of claims must have accepted the plan, not counting acceptances by insiders. Thus, as we saw in Chapter Eleven, the debtor may try to draft the plan so as to ensure that there is at least one impaired class of claims that will accept the plan. In this Chapter we revisit the classification issues that we discussed in Chapter Eleven and focus on a particularly important set of classification issues. May the plan classify apart from other unsecured claims the unsecured claim given to an undersecured nonrecourse lender by § 1111(b)? Must the plan do so? The circuits are split, as we discuss below, and the Supreme Court has not yet answered these questions. We also consider below some creative strategies that Foam Corporation or other chapter 11 debtors may use in order to satisfy § 1129(a)(10).

2. The Requirement That the Plan Be Fair and Equitable with Respect to Dissenting Classes

The second substantive requirement for cramdown is that the plan must be "fair and equitable" with respect to the dissenting class or classes. Section 1129(b)(1). The fair and equitable requirement includes but is not limited to the requirements explicitly set forth in § 1129(b)(2). Section 1129(b)(2) provides partial definitions of "fair and equitable" for each kind of class which may dissent: classes of secured claims (§ 1129(b)(2)(A)), classes of unsecured claims (§ 1129(b)(2)(B)), and classes of interests (§ 1129(b)(2)(C)).

a. Fair and equitable treatment of dissenting classes of secured claim(s)

Outside bankruptcy, a secured creditor is entitled to apply the value of the property in which it has a lien (minus the amount of any senior liens) to the payment of the secured debt, at least if the debt is in default. In bankruptcy, the automatic stay prevents the secured creditor from taking collateral that is encumbered by its lien, but the lien itself will be recognized (unless the trustee's avoiding powers eliminate it). If a plan places a secured claim in an impaired class, and if the holder of the claim rejects the plan, then the holder will be entitled to the protection of the best interests test—the plan must give that dissenter on account of its claim "property" with a present value at least equal to what the dissenter would obtain on account of the claim in a chapter 7 liquidation. Section 1129(a)(7)(A).[1] More importantly, the plan typically cannot be confirmed unless it meets the tougher fair and equitable standard of § 1129(b).

The fair and equitable standard will apply because the dissenter's *class* will usually reject the plan due to the dissenter's rejection of it. That follows because the secured creditor's claim typically will be in a class by itself, and

---

1. That is true if the secured creditor's class does not make the § 1111(b)(2) election. If the creditor's class does make the election, then the plan need only give the secured creditor property with a present value equal to the lesser of the value of its collateral or the amount of its allowed claim, even if that is less than the amount of value it would receive in a chapter 7 liquidation. See § 1129(a)(7)(B), discussed in Chapter Fourteen, supra, at the end of section B.4.

thus the secured creditor's rejection of the plan will cause the class to reject the plan. Ordinarily, each secured claim is in its own class, because generally each is not substantially similar to any other claim in the case. Recall that claims cannot be placed together in the same class unless they are substantially similar. Section 1122(a). Claims secured by liens on different collateral or by liens with different priority in the same collateral generally cannot be placed in the same class. See Resnick & Sommer, 7 COLLIER ON BANKRUPTCY ¶ 1122.03[4][c][i]. Usually each secured claim in a case differs from each other secured claim either with regard to collateral or priority, and hence each secured claim typically must be placed by the plan in a class of its own.[2]

Suppose the estate includes two parcels of real property, Greenacre and Purpleacre. If Galactic Bank has a first mortgage on Greenacre, Global Bank has a second mortgage on Greenacre, and National Bank has a first mortgage on Purpleacre, each claim must be classified separately. Galactic Bank and Global Bank have the same collateral but different priority; their claims are not substantially similar. Galactic Bank's and National Bank's mortgages have the same priority—first priority—but in different collateral, and thus their claims are not substantially similar. Global Bank and National Bank have different priorities in different collateral; their claims are even more dissimilar. With each claim in a separate class, and assuming the classes are impaired, each mortgagee can block consensual confirmation under § 1129(a) by rejecting the plan, thus creating an impaired dissenting class.

What must a plan do in order to be fair and equitable with respect to a dissenting class of secured claim(s)? With respect to dissenting classes of secured claims, the "fair and equitable" requirement includes giving each holder of a secured claim in the class at least one of three kinds of treatment, set forth in clauses (i), (ii), and (iii), respectively, of § 1129(b)(2)(A). The second option—§ 1129(b)(2)(A)(ii)—permits the debtor to sell the collateral free and clear of liens at a sale at which the secured creditor can credit bid (by setting off the debt against the amount of its bid under § 363(k)). The secured creditor's lien then attaches to any proceeds from the sale (if someone other than the secured creditor buys the property at the sale). Then the secured

---

2.   There are exceptions to this general rule. For example, materials and mechanics lien holders may all hold liens of equal priority on the same collateral—the real property which was improved as a result of materials or labor provided by the lien holders. Their claims will then be substantially similar and may be classified together.

Another exception to the general rule is provided by public bondholders. If the debtor issues secured debt securities (bonds), the bonds may end up being held by hundreds or thousands of investors. Each investor typically would have a secured claim with the same priority in the same collateral. Thus the public bondholders' claims would be substantially similar; they would be classified together in one class in any plan. (If the debtor issued two series of bonds with different collateral or different priority, then the plan ought to provide for two separate classes of bondholders' claims.)

There are also cases in which secured claims may be secured by different items of collateral which are identical or nearly identical. Two mortgagees with $100,000 first mortgages on two different vacant lots owned by a developer in an area of tract housing may be considered to have substantially similar claims if the lots are nearly identical in size and value.

creragtor's claim—with its new collateral, the proceeds received from the sale—must be given the treatment required by either § 1129(b)(2)(A)(i) or § 1129(b)(2)(A)(iii). Thus we come back to (A)(i) or (A)(iii).

(1) Section 1129(b)(2)(A)(i)—Retention of Lien and Provision for Cash Payments with Specified Present Value and in Specified Amount

Under 1129(b)(2)(A)(i), the plan must do two things: it must provide for the secured creditor to retain its lien, and it must provide for "cash payments" with a particular present value as of the effective date of the plan and in a specified total dollar amount. Thus, if the secured creditor is not paid cash on the effective date, the plan must provided for payment for the delay, so that the present value of the deferred payments equals the required amount. The key to understanding 1129(b)(2)(A)(i) is understanding the amounts involved: the amount of the allowed secured claim, the amount of the lien that the plan must allow the secured creditor to retain, the amount of the present value that the plan must provide on account of the secured claim as of the effective date, and the total number of dollars that the plan must pay on account of the secured claim.

If you read the statute carefully, you should reach at least two conclusions. If the creditor is oversecured, then each of those four amounts equals the amount of the debt owed to the creditor (including any postpetition fees or costs allowed under § 506(b)). If the creditor is undersecured—and assuming for the moment that the creditor either chooses not to make the § 1111(b)(2) election is not eligible to make it—then each of those amounts equals the value of the creditor's collateral. That is one reason why the determination of the value of a secured creditor's collateral is crucial to the chapter 11 process. How should collateral be valued? Consider the Supreme Court's answer to that question in the following case. It is a chapter 13 case, but it deals with valuation under § 506(a), which, at the time of the Court's decision, applied to all chapters of the Code.[3]

Associates Commercial Corporation v. Rash
United States Supreme Court, 1997
520 U.S. 953, 117 S. Ct. 1879, 138 L. Ed. 2d 148

GINSBURG, J., delivered the opinion of the Court, in which REHNQUIST, C.J., and O'CONNOR, KENNEDY, SOUTER, THOMAS, and BREYER, JJ., joined, and in all but n. 4 of which SCALIA, J., joined. STEVENS, J., filed a dissenting opinion * * *.

We resolve in this case a dispute concerning the proper application of § 506(a) of the Bankruptcy Code when a bankrupt debtor has exercised the "cram down" option for which Code § 1325(a)(5)(B) provides. Specifically, when a debtor, over

---

3. The 2005 BAPCPA turned the existing § 506(a) into § 506(a)(1) and added a new § 506(a)(2) providing specific rules governing valuation of personal property in chapter 7 and chapter 13 cases in which the debtors are individuals. In addition, the 2005 BAPCPA amended § 1325(a) by adding language at the end of the subsection providing that "section 506 shall not apply" to certain claims in chapter 13 cases.

a secured creditor's objection, seeks to retain and use the creditor's collateral in a Chapter 13 plan, is the value of the collateral to be determined by (1) what the secured creditor could obtain through foreclosure sale of the property (the "foreclosure-value" standard); (2) what the debtor would have to pay for comparable property (the "replacement-value" standard); or (3) the midpoint between these two measurements? We hold that § 506(a) directs application of the replacement-value standard.

I

In 1989, respondent Elray Rash purchased for $73,700 a Kenworth tractor truck for use in his freight-hauling business. Rash made a downpayment on the truck, agreed to pay the seller the remainder in 60 monthly installments, and pledged the truck as collateral on the unpaid balance. The seller assigned the loan, and its lien on the truck, to petitioner Associates Commercial Corporation (ACC).

In March 1992, Elray and Jean Rash filed a joint petition and a repayment plan under Chapter 13 of the Bankruptcy Code (Code). At the time of the bankruptcy filing, the balance owed to ACC on the truck loan was $41,171. Because it held a valid lien on the truck, ACC was listed in the bankruptcy petition as a creditor holding a secured claim. Under the Code, ACC's claim for the balance owed on the truck was secured only to the extent of the value of the collateral; its claim over and above the value of the truck was unsecured. See 11 U.S.C. § 506(a).

To qualify for confirmation under Chapter 13, the Rashes' plan had to satisfy the requirements set forth in § 1325(a) of the Code. The Rashes' treatment of ACC's secured claim, in particular, is governed by subsection (a)(5). Under this provision, a plan's proposed treatment of secured claims can be confirmed if one of three conditions is satisfied: The secured creditor accepts the plan, see 11 U.S.C. § 1325(a)(5)(A); the debtor surrenders the property securing the claim to the creditor, see § 1325(a)(5)(C); or the debtor invokes the so-called "cram down" power, see § 1325(a)(5)(B).

Under the cram down option, the debtor is permitted to keep the property over the objection of the creditor; the creditor retains the lien securing the claim, see § 1325(a)(5)(B)(i), and the debtor is required to provide the creditor with payments, over the life of the plan, that will total the present value of the allowed secured claim, i.e., the present value of the collateral, see § 1325(a)(5)(B)(ii). The value of the allowed secured claim is governed by § 506(a) of the Code.

The Rashes' Chapter 13 plan invoked the cram down power. It proposed that the Rashes retain the truck for use in the freight-hauling business and pay ACC, over 58 months, an amount equal to the present value of the truck. That value, the Rashes' petition alleged, was $28,500. ACC objected to the plan and asked the Bankruptcy Court to lift the automatic stay so ACC could repossess the truck. ACC also filed a proof of claim alleging that its claim was fully secured in the amount of $41,171. The Rashes filed an objection to ACC's claim.

The Bankruptcy Court held an evidentiary hearing to resolve the dispute over the truck's value. At the hearing, ACC and the Rashes urged different valuation benchmarks. ACC maintained that the proper valuation was the price the Rashes would have to pay to purchase a like vehicle, an amount ACC's expert estimated to be $41,000. The Rashes, however, maintained that the proper valuation was the net amount ACC would realize upon foreclosure and sale of the collateral, an amount their expert estimated to be $31,875. The Bankruptcy Court agreed with the Rashes and fixed the amount of ACC's secured claim at $31,875; that sum, the court found, was the net amount ACC would realize if it exercised its right to repossess and sell the truck. The Bankruptcy Court thereafter approved the plan, and the United States District Court for the Eastern District of Texas affirmed.

A panel of the Court of Appeals for the Fifth Circuit reversed. On rehearing en banc, however, the Fifth Circuit affirmed the District Court, holding that ACC's allowed secured claim was limited to $31,875, the net foreclosure value of the truck. In re Rash, 90 F.3d 1036 (1996). * * *

Courts of Appeals have adopted three different standards for valuing a security interest in a bankruptcy proceeding when the debtor invokes the cram down power to retain the collateral over the creditor's objection. In contrast to the Fifth Circuit's foreclosure-value standard, a number of Circuits have followed a replacement-value approach. See, e.g., In re Taffi, 96 F.3d 1190, 1191-1192 (C.A.9 1996) (en banc), cert. pending sub nom. Taffi v. United States, No. 96-881;[4] In re Winthrop Old Farm Nurseries, Inc., 50 F.3d 72, 74-75 (C.A.1 1995); In re Trimble, 50 F.3d 530, 531-532 (C.A.8 1995). Other courts have settled on the midpoint between foreclosure value and replacement value. See In re Hoskins, 102 F.3d 311, 316 (C.A.7 1996); cf. In re Valenti, 105 F.3d 55, 62 (C.A.2 1997) (bankruptcy courts have discretion to value at midpoint between replacement value and foreclosure value). We granted certiorari to resolve this conflict among the Courts of Appeals, and we now reverse the Fifth Circuit's judgment.

II

The Code provision central to the resolution of this case is § 506(a), which states:

> "An allowed claim of a creditor secured by a lien on property in which the estate has an interest ... is a secured claim to the extent of the value of such creditor's interest in the estate's interest in such property, ... and is an unsecured claim to the extent that the value of such creditor's interest ... is less than the amount of such allowed claim. Such value shall be determined in light of the purpose of the valuation and of the proposed disposition or use of such property ...." 11 U.S.C. § 506(a).

Over ACC's objection, the Rashes' repayment plan proposed, pursuant to § 1325(a)(5)(B), continued use of the property in question, i.e., the truck, in the debtor's trade or business. In such a "cram down" case, we hold, the value of the property (and thus the amount of the secured claim under § 506(a)) is the price a willing buyer in the debtor's trade, business, or situation would pay to obtain like property from a willing seller.

---

4.   [Footnote 2 in original:] In In re Taffi, the Ninth Circuit contrasted replacement value with fair-market value and adopted the latter standard, apparently viewing the two standards as incompatible. See 96 F.3d, at 1192. By using the term "replacement value," we do not suggest that a creditor is entitled to recover what it would cost the debtor to purchase the collateral brand new. Rather, our use of the term replacement value is consistent with the Ninth Circuit's understanding of the meaning of fair-market value; by replacement value, we mean the price a willing buyer in the debtor's trade, business, or situation would pay a willing seller to obtain property of like age and condition. See also infra, * * * n. 6.

Rejecting this replacement-value standard, and selecting instead the typically lower foreclosure-value standard, the Fifth Circuit trained its attention on the first sentence of § 506(a). In particular, the Fifth Circuit relied on these first sentence words: A claim is secured "to the extent of the value of such creditor's interest in the estate's interest in such property." See 90 F.3d, at 1044 (emphasis added) (citing § 506(a)). The Fifth Circuit read this phrase to instruct that the "starting point for the valuation [is] what the creditor could realize if it sold the estate's interest in the property according to the security agreement," namely, through "repossess[ing] and sell[ing] the collateral." Ibid.

We do not find in the § 506(a) first sentence words—"the creditor's interest in the estate's interest in such property"—the foreclosure-value meaning advanced by the Fifth Circuit. Even read in isolation, the phrase imparts no valuation standard: A direction simply to consider the "value of such creditor's interest" does not expressly reveal how that interest is to be valued.

Reading the first sentence of § 506(a) as a whole, we are satisfied that the phrase the Fifth Circuit considered key is not an instruction to equate a "creditor's interest" with the net value a creditor could realize through a foreclosure sale. The first sentence, in its entirety, tells us that a secured creditor's claim is to be divided into secured and unsecured portions, with the secured portion of the claim limited to the value of the collateral. To separate the secured from the unsecured portion of a claim, a court must compare the creditor's claim to the value of "such property," i.e., the collateral. That comparison is sometimes complicated. A debtor may own only a part interest in the property pledged as collateral, in which case the court will be required to ascertain the "estate's interest" in the collateral. Or, a creditor may hold a junior or subordinate lien, which would require the court to ascertain the creditor's interest in the collateral. The § 506(a) phrase referring to the "creditor's interest in the estate's interest in such property" thus recognizes that a court may encounter, and in such instances must evaluate, limited or partial interests in collateral. The full first sentence of § 506(a), in short, tells a court what it must evaluate, but it does not say more; it is not enlightening on how to value collateral.

The second sentence of § 506(a) does speak to the how question. "Such value," that sentence provides, "shall be determined in light of the purpose of the valuation and of the proposed disposition or use of such property." § 506(a). By deriving a foreclosure-value standard from § 506(a)'s first sentence, the Fifth Circuit rendered inconsequential the sentence that expressly addresses how "value shall be determined."

As we comprehend § 506(a), the "proposed disposition or use" of the collateral is of paramount importance to the valuation question. If a secured creditor does not accept a debtor's Chapter 13 plan, the debtor has two options for handling allowed secured claims: surrender the collateral to the creditor, see § 1325(a)(5)(C); or, under the cram down option, keep the collateral over the creditor's objection and provide the creditor, over the life of the plan, with the equivalent of the present value of the collateral, see § 1325(a)(5)(B). The "disposition or use" of the collateral thus turns on the alternative the debtor chooses—in one case the collateral will be surrendered to the creditor, and in the other, the collateral will be retained and used by the debtor. Applying a foreclosure-value standard when the cram down option is invoked attributes no significance to the different consequences of the debtor's choice to surrender the property or retain it. A replacement-value standard, on the other hand, distinguishes retention from surrender and renders meaningful the key words "disposition or use."

Tying valuation to the actual "disposition or use" of the property points away from a foreclosure-value standard when a Chapter 13 debtor, invoking cram down power, retains and uses the property. Under that option, foreclosure is averted by the debtor's choice and over the creditor's objection. From the creditor's perspective as well as the debtor's, surrender and retention are not equivalent acts.

When a debtor surrenders the property, a creditor obtains it immediately, and is free to sell it and reinvest the proceeds. We recall here that ACC sought that very advantage. If a debtor keeps the property and continues to use it, the creditor obtains at once neither the property nor its value and is exposed to double risks: The debtor may again default and the property may deteriorate from extended use. Adjustments in the interest rate and secured creditor demands for more "adequate protection," 11 U.S.C. § 361, do not fully offset these risks. See 90 F.3d, at 1066 (Smith, J., dissenting) ("vast majority of reorganizations fail ... leaving creditors with only a fraction of the compensation due them"; where, as here, "collateral depreciates rapidly, the secured creditor may receive far less in a failed reorganization than in a prompt foreclosure" (internal cross-reference omitted)).

Of prime significance, the replacement-value standard accurately gauges the debtor's "use" of the property. It values "the creditor's interest in the collateral in light of the proposed [repayment plan] reality: no foreclosure sale and economic benefit for the debtor derived from the collateral equal to ... its [replacement] value." In re Winthrop Old Farm Nurseries, 50 F.3d, at 75. The debtor in this case elected to use the collateral to generate an income stream. That actual use, rather than a foreclosure sale that will not take place, is the proper guide under a prescription hinged to the property's "disposition or use." See ibid.[5]

The Fifth Circuit considered the replacement-value standard disrespectful of state law, which permits the secured creditor to sell the collateral, thereby obtaining its net foreclosure value "and nothing more." See 90 F.3d, at 1044. In allowing Chapter 13 debtors to retain and use collateral over the objection of secured creditors, however, the Code has reshaped debtor and creditor rights in marked departure from state law. The Code's cram down option displaces a secured creditor's state-law right to obtain immediate foreclosure upon a debtor's

---

5.   [Footnote 4 in original:] We give no weight to the legislative history of § 506(a), noting that it is unedifying, offering snippets that might support either standard of valuation. The Senate Report simply repeated the phrase contained in the second sentence of § 506(a). See S. Rep. No. 95-989, 95th Cong. 2nd Sess. p. 68 (1978) U.S. Code Cong. & Admin. News 1978, pp. 5787, 5854. The House Report, in the Fifth Circuit's view, rejected a "replacement cost" valuation. See In re Rash, 90 F.3d 1036, 1056 (C.A.5 1996) (quoting H. Rep. No. 95-595, 95th Cong. 2nd Sess. p. 124 (1977) U.S. Code Cong. & Admin. News 1978, pp. 5963, 6085). That Report, however, appears to use the term " 'replacement cost' " to mean the cost of buying new property to replace property in which a creditor had a security interest. See ibid. In any event, House Report excerpts are not enlightening, for the provision pivotal here—the second sentence of § 506(a)—did not appear in the bill addressed by the House Report. The key sentence originated in the Senate version of the bill, compare H.R. 8200, 95th Cong., 1st Sess., § 506(a) (1977), with S. 2266, 95th Cong., 1st Sess., § 506(a) (1977), and was included in the final text of the statute after the House-Senate conference, see 124 Cong. Rec. 33997 (1978).

default. That change, ordered by federal law, is attended by a direction that courts look to the "proposed disposition or use" of the collateral in determining its value. It no more disrupts state law to make "disposition or use" the guide for valuation than to authorize the rearrangement of rights the cram down power entails.

Nor are we persuaded that the split-the-difference approach adopted by the Seventh Circuit provides the appropriate solution. See In re Hoskins, 102 F.3d, at 316. Whatever the attractiveness of a standard that picks the midpoint between foreclosure and replacement values, there is no warrant for it in the Code.[6] Section 506(a) calls for the value the property possesses in light of the "disposition or use" in fact "proposed," not the various dispositions or uses that might have been proposed. Cf. BFP v. Resolution Trust Corporation, 511 U.S. 531, 540, 114 S. Ct. 1757, 1762, 128 L. Ed. 2d 556 (1994) (court-made rule defining, for purposes of Code's fraudulent transfer provision, "reasonably equivalent value" to mean 70% of fair market value "represent[s][a] policy determinatio[n] that the Bankruptcy Code gives us no apparent authority to make"). The Seventh Circuit rested on the "economics of the situation," In re Hoskins, 102 F.3d, at 316, only after concluding that the statute suggests no particular valuation method. We agree with the Seventh Circuit that "a simple rule of valuation is needed" to serve the interests of predictability and uniformity. Id., at 314. We conclude, however, that § 506(a) supplies a governing instruction less complex than the Seventh Circuit's "make two valuations, then split the difference" formulation.

In sum, under § 506(a), the value of property retained because the debtor has exercised the § 1325(a)(5)(B) "cram down" option is the cost the debtor would incur to obtain a like asset for the same "proposed ... use."[7]

* * *

For the foregoing reasons, the judgment of the Court of Appeals is reversed, and the case is remanded for further proceedings consistent with this opinion.

It is so ordered.

[Dissenting opinion by Justice Stevens omitted.]

---

6. [Footnote 5 in original:] As our reading of § 506(a) makes plain, we also reject a ruleless approach allowing use of different valuation standards based on the facts and circumstances of individual cases. Cf. In re Valenti, 105 F.3d 55, 62-63 (C.A.2 1997) (permissible for bankruptcy courts to determine valuation standard case-by-case).

7. [Footnote 6 in original:] Our recognition that the replacement-value standard, not the foreclosure-value standard, governs in cram down cases leaves to bankruptcy courts, as triers of fact, identification of the best way of ascertaining replacement value on the basis of the evidence presented. Whether replacement value is the equivalent of retail value, wholesale value, or some other value will depend on the type of debtor and the nature of the property. We note, however, that replacement value, in this context, should not include certain items. For example, where the proper measure of the replacement value of a vehicle is its retail value, an adjustment to that value may be necessary: A creditor should not receive portions of the retail price, if any, that reflect the value of items the debtor does not receive when he retains his vehicle, items such as warranties, inventory storage, and reconditioning. Cf. 90 F.3d, at 1051-1052. Nor should the creditor gain from modifications to the property—e.g., the addition of accessories to a vehicle—to which a creditor's lien would not extend under state law.

NOTES

1. Is *Rash* consistent with BFP v. Resolution Trust Corp., reprinted above at page 364? In *BFP* the Court took into account the effect that the debtor's financial distress had on the value of the secured creditor's collateral; why not take it into account here and use foreclosure value?

2. Suppose the court on remand in *Rash* determines that Associates Commercial Corp. would incur expenses of $5,000 in repossessing and selling the tractor truck, if it were permitted to foreclose. Should the court deduct that amount from the tractor truck's $41,000 replacement value and thus determine that Commercial Associates' secured claim is $36,000? See Huntington Nat'l Bank v. Pees (In re McClurkin), 31 F.3d 401 (6th Cir. 1994). After the amendment of § 506(a) by the 2005 BAPCPA, the conclusion—in a chapter 7 or chapter 13 case— might differ depending on whether the debtor is an individual or a business entity. See § 506(a)(2).

3. If a chapter 11 debtor's plan is not confirmed, liquidation may result. What is the proposed use of the collateral if the secured creditor successfully opposes confirmation? If the secured creditor is in effect arguing for liquidation, would use of liquidation value be appropriate under the Court's decision?

4. Is chapter 11 sufficiently analogous to chapter 13 so that courts in chapter 11 cases are required to use a "replacement-value" measure rather than a liquidation value measure? What is the impact of § 506(a)(2) on this question?

5. Consider the Court's footnote 6. In what sense, if any, does "inventory storage" provide a benefit to retail buyers of automobiles. Do such buyers receive something of value from the dealer's expense of storing the inventory? Do they receive some value that the debtor who simply keeps his old automobile does not receive? Could Justice Ginsburg mean that a buyer from a dealer gets the benefit of choosing the automobile he or she wants from a selection automobiles? Is footnote 6 so broad and vague that a lower court could in effect give an item a foreclosure sale value while still paying lip service to the Justice Ginsburg's decision?

Now suppose that an undersecured creditor makes the § 1111(b)(2) election. How are we to determine the four amounts we need to determine in order to apply the fair and equitable standard? What is the amount of the allowable secured claim? How much present value must the plan provide for the undersecured creditor? How many total dollars? How large a lien must the creditor be permitted to retain? Note that the making of the § 1111(b)(2) election changes three out of those four amounts. Can you tell which three? How are they affected by the election?

In re Kvamme
United States Bankruptcy Court, District of North Dakota, 1988
93 B.R. 698

WILLIAM A. HILL, Bankruptcy Judge.

The matters under consideration are the confirmation of the Debtors' Fourth Amended Chapter 11 plan of reorganization, filed September 9, 1988, and a motion to dismiss filed by the Peoples State Bank of Velva (Bank). The Farmers Home Administration (FmHA) objects to confirmation of the plan, stating that its election under section 1111(b) has not been reflected in the plan. A hearing was held on September 20, 1988.

1.

The sole remaining issue regarding plan confirmation is whether the plan adequately treats FmHA's 1111(b) election. With regard to FmHA section V of the plan creates a Class 3 which gives FmHA a secured claim for the amount of the value of its collateral. The balance of the debt to FmHA is treated as an unsecured claim in Class 5. This treatment of FmHA is modified in a subsequent section of the plan. Section VI provides as follows:

> 3. The secured claim in Class 3 is held by Farmers Home Administration with a balance of $174,234.72. This has been divided into three areas:
>
> A. Cattle with a market value of $45,400.00 have been amortized over a period of 15 years at 9% interest with payments to commence as soon as the Plan is confirmed, with yearly payments on the same date each year in the amount of $5,632.27, and the balance to be paid in full after 15 years.
>
> B. Machinery with a market value of $5,600 has been amortized over a period of 7 years at 7% interest with payments commencing as soon as the Plan is confirmed and yearly payments on the same date each year thereafter in the amount of $1,112.67, the balance to be paid in full after 7 years.
>
> C. The secured interest that ASCS has will be paid at the time the grain is sold.
>
> The balance of A and B—$123,234.72—is no longer reclassified as unsecured and placed in Class 5 because of the § 1111(b) election. Instead, the claim is treated as entirely secured and treated as such. Pursuant to the election, FmHA shall retain a lien in the amount of $174,235.00

FmHA objects that the plan does not provide for payment of FmHA's total claim of $174,234.72. Section 1111(b)(1) provides that a class may elect to have its claims treated under section 1111(b)(2). Section 1111(b)(2) provides that, "If such an election is made, then notwithstanding section 506(a) of this title, such claim is a secured claim to the extent that such claim is allowed." Thus the amount of the allowed claim, rather than the value of the collateral, becomes the amount of the allowed secured claim. In re Hallum, 29 B.R. 343, 344 (Bankr. E.D. Tenn. 1983). This provision becomes important when read in conjunction with the cramdown provision of section 1129. In order to confirm a plan over the objection of a secured creditor, section 1129(b)(2)(A)(i)(II) requires:

> That each holder of a claim of such class receive on account of such claim deferred cash payments totaling at least the allowed amount of such claim, of a value, as of the effective date of the plan, of at least the value of such holder's interest in the estate's interest in such property.

Accordingly, once an 1111(b) election has been made the creditor must receive the greater of deferred payments equal to the full amount of its allowed claim without including the time value of money, or payments with a present value as of the date of the plan equal to at least the value of the creditors' interest in the estate's interest in the collateral. See In re Webster, 66 B.R. 46, 47 (Bankr. D.N.D. 1986) (citing 5 COLLIER ON BANKRUPTCY ¶ 1111.02[5] (15th ed. 1985). A plan which proposes to pay an electing creditor only the value of its collateral is not confirmable when the proposed payments do not total at least the full amount of the creditor's claim. See In re Hallum, 29 B.R. at 345.

The amount that is greater, between the total of the payments necessary to provide a creditor with the present value of the collateral and the total amount of a creditor's claim, switches depending upon the length of the term and the interest rate used to calculate the payments. For example, assume a piece of real estate worth $50,000.00 upon which a creditor electing under section 1111(b) holds a $120,000.00 secured claim. If the debtor proposes to pay the creditor the present value of its collateral $50,000.00 over twenty years at 10% interest the annual payments would be $5,873.00. Twenty payments of $5,873.00 total $117,460.00, which is less than the total amount of the creditor's claim. Under this scenario the debtor would be required to pay $6,000.00 annual payments ($120,000.00 total claim ÷ twenty annual payments = $6,000.00 annual payment) to comply with the "greater of the two" requirement. If, however, the terms of the payment are stretched out over twenty-five years the annual payments toward the present value of the collateral would be $5,508.00. Twenty-five payments of $5,508.00 total $137,700.00, which is more than the total amount of the creditor's claim. Thus under this second set of repayment terms the total of the payments necessary to pay the present value of the collateral is greater than the total allowed claim.

In the instant case the Debtors' plan proposes a string of payments to FmHA with a present value equal to the value of FmHA's interest in the collateral. The amount of these payments was calculated as follows:

	Fair Market Value	Interest Rate	Number of Annual Payments	Amount of Annual Payments
Cattle	$45,400.00	9.0%	15	$5,632.27
Machinery	$ 5,600.00	9.0%	7	$1,112.67

The present value of FmHA's collateral is, however, only one side of the comparison required by a section 1111(b) election. The other prong of the comparison is that the total payments received by FmHA must equal at least the total amount of its allowed secured claim, $174,234.72. The total of the payments proposed by the Debtors' plan is calculated as follows:

15 years x $5,632.27 = $84,484.05
7 years x $1,112.67 = $ 7,788.69
Total plan payments $92,272.74

The $92,272.74 in payments proposed under the plan falls short of FmHA's $174,234.72 allowed secured claim by $81,961.98. Accordingly, the court concludes that the Kvammes' plan does not adequately reflect FmHA's 1111(b) election.

2.

The other matter before the court is the motion to dismiss filed by the Bank. The Bank asserts that dismissal is appropriate under section 1112 of the Bankruptcy Code for, among other reasons, the Debtors' inability to effectuate a plan. Cause for dismissal is not limited to the specifically enumerated examples set out in section 1112 but is rather within the discretion of the bankruptcy court. The Kvammes have been under the protection of the bankruptcy court since November 24, 1986, without achieving plan confirmation. Their most recently proposed plan falls short of being confirmable by an 1111(b) payment deficiency of $81,961.98. On August 9, 1988, at a hearing on their Third Amended plan, the court warned the Debtors that they would have only one more opportunity to propose a confirmable plan. At the August hearing it was apparent that FmHA's objection regarding the plan treatment of its 1111(b) election was a serious obstacle to confirmation. Yet, the currently proposed Fourth Amended plan does not adjust the payments to FmHA to reflect the 1111(b) election. Congress did not intend for debtors to continue indefinitely in Chapter 11 when they do not appear to be able to achieve plan confirmation. In this case the Debtors have had ample time to propose a confirmable plan but have failed to do so.

Accordingly, for the reasons stated, confirmation of the Debtors' Fourth Amended plan of reorganization is DENIED and the motion to dismiss is GRANTED.

SO ORDERED.

Problem 15-1

Galactic Bank is owed $100,000 by DebCo, secured by a first mortgage on Greenacre, which is worth $145,000 (as determined by the court) and which is property of the estate in debtor DebCo's chapter 11 case. Global Bank is owed $85,000 by DebCo, secured by a second mortgage on Greenacre. DebCo's plan placed Galactic Bank's secured claim and Global Bank's secured claim in two separate classes, by themselves, and placed Global Bank's unsecured claim, if any, in the same class as all other general unsecured claims. DebCo's plan impaired all three of those classes. The plan provided that holders of unsecured claims would receive 15% payment in cash on the effective date in full satisfaction of their claims. (Possible treatments of the secured claims under the plan are discussed below.) Galactic Bank and Global Bank each rejected the plan, but the class of unsecured claims accepted it. DebCo asked the court to confirm the plan despite the rejections by the banks.

(a) Assume Global Bank did not make the § 1111(b)(2) election. What is the amount of each bank's allowed secured claim? What is the amount of the lien on Greenacre that the plan must permit each bank to retain? How much present value is each bank entitled to receive under the plan on account of its secured claim? What amount of total dollars—the sum total of all payments, not their present value—is the minimum that each bank is entitled to receive under the plan on account of its secured claim?

(b) Would an investor who might want to purchase Greenacre from DebCo be willing to pay full market value for it and at the same time agree that if it were to appreciate in value, then DebCo would be entitled to the appreciation? Is the possibility of appreciation factored into the $145,000 value of Greenacre? Assume (for purposes of this part (b) only) that (1) Greenacre is a commercial office building, (2) after payment of administrative expenses and the 15% cash to unsecured claim holders, the reorganized DebCo's only asset will be Greenacre, and (3) the reorganized DebCo's only source of funds will be rents from the building's tenants. Is it possible for the plan to give the banks the amount of present value to which they are entitled, on account of their secured claims, if DebCo retains ownership of the building? To put it another way, if Greenacre is worth $145,000 because that is the present value of all expected future net cash flows from operation of Greenacre, can the banks be given $145,000 in present value if they are not given all the future net cash flows? See Baird, *Remembering Pine Gate*, 38 J. MARSHALL L. REV. 5, 17 (2004).

(c) Was the class containing Global Bank's secured claim entitled to make the § 1111(b)(2) election? If the class made the election, would any of your answers to part (a) change? What would Global Bank give up by making the election? Consider not only the terms of DebCo's plan but also §§ 1126(c) and 1129(a)(8) & (10). What would Global Bank gain?

Problem 15-2

Assume the same facts as in Problem 15-1.

(a) Suppose DebCo's plan calls for payment of $45,000 cash to Global Bank on the effective date as full payment of Global Bank's secured claim. Would that indicate that DebCo thought the court's valuation of Greenacre was low? Would it perhaps indicate that DebCo thinks the real estate market has hit bottom and is likely to improve in the near future? Would it indicate that DebCo had other motivations, such as tax considerations? Would you advise Global Bank to make the § 1111(b)(2) election? If Global Bank made the election, and then DebCo modified its plan to provide that Global Bank's secured claim would be paid off over twenty years, could Global Bank revoke its election? See Rule 3014; In re Bloomingdale Partners, 155 B.R. 961 (Bankr. N.D. Ill. 1993).

(b) Assume DebCo's plan provides that the reorganized DebCo will pay Global Bank, on account of its secured claim, $4,500 interest on the first anniversary of the effective date of the plan, another $4,500 interest on the second anniversary of the effective date, and $49,500 (interest and principal) on the third anniversary of the effective date. The plan provides that after payment of the $49,500 "balloon payment," Global Bank will no longer have a lien on Greenacre, and Global Bank's secured claim will be fully satisfied. The court determines that 10% interest per annum is the appropriate discount rate to use to determine the present value of payments made to Global Bank on account of its secured claim. The court also determines that DebCo's plan is feasible; the court seems to believe that the property's value will remain stable for at least the next ten years, that the reorganized DebCo will be financially stable for at least that long, and that the reorganized DebCo will have little trouble selling Greenacre or refinancing it to raise the money needed to pay the balloon payment. If Global Bank does not make the

§ 1111(b)(2) election, is the plan fair and equitable with respect to the class consisting of Global Bank's secured claim? Is it fair and equitable if Global Bank does make the election? If Global Bank makes the election, what could DebCo do to make its plan fair and equitable with respect to Global Bank's class? (Hint: At 10% interest, payments of about $118 per year would pay off a $1,000 debt in twenty years.) Would you recommend that Global Bank make the § 1111(b)(2) election?

(c) Suppose the plan also provides that DebCo may sell Greenacre free of Global Bank's lien, at any time before the third anniversary of the effective date, on payment of $45,000 plus any accrued interest, and that such payment will constitute payment in full of Global Bank's secured claim. Will Global Bank's decision whether to make the § 1111(b)(2) election affect the confirmability of the plan?

Problem 15-3

Assume the same facts as in Problem 15-1.

(a) Suppose Global Bank's mortgage included a due on sale clause, enforceable under state law, which by its terms would require full payment of the mortgage if Greenacre were sold. You are Global Bank's attorney. You believe Greenacre is worth much more than the $145,000 that the court found it to be worth. You also believe that Greenacre may appreciate in the next few years, and that the reorganized DebCo will likely want to sell it within two or three years, because DebCo's principals are near retirement age. Would you recommend that Global Bank make the § 1111(b)(2) election? Suppose the debtor's plan provides for deletion of the due on sale clause from Global Bank's mortgage so that if and when Greenacre appreciates the reorganized debtor will be able to sell it subject to Global Bank's mortgage and reap the gain from the appreciation. Would such a provision impermissibly undercut the effectiveness of the § 1111(b)(2) election? See § 1123(a)(5)(E), (F), and (H), and (b)(5)-(6); IPC Atlanta Ltd. P'ship v. Fed. Home Mortgage Corp. (In re IPC Atlanta Ltd. P'ship), 163 B.R. 396 (Bankr. N.D. Ga.1994); In re Real Pro Fin. Serv., Inc., 120 B.R. 216 (Bankr. M.D. Fla.1990); In re Coastal Equities, Inc., 33 B.R. 898 (Bankr. S.D. Cal.1983); Epstein, Nickles & White, Bankruptcy § 10-27, at 778-79. If the mortgage did not include a due on sale clause, and Global Bank made the § 1111(b)(2) election, should the court require that the plan place a due on sale clause in the modified mortgage?

(b) Suppose the collateral were not real estate but equipment worth $145,000 with a useful remaining life of only four or five years. If you were the judge, would you allow DebCo's plan to pay the secured claim over ten years? Would you allow the plan to pay interest only for four years with a balloon payment at the end? See In re White, 36 B.R. 199 (Bankr. D. Kan. 1983). Assume the plan will provide for four equal yearly payments, and that an appropriate discount rate is 12% per annum. If Global Bank does not make the § 1111(b)(2) election, what amount would the plan have to provide Global Bank each year on account of its secured claim to treat its secured claim class fairly and equitably? (Hint: Mortgage tables or a financial calculator reveal that a $1,000 debt can be paid off at 12% interest by four equal annual payments of $329.) Would you advise Global Bank to make the § 1111(b)(2) election?

Once we have determined the amount of present value that must be provided to the secured creditor, we must determine whether the plan provides that amount of present value. To do so, we usually will need to determine the interest rate that must be paid on deferred payments.

The selection of an interest rate can have a dramatic effect on the amount that must be paid and on whether the plan will be feasible. The debtor will only have a certain amount of cash flow each year that can be paid to the secured creditor; if the payments are too high, the debtor may be unable to make them, and the court may then refuse to confirm the plan because of lack of feasibility under § 1129(a)(11).

Here are two cases to consider, one from the Supreme Court, in the chapter 13 context, resulting only in a plurality opinion, and the other an attempt by the Sixth Circuit to apply the Supreme Court's analysis to chapter 11. We present substantial portions of the plurality, concurrence, and dissenting opinion in the Supreme Court case, so that you can consider what approach might gain five votes in a chapter 11 case. Note that only two of the four dissenting Justices are still on the Court as of early 2006. Can you piece together a holding from the fractured 4-1-4 decision by the Court? Do you agree with the Sixth Circuit's analysis? Note that the secured creditor in the Sixth Circuit case argued that the "coerced loan" approach should not have been used; that is a reversal of the usual situation in which the secured creditor argues for use of the coerced loan (or market rate) approach, and the debtor or unsecured creditors' committee argues for use of the "formula" approach.

Till v. SCS Credit Corporation
United States Supreme Court, 2004
541 U.S. 465, 124 S. Ct. 1951, 158 L. Ed. 2d 787

Justice STEVENS announced the judgment of the Court and delivered an opinion, in which Justice SOUTER, Justice GINSBURG, and Justice BREYER join.

To qualify for court approval under Chapter 13 of the Bankruptcy Code, an individual debtor's proposed debt adjustment plan must accommodate each allowed, secured creditor in one of three ways: (1) by obtaining the creditor's acceptance of the plan; (2) by surrendering the property securing the claim; or (3) by providing the creditor both a lien securing the claim and a promise of future property distributions (such as deferred cash payments) whose total "value, as of the effective date of the plan, ... is not less than the allowed amount of such claim." [Section 1325(a)(5).] The third alternative is commonly known as the "cram down option" because it may be enforced over a claim holder's objection.

Plans that invoke the cram down power often provide for installment payments over a period of years rather than a single payment. In such circumstances, the amount of each installment must be calibrated to ensure that, over time, the creditor receives disbursements whose total present value[8] equals or exceeds that of the allowed claim. * * *

I

On October 2, 1998, petitioners Lee and Amy Till, residents of Kokomo, Indiana, purchased a used truck from Instant Auto Finance for $6,395 plus $330.75 in fees and taxes. They made a $300 down payment and financed the

---

8.   [Footnote 4 in original:] In the remainder of the opinion, we use the term "present value" to refer to the value as of the effective date of the bankruptcy plan.

balance of the purchase price by entering into a retail installment contract that Instant Auto immediately assigned to respondent, SCS Credit Corporation. Petitioners' initial indebtedness amounted to $8,285.24—the $6,425.75 balance of the truck purchase plus a finance charge of 21% per year for 136 weeks, or $1,859.49. Under the contract, petitioners agreed to make 68 biweekly payments to cover this debt; Instant Auto—and subsequently respondent—retained a purchase money security interest that gave it the right to repossess the truck if petitioners defaulted under the contract.

On October 25, 1999, petitioners, by then in default on their payments to respondent, filed a joint petition for relief under Chapter 13 of the Bankruptcy Code. At the time of the filing, respondent's outstanding claim amounted to $4,894.89, but the parties agreed that the truck securing the claim was worth only $4,000. * * *

Petitioners' proposed debt adjustment plan called for them to submit their future earnings to the supervision and control of the Bankruptcy Court for three years, and to assign $740 of their wages to the trustee each month. The plan charged the trustee with distributing these monthly wage assignments to pay, in order of priority: (1) administrative costs; (2) the IRS's priority tax claim; (3) secured creditors' claims; and finally, (4) unsecured creditors' claims.

The proposed plan also provided that petitioners would pay interest on the secured portion of respondent's claim at a rate of 9.5% per year. Petitioners arrived at this "prime-plus" or "formula rate" by augmenting the national prime rate of approximately 8% (applied by banks when making low-risk loans) to account for the risk of nonpayment posed by borrowers in their financial position. Respondent objected to the proposed rate, contending that the company was "entitled to interest at the rate of 21%, which is the rate ... it would obtain if it could foreclose on the vehicle and reinvest the proceeds in loans of equivalent duration and risk as the loan" originally made to petitioners.

At the hearing on its objection, respondent presented expert testimony establishing that it uniformly charges 21% interest on so-called "subprime" loans, or loans to borrowers with poor credit ratings, and that other lenders in the subprime market also charge that rate. Petitioners countered with the testimony of an Indiana University-Purdue University Indianapolis economics professor, who acknowledged that he had only limited familiarity with the subprime auto lending market, but described the 9.5% formula rate as "very reasonable" given that Chapter 13 plans are "supposed to be financially feasible." Moreover, the professor noted that respondent's exposure was "fairly limited because [petitioners] are under the supervision of the court." The bankruptcy trustee also filed comments supporting the formula rate as, among other things, easily ascertainable, closely tied to the "condition of the financial market," and independent of the financial circumstances of any particular lender. Accepting petitioners' evidence, the Bankruptcy Court overruled respondent's objection and confirmed the proposed plan.

The District Court reversed. It understood Seventh Circuit precedent to require that bankruptcy courts set cram down interest rates at the level the creditor could have obtained if it had foreclosed on the loan, sold the collateral, and reinvested the proceeds in loans of equivalent duration and risk. Citing respondent's unrebutted testimony about the market for subprime loans, the court concluded that 21% was the appropriate rate.

On appeal, the Seventh Circuit endorsed a slightly modified version of the District Court's "coerced" or "forced loan" approach. Specifically, the majority agreed with the District Court that, in a cram down proceeding, the inquiry should focus on the interest rate "that the creditor in question would obtain in making a new loan in the same industry to a debtor who is similarly situated, although not in bankruptcy." To approximate that new loan rate, the majority looked to the parties' prebankruptcy contract rate (21%). The court recognized, however, that using the contract rate would not "duplicat[e] precisely ... the present value of the collateral to the creditor" because loans to bankrupt, court-supervised debtors "involve some risks that would not be incurred in a new loan to a debtor not in default" and also produce "some economies." To correct for these inaccuracies, the majority held that the original contract rate should "serve as a presumptive [cram down] rate," which either the creditor or the debtor could challenge with evidence that a higher or lower rate should apply. Accordingly, the court remanded the case to the Bankruptcy Court to afford petitioners and respondent an opportunity to rebut the presumptive 21% rate.

Dissenting, Judge Rovner argued that the majority's presumptive contract rate approach overcompensates secured creditors because it fails to account for costs a creditor would have to incur in issuing a new loan. Rather than focusing on the market for comparable loans, Judge Rovner advocated either the Bankruptcy Court's formula approach or a "straightforward ... cost of funds" approach that would simply ask "what it would cost the creditor to obtain the cash equivalent of the collateral from an alternative source." Although Judge Rovner noted that the rates produced by either the formula or the cost of funds approach might be "piddling" relative to the coerced loan rate, she suggested courts should "consider the extent to which the creditor has already been compensated for ... the risk that the debtor will be unable to discharge his obligations under the reorganization plan ... in the rate of interest that it charged to the debtor in return for the original loan." We granted certiorari and now reverse.

II

The Bankruptcy Code provides little guidance as to which of the rates of interest advocated by the four opinions in this case—the formula rate, the coerced loan rate, the presumptive contract rate, or the cost of funds rate— Congress had in mind when it adopted the cram down provision. That provision, 11 U.S.C. § 1325(a)(5)(B), does not mention the term "discount rate" or the word "interest." Rather, it simply requires bankruptcy courts to ensure that the property to be distributed to a particular secured creditor over the life of a bankruptcy plan has a total "value, as of the effective date of the plan," that equals or exceeds the value of the creditor's allowed secured claim—in this case, $4,000.

That command is easily satisfied when the plan provides for a lump-sum payment to the creditor. Matters are not so simple, however, when the debt is to be discharged by a series of payments over time. A debtor's promise of future payments is worth less than an immediate payment of the same total amount because the creditor cannot use the money right away, inflation may cause the value of the dollar to decline before the debtor pays, and there is always some risk of nonpayment. The challenge for bankruptcy courts reviewing such repayment schemes, therefore, is to choose an interest rate sufficient to compensate the creditor for these concerns.

Three important considerations govern that choice. First, the Bankruptcy Code includes numerous provisions that, like the cram down provision, require a court to "discoun[t] … [a] stream of deferred payments back to the[ir] present dollar value," Rake v. Wade, 508 U.S. 464, 472, n. 8, 113 S. Ct. 2187, 124 L. Ed. 2d 424 (1993), to ensure that a creditor receives at least the value of its claim. We think it likely that Congress intended bankruptcy judges and trustees to follow essentially the same approach when choosing an appropriate interest rate under any of these provisions. Moreover, we think Congress would favor an approach that is familiar in the financial community and that minimizes the need for expensive evidentiary proceedings.

Second, Chapter 13 expressly authorizes a bankruptcy court to modify the rights of any creditor whose claim is secured by an interest in anything other than "real property that is the debtor's principal residence." 11 U.S.C. § 1322(b)(2). Thus, in cases like this involving secured interests in personal property, the court's authority to modify the number, timing, or amount of the installment payments from those set forth in the debtor's original contract is perfectly clear. Further, the potential need to modify the loan terms to account for intervening changes in circumstances is also clear: On the one hand, the fact of the bankruptcy establishes that the debtor is overextended and thus poses a significant risk of default; on the other hand, the postbankruptcy obligor is no longer the individual debtor but the court-supervised estate, and the risk of default is thus somewhat reduced.[9]

Third, from the point of view of a creditor, the cram down provision mandates an objective rather than a subjective inquiry. That is, although § 1325(a)(5)(B) entitles the creditor to property whose present value objectively equals or exceeds the value of the collateral, it does not require that the terms of the cram down loan match the terms to which the debtor and creditor agreed prebankruptcy, nor does it require that the cram down terms make the creditor subjectively indifferent between present foreclosure and future payment. Indeed, the very idea of a "cram down" loan *precludes* the latter result: By definition, a creditor forced to accept such a loan would prefer instead to foreclose.[10] Thus, a court choosing a cram down interest rate

---

9. [Footnote 12 in original:] Several factors contribute to this reduction in risk. First, as noted below, a court may only approve a cram down loan (and the debt adjustment plan of which the loan is a part) if it believes the debtor will be able to make all of the required payments. § 1325(a)(6). Thus, such loans will only be approved for debtors that the court deems creditworthy. Second, Chapter 13 plans must "provide for the submission" to the trustee "of all or such portion of [the debtor's] future … income … as is necessary for the execution of the plan," § 1322(a)(1), so the possibility of nonpayment is greatly reduced. Third, the Bankruptcy Code's extensive disclosure requirements reduce the risk that the debtor has significant undisclosed obligations. Fourth, as a practical matter, the public nature of the bankruptcy proceeding is likely to reduce the debtor's opportunities to take on additional debt. Cf. 11 U.S.C. § 525 (prohibiting certain Government grant and loan programs from discriminating against applicants who are or have been bankrupt).

10. [Footnote 14 in original:] This fact helps to explain why there is no readily apparent Chapter 13 "cram down market rate of interest": Because every cram down loan is imposed by a court over the objection of the secured creditor, there is no free market of willing cram down lenders. Interestingly, the same is *not* true in the Chapter 11 context, as numerous lenders advertise financing for Chapter 11 debtors

need not consider the creditor's individual circumstances, such as its prebankruptcy dealings with the debtor or the alternative loans it could make if permitted to foreclose. Rather, the court should aim to treat similarly situated creditors similarly,[11] and to ensure that an objective economic analysis would suggest the debtor's interest payments will adequately compensate all such creditors for the time value of their money and the risk of default.

III

These considerations lead us to reject the coerced loan, presumptive contract rate, and cost of funds approaches. Each of these approaches is complicated, imposes significant evidentiary costs, and aims to make each individual creditor whole rather than to ensure the debtor's payments have the required present value. For example, the coerced loan approach requires bankruptcy courts to consider evidence about the market for comparable loans to similar (though nonbankrupt) debtors—an inquiry far removed from such courts' usual task of evaluating debtors' financial circumstances and the feasibility of their debt adjustment plans. In addition, the approach overcompensates creditors because the market lending rate must be high enough to cover factors, like lenders' transaction costs and overall profits, that are no longer relevant in the context of court-administered and court-supervised cram down loans.

Like the coerced loan approach, the presumptive contract rate approach improperly focuses on the creditor's potential use of the proceeds of a foreclosure sale. In addition, although the approach permits a debtor to introduce some evidence about each creditor, thereby enabling the court to tailor the interest rate more closely to the creditor's financial circumstances and reducing the likelihood that the creditor will be substantially overcompensated, that right comes at a cost: The debtor must obtain information about the creditor's costs of overhead, financial circumstances, and lending practices to rebut the presumptive contract rate. Also, the approach produces absurd results, entitling "inefficient, poorly managed lenders" with lower profit margins to obtain higher cram down rates than "well managed, better capitalized lenders." 2 K. Lundin, Chapter 13 Bankruptcy § 112.1, p. 112-8 (3d ed. 2000). Finally, because the approach relies heavily on a creditor's prior dealings with the debtor, similarly situated creditors may end up with vastly different cram down rates.[12]

---

in possession. See, e.g., Balmoral Financial Corporation, http://www.balmoral.com/bdip.htm (all Internet materials as visited Mar. 4, 2004, and available in Clerk of Court's case file) (advertising debtor in possession lending); Debtor in Possession Financing: 1st National Assistance Finance Association DIP Division, http://www.loanmallusa.com/dip.htm (offering "to tailor a financing program ... to your business' needs and ... to work closely with your bankruptcy counsel"). Thus, when picking a cram down rate in a Chapter 11 case, it might make sense to ask what rate an efficient market would produce. In the Chapter 13 context, by contrast, the absence of any such market obligates courts to look to first principles and ask only what rate will fairly compensate a creditor for its exposure.

11. [Footnote 16 in original:] Cf. 11 U.S.C. § 1322(a)(3) ("The plan shall ... provide the same treatment for each claim within a particular class").

12. [Footnote 17 in original:] For example, suppose a debtor purchases two identical used cars, buying the first at a low purchase price from a lender who charges high interest, and buying the second at a much higher purchase price from a lender who charges zero-percent or nominal interest. Prebankruptcy, these two loans might well produce identical income streams for the two lenders. Postbankruptcy, however, the presumptive contract rate approach would entitle the first lender to a considerably higher cram down interest rate, even though the two secured debts are objectively indistinguishable.

The cost of funds approach, too, is improperly aimed. Although it rightly disregards the now-irrelevant terms of the parties' original contract, it mistakenly focuses on the creditworthiness of the *creditor* rather than the debtor. In addition, the approach has many of the other flaws of the coerced loan and presumptive contract rate approaches. For example, like the presumptive contract rate approach, the cost of funds approach imposes a significant evidentiary burden, as a debtor seeking to rebut a creditor's asserted cost of borrowing must introduce expert testimony about the creditor's financial condition. Also, under this approach, a creditworthy lender with a low cost of borrowing may obtain a lower cram down rate than a financially unsound, fly-by-night lender.

IV

The formula approach has none of these defects. Taking its cue from ordinary lending practices, the approach begins by looking to the national prime rate, reported daily in the press, which reflects the financial market's estimate of the amount a commercial bank should charge a creditworthy commercial borrower to compensate for the opportunity costs of the loan, the risk of inflation, and the relatively slight risk of default.[13] Because bankrupt debtors typically pose a greater risk of nonpayment than solvent commercial borrowers, the approach then requires a bankruptcy court to adjust the prime rate accordingly. The appropriate size of that risk adjustment depends, of course, on such factors as the circumstances of the estate, the nature of the security, and the duration and feasibility of the reorganization plan. The court must therefore hold a hearing at which the debtor and any creditors may present evidence about the appropriate risk adjustment. Some of this evidence will be included in the debtor's bankruptcy filings, however, so the debtor and creditors may not incur significant additional expense. Moreover, starting from a concededly *low* estimate and adjusting *upward* places the evidentiary burden squarely on the creditors, who are likely to have readier access to any information absent from the debtor's filing (such as evidence about the "liquidity of the collateral market," *post,* at 1973 (SCALIA, J., dissenting)). Finally, many of the factors relevant to the adjustment fall squarely within the bankruptcy court's area of expertise.

Thus, unlike the coerced loan, presumptive contract rate, and cost of funds approaches, the formula approach entails a straightforward, familiar, and objective inquiry, and minimizes the need for potentially costly additional evidentiary proceedings. Moreover, the resulting "prime-plus" rate of interest depends only on the state of financial markets, the circumstances of the bankruptcy estate, and the characteristics of the loan, not on the creditor's circumstances or its prior interactions with the debtor. For these reasons, the prime-plus or formula rate best comports with the purposes of the Bankruptcy Code.[14]

---

13. [Footnote 18 in original:] We note that, if the court could somehow be certain a debtor would complete his plan, the prime rate would be adequate to compensate any secured creditors forced to accept cram down loans.

14. [Footnote 19 in original:] The fact that Congress considered but rejected legislation that would endorse the Seventh Circuit's presumptive contract rate approach, H.R. 1085, 98th Cong., 1st Sess., § 19(2)(A) (1983); H.R. 1169, 98th Cong., 1st Sess., § 19(2)(A) (1983); H.R. 4786, 97th Cong., 1st Sess., § 19(2)(A) (1981), lends some support to our conclusion. It is perhaps also relevant that our conclusion is

We do not decide the proper scale for the risk adjustment, as the issue is not before us. The Bankruptcy Court in this case approved a risk adjustment of 1.5%, and other courts have generally approved adjustments of 1% to 3%. Respondent's core argument is that a risk adjustment in this range is entirely inadequate to compensate a creditor for the real risk that the plan will fail. There is some dispute about the true scale of that risk—respondent claims that more than 60% of Chapter 13 plans fail, but petitioners argue that the failure rate for *approved* Chapter 13 plans is much lower. We need not resolve that dispute. It is sufficient for our purposes to note that, under 11 U.S.C. § 1325(a)(6), a court may not approve a plan unless, after considering all creditors' objections and receiving the advice of the trustee, the judge is persuaded that "the debtor will be able to make all payments under the plan and to comply with the plan." *Ibid.* Together with the cram down provision, this requirement obligates the court to select a rate high enough to compensate the creditor for its risk but not so high as to doom the plan. If the court determines that the likelihood of default is so high as to necessitate an "eye-popping" interest rate, 301 F.3d, at 593 (Rovner, J., dissenting), the plan probably should not be confirmed.

V

The dissent's endorsement of the presumptive contract rate approach rests on two assumptions: (1) "subprime lending markets are competitive and therefore largely efficient"; and (2) the risk of default in Chapter 13 is normally no less than the risk of default at the time of the original loan. *Post,* at 1969. Although the Bankruptcy Code provides little guidance on the question, we think it highly unlikely that Congress would endorse either premise.

First, the dissent assumes that subprime loans are negotiated between fully informed buyers and sellers in a classic free market. But there is no basis for concluding that Congress relied on this assumption when it enacted Chapter 13. Moreover, several considerations suggest that the subprime market is not, in fact, perfectly competitive. To begin with, used vehicles are regularly sold by means of tie-in transactions, in which the price of the vehicle is the subject of negotiation, while the terms of the financing are dictated by the seller.[15] In addition, there is extensive federal and state regulation of subprime lending, which

---

endorsed by the Executive Branch of the Government and by the National Association of Chapter Thirteen Trustees. Brief for United States as *Amicus Curiae;* Brief for National Association of Chapter Thirteen Trustees as *Amicus Curiae.* If we have misinterpreted Congress' intended meaning of "value, as of the date of the plan," we are confident it will enact appropriate remedial legislation.

15. [Footnote 20 in original:] The dissent notes that "[t]ie-ins do not *alone* make financing markets noncompetitive; they only cause prices and interest rates to be considered *in tandem* rather than separately." This statement, while true, is nonresponsive. If a market prices the cost of goods and the cost of financing together, then even if that market is perfectly competitive, all we can know is that the *combined* price of the goods and the financing is competitive and efficient. We have no way of determining whether the allocation of that price between goods and financing would be the same if the two components were separately negotiated. But the only issue before us is the cram down interest rate (the cost of financing); the value of respondent's truck (the cost of the goods) is fixed. See *Rash,* 520 U.S., at 960, 117 S. Ct. 1879 (setting the value of collateral in Chapter 13 proceedings at the "price a willing buyer in the debtor's trade, business, or situation would pay to obtain like property from a willing seller"). The competitiveness of the market for cost-*cum*-financing is thus irrelevant to our analysis.

not only itself distorts the market, but also evinces regulators' belief that unregulated subprime lenders would exploit borrowers' ignorance and charge rates above what a competitive market would allow. * * *

Second, the dissent apparently believes that the debtor's prebankruptcy default—on a loan made in a market in which creditors commonly charge the maximum rate of interest allowed by law, and in which neither creditors nor debtors have the protections afforded by Chapter 13—translates into a high probability that the same debtor's confirmed Chapter 13 plan will fail. In our view, however, Congress intended to create a program under which plans that qualify for confirmation have a high probability of success. Perhaps bankruptcy judges currently confirm too many risky plans, but the solution is to confirm fewer such plans, not to set default cram down rates at absurdly high levels, thereby increasing the risk of default.

Indeed, as Justice THOMAS demonstrates, *post,* at 1966 (opinion concurring in judgment), the text of § 1325(a)(5)(B)(ii) may be read to support the conclusion that Congress did not intend the cram down rate to include *any* compensation for the risk of default. That reading is consistent with a view that Congress believed Chapter 13's protections to be so effective as to make the risk of default negligible. Because our decision in *Rash* assumes that cram down interest rates are adjusted to "offset," to the extent possible, the risk of default, 520 U.S., at 962-963, 117 S. Ct. 1879, and because so many judges who have considered the issue (including the authors of the four earlier opinions in this case) have rejected the risk-free approach, we think it too late in the day to endorse that approach now. Of course, if the text of the statute required such an approach, that would be the end of the matter. We think, however, that § 1325(a)(5)(B)(ii)'s reference to "value, as of the effective date of the plan, of property to be distributed under the plan" is better read to incorporate all of the commonly understood components of "present value," including any risk of nonpayment. Justice THOMAS' reading does emphasize, though, that a presumption that bankruptcy plans will succeed is more consistent with Congress' statutory scheme than the dissent's more cynical focus on bankrupt debtors' "financial instability and ... proclivity to seek legal protection," *post,* at 1969.

Furthermore, the dissent's two assumptions do not necessarily favor the presumptive contract rate approach. For one thing, the cram down provision applies not only to subprime loans but also to prime loans negotiated prior to the change in circumstance (job loss, for example) that rendered the debtor insolvent. Relatedly, the provision also applies in instances in which national or local economic conditions drastically improved or declined after the original loan was issued but before the debtor filed for bankruptcy. In either case, there is every reason to think that a properly risk-adjusted prime rate will provide a better estimate of the creditor's current costs and exposure than a contract rate set in different times.

Even more important, if all relevant information about the debtor's circumstances, the creditor's circumstances, the nature of the collateral, and the market for comparable loans were equally available to both debtor and creditor, then in theory the formula and presumptive contract rate approaches would yield the same final interest rate. Thus, we principally differ with the dissent not over what final rate courts should adopt but over which party (creditor or debtor) should bear the burden of rebutting the presumptive rate (prime or contract, respectively).

Justice SCALIA identifies four "relevant factors bearing on risk premium[:] (1) the probability of plan failure; (2) the rate of collateral depreciation; (3) the liquidity of the collateral market; and (4) the administrative expenses of enforcement." *Post,* at 1973. In our view, any information debtors have about any of these factors is likely to be included in their bankruptcy filings, while the remaining information will be far more accessible to creditors (who must collect information about their lending markets to remain competitive) than to individual debtors (whose only experience with those markets might be the single loan at issue in the case). Thus, the formula approach, which begins with a concededly low estimate of the appropriate interest rate and requires the creditor to present evidence supporting a higher rate, places the evidentiary burden on the more knowledgeable party, thereby facilitating more accurate calculation of the appropriate interest rate.

If the rather sketchy data uncovered by the dissent support an argument that Chapter 13 of the Bankruptcy Code should mandate application of the presumptive contract rate approach (rather than merely an argument that bankruptcy judges should exercise greater caution before approving debt adjustment plans), those data should be forwarded to Congress. We are not persuaded, however, that the data undermine our interpretation of the statutory scheme Congress has enacted.

The judgment of the Court of Appeals is reversed, and the case is remanded with instructions to remand the case to the Bankruptcy Court for further proceedings consistent with this opinion.

It is so ordered.

Justice THOMAS, concurring in the judgment.

* * * I agree that a "*promise* of future payments is worth less than an immediate payment" of the same amount, in part because of the risk of nonpayment. But this fact is irrelevant. The statute does not require that the value of the *promise* to distribute property under the plan be no less than the allowed amount of the secured creditor's claim. It requires only that "the value ... of *property* to be distributed under the plan," at the time of the effective date of the plan, be no less than the amount of the secured creditor's claim. 11 U.S.C. § 1325(a)(5)(B)(ii) (emphasis added). Both the plurality and the dissent ignore the clear text of the statute in an apparent rush to ensure that secured creditors are not undercompensated in bankruptcy proceedings. But the statute that Congress enacted does not require a debtor-specific risk adjustment that would put secured creditors in the same position as if they had made another loan. * * *

* * * The statute only requires the valuation of the "property to be distributed," not the valuation of the plan (*i.e.,* the promise to make the payments itself). Thus, in order for a plan to satisfy § 1325(a)(5)(B)(ii), the plan need only propose an interest rate that will compensate a creditor for the fact that if he had received the property immediately rather than at a future date, he could have immediately made use of the property. In most, if not all, cases, where the plan proposes simply a stream of cash payments, the appropriate risk-free rate should suffice.

* * *

This is not to say that a debtor's risk of nonpayment can never be a factor in determining the value of the property to be distributed. Although "property" is not defined in the Bankruptcy Code, nothing in § 1325 suggests that "property" is limited to cash. Rather, " 'property' can be cash, notes, stock, personal property or real property; in short, anything of value." 7 Collier on Bankruptcy ¶ 1129.03[7][b][i], p. 1129-44 (15th ed.2003) (discussing Chapter 11's cram down provision). And if the "property to be distributed" under a Chapter 13 plan is a note (i.e., a promise to pay), for instance, the value of that note necessarily includes the risk that the debtor will not make good on that promise. Still, accounting for the risk of nonpayment in that case is not equivalent to reading a risk adjustment requirement into the statute, as in the case of a note, the risk of nonpayment is part of the value of the note itself.

* * * [R]espondent overlooks the fact that secured creditors are already compensated in part for the risk of nonpayment through the valuation of the secured claim. In Associates Commercial Corp. v. Rash, 520 U.S. 953, 117 S. Ct. 1879, 138 L. Ed. 2d 148 (1997), we utilized a secured-creditor-friendly replacement-value standard rather than the lower foreclosure-value standard for valuing secured claims when a debtor has exercised Chapter 13's cram down option. We did so because the statute at issue in that case reflected Congress' recognition that "[i]f a debtor keeps the property and continues to use it, the creditor obtains at once neither the property nor its value and is exposed to double risks: The debtor may again default and the property may deteriorate from extended use." *Id.,* at 962, 117 S.Ct. 1879.

* * *

Although the Plan does not specifically state that "the property to be distributed" under the Plan is cash payments, the cash payments are the only "property" specifically listed for distribution under the Plan. Thus, although the plurality and the dissent imply that the "property to be distributed" under the Plan is the mere *promise* to make cash payments, the plain language of the Plan indicates that the "property to be distributed" to respondent is up to 36 monthly cash payments, consisting of a pro rata share of $740 per month.

The final task, then, is to determine whether petitioners' proposed 9.5% interest rate will sufficiently compensate respondent for the fact that instead of receiving $4,000 today, it will receive $4,000 plus 9.5% interest over a period of up to 36 months. Because the 9.5% rate is higher than the risk-free rate, I conclude that it will. I would therefore reverse the judgment of the Court of Appeals.

Justice SCALIA, with whom THE CHIEF JUSTICE, Justice O'CONNOR, and Justice KENNEDY join, dissenting.

My areas of agreement with the plurality are substantial. We agree that, although all confirmed Chapter 13 plans have been deemed feasible by a bankruptcy judge, some nevertheless fail. We agree that any deferred payments to a secured creditor must fully compensate it for the risk that such a failure will occur. Finally, we agree that adequate compensation may sometimes require an " 'eye-popping' " interest rate, and that, if the rate is too high for the plan to succeed, the appropriate course is not to reduce it to a more palatable level, but to refuse to confirm the plan.

Our only disagreement is over what procedure will more often produce accurate estimates of the appropriate interest rate. The plurality would use the prime lending rate—a rate we *know* is too low—and require the judge in every case to determine an amount by which to increase it. I believe that, in practice, this approach will systematically undercompensate secured creditors for the true risks of default. I would instead adopt the contract rate—i.e., the rate at which the creditor actually loaned funds to the debtor—as a presumption that the bankruptcy judge could revise on motion of either party. Since that rate is generally a good indicator of actual risk, disputes should be infrequent, and it will provide a quick and reasonably accurate standard.

I

The contract-rate approach makes two assumptions, both of which are reasonable. First, it assumes that subprime lending markets are competitive and therefore largely efficient. If so, the high interest rates lenders charge reflect not extortionate profits or excessive costs, but the actual risks of default that subprime borrowers present. * * * We have implicitly assumed market competitiveness in other bankruptcy contexts. See Bank of America Nat. Trust and Sav. Assn. v. 203 North LaSalle Street Partnership, 526 U.S. 434, 456-458, 119 S. Ct. 1411, 143 L. Ed. 2d 607 (1999). Here the assumption is borne out by empirical evidence * * *.

The second assumption is that the expected costs of default in Chapter 13 are normally no less than those at the time of lending. This assumption is also reasonable. Chapter 13 plans often fail. I agree with petitioners that the relevant statistic is the percentage of *confirmed* plans that fail, but even resolving that issue in their favor, the risk is still substantial. The failure rate they offer—which we may take to be a conservative estimate, as it is doubtless the lowest one they could find—is 37%. See Girth, The Role of Empirical Data in Developing Bankruptcy Legislation for Individuals, 65 Ind. L.J. 17, 40-42 (1989) (reporting a 63.1% success rate).[16] In every one of the failed plans making up that 37%, a bankruptcy judge had found that "the debtor will be able to make all payments under the plan," 11 U.S.C. § 1325(a)(6), and a trustee had supervised the debtor's compliance, § 1302. That so many nonetheless failed proves that bankruptcy judges are not oracles and that trustees cannot draw blood from a stone.

While court and trustee oversight may provide some marginal benefit to the creditor, it seems obviously outweighed by the fact that (1) an already-bankrupt borrower has demonstrated a financial instability and a proclivity to seek legal protection that other subprime borrowers have not, and (2) the costs of foreclosure are substantially higher in bankruptcy because the automatic stay bars repossession without judicial permission. * * *

The first of the two assumptions means that the contract rate reasonably reflects actual risk at the time of borrowing. The second means that this risk persists when the debtor files for Chapter 13. It follows that the contract rate is a decent estimate, or at least the lower bound, for the appropriate interest rate in cramdown.[17]

---

16. [Footnote 1 in original:] The true rate of plan failure is almost certainly much higher. The Girth study that yielded the 37% figure was based on data for a single division (Buffalo, New York) from over 20 years ago (1980-1982). See 65 Ind. L. J., at 41. A later study concluded that "the Buffalo division ha [d] achieved extraordinary results, far from typical for the country as a whole." Whitford, The Ideal of Individualized Justice: Consumer Bankruptcy as Consumer Protection, and Consumer Protection in Consumer Bankruptcy, 68 Am. Bankr. L.J. 397, 411, n. 50 (1994). * * *

17. [Footnote 2 in original:] The contract rate is only a presumption, however, and either party remains free to prove that a higher or lower rate is appropriate in a particular case. For example, if market interest rates generally have risen or fallen since the contract was executed, the contract rate could be adjusted by the same amount in cases where the difference was substantial enough that a party chose to make an issue of it.

The plurality disputes these two assumptions. It argues that subprime lending markets are not competitive because "vehicles are regularly sold by means of tie-in transactions, in which the price of the vehicle is the subject of negotiation, while the terms of the financing are dictated by the seller." Tie-ins do not *alone* make financing markets noncompetitive; they only cause prices and interest rates to be considered *in tandem* rather than separately. The force of the plurality's argument depends entirely on its claim that "the terms of the financing are dictated by the seller." *Ibid.* This unsubstantiated assertion is contrary to common experience. Car sellers routinely advertise their interest rates, offer promotions like "zero-percent financing," and engage in other behavior that plainly assumes customers are sensitive to interest rates and not just price.[18]

The plurality also points to state and federal regulation of lending markets. It claims that state usury laws evince a belief that subprime lending markets are noncompetitive. While that is one *conceivable* explanation for such laws, there are countless others. * * *

   * * *

As to the second assumption (that the expected costs of default in Chapter 13 are normally no less than those at the time of lending), the plurality responds, not that Chapter 13 *as currently administered* is less risky than subprime lending generally, but that it *would* be less risky, if only bankruptcy courts would confirm fewer risky plans. * * *

The plurality also claims that the contract rate overcompensates creditors because it includes "transaction costs and overall profits." But the same is true of the rate the plurality prescribes: The prime lending rate includes banks' overhead and profits. These are necessary components of *any* commercial lending rate, since creditors will not lend money if they cannot cover their costs and return a level of profit sufficient to prevent their investors from going elsewhere. The plurality's criticism might have force if there were reason to believe subprime lenders made exorbitant profits while banks did not—but, again, the data suggest otherwise.[19]

---

   18. [Footnote 4 in original:] I confess that this is "nonresponsive" to the argument made in the plurality's footnote (that the contract interest rate may not accurately reflect risk when set jointly with a car's sale price), see *ante,* at 1962, n. 20; it is in response to the quite different argument made in the plurality's text (that joint pricing shows that the subprime lending market is not competitive), see *ante,* at 1962. As to the *former* issue, the plurality's footnote makes a fair point. When the seller provides financing itself, there is a possibility that the contract interest rate might not reflect actual risk because a higher contract interest rate can be traded off for a lower sale price and vice versa. Nonetheless, this fact is not likely to bias the contract-rate approach in favor of creditors to any significant degree. If a creditor offers a promotional interest rate—such as "zero-percent financing"—in return for a higher sale price, the creditor bears the burden of showing that the true interest rate is higher than the contract rate. The opposite tactic—inflating the interest rate and decreasing the sale price—is constrained at some level by the buyer's option to finance through a third party, thus taking advantage of the lower price while avoiding the higher interest rate. (If a seller were to condition a price discount on providing the financing itself, the debtor should be entitled to rely on that condition to rebut the presumption that the contract rate reflects actual risk.) Finally, the debtor remains free to rebut the contract rate with any other probative evidence. While joint pricing may introduce some inaccuracy, the contract rate is still a far better initial estimate than the prime rate.

   19. [Footnote 6 in original:] Some transaction costs are avoided by the creditor in bankruptcy—for example, loan-origination costs such as advertising. But these are likely only a minor component of the interest rate. * * * Any transaction costs the creditor avoids in bankruptcy are thus far less than the additional ones he incurs.

Finally, the plurality objects that similarly situated creditors might not be treated alike. But the contract rate is only a presumption. If a judge thinks it necessary to modify the rate to avoid unjustified disparity, he can do so. For example, if two creditors charged different rates solely because they lent to the debtor at different times, the judge could average the rates or use the more recent one. The plurality's argument might be valid against an approach that *irrebuttably* presumes the contract rate, but that is not what I propose.

II

The defects of the formula approach far outweigh those of the contract-rate approach. The formula approach starts with the prime lending rate—a number that, while objective and easily ascertainable, is indisputably too low. It then adjusts by adding a risk premium that, unlike the prime rate, is neither objective nor easily ascertainable. If the risk premium is typically small relative to the prime rate—as the 1.5% premium added to the 8% prime rate by the court below would lead one to believe—then this subjective element of the computation might be forgiven. But in fact risk premiums, if properly computed, would typically be substantial. For example, if the 21% contract rate is an accurate reflection of risk in this case, the risk premium would be 13%—nearly two-thirds of the total interest rate. When the risk premium is the greater part of the overall rate, the formula approach no longer depends on objective and easily ascertainable numbers. The prime rate becomes the objective tail wagging a dog of unknown size.

As I explain below, the most relevant factors bearing on risk premium are (1) the probability of plan failure; (2) the rate of collateral depreciation; (3) the liquidity of the collateral market; and (4) the administrative expenses of enforcement. Under the formula approach, a risk premium must be computed in every case, so judges will invariably grapple with these imponderables. Under the contract-rate approach, by contrast, the task of assessing all these risk factors is entrusted to the entity most capable of undertaking it: the market. All the risk factors are reflected (assuming market efficiency) in the debtor's contract rate—a number readily found in the loan document. If neither party disputes it, the bankruptcy judge's task is at an end. There are straightforward ways a debtor *could* dispute it—for example, by showing that the creditor is now substantially oversecured, or that some other lender is willing to extend credit at a lower rate. But unlike the formula approach, which requires difficult estimation in every case, the contract-rate approach requires it only when the parties choose to contest the issue.

* * *

There is no better demonstration of the inadequacies of the formula approach than the proceedings in this case. Petitioners' economics expert testified that the 1.5% risk premium was "very reasonable" because Chapter 13 plans are "supposed to be financially feasible" and "the borrowers are under the supervision of the court." Nothing in the record shows how these two platitudes were somehow manipulated to arrive at a figure of 1.5%. It bears repeating that feasibility determinations and trustee oversight do not prevent at least 37% of confirmed Chapter 13 plans from failing. On cross-examination, the expert admitted that he had only limited familiarity with the subprime auto lending market and that he was not familiar with the default rates or the costs of collection in that market. In light of these devastating concessions, it is impossible to view the 1.5% figure as anything other than a smallish number picked out of a hat.

Based on even a rudimentary financial analysis of the facts of this case, the 1.5% figure is obviously wrong—not just off by a couple percent, but probably by roughly an order of magnitude.[20] For a risk premium to be adequate, a hypothetical, rational creditor must be indifferent between accepting (1) the proposed risky stream of payments over time and (2) immediate payment of its present value in a lump sum. Whether he is indifferent—i.e., whether the risk premium added to the prime rate is adequate—can be gauged by comparing benefits and costs: on the one hand, the expected value of the extra interest, and on the other, the expected costs of default.

Respondent was offered a risk premium of 1.5% on top of the prime rate of 8%. If that premium were fully paid as the plan contemplated, it would yield about $60. If the debtor defaulted, all or part of that interest would not be paid, so the expected value [assuming a 37% default rate] is only about $50. The prime rate itself already includes some compensation for risk; as it turns out, about the same amount, yielding another $50. Given the 1.5% risk premium, then, the total expected benefit to respondent was about $100. Against this we must weigh the expected costs of default. While precise calculations are impossible, rough estimates convey a sense of their scale.

The first cost of default involves depreciation. If the debtor defaults, the creditor can eventually repossess and sell the collateral, but by then it may be substantially less valuable than the remaining balance due—and the debtor may stop paying long before the creditor receives permission to repossess. * * *

The second cost of default involves liquidation. The $4,000 to which respondent would be entitled if paid in a lump sum reflects the *replacement* value of the vehicle, *i.e.,* the amount it would cost the debtor to purchase a similar used truck. See Associates Commercial Corp. v. Rash, 520 U.S. 953, 965, 117 S. Ct. 1879, 138 L. Ed. 2d 148 (1997). If the debtor defaults, the creditor cannot sell the truck for that amount; it receives only a lesser *foreclosure* value because collateral markets are not perfectly liquid and there is thus a spread between what a buyer will pay and what a seller will demand. The foreclosure value of petitioners' truck is not in the record, but, using the relative liquidity figures in *Rash* as a rough guide, respondent would suffer a further loss of about $450.

The third cost of default consists of the administrative expenses of foreclosure. While a Chapter 13 plan is in effect, the automatic stay prevents secured creditors from repossessing their collateral, even if the debtor fails to pay. The creditor's attorney must move the bankruptcy court to lift the stay. In the District where this case arose, the filing fee for such motions is now $150. And the standard attorney's fee for such motions, according to one survey, is $350 in Indiana and as high as $875 in other States. Moreover, bankruptcy judges will often excuse first offenses, so foreclosure may require multiple trips to court. The total expected administrative expenses in the event of default could reasonably be estimated at $600 or more.

---

20. [An order of magnitude is a factor of ten; thus Justice Scalia is arguing that the correct risk factor is about ten times as great as the 1.5% picked by the bankruptcy court.–Ed.]

I have omitted several other costs of default, but the point is already adequately made. The three figures above total $1,600. Even accepting petitioners' low estimate of the plan failure rate, a creditor choosing the stream of future payments instead of the immediate lump sum would be selecting an alternative with an expected cost of about $590 ($1,600 multiplied by 37%, the chance of failure) and an expected benefit of about $100 (as computed above). No rational creditor would make such a choice. The risk premium over prime necessary to make these costs and benefits equal is in the neighborhood of 16%, for a total interest rate of 24%.

Of course, many of the estimates I have made can be disputed. * * * When a risk premium is off by an order of magnitude, one's estimates need not be very precise to show that it cannot possibly be correct.

In sum, the 1.5% premium adopted in this case is far below anything approaching fair compensation. That result is not unusual, see, e.g., In re Valenti, 105 F.3d 55, 64 (C.A.2 1997) (recommending a 1%-3% premium over the *treasury* rate— i.e., approximately a 0% premium over prime); it is the entirely predictable consequence of a methodology that tells bankruptcy judges to set interest rates based on highly imponderable factors. Given the inherent uncertainty of the enterprise, what heartless bankruptcy judge can be expected to demand that the unfortunate debtor pay *triple* the prime rate as a condition of keeping his sole means of transportation? It challenges human nature.

* * *

The risk-free approach also leads to anomalous results. Justice THOMAS admits that, if a plan distributes a note rather than cash, the value of the "property to be distributed" must reflect the risk of default on the note. *Ante,* at 1966-1967. But there is no practical difference between obligating the debtor to make deferred payments under a plan and obligating the debtor to sign a note that requires those same payments. There is no conceivable reason why Congress would give secured creditors risk compensation in one case but not the other.

* * *

Today's judgment is unlikely to burnish the Court's reputation for reasoned decisionmaking. Eight Justices are in agreement that the rate of interest set forth in the debtor's approved plan must include a premium for risk. Of those eight, four are of the view that beginning with the contract rate would most accurately reflect the actual risk, and four are of the view that beginning with the prime lending rate would do so. The ninth Justice takes no position on the latter point, since he disagrees with the eight on the former point; he would reverse because the rate proposed here, being above the risk-free rate, gave respondent no cause for complaint. Because I read the statute to require full risk compensation, and because I would adopt a valuation method that has a realistic prospect of enforcing that directive, I respectfully dissent.

Bank of Montreal v. Official Committee of Unsecured Creditors (In re American Homepatient, Inc.)
United States Court of Appeals, Sixth Circuit, 2005
420 F.3d 559

* * *

American is a publicly-held company based in Brentwood, Tennessee. It specializes in providing home healthcare services and products and has more than 280 affiliates and subsidiaries in 35 states. Over the course of its operations, American borrowed a significant amount of money. Most of this debt was incurred between 1994 and 1998, when American invested in dozens of new branch offices. The lenders in this case are 24 entities that loaned money to American during this time frame. Although the parties disagree as to the exact total owed to the lenders, both sides acknowledge that the principal balance is in the range of $278 to $290 million.

Following American's voluntary filing for bankruptcy protection under Chapter 11 of the Bankruptcy Code in July of 2002, the company and its affiliates filed a Joint Plan of Reorganization. American filed a Second Amended Joint Plan of Reorganization in January of 2003. This amended plan was approved by all but the lenders in the present case. American then sought to have the plan confirmed pursuant to the Bankruptcy Code's cramdown provisions set forth in 11 U.S.C. § 1129(b), which allow a reorganization plan to go into effect notwithstanding the fact that it has not been accepted by all of the impaired classes.

The bankruptcy court held a five-day hearing on the lenders' claims. During this hearing, the court heard from various witnesses who testified as to the appropriate cramdown interest rate to be applied to the lenders' allowed secured claim. * * *

The bankruptcy court also heard testimony regarding the lenders' collateral value in order to determine the amount of the lenders' allowed secured claim. * * *

* * *

In its pre-*Till* assessment, the bankruptcy court relied on several Sixth Circuit cases calling for the application of the coerced loan theory in determining cramdown interest rates. Under the coerced loan theory, courts "treat any deferred payment of an obligation under a plan as a coerced loan and the rate of return with respect to such loan must correspond to the rate that would be charged or obtained by the creditor making a loan to a third party with similar terms, duration, collateral and risk." 7 Collier on Bankruptcy ¶ 1129.06[1][c][ii][B]. * * *

* * * In this analysis, it was most persuaded by David Rosen, one of American's expert witnesses. Rosen testified that, "under the 'coerced loan' theory, the appropriate level of interest to provide the Lenders with the present value of their claim is the six-year Treasury Bill [interest rate] plus 350 basis points." This resulted in the appropriate interest rate under the coerced loan theory being fixed by the bankruptcy court at 6.785% per annum.

The lenders, however, contend that application of the coerced loan theory was improper in light of *Till*, 541 U.S. 465, 124 S. Ct. 1951, 158 L. Ed.2d 787. In that Chapter 13 case, the Supreme Court evaluated the four widely used methods of calculating the cramdown interest rate (the coerced loan, presumptive contract rate, formula rate, and cost of funds approaches) and found that all but the formula rate suffered from serious flaws * * *.

* * *

Till, however, was a Chapter 13 bankruptcy case. So even though the plurality is clear that the formula approach is the preferable method for Chapter 13 cases, the opinion is less clear about cases in the Chapter 11 context. On the one hand, the plurality noted that "the Bankruptcy Code includes numerous provisions that, like the [Chapter 13] cram down provision, require a court to 'discoun[t] ... [a] stream of deferred payments back to the[ir] present dollar value' to ensure that a creditor receives at least the value of its claim." Id. at 474, 124 S. Ct. 1951 (quoting Rake v. Wade, 508 U.S. 464, 472 n. 8, 113 S. Ct. 2187, 124 L. Ed.2d 424 (1993)) (alterations in original). It further commented that "[w]e think it likely that Congress intended bankruptcy judges and trustees to follow essentially the same approach when choosing an appropriate interest rate under any of these provisions." Id. Some commentators have taken this to mean that *Till*'s analysis of Chapter 13 cramdown interest rates might be applicable to Chapter 11 cramdowns as well. See 7 Collier on Bankruptcy ¶ 1129.06[1][c][i].

In a footnote, however, the plurality noted that "there is no readily apparent Chapter 13 'cram down market rate of interest.'" Id. at 476 n. 14, 124 S. Ct. 1951. This follows from the fact that "[b]ecause every cram down loan is imposed by a court over the objection of the secured creditor, there is no free market of willing cram down lenders." Id. But

> [i]nterestingly, the same is not true in the Chapter 11 context, as numerous lenders advertise financing for Chapter 11 debtors in possession. *Thus, when picking a cram down rate in a Chapter 11 case, it might make sense to ask what rate an efficient market would produce.* In the Chapter 13 context, by contrast, the absence of any such market obligates courts to look to first principles and ask only what rate will fairly compensate a creditor for its exposure.

Id. (emphasis added). This footnote suggests that a formula approach like the one adopted by the plurality is not required in the Chapter 11 context.

At least one court that has examined cramdown interest rates post-*Till* has concluded that *Till* does not apply in a Chapter 11 context. See In re Prussia Assocs., 322 B.R. 572, 585, 589 (Bankr. E.D. Pa. 2005) (holding that "*Till* is instructive, but it is not controlling, insofar as mandating the use of the 'formula' approach described in *Till* in every Chapter 11 case," and noting that "[*Till* 's] dicta implies that the Bankruptcy Court in such circumstances (i.e., efficient markets) should exercise discretion in evaluating an appropriate cramdown interest rate by considering the availability of market financing").

Several outside commentators, however, have argued that *Till*'s formula approach should apply to Chapter 11 cases as well as to Chapter 13 cases, noting that the two are not all that dissimilar. See 7 Collier on Bankruptcy ¶ 1129.06[1][c][i] ("[T]he relevant market for involuntary loans in chapter 11 may be just as illusory as in chapter 13."); Ronald F. Greenspan & Cynthia Nelson, *'Un Till' We Meet Again: Why the Till Decision Might Not Be the Last Word on Cramdown Interest Rates*, Am. Bankr. Inst. J., Dec.-Jan. 2004, at 48 ("So we are left to wonder if footnote 14 nullifies *Till* in a chapter 11 context (or at least where efficient markets exist), modifies its application or is merely an irrelevant musing."); Thomas J. Yerbich, *How Do You Count the Votes—or Did* Till *Tilt the Game?*, Am. Bankr. Inst. J., July-Aug. 2004, at 10 ("There is no more of a 'free market of willing cramdown lenders' in a chapter 11 (or a chapter 12, for that matter) than in a chapter 13."). And at least one court has concluded that *Till* does apply in a Chapter 11 context. See Official Unsecured Creditor's Comm. of LWD, Inc. v. K & B Capital, LLC (In re LWD, Inc.), 2005 WL 567460 (Bankr. W.D. Ky. Feb.10, 2005).

Taking all of this into account, we decline to blindly adopt *Till*'s endorsement of the formula approach for Chapter 13 cases in the Chapter 11 context. Rather, we opt to take our cue from Footnote 14 of the opinion, which offered the guiding principle that "when picking a cram down rate in a Chapter 11 case, it might make sense to ask what rate an efficient market would produce." *Till*, 541 U.S. at 476 n. 14, 124 S. Ct. 1951. This means that the market rate should be applied in Chapter 11 cases where there exists an efficient market. But where no efficient market exists for a Chapter 11 debtor, then the bankruptcy court should employ the formula approach endorsed by the *Till* plurality. This nuanced approach should obviate the concern of commentators who argue that, even in the Chapter 11 context, there are instances where no efficient market exists.

While we accept Footnote 14's recommendation that the appropriate rate here is the one that "an efficient market would produce," we must still reconcile this principle with the coerced loan theory employed by the bankruptcy court. Indeed, the lenders make two related arguments against the bankruptcy court's determination of the appropriate interest rate, which they contend demonstrate that the court did not apply the rate that an efficient market would produce. They first claim that the 6.785% rate fixed by the bankruptcy court is not a realistic measure of what an efficient market would provide. According to the lenders' experts, an efficient market would have produced a rate of approximately 12%. One of their experts opined that this is because

> [i]t is not feasible, using conventional funding sources, to provide the $309 million in financing needed by the Company with 100% debt. There is, however, an established market that can provide financing of $309 million to the Company. This market would provide a combination of senior debt, mezzanine debt, and equity, with resulting yields priced in response to the inherent risks assumed by the holders of such instruments.

This dovetails with the lenders' second point of contention, which is that the bankruptcy court should have taken "loan-specific" criteria into account when adjusting the appropriate cramdown rate. In support of this argument, they cite to language in *Till* suggesting that the Supreme Court would look favorably on an analysis incorporating debtor-specific risks.

Our understanding of the bankruptcy court's methodology, however, is that it in fact sought to determine what an efficient market would have produced for the loan that the lenders provided, albeit under the rubric of the coerced loan theory. In its assessment of the coerced loan theory, the bankruptcy court court accepted Rosen's testimony to the effect that the loan in question was "senior debt loan in the health care field ... under a normalized capital structure." Rosen then proceeded to analyze the standard market rate for such a loan. The lenders' argument, on the other hand, is centered on the composite interest rate that a new loan (including "mezzanine" debt and equity) would command in the market, not what their loan to American (which was all senior debt) would require. But as the bankruptcy court properly noted:

> The Lenders' argument that the debtor could not obtain a "new loan" in the market place so highly leveraged might be so, but in actuality no new loan is being made here at all. Instead, the court is sanctioning the workout between the debtor and the Lenders. New funds are not being advanced without the consent of the claimants.

Indeed, the only type of debt contemplated by American's reorganization plan was senior secured debt. The inclusion of other types of financing-mezzanine debt and equity-is a pure hypothetical suggested by the lenders.

In addition, the bankruptcy court commented that, in its opinion, the 12.16% interest rate called for by the lenders would result in a "windfall." The court observed that

> [t]he lenders are not entitled to a premium on their return because the debtor filed for bankruptcy. The blended rate suggested by the Lenders goes beyond protecting the value of its claim from dilution caused by the delay in payment.... Any windfall because of bankruptcy is neither contemplated nor required under the Code. The court's role is not to reward the creditor for the "new loan" to a bankrupt debtor, but instead only to provide the creditor with the present value of its claim.

This observation, that the lenders' request would result in a windfall, is further highlighted by *Till*. In *Till*, the plurality acknowledged that lenders ought to be compensated for their risk. The opinion, however, cited with approval the fact that other courts starting from the prime rate "have generally approved adjustments of 1% to 3%." *Till*, 541 U.S. at 480, 124 S. Ct. 1951. It also commented that if a bankruptcy court "determines that the likelihood of default is so high as to necessitate an 'eye-popping' interest rate, the plan probably should not be confirmed." Id. at 480-81, 124 S. Ct. 1951 (citation omitted). The interest rate demanded by the lenders here—12.16%—is nearly eight percentage points higher than the 4.25% prime rate in effect on May 27, 2003, the date that the confirmation order was entered by the district court. As such, the 12.16% rate appears to fall under the "eye-popping" category described unfavorably by *Till*.

In sum, *Till* provides the lower courts with the guiding principle that "when picking a cram down rate in a Chapter 11 case, it might make sense to ask what rate an efficient market would produce." *Till*, 541 U.S. at 476 n. 14, 124 S. Ct. 1951. Although the lenders argue that the rate chosen by the bankruptcy court was not the rate produced by an efficient market, this is a question that was fully considered by that court. Its conclusion that the appropriate market rate would be 6.785% was reached only after carefully evaluating the testimony of various expert witnesses. The fact that the bankruptcy court utilized the rubric of the "coerced loan theory" that was criticized in *Till* provides no basis to reverse the bankruptcy court's decision because *Till* pointed out that, if anything, the coerced loan theory "*overcompensates* creditors ...." *Till*, 541 U.S. at 477, 124 S. Ct. 1951 (emphasis added). We therefore concur in the result reached by both the bankruptcy court and the district court on this issue.

* * *

Before *Till* was decided, courts tended to agree with COLLIER ON BANKRUPTCY, which, prior to 2004, stated that the rate should be "the prevailing market rate for a loan of a term equal to the payout period, with due consideration to the quality of the security and the risk of subsequent default." 5 King, COLLIER ON BANKRUPTCY, ¶ 1129.03(4)(f)(i) (15th ed. 1990) at 1129-85. In determining the market rate, however, courts used widely differing approaches as the Court notes in *Till*.

One approach was the formula approach noted in *Till*. Other courts sought to determine the appropriate rate based on information about the actual market rates for similar loans. Hardzog v. Fed. Land Bank (In re Hardzog), 901 F.2d 858, 860 (10th Cir.1990) (stating in chapter 12 case that approach of adding two percent to risk free rate "will probably not accurately reflect the market, and thus may unduly penalize the lender or borrower" and that "the market rate should be easily susceptible of determination by means of a hearing where each party is given the opportunity to submit evidence concerning the current market rate of interest for similar loans in the region"). The problem, however, is that there typically is no market in which loans of similar risk are made; for example, lenders seldom lend 100% of the value of real estate or other collateral.

As a result, some courts have used a blended rate approach. For the amount of the claim that could be borrowed in an ordinary commercial loan transaction (e.g., 75% of the value of the collateral), the court will use the market rate. For the other 25%, the court will use a higher rate reflective of the much higher return that a lender would demand for such a risky transaction. See In re Bloomingdale Partners, 155 B.R. 961 (Bankr. N.D. Ill. 1993) (market rate evidence suggested that rate on 75% of claim should be two percent over risk free rate, and rate on remaining 25% should be seven or eight percent over risk free rate). The court took a similar blended rate approach in In re Cellular Info. Sys., Inc., 171 B.R. 926 (Bankr. S.D.N.Y. 1994). Does this method ignore the fact that the other 25% is secured? Does this method include a profit component in the interest rate? Is it appropriate for a lender to make its usual profit on what is in effect a forced loan in chapter 11? How did the various opinions in *Till* treat the issue of profit? How did the Sixth Circuit in *American Homepatient* treat the issue of blended rates? Was the blended rate proposed in *American Homepatient* similar to the blended rate used in *Cellular Information Systems*?

In determining whether a dissenting secured claim class is treated fairly and equitably, another difficult issue arises if the collateral includes inventory. What is the consequence of the § 1129(b)(2)(A)(i)(I) requirement that the creditor retain its lien on the collateral? Does that mean that if the class that contains Kick Credit's secured claim dissents, then Foam Corporation's plan must provide that any foam, waterbeds, or children's pillows sold by Foam Corporation from its inventory must be sold subject to Kick Credit's lien? No one would buy from Foam Corporation on that basis, and thus Foam Corporation's business would fail in short order if such a plan were confirmed. Such a plan would not therefore be confirmable, because it would not be feasible. See § 1129(a)(11). Section 1129(b)(2)(A)(ii) presumably would permit the plan to provide that Foam Corporation could sell inventory free of Kick's lien, but it would also require that Kick's lien attach to the proceeds and that either § 1129(b)(2)(A)(i) or (iii) be satisfied. Section 1129(b)(2)(A)(i) would require that Kick retain its lien on the proceeds, which might then keep Foam Corporation from using any of the proceeds to operate its business. See In re Sparks, 171 B.R. 860 (Bankr. N.D. Ill. 1994) (refusing to confirm plan under which debtor would convert apartments to condominiums, mortgagee would be required to release liens on condominiums as debtor sold them, and debtor would use part of proceeds of sale of condominiums to finance operations). If Foam Corporation cannot use the proceeds of sales of its inventory and collection of its accounts receivable, it will not be able to pay its operating expenses and will fail. Thus, again, the plan would not be feasible and thus not be confirmable.

There seem to be two ways to deal with this problem. Courts may refuse to read the lien retention language of § 1129(b)(2)(A)(i) strictly, and thus permit sales of inventory and use of cash collateral as long as the plan provides for the secured creditor to receive replacement collateral (e.g., the new inventory) with a sufficient value to adequately protect its secured claim. See In re Roberts Rocky Mountain Equip. Co., 76 B.R. 784 (Bankr. D. Mont. 1987) (holding that § 1129(b)(2)(A)(i) was satisfied where SBA would retain lien on equipment, accounts receivable and inventory—presumably including after acquired property—and would receive new mortgage on real estate, even though plan permitted debtor to cancel life insurance policy which had also secured SBA loan); cf. Abbott Bank Thedford v. Hanna (In re Hanna), 912 F.2d 945 (8th Cir. 1990) (interpreting analogous provision of chapter 12 in particular context of liens on herds of cattle, a portion of which would need to be sold each year, but not permitting second mortgage on real property to serve as replacement lien for lien on cattle to be sold); In re Underwood, 87 B.R. 594 (Bankr. D. Neb. 1988) (same) (stating that use of cash collateral from sale of cattle would be permitted if secured claim were adequately protected during repayment period, but finding that plan provision requiring maintenance of collateral value at 110% of amount of secured claim did not provide adequate protection due to expected fluctuations in value of cattle), abrogated by *Hanna*, 912 F.2d 945, only with regard to interpretation of § 363(*l*). But see In re Stallings, 290 B.R. 777 (Bankr. D. Idaho 2003) (disagreeing with *Hanna*, noting that chapter 12 is stricter with regard to lien retention than is chapter 11—apparently because of absence of provision in chapter 12 analogous to § 1129(b)(2)(A)(iii)—and stating that such an approach probably is not even permissible in chapter 11).[21]

---

21. Cf. Corestates Bank, N.A. v. United Chem. Techs., Inc., 202 B.R. 33 (E.D. Pa. 1996) (interpreting § 1129(b)(2)(A)(i)(I) lien retention requirement strictly). In *Corestates Bank* (as in Foam Corporation's case), equipment was collateral for an equipment acquisition loan and also was collateral

The better approach is for a court to consider whether the plan provides the "indubitable equivalent" under § 1129(b)(2)(A)(iii) by providing for sufficient replacement collateral. See In re Underwood, supra, 87 B.R. 594 (applying indubitable equivalent analysis despite absence of indubitable equivalent option under chapter 12); cf. In re Nolen Tool Co., 50 B.R. 488 (Bankr. W.D. Ark. 1985) (finding that secured creditors with liens on accounts receivable did not receive indubitable equivalent where plan did not provide for their liens to attach to after-acquired property and where the extent to which their liens would continue in proceeds under § 552 was unclear); In re Loveridge Mach. & Tool Co., 36 B.R. 159 (Bankr. D. Utah 1983) (noting that secured creditor did not object to portion of plan which provided that its collateral of inventory and accounts receivable would be maintained at level of value previously agreed upon during the case).

Fourth, if the interest payments would be more than the debtor's cash flows for the first few years after reorganization, is it fair and equitable for a plan to provide that the debtor will not pay all of the interest during those years, so that the debt will actually grow during those years as unpaid interest accumulates? (The plan would then provide for a sale or refinancing of the collateral in several years to pay off the larger debt or for increased payments in later years to do so.) In other words, is "negative amortization" fair and equitable?

Note that negative amortization increases the risk that the secured creditor will never receive payment of the present value required by § 1129(b)(2)(A)(i). As the amount of the debt increases, the secured party becomes more vulnerable to losses from depreciation of the collateral. The extra risk ought to require that the interest rate be higher than if the interest were to be paid currently. Beyond that, at what point does negative amortization place such a risk on the secured party that the plan would not be fair and equitable in the ordinary meaning of those words?

---

for lines of credit (under the usual cross-collateralization). In reversing the bankruptcy court, the district court held that a plan was not fair and equitable where the secured creditor (whose class had not accepted the plan) would be forced to give up its lien on the equipment in exchange for full cash payment of the equipment acquisition loan on the plan's effective date, where the other loans for which the equipment was collateral would not be paid off immediately. The district court disregarded the debtor's argument that the remaining collateral would be worth double the amount of the unpaid loans and that the secured creditor was entitled to retain a lien only on an amount of collateral that would provide it adequate protection. Instead the district court held that the secured creditor must be permitted to retain a lien on the equipment until all the loans were paid off. Nowhere in the district or bankruptcy court opinions is it stated whether the amount that was owed on the equipment acquisition loan—and that was to be paid in full on the effective date—was equal to, greater than, or less than the value of the equipment. The bankruptcy court had noted in its reversed opinion that the debtor was not relying on the alternative "indubitable equivalence" provision of § 1129(b)(2)(A)(iii); on remand the debtor amended the plan to provide for the secured creditor to retain its lien on the collateral, and thus the bankruptcy court noted that it did not need to decide whether the cash payment was the indubitable equivalent of the lien on the equipment. See In re United Chem. Techs., Inc., No. 95-18221DAS, 1996 WL 571850 (Bankr. E.D. Pa. Oct 07, 1996).

In re Oaks Partners, Ltd.
United States Bankruptcy Court, N.D. Georgia, 1992
141 B.R. 453

JOYCE BIHARY, Bankruptcy Judge.

* * * On December 9, 1991, the Court entered an Order concerning certain key issues raised by First Union's objections to the confirmation of Debtor's Plan. In re Oaks Partners, Ltd., 135 B.R. 440, 22 B.C.D. 673 (Bankr. N.D. Ga. 1991). These issues included the appropriate cramdown rate of interest, the value of debtor's property serving as First Union's collateral, and the application of post-petition payments made by debtor to First Union during the pendency of this Chapter 11 case. * * *

At the January 8, 1992 hearing, counsel advised the Court that the significant remaining issues involved First Union's objections to debtor's classification of claims and to the negative amortization feature in Debtor's Plan. After hearing considerable argument with respect to the classification issues, the Court provided the parties with direction, suggesting that First Union's objections based on classification could be met by minor amendments to Debtor's Plan. Those amendments have been made * * * . Unfortunately, the factual presentation regarding the negative amortization feature of Debtor's Plan was not sufficiently clear for the Court to make any meaningful findings or rulings. Debtor had prepared some exhibits showing projected negative amortization, but had not shared them with First Union's counsel prior to the hearing. In addition, the Court advised counsel that the amount of negative amortization proposed was unreasonably high.

* * * On January 14, 1992, debtor filed a Third Modification of its Plan which: (i) increased the effective pay rate of interest on First Union's claim from 9.32% to 9.85%; (ii) eliminated debtor's obligation to pay an insider a fee of 1% of gross income for administrative services; (iii) eliminated the requirement in the plan to establish and maintain a reserve fund of $70,000.00 designed to cover emergency expenses; and (iv) increased the minimum amount that must be raised from limited partners to $600,000.00 from $450,000.00.

A. Objection to Negative Amortization

The significant remaining objection to Debtor's Plan is to the negative amortization feature. "Negative amortization" refers to the amount of deferred interest on the claim of First Union under Debtor's Plan. Debtor's Plan as now modified provides that First Union will be paid at the rate of 9.85%, while interest will accrue at the rate of 10.25% per annum or at such other rate as the Court may designate. * * * the Court still finds that 10 1/4 % is the appropriate cramdown interest rate. The effect of debtor's modifications is that there will be approximately $302,000.00 of deferred interest on First Union's claim during the first seven years under Debtor's Plan, and the deferred interest will not be fully paid until the end of the plan term in June, 2000. First Union objects and argues that this negative amortization feature of Debtor's Plan is not fair and equitable under 11 U.S.C. § 1129(b).

To put this discussion into focus, it is useful to remember that First Union has not accepted Debtor's Plan and is impaired under Debtor's Plan. Thus, debtor has requested that its plan be confirmed under the "cramdown" provisions in

§ 1129(b) of the Bankruptcy Code. Under § 1129(b)(1), a plan can be confirmed notwithstanding the impairment of and nonacceptance by a class of claims, if the plan does not discriminate unfairly and if it is fair and equitable with respect to such class of claims. Accordingly, the Court cannot confirm Debtor's Plan without a finding that the plan is fair and equitable with respect to First Union.

The recent Ninth Circuit case of Great Western Bank v. Sierra Woods Group, 953 F.2d 1174 (9th Cir.1992) summarizes the current state of the law regarding whether a plan that includes negative amortization is fair and equitable within the meaning of § 1129(b). The Court in *Sierra Woods* surveyed most, if not all, of the reported Chapter 11 cases on the subject and noted that certain patterns have emerged. First, all but one of the courts which have considered the issue have rejected a *per se* rule against negative amortization and have determined that compliance with the fair and equitable requirement must be decided on a case-by-case basis. Second, the courts have most often determined, after analyzing the particular facts of the case, that the negative amortization was not fair and equitable under the circumstances. The Ninth Circuit concluded that the fairness of a reorganization plan that includes negative amortization should be determined on a case-by-case basis and reversed the decisions below which involved, among other things, the conclusion that negative amortization was *per se* impermissible. This Court agrees with the Ninth Circuit and concludes that it cannot reject Debtor's Plan out of hand, because it contains some deferral of interest. However, the plan has to be scrutinized carefully.

The recent decision of In re Apple Tree Partners, L.P., 131 B.R. 380, 398 (Bankr. W.D. Tenn. 1991) sets forth the following list of ten factors relevant to the determination of whether the use of negative amortization is fair and equitable in a particular case.

1. Does the plan offer a market rate of interest and present value of the deferred payments;

2. Is the amount and length of the proposed deferral reasonable;

3. Is the ratio of debt to value satisfactory throughout the plan;

4. Are the debtor's financial projections reasonable and sufficiently proven, or is the plan feasible;

5. What is the nature of the collateral, and is the value of the collateral appreciating, depreciating, or stable;

6. Are the risks unduly shifted to the creditor;

7. Are the risks borne by one secured creditor or class of secured creditors;

8. Does the plan preclude the secured creditor's foreclosure;

9. Did the original loan terms provide for negative amortization; and

10. Are there adequate safeguards to protect the secured creditor against plan failure.

With regard to the first factor, the Court concludes that Debtor's Plan offers a market rate of interest (the cramdown rate), and the present value of the deferred payments is equal to the amount of First Union's claim. This is not surprising, since debtor amended its plan to provide for the accrual of interest at whatever rate the Court determined appropriate for cramdown under § 1129(b) of the Bankruptcy Code.

The issue posed by the second factor—whether the amount and length of the proposed interest deferral is reasonable—is more difficult to answer. There are no useful appellate guidelines for bankruptcy courts to follow in considering whether a particular amount is reasonable or unreasonable. Debtor argues that the amount of deferred interest is small in comparison to the total loan amount. The total amount of deferred interest will be $301,946.00 which is about 2.5% of First Union's $12,036,200.00 claim. First Union argues that $301,946.00 is a substantial sum of money and that requiring First Union to in effect increase its financing on this project by $301,946.00 is not fair. First Union also argues that seven years, the length of time over which interest is deferred, is not reasonable. The interest is not fully paid until the end of the plan which is about 8 1/2 years. The Court finds that this factor weighs in First Union's favor. While the amount of the interest deferral is now much lower than debtor's proposal on January 8, 1992 to defer interest in the amount of $893,698.00, the amount and length of time proposed now are still not reasonable.

The third and fifth numbered factors are interrelated and depend on the perceived worth of the collateral securing the creditor's claim. These factors consider the ratio of the debt to the collateral value during the term of the plan, and the nature of the collateral, including whether it is appreciating, depreciating, or relatively stable in value.

In this case, after applying debtor's post-petition payments to satisfy First Union's unsecured claim, the remaining balance of the claim will be equal to the value of the collateral, $12,036,200.00. Thus, there is an initial debt-to-value ratio of 100%. Debtor argues that the evidence indicates that this ratio will decrease during the Plan's term notwithstanding any projected negative amortization, due to the property's anticipated appreciation in value. While the property is well managed and now has a high occupancy rate, a finding that the property will increase in value during the period of negative amortization depends on a finding that certain capital improvements will be made. Roofing, exterior painting, and other extraordinary improvements have been budgeted by debtor to occur in Year 1 ($275,000.00), Year 2 ($175,000.00), and Year 3 ($28,575.00). The Court agrees with debtor that it is reasonable to conclude that these property improvements, reflecting an aggregate expenditure of more than $475,000.00, will improve the collateral value by an amount greater than the amount of deferred interest on First Union's claim. However, First Union points out that debtor has no obligation under the plan to make the capital improvements. First Union further argues that debtor's cash position, using debtor's own projections, are [sic] now very tight and that if debtor finds itself short of cash, it may defer capital improvements, as it has done in the past, in order to allow debtor to cover the minimum debt service to First Union and avoid default under the plan. If First Union is correct, there is a possibility that the improvements will not be made, and First Union could find itself with collateral that is not appreciating.

The fourth factor involves the feasibility of Debtor's Plan and the reasonableness of debtor's financial projections. The Court found as a part of the December 9, 1991 Order that debtor's feasibility analysis and projections appeared reasonable. First Union argues that the modifications in Debtor's Plan after December 9, 1991 which call for larger monthly payments to First Union render the plan infeasible, increase the risk of default and make it likely that debtor will not have money available to make the budgeted repairs to the property.

After carefully reviewing the evidence and the arguments by counsel, the Court still concludes that the plan is feasible within the meaning of § 1129(a)(11). This feasibility requirement does not involve a guaranty or a certainty, but a finding of reasonable probability of actual performance of the plan. Nonetheless, First Union is correct that the feasibility of Debtor's Plan has been affected by the recent modifications. Under the original projections presented to the Court at the confirmation hearing, debtor projected a cash shortfall from operations during the first two years of the plan of $235,278.00. This projected cash shortfall was to be covered by the $450,000.00 to be raised from the limited partners, leaving a cushion of approximately $215,000.00. Under Debtor's Plan, as modified, the projected cash shortfall over the first four years of the plan will amount to $531,771.00. Even if debtor is able to raise the $600,000.00 now required, there is only a cushion of $68,229.00. Furthermore, in order to raise the funds necessary to cover the increased cash requirement under Debtor's Plan, debtor has eliminated the reserve fund of $70,000.00 which was designed to provide funds to cover emergency expenses that might arise in the course of operations. The existence of the reserve fund was one of the elements offered by debtor at the confirmation hearing to support the reasonableness of its projections. Given the fact that the property presently is approximately 17 years old and the plan extends for an additional 8 ½ years, a reserve fund to cover emergency expenditures was warranted. Thus, while the projections on income and expenses have not changed and are reasonable, the larger monthly payments under the plan and the reduction of a cushion affect the feasibility of the plan. Simply put, the numbers here are very close and there is less room for error.

The sixth factor—whether the risks are unduly shifted to First Union— focuses on the fairness of the risks borne by the secured creditor who objects to having the interest payments deferred. The Court arrived at 10 1/4 % as the fair cramdown interest rate, after carefully evaluating the risks involved in the plan. Debtor's proposal to defer a portion of that interest payment shifts additional risks to First Union. In view of all that has been discussed above, the Court finds that deferring a part of the 10 1/4 % interest payment due First Union results in an undue shifting of risk to First Union. If the property needs another $302,000.00 in equity or debt, then it makes far greater sense for the owners to contribute the funds than for the Court to force First Union to in effect make an additional loan over its strenuous objection.

The seventh factor is whether the risks are borne by one secured creditor or a class of secured creditors. Here, the risks are borne by a single creditor.

The eighth and tenth factors involve whether the plan permits foreclosure and whether there are adequate safeguards to protect the creditor against plan failure. Thus, it is necessary to analyze what remedies exist for First Union in Debtor's Plan if (1) debtor does not raise the $600,000.00; (2) debtor does not make the monthly payments; and (3) debtor does not make the necessary repairs.

Debtor's Plan permits foreclosure if debtor misses a plan payment to First Union, but the foreclosure remedy is not available if debtor does not make the expected repairs. First Union argues that debtor is not required under its plan to make the necessary repairs and that First Union has no safeguard here. In fact, Debtor's Plan does not obligate debtor to perform repairs, despite testimony and statements that debtor expects to repair the roofs, perform exterior painting and make other improvements in the amount of some $475,000.00 during the first three years of the plan. Although debtor has budgeted significant sums for repairs, First Union is correct that Debtor's Plan does not provide First Union with the remedy of foreclosure or any other remedy if debtor does not make the repairs discussed at the confirmation hearing.

Finally, Debtor's Plan does not permit foreclosure if debtor fails to raise the $600,000.00. * * *

The ninth factor is whether the original loan terms provided for negative amortization. The parties do not dispute that the original loan terms here provided for negative amortization. Debtor argues that since the original loan contained a negative amortization feature, there is nothing unfair about requiring First Union to accept a deferral of interest once again in a new, extended forced Chapter 11 loan. First Union urges the Court to hold that this factor is irrelevant and should not be considered. This factor is of some relevance to the overall analysis, but the existence of the provision in the original consensual loan does not justify the inclusion of the provision in the forced context of a cramdown Chapter 11 plan, when the other factors weigh in the secured creditor's favor.

* * * In summary, Debtor's Plan still contains a substantial amount of negative amortization. While the recent modifications do not render the plan infeasible, they affect feasibility. The plan does not give First Union the right to foreclose if the repairs are not made, nor does it give First Union the right to foreclose if debtor is unable to raise the $600,000.00. Weighing all the factors, the Court cannot find that Debtor's Plan with this set of features is fair and equitable under § 1129(b). * * *

Both Debtor's Plan and First Union's Plan require further modification in order to meet the requirements of 11 U.S.C. § 1129. The Court is mindful that this case has dragged on, and the Court is as anxious as the parties to confirm one plan or the other. The alternatives to confirming one of the plans are dismissal of the case or conversion to a case under Chapter 7. Neither alternative would be in the interests of unsecured creditors who will receive payment under either plan. Thus, the Court is constrained to allow the parties one more opportunity to amend their plans, with the hope that one or more confirmable plan will be before the Court. Accordingly, both debtor and First Union are given seven (7) days from the entry of this Order to file modifications addressing those features of their current plans which the Court has identified as obstacles to confirmation. * * *

IT IS SO ORDERED.

ORDER OF CONFIRMATION

* * * Both debtor and First Union filed modifications on February 27, 1992. * * *

Debtor's modifications increase the minimum new investment by limited partners by an additional $75,000.00 (bringing the total required new investment to $675,000.00), eliminate the deferral of interest after the fourth year of the plan, and reduce the total amount of deferred interest to approximately $224,000.00.

Debtor's modifications also provide for the immediate exercise of remedies by First Union, including foreclosure, if debtor fails to raise the required new investment or fails to improve the property according to debtor's extraordinary improvement budget. To increase further the strength of First Union's remedies, Debtor's Plan now provides a mechanism such that instead of foreclosure, First Union at its option may demand a deed in lieu of foreclosure. It further provides that debtor will not be permitted in the future to delay or avoid First Union's remedies by seeking further reorganization or filing a new bankruptcy petition.

* * * the Court finds that Debtor's Plan of reorganization satisfies the requirements for confirmation under the Bankruptcy Code and should be confirmed instead of First Union's Plan of liquidation. * * *

* * * In light of the above findings and conclusions, it is hereby ordered that:

1. Debtor's Plan is hereby CONFIRMED;
2. All objections to confirmation of Debtor's Plan are hereby OVERRULED; and
3. Confirmation of First Union's Plan is hereby DENIED.

IT IS SO ORDERED.

(2) Section 1129(b)(2)(A)(iii)—Providing for Realization of the Indubitable Equivalent of the Secured Claim

The plan need not comply with § 1129(b)(2)(A)(i) to be fair and equitable with respect to a dissenting class of secured claims—it may instead comply with § 1129(b)(2)(A)(iii) by providing "for the realization by [the secured claim] holders of the indubitable equivalent of such claims." The phrase "indubitable equivalent" comes from Judge Learned Hand's opinion in In re Murel Holding Corp., 75 F.2d 941 (2d Cir. 1935).

Murel Holding was decided under § 77B of the old Bankruptcy Act, before Chapters X and XI were enacted. The debtors—owners of an apartment building—proposed to pay interest only on the first mortgagee's claim for ten years. The entire principal amount of the mortgage would then be due at the end of the ten years. The owners were to make an $11,000 loan to the debtor on a priming lien basis to pay for refurbishing some of the apartments. Cash flows might fall slightly short of enough to pay current taxes and interest until the refurbishment was completed, but supposedly then the rentals would be increased substantially. As a result, there supposedly would be sufficient cash flows from the apartment building to pay off overdue property taxes during the ten year period. Under § 77B, if the debtor's plan provided "adequate protection" of the mortgagee's interest, then the court would stay the mortgagee from foreclosing during the term of the plan. In holding that the district court erred in not vacating the stay, Judge Hand wrote:

> [W]e are to remember not only the underlying purposes of the section, but the constitutional limitations to which it must conform. It is plain that "adequate protection" must be completely compensatory; and that payment ten years hence is not generally the equivalent of payment now. Interest is indeed the common measure of the difference, but a creditor who fears the safety of his

principal will scarcely be content with that; he wishes to get his money or at least the property. We see no reason to suppose that the statute was intended to deprive him of that in the interest of junior holders, unless by a substitute of the most indubitable equivalence.

If therefore [the statute] may be applied to a situation like this, the stay so authorized, like any other, lies in the court's discretion; prima facie the creditor may go on to collect; if his hand is to be held up, the debtor must make a clear showing. The liens of the taxes and the first mortgage now are nearly $500,000 and the property is assessed for only $540,000; it has not been able to pay its way for several years. The [$11,000] amount to be advanced is a mere trifle compared with the debts; its effect is wholly speculative, based upon the expectations of those who have everything to gain and nothing to lose. The mortgagee is to be compelled to forego all amortization payments [payments on principal] for ten years and take its chances as to the fate of the lien at the end of that period, though it is now secured by a margin of only ten per cent. It does not seem to us that this setting authorized any stay; it should appear that the plan proposed has better hope of success; full details may not be necessary, but there must be some reasonable assurance that a suitable substitute will be offered. No doubt less will be required to hold up the [foreclosure] suit for a short time until the debtor shall have a chance to prepare * * * . But a stay should never be the automatic result of the petition itself, and we cannot see that there was anything else here of substance.

Id. at 942-43.

If the indubitable equivalent must be "completely compensatory," as Judge Hand wrote, it does not seem that a plan could provide the indubitable equivalent of a secured claim if it did not provide at least as much present value as the amount required by § 1129(b)(2)(A)(i)—present value equal to the lesser of the amount of the allowed secured claim or the value of the collateral securing it. Thus § 1129(b)(2)(A)(iii) will not allow the debtor to provide less present value than (A)(i) would require. Presumably also, if an undersecured creditor makes the § 1111(b)(2) election, "indubitable equivalence" of the secured claim would seem to require that the undersecured creditor be assured of receiving total value—eventually, not as a matter of present value—at least equal to the full amount of the debt. Thus § 1129(b)(2)(A)(iii) would not seem to allow the debtor's plan to provide less total, deferred value on account of the secured claim. The legislative history supports these conclusions. See 124 Cong. Rec. 32,407 & 34,007 (1978) (identical comments by House and Senate managers of bankruptcy bill that the indubitable equivalence standard was taken from Judge Hand's *Murel Holding Corp.* opinion and that "present cash payments less than the secured claim would not satisfy the [indubitable equivalence] standard because the creditor is deprived of an opportunity to gain from a future increase in value of the collateral"). What good, then, is subparagraph (A)(iii) to the debtor (or to any other plan proponent)?

The benefit of subparagraph (A)(iii) to the debtor is that it may allow the plan to ignore the other two requirements of subparagraph (A)(i):

—that secured creditors be given monetary payments (not stock or other property) on account of their secured claims, and

—that secured creditors be permitted to retain their liens on the collateral.

A plan does not have to provide monetary payments to the secured creditor to satisfy the indubitable equivalence standard. A plan does not have to permit the secured creditor to retain its lien on the same collateral; it can substitute different collateral, or pay the secured creditor with property so that the secured claim is satisfied. See Corestates Bank, N.A. v. United Chem. Tech., Inc., 202 B.R. 33 (E.D. Pa. 1996). However, a secured creditor cannot be forced to take unsecured promissory notes for its secured claim, nor can it be forced to take shares of stock or other ownership interests in the reorganized debtor. Klee, *All You Ever Wanted to Know About Cram Down Under the New Bankruptcy Code,* 53 AM. BANKR. L.J. 133, 156 (1979). "Unsecured notes * * * or equity securities of the debtor would not be the indubitable equivalent." 124 Cong. Rec. 32,407 & 34,007 (1978). As Judge Hand's opinion in *Murel Holding* suggests, whether a particular treatment provides indubitable equivalency depends on whether it completely compensates the secured creditor with respect to the secured claim and on the likelihood that the creditor will be paid. See Brite v. Sun Country Dev. (In re Sun Country Dev.), 764 F.2d 406, 409 (5th Cir. 1985); Metro. Life Ins. Co. v. San Felipe @ Voss, Ltd. (In re San Felipe @ Voss, Ltd.), 115 B.R. 526 (S.D. Tex. 1990). To be the indubitable equivalent of the secured claim, the treatment in the plan "must both compensate for present value and *insure the safety of the principal*." United States v. Arnold & Baker Farms (In re Arnold & Baker Farms), 177 B.R. 648, 661 (B.A.P. 9th Cir. 1994), (emphasis added by Bankruptcy Appellate Panel) (quoting from Crocker Nat'l Bank v. Am. Mariner Indus. (In re Am. Mariner Indus.), 734 F.2d 426, 433-34 (9th Cir. 1984), overruled on another issue, U.S. States Sav. Ass'n v. Timbers of Inwood Forest, 484 U.S. 365, 108 S. Ct. 626, 98 L. Ed. 2d 740 (1988)), aff'd, 85 F.3d 1415 (9th Cir. 1996). "[T]o the extent a debtor seeks to alter the collateral securing a creditor's loan, providing the 'indubitable equivalent' requires that the substitute collateral not increase the creditor's risk exposure" with respect to the principal owed. Arnold & Baker Farms v. United States (In re Arnold & Baker Farms), 85 F.3d 1415, 1422 (9th Cir. 1996) (quoting In re Keller, 157 B.R. 680, 683-84 (Bankr. E.D. Wash. 1993)); see Wiersma v. O.H. Kruse Grain & Milling (In re Wiersma), 324 B.R. 92, 111-12 (B.A.P. 9th Cir. 2005) (refusing to find indubitable equivalence where Idaho dairy farmer whose herd had been destroyed by tortfeasor, and who had received cash settlement subject to bank's lien, proposed to move to Georgia, start a new dairy farm, and give bank a lien on new cows to replace lien on cash) (citing *Arnold & Baker Farms* for proposition that creditor's risk must not be increased, and noting "the enormous risk to Bank inherent in new cows, not in Idaho, but in a startup operation in Georgia").

The court in *San Felipe @ Voss* held that a mortgagee with a first mortgage on the debtor's office building was given the indubitable equivalent of its secured claim where it received a combination of cash and stock in a *third* company, Warringtons PLC. Most of the stock—$7,775,000 worth—that the mortgagee was to receive would be restricted stock that could not be sold for six months, that could be sold only through a particular brokerage firm, and that could not be sold for a profit. Nevertheless, the court held that the mortgagee had received the indubitable equivalent of its first mortgage, which could therefore be eliminated by the plan. Warringtons was a stable company. Its stock had been stable in value and was listed on the London International Stock Exchange. The stock was worth 132.8% of the mortgagee's claim; as a backup in case the stock dropped in value during the six months, the mortgagee could obtain access to additional stock worth more than $800,000 and would have a $1 million guarantee from a third party. The court held that equity securities of the reorganized debtor could not be used to provide the indubitable equivalent, but that equity securities of another company—Warringtons—could, if they were sufficiently liquid and stable in value. The court held that the margin of value was sufficient to protect the mortgagee "against any depreciation that might realistically occur over a six-month period." 115 B.R. at 531.

Other courts might find that a shift from a first mortgage on real estate to a lien on common stock of a foreign company created too much extra risk that the mortgagee would not be paid in full—too much extra risk for the lien on the stock to provide the indubitable equivalent of a first mortgage on real property. The student should consider what risk factors the mortgagee was subject to under the plan and compare those to the risks of being an oversecured first mortgagee on an office building.

A plan could provide the indubitable equivalent of a secured claim by replacing part of the secured party's collateral with an annuity issued by a financially strong insurance company. See In re Keller, 157 B.R. 680, 684 (Bankr. E.D. Wash. 1993) (refusing for other reasons to confirm plan but suggesting that annuity could compensate for partial release of collateral which would leave secured creditor with collateral besides the annuity equal to 150% of the secured claim). One court held that a secured creditor with a lien on the cash proceeds of sale of its previous collateral could be forced to take, in exchange, a lien on other real property, a cogeneration facility that produced sulfuric acid and electricity. In re Mulberry Phosphates, Inc., 149 B.R. 702 (Bankr. M.D. Fla. 1993).

A plan that gives the secured creditor all of its collateral in full payment of the secured claim certainly provides the "indubitable equivalent" of the secured claim. See Sandy Ridge Dev. Corp. v. La. Nat'l Bank (In re Sandy Ridge Dev. Corp.), 881 F.2d 1346, limited on denial of rehearing, 889 F.2d 663 (5th Cir. 1989). The court in *Sandy Ridge* pointed out that "property is the indubitable equivalent of itself." Thus the secured creditor who receives all of its collateral receives the indubitable equivalent of its claim, and need not be given monetary payments.[22] Three related questions arise, however.

First, does the transfer of all of its collateral to the secured party satisfy the secured creditor's debt in the full amount of the value of the collateral, as determined by the court, even if the secured creditor receives less than that amount on sale of the collateral? Suppose a secured creditor owed $100,000 has collateral valued by the court at $80,000. The plan provides for surrender of the collateral to the secured creditor in full payment of the $80,000 secured claim. Assuming the debt is a recourse obligation, the secured creditor will have a $20,000 unsecured claim in the case. But suppose the secured creditor sells the collateral in a commercially reasonable way and receives only $70,000. Can the secured creditor go back to the bankruptcy court and seek to have its unsecured claim allowed in the amount of $30,000? Or did the surrender of the collateral satisfy $80,000 of claim, because that was the value placed on the collateral by the court, regardless of whether the collateral sells for that much? Most courts seem to assume that the full $80,000 would be satisfied. See e.g., *Sandy Ridge Dev. Corp.*, 881 F.2d at 1354; In re Hock, 169 B.R. 236 (Bankr. S.D. Ga. 1994). Others permit the secured party to seek reconsideration of its claim if a commercially reasonable resale yields less than the value as set by the court. See, e.g., In re Fursman Ranch, 38 B.R. 907 (Bankr. W.D. Mo. 1984) (permitting secured creditors who received part of their collateral under the plan in partial satisfaction of secured claim to seek reconsideration of claim if commercially reasonable sale yielded lower price than valuation set by court). What is needed to insure that the secured creditor's principal is protected? If the creditor gets the collateral, is there any need to protect principal beyond the time of delivery?

Second, may a plan transfer *part* of the collateral to the secured creditor, and thereby satisfy an amount of the secured claim equal to the court-determined value of the surrendered part of the collateral? Suppose a secured creditor owed $100,000 has collateral consisting of eight acres of land, valued by the court at $20,000 per acre. Suppose the plan provides for transfer of five acres to the secured creditor in full payment of its secured claim (and thus provides for the other three acres to revest in the debtor free of the secured creditor's lien.) Does the plan provide the secured creditor with the indubitable equivalent of the $100,000 claim that was secured by all

---

22. If the secured creditor is undersecured, if there is a junior lien on the property, and if title to the property is transferred to the secured creditor in satisfaction of its secured claim, there is a risk that the junior lien might end up senior to the secured creditor's new ownership interest. In such cases the plan must either provide that the secured creditor retain its lien on the property (without that lien being merged into the secured creditor's ownership interest) or else eliminate the junior lien under § 1123(a)(5)(E). Otherwise there would be a reversal of priority because the secured creditor—which held the senior lien—would receive title subject to the junior lien. The junior lienholder then could foreclose unless the secured creditor paid off the junior lien.

eight acres? Note that the secured creditor runs the risk that the property will sell for less than $20,000 per acre; thus the secured creditor's principal is placed at risk. Most courts seem to think that such a "dirt for debt" (or "eat dirt") plan could at least theoretically provide indubitable equivalence. Many courts, however, subject such plans to "extremely close scrutiny," because of the inherent difficulty in determining the precise value of land. Arnold & Baker Farms v. United States (In re Arnold & Baker Farms), 85 F.3d 1415 (9th Cir. 1996) (affirming reversal of order confirming "dirt for debt" plan, even though bankruptcy court's valuation was not clearly erroneous, because finding of value did not provide indubitable equivalence and did not insure safety of secured creditor's principal) (also stating that "we do not hold that the indubitable equivalence standard can never as a matter of law be satisfied when a creditor receives less than the full amount of the collateral originally bargained for ... "); see In re Walat Farms, Inc., 70 B.R. 330 (Bankr. E.D. Mich. 1987); cf. In re Fursman Ranch, supra, 38 B.R. 907 (permitting secured creditor to retain lien on all of its collateral pending sale of the part distributed to creditor by the plan, in case sale of that part did not satisfy entire secured claim). Other courts seem quite willing to take the chance that the court's valuation is incorrect or that the property will for some other reason not sell for enough money to provide full value to the secured creditor. They reason that application of the bankruptcy laws requires valuation, and that such valuations can be relied upon in this context as in others, as long as they are made conservatively. See, e.g., In re Atlanta S. Bus. Park, Ltd., 173 B.R. 444, 450-51 (Bankr. N.D. Ga. 1994); In re May, 174 B.R.832, 839-40 (Bankr. S.D. Ga. 1994) (holding that risk of incorrect valuation could be placed on secured creditor because "[a] court cannot be the guarantor of the values it sets" and because indubitable equivalence need only be proved by preponderance of the evidence). Cf. *Sandy Ridge Dev. Corp.*, 881 F.2d at 1354 (permitting plan to transfer undersecured mortgagee's entire collateral to mortgagee in satisfaction of amount of debt equal to bankruptcy court's valuation of property whether or not mortgagee ultimately obtained that much on sale of property). How would such courts react to a plan which provided that the secured creditor would receive a 5/8 undivided interest in the eight acres as tenant in common with the debtor in full satisfaction of its secured claim? What if the secured creditor received title to five acres and sold it for *more* than $20,000 per acre?

Third, what is the burden of proof on indubitable equivalence? One might think that sufficient protection would have to be shown "indubitably," which would mean perhaps a clear and convincing standard, rather than a preponderance of the evidence standard. That, or even the higher beyond a reasonable doubt standard, might be thought to be required because " 'Indubitable' means 'too evident to be doubted.' " Webster's Ninth New Collegiate Dictionary (1985)." *Arnold and Baker*, 85 F.3d at 1421. Most courts, however, agree with the court in *May* that the debtor need show indubitable equivalence only by a preponderance of the evidence. See, e.g., *Arnold and Baker*. But that does not mean that the evidence need merely show a 51% chance that the secured creditor's principal will be repaid. Rather, the debtor must show by a preponderance of the evidence that the safety of the secured creditor's principal is ensured. Id. Further, "[a]lthough the value of the [property to be distributed] is a finding of fact [to be] review[ed] for clear error, the ultimate conclusion of indubitable equivalence is a question of law [to be] review[ed] de novo because it requires analysis of the meaning of the statutory language in the context of the Bankruptcy Code's "cram down" scheme." Id., 85 F.3d at 1421.

> b. Fair and equitable treatment of dissenting classes of unsecured claims

A plan cannot be fair and equitable with respect to a dissenting class of unsecured claims unless it treats the class in one of two ways. First, the plan can provide for holders of claims in the dissenting class to receive property under the plan with a present value as of the effective date equal to the full allowed amount of their claims. Section 1129(b)(2)(B)(i). Second, if the plan does not provide such full payment, then holders of claims or interests in classes junior to the dissenting class must not receive or retain any property under the plan on account of their claims or interests. Section 1129(b)(2)(B)(ii). These requirements amount to an absolute priority rule: senior dissenting classes of unsecured claims must be paid or provided for in full or else junior classes get nothing.

Note that application of this absolute priority rule usually will require a going concern valuation of the debtor's assets. See Consol. Rock Prods. Co. v. Du Bois, 312 U.S. 510, 525, 61 S. Ct. 675, 685, 85 L. Ed. 982, 993 (1941) (holding that valuation of the enterprise based on prospective earnings was "essential for satisfaction of the absolute priority rule"). For example, consider DingCo's chapter 11 case, in which the allowed general unsecured claims total $100,000. SecCo, a noninsider secured creditor with a lien on a $20,000 truck used in DingCo's business, holds the only secured claim, in the amount of $15,000. DingCo impairs the class which contains SecCo's secured claim (by stretching out the payments by one year), but SecCo nevertheless accepts the plan. There is, as a result, an impaired class of claims which has accepted the plan not counting acceptances by insiders; thus § 1129(a)(10) is satisfied. The plan places all general unsecured claims in a single class. The plan provides that, on the effective date of the plan, holders of general unsecured claims will receive, on account of each $100 of unsecured claim, $5 cash, $50 in five-year promissory notes at a 9% interest rate, and one share of common stock in the reorganized DingCo. (Thus the general unsecured creditors will share pro rata a total of $5,000 cash, $50,000 in promissory notes, and 1,000 shares of stock.) The plan also provides that the existing stockholders' shares in DingCo will be cancelled but that a total of 1,000 shares of common stock in the reorganized

DingCo will be distributed to the existing stockholders, pro rata. The plan does not require the existing stockholders to contribute any new value in order to be entitled to the shares. Most of the general unsecured creditors do not like the plan, and thus their class votes to reject it.

What must the court do in order to determine whether the plan is fair and equitable with respect to the dissenting class? Stockholders are junior to creditors; thus the class consisting of the interests of the existing stockholders is junior to the class of general unsecured claims. The plan provides that DingCo's existing stockholders will receive property—shares of stock in the reorganized DingCo. Thus the plan cannot satisfy § 1129(b)(2)(B)(ii), because a class junior to the dissenting class of unsecured claims receives property under the plan. Thus, to be fair and equitable with respect to the dissenting class, the plan must satisfy § 1129(b)(2)(B)(i)—it must give holders of claims in the dissenting class property with a present value as of the effective date at least equal to the full amount of their claims. The cash, promissory notes, and stock are all property, but are they worth the full amount of the unsecured claims? In other words, will the unsecured creditors receive $100 in present value under the plan for each $100 of claim? For each $100 of claim, they will receive $5 in cash, a $50 promissory note, and a share of stock. The cash of course is worth its face amount of $5. Suppose the court finds that 9% is a fair market rate for the notes, so that the payments to be made under the notes have a present value equal to the face amount of the notes. If such a finding is made, then the $50 in promissory notes will represent $50 in present value, for a total thus far of $55 in present value. The question then is whether the one share of stock to be distributed to unsecured claim holders for each $100 of claim is worth at least $45—if it is, then the unsecured claim holders will receive $100 (or more) in present value under the plan for each $100 of claim, and § 1129(b)(2)(B)(i) will be satisfied. If a share of stock will be worth less than $45, the unsecured creditors will not receive full present value, the plan will not be fair and equitable with respect to their class, and the cramdown will fail.

We can determine the value of one share of stock in the reorganized DingCo by determining the value of all of the stock and then dividing that value by the number of shares that will be outstanding.[23] The value of all of the stock in the reorganized DingCo will simply be equal to the going concern value of its assets minus the present value of the payments which must be made on its debts. (Remember, the value of what a company has, minus the value that it must give to creditors, must equal the value that is left for shareholders.) Assume the court has found that the payments that must be made to SecCo on

---

23. That method works if there will only be one kind or class of stock and if no one will hold options to buy additional shares to be issued by DingCo; if either of those assumptions is incorrect, a more complex method must be used, but the general approach is the same. We also ignore the control premium that adds to the value of majority shares and the discount attributed to minority shares.

the debt secured by the truck will have a present value as of the effective date of $15,000. The court has also found that the promissory notes to be given to unsecured creditors (totaling $50,000) have a present value equal to their face amount, because the 9% interest rate is the fair market rate. Thus the total present value (as of the effective date) of payments to be made to creditors by the reorganized DingCo will be $65,000.

Suppose the court determines that the going concern (reorganization) value of the assets which the reorganized DingCo will hold is $85,000. The total value of all the shares in the reorganized DingCo then would be $20,000 ($85,000 minus $65,000). Under the plan there will be 2,000 shares outstanding (1,000 distributed to the unsecured creditors and 1,000 distributed to the existing stockholders). Each share would then be worth $10 ($20,000 divided by 2,000). The total value to be received by the unsecured creditors for each $100 of claim would then be only $65 ($5 cash, plus $50 in promissory notes, plus a $10 share of stock). Because that is less than $100, the plan does not provide for distribution of property with a present value equal to the full allowed amount of the unsecured claims, and thus it is not fair and equitable with respect to the dissenting class. The plan could not be confirmed over the dissent of the unsecured creditors' class.

Suppose on the other hand that the going concern value of the reorganized DingCo's assets will be $160,000. If that is so, then the total value of all of the shares in the reorganized DingCo will be $95,000 ($160,000 minus $65,000). Each share will be worth $47.50 ($95,000 divided by 2,000). Unsecured creditors would then receive property with a present value as of the effective date of $102.50 for each $100 of claim. That would be full present value (and a little more). Section 1129(b)(2)(B)(i) would be satisfied. Unless there were some other problem with the plan, the plan would satisfy the fair and equitable standard and could be crammed down over the dissent of the class of general unsecured claims. Would such a plan require payment of postpetition interest to the unsecured creditors in order to be fair and equitable?

Thus, to determine whether a plan is fair and equitable with respect to a dissenting class of unsecured claims, the court will generally need to determine the going concern value that the reorganized debtor will have. The student may ask, however, whether a valuation would be needed if the plan did not provide for distribution of shares of stock to the holders of unsecured claims in the dissenting class. The answer is that a valuation generally would still be needed. Suppose DingCo's plan provided that, for each $100 of claim, holders of general unsecured claims would receive on the effective date $5 cash and a $95 five-year promissory note at a 9% interest rate; thus $5,000 cash and notes with a total face amount of $95,000 would be distributed to the dissenting class. Suppose the plan also provided that the existing shareholders would retain all of the stock in the reorganized DingCo. It appears that the unsecured creditors will receive 100% payment; why would the going concern value of the reorganized DingCo matter? It would matter because (as explained in Chapter One in section E.4.d.(2)) the total value of all the stock issued by and debt owed by a company cannot be greater than its going concern value. All of the value of the stock and debt will come from the reorganized debtor's future cash flows; to the extent necessary those future cash flows will be used to make interest and principal payments on debts, and any remaining amount will benefit the stockholders and thus provide value to the shares. The value of the stock and debt thus comes from the future cash flows, and thus the value at any time of the stock and debt together cannot be worth more than the value of those cash flows. To put it another way, if an investor purchased all of the stock and debt of the reorganized debtor, the investor would simply obtain the benefit of all of the future cash flows; thus the value of the future cash flows is the same as the combined value of the stock and debt.[24]

That means the total value of the stock in the reorganized debtor and of the debt owed by the reorganized debtor cannot be greater than the going concern value that the reorganized debtor will have. If the going concern value of the reorganized DingCo will be only $85,000, the promissory notes given out by the plan cannot have the necessary present value of $95,000, so that the notes plus the $5,000 cash to be distributed would give the unsecured creditors present value equal to their full $100,000 of claims. Even if the stock in the reorganized debtor would be completely worthless, the most that the promissory notes could be worth would be $85,000. Thus the plan could not possibly be fair and equitable with respect to the dissenting class—it does not provide 100% present value to the dissenting class, and holders of interests in the junior class, the class of the stockholders' interests, receive property. See Norwest Bank Worthington v. Ahlers, 485 U.S. 197, 108 S. Ct. 963, 99 L. Ed. 2d 169 (1988) (holding that even supposedly worthless ownership interests are still property) (reprinted below). Thus the plan could not be confirmed. On the other hand, if the going concern value were determined to be more, for example, $160,000, then the promissory notes might well have the necessary present value of $95,000. (That would depend on whether the 9% interest rate was a fair market rate given the risks involved.)

Thus, if a class of unsecured claims dissents, the court needs to determine the going concern value that the reorganized debtor will have (unless the plan provides for a sale of all assets or for payment of the dissenting class in full in cash on the effective date). The plan will allocate that value going down in seniority of classes. Each class may be given whatever value the class is willing to accept (but not more than full value if any junior class dissents, as noted below). If the class does not accept the plan, then the plan must give it

---

24. However, if there is so much debt that the reorganized company is likely to again encounter financial difficulties, the total value of its stock and debt will be less than the value of the future expected cash flows. See Chapter One note 31.

the value required by the fair and equitable standard. Classes of secured claims are the most senior, in the sense that secured creditors have the right to be paid from the value of their collateral ahead of unsecured creditors. The plan must give each dissenting class of secured claims full present value, as discussed above, in Part A.2.a. of this Chapter. The plan must give each dissenting class of unsecured claims full present value or else ensure that no holder of a claim or interest in a junior class receives or retains any property. If there is not enough value to give the dissenting class of unsecured claims full payment, then the value has run out and any junior classes must take nothing.

Finally, there is a further, uncodified (but yet clearly established and very important) part of fair and equitable treatment. With a few possible exceptions, no class that is senior to a dissenting class may receive more than full present value under the plan. See Klee, *Cram Down II,* 64 AM. BANKR. L.J. 229, 231-32 (1990); Klee, *All You Ever Wanted to Know About Cram Down Under the New Bankruptcy Code,* 53 AM. BANKR. L.J. 133, 144-46 (1979). Consider a case in which the debtor had issued subordinated debentures which by their terms were subordinate to debts owed to financial institutions. For simplicity, assume that the only debts owed by the debtor are $100,000 in unsecured debts owed to financial institutions and $200,000 in unsecured debts owed to holders of the subordinated debentures. The debtor has no cash to distribute under its plan. The going concern value of the reorganized debtor will be $150,000. The plan classifies the institutional claims separately from the claims of the subordinated debenture holders, as it probably must. The plan provides that the institutional creditors will receive five-year promissory notes for $115,000 at a fair market rate of interest, that the subordinated debenture holders will receive all of the stock in the reorganized debtor, and that the existing stockholders will receive nothing and will have their existing shares of stock cancelled. Is the plan fair and equitable with respect to the subordinated debenture class? It meets the explicit statutory requirements in § 1129(b)(2)(B)(ii), because no class that is junior to the subordinated debenture class receives or retains any property. Do you think it is "fair and equitable" in the ordinary, common-sense meaning of that phrase?

Suppose there are three classes, a senior class of unsecured claims owed $10 million, a class of unsecured claims also owed $10 million but subordinated to the claims in the senior class, and a class of common stockholders' interests. Suppose also that the debtor's enterprise value is $17 million, enough to pay the senior class in full, but not to pay the subordinated debt class in full. And finally suppose that for some reason the holders of the claims in the senior class want the stockholders to continue their involvement with the reorganized company and are willing to share some of their value with the stockholders. Thus a plan is proposed that provides the senior class claimants $9 million in value, provides the subordinated claim class their full $7 million in value, and provides for the former stockholders to receive stock in the reorganized debtor worth $1 million. If the subordinated debt class rejects the plan, may it be confirmed? What if the senior class was not senior because of any subordination but rather because it consisted of the fully secured $10 million claim of a secured creditor with a lien on all the debtor's assets. Would that change your analysis? Consider the following case.

In re Armstrong World Industries, Inc.
United States Court of Appeals, Third Circuit, 2005
432 F.3d 507

ANNE E. THOMPSON,[25] District Judge.

* * *AWI designs, manufactures, and sells flooring products, kitchen and bathroom cabinets, and ceiling systems. Due to asbestos litigation liabilities, AWI and two of its subsidiaries filed for Chapter 11 bankruptcy in the United States Bankruptcy Court for the District of Delaware on December 6, 2000. The United States Trustee for the District of Delaware appointed two committees to represent AWI's unsecured creditors: (1) the Official Committee of Asbestos Personal Injury Claimants ("APIC"), and (2) the Official Committee of Unsecured Creditors ("UCC"). The Bankruptcy Court appointed Dean M. Trafelet as the Future Claimants' Representative ("FCR").

After holding negotiations with APIC, UCC, and FCR, AWI filed its Fourth Amended Plan of Reorganization (the "Plan") and Amended Disclosure Statement with the Bankruptcy Court in May 2003. Under the Plan, AWI's creditors were divided into eleven classes, and AWI's equity interest holders were placed into a twelfth class. Relevant to this appeal are Class 6, a class of unsecured creditors; Class 7, a class of present and future asbestos-related personal injury claimants; and Class 12, the class of equity interest holders who own AWI's common stock. The only member of Class 12 is Armstrong Worldwide, Inc. ("AWWD"), the parent company of AWI, which is in turn wholly owned by Armstrong Holdings, Inc. ("Holdings"). Classes 6 and 7 hold equal priority, and have interests senior to those of Class 12. All three are impaired classes because their claims or interests would be altered by the Plan.

The Plan provided that AWI would place approximately $1.8 billion of its assets into a trust for Class 7 pursuant to 11 U.S.C. § 524(g). Class 7's members would be entitled to an initial payment percentage from the trust of 20% of their allowed claims. Meanwhile, Class 6 would recover about 59.5% of its $1.651 billion in claims. The Plan would also issue new warrants to purchase AWI's new common stock, estimated to be worth $35 to $40 million, to AWWD or Holdings (Class 12). If Class 6 rejected the Plan, then the Plan provided that Class 7 would receive the warrants. However, the Plan also provided that Class 7 would automatically waive receipt of the warrants, which would then be issued to AWWD or Holdings (Class 12).
        * * *

---

25.   [Footnote * in original:] Honorable Anne E. Thompson, United States
District Judge for the District of New Jersey, sitting by designation.

* * * Although 88.03% of Class 6 claim holders voted for the Plan, only 23.21% of the amount of the claims voted to accept the Plan. As a result, Class 6 rejected the Plan. Classes 7 and 12 accepted the Plan, but Class 12's acceptance was rescinded under the Plan due to Class 6's rejection.

Following a hearing on November 17 and 18, 2003, the Bankruptcy Court recommended confirmation of the Plan to the District Court in its December 19, 2003 Proposed Findings and Conclusions. The Bankruptcy Court found that the absolute priority rule, as codified in section 1129(b)(2) of the Bankruptcy Code, was satisfied because the warrants were distributed to the holder of equity interests because of the waiver by Class 7, citing In re Genesis Health Ventures, Inc., 266 B.R. 591 (Bkrtcy. D. Del. 2001), and In re SPM Mfg. Corp., 984 F.2d 1305 (1st Cir. 1993). * * * Because the Plan included a channeling injunction under section 524(g) of the Bankruptcy Code, the District Court was required to affirm the Bankruptcy Court's Proposed Findings and Conclusions before the Plan could go into effect.

UCC filed objections to the Bankruptcy Court's Proposed Findings and Conclusions with the United States District Court for the District of Delaware. The District Court * * * issued a memorandum and order on February 23, 2005 denying confirmation of the Plan. The District Court found that (1) the issuance of warrants to the equity interest holders violated the absolute priority rule, and (2) no equitable exception to the absolute priority rule applied.

AWI now appeals the District Court's decision, and is joined by Appellees APIC and FCR, * * *.

* * *

The issues in this case require us to examine the "fair and equitable" requirement for a cram down, which invokes the absolute priority rule. The absolute priority rule is a judicial invention that predated the Bankruptcy Code. It arose from the concern that because a debtor proposed its own reorganization plan, the plan could be "too good a deal" for that debtor's owners. *LaSalle,* 526 U.S. at 444, 119 S. Ct. 1411. In its initial form, the absolute priority rule required that "creditors ... be paid before the stockholders could retain [equity interests] for any purpose whatever." Id. (quoting N. Pac. Ry. Co. v. Boyd, 228 U.S. 482, 508, 33 S. Ct. 554, 57 L. Ed. 931 (1913)) (emphasis added [sic]).

The absolute priority rule was later codified as part of the "fair and equitable" requirement of 11 U.S.C. § 1129(b). Under the statute, a plan is fair and equitable with respect to an impaired, dissenting class of unsecured claims if (1) it pays the class's claims in full, or if (2) it does not allow holders of any junior claims or interests to receive or retain any property under the plan "on account of" such claims or interests.

At the heart of this appeal is the Plan provision that distributes warrants to AWI's equity interest holders (Class 12) through Class 7 in the event that Class 6 rejects the Plan. Appellant AWI argues that this provision does not violate the absolute priority rule because (1) legislative history and historical context indicate that the rule does not prohibit the transfer of warrants to the equity interest holders under the current circumstances; (2) case law establishes that Class 7 can transfer part of its distribution under the Plan to another claimant; and (3) the Plan did not give the warrants to Class 12 "on account of" its equity interests. * * *

First, AWI suggests that this Court should apply a flexible interpretation of the absolute priority rule based on its legislative history and historical context. Because the absolute priority rule is now codified as part of the Bankruptcy Code, we will interpret it using standard principles of statutory construction. We begin by looking at the plain language of the statute. If the meaning is plain, we will make no further inquiry unless the literal application of the statute will end in a result that conflicts with Congress's intentions. In such a case, the intentions of Congress will control.

AWI contends that application of the absolute priority rule would be contrary to Congress's intentions because the rule was designed to prevent the " 'squeezing out' [of] *intermediate* unsecured creditors." See In re Wabash Valley Power Ass'n, 72 F.3d 1305, 1314 (7th Cir. 1995) (citing *N. Pac. Ry. Co.*, 228 U.S. 482, 33 S. Ct. 554, 57 L. Ed. 931) (emphasis added). AWI supports its claim with floor statements by Representative Don Edwards and Senator Dennis DeConcini, key legislators of the Bankruptcy Code. See Begier v. I.R.S., 496 U.S. 53, 64 n. 5, 110 S. Ct. 2258, 110 L. Ed. 2d 46 (1990) (considering these remarks as "persuasive evidence of congressional intent"). These statements indicate that "a senior class will not be able to give up value to a junior class over the dissent of an *intervening class* unless the *intervening class* receives the full amount, as opposed to value, of its claims or interests." 124 Cong. Rec. 32,408 & 34,007 (1978) (remarks of Rep. Edwards on Sept. 28, 1978 and remarks of Sen. DeConcini on Oct. 5, 1978, respectively) (emphasis added). AWI argues that this language demonstrates that the absolute priority rule was not meant to apply to the situation before us because Class 6 is not an intervening (or intermediate) class, and is not being squeezed out by Class 7's transfer of warrants to Class 12 under the Plan.

The absolute priority rule, as codified, ensures that "the holder of any claim or interest that is junior to the claims of [an impaired dissenting] class will not receive or retain under the plan on account of such junior claim or interest any property." 11 U.S.C. § 1129(b)(2)(B)(ii). The plain language of the statute makes it clear that a plan cannot give property to junior claimants over the objection of a more senior class that is impaired, but does not indicate that the objecting class must be an intervening class.

We find that the plain meaning of the statute does not conflict with Congress's intent. The legislative history shows that section 1129(b) was at least designed to address "give-up" situations where a senior class gave property to a class junior to the dissenting class. Other statements in the legislative history of section 1129(b), however, appear to apply the statute more broadly. For example, the House Report for H.R. 8200, the bill that was eventually enacted, states that section 1129(b) "codifies the absolute priority rule from the dissenting class on down." H.R. Rep. No. 95-595, at 413 (1978), reprinted in 1978 U.S.C.C.A.N. 5963, 6369. Despite amendments to the original version of H.R. 8200, the House Report has been considered an authoritative source of legislative history for section 1129(b). *See* 124 Cong. Rec. 32,408 & 34,007 (1978) (remarks of Rep. Edwards on Sept. 28, 1978 and remarks of Sen. DeConcini on Oct. 5, 1978, respectively) ("[T]he House report remains an accurate description of confirmation of section 1129(b)."). In addition, the floor statements of Representative Edwards and Senator DeConcini do not rule out the possibility that an impaired class may object to a co-equal class's distribution of property to a junior class. See id. ("As long as senior creditors have not been paid more than in full, and classes of equal claims are being treated so that the dissenting class of impaired unsecured claims is not being discriminated against unfairly, the plan may be confirmed if the impaired class of unsecured claims receives less than 100 cents on the dollar (or nothing at all) as long as no class junior to the dissenting class receives anything at all."). As a result, we will apply the plain meaning of the statute. Under this reading, the statute would be violated because the Plan would give property to Class 12, which has claims junior to those of Class 6. This finding does not end our consideration of this appeal, as AWI makes further arguments regarding exceptions to the absolute priority rule.

Second, AWI contends that Class 7 may distribute the property it will receive under the Plan to Class 12 without violating the absolute priority rule. AWI derives this result from application of the so-called *"MCorp-Genesis"* rule, which is based on a line of cases where creditors were allowed to distribute their proceeds from the bankruptcy estate to other claimants without offending section 1129(b). See *SPM,* 984 F.2d 1305 (permitting senior secured creditors to share bankruptcy proceeds with junior unsecured creditors while skipping over priority tax creditors in a Chapter 7 liquidation); *Genesis Health,* 266 B.R. at 602, 617-18 (allowing senior secured lenders to (1) give up a portion of their proceeds under the reorganization plan to holders of unsecured and subordinated claims, without including holders of punitive damages claims in the arrangement, and (2) allocate part of their value under the plan to the debtor's officers and directors as an employment incentive package); In re MCorp Fin., Inc., 160 B.R. 941, 948 (S.D. Tex. 1993) (permitting senior unsecured bondholders to allocate part of their claim to fund a settlement with the FDIC over the objection of the junior subordinated bondholders).

The District Court rejected this argument, and found that the *MCorp-Genesis* line of cases was distinguishable. It began its analysis with *SPM,* a First Circuit opinion cited by both the *MCorp* and *Genesis Health* courts to support the legality of the distribution schemes presented to them. *SPM,* 984 F.2d 1305. The District Court differentiated *SPM* from the current case in three ways: (1) *SPM* involved a distribution under Chapter 7, which did not trigger 11 U.S.C. 1129(b)(2)(B)(ii); (2) the senior creditor had a perfected security interest, meaning that the property was not subject to distribution under the Bankruptcy Code's priority scheme; and (3) the distribution was a "carve out," a situation where a party whose claim is secured by assets in the bankruptcy estate allows a portion of its lien proceeds to be paid to others. [S]ee generally Richard B. Levin, *Almost All You Ever Wanted to Know About Carve Out,* 76 Am. Bankr. L.J. 445 (2002). Similarly, *Genesis Health* involved property subject to the senior creditors' liens that was "carved out" for the junior claimants. In addition, the District Court found *MCorp* distinguishable on its facts because the senior unsecured creditor transferred funds to the FDIC to settle pre-petition litigation.

We adopt the District Court's reading of these cases, and agree that they do not stand for the unconditional proposition that creditors are generally free to do whatever they wish with the bankruptcy proceeds they receive. Creditors must also be guided by the statutory prohibitions of the absolute priority rule, as codified in 11 U.S.C. § 1129(b)(2)(B). Under the plan at issue here, an unsecured creditor class would receive and automatically transfer warrants to the holder of equity interests in the event that its co-equal class rejects the reorganization plan. We conclude that the absolute priority rule applies and is violated by this distribution scheme.

In addition, the structure of the Plan makes plain that the transfer between Class 7 and Class 12 was devised to ensure that Class 12 received the warrants, with or without Class 6's consent. The distribution of the warrants was only made to Class 7 if Class 6 rejected the Plan. In turn, Class 7 automatically waived the warrants in favor of Class 12, without any means for dissenting members of Class 7 to protest. Allowing this particular type of transfer would encourage parties to impermissibly sidestep the carefully crafted strictures of the Bankruptcy Code, and would undermine Congress's intention to give unsecured creditors bargaining power in this context. See H.R. Rep. No. 95-595, at 416, reprinted in 1978 U.S.C.C.A.N. 5963, 6372 ("[Section 1129(b)(2)(B)(ii)] gives intermediate creditors a great deal of leverage in negotiating with senior or secured creditors who wish to have a plan that gives value to equity.").

Third, AWI argues that the warrants would not be distributed to Class 12 on account of their equity interests, but rather would be given as consideration for settlement of their intercompany claims. UCC disputes the existence of any such settlement, alleging that such an arrangement should have been brought to the attention of the Bankruptcy Court. In response, AWI indicates that the settlement was detailed in the Plan's Disclosure Statement, which the Bankruptcy Court approved on June 2, 2003. The relevant portion of the Disclosure Statement reads as follows:

> In the ordinary course of business, such intercompany claims have been recorded on the books and records of Holdings, AWWD and AWI, and, assuming that all such intercompany claims are valid, the *net intercompany claim so recorded is in favor of Holdings in the approximate amount of $12 million.* In consideration of, among other things, AWI's agreement under the Plan to fund the reasonable fees and expenses associated with the Holdings Plan of Liquidation, the treatment of Holdings, AWWD, and their respective officers and directors as PI Protected Parties under the Asbestos PI Permanent Channeling Injunction, the simultaneous release by AWI of any claims (known and unknown) AWI has against Holdings and AWWD, and the *issuance of the New Warrants to AWWD,* and to avoid potentially protracted and complicated proceedings to determine the exact amounts, nature and status under the Plan of all such claims and to facilitate the expeditious consummation of the Plan and the completion of Holdings' winding up, Holdings and AWWD will, effective upon and subject to the occurrence of the Effective Date, release all such intercompany claims (known and unknown) against AWI or any of AWI's subsidiaries[.]

([E]mphasis added).

As stated earlier, section 1129(b)(2)(B)(ii) provides that holders of junior claims or interests "will not receive or retain [any property] under the plan *on account of* such junior claim or interest." 11 U.S.C. 1129(b)(2)(B)(ii) (emphasis added). In *LaSalle,* the Supreme Court interpreted "on account of" to mean "because of," or a "causal relationship between holding the prior claim or interest and receiving and retaining property." 526 U.S. at 450-51, 119 S. Ct. 1411. Although the Supreme Court did not decide what degree of causation would be necessary, its discussion on that topic revealed that the absolute priority rule, as codified, was not in fact absolute. First, it indicated that the "on account of" language would be redundant if section 1129(b) was read as a categorical prohibition against transfers to prior equity. Id. at 452-53, 119 S. Ct. 1411. Second, it noted that a "less absolute prohibition" stemming from the "on account of language" would "reconcile the two recognized policies underlying Chapter 11, of preserving going concerns and maximizing property available to satisfy creditors." Id. at 453-54, 119 S. Ct. 1411.

In keeping with these observations, we noted in *PWS* that the "on account of" language "confirms that there are some cases in which property can transfer to junior interests not 'on account of' those interests but for other reasons." 228 F.3d at 238. In *PWS,* the debtors released their legal claims against various parties to facilitate their reorganization, including an avoidance claim that would have allowed them to avoid certain aspects of a previous recapitalization. Id. at 232-35. The appellants in *PWS* argued that releasing the avoidance claim resulted in a prohibited transfer of value to equity interest holders who had participated in the recapitalization. We held that "without direct evidence of causation, releasing potential claims against junior equity does not violate the absolute priority rule in the particular circumstance [where] the claims are of only marginal viability and could be costly for the reorganized entity to pursue." Id. at 242.

AWI would analogize AWWD and Holdings's release of intercompany claims in exchange for warrants to the release of claims in *PWS.*[26] We disagree. According to the Disclosure Statement, the warrants have an estimated value of $35 to $40 million. In contrast, the intercompany claims were valued at approximately $12 million. This settlement would amount to a substantial benefit for Class 12, especially as the warrants were only part of the consideration for which the intercompany claims were released. Among other things, the intercompany claims were also ostensibly released in exchange for the simultaneous release of any claims by AWI against AWWD or Holdings and facilitation of the reorganization process. AWI gives no adequate explanation for this difference in value, leading us to conclude that AWWD or Holdings (Class 12) would receive the warrants on account of their status as equity interest holders. *See LaSalle,* 526 U.S. at 456, 119 S. Ct. 1411.

* * *

We recognize that the longer that the reorganization process takes, the less likely that the purposes of Chapter 11 (preserving the business as a going concern and maximizing the amount that can be paid to creditors) will be fulfilled. Nevertheless, we conclude that the absolute priority rule applies in this case. We will accordingly affirm the District Court's decision to deny confirmation of AWI's Plan.

---

c. Fair and equitable treatment of dissenting classes of interests

The uncodified requirement that no class senior to a dissenting class may receive more than full present value is especially important when the dissenting class is a class of interests. Note that under § 1129(b)(2)(C)(ii), a plan meets the explicit requirements for being fair and equitable with respect to a class of interests if no junior class receives or retains any property under

---

26. [Footnote 3 in original:] Because AWI does not assert any argument regarding a new value exception to the absolute priority rule, we do not address that issue.

the plan. If that were the only requirement, there would be a terrible problem for holders of common stock in a debtor corporation. *There are no classes that are junior to the common stock class of interests.* As a result, any plan would treat the class of the common stockholders' interests in a fair and equitable manner, even if the debtor were solvent—so that the stockholders' shares had substantial value—and the plan gave the stockholders nothing. Luckily, the uncodified requirement applies, that no class senior to the dissenting class may be provided for more than in full.

For example, if the debtor's going concern value is $300,000, and creditors' claims total only $200,000, the plan will not be fair and equitable with respect to the class of the common stockholders' interests if it gives present value of more than $200,000 to the creditors. Thus the class of common stockholders, if it rejects the plan, can ensure that it retains the $100,000 net worth of the debtor for itself.

If the debtor's capital structure is more complex, with not only common stock but also preferred stock, or with limited and general partners, then there will be more than one class of interests. Preferred stock gives its holders rights that are in one way superior to the rights of common stockholders, but in another way more limited. Preferred stock generally carries a fixed dividend entitlement. Suppose, for example, that DupCo issued 20,000 shares of preferred stock with a $1 per year fixed dividend to Friendly Insurance Co. for $20 per share. Before any dividends could be paid on the common stock during any year, a $1 dividend per share would have to be paid to Friendly Insurance on the preferred stock. Failure by DupCo to pay the dividend to Friendly Insurance would not be a default that could lead to bankruptcy, but it would at some point entitle Friendly Insurance to elect one or more members of DupCo's board of directors. The dividend preference generally is a cumulative preference; if DupCo did not pay dividends on the preferred stock for six years, then during the seventh year DupCo would have to pay the $6 in "arrearages" to Friendly Insurance plus the $1 for the current year before any dividends could be paid on the common stock. Preferred stock generally has a liquidation preference set at the time of issuance, which is the amount that must be paid to the preferred stockholders per share in a liquidation before any amount may be paid to common stockholders. The DupCo preferred stock might well have a liquidation preference of $20 per share plus any dividend arrearages. Preferred stock often is redeemable at the company's option for a price set at the time of issuance; the DupCo preferred might have a redemption price of $22 plus any dividend arrearages. All of these features affect the market value of preferred shares.

While it might seem that preferred shares are therefore "preferable" to common shares, note that preferred stockholders are entitled only to their fixed dividends. No matter how profitable DupCo may become, Friendly Insurance will only be entitled to a $1 per share dividend. Preferred stock is less risky than common stock, in that dividends are more likely to be paid and to be paid in an expected amount. But owners of common stock are entitled to all of the profits of the company after payment of the fixed dividend to the preferred stockholders; thus if the company does well, the common stockholders will reap most of the gain.[27]

Under § 1129(b)(2)(C), one way in which the plan may be fair and equitable with respect to a dissenting class of preferred stockholders' interests is for the plan to give the preferred stockholders present value equal to the greater of the three values discussed two paragraphs above: (1) the liquidation preference, (2) the redemption price, and (3) the value of the preferred stock. If the plan does not do so, then no holder of an interest in a junior class—the common stockholders—may receive or retain any property on account of its interest.

Again, a plan is not fair and equitable with respect to any dissenting class—including a class of preferred stockholders' interests—if a senior class receives more than full present value. It should be noted, however, that if a plan provides holders of claims or interests in a dissenting senior class with stock, notes, or other securities in the reorganized debtor that are equal in priority to the securities given to a junior class, an uncodified part of the fair and equitable standard requires that compensation be given to the senior class for its loss of seniority. See Consol. Rock Prods. Co. v. Du Bois, 312 U.S. 510, 61 S. Ct. 675, 85 L. Ed. 982 (1941); Klee, *Cram Down II,* 64 AM. BANKR. L.J. 229, 232-34 (1990). A plan should not be considered to violate the fair and equitable standard with respect to a dissenting junior class if a senior class receives more than 100% of its allowed claim as a result of compensation for loss of seniority.

3. The Requirement That the Plan Not Discriminate Unfairly Against Dissenting Classes

The fair and equitable requirement's absolute priority rule does not deal with how classes of equal priority may be treated. That issue is dealt with in § 1129(b)(1), which prohibits unfair discrimination against dissenting classes. Classes that have equal priority are almost always classes of unsecured claims, and our discussion is limited to such classes, although some courts have erroneously applied the "no unfair discrimination" standard to classes of secured claims with liens on different collateral or with different priorities.

Equality of treatment for similarly situated creditors—for all general unsecured creditors, at least—is a key policy of the bankruptcy laws. It is, for example, one of the foundations of the preference rules in § 547. Generally speaking, a creditor who receives a transfer from an insolvent debtor shortly

---

27. Some preferred stock—convertible preferred stock—carries with it the right to convert the preferred shares into common shares at a specified conversion rate (e.g., two shares of common for each share of preferred). Creditors who want the relative safety of preferred stock but who also want to participate in the "upside gains" if the reorganized company does very well can bargain to receive convertible preferred stock.

before bankruptcy must return the property if the transfer would enable the creditor to receive more value than it would receive in a chapter 7 liquidation. And of course in a chapter 7 liquidation there are strict rules that require distribution to similarly situated creditors on an equal basis. See § 726(a), (b).

In that context, what does it mean that the plan may not discriminate "unfairly" against a dissenting class? When would discrimination not be unfair? The answer seems to be that equal classes can be given different kinds of consideration by the plan, as long as holders of claims in the classes receive present value equal to roughly the same percentage of their claims. For example, if the holders of claims in one class receive 50% of their claims in cash on the effective date, while the holders of claims in an equal class receive promissory notes with a present value equal to 50% of their claims, the plan probably would not discriminate unfairly. Cf. In re Jim Beck, Inc., 207 B.R. 1010, 1016-17 (Bankr. W.D. Va. 1997) (holding that plan does not discriminate unfairly even though it cashes out one 50% shareholder and leaves the other 50% shareholder as the sole owner of the reorganized debtor), aff'd, 214 B.R. 305 (W.D. Va. 1997), aff'd without op., 162 F.3d 1155 (4th Cir. 1998); but see Markell, *A New Perspective on Unfair Discrimination in Chapter 11*, 72 AM. BANKR. L.J. 227 (1998) (arguing that provision of value to one class that carries materially greater risk than the value provided to a class of equal priority may constitute unfair discrimination).

By contrast, if holders of claims in two equal classes do not receive approximately the same percentage repayment in present value, the discrimination would seem to be unfair. The Code's legislative history reinforces the theme of equal distribution to general unsecured creditors with equal legal rights. It suggests that unfair discrimination consists of giving one class value equal to a lesser percentage of its claims than another equal class receives.

> One aspect of [the absolute priority] test that is not obvious is that whether one class is senior, equal, or junior to another class is relative and not absolute. Thus from the perspective of trade creditors holding unsecured claims, claims of senior and subordinated debentures [subordinated only to the senior debentures] may be entitled to share on an equal basis with the trade claims. However, from the perspective of the senior unsecured debt, the subordinated debentures are junior.
>
> This point illustrates the lack of precision in the first criterion which demands that a class not be unfairly discriminated against with respect to equal classes. From the perspective of unsecured trade claims, there is no unfair discrimination as long as the total consideration given all other classes of equal rank does not exceed the amount that would result from an exact aliquot distribution. Thus if trade creditors, senior debt, and subordinate debt are each owed $100 and the plan proposes to pay the trade debt $15, the senior debt $30, and the junior debt $0, the plan would not unfairly discriminate against the trade debt * * * .

H.R. Rep. No. 595, 95th Cong., 1st Sess. 416 (1977). Note that from the standpoint of the trade debt class, all $300 in claims are of equal priority; the trade creditors' $100 in claims constitutes one third of the total and is neither junior to nor senior to any part of the other $200 in claims. Thus, unfair discrimination would result from payment to the trade debt class of anything less than one third of the value that is paid on account of the $300 in claims. The House Report continues its analysis by considering the perspective of the senior debenture holders:

> Application of the test from the perspective of senior debt is best illustrated by the plan that proposes to pay trade debt $15, senior debt $25, and junior debt $0. Here the senior debt is being unfairly discriminated against with respect to the equal trade debt even though the trade debt receives less than the senior debt. The discrimination arises from the fact that the senior debt is entitled to the rights of the junior debt which in this example entitle the senior debt to share on a 2:1 basis with the trade debt.

Id. Thus it is clear that the rule of exact percentage shares is not simply a rule for protecting the trade creditors; it applies equally to debenture holders and apparently to any other unsecured claim holders' class that might exist. Note that the senior debenture class is in fact given the full benefit of its nonbankruptcy right to receive payments that would otherwise go to the subordinated debentures, and thus is entitled to two thirds of the value that the plan allocates to the $300 in claims. See § 510(a).

Some courts, however, have permitted plans to provide very different percentage recoveries to different classes of general unsecured claims whose claims seemed to be of equal priority. See, e.g., Creekstone Apartments Assocs. v. Resolution Trust Corp. (In re Creekstone Apartments Assocs., L.P.), 168 B.R. 639 (Bankr. M.D. Tenn. 1994) (holding that plan would not discriminate unfairly against undersecured creditor with 1111(b) unsecured claim by paying 10% of its claim but 100% of the unsecured claims in the trade creditor class because debtor needed to maintain good relations with trade creditors); In re Pattni Holdings, 151 B.R. 628 (Bankr. N.D. Ga.1992) (holding that plan did not discriminate unfairly against creditor with § 1111(b) unsecured claim by paying 25% cash to trade creditors and likely nothing at all to § 1111(b) creditor). In *Pattni* the court recited the four factors usually recited by courts as determining whether discrimination is unfair:

> Although the Code prohibits "unfair discrimination," it does not prohibit all discrimination. Factors used by many courts in determining the fairness of the discrimination include whether there is a reasonable basis for the discrimination, whether the debtor can confirm a plan without the discrimination, whether the discrimination is proposed in good faith, and the treatment of the class discriminated against.

151 B.R. at 631. For criticism of this four factor test, see Markell, *A New Perspective on Unfair Discrimination in Chapter 11*, 72 AM. BANKR. L.J. 227 (1998); Epstein, Nickles & White, BANKRUPTCY § 10-22. Obviously the

extent to which courts permit separate classification of different general unsecured claims affects the amount of discrimination that can be attempted; § 1123(a)(4) requires that the plan provide the same treatment for each claim or interest in a particular class, unless the holder of the claim or interest agrees to less favorable treatment.

Since unsecured deficiency claims created by § 1111(b)(1) in favor of nonrecourse secured lenders seem to be a favorite target of discrimination, note the discussion of the question whether such claims can be separately classified in the Seventh Circuit's *Woodbrook* decision and the Ninth Circuit's *Barakat* decision, both reprinted below in this Chapter. Note also that in *LaSalle*, reprinted below in this Chapter, the issue arose in the lower courts but had not been preserved for decision by the Supreme Court.

In re Greate Bay Hotel & Casino, Inc.
United States Bankruptcy Court, D. New Jersey, 2000
251 B.R. 213

JUDITH H. WIZMUR, Bankruptcy Judge.
　　* * *

The concept of unfair discrimination is not defined under the Bankruptcy Code. Various standards have been developed by the courts to test whether or not a plan unfairly discriminates. In re Dow Corning Corp., 244 B.R. 705, 710 (Bankr. E.D. Mich. 1999). See also G. Eric Brunstad, Jr. and Mike Sigal, "Competitive Choice Theory and the Unresolved Doctrines of Classification and Unfair Discrimination in Business Reorganizations Under the Bankruptcy Code", 55 BUS. LAW 1, 46-48 (Nov.1999) (describing various tests). The hallmarks of the various tests have been whether there is a reasonable basis for the discrimination, and whether the debtor can confirm and consummate a plan without the proposed discrimination. See, e.g., In re Ambanc La Mesa L.P., 115 F.3d 650, 656 (9th Cir. 1997), cert. denied, 522 U.S. 1110, 118 S. Ct. 1039, 140 L. Ed.2d 105 (1998); In re Jim Beck, Inc., 214 B.R. 305, 307 (W.D. Va. 1997), aff'd, 162 F.3d 1155 (4th Cir. 1998); In re Salem Suede, Inc., 219 B.R. 922, 933 (Bankr. D. Mass. 1998) ("if the plan protects the legal rights of a dissenting class in a manner consistent with the treatment of other classes whose legal rights are intertwined with those of the dissenting class, then the plan does not discriminate unfairly") (quoting Kenneth N. Klee, "All You Ever Wanted to Know About Cram Down under the New Bankruptcy Code", 53 AM BANKR. L.J. 133, 142 (1979)); In re Crosscreek Aparts., Ltd., 213 B.R. 521, 537 (Bankr. E.D. Tenn. 1997) ("at a minimum there must be a rational or legitimate basis for the discrimination and the discrimination must be necessary for the reorganization"); In re Aztec Co., 107 B.R. 585, 590 (Bankr. M.D. Tenn. 1989) (describing various tests and listing cases). Other courts apply the standard only in the context of subordinated claims or interests, In re Acequia, Inc., 787 F.2d 1352, 1364 (9th Cir. 1986), or require similarly situated creditors to receive their "exact aliquot distribution". In re Greystone III Joint Venture, 102 B.R. 560, 571 n. 16 (Bankr. W.D. Tex. 1989), aff'd, 127 B.R. 138 (W.D. Tex.1990), rev'd on other grounds, 995 F.2d 1274 (5th Cir. 1992).

More recently, one court has adopted a modified test for unfair discrimination, which gives rise to:

> a rebuttable presumption that a plan is unfairly discriminatory ... when there is: (1) a dissenting class; (2) another class of the same priority; and (3) a difference in the plan's treatment of the two classes that results in either (a) a materially lower percentage recovery for the dissenting class (measured in terms of the net present value of all payments), or (b) regardless of percentage recovery, an allocation under the plan of materially greater risk to the dissenting class in connection with its proposed distribution.

In re Dow Corning Corp., 244 B.R. 696, 702 (Bankr. E.D. Mich. 1999) (adopting the test proposed in Bruce A. Markell, "A New Perspective on Unfair Discrimination in Chapter 11", 72 AM BANKR. L.J. 227 (1998)).

    * * *

By our calculations, the deficiency claims of Old Noteholders in Class 2 are receiving 76% of their claims, while the general unsecured claims in Class 4 are receiving 80%. While the difference is not large, the disparity is nonetheless discriminatory. The question is whether or not the difference constitutes "unfair" discrimination.

Courts which have rejected confirmation on the basis of unfair discrimination have confronted plans proposing grossly disparate treatment (50% or more) to similarly situated creditors. See, e.g., In re Tucson Self- Storage, Inc., 166 B.R. 892 (9th Cir. BAP 1994) (providing for 100% for unsecured trade creditor and 10% to deficiency claim was unfair discrimination); * * *. But see In re 203 N. LaSalle St. Partnership, 126 F.3d 955, 969 (7th Cir. 1997) (paying unsecured trade creditors 100% and bank deficiency claim 16% not unfair because it was more than the bank would have received under a Chapter 7 liquidation); Jersey City Medical Center, 817 F.2d at 1057 (allowing payment of 100% of physicians claims and 30% of other unsecured claims where source of repayment was an issue).

There is no bright line test which establishes whether a given difference in percentage recovery results in unfair discrimination. Under the *Dow Corning* test cited above, confirmation would be denied only if there was a "materially lower" percentage recovery for the dissenting class or a "materially greater risk to the dissenting class in connection with its proposed distribution." In re Dow Corning Corp., 244 B.R. at 702. Like Judge Spector in *Dow Corning*, I adopt the test articulated in Bruce A. Markell, "A New Perspective on Unfair Discrimination", 72 AM. BANKR. L.J. 227 (1998), because the test "effectively targets the kind of discrimination or disparate treatment that is commonly understood as being 'unfair', namely that which causes injury or that unjustly favors one creditor over another." 244 B.R. at 702.

In this case, the dissenting class of Old Noteholders are not receiving a materially lower percentage recovery on their deficiency claim than the percentage recovery anticipated to be received by general unsecured creditors. The actual value being received by the Old Noteholders on their deficiency claims cannot be calculated with precision. There is substantial variation among the experts who testified at trial, including those who opined that the value received on account of the deficiency claims is higher than 80%. It is sufficient for these purposes to conclude that High River has met its burden to establish that the value being received on account of the deficiency claims is not "unfair."

Nor does the allocation of equity proposed by the High River plan on account of the deficiency claims of Old Noteholders impose a materially greater risk to the dissenting class. The disparity of risk imposed upon equally situated creditors may be evaluated by comparing the levels of risk accepted prepetition by each creditor with the levels of risk imposed in the plan. 72 AM. BANKR. L.J. at 253. For instance, it is generally recognized that "[t]rade creditors have short-term maturities; debenture holders have long-term expectations." Id. at 252. Correspondingly, in this case, the trade creditors are receiving an immediate cash payout, while the Old Noteholders are receiving a package of securities that conform to prepetition long-term expectations. No "unfairness" is discerned in this necessary disparity in treatment.

    * * *

[One party] also claims that the High River plan unfairly discriminates against Class 5 Intercompany Notes. However, the proscription in section 1129(b) against unfair discrimination is a "horizontal limit on nonconsensual confirmation … assuring equitable treatment among creditors who have the same level of priority." 72 AM. BANKR. L.J. at 227-228. As reflected above, the subordination agreements between the debtor and [the objecting party] change the level of priority [it] enjoy[s] to require any distribution received on account of the Intercompany Notes to be paid to the Old Noteholders. The objection * * * is overruled.

B. THE NEW VALUE "EXCEPTION" AND RELATED ISSUES

Norwest Bank Worthington v. Ahlers
United States Supreme Court, 1988
485 U.S. 197, 108 S.Ct. 963, 99 L.Ed.2d 169

[*Respondents Mr. and Mrs. Ahlers "obtained loans from [Norwest Bank], securing the loans with their farmland, machinery, crops, livestock, and farm proceeds." The Ahlers defaulted. When Norwest Bank sought to repossess their farm equipment, the Ahlers filed a chapter 11 petition. The debt exceeded $1 million, and Norwest was substantially undersecured. The farm did not generate enough cash flow to permit the Ahlers' plan to repay Norwest in full. Norwest's large unsecured claim would ensure that an impaired class of unsecured claims would reject any plan. The fair and equitable requirement, with its absolute priority rule, would thus seemingly have prevented confirmation of any plan under which the Ahlers retained their farm. The bankruptcy court granted Norwest relief from the automatic stay, a decision which was affirmed by the district court, which found the Ahlers' plan to be "utter[ly] unfeasibl[e]." The Eighth Circuit reversed, finding that the absolute priority rule would not be violated if the Ahlers kept their farm in exchange for future contributions of their "labor, experience, and expertise" to the operation of the farm. The Supreme Court granted certiorari.*]

Justice WHITE delivered the opinion of the Court.
    * * *

II

As the Court of Appeals stated, the absolute priority rule "provides that a dissenting class of unsecured creditors must be provided for in full before any junior class can receive or retain any property [under a reorganization] plan." 794

F.2d, at 401. The rule had its genesis in judicial construction of the undefined requirement of the early bankruptcy statute that reorganization plans be "fair and equitable." See Northern Pacific R. Co. v. Boyd, 228 U.S. 482, 504-505, 33 S. Ct. 554, 560, 57 L. Ed. 931 (1913); Louisville Trust Co. v. Louisville, N.A. & C.R. Co., 174 U.S. 674, 684, 19 S. Ct. 827, 830, 43 L. Ed. 1130 (1899). The rule has since gained express statutory force, and was incorporated into Chapter 11 of the Bankruptcy Code adopted in 1978. See 11 U.S.C. § 1129(b)(2)(B)(ii) (1982 ed., Supp. IV). Under current law, no Chapter 11 reorganization plan can be confirmed over the creditors' legitimate objections (absent certain conditions not relevant here) if it fails to comply with the absolute priority rule.

There is little doubt that a reorganization plan in which respondents retain an equity interest in the farm is contrary to the absolute priority rule. The Court of Appeals did not suggest otherwise in ruling for respondents, but found that such a plan could be confirmed over petitioners' objections because of an "exception" or "modification" to the absolute priority rule recognized in this Court's cases.

The Court of Appeals relied on the following dicta in Case v. Los Angeles Lumber Products Co., supra, 308 U.S., at 121-122, 60 S. Ct., at 10:

> "It is, of course, clear that there are circumstances under which stockholders may participate in a plan of reorganization of an insolvent debtor
>
> . . . .
>
> "[W]e believe that to accord 'the creditor of his full right of priority against the corporate assets' where the debtor is insolvent, the stockholder's participation must be based on a contribution in money or money's worth, reasonably equivalent in view of all the circumstances to the participation of the stockholder."

The Court of Appeals found this language applicable to this case, concluding that respondents' future contributions of "labor, experience, and expertise" in running the farm—because they have "value" and are "measurable"—are "money or money's worth" within the meaning of *Los Angeles Lumber*. 794 F.2d, at 402. We disagree.[28]

Los Angeles Lumber itself rejected an analogous proposition, finding that the promise of the existing shareholders to pledge their "financial standing and influence in the community" and their "continuity of management" to the reorganized enterprise was "[in]adequate consideration" that could not possibly

---

28. [Note 3 in original:] The United States, as *amicus curiae*, urges us to * * * hold that codification of the absolute priority rule has eliminated any "exception" to that rule suggested by *Los Angeles Lumber*. Relying on the statutory language and the legislative history, the United States argues that the 1978 Bankruptcy Code "dropped the infusion-of-new-capital exception to the absolute priority rule."

We need not reach this question to resolve the instant dispute. * * * we think it clear that even if the *Los Angeles Lumber* exception to the absolute priority rule has survived enactment of the Bankruptcy Code, this exception does not encompass respondents' promise to contribute their "labor, experience, and expertise" to the reorganized enterprise.

Thus, our decision today should not be taken as any comment on the continuing vitality of the *Los Angeles Lumber* exception—a question which has divided the lower courts since passage of the Code in 1978. Compare, e.g., In re Sawmill Hydraulics, Inc., 72 B.R. 454, 456, and n. 1 (Bkrtcy. Ct. CD Ill. 1987), with, e.g., In re Pine Lake Village Apartment Co., 19 B.R. 819, 833 (Bkrtcy. SDNY 1982). Rather, we simply conclude that even if an "infusion-of-'money-or-money's-worth' " exception to the absolute priority rule has survived the enactment of § 1129(b), respondents' proposed contribution to the reorganization plan is inadequate to gain the benefit of this exception.

be deemed "money's worth." 308 U.S., at 122, 60 S. Ct., at 10. No doubt, the efforts promised by the *Los Angeles Lumber* equity holders—like those of respondents—had "value" and would have been of some benefit to any reorganized enterprise. But ultimately, as the Court said in *Los Angeles Lumber,* "[t]hey reflect merely vague hopes or possibilities." Id., at 122-123, 60 S. Ct., at 11. The same is true of respondents' pledge of future labor and management skills.

Viewed from the time of approval of the plan, respondents' promise of future services is intangible, inalienable, and, in all likelihood, unenforceable. It "has no place in the asset column of the balance sheet of the new [entity]." *Los Angeles Lumber*, 308 U.S., at 122-123, 60 S. Ct., at 11. Unlike "money or money's worth," a promise of future services cannot be exchanged in any market for something of value to the creditors *today*. In fact, no decision of this Court or any Court of Appeals, other than the decision below, has ever found a promise to contribute future labor, management, or expertise sufficient to qualify for the *Los Angeles Lumber* exception to the absolute priority rule. In short, there is no way to distinguish between the promises respondents proffer here and those of the shareholders in *Los Angeles Lumber;* neither is an adequate contribution to escape the absolute priority rule.

Respondents suggest that, even if their proposed contributions to the reorganized farm do not fit within the *Los Angeles Lumber* dicta, they do satisfy some broader exception to the absolute priority rule. But no such broader exception exists. Even if Congress meant to retain the *Los Angeles Lumber* exception to the absolute priority rule when it codified the rule in Chapter 11—a proposition that can be debated, see n. 3, supra —it is clear that Congress had no intention to expand that exception any further. When considering adoption of the current Code, Congress received a proposal by the Bankruptcy Commission to modify the absolute priority rule to permit equity holders to participate in a reorganized enterprise based on their contribution of "continued management . . . essential to the business" or other participation beyond "money or money's worth." See H.R. Doc. No. 93-137, pt. 1, pp. 258-259 (1973). This proposal—quite similar to the Court of Appeals' holding in this case—prompted adverse reactions from numerous sources.[29] Congress ultimately rejected the proposed liberalization of the absolute priority rule and adopted the codification of the rule now found in 11 U.S.C. § 1129(b)(2)(B)(ii) (1982 ed. and Supp. IV). "This [section] codifies the absolute priority rule from the dissenting class on down." See H.R. Rep. No. 95-595, p. 413 (1977), U.S. Code Cong. & Admin. News 1978, pp. 5787, 6369. We think the statutory language and the legislative history of § 1129(b) clearly bar any expansion of any exception to the absolute priority rule beyond that recognized in our cases at the time Congress enacted the 1978 Bankruptcy Code.

In sum, we find no support in the Code or our previous decisions for the Court of Appeals' application of the absolute priority rule in this case. We conclude that the rule applies here, and respondents' promise of future labor warrants no exception to its operation.

---

29. [Note 5 in original:] See, e.g., Hearings on S. 235 and S. 236 before the Subcommittee on Improvements in Judicial Machinery of the Senate Committee on the Judiciary, 94th Cong., 1st Sess., pt. 2, p. 1044 (1975) (statement of Prof. Vernon [sic] Countryman); id., at 710 (statement of Phillip A. Loomis, Jr., Comm'r of the Securities and Exchange Comm'n); Brudney, The Bankruptcy Commission's Proposed "Modifications" of the Absolute Priority Rule, 48 Am. Bankr. L.J. 305, 336-339 (1974).

III

Respondents advance two additional arguments seeking to obviate the conclusion mandated by the absolute priority rule.

A

Respondents first advance a variety of "equitable arguments" which, they say, prevent the result we reach today. Respondents contend that the nature of bankruptcy proceedings—namely, their status as proceedings in "equity"—prevents petitioners from inequitably voting in the class of unsecured creditors, and requires that a "fair and equitable" reorganization plan in the best interests of all creditors and debtors be confirmed. Similarly, the Court of Appeals found it significant that—in its view—respondents' wholly unsecured creditors (as opposed to petitioners, who have partially secured claims) would fare better under the proposed reorganization plan than if the farm was liquidated. 794 F.2d, at 402.

The short answer to these arguments is that whatever equitable powers remain in the bankruptcy courts must and can only be exercised within the confines of the Bankruptcy Code. The Code provides that undersecured creditors can vote in the class of unsecured creditors, 11 U.S.C. § 506(a), the Code provides that a "fair and equitable" reorganization plan is one which complies with the absolute priority rule, 11 U.S.C. § 1129(b)(2)(B)(ii) (1982 ed. and Supp. IV), and the Code provides that it is up to the creditors—and not the courts—to accept or reject a reorganization plan which fails to provide them adequate protection or fails to honor the absolute priority rule, 11 U.S.C. § 1126 (1982 ed. and Supp. IV).

The Court of Appeals may well have believed that petitioners or other unsecured creditors would be better off if respondents' reorganization plan was confirmed. But that determination is for the creditors to make in the manner specified by the Code. 11 U.S.C. § 1126(c). Here, the principal creditors entitled to vote in the class of unsecured creditors (i.e., petitioners) objected to the proposed reorganization. This was their prerogative under the Code, and courts applying the Code must effectuate their decision.

B

Respondents further argue that the absolute priority rule has no application in this case, where the property which the junior interest holders wish to retain has no value to the senior unsecured creditors. In such a case, respondents argue, "the creditors are deprived of nothing if such a so-called 'interest' continues in the possession of the reorganized debtor." Here, respondents contend, because the farm has no "going concern" value (apart from their own labor on it), any equity interest they retain in a reorganization of the farm is worthless, and therefore is not "property" under 11 U.S.C. § 1129(b)(2)(B)(ii) (1982 ed. and Supp. IV).

We join with the consensus of authority which has rejected this "no value" theory. Even where debts far exceed the current value of assets, a debtor who retains his equity interest in the enterprise retains "property." Whether the value is "present or prospective, for dividends or only for purposes of control" a retained equity interest is a property interest to "which the creditors [are] entitled ... before the stockholders [can] retain it for any purpose whatever." Northern Pacific R. Co. v. Boyd, 228 U.S., at 508, 33 S. Ct., at 561. Indeed, even in a sole proprietorship, where "going concern" value may be minimal, there may still be some value in the control of the enterprise; obviously, also at issue is the interest in potential future profits of a now-insolvent business. And while the Code itself does not define what "property" means as the term is used in § 1129(b), the relevant legislative history suggests that Congress' meaning was quite broad. " '[P]roperty' includes both tangible and intangible property." See H.R. Rep. No. 95-595, at 413, U.S. Code Cong. & Admin. News 1978, at 6369.

Moreover, respondents' "no value" theory is particularly inapposite in this case. This argument appears not to have been presented to the Eighth Circuit, which implicitly concluded—to the contrary of respondents' position here—that the equity interest respondents desire to retain has some value. See 794 F.2d, at 402-403. Even cursory consideration reveals that the respondents' retained interest under the plan might be "valuable" for one of several reasons. For example, the Court of Appeals provided that respondents would be entitled to a share of any profits earned by the sale of secured property during the reorganization period, id., at 403, and n. 18—an interest which can hardly be considered "worthless." And there is great common sense in petitioners' contention that "obviously, there is some going concern value here, or the parties would not have been litigating over it for the last three years." Tr. of Oral Arg. 15-16.

Consequently, we think that the interest respondents would retain under any reorganization must be considered "property" under § 1129(b)(2)(B)(ii), and therefore can only be retained pursuant to a plan accepted by their creditors or formulated in compliance with the absolute priority rule. Since neither is true in this case, the Court of Appeals' judgment for respondents cannot stand. * * *

NOTES

1. For an insightful analysis of *Ahlers,* complete with a careful recounting of the history of the absolute priority rule, and a discussion of the constitutional "takings" issue that the Court did not address, see Ayer, *Rethinking Absolute Priority After Ahlers,* 87 MICH. L. REV. 963 (1989).

2. Do you agree with the Court's statement that the Ahlers' promise of future services was unenforceable and had "no place in the asset column of the [debtors'] balance sheet"? Cf. § 1129(a)(15) (added by 2005 BAPCPA).

3. Would it surprise you to learn that before the Court decided *Ahlers,* two circuit courts had assumed without analysis that the new value "exception" could be used and had applied it to permit confirmation of plans? See Teamsters Nat'l Freight Indus. Negotiating Comm. v. U.S. Truck Co. (In re U.S. Truck Co.), 800 F.2d 581, 588 (6th Cir. 1986); Official Creditors' Comm. ex rel. Class 8 Unsecured Creditors v. Potter Material Serv., Inc. (In re Potter Material Serv., Inc.), 781 F.2d 99, 101 (7th Cir. 1986). Was the Court in *Ahlers* unaware of these circuit cases? Why would the Court suggest that the lower courts were more divided on the issue of the survival of the new value "exception" than was apparently the case? Would it surprise you to learn that there apparently is no reported case under the pre-1978 Bankruptcy Act in which the new value "exception" was applied to permit confirmation of a plan? "Admittedly, no reported decision appears to exist under the Bankruptcy Act in which the exception applied, but there can be little doubt that the new value exception existed." Klee, *Cram Down II,* 64 AM. BANKR. L.J. 229, 241 (1990). See, e.g., Mason v. Paradise Irrigation Dist., 326 U.S. 536, 541-42, 66 S. Ct. 290, 90 L. Ed. 287 (1946).

Bank of America National Trust and Savings Association
v. 203 North Lasalle Street Partnership
United States Supreme Court, 1999
526 U.S. 434, 119 S. Ct. 1411,143 L. Ed. 2d 607

Justice SOUTER delivered the opinion of the Court.

The issue in this Chapter 11 reorganization case is whether a debtor's prebankruptcy equity holders may, over the objection of a senior class of impaired creditors, contribute new capital and receive ownership interests in the reorganized entity, when that opportunity is given exclusively to the old equity holders under a plan adopted without consideration of alternatives. We hold that old equity holders are disqualified from participating in such a "new value" transaction by the terms of 11 U.S.C. § 1129(b)(2)(B)(ii), which in such circumstances bars a junior interest holder's receipt of any property on account of his prior interest.

I

Petitioner, Bank of America National Trust and Savings Association (Bank), is the major creditor of respondent, 203 North LaSalle Street Partnership (Debtor or Partnership),an Illinois real estate limited partnership.[30] The Bank lent the Debtor some $93 million, secured by a nonrecourse first mortgage[31] on the Debtor's principal asset, 15 floors of an office building in downtown Chicago. In January 1995, the Debtor defaulted, and the Bank began foreclosure in a state court.

In March, the Debtor responded with a voluntary petition for relief under Chapter 11 of the Bankruptcy Code, which automatically stayed the foreclosure proceedings. The Debtor's principal objective was to ensure that its partners retained title to the property so as to avoid roughly $20 million in personal tax liabilities, which would fall due if the Bank foreclosed. The Debtor proceeded to propose a reorganization plan during the 120-day period when it alone had the right to do so, see 11 U.S.C. § 1121(b); see also § 1121(c) (exclusivity period extends to 180 days if the debtor files plan within the initial 120 days).[32] The Bankruptcy Court rejected the Bank's motion to terminate the period of exclusivity to make way for a plan of its own to liquidate the property, and instead extended the exclusivity period for cause shown, under § 1121(d).[33]

The value of the mortgaged property was less than the balance due the Bank, which elected to divide its undersecured claim into secured and unsecured deficiency claims under § 506(a) and § 1111(b).[34] Under the plan, the Debtor

---

30. [Footnote 2 in original:] The limited partners in this case are considered the Debtor's equity holders under the Bankruptcy Code, see 11 U.S.C. §§ 101(16), (17), and the Debtor Partnership's actions may be understood as taken on behalf of its equity holders.

31. [Footnote 3 in original:] A nonrecourse loan requires the Bank to look only to the Debtor's collateral for payment. But see n. 6, infra.

32. [Footnote 4 in original:] The Debtor filed an initial plan on April 13, 1995, and amended it on May 12, 1995. The Bank objected, and the Bankruptcy Court rejected the plan on the ground that it was not feasible. See § 1129(a)(11). The Debtor submitted a new plan on September 11, 1995.

33. [Footnote 5 in original:] The Bank neither appealed the denial nor raised it as an issue in this appeal.

34. [Footnote 6 in original:] Having agreed to waive recourse against any property of the Debtor other than the real estate, the Bank had no unsecured claim outside of Chapter 11. Section 1111(b), however, provides that nonrecourse secured creditors who are undersecured must be treated in Chapter 11 as if they had recourse.

separately classified the Bank's secured claim, its unsecured deficiency claim, and unsecured trade debt owed to other creditors. See § 1122(a).[35] The Bankruptcy Court found that the Debtor's available assets were prepetition rents in a cash account of $3.1 million and the 15 floors of rental property worth $54.5 million. The secured claim was valued at the latter figure, leaving the Bank with an unsecured deficiency of $38.5 million.

So far as we need be concerned here, the Debtor's plan had these further features:

(1) The Bank's $54.5 million secured claim would be paid in full between 7 and 10 years after the original 1995 repayment date.[36]

(2) The Bank's $38.5 million unsecured deficiency claim would be discharged for an estimated 16% of its present value.[37]

(3) The remaining unsecured claims of $90,000, held by the outside trade creditors, would be paid in full, without interest, on the effective date of the plan.[38]

(4) Certain former partners of the Debtor would contribute $6.125 million in new capital over the course of five years (the contribution being worth some $4.1 million in present value), in exchange for the Partnership's entire ownership of the reorganized debtor.

The last condition was an exclusive eligibility provision: the old equity holders were the only ones who could contribute new capital.[39]

The Bank objected and, being the sole member of an impaired class of creditors, thereby blocked confirmation of the plan on a consensual basis. See § 1129(a)(8). The Debtor, however, took the alternate route to confirmation of a reorganization plan, forthrightly known as the judicial "cramdown" process for imposing a plan on a dissenting class. Section 1129(b). See generally Klee, *All You Ever Wanted to Know About Cram Down Under the New Bankruptcy Code*, 53 AM. BANKR. L.J. 133 (1979).

---

35. [Footnote 7 in original:] Indeed, the Seventh Circuit apparently requires separate classification of the deficiency claim of an undersecured creditor from other general unsecured claims. See In re Woodbrook Associates, 19 F.3d 312, 319 (1994). Nonetheless, the Bank argued that if its deficiency claim had been included in the class of general unsecured creditors, its vote against confirmation would have resulted in the plan's rejection by that class. The Bankruptcy Court and the District Court rejected the contention that the classifications were gerrymandered to obtain requisite approval by a single class, and the Court of Appeals agreed. The Bank sought no review of that issue, which is thus not before us.

36. [Footnote 8 in original:] Payment consisted of a prompt cash payment of $1,149,500 and a secured, 7-year note, extendable at the Debtor's option.

37. [Footnote 9 in original:] This expected yield was based upon the Bankruptcy Court's projection that a sale or refinancing of the property on the 10th anniversary of the plan confirmation would produce a $19-million distribution to the Bank.

38. [Footnote 10 in original:] The Debtor originally owed $160,000 in unsecured trade debt. After filing for bankruptcy, the general partners purchased some of the trade claims. Upon confirmation, the insiders would waive all general unsecured claims they held.

39. [Footnote 11 in original:] The plan eliminated the interests of noncontributing partners. More than 60% of the Partnership interests would change hands on confirmation of the plan. The new Partnership, however, would consist solely of former partners, a feature critical to the preservation of the Partnership's tax shelter.

There are two conditions for a cramdown. First, all requirements of § 1129(a) must be met (save for the plan's acceptance by each impaired class of claims or interests, see § 1129(a)(8)). Critical among them are the conditions that the plan be accepted by at least one class of impaired creditors, see § 1129(a)(10), and satisfy the "best-interest-of-creditors" test, see § 1129(a)(7).[40] Here, the class of trade creditors with impaired unsecured claims voted for the plan,[41] and there was no issue of best interest. Second, the objection of an impaired creditor class may be overridden only if "the plan does not discriminate unfairly, and is fair and equitable, with respect to each class of claims or interests that is impaired under, and has not accepted, the plan." Section 1129(b)(1). As to a dissenting class of impaired unsecured creditors, such a plan may be found to be "fair and equitable" only if the allowed value of the claim is to be paid in full, § 1129(b)(2)(B)(i), or, in the alternative, if "the holder of any claim or interest that is junior to the claims of such [impaired unsecured] class will not receive or retain under the plan on account of such junior claim or interest any property," § 1129(b)(2)(B)(ii). That latter condition is the core of what is known as the "absolute priority rule."

The absolute priority rule was the basis for the Bank's position that the plan could not be confirmed as a cramdown. As the Bank read the rule, the plan was open to objection simply because certain old equity holders in the Debtor Partnership would receive property even though the Bank's unsecured deficiency claim would not be paid in full. The Bankruptcy Court approved the plan nonetheless, and accordingly denied the Bank's pending motion to convert the case to Chapter 7 liquidation, or to dismiss the case. The District Court affirmed, as did the Court of Appeals.

The majority of the Seventh Circuit's divided panel found ambiguity in the language of the statutory absolute priority rule, and looked beyond the text to interpret the phrase "on account of" as permitting recognition of a "new value corollary" to the rule. According to the panel, the corollary, as stated by this Court in Case v. Los Angeles Lumber Products Co., provides that the objection of an impaired senior class does not bar junior claim holders from receiving or retaining property interests in the debtor after reorganization, if they contribute new capital in money or money's worth, reasonably equivalent to the property's value, and necessary for successful reorganization of the restructured enterprise. The panel majority held that

> "when an old equity holder retains an equity interest in the reorganized debtor by meeting the requirements of the new value corollary, he is not receiving or retaining that interest 'on account of' his prior equitable ownership of the debtor. Rather, he is allowed to participate in the reorganized entity 'on account of' a new, substantial, necessary and fair infusion of capital." 126 F.3d, at 964.

In the dissent's contrary view, there is nothing ambiguous about the text: the "plain language of the absolute priority rule … does not include a new value exception." Id., at 970 (opinion of Kanne, J.). Since "[t]he Plan in this case gives

---

40. [Footnote 13 in original:] The "best interests" test applies to individual creditors holding impaired claims, even if the class as a whole votes to accept the plan.

41. [Footnote 14 in original:] Claims are unimpaired if they retain all of their prepetition legal, equitable, and contractual rights against the debtor. Section 1124.

[the Debtor's] partners the exclusive right to retain their ownership interest in the indebted property because of their status as ... prior interest holder[s]," id., at 973, the dissent would have reversed confirmation of the plan.

We granted certiorari, 523 U.S. 1106, 118 S. Ct. 1674, 140 L. Ed. 2d 812 (1998), to resolve a Circuit split on the issue. The Seventh Circuit in this case joined the Ninth in relying on a new value corollary to the absolute priority rule to support confirmation of such plans. See In re Bonner Mall Partnership, 2 F.3d 899, 910-916 (C.A.9 1993), cert. granted, 510 U.S. 1039, 114 S. Ct. 681, 126 L. Ed. 2d 648, vacatur denied and appeal dism'd as moot, 513 U.S. 18, 115 S. Ct. 386, 130 L. Ed. 2d 233 (1994). The Second and Fourth Circuits, by contrast, without explicitly rejecting the corollary, have disapproved plans similar to this one. See In re Coltex Loop Central Three Partners, L. P., 138 F.3d 39, 44-45 (C.A.2 1998); In re Bryson Properties, XVIII, 961 F.2d 496, 504 (C.A.4 1992), cert. denied, 506 U.S. 866, 113 S. Ct. 191, 121 L. Ed. 2d 134 (1992).[42] We do not decide whether the statute includes a new value corollary or exception, but hold that on any reading respondent's proposed plan fails to satisfy the statute, and accordingly reverse.

II

The terms "absolute priority rule" and "new value corollary" (or "exception") are creatures of law antedating the current Bankruptcy Code, and to understand both those terms and the related but inexact language of the Code some history is helpful. The Bankruptcy Act preceding the Code contained no such provision as subsection (b)(2)(B)(ii), its subject having been addressed by two interpretive rules. The first was a specific gloss on the requirement of § 77B (and its successor, Chapter X) of the old Act, that any reorganization plan be "fair and equitable." 11 U.S.C. § 205(e) (1934 ed., Supp. I) (repealed 1938) (§ 77B); 11 U.S.C. § 621(2) (1934 ed., Supp. IV) (repealed 1979) (Chapter X). The reason for such a limitation was the danger inherent in any reorganization plan proposed by a debtor, then and now, that the plan will simply turn out to be too good a deal for the debtor's owners. See H.R. Doc. No. 93-137, pt. I, p. 255 (1973) (discussing concern with "the ability of a few insiders, whether representatives of management or major creditors, to use the reorganization process to gain an unfair advantage"); ibid. ("[I]t was believed that creditors, because of management's position of dominance, were not able to bargain effectively without a clear standard of fairness and judicial control"); Ayer, *Rethinking Absolute Priority After Ahlers*, 87 MICH. L. REV. 963, 969-973 (1989). Hence the pre-Code judicial response known as the absolute priority rule, that fairness and equity required that "the creditors ... be paid before the stockholders could retain [equity interests] for any purpose whatever." Northern Pacific R. Co. v. Boyd, 228 U.S. 482, 508, 33 S. Ct. 554, 57 L. Ed. 931 (1913). See also Louisville Trust Co. v. Louisville, N.A. & C.R. Co., 174 U.S. 674, 684, 19 S. Ct. 827, 43 L. Ed. 1130 (1899) (reciting "the familiar rule that the stockholder's interest in the property is subordinate to the rights of creditors; first of secured and then of unsecured creditors" and concluding that "any arrangement of the parties by which the subordinate rights and interests of the stockholders are attempted to be secured at the expense of the prior rights of either class of creditors comes within judicial denunciation").

---

42. [Footnote 15 in original:] All four of these cases arose in the single-asset real estate context, the typical one in which new value plans are proposed.

The second interpretive rule addressed the first. Its classic formulation occurred in Case v. Los Angeles Lumber Products Co., in which the Court spoke through Justice Douglas in this dictum:

> "It is, of course, clear that there are circumstances under which stockholders may participate in a plan of reorganization of an insolvent debtor.... Where th[e] necessity [for new capital] exists and the old stockholders make a fresh contribution and receive in return a participation reasonably equivalent to their contribution, no objection can be made....
>
> "[W]e believe that to accord 'the creditor his full right of priority against the corporate assets' where the debtor is insolvent, the stockholder's participation must be based on a contribution in money or in money's worth, reasonably equivalent in view of all the circumstances to the participation of the stockholder." 308 U.S., at 121-122, 60 S. Ct. 1.

Although counsel for one of the parties here has described the *Case* observation as " 'black-letter' principle," it never rose above the technical level of dictum in any opinion of this Court, which last addressed it in Norwest Bank Worthington v. Ahlers, 485 U.S. 197, 108 S. Ct. 963, 99 L. Ed. 2d 169 (1988), holding that a contribution of " 'labor, experience, and expertise' " by a junior interest holder was not in the " 'money's worth' " that the *Case* observation required. Nor, prior to the enactment of the current Bankruptcy Code, did any court rely on the *Case* dictum to approve a plan that gave old equity a property right after reorganization. See Ayer, supra, at 1016; Markell, *Owners, Auctions, and Absolute Priority in Bankruptcy Reorganizations*, 44 STAN. L. REV. 69, 92 (1991). Hence the controversy over how weighty the *Case* dictum had become, as reflected in the alternative labels for the new value notion: some writers and courts (including this one, see *Ahlers*, supra, at 203, n. 3, 108 S. Ct. 963) have spoken of it as an exception to the absolute priority rule, while others have characterized it as a simple corollary to the rule, see, e.g., In re Bonner Mall Partnership, 2 F.3d, at 906; Ayer, supra, at 999.

Enactment of the Bankruptcy Code in place of the prior Act might have resolved the status of new value by a provision bearing its name or at least unmistakably couched in its terms, but the Congress chose not to avail itself of that opportunity. In 1973, Congress had considered proposals by the Bankruptcy Commission that included a recommendation to make the absolute priority rule more supple by allowing nonmonetary new value contributions. Although Congress took no action on any of the ensuing bills containing language that would have enacted such an expanded new value concept, each of them was reintroduced in the next congressional session. After extensive hearings, a substantially revised House bill emerged, but without any provision for nonmonetary new value contributions. After a lengthy mark-up session, the House produced H.R. 8200, 95th Cong., 1st Sess. (1977), which would eventually become the law. It had no explicit new value language, expansive or otherwise, but did codify the absolute priority rule in nearly its present form. See H.R. 8200, supra, § 1129(b)(2)(B)(iv) ("[T]he holders of claims or interests of any class of claims or interests, as the case may be, that is junior to such class will not receive or retain under the plan on account of such junior claims or interests any property").

For the purpose of plumbing the meaning of subsection (b)(2)(B)(ii) in search of a possible statutory new value exception, the lesson of this drafting history is equivocal. Although hornbook law has it that " 'Congress does not intend sub silentio to enact statutory language that it has earlier discarded,' " INS v. Cardoza–Fonseca, 480 U.S. 421, 442-443, 107 S. Ct. 1207, 94 L. Ed. 2d 434 (1987), the phrase "on account of" is not silentium, and the language passed by in this instance had never been in the bill finally enacted, but only in predecessors that died on the vine. None of these contained an explicit codification of the absolute priority rule, and even in these earlier bills the language in question stated an expansive new value concept, not the rule as limited in the *Case* dictum.

The equivocal note of this drafting history is amplified by another feature of the legislative advance toward the current law. Any argument from drafting history has to account for the fact that the Code does not codify any authoritative pre-Code version of the absolute priority rule. Compare § 1129(b)(2)(B)(ii) ("[T]he holder of any claim or interest that is junior to the claims of such [impaired unsecured] class will not receive or retain under the plan on account of such junior claim or interest any property") with *Boyd*, 228 U.S., at 508, 33 S. Ct. 554 ("[T]he creditors were entitled to be paid before the stockholders could retain [a right of property] for any purpose whatever"), and *Case*, 308 U.S., at 116, 60 S. Ct. 1 (" '[C]reditors are entitled to priority over stockholders against all the property of an insolvent corporation' " (quoting Kansas City Terminal R. Co. v. Central Union Trust Co. of N. Y., 271 U.S. 445, 455, 46 S. Ct. 549, 70 L. Ed. 1028 (1926))). See H.R. Rep. No. 95-595, supra, at 414, U.S. Code Cong.& Admin. News 1978, p. 6370. (characterizing § 1129(b)(2)(B)(ii) as a "partial codification of the absolute priority rule"); ibid. ("The elements of the [fair and equitable] test are new[,] departing from both the absolute priority rule and the best interests of creditors tests found under the Bankruptcy Act").

The upshot is that this history does nothing to disparage the possibility apparent in the statutory text, that the absolute priority rule now on the books as subsection (b)(2)(B)(ii) may carry a new value corollary. Although there is no literal reference to "new value" in the phrase "on account of such junior claim," the phrase could arguably carry such an implication in modifying the prohibition against receipt by junior claimants of any interest under a plan while a senior class of unconsenting creditors goes less than fully paid.

III

Three basic interpretations have been suggested for the "on account of" modifier. The first reading is proposed by the Partnership, that "on account of" harks back to accounting practice and means something like "in exchange for," or "in satisfaction of." On this view, a plan would not violate the absolute priority rule unless the old equity holders received or retained property in exchange for the prior interest, without any significant new contribution; if substantial money passed from them as part of the deal, the prohibition of subsection (b)(2)(B)(ii) would not stand in the way, and whatever issues of fairness and equity there might otherwise be would not implicate the "on account of" modifier.

This position is beset with troubles, the first one being textual. Subsection (b)(2)(B)(ii) forbids not only receipt of property on account of the prior interest but its retention as well. See also §§ 1129(a)(7)(A)(ii), (a)(7)(B), (b)(2)(B)(i), (b)(2)(C)(i), (b)(2)(C)(ii). A common instance of the latter would be a debtor's retention of an interest in the insolvent business reorganized under the plan. Yet it would be exceedingly odd to speak of "retain[ing]" property in exchange for the same property interest, and the eccentricity of such a reading is underscored by the fact that elsewhere in the Code the drafters chose to use the very phrase "in exchange for," § 1123(a)(5)(J) (a plan shall provide adequate means for implementation, including "issuance of securities of the debtor … for cash, for property, for existing securities, or in exchange for claims or interests"). It is unlikely that the drafters of legislation so long and minutely contemplated as the 1978 Bankruptcy Code would have used two distinctly different forms of words for the same purpose.

The second difficulty is practical: the unlikelihood that Congress meant to impose a condition as manipulable as subsection (b)(2)(B)(ii) would be if "on account of" meant to prohibit merely an exchange unaccompanied by a substantial infusion of new funds but permit one whenever substantial funds changed hands. "Substantial" or "significant" or "considerable" or like characterizations of a monetary contribution would measure it by the Lord Chancellor's foot, and an absolute priority rule so variable would not be much of an absolute. Of course it is true (as already noted) that, even if old equity holders could displace the rule by adding some significant amount of cash to the deal, it would not follow that their plan would be entitled to adoption; a contested plan would still need to satisfy the overriding condition of fairness and equity. But that general fairness and equity criterion would apply in any event, and one comes back to the question why Congress would have bothered to add a separate priority rule without a sharper edge.

Since the "in exchange for" reading merits rejection, the way is open to recognize the more common understanding of "on account of" to mean "because of." This is certainly the usage meant for the phrase at other places in the statute, see § 1111(b)(1)(A) (treating certain claims as if the holder of the claim "had recourse against the debtor on account of such claim"); § 522(d)(10)(E) (permitting debtors to exempt payments under certain benefit plans and contracts "on account of illness, disability, death, age, or length of service"); § 547(b)(2) (authorizing trustee to avoid a transfer of an interest of the debtor in property "for or on account of an antecedent debt owed by the debtor"); § 547(c)(4)(B) (barring trustee from avoiding a transfer when a creditor gives new value to the debtor "on account of which new value the debtor did not make an otherwise unavoidable transfer to … such creditor"). So, under the commonsense rule that a given phrase is meant to carry a given concept in a single statute, the better reading of subsection (b)(2)(B)(ii) recognizes that a causal relationship between holding the prior claim or interest and receiving or retaining property is what activates the absolute priority rule.

The degree of causation is the final bone of contention. We understand the Government, as amicus curiae, to take the starchy position not only that any degree of causation between earlier interests and retained property will activate the bar to a plan providing for later property, but also that whenever the holders of equity in the Debtor end up with some property there will be some causation;

when old equity, and not someone on the street, gets property the reason is res ipsa loquitur. An old equity holder simply cannot take property under a plan if creditors are not paid in full.[43]

There are, however, reasons counting against such a reading. If, as is likely, the drafters were treating junior claimants or interest holders as a class at this point (see *Ahlers*, 485 U.S., at 202, 108 S. Ct. 963),[44] then the simple way to have prohibited the old interest holders from receiving anything over objection would have been to omit the "on account of" phrase entirely from subsection (b)(2)(B)(ii). On this assumption, reading the provision as a blanket prohibition would leave "on account of" as a redundancy, contrary to the interpretive obligation to try to give meaning to all the statutory language.[45] One would also have to ask why Congress would have desired to exclude prior equity categorically from the class of potential owners following a cramdown. Although we have some doubt about the Court of Appeals's assumption (see 126 F.3d, at 966, and n. 12) that prior equity is often the only source of significant capital for reorganizations, see, e.g., Blum & Kaplan, *The Absolute Priority Doctrine in Corporate Reorganizations*, 41 U. CHI. L. REV. 651, 672 (1974); Mann, *Strategy and Force in the Liquidation of Secured Debt*, 96 MICH. L. REV. 159, 182-183, 192-194, 208-209 (1997), old equity may well be in the best position to make a go of the reorganized enterprise and so may be the party most likely to work out an equity-for-value reorganization.

A less absolute statutory prohibition would follow from reading the "on account of" language as intended to reconcile the two recognized policies underlying Chapter 11, of preserving going concerns and maximizing property

---

43. [Footnote 23 in original:] Our interpretation of the Government's position in this respect is informed by its view as amicus curiae in the Bonner Mall case: "the language and structure of the Code prohibit in all circumstances confirmation of a plan that grants the prior owners an equity interest in the reorganized debtor over the objection of a class of unpaid unsecured claims."

The Government conceded that, in the case before us, it had no need to press this more stringent view, since "whatever [the] definition of 'on account of,' a 100 percent certainty that junior equit[y] obtains property because they're junior equity will satisfy that." See Tr. of Oral Arg. 29 (internal quotation marks added).

44. [Footnote 24 in original:] It is possible, on the contrary, to argue on the basis of the immediate text that the prohibition against receipt of an interest "on account of" a prior unsecured claim or interest was meant to indicate only that there is no per se bar to such receipt by a creditor holding both a senior secured claim and a junior unsecured one, when the senior secured claim accounts for the subsequent interest. This reading would of course eliminate the phrase "on account of" as an express source of a new value exception, but would leave open the possibility of interpreting the absolute priority rule itself as stopping short of prohibiting a new value transaction.

45. [Footnote 25 in original:] Given our obligation to give meaning to the "on account of" modifier, we likewise do not rely on various statements in the House Report or by the bill's floor leaders, which, when read out of context, imply that Congress intended an emphatic, unconditional absolute priority rule. See, e.g., H.R. Rep. No. 95-595, p. 224 (1977) ("[T]he bill requires that the plan pay any dissenting class in full before any class junior to the dissenter may be paid at all"); id., at 413 ("[I]f [an impaired class is] paid less than in full, then no class junior may receive anything under the plan"); 124 Cong. Rec. 32408 (1978) (statement of Rep. Edwards) (cramdown plan confirmable only "as long as no class junior to the dissenting class receives anything at all"); id., at 34007 (statement of Sen. DeConcini) (same).

available to satisfy creditors. Causation between the old equity's holdings and subsequent property substantial enough to disqualify a plan would presumably occur on this view of things whenever old equity's later property would come at a price that failed to provide the greatest possible addition to the bankruptcy estate, and it would always come at a price too low when the equity holders obtained or preserved an ownership interest for less than someone else would have paid.[46] A truly full value transaction, on the other hand, would pose no threat to the bankruptcy estate not posed by any reorganization, provided of course that the contribution be in cash or be realizable money's worth, just as *Ahlers* required for application of *Case* 's new value rule. Cf. *Ahlers*, supra, at 203-205, 108 S. Ct. 963; *Case*, 308 U.S., at 121, 60 S. Ct. 1.

IV

Which of these positions is ultimately entitled to prevail is not to be decided here, however, for even on the latter view the Bank's objection would require rejection of the plan at issue in this case. It is doomed, we can say without necessarily exhausting its flaws, by its provision for vesting equity in the reorganized business in the Debtor's partners without extending an opportunity to anyone else either to compete for that equity or to propose a competing reorganization plan. Although the Debtor's exclusive opportunity to propose a plan under § 1121(b) is not itself "property" within the meaning of subsection (b)(2)(B)(ii), the respondent partnership in this case has taken advantage of this opportunity by proposing a plan under which the benefit of equity ownership may be obtained by no one but old equity partners. Upon the court's approval of that plan, the partners were in the same position that they would have enjoyed had they exercised an exclusive option under the plan to buy the equity in the reorganized entity, or contracted to purchase it from a seller who had first agreed to deal with no one else. It is quite true that the escrow of the partners' proposed investment eliminated any formal need to set out an express option or exclusive dealing provision in the plan itself, since the court's approval that created the opportunity and the partners' action to obtain its advantage were simultaneous. But before the Debtor's plan was accepted no one else could propose an alternative one, and after its acceptance no one else could obtain equity in the reorganized entity. At the moment of the plan's approval the Debtor's partners necessarily enjoyed an exclusive opportunity that was in no economic sense distinguishable from the advantage of the exclusively entitled offeror or option holder. This opportunity

---

46. [Footnote 26 in original:] Even when old equity would pay its top dollar and that figure was as high as anyone else would pay, the price might still be too low unless the old equity holders paid more than anyone else would pay, on the theory that the "necessity" required to justify old equity's participation in a new value plan is a necessity for the participation of old equity as such. On this interpretation, disproof of a bargain would not satisfy old equity's burden; it would need to show that no one else would pay as much. See, e.g., In re Coltex Loop Central Three Partners, L. P., 138 F.3d 39, 45 (C.A.2 1998) ("[O]ld equity must be willing to contribute more money than any other source" (internal quotation marks and citation omitted)); Strub, 111 Banking L. J., at 243 (old equity must show that the reorganized entity "needs funds from the prior owner-managers because no other source of capital is available"). No such issue is before us, and we emphasize that our holding here does not suggest an exhaustive list of the requirements of a proposed new value plan.

should, first of all, be treated as an item of property in its own right. Cf. In re Coltex Loop Central Three Partners, L. P., 138 F.3d, at 43 (exclusive right to purchase post-petition equity is itself property); In re Bryson Properties, XVII, 961 F.2d, at 504; Kham & Nate's Shoes No. 2, Inc. v. First Bank, 908 F.2d 1351, 1360 (C.A.7 1990); D. Baird, THE ELEMENTS OF BANKRUPTCY 261 (rev. ed. 1993) ("The right to get an equity interest for its fair market value is 'property' as the word is ordinarily used. Options to acquire an interest in a firm, even at its market value, trade for a positive price"). While it may be argued that the opportunity has no market value, being significant only to old equity holders owing to their potential tax liability, such an argument avails the Debtor nothing, for several reasons. It is to avoid just such arguments that the law is settled that any otherwise cognizable property interest must be treated as sufficiently valuable to be recognized under the Bankruptcy Code. See *Ahlers*, 485 U.S., at 207-208, 108 S. Ct. 963. Even aside from that rule, the assumption that no one but the Debtor's partners might pay for such an opportunity would obviously support no inference that it is valueless, let alone that it should not be treated as property. And, finally, the source in the tax law of the opportunity's value to the partners implies in no way that it lacks value to others. It might, indeed, be valuable to another precisely as a way to keep the Debtor from implementing a plan that would avoid a Chapter 7 liquidation.

Given that the opportunity is property of some value, the question arises why old equity alone should obtain it, not to mention at no cost whatever. The closest thing to an answer favorable to the Debtor is that the old equity partners would be given the opportunity in the expectation that in taking advantage of it they would add the stated purchase price to the estate. But this just begs the question why the opportunity should be exclusive to the old equity holders. If the price to be paid for the equity interest is the best obtainable, old equity does not need the protection of exclusiveness (unless to trump an equal offer from someone else); if it is not the best, there is no apparent reason for giving old equity a bargain. There is no reason, that is, unless the very purpose of the whole transaction is, at least in part, to do old equity a favor. And that, of course, is to say that old equity would obtain its opportunity, and the resulting benefit, because of old equity's prior interest within the meaning of subsection (b)(2)(B)(ii). Hence it is that the exclusiveness of the opportunity, with its protection against the market's scrutiny of the purchase price by means of competing bids or even competing plan proposals, renders the partners' right a property interest extended "on account of" the old equity position and therefore subject to an unpaid senior creditor class's objection.

It is no answer to this to say that the exclusive opportunity should be treated merely as a detail of the broader transaction that would follow its exercise, and that in this wider perspective no favoritism may be inferred, since the old equity partners would pay something, whereas no one else would pay anything. If this argument were to carry the day, of course, old equity could obtain a new property interest for a dime without being seen to receive anything on account of its old position. But even if we assume that old equity's plan would not be confirmed without satisfying the judge that the purchase price was top dollar, there is a further reason here not to treat property consisting of an exclusive opportunity as subsumed within the total transaction proposed. On the interpretation assumed here, it would, of course, be a fatal flaw if old equity acquired or retained the property interest without paying full value. It would thus be necessary for old equity to demonstrate its payment of top dollar, but this it could not satisfactorily do when it would receive or retain its property under a plan giving it exclusive rights and in the absence of a competing plan of any sort.[47] Under a plan granting an exclusive right, making no provision for competing bids or competing plans, any determination that the price was top dollar would necessarily be made by a judge in bankruptcy court, whereas the best way to determine value is exposure to a market. See Baird, ELEMENTS OF BANKRUPTCY at 262; Bowers, *Rehabilitation, Redistribution or Dissipation: The Evidence for Choosing Among Bankruptcy Hypotheses*, 72 WASH. U.L.Q. 955, 959, 963 n. 34, 975 (1994); Markell, 44 STAN. L. REV., at 73 ("Reorganization practice illustrates that the presence of competing bidders for a debtor, whether they are owners or not, tends to increase creditor dividends"). This is a point of some significance, since it was, after all, one of the Code's innovations to narrow the occasions for courts to make valuation judgments, as shown by its preference for the supramajoritarian class creditor voting scheme in § 1126(c), see *Ahlers*, supra, at 207, 108 S. Ct. 963 ("[T]he Code provides that it is up to the creditors—and not the courts—to accept or reject a reorganization plan which fails to provide them adequate protection or fails to honor the absolute priority rule").[48] In the interest of statutory coherence, a like disfavor for decisions untested by competitive choice ought to extend to valuations in administering subsection (b)(2)(B)(ii) when some form of market valuation may be available to test the adequacy of an old equity holder's proposed contribution.

Whether a market test would require an opportunity to offer competing plans or would be satisfied by a right to bid for the same interest sought by old equity, is a question we do not decide here. It is enough to say, assuming a new value corollary, that plans providing junior interest holders with exclusive opportunities free from competition and without benefit of market valuation fall within the prohibition of § 1129(b)(2)(B)(ii).

The judgment of the Court of Appeals is accordingly reversed, and the case is remanded for further proceedings consistent with this opinion.

It is so ordered.

---

47. [Footnote 27 in original:] The dissent emphasizes the care taken by the Bankruptcy Judge in examining the valuation evidence here, in arguing that there is no occasion for us to consider the relationship between valuation process and top-dollar requirement. While we agree with the dissent as to the judge's conscientious handling of the matter, the ensuing text of this opinion sets out our reasons for thinking the Act calls for testing valuation by a required process that was not followed here.

48. [Footnote 28 in original:] In *Ahlers*, we explained: "The Court of Appeals may well have believed that petitioners or other unsecured creditors would be better off if respondents' reorganization plan was confirmed. But that determination is for the creditors to make in the manner specified by the Code. 11 U.S.C. § 1126(c). Here, the principal creditors entitled to vote in the class of unsecured creditors (i.e., petitioners) objected to the proposed reorganization. This was their prerogative under the Code, and courts applying the Code must effectuate their decision." 485 U.S., at 207, 108 S. Ct. 963. The voting rules of Chapter 11 represent a stark departure from the requirements under the old Act. "Congress adopted the view that creditors and equity security holders are very often better judges of the debtor's economic viability and their own economic self- interest than courts, trustees, or the SEC.... Consistent with this new approach, the Chapter 11 process relies on creditors and equity holders to engage in negotiations toward resolution of their interests." Brunstad, Sigal, & Schorling, *Review of the Proposals of the National Bankruptcy Review Commission Pertaining to Business Bankruptcies: Part One*, 53 BUS. LAW. 1381, 1406, n. 136 (1998).

Justice THOMAS, with whom Justice SCALIA joins, concurring in the judgment.

I agree with the majority's conclusion that the reorganization plan in this case could not be confirmed. However, I do not see the need for its unnecessary speculations on certain issues and do not share its approach to interpretation of the Bankruptcy Code. I therefore concur only in the judgment. * * *

The meaning of the phrase "on account of" is the central interpretive question presented by this case. This phrase obviously denotes some type of causal relationship between the junior interest and the property received or retained—such an interpretation comports with common understandings of the phrase. See, e.g., THE RANDOM HOUSE DICTIONARY OF THE ENGLISH LANGUAGE 13 (2d ed.1987) ("by reason of," "because of"); WEBSTER'S THIRD NEW INTERNATIONAL DICTIONARY 13 (1976) ("for the sake of," "by reason of," "because of"). It also tracks the use of the phrase elsewhere in the Code. See, e.g., 11 U.S.C. §§ 365(f)(3), 510(b), 1111(b)(1)(A); see generally § 1129. Regardless how direct the causal nexus must be, the prepetition equity holders here undoubtedly received at least one form of property—the exclusive opportunity—"on account of" their prepetition equity interest. Since § 1129(b)(2)(B)(ii) prohibits the prepetition equity holders from receiving "any" property under the plan on account of their junior interest, this plan was not "fair and equitable" and could not be confirmed. That conclusion, as the majority recognizes, is sufficient to resolve this case. Thus, its comments on the Government's position taken in another case, and its speculations about the desirability of a "market test," are dicta binding neither this Court nor the lower federal courts.

* * * As we previously have recognized, the Code "was intended to modernize the bankruptcy laws, and as a result made significant changes in both the substantive and procedural laws of bankruptcy." United States v. Ron Pair Enterprises, Inc., 489 U.S. 235, 240, 109 S. Ct. 1026, 103 L. Ed. 2d 290 (1989) (citation omitted). The Code's overall scheme often reflects substantial departures from various pre-Code practices. Most relevant to this case, the Code created a system of creditor class approval of reorganization plans, unlike early pre-Code practice where plan confirmation depended on unanimous creditor approval and could be hijacked by a single holdout. See D. Baird, THE ELEMENTS OF BANKRUPTCY 262 (1993). Hence it makes little sense to graft onto the Code concepts that were developed during a quite different era of bankruptcy practice.

* * * No holding of this Court ever embraced the new value exception. As noted by the majority, the leading decision suggesting this possibility, Case v. Los Angeles Lumber Products Co., 308 U.S. 106, 60 S. Ct. 1, 84 L. Ed. 110 (1939), did so in dictum. And, prior to the Code's enactment, no court ever relied on the *Case* dictum to approve a plan. Given its questionable pedigree prior to the Code's enactment, a concept developed in dictum and employed by lower federal courts only after the Code's enactment is simply not relevant to interpreting this provision of the Code.[49] * * *

---

49. [Footnote 2 in original:] Nor do I think that the history of rejected legislative proposals bears on the proper interpretation of the phrase "on account of." As an initial matter, such history is irrelevant for the simple reason that Congress enacted the Code, not the legislative history predating it. Even if this history had some relevance, it would not support the view that Congress intended to insert a new value exception into the phrase "on account of." On the contrary, Congress never acted on bills that would have allowed nonmonetary new value contributions. Ante, at 1418.

Justice STEVENS, dissenting.

Prior to the enactment of the Bankruptcy Reform Act of 1978, this Court unequivocally stated that there are circumstances under which stockholders may participate in a plan of reorganization of an insolvent debtor if their participation is based on a contribution in money, or in money's worth, reasonably equivalent in view of all the circumstances to their participation. * * *

When read in the light of Justice Douglas' opinion in Case v. Los Angeles Lumber Products Co., 308 U.S. 106, 60 S. Ct. 1, 84 L. Ed. 110 (1939), the meaning of this provision is perfectly clear. Whenever a junior claimant receives or retains an interest for a bargain price, it does so "on account of" its prior claim. On the other hand, if the new capital that it invests has an equivalent or greater value than its interest in the reorganized venture, it should be equally clear that its participation is based on the fair price being paid and that it is not "on account of" its old claim or equity.

* * *

In every reorganization case, serious questions concerning the value of the debtor's assets must be resolved. Nevertheless, for the purpose of answering the legal question presented by the parties to this case, I believe that we should assume that all valuation questions have been correctly answered. * * *

* * * the decision is apparently driven by doubts concerning the procedures followed by the Bankruptcy Judge in making his value determinations, implicitly suggesting that the statute should be construed to require some form of competitive bidding in cases like this. * * *

* * * petitioner does not challenge the Bankruptcy Judge's valuation of the property or any of his other findings under § 1129 (other than the plan's compliance with § 1129(b)(2)(B)(ii)). Since there is no remaining question as to value, both the former partners (and the creditors, for that matter) are in the same position that they would have enjoyed if the Bankruptcy Court had held an auction in which this plan had been determined to be the best available. * * *

In this case, the partners had the exclusive right to propose a reorganization plan during the first 120 days after filing for bankruptcy. See § 1121(b). No one contends that that exclusive right is a form of property that is retained by the debtor "on account of" its prior status. The partners did indeed propose a plan which provided for an infusion of $6.125 million in new capital in exchange for ownership of the reorganized debtor. Since the tax value of the partnership depended on their exclusive participation, it is unsurprising that the partners' plan did not propose that unidentified outsiders should also be able to own an unspecified portion of the reorganized partnership. It seems both practically and economically puzzling to assume that Congress would have expected old equity to provide for the participation of unknown third parties, who would have interests different (and perhaps incompatible) with the partners', in order to comply with § 1129(b)(2)(B)(ii).

Nevertheless, even after proposing their plan, the partners had no vested right to purchase an equity interest in the postreorganization enterprise until the Bankruptcy Judge confirmed the plan. They also had no assurance that the court would refuse to truncate the exclusivity period and allow other interested parties to file competing plans. * * *

The moment the judge did confirm the partners' plan, the old equity holders were required by law to implement the terms of the plan. It was then, and only then, that what the Court characterizes as the critical "exclusive opportunity" came into existence. What the Court refuses to recognize, however, is that this "exclusive opportunity" is the function of the procedural features of this case: the statutory exclusivity period, the Bankruptcy Judge's refusal to allow the bank to file a competing plan, and the inescapable fact that the judge could confirm only one plan. * * *

Accordingly, I respectfully dissent.

NOTES

1. For a libel action arising from *LaSalle*, see Wilkow v. Forbes, Inc., 241 F.3d 552 (7th Cir. 2001) (article describing general partner who tried to confirm new value plan as "stiffing" the bank held nondefamatory under Illinois law).

2. Under the Supreme Court's analysis, what might the debtor have done to make a new value plan fair and equitable? Is there anything the bankruptcy judge could have done that might have made the plan fair and equitable? See In re Situation Mgmt. Sys., Inc., 252 B.R. 859 (Bankr. D. Mass. 2000); Lewis, *203 N. LaSalle Five Years Later: Answers to the Open Questions*, 38 J. MARSHALL L. REV. 61 (2004).

3. What benefit did Bank of America obtain from not making the § 1111(b)(2) election? Suppose Friendly Finance Co. held a $300,000 second mortgage on the same 15 floors of the office building on which Bank of America held the first mortgage. Friendly filed a document with the court in which it stated that it was electing to be treated as fully secured under § 1111(b)(2). Friendly then accepted the debtor's plan, which classified Friendly's claim in its own class and provided for payment of 25% of the $300,000 over three years. Would that have helped the debtor to confirm its plan?

4. Professor (and former dean and university president) Thomas Jackson argues (along with others) that, where the debtor is a business entity rather than a human being, the function of bankruptcy law should be to permit collective action by creditors that will avoid the inefficiencies caused when creditors scramble for priority in the state law race of diligence. Thus relative state law entitlements should generally be respected in bankruptcy, with bankruptcy primarily providing only a different, more efficient process for allowing creditors as a group to enjoy those entitlements. See Jackson, THE LOGIC AND LIMITS OF BANKRUPTCY LAW (1986). When there is only one creditor who, outside bankruptcy, would be entitled to all the value of the debtor's assets, there is an argument that use of bankruptcy—a collective proceeding—makes little sense, especially where the state law remedies that the creditor could use do not involve inefficiencies such as destruction of going concern value. Outside bankruptcy, was any creditor other than Bank of America entitled to any part of the value of the debtor's only asset, the 15 floors in the office building? Would a foreclosure by Bank of America under state law have destroyed the going concern value of those 15 floors? Would it have resulted in those 15 floors being torn down, with the bricks and boards and glass sold at auction? Would it likely have resulted in commercial tenants being turned out of the building? Would it have resulted in there being fewer jobs for janitors and maintenance workers? Does society benefit from allowing debtors whose only asset (or only substantial asset) is commercial real estate to use chapter 11 to hold off foreclosure by undersecured mortgagees? Does it matter whether the asset is a commercial office building,

shopping mall, hotel, or casino? Does society pay a price for allowing such debtors to use chapter 11? Do potential borrowers pay a price? Do state real property foreclosure laws provide sufficient protection to entrepreneurs who create value for society by developing real estate, and to limited partners and junior mortgagees who take the risks that make development possible? Is there a countervailing policy consideration against concentration of real estate ownership in foreclosing financial institutions?

5. Why did the Court suggest that under the government's "starchy" interpretation the phrase "on account of" would be superfluous? Does the Court's footnote 24 (footnote 28 of this Chapter) show that it would not be superfluous? Would omitting the phrase "on account of" have been an appropriate way for Congress to signal the elimination of the new value exception? Consider Foam Corporation's majority shareholder, Gruff, who also holds a $3.2 million unsecured claim. Would the phrase "on account of" in § 1129(b)(2)(B)(ii) have meaning as applied to Gruff even if there were no new value exception? What startling change in the law might result with regard to Gruff, if that phrase were deleted from the section? See In re Alta+Cast, LLC, No. 02-12982(MFW), 2004 WL 484881, at *4 (Bankr. D. Del. 2004) ("The Plan does not give the shareholders, qua shareholders, the right to invest in the reorganized Debtor. Instead, only creditors are given that opportunity. Although some of the creditors are also shareholders, the Plan is permitting them to invest only on account of their claims, not on account of their shareholder interests.").

6. As noted above, there apparently is no reported decision under the pre-1978 Bankruptcy Act that actually uses the new value exception to permit confirmation of a plan. Nevertheless, it was mentioned in several Supreme Court opinions. Was it an established enough part of pre-Code law for courts to conclude that Congress would have explicitly eliminated it if Congress did not intend it to be the law under the Bankruptcy Code?

7. Is Justice Stevens right (in his dissent) that the partners had nothing that could be described as property until the bankruptcy court confirmed the plan, and that confirmation of the plan did not give the old equity owners a right to buy the new equity but rather an obligation to buy it? If he is right, then should the focus be not on whether the exclusive opportunity to acquire the new equity is property but rather on whether there is a sufficient causal relation between the partners' ownership of the old equity and their acquisition of the new equity?

8. Suppose the board of directors of a debtor in possession which is a public company causes the debtor in possession to file a plan which permits only the shareholders to contribute new value for new common stock. Is the right to obtain new common stock "property"? What if the plan distributed options to purchase common stock (known as warrants) to the public shareholders? Would the warrants be property? See In re Armstrong World Industries, Inc., 432 F.3d 507 (3d Cir. 2005) (reprinted above in this chapter).

9. Suppose the plan in LaSalle had permitted creditors and partners alike to buy equity in the reorganized debtor on the same terms. Would the right to buy equity be property that the partners obtained on account of their prior partnership interests? If an auction were held, would the right to bid be a form of property? If so, must the old equity owners be barred from buying equity on equal terms with others or even from bidding for the equity? But are nonexclusive rights usually considered to be property? See Everex Sys. v. Cadtrak Corp. (In re CFLC, Inc.), 89 F.3d 673 (9th Cir. 1996) (holding that nonexclusive patent license is not property).

10. The partners in *LaSalle* have a personal tax problem that gives them an incentive to invest new value in the debtor. In effect their new investment creates extra value by saving them taxes. If there is somehow extra value, who is entitled to it? Is the Supreme Court's analysis of the value of the interest which the Ahlers attempted to retain and of who was entitled to it relevant? See Ayer, *Rethinking Absolute Priority After Ahlers,* 87 MICH. L. REV. 963 (1989). What about § 1129(d)? Cf. § 105(a). Does a high bid by the mortgagee indicate the true value of the property? If the mortgagee holds the vast majority of the unsecured debt, who will get the benefit of the high bid? See Condor One, Inc. v. Moonraker Assocs., Ltd. (In re Moonraker Assocs., Ltd.), 200 B.R. 950 (N.D. Ga. 1996) (discussing "roundhousing").

11. Consider two hypothetical cases posed by Professor Ayer. In the first, the debtor owes $100 to an undersecured lender who has a lien on all of the debtor's assets, and $50 to trade creditors. The court determines that the assets are worth $85. The debtor proposes a plan under which the secured lender will receive a secured promissory note worth $85 which will be secured by all the assets, the debtor's majority shareholder will contribute $10 to the debtor, the $10 contribution will be distributed pro rata to holders of the $65 in unsecured claims (the trade creditors and the secured lender as holder of an unsecured deficiency claim), and the shareholder will receive all of the shares in the reorganized debtor in exchange for the $10 contribution. If the shares are worth the $10 that the shareholder paid, what must the assets be worth? (Remember, assets minus liabilities equals shareholders' equity.) Is the plan fair and equitable with respect to the dissenting class consisting of the secured creditor's secured claim? See id. at 1014. It has been suggested that existing owners should be permitted to buy the equity in the reorganized debtor because their willingness to bid a particular amount will signal that they (with their inside knowledge) believe the equity to be worth at least the amount of their bid; hence others may be encouraged to consider bidding that much or more for the equity. See Markell, cited in *LaSalle*, 44 STAN. L. REV. at 110-11. Does Professor Ayer's hypothetical suggest that bidding by owners signals that the court has made a mistake in valuing collateral and hence that the plan should not be confirmed? Does it suggest that the new value exception only makes sense if the new value that is contributed remains in the business, at least where all of the debtor's assets are subject to a lien that exceeds their value?

   In Professor Ayer's second hypothetical, the debtor has only $100 in debts, all unsecured (and, although it does not seem to matter to the hypothetical, all owed to one creditor). Once again the court determines that the assets are worth $85. The plan proposes to give the unsecured creditor a promissory note worth $85 and to give all of the shares in the reorganized debtor to the existing shareholder in exchange for a contribution of $10. 87 MICH. L. REV. at 1014-15. Professor Ayer suggests that the shareholder's willingness to pay $10 for the equity means that the assets must have been worth more than $85 and thus the absolute priority rule is violated when some of that value is diverted to the shareholder. Id. at 1015. Do you agree? Why is this hypothetical different from the first hypothetical? If some or all of the $10 in this second hypothetical were used to pay expenses of administration rather than being retained in the reorganized debtor, would that indicate that the assets were worth more than $85? Would it necessarily show that value was being diverted to the shareholder that should have gone to the unsecured creditor under the absolute priority rule? If priority claims amount to $6, and therefore $6 of the $10 contribution is used to pay priority claims, with the other $4 remaining in the reorganized debtor, what does it appear that the assets were worth (not counting the $10 contribution)? Did the unsecured creditor receive all of the value to which it was entitled? Suppose the other $6 was used to pay the unsecured creditor $6 cash on the effective date of the plan, and the plan provided that the unsecured creditor would receive a promissory note worth only $79. Would the shareholders' willingness to pay $10 for the stock show that value was being impermissibly diverted to the shareholder?

12. Compare In re Union Fin. Serv., Inc., 303 B.R. 390 (Bankr. E.D. Mo. 2003) (holding that provision of $10 million cash and arrangement for financing crucial to the success of the reorganized debtor were sufficient new value), with In re Suncruz Casinos, LLC, 298 B.R. 833 (Bankr. S.D. Fla. 2003) (holding that even if new value exception exists, it was not satisfied by agreement of equity holders' affiliates to lease property to the debtor at market rental, which provided no value, and to allow use of "SunCruz" trade name, in which equity holders had no rights absent full payment of secured creditors).

13. Suppose Gruff owned all the stock of a holding company that in turn held all the stock of Foam Corporation. In Foam Corporation's chapter 11, would he as a result be subject to fewer limits on receiving property under the plan than the limits that apply to him as a direct stockholder in Foam Corporation? See In re 4 C Solutions, Inc., 302 B.R. 592 (Bankr. C.D. Ill. 2003).

In re Woodbrook Associates
United States Court of Appeals, Seventh Circuit, 1994
19 F.3d 312

Before POSNER, Chief Judge, CUMMINGS, Circuit Judge, and ZAGEL, District Judge.

ZAGEL, District Judge.

Woodbrook Associates ("Woodbrook"), is an Indiana real estate limited partnership whose sole asset is the Woodbrook Apartments constructed in 1980 in Indianapolis. The apartment complex was primarily funded by a first mortgage loan of $5,559,700.00, at 7.5 percent, insured by the United States Department of Housing and Urban Development (HUD). Woodbrook Apartments failed to generate the expected income levels, the partnership defaulted, and the original mortgage holder assigned the mortgage in 1988 to HUD.

In July 1990, HUD advertised Woodbrook Apartments for sale by private bid on September 5, 1990, stating that it would not bid over $3.4 million. On August 21, 1990, Woodbrook filed a voluntary Chapter 11 petition, and the advertised foreclosure sale was stayed.

Deci-Ma Management Corporation ("Deci-Ma Management") continued to serve as project manager of the apartments during the bankruptcy, as it had since the inception of the project.[50] Woodbrook then ceased paying net operating revenues to HUD, which had been less than the stipulated debt service.

---

50. [Note 1 in original:] The record is unclear as to how Deci-Ma Corporation served Woodbrook and its relationship to Deci-Ma Management. The district court found (and we agree) that Deci-Ma Corporation appears to be affiliated with Deci-Ma Management. Deci-Ma Corporation, however, has an unsecured claim of about $30,000, which presumably constitutes some sort of trade debt separate from the management fees owed to Deci-Ma Management.

Woodbrook filed a proposed Plan of Reorganization on April 19, 1991, eight months after the bankruptcy petition, and a substantially similar amended plan on June 14, 1991, by which time Woodbrook had possession of a net operating surplus of about $225,000 which it would otherwise have paid to HUD. The plan creates eight classes of claims and interests. Classes 1 and 2, as is typical, are reserved for expenses incurred by professionals and other administrative costs. Payments to creditors are structured as follows: HUD's secured claim (Class 3), valued at $3.6 million, is to be paid over 30 years at the mortgage interest rate of 7.5 percent; HUD will also be paid 5 percent of its unsecured deficiency claim (Class 4), plus all funds on hand at confirmation excluding $100,000 (reserved for repairs, working capital and bankruptcy fees, and expenses); Deci-Ma Management's unsecured claim (Class 5) will be paid in full over one year; Deci-Ma Corporation's unsecured claim (Class 6) will be paid monthly from any remaining cash flow from the debtor's operations until paid in full; other unsecured creditors (Class 7) will be paid in full 30 days after confirmation; and the general and limited partners of the debtor (Class 8) will retain their ownership interests in return for new capital contributions. The plan also provides in Article IV that, in the event the Bankruptcy Court determines the plan cannot be confirmed as a consequence of the proposed retention of ownership by the general and limited partners (Class 8), their interests will be deemed cancelled and void (presumably along with their obligation to contribute new capital) and the "property of the estate" will, instead, vest in Deci-Ma Corporation (Class 6), in satisfaction of its general unsecured claim. * * *

The next month, before any confirmation hearing or voting on the amended plan, HUD moved to dismiss the bankruptcy case, saying that HUD would not accept Woodbrook's proposed plan or any plan not providing for full payment of its claim. * * *

The bankruptcy court found, in part, that HUD would not accept any plan which did not provide for full payment of its claim; that general partner Charles Harvey had a beneficial interest in Deci-Ma Management and Deci-Ma Corporation; that HUD objected to Woodbrook's use of the money it kept; and that the plan could not be confirmed over HUD's objection. The court ultimately dismissed the bankruptcy case for cause, concluding that: (1) the plan could not be confirmed because it unfairly discriminated among unsecured creditors and violated the absolute priority rule; (2) the plan was not feasible because it relied on the use of funds in which HUD had a lien without HUD's consent; and (3) the proposal of an unconfirmable plan constituted an unreasonable delay and prejudiced the creditors.

* * * Woodbrook asked for leave to file an amended plan providing for full payment of HUD's claim of $6,208,273.24, plus interest, under terms which it believed would quell the court's concerns, but it did not say what those terms were. The bankruptcy court denied the Rule 9023 motion and did not permit Woodbrook to file a second amended plan. The district court affirmed, holding that Woodbrook would not be able to effectuate the proposed plan because it improperly classified unsecured claims in separate classes, violated the absolute priority rule, and did not meet the new value exception. * * *

DISMISSAL FOR CAUSE

A bankruptcy court has broad discretion under 11 U.S.C. sec. 1112(b) to dismiss a Chapter 11 case for cause. Woodbrook's bankruptcy case was dismissed under sec. 1112(b)(2), which authorizes dismissals for the inability to effectuate a plan. A sec. 1112(b)(2) dismissal is proper "if the court determines that it is unreasonable to expect that a plan can be confirmed in the [C]hapter 11 case." 5 CONRAD K. CYR ET AL., COLLIER ON BANKRUPTCY ¶ 1112.03[2][d][ii], at 1112-19-20 (15th ed. 1993).

    * * *

Nor can Woodbrook win on a claim that dismissal was premature. A Chapter 11 case can be dismissed at any time. Creditors need not wait until a debtor proposes a plan or until the debtor's exclusive right to file a plan has expired. Creditors, likewise, need not incur the added time and expense of a confirmation hearing on a plan they believe cannot be effectuated. The very purpose of § 1112(b) is to cut short this plan and confirmation process where it is pointless. The bankruptcy court found cause to dismiss the case under 11 U.S.C. § 1112(b), and it was not required to consider alternative remedies other than conversion to Chapter 7 in the best interest of the creditors. No one here claims (or claimed below) that conversion is in the best interest of the creditors. * * *

Did cause exist to dismiss Woodbrook's Chapter 11 case? Woodbrook argues that separate classification of HUD's sec. 1111(b) unsecured deficiency claim was proper because the amount and character of HUD's claim rendered it different from the unsecured claims of other creditors. HUD maintains that dismissal for cause was proper because Woodbrook engaged in "abusive" classification aimed at gerrymandering an affirmative vote. We review *de novo* the propriety of classification.

Woodbrook possesses considerable, but not complete, discretion to classify claims and interests in its Chapter 11 plan of reorganization. In re Holywell Corp., 913 F.2d 873, 880 (11th Cir. 1990). Some limits are necessary to offset a debtor's incentive to manipulate a classification scheme and ensure the affirmative vote of at least one impaired class, which is what the debtor needs to gain confirmation of the plan. Id.; In re U.S. Truck Co., Inc., 800 F.2d 581, 586 (6th Cir. 1986). What these limits may be is subject to debate. Section 1122(a) says: "a plan may place a claim or interest in a particular class only if such claim or interest is substantially similar to the other claims or interest of such class." 11 U.S.C. § 1122(a) [sic]. Section 1122 does not expressly forbid the separate classification of similar claims. Yet, the Fifth Circuit has coined a phrase referred to as the "one clear rule": "thou shalt not classify similar claims differently in order to gerrymander an affirmative vote on reorganization." Matter of Greystone III Joint Venture, 995 F.2d 1274, 1279 (5th Cir. 1991). *Greystone* condones separate classification "for reasons independent of the debtor's motivation to secure the vote of an impaired, assenting class of claims." Id.; accord *Lumber Exchange*, 968 F.2d at 649; In re Johnston, 140 B.R. 526, 529 (9th Cir. B.A.P. 1992).

The "one clear rule" is not easy to apply since it is not about "classifying similar claims"; it is about the debtor's purpose. Similarity is not a precise relationship, and the elements by which we judge similarity or resemblance shifts from time to time in bankruptcy. Some courts had permitted separate classification based simply on a readily perceived legal distinction between unsecured deficiency claims created by § 1111(b) and general unsecured claims. These courts noted that general unsecured claims are recourse claims cognizable under state law while § 1111(b) claims exist only within a Chapter 11 bankruptcy case and are not cognizable under state law. See, e.g., In re Aztec Co., 107 B.R. 585, 587 (Bankr. M.D. Tenn. 1989). This legal distinction has been eliminated by the Code (because a § 1111(b) deficiency claim is an unsecured claim in Chapter 11), and it has been rejected as the sole basis for separate classification by a majority of circuits. 11 U.S.C. § 1111(b)(1)(A); *Greystone*, 995 F.2d at 1279; John Hancock Mut. Life Ins. Co. v. Route 37 Business Park Assocs., 987 F.2d 154, 161 (3rd Cir. 1993); *Lumber Exchange*, 968 F.2d at 649. Other courts have permitted separate classification on the grounds that the vote of § 1111(b) claims "will be uniquely affected by the plan's proposed treatment of the secured claim held by the creditor"; a § 1111(b) claimant may vote its large deficiency claim to defeat any plan, obtain relief from the automatic stay and foreclose, while the general unsecured claimant has a strong incentive to vote to accept the plan because it may receive nothing from liquidating the debtor if the automatic stay is lifted. In re SM 104 Ltd., 160 B.R. 202, 218 & n. 35 (Bankr. S.D. Fla. 1993) (voting incentive rationale "is highly persuasive when viewed in light of the logic underlying § 1129(a)(10) . . . [which was] intended not to give the real estate lobby a veto power, but merely to require 'some indicia of creditor support' for confirmation of a proposed Chapter 11 plan"); *Aztec*, 107 B.R. at 587.[51] The voting incentive theory is worthy of careful study, but we need not reach the question of whether the voting incentive rationale supports the separate classification of HUD's claim.

Significant disparities do exist between the legal rights of the holder of a § 1111(b) claim and the holder of a general unsecured claim which render the two claims not substantially similar and which preclude the two from being classified together under § 1122(a). Thus, we cannot accept the proposition implicit in *Greystone* that separate classification of a § 1111(b) claim is nearly conclusive evidence of a debtor's intent to gerrymander an affirmative vote for confirmation. These disparities in rights stem from the most obvious difference between the two claims: a general unsecured claim exists in all chapters of the Code, while a § 1111(b) claim exists only as long as the case remains in Chapter 11 and, once converted to a Chapter 7 case, recovery is limited to its collateral. Compare 11 U.S.C. § 103(f) with 11 U.S.C. § 502(b)(1). This difference is amplified when the debtor is a partnership (as in this case) and the creditors face possible failure of its Chapter 11 case. Under such circumstances, the general unsecured creditors can seek equitable relief to prevent dissipation of the assets of the general partners, who upon conversion to Chapter 7, are liable for the debts of the partnership. Such equitable relief is not likely to be available to a § 1111(b) claimant, whose recovery is confined to its collateral.

---

51. [Note 4 in original:] But see *Route 37*, 987 F.2d at 161-62 (rejecting voting incentive rationale because "absent bad faith or illegality …, the Code is not concerned with a claim holder's reason for voting one way or another … [and because,] undoubtedly, most claim holders vote in accordance with their overall economic interests," not simply creditor interests).

This legal difference between the two claims also can lead to anomalous results when applying other sections of the Code to a class containing both § 1111(b) claimants and general unsecured claimants. First, section 1129(a)(7) requires that, for confirmation of a plan where a holder of a claim or interest in an impaired class rejects the plan, each claimant must "receive or retain . . . property of a value, as of the effective date of the plan, that is not less than the amount . . . receive[d] or retain[ed] if the debtor were liquidated under [C]hapter 7." 11 U.S.C. § 1129(a)(7). A § 1111(b) claimant is not entitled to payment under Chapter 7. Yet, because the § 1111(b) claimant has been classified with other general unsecured creditors and because § 1123(a)(4) mandates the same treatment of all claims in the class, the § 1111(b) claimant can block confirmation unless it receives payment of an amount equal to that of the general unsecured creditors. More importantly, there are anomalies in the application of § 1111(b) itself. Section 1111(b)(1)(A)(i), which requires that a § 1111(b)(2) election be made by "the class of which such [§ 1111(b)] claim is a part," means the general unsecured creditors, included in the class, must vote on whether the § 1111(b) claimants should make the § 1111(b)(2) election. The general unsecured creditors, consequently, can block approval of the election by a majority of votes. 11 U.S.C. § 1111(b)(1)(A)(i); Fed. R. Bankr. P. 3014. Finally, general unsecured creditors, who have no lien claims, can participate in the election process because the class comprised of the § 1111(b) claimants holds collateral that is not of inconsequential value. These anomalies are all clearly set out in Judge Ginsberg's well-reasoned opinion, In re SM 104 Ltd., 160 B.R. 202, 219-21 (Bankr. S.D. Fla. 1993).

The drafters of the Bankruptcy Code did not intend these results. We find that, at least where the debtor is a partnership comprised of a fully encumbered single asset, the legal rights of a § 1111(b) claimant are substantially different from those of a general unsecured claimant. Accordingly, we hold that §§ 1111(b) and 1122(a) not only permit but require separate classification of HUD's § 1111(b) unsecured deficiency claim in Class 4. Woodbrook's separate classification of HUD's § 1111(b) claim neither prevents confirmation of Woodbrook's plan nor serves as conclusive evidence in this case that Woodbrook manipulated the plan to obtain an affirmative vote. The bankruptcy court, however, found other barriers to confirmation.

ABSOLUTE PRIORITY RULE

To be confirmed under the cramdown provision of the Code, a plan must satisfy the absolute priority rule. That is, the claims or interests of a dissenting class of unsecured creditors must be fully satisfied before any junior class may retain any property under the reorganization plan. 11 U.S.C. § 1129(b)(2)(C); Norwest Bank Worthington v. Ahlers, 485 U.S. 197, 202, 108 S. Ct. 963, 966, 99 L. Ed. 2d 169 (1988). HUD says the proposed retention of ownership interest by the partners of the debtor, without payment in full of HUD's claim, violates the rule. Woodbrook counters that the partners' infusion of new capital contributions in exchange for their ownership interests places the plan outside the rule.

The new value precept permits old equity owners to participate in a plan, without full payment to the dissenting creditors, if they make a new contribution (1) in money or money's worth, (2) that is reasonably equivalent to the value of the new equity interests in the reorganized debtor, and (3) that is necessary for implementation of a feasible reorganization plan. Case v. Los Angeles Lumber Prods. Co., 308 U.S. 106, 121-22 (1939). Under this precept, old equity owners may purchase new equity interests in the reorganized debtor.

The new value precept, though mentioned in the Bankruptcy Commission's report to Congress, was not expressly codified in the Bankruptcy Code of 1978. *Report of the Commission on the Bankruptcy Laws of the United States*, H.R. Doc. No. 137, 93rd Cong., 1st Sess. pt. 2 at 241-42. Whether it survives the enactment of the new Code is the subject of much debate. The current trend is to treat the new value precept not as an exception (as it was commonly called) but as a corollary to the absolute priority rule preserved in the 1978 Code. See *Snyder*, 967 F.2d at 1130-31. The Supreme Court has yet to endorse or condemn such an interpretation of the Code, and we follow our prior decisions and again reserve ruling on the viability of the new value precept until another day. We reserve ruling because, even if we assume that this precept survives, we find the record supports the lower courts' conclusion that the proposed $100,000 contribution does not satisfy the new value criteria.

The district court reasoned that a proposed new capital infusion of $100,000 could not be considered "substantial" since it constituted, at most, 3.8 percent of the approximately $2.6 million of total unsecured debt. Simply put, "substantiality" requires that the contribution be real and necessary to the successful implementation of a feasible plan. Essentially, what the lower courts determined was that the proposed contribution, though in money, was a token cash infusion and not a fair price for the right to participate in the reorganized debtor. A token cash infusion violates the absolute priority rule because the old equity owners are receiving the opportunity to purchase the new equity interests at a bargain price "on account of" their prepetition ownership. See Matter of Stegall, 865 F.2d 140, 144 (7th Cir. 1989); *SM 104*, 160 B.R. at 226-27.

Whether the infusion of new capital is "substantial" is more a common sense determination than a mathematical calculation when the debtor comprises only a single real estate asset which is fully encumbered. And, as this Circuit noted in *Snyder*, this determination may not always hinge on a comparison of the proposed contribution to the total amount of unsecured debt. A court must make an informed judgment based on the facts of each case. We cannot say in this case, "where the disparity between the contribution and the unsecured debt is so extreme," that the lower courts' finding of insubstantiality is clearly erroneous. See *Snyder*, 967 F.2d at 1131-32 (refusing to disturb the bankruptcy and district courts' finding that the infusion of $30,000 in new capital, which was just 4.5 percent of the total amount due unsecured creditors, was not substantial). We agree with the courts below that the proposed token cash infusion does not constitute "new value" and violates the absolute priority rule. A Chapter 11 plan that violates the absolute priority rule cannot be confirmed over a creditor's legitimate objections.[52]

Woodbrook urges that Article IV saves the plan by voiding the partners' interests and vesting them in Deci-Ma Corporation in the event the bankruptcy

---

52. [Note 9 in original:] Woodbrook insists that whether the amount of capital infusion is substantial is a determination that must be made at the confirmation hearing. Dismissal here was not premature. A bankruptcy court need not engage in any further analysis of substantiality where the disparity between the proposed cash infusion and unsecured debt is so extreme. See *Snyder*, 967 F.2d at 1132.

court rejects the new value proposal. We disagree. The proposed "savings clause" may sound the plan's death knell. If Article IV is triggered, the 5 percent distribution to HUD is voided. The ultimate effect is to divest HUD of the 5 percent distribution towards its unsecured claim and vest the "property of the estate" in Deci-Ma Corporation in satisfaction of its unsecured claim. Deci-Ma Corporation's receipt of an equity interest without new cash infusion may violate the absolute priority rule. Furthermore, a fair reading of Article IV is that the new cash infusion is cancelled, and the cancellation of the new cash infusion confirms that the contribution is not necessary for the implementation of Woodbrook's plan and cannot qualify as "new value."

On the other hand, it may be that Deci-Ma Corporation's receipt of equity interests as payment of its unsecured claim does not violate the absolute priority rule since Deci-Ma Corporation is not a prepetition owner and that the new cash infusion is not cancelled but rather is to be distributed as cash on hand. But this does not help the debtor here. In any event, the operation of Article IV only brings to light another barrier to confirmation, i.e., the unfair treatment of or discrimination among unsecured creditors. 11 U.S.C. § 1129(b)(1). Clearly, the plan treats Deci-Ma Corporation and Deci-Ma Management more favorably at HUD's expense because of the connection to Harvey's wife and brother-in-law. Article IV preserves the equity interests and assets for insiders of the debtor. The meager 5 percent distribution, if any, on HUD's § 1111(b) unsecured deficiency claim, given the full payment of Deci-Ma Corporation's and Deci-Ma Management's unsecured claims, clearly suggests from our perspective, as it did from the perspective of the courts below, that this plan was the "three dollar bill." Such a plan, therefore, that unfairly discriminates among unsecured creditors cannot be confirmed.

HUD'S NEGATIVE VOTE

The bankruptcy court also determined that the plan could not be confirmed over HUD's objection. Under Woodbrook's amended plan, HUD would receive roughly 5 percent of its $2.6 million unsecured claim over three years, or $130,000; Deci-Ma Management would receive all of its unsecured claim within a year; and, Deci-Ma Corporation would receive Woodbrook's cash flow available after debt service until paid in full. HUD refused to accept the plan. This plan could be "crammed down" HUD's throat if at least one impaired class of creditors accepted the plan, not counting the acceptance by an insider. 11 U.S.C. § 1129(a)(10).

The difficulty here is that the only other impaired classes are Class 5 (Deci-Ma Management) and Class 6 (Deci-Ma Corporation). Charles Harvey, one of the debtor's partners, has a beneficial interest in both Deci-Ma Corporation and Deci-Ma Management. Charles Harvey's wife owns 48 percent of the capital stock in Deci-Ma Corporation and the "principal" of Deci-Ma Management is Harvey's brother-in-law. The definition of "insider" under the Bankruptcy Act § 101 is "extremely broad." 5 COLLIER ON BANKRUPTCY ¶ 1129.02, at 1129-35. Where the debtor is a partnership, insiders include "relatives of a general partner in, general partner of, or person in control of the debtor." 11 U.S.C. § 101(31)(C)(ii). Any affirmative vote from Deci-Ma Corporation and Deci-Ma Management must be discounted as an insider vote. Thus, as the bankruptcy court found, confirmation cannot be achieved over HUD's objection. Dismissal of Woodbrook's Chapter 11 case, under these circumstances, was in the creditor's best interest. See *Lumber Exchange*, 968 F.2d at 650 (dismissal is in the creditor's best interest where § 1111(b) claimant can block any plan that does not pay its claim in full and debtor comprised a single real estate asset).

DENIAL OF OPPORTUNITY TO AMEND PLAN

Finally, Woodbrook insists that any defects in the plan can be cured by amendment and that its offer to submit a plan paying HUD's claim in full plus interest renders dismissal for inability to effectuate a plan improper. "Chapter 11 provides a reasonable opportunity for corporate reorganization [;] it does not guarantee reorganization nor does it permit an indefinite suspension of creditors' rights and remedies pending the unsuccessful attempts of any party to effect a reorganization of debt." In re BGNX, Inc., 76 B.R. 851, 853 (Bankr. S.D. Fla. 1987) (in view of time elapsed and failure of proponents to obtain consent of United States, court converted Chapter 11 case to Chapter 7 liquidation after second proposed plan was unconfirmable). A special aspect of the practice of bankruptcy is that it functions on a fluid set of facts, i.e., the plan can always be changed. And, for the most part, bankruptcy courts permit the parties to submit numerous and alternative plans. Yet, bankruptcy courts are given a great deal of discretion to say when enough is enough.

Woodbrook was afforded an opportunity to amend its original plan. Woodbrook filed an amended plan two months after filing the original plan and ten months after filing for bankruptcy. The amended plan was substantially similar to the original plan. Essentially, Woodbrook had taken two bites at the apple and each time took a risk in formulating a plan that bordered on the fine line of unfair discrimination and feasible reorganization. The new amendment, Woodbrook's third bite at the apple, simply proposes to pay HUD's unsecured claim in full. This amendment looks less like an honest effort to devise an acceptable plan and more like a deathbed conversion, particularly where the proposed amendment is vague on important details such as funding for the plan. Under the circumstances, we find that the bankruptcy court did not abuse its discretion in denying Woodbrook an opportunity to amend the plan a second time. See *Hall*, 887 F.2d at 1044-45 (bankruptcy court did not abuse discretion in dismissing Chapter 11 case under § 1112(b)(2) and in not considering remedies other than dismissal "where the debtor's failure to file an acceptable plan after a reasonable time indicated its inability to do so"). * * *

For the foregoing reasons, the judgment of the district court affirming the bankruptcy court's dismissal of the debtor's bankruptcy case is AFFIRMED.

NOTES

1. Does the court's requirement of substantiality for the new value contribution make sense? What if the plan called for the old equity owners to contribute $100,000 in exchange for a 5% ownership interest? Does the substantiality requirement survive *203 N. LaSalle*?

2. Do you agree with the court that the class of unsecured claims into which the § 1111(b) deficiency claim is classified is the class that has the right to decide whether to make the 1111(b)(2) election? To what class does § 1111(b)(1)(A)(i) refer when it uses the term "the class of which such claim is a part"? Consider the Advisory Committee Note to Rule 3014:

> The secured creditor class must know the prospects of its treatment under the plan before it can intelligently determine its rights under § 1111(b). * * * Only if that plan is not confirmed may the class of secured creditors thereafter change its prior election.
>
> While this rule and the Code refer to a class of secured creditors it should be noted that ordinarily each secured creditor is in a separate and distinct class. In that event, the secured creditor has the sole power to determine application of § 1111(b) with respect to that claim.

Does the Code create classes of creditors or classes of claims? Even if the Advisory Committee's terminology is not completely consistent with the Code's, is the Advisory Committee's approach preferable to the *Woodbrook* court's approach? See In re D & W Realty Corp., 165 B.R. 127 (S.D.N.Y.1994); cf. In re B & B West 164th St. Corp., 147 B.R. 832, 838 (Bankr. E.D.N.Y. 1992).

3. Most courts disagree with the *Woodbrook* court's view that the § 1111(b) deficiency claim must be separately classified. In fact, most of the circuit level opinions dealing with the subject have refused to permit separate classification. See In re Suncruz Casinos, LLC, 298 B.R. 833 (Bankr. S.D. Fla. 2003). Consider the following excerpt from a Ninth Circuit case.

Barakat v. Life Ins. Co. of Virginia (In re Barakat)
United States Court of Appeals, Ninth Circuit, 1996
99 F.3d 1520

RESTANI, Judge.

* * *

Most courts have agreed that § 1122 contemplates some limits on the separate classification of similar claims. See, e.g., *Greystone III*, 995 F.2d at 1279 [5th Cir. 1992)]. Although noting that similar claims may be placed in different classes, the court in *Greystone* found that "[there is] one clear rule that emerges from otherwise muddled caselaw on § 1122 claims classification: thou shalt not classify similar claims differently in order to gerrymander an affirmative vote on a reorganization plan." 995 F.2d at 1279. This principle has been adopted by a majority of the Circuits that have addressed the issue. See, e.g., Boston Post Rd. Ltd. v. Federal Deposit Ins. Corp. (In re Boston Post Rd.), 21 F.3d 477, 483 (2d Cir.1994), cert. denied, __ U.S. __, 115 S. Ct. 897, 130 L. Ed. 2d 782 (1995); Travelers Ins. Co. v. Bryson Properties XVIII (In re Bryson Properties), 961 F.2d 496, 502 (4th Cir. 1992) ("[A]though separate classification of similar claims may not be prohibited, it 'may only be undertaken for reasons independent of the debtor's motivation to secure the vote of an impaired, assenting class of claims.' ") (quoting *Greystone III*, 948 F.2d at 139), cert. denied, 506 U.S. 866, 113 S. Ct. 191, 121 L. Ed. 2d 134 (1992); In re Holywell Corp., 913 F.2d 873, 880 (11th Cir. 1990) ("[I]f the classifications are designed to manipulate class voting ..., the plan cannot be confirmed."). But see ZRM-Oklahoma, 156 B.R. at 70 * * *.

Here, Debtor argues that separate classification of LICV's deficiency claim was not solely to manipulate class voting. Instead, Debtor contends that LICV's claim was not "substantially similar" to the other general unsecured claims. On this issue Debtor primarily relies upon In re Woodbrook Assocs., 19 F.3d 312 (7th Cir. 1994).

In *Woodbrook*, the court concluded that it was permissible to separately classify an unsecured deficiency claim created by § 1111(b) from general unsecured claims. The court noted that

> [s]ignificant disparities ... exist between the legal rights of the holder of a [§] 1111(b) claim and the holder of a general unsecured claim which render the two claims not substantially similar and which preclude the two from being classified together under [§]1122(a). Thus, we cannot accept the proposition ... that separate classification of a [§] 1111(b) claim is nearly conclusive evidence of a debtor's intent to gerrymander an affirmative vote for confirmation. These disparities in rights stem from the most obvious difference between the two claims: a general unsecured claim exists in all chapters of the Code, while a [§] 1111(b) claim exists only as long as the case remains in Chapter 11 and, once converted to a Chapter 7 case, recovery is limited to its collateral.

Id. at 318.

Although this Circuit has not addressed this issue, a number of courts declined to allow separate treatment based solely on the distinction that the claim is created by operation of law. See, e.g., Lumber Exchange Bldg. Ltd. Partnership v. Mutual Life Ins. Co. of New York (In re Lumber Exchange Bldg. Ltd.), 968 F.2d 647, 649 (8th Cir.1992) (rejecting argument that separate classification was warranted because creditor's unsecured recourse claim arose by operation of law under 11 U.S.C. § 1111(b)); *Greystone III*, 995 F.2d at 1279-80. In *Greystone III*, the court noted that § 1111(b) not only creates recourse claims where state antideficiency laws would abolish them, but also provides the undersecured creditor an election with respect to the treatment of its deficiency claim. 995 F.2d at 1279. Separate classification of similar claims by virtue of the legal rights of the holder of a § 1111(b) claim, the court concluded, would render the § 1111(b) election "meaningless," as "[p]lan proponents could effectively disenfranchise the holders of such [unsecured deficiency] claims by placing them in a separate class and confirming the plan over their objection by cramdown." Id. at 1280. Thus, the court found that, absent valid business justifications, separate classification of a Code-created deficiency claim was impermissible. Id.

In *Boston Post Rd.*, 21 F.3d at 483, the Second Circuit also held that separate classification for the purpose of preventing the undersecured creditor from rejecting the plan is contrary to the principles underlying the Bankruptcy Code, that is, that creditors holding greater debt should have a comparably greater voice in reorganization. The court stated:

> The purpose of the section 1111(b) election is to allow the undersecured creditor to weigh in its vote with the votes of the other unsecured creditors. Allowing the unsecured trade creditors to constitute their own class would effectively nullify the option that Congress provided to undersecured creditors to vote their deficiency as unsecured debt.

Id. Although the court noted that prohibiting the debtor from separately classifying deficiency claims will effectively bar single asset debtors from utilizing the Bankruptcy Code's cramdown provisions, the court was not persuaded that a single-asset debtor should be able to cramdown a plan that disadvantages the largest creditor. Id. Thus, absent a legitimate business or economic reason, separate classification is not permitted. Id.

* * * We agree with the principles enunciated in the *Greystone III* line of cases, that is, absent legitimate business or economic justification, it is impermissible for Debtor to classify LICV's deficiency claim separately from general unsecured claims.

* * * The bankruptcy court found that Debtor offered no business or economic justification for the separate classification of such a deficiency claim. The sole purpose of Debtor's separate classification was to obtain acceptance of the Plan. The bankruptcy court did not err in its finding that the claims were similar and that separate classification was not permitted. * * *

Problem 15-4

> Assume that in Debtor Corp.'s chapter 11 case, Morton, a nonrecourse mortgagee, is undersecured by $5 million. Assume there are $20,000 in unsecured trade claims in the case, and that in a chapter 7 liquidation $3,000 would be paid to the trade creditors (mostly from sale of some old furniture not covered by the mortgagee's lien). Assume there is a secured property tax claim class that is impaired and that will accept the plan. Assume that Morton does not make the § 1111(b)(2) election, that Morton and one small trade creditor are sure to vote against the plan, that the court will not permit Debtor Corp.'s plan to separately classify Morton's deficiency claim and the trade claims, and that the court will allow Debtor Corp.'s stockholders to contribute new value and keep their stock. How much present value must the plan provide to Morton on account of his unsecured claim in order to have a chance of being confirmed? Would your answer change if the court would permit the plan to separately classify Morton's unsecured claim? Would your answers to those questions change if the debtor were Debtor Partnership, a partnership with several very wealthy general partners? See § 723(a). Do you think your answers provide strong arguments that (1) the courts should permit separate classification of § 1111(b) unsecured claims, and (2) the courts should permit such classes to be discriminated against without such discrimination being considered to be unfair?

C. FOAM CORPORATION CONFIRMATION PROBLEMS

During mid-2006 Foam Corporation attempted to sell its eastern operations. Gruff and Simmons lent the debtor $1 million (on a superpriority and priming lien basis) to permit it to continue operations during this time.[53] Unfortunately, the foam market became even more competitive in the eastern United States; thus no buyers could be found who were willing to buy the operations for more than the liquidation value of the assets. In October, 2006, Kick Credit obtained relief from the stay to foreclose on the equipment and

---

53. Gruff was able to contribute $700,000 for this purpose because Tina Chemical and Swenson Chemical were enjoined under § 105(a) from seeking to enforce Gruff's guarantee of the large debts Foam Corporation owed to them. Tina and Swenson were extremely upset and agreed with each other to block any reorganization attempt.

inventory of the eastern operations. The sale netted only $900,000, which Kick Credit was permitted to apply to its $6.35 million claim. The same month First Bank obtained relief from the stay to foreclose its $700,000 mortgage on the Camden and Philadelphia real property; the foreclosure sales brought only $600,000, thus leaving a $100,000 deficiency. At the same time Foam Corporation rejected the leases covering the Detroit and Cleveland plants.

Foam Corporation had nearly run out of cash by that time, but with the eastern operations no longer causing a cash drain, Foam Corporation began to build its cash reserves back up.

The case has received a lot of publicity in Los Angeles; the Los Angeles Times ran several stories on job losses in the county and highlighted the job losses that would occur if Foam Corporation's reorganization failed. Thus the Los Angeles County officials wish to be seen as being very sympathetic to Foam Corporation's reorganization attempt.

It is now September 30, 2007. Foam Corporation is ready to propose a plan of reorganization. The § 1121(b) exclusivity period (the period of time within which Foam Corporation has the exclusive right as debtor in possession to file a proposed plan of reorganization) would have expired in mid-August, 2006 (120 days after the filing of the bankruptcy petition), but the court extended it several times, with the final extension expiring in mid-October, 2007. Under the terms of the court's order, if Foam Corporation files a plan by October 15, 2007, then no other party in interest will be permitted to file a plan until December 17, 2007. Foam Corporation has negotiated extensively with the unsecured creditors' committee, with Kick Credit, with Tina Chemical, with Swenson Chemical, with First Bank, and with individual creditors. Foam Corporation plans to file a proposed plan on October 15, 2007 which may include the terms noted below in the Problems. Foam Corporation anticipates that the effective date of the plan if it is confirmed will be roughly January 1, 2008. The claims of the various creditors are as follows:

Creditor	Total Claim	Secured Claim	Unsecured Claim
Institutional Creditors			
Kick Credit	$7 million[54]	$7 million	$ 0
First Bank	650,000	550,000	100,000
Subtotal	$7.65 million	$7.55 million	$ 100,000
Inside Creditors			
Gruff	$3.2 million	0	$3.2 million
(subordinated to trade debt & misc. to extent of $1 million)			

---

54. Including interest at 12% through 12/31/02 and attorneys' fees. $900,000 of the $6.35 million that was owed on the date of the petition was paid when Kick Credit obtained relief from the stay and foreclosed on the assets of the eastern operations.

Prepetition Tax Creditors

Los Angeles			
County	$ 20,000	$ 20,000	0
Fresno County	$ 15,000	$ 15,000	0

Claim Resulting from Rejected Leases for Cleveland and Detroit Plants

Imperial			
Insurance	$ 400,000	0	$ 400,000

Trade Creditors & Misc.

Tina	$3 million	0	$3 million
(guaranteed by Gruff)			
Swenson	$2 million	0	$2 million
(guaranteed by Gruff)			
Sixty trade creditors			
with total claims of	$3 million	0	$3 million
Ten misc. creditors'			
claims	$ 50,000		$ 50,000
Subtotal	$8.05 million	0	$8.05 million

Administrative Expense Claimants

Attorneys for			
—Debtor	$ 300,000	0	$ 300,000
—Unsecured			
Creditors'			
Committee	$ 100,000	0	$ 100,000
Accountants for			
—Debtor	$ 150,000	0	$ 150,000
—Unsecured			
Cred. Comm.	$ 15,000	0	$ 15,000
Postpetition			
Trade			
Payables	$1 million	0	$1 million
Loan by Gruff			
and Simmons	$1 million	$1 million	0
Postpetition			
property tax			
claims			
—Los Angeles			
County	$ 15,000	$ 15,000	0
—Fresno			
County	$ 10,000	$ 10,000	0

Prepetition Wage and Salary Claims[55]

Priority	$258,000	0	$258,000
General	$183,000	0	$183,000

Further information is given below in each Problem.

Problem 15-5

How much cash will Foam Corporation need to confirm a plan of reorganization? Add up your answers to a, b, and c below. How realistic is it to think Foam Corporation can build up the needed cash during the reorganization?

a. How much cash will Foam Corporation need to pay administrative expense claims on the effective date of the plan?

b. How much cash will Foam Corporation need to pay other priority claims on the effective date? Assume the workers who were terminated will vote overwhelmingly against any plan.

c. Assume the plan calls for cash payment on the effective date of 15% of the amount of the general unsecured claims. How much cash will Foam Corporation need to pay holders of general unsecured claims on the effective date?

Problem 15-6

Assume Tina Chemical, Swenson Chemical, Kick Credit, Imperial Insurance and First Bank will all vote to reject the plan of reorganization. Thus a consensual plan does not seem to be a realistic possibility, even though most of the trade creditors (other than Tina and Swenson) favor the plan. Foam Corporation needs to have at least one impaired class of claims accept the plan ("determined without including any acceptance of the plan by any insider") in order for it to be confirmed in a cramdown. See § 1129(a)(10) and (b)(1). How would you create at least one such class that is likely to accept the plan?

Problem 15-7

Gruff managed to persuade Swenson Chemical to hold its nose and vote for the plan. Tina Chemical, Kick Credit, Imperial Insurance, and First Bank still plan to vote to reject the plan. Foam Corporation expects that about 45 of the sixty other trade creditors will vote; about two thirds of them (holding claims totaling about $2 million) will vote to accept the plan, but the other third (holding claims totaling $650,000) will likely vote to reject the plan. Foam Corporation expects that seven or eight of the ten small "miscellaneous" creditors will vote (although Foam Corporation does not know how they will vote) and that all other holders of unsecured claims will vote. If all the general unsecured claims are classified together, will the class accept the plan for purposes of § 1129(a)(8)(A) and (a)(10)? Will Gruff's affirmative vote count for purposes of either of those sections? Should Gruff's, Tina Chemical's, or Swenson Chemical's vote be designated under § 1126(e)? Would it help to satisfy § 1129(a)(8) if First Bank's and Imperial Insurance's claims were classified separately in an institutional

---

55. 140 hourly employees who were terminated hold $170,000 of the priority wage claims. 160 hourly employees who are still employed by Foam Corporation hold $80,000 of the priority wage claims. Four current officers of Foam Corporation (including Gruff) hold the remaining $8,000 of priority wage claims and the entirety of the $183,000 of general wage claims.

creditor class? Would such a classification be permissible? If their claims are classified separately, and if the plan provides for them to receive property with a present value of 100% of their $500,000 in total claims so as to satisfy § 1129(b)(2)(B)(i), could TC (a dissenting trade creditor) object that the plan discriminated unfairly in favor of the institutional creditor class? Would it help to satisfy § 1129(a)(10) if the claims of Tina Chemical and Swenson Chemical were classified separately in a class for holders of claims guaranteed by Gruff? Would such a classification be permissible?

Problem 15-8

Assume the plan calls for general unsecured creditors to receive the following property on account of each $100 of claim:
(a) $12 cash;
(b) A 5 year promissory note at 7.5% interest with a face value of $30, interest payable quarterly, principal payable 10% at the end of each of the first four years and 60% at the end of five years;
(c) One share of common stock in the reorganized Foam Corporation.

Assume the reorganization value of Foam Corporation is $13 million (after payment of any cash that will be paid on the effective date of the plan), that the reorganized Foam Corporation will have debts equal to $9 million (on a present value basis), and that the reorganized Foam Corporation will have 800,000 shares of common stock outstanding. TC, a trade creditor, is willing to vote for the plan only if the value TC is to receive under the plan is at least equal to 45% of the amount of TC's claim. Is that criterion met?

Foam Corporation asserts that its reorganization value is $14.622 million (after payment of cash to be paid on the effective date of the plan). Kick Credit and certain other creditors assert that the reorganization value is much less, because Foam Corporation's sales will not grow as quickly as Foam Corporation projects and because a higher discount rate should be used in the discounted cash flow valuation. Assume Foam Corporation files a plan which includes the following terms:

CLASSES OF SECURED CLAIMS:

CLASS I:

The holder of the claim in Class I, consisting of the $7 million secured claim of Kick Credit, will receive a 10 year secured note at prime plus 2%, with 5% of the $7 million principal due at the end of each of the second through ninth years, and the remaining 60% due at the end of the tenth year. The note will be secured by a second lien on all the types of collateral which served as collateral for Kick Credit's original $6 million loan (including after acquired collateral) and, to the extent of the $350,000 workout loan plus interest and costs, by a first trust deed on the Los Angeles real estate.

CLASS II:

The holder of the claim in Class II, consisting of the secured claim of First Bank in the amount of $550,000, will receive a $550,000, fifteen year, fully amortized 8% note secured by a first trust deed on the Fresno real estate.

CLASS III:

The holder of the claim in Class III, consisting of the $20,000 secured real property prepetition tax claim of Los Angeles County, will retain its tax lien on the Los Angeles real estate and will receive payment of its claim in full with 5% interest in four equal annual installments, due on the first through fourth anniversaries of the effective date of the plan.

CLASS IV:

The holder of the claim in Class IV, consisting of the $15,000 secured real property prepetition tax claim of Fresno County, will receive payment of its claim in full in cash (with interest as required by § 511) on the effective date of the plan. Class IV is unimpaired.

CLASSES OF UNSECURED PRIORITY CLAIMS

CLASS V:

The holders of the claims in Class V, consisting of the $170,000 in priority wage claims of former employees of Foam Corporation (those who are no longer employees of Foam Corporation as of the time of filing of the plan), will receive payment of their claims in full on the effective date of the plan. Class V is unimpaired.

CLASS VI:

The holders of the claims in Class VI, consisting of the $88,000 in priority wage claims of current employees of Foam Corporation will receive payment of their claims in full with 9% interest (or such other rate of interest as the court may find necessary to provide full present value) in six equal monthly installments, beginning one month after the effective date of the plan.

CLASSES OF GENERAL UNSECURED CLAIMS

CLASS VII:

The holders of the claims in Class VII, consisting of the $500,000 of unsecured claims of the institutional creditors (First Bank and Imperial Insurance), will receive 12% of the amount of their claims in cash on the effective date of the plan and 8 year 7.5% promissory notes with face values equal in amount to 35% of the amount of their claims. Interest on the notes will be payable quarterly. One fifteenth of the principal will be paid at the end of each of the second through seventh years; the remaining 60% will be paid at the end of the eight years.

CLASS VIII:

The holders of the claims in Class VIII, consisting of the $11,433,000 of general unsecured claims other than those in Class VII, will receive 12% of the amount of their claims in cash on the effective date of the plan, 8 year 7.5% promissory notes equal in amount to 30% of the amount of their claims, and one share of cumulative preferred stock for each $100 of claim. Interest on the notes will be payable quarterly. One fifteenth of the notes' principal will be paid at the end of each of the second through seventh years; the remaining 60% will be paid at the end of the eight years. The preferred stock will have a liquidation preference of $5 per share and will carry a dividend of 50 cents per share per year. Dividends will accumulate if not paid; holders of preferred stock will be entitled to vote to elect one director in the event that the dividend is in arrears. Cash, notes, and preferred stock that would otherwise be distributed to Gruff on account of $1 million of his claim shall be distributed pro rata to the other holders of claims in the class pursuant to the subordination agreement entered into during the workout attempt. Gruff shall receive the cash, notes, and preferred stock to be distributed on account of the other $2.2 million of his claim; provided, however, that if Tina Chemical releases Gruff from his guaranty of the $3 million claim owed to Tina Chemical, then 3/5 of the cash, notes, and preferred stock that would otherwise have been distributed to Gruff on account of the $2.2 million in claim will be distributed to Tina Chemical together with $300,000 cash which Gruff will contribute; similarly, if Swenson Chemical releases Gruff from his guaranty of its $2 million claim, then it will receive 2/5 of the cash, notes, and preferred stock that otherwise would have been distributed to Gruff on account of the $2.2 million in claim together with $200,000 cash which Gruff will contribute.

THE CLASS OF INTERESTS

CLASS IX:
The holders of the common stock of Foam Corporation will retain their stock. No additional common stock is to be issued under this plan.

ADMINISTRATIVE CLAIMS

All administrative claims will be paid in full in cash on the effective date of the plan with the following exceptions:
—postpetition trade payables will be paid according to the terms of the obligations in the ordinary course of business;
—the $1 million postpetition loan from Gruff and Simmons will be satisfied by distribution to them of secured notes with a face amount of $1 million with the same terms as the notes distributed to Kick Credit (Class I) but secured by a first lien on all assets of Foam Corporation (including after acquired assets), junior only to the liens of Los Angeles County and Kick Credit on the Los Angeles real estate and First Bank on the Fresno real estate.

Problem 15-9

Assume Classes III, VI, VIII, and IX vote to accept the plan but that Classes I, II, and VII vote to reject it. Assume Class VIII's acceptance was by a narrow margin, that Classes III and IX accepted without dissent, and that Class VI accepted with almost no dissent.

(a) Should the court confirm the plan?

(b) The court refused to confirm the plan. At the hearing Foam Corporation proposed (pursuant to § 1127(e) & (f)) to modify the plan in one of the two ways set forth below.

    (1) If modification "A" is made and Class VII votes to accept the modified plan, can the modified plan be confirmed? If modification "B" is made, and if the same classes accept and reject the modified plan as accepted and rejected the original plan, should the modified plan be confirmed? If Foam Corporation believed when it filed its original plan

that Class VII would reject the original plan and that modification "B" below would then be attempted, would it have made more sense for Foam Corporation's plan to have placed the claims of Tina Chemical and Swenson Chemical in a separate class rather than placing the claims of First Bank and Imperial Insurance in a separate class?

(2) Is it permissible for the court to approve the modification and confirm the modified plan immediately without giving creditors an opportunity to change their votes, on the ground that the amendment does not materially affect the treatment of any creditors whose acceptances are needed for confirmation of the plan?

(3) Must Foam Corporation resolicit votes from creditors and, as part of that resolicitation, prepare and distribute an amended disclosure statement?

Possible modification "A":

The plan is modified so that the holders of claims in Class VII (First Bank and Imperial Insurance) receive notes with a face value of 88% of their claims, rather than the 35% provided for in the original plan, together with the same 12% cash provided for in the original plan.

Possible modification "B":

The plan is modified to provide that the holders of the interests in Class IX (the common stockholders Gruff and Simmons) receive nothing on account of their stock and their stock will be canceled. The plan is further modified to provide that Gruff and Simmons do not receive notes as payment of their $1 million postpetition loan to Foam Corporation but instead receive 100% of the common stock in the reorganized Foam Corporation as payment.

(c) Does the provision permitting Tina Chemical and Swenson Chemical to receive the distribution Gruff would otherwise receive on his $2.2 million unsecured claim (if they release him from his guarantee) render the plan nonconfirmable? See Chapter Sixteen below at section C.

D. CREDITORS' PLANS AND OTHER CREDITORS' REMEDIES RELATED TO THE PLAN PROCESS

We now briefly discuss creditors' remedies related to the plan process. If creditors can convince the court that the debtor is unlikely to be able to confirm a plan, they may have several available remedies, as the cases in this Chapter have illustrated. Even if the creditors cannot convince the court of that, they may convince the court to allow them to propose a creditors' plan as an alternative to the debtor's plan.

If there is not a reasonable possibility that a successful reorganization will be accomplished within a reasonable time, secured creditors can obtain relief from the stay to foreclose on collateral in which the debtor has no equity. See § 362(d)(2); Chapter Three of this text, supra at section C; U.S. Sav. Ass'n of Texas v. Timbers of Inwood Forest Assocs. Ltd., 484 U.S. 365, 375-76, 108 S. Ct. 626, 633, 98 L. Ed. 2d 740, 751 (1988) (reprinted above).

As we noted in Chapter Three, in the early stages of a case courts do not require debtors to present compelling evidence that reorganization will succeed. See Am. State Bank v. Grand Sports, Inc. (In re Grand Sports, Inc.), 86 B.R. 971 (Bankr. N.D. Ind. 1988). However, most courts apply a sliding scale; as the case goes on the debtor's burden becomes heavier and heavier. Id. When the debtor's attempt to confirm a plan fails, the court is likely to grant relief from the stay unless the debtor can make a strong showing that a different plan will be proposed and will be confirmable. See, e.g., In re Sparks, 171 B.R. 860, 869 (Bankr. N.D. Ill. 1994) (granting relief from stay where proposed plan could not be confirmed and where "there is no readily apparent alternative that can be proposed and confirmed within a reasonable time").

Where the debtor's only substantial asset is overencumbered real estate—as in *Lasalle*, *Woodbrook*, and *Barakat*, supra—the undersecured mortgagee often is implacably opposed to the reorganization. If the court is unwilling to allow separate classification of the mortgagee's deficiency claim, and if the deficiency claim is large compared to other claims, it may seem that the debtor will be unable to create an impaired class of claims that will accept any plan that the debtor might propose. Relief from stay may then be appropriate. See Calif. Fed. Bank v. Moorpark Adventure (In re Moorpark Adventure), 161 B.R. 254 (Bankr. C.D. Cal. 1993); In re B & B West 164th St. Corp., 147 B.R. 832 (Bankr. E.D.N.Y. 1992). In such cases, the mortgagee will often seek relief from the stay early in the case. Before granting relief from the stay, however, the court should carefully consider whether there may be a legitimate way—albeit creative—in which the debtor may be able to structure an accepting impaired class.

Woodbrook illustrates another creditor remedy where the debtor is unable to confirm a plan: dismissal of the case or conversion of it to chapter 7 pursuant to § 1112(b), which was substantially revised and expanded by the 2005 BAPCPA. Under § 1112(b)(1)-(2), where "cause" is established for dismissal or conversion, the court must dismiss or convert the case on request of a party in interest absent either (1) "unusual circumstances specifically identified by the court that establish that the requested conversion or dismissal is not in the best interest of creditors and the estate,"[56] or (2) a showing by the debtor or another party that there is a reasonable likelihood of timely confirmation of a plan.[57] Sixteen kinds of cause are catalogued (nonexhaustively) in § 1112(b)(4), including "substantial or continuing loss to or diminution of the estate" that is combined with an absence

---

56. See § 1112(b)(1).

57. See § 1112(b)(2). Where the ground for dismissal or conversion is "an act or omission of the debtor other than under" § 1112(b)(4)(A), discussed immediately below, then § 1112(b)(2) does not apply to prevent dismissal or conversion just because timely confirmation of a plan is reasonably likely; it also must be shown that the act or omission was reasonably justified and that it will be "cured" within a reasonable time. Those requirements may create great difficulties for nondebtor parties who are seeking to propose and confirm a plan. Dismissal or conversion can be avoided without such a showing of justification and timely cure if "unusual circumstances" exist as described in § 1112(b)(1); at least that should be the result if the convoluted statutory language is read correctly.

of a "reasonable likelihood of rehabilitation." Section 1112(b)(4)(A). Note that the possibility of confirming a liquidating plan will not save the debtor from dismissal or conversion of the case for § 1112(b)(4)(A) cause; liquidation is not "rehabilitation." In re Citi-Toledo Partners, 170 B.R. 602, 607 (Bankr. N.D. Ohio 1994). If the debtor has a negative cash flow from operations, or if the estate's assets are declining in value, there is certainly a sufficient loss or diminution. In re Schriock Constr., Inc., 167 B.R. 569 (Bankr. D.N.D. 1994). Some courts have even held that the erosion of the position of the creditors as they wait for payment without compensation for the delay is a sufficient loss or diminution, although this seems to be a misreading of the statute. See, e.g., Clarkson v. Cooke Sales and Serv. Co. (In re Clarkson), 767 F.2d 417 (8th Cir. 1985).

The court in *Woodbrook* relied on what then was § 1112(b)(2): "inability to effectuate a plan." Under that provision the question was "whether it is reasonable to expect that a plan could be confirmed within a reasonable amount of time." 5 Resnick & Sommer, COLLIER ON BANKRUPTCY ¶ 1112.04[5][b].[58] But the provision was deleted by the 2005 BAPCPA. The provision with the most similar language at first glance in the revised § 1112(b)(4) is subparagraph (M), but it actually deals with a very different issue involving effectuation of confirmed plans. It remains to be seen how courts will interpret the many subparagraphs of revised § 1112(b)(4), many of which deal with very specific misconduct that may occur during a chapter 11 case.

Note that § 1112(b)(4) provides that " 'cause' includes" the listed items. Thus the list in § 1112(b)(4) is nonexhaustive. The same is true of § 362(d)(1), which entitles a party in interest to relief from the automatic stay "for cause, including" lack of adequate protection. Thus there may be other kinds of "cause" not stated in the sections. In fact, the courts have held that lack of good faith in the filing of the petition is an unstated "cause" for purposes of both the former § 1112(b) and § 362(d)(1). See Trident Assocs. Ltd. P'ship v. Metro. Life Ins. Co. (In re Trident Assocs. Ltd. P'ship), 52 F.3d 127 (6th Cir. 1995); Epstein, Nickles & White, BANKRUPTCY §§ 2-15 and 3-29. Presumably lack of good faith will continue to be "cause" under the revised § 1112(b).

Recall that there is also a good faith requirement for confirmation of a plan: the plan must be "proposed in good faith." Section 1129(a)(3). As we saw in Chapter Fourteen, where the plan is proposed with a legitimate and honest purpose to reorganize—a subjective standard—*and* has a reasonable chance of success—an objective standard—the good faith standard is satisfied. Some courts find a lack of good faith *in the filing of a petition* only if there is *neither* a subjective honest intent to use chapter 11 for a legitimate purpose *nor* an objective reasonable prospect that reorganization will be successful. Carolin Corp. v. Miller, 886 F.2d 693 (4th Cir.1989). Other courts will find a lack of good faith simply on a finding of lack of subjective good faith—a lack of intent

---

58. As *Woodbrook* illustrates, the bankruptcy judge had considerable discretion in deciding when the debtor had had a sufficient opportunity to confirm a plan.

to use chapter 11 for a legitimate purpose. See In re Phoenix Piccadilly, Ltd., 849 F.2d 1393 (11th Cir.1988); State St. Houses, Inc. v. N.Y. State Urban Dev. Corp. (In re State St. Houses, Inc.), 356 F. 3d 1345 (11th Cir. 2004) (holding that 1994 enactment of § 362(d)(3) did not legislatively overrule *Phoenix Piccadilly* even with respect to single asset real estate cases). While the factors to be considered with respect to whether the petition was filed in good faith are the same under § 362(d)(1) and § 1112(b), some courts require stronger evidence of lack of good faith to justify the dismissal of the case than to justify granting relief from stay. See In re Dixie Broadcasting, Inc., 871 F.2d 1023 (11th Cir. 1989); cf. In re Star Broadcasting, Inc., 336 B.R. 825 (Bankr. N.D. Fla. 2006) (holding that debtor filed petition in bad faith to prevent buyer from going forward with suit seeking specific performance of contract for sale of debtor's FCC license, and granting relief from stay to allow suit to proceed, but denying motion to dismiss where the debtor had "substantial assets other than those involved in the district court litigation, [so that] it is not in the best interests of the creditors and the estate to dismiss the case at this time").

Many courts find that a petition is filed in bad faith if it is filed simply to delay foreclosure by a secured creditor, without any real hope of successfully reorganizing other than the hope that the real estate market will improve during the delay. In many cases, where the assets consist of apartment buildings or commercial real estate, there will be no loss of going concern value and probably no job loss simply because the mortgagee forecloses. Such cases are certainly far removed from the operating company's case—such as Foam Corporation's case—in which jobs are at stake and in which liquidation of productive assets on the auction block may cause real loss of going concern value. See In re Little Creek Dev. Co., 779 F.2d 1068 (5th Cir.1986).

The appearance of bad faith is compounded where, on the eve of foreclosure, the real estate is transferred to a new entity which then promptly files a chapter 11 petition. Where such a "new debtor syndrome" is found, courts often find bad faith. See Trident Assocs. Ltd. P'ship v. Metro. Life Ins. Co. (In re Trident Assocs. Ltd. P'ship), 52 F.3d 127 (6th Cir. 1995) ("Trident Associates exhibits the 'new debtor syndrome': it is a one-asset debtor created on the eve of foreclosure to isolate the property and MetLife from the rest of the Beztak real estate operations."); Antonini v. Neary (In re Gelso Invs. V, LLC), No. C 03-0312 SI, 2003 WL 22282346 (N.D. Cal. 2003); In re St. Stephen's 350 East 116th St., 313 B.R. 161 (Bankr. S.D.N.Y. 2004) (granting sanctions against attorney who filed "new debtor syndrome" cases and then abandoned them, and denying motion to set aside orders dismissing cases); In re Yukon Enters., Inc., 39 B.R. 919 (Bankr. C.D. Cal. 1984).

It is important to note that cases should not be dismissed simply because the debtor filed the petition in bad faith, if another party in interest seems willing and able to move the reorganization forward. The court can order appointment of a trustee if necessary, and one or more creditors may file plans that will result in a successful reorganization.

That brings us to the final creditors' remedy in this Chapter: the creditors' plan. Creditors who wish to take control of the reorganization process and bring it to an end they deem suitable—liquidation, in many cases—can seek to file and confirm a creditors' plan. There is nothing in chapter 11 that prevents a plan from providing for liquidation of the estate. Section 1123 explicitly authorizes liquidating plans. Section 1123(a)(5)(D) & (b)(4). Courts have even permitted confirmation of creditors' plans that call for liquidation of farmers' assets, despite the apparent intent of the Code to protect farmers from involuntary liquidation. See § 303(a) (prohibiting involuntary bankruptcy petition from being filed against a farmer); § 1112(c) (prohibiting the conversion of a farmer's chapter 11 case to chapter 7 except on the farmer's request); Tranel v. Adams Bank and Trust Co. (In re Tranel), 940 F.2d 1168 (8th Cir. 1991) (holding that creditors' liquidating plan could properly be confirmed in farmers' chapter 11 case); Jasik v. Conrad (In re Jasik), 727 F.2d 1379 (5th Cir. 1984) (same); Jorgensen v. Fed. Land Bank (In re Jorgensen), 66 B.R. 104 (B.A.P. 9th Cir. 1986) (same).

Exclusivity under § 1121 usually prevents creditors from quickly filing creditors' plans; it gives the debtor an opportunity to file a plan and to convince creditors to support it. However, if and when exclusivity expires, any party in interest can file a plan. See § 1121; Chapter Eleven of this text, supra. Creditors have standing as parties in interest to file plans. See § 1121(c). Even an entity that has purchased a claim against the debtor postpetition is a creditor with standing to file a plan. In re Rook Broadcasting, 154 B.R. 970 (Bankr. D. Idaho 1993).

As we have seen, debtors who propose plans sometimes have difficulty meeting the requirement in § 1129(a)(10) that at least one impaired class of claims accept the plan, not counting acceptances by insiders. In that respect creditors who propose plans—especially secured creditors—have an advantage over debtors. The creditors can impair their own class, vote in favor of their own plan, and often cause the class in which their claims are classified to accept the plan. Remember that each secured claim typically is classified separately; as a result, a secured creditor who proposes a plan can satisfy § 1129(a)(10), assuming the secured creditor is not an insider, simply by (1) voting for its own plan, and (2) drafting the plan so as to impair its own creditor's class. See, e.g., L & J Anaheim Assocs. v. Kawasaki Leasing Int'l, Inc. (In re L & J Anaheim Assocs.), 995 F.2d 940 (9th Cir. 1993) (holding that a plan filed by a secured creditor impaired the class in which the creditor's secured claim was placed by changing its state law foreclosure rights, even if the changes were beneficial to the secured creditor; unnecessary impairment may, however, go to the issue of good faith). Creditors are not generally considered to be insiders simply because they are the plan proponents. See In re Dwellco I Ltd. P'ship, 219 B.R. 5, 13 (Bankr. D. Conn. 1998); In re P.J. Keating Co., 168 B.R. 464 (Bankr. D. Mass. 1994); In re Union Meeting Partners, 160 B.R. 757 (Bankr. E.D. Pa. 1993).

Of course, for a creditors' plan to be confirmable, it must have been proposed in good faith. See § 1129(a)(3). Even though the main purpose of chapter 11 is to permit reorganization, liquidating plans can be proposed in good faith. See In re Landmark Park Plaza Ltd. P'ship, 167 B.R. 752 (Bankr. D. Conn. 1994) (permitting creditor to file liquidating plan because it would be filed in good faith, and shortening time for hearings on disclosure statement so that creditor's plan could be considered for confirmation at same time as debtor's plan, which was also a liquidating plan); In re River Vill. Assocs., 161 B.R. 127 (Bankr. E.D. Pa. 1993) (holding that plan providing for liquidation sale at which plan proponent could credit bid its mortgage debt was proposed in good faith), aff'd, 181 B.R. 795 (E.D. Pa. 1995). A takeover plan also may be proposed in good faith. See In re Consul Rests. Corp., 146 B.R. 979, 991-92 & 991 n.24 (Bankr. D. Minn. 1992); In re Evans Prods. Co., 65 B.R. 31 (Bankr. S.D. Fla.), aff'd, 65 B.R. 870 (S.D. Fla. 1986); see also In re Internet Navigator Inc., 289 B.R. 128 (Bankr. N.D. Iowa 2003) (confirming takeover plan rather than debtor's plan after holding, without specific discussion of good faith requirement, that both plans were confirmable).

Creditors' plans often provide for no distribution to be made to the debtor's owners and for their interests to be canceled. Such a plan cannot be fair and equitable if the debtor is solvent on a going concern basis—some class of claims must be paid at more than 100% in such a case, which, as we have seen, violates the fair and equitable standard with respect to a class of interests. See section A.2.c. supra in this Chapter. However, if the debtor is insolvent on a going concern basis, then there is not enough reorganization value to pay the creditors in full, and a plan eliminating the owners' interests can be fair and equitable. But see In re P.J. Keating Co., 168 B.R. 464 (Bankr. D. Mass. 1994) (questionable analysis arguing that the right to control the debtor gave value to an insolvent debtor's stock and thus entitled stockholders receive value under fair and equitable standard).

As we have seen, a chapter 11 plan can incorporate a settlement of the debtor's lender liability claims. See Chapter Ten of this text at the end of section A.1. In fact, lenders have used creditors' plans to settle the debtors' claims against themselves over the objection of the debtors. See, e.g., In re Andreuccetti, 975 F.2d 413 (7th Cir. 1992); In re In re Cellular Info. Sys., Inc., 171 B.R. 926 (Bankr. S.D.N.Y. 1994) (confirming plan filed by lender which incorporated a $14.5 million settlement of debtor's claims against lender); cf. In re Consul Rests. Corp., 146 B.R. 979, 991-92 (Bankr. D. Minn. 1992) (confirming plan under which franchisor took over debtor-franchisee and also settled action by debtor against franchisor). Of course, the court must find that the settlement is fair before it will confirm the plan.

Creditors may also be able to use the debtor's optimistic projections against the debtor in a creditors' plan—in effect to call the debtor's bluff. In *Cellular Information Systems* the debtor had made optimistic projections of its future cash flows. A creditor who thought the debtor's projections were very unrealistic filed a plan under which the debtor would be liquidated if its cash flows were more than 20% below the debtor's projections. The court confirmed the plan, holding that it was proposed in good faith even though the creditor did not expect the debtor to meet the cash flow requirements.

Two final procedural hurdles may stand in the way of confirmation of a creditors' plan. First, even if exclusivity expires so that creditors can file plans, it takes time to obtain approval of a disclosure statement, to solicit votes on the plan, and to hold a hearing on confirmation. See Rules 2002(b), 3017(a), and 3020(b) (providing for 25 days' notice to be given of the deadline for filing objections to the disclosure statement, of the hearing on approval of disclosure statement, of deadline for filing objections to the plan, and of the hearing on confirmation of the plan). Thus, unless the court shortens these time periods under Rule 9006(c), at least 50 days will pass from the date of filing of the creditors' plan to the date of the confirmation hearing on their plan. (Note that the time for filing objections can run concurrently with the notice time for the hearings, although that will leave the proponent no time to file a written response to objections filed on the day of the hearing.) Proposed disclosure statements usually require amendment before the court will approve them; that usually requires at least one additional hearing on the amended disclosure statement. If, before the creditors' plan is ready for confirmation, the court holds a confirmation hearing on the debtor's plan and determines that the debtor's plan is confirmable, the court is required by § 1129 to confirm it. See § 1129(a) & (b)(1) (each stating that the court "shall confirm" the plan if the requirements of the sections are met). Confirmation of the debtor's plan would moot the creditors' plan, because only one plan may be confirmed. See § 1129(c). Some courts are willing to grant orders shortening time, if necessary, so that a creditors' plan can be considered along with the debtor's plan at the confirmation hearing. See, e.g., In re Landmark Park Plaza Ltd. P'ship, 167 B.R. 752 (Bankr. D. Conn. 1994).

The second procedural hurdle is § 1129(c). It provides that only one plan can be confirmed, and that if there are two confirmable plans then "the court shall consider the preferences of creditors and equity security holders in determining which plan to confirm." The court is not bound by the preferences expressed by the parties, In re Rolling Green Country Club, 26 B.R. 729, 735 (Bankr. D. Minn. 1982), and the statute does not give the court guidance if most creditors prefer one plan and most interest holders prefer another. One court chose to confirm a creditors' liquidating plan where the debtor was insolvent on a going concern basis, the debtor had delayed in proposing a confirmable plan, the liquidating plan provided creditors with a higher payout, and liquidation of the real estate involved in the case would neither destroy going concern value nor eliminate jobs. See In re River Vill. Assocs., 161 B.R. 127 (Bankr. E.D. Pa. 1993). In another case involving a hotel and casino, the court confirmed a plan that (as compared to the competing plan not confirmed by the court) provided slightly higher likely recoveries for creditors, a "less leveraged" financial structure, a better cash position, substantially greater opportunity for future capital improvements, and less potential for problems with retaining the necessary gaming license. In re Greate Bay Hotel & Casino, Inc., 251 B.R. 213, 246-48 (Bankr. D.N.J. 2000). Where both plans contemplate the sale of the debtor's assets, the one for the higher price ordinarily will be preferred. In re Landmark Park Plaza Ltd. P'ship, supra, 167 B.R. 752. A debtor's plan that keeps the business alive as a going concern may be preferred over a liquidating plan, but not if the debtor's plan is subject to substantial uncertainty due to future contingencies. See In re Holywell Corp., 54 B.R. 41 (Bankr. S.D. Fla. 1985), aff'd, 59 B.R. 340 (S.D. Fla. 1986), affirmance by district court vacated and case remanded to district court for dismissal of appeal as moot, 838 F.2d 1547 (11th Cir. 1988). A creditors' plan providing for immediate payment of cash to creditors may be preferred over a plan that will provide less certain payment over time. See In re Internet Navigator Inc., 289 B.R. 128, 132-33 (Bankr. N.D. Iowa 2003).

E. HOW BUSINESSES SHOULD BE REORGANIZED: THE SCHOLARLY DEBATE

We have now seen the reorganization process from beginning to confirmation. It is a complex and expensive process. In the 1980s several scholars suggested it could be made simpler and more efficient by providing for a sale of the debtor's assets as a going concern—an auction—early in the case. In an article dealing with management and control of chapter 11 debtors, two bankruptcy scholars who had conducted extensive empirical research on large chapter 11 cases questioned the idea that a quick auction would be preferable to the present system.

LoPucki & Whitford, *Corporate Governance in the Bankruptcy of Large, Publicly Held Companies*
141 U. PA. L. REV. 669, 753-67 (1993)
Copyright © 1993 by the University of Pennsylvania Law Review;
Lynn M. LoPucki and William C. Whitford

In our view, the most fundamental problem of corporate governance is that of investment policy. So long as the company remains in reorganization, the risk of investment loss is borne largely by senior classes while the possibility of investment gain accrues largely to junior classes. This inclines the representatives of senior classes toward low risk investment and the representatives of junior classes toward high risk investments. In most cases, neither will have incentives that make them appropriate governors of investment policy. In the next part of this Article, we explain how we think these conflicting interests should be reconciled in contemporary reorganization cases. In this Part, we explore proposals to resolve the problem of investment policy by fusing the risk of loss with the possibility of gain through alteration of ownership interests shortly after filing, or even before a bankruptcy filing.

The most dramatic proposal of this nature calls for repeal of chapter 11.[59] It asserts that marketplace contracting then would result in shares that terminated on default precisely at the time the company became insolvent. Termination of the stock would

---

59. [Note 268 in original:] See Bradley & Rosenzweig, *Untenable Case*, supra note 10, [*The Untenable Case for Chapter 11*, 101 YALE L.J. 1043 (1992)]at 1078-89. Their proposal draws heavily on a proposal by Bebchuk. See Bebchuk, supra note 8, [*A New Approach to Corporate Reorganizations*, 101 HARV. L. REV. 775 (1988)]at 781-97. While the Bebchuk proposal differs in detail, it also presumes extraordinarily well functioning capital markets. See Lynn M. LoPucki, *Stakeholders in Bankruptcy: Some Comments*, 43 U. TORONTO L.J. (forthcoming summer 1993) (criticizing Bebchuk's proposal).

fuse the risk of loss with the possibility of gain in the hands of the class of creditors with the next lowest priority. One of us has critiqued this proposal in a separate publication.[60] Suffice it to say that we do not believe capital markets work well enough to make practical this vision of a world without bankruptcy reorganization.

Another proposal for fusing the risk of loss and the possibility of gain is to require sale of the company at an auction shortly after the filing of the bankruptcy case. The purchaser at such an auction would pay cash and take the company free of the claims of creditors in the bankruptcy case. * * *

Something like this change in reorganization practice was suggested several years ago by Professors Douglas Baird and Thomas Jackson in separate publications.[61] Each suggested that it might be more efficient to liquidate failed companies by auction to the highest bidder than to reorganize them. Because their proposals were motivated primarily by a desire to avoid the need for judicial valuation of the firm or, alternatively, negotiations over reorganizations plans that would deviate from the absolute priority rule, they did not explicitly address the issue of the timing of the sale. But if sales of assets are to avoid the troublesome corporate governance issues that are the subject of this Article, they must occur soon after the automatic stay takes effect. Recognizing this, Baird has recently "revisited" his proposal, advancing it explicitly as a solution to the corporate governance problems addressed in this Article and acknowledging that a sale shortly after filing would be necessary.[62]

Advocates of the proposal for an immediate, mandatory auction must solve the complex problem of "triggering" the filing of the reorganization case. In its current operation, the bankruptcy system relies heavily on voluntary filing. That is, management initiates the case. If filing led immediately and inevitably to a sale of the company, there is every reason to believe that the current process for triggering reorganization would fail. Purchasers usually replace the managers of the companies they purchase. Managers would know that filing for reorganization was generally equivalent to resigning their offices. The low filing rates under chapter X of the Bankruptcy Act suggest that in such circumstances managers choose not to bring their companies into bankruptcy. It was largely because of this triggering problem that Congress decided to return to the pre-1939 practice of allowing management to remain in office after the filing of a reorganization case.

This is not to say that managers must be assured that they will remain in office indefinitely. To the contrary, we found that under current practice, a substantial portion lose their jobs by the end of the case. But to the management of a company in financial crisis, the difference between immediate, virtually certain loss of control under a mandatory quick sale procedure and the slow squeeze that will force most of them from office under the current procedures is critical. To file for reorganization

---

60. [Note 269 in original:] See Lynn M. LoPucki, *Strange Visions in a Strange World: A Comment on Bradley and Rosenzweig*, 91 MICH L. REV. 79 (1992).

61. [Note 272 in original:] See Thomas H. Jackson, THE LOGIC AND LIMITS OF BANKRUPTCY LAW 209-24 (1986); Douglas G. Baird, *The Uneasy Case For Corporate Reorganizations*, 15 J. LEGAL STUD. 127, 136-45 (1986).

62. [Note 275 in original:] See Douglas G. Baird, *Revisiting Auctions in Chapter 11*, 36 *J.L. & ECON.* (forthcoming April 1993).

under the current practice is risky. But it is usually an acceptable alternative because it offers management the probability of a "soft landing." That is, even after filing, management probably will have the time and the leverage to negotiate a severance arrangement. But in a system where quick sale of the business was mandatory, the bulk of that leverage as well as the time in which to negotiate a deal would disappear. Ironically, therefore, without the delay built into current chapter 11 practice, the filing of many bankruptcy cases would be delayed. It is generally assumed that further delay in initiating bankruptcy for insolvent firms is likely to increase the overall losses suffered by creditors and shareholders.

A second problem with substituting a mandatory quick sale of the business for a reorganization is that the sale may not bring an appropriate price. The existence of bankruptcy reorganization procedures is commonly premised on the existence of a difference between the going concern value of the firm and its liquidation value, that is, the amount for which it can be sold. The purpose of establishing a reorganization procedure is to allow the claimants on the firm, creditors and shareholders together, to capture that difference for their own benefit by paying themselves with securities of the reorganized firm rather than the proceeds of an outright sale. Proponents of an immediate auction essentially call into question the fundamental assumption that for large, publicly traded firms there can be a substantial difference between the going concern and liquidation values. Given the prevalence of investment banking firms, and the widespread acceptance of the efficient capital markets hypothesis, these proponents doubt that a firm can be worth more as an continuing entity than what some outsider would be willing to pay for the firm in its entirety. The acquiring party might raise the necessary capital through borrowing or through the issue of a new stock offering.

Our interviewees were skeptical that large, publicly held companies in reorganization could be sold for their going concern value, particularly if the sales had to take place shortly after filing. Many of the businesses were suffering massive losses at the time they filed. Until such losses can be brought under control, reliable estimates of going concern value will be difficult to make. Potential purchasers will find it hard to acquire the information needed to evaluate the firm accurately, which will depress the price. Consistent with this view, when there was a sale of all or most of the assets of a firm in our study, it commonly occurred more than a year after filing. * * * Some of the delay was occasioned by disagreement among the various parties about whether to conduct a sale or to reorganize. But some of the delay was also occasioned by the perceived need to "structure" the firm so that the maximum bid could be received.

Auction theory[63] also lends credence to skepticism about the ability of a quick auction sale process to realize the full going concern value of the firm. Because many businesses are incurring losses, potential purchasers will need to develop a business plan for the company before they can estimate the level of profitability the reorganized company could achieve. They may need to obtain financing for the purchase and perhaps pay a commitment fee for that financing. An outsider will not incur these costs unless it has reason to believe that it can buy the assets at a price sufficiently below their going concern value (hereinafter called the "differential") to cover both the costs

---

63. [Note 295 in original:] A good introduction to, and bibliography of, auction theory appears in Bruce A. Markell, *Owners, Auctions, and Absolute Priority in Bankruptcy Reorganizations*, 44 STAN. L. REV. 69, 107-11 (1991).

of preparing a bid and the risk that it will not be accepted. There is reason to believe that the size of this differential is substantial. Today, firms that wish to attract bids for large blocks of assets often must offer incentives to persuade a potential purchaser to make the expenditures that are a prerequisite to bidding. The most common incentives are in the form of a contract for the seller to pay a "breakup" or "topping" fee to cover the cost of preparing a bid that is topped by a later bidder. That such incentives are often substantial suggests that the cost of preparing a bid, and therefore the amount of the "differential," is substantial. This amount could be captured by creditors and shareholders were they to reorganize the company rather than sell it at auction.

* * * To warrant reliance that the marketplace is going to yield an adequate price, at least two credible outside bidders must exist. Several of our interviewees expressed the view that capital markets are not sufficiently developed to produce enough bidders to ensure that the winning bid will approximate the going concern value of the firm less the "differential." Sizeable businesses were sold in many of our cases, but none of the purchases were financed through an initial public offering. The successful bidder was, in every instance, an already existing firm, usually one in the same line of business. This suggests that for most large businesses, only a limited number of potential buyers exists. Despite the questionable legality of such an agreement, the number of potential bidders may be further reduced by the formation of joint ventures among them. In five of the cases studied, the debtor was able to conclude a sale even though only one seriously interested buyer came forward. In those cases, the debtor's ability to decline to sell, and instead reorganize under an internal plan, must have been of critical importance in giving it the leverage needed to negotiate an adequate sale price.

A final reason why it may be less efficient to sell companies in chapter 7 than to reorganize them under chapter 11 is the possibly high direct cost of the former. Presumably the sale of a large, publicly held company in chapter 7 would be conducted in much the same way as in the absence of bankruptcy: the services of an investment banker would be employed. When the fees of the investment banker are considered, the cost of liquidating under chapter 7 may exceed the cost of reorganizing under chapter 11.[64]

In this Part, we have emphasized the need for the sale of assets to occur shortly after filing, because only a quick sale could render moot the problems of corporate governance. If, as originally proposed by Baird and Jackson, the sale could be made

---

64. [Note 308 in original:] Both Baird and Eisenberg suggest that the direct costs of auctioning a company may exceed the direct costs of reorganization because of the very high fees customarily charged by investment bankers. See Baird, supra note 275, at 9-10; Eisenberg, supra note 78, [*Baseline Problems in Assessing Chapter 11*, 43 U. TORONTO L.J. (1993)]at 33-34. Although that may be true, the reasons are not clear. Investment bankers already participate in many chapter 11 cases. In our study, creditors' committees hired investment bankers in at least 16 cases and equity committees did so in at least seven. Debtors consulted investment bankers even more frequently, but we did not systematically collect this information from debtors. When investment bankers do participate, typically one of their tasks is to investigate and advise on the available options, which includes selling the company in its entirety.

Consequently, it is possible that much of the work that an investment banker would have to do in an auction is already done in chapter 11, and it may be done by several sets of investment bankers rather than just one. If so, it is hard to see why investment bankers' fees in an auction should be higher that the direct costs of a reorganization. However, it is possible that an investment banker would have to do much more work to sell a company in a speedy auction than we realize. * * *

months or years after filing, several of the difficulties we have raised would be ameliorated. Managers' fear of chapter 11 would be reduced, because they would know that even after filing they still would have time to negotiate for a soft landing. Through the ability to conduct auctions with reserve and to offer bidding incentives, the debtor would have a better chance of prompting truly competitive bidding. If an auction were conducted after implementation of a business plan, a prospective purchaser may find it easier to obtain reliable information about the firm's prospects, reducing the extent to which information deficits lower the bid. The problem of shareholder-creditor conflict regarding investment policy during the period preceding the auction would remain. However, the sale price could be deemed to be the value of the company, thereby ameliorating the problem of allocating reorganization values between shareholders and creditors.[65]

We have pointed out a number of problems and costs inherent in requiring a quick sale of reorganizing firms. Problems and costs arise in the current process as well. Which set of problems and costs is greater is ultimately an empirical question for which we have no answer. The proposal for an immediate, mandatory, unitary sale of assets, however, would work a radical change in current reorganization practice. * * *

NOTE

The scholarly debate continued with Dean Douglas Baird noting that mandatory auctions would be desirable only if they brought forth a new kind of bidder with "ready access to capital markets" and a heightened ability to value firms, who would be willing to take substantial risks and act decisively. Baird, *Revisiting Auctions in Chapter 11*, 36 J.L. & ECON. 633, 652-53 (1993) ("*Revisiting Auctions*"). Meanwhile use of § 363(b) to sell all or substantially all the assets of chapter 11 debtors became accepted. Such sales often turned into auctions, with courts requiring an opportunity for higher bids to be made even where a sale had been negotiated.

The widespread use of § 363(b), and other approaches permitted by courts that seemed to some observers to sidestep the creditor-protective provisions of the Code, led to criticism. Chief among recent critics is Professor Lynn LoPucki, whose articles[66] and then 2005 book, COURTING FAILURE, made the provocative claim that a race to the bottom among bankruptcy courts seeking to have large cases filed in their districts had corrupted the chapter 11 process.[67] In his view, "case placers" such as bankruptcy law firms use the typically-wide choice of venue to choose a district in which bankruptcy courts will allow them to do what they believe is appropriate. In response, seeking to have large cases filed in their courts, bankruptcy judges grant "first day" orders that violate the Code (such as allowing payment of prepetition claims held by supposedly critical vendors), allow professional fees to get out of control, and permit streamlining of the chapter 11 process to the degree that companies emerge from chapter 11 insufficiently reorganized. The result is inefficient "chapter 22" cases, with an alarming number of large chapter 11 debtors reorganized in certain districts (particularly Delaware but also to some degree the

---

65. [Note 312 in original:] That is, sale of the company for cash would greatly reduce the leverages that are one reason that holders of underwater claims and interests can typically negotiate deviations from the absolute priority rule in their favor. The leverages are discussed in more detail in LoPucki & Whitford, *Preemptive Cram Down*, supra note 16, [65 AM. BANKR. L.J. 625 (1991)] at 628-33.

66. See, e.g., LoPucki & Doherty, *Why Are Delaware and New York Bankruptcy Reorganizations Failing?*, 55 Vand. L. Rev. 1933 (2002); LoPucki & Kalin, *The Failure of Public Company Bankruptcies in Delaware and New York: Empirical Evidence of a "Race to the Bottom,"* 54 Vand. L. Rev. 231 (2001).

67. See Problem 2-2 in Chapter Two above.

Southern District of New York and the Northern District of Illinois) soon finding themselves again in need of chapter 11 relief. Professor LoPucki's prodigious empirical studies of the chapter 11 cases of large public companies[68] lent weight to his startling claims.

Others have suggested, however, that Professor LoPucki has misinterpreted his data. Professors Kenneth Ayotte and David Skeel (author of the definitive DEBT'S DOMINION: A HISTORY OF BANKRUPTCY LAW IN AMERICA (2001)) argue, in their review of COURTING FAILURE, that the data support a finding that the bankruptcy processes in those districts have in fact been efficient and beneficial. Ayotte & Skeel, *An Efficiency-Based Explanation for Current Corporate Reorganization Practice*, 73 U. CHI. L. REV. 425 (2006) ("*An Efficiency-Based Explanation*"). They suggest that high failure rates may be due to rational, efficient choices by corporate managers seeking to maximize enterprise value by using a less expensive, but also less comprehensive, form of reorganization. For a response, see LoPucki & Doherty, *Delaware Bankruptcy Indefensible*, 73 U. CHI. L. REV. __ (forthcoming 2006). Professor Robert Rasmussen and Dean Baird agree with Professor LoPucki that Delaware reorganizations had a much higher recidivism rate than elsewhere, but they argue that the data are insufficient to prove a causal link between competition for cases and the high recidivism rate. See Baird & Rasmussen, *Beyond Recidivism*, 53 BUFF. L. REV. __ (forthcoming 2006 as part of a symposium issue focusing on Professor LoPucki's corruption hypothesis).

In *An Efficiency-Based Explanation*, Professors Ayotte and Skeel also question the absence of the "DIP financer" from the story told by Professor LoPucki. They suggest that the real potential for mischief lies not with debtors' managers or the bankruptcy professionals, but with the major prepetition secured creditors who typically become the DIP financers. The DIP financers then may use the control they obtain (or already had) as a result of financing agreements[69] to take value from other constituents by, for example, buying the debtor's assets on the cheap. The wealth of information about the debtor, and other advantages that such DIP financers have, may allow them to purchase the assets at an unfairly low value. Curiously, the DIP financers may be precisely the kind of bidders hoped for by Dean Baird, but Professors Ayotte and Skeel warn that the effect of their bidding may not be beneficial. Others (including Professor Rasmussen and Dean Baird) have noted that major secured creditors seem more and more to be in control of chapter 11 cases. See, e.g., Baird, *Revisiting Auctions*, at 76-77 ("The senior lenders are in control of the process."); Baird & Rasmussen, *The End of Bankruptcy*, 55 STAN. L. REV. 751, 784-85 (2002).

Professors Ayotte and Skeel "are cautiously optimistic that bankruptcy judges will themselves solve the loan-and-control problem without the need for congressional intervention," perhaps by imposing "a blanket or near-blanket prohibition against purchase of the debtor's assets by the debtor's postpetition financer." *An Efficiency-Based Explanation*, at 466, 467. LoPucki and Doherty respond that the bankruptcy judges cannot do anything about the loan-and-control problem. If a judge tried, the DIP lenders would simply insist that their debtors avoid that judge's court.

---

68. See, e.g., LoPucki & Whitford, *Bargaining Over Equity's Share in the Bankruptcy Reorganization of Large, Publicly Held Companies*, 139 U. PA. L. REV. 125, 126 (1990) ("report[ing] some of the results of an empirical study of the bankruptcy reorganization of large, publicly held companies"). Much of Prof. LoPucki's large Bankruptcy Research Database is available at http://lopucki.law.ucla.edu/.

69. See Skeel, *Creditors' Ball: The "New" New Corporate Governance in Chapter 11*, 152 U. PA. L. REV. 917 (2003). Creditor control is not a new phenomenon. See Skeel, DEBT'S DOMINION, at 64 (describing equity receiverships as the precursors to bankruptcy reorganization, and stating that "[t]he grip of Wall Street bankers and lawyers on receivership[s] only strengthened as the technique developed in the 1880s, 1890s, and thereafter"); Gilson & Vetsuypens, *Creditor Control in Financially Distressed Firms: Empirical Evidence*, 72 WASH. U. L.Q. 1005 (1994). Nor is creditor control only an issue for corporations in bankruptcy. Consider the story of Del-Met Corporation. See Limor v. Buerger (In re Del-Met Corp.), 322 B.R. 781 (Bankr. M.D. Tenn. 2005) (reprinted above in Chapter Ten of this text).

Creditor control may seem very appropriate, at least under a law and economics approach; after all, creditors are thought to be the "residual claimants" or "residual owners"— those whose money is at risk in the chapter 11 case.[70] But, as we note in section A of Chapter Six of this text, there are powerful reaons for giving the debtor substantial continuing control as the debtor in possession. Further, Professor LoPucki suggests that "most firms have no single class of residual owners. The Law and Economics scholars' search is for persons who do not exist." LoPucki, *The Myth of the Residual Owner: An Empirical Study*, 82 WASH. U. L.Q. 1341 (2004).[71]

Further, allowing the DIP lenders to take charge may not be in the broader interest of creditors. As Professor Elizabeth Warren noted almost twenty years ago, bankruptcy disputes often are less a matter of debtor versus creditor than of creditor versus creditor. Warren, *Bankruptcy Policy*, 54 U. CHI. L. REV. 775 (1987). "[H]istorically one of the prime purposes of the bankruptcy law has been to * * * protect the creditors from one another." Young v. Higbee Co., 324 U.S. 204, 210 (1945). An extensive empirical study by Professor Warren and Professor Jay Westbrook suggests that sophisticated institutional creditors may be working to consolidate their power at the expense of creditors who are not well-situated to protect their own rights, such as smaller creditors, tort victims, and utility providers. Warren & Westbrook, *Contracting Out of Bankruptcy: An Empirical Intervention*, 118 HARV. L. REV. 1197 (2005).

Professor Rasmussen and Dean Baird suggested in *The End of Bankruptcy*, as have other scholars, that the traditional chapter 11 process—the one you have followed in this book—is becoming an endangered species. See also Baird, *The New Face of Chapter 11*, 12 AM. BANKR. INST. L. REV. 69 (2004) ("*New Face*"). They suggest that this is true in the large cases due to the prevalence of (1) § 363(b) sales (and sales through plans) of all or substantially all of the assets of debtor companies and (2) prepackaged or prenegotiated cases. They suggest that this is true in small cases because there is little or nothing to reorganize; debtors have few assets (much less than $100,000 worth in most cases with little or none of it irreplaceable), and the value of the business resides in the debtor's personal skills and relationships, which creditors cannot reach.[72]

Important empirical research by Professor Edward Morrison in collaboration with Dean Baird backs up this picture with regard to the small cases. See Baird & Morrison, *Serial Entrepreneurs and Small Business Bankruptcies*, 105 COLUM. L. REV. 2310, 2310-11 (2005) ("The typical Chapter 11 cases are strikingly different from the cases one ordinarily hears about. Instead of Uniteds, Enrons, or Kmarts, we see small businesses. There are few assets beyond the entrepreneur's human capital, and these rarely have more value inside the business than outside. It is therefore a mistake to ask whether the corporate entity that is the subject of the bankruptcy case is worth saving. For small businesses, the relevant unit of analysis is the owner and operator of the business, not the business itself.") (footnote omitted).

---

70. See Baird & Jackson, *Bargaining After the Fall and the Contours of the Absolute Priority Rule*, 55 U. CHI. L. REV. 738,774-75 (1988); Gilson & Vetsuypens, supra note 69, at 1005-06.

71. Professor Rasmussen disagrees. Rasmussen, *The Search for Hercules: Residual Owners, Directors and Corporate Governance in Chapter 11*, 82 WASH. U. L.Q. 1445 (2004).

72. Baird, *New Face*, at 85 ("We have a travel agent or insurance broker who does business in corporate form. There are no employees. The business is run out of the home. The assets consist of little more than a telephone and a personal computer. The business has little connection with the corporate entity. The relationships belong to the individual.") Whether the relationships continue to belong to the individual under the 2005 BAPCPA is unclear. If the individual is personally liable for the business's debts (as guarantor or as partner or sole proprietor), the 2005 BAPCPA may force the individual in effect to use those relationships to earn money to pay creditors. See § 1129(a)(15) (discussed in Chapter Sixteen below at pages 941-42).

Others, including Professor A. Mechele Dickerson, suggest that the rumors of the traditional chapter 11 process's death are exaggerated. See Dickerson, *The Many Faces of Chapter 11: A Reply to Professor Baird*, 12 AM. BANKR. INST. L. REV. 109 (2004). The data also may suggest a long-term upward trend for public company reorganizations. See LoPucki, *Where Do You Get Off: A Reply to COURTING FAILURE's Critics*, 53 BUFF. L. REV. __ (forthcoming 2006). Nevertheless, all agree that the number of corporate chapter 11 cases—the cases on which Dean Baird's work is carefully focused—has fallen, suggesting, as Professor Morrison and Dean Baird argue, that chapter 11 is not responsive to the needs of small business entrepreneurs who use the corporate form.

Professors Robert Lawless and Elizabeth Warren argue from empirical studies that the number of business bankruptcy filings—more broadly defined—is much higher than generally thought. They argue, employing extensive empirical research, that there are likely about seven times as many business bankruptcy filings each year—filings made to deal primarily with business debt— than reported in the official data. Lawless & Warren, *The Myth of the Disappearing Business Bankruptcy*, 93 CAL. L. REV. 743 (2005). They suggest that the current official data gathering process misclassifies many small business cases as consumer cases. They also argue that the consumer-focused 2005 BAPCPA resulted in rules for chapter 7 and 13 that are ill-suited to the large number of small business cases that they believe are filed under those chapters. The financially-distressed self-employed person or small business sole proprietor often has not needed chapter 11. Debt relief under chapter 7 or 13 often allowed such a person to restart a failed business without missing much of a beat. That may not be the case after the 2005 BAPCPA.

If Professors Lawless and Warren are right that there are many more business bankruptcies than generally thought, there still is a question whether the needs of such business debtors differ from those of consumer debtors. That may turn on whether the debts in these overlooked business cases are primarily business debts—thus requiring an adjustment of relationships with potential ongoing suppliers, customers, and business lenders (the stuff of chapter 11 concern)—or primarily consumer debts. Their raw data on this point, as they admit, is not clear, id. at 774-75, and there may be reason to question their seeming conclusion that many of these filings involve primarily business debt. The businesses of self-employed persons, in particular, may fail not because of overwhelming business debt but because the business's profits (if any) are insufficient to pay for living expenses, leading to overwhelming consumer debt. That is not to say that business failure as a cause of bankruptcy in these cases would be irrelevant even if the debts turn out to be primarily consumer debts. The bankruptcies likely then would not be the result of the kind of culpable over-consumption that seems to have been the fixation of the drafters of the 2005 BAPCPA. See *Myth of the Disappearing Business Bankruptcy*, at 746-48. As Professors Lawless and Warren suggest, bankruptcy laws that have harsh results for the self-employed may discourage risk-taking and entrepreneurship.

Finally, the effects of globalization on business reorganization have escaped the attention neither of Congress nor of scholars. Professor LoPucki fears that the the 2005 BAPCPA's enactment of the Model Law on Cross-Border Insolvency as chapter 15 of the Bankruptcy Code will lead to world-wide corruption of bankruptcy courts. "Case placers" will engage in world-wide venue shopping for courts who will allow them to do what they want to do. See LoPucki, *Global and Out of Control?*, 79 AM. BANKR. L.J. 79 (2005) ; LoPucki, *Universalism Unravels*, 79 AM. BANKR. L.J. 143 (2005). By contrast, Professor Westbrook, who worked tirelessly for enactment of the Model Law, suggests that the principle of "modified universalism" embodied in the Model Law is "supported by the great majority of academic and practicing specialists in multinational bankruptcy." Westbrook, *Chapter 15 at Last*, 79 AM. BANKR. L.J. 713, 716 (2005).

There are other strands of bankruptcy scholarship, and much excellent and important work not mentioned here. We hope this note will lead the reader to further exploration.

Chapter Sixteen

Consequences of Confirmation — The Discharge And Related Postconfirmation Issues

Confirmation of the plan has five major effects. First, the provisions of the confirmed plan bind the debtor, the creditors, the interest holders, and various other entities. See § 1141(a). Second, except as provided in the plan or in the confirmation order, the property of the estate revests in the debtor free and clear of most claims and property interests. See § 1141(b) & (c). Third, confirmation generally discharges the debtor from preconfirmation debts, see § 1141(d)(1)(A), although amendments made by the 2005 BAPCPA delay individual debtors' receipt of discharges pending the making of sufficient payments under the plan, see § 1141(d)(5), and make a few debts nondischargeable in corporate chapter 11 cases, see § 1141(d)(6). Thus, for the most part, the preconfirmation debts are replaced by the obligations specified in the plan. Fourth, the automatic stay terminates, see § 362(c)(1) & (2)(C),[1] and the discharge injunction steps in to enjoin creditors from acting to collect the discharged debts as personal liabilities

---

[1]   Due to the 2005 BAPCPA, the picture is more complex where the chapter 11 debtor is an individual. Unless the plan or the order confirming the plan otherwise provides, confirmation of the plan causes the property of the estate to vest in the debtor. See § 1141(b). Section 362(c)(1) then triggers termination of the automatic stay with regard to acts against such property. But because the discharge of individual debtors is delayed by § 1141(d)(5) (enacted by BAPCPA) pending the making of sufficient payments under the plan, the discharge injunction of § 524(a)(2) will not yet be in effect. Creditors then may attempt to enforce their prepetition liens on the property that has revested in the debtor, or sue the debtor to collect on the as-yet not discharged debts, with the purpose of obtaining payment sooner (or in a greater amount) than provided for by the plan. Courts should prohibit attempts to collect from the debtor personally (including attempts to obtain new judicial liens) because the automatic stay should remain in effect with respect to actions against the debtor until the discharge is granted or the case is closed. See § 362(c)(2). Courts should prohibit attempts to enforce prepetition liens on property that has revested in the debtor because the provisions of the confirmed plan bind all the creditors under § 1141(a), even before a discharge is granted, and because under § 1123(a)(5)(E) &(b)(5) the plan will have modified the lienholders' rights. (Note that the discharge does not prevent enforcement of existing liens, but rather prohibits collection of a discharged debt as a personal liability of the debtor. See § 524(a)(2); Long v. Bullard, 117 U.S. 617, 6 S. Ct. 917, 29 L. Ed 1017 (1886); cf. Dewsnup v. Timm, 502 U.S. 410, 112 S. Ct. 773, 116 L. Ed. 2d 903 (1992). Thus the presence or absence of a discharge is not determinative of the rights of holders of existing liens.) Though it might show an excess of caution, counsel for individual debtors may wish to consider (1) providing in the plan that the property of the estate will not vest in the debtor until the discharge is granted or (2) seeking supplemental injunctive relief either under the terms of the plan or by way of the order confirming the plan to prevent creditor collection or foreclosure activity before the discharge is granted. Note that if the case must be kept open until sufficient payments have been made to permit grant of the discharge under § 1141(d)(5), the fees payable quarterly under 28 U.S.C. § 1930(a)(6)—which can be sizeable—may have to be paid quarter after quarter for several years after plan confirmation. Cf. Tighe v. Celeb. Home Entm't, Inc. (In re Celeb. Home Entm't, Inc.), 210 F. 3d 995 (9th Cir. 2000).

of the debtor. See § 524(a)(2). Fifth, unless implementation of the plan is stayed pending appeal, the debtor will proceed on the effective date to implement it by making required cash payments, issuing stock and debt instruments, transferring other property, and doing whatever else the plan requires. See § 1142.

We focus in this Chapter on issues related to the discharge. Thus we begin with an introduction to the discharge.

A. INTRODUCTION TO THE CHAPTER 11 DISCHARGE

The chapter 11 discharge under § 1141(d) discharges debts that arose before the date of confirmation. By contrast, note that the chapter 7 discharge under § 727 covers only debts that arose before the date of the order for relief.

Please read § 524(a), which details the effects of the discharge. As footnote 1 above in this chapter notes, the discharge affects personal liability and does not directly affect any existing lien. But the plan may modify an existing lien—such as by changing payment terms for the debt secured by the lien and (absent an election under § 1111(b)(2)) reducing the amount of the lien to the value of the collateral); the confirmed plan then will make those modifications binding on the lienholder. See §§ 1123(a)(5)(E) & (b)(5), 1141(a). Also please understand that the obtaining of new judicial liens with respect to a debt is a primary way in which a debt is enforced as a personal liability; it is only because a debt is enforceable as a personal liability that a judicial action can be brought in which new liens are obtained. Thus the § 524(a)(2) discharge injunction, by prohibiting the enforcement of any discharged debt as a personal liability of the debtor, prevents creditors from obtaining new judicial liens. Similarly, § 524(a)(1), by voiding as a matter of personal liability any judgment obtained at any time, before or after the grant of the discharge, with respect to a discharged debt, prevents such judgments from being the basis for imposition of new judicial liens on the discharged debtor's property. Note also that any post-discharge agreement by the debtor to grant a consensual lien to secure a discharged debt will be unenforceable. See § 524(c)(1).

Note also that in a chapter 7 case only individual debtors—human beings—receive discharges. Section 727(a)(1). Corporations and partnerships do not need chapter 7 discharges. A chapter 7 liquidation will end the business and strip the debtor of all of its valuable assets; there will be nothing left for a discharge to protect. (Only individuals are entitled to exemptions in bankruptcy, see § 522(b), and thus the chapter 7 trustee can liquidate all of a debtor corporation's or partnership's property.) Further, the chapter 7 discharge of an individual is designed to give the honest but unfortunate individual a "fresh start" so that he or she can go on with life unburdened with the mistakes of the past. There is no need to give a fresh start to the shell that is left after a corporation's or partnership's assets are liquidated.

In a chapter 11 case, however, the debtor corporation or partnership may continue in business after confirmation of the plan. If its debts were not discharged, typically it immediately would be in financial distress. The stock (or other ownership interests) and the notes (or other forms of indebtedness) distributed to the creditors and interest holders under the plan would be worth little or nothing. Without the prospect of a discharge, the plan in most cases could not even have been confirmed, because it would not have been feasible. See § 1129(a)(11). Thus the § 1141(d) discharge—unlike the § 727 discharge—is not limited to individual debtors.

Where the plan does not provide for creditors—holders of prepetition claims—to be paid 100% of their claims, the creditors may initially think that it is unfair for the chapter 11 debtor to receive a discharge of those prepetition debts. However, creditors can require that all of the value of the debtor's assets be distributed to them by voting against the plan; if a class of unsecured claims does not accept the plan, then, as we saw in the Chapter Fifteen of this text, the plan cannot be confirmed unless the plan either provides holders of claims in the class with present value equal to 100% of their allowed claims or else provides that junior classes get nothing. See § 1129(b)(2)(B). Thus, if they are not provided for in full, creditors have the right to become the owners of the debtor's business, with the old owners' interests being wiped out. If the creditors become the owners of the business, will it benefit them for the business to go into immediate financial distress after confirmation of the plan? Of course, it will not. The creditors usually receive debt owed by, and ownership interests in, the reorganized debtor; the discharge benefits the creditors by protecting the value and quality of that debt and of those ownership interests.

For the same reason, § 1141(d) discharges of business entities are not subject to the objections to discharge that can be raised in chapter 7 cases. Not all individuals are entitled to a "fresh start" in a chapter 7 case. Certain individuals are denied a discharge altogether under § 727(a)(2)-(11). The discharge is reserved for the honest but unfortunate debtor, and thus is not available to those who made fraudulent transfers (with actual fraudulent intent) within a year before the petition was filed, or who acted in various other dishonest ways before or after filing of the petition, or who seek to use bankruptcy too often. Id. If one or more of the grounds for objection to discharge in § 727(a) is established, then the individual debtor will not receive a discharge of any debts. Thus a successful *objection* to discharge results in the debtor not receiving a discharge in chapter 7.

In a chapter 11 case, by contrast, if the business remained subject to all of the preconfirmation debts, the business typically would not be able to continue. Whatever wrongful acts may have been committed by those in charge of the business in the past, it will do the creditors no good to deny the debtor a discharge. After the reorganization they likely will own all or a substantial part of the debtor's business and will be owed debts by the reorganized debtor—debts that will have value only if the reorganized debtor is in a position to pay interest and principal. A denial of discharge would harm the creditors' interests. Thus the § 727(a) grounds for objection to discharge do not apply by themselves to bar a discharge in a chapter 11 case.

However, if the plan provides for the debtor's assets to be liquidated—whether piecemeal or by sale of the business as a going concern—and if the debtor does not engage in business after the plan is consummated, then granting a discharge to the debtor will not benefit the creditors. They will not be looking to the reorganized debtor's business or assets for repayment; they also will not be counting on any value from any ownership interest in the worthless shell of a debtor. The shell that is left will have no need for a discharge, either. In such a case a debtor *that is not an individual* will not receive a discharge, because § 1141(d)(3)'s three requirements are met: (1) the plan provides for liquidation, (2) the debtor will not engage in business after consummation of the plan, and (3) the debtor would not have received a discharge if the case were in chapter 7 because under § 727(a)(1) only individual debtors are entitled to a discharge.[2]

Note that an *individual* debtor whose plan is confirmed eventually should receive a discharge under § 1141 unless all three requirements of § 1141(d)(3) are met. Even if the plan is a liquidating plan and the debtor does not engage in business after the plan's consummation, the honest but unfortunate debtor should still receive a fresh start; thus an individual debtor will receive a discharge in such a case (after making sufficient payments to satisfy § 1141(d)(5)) unless one of the § 727(a)(2)-(11) grounds for objection to discharge is established. See Dominguez v. Miller (In re Dominguez), 51 F.3d 1502 (9th Cir. 1995) (holding that provisions of § 1141(d)(3) are not self-executing with respect to denial of discharge to individual debtor and that timely complaint objecting to discharge must therefore be filed in order for individual debtor to be denied discharge). Theoretically, an individual debtor who committed serious wrongdoing—e.g., falsifying records or lying to the bankruptcy court—and who would be denied a discharge in a chapter 7 case could receive a discharge in chapter 11 (even though § 727(a)(3) or (4) would prevent the debtor from receiving a discharge if the case were in chapter 7). However, that is not likely to happen. If a debtor who is an individual engages in serious wrongdoing, the court is likely to dismiss the case, to convert it to chapter 7, or to deny confirmation of the debtor's plan on the grounds that the debtor/proponent did not comply with the provisions of the Code. If a plan proposed by another party is confirmed, it is likely to be a liquidating plan that will leave the debtor without a business—thus causing the first two requirements of § 1141(d)(3) to be met. See, e.g., *Dominguez*. If the debtor would not receive a discharge in a chapter 7 case, then the third requirement will be met, and the debtor can be denied a discharge despite confirmation of the plan.

---

2.   Note that a plan may call for the debtor's assets to be sold and for the reorganized debtor to use the proceeds to go back into business. In such a case, the reorganized business entity needs the protection of a discharge and will receive one, because § 1141(d)(3)(B) will not be satisfied. See In re Global Water Techs., Inc., 311 B.R. 896 (Bankr. D. Colo. 2004).

In addition, note that under § 1141(d)(2) individual debtors do not receive discharges in chapter 11 of debts that are *excepted* from discharge under § 523. It is important to understand the difference between an *objection* to discharge under § 727(a), and an *exception* to the discharge under § 523(a). A successful *objection* to discharge (under § 727(a) or 1141(d)(3)) results in the debtor receiving no discharge at all of any debts. By contrast, there are certain debts that are *excepted* from discharge in an individual's bankruptcy case. See § 523(a). For example, an individual who caused willful and malicious injury to another or to another's property can be denied a discharge of the debt resulting from that injury. See § 523(a)(6). If it is proved that one of the exceptions to discharge in § 523(a) applies to a particular debt, then that particular debt is *excepted* from the discharge, but the debtor can still receive a discharge of other debts. Note that corporations and partnerships—debtors other than individuals—are not affected by the § 523(a) exceptions. In chapter 11 they receive discharges even of debts for willful and malicious injury, of most debts incurred fraudulently, and of almost all other kinds of debt.[3]

Thus individuals who have substantial debts that are nondischargeable under § 523(a) may gain little from chapter 11. Such individuals should consider whether they are eligible to file under chapter 13. Successful completion of a chapter 13 plan results in a discharge somewhat broader than the discharge under the other chapters (though the 2005 BAPCPA narrowed the differences). See § 1328(a).

As stated in footnote 1 above, another disadvantage faced by individuals in chapter 11 is that their discharge is delayed. That disadvantage is intertwined with another. If any holder of an unsecured claim objects and would not receive present value under the plan equal to the 100% of the holder's claim, then the individual chapter 11 debtor's plan cannot be

---

3.   Tax claims listed in § 523(a)(1) typically qualify as priority tax claims and thus must be paid in full under § 1129(a)(9)(C) unless the taxing authority agrees otherwise; thus such tax obligations, although technically discharged, must be satisfied under the terms of the plan, and postconfirmation interest on them must (as a result of the 2005 BAPCPA) be paid at the same rate as outside bankruptcy, under § 511. In addition, § 1141(d)(6) (added by the 2005 BAPCPA) provides two exceptions from the discharge for a chapter 11 debtor that is a corporation: (1) certain fraudulently incurred debts owed to "domestic government unit[s]," and obligations owed to private party qui tam plaintiffs who have filed actions against the debtor corporation under the federal false claim act (31 U.S.C. § 3729) or a "similar State statute," and (2) taxes and customs duties, where the debtor "made a fraudulent return" or "willfully attempted in any manner to evade or to defeat such tax or such customs duty." Note that the list of tax claims that are excepted from the discharge by § 523(a)(1) in chapter 7 and chapter 11 cases of individuals includes tax claims that are priority claims under § 507(a)(8) but also includes certain other tax claims, including taxes like those listed in § 1141(d)(6), where fraud or tax evasion is involved. If the § 1141(d)(6) tax claims are too old (e.g., if the return for the tax year involved was due more than three years before the petition filing date) then they may not be priority claims. See § 507(a)(8)(A)(i). But now, even if they are not priority claims that must be paid in full under § 1129(a)(9)(C), they must be paid in full by the reorganized debtor or a settlement must be reached with the taxing authority—otherwise the taxing authority will use coercive means to collect the tax, which will not be discharged in the chapter 11 case.

confirmed unless the value to be distributed under the plan at least equals the debtor's projected disposable earnings for the next five years—or for "the period during which the plan provides payments" if that is longer than five years. See § 1129(a)(15). The discharge then is not granted until all payments under the plan are made. See § 1141(d)(5). The language of §§ 1129(a)(15) and 1141(d)(5) may contain enough ambiguities for a court to interpret them to reach a sensible and non-punitive result,[4] but that outcome is not certain. Suppose the plan provides for restructuring of a mortgage on an office building owned by the individual debtor, and the restructured mortgage provides for payments over thirty years. Must the plan distribute value equal to thirty years' worth of projected disposable earnings? Must entry of the discharge be delayed for thirty years?

In the rest of this Chapter, we consider three issues that are related to the discharge. First, only "debts" are discharged. To what extent is a right to an injunction—such as the right to specific enforcement of a covenant not to compete, or the right to an injunction requiring cleanup of toxic wastes—a debt that can be discharged?

Second, § 524(e) provides that "discharge of a debt of the debtor does not affect the liability of any other entity on, or the property of any other entity for, such debt." Does § 524(e) prohibit the court from extending, under § 105(a), the protections of the discharge to an entity other than the debtor? Does § 524(e) prevent the plan from binding a creditor to release a third party who is liable with the debtor?

Third, and finally, what are the due process limitations on the discharge? Can a claim be discharged where the creditor did not receive notice of the bar date for filing proofs of claim or notice of the date set for the confirmation hearing?

B. DISCHARGE OF THE RIGHT TO AN INJUNCTION

The right (outside of bankruptcy) to have the court exercise its equitable powers to enter an injunction may arise from contractual or noncontractual obligations. For example, the buyer typically has the right to specific enforcement of a contract for sale of land. (Note that an order of specific performance is simply a particular kind of injunction.) Employers and buyers of businesses often have the right to specific enforcement of covenants not to compete given by their employees or by the sellers of the businesses, respectively. Noncontractual examples include the right that a product manufacturer may have to enjoin others from infringing on its trademark or in

---

4.   For example, a court may be able to grant a discharge once creditors have received payments equal to what they would have received in a chapter 7 case, see § 1141(d)(5)(B), although that section seems designed to deal with a case in which the debtor is unable to complete the plan. It may also be the case that projected disposable income, based as it is it on the six months' income prior to the petition filing date (by way of the reference to § 1325(b)(2) in § 1129(a)(15) and the definition of "current monthly income" in § 101(10A)), may be very low in the case of an individual who has been operating a distressed business as a sole proprietor.

other ways competing unfairly; the right that a landowner may have to an injunction against the maintenance of a nuisance on nearby land; and the right that a private person or a governmental entity may have to an injunction to stop the discharge of toxic waste and to clean up toxic waste that has been spilled.

What is the effect of bankruptcy on these rights? The automatic stay generally prevents commencement or continuation of an action to obtain an injunction against the debtor, and the enforcement in an existing action of an injunction already entered against the debtor. However, as we saw in Chapter Three of this text, the automatic stay does not prevent a governmental unit from commencing or continuing an action to enforce its police or regulatory powers, and it does not prevent the enforcement of any resulting judgment, so long as it is not a money judgment. See § 362(b)(4); Penn Terra Ltd. v. Dep't of Envtl. Res., 733 F.2d 267 (3d Cir.1984) (reprinted in Chapter Three) (holding that order to comply with environmental protection laws was not a money judgment even though it required debtor to spend money, and thus that automatic stay did not prevent enforcement of order). Further, the court may grant relief from stay for cause in order to permit the obtaining or enforcement of an injunction.

In addition, the automatic stay protects the debtor only temporarily. Thus the question is whether something else will provide permanent protection. Steps taken during the bankruptcy case may provide permanent protection even before a plan is confirmed. For example, the right of a buyer to specifically enforce a contract for sale of land against the debtor/seller may be eliminated by the avoiding powers if the buyer is not in possession of the land and if the contract was not promptly recorded. Note that a bona fide purchaser of the land from the debtor would take free of the equitable rights of the buyer to the land under the unrecorded contract; the trustee or debtor in possession may therefore eliminate the buyer's right to the land using the power in § 544(a)(3) of a hypothetical bona fide purchaser of real property.

Another step that may provide permanent protection against an injunction requiring specific performance of an executory contract is the rejection of the contract under § 365. As we saw in Chapter Seven of this text, many courts follow the traditional understanding of contract rejection and hold that rejection eliminates any right to specific performance of the rejected contract. (But note that land sale buyers who are in possession of the land and licensees of intellectual property are given limited rights to enforce rejected contracts against the debtor under § 365(i) and (n).) The traditional understanding that rejection eliminates rights to specific performance has, however, been challenged by Michael Andrew and Jay Westbrook, as we saw in Chapter Seven. Under the Andrew/Westbrook approach, rejection of the contract does not eliminate the right to specific performance, but that right can be eliminated by the discharge—at least as a personal liability of the debtor—if the right to specific performance is a "claim."

Of course, even adherents to the traditional approach would agree that rejection cannot eliminate a right to specific performance of a *nonexecutory* contract. Thus, if the contract is not executory, or if the right to an injunction does not arise from a contract, § 365 will not help the debtor to eliminate the nondebtor's right to obtain and enforce an injunction.[5]

If nothing happens during the case to eliminate the right to an injunction, the question will be whether confirmation of the plan, and the resulting discharge under § 1141(d), will eliminate it. As noted above, the discharge operates to void judgments—including existing injunctions—against the debtor on discharged debts and to preclude any acts from being taken to collect those discharged debts, including the commencement or continuation of judicial proceedings. See § 524(a)(1) & (2).[6]

The discharge therefore will protect the debtor from having an injunction entered and enforced only if the right to the injunction was a discharged debt. The term "debt" is defined to mean "liability on a claim." Section 101(12). Thus we must ask whether the right to the injunction was a "claim." If so, then any liability the debtor faced as of the confirmation date to have an injunction entered and enforced—at least as a matter of the debtor's personal liability—was discharged.

A "right to an equitable remedy for breach of performance" is a claim "if such breach gives rise to a right to payment * * * ." Section 101(5)(B). What does that definition mean? Consider the following case.

In re Udell
United States Court of Appeals, Seventh Circuit, 1994
18 F.3d 403

SKINNER, District Judge [sitting by designation].
* * *

The Standard Carpetland USA, Inc. ("Carpetland") employed debtor-appellee Barry Stuart Udell ("Udell") in its Fort Wayne, Indiana store. The parties entered an employment contract that included a covenant not to compete. For three years after leaving Carpetland, Udell was not to engage in any business similar to Carpetland within 50 miles of Fort Wayne. The covenant gave Carpetland the right to both an injunction and liquidated damages:

> In the event of Udell's actual or threatened breach of the provisions of this paragraph 11, Carpetland shall be entitled to an injunction restraining Udell as well as reimbursement for reasonably [sic] attorneys fees incurred in securing said judgment and stipulated damages in the sum of $25,000.00.

---

5. Courts applying the functional test, however, might find a contract to be executory even where one party had fully performed, just so that the contract could be rejected. See Chapter Seven above in this text.

6. Note that judgments are voided only to the extent that they determine the personal liability of the debtor and that acts to collect the discharged debts are prohibited only to the extent that they are taken to collect discharged debts as personal liabilities of the debtor. Id. Thus it is possible to argue that the right to specific performance of a land sale contract creates a property interest that survives the discharge and permits the nondebtor buyer to move against the land and obtain title to it.

Soon after leaving Carpetland, Udell purchased a local carpet store which he claims does not compete in the same market as Carpetland. Udell sued Carpetland in the Superior Court for Allen County, Indiana, seeking damages for breach of the employment contract with respect to allegedly past due commissions and other compensation. Carpetland counterclaimed for damages and an injunction pursuant to the restrictive covenant. The state court granted Carpetland a preliminary injunction in June, 1992. Udell is appealing this order in the Indiana appellate courts.

Several days after the injunction issued, Udell filed a Chapter 13 bankruptcy petition. To enforce its preliminary injunction in the Indiana court, Carpetland filed a motion for emergency relief from the automatic stay prescribed by the Bankruptcy Code. Carpetland argued that its right to an injunction was not a "claim" under § 101(5)(B) of the Bankruptcy Code, 11 U.S.C. § 101 et seq., and therefore could not be discharged in Udell's bankruptcy. * * *

PROCEEDINGS IN THE LOWER COURTS

The bankruptcy court granted Carpetland relief for the purpose of enforcing the injunction entered in the state court. The court ruled that Carpetland's right to injunctive relief was not a claim dischargeable in bankruptcy. Under Indiana law, an injunction may issue only if the remedy of damages is inadequate. The state court had ruled in this case that an injunction is the proper remedy for Udell's breach, and under the strictures of Indiana law, this ruling necessarily encompasses a decision that the right to the injunction could not be satisfied by the payment of liquidated damages. Accordingly the breach that gives rise to the injunction does not "give rise to a right to payment" under § 101(5)(B). The bankruptcy court further ruled that relief from the automatic stay was warranted because "the potential harm to Carpetland by continuing the stay outweighs the potential harm to [Udell] which may flow from terminating it."

The district court reversed the grant of relief. It held that Carpetland's right to an injunction is a § 101(5)(B) "claim" dischargeable in bankruptcy because it also enables Carpetland to seek liquidated damages. Carpetland's restrictive covenant provides for an injunction and liquidated damages in the event of "threatened" as well as actual breaches. In the opinion of the district judge, a "threatened" breach is a future breach. Because a future breach gives rise here to liquidated damages, "the usual reason for granting ... injunctions, which is, that money damages for ... future violations are inadequate because of the inability to prove the extent of damages resulting from future breach of the restrictive employment covenants, does not apply." The district court acknowledged that Indiana law requires a showing of "irreparable harm incapable of reduction to monetary relief" before an injunction may issue. The court concluded, however, that "it is solely because the specific language employed by these parties contemplates liquidated damages for future breach that the right to payment arises in this case." * * *

DISCUSSION

For bankruptcy purposes, a "debt" is a liability on a "claim." 11 U.S.C. § 101(12). By fashioning a single definition of "claim" for the 1978 Bankruptcy Code, Congress intended to adopt the broadest available definition of that term. Under § 101(5) of the Code, a " 'claim' means"—

(A) right to payment … or

(B) right to an equitable remedy for breach of performance if such breach gives rise to a right to payment, whether or not such right to an equitable remedy is reduced to judgment, fixed, contingent, matured, unmatured, disputed, undisputed, secured, or unsecured[.]

Carpetland argues that our interpretation of § 101(5)(B) should focus on whether the equitable remedy itself gives rise to an alternative right to payment. Udell, on the other hand, argues that a right to an equitable remedy is a "claim" whenever the breach of performance also gives rise to a right to payment—*any* right to payment, even one that serves a separate remedial purpose from the equitable remedy. We must decide whether § 101(5)(B) requires any connection between the equitable and the legal remedies beyond the fact that both remedies arise from the same breach of performance.

In Ohio v. Kovacs, 469 U.S. 274, 105 S. Ct. 705, 83 L. Ed. 2d 649 (1985), the Supreme Court provided some general guidelines for the interpretation of § 101(5)(B). The State of Ohio had obtained a state court judgment against Kovacs for violations of environmental laws at a hazardous waste disposal site. The judgment included (1) an injunction to stop further pollution of the site, the air and public waters; (2) an injunction to clean up the site ("cleanup order"); and (3) an order to pay Ohio $75,000 for injury to wildlife. When Kovacs failed to comply with the judgment, Ohio obtained the appointment of a receiver who took possession of Kovacs' property and began to clean up the site. Kovacs filed for bankruptcy before the receiver had completed his task. The question presented was whether the cleanup order was a "claim" under § 101(4)(B)—now § 101(5)(B)—of the Bankruptcy Code.

The Court found that Ohio had effectively converted its cleanup order into a demand for money damages. After the appointment of the receiver, the only performance Ohio sought from Kovacs was "a money payment to effectuate the … clean up." Id. at 282, 105 S. Ct. at 709 (quoting from the Sixth Circuit's opinion below, In re Kovacs, 717 F.2d 984, 987 (1983)). Because the cleanup order had given rise to a right to payment, the order was a "claim" dischargeable in bankruptcy. The Court emphasized what it had not decided: whether the injunction against further pollution was also a "claim" under § 101(5)(B). Id. at 284, 105 S. Ct. at 710.

Kovacs is helpful in its analysis of the statute, even though the resolution of that case turned on the fact that Ohio had itself elected to convert its equitable right into a demand for a money judgment, the reverse of our present situation. The Court noted that "the key phrases 'equitable remedy,' 'breach of performance,' and 'right to payment' are not defined" in § 101(5)(B); it proceeded to examine its legislative history. Id. at 280, 105 S. Ct. at 708. We conclude that the Court deemed these provisions ambiguous and follow the Court's example by examining the legislative history of § 101(5)(B), "sparse as it is." Id. at 280, 105 S. Ct. at 708.

A sponsor of the Bankruptcy Reform Act stated with respect to the definition of "claim":

Section 101(4)(B) [now § 101(5)(B)] … is intended to cause the liquidation or estimation of contingent rights of payment for which there may be an *alternative* equitable remedy with the result that the equitable remedy will be susceptible to being discharged in bankruptcy. For example, in some States, a judgment for specific performance may be satisfied by an alternative right to payment, in the event performance is refused; in that event, the creditor entitled to specific performance would have a "claim" * * * . On the other hand, rights to an equitable remedy for a breach of performance *with respect to which* such breach does not give rise to a right to payment are not "claims" and would therefore not be susceptible to discharge in bankruptcy.

124 Cong. Rec. 32393 (1978) (remarks of Rep. Edwards) (emphasis added). The quoted part of the legislative history shows that one example of a "claim" is a right to an equitable remedy that can be satisfied by an "alternative" right to payment. If the right to payment is not an alternative remedy, it must at least arise "with respect to" the equitable remedy, not apart from it. Id. The proper inquiry under § 101(5)(B), then, is whether Carpetland's right to an injunction "gives rise" to an alternative or other corollary right to payment of liquidated damages.

Udell argues that Carpetland has improperly shifted our inquiry from whether the "breach" gives rise to a right to payment, to whether the "equitable remedy" gives rise to a right to payment. This, Udell claims, is to rewrite the statute. We disagree. There must first be a breach that gives rise to a right to an equitable remedy. Under applicable federal or state laws, that remedy may give rise to an "alternative" or other corollary right to payment. Both remedies, however, issue from the original breach; "such breach" as gives rise to the equitable remedy also gives rise to the right to payment.[7]

This reading of § 101(5)(B) is reinforced by *Home State Bank*, 501 U.S. at __, 111 S. Ct. at 2154, where the Court ruled that a creditor's right to foreclose on a [nonrecourse] mortgage is a "claim." Though the Court did not elaborate, in *Home State Bank* the equitable remedy of foreclosure necessarily gives rise to a right to payment—i.e., the proceeds from the sale of the debtor's property.

Also consistent with our reading are the decisions, including our own, that deal with the dischargeability in bankruptcy of environmental injunctions. In Matter of CMC Heartland Partners, 966 F.2d 1143, 1146-47 (7th Cir.1992), we held that a CERCLA injunction directing a property owner to clean up his land created an obligation that "run[s] with the land" and survives bankruptcy. In In re Chateaugay Corp., 944 F.2d 997 (2d Cir.1991), a case we cited in *CMC Heartland*, supra, the Court of Appeals for the Second Circuit distinguished between an injunction ordering the offender to remove accumulated wastes, and one ordering him to end further pollution from such wastes. The former "is a 'claim' if the creditor obtaining the order had the option, which CERCLA confers, to do the cleanup work itself and sue for response costs, thereby converting the injunction into a monetary obligation." The

---

7.   [Note 1 in original:] None of the courts that have interpreted § 101(5)(B) were troubled by any perceived conflict between the language of § 101(5)(B) and an inquiry, dictated by its legislative history, focusing on whether the equitable remedy gives rise to a right to payment. All of the courts below in *Kovacs* found that Ohio's cleanup order had given rise to a right to payment, rendering the order dischargeable in bankruptcy. The Supreme Court approved the reasoning repeatedly affirmed below: the "cleanup duty had been reduced to a monetary obligation." Id. at 280, 105 S. Ct. at 708 ("the rulings of the courts below were wholly consistent with the statute and its legislative history"). See also Matter of Davis, 3 F.3d 113, 116-17 (5th Cir.1993) (examining equitable remedies to see if "alternate remedies of money damages exist").

latter is not a "claim" because the creditor has "no option to accept payment in lieu of continued pollution"—i.e., the injunction does not give rise to a right to payment. Id. at 1008. See also In re Torwico Electronics, Inc., 8 F.3d 146 (3d Cir.1993) (citing *CMC Heartland* and *Chateaugay* with approval and holding that the state's cleanup order is not a "claim" because the state has no "right to payment under the statutory authority asserted or the Order imposed").

We recognize the appealing simplicity of Udell's "plain language" reading of § 101(5)(B). Udell asserts that "for an equitable remedy to be a claim, it must be the sole remedy available for breach of the agreement"; any right to payment arising from the same breach would turn the equitable remedy into a claim. The Supreme Court's approach in *Kovacs*, however, belies this reading of § 101(5)(B). In *Kovacs*, a single "breach of performance"—violations of environmental laws—had given rise to a judgment in three parts, two of them injunctive, and the third monetary. Udell's suggested "plain language" reading should have ended the case. Ohio already had a money judgment for injury to wildlife. This right to payment arose from the same breach as the cleanup order. For the Court, however, the cleanup order was a "claim," not because Ohio already had a $75,000 judgment arising from the same breach, but because Ohio's actions had effectively converted the cleanup order into money damages.

In light of *Kovacs*, *Home State Bank* and the legislative history of § 101(5)(B), we hold that a right to an equitable remedy for breach of performance is a "claim" if the same breach also gives rise to a right to a payment "with respect to" the equitable remedy.[8] If the right to payment is an "alternative" to the right to an equitable remedy, the necessary relationship clearly exists, for the two remedies would be substitutes for one another. This is the example of "claim" given in the legislative history. As the Supreme Court's decision in *Home State Bank* implies, relationships other than outright substitution may also suffice. For example, the right to foreclose on a mortgage, though not strictly an "alternative" to the right to the proceeds from the sale of the debtor's property, nonetheless gives rise to a corollary right to payment (and may in fact be considered as an alternative to money in the sense that the debtor can stop the foreclosure by paying the full debt). The two remedies are sufficiently related that the Supreme Court classified the right to foreclose as a "claim." See id. 501 U.S. at ___, 111 S. Ct. at 2154.

APPLICATION OF THE RULE TO THE PRESENT CASE

Indiana law determines the nature of Carpetland's contractual remedies, including whether the right to an injunction gives rise to a right to payment. See Butner v. United States, 440 U.S. 48, 54-55, 99 S. Ct. 914, 917-18, 59 L. Ed. 2d 136 (1979) (absent overriding federal interest, state law determines property rights in assets of bankrupt's estate).

With "the great weight of authority in this country," Indiana law permits (under proper circumstances) the award of an injunction in addition to liquidated

---

8. [Note 2 in original:] This interpretation of § 101(5)(B) is also consistent with a complementary provision of the Bankruptcy Code. Section 502(c)(2) of the Code provides for the "estimat[ion] for purpose of allowance" of "any right to payment *arising from a right to an equitable remedy* for breach of performance" (emphasis added).

damages. Duckwall v. Rees, 119 Ind. App. 474, 86 N.E.2d 460, 462 (1949) (en banc). The two remedies may be cumulative unless the liquidated damages were intended by the parties to be a substitute for performance:

> [W]here the sum specified [as liquidated damages] may be substituted for the performance of the act at the election of the person by whom the money is to be paid, or the act done, equity will deny specific performance and leave the aggrieved party to his remedy at law. Which of these types any given contract may be depends upon the intention of the parties as expressed in the whole instrument....

Id. While we have not found an Indiana case actually granting both remedies, the cases that deal with the subject in no way impeach this general statement. * * * In Seach v. Richards, Dieterle & Co., 439 N.E.2d 208 (Ind. App. 1982), the court upheld an injunction enforcing a covenant not to compete but reversed an award of liquidated damages as an unenforceable penalty because they were unrelated to actual damages. The court remanded the case for determination and award of any actual damages. Id. at 217. This opinion strongly supports the proposition that in Carpetland's case, an injunction and an award of liquidated damages are cumulative and not alternative. Udell cannot escape the restrictive covenant by paying $25,000 in liquidated damages. See also 5A Corbin on Contracts § 1213 at 436 (1964) ("if there is a promise to render one particular performance, with a provision for payment of a sum of money as ... liquidated damages for breach, without anything more, the contract is not an alternative contract" giving the promisor the option between performance or payment); Restatement (Second) of Contracts § 361 (1981) ("[m]erely by providing for liquidated damages, the parties are not taken to have fixed a price to be paid for the privilege not to perform").

The district judge found that a "threatened breach" is in effect a future breach, and that Carpetland's right to an injunction gives rise to a right to payment "solely because the specific language employed by these parties contemplates liquidated damages for *future* breach" (emphasis added). We disagree. A threatened breach is a present act. In Carpetland's case, a threatened breach could give rise to two independent remedies: (1) an injunction against the future realization of the threat, and (2) liquidated damages for the actual harm that has already accrued from the threat.[9] Carpetland's right to liquidated damages does not arise "with respect to" its right to an injunction, see 124 Cong. Rec. 32393; the two rights address entirely separate remedial concerns. As *Kovacs* shows, the fact that both remedies are triggered by a single act does not mean that the right to an injunction gives rise to a right to liquidated damages.

We further find that Carpetland's right to an injunction does not give rise in any other sense to the payment of liquidated damages. Lacking is the derivative relationship between the two remedies exemplified by *Home State Bank*, supra, where the equitable remedy of foreclosure was the means for realizing the right to the proceeds from the sale of the debtor's property. Id. 501 U.S. at ___, 111 S. Ct. at 2154.

Accordingly we rule that it was error for the district judge to reverse the order of the bankruptcy judge on the ground that the equitable relief sought by Carpetland was a "claim" dischargeable in bankruptcy. * * *

---

9.   [Note 5 in original:] We express no view as to the enforceability of the liquidated damages provision.

The order of the district court is reversed, and this case is remanded to the district court for consideration of whether the bankruptcy court abused its discretion by granting Carpetland relief from the stay. Costs to be awarded to Carpetland.

FLAUM, Circuit Judge, concurring in the result.

Even though I agree with the court's eventual outcome, I am unable to accept the court's approach which, in my view, dodges this statute's plain language in an effort to reach a sensible result.

* * *

To appreciate the patent absurdity of implementing the plain text of Section 101(5)(B) one must keep in mind that this is a bankruptcy statute. * * * If we were to apply the plain text of § 101(5)(B) to individuals restrained by court orders—e.g. trespassers, polluters, stalkers, batterers—theoretically, simply by filing bankruptcy, the violator could escape from any restraining order prompted by a breach that also gave rise to an award of money damages. Certainly the parade of horribles is extensive, and I need not belabor it further. Since the text of § 101(5)(B) presents one of those extremely unique circumstances of patent absurdity, we may turn to the purpose, context and policy of § 101(5)(B) to supplement its plain language. * * *

NOTES

1. If the legal remedy of damages is inadequate, thus making equitable remedies available, does it necessarily follow that damages—inadequate as they might be—are unavailable as a remedy? Suppose the state court determined that damages to Carpetland's business from Udell's present and future competition could be determined and awarded, even though the damages awarded might turn out to undercompensate or overcompensate Carpetland, because of the difficulty in determining the effect of present competition on Carpetland's profits and the even greater difficulty in determining what effect future competition would have. Would it be reasonable for the state court then to grant Carpetland an injunction because the legal remedy of damages, although available, is not adequate? Under such circumstances, would damages be an "alternative" remedy so that the right to an injunction would be a "claim" under the analysis in *Udell*? Compare Kennedy v. Medicap Pharmacies, Inc., 267 F.3d 493, 499 (6th Cir. 2001), with In re Nickels Midway Pier, LLC, 332 B.R. 262, 275-76 (Bankr. D.N.J. 2005).

2. The legislative history quoted in *Udell* suggests that if a judgment for specific performance is disobeyed, and if "the judgment for specific performance may be satisfied by an alternative right to payment," then the right to specific performance is a "claim." Is Representative Edwards referring to cases in which the defendant who disobeyed the order has the right to satisfy the judgment by paying money? Or is he referring to cases in which the plaintiff has the right to seek money as an alternative to forcing the defendant to obey the court's order? Are either of those interpretations consistent with the language of the statute?

3. The question whether a right to enforce a covenant not to compete survives the discharge and survives the rejection of any underlying executory contract has split the courts. See, e.g., Burger King Corp. v. Rovine Corp. (In re Rovine Corp.), 6 B.R. 661 (Bankr. W.D. Tenn. 1980) (rejection of Burger King franchise contract by debtor in possession/franchisee included rejection of covenant not to compete and therefore relieved estate and debtor of obligation not to compete); Oseen v. Walker (In re Oseen), 133 B.R. 527 (Bankr. D. Ida.

1991) (holding that because contract was not executory, covenant not to compete would remain as viable obligation of debtor unless it was a "claim" which could be discharged, but it was not a "claim" because violation could not adequately be compensated by damage award); In re Annabel, 263 B.R. 19 (Bankr. N.D.N.Y. 2001) (holding that rejection in chapter 7 case did not affect covenant's enforceability against debtor unless statutory § 365(g) breach gave rise to a dischargeable claim, and holding that it did not give rise to a claim, but noting that result might be different in chapter 11 case "where the Court would be required to consider the effect of the covenant not to compete on a debtor's ability to reorganize"); In re Kilpatrick, 160 B.R. 560 (Bankr. E.D. Mich.1993) (holding that rejection of contract did not constitute rescission and did not bar specific enforcement of covenant not to compete, but discharge of "claim" arising from covenant not to compete would bar enforcement). Was the contract in *Udell* executory? Should that matter?

Problem 16-1

During Foam Corporation's chapter 11 case, First Bank obtained relief from the automatic stay and foreclosed on Foam's Philadelphia plant. BipCo purchased the plant at the foreclosure sale. After Foam's plan of reorganization was confirmed, BipCo discovered that Foam Corporation had contaminated the Philadelphia property with toxic wastes. The Environmental Protection Agency then checked Foam's other plants and determined that the Denver plant was badly contaminated with toxic wastes, so badly that well water from the surrounding land was contaminated. The EPA determined that Foam Corporation was continuing to discharge toxic wastes in its operations at the Denver plant and that existing contamination in the soil was continuing to spread due to movement of underground water. The EPA sought an injunction requiring Foam to cease further discharges of toxic wastes in its operations and to clean up the contamination at both the Denver plant and the Philadelphia plant (now owned by BipCo). The EPA also sought fines of $100,000 from Foam for past contamination and $10,000 for each day that Foam continued to discharge toxic wastes in Denver. The EPA had the option to do the clean up work itself and charge Foam Corporation for the costs, but the EPA did not choose to do so. Does the discharge prevent the EPA from obtaining all or part of the relief it seeks? Consider *Udell* and the cases cited in it.

C. RELEASE OF THIRD PARTIES FROM LIABILITY

Section 524(e) provides that the "discharge of a debt does not affect the liability of any other entity on, or the property of any other entity for, such debt." Thus third parties who are liable along with the debtor on some or all of the debtor's debts—such as guarantors, joint tortfeasors, liability insurers, and (where the debtor is a partnership) general partners—generally will remain liable despite the debtor's receipt of a discharge. There may be times, however, when the ability to release third parties from liability would assist the debtor greatly in reorganizing. Guarantors, insurance companies, or general partners may be willing to contribute to contribute funds or other property to the reorganization for the benefit of all of the creditors if in return they can be released from liability—and without such contributions reorganization may be difficult or impossible. Does the court have authority to enjoin permanently actions against such third parties, or to confirm a plan that provides for their release from liability?[10]

Before we turn to that question, recall (as we saw in Chapter Three of this text) that under § 105(a) the court may *temporarily* enjoin actions against third parties—such as the debtor's key managers—in order to assist the debtor in reorganizing. The debtor's liability insurers probably will not need to seek a § 105(a) injunction; they usually will be protected by the automatic stay, because the automatic stay will prevent claimants from obtaining judgments against the debtor, and the obtaining of a judgment against the insured is usually a condition to the insurance company's obligation to pay claims. If it appears that claims against the insurance policy might exhaust the policy limits, the court will likely not grant relief from stay. Even tort claimants who obtained judgments prepetition may be stayed from obtaining payment out of the liability insurance; the automatic stay may apply if the insurance proceeds are treated as property of the estate, and in any case the court can enjoin payment temporarily under § 105(a) to preserve the value of the insurance policies where the claims against them may exhaust their limits. Thus some third parties may receive protection during the reorganization process, but what happens once the plan is confirmed?

The typical § 105(a) stay of actions against guarantors or against general partners who are key people in the reorganization will end when the plan is confirmed or soon after. After all, such stays are intended to let the key people attend to the reorganization of the debtor, which will have been accomplished when the plan is put into effect.

The debtor's liability insurers similarly will be at risk once the plan is confirmed. Note that under § 524(a)(2) the discharge injunction does not eliminate the discharged debts but rather protects the debtor from actions to collect them "as a personal liability of the debtor." What if a tort claimant brings an action against the reorganized debtor on a discharged debt, stating in the complaint that the action is solely for the purpose of recovering from the debtor's liability insurer and that any judgment will not be enforced

---

10. Some courts have relied on a supposed need to free the reorganized debtor from future claims for contribution or indemnity that might be asserted by co-tortfeasors as a basis for enjoining actions against those co-tortfeasors. See, e.g., Menard-Sanford v. Mabey (In re A.H. Robins Co.), 880 F.2d 694 (4th Cir. 1989). However, any such contingent claims would seem to be disallowed by § 502(e)(1)(B)—so that the co-tortfeasors could not claim a share of the distribution in the case—and then discharged under § 1141(d), see Greenblatt v. Richard Potasky Jeweler, Inc. (In re Richard Potasky Jeweler, Inc.), 222 B.R. 816, 827 n.20 (S.D. Ohio 1998). The reorganized debtor would not seem to be at any risk from such claims, unless they were held not to be in existence as of the date of confirmation. Outside of the Third Circuit (see supra page 486), as long as the injuries to the tort victims had occurred by the time of confirmation, it would seem that the co-tortfeasors would have dischargeable contingent claims as of the time of confirmation. Presumably all or almost all of the injuries that were going to occur from A.H. Robins' Dalkon Shield contraceptive device had occurred by the time of the confirmation of its plan. Certainly asbestos manufacturers would have a more realistic fear of co-tortfeasors' claims for contribution or indemnity that might come into existence postconfirmation.

against the debtor personally? Does the discharge injunction prohibit such a suit? Nearly all courts that have considered the issue have held that it does not; the claimant may proceed with the action. See, e.g., Houston v. Edgeworth (In re Edgeworth), 993 F.2d 51 (5th Cir. 1993); Hendrix v. Page (In re Hendrix), 986 F.2d 195 (7th Cir. 1993); Green v. Welsh, 956 F.2d 30 (2d Cir. 1992); Landsing Diversified Props.-II v. First Nat'l Bank (In re Western Real Estate Fund, Inc.), 922 F.2d 592, 601 n. 7 (10th Cir. 1990), modified, 932 F.2d 898 (10th Cir. 1991); Owaski v. Jet Fla. Sys., Inc. (In re Jet Fla. Sys., Inc.), 883 F.2d 970 (11th Cir. 1989); cf. In re Loewen Group, Inc., No. Civ.A. 98-6740, 2004 WL 1853137 (E.D. Pa. 2004) (allowing securities violation suit to proceed against debtor solely to establish liability so that co-defendants could be held responsible under "uncollectible share" provision of PSLRA). But see Citibank v. White Motor Corp. (In re White Motor Credit), 761 F.2d 270 (6th Cir. 1985); cf. DePippo v. Kmart Corp., 335 B.R. 290 (S.D.N.Y. 2005) (refusing to allow suit for racial discrimination claim to proceed against discharged debtor to reach insurance, where debtor had $2 million retained limit that debtor apparently would have to pay before insurance would have applied to cover any excess over $2 million); Greiner v. Colum. Gas Transmision Corp. (In re Colum. Gas Transmission Corp.), 219 B.R. 716 (S.D.W. Va. 1998) (refusing to allow suit to proceed where insurance would only be obligated to pay excess over $200,000 and only if debtor were "legally obligated to pay" the $200,000, because, inter alia, discharge prevented debtor from being legally obligated to pay that amount). and prevented personally injury tort claimant from holding that suit could refusing to allow .

The question then is whether the court has power to give permanent protection to third parties such as guarantors, partners, and liability insurance companies. If not, the third parties may not be willing to make the contributions of funds or other property that may be necessary for a successful reorganization.

Courts split several ways on the question whether a § 105(a) injunction or a plan provision may permissibly provide permanent protection to third parties—the equivalent of a release or discharge. See Gillman v. Cont'l Airlines (In re Cont'l Airlines), 203 F.3d 203 (3d Cir. 2000); In re Greate Bay Hotel & Casino, 251 B.R. 213 (Bankr. D.N.J. 2000) (striking third party release provisions from proposed plans and relying on severance provisions in plans to allow their consideration without the offending clauses). In *Gillman* the court canvassed the various approaches and then held that

> the provision in the Continental Debtors' plan releasing and permanently enjoining Plaintiffs' lawsuits against the non-debtor D&O defendants does not pass muster under even the most flexible tests for the validity of non-debtor releases. The hallmarks of permissible non-consensual releases—fairness, necessity to the reorganization, and specific factual findings to support these conclusions—are all absent here.

954   PART V

RESTRUCTURING DEBTS AND DIVIDING VALUE

Id. at 214. See also Neely, *The Continuing Debate Re: Non-Debtor Releases/Permanent Injunctions in Chapter 11*, in CHAPTER 11 BUSINESS REORGANIZATIONS 541 (Annual ALI-ABA Advanced Course of Study, No. SK092, 2005), available at SK092 ALI-ABA 541 (Westlaw) (hereinafter *"Continuing Debate"*).

Some courts take the very hard line position that they lack subject matter jurisdiction to consider the release of third parties. See In re Davis Broad., Inc., 176 B.R. 290 (M.D. Ga. 1994); In re Digital Impact, Inc., 223 B.R. 1 (Bankr. N.D. Okla. 1998); cf. In re Combustion Eng'g, Inc., 391 F.3d 190, 227 (3d Cir. 2004) (stating that (1) mere common ownership of debtor and affiliated companies that would be protected from asbestos suits by channeling injunction did not create "related to" subject matter jurisdiction in absence of indemnity relationship, shared insurance or other factors, and (2) that holding company's requirement that affiliated companies be protected as a condition to holding company's contribution to fund for payment of asbestos victims did not create jurisdiction, because parties' consent could not confer jurisdiction). Others hold simply that § 524(e) precludes the granting of permanent protection to nondebtor third parties. See Resorts Int'l, Inc. v. Lowenschuss (In re Lowenschuss), 67 F.3d 1394 (9th Cir. 1995) (affirming district court decision vacating third party release provisions and stating, "This court has repeatedly held, without exception, that § 524(e) precludes bankruptcy courts from discharging the liabilities of non-debtors."); Am. Hardwoods, Inc. v. Deutsche Credit Corp. (In re Am. Hardwoods, Inc.), 885 F.2d 621 (9th Cir. 1989) (holding that subject matter jurisdiction existed to grant third party release but that such an order was precluded by § 524(e)); Landsing Diversified Props.-II v. First Nat'l Bank (In re W. Real Estate Fund, Inc.), 922 F.2d 592, 601 n. 7 (10th Cir. 1990), modified, 932 F.2d 898 (10th Cir. 1991). Cf. Celotex Corp. v. Edwards, 514 U.S. 300, 115 S. Ct. 1493, 131 L. Ed. 2d 403 (1995) (discussed in footnote 6 below).

Some courts hold that a plan may incorporate an offer by a third party to provide extra consideration to creditors who elect individually to give a release to the third party. See In re Monroe Well Serv., Inc., 80 B.R. 324 (Bankr. E.D. Pa. 1987); cf. In re AOV Indus., 792 F.2d 1140 (D.C. Cir. 1986) (holding that plan impermissibly treated claims in the same class differently by requiring class members to give up any claims against third party in order to receive funds from third party, where one member of class held a claim against third party that was more valuable than claims held by other class members and thus was required to give up more). Other courts hold that any release given on confirmation of the plan is given pursuant to statute, not contract, and therefore is limited by § 524(e) to the debtor only. See Underhill v. Royal, 769 F.2d 1426 (9th Cir. 1985) (holding that court had no power to release third party); Union Carbide Corp. v. Newboles, 686 F.2d 593 (7th Cir. 1982) (same). Such courts might well refuse to give effect to any contract between creditors and a third party formed by way of the plan of reorganization. (However, as noted in the next paragraph, a later Seventh Circuit case seems to have limited the effect of *Union Carbide*.) Courts that deny existence of subject matter jurisdiction to grant third party releases may refuse to permit an agreements for such a release to be incorporated in a plan on the ground that parties may not by agreement confer subject matter jurisdiction on the court. See In re Digital Impact, Inc., 223 B.R. 1 (Bankr. N.D. Okla. 1998). There is also the possibility that if the third party release is to be effective as a matter of contract, rather than as a matter of a court's order, then consideration may be lacking. See id.

Some courts will go a step further than the courts in *Monroe Well Service* and *AOV Industries*, at least where the third party contributes funds to the reorganization, by permitting a plan to provide that any creditor voting to accept the plan will thereby release the third party. See In re Specialty Equip. Cos., 3 F.3d 1043, 1047 (7th Cir. 1993) (seemingly approving release provision; stating that nonconsensual release like the one at issue in *Union Carbide* "may be unwarranted in some circumstances;" noting that courts have approved "consensual and non-coercive" releases of third parties; but also holding that appeal was moot due to substantial consummation of plan); In re Boston Harbor Marina Co., 157 B.R. 726 (Bankr. D. Mass.1993) (denying confirmation because plan provided for release of third parties by all members of accepting classes, not just by creditors who accepted plan).

Other courts take the final step of permitting the plan (or a separate injunction entered by the court under § 105(a)) to force even creditors who vote against the plan to release third parties, as long as the release is important or necessary to reorganization. See SEC v. Drexel Burnham Lambert Group, Inc. (In re Drexel Burnham Lambert Group, Inc.), 960 F.2d 285 (2d Cir. 1992); Menard-Sanford v. Mabey (In re A.H. Robins Co.), 880 F.2d 694 (4th Cir. 1989); MacArthur Co. v. Johns-Manville Corp. (In re Johns-Manville Corp.), 837 F.2d 89 (2d Cir. 1988); In re Heron, Burchette, Ruckert & Rothwell, 148 B.R. 660 (Bankr. D.D.C. 1992). Cf. In re Dow Corning Corp., 280 F.3d 648 (6th Cir. 2002) (setting up seven factors, all of which must be present, before non-consenting creditor could be enjoined, including requirements of identity of interest between debtor and third party (ordinarily due to indemnity relationship) and provision of opportunity for non-settling claimants to recover in full); Feld v. Zale Corp. (In re Zale Corp.), 62 F.3d 746 (5th Cir. 1995) (holding that where plan did not provide another source of recovery, such as a trust to which claims are channeled, bankruptcy court lacked power under § 105 to enter permanent injunction prohibiting action against nondebtor).

Even if the bankruptcy court errs in approving a release of a third party, that error is reviewable only on direct appeal; the court's decision cannot be collaterally attacked. If it is not reversed on appeal, the decision of the bankruptcy judge, however erroneous it might have been, will, under res judicata principles, bar any action against the third party. That is true even if the bankruptcy court did not have subject matter jurisdiction, because the bankruptcy court had jurisdiction to determine its jurisdiction. See Stoll v.

Gottlieb, 305 U.S. 165, 59 S. Ct. 134, 83 L. Ed. 104 (1938) (holding that confirmation of plan providing for release of guarantor barred later state court suit against guarantor under res judicata principles even assuming bankruptcy court did not have subject matter jurisdiction, where issue of subject matter jurisdiction was litigated in the bankruptcy court); Stratosphere Litigation L.L.C. v. Grand Casinos, Inc., 298 F.3d 1137 (9th Cir. 2002); Trulis v. Barton, 107 F.3d 685 (9th Cir. 1995) (holding that district court abused its discretion by refusing to impose sanctions under 28 U.S.C. § 1927 for unsuccessful collateral attack on third party release provided by unappealed confirmed plan); Republic Supply Co. v. Shoaf, 815 F.2d 1046 (5th Cir. 1987) (holding that confirmation of plan that purported to release guarantor was res judicata in action against guarantor where claimant had questioned bankruptcy court's authority to release guarantor); . As the court in *Republic Supply* notes, since deciding Stoll v. Gottlieb, the Supreme Court has determined that a court's judgment is entitled to res judicata effect even if the court had no subject matter jurisdiction and even if the issue of subject matter jurisdiction was not litigated before entry of the judgment. All that is needed is that the party had an *opportunity* to assert the lack of subject matter jurisdiction.[11]

Further, even a direct appeal of a third party release provision may not provide the appellant with effective review of the bankruptcy court's action. If the appellant is unable (as is often the case) to obtain a stay of the confirmation order pending appeal, the plan may quickly be put into effect, with property sold to bona fide purchasers, moneys paid out to creditors, liens cancelled, stock issued, new investments funneled into the reorganized debtor, and other steps taken that could not, in fairness to all the parties involved, be undone. If the third party release is an integral part of the plan—if for example third parties contribute funds or property in reliance on the releases—then the appellate court will dismiss the appeal as moot. See, e.g., In re Specialty Equipment Cos., 3 F.3d 1043 (7th Cir. 1993).

---

11. The Supreme Court dealt with a related issue involving a third party that was liable for the debtor's debt in Celotex Corp. v. Edwards, 514 U.S. 300, 115 S. Ct. 1493, 131 L. Ed. 2d 403 (1995). Edwards had obtained a prepetition judgment against Celotex in the federal district court for the Northern District of Texas. In order to stay enforcement of the judgment pending appeal, Celotex posted a supersedeas bond, with an insurance company promising to pay the judgment if it was affirmed. The Fifth Circuit affirmed the judgment, with its decision becoming final the same day that Celotex filed its bankruptcy petition in the Middle District of Florida (part of the Eleventh Circuit). The bankruptcy court then preliminarily enjoined Edwards from collecting the judgment from the insurance company, thus protecting a third party that was liable on the debtor's debt. The district court for the Northern District of Texas nonetheless permitted Edwards to seek payment from the insurance company. The Fifth Circuit affirmed the district court's decision allowing Edwards to proceed, but the Supreme Court reversed. The preliminary injunction was not a final judgment and thus the Court did not discuss res judicata; the Court did, however, hold, citing *American Hardwoods*, supra, that the bankruptcy court had subject matter jurisdiction to enter the injunction. Because the injunction did not have "only a frivolous pretense to validity," the judgment creditor had to obey it until and unless it was reversed on direct appeal from the bankruptcy court—on appeal to the district court for the Middle District of Florida and then, if necessary, to the Eleventh Circuit. 115 S. Ct. at 1501.

Sometimes a claim asserted by creditors or interest holders against a third party is actually property of the estate. For example, outside bankruptcy, shareholders who claim that an officer or director breached fiduciary duties may sue the officer or director on behalf of the corporation in a derivative action. Nevertheless, if the claim belongs to the corporation, then when the corporation files a bankruptcy petition the claim becomes property of the estate, and the shareholders may not exercise control over it. See § 362(a)(3). If the trustee or debtor in possession, with court approval, settles the claim, the claim will be eliminated, and the court can certainly to enjoin the shareholders from proceeding against the officer or director on the nonexistent claim. See Sobchak v. Am. Nat'l Bank & Trust Co. (In re Ionosphere Clubs, Inc.), 17 F.3d 600 (2d Cir. 1994). Sometimes courts mistakenly apply the same analysis to this issue that they apply to whether a plan may release a third party. See Neely, supra, *Continuing Debate*, at 574; see, e.g., In re Coram Healthcare, Corp., 315 B.R. 321 (Bankr. D. Del. 2004).

Similarly, it would seem that the debtor in possession should be permitted, with the court's approval, to reach a settlement with the debtor's liability insurers under which the insurers contribute to the reorganization for the benefit of tort claimants who might have claims against the insurance policies, and in exchange receive a release of any further obligation to anyone on the insurance policies. The debtor's insurance policies become property of the estate, and it would seem that a settlement with the insurance companies would be an appropriate way of realizing the value of the policies for the estate. That approach has been taken in several cases, particularly in cases involving mass torts. See Menard-Sanford v. Mabey (In re A.H. Robins Co.), 880 F.2d 694 (4th Cir.1989); MacArthur Co. v. Johns-Manville Corp. (In re Johns-Manville Corp.), 837 F.2d 89 (2d Cir. 1988); Unarco Bloomington Factory Workers v. UNR Indus., 124 B.R. 268 (N.D. Ill. 1990).

On the other hand, the debtor (and subsequently the estate) as owner of the liability policies is not the only person with rights in the policies. Under state insurance law (and third party beneficiary contract law), the debtor and the insurance companies would have no right to collusively deny the protection of the policies to persons injured by the debtor's torts; the insurance companies could not pay the debtor for a release of their obligations to the tort claimants. Tort claimants have a right to payment from the liability insurers—a right contingent on the obtaining of a judgment against the debtor and on the policy limits not having been exhausted—but a right nonetheless. That may justify the bankruptcy court in requiring that the tort claimants receive priority over other creditors as to the proceeds of any settlement with the liability insurers. Otherwise the effect will be to grant a release to a third party for the benefit of creditors to whom the third party was not liable. That would seem to violate the policy of § 524(e).

In 1994 Congress added subsections (g) and (h) to § 524 to validate the injunctions entered in the Manville and UNR cases, which involved massive numbers of claims for asbestos-related injuries, and to permit other asbestos manufacturers to confirm similar plans. Of course, the most unusual aspect of the Manville and UNR plans was their creation of trusts to which asbestos claimants would be required to look for recovery and the entry of channeling injunctions requiring even people who would develop asbestos related disease in the future to look only to the trusts for payment. (See discussion in Chapter 9 of this text above.) In addition, however, the injunctions protected officers, directors, insurance companies, and others from being sued, and instead channeled claims against them to the trusts. Those provisions would seem to be validated by § 524(g)(4)(A)(ii) and (h)(1). It has been held that § 105(a) cannot be used to provide third party releases in cases involving asbestos liability where the requirements of § 524(g) are not met. In re Combustion Eng'g, Inc., 391 F.3d 190 (3d Cir. 2004).

D. DUE PROCESS LIMITATIONS ON THE DISCHARGE

Finally, we consider the limits placed on the discharge by the constitutional requirement of due process. We saw in Chapter Nine that due process concerns militate against too broad a reading of the term "claim." If people who have no way of knowing that they will be injured in the future were nevertheless considered to have claims, they would have no way to know that they needed to participate in the case, and their rights would be affected without their having a real opportunity to participate in the case. See In re Piper Aircraft Corp., 162 B.R. 619 (Bankr. S.D. Fla.1994) (reprinted in Chapter Nine), aff'd, 168 B.R. 434 (S.D. Fla. 1994). Whether people who develop asbestos-related disease in the future from asbestos manufactured by Manville or UNR will be bound by their plans of reorganization is an open question. Such people may have had reason to know that they could become ill from past exposure, and the courts in the Manville and UNR cases appointed able representatives for such future health claimants; perhaps that was due process.

Another due process issue arises when a creditor alleges that it did not have sufficient notice of the bar date for filing of claims or of the confirmation hearing and that due process would be violated if the creditor's claim were discharged.

Reliable Electric Co., Inc. v. Olson Construction Company
United States Court of Appeals, Tenth Circuit, 1984
726 F.2d 620

BARRETT, Circuit Judge.
* * *

Between June, 1979, and December, 1979, Reliable was the electrical subcontractor on a construction project; Olson was the general contractor. On December 26, 1979, Reliable withdrew from the project because it felt Olson had breached the subcontract. On January 30, 1980, Reliable filed a petition for voluntary Chapter 11 reorganization in the United States Bankruptcy Court.

Reliable filed a schedule of creditors on February 14, 1980, and amended that schedule on August 28, 1980. Within the schedule, Olson was listed under "Accounts Receivable," but never as a "Creditor."

Sometime between January, 1980, and November, 1980, Jon Clarke, Reliable's attorney, telephoned Charles H. Haines, Jr., Olson's attorney, and informed Mr. Haines that Reliable had instituted Chapter 11 proceedings. However, Olson did not receive any further information from Reliable concerning the proceedings. On November 9, 1980, Reliable filed suit against Olson in Colorado State District Court seeking damages for breach of the subcontract. On or about December 16, 1980, Olson removed the cause to federal bankruptcy court. Thereafter, on December 23, 1980, Olson responded to Reliable's complaint through an Answer and Counterclaim for damages based upon Reliable's alleged prepetition breach of the subcontract.

On January 6, 1981, Reliable filed its Third Amended Plan of Reorganization. The Disclosure Statement attached to this Plan stated that both documents were sent to all of Reliable's known creditors. On January 13, 1981, the bankruptcy court mailed a notice to the scheduled creditors informing them of the time for filing acceptances or rejections of the Plan, of the confirmation hearing, and of the time for filing objections to confirmation. The confirmation hearing was conducted on March 9, 1981, after which the court entered an order confirming Reliable's Third Amended Plan. On March 12, 1981, the court mailed to the scheduled creditors notice of the confirmation order and discharge of Reliable. Because Olson was not a scheduled creditor, it did not receive any of these notices.

On August 6, 1981, trial was held on the subcontract dispute between Reliable and Olson. On August 10, 1981, the bankruptcy court entered judgment dismissing Reliable's complaint and granting Olson recovery against Reliable in the amount of $10,378.00. Reliable then filed a claim in the Chapter 11 proceeding on behalf of Olson for $10,378.00 pursuant to Bankruptcy Interim Rule 3004. Reliable also filed a motion in the same proceeding to allow the claim of Olson. Further, Reliable filed a motion in the subcontract litigation to amend the judgment, requesting that the court specifically find the $10,378.00 judgment for Olson be determined a prepetition debt subject to compromise and payment as a general unsecured claim under the confirmed Plan of Reorganization and, thus, subject to discharge. The bankruptcy court issued an order, containing findings of fact and conclusions of law, denying Reliable's motions. The court found that because Reliable failed to schedule Olson as a creditor and failed to notify Olson of the confirmation hearing and because Olson's claim would be substantially impaired without due process of law if it were forced to comply with the Plan, Olson's claim was not subject to the confirmed Plan and, therefore, not discharged. The district court denied Reliable's petition for review of the bankruptcy court's ruling.

The issues on appeal are (1) whether Reliable's failure to give Olson reasonable notice of the bankruptcy confirmation hearing constituted a denial of due process, and (2) if we find a denial of due process, whether the district court erred by finding Olson's claim not to be subject to the Plan and, thus, not dischargeable.

I.

11 U.S.C. § 1128(a) provides: "After notice, the court shall hold a hearing on confirmation of a plan." This section requires notice to be given to all parties in interest. 5 Collier on Bankruptcy Para. 1128.01[2] (15th ed. 1983). After Olson filed the counterclaim against Reliable on December 23, 1980, Reliable was put on notice of Olson's status as a potential creditor. Despite this, no formal notice of any kind regarding the reorganization proceedings, or the time and manner of filing a claim, was ever given to Olson prior to the confirmation hearing. The apparent notice given to Olson prior to the counterclaim filing was inadequate notice of the confirmation hearing. Although Olson's attorney was generally aware of Reliable's involvement in reorganization proceedings, Olson was essentially denied the opportunity to be heard at the confirmation hearing.

The Supreme Court has repeatedly held that "[a]n elementary and fundamental requirement of due process in any proceeding which is to be accorded finality is notice reasonably calculated, under all the circumstances, to apprise interested parties of the pendency of the action and afford them an opportunity to present their objections." Mullane v. Central Hanover Trust Co., 339 U.S. 306, 314, 70 S. Ct. 652, 657, 94 L. Ed. 865 (1950) * * * As specifically applied to bankruptcy reorganization proceedings, the Court has held that a creditor, who has general knowledge of a debtor's reorganization proceeding, has no duty to inquire about further court action. The creditor has a "right to assume" that he will receive all of the notices required by statute before his claim is forever barred. New York v. New York, New Haven & Hartford R.R. Co., 344 U.S. 293, 297, 73 S. Ct. 299, 301, 97 L. Ed. 333 (1953). See also In re Intaco Puerto Rico, Inc., 494 F.2d 94, 99 (1st Cir. 1974); In re Harbor Tank Storage Co., Inc., 385 F.2d 111, 115 (3d Cir. 1967). Thus, Olson acted reasonably when it expected the same formal notice of the confirmation hearing which was sent to other identifiable creditors. Inasmuch as Olson was deprived of the opportunity to comment on Reliable's Third Amended Plan of Reorganization, it was denied due process of law.

II.

Reliable's primary contention is that, even if Olson was not given the requisite notice, Olson is still subject to the confirmed Plan as are all of the other creditors. Reliable argues that 11 U.S.C. § 1141(d) discharges *all* claims, whether a proof of claim has been filed, whether such claim is allowed, or whether the claimholder has accepted the plan. Further, Reliable contends that an "all-encompassing" discharge is necessary to meet the purpose of reorganization to give the debtor a "fresh start." Thus, Reliable urges that the only remedy available to Olson is to file a late claim under the confirmed Plan.

Sections 1141(c) and (d) ostensibly allow *any* claim to be discharged even though the claimholder has not received notice of the proceeding or of the confirmation hearing. However, we hold that notwithstanding the language of section 1141, the discharge of a claim without reasonable notice of the confirmation hearing is violative of the fifth amendment to the United States Constitution. See 5 Collier on Bankruptcy Para. 1141.01[b], at 1141-12. In our view, this holding is supported by the Supreme Court's decisions in *Mullane*, supra, and *New York*, supra, and by two other circuit court opinions which applied this reasoning specifically to bankruptcy reorganization proceedings. See In re Intaco, supra; In re Harbor Tank, supra. Inasmuch as we have held the notice by Reliable to Olson was deficient, the district court's decision was not contrary to law; Olson's claim cannot be bound to the Plan and, thus, it is not dischargeable.

A fundamental right guaranteed by the Constitution is the opportunity to be heard when a property interest is at stake. Specifically, the reorganization process depends upon all creditors and interested parties being properly notified of all vital steps in the proceeding so they may have the opportunity to protect their interests.[12] We will not require Olson to subject its claim to a confirmed reorganization plan that it had no opportunity to dispute.[13]

WE AFFIRM.

NOTES

1.   Olson knew Reliable was in chapter 11. Is it too much to expect Olson to have inquired about what was happening in the case? For views that contrast with *Reliable Electric*, see Sequa Corp. v. Christopher (In re Christopher), 28 F.3d 512 (5th Cir.1994), and Lawrence Tractor Co. v. Gregory (In re Gregory), 705 F.2d 1118, 1123 (9th Cir.1983) (holding in chapter 13 case that notice of existence of bankruptcy case place creditor "under constructive or inquiry notice that its claim may be affected, and it ignores the proceedings * * * at its peril"). In *Christopher* a chapter 11 debtor entered into business dealings with Sequa, which knew he was in chapter 11. The dealings resulted in Sequa filing suit in state court against the debtor for damages, including damages for alleged fraud. The debtor then failed to give Sequa notice of the deadline for filing objections to the debtor's plan and notice of the confirmation hearing. The court distinguished the Supreme Court's *New York* decision (discussed in *Reliable Electric*) as being a statutory decision based on a specific old Bankruptcy Act requirement of notice rather than a constitutional decision. The court noted that all of the parties agreed that nothing in the Bankruptcy Code explicitly required notice to be given to a postpetition claimant like Sequa. The court held that Sequa's knowledge of the chapter 11 case was sufficient to place the burden on it of inquiring about deadlines; thus Sequa's claim was discharged. *Reliable*

---

12. [Note 5 in original:] Reliable asserts that even if Olson had voted to reject the Third Amended Plan, the Plan would still have been approved. This overwhelming approval of the Plan by other creditors does not justify depriving Olson of its guaranteed due process right. See Coe v. Armour Fertilizer Works, 237 U.S. 413, 424, 35 S. Ct. 625, 629, 59 L. Ed. 1027 (1915).

13. [Note 6 in original:] * * * Further, Reliable attempts to distinguish *New York*, In re Intaco and In re Harbor Tank on the basis that those decisions did not hold that a defective notice of a confirmation hearing rendered the creditor's claim nondischargeable; those cases held only that the creditor without sufficient notice may untimely file a claim over the debtor's objection. Such distinction does not affect the application of those cases to the facts presented in the instant case. First, Reliable, not Olson, filed the request that Olson's claim be allowed under the Plan. Second, Reliable had already fully distributed the payable assets to Class 4 unsecured creditors (the group Olson would belong to) at the time it moved to force Olson's claim to be subject to the Plan. Under these circumstances, we agree with the bankruptcy court that "Olson's claim against Reliable will be substantially impaired if Olson must share in the distribution of the debtor's assets on the percentage basis allowed to other unsecured creditors of the debtor in the reorganization plan." Due process does not allow such a result without reasonable notice and an opportunity to be heard.

Finally, Reliable argues strenuously that for us to uphold the finding of the district court would defeat the purpose of Chapter 11--to give the bankrupt debtor a "fresh start." As we noted in the text of this opinion, sections 1141(c) and (d) do appear to be "all-encompassing" as applied to creditor's claims. Even so, Olson's guaranteed right to due process is paramount under the circumstances presented in this case.

Electric is criticized in Klee & Merola, *Ignoring Congressional Intent: Eight Years of Judicial Legislation*, 62 AM. BANKR. L.J. 1, 22-27 (1988).

2. Other cases holding claims nondischargeable because of failure to give notice of particular deadlines or hearings include Dalton Dev. Project #1 v. Unsecured Cred. Comm. (In re Unioil), 948 F.2d 678 (10th Cir.1991) (holding that postpetition claim was not discharged because claimant did not receive formal notice of claims bar date, of deadline for filing objections to plan, and of confirmation hearing); and Spring Valley Farms, Inc. v. Crow (In re Spring Valley Farms, Inc.), 863 F.2d 832 (11th Cir.1989) (holding that claims were not discharged where debtor knew of claims, creditors knew of chapter 11 case but did not have actual knowledge of claims bar date, and debtor did not give creditors the mandatory notice of claims bar date). Cf. Broomall Indus. v. Data Design Logic Sys., Inc., 786 F.2d 401 (Fed. Cir. 1986) (denying summary judgment sought by debtor even though claimant who may not have known of bankruptcy case intentionally held off asserting patent infringement claim for several years). Where the debtor is an individual, the court may apply a different standard, allowing a creditor's debt to be discharged, even if the creditor does not receive notice of particular important dates, if the creditor simply knew that the debtor was in bankruptcy. See *Spring Valley*, 863 F.2d 832, 833-34. Is there a principled basis for varying the constitutional requirements of due process based on whether the debtor is an individual? Is this approach consistent with Congress' intent that corporations and partnerships receive broader discharges than individuals in chapter 11?

3. Publication provides sufficient notice to satisfy due process where the claimant is "unknown," but a "known" claimant is entitled to actual notice of the confirmation hearing. See, e.g., Berger v. Trans World Airlines, Inc. (In re Trans World Airlines, Inc.), 96 F.3d 687 (3d Cir. 1996) (also distinguishing *Reliable Electric* on ground that *Reliable Electric* had not considered effect of bar date). "A creditor will be deemed to be 'known' to the debtor if the debtor has either actual knowledge of its existence or if its identity 'can be identified through reasonably diligent efforts.' " Id. at 690 (quoting Chemetron Corp. v. Jones, 72 F.3d 341, 346 (3d Cir. 1995)). On a further appeal after remand in *Chemetron*, the Third Circuit held that the "unknown creditors" as to whom publication was sufficient notice had not demonstrated excusable neglect. Thus their toxic tort claims, filed four years after the bar date, could not be allowed. However, one of the toxic tort claimants had not been born until two years after confirmation of the plan. The unborn claimant could not have received notice from the publication, and thus discharge of his claim would violate due process. At least that result was required where no representative had been appointed in the case to represent such unborn, future claimants. Jones v. Chemetron Corp., 212 F.3d 199 (3d Cir. 2000).

4. Under § 1141(c), with exceptions for nondischarged debts, "except as otherwise provided in the plan or in the order confirming the plan, after confirmation of the plan, the property dealt with by the plan is free and clear of all claims and interests." Thus "[a] confirmed bankruptcy plan may extinguish a lien." Am. Bank & Trust Co. v. Jardine Ins. Servs. Tex., Inc. (In re Barton Indus., Inc.), 104 F.3d 1241 (9th Cir. 1997). If a plan fails to provide for a valid lien to continue, the holder of the affected secured claim could, in most cases, block confirmation by voting against the plan (which ordinarily would cause its class to reject the plan), and then by objecting that the secured claim class was not receiving fair and equitable treatment. See § 1129(b)(2)(A). What kind of notice does due process be given to such a secured creditor before § 1141(c) will be permitted to extinguish its lien? Compare *Barton Industries* with Universal Suppliers, Inc. v. Reg'l Bldg. Sys., Inc. (In re Reg'l Bldg. Sys., Inc.), 254 F.3d 528 (4th Cir. 2001).

APPENDIX

Appendix A: Deborah Bell's Explanation of Foam Corporation's Financial Statements

Deborah Bell, Foam Corp.'s chief financial officer, handed William Gruff, Foam's chief executive officer, a copy of the financial statement summaries set forth on pages 52-53 above. She explained that the full-blown financial statements would include more detail and would be followed by several pages of notes. Even so, the summaries follow the same pattern that the detailed statements follow; if Gruff could understand the summaries, he would be prepared for the more arduous task of working through the detailed statements, if that should be necessary.

Financial statements are prepared by a company's own internal accounting personnel or by outside accountants hired to do the job. Once the statements have been prepared, independent accountants are usually hired to "audit" the statements, if the company is of substantial size or has issued publicly held stock securities. The auditors review the statements to see if they follow generally accepted accounting principles ("GAAP"), established by the Financial Accounting Standards Board ("FASB").[1] The auditors do not check the accuracy of everything in the statements, but they do sample and analytically review the financial records to the extent necessary for the auditors to be satisfied that the financial statements either do or do not fairly present the company's financial position and operating results in accordance with "GAAP." Once the audit is complete, the accountants will issue a report based on their examination. If their examination concludes that the financial statements fairly present the company's financial position and results of operation, an unqualified report will be issued to convey the results of the examination. The financial statements Bell brought to Gruff were unaudited.

Bell said it was important to note that the financial statements are "consolidated;" that is, that they were prepared on a "consolidated basis." Consolidated financial statements treat a corporation and its subsidiaries as if they were one enterprise. All of their assets and liabilities are listed on the financial statements as if they were all owned and owed by one company. Thus, even though U Foam is legally a separate person, the financial statements lump together U Foam's and Foam Corporation's assets and liabilities.

Bell then explained three of the basic financial statements:

a. The Balance Sheet

The balance sheet provides a snapshot at a moment in time, in this case 12/31/2005. The snapshot shows three things: (1) what Foam Corporation owns (the assets), (2) what Foam Corporation owes (the liabilities), and (3) what is left over for Foam Corporation's shareholders (shareholders' equity). Creditors are entitled to be paid ahead of shareholders out of the corporation's assets, so shareholders' equity equals the dollar amount of the assets minus the amount of

---

1. The FASB may delegate to the Accounting Standards Executive Committee ("AcSEC") of the American Institute of Certified Public Accountants ("AICPA") the right to develop standards in some specialized areas. For example, AcSEC was responsible for issuing Statement of Position 90-7 ("SOP 90-7") dealing with financial reporting by companies in chapter 11 and on emergence from chapter 11. Prior to the AcSEC's issuance of SOP 90-7, it was reviewed by the FASB, as is true with most statements issued by AcSEC. The Securities and Exchange Commission ("SEC") has delegated to the FASB the requirements to establish accounting standards, but the SEC does issue regulations regarding accounting disclosures.

the liabilities (SE = A - L). A little basic arithmetic shows that the dollar amount of the assets must then equal the total of the liabilities and shareholders' equity (A = L + SE). (For example, if assets are listed at $10, and liabilities are $6, then shareholders' equity by definition is the difference, $4. The sum of the $6 in liabilities and $4 in shareholders' equity equals the $10 in assets.) That is why this statement is called a "balance" sheet; the dollar amount of assets shown on the left side of the balance sheet must "balance" (be equal to) the total of the liabilities and shareholders' equity shown on the right side. Note that Foam Corporation's balance sheet does balance; the total is $14,900,000 on both sides.

Another way of thinking about the balance sheet is to think of the left side as showing what Foam Corporation has, and the right side as showing who is entitled to how much of it. The creditors are entitled to as much of the value of Foam Corporation as they need to pay off their debts in full, and the shareholders are entitled to whatever is left over.

Of course, this balance sheet shows that Foam Corporation does not have as much in assets as it has in debts; Foam Corporation is insolvent, according to the balance sheet. Look for the "(4,600)" on the right side of the balance sheet just above the total of "$14,900." (Note that numbers in parentheses represent negative numbers.) That means the shareholders' equity is negative in the amount of 4,600 thousand dollars ($4.6 million). The shareholders are "in the hole" or "under water" that much. Foam Corporation would need to earn more than $4.6 million in profits in order to have more assets than liabilities, so there would be something left over for the shareholders.

The balance sheet shows $14.9 million for Foam Corporation's assets, but that must be taken with caution. The $14.9 million is the "book value" of Foam Corporation's assets, meaning that the assets are listed or carried in Foam Corporation's accounting records at that value, but the market value of the assets may be more or less than that. For example, there is nothing on the balance sheet for "value of well-trained work force" even though the money spent to train the workers helps to give value to Foam Corporation's assets as a going business. Another example is that Foam Corporation's equipment and real estate ("property, plant, and equipment") appears on the balance sheet at an amount equal to what Foam Corporation paid for it, minus depreciation. The equipment may have been made nearly obsolete by advances in technology or it may not be usable if new pollution regulations under consideration are adopted; in either case its actual value may be much less than the "book value" shown on the balance sheet. Fluctuations in the real estate market may cause Foam Corporation's real estate to be worth much more or much less than what Foam Corporation paid for it; the balance sheet will not show the present market value of the land. (However, if there has been an impairment (decline) in the value of an asset, the financial statements, under certain circumstances, may be modified to reflect that decline.) A balance sheet does not purport to show the value of a business enterprise but, together with other financial statements and other information, should provide information that is useful to those who desire to make their own estimates of the enterprise's value.[2]

---

2.   FASB, *Statement of Financial Accounting Concepts No. 5: Recognition and Measurement in Financial Statements* (Norwak, Ct.: FASB, 1984), ¶¶ 26-27.

Bell explained that they would need to look more closely at the balance sheet. First, though, she said she would introduce Gruff to the statement of operations, because "the balance sheet and statement of operations are so interrelated that it is hard to understand one without the other."

b. The Statement of Operations (or Income Statement)

The balance sheet is a snapshot as of a particular date of what Foam Corporation has and who is entitled to it. By contrast, the statement of operations covers a period of time, in this case the calendar year 2005. The statement of operations shows what Foam Corporation's profit or loss was for that period. (Often the statement of operations is called the "income statement;" Foam Corporation did not earn income but instead lost $5 million during 2005, so the term "statement of operations" is more appropriate than "income statement.")

(1) Revenue

The first part of the statement of operations shows the amount of money to which Foam Corporation became entitled during 2005, Foam Corporation's "revenue." In Foam Corporation's case, its only source of revenue was sales of its products, so the only entry for revenue is the amount of Foam Corporation's "net sales," $30 million. (The term "net" means that it does not include sales where the customer returned the product to Foam Corporation or where for some other reason the customer is not likely to pay for the products.)

Foam Corporation became *entitled* to $30 million for sales of its products, and likely will eventually collect the whole $30 million, but that does not mean Foam Corporation actually collected the $30 million during 2005. Foam Corporation sells its products on credit to its customers, and some of the $30 million was not due yet from the customers (or at least they had not yet paid it) as of 12/31/95. GAAP requires the use of a concept called "accrual" under an item is considered revenue when Foam Corporation has done all or virtually all that it has to do to earn the revenue and when an exchange transaction such as a sale has occurred. For example, if Foam Corporation contracts to sell five tons of foam cushions to a customer, Foam Corporation has earned the contract price when Foam Corporation ships the goods; at that point the amount of that sale will go into revenue for purposes of the financial statements, even if the customer has thirty or sixty days to pay for the foam.

(2) Expenses

The statement of operations goes on to list the various expenses that Foam Corporation incurred during 2005. Expenses are defined as outflows or other using up of assets or incurring of liabilities (or a combination of both) during a period from delivering or producing goods, rendering services, or carrying out other activities that constitute the entity's ongoing major or central operations.[3]

---

3.   FASB, *Statement of Financial Accounting Concepts No. 6: Elements of Financial Statements of Business Enterprises* (Norwak, Ct.: FASB, 1985), ¶ 80.

Foam Corporation's largest expense for 2005 was $20 million for "cost of goods sold." The accrual method is used for determining the expenses associated with the goods that are sold, just as the accrual method was used for revenue from sale of the goods. The cost of producing an item of inventory is not considered to be an expense until the item is sold. For example, the cost of buying ten tons of chemicals for foam production will not be considered an expense until Foam Corporation sells the foam that it makes from the chemicals. After all, Foam Corporation did not lose the money it spent on the chemicals; rather the money was used to buy another asset, the chemicals, which Foam Corporation still has; when the chemicals are turned into foam, Foam Corporation will still have the foam. Foam Corporation does not actually lose the value of the chemicals until the foam made with the chemicals leaves Foam Corporation's hands.

Bell told Gruff that she was not trying to turn Gruff into an accountant, but she hoped he could see that it made sense to try to match up expenses with the revenue generated as a result of those expenses, so that a company could see whether it was making money—she explained that the accrual method is designed to do that.

Thus the $20 million figure for cost of goods sold represents the cost to Foam Corporation of the goods (chemicals), services (labor, engineering consultants, etc.), and use of property, plant, and equipment that went into producing the goods that were shipped during 2005. (The cost of using property, plant, and equipment owned by Foam Corporation is called depreciation, which is discussed below; the cost of using property, plant, and equipment owned by others and leased by the debtor is the amount of the rent for 2005.)

The next item of expense for 2005 was selling expenses of $6 million. Selling expensesincluded salary and commissions of salespersons, reimbursement of travel expenses for salespersons, and other expenses related to the sale of Foam Corporation's products.

General and administrative expenses for 2005 were $8 million and included the salaries of Gruff and the other managers, professional fees incurred for legal and accounting work, salaries of Foam Corporation's bookkeepers, and all the costs of administering a company, down to the cost of paying for the janitorial services to keep the offices clean.[4]

The expenses we have discussed thus far—cost of goods sold, selling expenses, and general and administrative expenses—are called the "operating expenses." These are the expenses that are incurred in operating the business; it may be possible to reduce these expenses in the future, but they are the kind of expenses that must be incurred for the business to continue operations. "Operating profit" (or loss) is the difference between revenue from operations and the operating expenses. Foam Corporation's loss from operations in 2005 was $4 million as shown below (all numbers in thousands):

---

4. Janitorial services to keep the factories clean, on the other hand, are allocated as part of the cost of goods sold. If the same janitor works in both factory and administrative office areas, then the janitor's wages are divided between "cost of goods sold" and "general and administrative expense." Allocating costs among different kinds of expenses—"cost accounting"—can be very involved.

Net sales		$30,000
Cost of goods sold	$20,000	
Selling expenses	6,000	
General and administrative expenses	8,000	
Total operating expenses	34,000	
Net loss from operations		$ (4,000)

Note that operating profit or loss was determined without considering income taxes.

Beyond operating expenses, Foam Corporation had additional expenses, which are listed in the statement of operations. Interest on Foam Corporation's various debts totaled $1.5 million during 2005.[5] Foam Corporation also sold some surplus equipment during 2005 for $600,000 less than its book value, so Foam Corporation had a $600,000 loss on the sale, which is considered an expense. (Foam Corporation is not in the business of selling equipment so the money from the sale is not included in revenue, and the cost of the equipment is not included in cost of goods sold. Instead, gains or losses from sale of equipment are treated as incidental gains or losses.[6]) Foam Corporation had a "negative expense" of $1.1 million in the form of an entitlement to a tax refund of some of the income taxes Foam Corporation paid in past years. Foam Corporation is entitled to the refund due to the losses Foam Corporation suffered in 2005. (Taxes are considered an expense, so the right to a tax refund is a "negative expense," which of course is beneficial to the company; tax refunds are not included in the revenue portion of the statement of operations because Foam Corporation is not in the business of generating tax refunds.)

All together, Foam Corporation's expenses exceeded its revenues by $5 million, so Foam Corporation lost $5 million in 2005.

Gruff interrupted Bell to ask where the expense for depreciation was on the statement of operations, and "What is depreciation anyway?" Bell said it would be best to answer that question by going back to the balance sheet and going through it line by line. She asked Gruff to be patient and promised she would eventually answer his question.

c. Balance Sheet Revisited

(1) Assets

The left side of the balance sheet lists assets. The concept of an "asset" seems simple enough—something of value owned by someone, in this case Foam Corporation. GAAP defines assets using a more obscure definition: a probable future economic benefit obtained or controlled by a particular entity as a result of past transactions or events. Furthermore, assets are divided into two major categories, current and noncurrent.

---

5. Note that under the accrual method there is a $1.5 million interest expense whether or not Foam Corporation actually paid the interest during 2005. However, if Foam were in chapter 11, interest would generally not accrue unless the debt was secured by property with a value in excess of the debt, or unless Foam was solvent and able to pay all debts plus interest. Note also that payment of all or part of the principal amount of a debt is not considered to be an expense. The payment uses up an asset—cash—but it eliminates just as great an amount of the liabilities, and it does not have a net negative effect on the net worth of the company.

6. However, if Foam Corporation had filed a bankruptcy petition at the time of the sale of the equipment, the gain or loss on sale would be a "reorganization item."

(a) Current Assets

Current assets include cash and other assets that are reasonably expected to be realized in cash, sold, or consumed by the business within a year (or during the normal operating cycle of the business if it typically takes the business more than a year to go through the cycle of investment, production, and sale of an item of goods or services). As Foam Corporation's balance sheet illustrates, current assets are listed first. Included in current assets are:

1. Cash or its equivalent. Foam Corporation has $800,000 of cash as of 12/31/05.
2. Marketable securities (stock, bonds, etc.) issued by other companies. Foam Corporation has no marketable securities so the balance sheet omits this category.
3. Receivables due within a year, including accounts receivable (money owed by Foam Corporation's customers but not evidenced by a promissory note for goods delivered or services rendered) and short term promissory notes (which typically would be for money owed by customers but could be for other debts owed to Foam Corporation). The balance sheet shows that Foam Corporation had $6.3 million in receivables as of 12/31/05, all of which happened to be accounts receivable. Receivables are shown on the balance sheet at their net "realizable" value; allowance has been made for customers who will not pay, so the $6.3 million is the amount Foam Corporation expects that it will actually collect.[7]
4. Inventories, including supplies, raw materials, work-in-process, and finished goods. Foam Corporation has inventory listed at $2.7 million on the balance sheet. Items of inventory are valued for financial statement purposes at the lower of what they cost Foam Corporation or their market value. (Due to inflation, the lower of cost or market value is usually cost, unless the items have become unpopular or obsolete or have deteriorated.) In a distress sale, inventory often brings far less than its book value. This is especially true of unfinished "work-in-process."
5. Prepaid expenses, such as prepaid insurance or prepayment for supplies which have not yet been delivered. Gruff exclaimed in exasperation that he did not see how an "expense" could be an asset. Bell explained that the asset consists of the value of the insurance coverage or supplies which have already been paid for and which Foam Corporation will benefit from in the future. Of course the payment that Foam Corporation made reduced one kind of asset (cash), but the payment entitled Foam Corporation to receive a benefit in the future, and that benefit is an asset. Foam Corporation in fact paid $100,000 for insurance coverage that will extend past 12/31/05 (the date of the balance sheet) and for supplies and miscellaneous services that it will obtain after 12/31/05, so Foam Corporation has an asset, prepaid expenses, listed on the balance sheet at $100,000.

---

7. Bell pointed out that if Foam Corporation were to cease its business operations, the accounts receivable would become much harder to collect. Customers who did not look forward to a continuing relationship would have less reason to pay and more reason to find fault with the goods that were delivered. Other customers would hope that the debts they owed might be overlooked in the turmoil resulting from Foam Corporation's demise. Costs of collection could eat up a substantial part of the value of the accounts.

Bell asked if Gruff had any questions, and he asked, "You said the value for inventory on the balance sheet depends on what it cost us to make it. How do we know at any time how much it cost us to produce the items that are in our inventory? Because of inflation, the items we produced in May probably cost us more than the items we produced in January. That means we can't just count up how many waterbeds we have in our warehouse, for example, and just multiply that number by a fixed cost; we would need to know which items are still in our inventory and how much it cost us to make each of them in order to know what to put on the 'Inventory' line in the balance sheet. How can we keep track of exactly which items are sold and which are still in the warehouse?"

Bell responded that it could be done with modern computer inventory systems, but that in the past it would have been very difficult to do. As a result, accountants worked out several physical flow approaches (which are still used) that did not require a company to keep track of exactly which items were sold.

One approach was to use the "first-in-first-out" (FIFO—pronounced "FIE-foe") method. The accountants would pretend that the oldest inventory in the warehouse was always the inventory that was shipped out; they did not care whether the shipping clerk actually took the oldest or not. A company which uses the FIFO method pretends the warehouse is like a pipeline; the new inventory goes in one end of the pipe and does not come out the other end to be sold until all the older inventory has come out first and been sold.

The problem with the FIFO method is that it tends to overstate income during inflationary periods. Suppose it cost a company $1 to make an item during 2005, and $1.10 during 2006; suppose the company makes and sells 100 items per year and keeps an inventory of 50 at all times. Under the FIFO method the first 50 items sold in 2006 would be the 50 items made in 2005 that were in inventory at the end of 2005. The company would be selling those items at inflated 2006 prices, for, say $1.75 per item. If we consider the expense associated with those items to be the old $1 cost of production, as we would under the FIFO method, then each sale will generate a gain of 75 cents (not counting the costs of selling the items). At the same time, though, the company is having to spend $1.10 to make new items to replace the old ones; to get back to having 50 items in inventory, the company will have to spend the $1.10 per item, so in a sense it costs the company $1.10 per item to sell the old ones.

Another physical flow approach assumes that the newest items of inventory are sold first. This approach is called the last-in-first-out (LIFO) method. A company which uses the LIFO method pretends that the warehouse is like a long narrow room with only one door, located at one of the narrow ends. New inventory is put in the door, in front of the inventory that is already in the warehouse. When the shipping clerk gets inventory out of the warehouse to ship to a customer, the clerk does not struggle to take the old inventory from the back, but instead takes whatever is in front, which of course is the newest inventory. (This is something like what happens with the bread or yogurt at a poorly run grocery store.)

Going back to our example, the items sold in 2006 would be presumed to be the newest ones. That would mean that their cost would be the up-to-date $1.10. Thus each sale at $1.75 would generate only 65 cents of income. This approach takes into account the cost of replacing the items that are sold, and most accountants think it is superior to the FIFO method. LIFO also results in the inventory being valued on the balance sheet at a lower figure than under a FIFO method during times of inflation; the inventory in the warehouse is considered to be the oldest, and hence the lowest cost, inventory.

A third physical flow assumption is that of average costs. Under this approach it is assumed that all inventory items are mixed together, just as liquid products such as chemical solvents would be mixed together if they were placed in the same storage tank. When the company ships products, it is assumed to ship a combination of inventory from various purchases or production batches.

(b) Noncurrent Assets

Bell continued by explaining that noncurrent assets are assets the value of which Foam Corporation will probably not fully obtain in cash within a year. Noncurrent assets include:

1. Investments and funds. Included in this category are assets normally acquired for financial or investment purposes, rather than for business operations. They include long term loans made by Foam Corporation (for example, Foam Corporation might have lent one of its officers $15,000 to help with the down payment on a home), cash surrender value of life insurance policies, and funds set aside for future expansion. Also included would be investments in land for future plant expansion. Foam Corporation does not have any investments, so the balance sheet omits this category.[8]

2. Tangible operating assets. To be classified in this section, the asset must have physical substance and be held for productive use in business operations. Assets in this category are frequently labeled "property, plant, and equipment" (as on Foam Corporation's balance sheet) or "property and equipment." Tangible operating assets include land, buildings, machinery, equipment, tools, fixtures, and leasehold improvements. Leasehold improvements represent expenditures made by the lessee to improve property that is being rented; at the end of the lease, the improvements (assuming they cannot be removed) will revert to the landlord. Tangible operating assets are shown on the balance sheet at a value equal to what they cost Foam Corporation, $6.5 million, minus depreciation.

3. Intangible assets. This category includes long term rights and privileges of a nonphysical nature. Goodwill, patents, copyrights, and trademarks are the major kinds of intangible operating assets. Patents run for seventeen years, copyrights even longer, and trademarks theoretically have an unlimited life span. Each of these forms of long term, intangible assets may help a company make money. Foam Corporation shows two kinds on its balance sheet: patents and trademarks, for a total book value of $1 million, less amortization.

---

8. Of course Foam Corporation owns the stock of U Foam, which is an investment. However, the financial statements are consolidated, meaning that they treat Foam Corporation and U Foam as one enterprise, so the U Foam stock is not listed as an asset of Foam Corporation. The value of Foam Corporation's investment in U Foam stock is already reflected in the balance sheet, because U Foam's assets are counted in the balance sheet the same as if Foam Corporation owned them. If the U Foam stock were shown on the balance sheet as an asset, the value of the U Foam assets would be counted twice.

Gruff said Foam Corporation's numerous patents and trademarks were worth more than the $1 million (less amortization) shown on the balance sheet. He said the waterbed patent for the kind of waterbed invented by Foam Corporation's engineers and the "Waveless" waterbed trademark developed by Foam Corporation's marketing staff were worth more than $1 million by themselves.

Bell explained that the values of the waterbed patent and of the "Waveless" trademark were not included on the balance sheet because Foam Corporation did not buy them. Current GAAP does not permit subjective valuations of assets; thus they permit a company to show an intangible asset on its books only if the asset was acquired in a transaction that establishes a market value for it as of the time of the transaction.

Foam Corporation purchased several trademarks and patents from their owners, so Foam Corporation is entitled to show those trademarks and patents on its balance sheet at the amount Foam Corporation paid for them (less amortization). Of course Foam Corporation also developed several trademarks and patents "in house," which Foam Corporation owns, including the waterbed patent and the "Waveless" waterbed trademark, but Foam Corporation is not permitted to show those trademarks and patents on its balance sheet. Who could say objectively what, if anything, they are worth, when they were not purchased in an arms' length transaction?

Of course that means the true value of a company's intellectual property (patents, trademarks, copyrights, trade secrets) may differ greatly from the book value shown on the balance sheet.

Goodwill—the last major kind of intangible operating asset—is treated similarly to intellectual property. Goodwill is the difference between the value of a company's assets as a going concern and the total value of the assets (other than goodwill) as shown on the balance sheet. Accountants do not permit companies to set their own valuation for their going concern value and then put the resulting goodwill on their balance sheets. Again it would be very difficult to police the process and make sure that the goodwill was legitimate. Besides, the going concern value of a company is based on how much money it can make; potential investors can review the statement of operations and the statement of cash flows (discussed below) and determine for themselves how much they think the company is worth as a going concern. There is no need to allow the company itself to make that judgment and thus manufacture an asset for the balance sheet.

Once again, however, if the amount of the goodwill is set by a market transaction, it can be listed on the balance sheet. U Foam has the assets Foam Corporation purchased from another company as a going concern for $2 million; that market transaction is good evidence that the assets were worth $2 million. The assets were appraised item by item and that appraised valuation was used as the book value of the assets when they were added to Foam Corporation's consolidated balance sheet. The item by item appraisal totaled only $1.5 million, so Foam Corporation paid $500,000 extra to buy the assets as a going concern. That $500,000 extra then was added to the asset side of Foam Corporation's balance sheet as "goodwill;" it is part of the $1 million listed for "Goodwill, Patents, and Trademarks."

Bell said she could now explain the concepts of depreciation and amortization. Assume Foam Corporation purchased a chemical mixing machine for $100,000 at the beginning of 2006. It would not make sense to consider the whole $100,000 to be an expense of doing business in 2006. The machine will last for ten years, and so the $100,000 in value is not used up during 2006; at the end of 2006 most of the value is still there in the form of a slightly used machine. If the whole $100,000 were considered an expense in 2006, Foam Corporation's profits for 2006 would be artificially reduced. Similarly, if the whole $100,000 were considered an expense in 2006, there would be no expense in 2007 or 2008 or later years connected with using the machine, even though use of it in each of those years is causing it slowly to wear out.

The accountants therefore require Foam Corporation to spread out the cost of purchasing the machine over the number of years that the machine will probably last; they require Foam Corporation to "depreciate" the machine, by taking a yearly amount of "depreciation expense" rather than taking the entire purchase price as an expense in the year of the purchase. That allows us to match up the cost of acquiring and using the machine with the period of time in which the machine is helping Foam Corporation to make money. Thus Foam Corporation is required to "capitalize" the $100,000 purchase in 2006; the purchase is not an "expense" but rather is just a change in the form of Foam Corporation's assets. Foam Corporation's cash goes down by $100,000; Foam Corporation's property, plant, and equipment on its balance sheet goes up by $100,000, and the mere purchase of the machine is not considered to have been an expense of doing business.

Of course, over time, it does cost Foam Corporation the full $100,000 to use the machine (assuming it is worthless when it is worn out, so that Foam Corporation has nothing left to show for its original $100,000). GAAP provides various ways of spreading that $100,000 expense over time based on several factors including those based on time as discussed below and those based on the use of the asset. We will only consider the simplest way of calculating depreciation, the straight line method. Under the straight line method, Foam Corporation decides how long it thinks the machine will last—say, ten years—and then divides the purchase price by that number of years, to get the yearly expense of having purchased and used the machine. Thus Foam Corporation will consider that it has a $10,000 expense of using the machine for each of the ten years. The total expense over ten years then is $100,000, which is the amount the machine cost Foam Corporation.

At the end of 2006, after Foam Corporation has used the new machine for a full year, Foam Corporation's cost of producing inventory during 2006 will include $10,000 of depreciation on the machine. As the inventory produced in 2006 is sold, the cost of producing the inventory will be reported as an expense, and part of that cost will be depreciation expense on the machines used to produce the inventory.[9] Assuming at least some of the inventory produced with the new machine is sold during 2006, the "cost of goods sold" on the 2006 statement of operations will be higher than if there were no depreciation expense on the new machine.

Because Foam Corporation considers that it has cost it $10,000 of the original $100,000 investment to use the machine during 2006, for accounting purposes Foam Corporation will consider that the machine is worth $100,000 minus the $10,000

---

9.   Depreciation on a personal computer used by Gruff in his management function would be included as part of the "general and administrative expense."

depreciation at the end of 2006. Thus the "book value" of the machine on Foam Corporation's balance sheet as of 12/31/06 will be $90,000. At the end of 2007, its book value will be $100,000 minus $20,000 (two years' worth of depreciation), and so forth. At the end of the tenth year, 12/31/2015, the book value will be zero.

Bell then emphasized three points. First, she hoped Gruff could see that depreciation expense was a way of showing that Foam Corporation uses up tangible operating assets over time, so that the initial investment in them bit by bit becomes an expense of doing business; thus a part of the value on the balance sheet is used up and converted into an expense each year on the statement of operations. Second, she stressed that depreciation is just a way of figuring out how to allocate the original cost of the machine (or any other asset that gets used up slowly) over the time it is used. Depreciation does not necessarily equal any actual reduction in the market value of the machine or building or whatever it is that is being depreciated on the books. (Sometimes assets last longer than their expected useful life or wear out sooner. Sometimes the market goes up or down, affecting the market value of the machine or building.) Third, she said that land is not depreciated, because it is not used up; buildings are depreciated because they wear out, but land is (at least for accountants) forever. Thus the part of the price of a purchase of real estate that is allocated to the raw land is not depreciated and will stay on the balance sheet forever (or for as long as the company owns the land).

Bell then explained that the term "amortization" is used instead of depreciation when the asset that is being used is intangible. Thus if Foam Corporation buys a patent that was issued several years before the purchase, and that will expire after thirteen more years, the purchase price will be "amortized" (spread out) over the set period of thirteen years (assuming Foam Corporation expects the patent to be valuable until the end). Similarly, leasehold improvements made by Foam Corporation, if they cannot be removed at the end of the lease, are amortized over the remaining number of years of the lease (assuming they will be useful for at least that long). Intangible assets that do not have a finite life, such as some trade names and goodwill, are not amortized, just as land is not amortized. However, they are tested for impairment at least annually; if their value is less than the book value, an impairment loss is reported, and the asset's book value is reduced.

Going back to Foam Corporation's balance sheet, it shows as of 12/31/05 total tangible operating assets and intangible assets of $7.5 million, minus $3.6 million in depreciation and amortization. That means that the property, plant, equipment, patents, and trademarks that Foam Corporation had as of 12/31/05 cost Foam Corporation $7.5 million to acquire in market transactions. It also means that, as of 12/31/00, there had been $3.6 million in total depreciation and amortization costs that had accrued over the years on those items. That left a net book value of $3.9 million for Foam Corporation's tangible and intangible operating assets, as of 12/31/00.

(2) Liabilities

Liabilities are debts or obligations of the business. From an accounting perspective, liabilities are (1) probable future sacrifices of economic benefits or resources, (2) arising from present obligations to transfer assets or provide services in the future, (3) as a result of past transactions or events. Liabilities represent the interest that creditors have in the business, because they are entitled to be paid out of the value of the business. Just as there are current and noncurrent assets, there are current and long term liabilities.

(a) Current Liabilities

Current liabilities are those liabilities that will likely need to be satisfied within a year out of current assets or by getting other short term credit. (Current assets are those assets likely to be turned into cash within a year; consequently, the source of any cash needed to satisfy the liabilities due within a year will likely be the current assets.) Current liabilities include obligations owed to the trade creditors (those who supplied goods and services to Foam Corporation on credit for its business needs); if these liabilities are not evidenced by promissory notes they will be called "accounts payable" or "trade payables." (Note that one company's trade payable is another company's account receivable.) The balance sheet shows that Foam Corporation owes $8 million in trade payables as of 12/31/05.

In addition to trade payables, current liabilities will include short term notes payable, accrued expenses such as unpaid wages and unpaid royalties for previous periods, the portion of the principal amount of long term debt due within one year that will have to be paid out of current assets,[10] taxes that will have to be paid within the year, and collections received in advance of the sale of goods or rendering of services.[11]

Foam Corporation's scheduled mortgage payments to First Bank during 2006 will pay not only interest on the mortgages covering the Fresno, Camden, and Philadelphia plants, but also $21,000 of principal. Thus the balance sheet shows the $21,000 as a current liability and the remainder of the mortgage amounts—$1,229,000—as a long term liability.[12] The entire $6 million Foam Corporation owes to Kick Credit is a current liability, because Kick Credit has

10. If the portion of a long term liability that is due within a year will be paid from a noncurrent asset special fund, such as a bond sinking fund, it should not be included in current liabilities.

11. Gruff exclaimed, "How can a collection of money be a liability?" Bell explained that if Foam Corporation collects the price for a shipment of foam but has not yet shipped it, then Foam Corporation has both an asset and a liability. The asset is the cash that was received; it will show up on the balance sheet as part of cash. The liability is the obligation to ship foam, which is a present obligation that will require Foam Corporation to part with an asset in the future; that present obligation will reduce Foam Corporation's inventory of foam when Foam Corporation ships the foam, so it is a present liability just as an obligation to pay money in the future is a present liability.

12. Foam Corporation is making monthly payments to First Bank (on its mortgages) that equal interest due on the mortgages plus a small amount of principal, so that in another twenty years the mortgages will be paid off. The interest part of each payment that will be due in the next year (or later) will not be considered a liability, because Foam Corporation has not yet gotten the benefit of having the use of First Bank's money for the year; Foam Corporation may not end up having to pay the interest at all if the mortgages by some chance are paid off early--or if Foam Corporation files for bankruptcy and First Bank is not oversecured. See §§ 502(b)(2) and 506(b).

The amount of principal due within the next year is considered a current liability; the rest of the principal amount of the mortgages is a long term liability. As the student can confirm by using a book of financial tables or a financial calculator, payments on $1.25 million paid off over twenty years at 10% interest are slightly more than $12,000 per month, or almost $145,000 per year. The same book or calculator will reveal that in the first of the twenty years, only $21,000 of the $145,000 in payments goes to pay off principal; the rest just pays the interest.

accelerated the term loan and the line of credit and demanded payment within 60 days. Foam Corporation also owes $1 million in withholding taxes to the federal government that is due now; Foam Corporation withheld that much from its employees' paychecks for their tax obligations but has not yet paid it over to the government. (If the withholding taxes are not paid to the government, Foam Corporation's officers could be held personally liable; due to its cash shortage, Foam Corporation should consider paying the withholding taxes with the $1.1 million tax refund Foam Corporation has coming from the government, by setting off the two amounts against each other.) When miscellaneous ("other") current liabilities of $50,000 are added in, the total current liabilities are $15,071,000.

Current liabilities are generally paid out of current assets. One result of Foam Corporation's financial problems is that it does not have enough current assets (only $11 million) to cover its current liabilities of over $15 million. This relationship—current assets divided by current liabilities—is called the "current ratio." The current ratio for Foam Corporation as of 12/31/05 is 11 to about 15, or approximately .73 to 1. A current ratio of 2 to 1—that is, current assets equaling twice the amount of the current liabilities—is often considered good. Certainly a ratio of less than 1 to 1 (as in Foam Corporation's case) may be an indication of real financial problems.

(b) Long term liabilities

Long term liabilities are obligations that will not require the use of current assets within the next year. These include debts based on the issuance of securities or other instruments (such as notes, mortgages, or bonds) that mature in more than one year, deferred revenue (advance collections for goods and services that the company will not have to supply until at least a year in the future), and long term pension obligations. Foam Corporation's long term liabilities consist of the portion of the $1.25 million mortgage debt owed to First Bank that is not due during 2006—$1.229 million—and the $3.2 million Foam Corporation owes to Gruff under long term promissory notes, for a total of $4,429,000.

When Foam Corporation's $15,071,000 of current liabilities and $4,429,000 of long term liabilities are added together, Foam Corporation has total liabilities of $19.5 million as of 12/31/05.

(3) Shareholders' Equity

Shareholders' equity—sometimes called owners' equity or net worth—represents the value of the shareholders' interest in the company. Creditors are entitled to the value of the company's assets (at least their liquidation value) ahead of shareholders, so shareholders' equity is equal to whatever value of assets is left after subtracting the amount of the liabilities. Thus, by definition, what is owed to creditors (the liabilities) plus what is left over for shareholders (shareholders' equity) has to equal the amount of the assets.

Foam Corporation's assets have a book value of $14.9 million, and its liabilities are on the books in the amount of $19.5 million. That means that, as a matter of book values, Foam Corporation is insolvent by $4.6 million. The shareholders' equity—the shareholders' interest in Foam Corporation—is a negative $4.6 million.

The book value of the assets probably is not the same as either their liquidation value or their going concern value, so we cannot tell from the balance sheet whether Foam Corporation is insolvent on a liquidation or going concern basis. Nevertheless, the balance sheet suggests Foam Corporation is in serious trouble.

The shareholders' equity portion of the balance sheet reflects the two ways in which shareholders build up value in the company. Practically speaking, a company can get assets three ways, two of which represent value or potential value for shareholders.

First, the company can borrow money, which then becomes an asset (and which can be converted into other kinds of assets when the company spends the money to buy them). Similarly, the company can obtain assets on credit by promising to pay for them in the future. The borrowing of money or obtaining of credit creates a liability that balances the assets, so there is no net value for shareholders—at least not until the company does something with the assets to earn a profit. (Imagine a corporation which had no assets and no liabilities, and thus of course no shareholders' equity. If it manages to borrow $100, it will have assets of $100, liabilities of $100, and still no value left over for shareholders.)

Second, the company can obtain money or other assets from its shareholders, not as loans but as contributions of capital. Imagine again a company with no assets and no liabilities. If the shareholders contribute $150 to the corporation as capital, the corporation will now have $150 in assets, no liabilities, and thus $150 in shareholders' equity. Note that under corporation law, the corporation has no duty to repay the $150 to the shareholders; they did not loan the money to the corporation. The shareholders generally cannot sue the corporation for failing to return their money or failing to pay them dividends. The shareholders take the risk that the company may lose money, and if it does, they suffer loss. On the other hand, they stand to gain if the company makes a profit, and they may gain much more than if they had simply lent the money to the company at a particular interest rate. They are owners, with the risks and benefits of ownership. (An owner can *also* be a creditor; note that Gruff not only owns stock in Foam Corporation but also lent it $3.2 million.)

Foam Corporation's balance sheet shows "Common Stock" of $5 million. That means the common shareholders (Gruff and Simmons or whoever the stockholders may have been in the past) have contributed $5 million total as capital since Foam Corporation was formed.[13] If Foam Corporation never made a profit and never suffered a loss, all of its assets would have to derive directly or indirectly from one of these first two sources: either Foam Corporation got them by incurring a liability (borrowing money or getting them on credit), or else Foam Corporation got them with the money that the stockholders contributed. The stockholders' equity would then remain at $5 million. The assets gotten by way of incurring liabilities would just balance the liabilities incurred to obtain assets, and the only value of assets left over for the stockholders would be the amount they contributed, the $5 million.

Making a profit is the third way a company can acquire assets. When a company makes a profit, the shareholders' equity is increased. Imagine again a company to which its shareholders contributed $150 as capital; assume the

---

13. Often the contribution by shareholders is divided between a common stock account and an additional paid-in capital account, both representing equity.

company has not incurred any liabilities, that it begins operations, and that at the end of the year its statement of operations shows that it has made a profit of $50, all still without incurring any liabilities. If the company does not pay any dividends out to its shareholders, the company will now have assets of $200, the original $150 worth of assets plus the $50 profit. The $50 profit from the statement of operations will then appear in the shareholders' equity section of the balance sheet under the heading "retained earnings." The company earned the $50 profit and retained it, by not paying it out as dividends. If the next year the company makes $40 in profits as shown on the statement of operations, again incurs no liabilities, and again pays no dividends, assets will grow to $240, retained earnings will grow to $90, and shareholders' equity will of course equal the whole $240. If the company then pays $15 cash out in dividends, assets and shareholders' equity will drop to $225, and retained earnings will drop to $75. If at the start of the next year the company borrows $100 and buys some equipment with it, assets will grow immediately to $325, liabilities will immediately be $100, shareholders' equity will stay at $225, and retained earnings will stay at $75. If during that year the company pays interest on the $100 debt, incurs no additional liabilities, pays no dividends, but suffers a loss of $20 as shown on the statement of operations, assets will have shrunk to $305, liabilities will stay at $100, shareholders' equity will therefore be reduced to $205, and retained earnings will therefore be reduced to $55. (Throughout all of this, the "common stock" entry in the shareholders' equity section will remain unchanged at $150, because that entry reflects the historical fact that the shareholders contributed $150 in capital.)

It is important to understand that a retained earnings figure of $55 on a balance sheet does not represent a pot of money with $55 in it. The extra value in the company as a result of the $55 in retained earnings will be found on the left side of the balance sheet, in the assets. Rather than representing a pot of money, the retained earnings figure (sometimes called the retained earnings "account") simply is a way of keeping track of how much profit has been made by the company and kept in the company over the years.

Unfortunately, Foam Corporation does not have any retained earnings. In earlier years Foam Corporation was profitable and had retained earnings, but due to payment of dividends and, more importantly, the suffering of huge losses, all the retained earnings were wiped out. In fact, Foam Corporation has lost so much money that its retained earnings entry is a negative $9.6 million that is referred to as a "deficit." That means Foam Corporation has paid out to shareholders or lost $9.6 million more over the years than it has made in profits. That does not change the fact that Gruff and Simmons contributed $5 million to Foam Corporation as capital, so the common stock entry still reads $5 million, but the $9.6 million in losses means that Foam Corporation has lost more money than its stockholders originally put in, $4.6 million more.

Foam Corporation still has a lot of assets, $14.9 million worth at book value, but it does not have enough assets to cover its liabilities. Foam Corporation lost Gruff's and Simmons' $5 million, and $4.6 million more that Foam Corporation got from its creditors. Based on book value, Foam Corporation is insolvent in the amount of $4.6 million.

At this point, Gruff was stunned. Bell then said she would finish up by explaining briefly the last major financial statement and the notes that should accompany the financial statements.

d. The Statement of Cash Flows

What creditors really will want to know is whether Foam Corporation can generate cash to make payments on its debts. How much cash Foam Corporation can generate will also determine what its assets are worth on a going concern basis. The statement of cash flows deals with the question of cash generation.

Gruff wondered why a statement of cash flows was needed when the statement of operations will show whether the company is making a profit or losing money. The answer is that the statement of operations shows whether Foam Corporation made a profit or a loss for 2005, but it does not show how much *cash* Foam Corporation generated or lost in 2005. Even when a company is making a profit, it still needs to be sure that it has enough cash to pay its obligations. A company in Foam Corporation's situation has a critical need for cash and must have as much information as possible about its cash situation.

The last three lines of the statement of cash flows tell a chilling story for Foam Corporation. It started 2005 with $2.9 million in cash and cash equivalents, but ended 2005 with only $800,000 in cash and cash equivalents. At that rate of cash outflow, $2.1 million per year, Foam Corporation's remaining $800,000 will run out before the middle of 2006. When there is no more cash, Foam Corporation will not be able to pay its employees or buy raw materials; it will be out of business by mid-2006 unless something is done.

The statement of cash flows is an important part of the set of financial statements precisely because it tracks what is happening to cash. The statement of operations can tell a company whether it is making a profit or suffering losses, but it does not provide a clear picture of the cash situation.

In part this is because of the accrual method of accounting for revenue, which is used on the statement of operations. If customers are paying for goods that have been shipped, but are gradually taking longer and longer to pay, the amount of cash taken in will slow down. That will not show up on the statement of operations; on the statement of operations the revenue is considered earned when the goods are shipped.

The accrual method for expenses, which is also used on the statement of operations, can also distort the cash flow picture. Expenses associated with making products are not recognized on the statement of operations *until the products are sold.* For example, if a company is making more products than it can sell, its statement of operations may not show any problem; it may be spending huge amounts of money to make the products which are piling up in the warehouse, but that spending does not show up as an expense on the statement of operations because the products are not being sold.[14] If the company is not careful, it will spend so much of its cash resources in building up inventory that it will run out of cash to pay its bills. Then it may have to try to sell the inventory or other assets quickly (at a low price) to avoid ruin. Close attention to cash flows (and to the amount of inventory) can help the company to recognize and deal with the situation in time.

---

14. The spending does show up on the balance sheet. The company has to use cash or borrow cash (or obtain goods and services on credit) in order to make the products, so the balance sheet will show a reduction in cash or an increase in liabilities. On the other hand the balance sheet will also show an increase in book value of inventory, and that increase will balance the decrease in cash or increase in liabilities. As a result, retained earnings and shareholders' equity will not be changed, so they will not signal the existence of an inventory build up problem.

Depreciation and amortization expense also prevent the statement of operations from providing a clear picture of cash flow. Depreciation and amortization are expenses that reduce the profit (or increase the loss) on the statement of operations. However, they do not use cash; no cash flows out of Foam Corporation just because an accountant makes an entry for depreciation, for example with respect to a machine Foam Corporation purchased three years ago. The cash to purchase the machine flowed out three years ago. That cash is gone; the accountant's entry does not cause more cash to flow out from Foam Corporation. Depreciation is a way of allocating the expense of that purchase to the periods in which the machine is used, but the allocation does not require any more cash this year. Thus a company may show no profit on its statement of operations but yet have plenty of cash flowing in to pay bills, because of a high level of depreciation expense. It may be that eventually cash will need to be used to replace the machine when it wears out, but that may not be for another six or seven years; a company worried about paying its bills will be happy to find that it has more cash than the statement of operations might have suggested to meet the more immediate need. If the company does not survive, it will not need to worry about replacing the machine in six or seven years. If the company reduces the size of its operations, it may never need to spend the cash to replace the machine. The depreciation expense may thus turn out to be irrelevant to Foam Corporation's situation.

The statement of cash flows is organized into three major categories based on an enterprise's (1) operations, (2) investing transactions, and (3) financing transactions.

(1) Cash Flows from Operating Activities

Cash inflows from operating activities may be thought of as the cash equivalent of revenues. (Remember, revenues are determined on the accrual basis.) The cash inflows include cash receipts from sale of goods and services, including cash received from collection of accounts receivable. Also included in cash inflows are interest and dividends received by the company from others, and any other cash receipts from transactions which are not investing or financing transactions, as described below. In 2005 Foam Corporation's cash inflows from operating activities consisted of $29 million in payments by customers and a $1.5 million tax refund paid by the IRS for the 2004 tax year.

Cash outflows from operating activities are the cash equivalent of expenses. (Remember, expenses are determined on the accrual basis.) The cash outflows include cash payments to suppliers and employees to acquire services, raw materials, and merchandise, including payments on trade payables; cash payments to the government for taxes; cash payments to creditors as interest on debts; and other cash payments from transactions which are not investing or financing transactions, as described below. In 2005, Foam Corporation's cash outflows from operating activities consisted of $33 million paid to suppliers and employees, and $1.4 million of interest paid to creditors (primarily to Kick Credit and First Bank).

Thus, in 2005, Foam Corporation did not have a positive cash flow from operations; cash inflows were $30.5 million and cash outflows were $34.4 million. Foam Corporation therefore had a negative $3.9 million cash flow from operations. That is somewhat better than the $5 million loss figure from the statement of operations, because of Foam Corporation's delays in paying its suppliers and because depreciation expense does not affect cash flows. $3.9 million per year is still a huge cash outflow that cannot be sustained.

The total negative cash flow for the year was only $2.1 million,[15] so Foam Corporation must have gotten $1.8 million in positive cash flow from somewhere, which partially offset the massive $3.9 million in negative cash flow from operations. As we will see, investing and financing activities provided $1.8 million in positive cash flow, but such positive cash flow cannot be counted on for the future. If creditors cannot be convinced that Foam Corporation will take strong and effective action to turn around the massive negative cash flow from operations, they will seek to liquidate Foam Corporation.

(2) Cash Flows from Investing Activities

Cash inflows from investing activities include cash received from:

1. Collection of loans made by the enterprise.
2. Sales of equity interests of other enterprises (for example, if Foam Corporation sold its stock in U Foam that would generate cash from an investing activity).
3. Sales of property, plant, and equipment and other productive assets.

Cash outflows resulting from investing activities include:

1. Disbursements for loans made by the enterprise.
2. Payments to acquire debt instruments (such as bonds) or equity interests of other entities.
3. Payments to acquire property, plant, and equipment and other productive assets.

The only investing transaction of Foam Corporation for 2005 was the sale of surplus equipment for $800,000.[16]

(3) Cash Flows from Financing Activities

The final category of information on the cash flow statement involves cash inflows and outflows relating to financing activities. Cash inflows related to financing activities include proceeds from issuance of equity instruments (stock, if the issuer is a corporation like Foam Corporation) and also proceeds from borrowing. The borrowing may be carried out by issuance of bonds, mortgages, notes, or in other ways.

Cash outflows related to financing activities include payments of dividends or other payments to owners, including money spent to buy back stock; repayments of amounts borrowed; and other principal payments to creditors who have extended long term credit (such as repayment by an auto dealer of credit extended by an auto manufacturer for purchase of autos).

Under Foam Corporation's revolving line of credit arrangement with Kick Credit, during 2005 Foam Corporation continuously paid off part of the line of credit (as Foam Corporation's customers sent in payments on their accounts to the lock box controlled by Kick Credit). During 2005 Kick Credit also weekly or daily made new loans to Foam Corporation as new accounts were generated by the shipment of products to Foam Corporation's customers. The net result of all this

---

15. See the third line from the bottom of the statement of cash flows.

16. Note that if Foam Corporation had not sold the equipment it would have been completely out of cash and cash equivalents as of the end of 2005. Sale of surplus assets can be an important source of cash for a business in financial distress. However, in many situations, sale of surplus assets does not provide the needed cash, and divisions or segments of the business must be sold.

paying and relending was that Foam Corporation borrowed an extra $1 million from Kick Credit during 2005—the debt owing to Kick Credit increased from $5 million at the end of 1999 to $6 million at the end of 2005.

That explains why Foam Corporation's cash and cash equivalents decreased by "only" $2.1 million in 2005 instead of by the entire $3.9 million in negative cash flow from operations. Foam Corporation raised $1.8 million by selling surplus equipment for $800,000 and by borrowing an extra $1 million from Kick Credit.

e. The Notes to the Financial Statements

Finally, Bell explained that the basic financial statements are followed by notes, which she did not bring to Gruff. However, the notes provide important information about the financial position and operating results of a company. The notes provide more detail about and clarification of many of the matters in the basic financial statements. The objective of the notes is to provide detailed financial information about selected accounts and to provide additional explanation necessary for full disclosure that cannot conveniently be presented in the basic financial statements themselves.

Appendix B: Cost of Capital

Free cash flows are discounted by a rate equal to the "cost of capital" to determine the going concern value of an enterprise. Suppose that when a new company is formed it obtains its capital by selling all of its common stock to investors for $400,000 and by selling debentures (debt securities) for $600,000. Thus the company will have $1,000,000 in assets, $600,000 in debt, and $400,000 in stockholders' equity. The company then uses its $1,000,000 in assets in a business venture. If the return on that venture is less than the stockholders and creditors expected, then the value of the assets as a going concern will be less than the $1,000,000 they invested. If the return is greater than they expected, then the value of the assets as a going concern will be more than $1,000,000. The cost of capital to the new company is the rate of return expected by the investors (stockholders and creditors); if the company makes that rate of return on its $1,000,000 in assets, then its value will remain unchanged at $1,000,000.

The cost of capital is often determined by calculating the weighted average of the costs of debt and equity. In other words, those who lend money to the company will expect a particular return in the form of interest; those who invest in the company by becoming equity owners will expect a higher return because their investment is riskier than the investment of those who lend money. The return the company must make on its assets to meet those expectations is the weighted average of the returns expected by the lenders and equity owners. Consider the following example, where the planned financial structure is 60 percent debt and 40 percent equity, just as in the example in the previous paragraph. In this example, we assume that in order to attract lenders to lend, the debtor must promise to pay 8% interest per year, and that in order to attract people to buy its stock, the debtor must convince them that they are likely to make 18% per year on their investment:

	Weight		Cost		Weighted Cost
Debt	60%	x	8%	=	4.8%
Equity	40%	x	18%	=	+7.2%
	Weighted average cost of capital				12.0%

If the debtor makes a return of 12%, then it will have met the expectations of both lenders and stockholders; it can pay lenders 8% and have 18% profit on the stockholders' investment left for the stockholders. The market value of its debt and of its stock will then neither go up nor down (assuming there are no economic or other changes that would influence the interest rate or the rate of return expected by holders of equity.) If the debtor does not pay out the 18% return to the stockholders but rather keeps it in the company, the amount of stockholders' equity will increase, and thus the price of the stock will go up.

For a chapter 11 debtor, the weights in the formula should be based on the expected capital structure of the entity as it emerges from bankruptcy. The rate that would generally be used for the cost of debt is the marginal rate at which the debtor will be able to borrow when it emerges from bankruptcy, based on the nature of the debt—secured, subordinated, or other—that will be issued. In a bankruptcy case this rate should be estimated according to the debt and equity structure that will emerge from bankruptcy rather than the existing capital structure.

Another factor to include in the formula for the cost of capital is the effect of tax savings on the effective interest rate paid for borrowing. Because interest payments are deductible from income for income tax purposes, it does not cost $1 to pay $1 of interest. The cost of debt is therefore the interest rate that must be paid minus the effect of the tax savings, as shown in the following formula (where "x" means "times"):

Cost of debt = Marginal long term interest rate x (1- tax rate)

For example, if a reorganized debtor's long term interest rate on bonds to be issued is 9%, and if it will be paying income tax at a 33.3% rate, then the cost of debt is 9% times (1 - .333), which is 9% times .667, or 6%. Thus, the cost of debt reflects the tax savings of one third of the amount of the interest that will be paid.

The cost of equity, or common stock, is not as easy to determine. In theory it is the implicit rate of return necessary to attract investors to purchase the entity's common stock. It is the return that must be earned on new projects (financed with profits or with new issuances of common stock) to leave the value of the shareholders' equity unchanged.

Several approaches may be used to estimate the cost of equity in chapter 11 proceedings. One of the more common methods is the capital asset pricing model ("CAPM").[1] The cost of capital is defined by the CAPM as:

Cost of equity = Risk free rate + β(Equity risk premium)[2]

The first component of the equation is the risk-free rate. The risk-free rate consists of the real interest rate plus an allowance for expected inflation. There are no "pure" risk-free securities issued in the U.S. While it may be claimed that there is no default risk in government securities, long term treasury bonds are subject to capital losses if interest rates rise or capital gains in interest rates decline. While a pure risk-free rate cannot be found, most practitioners use the rate on long-term treasury bonds as a proxy for the risk free rate. Also included in the rate for treasury bonds is the premium for expected inflation.

The second part of the equation for the cost of equity is β—the "beta coefficient" or "beta." The beta coefficient is a measurement of how risky a particular stock is compared to the stock market as a whole. A stock that goes up in price faster than the average stock when the market goes up, and that goes down faster than the average stock when the market goes down, will have a beta coefficient of greater than 1, indicating it is more volatile—or riskier—than the average stock. A stock that goes up in price more slowly than the average stock when the market goes up, and that goes down more slowly than the average stock when the market goes down, will have a beta of less than 1, indicating it is less volatile or risky than the average stock. A stock whose price tends to go up and down in the same proportion as the stock market as a whole will have a beta of 1, indicating it carries the same volatility or risk as the average. Most people are "risk

---

1.   The capital asset pricing model, or CAPM, is a widely accepted model used to estimate a company's equity cost of capital. CAPM is part of a larger body of economic theory known as modern portfolio theory which was developed in 1952 by economist Harry Markowitz. CAPM attempts to provide a measure of the market relationships based on the theory of expected returns if investors behave in the manner prescribed by portfolio theory. Another approach is to use the buildup method. The buildup method is based on the summation of a risk-free rate plus additional reward premiums for taking on additional types of risk. It is used frequently for nonpublic companies.

2.   When two terms such as "β" and "(Equity risk premium)" are placed next to each other in a formula, they are to be multiplied together. Thus "β(Equity risk premium)" equals β times the equity risk premium.

averse"—they would rather have a sure thing with less variability in the outcome. Thus a stock with a high beta has to provide a higher expected average return than a stock with a low beta, if they are to be equally attractive to investors.

Betas are generally determined by running a linear regression between past returns on the stock and past returns on some market index such as the Standard & Poor's 500. Betas determined in this manner are referred to as historical betas. They provide information about how risky—or volatile—the investment has been in the past. Because historical beta values may be of limited use in bankruptcy proceedings, several approaches have been used to adjust historical betas for bankruptcy purposes. Rosenbaum and other researchers have developed a "fundamental beta" based on the theory that certain fundamental characteristics—such as the industry in which the entity operates, the capital structure, and sales and earnings variability—provide a better basis for estimating betas.[3]

In the case of a bankrupt entity, any reliance on historical data in the development of the beta must be carefully evaluated; in many bankruptcy cases betas based on historical data are of no value. In dealing with companies in chapter 11, the beta is generally determined by looking at betas of similarly sized companies within the industry of the debtor. For entities that have borrowed funds during the bankruptcy proceeding or that will be obtaining new debt funds, the interest rate associated with those transactions in relationship to the rate given similar companies within the same industry might give some indication of the risk the market associates with the entity that will emerge from bankruptcy.

The next factor needed to calculate the cost of equity is the equity risk premium. Ibbotson Associates, Bloomberg, and other financial services firms regularly publish their estimates of the equity risk premium. The equity risk premium is determined by subtracting the risk free rate from the expected return of the stock market as a whole.

One of the underlying assumptions behind CAPM is that investors hold well-diversified portfolios. However, because it is hard to diversify all the risk of a small, privately-held company, the traditional CAPM formula is extended out to the Modified Capital Asset Pricing Model ("MCAPM") to capture the unsystematic risk associated with smaller companies, as shown below:

$$E(R) = R(f) + \beta(ERP) + RP(s) + Alpha$$

Where:

E(R)	=	Expected return on an individual security (cost of equity)
R(f)	=	Rate of return available on a risk-free security (as of the valuation date)
β	=	Beta, systematic risk of a company in relation to the market as a whole
ERP	=	Equity risk premium for the market
RP(s)	=	Risk premium for small size
Alpha	=	Risk premium for specific company or unsystematic risk

The MCAPM is simply the traditional CAPM with an additional adjustment first for size and then for unsystematic or company specific risk.[4] Examples of key company

---

3.   Rosenberg & Guy, *Beta and Investment Fundamentals*, FIN. ANAL. J., May-June 1976, at 60-72.

4.   While company size is a part of the company specific risk, because there are published estimates of the adjustments for size, the risk associated with size is separated from the company specific risk.

specific risks include key person dependence, key supplier dependence, customer concentration, and changing technology. For companies in chapter 11 another example of specific company risk is that the reorganized debtor may have to change several aspects of its operations as it attempts to develop new strategies that will allow it to be profitable again. Thus the risks associated with a reorganized company may be more like a new venture than a continuing business.

Jefferies & Co., the financial advisor for the Creditor's Committee in In re Exide Technologies, 303 B.R. 48, (Bankr. D. Del. 2003) (discussed in Chapter Twelve above), estimated the cost of capital for Exide to be between 10.5 percent and 11.5 percent as shown in Exhibit B-1, on the next page. The first part of the exhibit shows the marginal cost of debt (cost for Exide to borrow on its emergence from chapter 11) as 5.9 percent. The cost of equity capital was determined to be between 13.3 percent and 14.3 percent. Recall that we described the following equation to determine the cost of equity:

$$E(R) = R(f) + \beta(ERP) + RP(s) + Alpha$$

Using the information in Exhibit B-1, the cost of equity is 13.3% as shown below:

$R(f) = 4.3\%$; $\beta=1.14\%$; $ERP = 7\%$; $RP(s) = 0$; Alpha $= 1.0\%$ or 2.0%
Assume Alpha $= 1\%$.
$E(R) = 4.3\% + 1.14(7.0\%) + 0 + 1.0\%$
$E(R) = 13.3\%$

An additional risk factor that must be considered for reorganized private companies is reflected in an adjustment to the value of the reorganized entity due to lack of marketability. This adjustment is generally made to the reorganization value once it has been determined; however, some appraisers for chapter 11 companies make the adjustment by adjusting the cost of equity.

Students are cautioned against drawing a quick conclusion that the use of debt as a part of the financial structure will necessarily lead to a lower cost of capital. The existence of debt will "leverage" the equity and make it a riskier investment with a higher beta; thus equity investors will demand a higher rate of return when a business has substantial debt than when it does not. This increases the cost of equity capital beyond the cost it would have if the business did not have substantial debt. Therefore the use of debt financing, as compared to the use of 100% equity financing, will reduce the cost of capital for the part of the financial structure represented by debt, but will increase the cost of capital for the part of the financial structure represented by equity.

The question whether the use of debt financing reduces the cost of capital is beyond the scope of this text. However, many experts agree that where debt/equity ratios approach the extremes (100% debt or 100% equity), the cost of capital may be increased—and thus the enterprise's value reduced—due to (1) the risks associated with high debt, or (2) the tax benefits lost when there is little debt and thus little deductible interest. A more interesting question is whether changes in the debt/equity ratio within the broad middle range (e.g., 40% to 60% debt and thus 60% to 40% equity) have any effect on the cost of capital (and thus on the value of the enterprise). Interested students may wish to consult Krawiec, *Derivatives, Corporate Hedging, and Shareholder Wealth: Modigliani-Miller Forty Years Later*, 1998 U. ILL. L. REV. 1039; Miller, *The Modigliani-Miller Propositions after Thirty Years*, 2 J. ECON. PERSP. 99 (1988).

DISCOUNTED CASH FLOW VALUATION ANALYSIS

Weighted Average Cost of Debt Calculation

The analysis below is based upon the Company's projected capital structure upon emergence as per the Business Plan and Commitment Letter from the Company's senior secured lenders.

	Amount (in millions)	Interest Rate[1]
US Term Loan	$200.0	5.9%
European Term Loan	300.0	5.9%
Capital Leases and Other Debt	1.2	4.9%
Capital Lease- Europe	20.8	4.9%
Other Debt- Europe	10.6	7.8%
	$532.5	5.9%

[1]Interest rates assume normalized LIBOR rate of approximately 1.9%, or approximately 50 basis points above current levels.

Discount Rate Derivation

		Company Risk Premium	
Inputs		**1%**	**2%**
Risk-free Interest Rate (Twenty-year long-term treasury rate)	Rf	4.3%	4.3%
Market Risk Premium	Rm	7.0%	7.0%
Unlevered Asset Beta of Comparables	Ba	0.94	0.94
Comparables Tax Rate	t	40.0%	40.0%
Weight of Total Equity of Comparables	We	73.2%	73.2%
Weight of Net Debt of Comparables	Wd	26.8%	26.8%
Levered Equity Beta of Comparables (Ba*(1+(Wd/We*(1-t)))	Be	1.14	1.14
Cost of Equity:			
Levered Equity Beta of Comparables	Be	1.14	1.14
Multiply: Market Risk Premium	Rm	7.0%	7.0%
Industry Risk Premium		8.0%	8.0%
Plus: Company Risk Premium	Rc	1.0%	2.0%
Plus: Risk-Free Interest Rate	Rf	4.3%	4.3%
Cost of Equity (Rc+Rf+Rp+Be*(Rm))	**Ke**	**13.3%**	**14.3%**
Pre-tax cost of debt	Kd	5.9%	5.9%
Multiply: Assumed Tax Rate	t	40.0%	40.0%
Cost of Debt (kd*(1-t))		**3.5%**	**3.5%**
Calculation of WACC:			
WACC ((Ke*We)+(Kd*Wd)) (Rounded)		**10.5%**	**11.5%**

Source: Blackstone Exhibits to *ExideTechnologies,* 303 B.R. 48 (Bankr. D. Del. 2003)

Appendix C: The Concept of Present Value

In decisions involving the receipt of cash in different future years, consideration should be given to the time value of money. A dollar today is worth more than a dollar to be received tomorrow. One method often used to adjust for this time difference in the value of money is to consider the current value—or "present value"—of future cash flows. Using the concept of present value, the reader of financial information is able to compare cash flows that will be received at different points in time by calculating the amount of the cash payment that would need to be received today in order to provide the same value as the future cash flows.[5]

For example, at an interest rate (technically a discount rate) of 10 percent, the present value of $3,000 to be received at the end of three years is $2,253. This value is determined by multiplying the present value factor of .751 times the $3,000 of cash inflow expected at the end of year three. The present value factor of .751 is located in Table C-1 (located immediately after this Appendix C) for a period of three years and an interest rate of 10 percent per year. There are several observations that can be made from Table C-1, the present value of $1 to be received in the future. First note that all of the value are less than 1, indicating that one dollar to be received in the future is worth less than one dollar to be received today. Note also that the further down the table it is, the lower the factor becomes, because the longer it takes to collect a dollar the less value it has. Another observation is that as the discount rate is increased, the values become smaller, indicating that as the rate increases, the present value of a dollar to be received in the future decreases.

Table C-2 shows the present value of an annuity—the present value of a series of equal cash flow streams to be received at specified future time intervals. For example, if $1,000 is to be received at the end of each year for the next three years, and if the appropriate discount rate is 10 percent, the present value of the cash flows is the sum of each cash flow times the present value factor at the end of each year (see Table C-1) as shown below:

Year 1	$1,000 x .909	=	$909
Year 2	$1,000 x .826	=	$826
Year 3	$1,000 x .751	=	$751
Total	$1,000 x 2.486	=	$2,486

The present value could also have been calculated by using the present value factor for three years from Table C-1 at an interest rate of 10 percent. Note that the 2.486 value in Table C-2 for the third period at an interest rate of 10 percent is equal to the sum of the present value factors for years one through three: .909 + .826 + .751 = 2.486. Thus, Table C-2 shows the cumulative present value factor of a series of cash flows.

---

5.   Here is the equation for calculating the present value PV of a single payment of F dollars to be received n periods in the future, where i equals the discount rate (expressed as a decimal) per period:

$$PV = \frac{F}{(1+i)^n}$$

For example, if F is $1, n is 3 years, and i is 10% per year, then $PV = 1/(1+.1)^3 = 1/(1.1)^3 = .751315$, which rounds off to the .751 figure found in Table A on the next page, at the intersection of the row for 3 periods, and the column for 10%. Thus an investor would be willing to pay 75.1 cents today in exchange for the right to be paid $1 three years from now, if the investor wants a 10% return per year. (Or, more realistically, an investor would pay $751 today in exchange for the right to be paid $1,000 three years from now.)

Table C-1
Present Value of $1

Periods	0.5%	1%	1.5%	2%	3%	4%	5%	6%	7%	8%	9%	10%	12%	14%	16%	18%	20%
1	0.995	0.990	0.985	0.980	0.971	0.962	0.952	0.943	0.935	0.926	0.917	0.909	0.893	0.877	0.862	0.847	0.833
2	0.990	0.980	0.971	0.961	0.943	0.925	0.907	0.890	0.873	0.857	0.842	0.826	0.797	0.769	0.743	0.718	0.694
3	0.985	0.971	0.956	0.942	0.915	0.889	0.864	0.840	0.816	0.794	0.772	0.751	0.712	0.675	0.641	0.609	0.579
4	0.980	0.961	0.942	0.924	0.888	0.855	0.823	0.792	0.763	0.735	0.708	0.683	0.636	0.592	0.552	0.516	0.482
5	0.975	0.951	0.928	0.906	0.863	0.822	0.784	0.747	0.713	0.681	0.650	0.621	0.567	0.519	0.476	0.437	0.402
6	0.971	0.942	0.915	0.888	0.837	0.790	0.746	0.705	0.666	0.630	0.596	0.564	0.507	0.456	0.410	0.370	0.335
7	0.966	0.933	0.901	0.871	0.813	0.760	0.711	0.665	0.623	0.583	0.547	0.513	0.452	0.400	0.354	0.314	0.279
8	0.961	0.923	0.888	0.853	0.789	0.731	0.677	0.627	0.582	0.540	0.502	0.467	0.404	0.651	0.605	0.266	0.233
9	0.956	0.914	0.875	0.837	0.766	0.706	0.645	0.592	0.544	0.500	0.460	0.424	0.361	0.308	0.263	0.225	0.194
10	0.951	0.905	0.862	0.820	0.744	0.676	0.614	0.558	0.508	0.463	0.422	0.386	0.322	0.270	0.227	0.191	0.162
11	0.947	0.896	0.849	0.804	0.722	0.650	0.585	0.527	0.475	0.429	0.388	0.350	0.287	0.237	0.195	0.162	0.135
12	0.942	0.887	0.836	0.788	0.701	0.625	0.557	0.497	0.444	0.397	0.356	0.319	0.257	0.208	0.168	0.137	0.112
13	0.937	0.879	0.824	0.773	0.681	0.604	0.530	0.469	0.415	0.368	0.326	0.290	0.229	0.182	0.145	0.116	0.093
14	0.933	0.870	0.812	0.758	0.661	0.577	0.505	0.442	0.388	0.340	0.299	0.263	0.205	0.160	0.12	0.099	0.078
15	0.928	0.861	0.800	0.743	0.642	0.555	0.481	0.417	0.362	0.315	0.275	0.239	0.183	0.140	0.108	0.084	0.065
16	0.923	0.853	0.788	0.728	0.623	0.523	0.458	0.394	0.339	0.292	0.252	0.218	0.163	0.123	0.093	0.071	0.054
18	0.914	0.836	0.765	0.700	0.587	0.494	0.416	0.350	0.296	0.250	0.212	0.180	0.130	0.095	0.069	0.051	0.038
20	0.905	0.820	0.742	0.673	0.554	0.456	0.377	0.312	0.258	0.215	0.178	0.149	0.104	0.073	0.051	0.037	0.026
22	0.896	0.803	0.721	0.647	0.522	0.422	0.342	0.278	0.226	0.184	0.150	0.123	0.083	0.056	0.038	0.026	0.018
24	0.887	0.788	0.700	0.622	0.492	0.390	0.310	0.247	0.197	0.158	0.126	0.102	0.066	0.043	0.028	0.019	0.013
26	0.878	0.772	0.679	0.598	0.464	0.361	0.281	0.220	0.172	0.135	0.106	0.084	0.053	0.033	0.021	0.014	0.009
28	0.870	0.757	0.659	0.574	0.437	0.333	0.255	0.196	0.150	0.116	0.090	0.069	0.042	0.026	0.016	0.010	0.006
30	0.861	0.742	0.640	0.552	0.412	0.308	0.231	0.174	0.131	0.099	0.075	0.057	0.033	0.020	0.012	0.007	0.004
32	0.852	0.727	0.621	0.531	0.388	0.285	0.210	0.155	0.115	0.085	0.063	0.047	0.027	0.15	0.009	0.005	0.003
34	0.844	0.713	0.603	0.510	0.366	0.264	0.190	0.138	0.100	0.073	0.053	0.039	0.021	0.012	0.006	0.004	0.002
36	0.836	0.699	0.585	0.490	0.345	0.244	0.173	0.123	0.088	0.063	0.045	0.032	0.017	0.009	0.005	0.003	0.001
40	0.819	0.672	0.551	0.453	0.307	0.208	0.142	0.097	0.067	0.046	0.032	0.022	0.011	0.005	0.003	0.001	0.001
44	0.803	0.645	0.519	0.418	0.272	0.178	0.117	0.077	0.051	0.034	0.023	0.015	0.007	0.003	0.001	0.001	<.001
48	0.787	0.620	0.489	0.387	0.242	0.152	0.096	0.061	0.039	0.025	0.016	0.010	0.004	0.002	0.001	<.001	<.001

Table C-2
Present Value of an Ordinary Annuity of $1

Payments	0.5%	1%	1.5%	2%	3%	4%	5%	6%	7%	8%	9%	10%	12%	14%	16%	18%	20%
1	0.995	0.990	0.985	0.971	0.962	0.952	0.943	0.952	0.943	0.926	0.917	0.909	0.893	0.877	0.862	0.847	0.833
2	1.985	1.970	1.956	1.942	1.913	1.886	1.859	1.833	1.808	1.783	1.759	1.736	1.690	1.647	1.605	1.566	1.528
3	2.970	2.941	2.912	2.884	2.829	2.775	2.723	2.673	2.624	2.577	2.531	2.487	2.402	2.322	2.246	2.174	2.106
4	3.950	3.902	3.854	3.808	3.717	3.630	3.546	3.465	3.387	3.312	3.240	3.170	3.037	2.914	2.798	2.690	2.589
5	4.926	4.853	4.783	4.713	4.580	4.452	4.329	4.212	4.100	3.993	3.890	3.791	3.605	3.433	3.274	3.127	2.991
6	5.896	5.795	5.697	5.601	5.417	5.242	5.076	4.917	4.767	4.623	4.486	4.355	4.111	3.889	3.685	3.498	3.326
7	6.862	6.728	6.598	6.472	6.230	6.002	5.786	5.582	5.389	5.206	5.033	4.868	4.564	4.288	4.039	3.812	3.605
8	7.823	7.652	7.486	7.325	7.020	6.733	6.463	6.210	5.971	5.747	5.535	5.335	4.968	4.639	4.344	4.078	3.837
9	8.779	8.566	8.361	8.162	7.786	7.432	7.108	6.802	6.515	6.247	5.995	5.759	5.328	4.946	4.607	4.303	4.031
10	9.730	9.471	9.222	8.983	8.530	8.111	7.722	7.360	7.024	6.710	6.418	6.145	5.650	5.216	4.833	4.494	4.192
11	10.677	10.368	10.071	9.787	9.253	8.760	8.306	7.887	7.499	7.139	6.805	6.495	5.937	5.453	5.029	4.656	4.327
12	11.619	11.255	10.908	10.575	9.954	9.385	8.863	8.384	7.943	7.536	7.161	6.814	6.194	5.660	5.197	4.793	4.439
13	12.556	12.134	11.732	11.348	10.635	9.986	9.394	8.853	8.358	7.904	7.487	7.103	6.424	5.842	5.342	4.910	4.533
14	13.489	13.004	12.543	12.106	11.296	10.563	9.899	9.295	8.745	8.244	7.786	7.367	6.628	6.002	5.468	5.008	4.611
15	14.417	13.865	13.343	12.849	11.938	11.118	10.380	9.712	9.108	8.559	8.061	7.606	6.811	6.142	5.575	5.092	4.675
16	15.340	14.718	14.131	13.578	12.561	11.652	10.838	10.106	9.447	8.851	8.313	7.824	6.974	6.265	5.668	5.162	4.730
18	17.173	16.398	15.673	14.992	13.754	12.659	11.690	10.828	10.059	9.372	8.756	8.201	7.250	6.467	5.818	5.273	4.812
20	18.987	18.046	17.169	16.351	14.877	13.590	12.462	11.470	10.594	9.818	9.129	8.514	7.469	6.623	5.929	5.353	4.870
22	20.784	19.660	18.621	17.658	15.937	14.451	13.163	12.042	11.061	10.201	9.442	8.772	7.645	6.743	6.011	5.410	4.909
24	22.563	21.243	20.030	18.914	16.936	15.247	13.799	12.550	11.469	10.529	9.707	8.985	7.784	6.835	6.073	5.451	4.937
26	24.324	22.795	21.399	20.121	17.877	15.983	14.375	13.003	11.826	10.810	9.929	9.161	7.896	6.906	6.118	5.480	4.956
28	26.068	24.316	22.727	21.281	18.764	16.663	14.898	13.406	12.137	11.051	10.116	9.307	7.984	6.961	6.152	5.502	4.970
30	27.794	25.808	24.016	22.396	19.600	17.292	15.372	13.765	12.409	11.258	10.274	9.427	8.055	7.003	6.177	5.517	4.979
32	29.503	27.270	25.267	23.468	20.389	17.874	15.803	14.084	12.647	11.435	10.406	9.526	8.112	7.035	6.196	5.528	4.985
34	31.196	28.703	26.482	24.499	21.132	18.411	16.193	14.368	12.854	11.587	10.609	9.609	8.157	7.060	6.210	5.536	4.990
36	32.871	30.108	27.661	25.489	21.832	18.908	16.547	14.623	13.035	11.717	10.612	9.677	8.192	7.073	6.220	5.541	4.993
40	36.172	32.835	29.916	27.355	23.115	19.793	17.159	15.046	13.332	11.925	10.757	9.779	8.244	7.105	6.233	5.548	4.997
44	39.408	35.455	32.041	29.080	24.254	20.549	17.663	15.383	13.558	12.077	10.861	9.849	8.276	7.120	6.241	5.552	4.998
48	42.580	37.974	34.043	30.673	25.267	21.195	18.077	15.650	13.730	12.189	10.934	9.897	8.297	7.130	6.245	5.554	4.999

Index